# CIVIL PROCEDURE HANDBOOK

# CIVIL PROCEDURE HANDBOOK

DR VICTORIA WILLIAMS

OXFORD
UNIVERSITY PRESS

OXFORD
UNIVERSITY PRESS

Great Clarendon Street, Oxford OX2 6DP

Oxford University Press is a department of the University of Oxford. It furthers the University's objective of excellence in research, scholarship, and education by publishing worldwide in

Oxford New York

Auckland Cape Town Dar es Salaam Hong Kong Karachi Kuala Lumpur Madrid Melbourne Mexico City Nairobi New Delhi Shanghai Taipei Toronto

With offices in

Argentina Austria Brazil Chile Czech Republic France Greece Guatemala Hungary Italy Japan Poland Portugal Singapore South Korea Switzerland Thailand Turkey Ukraine Vietnam



Published in the United States by Oxford University Press Inc., New York



First published 2007



British Library Cataloguing in Publication Data
Data available

Library of Congress Cataloging-in-Publication Data

Williams, Victoria, 1969–
Civil procedure handbook 2007 / Victoria Williams. — 4th ed.
p. cm.
Includes bibliographical references and index.
ISBN 978–0–19–923194–2 (alk. paper)
1. Civil procedure—England. 2. Civil procedure—Wales. I. Title.
KD7325.W554 2007
347.42′05—dc22 2007028188

Typeset by RefineCatch Limited, Bungay, Suffolk
Printed in Great Britain
on acid-free paper by
Ashford Colour Press Ltd., Gosport, Hampshire

ISBN 978–0–19–923149–2

1 3 5 7 9 10 8 6 4 2

# Preface to the First–Fourth Editions (2004–2007)

Keeping track of numerous[1] cumulative updates since the Civil Procedure Rules came into force is quite difficult for anyone. Against that backdrop the Civil Procedure Handbook aims to be, as its title suggests, a helpful handbook which sets out in an uncluttered style the CPR, schedules and protocols as they stand at a known and specified point in time as close to publication date as possible whilst taking into account all the rule updates which have been formally approved.

In the text I have endeavoured to ensure that the rules, schedules and protocols appear in their official form. Where numbered footnotes appear they are selected from official footnotes rather than reflecting any expression of opinion or analysis by me. However there are occasions, which should be clear from their context, where the text of the official rules contains minor errors such as references to repealed forms. Generally this is pointed out with an asterisked footnote, and I am grateful to the team at Oxford University Press for recording such errors. The one notable addition, provided in the Introduction and which is not 'official CPR', is a list of transitional Regulations which relate to various historic amendments.

To keep the length manageable there are some annexes to rules, forms and EU Regulations which are not reproduced, but in each instance I have reminded the reader that the DCA website or the Court Service website, as the case may be, are an excellent way to access that material. Likewise I have not included the mass of official court forms but have referred the reader to the appropriate website.

Unless otherwise stated, all the text is in force at date of publication. Any changes to rules which have been approved but which are yet to come into force are clearly denoted in the text, with their commencement dates.

My thanks go to Oxford University Press, and to Annie McCloud at home.

Fourth Edition (2007)

*The fourth edition of this text endeavours to state the Rules, Practice Directions and Pre-Action Protocols of the Civil Procedure Rules as at their 44th update, including all rules, and amendments published and in force at 6 April 2007, including the Civil Procedure (Amendment No.3) Rules (SI 2006/3435).*

*Note: for transitional provisions relating to the Civil Procedure Rules please see the DCA website at <http://www.justice.gov.uk/civil/procrules_fin/index.htm>.*

**Dr Victoria Williams**
2 Gray's Inn Square Chambers, Gray's Inn, London,
April 2007

[1] Forty-four as at April 2007.

# Contents



[* The forms listed here are not reproduced in this work, but may be accessed via the court service website at <http://www.courtservice.gov.uk>]

* For Practice Direction see PD to RSC Ord.46.
† For Practice Direction see PD to RSC Ord.52.

# Table of UK Cases

# Table of Statutes

# Table of Statutory Instruments

# Procedural Checklists*



* These checklists are taken from *Blackstone's Civil Practice 2008* (Oxford University Press) with the kind permission of the editors. They are also available from CS Group Laserform as a unique electronic product, LitPro. Please see <http://www.laserform.co.uk> for more details.

## Procedural checklist 1 Pre-action Protocol for Personal Injury Claims

All references are to the Pre-Action Protocol for Personal Injury Claims unless otherwise indicated.

| | |
|---|---|
| Soon after being retained | Solicitor should consider whether an informal notification of the possible claim should be made to the defendant. This will not start the protocol timetable (para. 2.6). |
| Letter of claim | This should be sent at least 6 months before the expiry of limitation period to give time for compliance before limitation expires. Two copies of the letter should be sent to the defendant, or one to the defendant and one to the insurer (paras 2.7 and 3.1). For detailed contents of the letter, see paras 3.2 to 3.5 and annex A. |
| 21 days from letter of claim | Defendant should reply with name of insurer, or the insurer should acknowledge (para. 3.6). The period is up to 42 days if the accident was outside England and Wales (para. 3.8). |
| Failure to acknowledge | If there is no acknowledgment within 21 days, proceedings may be issued (para. 3.6). |
| 3 months from acknowledging letter of claim | Defendant should have completed investigations. Defendant must reply stating if liability is admitted or denied (paras 2.12 and 3.7). If liability is denied or if contributory negligence is alleged, the defendant should give reasons and provide documents on liability (paras 3.7, 3.10 to 3.12). Standard disclosure lists are in annex B. No charge is to be made for providing copy documents (para. 3.13). |
| Before issuing proceedings | If contributory negligence has been alleged, the claimant should respond to those allegations (para. 3.12). |
| As soon as possible after defendant's response | Claimant sends defendant a schedule of special damages and documents in support. This is particularly important where liability has been admitted (para. 3.14). Both sides must consider the claimant's rehabilitation needs (para. 4.1). |
| No time limit, but usually shortly after the defendant's response | Either party may send the other a list of suggested experts for each field of expertise (para. 3.15). The letter should also state the basis of the proposed instruction (otherwise this procedure results in the joint selection of experts rather than joint instruction). |
| No time limit | Claimant organises access to relevant medical records (para. 3.16). |
| 14 days after list of experts | Other side may raise objections to the suggested experts (para. 3.17). |
| Objection to all suggested experts | Both parties are free to instruct their own experts. This may be penalised in costs later if either side has acted unreasonably (para. 3.18). |
| No complete objection | First party selects an expert from those left, and sends a letter of instruction in accordance with the standard letter (annex C). |
| Receipt of report | First party decides whether to send copy to the other side. Both parties consider sending questions to clarify the report to the expert. The second party should send its questions via the first party's solicitors (para. 3.20). |
| Before proceedings | Both parties should consider sending Part 36 offers to the other side. Both parties should also consider whether mediation or ADR might be appropriate (paras 2.16, 5.2, and 8.7). |
| 14 days before issue | Claimant should ask the defendant's insurers to nominate solicitors, and both parties should carry out a stocktake of the issues and evidence (para. 2.17). |

## Procedural checklist 2 Pre-action procedure where no protocol applies

All references are to PD Pre-Action Protocols unless otherwise indicated.

| | |
|---|---|
| First step | Letter of claim is sent to the defendant giving details of the claim and other matters set out in para. 4.3 including time for a detailed response (usually one month), and enclosing copies of the essential documents the claimant relies upon and, if the defendant is not represented, a copy of the PD Pre-action Protocols. |
| Within next 21 days | Defendant acknowledges letter of claim, stating when a detailed response will be sent, and reasons for any extra time required (para. 4.4). |
| One month from letter of claim | Defendant provides full written response accepting the claim and making proposals for settlement, or denying the claim with detailed reasons and enclosing essential documents and other matters set out in para. 4.6. |
| Promptly thereafter | The parties should consider ADR and engage in appropriate genuine and reasonable negotiations with a view to settling the claim economically and without court proceedings (paras 4.2(d), 4.7 and 8.7). |
| Expert evidence | If expert evidence is required, the parties should if possible engage an agreed expert (paras 4.9 and 4.10). |

## Procedural checklist 3 Issue and service where service of the claim form is to be effected by the court

Where the court is to effect service the procedure is as follows:

(a) The claimant sends or takes to court one copy of the claim form and, if necessary, a notice of funding of claim or copy LSC certificate for the court, and a copy for each defendant to be served, together with the issue fee (CPFO, fee 1). Claimants in the RCJ can get the court to seal a 'claimant's copy' claim form, if convenient.

(b) The court issues the claim form by entering the issue date on the claim form, affixing the court seal to the claim form and allocating a number to the claim. It creates a case management file, in which it files its copy of the claim form and, if supplied, notice of funding of claim or LSC certificate. The claimant's copy of the claim form (if any) will be returned.

(c) The court serves the claim form and, if supplied, notice of funding of claim. It is for the court to decide which method of service to choose, although the method will normally be by first-class post (CPR, r. 6.3(2); PD 6, para. 8.1).

(d) Where particulars of claim are contained in the claim form or are to be served with it, court staff will add to the documents for service forms for admitting and for defending the claim and for acknowledging service (CPR, r. 7.8(1)). Where the particulars of claim are to be served later, these documents do not accompany the claim form.

(e) The court will send the claimant a notice of issue (form N205A, N205B or N205C), which will include the date when the claim form is deemed to be served under r. 6.7 (r. 6.14).

(f) Where the court sends the claim form by post and it is returned to the court, or where the court attempts to serve by its bailiff and is unable to do so, it must notify the claimant (rr. 6.11 and 6.11A).

(g) A claimant who receives a notice of ineffectual bailiff service should take steps to effect service of the claim form himself. If the court sent the claim form by first-class post to the correct address for service, there is an irrebuttable presumption of dues service (r. 6.7).

## Procedural checklist 4 Issue and service where service of the claim form is to be effected by the claimant

Where the claimant is to effect service the procedure is as follows:

(a) The claimant sends or takes to court one copy of the claim form for the court, and a copy for each defendant to be served, together with the issue fee. Claimants in the RCJ can get the court to seal a 'claimant's copy' claim form, if convenient. There must be a notification to the court that the claimant wishes to effect service. If necessary, a notice of funding of claim or copy LSC certificate must be filed.
(b) The court issues the claim form by entering the issue date on the claim form, affixing the court seal to the claim form and allocating a number to the claim. It creates a case management file, which will include the court's copy of the claim form and, if supplied, notice of funding of claim or copy LSC certificate.
(c) The claimant's copy of the claim form (if any) and the copies for service on the defendants will be returned.
(d) The claimant will effect service, in one of the ways specified in CPR, r. 6.2. If a notice of funding of claim form N251 was filed, it must be served with the claim form. Where particulars of claim are contained in the claim form or are to be served with it, the claimant must add to the documents for service forms for acknowledging service, for admitting and for defending the claim (r. 7.8(1)). Where the particulars of claim are to be served later, these documents do not accompany the claim form.
(e) The claimant must file a certificate of service (form N215) within seven days of service of the claim form, giving the details set out in table 15.1 (r. 6.14(2)(a)).

## Procedural checklist 5 Claim under standard Part 8 procedure

| | |
|---|---|
| Issue | Issue claim on form N208 (PD 8, para. 2.2). File claimant's notice of funding of claim (form N251), where appropriate (PD 43–48, para. 19.2(2)(a)). At same time, file evidence in support of claim (CPR, r. 8.5(1); PD 8, para. 5.1). |
| Fee | Part 8 claims are likely to be non-money claims for which the fee is £400 in the High Court, £150 in a county court (CPFO, fee 1.4). |
| Service | Serve claim form (form N208), form for acknowledging service (form N210), notice of funding of claim (form N251), and evidence in support of claim (CPR, r. 8.5(4)). Forms for defending or admitting the claim are not required (rr. 7.8(2) and 8.9(b)(ii)). Usual rules for service, set out in CPR, Part 6, apply. |
| Time for service | The claim must be served within four months after issue, if it is served in the jurisdiction, or six months after issue, if it is served out of the jurisdiction (r. 7.5). |
| Acknowledgment | Defendant should file acknowledgment (form N210), verified by a statement of truth (r. 8.2A) within 14 days after service of claim form, and serve copies of form N210 on other parties at the same time (r. 8.3(1)). Alternatively, the defendant may acknowledge service informally by letter (PD 8, para. 3.2). At the same time the defendant should file and serve notice of funding of claim (form N251), where appropriate (PD 43–48, para. 19.2(3)). |
| Objecting to Part 8 procedure | At same time as filing acknowledgment, defendant may file and serve statement of reasons for objecting to Part 8 procedure (CPR, r. 8.8(1); PD 8, para. 3.6). |

| | |
|---|---|
| Responding to claim | At the same time as acknowledging service, the defendant should file and serve evidence in opposition to the claim (CPR, r. 8.5(3) and (4)). If he fails to do this, he may participate in the hearing only if the court gives permission. However, judgment in default may not be entered against him (rr. 8.1(5) and 8.4). |
| Evidence in reply | Within 14 days after service of defendant's evidence, claimant may file and serve evidence in reply (r. 8.5(5) and (6)). |
| Form of evidence | Evidence may be in the form of an affidavit or witness statement, or in the case of the claimant's evidence in support, in the claim form itself, provided it is verified by a statement of truth (PD 8, para. 5.2). |
| Extending time for service of evidence | Parties may agree in writing extensions of time for service of the defendant's evidence, and of the claimant's evidence in reply, of up to 14 days. A copy of the agreement to extend time for the defendant's evidence must be filed with his acknowledgment (PD 8, para. 5.6). Any longer extensions may only be granted by the court (PD 8, para. 5.5). |
| Case management | Part 8 claims are automatically allocated to the multi-track and parties do not need to complete allocation questionnaires (CPR, r. 8.9(c)). No allocation fee is payable in a Part 8 claim (CPFO, notes following fee 2.2). Directions (including fixing a hearing date) will be given by the court either when the claim is issued or after the acknowledgment has been filed (PD 8, para. 4). |
| Listing fee | A listing fee of £600 (High Court) or £500 (county court) is payable, usually by the claimant on the defendant filing a pre-trial checklist (CPFO, fee 2.2). |
| Hearing | Most claims will be disposed of with a hearing on the written evidence. |

## Procedural checklist 6 Application for joinder

| | |
|---|---|
| Timing | If joinder is sought before service of claim form, the court's permission is not required. If joinder is sought after service of the claim form, application must be made for the court's permission. |
| Application notice | Form N244. Apply for new party to be added as Claimant/Defendant, or for new party to be substituted for existing party, or for existing party to be removed and also, in each case, for permission to amend statement of case. Attach draft of order sought and draft of proposed amended statement of case. Set out brief reasons for application. |
| Consent of new party | Where party to be added or substituted is claimant, file and serve, with the application notice, the signed written consent of the new party (PD 19, para. 2.1). |
| Evidence | Application to add or substitute a party must be supported by evidence setting out the proposed new party's interest in or connection with the claim (PD 19, para. 1.3). The evidence must be filed and served with the application notice. |
| Fee | £100 (High Court) or £65 (county court) (CPFO, fee 2.5); for consent application £50 (High Court) or £35 (county court) (CPFO, fee 2.6). |

| | |
|---|---|
| Service | The application notice, attachments and evidence in support must be served on all existing parties and any proposed new party as soon as practicable after filing and at least three clear days before the hearing date (CPR, r. 23.7). |
| Costs | In contested applications, parties should file and serve costs schedules in form N260 24 hours before hearing (PD 43–48, para. 13.5(4)). |
| Hearing | Consent applications may be dealt with without a hearing. |
| After the hearing | Comply with directions. If permission is given, these will normally require the applicant to file the amended claim form and particulars of claim within 14 days of the order (a fee of £50 (High Court) or £35 (county court) is payable (CPFO, fee 1.5)), to serve the new defendant with the existing statements of case, the amended claim form and particulars of claim, a response pack and a copy of the order. |
| Limitation | A new defendant does not become a party to the proceedings for the purpose of the Limitation Act 1980 until served with the claim form (PD 19, para. 3.3). |

## Procedural checklist 7 Interpleader proceedings: High Court

### (a) Sheriff or enforcement officer's interpleader: preliminary steps

| | |
|---|---|
| Notice to enforcement officer | The person claiming ownership of goods taken or intended to be taken by the enforcement officer should notify the enforcement officer of his claim, and give his address for service (RSC, ord. 17, r. 2(1) in CPR, sch. 1). |
| Enforcement officer's notice to judgment creditor | Enforcement officer must notify judgment creditor immediately of claim (RSC, ord. 17, r. 2(2) in CPR, sch. 1). |
| Response from judgment creditor | Within seven days, judgment creditor must inform the enforcement officer whether he admits or disputes the claim (RSC, ord. 17, r. 2(2) in CPR, sch. 1). Where the claim is disputed, the enforcement officer may apply for interpleader relief. |

### (b) Interpleader application

| | |
|---|---|
| Application | Application for interpleader relief in existing proceedings is made by application notice (form N244,) and where there are no pending proceedings, by Part 8 claim form (form N208) (RSC, ord. 17, r. 3(1) in CPR, sch. 1). |
| Fee | £100 where claim is made by application notice (CPFO, fee 2.5); £400 where claim is made by Part 8 claim form (where claim is for goods, not proceeds of sale) (CPFO, fee 1.4). |
| Evidence in support | Where the enforcement officer is interpleader claimant, no evidence in support is required. Otherwise, evidence must be filed and served showing that the interpleader claimant:<br>• claims no interest in the subject matter in dispute, other than for charges or costs;<br>• does not collude with any of the claimants to the subject matter; and<br>• is willing to pay or transfer that subject matter into court or to dispose of it as the court may direct (RSC, ord. 17, r. 3(4) in CPR, sch. 1). |
| Service | The claim form or application notice must be served on all persons asserting a claim to the property. |

| | |
|---|---|
| Claimant's response | Where the claim relates to goods seized in execution, the claimant then has 14 days in which to serve a witness statement or affidavit on the enforcement officer and the judgment creditor. This must identify the property claimed and the grounds for asserting rights in the property (RSC, ord. 17, r. 3(6) in CPR, sch. 1). |

## Procedural checklist 8 Interpleader proceedings: county court

### (a) Bailiff's interpleader

| | |
|---|---|
| Notice to bailiff | The person claiming ownership of goods taken or intended to be taken in execution (the 'interpleader claimant') should notify the bailiff of his claim, give his address for service, and the grounds for the claim (CCR, ord. 33, r. 1(1) in CPR, sch. 2). |
| Security | Except where the claim is for the value or proceeds of goods, the interpleader claimant must make a deposit or provide security for the claim (CCR, ord. 33, r. 1(2)(b) in CPR, sch. 2). |
| Notice to judgment creditor | Court will notify judgment creditor of claim (CCR, ord. 33, r. 1(2)(a) in CPR, sch. 2). |
| Response from judgment creditor | Within four days, judgment creditor must inform the court whether he admits or disputes the claim (CCR, ord. 33, r. 2 in CPR, sch. 2). |
| Issue of interpleader proceedings | Where the claim is disputed, the court will issue an interpleader notice (form N88 or N88(1)), fix a date for the hearing and serve the notice on the judgment creditor and the interpleader claimant at least 14 days before the hearing date (CCR, ord. 33, r. 4 in CPR, sch. 2). |

### (b) Stakeholder's interpleader

| | |
|---|---|
| Jurisdiction | A person ('the applicant'), who is being, or expects to be, sued by two or more persons (the 'interpleader claimant') making opposing claims to a debt, money or goods for which the applicant is liable, may apply for interpleader relief (CCR, ord. 33, r. 6(1) in CPR, sch. 2). |
| Application | Application is made by filing a witness statement or affidavit showing that the applicant:<br>• claims no interest in the subject matter in dispute, other than for charges or costs;<br>• does not collude with any of the interpleader claimants; and<br>• is willing to pay or transfer that subject matter into court or to dispose of it as the court may direct (CCR, ord. 33, r. 6(3) in CPR, sch. 2). |
| Number of copies | One copy of the affidavit or witness statement should be filed for the court together with an additional copy for each competing interpleader claimant (CCR, ord. 33, r. 6(3) in CPR, sch. 2). |
| Time for application | Where the applicant is a defendant in a pending claim, the application should be filed within 14 days after service of the claim form. |
| Interpleader notice | Where there are no pending proceedings, the court will issue an interpleader notice (form N89). |
| Pre-trial review | The court will fix a date for a pre-trial review on receipt of the application. |
| Service | The court will serve notice of the application, form N89 (where appropriate) and copies of the affidavit or witness statement on all parties and interpleader claimants at least 21 days before the date for the pre-trial review. |

| | |
|---|---|
| Interpleader claimant's response | Within 14 days after service, the interpleader claimant must either file a notice that no interpleader claim is to be made or file particulars of the grounds for a claim. Copies for all parties should be filed. The court will serve the parties (CCR, ord. 33, r. 10 in CPR, sch. 2). |

## Procedural checklist 9 Approval of settlement or compromise to which a child or patient is party, where sole purpose of claim is to obtain court approval

| | |
|---|---|
| Part 8 claim form | Issue Part 8 claim form, including request for approval of the settlement and either set out the terms of the settlement or attach a draft consent order in form N292 (PD 21, para. 6.1). |
| Contents of Part 8 claim form | The claim form must include the following information (PD 21, para. 6.2):<br>• whether and to what extent the defendant admits liability;<br>• the age and occupation (if any) of the child or patient;<br>• the litigation friend's approval of the proposed settlement;<br>• in a personal injury case only, the circumstances of the accident, any medical reports, a schedule of damages, any evidence or police reports in any related criminal proceedings or inquest and details of any prosecution;<br>• where the settlement provides for periodical payments, the terms of the settlement or compromise. Alternatively the draft consent order should be attached to the claim form. |
| Part 8 Procedure | See procedural checklist 5. |
| Opinion on the merits | An opinion on the merits by counsel or solicitor should be supplied to the court (PD 21, para. 6.3). |
| Hearing | The application will normally be heard by a master or district judge (PD 21, para. 6.5). However, in the Chancery Division the application will be heard by a judge if the amount exceeds £100,000 (PD 2B, para. 5.1(a)). |
| Privacy | The hearing of the application to approve the settlement may be in private where it involves the interests of a child or patient (CPR, r. 39.2(3)(d); PD 39, para. 1.6). |

## Procedural checklist 10 Application to extend time for service of claim form

| | |
|---|---|
| Application notice | Form N244. The application is for the period within which the claim form may be served to be extended to a specific date. Brief reasons for the application should be included in form N244. |
| Evidence in support | Evidence in support must be filed with form N244 and will usually either be set out in the notice of application itself or in a witness statement. The evidence must state all the circumstances relied on; the date of issue of the claim; the expiry date of any extension already granted under CPR, r. 7.6; and a full explanation of why the claim form has not been served (PD 7, para. 8.2). Where the application is without notice, the evidence must also state why notice has not been given (CPR, r. 25.3( 3)). |

| | |
|---|---|
| Without notice | Application will usually be made without notice, as the defendant is not yet on the record (CPR, r. 7.6(4)(b)). Because the application is without notice to the defendant, the claimant must make full and frank disclosure of all relevant facts. |
| Fee | £50 (High Court) or £35 (county court) (CPFO, fee 2.6). |
| Hearing | As the application is made without notice, there will not normally be a hearing. However, where the application is made shortly before expiry of the period for service of the claim form and where the cause of action has become time-barred since the date of issue of the claim form, it is desirable that the application should be dealt with by an urgent hearing. |
| Service of order | A copy of any order made without notice to the defendant, whether extending time for service of the claim form or refusing to do so, must be served on the defendant, together with form N244 and any evidence in support. The order should contain a statement of the defendant's right to apply to set aside or vary the order within seven clear days of service of the order (CPR, r. 23.9). |

## Procedural checklist 11 Application for permission to serve claim form out of jurisdiction

| | |
|---|---|
| Claim form | Claimant has the choice of whether to issue the claim form before seeking permission to serve outside the jurisdiction. |
| Application | If a claim form is issued first, the application is for permission to serve outside the jurisdiction, and fee 2.6 (see 'Fee' below) is payable on the application. If a claim form is not issued first, the application is for permission to issue and to serve the claim form, and fee 1.7 (see 'Fee' below) is payable on the application. |
| Application notice | Form N244. Apply for permission under CPR, r. 6.20, to serve the defendant at his address out of the jurisdiction because [state grounds of r. 6.20 relied on; Claimant believes his claim has a reasonable prospect of success; state Defendant's address, or where it is believed he may be found. Where r. 6.20(3) is relied on state also that it is believed that there is a real issue which it is reasonable for the court to try]. Indicate that the claimant wishes to have the matter dealt with without a hearing, and that no notice should be given to the defendant. |
| Evidence in support | Evidence in form of witness statement must be filed with form N244. Evidence must show which paragraph of r. 6.20 applies to the claim; that the claimant has a reasonable prospect of success; why England and Wales is the proper place to bring the claim and state the defendant's address, or at least the country in which he may be found. Where r. 6.20(3) is relied on set out evidence for belief that there is a real issue which it is reasonable for the court to try (r. 6.21). |
| Without notice to defendant | Application will be made without notice to the defendant. In the RCJ, leave the application notice and supporting evidence in the Master's Secretary's Department, room E16. The papers will be placed before a master or district judge, who will note the order on the papers and on the court file. Because the application is made without notice to the defendant, the claimant must make full and frank disclosure of all relevant facts. |
| Fee | £50 (High Court) or £35 (county court) (CPFO, fees 1.7 and 2.6). |
| Hearing | As the application is made without notice, there will not normally be a hearing. |

## Procedural checklist 12 Admitting a claim and requesting time to pay

| Type of claim and admission | Step to be taken by defendant | Step to be taken by claimant where claimant accepts defendant's offer | Step to be taken by claimant where claimant rejects defendant's offer |
|---|---|---|---|
| Specified sum. Admitted in whole; defendant seeking time to pay (CPR, r. 14.9). | Return form N9A to claimant (r. 14.4(2)) within 14 days after service of the particulars of claim (r. 14.2). | File request for judgment, form N225, reflecting defendant's offer for payment. No fee is payable (CPFO, notes to fee 2.6). Court will enter judgment for the amount of the claim and costs, and for payment at the time and rate specified in defendant's request for time to pay (r. 14.9). | File request for judgment form N225, and N9A giving notice that claimant does not accept defendant's offer. No fee is payable (CPFO, notes to fee 2.6). Court will enter judgment for the amount of the claim and decide time and rate for payment (r. 14.10(2) and (4)), and will issue decision on form N30(2). Either party can object to the determination within 14 days after receipt of form N30(2). |
| Specified sum. Admitted in whole; defendant not seeking time to pay (r. 14.4). | Return form N9A to claimant (r. 14.4(2)) within 14 days after service of the particulars of claim (r. 14.2). | Claimant files request for judgment (form N225) and specifies the times and rates for payment. No fee is payable (CPFO, notes to fee 2.6). The court enters judgment as requested by claimant (r. 14.4(4) to (6)). | — |
| Specified sum. Admitted in part, but defendant seeks time to pay (r. 14.5). | Return forms N9A and N9B to the court (r. 14.5(2)) within 14 days after service of the particulars of claim (r. 14.2). Court sends forms N9A, N9B and N255A to claimant, requiring claimant to notify response to the court within 14 days (r. 14.53)). If defendant does not reply within 14 days, claim stayed (r. 14.5(5)(). | Within 14 days of receipt of forms N9A, N9B and N255A, from court, file request for judgment (form N255A), reflecting defendant's offer for payment. Court will enter judgment for the amount admitted and costs, and for payment at the time and rate specified in defendant's request for time to pay (r. 14.9). | Within 14 days of receipt of court notice, file request for judgment (form N255A), giving notice either:<br>• that claimant does not accept defendant's partial admission, in which case the claim will proceed as a defended claim, or<br>• that claimant accepts the partial admission in settlement of the claim but does not accept defendant's proposals for payment. The court |

| Type of claim and admission | Step to be taken by defendant | Step to be taken by claimant where claimant accepts defendant's offer | Step to be taken by claimant where claimant rejects defendant's offer |
|---|---|---|---|
| | | | will then enter judgment for the amount admitted and will calculate a rate of payment. It will notify the parties of its decision in form N30(2). Either party can object to the determination within 14 days after receipt of form N30(2) (rr. 14.10 to (14.13). |
| Specified sum. Admitted in part; defendant does not seek time to pay (r. 14.5). | Return forms N9A and N9B to the court (r. 14.5(2)) within 14 days after service of the particulars of claim (r. 14.2). Court sends forms N9A, N9B and N255A, requiring claimant to notify response to court within 14 days (r. 4.5(3)). If defendant does not reply within 14 days, claim stayed (r. 14.5(5)). | Within 14 days of receipt of forms N9A, N9B and N255A, file request for judgment (form N225A), reflecting defendant's offer for payment. No fee is payable (CPFO, notes to fee 2.6). Court enters judgment for amount offered by defendant and costs to be paid by the date or at the rate specified in form N255A (r. 14.5(7) to (9)). | File form N255A at court, indicating that partial admission is rejected and case will proceed as a defended claim. |
| Unspecified sum. Defendant admits liability without saying how much is admitted (r. 14.6). | Return form N9C to court (r. 14.6(2)) within 14 days after service of the particulars of claim (r. 14.2). Court will forward form N9C to claimant, together with form N226 (notice of admission) (r. 14.6(3)). If claimant does not respond within 14 days, claim will be stayed (r. 14.6(5)). | Within 14 days of receipt of forms N9C and N226, file completed N226 asking the court to enter judgment for an amount to be decided by the court and costs. No fee is payable (CPFO, notes to fee 2.6). Court will enter judgment and give directions, either allocating the claim to the small claims track or directing a disposal hearing (r. 14.6(6)). | — |
| Unspecified sum. Defendant admits liability and offers a | Return form N9C to court (r. 14.7(2)) within 14 days after service of | Within 14 days of receipt of notice from the court, file form | Within 14 days of receipt of notice from the court, file form |

| Type of claim and admission | Step to be taken by defendant | Step to be taken by claimant where claimant accepts defendant's offer | Step to be taken by claimant where claimant rejects defendant's offer |
|---|---|---|---|
| fixed sum in settlement of it, without seeking time to pay (r. 14.7). | the particulars of claim (r. 14.2). Court will forward form N9C to claimant, together with form N226 (notice of admission). | N226, accepting the offer. No fee is payable (CPFO, notes to fee 2.6). Court will enter judgment in accordance with the offer (r. 14.7(6) to (8)). Failing to file N226 results in a stay (r. 14.7( 4)). | N226, notifying court that offer of sum in settlement of claim rejected. No fee is payable (CPFO, notes to fee 2.6). Judgment will be entered for an amount to be decided by the court and costs. The court will give case management directions (r. 14.7(9)). |
| Unspecified sum. Defendant admits liability, offers a fixed sum in settlement and asks to pay by instalments or at a future date (r. 14.7). | Return form N9C to court (r. 14.7(2)) within 14 days after service of the particulars of claim (r. 14.2). Court will forward form N9C to claimant, together with form N226 (notice of admission). If claimant does not respond within 14 days, claim will be stayed (r. 14.7(4)). | If the offer is accepted in full, including the proposals for payment, file request for payment (form N226) and court will enter judgment for amount offered and costs at the time and rate specified in defendant's request for time to pay (r. 14.9). No fee is payable (CPFO, notes to fee 2.6). | If claimant rejects the amount offered, file request for judgment form N226. No fee is payable (CPFO, notes to fee 2.6). Court enters judgment for an amount to be decided by the court and costs (r. 14.7(9)).<br>If claimant accepts the amount offered, but not the proposals for payment, file form N226. The court will enter judgment and calculate the rate of payment, and will notify the parties of its decision in form N30(2). Either party can object within 14 days after receipt of form N30(2) (r. 14.10). |

## Procedural checklist 13 Time limits for responding to claim by acknowledging service and/or filing a defence

| Step to be taken | Place of service of claim form | Time limit |
|---|---|---|
| Acknowledgment to be filed at court | Within the jurisdiction. | 14 days after service of particulars of claim (whether or not particulars of claim served with claim form) (CPR, r. 10.3(1)). |

| Step to be taken | Place of service of claim form | Time limit |
|---|---|---|
| | Out of the jurisdiction under r. 6.19(1) in Scotland, Northern Ireland, or in a European territory of another contracting State, or under r. 6.19(1A) in another EU State (apart from Denmark). | 21 days after service of particulars of claim (r. 6.22(2)). |
| | Out of the jurisdiction under r. 6.19(1) in any other territory of a contracting State. | 31 days after service of particulars of claim (r. 6.22(3)). |
| | Out of the jurisdiction with permission under r. 6.20. | Court will specify the time for acknowledging service, calculated by reference to the table at the end of PD 6B (r. 6.21(4); PD 6B, paras 7.2(1) and 7.3). |
| Filing of defence at court, where no acknowledgment filed | Within the jurisdiction. | 14 days after service of particulars of claim (CPR, r. 15.4(1)(a)). |
| | Out of the jurisdiction under r. 6.19(1) in Scotland, Northern Ireland, or in a European territory of another contracting State, or under r. 6.19(1A) in another EU State (apart from Denmark). | 21 days after service of particulars of claim (r. 6.23(2)). |
| | Out of the jurisdiction under r. 6.19(1) in any other territory of a contracting State. | 31 days after service of particulars of claim (r. 6.23(3)). |
| | Out of the jurisdiction with permission under r. 6.20. | Court will specify the time for acknowledging service, calculated by reference to the table at the end of PD 6B (r. 6.21(4) PD 6B, paras 7.2(3) and 7.4(1)). |
| Filing of defence at court, following filing of acknowledgment | Within the jurisdiction. | 28 days after service of particulars of claim (CPR, r. 15.4(1)(b)). |
| | Out of the jurisdiction under r. 6.19(1) in Scotland, Northern Ireland, or in a European territory of another contracting State, or under r. 6.19(1A) in another EU State (apart from Denmark). | 35 days after service of particulars of claim (r. 6.23(2)). |
| | Out of the jurisdiction under r. 6.19(1) in any other territory of a contracting State. | 45 days after service of particulars of claim (r. 6.23(3)). |
| | Out of the jurisdiction with permission under r. 6.20. | Court will specify the time for acknowledging service, calculated by reference to the table at the end of PD 6B, plus an additional 14 days (PD 6B, paras 7.2(3) and 7.4(2)). |

## Procedural checklist 14 Procedure for disputing the court's jurisdiction

| | |
|---|---|
| Acknowledgment | File acknowledgment of service within 14 days after service of particulars of claim, if served in the jurisdiction, within 21 days after service of the particulars of claim, if served in Europe under CPR, r. 6.19, or within the period given in the court order, if served out of the jurisdiction with the court's permission, under r. 6.21 (r. 11(2)). Tick only the 'intention to contest the jurisdiction' box. See procedural checklist 13. |

| | |
|---|---|
| Application—time | Within 14 days after filing an acknowledgment make an application under Part 23 for an order that the court has no jurisdiction to try the claim (r. 11(4)). |
| Extension of time | If more time is needed, apply under r. 3.1(2)(a) for an extension of the time limit laid down in r. 11(4). An extension of time for service of the defence will not carry with it an extension of time for an application to dispute the jurisdiction (*Montrose Investments Ltd v Orion Nominees Ltd* [2001] CP Rep 109). |
| Application notice | Form N244. Where service out of the jurisdiction is contested, application is for any order giving permission for service out of the jurisdiction under r. 6.20 to be set aside, for service of the claim form to be set aside and for the proceedings to be stayed. |
| Evidence in support | Must be filed and served with form N244. |
| Fee | £100 (High Court) or £65 (county court) (CPFO, fee 2.5). |
| Service | On defendant as soon as practicable after filing application notice, and at least three days before hearing (CPR, r. 23.7(1)). |
| Costs | Both parties should file and serve costs schedules in form N260 24 hours before hearing (PD 43–48, para. 13.5(4)). |
| Defence | No need to file defence before hearing (CPR, r. 11(9)(a)). If the application is unsuccessful, the court must give directions for filing and service of the defence (r. 11.7(c)). Claimant cannot enter default judgment (r. 12.3). |

## Procedural checklist 15 Request for entry of judgment in default

| | |
|---|---|
| Claim form | Serve claim form on defendant in accordance with CPR, r. 6.2. |
| Certificate of service of claim form | If claim form is served by claimant rather than court, file certificate of service of claim form, within seven days after service of claim form (r. 6.14(2)). |
| Particulars of claim | Serve particulars of claim, either with claim form or within 14 days after service of claim form, and within period of validity of the claim form (r. 7.4(1) and (2)). |
| Certificate of service of particulars of claim | Where the particulars of claim are served separately from the claim form, within seven days of service of the particulars on the defendant, file a copy of the particulars and a certificate that they have been served (rr. 6.10 and (7.4(3)). |
| Failure to respond: request for judgment | Wait 14 days after service of particulars of claim (whether served with claim form or later) (rr. 10.3 and 15.4). (For time limits where service effected out of the jurisdiction, see procedural checklist 13.) If neither acknowledgment of service nor defence filed by then, file request for default judgment in form N205A or N225 (for specified sum) or N205B or N227 (for unspecified sum) (r. 12.4(1)(a); PD 12, para. 3). No fee is payable (CPFO, notes to fee 2.6). |
| Failure to file defence: request for judgment | If acknowledgment filed within 14 days after service of particulars of claim, wait until 28 days after service of particulars of claim (CPR, rr. 10.3 and 15.4). (For time limits where service effected out of the jurisdiction, see procedural checklist 13.) If defence not filed by then, file request for default judgment in form N205A or N225 (for specified sum) or N205B or N227 (for unspecified sum) (r. 12.4(1)(b); PD 12, para. 3). No fee is payable (CPFO, notes to fee 2.6). |

| | |
|---|---|
| Calculating time | The periods of 14 and 28 days above should be calculated to exclude the date of service of the particulars of claim but to include the date of filing of the acknowledgment or service of the particulars of claim (CPR, r. 2.8(3)(b)), and must take into account the deemed dates of service in r. 6.7 (see **15.36**). |

## Procedural checklist 16 Application for entry of judgment in default

| | |
|---|---|
| When required | Claims for costs (other than fixed costs); claims for delivery up (where the defendant has not offered the alternative of paying the value of the goods claimed); claims by one spouse or civil partner against the other in tort and claims against children and patients. Also, the following cases where the defendant has not filed an acknowledgment: claims where service has been effected out of the jurisdiction under CPR, r. 6.19, or on a defendant domiciled in a Convention territory or Regulation State; claims against States, diplomats and bodies granted immunity under the International Organisations Acts 1968 and 1981. |
| Preliminary steps | • Serve claim form and particulars of claim and file certificates of service (procedural checklist 15).<br>• In an application against a child or patient, apply for a litigation friend to be appointed under CPR, r. 21.6. |
| Time | Wait 14 days after service of particulars of claim (whether served with claim form or later) (rr. 10.3 and 15.4). If neither acknowledgment of service nor defence filed by then, make application under Part 23. If acknowledgment filed within 14 days after service of particulars of claim, wait until 28 days after service of particulars of claim (rr. 10.3 and 15.4) before making application under Part 23. Time limits to be calculated as in procedural checklist 15. (For time limits where service effected out of the jurisdiction, see procedural checklist 13.) |
| Application notice | Form N244. Application is for judgment to be entered against the defendant on the ground that he has not filed an acknowledgment of service or defence, as the case may be. Where application not on notice, state on form N244 that claimant wishes to have the matter dealt with without a hearing. Where the defendant is an individual, state his/her date of birth, if known. |
| Evidence in support | An application must be supported by evidence if it is for default judgment<br>• against a child or patient;<br>• in a claim in tort between spouses or civil partners;<br>• against a State;<br>• against a defendant who was served outside the jurisdiction, or inside the jurisdiction when domiciled in a Convention territory or Regulation State, and who has not acknowledged service (see r. 12.11(4)(a))<br>(r. 12.11(3) and PD 12, para. 4). |
| Service of evidence | Evidence in support need not be served on defendant who failed to file an acknowledgment of service (CPR, r. 12.11(2)). |
| Notice | Generally the application is with notice, but will be without notice where the claim was served under the Civil Jurisdiction and Judgments Act 1982 or the Jurisdiction and Judgments Regulation or where application is made against a State and in either case the defendant has failed to file an acknowledgment (CPR, r. 12.11(4) and (5)). |

| | |
|---|---|
| Fee | £100 (High Court); £65 (county court) (CPFO, fee 2.5); £55 (High Court); £35 (county court) where application without notice (CPFO, fee 2.6). |
| Service of N244 | Where application on notice, serve defendant as soon as practicable after filing application notice, and at least three days before hearing (CPR, r. 23.7(1)). |
| Costs | Where application on notice, both parties should file and serve costs schedules in form N260 24 hours before hearing (PD 43–48, para. 13.5(4)). The court will not summarily assess the costs of a child or patient, unless the solicitor acting or the child or patient has waived the right to further costs (PD 43–48, para. 13.11(1)). |
| Hearing | Normally before master or district judge. Where the application is made without notice, there will not normally be a hearing. |

## Procedural checklist 17 Counterclaim (Part 20)

| | |
|---|---|
| Timing | Generally, at the same time as filing the defence in order to avoid the need for permission (CPR, r. 20.4(2)). Can be made up to trial, but obtaining permission gets progressively more difficult. |
| Forms | N211. Simple counterclaims can be made on forms N9B or N9D. |
| Title | Must comply with PD 20, paras 7.1 to 7.11. |
| Issue | Issue fee is payable when the counterclaim is filed (CPFO, fees and 1.5 and 1.6). |
| Pleading | Particulars of the counterclaim, verified by a statement of truth, can be set out in a counterclaim, but if the defendant also intends to defend the main proceedings, the defence and counterclaim should normally form one document with the counterclaim following the defence (PD 20, para. 6.1). |
| Counterclaim against a person other than the claimant | Most counterclaims are made against the claimant, but it is possible to bring a counterclaim against a person other than a claimant (CPR, r. 20.5). Permission is always required (r. 20.5(1)), and, unless the court otherwise directs, the application is made without notice (r. 20.5(2)). The new party is added as an additional party (r. 20.5(1)). |
| Permission to issue | Required if a defendant wishes to file a counterclaim after filing a defence (r. 20.4(2)). Issue application notice with written evidence in support:<br>• stating the stage the main proceedings have reached;<br>• stating the nature of the counterclaim;<br>• summarising the facts on which the counterclaim is based;<br>• stating the name and address of the defendant to the counterclaim;<br>• explaining any delay where this is a factor; and<br>• providing a timetable of the steps in the claim to date.<br>As rr. 20.5(2) and 20.7(5) do not apply to this situation, the application is made on notice to the claimant. |
| Documents to be served | Claim form; counterclaim or defence and counterclaim. |
| Service | CPR, Part 6, applies. |
| Response | Acknowledgment of service (Part 10) does not apply (r. 20.4(3)). The claimant should file and serve a defence to counterclaim or a reply and defence to counterclaim within 14 days of deemed service of the counterclaim (rr. 15.4(1), 20.3(1); PD 20, para. 6.2). |

| | |
|---|---|
| Default judgment | May be entered (CPR, r. 12.3(2); PD 20, para. 3). |
| Directions | The effect of rr. 20.3(2)(c) and 20.13, together with PD 20, para. 5.1, is that the relevant directions governing counterclaims are (unless the court gives special directions for the counterclaim) those given in the main proceedings. |

## Procedural checklist 18 Additional claim (against third party)

| | |
|---|---|
| Timing | Generally, before or at the same time as filing the defence in order to avoid the need for permission (CPR, r. 20.7(3)). Can be made up to trial, but obtaining permission gets progressively more difficult. |
| Form | Additional claim form, form N211. |
| Title of claim | Must comply with PD 20, paras 7.1 to 7.11. |
| Issue | Issue fee is the same as for Part 7 claim forms (see CPFO, fee 1).<br>Issue takes place when the claim form is sealed and on the date entered by the court on the claim form (CPR, r. 20.7(2) and r. 7.2(2)). |
| Pleading | Particulars of the additional claim must be contained in or served with the claim form (r. 20.7(4)), and must be verified by a statement of truth in the form '[ I believe] [the defendant believes] that the facts stated in this statement of case are true.' (PD 20, para 4.2). |
| Permission to issue | Required if a defendant wishes to issue an additional claim after filing a defence (CPR, r. 20.7(3)).<br>Issue application notice (see procedural checklist 19) with written evidence in support:<br>• stating the stage the main proceedings have reached;<br>• stating the nature of the additional claim, question or relief;<br>• summarising the facts on which the additional claim is based;<br>• stating the name and address of the third party;<br>• explaining any delay where this is a factor; and<br>• providing a timetable of the steps in the claim to date.<br>Unless the court otherwise directs, the application is made without notice (r. 20.7(5)). |
| Documents to be served on third party | Additional claim form (N211);<br>notes for defendant on replying to the additional claim form (N211C);<br>particulars of the additional claim (either contained in or served with the claim form) (r. 20.7(4));<br>forms for defending and admitting the claim (forms N9A and N9B or N9C and N9D as appropriate);<br>form for acknowledging service (form N213) (r. 20.12(1));<br>copies of every statement of case previously served (r. 20.12(1)(d)(i));<br>notice of public funding or of any CFA (form N251); and<br>such other documents as the court may direct (r. 20.12(1)(ii)). |
| Service | CPR, Part 6, applies. |
| Time to serve | An additional claim issued without permission must be served within 14 days after the additional claim is issued by the court (r. 20.8(1)(b)).<br>Any order for permission will give directions for service (r. 20.8(3)). |
| Effect of service | Third party becomes a party to the proceedings on being served (r. 20.10(1)). |

| | |
|---|---|
| Service on other parties | Copies of the additional claim form must be served on all existing parties (r. 20.12(2)). |
| Response | Third party must acknowledge service or file a defence within 14 days of deemed service (r. 6.7, 9.2, 10.3, 14.2, 15.4 and 20.3(1)). |
| Defence | A defence to the additional claim must be filed within 14 days of deemed service of the additional claim, or within 28 days if an acknowledgment of service is filed (r. 15.4). Time may be extended by consent for up to 28 days (r. 15.5). A copy of the defence to the additional claim must be served on every other party (r. 15.6). It must be verified by a statement of truth (PD 15, paras 2.1, 2.2). |
| Default judgment | Subject to r. 20.11(2), default judgment is not available (r. 20.3(3)). Instead, if there is no response within the prescribed period, the third party is deemed to admit the additional claim and is bound by any judgment or decision in the main proceedings (r. 20.11(2)(a)). If default judgment is given against the defendant and if the defendant satisfies that judgment, the defendant can enter default judgment for a contribution or indemnity against the third party by filing a request (r. 20.11(3)). Otherwise, default judgment against a third party is possible only with permission (r. 20.11(3), (4)). |
| Directions | After a defence to an additional claim is filed the court will list the matter for case management directions (r. 20.13(1) and PD 20, para 5.1). The court:<br>• will ensure, so far as practicable, that the main proceedings and additional claim are managed together (r. 20.13(2));<br>• may treat the hearing as a summary judgment hearing (PD 20, para. 5.3);<br>• may dismiss the additional claim;<br>• may require the additional claim to be dealt with separately from the main proceedings (CPR, r. 20.9(1)(c));<br>• may give directions about the way the claim should be dealt with (PD 20, para. 5.3);<br>• may give directions as to the third party's involvement at trial; and<br>• may give directions about the extent to which the third party will be bound by any judgment or decision in the main proceedings. |

## Procedural checklist 19 Interim application without notice

| | |
|---|---|
| Application notice | Issue and file form N244, stating whether a hearing is sought (CPR, r. 23.6). County court interim injunction applications should be on form N16A. |
| Evidence in support | Normally required. In addition to covering evidence required for the order sought (PD 25, para. 3.3), written evidence must:<br>• state reasons why notice was not given (CPR, r. 25.3(3));<br>• where secrecy is not essential, state what steps have been taken to give informal notice to the respondent (PD 25, para. 4.3(3)).<br>Usually in the form of witness statements, but affidavits are required for freezing and search orders (PD 25, para. 3.1).<br>Applicant is under a duty of full and frank disclosure, which includes a duty to disclose adverse matters which could be discovered on making reasonable inquiries. |
| Fee | £50 (High Court); £35 (county court) (CPFO, fee 2.6). |

| | |
|---|---|
| Draft order | Usually required for without notice applications as most are complex. If application is for an interim injunction, use form PF 39 CH (intended actions) or PF 40 CH (after issue). Freezing and search orders should follow the standard forms in PD 25. |
| Undertakings | Should be incorporated into the order as required (e.g., to issue and serve a claim form (CPR, r. 25.2(3)), to file and serve written evidence, to pay damages (injunctions)). |
| Skeleton argument | Required for most High Court applications dealt with by judges. Should state how the requirements for the relief sought are satisfied. File two clear days before the hearing (if possible). |
| Arrange hearing | Urgent applications: emergency telephone number for the High Court is (020) 7947 6000. See PD 25, para. 4.5. |
| Hearing | Explain, among other things:<br>• why without notice;<br>• whether any informal notice has been given, and why;<br>• points relevant to the duty of full and frank disclosure;<br>• any variations on standard-form orders. |
| Note of hearing | Advocate should produce note of the hearing. |
| Order | Should include a statement of the respondent's right to apply to set aside (CPR, r. 23.9(3)). It also often provides for listing a hearing to review to be heard on notice. Application notice, evidence in support and note of the hearing should be served with the order. |

## Procedural checklist 20 Interim application with notice

| | |
|---|---|
| Timing | As soon as it becomes apparent that it is desirable or necessary (PD 23, para. 2.7).<br>Other than urgent applications, they can only be made once applicant has come on the record. Applications can be made after judgment (CPR, r. 25.2). |
| Application notice | Form N244, which must be filed (r. 23.3). It must state the order sought and the reason for applying (r. 23.6) and provide a time estimate. County court interim injunction applications should be on form N16A. |
| Draft order | Not required for simple applications. Drafts of more complex orders should be brought to the hearing (PD 23, para. 12.1) together with a copy on 3.5 inch disk. |
| Evidence in support | Consider whether evidence is required. If so, consider whether to use part C of N244, witness statements, affidavits or statements of case. Must be served and filed (if not already done) with the N244. |
| Combined applications | Are encouraged (CPR, r. 1.4(2)(i)), and should be combined with any existing case management hearing (PD 23, para. 2.8). |
| Fee | £100 (High Court); £65 (county court) (CPFO, fee 2.5). |
| Service | On respondent as soon as practicable after N244 is filed, and at least three clear days before hearing (CPR, r. 23.7(1)) (unless some other period is prescribed, such as for summary judgment and interim payments). |

| | |
|---|---|
| Cross-applications | Respondent may issue a cross-application returnable at the same hearing date as the applicant's application. This may require relisting of both applications if the original time estimate is insufficient for both. |
| Directions | Sometimes directions are made for filing and serving evidence and skeleton arguments in the application (PD 23, para. 9.2). |
| Respondent's written evidence | Serve and file in accordance with directions, if any, or as soon as possible (PD 23, para. 9.4) and in sufficient time to avoid the need to adjourn. |
| Applicant's evidence in reply | Serve and file in accordance with directions, if any, or as soon as possible (PD 23, para. 9.5) and in sufficient time to avoid the need to adjourn. |
| Application bundles | In substantial applications bundles of material documents should be prepared (usually at least two clear days before the hearing). |
| Skeleton arguments | Not mandatory for applications before circuit judges, masters and district judges, but if used should be served and filed the day before the hearing. Usually required for applications before High Court judges, where they should be filed two clear days before the hearing. |
| Costs schedules | Both parties should file and serve costs schedules in form N260 24 hours before the hearing (PD 43–48, para. 13.5(4)). (But see PD 43–48, paras 13.9 and 13.11, where the receiving party is publicly funded, or a child or patient.) |
| Hearing | Most applications should be listed for hearing by a master or district judge. Injunctions should usually be heard by judges. Freezing and search orders should normally be dealt with by High Court judges. Most applications are heard in chambers even if technically they are dealt with in public. The court may review the case and give case management directions (PD 23, para. 2.9). |
| Costs orders | If the hearing is less than a day, usually there will be a summary assessment (PD 43–48, para. 13.2(2)). |

## Procedural checklist 21 Application for striking out

| | |
|---|---|
| General procedure | Follow procedural checklist 20. |
| Application notice | E.g.: 'for an order that the Particulars of Claim be struck out under CPR, r. 3.4, and judgment be entered for the Defendant with costs because the Particulars of Claim disclose no reasonable grounds for bringing the claim [is an abuse of the court's process] [is likely to obstruct the just disposal of the proceedings]' |
| Combined application | It is common to combine the various grounds in CPR, r. 3.4 in a single application, and also to seek summary judgment in the alternative. |
| Fee to costs orders | See procedural checklist 20. |
| Claim totally without merit | If the court strikes out a claimant's statement of case and considers it is totally without merit, it must record that fact in the order (r. 3.4(5)), and consider making a civil restraint order. |

| Procedural checklist 22 | Application by party for summary judgment |
|---|---|
| Timing | After acknowledgment of service or filing defence (**34.2**). Generally before filing allocation questionnaire (PD 26, para. 5.3(1)). |
| Application notice | Form N244. Apply for 'summary judgment under CPR, Part 24 and costs because the [claimant has no real prospect of succeeding on the claim / issue] or [defendant has no real prospect of successfully defending the claim / issue] and the Applicant knows of no other reason why disposal of the claim or issue should await trial' (PD 24, para. 2(3)). If the application relates to specific issues, these must be identified (CPR, r. 24.4(3)(b)). Also add to the N244: 'Take Notice that if the Respondent wishes to rely on written evidence at the hearing, he must file and serve the written evidence at least 7 days before the summary judgment hearing' (PD 24, para. 2(5)). |
| Evidence in support | Must be served and filed with the N244. |
| Combined applications | It is common to combine a summary judgment application with an application for striking out under CPR, r. 3.4, or for interim payment under r. 25.7. |
| Fee | £100 (High Court); £65 (county court) (CPFO, fee 2.5). |
| Service | On respondent at least 14 days before hearing (CPR, r. 24.4(3)). |
| Respondent's written evidence | Serve and file at least seven days before hearing (r. 24.5(2)). |
| Applicant's evidence in reply | File and serve at least three days before the hearing (r. 24.5(2)). |
| Main proceedings | No need to file defence (r. 24.4(2)). Claimant cannot enter default judgment if defendant is applying for summary judgment (r. 12.3(3)(a)(ii)). Court will not normally allocate to a track before hearing application to strike out (PD 26, para. 5.3(2)). |
| Costs | Both parties should file and serve costs schedules in form N260 24 hours before the hearing (PD 43–48, para. 13.5(4)). |
| Hearing | Normally before master or district judge (PD 24, para. 3(1)). In addition to determining the application, the court usually gives directions (CPR, r. 24.6). |

| Procedural checklist 23 | Proposal by court for order for summary judgment |
|---|---|
| Notice of date for hearing | At least 14 days before the hearing. |
| Written evidence | Both sides file and (unless the court otherwise orders) serve written evidence at least seven days before the hearing (CPR, r. 24.5(3)(a)). |
| Evidence in reply | Both sides may file and (unless the court otherwise orders) serve written evidence in reply at least three days before the hearing (r. 24.5(3)(b)). |
| Costs | Both parties should file and serve costs schedules in form N260 24 hours before the hearing (PD 43–48, para. 13.5(4)). |

## Procedural checklist 24 Application for an order for interim payment

| | |
|---|---|
| Timing | After period for filing acknowledgment of service (CPR, r. 25.6(1)). More than one application can be made (r. 25.6(2)). |
| Application notice | Form N244. Apply for 'an interim payment under CPR, r. 25.7, and costs because the [defendant has admitted liability] [the claimant has obtained judgment for damages to be assessed] [if the claim went to trial the claimant would obtain judgment for a substantial amount of money (other than costs) against the defendant] [the claim is for possession of land and if the claim went to trial the defendant would be held liable to pay the claimant a sum of money for occupation and use of the land while the claim is pending]'. |
| Evidence in support | Must be served and filed with the N244. It must deal with the matters set out in PD 25B, para. 2.1, and exhibit all documents in support, including (in personal injuries claims) medical reports (para. 2.2). |
| Combined applications | Interim payment applications are commonly combined with applications for summary judgment. |
| Fee | £100 (High Court); £65 (county court) (CPFO, fee 2.5). |
| Service | On respondent at least 14 days before hearing (CPR, r. 25.6(3)). |
| Respondent's written evidence | Serve and file at least seven days before hearing (r. 25.6(4)). |
| Applicant's evidence in reply | File and serve at least three days before the hearing (r. 25.6(5)). |
| Costs | Both parties should file and serve costs schedules in form N260 24 hours before the hearing (PD 43–48, para. 13.5(4)). |
| Hearing | Normally before master or district judge (PD 24, para. 3(1)). In addition to determining the application, the court may give directions (PD 23, para. 2.9). |
| Instalments | If an interim payment is payable by instalments, the order must comply with PD 25B, para. 3. |
| Trial | The fact that an interim payment has been made should not be mentioned to the trial judge until all questions on liability and quantum have been decided (CPR, r. 25.9), unless the defendant agrees. |
| Final judgment | Where an interim payment has previously been made, the final judgment must include details in a preamble, deduct the interim payments from the amount of the judgment, and make any necessary adjustments or orders for repayment (PD 25B, para. 5; PD 40B, para. 6). |

## Procedural checklist 25 Standard disclosure

| | |
|---|---|
| When first retained | Inform clients of their duty to retain disclosable documents (*Rockwell Machine Tool Co. Ltd v E. P. Barrus (Concessionaires) Ltd* [1968] 1 WLR 693). |
| Pre-action | Preliminary disclosure of documents should often take place in accordance with PD Protocols and any pre-action protocol applicable to the claim. This is not standard disclosure, but a means of providing the other side with the key documents to inform them of the nature and strength of the case. |

| | |
|---|---|
| Timing for standard disclosure | In accordance with directions made by the court. In most fast track and multi-track claims directions are made when the claim is allocated to a track (CPR, rr. 28.2(1), 28.3, 29.2(1)(a) and PD 29, para.4) or at the first case management conference (CPR, r. 29.2(1)(b)) and these typically include directions for standard disclosure. |
| Normal directions | (1) Standard disclosure by 4 weeks after directions (PD 28, para. 3.12).<br>(2) Requests for inspection of listed documents within 7 days thereafter (CPR, r. 31.15(a)).<br>(3) Inspection of documents, or provision of copies, within 7 days thereafter (r. 31.15(b) and (c)). |
| Documents to be disclosed | Standard disclosure covers (r. 31.6) documents in a party's control (r. 31.8):<br>(a) on which the disclosing party relies;<br>(b) which adversely affect his own case;<br>(c) which adversely affect another party's case;<br>(d) which support another party's case; and<br>(e) which are specified by a PD (at present there is no relevant PD). |
| Documents | Anything on which information of any description is recorded (r. 31.4). Includes papers (whether written, pictures or photographs); video and sound recordings; computer records, files, mobile phone texts and emails; metadata; inscriptions on metal, wood and stone. |
| Control | A document is in a party's control (r. 31.8) if:<br>(a) it is or was in his physical possession;<br>(b) he has or has had a right to possession of it; or<br>(c) he has or has had a right to inspect or take copies of it. |
| Search | Each party must make a reasonable search for disclosable documents (r. 31.7). |
| Method of giving disclosure | Usually by serving a list of documents (r. 31.10(2), form N265).<br>Parties may agree in writing to give disclosure without making a list or without a disclosure statement (r. 31.10(8)).<br>Parties may agree in writing, or the court may direct, that disclosure and/or inspection should take place in stages (r. 31.13). |
| List of documents | The list (N265) must (r. 31.10):<br>(a) Identify the documents concisely and in a convenient order.<br>(b) Identify privileged documents, stating the grounds on which it is claimed there is a right or duty to withhold inspection (r. 31.19(3)).<br>(c) Identify documents no longer in the party's control, stating what has happened to them.<br>(d) Include a disclosure statement in the form set out in the annex to PD 31 (PD 31, para. 4.1). |
| Signing disclosure statement | (a) Should normally be signed by the party (r. 31.10(6): exceptions are set out in r. 31.10(7) to (9)).<br>(b) Legal representative must ensure person signing understands the duty of disclosure in Part 31 (PD 31, para. 4.4).<br>(c) Companies, firms etc. sign by a duly authorised officer. The disclosure statement must include that person's name and address, the office or position held, and explain why he or she is an appropriate person to make the statement (CPR, r. 31.10(7) and PD 31, para. 4.3).<br>(d) An insurer, or the Motor Insurers' Bureau, may sign if they have a financial interest in the claim (PD 31, para. 4.7). |
| Inspection | The party seeking to inspect must give written notice (by letter) (CPR, r. 31.15(a)), which must be complied with within 7 days. |

| | |
|---|---|
| | (a) Inspection may take place by attendance at the other side's offices or solicitor's office (r. 31.15(b)).<br>(b) Inspection usually takes place by making a written request for photocopies, with the inspecting party undertaking to pay reasonable copying costs (r. 31.15(c)). |
| Continuing duty | Each party has a continuing duty to disclose documents subsequently coming into their control. If this happens they must immediately notify the other parties (r. 31.11) by serving a supplemental list (PD 31, para. 3.3). |

## Procedural checklist 26 Specific disclosure

| | |
|---|---|
| Timing | Usually after standard disclosure.<br>A request for the documents to be sought in the application should be made first by letter. |
| Application | Application notice (form N244).Wording for Part A:<br>'. . . intend to apply for an order (a draft of which is attached) that the [claimant/defendant] do give specific disclosure of documents because [the claimant/defendant] [has failed to give full standard disclosure] [further disclosure is necessary in order to investigate this claim fully]'. |
| Form of order | (1) The [claimant/defendant] do give specific disclosure of documents by filing and serving a supplementary list of documents in form N265 by 4 p.m. on [date] specifying whether each of the [documents] and/or [classes of documents] specified in the schedule to this order are presently in its control, and if not, specifying which of those [documents] and/or [classes of documents] are no longer in its control (and indicating what has happened to such documents), and also specifying which of those [documents] and/or [classes of documents] it claims a right or duty to withhold inspection of.<br>(2) The [claimant/defendant] do make any request for inspection in writing within 7 days after service of the list of documents.<br>(3) The [claimant/defendant] do provide the [claimant/defendant] with copies of the requested documents within 7 days of receipt of the request.<br>A schedule attached to the application, or to a draft order, should set out concisely and in a convenient order the documents and classes of documents sought from the other side. |
| Written evidence | Is required (PD 31, para. 5.2), and is typically given in a witness statement (although Part C of the N244 can be used). The evidence should:<br>(a) Exhibit the lists of documents provided by the other side.<br>(b) Exhibit relevant correspondence.<br>(c) Deal with each document or class of document in the schedule to the application:<br>(i) Explaining why it is believed to be in the control of the other side; and<br>(ii) Explaining why it should be disclosed (because it is relevant to an issue in the case, and should have been disclosed under standard disclosure, or because it is a 'train of inquiry' document, explaining the value of the document in investigating the claim). |

| | |
|---|---|
| Issue application | See procedural checklist 20, and CPR, Part 23. Fee £100 (High Court); £65 (county court) (CPFO, fee 2.5). |
| Serve application | At least 3 clear days before the return day (CPR, rr. 23.7(1) and 2.8(3)). |

## Procedural checklist 27 Non-party disclosure

| | |
|---|---|
| Timing | At any time after proceedings are issued (Supreme Court Act 1981, s. 34(2); County Courts Act 1984, s. 53(2); CPR, r. 31.17(1)).<br>A request for the documents to be sought in the application should be made first by letter. |
| Application | Application notice (form N244). Wording for Part A:<br>'. . . intend to apply for an order pursuant to the [Supreme Court Act 1981, s. 34(2)] [County Courts Act 1984, s. 53(2)] that [name of person with the documents] give non-party disclosure of documents because it has in its control documents which are likely to support the [claimant's/defendant's] case and disclosure is necessary in order to dispose fairly of the claim or to save costs'. |
| Form of order | (1) [Name of person with the documents] do by 4 p.m. on [date] serve on the [claimant's/defendant's] solicitors a list of documents in form N265 specifying whether each of the [documents] and / or [classes of documents] specified in the schedule to this order are presently in its control, and if not, specifying which of those [documents] and/or [classes of documents] are no longer in its control (and indicating what has happened to such documents), and also specifying which of those [documents] and/or [classes of documents] it claims a right or duty to withhold inspection of.<br>(2) The [claimant/defendant] do make any request for inspection of the documents disclosed by [name of person with the documents] in writing within 7 days after service of the list of documents.<br>(3) [Name of person with the documents] do provide the [claimant/defendant] with copies of the requested documents within 7 days of receipt of the request.<br>A schedule attached to the application, or to a draft order, should set out concisely and in a convenient order the documents and classes of documents sought from the non-party. |
| Written evidence | Is required (r. 31.17(2)), and is typically given in a witness statement (although Part C of the N244 can be used). The evidence should:<br>(a) Exhibit relevant correspondence.<br>(b) Deal with each document or class of document in the schedule to the application:<br>(i) explaining why it is believed to be in the control of the non-party;<br>(ii) explaining how it is likely to support the case of the applicant or adversely affect the case of another party (r. 31.17(3)(a));<br>(iii) explaining why disclosure is necessary in order to dispose fairly of the claim or to save costs (r. 31.17(3)(b)). |
| Issue application | See procedural checklist 20, and Part 23. Fee £100 (High Court); £65 (county court) (CPFO, fee 2.5). |
| Serve application | At least 3 clear days before the return day (rr. 23.7(1) and 2.8(3)). |

## Procedural checklist 28 Trial preparation

| Item | Timing | Action |
|---|---|---|
| Witness availability | Before listing for trial | Communicate with lay and expert witnesses, and also counsel, to obtain available dates (and reasons). |
| Witness abroad or incapacitated | Several months before trial | Consider best means of adducing evidence from the witness:<br>(a) Hearsay statement.<br>(b) Letter of request.<br>(c) Video link.<br>(d) Deposition. |
| Listing for trial | In accordance with case management directions | |
| Inform witnesses | Receipt of trial date or window | Write to lay and expert witnesses confirming trial date or window and seeking confirmation of the witness's availability. |
| Pre-trial review (if directed in case management directions) | 8–10 weeks before trial | Most common in multi-track claims.<br>Brief trial advocate to attend.<br>May result in further directions, settling a statement of issues, and fixing a trial timetable. |
| Statement of issues | As directed | May need to be settled and agreed between the parties after a pre-trial review. |
| Brief counsel | Sufficient time before trial | Prepare counsel's brief and supporting trial bundles or papers for the trial bundle.<br>Agree fees with counsel's clerk.<br>Even for simple cases counsel should be briefed at least a week in advance because counsel has to prepare a skeleton argument. In complex claims a period of months may be required. Counsel will also often advise on further pre-trial preparation that may be required. |
| Witness summonses | At least 2 weeks before trial | Issue witness summonses for unwilling witnesses (form N20). Fee £50 (High Court); £35 (county court) (CPFO, fee 2.7).<br>Serve at least 7 clear days (rr. 2.8(2) and 34.5(1)) before the date the witness is required to attend, bearing in mind deemed dates of service (r. 6.7).<br>Include witness expenses. |
| Reading guide and time estimate | Before lodging trial bundle | In QBD and ChD reading lists and time estimates signed by counsel must be lodged with trial bundles (Practice Direction (Royal Courts of Justice: Reading Lists and Time Estimates) [2000] 1 WLR 208). |
| Trial bundles | c. 14 days before trial | Defendants should notify claimant of documents they wish to be included. |
| | 3 to 7 days before trial | Copies for judge, witness box and all parties. |
| | At least 7 days before ChD trials | Paginated and prepared in accordance with PD 39. |

| | | |
|---|---|---|
| Skeleton argument (required in the High Court, often directed or desirable in the county courts) | As directed 2 clear days before HC trials | Usually simultaneous exchange, but directions may provide for sequential exchange. Lodge at list office (Queen's Bench Guide, para. 7.11.11) or with judge's clerk (Chancery Guide, para. 7.26). |
| Authorities | 4 p.m. day before trial<br>9 a.m. trial day | Advocates should exchange lists of authorities (e.g., Chancery Guide, para. 7.33).<br>Provide usher with list of authorities (Queen's Bench Guide, para. 7.11.8; Chancery Guide, para. 7.32). |
| Adjournment | As soon as need arises | Immediately inform court and other parties in writing, seeking adjournment. If not dealt with administratively, issue application in accordance with Part 23 (see r. 3.1(2)(b)). |
| Statement of costs (fast track trials) | 24 hours before trial | Form N260. PD 43–48, para. 13.2. |

## Procedural checklist 29 Offer to settle (from 6 April 2007)

| | |
|---|---|
| Timing | Can be made before or after issue of proceedings. Should be made once an appraisal has been made of the merits and value of the claim. Should be made, if possible, more than 21 days before the trial. |
| Method | Form N242A is the prescribed form, but is not obligatory, and the offer can be made by letter. |
| Relevant period | Normally, the period of not less than 21 days after the offer is made specified as the period within which the defendant will be liable for the claimant's costs if the Part 36 offer is accepted. If the offer is made less than 21 days before trial, the relevant period ends with the end of the trial or such other period as the court determines (CPR,r. 36.3(1)(c)). |
| Form | (a) Must be in writing (r. 36.2(2)(a)).<br>(b) Must state on its face that it is intended to have the consequences of Part 36 r. 36.2(2)(b)).<br>(c) If made at least 21 days before trial, it must specify a period of not less than 21 days within which the defendant will be liable for the claimant's costs in accordance with r. 36.10 if the offer is accepted (r. 36.2(2)(c)).<br>(d) Must state whether it relates to the whole claim or part or to an issue, and if so, which (r. 36.2(2)(d)).<br>(e) Must state whether it takes into account any counterclaim (r. 36.2(2)(e)).<br>(f) Needs to state the proposed terms of compromise. |
| Additional requirements | (a) Money claims. Must offer a single sum of money (r. 36.4(1)), which is treated as inclusive of interest until the end of the relevant period (r. 36.3(3)).<br>(b) Personal injury claims. Must set out the position on deductible benefits (see r. 36.15), unless the offer is made after the certificate of benefits has been requested but before it arrives. In the latter situation, the defendant is required to clarify the offer within 7 days after receipt of the certificate (r. 36.15(7)).<br>(c) Personal injury claims for future pecuniary loss. There are additional requirements in r. 36.15.<br>(d) Provisional damages claims. There are additional requirements in r. 36.6. |

| | |
|---|---|
| Making a Part 36 offer | A Part 36 offer is made when it is served on the offeree (r. 36.7(1)). The offer should be served on the legal representative of a person who is legally represented (PD 36, para. 1.2). A certificate of service in form N215 should be filed. |
| Clarification | Can be sought, using the Part 23 procedure. See procedural checklist 20. |
| Withdrawal | Permission is required to withdraw or reduce a Part 36 offer during the relevant period (r. 36.3(5)). Thereafter, permission is not required, but the offer can be withdrawn or reduced only if it has not been accepted (r. 36.3(6)). |
| Acceptance | By serving written notice of acceptance on the offeror (r. 36.9(1)) and filing notice of acceptance at court (PD 36, para. 3.1). |
| Late acceptance | If a Part 36 offer has not been withdrawn, it may be accepted even after the relevant period (r. 36.9(2)). |
| Effect of acceptance | (a) The claim is stayed (r. 36.11(1)).<br>(b) If accepted within the relevant period, the defendant is liable to pay the claimant's standard-basis costs to the date of acceptance (r. 36.10(1) and (3)). This is subject to four exceptions.<br>(c) If accepted after the relevant period, the parties may agree costs, but if they do not, the court will make an order for costs (r. 36.10(4)(b)). |
| Trial | A Part 36 offer is treated as 'without prejudice save as to costs' (r. 36.13(1)). It must not be communicated to the trial judge, and must not be included in the trial papers, until the case has been decided (r. 36.13(2)). |
| Non-acceptance | The question is whether the offeree can obtain a result on judgment which is more advantageous than the terms of the offer (r. 36.14).<br>If not:<br>(a) if the offer was made by the defendant, the claimant will normally be ordered to pay the defendant's costs from the end of the relevant period (r. 36.14(2));<br>(b) if the offer was made by the claimant, the court has a discretion to order enhanced interest at up to 10 per cent above base rate, indemnity-basis costs, and enhanced interest on those cost, from the end of the relevant period r. 36.14(3)). |
| Appeal proceedings | Appeal proceedings Need a separate Part 36 offer. A Part 36 offer made in the proceedings at first instance only relates to the proceedings at first instance r. 36.3(4)). |

## Procedural checklist 30 Part 36 payment (before 6 April 2007)

| | |
|---|---|
| Timing | As soon as possible after issue of proceedings. Should be made once an appraisal can be made of the merits and value of the claim. Should be made, if possible, more than 21 days before trial. |
| Money claims | Part 36 payments can only be made in money claims. In claims seeking money and other types of relief, Part 36 protection may be sought by making a Part 36 payment in respect of the money claim, and a Part 36 offer in respect of the other relief. |
| Method | Part 36 notice of payment in, and lodging money in court. |

| | |
|---|---|
| Form | Must be in form N242A, which (CPR, r. 36.6(2)):<br>(a) Must state the amount paid in.<br>(b) Must state if it relates to the whole claim or to part, and if to part, it must state to which part or issue.<br>(c) Must state whether it includes any counterclaim.<br>(d) May be made by reference to an interim payment.<br>(e) May state whether the offer is inclusive of interest. Unless it states to the contrary, the notice will be taken as inclusive of all interest to the last date for acceptance (r. 36.22(1)). If it is expressed not to be inclusive of interest, the offer must (r. 36.22(2)) state whether interest is offered, and if so, the amount offered, the rates offered and the periods covered.<br>(f) In personal injuries claims, the notice should provide a breakdown of the global amount into the amounts allowed for each of the heads of damage (*Williams v Devon County Council* [2003] EWCA Civ 365, [2003] PIQR Q68, considering r.36.23).<br>(g) Must be signed by the offeror or his legal representative (PD 36, para. 5.1). |
| Service | Is effected by the offeror, who must file a certificate of service (form N215), see CPR, r. 36.6(3). |
| Making a Part 36 payment | A Part 36 offer is made when written notice of the payment is served on the offeree (r. 36.8(2)). |
| Clarification | Can be sought, using the Part 23 procedure. See procedural checklist 21. |
| Withdrawal or reduction | Requires permission (sought under Part 23). |
| Acceptance | Form N243A/Form 201, which is a notice of acceptance and request for payment form. |
| Acceptance during trial | Permission is sought from the trial judge. |
| Permission to accept | (1) Part 36 payment made less than 21 days before trial.<br>(2) Acceptance sought more than 21 days after service of Part 36 notice.<br>(3) Part 36 payment made on behalf of some only of the defendants.<br>(4) Offeree is a child or a patient.<br>Permission is sought on notice on form N244 with written evidence in support (see Part 23). |
| Acceptance without permission | The claimant is entitled to costs of the claim up to the date of serving notice of acceptance (r. 36.13(1)). |
| Trial bundles | No reference to the Part 36 payment must be made in any of the papers in the trial bundles. |
| Trial | Fact or amount of Part 36 payment not to be referred to until all decisions on liability and quantum have been decided (r. 36.19(2)). |
| Final order | Should include payment out of the money in court and interest in accordance with the judge's decision. |

## Procedural checklist 31 Summary assessment of costs

| | |
|---|---|
| When required | Unless the court orders otherwise, costs will be assessed summarily (PD 43–48, para. 13.2):<br>(1) At the conclusion of a trial on the fast track;<br>(2) At the conclusion of an interim hearing lasting no more than one day. In these cases the summary assessment covers the interim costs only, unless the whole proceedings are disposed of, in which event the summary assessment may deal with the costs of the whole claim; and<br>(3) At the conclusion of interim hearings within appeals and appeals listed for one day or less (see also PD 52, para.14). |
| Statement of costs | Form N260. Should be filed and served 24 hours before the hearing (PD 43–48, para. 13.5(4)). |
| Failure to serve statement of costs 24 hours in advance | Court may:<br>(1) give the paying party a brief (minutes or hours) adjournment, and then proceed with the summary assessment;<br>(2) stand over for a detailed assessment;<br>(3) stand over for a summary assessment at a later date;<br>(4) if both sides agree, stand over for a summary assessment to be dealt with in writing. |

## Procedural checklist 32 Arbitration claim

| | |
|---|---|
| Commence an arbitration claim under CPR, Part 62, using arbitration claim form N8. | Claim form must:<br>• include a concise statement of remedy claimed;<br>• include any questions on which the claimant seeks the decision of the court;<br>• give details of any arbitration award challenged by the claimant;<br>• show statutory requirements have been met;<br>• specify under which section of the Arbitration Act 1996 the claim is made;<br>• identify against which (if any) defendants a cost order is sought;<br>• specify either:<br>– the persons on whom the arbitration claim form is to be served; or<br>– that the claim is made without notice.<br>(CPR, r. 62.4(1)).<br>Where required, evidence in support must be filed with the arbitration claim form. |
| Issue | Claim form may be issued in one of the following courts:<br>• Admiralty and Commercial Registry at the Royal Courts of Justice (Commercial List);<br>• Technology and Construction Court Registry (TCC List);<br>• district registry of the High Court (where a Mercantile Court is established) (Mercantile List);<br>• district registry of the High Court (arbitration claim form must be marked 'Technology and Construction Court' in the top right-hand corner) (TCC List);<br>• Central London Civil Justice Centre (Mercantile List).<br>(PD 62, para. 2.3(1)).<br>Claim form relating to a landlord and tenant or partnership dispute must be issued in the High Court, Chancery Division (PD 62, para. 2.3(2)). |

| | |
|---|---|
| Service | Claim form must be served by the claimant within one month from the date of issue (CPR, r. 62.4(2)).<br>Once served, the claimant must file the certificate of service within seven days of service (PD 62, para. 3.2). |
| Service out of the jurisdiction | The court can give permission to serve a claim form out of the jurisdiction in the following circumstances:<br>• When a claimant seeks to challenge an arbitration award or appeal on a question of law arising out of an award made within England and Wales.<br>• The claim is for an order under the Arbitration Act 1996, s. 44. The court can give permission for service out of the jurisdiction notwithstanding the only remedy sought is in respect of proceedings taking place outside England and Wales.<br>• Any other situation where the claimant seeks a remedy or requires a question to be determined by the court which affects an arbitration (pending or anticipated), an arbitration agreement or an arbitration award. Seat of the arbitration must be in England and Wales. Where the seat is not in England and Wales the court can still give permission as long as the seat has not been designated or, by reason of connection with England and Wales or Northern Ireland, the court is satisfied it is appropriate to do so.<br>(CPR, r. 62.5(1).)<br>Application must be supported by written evidence and:<br>• state the grounds on which the application is made;<br>• show in what place or country the person to be served is, or probably may be, found<br>(CPR, r. 62.5(2)).<br>CPR, rr. 6.24 to 6.29 (which regulate service of claim forms abroad), apply to the service of arbitration claim forms out of the jurisdiction (r. 62.5(3)).<br>The order giving permission to serve out of the jurisdiction must specify the period within which the defendant has to file the acknowledgment of service (r. 62.5(4)). |
| Acknowledgment of service | Generally within 14 days after service of the arbitration claim form (r. 10.3(1)(b)) by using form N15 or, alternatively in the commercial court, form N210(CC) (Admiralty and Commercial Courts Guide, para. O5.1(b)). |
| Defendant's written evidence | Must be filed and served within 21 days after the date by which the defendant is required to acknowledge service or, if not required to file an acknowledgment, within 21 days after the service of the arbitration claim form (PD 62, para. 6.2). |
| Claimant's written evidence in reply | Evidence in reply to the defendant's written evidence must be filed or served within seven days after service of the defendant's evidence (PD 62, para. 6.3). |
| Preparation for hearing | Agreed indexed and paginated bundles of all evidence and other documents to be used at the hearing should be prepared by the claimant (PD 62, para 6.4).<br>Estimates for length and a complete set of documents should be filed no later than five days before the hearing date (PD 62, para. 6.5). |
| Main hearing | The claimant must file and serve no later than 2 days before the hearing:<br>• chronology of relevant events cross-referenced to a bundle of documents; |

- list of persons involved; and
- skeleton argument

(PD 62, para. 6.6).

The defendant must file and serve its skeleton argument not later than the day before the hearing date. The skeleton argument must list:

- issues which arise for decision;
- the grounds for relief to be relied upon;
- submissions of fact to be made with references to the evidence; and
- submissions of law with references to the relevant authorities (PD 62, para. 6.7).

Hearing generally in private save for claims to determine a preliminary point of law (Arbitration Act 1996, s. 45) or appeal on a question of law arising out of an award (Arbitration Act 1996, s. 69) (CPR, r. 62.10(3)).

## Procedural checklist 33 Appeals within the county courts and High Court

| | |
|---|---|
| Timing | At the end of the hearing in the lower court, permission to appeal should be sought.<br>Any request for the provision of a transcript at public expense (on the ground of poor financial circumstances) should be made at the hearing (PD 52, paras 5.17 and 5.18).<br>An appellant's notice in form N161 must be filed (unless time is extended) no later than 21 days from the date of the decision of the lower court (CPR, r. 52.4(2)(b)). (Before 6 April 2006 it was 14 days.) |
| Permission | Required for all civil appeals (r. 52.3) other than those involving personal liberty and from decisions of authorised court officers in detailed assessments. |
| Seeking permission | Initially sought orally from the lower court (r. 52.3(2)). If refused, can renew application for permission to the appeal court (r. 52.3(3)). Permission from the appeal court is initially sought in the appellant's notice (form N161), and is normally considered without a hearing (PD 52, para. 4.11). |
| Reconsideration of permission | Where the appeal court refuses permission without a hearing, it may reconsider granting permission at a hearing (CPR, r. 52.3(4)). If represented, the appellant's advocate must file and serve a brief written statement at least 4 days before the hearing identifying the points proposed to be raised and his reasons why permission should be granted (PD 52, para. 4.14A). There is no jurisdiction to consider an appeal from an appeal court's refusal to grant permission (Access to Justice Act 1999, s. 54(4)). |
| Appeal court | (1) From county court district judge appeal to circuit judge.<br>(2) From county court circuit judge appeal to High Court judge.<br>(3) From High Court master, district judge or registrar appeal to High Court judge.<br>The above applies equally to deputies and part-time judges fulfilling the above roles.<br>By way of exceptions to the above<br>(a) Final decisions in multitrack claims are appealed to the Court of Appeal (Destination of Appeals Order, art. 4).<br>(b) Final decisions in specialist claims are appealed to the Court of Appeal (Destination of Appeals Order, art. 4). |

| | |
|---|---|
| | (c) Second appeals are appealed to the Court of Appeal (Destination of Appeals Order, art. 5). This applies where a county court district judge's decision is appealed to the circuit judge, whose decision is subject to a second appeal (which is taken to the Court of Appeal). |
| Extending time to appeal | Can only be granted by the appeal court (not by consent) (CPR, r. 52.6), although the lower court can direct some period other than 21 days for filing the appellant's notice (r. 52.4(2)(a)). Applications to extend time are made in the appellant's notice (PD 52, para. 5.2). |
| Appellant's notice | Form N161. Must be filed with the appeal court no more than 21 days after the decision of the lower court (or as directed or extended) (CPR, r. 52.4(2)(b)). It must:<br>(a) set out the grounds of the appeal;<br>(b) give reasons why the lower court's decision is wrong or unjust through serious procedural or other irregularity and state whether each ground is on a point of law or against a finding of fact (PD 52, para. 3.2);<br>(c) include any application for permission to appeal (para. 5.1);<br>(d) include any application to appeal out of time (para. 5.2);<br>(e) include information about any issue raised or remedy sought under the Human Rights Act 1998 (para. 5.1A).<br>The N161 may include applications for interim relief (para. 5.5), including any stay of execution. |
| Fee | £100 for small claims appeal; £120 for other appeals in the county courts (CPFO, fee 2.4); £200 for appeals in the High Court (CPFO, fee 2.3). |
| Documents to be filed | At the same time as filing the appellant's notice, the appellant must file (PD 52, para. 5.6):<br>(a) two additional copies of the appellant's notice for the court and one for each respondent;<br>(b) the same number of copies of the appellant's skeleton argument;<br>(c) a sealed copy of the order of the court below;<br>(d) any orders giving or refusing permission to appeal together with the reasons for each decision;<br>(e) any written evidence in support of any interim application within the appeal;<br>(f) a paginated appeal bundle complying with PD 52, para. 5.6A; and<br>(g) a transcript (or agreed note) of the judgment under appeal (PD 52, para. 5.12).<br>Where it is not possible to file any of the above, the appellant must state which items are not being filed and why (PD 52, para. 5.7). For small claims appeals, see PD 52, para. 5.8. |
| Skeleton argument | Form N163. Should be filed with the appellant's notice, or, if impractical, within 14 days of filing the notice (PD 52, para. 5.9). |
| Transcripts of evidence | Are requested, if required, after permission to appeal is granted. Transcripts of judgments are required before permission. |
| Service of appellant's notice | As soon as practicable, and within 7 days of being filed the appellant must serve the appellant's notice and skeleton argument on the respondents (CPR, r. 52.4(3); PD 52, para. 5.21). The appellant must then file a certificate of service (form N215). |

| | |
|---|---|
| Service of skeleton argument | With appellant's notice, unless impracticable, when within 14 days of filing appellant's notice (PD 52, para. 5.9(2)). |
| Service of supporting documents | Appeal bundles, orders in the court below and for permission etc.:<br>(a) where permission to appeal is being sought, need not be served unless and until permission is given;<br>(b) where permission is granted by the lower court (or not required), supporting documents must be served with the appellant's notice (PD 52, para. 5.24). Where permission is granted by the appeal court, service is required within 7 days of receiving the order granting permission (para. 6.2). |
| Permission granted | Court sends order and any directions to the parties (PD 52, para. 6.3(2)) together with date for the appeal hearing or listing window. The appellant must add the order and other documents to the appeal bundle (para. 6.3A). Appeal questionnaires are optional in the High Court. |
| Respondent's notice | Respondent's notice (form N162) is required (r. 52.5(2)) where the respondent:<br>(a) seeks permission to appeal against the decision in the court below;<br>(b) wishes the appeal court to uphold the decision of the court below for different or additional reasons to those given by the court below.<br>In circumstances (a) and (b), there is a fee of £100 for a small claims appeal or £120 for any other appeal in the county court (CPFO, fee 2.4); £200 in the High Court (CPFO, fee 2.3). |
| Filing respondent's notice | As directed, otherwise within 14 days of:<br>(a) service of appellant's notice if permission to appeal was not required or if permission was given to the appellant by the court below;<br>(b) service of notification of permission to appeal; or<br>(c) service of notification that permission and the substantive appeal are to be heard together.<br>With the respondent's notice, the respondent must file two additional copies of the notice for the court and one for every other party (PD 52, para. 7.10). |
| Additional documents | The respondent must make every effort to agree any additional documents for the appeal bundle with the appellant. If they cannot agree, the respondent should prepare a supplementary bundle, to be served and filed with the respondent's notice (PD 52, paras. 7.11 and 7.12). |
| Service of respondent's notice | As soon as practicable, and within 7 days of being filed (r. 52.5(6)). |
| Respondent's skeleton argument | May be included in the respondent's notice, or served within 14 days of filing the respondent's notice (PD 52, para. 7.7). |
| Authorities | In the county court authorities must be brought to the hearing. In the High Court lists of authorities must be provided to the head usher by 5.30 p.m. on the working day before the hearing or copies should be included in the appeal bundles (Queen's Bench Guide, para. 7.11.9). |
| Summary assessment of costs | In appeals from case management decisions and appeals listed for one day or less, statements of costs should be filed 24 hours before the appeal hearing (PD 52, para. 14.1). |

## Procedural checklist 34 Appeals to the Court of Appeal

| | |
|---|---|
| Timing | At the end of the hearing in the lower court, permission to appeal should be sought. Any request for the provision of a transcript at public expense (on the ground of poor financial circumstances) should be made at the hearing (PD 52, paras 5.17 and 5.18).<br>An appellant's notice in form N161 must be filed (unless time is extended) no later than 21 days from the date of the decision of the lower court (CPR, r. 52.4(2)(b)). (Before 6 April 2006 it was 14 days.) |
| Permission | Required for all civil appeals (r. 52.3) other than those involving personal liberty and from decisions of authorised court officers in detailed assessments. |
| Fee | £200 if permission or an extension of time is required (CPFO, fee 12.1(a)); £400 if permission is not required or was granted by the lower court (CPFO, fee 12.1(b)). |
| Seeking permission | Initially sought orally from the lower court (r. 52.3(2)). If refused, can renew application for permission to the appeal court (r. 52.3(3)). Except that in second appeals to the Court of Appeal permission can only be sought from the Court of Appeal (r. 52.13(1)(c)). Permission from the Court of Appeal is initially sought in the appellant's notice (form N161), and is normally considered without a hearing (PD 52, para. 4.11). |
| Reconsideration of permission | Where the Court of Appeal refuses permission without a hearing, it may reconsider granting permission at a hearing (CPR, r. 52.3(4)). If represented, the appellant's advocate must file and serve a brief written statement at least 4 days before the hearing identifying the points proposed to be raised and his reasons why permission should be granted (PD 52, para. 4.14A). There is no jurisdiction to consider an appeal from a refusal by the Court of Appeal to grant permission (Access to Justice Act 1999, s. 54(4)). |
| Appeals taken to the Court of Appeal | (a) Final decisions in multi-track claims (Destination of Appeals Order, art. 4).<br>(b) Final decisions in specialist claims (Destination of Appeals Order, art. 4).<br>(c) Second appeals in the county courts (Destination of Appeals Order, art. 5). This applies where a county court district judge's decision is appealed to the circuit judge, whose decision is subject to a second appeal (which is taken to the Court of Appeal).<br>(d) Appeals from High Court judges. |
| Extending time to appeal | Can only be granted by the appeal court (not by consent) (CPR, r. 52.6), although the lower court can direct some period other than 21 days for filing the appellant's notice (r. 52.4(2)(a)). Applications to extend time are made in the appellant's notice (PD 52, para. 5.2). |
| Appellant's notice | Form N161. Must be filed with the appeal court no more than 21 days after the decision of the lower court (or as directed or extended) (CPR, r. 52.4(2)(b)). It must:<br>(a) set out the grounds of the appeal;<br>(b) give reasons why the lower court's decision is wrong or unjust through serious procedural or other irregularity and state whether each ground is on a point of law or against a finding of fact (PD 52, para. 3.2);<br>(c) include any application for permission to appeal (para. 5.1); |

| | |
|---|---|
| | (d) include any application to appeal out of time (para. 5.2);<br>(e) include information about any issue raised or remedy sought under the Human Rights Act 1998 (para. 5.1A).<br>The N161 may include applications for interim relief (para. 5.5), including any stay of execution. |
| Documents to be filed | At the same time as filing the appellant's notice, the appellant must file (PD 52, para. 5.6):<br>(a) an appeal bundle complying with PD 52, para. 5.6A;<br>(b) two additional copies of the appellant's notice for the court and one for each respondent;<br>(c) the same number of copies of the appellant's skeleton argument;<br>(d) a sealed copy of the order of the court below;<br>(e) any orders giving or refusing permission to appeal together with the reasons for each decision;<br>(f) any written evidence in support of any interim application within the appeal; and<br>(g) a copy of the order allocating the case to a track (if any).<br>Where it is not possible to file any of the above, the appellant must state which items are not being filed and why (PD 52, para. 5.7). If the bundles exceed 500 pages, a core bundle not exceeding 150 pages must be filed and served (PD 52, para. 15.2) within 28 days of receipt of the order granting permission to appeal. |
| Skeleton argument | Form N163. Should be filed with the appellant's notice. |
| Transcripts | Transcripts of evidence are requested, if required, after permission to appeal is granted. Transcripts of judgments are required before permission. |
| Service of appellant's notice | As soon as practicable, and within 7 days of being filed (CPR, r. 52.4(3)). Served by the appellant (PD 52, para. 15.1(2)), who must file a certificate of service (para. 5.21(2)). |
| Service of skeleton argument | With appellant's notice, unless impracticable, when within 14 days of filing appellant's notice (PD 52, para. 5.9(2)). The advocate's time estimate should be included in paragraph 1(PD 52, para. 5.10(7)). |
| Service of supporting documents | Appeal bundles, orders in the court below and for permission etc.:<br>(a) where permission to appeal is being sought, need not be served unless and until permission is given;<br>(b) where permission is granted by the lower court (or not required), supporting document must be served with the appellant's notice (PD 52, para. 5.24). Where permission is granted by the appeal court, service is required within 7 days of receiving the order granting permission (para. 6.2). |
| Permission granted | Court sends order and any directions to the parties (PD 52, para. 6.3(2)) together with listing details and an appeal questionnaire to the appellant. |
| Appeal questionnaires | Must be returned to court within 14 days together with £400 fee, unless fee 12.1(b) has been paid (CPFO, fee 12.1(c)).<br>Must include:<br>(a) appellant's advocate's time estimate;<br>(b) confirmation that lower court transcript has been requested;<br>(c) confirmation that appeal bundles are being prepared;<br>(d) confirmation that copies of the questionnaire have been sent to the respondents; and<br>(e) confirmation that appeal bundles have been served on the respondents. |

| | |
|---|---|
| Listing | |
| Respondent's notice | Form N162. Is required (r. 52.5(2)) where the respondent:<br>(a) seeks permission to appeal against the decision in the court below;<br>(b) wishes the appeal court to uphold the decision of the court below for different or additional reasons to those given by the court below.<br>In circumstances (a) and (b), there is a fee of £200 (CPFO, fee 12.2). |
| Filing respondent's notice | As directed, otherwise within 14 days of:<br>(a) service of appellant's notice if permission to appeal was not required or if permission was given to the appellant by the court below;<br>(b) service of notification of permission to appeal; or<br>(c) service of notification that permission and the substantive appeal are to be heard together.<br>With the respondent's notice, the respondent must file two additional copies of the notice for the court and one for every other party (PD 52, para. 7.10). |
| Additional documents | The respondent must make every effort to agree any additional documents for the appeal bundle with the appellant. If they cannot agree, the respondent should prepare a supplementary bundle, to be served and filed with the respondent's notice (PD 52, para. 7.11 and 7.12). |
| Service of respondent's notice | As soon as practicable, and within 7 days of being filed (r. 52.5(6)). |
| Respondent's skeleton argument | May be included in the respondent's notice, or served within 14 days of filing the respondent's notice (PD 52, para. 7.7). |
| Authorities | When notified of the date fixed for the hearing, the appellant's advocate must file a bundle containing copies of the principal authorities relied upon by both sides (PD 52, para. 15.11). |
| Final deadline | All the documents needed for an appeal must be filed at least 7 days before the hearing (PD 52, para. 15.11B(1)). A party failing to comply may be summoned before the presiding lord justice. |
| Summary assessment of costs | In appeals from case management decisions and appeals listed for one day or less, statements of costs (form N260) should be filed 24 hours before the appeal hearing (PD 52, para. 14.1). |

## Procedural checklist 35 Claim for judicial review

| | |
|---|---|
| Pre-action protocol | The Pre-action Protocol for Judicial Review requires that, before making a claim, the claimant should send a letter to the defendant identifying issues in dispute and establishing whether litigation can be avoided. Copies of the letter should be sent to all interested parties for information. Defendant should normally respond within 14 days to the letter before claim. Response should be sent to all interested parties identified by claimant and contain details of any other parties who the defendant considers also have an interest. |
| Timing | Claim form must be filed promptly and in any event not later than three months after the grounds to make the claim first arose (CPR, r. 54.5(1)). There must be good reason before this time limit will be extended. This time limit may not be extended by agreement between the parties (r. 54.5(2)). |

| | |
|---|---|
| Claim form | Form N461. The claim form must specify:<br>• the name and address of any person considered to be an interested party,<br>• that permission is sought to proceed with a judicial review claim, and<br>• any remedy (including any interim remedy) being claimed.<br>The claim form must include or be accompanied by:<br>• a detailed statement of the claimant's grounds for bringing the claim,<br>• a statement of facts relied on,<br>• any application to extend the time limit for filing the claim form, and<br>• any application for directions (PD 54, para. 5.6).<br>In addition the claim form must be accompanied by:<br>• any written evidence in support of the claim or application to extend time,<br>• a copy of any order that the claimant seeks to have quashed,<br>• where the claim relates to a decision of a court or tribunal, an approved copy of the reasons for reaching that decision,<br>• copies of any relevant statutory material, and<br>• a list of essential documents for advance reading by the court (with page references to the passages relied on) (PD 54, para. 5.7).<br>Where it is not possible to file all the above documents, the claimant must indicate which documents have not been filed and the reasons why they are not currently available (PD 54, para. 5.8). |
| Urgent procedure | Form N463. Claimant must state the reasons for urgency, the proposed timescale for consideration of the permission application, and the date by which the full hearing of the merits should take place if permission is granted. A claimant who applies for an interim injunction must also provide a draft order and a statement of the grounds on which the injunction is sought. The application must be served by fax and post, along with the claim form, on the defendant and interested parties. The defendant and interested parties must be advised that they may make representations on the application. |
| Fee | £50 when claim form is issued and a further £180 if permission to proceed is granted (CPFO, fee 1.8). |
| Service | The claim form must be served on the defendant and any person the claimant considers to be an interested party within seven days of issue (CPR, r. 54.7). |
| Acknowledgment of service | Form N462. Any person served with the claim form must file an acknowledgment of service (A/S) in the Administrative Court Office within 21 days after service of the claim form. Where person filing A/S intends to contest the claim, the A/S must set out a summary of his grounds for doing so. The A/S must also be served on the claimant and interested persons not later than seven days after it is filed (CPR, r. 54.8). |
| Permission | The court's permission to proceed is required in a judicial review claim (CPR, r. 54.4). If permission is granted, the court may give directions (r. 54.10). The court will serve the permission decision on the claimant and defendant and on any other person who filed an A/S (r. 54.11). |
| Defendant's and other interested parties' detailed grounds of opposition/support | The defendant and any other interested person has 35 days after service of the permission order to file detailed grounds for contesting the claim or supporting it on additional grounds (CPR, r. 54.14). |

| | |
|---|---|
| Skeleton arguments | The claimant must file and serve a skeleton argument not less than 21 working days before the date of the hearing (or the warned date) (PD 54, para. 15.1). The defendant and other relevant parties wishing to make representations must file and serve a skeleton argument not less than 14 working days before the hearing (or warned date) (PD 54, para. 15.2). |
| Substantive hearing | Substantive judicial review applications in civil matters are generally heard by a single judge sitting in open court. The court may determine the claim without a hearing where all parties agree (CPR, r. 54.18). |

## Procedural checklist 36 Application by a creditor whose debt is presently payable to wind up a company incorporated in England and Wales

| | |
|---|---|
| Pre-action | Check that the amount of the creditor's claim is at least £750 and that there is no substantial dispute about the amount or about whether it is due and payable. Check that there is no substantial cross-claim which would reduce the balance owed to the creditor to less than £750. Check that an appropriately clear demand for payment has been made and that no payment has been received. Consider whether serving a statutory demand (form 4.1) or other action short of petitioning might induce payment. |
| Preparation | Check the company's correct name and details required for the petition (form 4.2) at Companies House. Check at the Central Registry of Winding-up Petitions that no other petition has been presented (go to the RCJ Companies Court General Office or telephone (020) 7947 7328). If a petition has already been presented, do not present a second petition, but notify the existing petitioner of intention to support.<br>In order to complete the petition and verifying evidence, ascertain whether the company appears to be an insurance undertaking, credit institution, investment undertaking providing services involving the holding of funds or securities for third parties, or a collective investment undertaking, and ascertain whether the company's centre of main interests is outside the United Kingdom. |
| Appropriate court | High Court, or, if company's paid-up capital is £120,000 or less, the county court with insolvency jurisdiction for the district where the company's registered office is located. In the London area only the High Court has jurisdiction.<br>If the company's centre of main interests is in another EU State and it has no establishment in the United Kingdom, proceedings must be started in the country where the centre of main interests is located, not in England and Wales. |
| Form of petition | Form 4.2, which must be verified by witness statement or affidavit complying with IR 1986, r. 4.12. At least three copies will be required for filing (one for the court, one for service on the company, one to be exhibited to the affidavit of service). Extra copies are required if the company has a liquidator in a voluntary winding up, an administrator, an administrative receiver or a supervisor of a voluntary arrangement. |
| Fees | A court fee of £190 and a deposit of £655 for the official receiver's fee must be paid when filing. |

| | |
|---|---|
| Filing | All required copies are sealed and endorsed with the venue for hearing the petition. One copy is retained by the court, the others are returned to the petitioner. |
| Service | On the company at its registered office:<br>• by handing it to a person who there and then acknowledges him or herself to be, or to the best of the server's knowledge, information and belief is, a director or other officer, or employee, of the company, or<br>• by handing it to a person who there and then acknowledges him or herself to be authorised to accept service on the company's behalf, or<br>• if no individual meeting these criteria is available, by depositing it at or about the registered office in such a way that it is likely to come to the notice of a person attending at the office.<br>If service at the registered office is not practicable.<br>Copies of the petition must also be sent (by post) to the company's voluntary liquidator, administrator, supervisor of a voluntary arrangement or administrative receiver. |
| Evidence of service | Evidence of service on the company (form 4.4 if service was at registered office, form 4.5 otherwise) must be filed immediately after service exhibiting a sealed copy of petition. |
| Advertisement | Petition must be advertised in the *London Gazette* (fee £60 + VAT, or £45 + VAT if submitted electronically), but not until seven business days after service on the company. There must be no other publicity for the petition until this advertisement appears. Advertisement must appear at least seven days before the date appointed for hearing the petition. |
| Track | Automatically multi-track. |
| Provisional liquidator | An application may be made for the appointment of a provisional liquidator. |
| Evidence | The petition and verifying affidavit are evidence, and will usually be the only evidence in the case. The company may file evidence in opposition, a copy of which must be sent to the petitioner, not less than seven days before the hearing. No further evidence may be filed unless the court directs. |
| Certificate of compliance | Certificate of compliance (form 4.7) must be filed, with a copy of the advertisement, by 4.30 p.m. on Friday before hearing (at least five days before hearing in county courts). |
| List of persons appearing | Form 4.10 must be completed and handed to the court before the hearing commences. |
| Heard by | Registrar or district judge in public. |
| Decision | Court may make order applied for, dismiss the petition, adjourn (conditionally or unconditionally), make an interim order, or any other order it thinks fit. Registrar or district judge may refer case to judge. |
| Perfection | If court makes winding-up order, it will notify the official receiver, who becomes liquidator. All documents necessary to enable the order to be completed must be left at the court by the next business day. Court draws up the order. Official receiver notifies the order in the *London Gazette*. |

## Procedural checklist 37 Application by a creditor whose debt is presently payable for a bankruptcy order

| | |
|---|---|
| Pre-action | Check that the amount of the creditor's claim is at least £750 and that there is no substantial dispute about the amount. Check that the claim is unsecured and is for a liquidated debt payable immediately and there is no substantial dispute that it is due and payable. Check that there is no substantial cross-claim which would reduce the balance owed to the creditor to less than £750. Check that an appropriately clear demand for payment has been made and that no payment has been received. If judgment has been obtained for the debt, consider whether to execute: partly or wholly unsatisfied execution is a ground for a bankruptcy petition. |
| Statutory demand | Unless there is a partly or wholly unsatisfied execution for the debt, a statutory demand must be served on the debtor. Prescribed form is form 6.1, or form 6.2 if the debt is a judgment debt for which execution has not been issued. If practicable, there must be personal service of a statutory demand, by leaving it with the debtor (CPR, r. 6.4(3)). If prompt personal service is not possible, service may be by first-class post or insertion through a letter box. If the debt is a judgment debt, service may be by newspaper advertisement if the debtor has absconded or is avoiding service and there is no real prospect of successful execution. Evidence of service, using form 6.11 or, for substituted service, 6.12, must be filed with the petition.<br>The debtor has three weeks to comply with the statutory demand and may apply for it to be set aside.<br>A petition may be presented before the three weeks expire if there is a serious possibility that the debtor's property or the value of any of it will be significantly diminished during the three weeks. The petition must state that possibility. |
| Preparation | In order to complete the petition, ascertain whether the debtor appears to be carrying on business as an insurance undertaking, credit institution, investment undertaking providing services involving the holding of funds or securities for third parties, or a collective investment undertaking, and ascertain whether the debtor's centre of main interests is outside the United Kingdom. |
| Appropriate court | County court which has insolvency jurisdiction for the district in which the debtor resided or carried on business in the previous six months. In the London area, the High Court. If residence and business are in different districts, jurisdiction is normally determined by place of business.<br>If the debtor's centre of main interests is in another EU State and the debtor has no establishment in the United Kingdom, proceedings must be started in the country where the centre of main interests is located, not in England and Wales. |
| Form of petition | Form 6.7, or form 6.9 if the petition is based on partially or wholly unsatisfied execution. The petition must be verified by witness statement or affidavit in form 6.13. Three copies will be required for filing (one for the court, one for service on the debtor, one to be exhibited to the affidavit of service). |
| Fees | A court fee of £190 and a deposit of £390 for the official receiver's fee must be paid when filing. |

| | |
|---|---|
| Filing | Three copies of the petition must be filed and, if the petition relies on non-compliance with a statutory demand, written evidence of service of the demand. All three copies of the petition are sealed and endorsed with the venue for hearing the petition. One copy is retained by the court, the others are returned to the petitioner. |
| Service | Personal service of the petition by leaving it with the debtor (CPR, r. 6.4(3)) is required. PD Insolvency Proceedings, para. 11.4, sets out the steps which should be taken before concluding that personal service cannot be effected so that an application for substituted service is justified. Application for substituted service is by ordinary application. |
| Evidence of service | Evidence of service on the debtor (form 6.17 for personal service; form 6.18 for substituted service) must be filed immediately after service exhibiting a sealed copy of the petition. |
| Track | Automatically multi-track. |
| Interim receiver | An application may be made by the debtor or any creditor for the appointment of an interim receiver. |
| Evidence | The petition and verifying affidavit are evidence, and will usually be the only evidence in the case. If the debtor intends to oppose the petition, he or she must, not later than seven days before the hearing, file in court a notice specifying the grounds of objection and send a copy to the petitioner. |
| List of persons appearing | Form 6.20 must be completed and handed to the court before the hearing commences. |
| Decision | Court may make order applied for if satisfied that the statements in the petition are true, and that the debt on which it is founded has not been paid, or secured or compounded for. |
| Perfection | The court settles a bankruptcy order. Two sealed copies are sent to the official receiver, who sends one to the bankrupt. Official receiver notifies the order in the *London Gazette*. |

# Guide to Civil Proceedings Fees—From 6 April 2007

The new Civil Proceedings Fees Order combines Supreme Court and county court fees—

For easy reference Civil Proceedings fees have been broken down into:

Supreme Court fees—(pages lxvii to lxxv)

County Court fees—(pages lxxvii to lxxxvi)

Endnotes (page lxxxvi)

## GUIDE TO CIVIL PROCEEDINGS FEES FROM 6 APRIL 2007 SUPREME COURT FEES ONLY

Includes exemption and remission—please read the notes at the end of this schedule under Further Information

### Fees Taken in the High Court

| Fee No. | Schedule 1 Column 1 | Schedule 1 Column 2 |
|---|---|---|
| | The number and description of fees have been taken from the Civil Proceedings Fees Order 2004 | |
| 1.1 | **On the commencement of originating proceedings in the High Court** (including originating proceedings issued after leave to issue is granted) to recover a sum of money where the sum claimed: | |
| 1.1(a) | does not exceed £50,000 | £400 |
| 1.1(b) | exceeds £50,000 but does not exceed £100,000 | £700 |
| 1.1(c) | exceeds £100,000 but does not exceed £150,000 | £900 |
| 1.1(d) | exceeds £150,000 but does not exceed £200,000 | £1,100 |
| 1.1(e) | exceeds £200,000 but does not exceed £250,000 | £1,300 |
| 1.1(f) | exceeds £250,000 but does not exceed £300,000 | £1,500 |
| 1.1(g) | exceeds £300,000 or not limited | £1,700 |
| 1.2 & 1.3 | **Refer to fees taken in the County Court**<br>**Fees 1.1**<br>Where the claimant is making a claim for interest on a specified sum of money, the sum claimed for the purposes of calculating fees 1.1 shall be taken to include the interest in addition to that specified sum. | |
| 1.4 | **On the commencement of originating proceedings** for any other remedy or relief (including originating proceedings issued after leave to issue is granted): | £400 |
| Notes | **Fees 1.1, and 1.4 Recovery of land or goods**<br>Where a claim for money is additional or alternative to a claim for recovery of land or goods, only fee 1.4 shall be payable.<br>**Fees 1. 1, and 1.4 Claims other than recovery of land or goods**<br>Where a claim for money is additional to a non-money claim (other than a claim for recovery of land or goods) then fee 1.1 as appropriate shall be payable in addition to fee 1.4. Where a claim for money is alternative to a non-money claim (other than a claim for recovery of land or goods), only fee 1.1 shall be payable in the High Court, and, or fee 1.4 shall be payable, whichever is the greater.<br>**Fees 1.1 and 1.4 Generally**<br>Where more than one non-money claim is made in the same proceedings, fee 1.4 shall be payable once only, in addition to any fee which may be payable under fee 1.1 as appropriate. | |

## Fees Taken in the High Court (*Contd.*)

| Fee No. | Schedule 1 Column 1 | Schedule 1 Column 2 |
|---|---|---|
| | **Fees 1.1 and fee 1.4** shall not be payable where fee 1.7(b), fee 1.8(a) (in the High Court only), fee 9.1 (in the High Court only) or fee 3 apply. | |
| | **Fees 1.1 as appropriate and 1.4 Amendment of claim or counterclaim** Where the claim or counterclaim is amended, and the fee paid before amendment is less than that which would have been payable if the document, as amended, had been so drawn in the first instance, the party amending the document shall pay the difference. | |
| 1.5 | **On the filing of proceedings against a party or parties not named in the originating proceedings:** | £50 |
| **Notes** | Fee 1.5 shall be payable by a defendant who adds or substitutes a party or parties to the proceedings or by a claimant who adds or substitutes a defendant or defendants. | |
| 1.6 | **On the filing of a counterclaim** | The same fee as if the relief or remedy sought were the subject of separate proceedings |
| **Notes** | **Fee 1.6** No fee is fee is payable on a counterclaim which a defendant is required to make under the CPR because he contends that he has a claim or is entitled to any remedy relating to a grant of probate of a will, or letters of administration of an estate, of a deceased person. | |
| 1.7 (a) | **On an application for leave to issue originating proceedings:** | £50 |
| 1.7 (b) | **On an application for an order under Part III of the Solicitors Act 1974[1] for the assessment of costs payable to a solicitor by his client or on the commencement of costs-only proceedings** | £50 |
| 1.8 | **Judicial Review (applies to High Court only)** | |
| 1.8(a) | **On the commencement of the judicial review procedure** Where the court has made an order giving permission to proceed with a claim for judicial review, there shall be payable by the claimant within 7 days of service on the claimant of that order: | £50 |
| 1.8(b) | **if the judicial review procedure has been commenced** | £180 |
| 1.8(c) | **if the claim for judicial review was commenced otherwise** than by using the judicial review procedure | £50 |
| 2 | **General Fees** | |
| 2.1 | **On the claimant filing an allocation questionnaire**; or<br>• where the court dispenses with the need for an allocation questionnaire, within 14 days of the date of despatch of the notice of allocation to track; or<br>• where the CPR or a Practice Direction provide for automatic allocation or provide that the rules on allocation shall not apply, within 28 days of the filing of the defence (or the filing of the last defence if there is more than one defendant), or within 28 days of the expiry of the time permitted for filing all defences if sooner | £200 |
| **Notes** | **Fee 2.1** shall be payable by the claimant except where the action is proceeding on the counterclaim alone, when it shall be payable by the defendant—<br>• on the defendant filing an allocation questionnaire; or<br>• where the court dispenses with the need for an allocation questionnaire, within 14 days of the date of despatch of the notice of allocation to track; or | |

- where the CPR or a Practice Direction provide for automatic allocation or provide that the rules on allocation shall not apply, within 28 days of the filing of the defence to the counterclaim (or the filing of the last defence to the counterclaim if there is more than one party entitled to file a defence to a counterclaim), or within 28 days of the expiry of the time permitted for filing all defences to the counterclaim if sooner

2.2 **On the claimant filing a listing questionnaire; or where the court fixes the trial date or trial week** without the need for a listing questionnaire, within 14 days of the date of despatch of the notice (or the date when oral notice is given if no written notice is given) of the trial week or the trial date if no trial week is fixed — £600

Notes Fee 2.2 shall be payable by the claimant except where the action is proceeding on the counterclaim alone, when it shall be payable by the defendant—

- on the defendant filing a listing questionnaire; or
- where the court fixes the trial date or trial week without the need for a listing questionnaire, within 14 days of the date of despatch of the notice (or the date when oral notice is given if no written notice is given) of the trial week or the trial date if no trial week is fixed.

Where the court receives notice in writing—

- before the trial date has been fixed or,
- where a trial date has been fixed, at least 14 days before the trial date,

from the party who paid fee 2.2 that the case is settled or discontinued, fee 2.2 shall be refunded.

**Fees 2.1 and 2.2 Generally**

Fees 2.1 and 2.2 shall:

- be payable as appropriate where the court allocates a case to track for a trial of the assessment of damages;
- not be payable in relation to claims managed under a GLO after that GLO is made;
- be payable once only in the same proceedings.

Fee 2.1 shall not be payable where the procedure in Part 8 of the CPR is used.

2.3 **On filing:** — £200

- an appellant's notice, or
- a respondent's notice where the respondent is appealing or wishes to ask the appeal court to uphold the order of the lower court for reasons different from or additional to those given by the lower court.

Notes Fee 2.3 does not apply on appeals against a decision made in detailed assessment proceedings.

2.5 **On an application on notice where no other fee is specified** — £100

2.6 **On an application by consent or without notice for a judgment or order** where no other fee is specified — £50

Notes For the purpose of fee 2.6 a request for a judgment or order on admission or in default shall not constitute an application and no fee shall be payable.

Fee 2.6 shall not be payable in relation to an application by consent for an adjournment of a hearing where the application is received by the court at least 14 days before the date set for that hearing

Fees 2.5 and 2.6 shall not be payable when an application is made in an appeal notice or is filed at the same time as an appeal notice.

2.7 **On an application for a summons or order for a witness to attend court to be examined on oath or an order for evidence to be taken by deposition**, other than an application for which fee 6.2 enforcement in the High Court or for which fee 7.3 is payable — £50

## Fees Taken in the High Court (*Contd.*)

| Fee No. | Schedule 1 Column 1 | Schedule 1 Column 2 |
|---|---|---|
| 2.8 | **On an application to vary a judgment or suspend enforcement** (where more than one remedy is sought in the same application only one fee shall be payable) | £50 |
| 2.9 | **Register of** judgments etc kept under section 98 of the Courts Act 2003<br>On a request for the issue of a certificate of satisfaction | £15 |
| 3 | **Companies Act 1985[2] and Insolvency Act 1986[3]** | |
| 3.1 | **On entering a bankruptcy petition:** | |
| 3.1(a) | if presented by a debtor or the personal representative of a deceased debtor | £150 |
| 3.1(b) | if presented by a creditor or other person | £190 |
| 3.2 | **On entering a petition for an administration order** | £150 |
| 3.3 | **On entering any other petition**<br>One fee only is payable where more than one petition is presented in relation to a partnership. | £190 |
| 3.4 | **Certificate of Discharge** | |
| 3.4(a) | On a request for a certificate of discharge from bankruptcy | £60 |
| 3.4(b) | and after the first certificate for each copy | £1 |
| 3.5 | **On an application under the Companies Act 1985 or the Insolvency Act 1986** other than one brought by petition and where no other fee is specified. | £130 |
| Notes | **Fee 3.5** is not payable where the application is made in existing proceedings | |
| 3.6 | **On an application for the conversion of a voluntary arrangement** into a winding up or bankruptcy under Article 37 of Council Regulation (EC) No 1346/2000 | £130 |
| 3.7 | **On an application, for the purposes of Council Regulation (EC) No 1346/2000**, for an order confirming creditors' voluntary winding up (where the company has passed a resolution for voluntary winding up, and no declaration under section 89 of the Insolvency Act 1986 has been made) | £30 |
| 3.8 | **On filing**<br>• a notice of intention to appoint an administrator under paragraph 14 of Schedule B1 to the Insolvency Act 1986 or in accordance with paragraph 27 of that Schedule; or<br>• a notice of appointment of an administrator in accordance with paragraphs 18 or 29 of that Schedule. | £30 |
| Notes | **Fee 3.8** Where a person pays fee 3.8 on filing a notice of intention to appoint an administrator, no fee shall be payable on that same person filing a notice of appointment of that administrator. | |
| 3.9 | **On submitting a nominee's report under section 2(2) of the Insolvency Act 1986[4] or** | £30 |
| 3.10 | **On filing documents in accordance with paragraph 7(1) of Schedule A1 to the Insolvency Act 1986** | £30 |
| 3.11 | **On an application by consent or without notice** where no other fee is specified | £30 |
| 3.12 | **On an application with notice** where no other fee is specified | £60 |
| Notes | **Requests and applications with no fee**<br>No fee is payable on a request or on an application to the Court by the Official Receiver when applying only in the capacity of Official Receiver to the case (and not as trustee or liquidator), or on an application to set aside a statutory demand. | |

| | | |
|---|---|---|
| 4 | **Copy Documents** (High Court, Court of Appeal) | |
| 4.1 | **On a request for a copy of any document** (other then where fee 4.2 applies): | |
| 4.1(a) | for the first page (except the first page of a subsequent copy of the same document supplied at the same time) | £1 |
| 4.1(b) | per page in any other case | 20p |
| Notes | Fee 4.1 shall be payable<br>• for a faxed copy or for examining a plain copy and marking it as an examined copy.<br>• whether or not the copy is issued as an office copy. | |
| 4.2 | **On a request for a copy of a document required in connection with proceedings** and supplied by the party making the request at the time of copying, for each page. | 20p |
| 4.3 | **On a request for a copy of a document on a computer disk or in other electronic form**, for each such copy. | £3 |
| 5 | **Determination of costs** | |
| 5.1 | **On the filing of a request for detailed assessment** where the party filing the request is legally aided or is funded by the LSC and no other party is ordered to pay the costs of the proceedings | £120 |
| 5.2 | **On the filing of a request for a detailed assessment hearing in any case where fee 5.1 does not apply; or on the filing of a request for a hearing date for the assessment of costs payable to a solicitor by his client pursuant to an order under Part III of the Solicitors Act 1974**<br>Where there is a combined party and party and legal aid, or a combined party and party and LSC, or a combined party and party, legal aid and LSC determination of costs, fee 5.2 shall be attributed proportionately to the party and party, legal aid, or LSC (as the case may be) portions of the bill on the basis of the amount allowed. | £600 |
| 5.3 | **On a request for the issue of a default costs certificate** | £50 |
| 5.4 | **On an appeal against a decision made in detailed assessment proceedings** | £200 |
| 5.5 | **On applying for the court's approval of a certificate of costs payable from the Community Legal Service Fund.** | £50 |
| Notes | Fee 5.5 is payable at the time of applying for the court's approval and is recoverable only against the Community Legal Service Fund. | |
| 5.6 | **On a request or application to set aside a default costs certificate** | £100 |
| 6 | **Enforcement** | |
| 6.1 | **On sealing a writ of execution/possession/delivery**<br>Where the recovery of a sum of money is sought in addition to a writ of possession and delivery, no further fee is payable. | £50 |
| 6.2 | **On an application for an order requiring a judgment debtor or other person to attend court to provide information in connection with enforcement of a judgment or order.** | £50 |
| 6.3(a) | **On an application for a third party debt order or the appointment of a receiver by way of equitable execution** | £100 |
| Notes | Fee 6.3 (a) shall be payable in respect of each third party against whom the order is sought. | |
| 6.3(b) | **On an application for a charging order** | £100 |
| Notes | Fee 6.3(b) shall be payable in respect of each application issued | |
| 6.4 | **On an application for a judgment summons** | £100 |
| 6.5 | **On a request or application to register a judgment or order, or for leave to enforce an arbitration award, or for a certificate or a certified copy of a judgment or order for use abroad** | £50 |
| 7 & 8 | **Refers to County Court Fees for Enforcement and Sale** | |
| 9 | **Miscellaneous proceedings or matters** | |

## Fees Taken in the High Court (*Contd.*)

| Fee No. | Schedule 1 Column 1 | Schedule 1 Column 2 |
|---|---|---|
| | **Bills of Sale** | |
| 9.1 | **On filing any document under the Bills of Sale Acts 1878() and the Bills of Sale Act (1878)[5] Amendment Act 1882[6] or on an application under Section 15 of the Bills of Sale Act 1878 for an order that a memorandum of satisfaction be written on a registered copy of the bill** | £10 |
| | **Searches** | |
| 9.2 | **For an official certificate** of the result of a search for each name, in any register or index held by the court; or in the Court Funds Office, for an official certificate of the result of a search of unclaimed balances for a specified period of up to 50 years | £5 |
| 9.3 | **On a search in person of the bankruptcy and companies records,** including inspection, for each 15 minutes or part of 15 minutes | £5 |
| | **Judge sitting as arbitrator** | |
| 9.4 | **On the appointment of—** | |
| 9.4(a) | a judge of the Commercial Court as an arbitrator or umpire under section 93 of the Arbitration Act 1996(c); or | £1,800 |
| 9.4(b) | a judge of the Technology and Construction Court as an arbitrator or umpire under section 93 of the Arbitration Act 1996 | £1,400 |
| Notes | Where fee 9.4 has been paid on the appointment of a judge of the Commercial Court or a judge of the Technology and Construction Court as an arbitrator or umpire but the arbitration does not proceed to a hearing or an award, the fee shall be refunded. | |
| 9.5 | **For every day or part of a day** (after the first day) of the hearing before— | |
| 9.5(a) | a judge of the Commercial Court; or | £1,800 |
| 9.5(b) | a judge of the Technology and Construction Court, so appointed as arbitrator or umpire | £1,400 |
| 10 | **Fees payable in Admiralty Matters** | |
| | **In the Admiralty Registrar and Marshal's Office—** | |
| 10.1 | **On the issue of a warrant for the arrest of a ship or goods** | £100 |
| 10.2 | **On the sale of a ship or goods—** | |
| | Subject to a minimum fee of £200 | |
| 10.2(a) | for every £100 or fraction of £100 of the price up to £100,000 | £1 |
| 10.2(b) | for every £100 or fraction of £100 of the price exceeding £100,000<br>Where there is/are sufficient proceeds of sale in court, fee 10.2 shall be taken by transfer from the proceeds of sale in court. | 50p |
| 10.3 | **On entering a reference for hearing by the Registrar** | £50 |
| 11 | **Affidavits (in the High Court and Court of Appeal only)** | |
| 11.1 | **On taking an affidavit or an affirmation or attestation** upon honour in lieu of an affidavit or a declaration except for the purpose of receipt of dividends from the Accountant General and for a declaration by a shorthand writer appointed in insolvency proceedings<br>• for each person making any of the above | £5 |
| 11.2 | **For each exhibit** referred to in an affidavit, affirmation, attestation or declaration for which fee 11.1 is payable | £2 |
| 12 | **Fees payable in appeals to the Court of Appeal** | |
| 12.1(a) | **Where in an appeal notice** permission to appeal or an extension of time for appealing is applied for (or both are applied for)—<br>• on filing an appellant's notice, or<br>• where the respondent is appealing, on filing a respondent's notice | £200 |

| | | |
|---|---|---|
| 12.1(b) | **Where permission to appeal** is not required or has been granted by the lower court'<br>on filing an appellant's notice, or<br>on filing a respondent's notice where the respondent is appealing | £400 |
| 12.1(c) | **On the appellant filing an appeal questionnaire** (unless the appellant has paid fee 12.1(b), or on the respondent filing an appeal questionnaire (unless the respondent has paid fee 12.1(b)) | £400 |
| 12.2 | **On filing a respondent's notice** where the respondent wishes to ask the appeal court to uphold the order of the lower court for reasons different from or additional to those given by the lower court | £200 |
| 12.3 | **On filing an application notice** | £200 |
| Notes | Fee **12.3** shall not be payable for an application made in an appeal notice. | |

# Further Information (High Court)

# The following wording is taken from the Civil Proceedings Fees Order 2004 [2004/3121 (L.23)]

## Citation and commencement

1 (1) This Order may be cited as the Civil Proceedings Fees Order 2004 and shall come into force on the 4 January 2005.

(2) In this Order

(a) a fee referred to by number means the fee so numbered in Schedule 1 to this Order;

(b) "CCBC" means County Court Bulk Centre;

(c) "CPC" means Claim Production Centre;

(d) "the CPR" means the Civil Procedure Rules 1998;[7]

(e) expressions also used in the CPR have the same meaning as in those Rules;

(f) "family proceedings" means family proceedings in the High Court or in a county court as appropriate;

(g) "LSC" means the Legal Services Commission established under section 1 of the Access to Justice Act 1999;[8]

(h) "Funding Code" means the code approved under section 9 of the Access to Justice Act 1999;[9]

(i) "GLO" means a Group Litigation Order.

## Fees to be taken

2 The fees set out in column 2 of Schedule 1 to this Order shall be taken in the Supreme Court and in county courts respectively in respect of the items described in column 1 in accordance with and subject to the directions specified in column 1.

3 The provisions of this Order shall not apply to—

(a) non-contentious probate business;

(b) proceedings in the Court of Protection, except in so far as fees 1, 2, 3, 6, 9 and 10 in Schedule 1 (High Court only) are applicable;

(c) the enrolment of documents;

(d) criminal proceedings (except proceedings on the Crown side of the Queen's Bench Division to which the fees contained in Schedule 1 are applicable);

(e) proceedings by sheriffs, under-sheriffs, deputy-sheriffs or other officers of the sheriff; and

(f) family proceedings.

## Exemptions, reductions, remissions and refunds

4 (1) No fee shall be payable under this Order by a party who, at the time when a fee would otherwise become payable—

(a) is in receipt of any qualifying benefit, and

(b) is not in receipt of, as appropriate, either—

(i) representation under Part IV of the Legal Aid Act 1988[10] for the purposes of the proceedings; or

(ii) funding provided by the LSC for the purposes of the proceedings and for which a certificate has been issued under the Funding Code certifying a decision to fund services for that party.

(2) The following are qualifying benefits for the purposes of paragraph (1)(a) above—

(a) income support under the Social Security Contributions and Benefits Act 1992;[11]

(b) working tax credit, provided that—

(i) child tax credit is being paid to the party, or otherwise following a claim for child tax credit made jointly by the members of a couple (as defined in section 3(5A) of the Tax Credits Act 2002[12] which includes the party; or

(ii) there is a disability element or severe disability element (or both) to the tax credit received by the party;

**and** that the gross annual income taken into account for the calculation of the working tax credit is £16,017 or less;

(c) income-based jobseeker's allowance under the Jobseekers Act 1995;[13] and

(d) guarantee credit under the State Pension Credit Act 2002.[14]

(3) In the county courts paragraph (1) shall not apply to fee 7.8 (fee payable on a consolidated attachment of earnings order or an administration order).

5 Where it appears to the Lord Chancellor that the payment of any fee prescribed by this Order would, owing to the exceptional circumstances of the particular case, involve undue financial hardship, he may reduce or remit the fee in that case.

6 (1) Subject to paragraph (2), where a fee has been paid at a time—

(a) when, under article 4, it was not payable, the fee shall be refunded;

(b) where the Lord Chancellor, if he had been aware of all the circumstances, would have reduced the fee under article 4, the amount by which the fee would have been reduced shall be refunded; and

(c) where the Lord Chancellor, if he had been aware of all the circumstances, would have remitted the fee under article 4, the fee shall be refunded.

(2) No refund shall be made under paragraph (1) unless the party who paid the fee applies within 6 months of paying the fee.

(3) The Lord Chancellor may extend the period of 6 months referred to in paragraph (2) if he considers that there is good reason for an application being made after the end of the period of 6 months.

7 Where by any convention entered into by Her Majesty with any foreign power it is provided that no fee shall be required to be paid in respect of any proceedings, the fees specified in this Order shall not be taken in respect of those proceedings.

## Revocations

8 The Orders specified below, in so far as they were made under sections 414 and 415 of the Insolvency Act 1986 and section 128 of the Finance Act 1990, shall be revoked.

| Orders Revoked | Reference |
|---|---|
| The Supreme Court Fees Order 1999 | SI 1999/687 |
| The Supreme Court Fees (Amendment) Order 1999 | SI 1999/2569 |
| The Supreme Court Fees (Amendment) Order 2000 | SI 2000/641 |
| The Supreme Court Fees (Amendment) Order 2003 | SI 2003/646 |
| The Supreme Court Fees (Amendment) Order 2004 | SI 2004/2100 |
| The Supreme Court Fees (Amendment No.2) Order 2000 | SI 2000/937 |
| The Supreme Court Fees (Amendment No.2) Order 2003 | SI 2003/717 |
| The County Court Fees Order 1999 | SI 1999/689 |
| The County Court Fees (Amendment) Order 1999 | SI 1999/2548 |
| The County Court Fees (Amendment) Order 2000 | SI 2000/639 |
| The County Court Fees (Amendment) Order 2003 | SI 2003/648 |
| The County Court Fees (Amendment) Order 2004 | SI 2004/2098 |
| The County Court Fees (Amendment No.2) Order 2000 | SI 2000/939 |
| The County Court Fees (Amendment No.2) Order 2003 | SI 2003/718 |
| The County Court Fees (Amendment No.4) Order 2000 | SI 2000/2310 |

(b) where [illegible] disability element [illegible] disability element [illegible] for [illegible] the payment [illegible] received by the party;

and that the gross annual income taken into account [illegible] the calculation of the working tax credit [illegible] Order;

(c) income-based jobseeker's allowance under the Jobseekers Act 1995; and

(d) guarantee credit under the State Pension Credit Act 2002.

(4) In the county courts, sub-paragraph (2) shall not apply to fee 7.5 (the issue of [illegible] attachment of earnings order or consolidated attachment of earnings order [illegible] arrears).

5. Where it appears to the Lord Chancellor that the payment of any fee prescribed by this Order would, owing to the exceptional circumstances of the particular case, involve undue financial hardship, he may reduce or remit the fee in that case.

6. (1) Subject to paragraph (3), where a fee has been paid at a time—

(a) when, under article 4, it was not payable, the fee shall be refunded;

(b) where the Lord Chancellor, if he had been aware of all the circumstances, would have reduced the fee under article 5, the amount by which the fee would have been reduced shall be refunded; and

(c) where the Lord Chancellor, if he had been aware of all the circumstances, would have remitted the fee under article 5, the fee shall be refunded.

(2) No refund shall be made under paragraph (1) unless the party who paid the fee applies within 6 months of paying the fee.

(3) The Lord Chancellor may extend the period of 6 months referred to in paragraph (2) if he considers that there is a good reason for an application being made after the end of the period of 6 months.

7. Where by any convention entered into by Her Majesty with any foreign power it is provided that no fee shall be required to be paid in respect of any proceedings, the fees specified in this Order shall not be taken in respect of those proceedings.

## Revocations

8. The Orders specified in the Table [illegible] section [illegible] of the Insolvency Act 1986 and section 128 of the Insolvency Act 1986, shall be revoked.

| Orders Revoked | Reference |
|---|---|
| [illegible] | [illegible] |
| The Supreme Court Fees (Amendment) Order [illegible] | SI 2005/[illegible] |
| The Supreme Court Fees (Amendment) Order [illegible] | SI 2005/[illegible] |
| The Supreme Court Fees (Amendment) Order 2005 | SI 2005/[illegible] |
| The Supreme Court Fees (Amendment) Order 2006 | SI 2006/[illegible] |
| The Supreme Court Fees (Amendment No. 2) Order 2006 | SI 2006/[illegible] |
| The Supreme Court Fees (Amendment No. [illegible]) Order 2006 | SI 2006/[illegible] |
| The County Court Fees Order 1999 | SI 1999/689 |
| The County Court Fees (Amendment) Order 1999 | SI 1999/2548 |
| The County Court Fees (Amendment) Order 2000 | SI 2000/639 |
| The County Court Fees (Amendment) Order 2003 | SI 2003/[illegible] |
| The County Court Fees (Amendment) Order 2005 | SI 2005/[illegible] |
| The County Court Fees (Amendment No. 2) Order 2005 | SI 2005/[illegible] |
| The County Court Fees (Amendment No. 2) Order 2006 | SI 2006/[illegible] |
| The County Court Fees (Amendment No. [illegible]) Order 2006 | SI 2006/[illegible] |

# Guide to Civil Proceedings Fees from 6 April 2007
# County Court Fees Only

Includes exemption and remission—please read the notes at the end of this schedule under Further Information

### Fees Taken in the County Court

| Fee No. | Schedule 1 Column 1 | Schedule 1 Column 2 |
|---|---|---|
| | The number and description of fees have been taken from the Civil Proceedings Fees Order 2004 | |
| 1.1 | **Refer to Guide to fees taken in the High Court** | |
| 1.2 | **On the commencement of originating proceedings in the County Court** (including originating proceedings issued after leave to issue is granted) to recover a sum of money, except in CPC cases brought by Centre users: | |
| 1.2(a) | does not exceed £300 | £30 |
| 1.2(b) | exceeds £300 but not £500 | £50 |
| 1.2(c) | exceeds £500 but not £1,000 | £80 |
| 1.2(d) | exceeds £1,000 but not £5,000 | £120 |
| 1.2(e) | exceeds £5,000 but not £15,000 | £250 |
| 1.2(f) | exceeds £15,000 but not £50,000 | £400 |
| 1.2(g) | exceeds £50,000 but not £100,000 | £700 |
| 1.2(h) | exceeds £100,000 but not £150,000 | £900 |
| 1.2(i) | exceeds £150,000 but not £200,000 | £1,100 |
| 1.2(j) | exceeds £200,000 but not 250,000 | £1,300 |
| | 1.2(k) exceeds £250,000 but not £300,000 | £1,500 |
| 1.2(l) | exceeds £300,000 or not limited | £1,700 |
| 1.3 | **On the commencement of originating proceedings in the County Court** to recover a sum of money in Claims Production Centre cases brought by Centre users, where the sum claimed: | |
| 1.3(a) | does not exceed £300 | £20 |
| 1.3(b) | exceeds £300 but not £500 | £40 |
| 1.3(c) | exceeds £500 but not £1,000 | £70 |
| 1.3(d) | exceeds £1,000 but not £5,000 | £110 |
| 1.3(e) | exceeds £5,000 but not £15,000 | £240 |
| 1.3(f) | exceeds £15,000 but not £50,000 | £390 |
| 1.3(g) | exceeds £50,000 but not £100,000 | £690 |
| **Notes** | Fee 1.3 Claims above £99,999.99 cannot be issued through the Claim Production Centre. Parties should issue the claim in the relevant court.<br>**Fees 1.2 and 1.3**<br>Where the claimant is making a claim for interest on a specified sum of money, the sum claimed for the purposes of calculating fees 1.2 and 1.3 shall be taken to include the interest in addition to that specified sum. | |
| 1.4 | **On the commencement of originating proceedings** for any other remedy or relief (including originating proceedings issued after leave to issue is granted): | £150 |

**Fees Taken in the County Court** (*Cont.*)

| Fee No. | Schedule 1 Column 1 | Schedule 1 Column 2 |
|---|---|---|
| Notes | **Fees 1.2 and 1.4 Recovery of land or goods** Where a claim for money is additional or alternative to a claim for recovery of land or goods, only fee 1.4 shall be payable.<br>**Fees 1.2 and 1.4 Claims other than recovery of land or goods** Where a claim for money is additional to a non-money claim (other than a claim for recovery of land or goods) then fee 1.2 as appropriate shall be payable in addition to fee 1.4. Where a claim for money is alternative to a non money claim (other than a claim for recovery of land or goods), and, in the County Court, fee 1.2 or fee 1.4 shall be payable, whichever is the greater.<br>**Fees1.2 as appropriate and 1.4 Generally** Where more than one non-money claim is made in the same proceedings, fee 1.4 shall be payable once only, in addition to any fee which may be payable under fee 1.2 as appropriate.<br>**Fees fee 1.2 as appropriate and fee 1.4** shall not be payable where fee 1.7(b), fee 1.8(a) (in the High Court only), fee 9.1 (in the High Court only) or fee 3 apply.<br>**Fees 1.2 as appropriate and 1.4 Amendment of claim or counterclaim** Where the claim or counterclaim is amended, and the fee paid before amendment is less than that which would have been payable if the document, as amended, had been so drawn in the first instance, the party amending the document shall pay the difference. | |
| 1.5 | **On the filing of proceedings against a party or parties not named in the originating proceedings:** | £35 |
| Notes | Fee 1.5 shall be payable by a defendant who adds or substitutes a party or parties to the proceedings or by a claimant who adds or substitutes a defendant or defendants. | |
| 1.6 | **On the filing of a counterclaim** | The same fee as if the relief or remedy sought were the subject of separate proceedings |
| Notes | **Fee 1.6** No fee is fee is payable on a counterclaim which a defendant is required to make under the CPR because he contends that he has a claim or is entitled to any remedy relating to a grant of probate of a will, or letters of administration of an estate, of a deceased person. | |
| 1.7(a) | **On an application for leave to issue originating proceedings:** | £35 |
| 1.7(b) | **On an application for an order under Part III of the Solicitors Act 1974[1] for the assessment of costs payable to a solicitor by his client or on the commencement of costs-only proceedings** | £35 |
| 1.8 | **Judicial Review**—refer to fees taken in the High Court | |
| 2 | **General Fees** | |
| 2.1 | **On the claimant filing an allocation questionnaire**; or<br>• where the court dispenses with the need for an allocation questionnaire, within 14 days of the date of despatch of the notice of allocation to track; or<br>• where the CPR or a Practice Direction provide for automatic allocation or provide that the rules on allocation shall not apply, within 28 days of the filing of the defence (or the filing of the last defence if there is more than one defendant), or within 28 days of the expiry of the time permitted for filing all defences if sooner | £100 |

Notes Fee 2.1 shall be payable by the claimant except where the action is proceeding on the counterclaim alone, when it shall be payable by the defendant -

- on the defendant filing an allocation questionnaire; or
- where the court dispenses with the need for an allocation questionnaire, within 14 days of the date of despatch of the notice of allocation to track; or
- where the CPR or a Practice Direction provide for automatic allocation or provide that the rules on allocation shall not apply, within 28 days of the filing of the defence to the counterclaim (or the filing of the last defence to the counterclaim if there is more than one party entitled to file a defence to a counterclaim), or within 28 days of the expiry of the time permitted for filing all defences to the counterclaim if sooner

2.2 **On the claimant filing a listing questionnaire; or where the court fixes the trial date or trial week** without the need for a listing questionnaire, within 14 days of the date of despatch of the notice (or the date when oral notice is given if no written notice is given) of the trial week or the trial date if no trial week is fixed

- if the case is on the **multi-track** £500
- in any **other case** £275

Notes Fee 2.2 shall be payable by the claimant except where the action is proceeding on the counterclaim alone, when it shall be payable by the defendant -

- on the defendant filing a listing questionnaire; or
- where the court fixes the trial date or trial week without the need for a listing questionnaire, within 14 days of the date of despatch of the notice (or the date when oral notice is given if no written notice is given) of the trial week or the trial date if no trial week is fixed.

**Where the court receives notice in writing—**

- before the trial date has been fixed or,
- where a trial date has been fixed, at least 14 days before the trial date,

from the party who paid fee 2.2 that the case is settled or discontinued, fee 2.2 shall be refunded.

**Fees 2.1 and 2.2 Generally**

**Fees 2.1 and 2.2**

- shall be payable once only in the same proceedings.
- shall be payable as appropriate where the court allocates a case to a track for a trial of the assessment of damages.
- shall not be payable in relation to claims managed under a GLO after that GLO is made

Fee 2.1 shall not be payable

- where the procedure in Part 8 of the CPR is used.
- in proceedings where the only claim is a claim to recover a sum of money and the sum claimed does not exceed **£1,500.**

Fee 2.2 shall not be payable in respect of a small claims hearing.

2.4 **On filing—**

- an appellant's notice, or
- a respondent's notice where the respondent is appealing or wishes to ask the appeal court to uphold the order of the lower court for reasons different from or additional to those given by the lower court:

2.4(a) in a claim allocated to the small claims track £100

2.4(b) in all other claims £120

## Fees Taken in the County Court (*Cont.*)

| Fee No. | Schedule 1 Column 1 | Schedule 1 Column 2 |
|---|---|---|
| Notes | Fee 2.4 and 2.5 do not apply on appeals against a decision made in detailed assessment proceedings. | |
| 2.5 | **On an application on notice where no other fee is specified** | £65 |
| 2.6 | **On an application by consent or without notice for a judgment or order** where no other fee is specified<br>For the purpose of fee 2.7 a request for a judgment or order on admission or in default shall not constitute an application and no fee shall be payable. | £35 |
| Notes | Fee 2.6 shall not be payable in relation to an application by consent for an adjournment of a hearing where the application is received by the court at least 14 days before the date set for that hearing<br>Fees 2.5 and 2.6 shall not be payable when an application is made in an appeal notice or is filed at the same time as an appeal notice. | |
| 2.7 | **On an application for a summons or order for a witness to attend court to be examined on oath or an order for evidence to be taken by deposition**, other than an application for which fee 6.2 enforcement in the High Court or for which fee 7.3 is payable | £35 |
| 2.8 | **On an application to vary a judgment or suspend enforcement** (where more than one remedy is sought in the same application only one fee shall be payable) | £35 |
| 2.9 | **Register of** judgments etc kept under section 98 of the Courts Act 2003<br>On a request for the issue of a certificate of satisfaction | £15 |
| 3 | **Companies Act 1985[2] and Insolvency Act 1986[3]** | |
| 3.1 | **On entering a bankruptcy petition:** | |
| 3.1(a) | if presented by a debtor or the personal representative of a deceased debtor | £150 |
| 3.1(b) | if presented by a creditor or other person | £190 |
| 3.2 | **On entering a petition for an administration order** | £150 |
| 3.3 | **On entering any other petition**<br>One fee only is payable where more than one petition is presented in relation to a partnership. | £190 |
| 3.4 | **Certificate of Discharge from Bankruptcy** | |
| 3.4(a) | On a request for a certificate of discharge from bankruptcy | £60 |
| 3.4(b) | And after the first certificate for each copy | £1 |
| 3.5 | **On an application under the Companies Act 1985 or the Insolvency Act 1986** other than one brought by petition and where no other fee is specified.<br>**Fee 3.5** is not payable where the application is made in existing proceedings | £130 |
| 3.6 | **On an application for the conversion of a voluntary arrangement** into a winding up or bankruptcy under Article 37 of Council Regulation (EC) No 1346/2000 | £130 |
| 3.7 | **On an application, for the purposes of Council Regulation** (EC) **No 1346/2000**, for an order confirming creditors' voluntary winding up (where the company has passed a resolution for voluntary winding up, and no declaration under section 89 of the Insolvency Act 1986 has been made). | £30 |
| 3.8 | **On filing**<br>• a notice of intention to appoint an administrator under paragraph 14 of Schedule B1 to the Insolvency Act 1986 or in accordance with paragraph 27 of that Schedule; or | £30 |

| | | |
|---|---|---|
| | • a notice of appointment of an administrator in accordance with paragraphs 18 or 29 of that Schedule | |
| Notes | Fee 3.8 Where a person pays fee 3.8 on filing a notice of intention to appoint an administrator, no fee shall be payable on that same person filing a notice of appointment of that administrator. | |
| 3.9 | **On submitting a nominee's report under section 2(2) of the Insolvency Act 1986**[4] or | £30 |
| 3.10 | **On filing documents in accordance with paragraph 7(1) of Schedule A1 to the Insolvency Act 1986** | £30 |
| 3.11 | **On an application by consent or without notice** within existing proceedings where no other fee is specified | £30 |
| 3.12 | **On an application with notice** within existing proceedings where no other fee is specified | £60 |
| Notes | **Requests and applications with no fee**—no fee is payable on a request or on an application to the Court by the Official Receiver when applying only in the capacity of Official Receiver to the case (and not as trustee or liquidator), or on an application to set aside a statutory demand. | |
| 4 | **Copy Documents** | |
| 4.1 | **On a request for a copy of any document** (other then where fee 4.2 applies): | |
| 4.1(a) | for the first page (except the first page of a subsequent copy of the same document supplied at the same time) | £1 |
| 4.1(b) | per page in any other case | 20p |
| Notes | Fee 4.1 shall be payable for a faxed copy or for examining a plain copy and marking it as an examined copy.<br>Fee 4.1 shall be payable whether or not the copy is issued as an office copy. | |
| 4.2 | **On a request for a copy of a document required in connection with proceedings** and supplied by the party making the request at the time of copying, for each page. | 20p |
| 4.3 | **On a request for a copy of a document on a computer disk or in other electronic form**, for each such copy. | £3 |
| 5 | **Determination of costs** | |
| 5.1 | **On the filing of a request for detailed assessment** where the party filing the request is legally aided or is funded by the LSC and no other party is ordered to pay the costs of the proceedings | £105 |
| 5.2 | **On the filing of a request for a detailed assessment hearing in any case where fee 5.1 does not apply; or on the filing of a request for a hearing date for the assessment of costs payable to a solicitor by his client pursuant to an order under Part III of the Solicitors Act 1974**<br>Where there is a combined party and party and legal aid, or a combined party and party and LSC, or a combined party and party, legal aid and LSC determination of costs, fee 5.2 shall be attributed proportionately to the party and party, legal aid, or LSC (as the case may be) portions of the bill on the basis of the amount allowed. | £300 |
| 5.3 | **On a request for the issue of a default costs certificate** | £45 |
| 5.4 | **On an appeal against a decision made in detailed assessment proceedings** | £105 |
| 5.5 | **On applying for the court's approval of a certificate of costs payable from the Community Legal Service Fund.** | £35 |
| Notes | Fee 5.5 is payable at the time of applying for the court's approval and is recoverable only against the Community Legal Service Fund. | |
| 5.6 | **On a request or application to set aside a default costs certificate** | £65 |
| 6 | **Refer to Enforcement in the High Court** | |
| 7 | **Enforcement** | |

## Fees Taken in the County Court (*Cont.*)

| Fee No. | Schedule 1 Column 1 | Schedule 1 Column 2 |
|---|---|---|
| 7.1 | **On an application for or in relation to enforcement of a judgment or order of a county court or through a county court:** | |
| 7.1(a) | In cases other than CCBC cases brought by Centre users, by the issue of a warrant of execution against goods except a warrant to enforce payment of a fine; | (a) Where the amount for which the warrant issues does not exceed £125 . . . . . . £35 |
| 7.1(b) | | (b) Where the amount for which the warrant issues exceeds £125 . . . . . . £55 |
| 7.1(c) | In CCBC cases brought by Centre users, by the issue of a warrant of execution against goods except a warrant to enforce payment of a fine | (c) Where the amount for which the warrant issues does not exceed £125 . . . . . . £25 |
| 7.1(d) | | (d) Where the amount for which the warrant issues exceeds £125 . . . . . . £45 |
| 7.2 | **On a request for a further attempt at execution of a warrant** at a new address following a notice of the reason for non-execution (except a further attempt following suspension and CCBC cases brought by Centre users) | £25 |
| 7.3 | **On an application for an order requiring a judgment debtor or** other person to attend court to provide information in connection with enforcement of a judgment or order | £45 |
| 7.4(a) | **On an application for a third party debt order or** the appointment of a receiver by way of equitable execution | £55 |
| Notes | Fee 7.4(a) shall be payable in respect of each third party against whom the order is sought | |
| 7.4(b) | **On an application for a charging order** | £55 |
| Notes | Fee 7.4(b) shall be payable in respect of each application issued | |
| 7.5 | **On an application for a judgment summons** | £95 |
| 7.6 | **On the issue of a warrant of possession or a warrant of delivery** Where the recovery of a sum of money is sought in addition, no further fee is payable. | £95 |
| 7.7 | **On an application for an attachment of earnings order** (other than a consolidated attachment of earnings order) to secure payment of a judgment debt | £65 |
| Notes | Fee 7.7 is payable for each defendant against whom an order is sought. Fee 7.7 is not payable where the attachment of earnings order is made on the hearing of a judgment summons. | |
| 7.8 | **On a consolidated attachment of earnings order or on an administration order** | For every £1 or part of a £1 of the money paid into court in respect of debts due to creditors . . . . 10p |

| | | |
|---|---|---|
| Notes | Fee 7.8 shall be calculated on any money paid into court under any order at the rate in force at the time when the order was made (or, where the order has been amended, at the time of the last amendment before the date of payment). | |
| 7.9 | **On the application for the recovery of a tribunal award** | £35 |
| 7.10 | **On a request for an order to recover a sum that is:**<br>• a specified debt within the meaning of the Enforcement of Road Traffic Debts Order 1993[15] as amended from time to time; or<br>• pursuant to an enactment, treated as a specified debt for the purposes of that Order<br>**No fee is payable on:**<br>• an application for an extension of time to serve a statutory declaration in connection with any such order; or<br>• a request to issue a warrant of execution to enforce any such order | £5 |
| 8 | Sale | |
| 8.1 | **For removing or taking steps to remove goods to a place of deposit**<br>Fee 8.1 is to include the reasonable expenses of feeding and caring for any animals. | The reasonable expenses incurred |
| 8.2 | **For advertising a sale by public auction pursuant to section 97 of the County Courts Act 1984**[16] | The reasonable expenses incurred |
| 8.3 | **For the appraisement of goods** | 5p in the £1 or part of a £1 of the appraised value |
| 8.4 | **For the sale of goods** (including advertisements, catalogues, sale and commission and delivery of goods) | 15p in the £1 or part of a £1 on the amount realised by the sale or such other sum as the district judge may consider to be justified in the circumstances |
| 8.5 | **Where no sale takes place by reason of an execution being withdrawn, satisfied or stopped** | (a) 10p in the £1 or part of a £1 on the value of the goods seized, the value to be the appraised value where the goods have been appraised or such other sum as the district judge may consider to be justified in the circumstances; and in addition (b) any sum payable under fee 8.1, 8.2 or 8.3 |
| 9 to 12 | **Refer to High Court fees for Bills of Sale, Admiralty and Affidavits** | |

# Further Information (County Court)

# The following wording is taken from the Civil Proceedings Fees Order 2004 [2004/3121 (L.23)]

## Citation and commencement

1 (1) This Order may be cited as the Civil Proceedings Fees Order 2004 and shall come into force on the 4 January 2005.

(2) In this Order

(a) a fee referred to by number means the fee so numbered in Schedule 1 to this Order;

(b) "CCBC" means County Court Bulk Centre;

(c) "CPC" means Claim Production Centre;

(d) "the CPR" means the Civil Procedure Rules 1998;[7]

(e) expressions also used in the CPR have the same meaning as in those Rules;

(f) "family proceedings" means family proceedings in the High Court or in a county court as appropriate;

(g) "LSC" means the Legal Services Commission established under section 1 of the Access to Justice Act 1999;[8]

(h) "Funding Code" means the code approved under section 9 of the Access to Justice Act 1999;[9]

(i) "GLO" means a Group Litigation Order.

## Fees to be taken

2 The fees set out in column 2 of Schedule 1 to this Order shall be taken in the Supreme Court and in county courts respectively in respect of the items described in column 1 in accordance with and subject to the directions specified in column 1.

3 The provisions of this Order shall not apply to—

(a) non-contentious probate business;

(b) proceedings in the Court of Protection, except in so far as fees 1, 2, 3, 6, 9 and 10 in Schedule 1 (High Court only) are applicable;

(c) the enrolment of documents;

(d) criminal proceedings (except proceedings on the Crown side of the Queen's Bench Division to which the fees contained in Schedule 1 are applicable);

(e) proceedings by sheriffs, under-sheriffs, deputy-sheriffs or other officers of the sheriff; and

(f) family proceedings.

## Exemptions, reductions, remissions and refunds

4 (1) No fee shall be payable under this Order by a party who, at the time when a fee would otherwise become payable—

(a) is in receipt of any qualifying benefit, and

(b) is not in receipt of, as appropriate, either—

(i) representation under Part IV of the Legal Aid Act 1988[10] for the purposes of the proceedings; or

(ii) funding provided by the LSC for the purposes of the proceedings and for which a certificate has been issued under the Funding Code certifying a decision to fund services for that party.

(2) The following are qualifying benefits for the purposes of paragraph (1)(a) above—

(a) income support under the Social Security Contributions and Benefits Act 1992;[11]

(b) working tax credit, provided that—

(i) child tax credit is being paid to the party, or otherwise following a claim for child tax credit made jointly by the members of a couple (as defined in section 3(5A) of the Tax Credits Act 2002[12] which includes the party; or

(ii) there is a disability element or severe disability element (or both) to the tax credit received by the party;

**and** that the gross annual income taken into account for the calculation of the working tax credit is £16,017 or less;

(c) income-based jobseeker's allowance under the Jobseekers Act 1995;[13] and

(d) guarantee credit under the State Pension Credit Act 2002.[14]

(3) In the county courts paragraph (1) shall not apply to fee 7.8 (fee payable on a consolidated attachment of earnings order or an administration order).

5 Where it appears to the Lord Chancellor that the payment of any fee prescribed by this Order would, owing to the exceptional circumstances of the particular case, involve undue financial hardship, he may reduce or remit the fee in that case.

6 (1) Subject to paragraph (2), where a fee has been paid at a time—

(a) when, under article 4, it was not payable, the fee shall be refunded;

(b) where the Lord Chancellor, if he had been aware of all the circumstances, would have reduced the fee under article 4, the amount by which the fee would have been reduced shall be refunded; and

(c) where the Lord Chancellor, if he had been aware of all the circumstances, would have remitted the fee under article 4, the fee shall be refunded.

(2) No refund shall be made under paragraph (1) unless the party who paid the fee applies within 6 months of paying the fee.

(3) The Lord Chancellor may extend the period of 6 months referred to in paragraph (2) if he considers that there is good reason for an application being made after the end of the period of 6 months.

7 Where by any convention entered into by Her Majesty with any foreign power it is provided that no fee shall be required to be paid in respect of any proceedings, the fees specified in this Order shall not be taken in respect of those proceedings.

## Revocations

8 The Orders specified below, in so far as they were made under sections 414 and 415 of the Insolvency Act 1986 and section 128 of the Finance Act 1990, shall be revoked.

| Orders Revoked | Reference |
|---|---|
| The Supreme Court Fees Order 1999 | SI 1999/687 |
| The Supreme Court Fees (Amendment) Order 1999 | SI 1999/2569 |
| The Supreme Court Fees (Amendment) Order 2000 | SI 2000/641 |
| The Supreme Court Fees (Amendment) Order 2003 | SI 2003/646 |
| The Supreme Court Fees (Amendment) Order 2004 | SI 2004/2100 |
| The Supreme Court Fees (Amendment No.2) Order 2000 | SI 2000/937 |
| The Supreme Court Fees (Amendment No.2) Order 2003 | SI 2003/717 |
| The County Court Fees Order 1999 | SI 1999/689 |
| The County Court Fees (Amendment) Order 1999 | SI 1999/2548 |
| The County Court Fees (Amendment) Order 2000 | SI 2000/639 |
| The County Court Fees (Amendment) Order 2003 | SI 2003/648 |
| The County Court Fees (Amendment) Order 2004 | SI 2004/2098 |
| The County Court Fees (Amendment No.2) Order 2000 | SI 2000/939 |
| The County Court Fees (Amendment No.2) Order 2003 | SI 2003/718 |
| The County Court Fees (Amendment No.4) Order 2000 | SI 2000/2310 |

## Endnotes

1. 1974 c.47.
2. 1985 c.6.
3. 1986 c.45.
4. Section 2(2) was amended by section 2(a) of and Schedule 2, paragraphs 1 and 3(a) to the Insolvency Act 2000 (c.39).
5. 1878 c.31, section 15 was repealed, in relation to bills of sale given as security for payment of money in so far as inconsistent with the Bills of Sale Act (1878) Amendment Act 1882, by sections 3 and 15 of that Act.
6. 1882 c.43.
7. SI 1998/3132.
8. 1999 c.22. Section 1 was amended by article 9 of and Schedule 2, paragraph 11(1)(a) to the Secretary of State for Constitutional Affairs Order 2003 (SI 2003/1887).
9. Section 9 was amended by article 9 of and Schedule 2, paragraph 11(1)(a) to the Secretary of State for Constitutional Affairs Order 2003 (SI 2003/1887).
10. 988 c.34, Part IV was repealed by section 106 of and Part I of Schedule 15 to the Access to Justice Act 1999 (c.22), from 1 April 2000 subject to the transitional and savings provisions in article 5 of the Access to Justice Act 1999 (Commencement No.3, Transitional Provisions and Savings) Order 2000 (SI 2000/774), in respect of an application for legal aid signed before 1 April 2000 and received by the Legal Aid Board by the 2 May 2000.
11. 1992 c. 4.
12. 2002 c.21. Section 3(5A) is substituted for section 3(5) and (6) by the Civil Partnership Act 2004, Schedule 24 paragraph 144(3).
13. 1995 c.18.
14. 2002 c.16.
15. SI 1993/2073.
16. 1984 c.28.

# Section 1

## CIVIL PROCEDURE RULES 1998 AND PRACTICE DIRECTIONS AS AMENDED

# Foreword*

'It is now some years since the publication of Lord Woolf's report on the civil justice system in England and Wales, "Access to Justice". This report set out a new vision for the administration of civil justice. It envisaged a civil justice system which was comprehensible to its users; where claims were dealt with in a manner proportionate to their substance; which contained greatly reduced opportunities to use the law as a tactical weapon to obstruct progress and inflate costs; which provided access to justice for all, and most importantly, which was just in the results it delivered.

In the original foreword to the Civil Procedure Rules, my predecessor, Lord Irvine of Lairg, set out the formidable task ahead of the then newly formed Civil Procedure Rule Committee. All of these intentions were to be enacted through a new set of rules which would govern the operation of both the High Court and the county court, unifying the civil justice procedures. The ongoing changes to the rules reflect the continuing civil justice reforms.

I am pleased to see that Lord Woolf's vision is still apparent throughout these rules, especially his concept of the rules themselves and their role in breaking down artificial distinctions in the civil justice system. The number of interconnecting provisions between the High Court and the county court has indeed been substantially reduced in the intervening years, as have those provisions which apply only to one or the other of those courts. The range of special provisions for specific types of case has also been reduced, replaced wherever possible with procedures which apply to the broadest possible range of cases. Perhaps most noticeably, the language of the rules is clear, non-technical and easily comprehensible.

The rules are also the vehicle for a number of new initiatives. Developments in technology have provided a major new route into the civil justice system, and projects such as Money Claims Online and Possession Claims Online are slowly but surely changing the way litigants resolve their claims. Lord Woolf's desire for greater proportionality is being borne out in the groundbreaking work on alternative dispute resolution (ADR), offering litigants easier access to the quickest and most appropriate method of resolving their dispute. The introduction of fixed recoverable costs and success fees in some types of personal injury cases has introduced much needed stability and certainty into the cost regime. Supplementing this is the developing work on the civil debt strategy with its strong emphasis on early and effective advice, which aims to avoid unnecessary court action where appropriate and to promote the speedy resolution of cases that must come to court.

The title of Lord Woolf's report, "Access to Justice", became the phrase that marked a paradigm shift in the administration of civil justice. That every citizen and business in England and Wales now has the ability to approach our legal system and ask for justice without always needing expert knowledge and aware of the continuing drive to control costs is something we should be proud of, and we must ensure that these ideals are never lost in the business of reviewing, changing and implementing these rules.

For this work, I wish to extend my thanks to the members of the Civil Procedure Rule Committee, past and present, who work tirelessly to ensure that the Civil Procedure Rules remain adherent to the ideals outlined above. Keeping the rules responsive to the constant and ongoing changes in the legal system, the law and society as a whole is no easy matter, and I am grateful for the committee's dedication to their task.

Lord Falconer of Thoroton'

---

* This Foreword was published generally by the DCA as part of the current release of the CPR and was not produced for the purposes of this work. It is reproduced here for completeness.

# Introduction

## Civil Procedure Rules 1998 Preamble

The Civil Procedure Rule Committee, having power under section 2 of the Civil Procedure Act 1997 to make rules of court under section 1 of that Act, make the following rules which may be cited as the Civil Procedure Rules 1998.

## Notes on Practice Directions

1 The practice directions to the Civil Procedure Rules apply to civil litigation in the Queen's Bench Division and the Chancery Division of the High Court and to litigation in the county courts other than family proceedings. Where relevant they also apply to appeals to the Civil Division of the Court of Appeal.

2 The practice directions are made:
   (1) for the Queen's Bench Division by the Lord Chief Justice as president of that Division;
   (2) for the Civil Division of the Court of Appeal by the Master of the Rolls as president of that Division;
   (3) for the Chancery Division by the Vice-Chancellor as vice-president of that Division; and
   (4) for the county courts by the Lord Chancellor or a person authorised to act on his behalf under s. 74A of the County Courts Act 1984.

3 From April 1999 to July 2000 the Lord Chancellor authorised the Vice-Chancellor, Sir Richard Scott (as he then was) under s. 74A of the 1984 Act. The Vice-Chancellor made all practice directions for county courts during that time.

4 From July 2000 to September 2003 the Lord Chancellor authorised Lord Justice May to make these practice directions. Lord Justice May made all practice directions for county courts during that time.

5 From September 2003 the Lord Chancellor has authorised Lord Justice Dyson to make practice directions for the county courts.

## List of Transitional Regulations

The following list of Regulations is given to assist the reader but does not form part of the CPR text.

1 The following transitional provision is made by SI 2000/2092, r. 29:
   Where a person has, before 2nd October 2000, filed a notice of appeal in a claim allocated to the small claims track—
   (a) Part 52 shall not apply to the appeal to which that notice relates; and
   (b) rules 27.12 and 27.13 shall apply to that appeal as if they had not been revoked.

2 The following transitional provision is made by SI 2000/1317, r. 39:
   (1) This rule applies where a person has—
      (a) entered into a funding arrangement, and
      (b) started proceedings in respect of a claim the subject of that funding arrangement, before the date on which these Rules come into force [i.e., 3 July 2000].
   (2) Any requirement imposed—
      (a) by any provision of the Civil Procedure Rules 1998 amended by these Rules, or
      (b) by a practice direction
      in respect of that funding arrangement may be complied with within 28 days of the coming into force of these Rules, and that compliance shall be treated as compliance with the relevant rule or practice direction.
   (3) For the purpose of this rule, 'funding arrangement' means an arrangement where a person has—

(a) entered into a conditional fee agreement which provides for a success fee within the meaning of section 58(2) of the Courts and Legal Services Act 1990;
(b) taken out an insurance policy to which section 29 of the Access to Justice Act 1999 (recovery of insurance premiums by way of costs) applies; or
(c) made an agreement with a membership organisation prescribed for the purpose of section 30 of the Access to Justice Act 1999 (recovery where body undertakes to meet cost liabilities) to meet his legal costs.

3 The following transitional provision is made by SI 2000/221, r. 39, as substituted by SI 2000/940, r. 2:
Where a person has filed a notice of appeal or applied for permission to appeal before 2 May 2000—
(a) rule 19 of these Rules shall not apply to the appeal to which that notice or application relates; and
(b) the rules of court relating to appeals in force immediately before 2 May 2000 shall apply to that appeal as if they had not been revoked.

4 The following transitional provision is made by SI 2000/2092, r. 30:
Where a person has, before 2nd October 2000, filed an application for permission to make an application for judicial review in accordance with RSC Order 53—
(a) Part 54 shall not apply to that application for permission or the application for judicial review to which it relates; and
(b) RSC Order 53 shall apply to those applications as if it had not been revoked.

5 The following transitional provision is made by SI 2001/256, r. 31:
Where a claim form—
(a) relates to proceedings to which Part 55 or Part 56 would apply if it was issued on or after the date of entry into force of rules 17 and 18 of these Rules [i.e., 15 October 2001], but
(b) is issued before that date,
those rules shall not apply, and the rules of court in force immediately before that date shall apply as if they had not been amended or revoked.

6 The following transitional provision is made by SI 2001/1388, r. 19:
Where a claim form—
(a) relates to proceedings to which Part 57 would apply if it was issued on or after 15th October 2001, but
(b) is issued before that date,
that Part shall not apply to the proceedings, and the rules of court in force immediately before that date shall apply as if they had not been amended or revoked.

7 The following transitional provision is made by SI 2001/2792, r. 24:
(1) Parts 70 to 73 shall not apply to any enforcement proceedings specified in paragraph (2) which are issued before 25th March 2002, and the rules of court in force immediately before that date shall apply to those proceedings as if they had not been amended or revoked.
(2) The enforcement proceedings to which this rule applies are—
  (a) an application for an order for oral examination;
  (b) an application for a garnishee order;
  (c) an application by a judgment creditor for an order for the payment to him of money standing in court to the credit of a judgment debtor;
  (d) an application for a charging order;
  (e) a claim for the enforcement of a charging order by sale of the property charged; and
  (f) an application for a stop order.

8 The following transitional provision is made by SI 2001/4015, r. 43:
(1) Where proceedings for the possession of land are issued before 25th March 2002, rule 42(b) shall not apply, and CCR Order 38 shall apply as if it had not been amended.

(2) Where on or after 25th March 2002 fixed costs are to be awarded in enforcement proceedings which, pursuant to rule 24 of the Civil Procedure (Amendment No. 4) Rules 2001, continue to be governed by rules in Schedule 1 or Schedule 2 to the Civil Procedure Rules 1998 rather than rules in Parts 70 to 73, the rules governing enforcement costs in force immediately before 25th March 2002 shall continue to apply as if they had not been revoked.

9 The following transitional provision is made by SI 2002/2058, r. 34:
Where before 2nd December 2002 proceedings have begun under rule 47.6(1) for the detailed assessment of the costs of a litigant in person, rule 48.6 shall continue to apply to those proceedings as if it had not been amended.

10 The following transitional provision is made by SI 2003/1242, r. 6:
Rule 5(b) of these Rules has effect only where the conditional fee agreement which is in issue was entered into on or after 2nd June 2003.

11 The following transitional provision is made by SI 2003/2113, r. 18:
Section II of Part 45 shall not apply to any costs-only proceedings arising out of a dispute, where the road traffic accident which gave rise to the dispute occurred before 6th October 2003.

12 See the DCA website for details of the transitional provisions relating to Updates 35 onwards. (A table of Statutory Instruments is also included in this work and reference should be had in particular to the various Civil Procedure Rules (Amendment) Regulations listed there.)

# CPR Part 1 Overriding Objective



## 1.1 The Overriding Objective

(1) These Rules are a new procedural code with the overriding objective of enabling the court to deal with cases justly.

(2) Dealing with a case justly includes, so far as is practicable—

- (a) ensuring that the parties are on an equal footing;
- (b) saving expense, subject to rule 76.2;
- (c) dealing with the case in ways which are proportionate—
  - (i) to the amount of money involved;
  - (ii) to the importance of the case;
  - (iii) to the complexity of the issues; and
  - (iv) to the financial position of each party;
- (d) ensuring that it is dealt with expeditiously and fairly; and
- (e) allotting to it an appropriate share of the court's resources, while taking into account the need to allot resources to other cases.

## 1.2 Application by the Court of the Overriding Objective

The court must seek to give effect to the overriding objective when it—

- (a) exercises any power given to it by the Rules; or
- (b) interprets any rule.

## 1.3 Duty of the Parties

The parties are required to help the court to further the overriding objective.

## 1.4 Court's Duty to Manage Cases

(1) The court must further the overriding objective by actively managing cases.

(2) Active case management includes—

- (a) encouraging the parties to co-operate with each other in the conduct of the proceedings;
- (b) identifying the issues at an early stage;
- (c) deciding promptly which issues need full investigation and trial and accordingly disposing summarily of the others;
- (d) deciding the order in which issues are to be resolved;
- (e) encouraging the parties to use an alternative dispute resolution(GL)* procedure if the court considers that appropriate and facilitating the use of such procedure;
- (f) helping the parties to settle the whole or part of the case;
- (g) fixing timetables or otherwise controlling the progress of the case;
- (h) considering whether the likely benefits of taking a particular step justify the cost of taking it;
- (i) dealing with as many aspects of the case as it can on the same occasion;
- (j) dealing with the case without the parties needing to attend at court;
- (k) making use of technology; and
- (l) giving directions to ensure that the trial of a case proceeds quickly and efficiently.

* Editorial note: the expression (GL) refers to expressions for which there is an entry in the CPR glossary.

# CPR Part 2 Application and Interpretation of the Rules



## 2.1 Application of the Rules

(1) Subject to paragraph (2), these Rules apply to all proceedings in—
   (a) county courts;
   (b) the High Court; and
   (c) the Civil Division of the Court of Appeal.

(2) These Rules do not apply to proceedings of the kinds specified in the first column of the following table (proceedings for which rules may be made under the enactments specified in the second column) except to the extent that they are applied to those proceedings by another enactment—

| | Proceedings | Enactments |
|---|---|---|
| 1. | Insolvency proceedings | Insolvency Act 1986, ss. 411 and 412 |
| 2. | Non-contentious or common form probate proceedings | Supreme Court Act 1981, s. 127 |
| 3. | Proceedings in the High Court when acting as a Prize Court | Prize Courts Act 1894, s. 3 |
| 4. | Proceedings before the judge within the meaning of Part VII of the Mental Health Act 1983. | Mental Health Act 1983, s. 106 |
| 5. | Family proceedings | Matrimonial and Family Proceedings Act 1984, s. 40 |
| 6. | Adoption proceedings | Adoption Act 1976, s. 66 or Adoption and Children Act 2002, s. 141 |
| 7. | Election petitions in the High Court | Representation of the People Act 1983, s. 182 |

## 2.2 The Glossary

(1) The glossary at the end of these Rules is a guide to the meaning of certain legal expressions used in the Rules, but is not to be taken as giving those expressions any meaning in the Rules which they do not have in the law generally.

(2) Subject to paragraph (3), words in these Rules which are included in the glossary are followed by '(GL)'.

(3) The words 'counterclaim', 'damages', 'practice form' and 'service', which appear frequently in the Rules, are included in the glossary but are not followed by '(GL)'.

## 2.3 Interpretation

(1) In these Rules—
'child' has the meaning given by rule 21.1(2);

'civil restraint order' means an order restraining a party—

(a) from making any further applications in current proceedings (a limited civil restraint order);

(b) from issuing certain claims or making certain applications in specified courts (an extended civil restraint order); or

(c) from issuing any claim or making any application in specified courts (a general civil restraint order);

'claim for personal injuries' means proceedings in which there is a claim for damages in respect of personal injuries to the claimant or any other person or in respect of a person's death, and 'personal injuries' includes any disease and any impairment of a person's physical or mental condition;

'claimant' means a person who makes a claim;

'CCR' is to be interpreted in accordance with Part 50;

'court officer' means a member of the court staff,

'defendant' means a person against whom a claim is made;

'defendant's home court' means—

(a) if the claim is proceeding in a county court, the county court for the district in which the defendant resides or carries on business; and

(b) if the claim is proceeding in the High Court, the district registry for the district in which the defendant resides or carries on business or, where there is no such district registry, the Royal Courts of Justice;

(Rule 6.5 provides for a party to give an address for service.)

'filing', in relation to a document, means delivering it, by post or otherwise, to the court office;

'judge' means, unless the context otherwise requires, a judge, Master or district judge or a person authorised to act as such;

'jurisdiction' means, unless the context requires otherwise, England and Wales and any part of the territorial waters of the United Kingdom adjoining England and Wales;

'legal representative' means a barrister or a solicitor, solicitor's employee or other authorised litigator (as defined in the Courts and Legal Services Act 1990) who has been instructed to act for a party in relation to a claim.

'litigation friend' has the meaning given by Part 21;

'patient' has the meaning given by rule 21.1(2);

'RSC' is to be interpreted in accordance with Part 50;

'statement of case'—

(a) means a claim form, particulars of claim where these are not included in a claim form, defence, Part 20 claim, or reply to defence; and

(b) includes any further information given in relation to them voluntarily or by court order under rule 18.1;

'statement of value' is to be interpreted in accordance with rule 16.3;

'summary judgment' is to be interpreted in accordance with Part 24.

(2) A reference to a 'specialist list' is a reference to a list(GL) that has been designated as such by a rule or practice direction.

(3) Where the context requires, a reference to 'the court' means a reference to a particular county court, a district registry, or the Royal Courts of Justice.

## 2.4 Power of Judge, Master or District Judge to Perform Functions of the Court

Where these Rules provide for the court to perform any act then, except where an enactment, rule or practice direction provides otherwise, that act may be performed—

(a) in relation to proceedings in the High Court, by any judge, Master or district judge of that Court; and

(b) in relation to proceedings in a county court, by any judge or district judge.

## 2.5 Court Staff

(1) Where these Rules require or permit the court to perform an act of a formal or administrative character, that act may be performed by a court officer.
(2) A requirement that a court officer carry out any act at the request of a party is subject to the payment of any fee required by a fees order for the carrying out of that act.

(Rule 3.2 allows a court officer to refer to a judge before taking any step.)

## 2.6 Court Documents to be Sealed

(1) The court must seal[(GL)] the following documents on issue—
 (a) the claim form; and
 (b) any other document which a rule or practice direction requires it to seal.
(2) The court may place the seal on the document—
 (a) by hand; or
 (b) by printing a facsimile of the seal on the document whether electronically or otherwise.
(3) A document purporting to bear the court's seal[(GL)] shall be admissible in evidence without further proof.

## 2.7 Court's Discretion as to Where it Deals With Cases

The court may deal with a case at any place that it considers appropriate.

## 2.8 Time

(1) This rule shows how to calculate any period of time for doing any act which is specified—
 (a) by these Rules;
 (b) by a practice direction; or
 (c) by a judgment or order of the court.
(2) A period of time expressed as a number of days shall be computed as clear days.
(3) In this rule 'clear days' means that in computing the number of days—
 (a) the day on which the period begins; and
 (b) if the end of the period is defined by reference to an event, the day on which that event occurs are not included.

*Examples*

(i) Notice of an application must be served at least 3 days before the hearing. An application is to be heard on Friday 20 October.
The last date for service is Monday 16 October.

(ii) The court is to fix a date for a hearing.
The hearing must be at least 28 days after the date of notice. If the court gives notice of the date of the hearing on 1 October, the earliest date for the hearing is 30 October.

(iii) Particulars of claim must be served within 14 days of service of the claim form.
The claim form is served on 2 October.
The last day for service of the particulars of claim is 16 October.

(4) Where the specified period—
 (a) is 5 days or less; and
 (b) includes—
  (i) a Saturday or Sunday; or
  (ii) a Bank Holiday, Christmas Day or Good Friday, that day does not count.

*Example*

Notice of an application must be served at least 3 days before the hearing. An application is to be heard on Monday 20 October.
The last date for service is Tuesday 14 October.

(5) When the period specified—
  (a) by these Rules or a practice direction; or
  (b) by any judgment or court order,
  for doing any act at the court office ends on a day on which the office is closed, that act shall be in time if done on the next day on which the court office is open.

## 2.9 Dates for Compliance to be Calendar Dates and to Include Time of Day

(1) Where the court gives a judgment, order or direction which imposes a time limit for doing any act, the last date for compliance must, wherever practicable—
  (a) be expressed as a calendar date; and
  (b) include the time of day by which the act must be done.
(2) Where the date by which an act must be done is inserted in any document, the date must, wherever practicable, be expressed as a calendar date.

## 2.10 Meaning of 'Month' in Judgments, etc.

Where 'month' occurs in any judgment, order, direction or other document, it means a calendar month.

## 2.11 Time Limits May be Varied by Parties

Unless these Rules or a practice direction provide otherwise or the court orders otherwise, the time specified by a rule or by the court for a person to do any act may be varied by the written agreement of the parties.

(Rules 3.8 (sanctions have effect unless defaulting party obtains relief), 28.4 (variation of case management timetable—fast track) and 29.5 (variation of case management timetable—multi-track) provide for time limits that cannot be varied by agreement between the parties.)

# PD 2 Practice Direction — Court Offices

This practice direction supplements CPR Part 2.

## Central Office of the High Court at the Royal Courts of Justice

1 The Central Office shall be divided into such departments, and the business performed in the Central Office shall be distributed among the departments in such manner, as is set out in the Queen's Bench Division Guide.

## Business in the Offices of the Supreme Court

2.1 (1) The offices of the Supreme Court shall be open on every day of the year except:
(a) Saturdays and Sundays,
(b) Good Friday and the day after Easter Monday,
(c) Christmas Day and, if that day is a Friday or Saturday, then 28 December,
(d) Bank Holidays in England and Wales under the Banking and Financial Dealings Act 1971, and
(e) such other days as the Lord Chancellor, with the concurrence of the Lord Chief Justice, the Master of the Rolls, the President of the Family Division and the Vice-Chancellor ('the Heads of Division') may direct.

(2) The hours during which the offices of the Supreme Court at the Royal Courts of Justice and at the Principal Registry of the Family Division at First Avenue House, 42–49 High Holborn, London WC1V 6NP shall be open to the public shall be as follows:
(a) from 10 a.m. to 4.30 p.m.;
(b) such other hours as the Lord Chancellor, with the concurrence of the Heads of Division, may from time to time direct.

(3) Every district registry shall be open on the days and during the hours that the Lord Chancellor from time to time directs and, in the absence of any such directions, shall be open on the same days and during the same hours as the county court offices of which it forms part are open.

2.2 One of the masters of the Queen's Bench Division (the 'Practice Master') shall be present at the Central Office on every day on which the office is open for the purpose of superintending the business performed there and giving any directions which may be required on questions of practice and procedure.

## County Courts

3.1 Every county court shall have an office or, if the Lord Chancellor so directs, two or more offices, situated at such place or places as he may direct, for the transaction of the business of the court.

3.2 (1) Every county court office, or if a court has two or more offices at least one of those offices, shall be open on every day of the year except:
(a) Saturdays and Sundays,
(b) the day before Good Friday from noon onwards and Good Friday,
(c) the Tuesday after the Spring bank holiday,
(d) Christmas Day and, if that day is a Friday or Saturday, then 28 December,
(e) bank holidays and
(f) such other days as the Lord Chancellor may direct.

(2) In this paragraph 'bank holiday' means a bank holiday in England and Wales under the Banking and Financial Dealings Act 1971 and 'Spring bank holiday' means the

bank holiday on the last Monday in May or any day appointed instead of that day under section 1(2) of that Act.

3.3 Subject to para. 3.2(1)(b), the hours during which any court office is open to the public shall be from 10 a.m. to 4 p.m. or such other hours as the Lord Chancellor may from time to time direct.

# PD 2B Practice Direction — Allocation of Cases to Levels of Judiciary

1.1 Rule 2.4 provides that judges, masters and district judges may exercise any function of the court except where an enactment, rule or practice direction provides otherwise. This practice direction sets out the matters over which masters and district judges do not have jurisdiction or which they may deal with only on certain conditions. It does not affect jurisdiction conferred by other enactments. Reference should also be made to other relevant practice directions (e.g. PD 24, para. 3, and PD 26, paras 12.1–10). References to circuit judges include recorders and assistant recorders and references to masters and district judges include deputies.

1.2 Wherever a master or district judge has jurisdiction, he may refer the matter to a judge instead of dealing with it himself.

## THE HIGH COURT

### Injunctions

2.1 Search orders (r. 25.1(1)(h)), freezing orders (r. 25.1(1)(f)), an ancillary order under r. 25.1(1)(g) and orders authorising a person to enter land to recover, inspect or sample property (r. 25.1(1)(d)) may only be made by a judge.

2.2 Except where paras 2.3 and 2.4 apply, injunctions and orders relating to injunctions, including orders for specific performance where these involve an injunction, must be made by a judge.

2.3 A master or a district judge may only make an injunction:

(a) in terms agreed by the parties;
(b) in connection with or ancillary to a charging order;
(c) in connection with or ancillary to an order appointing a receiver by way of equitable execution; or
(d) in proceedings under rule 66.7 (order restraining person from receiving sum due from the Crown).

2.4 A master or district judge may make an order varying or discharging an injunction or undertaking given to the court if all parties to the proceedings have consented to the variation or discharge.

### Other Pre-trial Orders and Interim Remedies

3.1 A master or district judge may not make orders or grant interim remedies:

(a) relating to the liberty of the subject;
(b) relating to criminal proceedings or matters except procedural applications in appeals to the High Court (including appeals by case stated) under any enactment;
(c) relating to a claim for judicial review, except that interim applications in claims for judicial review may be made to masters of the Queen's Bench Division;
(d) relating to appeals from masters or district judges;
(e) in appeals against costs assessment under Parts 43 to 48, except on an appeal under r. 47.20 against the decision of an authorised court officer;
(f) in applications under s. 42 of the Supreme Court Act 1981 by a person subject to a civil or a criminal or an all proceedings order (vexatious litigant) for permission to start or continue proceedings;
(g) in applications under the Mental Health Act 1983, s. 139, for permission to bring proceedings against a person.

3.2 This practice direction is not concerned with family proceedings. It is also not concerned with proceedings in the Family Division except to the extent that such proceedings can be dealt with in the Chancery Division or the Family Division e.g. proceedings under the Inheritance (Provision for Family and Dependants) Act 1975 or under s. 14 of the Trusts of Land and Appointment of Trustees Act 1996. District judges (including district judges of the Principal Registry of the Family Division) have jurisdiction to hear such proceedings, subject to any direction given by the President of the Family Division.

## Trials and Assessments of Damages

4.1 A master or district judge may, subject to any practice direction, try a case which is treated as being allocated to the multi-track because it is proceeding under Part 8 (see r. 8.9(c)). He may try a case which has been allocated to the multi-track under Part 26 only with the consent of the parties. Restrictions on the trial jurisdiction of masters and district judges do not prevent them from hearing applications for summary judgment or, if the parties consent, for the determination of a preliminary issue.

4.2 A master or a district judge may assess the damages or sum due to a party under a judgment without limit as to the amount.

## Chancery Proceedings

5.1 In proceedings in the Chancery Division, a master or a district judge may not deal with the following without the consent of the Chancellor:

(a) approving compromises (other than applications under the Inheritance (Provision for Family and Dependants) Act 1975) (i) on behalf of a person under disability where that person's interest in a fund, or if there is no fund, the maximum amount of the claim, exceeds £100,000 and (ii) on behalf of absent, unborn and unascertained persons;

(b) making declarations, except in plain cases;

(c) making final orders under s. 1(1) of the Variation of Trusts Act 1958, except for the removal of protective trusts where the interest of the principal beneficiary has not failed or determined;

(d) where the proceedings are brought by a Part 8 claim form seeking determination of any question of law or as to the construction of a document which is raised by the claim form;

(e) giving permission to executors, administrators and trustees to bring or defend proceedings or to continue the prosecution or defence of proceedings, and granting an indemnity for costs out of the trust estate, except in plain cases;

(f) granting an indemnity for costs out of the assets of a company on the application of minority shareholders bringing a derivative [claim], except in plain cases;

(g) making an order for rectification, except for:
  (i) rectification of the register under the Land Registration Act 1925; or
  (ii) alteration or rectification of the register under the Land Registration Act 2002, in plain cases;

(h) making orders to vacate entries in the register under the Land Charges Act 1972, except in plain cases;

(i) making final orders on applications under s. 19 of the Leasehold Reform Act 1967, s. 48 of the Administration of Justice Act 1985 and ss. 21 and 25 of the Law of Property Act 1969;

(j) making final orders under the Landlord and Tenant Acts 1927 and 1954, except; (i) by consent, and (ii) orders for interim rents under sections 24A to 24D of the 1954 Act; (iii) on applications to authorise agreements under s. 38(4) of the 1954 Act;

(k) making orders in proceedings in the Patents Court except (i) by consent, (ii) to extend time, (iii) on applications for permission to serve out of the jurisdiction and (iv) on applications for security for costs.

5.2 A master or district judge may only give directions for early trial after consulting the judge in charge of the relevant list.

5.3 Where a winding-up order has been made against a company, any proceedings against the company by or on behalf of debenture holders may be dealt with, at the Royal Courts of Justice, by a registrar and, in a district registry with insolvency jurisdiction, by a district judge.

## Assignment of Claims to Masters and Transfer Between Masters

6.1 The Senior Master and the Chief Master will make arrangements for proceedings to be assigned to individual masters. They may vary such arrangements generally or in particular cases, for example, by transferring a case from a master to whom it had been assigned to another master.

6.2 The fact that a case has been assigned to a particular master does not prevent another master from dealing with that case if circumstances require, whether at the request of the assigned master or otherwise.

## Freezing Orders: Cross-examination of Deponents About Assets

7 Where the court has made a freezing order under r. 25.1(1)(f) and has ordered a person to make a witness statement or affidavit about his assets and to be cross-examined on its contents, unless the judge directs otherwise, the cross-examination will take place before a master or a district judge, or if the master or district judge directs, before an examiner of the court.

## Human Rights

7A A deputy High Court judge, a master or district judge may not try:
- (1) a case in a claim made in respect of a judicial act under the Human Rights Act 1998; or
- (2) a claim for a declaration of incompatibility in accordance with s. 4 of the Human Rights Act 1998.

# COUNTY COURTS

## Injunctions, Anti-social Behaviour Order and Committal

8.1 Injunctions which a county court has jurisdiction to make may only be made by a circuit judge, except:
- (a) where the injunction is to be made in proceedings which a district judge otherwise has jurisdiction to hear (see para. 11.1 below);
- (b) where the injunction is sought in a money claim which has not yet been allocated to a track, where the amount claimed does not exceed the fast track financial limit;
- (c) in the circumstances provided by para. 2.3;
- (d) where the injunction is to be made under any of the following provisions—
  - (i) section 153A, 153B or 153D of the Housing Act 1996; or
  - (ii) section 3 of the Protection from Harassment Act 1997.

8.1A A district judge has jurisdiction to make an order under—
- (1) section 1B or 1D of the Crime and Disorder Act 1998 (anti-social behaviour); and
- (2) section 4 or 9 of the Violent Crime Reduction Act 2006 (drinking banning order).

8.2 A district judge may make orders varying or discharging injunctions in the circumstances provided by para. 2.4.

8.3 A district judge may not make an order committing a person to prison except where an enactment authorises this: see s. 23 of the Attachment of Earnings Act 1971, ss. 14 and 118 of the County Courts Act 1984, ss. 152–157 of the Housing Act 1996, and the relevant rules.

## Homelessness Appeals

9 A district judge may not hear appeals under s. 204 or s. 204A of the Housing Act 1996.

## Other Pre-trial Orders and Interim Remedies

10.1 In addition to the restrictions on jurisdiction mentioned at paras 8.1–3, para. 3.1(d) and (e) above applies.

## Trials and Assessments of Damages

11.1 A district judge has jurisdiction to hear the following:
- (a) any claim which has been allocated to the small claims track or fast track or which is treated as being allocated to the multi-track under r. 8.9(c) and the table at Section B of the Practice Direction to Part 8, except claims:
  - (i) under the Landlord and Tenant Act 1927, part I;
  - (ii) for a new tenancy under Section 24 or for the termination of a tenancy under Section 29(2) of the Landlord and Tenant Act 1954;
  - (iii) for an order under the Landlord and Tenant Act 1987, s. 38 or 40;
  - (iv) under the Agricultural Holdings Act 1986, s. 27, or sch. 11, para. 26 or 27;
  - (v) under the Matrimonial Causes Act 1973, s. 45(2), for a declaration of legitimation by virtue of the Legitimacy Act 1976;
  - (vi) under the Fair Trading Act 1973, s. 35, 38 or 40;
  - (vii) under the Mental Health Act 1983, part II;
- (b) proceedings for the recovery of land; proceedings under section 82A(2) of the Housing Act 1985 or Section 6A(2) of the Housing Act 1988 (demotion claims) or proceedings in a County Court under Chapter 1A of the Housing Act 1996 (demoted tenancies);
- (c) the assessment of damages or other sum due to a party under a judgment without any financial limit;
- (d) with the permission of the designated civil judge in respect of that case, any other proceedings.

11.2 A case allocated to the small claims track may only be assigned to a circuit judge to hear with his consent.

## Freezing Orders: Cross-examination of Deponents About Assets

12 To the extent that a county court has power to make a freezing order, para. 7 applies as appropriate.

## Distribution of Business Between Circuit Judge and District Judge

13 Where both the circuit judge and the district judge have jurisdiction in respect of any proceedings, the exercise of jurisdiction by the district judge is subject to any arrangements made by the designated civil judge for the proper distribution of business between circuit judges and district judges.

14.1 In district registries of the High Court and in the county court, the designated civil judge may make arrangements for proceedings to be assigned to individual district judges. He may vary such arrangements generally or in particular cases.

14.2 The fact that a case has been assigned to a particular district judge does not prevent another district judge from dealing with the case if the circumstances require.

## Human Rights

15 A district judge may not try a case in which an allegation of indirect discrimination is made against a public authority that would, if the court finds that it occurred, be unlawful under the Race Relations Act 1976, s. 19B.

# CPR Part 3 The Court's Case Management Powers



### 3.1 The Court's General Powers of Management

(1) The list of powers in this rule is in addition to any powers given to the court by any other rule or practice direction or by any other enactment or any powers it may otherwise have.

(2) Except where these Rules provide otherwise, the court may—

(a) extend or shorten the time for compliance with any rule, practice direction or court order (even if an application for extension is made after the time for compliance has expired);

(b) adjourn or bring forward a hearing;

(c) require a party or a party's legal representative to attend the court;

(d) hold a hearing and receive evidence by telephone or by using any other method of direct oral communication;

(e) direct that part of any proceedings (such as a counterclaim) be dealt with as separate proceedings;

(f) stay(GL) the whole or part of any proceedings or judgment either generally or until a specified date or event;

(g) consolidate proceedings;

(h) try two or more claims on the same occasion;

(i) direct a separate trial of any issue;

(j) decide the order in which issues are to be tried;

(k) exclude an issue from consideration;

(l) dismiss or give judgment on a claim after a decision on a preliminary issue;

(ll) order any party to file and serve an estimate of costs;

(m) take any other step or make any other order for the purpose of managing the case and furthering the overriding objective.

(3) When the court makes an order, it may—

(a) make it subject to conditions, including a condition to pay a sum of money into court; and

(b) specify the consequence of failure to comply with the order or a condition.

(4) Where the court gives directions it may take into account whether or not a party has complied with any relevant pre-action protocol(GL).

(5) The court may order a party to pay a sum of money into court if that party has, without good reason, failed to comply with a rule, practice direction or a relevant pre-action protocol.

(6) When exercising its power under paragraph (5) the court must have regard to—

(a) the amount in dispute; and
(b) the costs which the parties have incurred or which they may incur.

(6A) Where a party pays money into court following an order under paragraph (3) or (5), the money shall be security for any sum payable by that party to any other party in the proceedings.

(7) A power of the court under these Rules to make an order includes a power to vary or revoke the order.

## 3.2 Court Officer's Power to Refer to a Judge

Where a step is to be taken by a court officer—
(a) the court officer may consult a judge before taking that step;
(b) the step may be taken by a judge instead of the court officer.

## 3.3 Court's Power to Make Order of its Own Initiative

(1) Except where a rule or some other enactment provides otherwise, the court may exercise its powers on an application or of its own initiative.
(Part 23 sets out the procedure for making an application.)

(2) Where the court proposes to make an order of its own initiative—
(a) it may give any person likely to be affected by the order an opportunity to make representations; and
(b) where it does so it must specify the time by and the manner in which the representations must be made.

(3) Where the court proposes—
(a) to make an order of its own initiative; and
(b) to hold a hearing to decide whether to make the order,
it must give each party likely to be affected by the order at least 3 days' notice of the hearing.

(4) The court may make an order of its own initiative, without hearing the parties or giving them an opportunity to make representations.

(5) Where the court has made an order under paragraph (4)—
(a) a party affected by the order may apply to have it set aside varied or stayed(GL); and
(b) the order must contain a statement of the right to make such an application.

(6) An application under paragraph (5)(a) must be made—
(a) within such period as may be specified by the court; or
(b) if the court does not specify a period, not more than 7 days after the date on which the order was served on the party making the application.

(7) If the court of its own initiative strikes out a statement of case or dismisses an application (including an application for permission to appeal or for permission to apply for judicial review), and it considers that the claim or application is totally without merit—
(a) the court's order must record that fact; and
(b) the court must at the same time consider whether it is appropriate to make a civil restraint order.

## 3.4 Power to Strike Out a Statement of Case

(1) In this rule and rule 3.5, reference to a statement of case includes reference to part of a statement of case.

(2) The court may strike out(GL) a statement of case if it appears to the court—
(a) that the statement of case discloses no reasonable grounds for bringing or defending the claim;
(b) that the statement of case is an abuse of the court's process or is otherwise likely to obstruct the just disposal of the proceedings; or
(c) that there has been a failure to comply with a rule, practice direction or court order.

(3) When the court strikes out a statement of case it may make any consequential order it considers appropriate.

(4) Where—
(a) the court has struck out a claimant's statement of case;
(b) the claimant has been ordered to pay costs to the defendant; and
(c) before the claimant pays those costs, he starts another claim against the same defendant, arising out of facts which are the same or substantially the same as those relating to the claim in which the statement of case was struck out,
the court may, on the application of the defendant, stay(GL) that other claim until the costs of the first claim have been paid.
(5) Paragraph (2) does not limit any other power of the court to strike out(GL) a statement of case.
(6) If the court strikes out a claimant's statement of case and it considers that the claim is totally without merit—
(a) the court's order must record that fact; and
(b) the court must at the same time consider whether it is appropriate to make a civil restraint order.

### 3.5 Judgment Without Trial after Striking Out

(1) This rule applies where—
(a) the court makes an order which includes a term that the statement of case of a party shall be struck out if the party does not comply with the order; and
(b) the party against whom the order was made does not comply with it.
(2) A party may obtain judgment with costs by filing a request for judgment if—
(a) the order referred to in paragraph (1)(a) relates to the whole of a statement of case; and
(b) where the party wishing to obtain judgment is the claimant, the claim is for—
(i) a specified amount of money;
(ii) an amount of money to be decided by the court;
(iii) delivery of goods where the claim form gives the defendant the alternative of paying their value; or
(iv) any combination of these remedies.
(3) Where judgment is obtained under this rule in a case to which paragraph (2)(b)(iii) applies, it will be judgment requiring the defendant to deliver the goods, or (if he does not do so) pay the value of the goods as decided by the court (less any payments made).
(4) The request must state that the right to enter judgment has arisen because the court's order has not been complied with.
(5) A party must make an application in accordance with Part 23 if he wishes to obtain judgment under this rule in a case to which paragraph (2) does not apply.

### 3.6 Setting Aside Judgment Entered after Striking Out

(1) A party against whom the court has entered judgment under rule 3.5 may apply to the court to set the judgment aside.
(2) An application under paragraph (1) must be made not more than 14 days after the judgment has been served on the party making the application.
(3) If the right to enter judgment had not arisen at the time when judgment was entered, the court must set aside(GL) the judgment.
(4) If the application to set aside(GL) is made for any other reason, rule 3.9 (relief from sanctions) shall apply.

### 3.7 Sanctions for Non-payment of Certain Fees

(1) This rule applies where—
(a) an allocation questionnaire or a pre-trial checklist (listing questionnaire) is filed without payment of the fee specified by the relevant Fees Order;
(b) the court dispenses with the need for an allocation questionnaire or a pre-trial checklist or both;

(c) these Rules do not require an allocation questionnaire or a pre-trial checklist to be filed in relation to the claim in question; or
(d) the court has made an order giving permission to proceed with a claim for judicial review.

(Rule 26.3 provides for the court to dispense with the need for an allocation questionnaire and rules 28.5 and 29.6 provide for the court to dispense with the need for a pre-trial checklist.)

(Rule 54.12 provides for the service of the order giving permission to proceed with a claim for judicial review.)

(2) The court will serve a notice on the claimant requiring payment of the fee specified in the relevant Fees Order if, at the time the fee is due, the claimant has not paid it or made an application for exemption or remission.
(3) The notice will specify the date by which the claimant must pay the fee.
(4) If the claimant does not—
(a) pay the fee; or
(b) make an application for an exemption from or remission of the fee,
by the date specified in the notice—
(i) the claim will automatically be struck out without further order of the court; and
(ii) the claimant shall be liable for the costs which the defendant has incurred unless the court orders otherwise.

(Rule 44.12 provides for the basis of assessment where a right to costs arises under this rule.)

(5) Where an application for exemption from or remission of a fee is refused, the court will serve notice on the claimant requiring payment of the fee by the date specified in the notice.
(6) If the claimant does not pay the fee by the date specified in the notice—
(a) the claim will automatically be struck out without further order of the court; and
(b) the claimant shall be liable for the costs which the defendant has incurred unless the court orders otherwise.
(7) If—
(a) a claimant applies to have the claim reinstated; and
(b) the court grants relief,
the relief shall be conditional on the claimant either paying the fee or filing evidence of exemption from payment or remission of the fee within the period specified in paragraph (8).
(8) The period referred to in paragraph (7) is—
(a) if the order granting relief is made at a hearing at which a claimant is present or represented, 2 days from the date of the order;
(b) in any other case, 7 days from the date of service of the order on the claimant.

3.7A(1) This rule applies where a defendant files a counterclaim without [E1]—
(a) payment of the fee specified by the relevant Fees Order; or
(b) making an application for an exemption from or remission of the fee.
(2) The court will serve a notice on the defendant requiring payment of the fee specified in the relevant Fees Order if, at the time the fee is due, the defendant has not paid it or made an application for exemption or remission.
(3) The notice will specify the date by which the defendant must pay the fee.
(4) If the defendant does not—
(a) pay the fee; or
(b) make an application for an exemption from or remission of the fee,
by the date specified in the notice, the counterclaim will automatically be struck out without further order of the court.
(5) Where an application for exemption from or remission of a fee is refused, the court will serve notice on the defendant requiring payment of the fee by the date specified in the notice.

(6) If the defendant does not pay the fee by the date specified in the notice, the counterclaim will automatically be struck out without further order of the court.

(7) If—
   (a) the defendant applies to have the counterclaim reinstated; and
   (b) the court grants relief,
   the relief will be conditional on the defendant either paying the fee or filing evidence of exemption from payment or remission of the fee within the period specified in paragraph (8).

(8) The period referred to in paragraph (7) is—
   (a) if the order granting relief is made at a hearing at which the defendant is present or represented, 2 days from the date of the order;
   (b) in any other case, 7 days from the date of service of the order on the defendant.

### 3.7B Sanctions for dishonouring cheque

(1) This rule applies where any fee is paid by cheque and that cheque is subsequently dishonoured.

(2) The court will serve a notice on the paying party requiring payment of the fee which will specify the date by which the fee must be paid.

(3) If the fee is not paid by the date specified in the notice—
   (a) where the fee is payable by the claimant, the claim will automatically be struck out without further order of the court;
   (b) where the fee is payable by the defendant, the defence will automatically be struck out without further order of the court,
   and the paying party shall be liable for the costs which any other party has incurred unless the court orders otherwise.

(Rule 44.12 provides for the basis of assessment where a right to costs arises under this rule.)

(4) If—
   (a) the paying party applies to have the claim or defence reinstated; and
   (b) the court grants relief,
   the relief shall be conditional on that party paying the fee within the period specified in paragraph (5).

(5) The period referred to in paragraph (4) is—
   (a) if the order granting relief is made at a hearing at which the paying party is present or represented, 2 days from the date of the order;
   (b) in any other case, 7 days from the date of service of the order on the paying party.

(6) For the purposes of this rule, 'claimant' includes a Part 20 claimant and 'claim form' includes a Part 20 claim.

### 3.8 Sanctions have Effect Unless Defaulting Party Obtains Relief

(1) Where a party has failed to comply with a rule, practice direction or court order, any sanction for failure to comply imposed by the rule, practice direction or court order has effect unless the party in default applies for and obtains relief from the sanction.

(Rule 3.9 sets out the circumstances which the court may consider on an application to grant relief from a sanction.)

(2) Where the sanction is the payment of costs, the party in default may only obtain relief by appealing against the order for costs.

(3) Where a rule, practice direction or court order—
   (a) requires a party to do something within a specified time, and
   (b) specifies the consequence of failure to comply,
   the time for doing the act in question may not be extended by agreement between the parties.

### 3.9 Relief from Sanctions

(1) On an application for relief from any sanction imposed for a failure to comply with any

rule, practice direction or court order the court will consider all the circumstances including—

(a) the interests of the administration of justice;
(b) whether the application for relief has been made promptly;
(c) whether the failure to comply was intentional;
(d) whether there is a good explanation for the failure;
(e) the extent to which the party in default has complied with other rules, practice directions, court orders and any relevant pre-action protocol(GL);
(f) whether the failure to comply was caused by the party or his legal representative;
(g) whether the trial date or the likely trial date can still be met if relief is granted;
(h) the effect which the failure to comply had on each party; and
(i) the effect which the granting of relief would have on each party.

(2) An application for relief must be supported by evidence.

## 3.10 General Power of the Court to Rectify Matters Where There has been an Error of Procedure

Where there has been an error of procedure such as a failure to comply with a rule or practice direction—

(a) the error does not invalidate any step taken in the proceedings unless the court so orders; and
(b) the court may make an order to remedy the error.

## 3.11 Power of the Court to Make Civil Restraint Orders

A practice direction may set out—

(a) the circumstances in which the court has the power to make a civil restraint order against a party to proceedings;
(b) the procedure where a party applies for a civil restraint order against another party; and
(c) the consequences of the court making a civil restraint order.

# PD 3 Practice Direction — Striking Out a Statement of Case

This practice direction supplements CPR rule 3.4.

## Introductory

1.1 Rule 1.4(2)(c) includes as an example of active case management the summary disposal of issues which do not need full investigation at trial.

1.2 The rules give the court two distinct powers which may be used to achieve this. Rule 3.4 enables the court to strike out the whole or part of a statement of case which discloses no reasonable grounds for bringing or defending a claim (rule 3.4(2)(a)), or which is an abuse of the process of the court or otherwise likely to obstruct the just disposal of the proceedings (rule 3.4(2)(b)). Rule 24.2 enables the court to give summary judgment against a claimant or defendant where that party has no real prospect of succeeding on his claim or defence. Both those powers may be exercised on an application by a party or on the court's own initiative.

1.3 This practice direction sets out the procedure a party should follow if he wishes to make an application for an order under rule 3.4.

1.4 The following are examples of cases where the court may conclude that particulars of claim (whether contained in a claim form or filed separately) fall within rule 3.4(2)(a):

(1) Those which set out no facts indicating what the claim is about, for example 'Money owed £5000',

(2) those which are incoherent and make no sense,

(3) those which contain a coherent set of facts but those facts, even if true, do not disclose any legally recognisable claim against the defendant.

1.5 A claim may fall within rule 3.4(2)(b) where it is vexatious, scurrilous or obviously ill-founded.

1.6 A defence may fall within rule 3.4(2)(a) where:

(1) it consists of a bare denial or otherwise sets out no coherent statement of facts, or

(2) the facts it sets out, while coherent, would not even if true amount in law to a defence to the claim.

1.7 A party may believe he can show without a trial that an opponent's case has no real prospect of success on the facts, or that the case is bound to succeed or fail, as the case may be, because of a point of law (including the construction of a document). In such a case the party concerned may make an application under rule 3.4 or Part 24 (or both) as he thinks appropriate.

1.8 The examples set out above are intended only as illustrations.

1.9 Where a rule, practice direction or order states 'shall be struck out or dismissed' or 'will be struck out or dismissed' this means that the striking out or dismissal will be automatic and that no further order of the court is required.

## Claims Which Appear to Fall Within Rule 3.4(2)(a) or (b)

2.1 If a court officer is asked to issue a claim form which he believes may fall within rule 3.4(2)(a) or (b) he should issue it, but may then consult a judge (under rule 3.2) before returning the claim form to the claimant or taking any other step to serve the defendant. The judge may on his own initiative make an immediate order designed to ensure that the claim is disposed of or (as the case may be) proceeds in a way that accords with the rules.

2.3 The judge may allow the claimant a hearing before deciding whether to make such an order.

2.4 Orders the judge may make include:
(1) an order that the claim be stayed until further order,
(2) an order that the claim form be retained by the court and not served until the stay is lifted,
(3) an order that no application by the claimant to lift the stay be heard unless he files such further documents (for example a witness statement or an amended claim form or particulars of claim) as may be specified in the order.

2.5 Where the judge makes any such order or, subsequently, an order lifting the stay he may give directions about the service on the defendant of the order and any other documents on the court file.

2.6 The fact that a judge allows a claim referred to him by a court officer to proceed does not prejudice the right of any party to apply for any order against the claimant.

## Defences Which Appear to Fall Within Rule 3.4(2)(a) or (b)

3.1 A court officer may similarly consult a judge about any document filed which purports to be a defence and which he believes may fall within rule 3.4(2)(a) or (b).

3.2 If the judge decides that the document falls within rule 3.4(2)(a) or (b) he may on his own initiative make an order striking it out. Where he does so he may extend the time for the defendant to file a proper defence.

3.3 The judge may allow the defendant a hearing before deciding whether to make such an order.

3.4 Alternatively the judge may make an order under rule 18.1 requiring the defendant within a stated time to clarify his defence or to give additional information about it. The order may provide that the defence will be struck out if the defendant does not comply.

3.5 The fact that a judge does not strike out a defence on his own initiative does not prejudice the right of the claimant to apply for any order against the defendant.

## General Provisions

4.1 The court may exercise its powers under rule 3.4(2)(a) or (b) on application or on its own initiative at any time.

4.2 Where a judge at a hearing strikes out all or part of a party's statement of case he may enter such judgment for the other party as that party appears entitled to.

## Applications for Orders Under Rule 3.4(2)

5.1 Attention is drawn to Part 23 (General Rules about Applications) and to the practice direction that supplements it. The practice direction requires all applications to be made as soon as possible and before allocation if possible.

5.2 While many applications under rule 3.4(2) can be made without evidence in support, the applicant should consider whether facts need to be proved and, if so, whether evidence in support should be filed and served.

## Applications for Summary Judgment

6.1 Applications for summary judgment may be made under Part 24. Attention is drawn to that Part and to the practice direction that supplements it.

## Vexatious Litigants

7.1 This Practice Direction applies where a 'civil proceedings order' or an 'all proceedings order' (as respectively defined under section 42(1A) of the Supreme Court Act 1981) is in force against a person ('the litigant').

7.2 An application by the litigant for permission to begin or continue, or to make any application in, any civil proceedings shall be made by application notice issued in the High Court and signed by the litigant.

7.3 The application notice must state:

(1) the title and reference number of the proceedings in which the civil proceedings order or the all proceedings order, as the case may be, was made,
(2) the full name of the litigant and his address,
(3) the order the applicant is seeking, and
(4) briefly, why the applicant is seeking the order.

7.4 The application notice must be filed together with any written evidence on which the litigant relies in support of his application.

7.5 Either in the application notice or in written evidence filed in support of the application, the previous occasions on which the litigant made an application for permission under section 42(1A) of the said Act must be listed.

7.6 The application notice, together with any written evidence, will be placed before a High Court judge who may:
(1) without the attendance of the applicant make an order giving the permission sought;
(2) give directions for further written evidence to be supplied by the litigant before an order is made on the application;
(3) make an order dismissing the application without a hearing; or
(4) give directions for the hearing of the application.

7.7 Directions given under paragraph 7.6(4) may include an order that the application notice be served on the Attorney-General and on any person against whom the litigant desires to bring the proceedings for which permission is being sought.

7.8 Any order made under paragraphs 7.6 or 7.7 will be served on the litigant at the address given in the application notice. CPR Part 6 will apply.

7.9 A person may apply to set aside the grant of permission if:
(1) the permission allowed the litigant to bring or continue proceedings against that person or to make any application against him, and
(2) the permission was granted other than at a hearing of which that person was given notice under paragraph 7.7.

7.10 Any application under paragraph 7.9 must be made in accordance with CPR Part 23.

# PD 3B Practice Direction — Sanctions for Non-payment of Fees

This practice direction supplements CPR rule 3.7.

1 If a claim is struck out under rule 3.7, the court will send notice that it has been struck out to the defendant.

2 The notice will also explain the effect of rule 25.11. This provides that any interim injunction will cease to have effect 14 days after the date the claim is struck out under rule 3.7. Paragraph (2) provides that if the claimant applies to reinstate the claim before the interim injunction ceases to have effect, the injunction will continue until the hearing of the application unless the court orders otherwise. If the claimant makes such an application, the defendant will be given notice in the ordinary way under rule 23.4.

# PD 3C Practice Direction — Civil Restraint Orders

This practice direction supplements CPR rule 3.11.

## Introduction

1 This practice direction applies where the court is considering whether to make—
   (a) a limited civil restraint order;
   (b) an extended civil restraint order; or
   (c) a general civil restraint order,
   against a party who has issued claims or made applications which are totally without merit.

Rules 3.3(7), 3.4(6) and 23.12 provide that where a statement of case or application is struck out or dismissed and is totally without merit, the court order must specify that fact and the court must consider whether to make a civil restraint order. Rule 52.10(6) makes similar provision where the appeal court refuses an application for permission to appeal, strikes out an appellant's notice or dismisses an appeal.

## Limited Civil Restraint Orders

2.1 A limited civil restraint order may be made by a judge of any court where a party has made 2 or more applications which are totally without merit.

2.2 Where the court makes a limited civil restraint order, the party against whom the order is made—
   (1) will be restrained from making any further applications in the proceedings in which the order is made without first obtaining the permission of a judge identified in the order;
   (2) may apply for amendment or discharge of the order provided he has first obtained the permission of a judge identified in the order; and
   (3) may apply for permission to appeal the order and if permission is granted, may appeal the order.

2.3 Where a party who is subject to a limited civil restraint order—
   (1) makes a further application in the proceedings in which the order is made without first obtaining the permission of a judge identified in the order, such application will automatically be dismissed—
      (a) without the judge having to make any further order; and
      (b) without the need for the other party to respond to it;
   (2) repeatedly makes applications for permission pursuant to that order which are totally without merit, the court may direct that if the party makes any further application for permission which is totally without merit, the decision to dismiss the application will be final and there will be no right of appeal, unless the judge who refused permission grants permission to appeal.

2.4 A party who is subject to a limited civil restraint order may not make an application for permission under paragraphs 2.2(1) or 2.2(2) without first serving notice of the application on the other party in accordance with paragraph 2.5.

2.5 A notice under paragraph 2.4 must—
   (1) set out the nature and grounds of the application; and
   (2) provide the other party with at least 7 days within which to respond.

2.6 An application for permission under paragraphs 2.2(1) or 2.2(2)—
   (1) must be made in writing;
   (2) must include the other party's written response, if any, to the notice served under paragraph 2.4; and
   (3) will be determined without a hearing.

2.7 An order under paragraph 2.3(2) may only be made by—
(1) a Court of Appeal judge;
(2) a High Court judge or master; or
(3) a designated civil judge or his appointed deputy.

2.8 Where a party makes an application for permission under paragraphs 2.2(1) or 2.2(2) and permission is refused, any application for permission to appeal—
(1) must be made in writing; and
(2) will be determined without a hearing.

2.9 A limited civil restraint order—
(1) is limited to the particular proceedings in which it is made;
(2) will remain in effect for the duration of the proceedings in which it is made, unless the court otherwise orders; and
(3) must identify the judge or judges to whom an application for permission under paragraphs 2.2(1), 2.2(2) or 2.8 should be made.

## Extended Civil Restraint Orders

3.1 An extended civil restraint order may be made by—
(1) a judge of the Court of Appeal;
(2) a judge of the High Court; or
(3) a designated civil judge or his appointed deputy in the county court,
where a party has persistently issued claims or made applications which are totally without merit.

3.2 Unless the court otherwise orders, where the court makes an extended civil restraint order, the party against whom the order is made—
(1) will be restrained from issuing claims or making applications in—
(a) any court if the order has been made by a judge of the Court of Appeal;
(b) the High Court or any county court if the order has been made by a judge of the High Court; or
(c) any county court identified in the order if the order has been made by a designated civil judge or his appointed deputy,
concerning any matter involving or relating to or touching upon or leading to the proceedings in which the order is made without first obtaining the permission of a judge identified in the order;
(2) may apply for amendment or discharge of the order provided he has first obtained the permission of a judge identified in the order; and
(3) may apply for permission to appeal the order and if permission is granted, may appeal the order.

3.3 Where a party who is subject to an extended civil restraint order—
(1) issues a claim or makes an application in a court identified in the order concerning any matter involving or relating to or touching upon or leading to the proceedings in which the order is made without first obtaining the permission of a judge identified in the order, the claim or application will automatically be struck out or dismissed—
(a) without the judge having to make any further order; and
(b) without the need for the other party to respond to it;
(2) repeatedly makes applications for permission pursuant to that order which are totally without merit, the court may direct that if the party makes any further application for permission which is totally without merit, the decision to dismiss the application will be final and there will be no right of appeal, unless the judge who refused permission grants permission to appeal.

3.4 A party who is subject to an extended civil restraint order may not make an application for permission under paragraphs 3.2(1) or 3.2(2) without first serving notice of the application on the other party in accordance with paragraph 3.5.

3.5 A notice under paragraph 3.4 must—

(1) set out the nature and grounds of the application; and
(2) provide the other party with at least 7 days within which to respond.

3.6 An application for permission under paragraphs 3.2(1) or 3.2(2)—
(1) must be made in writing;
(2) must include the other party's written response, if any, to the notice served under paragraph 3.4; and
(3) will be determined without a hearing.

3.7 An order under paragraph 3.3(2) may only be made by—
(1) a Court of Appeal judge;
(2) a High Court judge; or
(3) a designated civil judge or his appointed deputy.

3.8 Where a party makes an application for permission under paragraphs 3.2(1) or 3.2(2) and permission is refused, any application for permission to appeal—
(1) must be made in writing; and
(2) will be determined without a hearing.

3.9 An extended civil restraint order—
(1) will be made for a specified period not exceeding 2 years;
(2) must identify the courts in which the party against whom the order is made is restrained from issuing claims or making applications; and
(3) must identify the judge or judges to whom an application for permission under paragraphs 3.2(1), 3.2(2) or 3.8 should be made.

3.10 The court may extend the duration of an extended civil restraint order, if it considers it appropriate to do so, but it must not be extended for a period greater than 2 years on any given occasion.

3.11 If he considers that it would be appropriate to make an extended civil restraint order—
(1) a master or a district judge in a district registry of the High Court must transfer the proceedings to a High Court judge; and
(2) a circuit judge or a district judge in a county court must transfer the proceedings to the designated civil judge.

## General Civil Restraint Orders

4.1 A general civil restraint order may be made by—
(1) a judge of the Court of Appeal;
(2) a judge of the High Court; or
(3) a designated civil judge or his appointed deputy in a county court,
where the party against whom the order is made persists in issuing claims or making applications which are totally without merit, in circumstances where an extended civil restraint order would not be sufficient or appropriate.

4.2 Unless the court otherwise orders, where the court makes a general civil restraint order, the party against whom the order is made—
(1) will be restrained from issuing any claim or making any application in—
(a) any court if the order has been made by a judge of the Court of Appeal;
(b) the High Court or any county court if the order has been made by a judge of the High Court; or
(c) any county court identified in the order if the order has been made by a designated civil judge or his appointed deputy,
without first obtaining the permission of a judge identified in the order;
(2) may apply for amendment or discharge of the order provided he has first obtained the permission of a judge identified in the order; and
(3) may apply for permission to appeal the order and if permission is granted, may appeal the order.

4.3 Where a party who is subject to a general civil restraint order—
(1) issues a claim or makes an application in a court identified in the order without

first obtaining the permission of a judge identified in the order, the claim or application will automatically be struck out or dismissed—
(a) without the judge having to make any further order; and
(b) without the need for the other party to respond to it;
(2) repeatedly makes applications for permission pursuant to that order which are totally without merit, the court may direct that if the party makes any further application for permission which is totally without merit, the decision to dismiss that application will be final and there will be no right of appeal, unless the judge who refused permission grants permission to appeal.

4.4 A party who is subject to a general civil restraint order may not make an application for permission under paragraphs 4.2(1) or 4.2(2) without first serving notice of the application on the other party in accordance with paragraph 4.5.

4.5 A notice under paragraph 4.4 must—
(1) set out the nature and grounds of the application; and
(2) provide the other party with at least 7 days within which to respond.

4.6 An application for permission under paragraphs 4.2(1) or 4.2(2)—
(1) must be made in writing;
(2) must include the other party's written response, if any, to the notice served under paragraph 4.4; and
(3) will be determined without a hearing.

4.7 An order under paragraph 4.3(2) may only be made by—
(1) a Court of Appeal judge;
(2) a High Court judge; or
(3) a designated civil judge or his appointed deputy.

4.8 Where a party makes an application for permission under paragraphs 4.2(1) or 4.2(2) and permission is refused, any application for permission to appeal—
(1) must be made in writing; and
(2) will be determined without a hearing.

4.9 A general civil restraint order—
(1) will be made for a specified period not exceeding 2 years;
(2) must identify the courts in which the party against whom the order is made is restrained from issuing claims or making applications; and
(3) must identify the judge or judges to whom an application for permission under paragraphs 4.2(1), 4.2(2) or 4.8 should be made.

4.10 The court may extend the duration of a general civil restraint order, if it considers it appropriate to do so, but it must not be extended for a period greater than 2 years on any given occasion.

4.11 If he considers that it would be appropriate to make a general civil restraint order—
(1) a master or a district judge in a district registry of the High Court must transfer the proceedings to a High Court judge; and
(2) a circuit judge or a district judge in a county court must transfer the proceedings to the designated civil judge.

## General

5.1 The other party or parties to the proceedings may apply for any civil restraint order.

5.2 An application under paragraph 5.1 must be made using the Part 23 procedure unless the court otherwise directs and the application must specify which type of civil restraint order is sought.

5.3 Examples of a limited civil restraint order, an extended civil restraint order and a general civil restraint order are annexed to this practice direction. These examples may be modified as appropriate in any particular case.

| | |
|---|---|
| FORM N19 | Limited Civil Restraint Order* |
| FORM N19A | Extended Civil Restraint Order |
| FORM N19B | General Civil Restraint Order |

* These forms are not reproduced in this work but may be accessed via the Court Service website at <http://www.courtservice.gov.uk>.

# CPR Part 4 Forms

4—(1) The forms set out in a practice direction shall be used in the cases to which they apply.

(2) A form may be varied by the court or a party if the variation is required by the circumstances of a particular case.

(3) A form must not be varied so as to leave out any information or guidance which the form gives to the recipient.

(4) Where these Rules require a form to be sent by the court or by a party for another party to use, it must be sent without any variation except such as is required by the circumstances of the particular case.

(5) Where the court or a party produces a form shown in a practice direction with the words 'Royal Arms', the form must include a replica of the Royal Arms at the head of the first page.

# PD 4 Practice Direction — Forms*

This practice direction supplements CPR Part 4.

## Scope of this Practice Direction

1.1 This practice direction lists the forms to be used in civil proceedings on or after 26 April 1999, when the Civil Procedure Rules (CPR) came into force.

1.2 The forms may be modified as the circumstances require, provided that all essential information, especially information or guidance which the form gives to the recipient, is included.

1.3 This practice direction contains 3 tables—
- Table 1 lists forms required by CPR, Parts 1 to 75
- Table 2 lists High Court forms in use before 26 April 1999 which have remained in use on or after that date (see 4 below)
- Table 3 lists county court forms in use before 26 April 1999 that will remain in use on or after that date (see 5 below)

1.4 Former prescribed forms are shown as 'No. 00'. The former practice forms where they are appropriate for use in either the Chancery or Queen's Bench Division (or where no specific form is available for use in the county court, in that court also) are prefixed 'PF' followed by the number. Where the form is used mainly in the Chancery or Queen's Bench Division, the suffix CH or QB follows the form number.

## Other Forms

2.1 Other forms may be authorised by practice directions. For example the forms relating to Part 61 Admiralty claims are authorised by, and annexed to, the Admiralty Claims practice direction.

### Table 1

*Contents*

3.1 This table lists the forms that are referred to and required by rules or practice directions supplementing particular Parts of the CPR. A practice direction and its paragraphs are abbreviated by reference to the Part of the CPR which it supplements and the relevant paragraph of the practice direction, for example PD 34 1.2. For ease of reference, forms required for claims in the Commercial Court, Technology and Construction Court and for Admiralty claims and arbitration claims, are separately listed.

3.2 There are Court Funds Office forms referred to in Part 37. These are not listed below. They are Form 201 (Request for payment out of money in court to satisfy a Part 36 offer) and Form 202 (Notice of Defendant's consent to payment out of money in court to satisfy a Part 36 offer). It should also be noted that use of Form N242A – Offer to settle – Part 36, referred to in paragraph 1.1 of the Practice Direction supplementing Part 36 and in the table below, is not mandatory,

| No. | Title |
|---|---|
| N1 | Part 7 (general) claim form (PD 7, para. 3.1) |
| N1A | Notes for claimant |
| N1C | Notes for defendant |
| N1(FD) | Notes for defendant (Consumer Credit Act cases) |
| N2 | Claim form (probate claim) (PD 57, para. 2.1) |
| N2A | Claimant's notes for guidance (probate claim) |

* The forms listed here are not reproduced in this work but may be accessed via the Court Service website at <http://www.courtservice.gov.uk>.

| No. | Title |
|---|---|
| N2B | Defendant's notes for guidance (probate claim) |
| N3 | Acknowledgement of service (probate claim) (Rule 57.4(1)) |
| N5 | Claim form for possession of property (PD 55, para. 1.5) |
| N5A | Claim form for relief against forfeiture (PD 55, para. 1.5) |
| N5B | Claim form for possession of property (accelerated procedure) (assured shorthold tenancy) (PD 55, para. 1.5) |
| N5C | Notes for the claimant (accelerated possession procedure) |
| N6 | Claim form for demotion of tenancy (PD 65, para. 5.2) |
| N7 | Notes for defendant (mortgaged residential premises) |
| N7A | Notes for defendant (rented residential premises) |
| N7B | Notes for defendant—forfeiture of the lease (residential premises) |
| N7D | Notes for defendant—demotion claim |
| N8 | Claim form (arbitration) |
| N8A | Arbitration claim (notes for claimant) |
| N8B | Arbitration claim (notes for defendant) |
| N9 | Acknowledgment of service/response pack (PD 10, para. 2) |
| N9A | Admission and statement of means (specified amount) (PD 14, para. 2.1) |
| N9B | Defence and counterclaim (specified amount) (PD 15, para. 1.3) |
| N9C | Admission and statement of means (unspecified amount and non money claims) (PD 14, para. 2.1) |
| N9D | Defence and counterclaim (unspecified amount and non money claims) (PD 15, para. 1.3) |
| N10 | Notice that acknowledgment of service has been filed (Rule 10.4) |
| N11 | Defence form (PD 55, para. 1.5) |
| N11B | Defence form (accelerated possession procedure) (assured shorthold tenancy) (PD 55, para. 1.5) |
| N11D | Defence form (demotion of tenancy) (PD 65, para. 5.2) |
| N11M | Defence form (mortgaged residential premises) (PD 55, para. 1.5) |
| N11R | Defence form (rented residential premises) (PD 55, para. 1.5) |
| N15 | Acknowledgment of service (arbitration) |
| N16 | General form of injunction |
| N16(1) | General form of injunction (formal parts only) |
| N16A | General form of application for injunction |
| N17 | Judgment for claimant (amount to be decided by court) |
| N19 | Limited civil restraint order |
| N19A | Extended civil restraint order |
| N19B | General civil restraint order |
| N20 | Witness summons (PD 34, para. 1.2) |
| N21 | Order for Examination of Deponent before the hearing (PD 34, para. 4.1) |
| N24 | Blank form of order or judgment |
| N26 | Order for possession |
| N26A | Order for possession (accelerated possession procedure) (assured shorthold tenancy) |
| N27 | Order for possession on forfeiture (for rent arrears) |
| N27(2) | Order for possession on forfeiture (for rent arrears) (suspended) |
| N28 | Order for possession (rented premises) (suspended) |
| N28A | Order for possession (rented premises) (postponed) |
| N30 | Judgment for claimant (default HC) |
| N30 | Judgment for claimant (default CC) |
| N30(1) | Judgment for claimant (acceptance HC) |
| N30(1) | Judgment for claimant (acceptance CC) |
| N30(2) | Judgment for claimant (after determination HC) |
| N30(2) | Judgment for claimant (after determination CC) |
| N30(3) | Judgment for claimant (after re-determination HC) |

(*cont.*)

| No. | Title |
|---|---|
| N30(3) | Judgment for claimant (after re-determination CC) |
| N5 | Claim form for possession of property (PD 55, para. 1.5) |
| N32 | Judgment for return of goods |
| N32(1) HP/CCA | Judgment for delivery of goods |
| N32(2) HP/CCA | Judgment for delivery of goods (suspended) |
| N32(3) HP/CCA | Judgment for delivery of goods |
| N32(4) | Variation order (return of goods) |
| N32(5) HP/CCA | Order for balance of purchase price |
| N33 | Judgment for delivery of goods |
| N34 | Judgment for claimant (after amount decided by court HC) |
| N34 | Judgment for claimant (after amount decided by court CC) |
| N37 | Hardship Payment Order |
| N39 | Order to attend court for questioning |
| N40A(CC) | Warrant of arrest |
| N40B(CC) | Warrant of committal |
| N40A(HC) | Warrant of arrest |
| N40B(HC) | Warrant of committal |
| N54 | Notice of eviction |
| N79A | Suspended committal order (for disobedience) |
| N84 | Interim Third Party debt order |
| N85 | Final Third Party debt order |
| N86 | Interim Charging Order |
| N87 | Final Charging order |
| N110A | Anti-social behaviour injunction—power of arrest (Housing Act 1996, Anti-Social Behaviour Act 2003, Police and Justice Act 2006) |
| N113 | Anti-social behaviour (Order under section 1B(4) of the Crime and Disorder Act 1998) |
| N119 | Particulars of claim for possession (rented residential premises) (PD 55, para. 2.1) |
| N119A | Notes for guidance on completing particulars of claim form (rented residential premises) |
| N120 | Particulars of claim for possession (mortgaged residential premises) (PD 55, para. 2.1) |
| N121 | Particulars of claim for possession (trespassers) (PD 55, para. 2.1) |
| N122 | Particulars of claim for demotion of tenancy (PD65, para. 5.2) |
| N130 | Application for an interim possession order |
| N133 | Witness statement of the defendant to oppose the making of an interim possession order |
| N134 | Interim possession order |
| N136 | Order for possession |
| N142 | Guardianship order (Housing Act 1996, Mental Health Act 1983) |
| N143 | (Interim) Hospital order (Housing Act 1996, Mental Health Act 1983) |
| N144 | Recognizance of defendant (Housing Act 1996) |
| N145 | Recognizance of surety (Housing Act 1966) |
| N146 | Warrant of arrest (Housing Act 1996) |
| N147 | Remand Order (Housing Act 1996) (bail granted) |
| N148 | Remand Order (Housing Act 1996) (bail not granted) |
| N149 | Allocation questionnaire (small claims track) (PD2B 2.1) |
| N150 | Allocation questionnaire (PD 26, para. 2.1) |
| N150A | Master/DJ's directions on allocation |
| N151 | Allocation Questionnaire (amount to be decided by court) |
| N151A | Master/DJ's directions on allocation |
| N152 | Notice that [defence][counterclaim] has been filed (PD 26, para. 2.5) |
| N153 | Notice of allocation or listing hearing (PD 26, para. 6.2) |

| No. | Title |
|---|---|
| N154 | Notice of allocation to fast track (PD 26, paras 4.2 and 9) |
| N155 | Notice of allocation to multi–track (PD 26, paras 4.2 and 10) |
| N156 | Order for further information (for allocation) (PD 26, para. 4.2(2)) |
| N157 | Notice of allocation to small claims track (PD 26, paras 4.2 and 8) |
| N158 | Notice of allocation to small claims track (preliminary hearing) (PD 26, paras 4.2 and 8) |
| N159 | Notice of allocation to small claims track (no hearing) (PD 26, paras 4.2 and 8) |
| N160 | Notice of allocation to small claims track (with parties' consent) (PD 26, paras 4.2 and 8) |
| N161 | Appellant's Notice (PD 52, para. 5.1) |
| N161A | Guidance Notes on completing the Appellant's Notice |
| N161B | Important Notes for Respondent |
| N162 | Respondent's Notice (PD 52, para. 7.3) |
| N162A | Guidance Notes on completing the Respondent's Notice |
| N163 | Skeleton Argument (PD 52, paras 5.9 and 7.10) |
| N164 | Appellant's notice (small claims track only) (PD52 5.8(1A)) |
| N170 | Listing questionnaire (Pre-trial check list) (PD 28, para. 6.1) |
| N171 | Notice of date for return of listing questionnaire (PD 26, para. 6.1 and PD 28, para. 8.1) |
| N172 | Notice of trial date |
| N173 | Notice of non-payment of fee (r. 3.7) |
| N205A | Notice of issue (specified amount) |
| N205B | Notice of issue (unspecified amount) |
| N205C | Notice of issue (non-money claim) |
| N205D | Notice of issue (probate claim) |
| N206A | Notice of issue (accelerated possession procedure) (assured shorthold tenancy) |
| N206B | Notice of issue (possession claim) |
| N206D | Notice of issue (demotion claim) |
| N208 | Part 8 claim form (PD 8, para. 2.2) |
| N208A | Part 8 notes for claimant |
| N208C | Part 8 notes for defendant |
| N209 | Part 8 notice of issue |
| N210 | Part 8 acknowledgment of service (PD 8, para. 3.2) |
| N210A | Part 8 acknowledgment of service (costs-claim only) (PD 43–48, para. 17.9) |
| N211 | Part 20 claim form (r. 20.7) |
| N211A | Part 20 notes for claimant |
| N211C | Part 20 notes for defendant |
| N212 | Part 20 notice of issue |
| N213 | Part 20 acknowledgment of service (r. 20.12) |
| N215 | Certificate of service (r. 6.10) |
| N216 | Notice of returned document (r. 6.11) |
| N217 | Order for substituted service (r. 6.8) |
| N218 | Notice of service on a partner (PD 6, para. 4.2) |
| N225 | Request for judgment and reply to admission (specified amount) (PD 12, para. 3) |
| N225A | Notice of part admission (specified amount) (r. 14.5) |
| N226 | Notice of admission (unspecified amount) (r. 14.7) |
| N227 | Request for judgment by default (amount to be decided by the court) (r. 12.5) |
| N228 | Notice of admission (return of goods) (PD 7, para. 8.5) |
| N235 | Certificate of suitability of litigation friend (PD 21, para. 2.3) |
| N236 | Notice of defence that amount claimed has been paid (r. 15.10) |
| N242 | Notice of payment into court (under order—Part 37) |

(*cont.*)

| No. | Title |
| --- | --- |
| N242A | Notice of offer to settle — Part 36 |
| N244 | Application notice (PD 23, para. 2.1) |
| N244A | Notice of hearing of application (PD 23, para. 2.2) |
| N251 | Notice of funding of case or claim |
| N252 | Notice of commencement of assessment (PD 43–48, para. 2.3) |
| N253 | Notice of amount allowed on provisional assessment (PD 43–48, para. 6.5) |
| N254 | Request for default costs certificate (PD 43–48, para. 3.1) |
| N255 | Default costs certificate HC (PD 43–48, para. 3.3) |
| N255 | Default costs certificate CC (PD 43–48, para. 3.3) |
| N256 | Final costs certificate HC (PD 43–48, para. 5.11) |
| N256 | Final costs certificate CC (PD 43–48, para. 5.11) |
| N257 | Interim costs certificate (PD 43–48, para. 5.11) |
| N258 | Request for detailed assessment hearing (non-legal aid) (PD 43–48, para. 4.3) |
| N258A | Request for detailed assessment hearing (legal aid only) |
| N258B | Request for detailed assessment (costs payable out of a fund other than the Community Legal Service Fund) |
| N258C | Request for detailed assessment hearing pursuant to an order under Part III of the Solicitor's Act 1974. |
| N259 | Notice of Appeal (PD 43–48, para. 48.1) |
| N260 | Statement of costs (summary assessment) (PD 43–48, para. 3.2) |
| N265 | List of documents (PD 31, para. 3.1) |
| N266 | Notice to admit facts/admission of facts (r. 32.18) |
| N268 | Notice to prove documents at trial (r. 32.19) |
| N271 | Notice of transfer of proceedings (r. 30) |
| N279 | Notice of discontinuance (r. 38.3) |
| N292 | Order on settlement on behalf of child or patient (PD 21, para. 11.3) |
| N294 | Claimant's application for a variation order |
| N316 | Application for order that debtor attend court for questioning (PD 71, para. 1.1) |
| N316A | Application that an officer of a company attend court for questioning (PD 71, para. 1.1) |
| N322 | Order for recovery of an award |
| N322A | Application to enforce an award (PD 70, para. 4.1) |
| N322H | Request to register a High Court Judgment or order for enforcement |
| N349 | Application for third party debt order (PD 72, para. 1.1) |
| N367 | Notice of hearing to consider why fine should not be imposed (r. 34.10) |
| N379 | Application for changing order on land or property (PD 73, para. 1.1) |
| N380 | Application for changing order on securities (PD 73, para. 1.1) |
| N434 | Notice of change of solicitor (r. 42.2) |
| N446 | Request for re-issue of enforcement or an order to obtain information from judgment debtor (not warrant) |
| N460 | Reasons for allowing or refusing permission to appeal |
| N461 | Judicial review claim form (PD 54) |
| N461 (notes) | Guidance notes on completing the judicial review claim form |
| N462 | Judicial review acknowledgment of service (PD 54) |
| N463 | Judicial review — application for urgent consideration |
| No. 32 | Order for examination within jurisdiction of witness before trial (r. 34.8) |
| No. 33 | Application for issue of letter of request to judicial authority out of jurisdiction (r. 34.13) |
| No. 34 | Order for issue of letter of request to judicial authority out of jurisdiction (r. 34.13) |
| No. 35 | Letter of request for examination of witness out of jurisdiction (r. 34.13) |
| No. 37 | Order for appointment of examiner to take evidence of witness out of jurisdiction (r. 34.13(4)) |

| No. | Title |
|---|---|
| No. 41 | Default judgment in claim relating to detention of goods (r. 12.4(1)(c)) |
| No. 44 | Part 24 judgment for claimant |
| No. 44A | Part 24 judgment for defendant |
| No. 45 | Judgment after trial before judge without jury (PD 40B, para. 14) |
| No. 46 | Judgment after trial before judge with jury (PD 40B, para. 14) |
| No. 47 | Judgment after trial before a judge of the Technology & Construction Court or a master or district judge (PD 40B, para. 14) |
| No. 48 | Order after trial of issue directed to be tried under rule 3.1(2)(i) |
| No. 49 | Judgment against personal representatives (PD 40B, para. 14.3) |
| No. 52 | Notice of claim (r. 19.8A(4)(a)) |
| No. 52A | Notice of judgment or order to an interested party |
| No. 82 | Application for appointment of a receiver |
| No. 83 | Order directing application for appointment of receiver and granting injunction meanwhile |
| No. 84 | Order for appointment of receiver by way of equitable execution (Supreme Court Act 1981, s. 37) |
| No. 93 | Order under the Evidence (Proceedings in Other Jurisdictions) Act 1975 |
| No. 94 | Order for production of documents in marine insurance action [r. 58.14] |
| No. 109 | Order for reference to the European Court |
| No. 111 | Certificate of money provisions contained in a judgment for registration in another part of the United Kingdom (Civil Jurisdiction and Judgments Act 1982, sch. 6) |
| No. 112 | Certificate issued under the Civil Jurisdiction and Judgments Act 1982, sch. 7 in respect of non-money provisions for registration in another part of the United Kingdom |
| PF 1 | Application for time (r. 3.1(2)(a)) |
| PF 2 | Order for time (r. 3.1(2)(a)) |
| PF 3 | Application for an extension of time for serving a claim form (r. 7.6) |
| PF 4 | Order for an extension of time for serving a claim form (r. 7.6) |
| PF 6(A) | Application for permission to serve claim form out of jurisdiction (r. 6.21) |
| PF 6(B) | Order for service out of the jurisdiction (r. 6.21(4)) |
| PF 7QB | Request for service of document abroad (rr. 6.26(2)(a) and 6.27(2)(a)) |
| PF 8 | Standard 'unless' order (r. 26.5(5), Part 26 PD, para 2.5 and N150A) |
| PF 11 | Application for Part 24 judgment (whole claim) (r. 24.2) |
| PF 12 | Application for Part 24 judgment (one or some of several claims) (r. 24.2) |
| PF 13 | Order under Part 24 (No 1) |
| PF 14 | Order under Part 24 (No 2) |
| PF 15 | Order under Part 24 for amount found due upon detailed assessment of solicitor's bill of costs |
| PF 16 | Notice of court's intention to make an order of its own initiative (r. 3.3(2) and (3)) |
| PF 17 | Order made on court's own initiative without a hearing (r. 3.3(4) and (5)) |
| PF 19 | Group litigation order (r. 19.1) |
| PF 20 | Application for Part 20 directions |
| PF 21 | Order for Part 20 directions |
| PF 21A | Order to add person as defendant to counterclaim (r. 20.5) |
| PF 22 | Notice claiming contribution or indemnity against another defendant (r. 20.6) |
| PF 43 | Application for security for costs (r. 25.12, also Companies Act 1985 s. 726) |
| PF 44 | Order for security for costs (r. 25.12, also Companies Act 1985 s. 726) |
| PF 48 | Court record available for use before and at hearing |
| PF 49 | Request to parties to state convenient dates for hearing of 1st CMC |
| PF 50 | Application for directions (Part 29) |

(*cont.*)

| No. | Title |
|---|---|
| PF 52 | Order for case management directions in the multi-track (Part 29) |
| PF 53 | Order for separate trial of an issue (r. 3.1(2)(i)) |
| PF 56 | Request for further information or clarification with provision for response (PD 18 1.6(2)) |
| PF 57 | Application for further information or clarification (PD 18, para. 5) |
| PF 58 | Order for further information or clarification (r. 18.1) |
| PF 63 | Interim order for receiver in pending claim |
| PF 67 | Evidence in support of application to make order of House of Lords an order of the High Court (PD 40B, para. 13.2) |
| PF 68 | Order making an order of the House of Lords an order of the High Court (PD 40B 13.3) |
| PF 72 | List of exhibits handed in at trial (PD 39, para 7) |
| PF 74 | Order for trial of whole claim or of an issue by master or district Judge (PD 2B, para. 4.1) |
| PF 78 QB | Solicitor's undertaking as to expenses (re letter of request) (r. 34.13 (6)(b) and PD 34, para. 5.3.(5)) |
| PF 83 | Judgment (non attendance of party) (r. 39.3) |
| PF 84A | Order on application arising from a failure to comply with an order or condition (r. 3.1(3)) |
| PF 84B | Judgment on application arising from a failure to comply with an order (rr. 3.5(1) and (4)) |
| PF 85A | Request for judgment (r. 3.5(2)) |
| PF 85B | Judgment on request arising from a failure to comply with an order (r. 3.5(2)) |
| PF 113 | Evidence in support of application for service by an alternative method (PD 6, para. 9.1) |
| PF 130 | Form of advertisement (r. 6.8) |
| PF 147 | Application for order declaring solicitor ceased to act (death etc.) |
| PF 148 | Order declaring solicitor has ceased to act |
| PF 149 | Application by solicitor that he has ceased to act |
| PF 150 | Order that solicitor has ceased to act |
| PF 152 QB | Evidence in support of application for examination of witness under the Evidence (Proceedings in Other Jurisdictions) Act 1975 |
| PF 153 QB | Certificate witness under the Evidence (Proceedings in Other Jurisdictions) Act 1975 |
| PF 154 QB | Order for registration of foreign judgment under the Foreign Judgments (Reciprocal Enforcement) Act 1933 |
| PF 155 | Certificates under s.10 of the Foreign Judgments (Reciprocal Enforcement) Act 1933 |
| PF 156 QB | Evidence in support of application for registration of a Community judgment |
| PF 157 QB | Order for registration of a Community judgment |
| PF 158 QB | Notice of registration of a Community judgment |
| PF 159 QB | Evidence in support of application for registration of a judgment of another Contracting State or Regulation State |
| PF 160 QB | Order for registration of a judgment of another Contracting State or Regulation State under s.4 of the Civil Jurisdiction and Judgments Act 1982 |
| PF 161 QB | Notice of registration of a judgment of another Contracting State or Regulation State |
| PF 163 QB | Evidence in support of application for certified copy of a judgment for enforcement in another Contracting State or Regulation State |
| PF 164 | Evidence in support of application for certificate as to money provisions of a judgment of the High Court for registration elsewhere in the United Kingdom |
| PF 165 | Evidence in support of application for registration of a judgment of a court in another part of the United Kingdom containing non-money provisions |

| No. | Title |
|---|---|
| PF 166 QB | Certificate as to finality etc. of Arbitration Award for enforcement abroad (Arbitration Act 1996, s.58) |
| PF 167 QB | Order to stay proceedings under the Arbitration Act 1996, s. 9 (PD 49G, para. 6) |
| PF 168 | Order to transfer claim from the High Court to county court (County Courts Act 1984; High and County Courts Jurisdiction Order 1991; r. 30.3) |
| PF 170A | Application for child or patient's settlement in personal injury or Fatal Accidents Act claims before proceedings begun (r. 21.10(2); PD 21, paras 6 and 7) |
| PF 170B | Application for child or patient's settlement in personal injury or fatal accident claims in existing proceedings (r. 21.10(2); PD 21, paras 6 and 7) |
| PF 172 QB | Request for directions in respect of funds in court or to be brought into court (r. 21.11) |
| PF 197 | Application for order for transfer from the Royal Courts of Justice to a district registry or vice versa or from one district registry to another (r. 30.2(4)) |
| PF 198 | Order under PF 197 |
| PF 205 | Evidence in support of application for permission to execute for earlier costs of enforcement under the Courts and Legal Services Act 1990, s.15(3) and (4) |
| PF 244 | Application Notice (RCJ only) (Part 23) |
| PF 12 CH | Advertisement for creditors |
| PF 13 CH | Advertisement for claimants other than creditors |
| PF 14 CH | [Witness statement] [Affidavit] verifying list of creditors' claims |
| PF 15 CH | List of claims by persons claiming to be creditors following advertisement (Exhibit A referred to in [witness statement][affidavit] in PF 14 CH). |
| PF 16 CH | List of claims by persons claiming to be creditors other than those sent in following advertisement (Exhibit B referred to in [witness statement][affidavit] in PF 14 CH) |
| PF 17 CH | List of sums of money which may be due in respect of which no claim has been received (Exhibit C referred to in [witness statement] [affidavit] in PF 14 CH) |
| PF 18 CH | Notice to creditor to prove claim |
| PF 19 CH | Notice to creditor or other claimant to produce documents or particulars in support of claim |
| PF 20 CH | Notice to creditor of allowance of claim |
| PF 21 CH | Notice to creditor of disallowance of claim in whole or in part |
| PF 22 CH | Order for administration: beneficiaries' action reconstituted as creditors' claim (Van Oppen order) |
| PF 23 CH | [Witness statement] [Affidavit] verifying list of claims other than creditors' claims |
| PF 24 CH | List of claims not being creditors' claims sent following advertisement (Exhibit D referred to in [witness statement] [affidavit] in PF 23 CH) |
| PF 25 CH | List of claims not being creditors' claims other than those sent in following advertisement (Exhibit E referred to in [witness statement] [affidavit] in PF 23 CH) |
| PF 26 CH | Notice to claimant other than a creditor to prove claim |
| PF 27 CH | [Witness statement] [Affidavit] verifying accounts and answering usual enquiries in administration claim (CPR r. 32.8 and 32.16) |
| PF 28 CH | Executors (or administrators account) (account A in PF 27 CH) |
| PF 29 CH | Master's order stating the results of proceedings before him on the usual accounts and inquiries in an administration claim |
| PF 30 CH | Security of receiver or administrator pending determination of a probate claim (PD 44) |
| PF 31 CH | Consent to act as trustee (r. 33.8) |

*(cont.)*

| No. | Title |
|---|---|
| PF 32 CH | [Witness statement] [Affidavit] in support of application for appointment of new litigation friend of child claimant (r. 21.6(4)) |
| PF 33 CH | Order for distribution of a Lloyd's estate |
| PF 34 CH | Order in inquiry as to title in proceedings to enforce charging order where the defendant's title is not disclosed |
| PF 36 CH | Order appointing administrator pending determination of probate claim (PD 44) |
| PF 38 CH | Order in probate claim approving compromise (PD 44) |
| **Commercial Court forms (CPR Part 58)** | |
| N1(CC) | Claim form (PD 58, para. 2.4) |
| N1c(CC) | Notes for the defendant |
| N9(CC) | Acknowledgment of service (PD 58, para. 5.1) |
| N208(CC) | Claim form (Part 8) (PD 58, para. 2.4) |
| N208c(CC) | Notes for the defendant |
| N210(CC) | Acknowledgment of service (Part 8) (PD 58, para. 5.2) |
| N211(CC) | Claim Form (Part 20) (PD 58, para. 12) |
| N211c(CC) | Notes for defendant (Part 20) |
| N213(CC) | Acknowledgment of service (Part 20) |
| N244(C) | Application Notice (PD 58, para. 10.7(2)) |
| N265(CC) | List of documents |
| **Technology and Construction forms (Part 60)** | |
| TCC/CM1 | Case management information sheet (PD 60, para. 8.2) |
| TCC/PTR1 | Pre-trial review questionnaire (PD 60, para. 9.1) |
| **Admiralty forms (Part 61)** | |
| ADM1 | Claim form (Admiralty claim *in rem*) (PD 61, para. 3.1) |
| ADM1A | Claim form (Admiralty claim) (PD 61, para. 12.3) |
| ADM1C | Notes for the defendant on replying to an *in rem* claim form |
| ADM2 | Acknowledgment of service for admiralty claims *in rem* (PD 61, para. 3.4) |
| ADM3 | Collision statement of case (PD 61, para. 4.1) |
| ADM4 | Application and undertaking for arrest and custody (PD 61, para. 5.1(1)) |
| ADM5 | Declaration in support of an application for warrant of arrest (PD 61, para. 5.1(2)) |
| ADM6 | Notice to consular officer of intention to apply for warrant of arrest (PD 61, para. 5.4) |
| ADM7 | Request for caution against arrest (PD 61, para. 6.2) |
| ADM9 | Warrant of arrest (PD 61, para. 5.5(1)) |
| ADM10 | Standard directions to Admiralty Marshal (PD 61, para. 5.6) |
| ADM11 | Request for caution against release (PD 61, para. 7.1) |
| ADM12 | Request for undertaking for release (PD 61, para. 7.4) |
| ADM12a | Request for withdrawal and caution against release (PD 61, para. 7.5) |
| ADM13 | Application for judgment in default (PD 61, para. 8.1) |
| ADM14 | Order for sale of a ship (PD 61, para. 9.2) |
| ADM15 | Claim form (Admiralty limitation claim) (PD 61, para. 10.1(1)) |
| ADM15B | Notes for defendant on replying to an Admiralty limitation claim |
| ADM16 | Notice of admission of right of claimant to limit liability (PD 61, para. 10.3)) |
| ADM16a | Defence to Admiralty limitation claim (PD 61, para. 10.2)) |
| ADM16b | Acknowledgment of service (Admiralty limitation claim) (PD 61, para. 10.4)) |
| ADM17 | Application for restricted limitation decree (PD 61, para. 10.5)) |
| ADM17a | Application for general limitation decree (PD 61, para. 10.6)) |
| ADM18 | Restricted limitation decree (PD 61, para. 10.5)) |
| ADM19 | General limitation decree |
| ADM20 | Defendant's claim in limitation (PD 61, para. 10.14)) |
| ADM21 | Declaration as to liability of a defendant to file and serve statement of case under a decree of limitation (PD 61, para. 10.16)) |

| No. | Title |
|---|---|
| **Arbitration forms (Part 62)** | |
| N8 | Claim form (arbitration) (PD 62, para. 2.1) |
| N8A | Notes for claimant (arbitration) |
| N8B | Notes for defendant (arbitration) |
| N15 | Acknowledgment of service (arbitration claim) |

## Table 2 Practice Forms

*Contents*

4.1 This table lists the practice forms that may be used under this practice direction. It contains forms that were previously:

- Prescribed forms contained in Appendix A to the Rules of the Supreme Court 1965
- Queen's Bench masters' practice forms
- Chancery masters' practice forms

4.2 Where a rule permits, a party intending to use a witness statement as an alternative to an affidavit should amend any form in this Table to be used in connection with that rule so that 'witness statement' replaces 'affidavit' wherever it appears in the form.

4.3 The forms in this list are reproduced in an Appendix to the Chancery and Queen's Bench Guides, in practitioners' text books and on the Court Service website (<http://www.courtservice.gov.uk>).

| No. | Title |
|---|---|
| No. 53 | Writ of *fieri facias* (sch. 1, RSC, ord. 45, r. 12) |
| No. 54 | Writ of *fieri facias* on order for costs (sch. 1, RSC, ord. 45, r. 12) |
| No. 55 | Notice of seizure (sch. 1, RSC, ord. 45, r. 2) |
| No. 56 | Writ of *fieri facias* after levy of part (sch. 1, RSC, ord. 45, r. 12) |
| No. 57 | Writ of *fieri facias* against personal representatives (sch. 1, RSC, ord. 45, r. 12) |
| No. 58 | Writ of *fieri facias de bonis ecclesiasticis* (sch. 1, RSC, ord. 45, r. 12) |
| No. 59 | Writ of *sequestrari de bonis ecclesiasticis* (sch. 1, RSC, ord. 45, r. 12) |
| No. 62 | Writ of *fieri facias* to enforce Northern Irish or Scottish judgment (sch. 1, RSC, ord. 45, r. 12) |
| No. 63 | Writ of *fieri facias* to enforce foreign registered judgment (sch. 1, RSC, ord. 45, r. 12) |
| No. 64 | Writ of delivery: delivery of goods, damages and costs (sch. 1, RSC, ord. 45, r. 4) |
| No. 65 | Writ of delivery: delivery of goods or value, damages and costs (sch. 1, RSC, ord. 45, r. 12(2)) |
| No. 66 | Writ of possession (sch. 1, RSC, ord. 45, r. 12(3)) |
| No. 66A | Writ of possession (sch. 1, RSC, ord. 113, r. 7) |
| No. 67 | Writ of sequestration (sch. 1, RSC, ord. 45, r. 12(4), and ord. 46, r. 5) |
| No. 68 | Writ of restitution (sch. 1, RSC, ord. 46, rr. 1 and 3) |
| No. 69 | Writ of assistance (sch. 1, RSC, ord. 46, rr. 1 and 3) |
| No. 71 | Notice of renewal of writ of execution (sch. 1, RSC, ord. 46, r. 8) |
| No. 85 | Order of committal or other penalty upon finding of contempt of court (sch. 1, RSC, ord. 52) |
| No. 87 | Claim form for writ of *habeas corpus ad subjiciendum* |
| No. 88 | Notice of adjourned application for writ of habeas corpus |
| No. 89 | Writ of *habeas corpus ad subjiciendum* |
| No. 90 | Notice to be served with writ of *habeas corpus ad subjiciendum* |
| No. 91 | Writ of *habeas corpus ad testificandum* |
| No. 92 | Writ of *habeas corpus ad respondendum* |
| No. 95 | Certificate of order against the Crown (sch. 1, RSC, ord. 77, r. 15, and Crown Proceedings Act 1947, s. 25) |

*(cont.)*

| No. | Title |
|---|---|
| No. 96 | Certificate of order against the Crown (sch. 1, RSC, ord. 77, r. 15, and Crown Proceedings Act 1947, s. 25) |
| No. 97 | Claim form to grant bail (criminal proceedings) (sch. 1, RSC, ord. 79, r. 9(1)) |
| No. 97A | Claim form to vary arrangements for bail (criminal proceedings) (sch. 1, RSC, ord. 79, r. 9(1)) |
| No. 98 | Order to release prisoner on bail (sch. 1, RSC, ord. 79, r. 9(6), (6A) and (6B)) |
| No. 98A | Order varying arrangements for bail (sch. 1, RSC, ord. 79, r. 9(10)) |
| No. 99 | Order of Court of Appeal to admit prisoner to bail |
| No. 100 | Notice of bail (sch. 1, RSC, ord. 79, r. 9(7)) |
| No. 101 | Witness summons — Crown Court |
| No. 103 | Witness summons — Crown Court |
| No. 104 | Attachment of earnings order (Attachment of Earnings Act 1971) |
| No. 105 | Notice under the Attachment of Earnings Act 1971, s. 10(2) |
| No. 110 | Certificate under s.12 of the Civil Jurisdiction and Judgments Act 1982 |
| PF 23 QB | Notice by sheriff of claim to goods taken in execution (sch. 1, RSC, ord. 17, r. 2(2)) |
| PF 24 QB | Notice by execution creditor of admission or dispute of title of interpleader/claimant (sch. 1, RSC, ord. 17, r. 2(2)) |
| PF 25 QB | Interpleader application (sch. 1, RSC, ord. 17, r. 3) |
| PF 26 QB | Interpleader application by sheriff (sch. 1, RSC, ord. 17, r. 3) |
| PF 27 QB | Evidence in support of interpleader application (sch. 1, RSC, ord. 17, r. 3(4)) |
| PF 28 QB | Interpleader order (1) claim barred where sheriff interpleads (sch. 1, RSC, ord. 17) |
| PF 29 QB | Interpleader order (1a) sheriff to withdraw (sch. 1, RSC, ord. 17) |
| PF 30 QB | Interpleader order (2) interpleader claimant substituted as defendant (sch. 1, RSC, ord. 17) |
| PF 31 QB | Interpleader order (3) trial of issue (sch. 1, RSC, ord. 17) |
| PF 32 QB | Interpleader order (4) conditional order for sheriff to withdraw and trial of issue (sch. 1, RSC, ord. 17) |
| PF 34 QB | Interpleader order (6) summary disposal (sch. 1, RSC, ord. 17, r. 5(2)) |
| PF 86 | *Praecipe* for writ of *fieri facias* (sch. 1, RSC, ord. 45, r. 12(1) and ord. 46, r. 6) |
| PF 87 | *Praecipe* for writ of sequestration (sch. 1, RSC, ord. 45, r. 12(4) and ord. 46, r. 6) |
| PF 88 | *Praecipe* for writ of possession (sch. 1, RSC, ord. 45, r. 12(3); ord. 46, r. 6 and ord. 113, r. 7) |
| PF 89 | *Praecipe* for writ of possession and *fieri facias* combined (sch. 1, RSC, ord. 45, r. 12 and ord. 46, r. 6) |
| PF 90 | *Praecipe* for writ of delivery (sch. 1, RSC, ord. 45, r. 12(2) and ord. 46, r. 6) |
| PF 97 QB | Order for sale by sheriff by private contract (sch. 1, RSC, ord. 47, r. 6) |
| PF 102 | Bench warrant (sch. 1, RSC, ord. 52) |
| PF 103 | Warrant of committal (general) (sch. 1, RSC, ord. 52) (not for orders to obtain information—use forms N40A and N40B) |
| PF 104 | Warrant of committal (contempt in face of court) (sch. 1, RSC, ord. 52) |
| PF 105 | Warrant of committal (failure of witness to attend) (sch. 1, RSC, ord. 52) |
| PF 106 | Warrant of committal (of prisoner) (sch. 1, RSC, ord. 52) |
| PF 141 | Witness statement/affidavit of personal service of judgment or order (sch. 1, RSC, ord. 45, r. 7) |
| PF 177 | Order for written statement as to partners in firm (sch. 1, RSC, ord. 81, r. 2) |
| PF 179 QB | Evidence on registration of a bill of sale (Bills of Sale Act 1878; sch. 1, RSC, ord. 95) |
| PF 180 QB | Evidence on registration of an absolute bill of sale, settlement and deed of gift (sch. 1, RSC, ord. 95) |

| No. | Title |
|---|---|
| PF 181 QB | Evidence in support of an application for re-registration of a bill of sale (Bills of Sale Act 1878, s. 11; sch. 1, RSC, ord. 95) |
| PF 182 QB | Order for extension of time to register or re-register a bill of sale (Bills of Sale Act 1878, s. 14; sch. 1, RSC, ord. 95) |
| PF 183 QB | Evidence for permission to enter a memorandum of satisfaction on a bill of sale (Bills of Sale Act 1878, s. 15; sch. 1, RSC, ord. 95; PD RSC Ord. 95, 1) |
| PF 184 QB | Claim form for entry of satisfaction on a registered bill of sale (Bills of Sale Act 1878, s. 15; sch. 1, RSC, ord. 95, r. 2; PD RSC Ord. 95, 3) |
| PF 185 QB | Order for entry of satisfaction on a registered bill of sale (Bills of Sale Act 1878, s. 14; sch. 1, RSC, ord. 95, r. 2) |
| PF 186 QB | Evidence on registration of assignment of book debts (Insolvency Act 1986, s. 344; sch. 1, RSC, ord. 95, r. 6(2)) |
| PF 187 | Claim form for solicitor's charging order (Solicitors Act 1974, s. 73; sch. 1, RSC, ord. 106, r. 2) |
| PF 188 | Charging order: solicitor's costs (Solicitors Act 1974, s. 73; sch. 1, RSC, ord. 106, r. 2) |
| PF 6 CH | Certificate on application for permission to issue execution on suspended order for possession where defendant in default of acknowledgement of service (sch. 1, RSC, ord. 46, rr. 2 and 4 and CPR, Part 23) |
| PF 7 CH | Inquiry for persons entitled to the property of an intestate (sch. 1, RSC, ord. 85) |
| PF 8 CH | Application notice after master's findings on kin enquiry (*Benjamin* order) giving permission to distribute estate upon footing (sch. 1, RSC, ord. 85) |
| PF 9 CH | Order giving leave to distribute estate upon footing (*Benjamin*) (sch. 1, RSC, ord. 85) |
| PF 10 CH | Judgment in beneficiaries' administration claim (sch. 1, RSC, ord. 85) |
| PF 11 CH | Judgment in creditors' administration claim (sch. 1, RSC, ord. 85) |

## Table 3

*Contents*

5.1 This table lists county court forms in use before 26 April 1999 that have continued to be used on or after that date.*

5.2 Where a rule permits, a party intending to use a witness statement as an alternative to an affidavit should amend any form in this Table to be used in connection with that rule so that 'witness statement' replaces 'affidavit' wherever it appears in the form.

| No. | Title |
|---|---|
| N27 | Judgment for claimant in action of forfeiture for non-payment of rent |
| N35 | Variation order |
| N35A | Variation order (determination) |
| N41 | Order suspending judgment or order, and/or warrant of execution/committal |
| N41A | Order suspending warrant (determination) |
| N42 | Warrant of execution |
| N46 | Warrant of delivery and execution for damages and costs |
| N48 | Warrant of delivery, where, if goods are not returned, levy is to be made for their value |
| N49 | Warrant for possession of land |
| N50 | Warrant of restitution (CCR, ord. 26, r. 17) |

(*cont.*)

* Note: obsolete forms are omitted. The forms listed here are not reproduced in this work. but may be accessed via the Court Service website at <http://www.courtservice.gov.uk>.

| No. | Title |
|---|---|
| N51 | Warrant of restitution (CCR, ord. 24, r. 6(1)) |
| N52 | Warrant of possession under CCR, ord. 24 |
| N53 | Warrant of execution or committal to district judge of foreign court |
| N55 | Notice of application for attachment of earnings order |
| N55A | Notice of application for attachment of earnings order (maintenance) |
| N56 | Form for replying to an attachment of earnings application (statement of means) |
| N58 | Order for defendant's attendance at an adjourned hearing of an attachment of earnings application (maintenance) |
| N59 | Warrant of committal under the Attachment of Earnings Act 1971, s. 23(1) |
| N60 | Attachment of earnings order (judgment debt) |
| N61 | Order for production of statement of means |
| N61A | Order to employer for production of statement of earnings |
| N62 | Summons for offence under Attachment of Earnings Act 1971 |
| N63 | Notice to show cause (Attachment of Earnings Act 1971, s. 23) |
| N64 | Suspended attachment of earnings order |
| N64A | Suspended attachment of earnings order (maintenance) |
| N65A | Attachment of earnings arrears order |
| N65 | Attachment of earnings order (priority maintenance) |
| N66 | Consolidated attachment of earnings order |
| N66A | Notice of application for consolidated attachment of earnings order |
| N67 | Judgment summons under the Debtors Act 1869 |
| N68 | Certificate of service (judgment summons) |
| N69 | Order for debtor's attendance at an adjourned hearing of judgment summons |
| N70 | Order of commitment under the County Courts Act 1984, s. 110 |
| N71 | Order revoking an order of commitment under the County Courts Act 1984, s. 110 |
| N72 | Notice to defendant where a committal order made but directed to be suspended under Debtors Act 1869 |
| N73 | New order on judgment summons |
| N74 | Warrant of committal judgment summons under the Debtors Act 1869 |
| N75 | Endorsement on a warrant of committal sent to a foreign court |
| N76 | Certificate to be endorsed on duplicate warrant of committal issued for re-arrest of debtor |
| N77 | Notice as to consequences of disobedience to court order |
| N78 | Notice to show good reason why an order for your committal to prison should not be made (Family proceedings only) |
| N79 | Committal of other order, upon proof of disobedience of a court order or breach of undertaking |
| N80 | Warrant for committal to prison |
| N81 | Notice to solicitor to show cause why an undertaking should not be enforced by committal to prison |
| N82 | Order for committal for failure by solicitor to carry out undertaking |
| N83 | Order for discharge from custody under warrant of committal |
| N88 | Interpleader summons to execution creditor |
| N88(1) | Interpleader summons to claimant claiming goods or rent under an execution |
| N89 | Interpleader summons to persons making adverse claims to debt |
| N90 | Summons for assaulting an officer of the court or rescuing goods |
| N91 | Order of commitment and/or imposing a fine for assaulting an officer of the court or rescuing goods |
| N92 | Request for administration order |
| N93 | List of creditors furnished under the Act of 1971 |
| N94 | Administration order |

| No. | Title |
|---|---|
| N95 | Order revoking an administration order |
| N95A | Order suspending or varying an administration order |
| N110 | Power of arrest attached to injunction under the Domestic Violence and Matrimonial Proceedings Act 1976, s. 2 |
| N112 | Order for Arrest under County Courts Act 1984, s. 110 |
| N112A | Power of arrest under Attachment of Earnings Act 1971, s. 23 |
| N117 | General form of undertaking |
| N118 | Notice to defendant where committal order made but directed to be suspended |
| N130 | Application for possession including application for interim possession order |
| N133 | Affidavit to occupier to oppose the making of an interim possession order |
| N134 | Interim possession order |
| N136 | Order for possession |
| N138 | Injunction order |
| N139 | Application for warrant of arrest |
| N140 | Warrant of arrest |
| N206 | Notice of Issue of fixed date claim |
| N207 | Plaint note (Adoption freeing for Adoption) |
| N200 | Petition—Note old number was N208 |
| N201 | Request for entry of appeal—Note old number was N209 |
| N202 | Order for party to sue or defend on behalf of others having the same interest — Note old number was N210 |
| N203 | Notice to persons on whose behalf party has obtained leave to sue or defend — Note old number was N211 |
| N204 | Notice to person against whom party has obtained leave to sue or defend on behalf of others — Note old number was N212 |
| N224 | Request for service out of England and Wales through the court |
| N245 | Application for suspension of a warrant and/or variation of an instalment order |
| N246 | Claimant's reply to defendant's application to vary instalment order |
| N246A | Claimant's reply to defendant's application to suspend warrant of execution |
| N270 | Notes for guidance (application for administration order) |
| N276 | Notice of hearing of interpleader proceedings transferred from High Court |
| N277 | Notice of pre-trial review of interpleader proceedings transferred from the High Court |
| N280 | Order of reference of proceedings or questions for inquiry and report |
| N285 | General form of affidavit |
| N288 | Order to produce prisoner |
| N289 | Judgment for defendant |
| N293 | Certificate or judgment or order |
| N293A | Combined certificate of judgment and request for writ of fieri facias |
| N295 | Order for sale of land |
| N296 | Notice of judgment or order to party directed to be served with notice |
| N297 | Order for accounts and inquiries in creditors' administration action |
| N298 | Order for Administration |
| N299 | Order for foreclosure nisi of legal mortgage of land |
| N300 | Order for sale in action by equitable mortgagee |
| N302 | Judgment in action for specific performance (vendor's action title accepted) |
| N303 | Order for dissolution of partnership |
| N304 | Notice to parties to attend upon taking accounts |
| N305 | Notice to creditor to prove his claim |
| N306 | Notice to creditor of determination of claim |
| N307 | District judge's order (accounts and inquiries) |
| N309 | Order for foreclosure absolute |

*(cont.)*

| No. | Title |
|---|---|
| N310 | Partnership order on further consideration |
| N311 | Administrative action order on further consideration |
| N313 | Endorsement on certificate of judgment (transfer) |
| N317 | Bailiff's report |
| N317A | Bailiff's report to the claimant |
| N319 | Notice of execution of warrant of committal |
| N320 | Request for return of, or to, warrant |
| N322 | Order for recovery of money awarded by tribunal |
| N323 | Request for warrant of execution |
| N324 | Request for warrant of goods |
| N325 | Request for warrant for possession of land |
| N326 | Notice of issue of warrant of execution |
| N327 | Notice of issue of warrant of execution to enforce a judgment or order |
| N328 | Notice of transfer of proceedings to the High Court |
| N329 | Notes for guidance on completion of N79 |
| N330 | Notice of sale or payment under execution in respect of a judgment for a sum exceeding £500 |
| N331 | Notice of withdrawal from possession or payment of moneys on notice of receiving or winding up order |
| N332 | Inventory of goods removed |
| N333 | Notice of time when and where goods will be sold |
| N334 | Request to hold walking possession and authority to re-enter |
| N336 | Request and result of search in the attachment of earnings index |
| N337 | Request for attachment of earnings order |
| N338 | Request for statement of earnings |
| N339 | Discharge of attachment of earnings order |
| N340 | Notice as to payment under attachment of earnings order made by the High Court |
| N341 | Notice of intention to vary attachment of earnings order under the Attachment of Earnings Act 1971, s. 10(2) |
| N342 | Request for judgment summons |
| N343 | Notice of result of hearing of a judgment summons issued on a judgment or order of the High Court |
| N344 | Request for warrant of committal on judgment summons |
| N345 | Certificate of payment under the Debtors Act 1869 |
| N353 | Order appointing receive of real and personal property |
| N354 | Order appointing receiver of partnership |
| N355 | Interim order for appointment of receiver |
| N356 | Order for appointment of receiver by way of equitable execution |
| N358 | Notice of claim to goods taken in execution |
| N359 | Notice to claimant to goods taken in execution to make deposit or give security |
| N360 | Affidavit in support of interpleader summons other than an execution |
| N361 | Notice of application for relief in pending action |
| N362 | Order on interpleader summons under an execution where the claim is not established |
| N363 | Order on interpleader summons under an execution where the claim is established |
| N364 | Order on interpleader summons (other than execution) where there is an action |
| N365 | Order on interpleader summons (other than execution) where there is no action |
| N366 | Summons for neglect to levy execution |
| N368 | Order fining a witness for non-attendance |

| No. | Title |
|---|---|
| N370 | Order of commitment or imposing a fine for insult or misbehaviour |
| N372 | Order for rehearing |
| N373 | Notice of application for an administration order |
| N374 | Notice of intention to review an administration order |
| N374A | Notice of intention to revoke an administration order |
| N375 | Notice of further creditor's claim |
| N376 | Notice of hearing administration order (by direction of the court) |
| N377 | Notice of dividend |
| N388 | Notice to probate registry to produce documents |
| N390 | Notice that a claim has been entered against the Crown |
| N391 | Crown Proceedings Act 1947 affidavit in support of application directing payment by Crown to judgment creditor |
| N392 | Crown Proceedings Act 1947 notice of application for order directing payment by the Crown to the judgment creditor |
| N432 | Affidavit on payment into court, the Trustee Act 1925, s. 63 |
| N436 | Order for sale of land under charging order |
| N437 | District judge's report |
| N438 | Notice to charge holder under Matrimonial Homes Act 1983 |
| N440 | Notice of application for time order by debtor or hirer—Consumer Credit Act 1974 |
| N441 | Notification of request for certificate of satisfaction or cancellation |
| N441A | Certificate of satisfaction or cancellation of judgment debt |
| N444 | Details of sale under a warrant of execution |
| N445 | Request for re-issue of warrant |
| N447 | Notice to claimant of date fixed for adjourned hearing |
| N448 | Request to defendant for employment details, attachment of earnings |
| N449 | Notice to employer, failure to make deductions under attachment of earnings order |

# CPR Part 5 Court Documents



## 5.1 Scope of this Part

This part contains general provisions about—
(a) documents used in court proceedings; and
(b) the obligations of a court officer in relation to those documents.

## 5.2 Preparation of Documents

(1) Where under these Rules, a document is to be prepared by the court, the document may be prepared by the party whose document it is, unless—
  (a) a court officer otherwise directs; or
  (b) it is a document to which—
    (ii) CCR Order 25, rule 8(9) (reissue of warrant where condition upon which warrant was suspended has not been complied with); or
    (iii) CCR Order 28, rule 11(1) (issue of warrant of committal), applies.
(2) Nothing in this rule shall require a court officer to accept a document which is illegible, has not been duly authorised, or is unsatisfactory for some other similar reason.

## 5.3 Signature of Documents by Mechanical Means

Where any of these Rules or any practice direction requires a document to be signed, that requirement shall be satisfied if the signature is printed by computer or other mechanical means.

## 5.4 Register of claims

(1) A court or court office may keep a publicly accessible register of claims which have been issued out of that court or court office.
(2) Any person who pays the prescribed fee may, during office hours, search any available register of claims.
(The practice direction contains details of available registers.)

## 5.4A Supply of documents to Attorney-General from court records

(1) The Attorney-General may search for, inspect and take a copy of any documents within a court file for the purpose of preparing an application or considering whether to make an application under section 42 of the Supreme Court Act 1981 or section 33 of the Employment Tribunals Act 1996 (restriction of vexatious proceedings).
(2) The Attorney-General must, when exercising the right under paragraph (1)—
  (a) pay any prescribed fee; and
  (b) file a written request, which must—
    (i) confirm that the request is for the purpose of preparing an application or considering whether to make an application mentioned in paragraph (1); and
    (ii) name the person who would be the subject of the application.

## 5.4B Supply of documents to a party from court records

(1) A party to proceedings may, unless the court orders otherwise, obtain from the records of the court a copy of any document listed in paragraph 4.2A of the Practice Direction.

(2) A party to proceedings may, if the court gives permission, obtain from the records of the court a copy of any other document filed by a party or communication between the court and a party or another person.

## 5.4C Supply of documents to a non-party from court records

(1) The general rule is that a person who is not a party to proceedings may obtain from the court records a copy of—
   (a) a statement of case, but not any documents filed with or attached to the statement of case, or intended by the party whose statement it is to be served with it;
   (b) a judgment or order given or made in public (whether made at a hearing or without a hearing).

(1A) Where a non-party seeks to obtain a copy of a statement of case filed before 2nd October 2006—
   (a) this rule does not apply; and
   (b) the rules of court relating to access by a non-party to statements of case in force immediately before 2nd October 2006 apply as if they had not been revoked.

(The rules relating to access by a non-party to statements of case in force immediately before 2nd October 2006 were contained in the former rule 5.4(5) to 5.4(9). The Practice Direction to this Part sets out the relevant provisions as they applied to statements of case.)

(2) A non-party may, if the court gives permission, obtain from the records of the court a copy of any other document filed by a party, or communication between the court and a party or another person.

(3) A non-party may obtain a copy of a statement of case or judgment or order under paragraph (1) only if—
   (a) where there is one defendant, the defendant has filed an acknowledgment of service or a defence;
   (b) where there is more than one defendant, either—
      (i) all the defendants have filed an acknowledgment of service or a defence;
      (ii) at least one defendant has filed an acknowledgment of service or a defence, and the court gives permission;
   (c) the claim has been listed for a hearing; or
   (d) judgment has been entered in the claim.

(4) The court may, on the application of a party or of any person identified in a statement of case—
   (a) order that a non-party may not obtain a copy of a statement of case under paragraph (1);
   (b) restrict the persons or classes of persons who may obtain a copy of a statement of case;
   (c) order that persons or classes of persons may only obtain a copy of a statement of case if it is edited in accordance with the directions of the court; or
   (d) make such other order as it thinks fit.

(5) A person wishing to apply for an order under paragraph (4) must file an application notice in accordance with Part 23.

(6) Where the court makes an order under paragraph (4), a non-party who wishes to obtain a copy of the statement of case, or to obtain an unedited copy of the statement of case, may apply on notice to the party or person identified in the statement of case who requested the order, for permission.

## 5.4D Supply of documents from court records—general

(1) A person wishing to obtain a copy of a document under rule 5.4B or rule 5.4C must pay any prescribed fee and—

(a) if the court's permission is required, file an application notice in accordance with Part 23; or
(b) if permission is not required, file a written request for the document.

(2) An application for an order under rule 5.4C(4) or for permission to obtain a copy of a document under rule 5.4B or rule 5.4C (except an application for permission under rule 5.4C(6)) may be made without notice, but the court may direct notice to be given to any person who would be affected by its decision.

(3) Rules 5.4, 5.4B and 5.4C do not apply in relation to any proceedings in respect of which a rule or practice direction makes different provision.

## 5.5 Filing and Sending Documents

(1) A practice direction may make provision for documents to be filed or sent to the court by—
(a) facsimile; or
(b) other electronic means.

(2) Any such practice direction may—
(a) provide that only particular categories of documents may be filed or sent to the court by such means;
(b) provide that particular provisions only apply in specific courts; and
(c) specify the requirements that must be fulfilled for any document filed or sent to the court by such means.

# PD 5 Practice Direction — Court Documents

This practice direction supplements CPR Part 5.

## Signature of Documents by Mechanical Means

1 Where, under rule 5.3, a replica signature is printed electronically or by other mechanical means on any document, the name of the person whose signature is printed must also be printed so that the person may be identified. This paragraph does not apply to claim forms issued through the Claims Production Centre.

## Form of Documents

2.1 Statements of case and other documents drafted by a legal representative should bear his/her signature and if they are drafted by a legal representative as a member or employee of a firm they should be signed in the name of the firm.

2.2 Every document prepared by a party for filing or use at the court must:

(1) Unless the nature of the document renders it impracticable, be on A4 paper of durable quality having a margin, not less than 3.5 centimetres wide,

(2) be fully legible and should normally be typed,

(3) where possible be bound securely in a manner which would not hamper filing or otherwise each page should be endorsed with the case number,

(4) have the pages numbered consecutively,

(5) be divided into numbered paragraphs,

(6) have all numbers, including dates, expressed as figures, and

(7) give in the margin the reference of every document mentioned that has already been filed.

2.3 A document which is a copy produced by a colour photostat machine or other similar device may be filed at the court office provided that the coloured date seal of the court is not reproduced on the copy.

## Supply of Documents to New Parties

3.1 Where a party is joined to existing proceedings, the party joined shall be entitled to require the party joining him to supply, without charge, copies of all statements of case, written evidence and any documents appended or exhibited to them which have been served in the proceedings by or upon the joining party which relate to any issues between the joining party and the party joined, and copies of all orders made in those proceedings. The documents must be supplied within 48 hours after a written request for them is received.

3.2 If the party joined is not supplied with copies of the documents requested under paragraph 3.1 within 48 hours, he may apply under Part 23 for an order that they be supplied.

3.3 The party by whom a copy is supplied under paragraph 3.1 or, if he is acting by a solicitor, his solicitor, shall be responsible for it being a true copy.

## Supply of Documents from Court Records

4.1 Registers of claims which have been issued are available for inspection at the following offices of the High Court at the Royal Courts of Justice:

(1) the Central Office of the Queen's Bench Division;

(2) Chancery Chambers.

4.2 No registers of claims are at present available for inspection in county courts or in District Registries or other offices of the High Court.

4.3 An application under rule 5.4B(2), 5.4C(2) or 5.4C(3)(b)(ii) for permission to obtain a copy of a document, even if made without notice, must be made under CPR Part 23 and the application notice must identify the document or class of document in respect of which permission is sought and the grounds relied upon.

4.4 An application under rule 5.4C(4) by a party or a person identified in a claim form must be made—

(1) under CPR Part 23; and
(2) to a Master or district judge, unless the court directs otherwise.

4.5 Rule 5.4B allows a person who is a party to proceedings to obtain copies of documents from court records. A person is a party to proceedings who has been named as a party on a statement of case irrespective of whether they have been served with that statement of case.

## Supply of Documents from Court Records—Statements of Case Filed before 2nd October 2006

4A.1 Rule 5.4C(1A) provides that the rules of court relating to access by a non-party to statements of case in force immediately before 2nd October 2006 apply to statements of case filed before that date as if they had not been revoked. For ease of reference, those rules are set out in the following paragraphs as they applied to statements of case, along with the relevant supplementary provisions previously contained in this practice direction.

4A.2 A person who is not a party to proceedings may—

(1) unless the court orders otherwise, obtain from the records of the court a copy of a claim form, but not any documents filed with or attached to or intended by the claimant to be served with such claim form, subject to paragraph 4A.3 and to any order of the court under paragraph 4A.4; and
(2) if the court gives permission, obtain from the records of the court a copy of any other statement of case.

4A.3 A person may obtain a copy of a claim form under paragraph 4A.2(1) only if—

(1) where there is one defendant, the defendant has filed an acknowledgment of service or a defence;
(2) where there is more than one defendant, either—
   (a) all the defendants have filed an acknowledgment of service or a defence;
   (b) at least one defendant has filed an acknowledgment of service or a defence, and the court gives permission;
(3) the claim has been listed for a hearing; or
(4) judgment has been entered in the claim.

4A.4 The court may, on the application of a party or any person identified in the claim form—

(1) restrict the persons or classes of persons who may obtain a copy of the claim form;
(2) order that persons or classes of persons may only obtain a copy of the claim form if it is edited in accordance with the directions of the court; or
(3) make such other order as it thinks fit.

4A.5 A person wishing to obtain a copy of a document under paragraph 4A.2 must pay any prescribed fee and—

(a) if the court's permission is required, file an application notice in accordance with Part 23; or
(b) if permission is not required, file a written request for the document.

4A.6 An application for permission to obtain a copy of a statement of case, or for an order under paragraph 4A.4, may be made without notice, but the court may direct notice to be given to any person who would be affected by its decision.

4A.7 An application under paragraph 4A.3(2)(b) for permission to obtain a copy of a claim form must be made under Part 23.

4A.8 An application notice under paragraph 4A.2(2) or paragraph 4A.3(2)(b) must identify the document or class of document in respect of which permission is sought and the grounds relied upon.

4A.9 An application under paragraph 4A.4 by a party or a person identified in a claim form must be made—
(a) under Part 23; and
(b) to a Master or district judge, unless the court directs otherwise.

## Documents for Filing at Court

5.1 The date on which a document was filed at court must be recorded on the document. This may be done by a seal or a receipt stamp.

5.2 Particulars of the date of delivery at a court office of any document for filing and the title of the proceedings in which the document is filed shall be entered in court records, on the court file or on a computer kept in the court office for the purpose. Except where a document has been delivered at the court office through the post, the time of delivery should also be recorded.

5.3 Filing by Facsimile
(1) Subject to paragraph (6) below, a party may file a document at court by sending it by facsimile ('fax').
(2) Where a party files a document by fax, he must not send a hard copy in addition.
(3) A party filing a document by fax should be aware that the document is not filed at court until it is delivered by the court's fax machine, whatever time it is shown to have been transmitted from the party's machine.
(4) The time of delivery of the faxed document will be recorded on it in accordance with paragraph 5.2.
(5) It remains the responsibility of the party to ensure that the document is delivered to the court in time.
(6) If a fax is delivered after 4 p.m. it will be treated as filed on the next day the court office is open.
(7) If a fax relates to a hearing, the date and time of the hearing should be prominently displayed.
(8) Fax should not be used to send letters or documents of a routine or non-urgent nature.
(9) Fax should not be used, except in an unavoidable emergency, to deliver:
(a) a document which attracts a fee;
(b) *Omitted*
(c) a document relating to a hearing less than two hours ahead;
(d) trial bundles or skeleton arguments.
(10) Where (9)(a) or (b) applies, the fax should give an explanation for the emergency and include an undertaking that the fee or money has been dispatched that day by post or will be paid at the court office counter the following business day.
(11) Where courts have several fax machines, each allocated to an individual section, fax messages should only be sent to the machine of the section for which the message is intended.

5.4 Where the court orders any document to be lodged in court, the document must, unless otherwise directed, be deposited in the office of that court.

5.5 A document filed, lodged or held in any court office shall not be taken out of that office without the permission of the court unless the document is to be sent to the office of another court (for example, under CPR Part 30 (transfer)), except in accordance with CPR rule 39.7 (impounded documents) or in accordance with paragraph 5.6 below.

5.6 (1) Where a document filed, lodged or held in a court office is required to be produced to any court, tribunal or arbitrator, the document may be produced by sending it by registered post (together with a certificate as in paragraph 5.6(8)(b)) to the court, tribunal or arbitrator in accordance with the provisions of this paragraph.
(2) Any court, tribunal or arbitrator or any party requiring any document filed, lodged or held in any court office to be produced must apply to that court office by sending a completed request (as in paragraph 5.6(8)(a)), stamped with the prescribed fee.

(3) On receipt of the request the court officer will submit the same to a master in the Royal Courts of Justice or to a district judge elsewhere, who may direct that the request be complied with. Before giving a direction the master or district judge may require to be satisfied that the request is made in good faith and that the document is required to be produced for the reasons stated. The master or district judge giving the direction may also direct that, before the document is sent, an official copy of it is made and filed in the court office at the expense of the party requiring the document to be produced.

(4) On the direction of the master or district judge the court officer shall send the document by registered post addressed to the court, tribunal or arbitrator, with:
  (a) an envelope stamped and addressed for use in returning the document to the court office from which it was sent;
  (b) a certificate as in paragraph 5.6(8)(b);
  (c) a covering letter describing the document, stating at whose request and for what purpose it is sent, referring to this paragraph of the practice direction and containing a request that the document be returned to the court office from which it was sent in the enclosed envelope as soon as the court or tribunal no longer requires it.

(5) It shall be the duty of the court, tribunal or arbitrator to whom the document was sent to keep it in safe custody, and to return it by registered post to the court office from which it was sent, as soon as the court, tribunal or arbitrator no longer requires it.

(6) In each court office a record shall be kept of each document sent and the date on which it was sent and the court, tribunal or arbitrator to whom it was sent and the date of its return. It shall be the duty of the court officer who has signed the certificate referred to in para. 5.6(8)(b) below to ensure that the document is returned within a reasonable time and to make inquiries and report to the master or district judge who has given the direction under paragraph (3) above if the document is not returned, so that steps may be taken to secure its return.

(7) Notwithstanding the preceding paragraphs, the master or district judge may direct a court officer to attend the court, tribunal or arbitrator for the purpose of producing the document.

(8) (a) I, of, an officer of the Court/Tribunal at /an arbitrator of /the Claimant/Defendant/Solicitor for the Claimant/Defendant *[describing the Applicant* so as to show that he is a proper person to make the request] in the case of v. [19 No. ]
REQUEST that the following document [or documents] be produced to the Court/Tribunal/arbitrator on the day of 19 [and following days] and I request that the said document [or documents] be sent by registered post to the proper officer of the Court/Tribunal/arbitrator for production to that Court/Tribunal/arbitrator on that day.
(Signed).
Dated the day of 1999/2

  (b) I, A.B., an officer of the Court of certify that the document sent herewith for production to the Court/Tribunal/arbitrator on the day of 1999/2 in the case of v. and marked 'A.B.' is the document requested on the day of 1999/2 and I FURTHER CERTIFY that the said docment has been filed in and is produced from the custody of the Court.
(Signed)
Dated the day of 1999/2

## Enrolment of Deeds and Other Documents

6.1 (1) Any deed or document which by virtue of any enactment is required or authorised to be enrolled in the Supreme Court may be enrolled in the Central Office of the High Court.

(2) Attention is drawn to the Enrolment of Deeds (Change of Name) Regulations 1994 which are reproduced in the appendix to this practice direction.

6.2 The following paragraph of the practice direction describes the practice to be followed in any case in which a child's name is to be changed and to which the 1994 Regulations apply.

6.3 (1) Where a person has by any order of the High Court, county court or Family Proceedings Court been given parental responsibility for a child and applies to the Central Office, Filing Department, for the enrolment of a deed poll to change the surname (family name) of a child who is under the age of 18 years (unless a child who is or has been married), the application must be supported by the production of the consent in writing of every other person having parental responsibility.

(2) In the absence of that consent, the application will be adjourned generally unless and until permission is given in the proceedings, in which the said order was made, to change the surname of the child and the permission is produced to the Central Office.

(3) Where an application is made to the Central Office by a person who has not been given parental responsibility for a child by any order of the High Court, county court or Family Proceedings Court for the enrolment of a deed poll to change the surname of the child who is under the age of 18 years (unless the child is or has been married), permission of the court to enrol the deed will be granted if the consent in writing of every person having parental responsibility is produced or if the person (or, if more than one, persons) having parental responsibility is dead or overseas or despite the exercise of reasonable diligence it has not been possible to find him or her for other good reason.

(4) In cases of doubt the Senior Master or, in his absence, the practice master will refer the matter to the Master of the Rolls.

(5) In the absence of any of the conditions specified above the Senior Master or the Master of the Rolls, as the case may be, may refer the matter to the Official Solicitor for investigation and report.

## APPENDIX

Regulations made by the Master of the Rolls, Sir Thomas Bingham MR on March 3, 1994 (SI 1994/604) under s. 133(1) of the Supreme Court Act 1981.

1 (1) These regulations may be cited as the Enrolment of Deeds (Change of Name) Regulations 1994 and shall come into force on 1 April 1994.

(2) These Regulations shall govern the enrolment in the Central Office of the Supreme Court of deeds evidencing change of name (referred to in these Regulations as 'deeds poll').

2 (1) A person seeking to enrol a deed poll ('the applicant') must be a Commonwealth citizen as defined by section 37(1) of the British Nationality Act 1981.

(2) If the applicant is a British citizen, a British Dependent Territories citizen or a British Overseas citizen, he must be described as such in the deed poll, which must also specify the section of the British Nationality Act under which the relevant citizenship was acquired.

(3) In any other case, the applicant must be described as a Commonwealth citizen.

(4) The applicant must be described in the deed poll as single, married, widowed or divorced.

3 (1) As proof of the citizenship named in the deed poll, the applicant must produce

(a) a certificate of birth; or

(b) a certificate of citizenship by registration or naturalisation or otherwise; or
(c) some other document evidencing such citizenship.

(2) In addition to the documents set out in paragraph (1), an applicant who is married must—
(a) produce his certificate of marriage; and
(b) show that the notice of his intention to apply for the enrolment of the deed poll has been given to his spouse by delivery or by post to his spouse's last known address; and
(c) show that he has obtained the consent of his spouse to the proposed change of name or that there is good reason why such consent should be dispensed with.

4 (1) The deed poll and the documents referred to in regulation 3 must be exhibited to a statutory declaration by a Commonwealth citizen who is a householder in the United Kingdom and who must declare that he is such in the statutory declaration.

(2) The statutory declaration must state the period, which should ordinarily not be less than 10 years, during which the householder has known the applicant and must identify the applicant as the person referred to in the documents exhibited to the statutory declaration.

(3) Where the period mentioned in paragraph (2) is stated to be less than 10 years, the Master of the Rolls, may, in his absolute discretion decide whether to permit the deed poll to be enrolled and may require the applicant to provide more information before so deciding.

5 If the applicant is resident outside the United Kingdom, he must provide evidence that such residence is not intended to be permanent and the applicant may be required to produce a certificate by a solicitor or as to the nature and probable duration of such residence.

6 The applicant must sign the deed poll in both his old and new names.

7 Upon enrolment the deed poll shall be advertised in the London Gazette by the clerk in charge for the time being of the Filing and Record Department at the Central Office of the Supreme Court.

8 (1) Subject to the following provisions of this regulation, these Regulations shall apply in relation to a deed poll evidencing the change of name of a child as if the child were the applicant.

(2) Paragraphs (3) to (8) shall not apply to a child who has attained the age of 16, is female and is married.

(3) If the child is under the age of 16, the deed poll must be executed by a person having parental responsibility for him.

(4) If the child has attained the age of 16, the deed poll must, except in the case of a person mentioned in paragraph (2), be executed by a person having parental responsibility for the child and be endorsed with the child's consent signed in both his old and new names and duly witnessed.

(5) The application for enrolment must be supported—
(a) by an affidavit showing that the change of name is for the benefit of the child, and
(i) that the application is submitted by all persons having parental responsibility for the child; or
(ii) that it is submitted by one person having parental responsibility for the child with the consent of every other person; or
(iii) that it is submitted by one person having parental responsibility for the child without the consent of every other such person, or by some other person whose name and capacity are given, for reasons set out in the affidavit;

and
(b) by such other evidence, if any, as the Master of the Rolls may require in the particular circumstances of the case.

(6) Regulation 4(2) shall not apply but the statutory declaration mentioned in regulation 4(1) shall state how long the householder has known the deponent under paragraph (5)(a) and the child respectively.

(7) Regulation 6 shall not apply to a child who has not attained the age of 16.

(8) In this regulation 'parental responsibility' has the meaning given in section 3 of the Children Act 1989.

9 The Enrolment of Deeds (Change of Name) Regulations 1983 and the Enrolment of Deeds (Change of Name) (Amendment) Regulations 1990 are hereby revoked.

# PD 5B Practice Direction — Pilot Scheme for Communication and Filing of Documents by Email[1]

This practice direction supplements CPR rule 5.5.

## General

1.1 Section I of this practice direction provides for parties to claims in specified courts to:
(1) communicate with the court by email; and
(2) file specified documents by email.

1.2 Section II of this practice direction provides for parties to claims in specified courts to file specified documents electronically via an online forms service.

1.3 Section III of this practice direction contains general provisions which apply to both Section I and Section II.

1.4 This practice direction does not allow:
(1) communication with the court or the filing of documents by email; or
(2) use of the online forms service,
in proceedings to which the Civil Procedure Rules do not apply.

## I COMMUNICATION AND FILING OF DOCUMENTS BY EMAIL

### Interpretation

2.1 For the purposes of this Section:
(1) a specified court is a court or court office which has published an email address for the filing of documents on the Court Service website <http://www.courtservice.gov.uk> ('the Court Service website'); and
(2) a specified document is a document listed on the Court Service website as a document that may be sent to or filed in that court by email.

### Communications and Documents which May Be Sent by Email

3.1 Subject to para 3.2, a party to a claim in a specified court may send a specified document to the court by email.

3.2 Subject to paragraph 3.2A, a party must not use email to take any step in a claim for which a fee is payable.

3.2A A party may make an application using email in the Preston Combined Court, where he is permitted to do so by PREMA (Preston Email Application Service) User Guide and Protocols.

3.3 Subject to paragraph 3.3A and paragraph 15.1A of the practice direction which supplements Part 52, if—
(a) a fee is payable on the filing of a particular document; and
(b) a party purports to file that document by email,
the court shall treat the document as not having been filed.

3.3A A party may file by email an application notice in the Preston Combined Court where he is permitted to do so by PREMA (Preston Email Application Service) User Guide and Protocols.

(Paragraph 15.1A of the practice direction which supplements CPR Part 52 provides for filing by email an appeal notice or application notice in proceedings in the Court of Appeal, Civil Division.)

(Rule 6.2(1)(e) permits service by email in accordance with the relevant practice direction. PD 6, para. 3, sets out the circumstances in which a party may serve a document by email.)

---

[1] In force 1 May 2004.

## Technical Specifications of Email

4.1 The email message must contain the name, telephone number and email address of the sender and should be in plain text or rich text format rather than HTML.

4.2 Correspondence and documents may be sent as either text in the body of the email, or as attachments, except as mentioned in para. 4.3.

4.3 Documents required to be in a practice form must be sent in that form as attachments.

4.4 Court forms may be downloaded from the Court Service website.

4.5 Attachments must be sent in a format supported by the software used by the specified court to which it is sent. The format or formats which may be used in sending attachments to a particular specified court are listed on the Court Service website.

4.6 An attachment which is sent to a specified court in a format not listed on the Court Service website as appropriate for that court will be treated as not having been received by the court.

4.7 The length of attachments and total size of email must not exceed the maximum which a particular specified court has indicated that it can accept. This information is listed on the Court Service website.

4.8 Where proceedings have been commenced, the subject line of the email must contain the following information:

(1) the case number;

(2) the parties' names (abbreviated if necessary); and

(3) the date and time of any hearing to which the email relates.

# II ONLINE FORMS SERVICE

## Scope and Interpretation

5.1 Reference to an online forms service is reference to a service available at <http://www.courtservice.gov.uk> ('the forms website'). The forms website contains certain documents which a user may complete online and then submit electronically to a specified court.

5.2 For the purposes of this Section:

(1) a specified court is a court or court office listed on the Court Service website as able to receive documents filed electronically via the online forms service; and

(2) a specified document is a document which is available for completion on the forms website.

(Paragraph 15.1B of the Practice Direction which supplements CPR Part 52 provides for certain notices to be filed electronically at the Court of Appeal, Civil Division using the online forms service on the Court of Appeal, Civil Division website.)

## Filing of Documents Online

6.1 A party to a claim in a specified court may send a specified document to the court using the online forms service.

6.2 A party may use the online forms service to take a step in a claim for which a fee is payable. The fee must be paid, using the facilities available at the online forms service, before the application, or other document attracting a fee, is forwarded to the specified court.

6.3 The online forms service will assist the user in completing a document accurately but the user is responsible for ensuring that the rules and practice directions relating to the document have been complied with. Transmission by the service does not guarantee that the document will be accepted by the specified court.

## III GENERAL PROVISIONS

### Interpretation

7 In this Section:

(1) filing or sending a document 'electronically', means filing or sending it in accordance with Section I or Section II; and

(2) a reference to 'transmission' means, unless the context otherwise requires:

(a) in relation to Section I, the email sent by the party to the court; and

(b) in relation to Section II, the electronic transmission of the form by the online forms service to the court.

### Provisions Relating to the Filing of Documents Electronically

8.1 Where a party files a document electronically, he must not send a hard copy of that document to the court.

8.2 A document is not filed until the transmission is received by the court, whatever time it is shown to have been sent.

8.3 The time of receipt of a transmission will be recorded electronically on the transmission as it is received.

8.4 If a transmission is received after 4 p.m.:

(1) the transmission will be treated as received; and

(2) any document attached to the transmission will be treated as filed,

on the next day the court office is open.

8.5 A party:

(1) sending an email in accordance with Section I; or

(2) using the online forms service in accordance with Section II,

is responsible for ensuring that the transmission or any document attached to it is filed within any relevant time limits.

8.6 The court will normally reply by email where:

(1) the response is to a message transmitted electronically; and

(2) the sender has provided an email address.

8.7 Parties are advised not to transmit electronically any correspondence or documents of a confidential or sensitive nature, as security cannot be guaranteed.

8.8 If a document transmitted electronically requires urgent attention, the sender should contact the court by telephone.

8.9 A document that is required by a rule or practice direction to be filed at court is not filed when it is sent to the judge by email.

### Statement of Truth in Documents Filed Electronically

9 Where a party wishes to file a document containing a statement of truth electronically, that party should retain the document containing the original signature and file with the court a version of the document satisfying one of the following requirements:

(1) the name of the person who has signed the statement of truth is typed underneath the statement;

(2) the person who has signed the statement of truth has applied a facsimile of his signature to the statement in the document by mechanical means; or

(3) the document that is filed is a scanned version of the document containing the original signature to the statement of truth.

# CPR Part 6 Service of Documents



## I GENERAL RULES ABOUT SERVICE

### 6.1 Part 6 Rules About Service Apply Generally

The rules in this Part apply to the service of documents, except where—
(a) any other enactment, a rule in another Part, or a practice direction makes a different provision; or
(b) the court orders otherwise.
(For service in possession claims, see Part 55.)

### 6.2 Methods of Service—General

(1) A document may be served by any of the following methods—
(a) personal service, in accordance with rule 6.4;

(b) first class post (or an alternative service which provides for delivery on the next working day);
(c) leaving the document at a place specified in rule 6.5;
(d) through a document exchange in accordance with the relevant practice direction; or
(e) by fax or other means of electronic communication in accordance with the relevant practice direction.
(Rule 6.8 provides for the court to permit service by an alternative method.)

(2) A company may be served by any method permitted under this Part as an alternative to the methods of service set out in—
(a) section 725 of the Companies Act 1985 (service by leaving a document at or posting it to an authorised place);
(b) section 695 of that Act (service on overseas companies); and
(c) section 694A of that Act (service of documents on companies incorporated outside the UK and Gibraltar and having a branch in Great Britain).

## 6.3 Who is to Serve

(1) The court will serve a document which it has issued or prepared except where—
(a) a rule provides that a party must serve the document in question;
(b) the party on whose behalf the document is to be served notifies the court that he wishes to serve it himself;
(c) a practice direction provides otherwise;
(d) the court orders otherwise; or
(e) the court has failed to serve and has sent a notice of non-service to the party on whose behalf the document is to be served in accordance with rule 6.11.

(2) Where the court is to serve a document, it is for the court to decide which of the methods of service specified in rule 6.2 is to be used.

(3) Where a party prepares a document which is to be served by the court, that party must file a copy for the court, and for each party to be served.

## 6.4 Personal Service

(1) A document to be served may be served personally, except as provided in paragraphs (2) and (2A).

(2) Where a solicitor—
(a) is authorised to accept service on behalf of a party; and
(b) has notified the party serving the document in writing that he is so authorised,
a document must be served on the solicitor, unless personal service is required by an enactment, rule, practice direction or court order.

(2A) In civil proceedings by or against the Crown, as defined in rule 66.1(2), documents required to be served on the Crown may not be served personally.

(3) A document is served personally on an individual by leaving it with that individual.

(4) A document is served personally on a company or other corporation by leaving it with a person holding a senior position within the company or corporation.
(The service practice direction sets out the meaning of 'senior position'.)

(5) A document is served personally on a partnership where partners are being sued in the name of their firm by leaving it with—
(a) a partner; or
(b) a person who, at the time of service, has the control or management of the partnership business at its principal place of business.

## 6.5 Address for Service

(1) Except as provided by Section III of this Part (service out of the jurisdiction) a document must be served within the jurisdiction.
('Jurisdiction' is defined in rule 2.3.)

(2) A party must give an address for service within the jurisdiction. Such address must include a full postcode, unless the court orders otherwise.

(Paragraph 2.4 of the practice direction to Part 16 contains provision about the content of an address for service.)

(3) Where a party—
(a) does not give the business address of his solicitor as his address for service; and
(b) resides or carries on business within the jurisdiction,
he must give his residence or place of business as his address for service.

(4) Any document to be served—
(a) by first class post (or an alternative service which provides for delivery on the next working day);
(b) by leaving it at the place of service;
(c) through a document exchange; or
(d) by fax or by other means of electronic communication,
must be sent or transmitted to, or left at, the address for service given by the party to be served.

(5) Where—
(a) a solicitor is acting for the party to be served; and
(b) the document to be served is not the claim form; the party's address for service is the business address of his solicitor.

(Rule 6.13 specifies when the business address of a defendant's solicitor may be the defendant's address for service in relation to the claim form.)

(6) Where—
(a) no solicitor is acting for the party to be served; and
(b) the party has not given an address for service,
the document must be sent or transmitted to, or left at, the place shown in the following table.

(Rule 6.2(2) sets out the statutory methods of service on a company.)

| Nature of party to be served | Place of service |
|---|---|
| Individual | • Usual or last known residence. |
| Proprietor of a business | • Usual or last known residence; or<br>• Place of business or last known place of business. |
| Individual who is suing or being sued in the name of a firm | • Usual or last known residence; or<br>• Principal or last known place of business of the firm. |
| Corporation incorporated in England and Wales other than a company | • Principal office of the corporation; or<br>• Any place within the jurisdiction where the corporation carries on its activities and which has a real connection with the claim. |
| Company registered in England and Wales | • Principal office of the company; or<br>• Any place of business of the company within the jurisdiction which has a real connection with the claim. |
| Any other company or corporation | • Any place within the jurisdiction where the corporation carries on its activities; or<br>• Any place of business of the company within the jurisdiction. |

(7) This rule does not apply where an order made by the court under rule 6.8 (service by an alternative method) specifies where the document in question may be served.

(Rule 42.1 provides that if the business address of his solicitor is given that solicitor will be treated as acting for that party.)

(8) In civil proceedings by or against the Crown, as defined in rule 66.1(2)—
- (a) service on the Attorney General must be effected on the Treasury Solicitor;
- (b) service on a government department must be effected on the solicitor acting for that department as required by section 18 of the Crown Proceedings Act 1947.

(The practice direction to Part 66 gives the list published under section 17 of that Act of the solicitors acting for the different government departments on whom service is to be effected, and of their addresses.)

## 6.6 Service of Documents on Children and Patients

(1) The following table shows the person on whom a document must be served if it is a document which would otherwise be served on a child or a patient—

| Type of document | Nature of party | Person to be served |
|---|---|---|
| Claim form | Child who is not also a patient | • One of the child's parents or guardians;<br>or<br>• If there is no parent or guardian, the person with whom the child resides or in whose care the child is. |
| Claim form | Patient | • The person authorised under Part VII of the Mental Health Act 1983 to conduct the proceedings in the name of the patient or on his behalf;<br>or<br>• If there is no person so authorised, the person with whom the patient resides or in whose care the patient is. |
| Application for an order appointing a litigation friend, where a child or patient has no litigation friend | Child or patient | See rule 21.8. |
| Any other document | Child or patient | The litigation friend who is conducting proceedings on behalf of the child or patient. |

(2) The court may make an order permitting a document to be served on the child or patient, or on some person other than the person specified in the table in this rule.

(3) An application for an order under paragraph (2) may be made without notice.

(4) The court may order that, although a document has been served on someone other than the person specified in the table, the document is to be treated as if it had been properly served.

(5) This rule does not apply where the court has made an order under rule 21.2(3) allowing a child to conduct proceedings without a litigation friend.

(Part 21 contains rules about the appointment of a litigation friend.)

## 6.7 Deemed Service

(1) A document which is served in accordance with these rules or any relevant practice direction shall be deemed to be served on the day shown in the following table—

| Method of Service | Deemed day of service |
|---|---|
| First class post (or an alternative service which provides for delivery on the next working day) | The second day after it was posted. |
| Document exchange | The second day after it was left at the document exchange. |
| Delivering the document to or leaving it at a permitted address | The day after it was delivered to or left at the permitted address. |
| Fax | • If it is transmitted on a business day before 4 p.m., on that day; or<br>• In any other case, on the business day after the day on which it is transmitted. |
| Other electronic method | The second day after the day on which it is transmitted. |

(2) If a document is served personally—
(a) after 5 p.m., on a business day; or
(b) at any time on a Saturday, Sunday or a Bank Holiday,
it will be treated as being served on the next business day.
(3) In this rule—
'business day' means any day except Saturday, Sunday or a bank holiday; and
'bank holiday' includes Christmas Day and Good Friday.

## 6.8 Service by an Alternative Method

(1) Where it appears to the court that there is a good reason to authorise service by a method not permitted by these Rules, the court may make an order permitting service by an alternative method.
(2) An application for an order permitting service by an alternative method—
(a) must be supported by evidence; and
(b) may be made without notice.
(3) An order permitting service by an alternative method must specify—
(a) the method of service; and
(b) the date when the document will be deemed to be served.

## 6.9 Power of Court to Dispense with Service

(1) The court may dispense with service of a document.
(2) An application for an order to dispense with service may be made without notice.

## 6.10 Certificate of Service

Where a rule, practice direction or court order requires a certificate of service, the certificate must state the details set out in the following table—

| Method of service | Details to be certified |
|---|---|
| Post | Date of posting |
| Personal | Date of personal service |
| Document exchange | Date of delivery to the document exchange |
| Delivery of document to or leaving it at a permitted place | Date when the document was delivered to or left at the permitted place |
| Fax | Date and time of transmission |
| Method of service | Details to be certified |
| Other electronic means | Date of transmission and the means used |
| Alternative method permitted by the court | As required by the court |

### 6.11 Notification of Outcome of Postal Service by the Court

Where—

(a) a document to be served by the court is served by post; and
(b) such document is returned to the court,

the court must send notification to the party who requested service stating that the document has been returned.

### 6.11A Notice of Non-service by Bailiff

Where—

(a) the court bailiff is to serve a document; and
(b) the bailiff is unable to serve it,

the court must send notification to the party who requested service.

## II SPECIAL PROVISIONS ABOUT SERVICE OF THE CLAIM FORM

### 6.12 General Rules About Service Subject to Special Rules About Service of Claim Form

The general rules about service are subject to the special rules about service contained in rules 6.13 to 6.16.

### 6.13 Service of Claim Form by the Court—Defendant's Address for Service

(1) Where a claim form is to be served by the court, the claim form must include the defendant's address for service.
(2) For the purposes of paragraph (1), the defendant's address for service may be the business address of the defendant's solicitor if he is authorised to accept service on the defendant's behalf but not otherwise.

(Rule 6.5 contains general provisions about the address for service.)
(Paragraph 2.4 of the practice direction to Part 16 contains provision about the content of an address for service.)

### 6.14 Certificate of Service Relating to the Claim Form

(1) Where a claim form is served by the court, the court must send the claimant a notice which will include the date when the claim form is deemed to be served under rule 6.7.
(2) Where the claim form is served by the claimant—
    (a) he must file a certificate of service within 7 days of service of the claim form; and
    (b) he may not obtain judgment in default under Part 12 unless he has filed the certificate of service.

(Rule 6.10 specifies what a certificate of service must show.)

### 6.15 Service of Claim Form by Contractually Agreed Method

(1) Where—
    (a) a contract contains a term providing that, in the event of a claim being issued in relation to the contract, the claim form may be served by a method specified in the contract; and
    (b) a claim form containing only a claim in respect of that contract is issued,
    the claim form shall, subject to paragraph (2), be deemed to be served on the defendant if it is served by a method specified in the contract.
(2) Where the claim form is served out of the jurisdiction in accordance with the contract, it shall not be deemed to be served on the defendant unless—
    (a) permission to serve it out of the jurisdiction has been granted under rule 6.20; or
    (b) it may be served without permission under rule 6.19.

## 6.16 Service of Claim Form on Agent of Principal Who is Overseas

(1) Where—
   (a) the defendant is overseas; and
   (b) the conditions specified in paragraph (2) are satisfied,
   the court may, on an application only, permit a claim form relating to a contract to be served on a defendant's agent.
(2) The court may not make an order under this rule unless it is satisfied that—
   (a) the contract to which the claim relates was entered into within the jurisdiction with or through the defendant's agent; and
   (b) at the time of the application either the agent's authority has not been terminated or he is still in business relations with his principal.
(3) An application under this rule—
   (a) must be supported by evidence; and
   (b) may be made without notice.
(4) An order under this rule must state a period within which the defendant must respond to the particulars of claim.
(Rule 9.2 sets out how a defendant may respond to particulars of claim.)
(5) The power conferred by this rule is additional to the power conferred by rule 6.8 (service by an alternative method).
(6) Where the court makes an order under this rule, the claimant must send to the defendant copies of—
   (a) the order; and
   (b) the claim form.

# III SPECIAL PROVISIONS ABOUT SERVICE OUT OF THE JURISDICTION

## 6.17 Scope of this Section

This Section contains rules about—
(a) service out of the jurisdiction;
(b) how to obtain the permission of the court to serve out of the jurisdiction; and
(c) the procedure for serving out of the jurisdiction.
(Rule 2.3 defines 'jurisdiction'.)

## 6.18 Definitions

For the purposes of this Part—
(a) 'the 1982 Act' means the Civil Jurisdiction and Judgments Act 1982;
(b) 'the Hague Convention' means the Convention on the service abroad of judicial and extra-judicial documents in civil or commercial matters signed at the Hague on November 15, 1965;
(c) 'Contracting State' has the meaning given by section 1(3) of the 1982 Act;
(d) 'Convention territory' means the territory or territories of any Contracting State to which the Brussels or Lugano Conventions (as defined in section 1(1) of the 1982 Act) apply;
(e) 'Civil Procedure Convention' means the Brussels and Lugano Conventions and any other Convention entered into by the United Kingdom regarding service outside the jurisdiction;
(ea) 'the Service Regulation' means Council Regulation (EC) No 1348/2000 of 29 May 2000 on the service in the Member States of judicial and extrajudicial documents in civil or commercial matters;
(f) 'United Kingdom Overseas Territory' means those territories as set out in the relevant practice direction.
(g) 'domicile' is to be determined—
   (i) in relation to a Convention territory, in accordance with sections 41 to 46 of the 1982 Act;

(ii) in relation to a Regulation State, in accordance with the Judgments Regulation and paragraphs 9 to 12 of Schedule 1 to the Civil Jurisdiction and Judgments Order 2001;

(h) 'claim form' includes petition and application notice; and

(i) 'claim' includes petition and application.

(j) 'the Judgments Regulation' means Council Regulation (EC) No. 44/2001 of 22nd December 2000 on jurisdiction and the recognition and enforcement of judgments in civil and commercial matters; and

(k) 'Regulation State' has the same meaning as 'Member State' in the Judgments Regulation, that is all Member States except Denmark.

(Rule 6.30 provides that where an application notice is to be served out of the jurisdiction under this Part, rules 6.21(4), 6.22 and 6.23 do not apply.)

## 6.19 Service Out of the Jurisdiction Where the Permission of the Court is Not Required

(1) A claim form may be served on a defendant out of the jurisdiction where each claim included in the claim form made against the defendant to be served is a claim which the court as power to determine under the 1982 Act and—

(a) no proceedings between the parties concerning the same claim are pending in the courts of any other part of the United Kingdom or any other Convention territory; and

(b) (i) the defendant is domiciled in the United Kingdom or in any Convention territory;

(ii) Article 16 of Schedule 1 or 3C to the 1982 Act, or paragraph 11 of Schedule 4 to that Act, refers to the proceedings; or

(iii) the defendant is a party to an agreement conferring jurisdiction to which Article 17 of Schedule 1 or 3C to the 1982 Act, or paragraph 12 of Schedule 4 to that Act, refers.

(1A) A claim form may be served on a defendant out of the jurisdiction where each claim included in the claim form made against the defendant to be served is a claim which the court has power to determine under the Judgments Regulation and—

(a) no proceedings between the parties concerning the same claim are pending in the courts of any other part of the United Kingdom or any other Regulation State; and

(b) (i) the defendant is domiciled in the United Kingdom or in any Regulation State;

(ii) Article 22 of the Judgments Regulation refers to the proceedings; or

(iii) the defendant is a party to an agreement conferring jurisdiction to which Article 23 of the Judgments Regulation refers.

(2) A claim form may be served on a defendant out of the jurisdiction where each claim included in the claim form made against the defendant to be served is a claim which, under any other enactment, the court has power to determine, although—

(a) the person against whom the claim is made is not within the jurisdiction; or

(b) the facts giving rise to the claim did not occur within the jurisdiction.

(3) Where a claim form is to be served out of the jurisdiction under this rule, it must contain a statement of the grounds on which the claimant is entitled to serve it out of the jurisdiction.

## 6.20 Service Out of the Jurisdiction Where the Permission of the Court is Required

In any proceedings to which rule 6.19 does not apply, a claim form may be served out of the jurisdiction with the permission of the court if—

*General grounds*

(1) a claim is made for a remedy against a person domiciled within the jurisdiction;

(2) a claim is made for an injunction ordering the defendant to do or refrain from doing an act within the jurisdiction;

(3) a claim is made against someone on whom the claim form has been or will be served (otherwise than in reliance on this paragraph) and—

(a) there is between the claimant and that person a real issue which it is reasonable for the court to try; and

(b) the claimant wishes to serve the claim form on another person who is a necessary or proper party to that claim;

(3A) a claim is a Part 20 claim and the person to be served is a necessary or proper party to the claim against the Part 20 claimant;

*Claims for interim remedies*

(4) a claim is made for an interim remedy under section 25(1) of the 1982 Act;

*Claims in relation to contracts*

(5) a claim is made in respect of a contract where the contract—

(a) was made within the jurisdiction;

(b) was made by or through an agent trading or residing within the jurisdiction;

(c) is governed by English law; or

(d) contains a term to the effect that the court shall have jurisdiction to determine any claim in respect of the contract;

(6) a claim is made in respect of a breach of contract committed within the jurisdiction;

(7) a claim is made for a declaration that no contract exists where, if the contract was found to exist, it would comply with the conditions set out in paragraph (5);

*Claims in tort*

(8) a claim is made in tort where—

(a) damage was sustained within the jurisdiction; or

(b) the damage sustained resulted from an act committed within the jurisdiction;

*Enforcement*

(9) a claim is made to enforce any judgment or arbitral award;

*Claims about property within the jurisdiction*

(10) the whole subject matter of a claim relates to property located within the jurisdiction;

*Claims about trusts etc.*

(11) a claim is made for any remedy which might be obtained in proceedings to execute the trusts of a written instrument where—

(a) the trusts ought to be executed according to English law; and

(b) the person on whom the claim form is to be served is a trustee of the trusts;

(12) a claim is made for any remedy which might be obtained in proceedings for the administration of the estate of a person who died domiciled within the jurisdiction;

(13) a claim is made in probate proceedings which includes a claim for the rectification of a will;

(14) a claim is made for a remedy against the defendant as constructive trustee where the defendant's alleged liability arises out of acts committed within the jurisdiction;

(15) a claim is made for restitution where the defendant's alleged liability arises out of acts committed within the jurisdiction;

*Claims by HM Revenue and Customs*

(16) a claim is made by the Commissioners for HM Revenue and Customs relating to duties or taxes against a defendant not domiciled in Scotland or Northern Ireland;

*Claim for costs order in favour of or against third parties*

(17) a claim is made by a party to proceedings for an order that the court exercise its power under section 51 of the Supreme Court Act 1981 to make a costs order in favour of or against a person who is not a party to those proceedings;

(Rule 48.2 sets out the procedure where the court is considering whether to exercise its discretion to make a costs order in favour of or against a non-party.)

*Admiralty claims*

(17A) a claim is—

(a) in the nature of salvage and any part of the services took place within the jurisdiction; or

(b) to enforce a claim under section 153, 154 or 175 of the Merchant Shipping Act 1995;

*Claims under various enactments*

(18) a claim is made under an enactment specified in the relevant practice direction.

## 6.21 Application for Permission to Serve Claim Form Out of Jurisdiction

(1) An application for permission under rule 6.20 must be supported by written evidence stating—

(a) the grounds on which the application is made and the paragraph or paragraphs of rule 6.20 relied on;

(b) that the claimant believes that his claim has a reasonable prospect of success; and

(c) the defendant's address or, if not known, in what place or country the defendant is, or is likely, to be found.

(2) Where the application is made in respect of a claim referred to in rule 6.20(3), the written evidence must also state the grounds on which the witness believes that there is between the claimant and the person on whom the claim form has been, or will be served, a real issue which it is reasonable for the court to try.

(2A) The court will not give permission unless satisfied that England and Wales is the proper place in which to bring the claim.

(3) Where—

(a) the application is for permission to serve a claim form in Scotland or Northern Ireland; and

(b) it appears to the court that the claimant may also be entitled to a remedy there, the court, in deciding whether to give permission, shall—

(i) compare the cost and convenience of proceeding there or in the jurisdiction; and

(ii) (where relevant) have regard to the powers and jurisdiction of the Sheriff court in Scotland or the county courts or courts of summary jurisdiction in Northern Ireland.

(4) An order giving permission to serve a claim form out of the jurisdiction must specify the periods within which the defendant may—

(a) file an acknowledgment of service;

(b) file or serve an admission; and

(c) file a defence.

(The second practice direction to this Part [PD 6B] sets out how the periods referred to in paragraphs (a), (b) and (c) are calculated.)

(Part 11 sets out the procedure by which a defendant may dispute the court's jurisdiction.)

## 6.22 Period for Acknowledging Service or Admitting the Claim Where the Claim Form is Served Out of the Jurisdiction Under Rule 6.19

(1) This rule sets out the period for filing an acknowledgment of service or filing or serving an admission where a claim form has been served out of the jurisdiction under rule 6.19. (Part 10 contains rules about the acknowledgment of service and Part 14 contains rules about admissions)

(2) If the claim form is to be served under rule 6.19(1) or (1A) in Scotland, Northern Ireland or in the European territory of another Contracting State or Regulation State the period is—

(a) where the defendant is served with a claim form which states that particulars of claim are to follow, 21 days after the service of the particulars of claim; and
(b) in any other case, 21 days after service of the claim form.

(3) If the claim form is to be served under rule 6.19(1) in any other territory of a Contracting State the period is—
(a) where the defendant is served with a claim form which states that particulars of claim are to follow, 31 days after the service of the particulars of claim; and
(b) in any other case, 31 days after service of the claim form.

(4) If the claim form is to be served under—
(a) rule 6.19(1) or (1A) in a country not referred to in paragraphs (2) or (3); or
(b) rule 6.19(2),
the period is set out in the relevant practice direction.

## 6.23 Period for Filing a Defence Where the Claim Form is Served Out of the Jurisdiction Under Rule 6.19

(1) This rule sets out the period for filing a defence where a claim form has been served out of the jurisdiction under rule 6.19.
(Part 15 contains rules about the defence.)

(2) If the claim form is to be served under rule 6.19(1) or (1A) in Scotland, Northern Ireland or in the European territory of another Contracting State or Regulation State the period is—
(a) 21 days after service of the particulars of claim; or
(b) if the defendant files an acknowledgment of service, 35 days after service of the particulars of claim.

(3) If the claim form is to be served under rule 6.19(1) in any other territory of a Contracting State the period is—
(a) 31 days after service of the particulars of claim; or
(b) if the defendant files an acknowledgment of service, 45 days after service of the particulars of claim.

(4) If the claim form is to be served under—
(a) rule 6.19(1) or (1A) in a country not referred to in paragraphs (2) or (3); or
(b) rule 6.19(2),
the period is set out in the relevant practice direction.

## 6.24 Method of Service—General Provisions

(1) Where a claim form is to be served out of the jurisdiction, it may be served by any method—
(a) permitted by the law of the country in which it is to be served;
(b) provided for by—
(i) rule 6.25 (service through foreign governments, judicial authorities and British Consular authorities);
(ii) rule 6.26A (service in accordance with the Service Regulation); or
(iii) rule 6.27 (service on a State); or
(c) permitted by a Civil Procedure Convention.

(2) Nothing in this rule or in any court order shall authorise or require any person to do anything in the country where the claim form is to be served which is against the law of that country.

## 6.25 Service Through Foreign Governments, Judicial Authorities and British Consular Authorities

(1) Where a claim form is to be served on a defendant in any country which is a party to the Hague Convention, the claim form may be served—

(a) through the authority designated under the Hague Convention in respect of that country; or
(b) if the law of that country permits—
(i) through the judicial authorities of that country, or
(ii) through a British Consular authority in that country.

(2) Where—
(a) paragraph (4) (service in Scotland etc., other than under the Hague Convention) does not apply; and
(b) a claim form is to be served on a defendant in any country which is a party to a Civil Procedure Convention (other than the Hague Convention) providing for service in that country,

the claim form maybe served, if the law of that country permits—
(i) through the judicial authorities of that country; or
(ii) through a British Consular authority in that country (subject to any provisions of the applicable convention about the nationality of persons who may be served by such a method).

(3) Where—
(a) paragraph (4) (service in Scotland etc., other than under the Hague Convention) does not apply; and
(b) a claim form is to be served on a defendant in any country with respect to which there is no Civil Procedure Convention providing for service in that country,

the claim form may be served, if the law of that country so permits—
(i) through the government of that country, where that government is willing to serve it; or
(ii) through a British Consular authority in that country.

(4) Except where a claim form is to be served in accordance with paragraph (1) (service under the Hague Convention), the methods of service permitted by this rule are not available where the claim form is to be served in—
(a) Scotland, Northern Ireland, the Isle of Man or the Channel Islands;
(b) any Commonwealth State; or
(c) any United Kingdom Overseas Territory.

(5) This rule does not apply where service is to be effected in accordance with the Service Regulation.

## 6.26 Procedure Where Service is to be Through Foreign Governments, Judicial Authorities and British Consular Authorities

(1) This rule applies where the claimant wishes to serve the claim form through—
(a) the judicial authorities of the country where the claim form is to be served;
(b) a British Consular authority in that country;
(c) the authority designated under the Hague Convention in respect of that country; or
(d) the government of that country.

(2) Where this rule applies, the claimant must file—
(a) a request for service of the claim form by the method in paragraph (1) that he has chosen;
(b) a copy of the claim form;
(c) any translation required under rule 6.28; and
(d) any other documents, copies of documents or translations required by the relevant practice direction.

(3) When the claimant files the documents specified in paragraph (2), the court officer will—
(a) seal(GL) the copy of the claim form; and
(b) forward the documents to the Senior Master.

(4) The Senior Master will send documents forwarded under this rule—

(a) where the claim form is being served through the authority designated under the Hague Convention, to that authority; or
(b) in any other case, to the Foreign and Commonwealth Office with a request that it arranges for the claim to be served by the method indicated in the request for service filed under paragraph (2) or, where that request indicates alternative methods, by the most convenient method.

(5) An official certificate which—
(a) states that the claim form has been served in accordance with this rule either personally, or in accordance with the law of the country in which service was effected;
(b) specifies the date on which the claim form was served; and
(c) is made by—
(i) a British Consular authority in the country where the claim form was served;
(ii) the government or judicial authorities in that country; or
(iii) any other authority designated in respect of that country under the Hague Convention, shall be evidence of the facts stated in the certificate.

(6) A document purporting to be an official certificate under paragraph (5) shall be treated as such a certificate, unless it is proved not to be.

(7) This rule does not apply where service is to be effected in accordance with the Service Regulation.

## 6.26A Service in Accordance with the Service Regulation

(1) This rule applies where a claim form is to be served in accordance with the Service Regulation.

(2) The claimant must file the claim form and any translations or other documents required by the Service Regulation.

(3) When the claimant files the documents referred to in paragraph (2), the court officer will—
(a) seal(GL) the copy of the claim form; and
(b) forward the documents to the Senior Master.

(4) Rule 6.31 does not apply.

(The Service Regulation is annexed to the relevant practice direction.)

## 6.27 Service of Claim Form on State Where Court Permits Service Out of the Jurisdiction

(1) This rule applies where a claimant wishes to serve the claim form on a State.

(2) The claimant must file in the Central Office of the Royal Courts of Justice—
(a) a request for service to be arranged by the Foreign and Commonwealth Office;
(b) a copy of the claim form; and
(c) any translation required under rule 6.28.

(3) The Senior Master will send documents filed under this rule to the Foreign and Commonwealth Office with a request that it arranges for the claim form to be served.

(4) An official certificate by the Foreign and Commonwealth Office stating that a claim form has been duly served on a specified date in accordance with a request made under this rule shall be evidence of that fact.

(5) A document purporting to be such a certificate shall be treated as such a certificate, unless it is proved not to be.

(6) Where—
(a) section 12(6) of the State Immunity Act 1978 applies; and
(b) the State has agreed to a method of service other than through the Foreign and Commonwealth Office,

the claim may be served either by the method agreed or in accordance with this rule.

(Section 12(6) of the State Immunity Act 1978 provides that section 12(1) of that Act, which prescribes a method for serving documents on a State, does not prevent the service of a claim form or other document in a manner to which the State has agreed.)

(7) In this rule 'State' has the meaning given by section 14 of the State Immunity Act 1978.

## 6.28 Translation of Claim Form

(1) Except where paragraph (4) or (5) applies, every copy of the claim form filed under rule 6.26 (service through judicial authorities, foreign governments etc.) or 6.27 (service on State) must be accompanied by a translation of the claim form.

(2) The translation must be—

(a) in the official language of the country in which it is to be served; or

(b) if there is more than one official language of that country, in any official language which is appropriate to the place in the country where the claim form is to be served.

(3) Every translation filed under this rule must be accompanied by a statement by the person making it that it is a correct translation, and the statement must include—

(a) the name of the person making the translation;

(b) his address; and

(c) his qualifications for making a translation.

(4) The claimant is not required to file a translation of a claim form filed under rule 6.26 (service through judicial authorities, foreign governments etc.) where the claim form is to be served—

(a) in a country of which English is an official language; or

(b) on a British subject,

unless a Civil Procedure Convention expressly requires a translation.

(5) The claimant is not required to file a translation of a claim form filed under rule 6.27 (service on State) where English is an official language of the State where the claim form is to be served.

## 6.29 Undertaking to be Responsible for Expenses of the Foreign and Commonwealth Office

Every request for service filed under rule 6.26 (service through judicial authorities, foreign governments etc.) or rule 6.27 (service on State) must contain an undertaking by the person making the request—

(a) to be responsible for all expenses incurred by the Foreign and Commonwealth Office or foreign judicial authority; and

(b) to pay those expenses to the Foreign and Commonwealth Office or foreign judicial authority on being informed of the amount.

## 6.30 Service of Documents Other than the Claim Form

(1) Where an application notice is to be served out of the jurisdiction under this Section of this Part—

(a) rules 6.21(4), 6.22 and 6.23 do not apply; and

(b) where the person on whom the application notice has been served is not a party to proceedings in the jurisdiction in which the application is made, that person may make an application to the court under rule 11(1) as if he were a defendant and rule 11(2) does not apply.

(Rule 6.21(4) provides that an order giving permission to serve a claim form out of the jurisdiction must specify the periods within which the defendant may (a) file an acknowledgment of service, (b) file or serve an admission, and (c) file a defence.)

(Rule 6.22 provides rules for the period for acknowledging service or admitting the claim where the claim form is served out of the jurisdiction under rule 6.19.)

(Rule 6.23 provides rules for the period for filing a defence where the claim form is served out of the jurisdiction under rule 6.19.)

(The practice direction supplementing this Section of this Part [PD 6B] provides that where an application notice is to be served out of the jurisdiction in accordance with this Section of this Part, the court must have regard to the country in which the application notice is to be served in setting the date for the hearing of the application and giving any direction about service of the respondent's evidence.)

(Rule 11(1) provides that a defendant may make an application to the court to dispute the court's jurisdiction to try the claim or argue that the court should not exercise its jurisdiction. Rule 11(2) provides that a defendant who wishes to make such an application must first file an acknowledgment of service in accordance with Part 10.)

(2) Unless paragraph (3) applies, where the permission of the court is required for a claim form to be served out of the jurisdiction the permission of the court must also be obtained for service out of the jurisdiction of any other document to be served in the proceedings.

(3) Where—
(a) the court gives permission for a claim form to be served out of the jurisdiction; and
(b) the claim form states that particulars of claim are to follow,
the permission of the court is not required to serve the particulars of claim out of the jurisdiction.

### 6.31 Proof of Service

Where—
(a) a hearing is fixed when the claim is issued;
(b) the claim form is served on a defendant out of the jurisdiction; and
(c) that defendant does not appear at the hearing,
the claimant may take no further steps against that defendant until the claimant files written evidence showing that the claim form has been duly served.

## IV SERVICE OF FOREIGN PROCESS

### 6.32 Scope and Definitions

(1) This Section of this Part—
(a) applies to the service in England or Wales of any court process in connection with civil or commercial proceedings in a foreign court or tribunal; but
(b) does not apply where the Service Regulation applies.
(The Service Regulation is annexed to the relevant practice direction.)

(2) In this Section—
(a) 'convention country'—
(i) means a foreign country in relation to which there is a civil procedure convention providing for service in that country of process of the High Court; and
(ii) includes a country which is a party to the Convention on the Service Abroad of Judicial and Extra-Judicial Documents in Civil or Commercial Matters signed at the Hague on 15 November 1965; and
(b) 'process server' means—
(i) a process server appointed by the Lord Chancellor to serve documents to which this Section applies, or
(ii) his authorised agent.

### 6.33 Request for Service

Process will be served where the Senior Master receives—
(a) a written request for service—
(i) where the foreign court or tribunal is in a convention country, from a consular or other authority of that country; or
(ii) from the Secretary of State for Foreign and Commonwealth Affairs, with a recommendation that service should be effected;

(b) a translation of that request into English;
(c) two copies of the process to be served; and
(d) unless the foreign court or tribunal certifies that the person to be served understands the language of the process, two copies of a translation of it into English.

### 6.34 Method of Service

The process must be served as directed by the Senior Master.

### 6.35 After Service

(1) The process server must—
  (a) send the Senior Master a copy of the process, and
    (i) proof of service; or
    (ii) a statement why the process could not be served; and
  (b) if the Senior Master directs, specify the costs incurred in serving or attempting to serve the process.
(2) The Senior Master will send the following documents to the person who requested service—
  (a) a certificate, sealed with the seal of the Supreme Court for use out of the jurisdiction, stating—
    (i) when and how the process was served or the reason why it has not been served; and
    (ii) where appropriate, an amount certified by a costs judge to be the costs of serving or attempting to serve the process; and
  (b) a copy of the process.

# PD 6 Practice Direction — Service

This practice direction supplements CPR Part 6.

## METHODS OF SERVICE

1.1 The various methods of service are set out in rule 6.2.
1.2 The following provisions apply to the specific methods of service referred to.

### Service by Non-electronic Means

*Service by document exchange*

2.1 Service by document exchange (DX) may take place only where:
- (1) the party's address for service[1] includes a numbered box at a DX, or
- (2) the writing paper of the party who is to be served or of his legal representative[2] sets out the DX box number, and
- (3) the party or his legal representative has not indicated in writing that they are unwilling to accept service by DX.

2.2 Service by DX is effected by leaving the document addressed to the numbered box:
- (1) at the DX of the party who is to be served, or
- (2) at a DX which sends documents to that party's DX every business day.

### Service by Electronic Means

*Service by facsimile*

3.1 Subject to the provisions of para. 3.3 below, where a document is to be served by electronic means:
- (1) the party who is to be served or his legal representative must previously have expressly indicated in writing to the party serving:
  - (a) that he is willing to accept service by electronic means; and
  - (b) the fax number, email address or electronic identification to which it should be sent; and
- (2) the following shall be taken as sufficient written indication for the purposes of para. 3.1(1):
  - (a) a fax number set out on the writing paper of the legal representative of the party who is to be served; or
  - (b) a fax number, email address or electronic identification set out on a statement of case or a response to a claim filed with the court.

3.2 Where a party seeks to serve a document by electronic means he should first seek to clarify with the party who is to be served whether there are any limitations to the recipient's agreement to accept service by such means including the format in which documents are to be sent and the maximum size of attachments that may be received.

3.3 An address for service given by a party must be within the jurisdiction and any fax number must be at the address for service. Where an email address or electronic identification is given in conjunction with an address for service, the email address or electronic identification will be deemed to be at the address for service.

3.4 Where a document is served by electronic means, the party serving the document need not in addition send a hard copy by post or document exchange.

---

[1] See rule 6.5.

[2] See rule 2.3 for the definition of legal representative.

## Service on Certain Individuals

*Personal service on partners*

4.1 Where partners are sued in the name of a partnership, service should be in accordance with rule 6.4(5) and the table set out in rule 6.5(5) where it refers to an 'individual who is suing or being sued in the name of a firm'.

4.2 A claim form or particulars of claim which are served by leaving them with a person at the principal or last known place of business of the partnership, must at the same time have served with them a notice as to whether that person is being served:
(1) as a partner,
(2) as a person having control or management of the partnership business, or
(3) as both.

*Service on members of H.M. Forces and United States Air Force*

5 The Lord Chancellor's Office issued a memorandum on 26 July 1979 as to service on members of H.M. Forces and guidance notes as to service on members of the United States Air Force. The provisions annexed to this practice direction are derived from that memorandum and guidance notes.

## Service Generally

*Personal service on a company or other corporation*

6.1 Personal service on a registered company or corporation in accordance with rule 6.4(4) service is effected by leaving a document with 'a person holding a senior position'.

6.2 Each of the following persons is a person holding a senior position:
(1) in respect of a registered company or corporation, a director, the treasurer, secretary, chief executive, manager or other officer of the company or corporation, and
(2) in respect of a corporation which is not a registered company, in addition to those persons set out in (1), the mayor, chairman, president, town clerk or similar officer of the corporation.

## Change of Address

7 A party or his legal representative who changes his address for service shall give notice in writing of the change as soon as it has taken place to the court and every other party.

## Service by the Court

8.1 Where the court effects service of a document in accordance with rule 6.3(1) and (2), the method will normally be by first class post.

8.2 *Omitted.*

8.3 Where the court effects service of a claim form, delivers a defence to a claimant or notifies a claimant that the defendant has filed an acknowledgment of service, the court will also serve or deliver a copy of any notice of funding that has been filed provided:
(a) it was filed at the same time as the claim form, defence or acknowledgment of service, and
(b) copies were provided for service.

## Content of Evidence

*The following applications relating to service require evidence in support*

9.1 An application for an order for service by an alternative method[3] should be supported by evidence stating:
(1) the reason an order for an alternative method of service is sought, and
(2) what steps have been taken to serve by other permitted means.

---

[3] See rule 6.8.

9.2 An application for service of a claim form relating to a contract on the agent of a principal who is overseas should be supported by evidence setting out:

(1) full details of the contract and that it was entered into within the jurisdiction with or through an agent who is either an individual residing or carrying on business within the jurisdiction, or a registered company or corporation having a registered office or a place of business within the jurisdiction,

(2) that the principal for whom the agent is acting was, at the time the contract was entered into and is at the time of making the application, neither an individual, registered company or corporation as described in (1) above, and

(3) why service out of the jurisdiction cannot be effected.

## ANNEX SERVICE ON MEMBERS OF H.M. FORCES

1. The following information is for litigants and legal representatives who wish to serve legal documents in civil proceedings in the courts of England and Wales on parties to the proceedings who are (or who, at the material time, were) regular members of Her Majesty's Forces.
2. The proceedings may take place in the county court or the High Court, and the documents to be served may be both originating claims, interim applications and pre-action applications. Proceedings for divorce or maintenance and proceedings in the Family Courts generally are subject to special rules as to service which are explained in a practice direction issued by the Senior District Judge of the Principal Registry on 26 June 1979.
3. In these instructions, the person wishing to effect service is referred to as the 'claimant' and the person to be served is referred to as the 'serviceman'; the expression 'overseas' means outside the United Kingdom.

### Enquiries as to Address

4. As a first step, the claimant's legal representative will need to find out where the serviceman is serving, if he does not already know. For this purpose he should write to the appropriate officer of the Ministry of Defence as specified in paragraph 10 below.
5. The letter of enquiry should in every case show that the writer is a legal representative and that the enquiry is made solely with a view to the service of legal documents in civil proceedings.
6. In all cases the letter should give the full name, service number, rank or rating, and Ship, Arm or Trade, Regiment or Corps and Unit or as much of this information as is available. Failure to quote the service number and the rank or rating may result either in failure to identify the serviceman or in considerable delay.
7. The letter should contain an undertaking by the legal representative that, if the address is given, it will be used solely for the purpose of issuing and serving documents in the proceedings and that so far as is possible the legal representative will disclose the address only to the court and not to his client or to any other person or body. A legal representative in the service of a public authority or private company should undertake that the address will be used solely for the purpose of issuing and serving documents in the proceedings and that the address will not be disclosed so far as is possible to any other part of his employing organisation or to any other person but only to the court. Normally on receipt of the required information and undertaking the appropriate office will give the service address.
8. If the legal representative does not give the undertaking, the only information he will receive will be whether the serviceman is at that time serving in England or Wales, Scotland, Northern Ireland or overseas.
9. It should be noted that a serviceman's address which ends with a British Forces Post Office address and reference (BFPO) will nearly always indicate that he is serving overseas.

10. The letter of enquiry should be addressed as follows:

(a) *Royal Navy Officers*
The Naval Secretary
Room 161
Victory Building
HM Naval Base
Portsmouth Hants PO1 3LS

*RN Ratings*
Commodore Naval Drafting
Centurion Building
Grange Road
Gosport
Hants PO13 9XA

*RN Medical and Dental Officers*
The Medical Director General (Naval)
Room 114 Victory Building
HM Naval Base
Portsmouth
Hants PO1 3LS

*Officers of Queen Alexandra's Royal Naval Nursing Service*
The Matron-in-Chief
QARNNS
Room 129
Victory Building
HM Naval Base
Portsmouth
Hants PO1 3LS

*Naval Chaplains*
Director General Naval
Chaplaincy Service
Room 201
Victory Building
HM Naval Base
Portsmouth
Hants PO1 3LS

(b) *Royal Marine Officers and Ranks*
Personnel section
West Battery
Whale Island
Portsmouth
Hants PO2 8DX

*RM Ranks HQRM*
(DRORM)
West Battery
Whale Island
Portsmouth
Hants PO2 8DX

(c) *Army Officers and Other Ranks*
Ministry of Defence
Army Personnel Centre
Secretariat, Public Enquiries
RM CD424

Kentigern House
65 Brown Street
Glasgow G2 8EH

(d) *Royal Air Force Officers and Other Ranks*
Personnel Management Agency (RAF)
Building 248
RAF Innsworth
Gloucester GL3 1EZ

## Assistance in Serving Documents on Servicemen

11. Once the claimant's legal representative has learnt the serviceman's address he may use that address as the address for service by post, in cases where this method of service is allowed by the Civil Procedure Rules. There are, however, some situations in which service of the proceedings, whether in the High Court or in the county court, has to be effected personally; in these cases an appointment will have to be sought, through the Commanding Officer of the Unit, Establishment or Ship concerned, for the purpose of effecting service. The procedure for obtaining an appointment is described below, and it applies whether personal service is to be effected by the claimant's legal representative or his agent or by a court bailiff, or, in the case of proceedings served overseas (with the leave of the court) through the British Consul or the foreign judicial authority.
12. The procedure for obtaining an appointment to effect personal service is by application to the Commanding Officer of the Unit, Establishment or Ship in which the serviceman is serving. The Commanding Officer may grant permission for the document server to enter the Unit, Establishment or Ship but if this is not appropriate he may offer arrangements for the serviceman to attend at a place in the vicinity of the Unit, Establishment or Ship in order that he may be served. If suitable arrangements cannot be made the legal representative will have evidence that personal service is impracticable, which may be useful in an application for service by an alternative method.

## General

13. Subject to the procedure outlined in paragraphs 11 and 12, there are no special arrangements to assist in the service of process when a serviceman is outside the United Kingdom. The appropriate office will however give an approximate date when the serviceman is likely to return to the United Kingdom.
14. It sometimes happens that a serviceman has left the service by the time that the enquiry is made. If the claimant's legal representative confirms that the proceedings result from an occurrence when the serviceman was in the Forces and he gives the undertaking referred to in paragraph 7, the last known private address after discharge will normally be provided. In no other case however will the Department disclose the private address of a member of H.M. Forces.

## Service on Members of United States Air Force

15. In addition to the information contained in the memorandum of 26 July 1979, the Lord Chancellor's Office, some doubts having been expressed as to the correct procedure to be followed by persons having civil claims against members of the United States Air Force in this country, issued the following notes for guidance with the approval of the appropriate United States authorities:
16. Instructions have been issued by the U.S. authorities to the commanding officers of all their units in this country that every facility is to be given for the service of documents in civil proceedings on members of the U.S. Air Force. The proper course to be followed by a creditor or other person having a claim against a member of the U.S. Air Force is for him to communicate with the commanding officer or, where the unit concerned has a legal officer, with the legal officer of the defendant's unit requesting him to provide facilities for the service of documents on the defendant. It is not possible for the U.S.

authorities to act as arbitrators when a civil claim is made against a member of their forces. It is, therefore, essential that the claim should either be admitted by the defendant or judgment should be obtained on it, whether in the High Court or a county court. If a claim has been admitted or judgment has been obtained and the claimant has failed to obtain satisfaction within a reasonable period, his proper course is then to write to: Office of the Staff Judge Advocate, Headquarters, Third Air Force, R.A.F. Mildenhall, Suffolk, enclosing a copy of the defendant's written admission of the claim or, as the case may be, a copy of the judgment. Steps will then be taken by the Staff Judge Advocate to ensure that the matter is brought to the defendant's attention with a view to prompt satisfaction of the claim.

# PD 6B Practice Direction — Service out of the Jurisdiction

This practice direction supplements Section III of CPR Part 6.

## Service in Other Member States of the European Union

A1.1 Where service is to be effected in another Member of State of the European Union, Council Regulation (EC) No. 1348/2000 of 29 May 2000 on the service in the Member States of judicial and extrajudicial documents in civil or commercial matters ('the Service Regulation') applies.

A1.2 The Service Regulation is annexed to this Practice Direction.

(Article 20(1) of the Service Regulation provides that the Regulation prevails over other provisions contained in bilateral or multilateral agreements or arrangements concluded by the Member States and in particular art. IV of the protocol to the Brussels Convention of 1968 and the Hague Convention of 15 November 1965.)[1]

## Service Out of the Jurisdiction Where Permission of the Court is Not Required

1.1 The usual form of words of the statement required by r. 6.19(3) where the court has power to determine the claim under the 1982 Act should be:

I state that the High Court of England and Wales has power under the Civil Jurisdiction and Judgments Act 1982 to hear this claim and that no proceedings are pending between the parties in Scotland, Northern Ireland or another Convention territory of any contracting State as defined by section 1(3) of the Act.

1.2 However, in proceedings to which r. 6.19(1)(b)(ii) applies, the statement should be:

I state that the High Court of England and Wales has power under the Civil Jurisdiction and Judgments Act 1982, the claim having as its object rights *in rem* in immovable property or tenancies in immovable property (or otherwise in accordance with the provisions of Article 16 of Schedule 1 or 3C to that Act or paragraph 11 of Schedule 4 to that Act) to which any of those provisions applies, to hear the claim and that no proceedings are pending between the parties in Scotland, Northern Ireland or another Convention territory of any contracting State as defined by section 1(3) of the Act.

1.3 And in proceedings to which r. 6.19(1)(b)(iii) applies, the statement should be:

I state that the High Court of England and Wales has power under the Civil Jurisdiction and Judgments Act 1982, the defendant being a party to an agreement conferring jurisdiction to which Article 17 of Schedule 1 or 3C to that Act or paragraph 12 of Schedule 4 to that Act applies, to hear the claim and that no proceedings are pending between the parties in Scotland, Northern Ireland or another Convention territory of any contracting State as defined by section 1(3) of the Act.

1.3A The usual form of words of the statement required by r. 6.19(3) where the Judgments Regulation applies should be:

I state that the High Court of England and Wales has power under Council Regulation (EC) No. 44/2001 of 22 December 2000 (on jurisdiction and the recognition and enforcement of judgments in civil and commercial matters) to hear this claim and that no proceedings are pending between the parties in Scotland, Northern Ireland or any other Regulation State as defined by section 1(3) of the Civil Jurisdiction and Judgments Act 1982.

1.3B However, in proceedings to which r. 6.19(1A)(b)(ii) applies, the statement should be:

---

[1] Not reproduced in this work.

I state that the High Court of England and Wales has power under Council Regulation (EC) No. 44/2001 of 22 December 2000 (on jurisdiction and the recognition and enforcement of judgments in civil and commercial matters), the claim having as its object rights *in rem* in immovable property or tenancies in immovable property (or otherwise in accordance with the provisions of Article 22 of that Regulation) to which Article 22 of that Regulation applies, to hear this claim and that no proceedings are pending between the parties in Scotland, Northern Ireland or any other Regulation State as defined by section 1(3) of the Civil Jurisdiction and Judgments Act 1982.

1.3C And in proceedings to which r. 6.19(1A)(b)(iii) applies, the statement should be:

I state that the High Court of England and Wales has power under Council Regulation (EC) No. 44/2001 of 22 December 2000 (on jurisdiction and the recognition and enforcement of judgments in civil and commercial matters), the defendant being a party to an agreement conferring jurisdiction to which Article 23 of that Regulation applies, to hear this claim and that no proceedings are pending between the parties in Scotland, Northern Ireland or any other Regulation State as defined by section 1(3) of the Civil Jurisdiction and Judgments Act 1982.

1.3D In proceedings to which Rule 6.19(2) applies, the statement should be:

'I state that the High Court of England and Wales has power to hear this claim under [state the provisions of the relevant enactment] which satisfies the requirements of rule 6.19(2), and that no proceedings are pending between the parties in Scotland or Northern Ireland, or in another Contracting State or Regulation State as defined by section 1(3) of the Civil Jurisdiction and Judgments Act 1982.'

1.4 A claim form appearing to be for service on a defendant under the provisions of r. 6.19 which does not include a statement in the form of 1.1, 1.2, 1.3, 1.3A, 1.3B or 1.3C above will be marked on issue 'Not for service out of the jurisdiction'.

1.5 Where a claim form is served without particulars of claim, it must be accompanied by a copy of form N1C (notes for defendants).

## Service out of the Jurisdiction Where Permission is Required

*Documents to be filed under rule 6.26(2)(d)*

2.1 A complete set of the following documents must be provided for each party to be served out of the jurisdiction:

(1) a copy of particulars of claim if not already incorporated in or attached to the claim;
(2) a duplicate of the claim form of the particulars of claim and of any documents accompanying the claim and of any translation required by r. 6.28;
(3) forms for responding to the claim;
(4) any translation required under r. 6.28 and paras 4.1 and 4.2, in duplicate.

2.2 The documents to be served in certain countries require legalisation and the Foreign Process Section (Room E02), Royal Courts of Justice will advise on request. Some countries require legalisation and some require a formal letter of request, see form No. 34 which must be signed by the Senior Master of the Queen's Bench Division irrespective of the Division of the High Court or any county court in which the order was made.

## Service in Scotland, Northern Ireland, the Channel Islands, the Isle of Man, Commonwealth Countries and United Kingdom Overseas Territories

3.1 Where rule 6.25(4) applies, service should be effected by the claimant or his agent direct except in the case of a Commonwealth State where the judicial authorities have required service to be in accordance with rule 6.24(1)(b)(i). These are presently Malta and Singapore.

3.2 For the purposes of r. 6.25(4)(c), the following countries are United Kingdom Overseas Territories:

(a) Anguilla;
(b) Bermuda;
(c) British Antarctic Territory;
(d) British Indian Ocean Territory;
(e) Cayman Islands;
(f) Falkland Islands;
(g) Gibraltar;
(h) Montserrat;
(i) Pitcairn, Henderson, Ducie and Oeno;
(j) St Helena and Dependencies;
(k) South Georgia and the South Sandwich Islands;
(l) Sovereign Base Areas of Akrotiri and Dhekelia;
(m) Turks and Caicos Islands; and
(n) Virgin Islands.

## Translations

4.1 Rule 6.28 applies to particulars of claim not included in a claim form as well as to claim forms.

4.2 Where a translation of a claim form is required under r. 6.28, the claimant must also file a translation of all the forms that will accompany the claim form.

(It should be noted that English is not an official language in the Province of Quebec.)

## Service with the Permission of the Court under Certain Acts

5.1 Rule 6.20(18) provides that a claim form may be served out of the jurisdiction with the court's permission if the claim is made under an enactment specified in the relevant practice direction.

5.2 These enactments are:

(1) the Nuclear Installations Act 1965,
(2) the Social Security Contributions and Benefits Act 1992,
(3) the Directive of the Council of the European Communities dated 15 March 1976 No. 76/308/EEC where service is to be effected in a member State of the European Union,
(4) the Drug Trafficking Offences Act 1994,[2]
(7) Part VI of the Criminal Justice Act 1988,
(8) The Inheritance (Provision for Family and Dependants) Act 1975,
(9) Part II of the Immigration and Asylum Act 1999,
(10) Schedule 2 to the Immigration Act 1971,
(11) the Financial Services and Markets Act 2000.
(12) The Pensions Act 1995,
(13) The Pensions Act 2004.

5.3 Under the State Immunity Act 1978, the foreign State being served is allowed an additional two months over the normal period for filing an acknowledgment of service or defence or for filing or serving an admission allowed under paras 7.3 and 7.4.

## Service of Petitions, Application Notices and Orders

6.1 The provisions of Section III of Part 6 (special provisions about service out of the jurisdiction) apply to service out of the jurisdiction of a petition, application notice or order. (Rule 6.30(1) contains special provisions relating to application notices.)

6.2 Where an application notice is to be served out of the jurisdiction in accordance with Section III of Part 6 the court must have regard to the country in which the application notice is to be served in setting the date for the hearing of the application and giving any direction about service of the respondents evidence.

[2] This appears to be a reference to the Drug Trafficking Act 1994.

6.3 Where the permission of the court is required for a claim form to be served out of the jurisdiction the permission of the court, unless r. 6.30(3) applies, must also be obtained for service out of the jurisdiction of any other document to be served in the proceedings and the provisions of this practice direction will, so far as applicable to that other document, apply.

6.4 When particulars of claim are served out of the jurisdiction any statement as to the period for responding to the claim contained in any of the forms required by r. 7.8 to accompany the particulars of claim must specify the period prescribed under r. 6.22 or 6.23 or (as the case may be) by the order permitting service out of the jurisdiction (see r. 6.21(4)).

## Period for Responding to a Claim Form

7.1 Where a claim has been served out of the jurisdiction without permission under r. 6.19:

(1) r. 6.22 sets out the period for filing an acknowledgment of service or filing or serving an admission; and where r. 6.22(4) applies, the period will be calculated in accordance with para. 7.3 having regard to the table below;

(2) r. 6.23 sets out the period for filing a defence and where r. 6.23(4) applies, the period will be calculated in accordance with para. 7.4 having regard to the table below.

7.2 Where an order grants permission to serve a claim form out of the jurisdiction, the periods within which the defendant may:

(1) file an acknowledgment of service;

(2) file or serve an admission;

(3) file a defence,

will be calculated in accordance with paras 7.3 and 7.4 having regard to the table below. (Rule 6.21(4) requires an order giving permission for a claim form to be served out of the jurisdiction to specify the period within which the defendant may respond to the claim form.)

7.3 The period for filing an acknowledgment of service under Part 10 or filing or serving an admission under Part 14 is:

(1) where the defendant is served with a claim form which states that particulars of claim are to follow, the number of days listed in the table after service of the particulars of claim; and

(2) in any other case, the number of days listed in the table after service of the claim form.

For example: where a defendant has been served with a claim form (accompanied by particulars of claim) in the Bahamas, the period for acknowledging service or admitting the claim is 22 days after service.

7.4 The period for filing a defence under Part 15 is:

(1) the number of days listed in the table after service of the particulars of claim; or

(2) where the defendant has filed an acknowledgment of service, the number of days listed in the table plus an additional 14 days after the service of the particulars of claim.

For example, where a defendant has been served with particulars of claim in Gibraltar and has acknowledged service, the period for filing a defence is 45 days after service of the particulars of claim.

## Period for Responding to an Application Notice

8.1 Where an application notice or order needs to be served out of the jurisdiction, the period for responding to service is seven days less than the number of days listed in the table.

## Address for Service and Further Information

10.1 A defendant is required by r. 6.5(2) to give an address for service within the jurisdiction.

10.2 Further information concerning service out of the jurisdiction can be obtained from the Foreign Process Section, Room E02, Royal Courts of Justice, Strand, London WC2A 2LL (telephone (020) 7947 6691).

**Table**

| Place or country | Number of days |
|---|---|
| Abu Dhabi | 22 |
| Afghanistan | 23 |
| Albania | 25 |
| Algeria | 22 |
| Angola | 22 |
| Anguilla | 31 |
| Antigua | 23 |
| Antilles (Netherlands) | 31 |
| Argentina | 22 |
| Armenia | 21 |
| Ascension | 31 |
| Australia | 25 |
| Austria | 21 |
| Azores | 23 |
| Bahamas | 22 |
| Bahrain | 22 |
| Balearic Islands | 21 |
| Bangladesh | 23 |
| Barbados | 23 |
| Belarus | 21 |
| Belgium | 21 |
| Belize | 23 |
| Benin | 25 |
| Bermuda | 31 |
| Bhutan | 28 |
| Bolivia | 23 |
| Bosnia-Hercegovina | 21 |
| Botswana | 23 |
| Brazil | 22 |
| Brunei | 25 |
| Bulgaria | 23 |
| Burkina Faso | 23 |
| Burma | 23 |
| Burundi | 22 |
| Cameroon | 22 |
| Canada | 22 |
| Canary Islands | 22 |
| Cape Verde Islands | 25 |
| Caroline Islands | 31 |
| Cayman Islands | 31 |
| Central African Republic | 25 |
| Chad | 25 |
| Chile | 22 |
| China | 24 |
| Christmas Island | 27 |
| Cocos (Keeling) Islands | 41 |
| Colombia | 22 |
| Comoros | 23 |

*(cont.)*

| Place or country | Number of days |
|---|---|
| Congo (People's Republic)* | 25 |
| Corsica | 21 |
| Costa Rica | 23 |
| Croatia | 21 |
| Cuba | 24 |
| Cyprus | 31 |
| Cyrenaica (see Libya) | 21 |
| Czech Republic | 21 |
| Denmark | 21 |
| Djibouti | 22 |
| Dominica | 23 |
| Dominican Republic | 23 |
| Dubai | 22 |
| Ecuador | 22 |
| Egypt (Arab Republic) | 22 |
| El Salvador (Republic of) | 25 |
| Equatorial Guinea | 23 |
| Estonia | 21 |
| Ethiopia | 22 |
| Falkland Islands and Dependencies | 31 |
| Faroe Islands | 31 |
| Fiji | 23 |
| Finland | 24 |
| France | 21 |
| French Guiana | 31 |
| French Polynesia | 31 |
| French West Indies | 31 |
| Gabon | 25 |
| Gambia | 22 |
| Georgia | 21 |
| Germany | 21 |
| Ghana | 22 |
| Gibraltar | 31 |
| Greece | 21 |
| Greenland | 31 |
| Grenada | 24 |
| Guatemala | 24 |
| Guernsey | 18 |
| Guyana | 22 |
| Haiti | 23 |
| Holland (Netherlands) | 21 |
| Honduras | 24 |
| Hong Kong | 31 |
| Hungary | 22 |
| Iceland | 22 |
| India | 23 |
| Indonesia | 22 |
| Iran | 22 |
| Iraq | 22 |
| Ireland (Republic of) | 21 |
| Ireland (Northern) | 21 |
| Isle of Man | 18 |

[* Now Republic of Congo.]

| Place or country | Number of days |
|---|---|
| Israel | 22 |
| Italy | 21 |
| Ivory Coast | 22 |
| Jamaica | 22 |
| Japan | 23 |
| Jersey | 18 |
| Jordan | 23 |
| Kampuchea | 38 |
| Kazakhstan | 21 |
| Kenya | 22 |
| Kirgizstan | 21 |
| Korea (North) | 28 |
| Korea (South) | 24 |
| Kuwait | 22 |
| Laos | 30 |
| Latvia | 31 |
| Lebanon | 22 |
| Lesotho | 23 |
| Liberia | 22 |
| Libya | 21 |
| Liechtenstein | 21 |
| Lithuania | 21 |
| Luxembourg | 21 |
| Macau | 31 |
| Macedonia | 21 |
| Madagascar | 23 |
| Madeira | 31 |
| Malawi | 23 |
| Malaya | 24 |
| Maldive Islands | 26 |
| Mali | 25 |
| Malta | 21 |
| Mariana Islands | 26 |
| Marshall Islands | 32 |
| Mauritania | 23 |
| Mauritius | 22 |
| Mexico | 23 |
| Moldova | 21 |
| Monaco | 21 |
| Montserrat | 31 |
| Morocco | 22 |
| Mozambique | 23 |
| Nauru Island | 36 |
| Nepal | 23 |
| Netherlands | 21 |
| Nevis | 24 |
| New Caledonia | 31 |
| New Hebrides (now Vanuatu) | 29 |
| New Zealand | 26 |
| New Zealand Island Territories | 50 |
| Nicaragua | 24 |
| Niger (Republic of) | 25 |
| Nigeria | 22 |
| Norfolk Island | 31 |

*(cont.)*

| Place or country | Number of days |
|---|---|
| Norway | 21 |
| Oman (Sultanate of) | 22 |
| Pakistan | 23 |
| Panama (Republic of) | 26 |
| Papua New Guinea | 26 |
| Paraguay | 22 |
| Peru | 22 |
| Philippines | 23 |
| Pitcairn Island | 31 |
| Poland | 21 |
| Portugal | 21 |
| Portuguese Timor | 31 |
| Puerto Rico | 23 |
| Qatar | 23 |
| Reunion | 31 |
| Romania | 22 |
| Russia | 21 |
| Rwanda | 23 |
| Sabah | 23 |
| St Helena | 31 |
| St Kitts–Nevis | 24 |
| St Lucia | 24 |
| St Pierre and Miquelon | 31 |
| St Vincent and the Grenadines | 24 |
| Samoa (USA Territory) (see also Western Samoa) | 30 |
| Sarawak | 28 |
| Saudi Arabia | 24 |
| Scotland | 21 |
| Senegal | 22 |
| Seychelles | 22 |
| Sharjah | 24 |
| Sierra Leone | 22 |
| Singapore | 22 |
| Slovakia | 21 |
| Slovenia | 21 |
| Society Islands (French Polynesia) | 31 |
| Solomon Islands | 29 |
| Somali Democratic Republic* | 22 |
| South Africa (Republic of) | 22 |
| South Georgia (Falkland Island Dependencies) | 31 |
| South Orkneys | 21 |
| South Shetlands | 21 |
| Spain | 21 |
| Spanish Territories of North Africa | 31 |
| Sri Lanka | 23 |
| Sudan | 22 |
| Suriname | 22 |
| Swaziland | 22 |
| Sweden | 21 |
| Switzerland | 21 |
| Syria | 23 |
| Taiwan | 23 |
| Tajikistan | 21 |

[* At present, this country is generally referred to as Somalia.]

| Place or country | Number of days |
|---|---|
| Tanzania | 22 |
| Thailand | 23 |
| Tibet | 34 |
| Tobago | 23 |
| Togo | 22 |
| Tonga | 30 |
| Tortola | 31 |
| Trinidad and Tobago | 23 |
| Tristan da Cunha | 31 |
| Tunisia | 22 |
| Turkey | 21 |
| Turkmenistan | 21 |
| Turks and Caicos Islands | 31 |
| Uganda | 22 |
| Ukraine | 21 |
| United States of America | 22 |
| Uruguay | 22 |
| Uzbekistan | 21 |
| Vanuatu | 29 |
| Vatican City State | 21 |
| Venezuela | 22 |
| Vietnam | 28 |
| Virgin Islands—British (Tortola) | 31 |
| Virgin Islands—USA | 24 |
| Wake Island | 25 |
| Western Samoa | 34 |
| Yemen (Republic of) | 30 |
| Yogoslavia (except for Bosnia-Hercegovina, Croatia, Macedonia and Slovenia)† | 21 |
| Zaire‡ | 25 |
| Zambia | 23 |
| Zimbabwe | 22 |

## COUNCIL REGULATION (EC) NO. 1348/2000

This Regulation is annexed to PD 6B but is not reproduced in this work. It may be accessed via the DCA website at <http://www.dca.gov.uk>.

[† The country referred to in this entry is now Serbia and Montenegro. It includes Kosovo (which is under United Nations administration) and the autonomous province of Vojvodina. There are separate entries in this table for Bosnia-Hercegovina, Croatia, Macedonia and Slovenia.]

[‡ Now Democratic Republic of the Congo.]

# CPR Part 7 How to Start Proceedings — The Claim Form



## 7.1 Where to Start Proceedings

Restrictions on where proceedings may be started are set out in the relevant practice direction.

## 7.2 How to Start Proceedings

(1) Proceedings are started when the court issues a claim form at the request of the claimant.
(2) A claim form is issued on the date entered on the form by the court.
(A person who seeks a remedy from the court before proceedings are started or in relation to proceedings which are taking place, or will take place, in another jurisdiction must make an application under Part 23.)
(Part 16 sets out what the claim form must include.)
(The costs practice direction sets out the information about a funding arrangement to be provided with the claim form where the claimant intends to seek to recover an additional liability)
('Funding arrangement' and 'additional liability' are defined in rule 43.2.)

7.2A The practice direction supplementing this Part makes provision for procedures to be followed when claims are brought by or against a partnership within the jurisdiction.

## 7.3 Right to Use One Claim Form to Start Two or More Claims

A claimant may use a single claim form to start all claims which can be conveniently disposed of in the same proceedings.

## 7.4 Particulars of Claim

(1) Particulars of claim must—
 (a) be contained in or served with the claim form; or
 (b) subject to paragraph (2) be served on the defendant by the claimant within 14 days after service of the claim form.
(2) Particulars of claim must be served on the defendant no later than the latest time for serving a claim form.
(Rule 7.5 sets out the latest time for serving a claim form.)
(3) Where the claimant serves particulars of claim separately from the claim form in accordance with paragraph (1)(b), he must, within 7 days of service on the defendant, file a copy of the particulars together with a certificate of service.
(Part 16 sets out what the particulars of claim must include.)
(Part 22 requires particulars of claim to be verified by a statement of truth.)
(Rule 6.10 makes provision for a certificate of service.)

## 7.5 Service of a Claim Form

(1) After a claim form has been issued, it must be served on the defendant.

(2) The general rule is that a claim form must be served within 4 months after the date of issue.
(3) The period for service is 6 months where the claim form is to be served out of the jurisdiction.

## 7.6 Extension of Time for Serving a Claim Form

(1) The claimant may apply for an order extending the period within which the claim form may be served.
(2) The general rule is that an application to extend the time for service must be made—
  (a) within the period for serving the claim form specified by rule 7.5; or
  (b) where an order has been made under this rule, within the period for service specified by that order.
(3) If the claimant applies for an order to extend the time for service of the claim form after the end of the period specified by rule 7.5 or by an order made under this rule, the court may make such an order only if—
  (a) the court has been unable to serve the claim form; or
  (b) the claimant has taken all reasonable steps to serve the claim form but has been unable to do so; and
  (c) in either case, the claimant has acted promptly in making the application.
(4) An application for an order extending the time for service—
  (a) must be supported by evidence; and
  (b) may be made without notice.

## 7.7 Application by Defendant for Service of Claim Form

(1) Where a claim form has been issued against a defendant, but has not yet been served on him, the defendant may serve a notice on the claimant requiring him to serve the claim form or discontinue the claim within a period specified in the notice.
(2) The period specified in a notice served under paragraph (1) must be at least 14 days after service of the notice.
(3) If the claimant fails to comply with the notice, the court may, on the application of the defendant—
  (a) dismiss the claim; or
  (b) make any other order it thinks just.

## 7.8 Form for Defence etc. Must be Served with Particulars of Claim

(1) When particulars of claim are served on a defendant, whether they are contained in the claim form, served with it or served subsequently, they must be accompanied by—
  (a) a form for defending the claim;
  (b) a form for admitting the claim; and
  (c) a form for acknowledging service.
(2) Where the claimant is using the procedure set out in Part 8 (alternative procedure for claims)—
  (a) paragraph (1) does not apply; and
  (b) a form for acknowledging service must accompany the claim form.

## 7.9 Fixed Date and Other Claims

A practice direction—
  (a) may set out the circumstances in which the court may give a fixed date for a hearing when it issues a claim;
  (b) may list claims in respect of which there is a specific claim form for use and set out the claim form in question; and
  (c) may disapply or modify these Rules as appropriate in relation to the claims referred to in paragraphs (a) and (b).

### 7.10 Production Centre for Claims

(1) There shall be a Production Centre for the issue of claim forms and other related matters.
(2) The relevant practice direction makes provision for—
  (a) which claimants may use the Production Centre;
  (b) the type of claims which the Production Centre may issue;
  (c) the functions which are to be discharged by the Production Centre;
  (d) the place where the Production Centre is to be located; and
  (e) other related matters.
(3) The relevant practice direction may disapply or modify these Rules as appropriate in relation to claims issued by the Production Centre.

### 7.11 Human Rights

(1) A claim under section 7(1)(a) of the Human Rights Act 1998 in respect of a judicial act may be brought only in the High Court.
(2) Any other claim under section 7(1)(a) of that Act may be brought in any court.

### 7.12 Electronic Issue of Claims

(1) A practice direction may make provision for a claimant to start a claim by requesting the issue of a claim form electronically.
(2) The practice direction may, in particular—
  (a) specify—
    (i) the types of claim which may be issued electronically; and
    (ii) the conditions which a claim must meet before it may be issued electronically;
  (b) specify—
    (i) the court where the claim will be issued; and
    (ii) the circumstances in which the claim will be transferred to another court;
  (c) provide for the filing of other documents electronically where a claim has been started electronically;
  (d) specify the requirements that must be fulfilled for any document filed electronically; and
  (e) provide how a fee payable on the filing of any document is to be paid where that document is filed electronically.
(3) The practice direction may disapply or modify these Rules as appropriate in relation to claims started electronically.

# PD 7 Practice Direction — How to Start Proceedings — The Claim Form

This practice direction supplements CPR Part 7.

## General

1 Subject to the following provisions of this practice direction, proceedings which both the High Court and the county courts have jurisdiction to deal with may be started in the High Court or in a county court.

## Where to Start Proceedings

2.1 Proceedings (whether for damages or for a specified sum) may not be started in the High Court unless the value of the claim is more than £15,000.

2.2 Proceedings which include a claim for damages in respect of personal injuries must not be started in the High Court unless the value of the claim is £50,000 or more (art. 9 of the High Court and County Courts Jurisdiction Order 1991 (SI 1991/724 as amended) describes how the value of a claim is to be determined).

2.3 A claim must be issued in the High Court or a county court if an enactment so requires.

2.4 Subject to paragraphs 2.1 and 2.2 above, a claim should be started in the High Court if by reason of:
(1) the financial value of the claim and the amount in dispute, and/or
(2) the complexity of the facts, legal issues, remedies or procedures involved, and/or
(3) the importance of the outcome of the claim to the public in general,
the claimant believes that the claim ought to be dealt with by a High Court judge. (CPR Part 30 and PD 30 contain provisions relating to the transfer to the county court of proceedings started in the High Court and vice versa.)

2.5 A claim relating to Chancery business (which includes any of the matters specified in the Supreme Court Act 1981, sch. 1, para. 1) may, subject to any enactment, rule or practice direction, be dealt with in the High Court or in a county court. The claim form should, if issued in the High Court, be marked in the top right-hand corner 'Chancery Division' and, if issued in the county court, be marked 'Chancery Business'. (For the equity jurisdiction of county courts, see the County Courts Act 1984, s. 23.)

2.6 A claim relating to any of the matters specified in the Supreme Court Act 1981, sch. 1, para. 2(a) and (b) must be dealt with in the High Court and will be assigned to the Queen's Bench Division.

2.7 Practice directions applying to particular types of proceedings, or to proceedings in particular courts, will contain provisions relating to the commencement and conduct of those proceedings.

2.8 A claim in the High Court for which a jury trial is directed will, if not already being dealt with in the Queen's Bench Division, be transferred to that Division.

2.9 The following proceedings may not be started in a county court unless the parties have agreed otherwise in writing:
(1) a claim for damages or other remedy for libel or slander, and
(2) a claim in which the title to any toll, fair, market or franchise is in question.

2.10 (1) The normal rules apply in deciding in which court and specialist list a claim that includes issues under the Human Rights Act 1998 should be started. They also apply in deciding which procedure to use to start the claim: Part 7, Part 8 or Part 54 (judicial review).
(2) The exception is a claim for damages in respect of a judicial act, which should be commenced in the High Court. If the claim is made in a notice of appeal then

it will be dealt with according to the normal rules governing where that appeal is heard.

(A county court cannot make a declaration of incompatibility in accordance with s. 4 of the Human Rights Act 1998. Legislation may direct that such a claim is to be brought before a specified tribunal.)

## The Claim Form

3.1 A claimant must use form N1 or form N208 (the Part 8 claim form) to start a claim (but see paragraphs 3.2 and 3.4 below).

3.2 Rule 7.9 deals with fixed date claims and rule 7.10 deals with the Production Centre for the issue of claims; there are separate practice directions supplementing rules 7.9 and 7.10.

3.3 If a claimant wishes his claim to proceed under Part 8, or if the claim is required to proceed under Part 8, the claim form should so state. Otherwise the claim will proceed under Part 7. But note that in respect of claims in specialist proceedings (listed in Part 49) and claims brought under the RSC or CCR set out in the schedules to the CPR (see Part 50) the CPR will apply only to the extent that they are not inconsistent with the rules and practice directions that expressly apply to those claims.

3.4 Other practice directions may require special forms to be used to commence particular types of proceedings, or proceedings in particular courts.

3.5 Where a claim which is to be served out of the jurisdiction is one which the court has power to deal with under the Civil Jurisdiction and Judgments Act 1982, the claim form and, when they are contained in a separate document, the particulars of claim should be endorsed with a statement that the court has power under that Act to deal with the claim and that no proceedings based on the same claim are pending between the parties in Scotland, Northern Ireland or another Convention territory.[1]

3.5A Where a claim which is to be served out of jurisdiction is one which the court has power to deal with under Council Regulation (EC) No. 44/2001 of 22 December 2000 on jurisdiction and the recognition and enforcement of judgments in civil and commercial matters, the claim form and, when they are contained in a separate document, the particulars of claim must be endorsed with a statement that the court has power under that Regulation to deal with the claim and that no proceedings based on the same claim are pending between the parties in Scotland, Northern Ireland or another Regulation State.[2]

3.6 If a claim for damages or for an unspecified sum is started in the High Court, the claim form must:

(1) state that the claimant expects to recover more than £15,000 (or £50,000 or more if the claim is for personal injuries) or

(2) state that some enactment provides that the claim may only be commenced in the High Court and specify that enactment or

(3) state that the claim is to be in one of the specialist High Court lists (see CPR Parts 49 and 58 to 62) and specify that list.

3.7 If the contents of a claim form commencing specialist proceedings complies with the requirements of the specialist list in question the claim form will also satisfy paragraph 3.6 above.

3.8 If a claim for damages for personal injuries is started in the county court, the claim form must state whether or not the claimant expects to recover more than £1000 in respect of pain, suffering and loss of amenity.

3.9 If a claim for housing disrepair which includes a claim for an order requiring repairs or

[1] 'Convention territory' means the territory or territories of any Contracting State as defined by section 1(3) of the Civil Jurisdiction and Judgments Act 1982, to which the Brussels Convention or Lugano Convention apply.

[2] 'Regulation State' means all member States except Denmark.

other work to be carried out by the landlord is started in the county court, the claim form must state:

(1) whether or not the cost of the repairs or other work is estimated to be more than £1000, and

(2) whether or not the claimant expects to recover more than £1000 in respect of any claim for damages.[3]

If either of the amounts mentioned in (1) and (2) is more than £1000, the small claims track will not be the normal track for that claim.

(PD 43–48 contains details of the information required to be filed with a claim form to comply with r. 44.15 (providing information about funding arrangements).)

## Title of Proceedings

4.1 The claim form and every other statement of case, must be headed with the title of the proceedings. The title should state:

(1) the number of proceedings,
(2) the court or division in which they are proceeding,
(3) the full name of each party,
(4) his status in the proceedings (i.e. claimant/defendant).

(Paragraph 2.6 of the practice direction to Part 16 sets out what is meant by a full name in respect of each type of claimant)

4.2 Where there is more than one claimant and/or more than one defendant, the parties should be described in the title as follows:

(1) AB
(2) CD
(3) EF *Claimants*
and
(1) GH
(2) IJ
(3) KL *Defendants*

## Start of Proceedings

5.1 Proceedings are started when the court issues a claim form at the request of the claimant (see rule 7.2) but where the claim form as issued was received in the court office on a date earlier than the date on which it was issued by the court, the claim is 'brought' for the purposes of the Limitation Act 1980 and any other relevant statute on that earlier date.

5.2 The date on which the claim form was received by the court will be recorded by a date stamp either on the claim form held on the court file or on the letter that accompanied the claim form when it was received by the court.

5.3 An enquiry as to the date on which the claim form was received by the court should be directed to a court officer.

5.4 Parties proposing to start a claim which is approaching the expiry of the limitation period should recognise the potential importance of establishing the date the claim form was received by the court and should themselves make arrangements to record the date.

5.5 Where it is sought to start proceedings against the estate of a deceased defendant where probate or letters of administration have not been granted, the claimant should issue the claim against 'the personal representatives of A.B. deceased'. The claimant should then, before the expiry of the period for service of the claim form, apply to the court for the appointment of a person to represent the estate of the deceased.

[3] See rules 16.3(4) and 26.6.

### Claims by and against partnerships within the jurisdiction

5A.1 Paragraphs 5A and 5B apply to claims that are brought by or against two or more persons who—
(1) were partners; and
(2) carried on that partnership business within the jurisdiction, at the time when the cause of action accrued.

5A.2 For the purposes of this paragraph, 'partners' includes persons claiming to be entitled as partners and persons alleged to be partners.

5A.3 Where that partnership has a name, unless it is inappropriate to do so, claims must be brought in or against the name under which that partnership carried on business at the time the cause of action accrued.

### Partnership membership statements

5B.1 In this paragraph a 'partnership membership statement' is a written statement of the names and last known places of residence of all the persons who were partners in the partnership at the time when the cause of action accrued, being the date specified for this purpose in accordance with paragraph 5B.3.

5B.2 If the partners are requested to provide a copy of a partnership membership statement by any party to a claim, the partners shall do so within 14 days of receipt of the request.

5B.3 In that request the party seeking a copy of a partnership membership statement must specify the date when the relevant cause of action accrued.

(Signing of the acknowledgment of service in the case of a partnership is dealt with in Paragraph 4.4 of the Practice Direction supplementing Part 10.)

### Persons carrying on business in another name

5C.1 This paragraph applies where—
(1) a claim is brought against an individual;
(2) that individual carries on a business within the jurisdiction (but need not himself be within the jurisdiction); and
(3) that business is carried on in a name other than his own name ('the business name').

5C.2 The claim may be brought against the business name as if it were the name of a partnership.

### Particulars of Claim

6.1 Where the claimant does not include the particulars of claim in the claim form, particulars of claim may be served separately:
(1) either at the same time as the claim form, or
(2) within 14 days after service of the claim form[4] provided that the service of the particulars of claim is within four months after the date of issue of the claim form[5] (or six months where the claim form is to be served out of the jurisdiction).[6]

6.2 If the particulars of claim are not included in or have not been served with the claim form, the claim form must contain a statement that particulars of claim will follow.[7] (These paragraphs do not apply where the Part 8 procedure is being used. For information on matters to be included in the claim form or the particulars of claim, see Part 16 (statements of case) and PD 16.)

[4] See rule 7.4(1)(b).
[5] See rules 7.4(2) and 7.5(2).
[6] See rule 7.5(3).
[7] See rule 16.2(2).

## Statement of Truth

7.1 Part 22 requires the claim form and, where they are not included in the claim form, the particulars of claim, to be verified by a statement of truth.

7.2 The form of the statement of truth is as follows:

'[I believe] [the claimant believes] that the facts stated in [this claim form] [these particulars of claim] are true.'

7.3 Attention is drawn to rule 32.14 which sets out the consequences of verifying a statement of case containing a false statement without an honest belief in its truth.

(For information regarding statements of truth see Part 22 and PD 22.)

## Extension of Time

8.1 An application under rule 7.6 (for an extension of time for serving a claim form under rule 7.6(1)) must be made in accordance with Part 23 and supported by evidence.

8.2 The evidence should state:

(1) all the circumstances relied on,

(2) the date of issue of the claim,

(3) the expiry date of any rule 7.6 extension, and

(4) a full explanation as to why the claim has not been served.

(For information regarding (1) written evidence see Part 32 and PD 32 and (2) service of the claim form see Part 6 and PD 6.)

# PD 7B Practice Direction — Consumer Credit Act Claim

This practice direction supplements CPR rule 7.9.

1.1 In this practice direction 'the Act' means the Consumer Credit Act 1974, a section referred to by number means the section with that number in the Act, and expressions which are defined in the Act have the same meaning in this practice direction as they have in the Act.

1.2 'Consumer Credit Act procedure' means the procedure set out in this practice direction.

## When to Use the Consumer Credit Act Procedure

2.1 A claimant must use the Consumer Credit Act procedure where he makes a claim under a provision of the Act to which paragraph 3 of this practice direction applies.

2.2 Where a claimant is using the Consumer Credit Act procedure the CPR are modified to the extent that they are inconsistent with the procedure set out in this practice direction.

2.3 The court may at any stage order the claim to continue as if the claimant had not used the Consumer Credit Act procedure, and if it does so the court may give any directions it considers appropriate.

2.4 This practice direction also sets out matters which must be included in the particulars of claim in certain types of claim, and restrictions on where certain types of claim may be started.

## The Provisions of the Act

3.1 Subject to paragraph 3.2 and 3.3 this practice direction applies to claims made under the following provisions of the Act:

(1) section 141 (claim by the creditor to enforce regulated agreement relating to goods etc.),

(2) section 129 (claim by debtor or hirer for a time order),

(3) section 90 (creditor's claim for an order for recovery of protected goods),

(4) section 92(1) (creditor's or owner's claim to enter premises to take possession of goods),

(5) section 140B(2)(a) (debtor's or surety's application for an order relating to an unfair relationship);

(5A) section 139(1)(a) (debtor's claim for a credit agreement to be reopened as extortionate); and

(6) creditor's or owner's claim for a court order to enforce a regulated agreement relating to goods or money where the court order is required by—

(a) section 65(1) (improperly-executed agreement),

(b) section 86(2) of the Act (death of debtor or hirer where agreement is partly secured or unsecured),

(c) section 111(2) (default notice etc. not served on surety),

(d) section 124(1) or (2) (taking of a negotiable instrument in breach of terms of section 123), or

(e) section 105(7)(a) or (b) (security not expressed in writing, or improperly executed).

3.2 This practice direction does not apply to any claim made under the provisions listed in paragraph 3.1 above if that claim relates to the recovery of land.

3.3 This practice direction also does not apply to a claim made by the creditor under section 141 of the Act to enforce a regulated agreement where the agreement relates only to money. Such a claim must be started by the issue of a Part 7 claim form.

## Restrictions on Where to Start Some Consumer Credit Act Claims

4.1 Where the claim includes a claim to recover goods to which a regulated hire purchase agreement or conditional sale agreements relates, it may only be started in the county court for the district in which the debtor, or one of the debtors:
(1) resides or carries on business, or
(2) resided or carried on business at the date when the defendant last made a payment under the agreement.

4.2 In any other claim to recover goods, the claim may only be started in the court for the district:
(1) in which the defendant, or one of the defendants, resides or carries on business, or
(2) in which the goods are situated.

4.3 A claim of a debtor or hirer for an order under section 129(1)(b) of the Act (a time order) may only be started in the court where the claimant resides or carries on business.
(Costs rule 45.1(2)(b) allows the claimant to recover fixed costs in certain circumstances where such a claim is made.)
(Paragraph 7 sets out the matters the claimant must include in his particulars of claim where he is using the Consumer Credit Act procedure.)

## The Consumer Credit Act Procedure

5.1 In the types of claim to which paragraph 3 applies the court will fix a hearing date on the issue of the claim form.

5.2 The particulars of claim must be served with the claim form.

5.3 Where a claimant is using the Consumer Credit Act procedure, the defendant to the claim is not required to:
(1) serve an acknowledgment of service, or
(2) file a defence, although he may choose to do so.

5.4 Where a defendant intends to defend a claim, his defence should be filed within 14 days of service of the particulars of claim. If the defendant fails to file a defence within this period, but later relies on it, the court may take such a failure into account as a factor when deciding what order to make about costs.

5.5 Part 12 (default judgment) does not apply where the claimant is using the Consumer Credit Act procedure.

5.6 Each party must be given at least 28 days' notice of the hearing date.

5.7 Where the claimant serves the claim form, he must serve notice of the hearing date at the same time, unless the hearing date is specified in the claim form.

## Powers of the Court at the Hearing

6.1 On the hearing date the court may dispose of the claim.

6.2 If the court does not dispose of the claim on the hearing date:
(1) if the defendant has filed a defence, the court will:
(a) allocate the claim to a track and give directions about the management of the case, or
(b) give directions to enable it to allocate the claim to a track,
(2) if the defendant has not filed a defence, the court may make any order or give any direction it considers appropriate.

6.3 Rule 26.5(3) to (5) and rules 26.6 to 26.10 apply to the allocation of a claim under paragraph 6.2.

## Matters Which Must be Included in the Particulars of Claim

7.1 Where the Consumer Credit Act procedure is used, the claimant must state in his particulars of claim that the claim is a Consumer Credit Act claim.

7.2 A claimant making a claim for the delivery of goods to enforce a hire purchase agreement or conditional sale agreement which is:

(1) a regulated agreement for the recovery of goods, and
(2) let to a person other than a company or other corporation,
must also state (in this order) in his particulars of claim:
(a) the date of the agreement,
(b) the parties to the agreement,
(c) the number or other identification of the agreement (with enough information to allow the debtor to identify the agreement),
(d) where the claimant was not one of the original parties to the agreement, the means by which the rights and duties of the creditor passed to him,
(e) the place where the agreement was signed by the defendant (if known),
(f) the goods claimed,
(g) the total price of the goods,
(h) the paid up sum,
(i) the unpaid balance of the total price,
(j) whether a default notice or a notice under section 76(1) or section 88(1) of the Act has been served on the defendant, and, if it has, the date and the method of service,
(k) the date on which the right to demand delivery of the goods accrued,
(l) the amount (if any) claimed as an alternative to the delivery of goods, and
(m) the amount (if any) claimed in addition to:
(i) the delivery of the goods, or
(ii) any claim under sub paragraph (l) above with the grounds of each such claim.

7.3 A claimant who is a debtor or hirer making a claim for an order under section 129(1)(b) of the Act (a time order) must state (in the following order) in his particulars of claim:
(1) the date of the agreement,
(2) the parties to the agreement,
(3) the number or other means of identifying the agreement,
(4) details of any sureties,
(5) if the defendant is not one of the original parties to the agreement then the name of the original party to the agreement,
(6) the names and addresses of the persons intended to be served with the claim form,
(7) the place where the claimant signed the agreement,
(8) details of the notice served by the creditor or owner giving rise to the claim for the time order,
(9) the total unpaid balance the claimant admits is due under the agreement, and:
(a) the amount of any arrears (if known), and
(b) the amount and frequency of the payments specified in the agreement,
(10) the claimant's proposals for payments of any arrears and of future instalments together with details of his means,
(11) where the claim relates to a breach of the agreement other than for the payment of money the claimant's proposals for remedying it.

7.4 (1) This paragraph applies where a claimant is required to obtain a court order to enforce a regulated agreement by:
(a) section 65(1) (improperly-executed agreement),
(b) section 105(7)(a) or (b) (security not expressed in writing, or improperly executed),
(c) section 111(2) (default notice etc. not served on surety),
(d) section 124(1) or (2) (taking of a negotiable instrument in breach of terms of section 123), or
(e) section 86(2) of the Act (death of debtor or hirer where agreement is partly secured or unsecured).
(2) The claimant must state in his particulars of claim what the circumstances are that require him to obtain a court order for enforcement.

## Admission of Certain Claims for Recovery of Goods Under Regulated Agreements

8.1 In a claim to recover goods to which section 90(1)[1] applies:
(1) the defendant may admit the claim, and
(2) offer terms on which a return order should be suspended under section 135(1)(b).

8.2 He may do so by filing a request in form N9C.

8.3 He should do so within the period for making an admission specified in rule 14.2(b). If the defendant fails to file his request within this period, and later makes such a request, the court may take the failure into account as a factor when deciding what order to make about costs.

8.4 On receipt of the admission, the court will serve a copy on the claimant.

8.5 The claimant may obtain judgment by filing a request in form N228.

8.6 On receipt of the request for judgment, the court will enter judgment in the terms of the defendant's admission and offer and for costs.

8.7 If:
(1) the claimant does not accept the defendant's admission and offer, and
(2) the defendant does not appear on the hearing date fixed when the claim form was issued,

the court may treat the defendant's admission and offer as evidence of the facts stated in it for the purposes of sections 129(2)(a)[2] and 135(2).[3]

## Additional Requirements About Parties to the Proceedings

9.1 The court may dispense with the requirement in section 141(5) (all parties to a regulated agreement and any surety to be parties to any proceedings) in any claim relating to the regulated agreement, if:
(1) the claim form has not been served on the debtor or the surety, and
(2) the claimant either before or at the hearing makes an application (which may be made without notice) for the court to make such an order.

9.2 In a claim relating to a regulated agreement where:
(1) the claimant was not one of the original parties to the agreement, and
(2) the former creditor's rights and duties under the agreement have passed to him by:
(a) operation of law, or
(b) assignment,

the requirement of section 141(5) (all parties to a regulated agreement and any surety to be parties to any proceedings) does not apply to the former creditor, unless the court otherwise orders.

9.3 Where a claimant who is a creditor or owner makes a claim for a court order under section 86(2) (death of debtor or hirer where agreement is partly secured or unsecured)

---

[1] Section 90(1) provides that:
'At any time when—
(a) the debtor is in breach of a regulated hire-purchase or a regulated conditional sale agreement relating to goods, and
(b) the debtor has paid to the creditor one-third or more of the total price of the goods, and
(c) the property in the goods remains in the creditor, the creditor is not entitled to recover possession of the goods from the debtor except on an order of the court.'

[2] Section 129(2) provides that:
'A time order shall provide for one or both of the following, as the court considers just—
(a) the payment by the debtor or hirer or any surety of any sum owed under a regulated agreement or a security by such instalments, payable at such times, as the court, having regard to the means of the debtor or hirer and any surety, considers reasonable;
(b) the remedying by the debtor or hirer of any breach of a regulated agreement (other than non-payment of money) within such period as the court may specify.'

[3] Section 135(2) provides that:
'The court shall not suspend the operation of a term [in an order relating to a regulated agreement] requiring the delivery up of goods by any person unless satisfied that the goods are in his possession or control.'

the personal representatives of the deceased debtor or hirer must be parties to the proceedings in which the order is sought, unless no grant of representation has been made to the estate.

9.4 Where no grant of representation has been made to the estate of the deceased debtor or hirer, the claimant must make an application in accordance with Part 23 for directions about which persons (if any) are to be made parties to the claim as being affected or likely to be affected by the enforcement of the agreement.

9.5 The claimant's application under paragraph 9.4:
(a) may be made without notice, and
(b) should be made before the claim form is issued.

## Notice to be Given to Reopen a Consumer Credit Agreement

10.1 Paragraph 10.2 applies where—
(1) a debtor or any surety intends to seek an order relating to an unfair relationship between a creditor and that debtor, arising out of a credit agreement (taken together with any related agreement);
(2) a claim relating to that agreement or any related agreement has already begun; and
(3) section 140B(2)(b) or section 140B(2)(c) applies.

10.2 The debtor or surety must serve written notice of his intention on the court and every other party to the claim within 14 days of the service of the claim form on him.

10.2A Where a debtor or any surety intends to apply for a credit agreement to be reopened after a claim on or relating to the agreement has already begun, and—
(1) section 139(1)(b); or
(2) section 139(1)(c),
applies, the debtor or surety must serve written notice of his intention on the court and every other party to the proceedings within 14 days of the service of the claim form on him.

10.3 If the debtor or surety (as the case may be) serves a notice under paragraph 10.2 or 10.2A he will be treated as having filed a defence for the purposes of the Consumer Credit Act procedure.

# PD 7C Practice Direction — Production Centre

This practice direction supplements CPR rule 7.10.

## General

1.1 In this practice direction
'the Centre' means the Production Centre,
'Centre user' means a person who is for the time being permitted to issue claims through the Centre, and includes a solicitor acting for such a person,
'officer' means the officer in charge of the Centre or another officer of the Centre acting on his behalf,
'national creditor code' means the number or reference allotted to a Centre user by the officer,
'Code of Practice' means any code of practice which may at any time be issued by the Court Service relating to the discharge by the Centre of its functions and the way in which a Centre user is to conduct business with the Centre,
'data' means any information which is required to be given to the court or which is to be contained in any document to be sent to the court or to any party.

1.2 For any purpose connected with the exercise of its functions, the Centre will be treated as part of the office of the court whose name appears on the claim form to which the functions relate, or in whose name the claim form is requested to be issued and, the officer will be treated as an officer of that court.

1.3 (1) The functions of the Centre include the provision of a facility which, through the use of information technology, enables a Centre user to have claim forms issued and served, whether or not those claim forms are to be treated as issued in the Northampton County Court or in another county court.
(2) If a Centre user issues claim forms in the name of Northampton County Court, the functions of the Centre also include:
(a) the handling of defences and admissions,
(b) the entry of judgment in default, on admission, on acceptance, or on determination,
(c) the registration of judgments,
(d) the issue of warrants of execution,
(e) where the defendant is an individual, the transfer to the defendant's home court of any case that is to continue following the filing of a defence or where a hearing is required before judgment; or, where the defendant is not an individual, the transfer to the court for the area of the claimant's, or where he is represented, his solicitor's, address, and
(f) the transfer to the defendant's home court of any case for oral examination or where enforcement of a judgment (other than by warrant of execution, charging order or third party debt order) is to follow.

1.4 (1) Where the officer is to take any step, any rule or practice direction which requires a document to be filed before he does so will be treated as complied with if the data which that document would contain is delivered to the Centre in computer readable form in accordance with the Code of Practice.
(2) Data relating to more than one case may be included in a single document or delivery of data.
(3) Rule 6.3(3) (copies of documents to be served by court) does not apply to any document which is to be produced by electronic means from data supplied by a Centre user.

(4) PD 16, [para. 7.3*], which requires documentation to be attached to the particulars of contract claims, does not apply to claims to be issued by the Centre.
(5) PD 22 (statements of truth) is modified as follows:
(a) a single statement of truth may accompany each batch of requests to issue claim forms and may be in electronic form,
(b) the form of such a statement should be as follows: 'I believe that the facts stated in the attached claim forms are true.', and
(c) the signature of the appropriate person (as to which see PD 22, para. 3) may be in electronic form.

## Claims Which May Not be Issued Through the Centre

2.1 The Centre will not issue any claim form which is to be issued in the High Court.
2.2 The Centre will only issue a claim form if the claim is for a specified sum of money less than £100,000.
2.3 The Centre will not issue any of the following types of claim:
(1) a claim against more than two defendants,
(2) a claim against two defendants where a different sum is claimed against each of them,
(3) a claim where particulars of claim separate from the claim form are required,
(4) a claim against the Crown,
(5) a claim for an amount in a foreign currency,
(6) a claim where either party is known to be a child or patient within Part 21 of the Civil Procedure Rules,
(7) a claim where the claimant is a legally assisted person within the meaning of the Legal Aid Act 1988,
(8) a claim where the defendant's address for service as it appears on the claim form is not in England or Wales.
(9) a claim which is to be issued under Part 8 of the Civil Procedure Rules.

## Centre Users

3.1 Only a Centre user may issue or conduct claims through the Centre.
3.2 The officer may permit any person to be a Centre user.
3.3 The officer may withdraw the permission for any person to be a Centre user.
3.4 A Centre user must comply with the provisions of the Code of Practice in his dealings with the Centre.
3.5 The officer will allot a national creditor code to each Centre user.

## The Code of Practice

4.1 The Code of Practice will contain provisions designed to ensure that the Centre can discharge its functions efficiently, and it may in particular provide for:
(1) the forms of magnetic media that may be used,
(2) the circumstances in which data may or must be supplied in magnetic form,
(3) the circumstances in which data may or must be supplied in a document and the form that such a document must take,
(4) how often data may be supplied,
(5) the numbering of cases and data relating to cases,
(6) data to be given to the Centre by the Centre user about cases which have been settled or paid or are otherwise not proceeding, and
(7) accounting arrangements and the method of payment of fees.
4.2 The Court Service may change the Code of Practice from time to time.

[* The text issued by the Department for Constitutional Affairs mistakenly refers to paragraph 8.3.]

## Other Modifications to the Civil Procedure Rules

*Powers of the officer to make orders*

5.1 The officer may make the following orders:

(1) an order to set aside a default judgment where, after that judgment has been entered, the claim form in the case is returned by the Post Office as undelivered,

(2) an order to set aside a judgment on application by a Centre user,

(3) an order to transfer a case to another county court for enforcement or for a judgment debtor to attend court for questioning.

*Procedure on the filing of a defence*

5.2 (1) This paragraph applies where a Centre user has issued a claim in the Northampton County Court and the defendant has filed a defence to the claim or to part of the claim.

(2) On the filing of the defence the officer will serve a notice on the Centre user requiring the Centre user to notify him within 28 days whether he wishes the claim to proceed.

(3) If the Centre user does not notify the officer within the time specified in the notice that he wishes the claim to proceed the claim will be stayed, and the officer will notify the parties accordingly.

(4) The proceedings will not be transferred as provided by para. 1.3(2)(e) until the Centre user notifies the officer that he wishes the claim to continue.

# PD 7D Practice Direction — Claims for the Recovery of Taxes

This practice direction supplements CPR rule 7.9.

## Scope

1.1 This practice direction applies to claims by HM Revenue and Customs for the recovery of:

(a) income tax,

(b) corporation tax,

(c) capital gains tax,

(d) interest, penalties and surcharges on income tax, corporation tax or capital gains tax which by virtue of s. 69 of the Taxes Management Act 1970 are to be treated as if they are taxes due and payable,

(e) national insurance contributions and interest, penalties and surcharges thereon.

## Procedure

2.1 If a defence is filed, the court will fix a date for the hearing.

2.2 Part 26 (case management—preliminary stage) apart from r. 26.2 (automatic transfer) does not apply to claims to which this practice direction applies.

## At the Hearing

3.1 On the hearing date the court may dispose of the claim.

(Section 70 of the Taxes Management Act 1970 and s. 118 of the Social Security Administration Act 1992 provide that a certificate of an officer of the Commissioners for HM Revenue and Customs is sufficient evidence that a sum mentioned in such a certificate is unpaid and due to the Crown.)

3.2 But exceptionally, if the court does not dispose of the claim on the hearing date it may give case management directions, which may, if the defendant has filed a defence, include allocating the case.

# PD 7E Practice Direction — Money Claim Online

## General

1.1 This practice direction provides for a scheme in which, in the circumstances set out in this practice direction, a request for a claim form to be issued and other specified documents may be filed electronically ('Money Claim Online').

1.2 This practice direction enables claimants and their representatives:
- (1) to start certain types of county court claims by requesting the issue of a claim form electronically via the Court Service website; and
- (2) where a claim has been started electronically:
  - (a) to file electronically a request for:
    - (i) judgment in default:
    - (ii) judgment on acceptance of an admission of the whole of the amount claimed; or
    - (iii) the issue of a warrant of execution; and
  - (b) to view an electronic record of the progress of the claim.

1.3 This practice direction also enables defendants and their representatives:
- (1) to file electronically:
  - (a) an acknowledgment of service;
  - (b) a part admission;
  - (c) a defence; or
  - (d) a counterclaim (if filed together with a defence).
- (2) to view an electronic record of the progress of the claim.

1.4 Claims started using Money Claim Online will be issued by Northampton County Court and will proceed in that court unless they are transferred to another court. The address for filing any document, application or request (other than one which is filed electronically in accordance with this practice direction) is Northampton County Court, St Katharine's House, 21–27 St Katharine's Street, Northampton NN1 2LH, DX 702885 Northampton 7, fax No. 0845 6015889.

## Security

2. The Court Service will take such measures as it thinks fit to ensure the security of steps taken or information stored electronically. These may include requiring users of Money Claim Online:
- (1) to enter a customer identification and password;
- (2) to provide personal information for identification purposes; and
- (3) to comply with any other security measures,

before taking any of the steps mentioned in para. 1.2 or 1.3.

## Fees

3.1 Where this practice direction provides for a fee to be paid electronically, it may be paid by:
- (1) credit card;
- (2) debit card; or
- (3) any other method which the Court Service may permit.

3.2 A step may only be taken using Money Claim Online on payment of the prescribed fee. The County Court Fees Order 1999 provides that parties may, in certain circumstances, be exempt from payment of fees, or may be entitled to apply for fees to be remitted or reduced. The Court Service website contains guidance as to when this entitlement arises. A claimant who wishes to claim exemption from payment of fees, or to apply for remission or reduction of fees, may not use Money Claim Online and should issue his claim at a court office.

## Types of Claims Which May be Started Using Money Claim Online

4. A claim may be started using Money Claim Online if it meets all the following conditions:
   (1) the only remedy claimed is a specified amount of money:
      (a) less than £100,000 (excluding any interest or costs claimed); and
      (b) in sterling;
   (2) the procedure under Part 7 is used;
   (3) the claimant is not:
      (a) a child or patient; or
      (b) funded by the Legal Services Commission;
   (4) the claim is against:
      (a) a single defendant; or
      (b) two defendants, if the claim is for a single amount against each of them;
   (5) the defendant is not:
      (a) the Crown; or
      (b) a person known to be a child or patient; and
   (6) the defendant's address for service is within England and Wales.

## Starting a Claim

5.1 A claimant may request the issue of a claim form by:
   (1) completing and sending an online claim form; and
   (2) electronically paying the appropriate issue fee,
   at <http://www.courtservice.gov.uk/mcol> or <http://www.moneyclaim.gov.uk>.

5.2 The particulars of claim:
   (1) must be included in the online claim form and may not be filed separately; and
   (2) must be limited in size to not more than 1080 characters (including spaces).

5.3 PD 16, para. 7.3, which requires documents to be filed with the particulars of claim in contract claims, does not apply to claims started using an online claim form.

5.4 When an online claim form is received by the Money Claim Online website, an acknowledgment of receipt will automatically be sent to the claimant. The acknowledgment of receipt does not constitute a notice that the claim form has been issued.

5.5 When the court issues a claim form following the submission of an online claim form, the claim is 'brought' for the purposes of the Limitation Act 1980 and any other enactment on the date on which the online claim form is received by the court's computer system. The court will keep a record, by electronic or other means, of when online claim forms are received.

5.6 When the court issues a claim form, it will:
   (1) serve a printed version of the claim form on the defendant; and
   (2) send the claimant notice of issue by post.

5.7 The claim form shall have printed on it a unique customer identification number or a password by which the defendant may access the claim on the Court Service website.

5.8 The claim form shall be deemed to be served on the fifth day after the claim was issued irrespective of whether that day is a business day or not.

5.9 Where a period of time within which an acknowledgment of service or a defence must be filed ends on a day when the court is closed, the defendant may file his acknowledgment or defence on the next day that the court is open.

## Online Response

6.1 A defendant wishing to file:
   (1) an acknowledgment of service of the claim form under Part 10;
   (2) a part admission under r. 14.5;

(3) a defence under Part 15; or

(4) a counterclaim (to be filed together with a defence),

may, instead of filing a written form, do so by completing and sending the relevant online form at <http://www.courtservice.gov.uk/mcol> or <http://www.moneyclaim.gov.uk>.

6.2 Where a defendant files an online form:

(1) he must not send a hard copy in addition;

(2) the form is not filed until it is received by the court, whatever time it is shown to have been sent;

(3) an online form received after 4 p.m. will be treated as filed on the next day the court office is open; and

(4) where a time limit applies, it remains the responsibility of the defendant to ensure that the online form is filed in time.

## Acknowledgment of Service

7.1 Attention is drawn to Part 10 and PD 10, which contain rules about acknowledgment of service.

## Admission

8.1 Attention is drawn to Part 14 and PD 14, which contain rules about admissions.

## Defence

9.1 Attention is drawn to Part 15 and PD 15, which contain rules about defences.

## Counterclaim

10.1 Where a counterclaim is filed using an online form, any fee payable shall be taken by the court to which the claim is transferred under para. 14.1.

10.2 Attention is drawn to Part 20 and PD 20, which contain provisions about counterclaims.

## Statement of Truth

11.1 Part 22 requires any statement of case to be verified by a statement of truth. This applies to any online forms.

11.2 The statement of truth in an online statement of case must be in the form:

[I believe] [The claimant believes] that the facts stated in this claim form are true.

or

[I believe] [The defendant believes] that the facts stated in this defence are true. as appropriate.

11.3 Attention is drawn to:

(1) PD 22, para. 3, which provides who may sign a statement of truth; and

(2) r. 32.14, which sets out the consequences of making, or causing to be made, a false statement in a document verified by a statement of truth, without an honest belief in its truth.

## Signature

12.1 Any provision of the CPR which requires a document to be signed by any person is satisfied by that person entering his name on an online form.

## Request for Judgment or Issue of Warrant

13.1 If, in a claim started using Money Claim Online:

(1) the claimant wishes to apply for judgment in default in accordance with Part 12; or

(2) the defendant has filed or served an admission of the whole of the claim in accordance with r. 14.4,

the claimant may request judgment to be entered in default or on the admission (as the case may be) by completing and sending an online request form at: <http://www.courtservice.gov.uk/mcol> or <http://www.moneyclaim.gov.uk>.

13.2 Where:

(1) judgment has been entered following a request under para. 13.1; and

(2) the claimant is entitled to the issue of a warrant of execution without requiring the permission of the court,

the claimant may request the issue of a warrant of execution by:

(a) completing and sending an online request form; and

(b) electronically paying the appropriate fee,

at <http://www.courtservice.gov.uk/mcol> or <http://www.moneyclaim.gov.uk>.

(CCR, ord. 26 in CPR, sch. 2, contains rules about warrants of execution. Among other matters, CCR, ord. 26, r. 1, contains restrictions on when a warrant of execution may be issued if the court has made an order for payment of a sum of money by instalments, and CCR, ord. 26, r. 5, sets out certain circumstances in which a warrant of execution may not be issued without the permission of the court.)

13.3 A request under para. 13.1 or 13.2 will be treated as being filed:

(1) on the day the court receives the request, if it receives it before 10 a.m. on a working day; and

(2) otherwise, on the next working day after the court receives the request.

## Transfer of Claim

14.1 Where the defendant is an individual and Northampton County Court is not his home court, the court will transfer the claim to the defendant's home court:

(1) under r. 13.4, if the defendant applies to set aside or vary judgment;

(2) under r. 14.12, if there is to be a hearing for a judge to determine the time and rate of payment;

(3) under r. 26.2, if a defence is filed to all or part of the claim; or

(4) if either party makes an application which cannot be dealt with without a hearing.

14.2 Where the defendant is not an individual, if:

(1) the claimant's address for service on the claim form is not within the district of Northampton County Court; and

(2) one of the events mentioned in para. 14.1 arises,

the court will transfer the claim to the county court for the district in which the claimant's address for service on the claim form is situated.

## Viewing the Case Record

15.1 A facility will be provided for parties or their representatives to view an electronic record of the status of claims started using Money Claim Online.

15.2 The record of each claim will be reviewed and, if necessary, updated at least once each day until the claim is transferred from Northampton County Court.

# CPR Part 8 Alternative Procedure for Claims



## 8.1 Types of Claim in Which Part 8 Procedure May be Followed

(1) The Part 8 procedure is the procedure set out in this Part.

(2) A claimant may use the Part 8 procedure where—

- (a) he seeks the court's decision on a question which is unlikely to involve a substantial dispute of fact; or
- (b) paragraph (6) applies.

(3) The court may at any stage order the claim to continue as if the claimant had not used the Part 8 procedure and, if it does so, the court may give any directions it considers appropriate.

(4) Paragraph (2) does not apply if a practice direction provides that the Part 8 procedure may not be used in relation to the type of claim in question.

(5) Where the claimant uses the Part 8 procedure he may not obtain default judgment under Part 12.

(6) A rule or practice direction may, in relation to a specified type of proceedings—

- (a) require or permit the use of the Part 8 procedure; and
- (b) disapply or modify any of the rules set out in this Part as they apply to those proceedings.

(Rule 8.9 provides for other modifications to the general rules where the Part 8 procedure is being used.)

## 8.2 Contents of the Claim Form

Where the claimant uses the Part 8 procedure the claim form must state—

- (a) that this Part applies;
- (b) (i) the question which the claimant wants the court to decide; or
  - (ii) the remedy which the claimant is seeking and the legal basis for the claim to that remedy;
- (c) if the claim is being made under an enactment, what that enactment is;
- (d) if the claimant is claiming in a representative capacity, what that capacity is; and
- (e) if the defendant is sued in a representative capacity, what that capacity is.

(Part 22 provides for the claim form to be verified by a statement of truth.)

(Rule 7.5 provides for service of the claim form.)

(The costs practice direction [PD 43–48] sets out the information about a funding arrangement to be provided with the claim form where the claimant intends to seek to recover an additional liability.)

('Funding arrangement' and 'additional liability' are defined in rule 43.2.)

## 8.2A Issue of Claim Form Without Naming Defendants

(1) A practice direction may set out the circumstances in which a claim form may be issued under this Part without naming a defendant.

(2) The practice direction may set out those cases in which an application for permission must be made by application notice before the claim form is issued.
(3) The application notice for permission—
  (a) need not be served on any other person; and
  (b) must be accompanied by a copy of the claim form that the applicant proposes to issue.
(4) Where the court gives permission it will give directions about the future management of the claim.

## 8.3 Acknowledgment of Service

(1) The defendant must—
  (a) file an acknowledgment of service in the relevant practice form not more than 14 days after service of the claim form; and
  (b) serve the acknowledgment of service on the claimant and any other party.
(2) The acknowledgment of service must state—
  (a) whether the defendant contests the claim; and
  (b) if the defendant seeks a different remedy from that set out in the claim form, what that remedy is.
(3) The following rules of Part 10 (acknowledgment of service) apply—
  (a) rule 10.3(2) (exceptions to the period for filing an acknowledgment of service); and
  (b) rule 10.5 (contents of acknowledgment of service).

(The costs practice direction [PD 43–48] sets out the information about a funding arrangement to be provided with the acknowledgment of service where the defendant intends to seek to recover an additional liability.)

('Funding arrangement' and 'additional liability' are defined in rule 43.2.)

## 8.4 Consequence of Not Filing an Acknowledgment of Service

(1) This rule applies where—
  (a) the defendant has failed to file an acknowledgment of service; and
  (b) the time period for doing so has expired.
(2) The defendant may attend the hearing of the claim but may not take part in the hearing unless the court gives permission.

## 8.5 Filing and Serving Written Evidence

(1) The claimant must file any written evidence on which he intends to rely when he files his claim form.
(2) The claimant's evidence must be served on the defendant with the claim form.
(3) A defendant who wishes to rely on written evidence must file it when he files his acknowledgment of service.
(4) If he does so, he must also, at the same time, serve a copy of his evidence on the other parties.
(5) The claimant may, within 14 days of service of the defendant's evidence on him, file further written evidence in reply.
(6) If he does so, he must also, within the same time limit, serve a copy of his evidence on the other parties.
(7) The claimant may rely on the matters set out in his claim form as evidence under this rule if the claim form is verified by a statement of truth.

## 8.6 Evidence—General

(1) No written evidence may be relied on at the hearing of the claim unless—
  (a) it has been served in accordance with rule 8.5; or
  (b) the court gives permission.
(2) The court may require or permit a party to give oral evidence at the hearing.

(3) The court may give directions requiring the attendance for cross-examination(GL) of a witness who has given written evidence.

(Rule 32.1 contains a general power for the court to control evidence.)

## 8.7 Part 20 Claims

Where the Part 8 procedure is used, Part 20 (counterclaims and other additional claims) applies except that a party may not make a Part 20 claim (as defined by rule 20.2) without the court's permission.

## 8.8 Procedure Where Defendant Objects to Use of the Part 8 Procedure

(1) Where the defendant contends that the Part 8 procedure should not be used because—
- (a) there is a substantial dispute of fact; and
- (b) the use of the Part 8 procedure is not required or permitted by a rule or practice direction,

he must state his reasons when he files his acknowledgment of service.

(Rule 8.5 requires a defendant who wishes to rely on written evidence to file it when he files his acknowledgment of service.)

(2) When the court receives the acknowledgment of service and any written evidence it will give directions as to the future management of the case.

(Rule 8.1(3) allows the court to make an order that the claim continue as if the claimant had not used the Part 8 procedure.)

## 8.9 Modifications to the General Rules

Where the Part 8 procedure is followed—

(a) provision is made in this Part for the matters which must be stated in the claim form and the defendant is not required to file a defence and therefore—
- (i) Part 16 (statements of case) does not apply;
- (ii) Part 15 (defence and reply) does not apply;
- (iii) any time limit in these Rules which prevents the parties from taking a step before a defence is filed does not apply;
- (iv) the requirement under rule 7.8 to serve on the defendant a form for defending the claim does not apply;

(b) the claimant may not obtain judgment by request on an admission and therefore—
- (i) rules 14.4 to 14.7 do not apply; and
- (ii) the requirement under rule 7.8 to serve on the defendant a form for admitting the claim does not apply; and

(c) the claim shall be treated as allocated to the multi-track and therefore Part 26 does not apply.

# PD 8 Practice Direction—Alternative Procedure for Claims

This practice direction supplements CPR Part 8 and Schedule 1 & Schedule 2 to the CPR.

## Terminology

1.1 In this Practice Direction, "Schedule rules" means provisions contained in the Schedules to the CPR, which were previously contained in the Rules of the Supreme Court (1965) or the County Court Rules (1981).

## Application of this Practice Direction

2.1 Section A contains general provisions about claims and applications to which Part 8 applies. Section B comprises a table listing claims, petitions and applications under various enactments which must be made under Part 8. Section C contains certain additions and modifications to the Part 8 procedure that apply to the particular claims and applications identified.

2.2 Some of the claims and applications listed in the table in Section B are dealt with in the Schedule Rules in the CPR. The table in Section B contains cross-reference to the relevant Schedule Rules.

## SECTION A

## GENERAL PROVISIONS APPLICABLE TO PART 8 CLAIMS

### Types of claim in which the Part 8 procedure may be used

3.1 The types of claim for which the Part 8 procedure may be used include—
- (1) a claim by or against a child or patient, as defined in rule 21.1(2), which has been settled before the commencement of proceedings and the sole purpose of the claim is to obtain the approval of the court to the settlement; or
- (2) a claim for provisional damages which has been settled before the commencement of proceedings and the sole purpose of the claim is to obtain a consent judgment.

3.2 (1) The Part 8 procedure must be used for those claims, petitions and applications listed in the table in Section B.
- (2) Where a claim is listed in the table in Section B and is identified as a claim to which particular provisions of Section C apply, the Part 8 procedure shall apply subject to the additions and modifications set out in the relevant paragraphs in Section C.

3.3 The Part 8 procedure must also be used for any claim or application in relation to which an Act, rule or practice direction provides that the claim or application is brought by originating summons, originating motion or originating application.

3.4 Where it appears to a court officer that a claimant is using the Part 8 procedure inappropriately, he may refer the claim to a judge for the judge to consider the point.

3.5 The court may at any stage order the claim to continue as if the claimant had not used the Part 8 procedure and, if it does so, the court will allocate the claim to a track and give such directions as it considers appropriate.

### Issuing the Claim

4.1 Part 7 and the practice direction which supplements it contain a number of rules and directions applicable to all claims, including those to which Part 8 applies. Those rules and directions should be applied where appropriate.

4.2 Where a claimant uses the Part 8 procedure, the claim form (practice form N208) should be used and must state the matters set out in rule 8.2 and, if rule 8.1(6) applies, must comply with the requirements of the rule or practice direction in question. In particular, the claim form must state that Part 8 applies; a Part 8 claim form means a claim form which so states.

(The Costs Practice Direction supplementing Parts 43 to 48 contains details of the information required to be filed with a claim form to comply with rule 44.15 (providing information about funding arrangements).)

## Responding to the Claim

5.1 The provisions of Part 15 (defence and reply) do not apply where the claim form is a Part 8 claim form.

5.2 Where a defendant who wishes to respond to a Part 8 claim form is required to file an acknowledgment of service, that acknowledgment of service should be in practice form N210.

5.3 Where a defendant objects to the use of the Part 8 procedure, and his statement of reasons includes matters of evidence, the acknowledgment of service must be verified by a statement of truth.

## Managing the Claim

6.1 The court may give directions immediately a Part 8 claim form is issued either on the application of a party or on its own initiative. The directions may include fixing a hearing date where—

(1) there is no dispute, such as in child and patient settlements; or

(2) where there may be a dispute, but a hearing date could conveniently be given.

6.2 Where the court does not fix a hearing date when the claim form is issued, it will give directions for the disposal of the claim as soon as practicable after the defendant has acknowledged service of the claim form or, as the case may be, after the period for acknowledging service has expired.

6.3 Certain applications may not require a hearing.

6.4 The court may convene a directions hearing before giving directions.

## Evidence

7.1 A claimant must file the written evidence on which he relies when his Part 8 claim form is issued (unless the evidence is contained in the claim form itself).

7.2 Evidence will normally be in the form of a witness statement or an affidavit but a claimant may rely on the matters set out in his claim form provided that it has been verified by a statement of truth.

(For information about (1) statements of truth see Part 22 and the practice direction that supplements it, and (2) written evidence see Part 32 and the practice direction that supplements it.)

7.3 A defendant wishing to rely on written evidence must file it with his acknowledgment of service.

7.4 A party may apply to the court for an extension of time to serve and file evidence under rule 8.5 or for permission to serve and file additional evidence under rule 8.6(1).

(For information about applications see Part 23 and the practice direction that supplements it.)

7.5 (1) The parties may, subject to the following provisions, agree in writing on an extension of time for serving and filing evidence under rule 8.5(3) or rule 8.5(5).

(2) An agreement extending time for a defendant to file evidence under rule 8.5(3)—

(a) must be filed by the defendant at the same time as he files his acknowledgement of service; and

(b) must not extend time by more than 14 days after the defendant files his acknowledgement of service.

(3) An agreement extending time for a claimant to file evidence in reply under rule 8.5(5) must not extend time to more than 28 days after service of the defendant's evidence on the claimant.

## Hearing

8.1 The court may on the hearing date—
(1) proceed to hear the case and dispose of the claim;
(2) give case management directions.

8.2 Case management directions may include the specific allocation of a case to a track.

8.3 CPR rules 26.5(3) to (5) and rules 26.6 to 26.10 apply to the allocation of a claim under paragraph 8.2.

# SECTION B

## Claims and Applications that Must be Made under Part 8

9.1 The claimant must use the Part 8 procedure if the claim is listed in the table below.

9.2 Section C of this Practice Direction contains special provisions modifying the Part 8 procedure, and where it does so, those provisions should be followed. The table below refers to the relevant paragraph of Section C where it applies.

9.3 Some of the claims and applications listed in the table below are dealt with in the Schedule Rules, and those rules modify the Part 8 procedure. A cross-reference to the relevant Schedule Rule is contained in the table below.

| Type of Claim or Application | Paragraph of Section C | Schedule Rule |
|---|---|---|
| Application under section 15 of the Bills of Sale Act 1878 (Entry of satisfaction) | Paragraph 11 | |
| Application under the proviso to section 7 of the Bills of Sale Act (1878) Amendment Act 1882 (Restraining removal on sale of goods seized) | | |
| Application under the Public Trustee Act 1906 (free-standing proceedings) | Paragraph 12 | |
| Applications under section 2(3) of the Public Order Act 1936 | Paragraph 13 | |
| Proceedings under jurisdiction conferred by section 1 of the Railway and Canal Commission (Abolition) Act 1949 | Paragraph 14 | |
| Administration Act 1960 (Applications under the Act) | | RSC O.109 r.1(3) |
| Administration of Justice Act 1960 (Appeals under section 13 of the Act) | | RSC O.109, r.2(4) |
| Proceedings under section 14 of the Commons Registration Act 1965 | | |
| Application under the Mines (Working Facilities and Support) Act 1966 | Paragraph 15 | |
| The Local Government Act 1972 (claims under section 92—proceedings for disqualification) | | |
| Proceedings under the Control of Misleading Advertisements Regulations 1988 | | |
| Applications under section 42 of the Supreme Court Act 1981 | Paragraph 16 | |
| Application for detailed assessment of returning officer's account under the Representation of the People Act 1983 | Paragraph 17 | |

| | | |
|---|---|---|
| Proceedings in the High Court under Representation of the People Acts | | |
| Applications under Part II of the Mental Health Act 1983 | Paragraph 18 | |
| Applications under section 13 of the Coroners Act 1988 | Paragraph 19 | |
| Application for an injunction to prevent Environmental Harm under section 187B or 214A of the Town and Country Planning Act 1990; section 44A of the Planning (Listed Buildings and Conservation Areas) Act 1990; or section 26AA of the Planning (Hazardous Substances) Act 1990 | Paragraph 20 | |
| Confiscation and Forfeiture in Connection with Criminal Proceedings (I. Drug Trafficking Act 1994 and Criminal Justice (International Co-operation) Act 1990—Application for a confiscation order) | | RSC O.115, r.2B(1) |
| Confiscation and Forfeiture in Connection with Criminal Proceedings (I. Drug Trafficking Act 1994 and Criminal Justice (International Co-operation) Act 1990—Application for a restraint order or charging order) | | RSC O.115, r.3(1) |
| Confiscation and Forfeiture in Connection with Criminal Proceedings (I. Drug Trafficking Act 1994 and Criminal Justice (International Co-operation) Act 1990—Realisation of property) | | RSC O.115, r.7(1) |
| The Criminal Procedure and Investigations Act 1996 (Application under section 54(3)). | | RSC O.116, r.5(1) |
| Confiscation and Forfeiture in Connection with Criminal Proceedings (III. Terrorism Act 2000—Application for a restraint order) | | RSC O.115, r.26(1) |
| Proceedings under the Financial Services and Markets Act 2000) | Paragraph 21 | |
| Interpleader (Mode of application) | | RSC O.17 r.3(1) |
| Criminal Proceedings (Estreat of recognizances) | | RSC O.79, r.8(2) |
| Criminal Proceedings (Bail) | | RSC O.79, r.9(2) |
| Application under an enactment giving the High Court jurisdiction to quash or prohibit any order, scheme, certificate or plan, any amendment or approval of a plan, any decision of a Minister or government department or any action on the part of a Minister or government department | Paragraph 22 | |

## SECTION C

### Special Provisions

10.1 The following special provisions apply to the applications indicated.

## Applications under Section 15 of the Bills of Sale Act 1878

11.1 This paragraph applies where an application is made under section 15 of the Bills of Sale Act 1878 for an order that a memorandum of satisfaction be written on a registered copy of a bill of sale.

11.2 If the person entitled to the benefit of the bill of sale has not consented to the satisfaction, the claim form—
(1) must be served on that person; and
(2) must be supported by evidence that the debt (if any) for which the bill of sale was made has been satisfied or discharged.

11.3 If the person entitled to the benefit of the bill of sale has consented to the satisfaction, the application may be made by—
(1) claim form under Part 8; or
(2) witness statement.

11.4 Where paragraph 11.3 applies and the application is made by Part 8 claim form, the claim form—
(1) must contain details of the consent;
(2) must be supported by a witness statement by a person who witnessed the consent verifying the signature on it; and
(3) must not be served on any person other than the person entitled to the benefit of the bill of sale.

11.5 Where paragraph 11.3 applies and the application is made by witness statement—
(1) Part 23 will apply to the application;
(2) the witness statement will constitute the application notice under that Part;
(3) the witness statement does not need to be served on any other person; and
(4) the application will normally be dealt with without a hearing.

## Application under the Public Trustee Act 1906

12.1 An application under the Public Trustee Act 1906 must be made—
(1) where no proceedings have been issued, by a Part 8 claim;
(2) in existing proceedings, by a Part 23 application.

12.2 Without prejudice to sections 10(2) and 13(7) of the Public Trustee Act 1906, the jurisdiction of the High Court under the Act is exercised by a single judge of the Chancery Division sitting in private.

## Application under Section 2(3) of the Public Order Act 1936

13.1 The Attorney General may determine the persons who should be made defendants to an application under section 2(3) of the Public Order Act 1936.

13.2 If the court directs an inquiry under section 2(3), it may appoint the Official Solicitor to represent any interests it considers are not sufficiently represented and ought to be represented.

## Proceedings under Section 1 of the Railway and Canal Commission (Abolition) Act 1949

14.1 Paragraphs 15.3 to 15.14 apply, with appropriate modifications, to proceedings in which jurisdiction has been conferred on the High Court by section 1 of the Railway and Canal Commission (Abolition) Act 1949, except to the extent that—
(1) an Act;
(2) a rule;
(3) a practice direction,
provides otherwise.

## Application under the Mines (Working Facilities and Support) Act 1966

15.1 In this paragraph—

(1) 'the Act' means the Mines (Working Facilities and Support) Act 1966;
(2) 'the applicant' means the person who has applied for the grant of a right under the Act.

15.2 This paragraph applies where the Secretary of State refers an application to the High Court under any provision of the Act.

15.3 The Secretary of State must—
(1) file a reference signed by him or a person authorised to sign on his behalf in the Chancery Division of the High Court;
(2) file, along with the reference, any documents and plans deposited with him by the applicant in support of his application; and
(3) within 3 days of filing the reference, give notice to the applicant that the reference has been filed.

15.4 Within 10 days of receiving the notice referred to in paragraph 15.3(3), the applicant must issue a claim form.

15.5 The claim form—
(1) must identify the application under the Act and the remedy sought; and
(2) need not be served on any other party.

15.6 Within 7 days of the claim form being issued, the applicant must—
(1) apply for the claim to be listed for a hearing before a Master; and
(2) give notice of the hearing date to the Secretary of State.

15.7 The applicant must, not less than 2 days before the date fixed for a hearing, file at court—
(1) a witness statement in support of the claim, giving details of all persons known to the applicant to be interested in, or affected by, the application; and
(2) a draft of any proposed advertisement or notice of the application.

15.8 At the hearing, the Master will—
(1) fix a date by which any notice of objection under paragraph 15.9 must be filed;
(2) fix a date for a further hearing of the claim; and
(3) give directions about—
(a) any advertisement that is to be inserted or notice of the application and hearing date that is to be given; and
(b) what persons are to be served with a copy of the application or any other document in the proceedings.

15.9 Any person who wishes to oppose the application must, within the time fixed by the court under paragraph 15.8, serve notice of objection on the applicant, stating—
(a) his name and address;
(b) the name and address of his solicitor, if any;
(c) the grounds of his objection;
(d) any alternative method for effecting the objects of the application that he alleges may be used; and
(e) the facts on which he relies.

15.10 Any document that is required to be served on the person who has given notice of objection ('the objector') may be served by posting it to the following address—
(1) where the notice of objection gives the name and address of a solicitor, to the solicitor;
(2) in any other case, to the objector at the address stated in the notice of objection.

15.11 The objector may appear, or be represented at any further hearing, and may take such part in the proceedings as the court allows.

15.12 The applicant must, not less than two days before the date set for the further hearing, file at court—
(1) any notices of objection served on him;
(2) a list of objectors, together with—
(a) their names and addresses;

(b) the names and addresses of their solicitors, if any; and
(c) a summary of their respective grounds of objection.

15.13 If the objector does not appear, or is not represented, at the further hearing—
(1) his notice of objection will have no effect; and
(2) he will not be entitled to take any further part in the proceedings unless the court orders otherwise.

15.14 At the further hearing, the court will—
(1) give directions about the future conduct of the claim, including
(a) any further information the applicant is required to give in relation to any of the grounds or facts relied on in support of the application;
(b) any further information the objector is required to give in relation to any of the grounds or facts relied on in opposition to the application;
(c) whether the applicant may serve a reply to any notice of objection;
(d) whether any particular fact should be proved by a witness statement;
(e) whether any statements of case or points of claim or defence are to be served; and
(2) adjourn the claim for hearing before a judge.

## Application under Section 42 of the Supreme Court Act 1981

16.1 An application under section 42 of the Supreme Court Act 1981 is heard and determined by a Divisional Court.

16.2 The claim form must be filed at the Administrative Court and—
(1) be accompanied by a witness statement in support; and
(2) be served on the person against whom the order is sought.

## Application for Detailed Assessment of a Returning Officer's Account

17.1 An application by the Secretary of State under section 30 of the Representation of the People Act 1983 for the detailed assessment of a returning officer's account must be made by claim form.

17.2 When it issues the claim form, the court will fix a date for the hearing of the detailed assessment to be dealt with if the application is granted.

17.3 The returning officer may, on the application, apply to the court to examine any claim made against him in respect of matters charged in the account.

17.4 To make an application under paragraph 17.3, the returning officer must file an application within 7 days of being served with a copy of the application for detailed assessment.

17.5 When an application is filed under paragraph 17.3, the court will—
(a) fix a date for the hearing;
(b) give notice of the hearing date to the returning officer; and
(c) serve a copy of the application and notice of hearing on the claimant.

17.6 The examination and detailed assessment may take place on the same day, provided that the examination is determined before the detailed assessment is concluded.

17.7 The district judge may hear and determine—
(a) an application for detailed assessment;
(b) any application under paragraph 17.3.

17.8 The court will serve a copy of the order made in the application on—
(a) the Secretary of State;
(b) the returning officer; and
(c) in an application under paragraph 17.3, the claimant.

## Application under Mental Health Act 1983

18.1 In this paragraph—
(1) a section referred to by a number refers to the section so numbered in the Mental Health Act 1983 and 'Part II' means Part II of that Act;

(2) 'hospital manager' means the manager of a hospital as defined in section 145(1) of the Act; and
(3) 'place of residence' means, in relation to a patient who is receiving treatment as an in-patient in a hospital or other institution, that hospital or institution.

18.2 The claim form must be filed—
(1) in the court for the district in which the patient's place of residence is situated; or
(2) in the case of an application under section 30, in the court that made the order under section 29 which the application seeks to discharge or vary.

18.3 Where an application is made under section 29 for an order that the functions of the nearest relative of the patient are to be exercisable by some other person—
(1) the nearest relative must be made a respondent, unless
(a) the application is made on the grounds that the patient has no nearest relative or that it is not reasonably practicable to ascertain whether he has a nearest relative; or
(b) the court orders otherwise; and
(2) the court may order that any other person shall be made a respondent.

18.4 Subject to paragraph 18.5, the court may accept as evidence of the facts relied upon in support of the application, any report made—
(1) by a medical practitioner; or
(2) by any of the following acting in the course of their official duties—
(a) a probation officer;
(b) an officer of a local authority;
(c) an officer of a voluntary body exercising statutory functions on behalf of a local authority; or
(d) an officer of a hospital manager.

18.5 The respondent must be informed of the substance of any part of the report dealing with his fitness or conduct that the court considers to be material to the determination of the claim.

18.6 An application under Part II shall be heard in private unless the court orders otherwise.

18.7 The judge may, for the purpose of determining the application, interview the patient. The interview may take place in the presence of, or separately from, the parties. The interview may be conducted elsewhere than at the court. Alternatively, the judge may direct the district judge to interview the patient and report to the judge in writing.

## Applications under Section 13 of the Coroners Act 1988

19.1 An application under section 13 of the Coroners Act 1988 is heard and determined by a Divisional Court.

19.2 The application must, unless made by the Attorney General, be accompanied by the Attorney General's fiat.

19.3 The claim form must—
(1) state the grounds for the application;
(2) be filed at the Administrative Court; and
(3) be served upon all persons directly affected by the application within six weeks of the grant of the Attorney General's fiat.

## Application for Injunction to Prevent Environmental Harm

20.1 This paragraph relates to applications under—
(1) section 187B or 214A of the Town and Country Planning Act 1990;
(2) section 44A of the Planning (Listed Buildings and Conservation Areas) Act 1990; or
(3) section 26AA of the Planning (Hazardous Substances) Act 1990.

20.2 An injunction may be granted under those sections against a person whose identity is unknown to the applicant.

20.3 In this paragraph, an injunction refers to an injunction under one of those sections and 'the defendant' is the person against whom the injunction is sought.

20.4 In the claim form, the applicant must describe the defendant by reference to—
(1) a photograph;
(2) a thing belonging to or in the possession of the defendant; or
(3) any other evidence.

20.5 The description of the defendant under paragraph 20.4 must be sufficiently clear to enable the defendant to be served with the proceedings.

(The court has power under Part 6 to dispense with service or make an order permitting service by an alternative method.)

20.6 The application must be accompanied by a witness statement. The witness statement must state—
(1) that the applicant was unable to ascertain the defendant's identity within the time reasonably available to him;
(2) the steps taken by him to ascertain the defendant's identity;
(3) the means by which the defendant has been described in the claim form; and
(4) that the description is the best the applicant is able to provide.

20.7 When the court issues the claim form it will—
(1) fix a date for the hearing; and
(2) prepare a notice of the hearing date for each party.

20.8 The claim form must be served not less than 21 days before the hearing date.

20.9 Where the claimant serves the claim form, he must serve notice of the hearing date at the same time, unless the hearing date is specified in the claim form.

(CPR rules 3.1(2) (a) and (b) provide for the court to extend or shorten the time for compliance with any rule or practice direction, and to adjourn or bring forward a hearing.)

20.10 The court may on the hearing date—
(1) proceed to hear the case and dispose of the claim; or
(2) give case management directions.

## Proceedings under the Financial Services and Markets Act 2000

21.1 This paragraph applies to proceedings in the High Court under the Financial Services and Markets Act 2000.

21.2 Proceedings in the High Court under the Act (other than applications for a mandatory order) and actions for damages for breach of a statutory duty imposed by the Act shall be assigned to the Chancery Division.

21.3 Such proceedings and actions must be begun by claim form (except for applications by petition by the Financial Services Authority under section 367 of the Act).

21.4 The Financial Services Authority may make representations to the court where there is a question about the meaning of any rule or other instrument made by, or with the approval or consent of, the Financial Services Authority.

## Application to Quash Certain Orders, Schemes, etc

22.1 This paragraph applies where the High Court has jurisdiction under any enactment, on the application of any person to quash or prohibit any—
(1) order, scheme, certificate or plan of;
(2) amendment or approval of a plan of;
(3) decision of;
(4) action on the part of,
a Minister or government department.

22.2 The jurisdiction shall be exercisable by a single judge of the Queen's Bench Division.

22.3 The claim form must be filed at the Administrative Court and served within the time limited by the relevant enactment for making the application.

22.4 Subject to paragraph 22.6, the claim form must be served on the appropriate Minister or government department and on the person indicated in the following table.

| | |
|---|---|
| If the application relates to—<br>(i) a compulsory purchase order made by an authority other than the appropriate Minister or government department; or<br>(ii) a clearance order under the Housing Act 1985. | The authority that made the order. |
| If the application relates to a scheme or order—<br>(i) to which Section 2 of the Highways Act 1980 applies; and<br>(ii) which was made by an authority other than the Secretary of State. | The authority that made the scheme or order. |
| If the application relates to a structure plan, local plan or other development plan within the meaning of the Town and Country Planning Act 1990. | The local planning authority who prepared the plan. |
| If the application relates to any decision or order, or any action on the part of a Minister of the Crown to which—<br>(i) section 21 of the Land Compensation Act 1961; or<br>(ii) section 288 of the Town and Country Planning Act 1990, applies. | (a) The authority directly concerned with such decision, order or action; or<br>(b) if that authority is the applicant, on every person who would, if he were aggrieved by the decision, order or action, be entitled to apply to the High Court under section 21 of the Land Compensation Act or section 288 of the Town and Country Planning Act, as the case may be. |
| If the application relates to a scheme to which Schedule 32 of the Local Government, Planning and Land Act 1980 applies. | The body which adopted the scheme. |

22.5 In paragraph 22.4, 'the appropriate Minister or government department' means the Minister of the Crown or government department—
(1) by whom the order, scheme, certificate, plan, amendment, approval or decision in question was or may be made, authorised, confirmed, approved or given;
(2) on whose part the action in question was or may be taken.

22.6 Where the application relates to an order made under the Road Traffic Regulation Act 1984, the claim form must be served—
(1) if the order was made by a Minister of the Crown, on that Minister;
(2) if the order was made by a local authority with the consent, or following a direction, of a Minister of the Crown, on that authority and also on that Minister;
(3) in any other case, on the local authority by whom the order was made.

22.7 Evidence at the hearing of an application under this paragraph is by witness statement.

22.8 The applicant must—
(1) file a witness statement in support of the application in the Administrative Court within 14 days after service of the claim form; and
(2) serve a copy of the witness statement and of any exhibit on the respondent at the time of filing.

22.9 The respondent must—
(1) file any witness statement in opposition to the application in the Administrative Court within 21 days after service on him of the applicant's witness statement; and
(2) serve a copy of his witness statement and of any exhibit on the applicant at the time of filing.

22.10 A party must, when filing a witness statement, file a further copy of the witness statement, including exhibits, for the use of the court.

22.11 Unless the court otherwise orders, the application will not be heard earlier than 14 days after the time for filing a witness statement by the respondent has expired.

# CPR Part 9 Responding to Particulars of Claim — General



## 9.1 Scope of this Part

(1) This Part sets out how a defendant may respond to particulars of claim.
(2) Where the defendant receives a claim form which states that particulars of claim are to follow, he need not respond to the claim until the particulars of claim have been served on him.

## 9.2 Defence, Admission or Acknowledgment of Service

When particulars of claim are served on a defendant, the defendant may—
(a) file or serve an admission in accordance with Part 14;
(b) file a defence in accordance with Part 15,
(or do both, if he admits only part of the claim); or
(c) file an acknowledgment of service in accordance with Part 10.

# CPR Part 10 Acknowledgment of Service



## 10.1 Acknowledgment of Service

(1) This Part deals with the procedure for filing an acknowledgment of service.
(2) Where the claimant uses the procedure set out in Part 8 (alternative procedure for claims) this Part applies subject to the modifications set out in rule 8.3.
(3) A defendant may file an acknowledgment of service if—
 (a) he is unable to file a defence within the period specified in rule 15.4; or
 (b) he wishes to dispute the court's jurisdiction.

(Part 11 sets out the procedure for disputing the court's jurisdiction.)

## 10.2 Consequence of Not Filing an Acknowledgment of Service

If—
(a) a defendant fails to file an acknowledgment of service within the period specified in rule 10.3; and
(b) does not within that period file a defence in accordance with Part 15 or serve or file an admission in accordance with Part 14,

the claimant may obtain default judgment if Part 12 allows it.

## 10.3 The Period for Filing an Acknowledgment of Service

(1) The general rule is that the period for filing an acknowledgment of service is—
 (a) where the defendant is served with a claim form which states that particulars of claim are to follow, 14 days after service of the particulars of claim; and
 (b) in any other case, 14 days after service of the claim form.
(2) The general rule is subject to the following rules—
 (a) Rule 6.22 (which specifies how the period for filing an acknowledgment of service is calculated where the claim form is served out of the jurisdiction);
 (b) rule 6.16(4) (which requires the court to specify the period for responding to the particulars of claim when it makes an order under that rule); and
 (c) rule 6.21(4) (which requires the court to specify the period within which the defendant may file an acknowledgment of service calculated by reference to Practice Direction 6B when it makes an order giving permission to serve a claim form out of the jurisdiction).

## 10.4 Notice to Claimant That Defendant has Filed an Acknowledgment of Service

On receipt of an acknowledgment of service, the court must notify the claimant in writing.

## 10.5 Contents of Acknowledgment of Service

An acknowledgment of service must—
(a) be signed by the defendant or his legal representative; and
(b) include the defendant's address for service.

(Rule 6.5 provides that an address for service must be within the jurisdiction.)
(Rule 19.8A modifies this Part where a notice of claim is served under that rule to bind a person not a party to the claim.)

# PD 10 Practice Direction — Acknowledgment of Service

This practice direction supplements CPR Part 10.

## Responding to the Claim

1.1 Part 9 sets out how a defendant may respond to a claim.

1.2 Part 10 sets out the provisions for acknowledging service (but see rule 8.3 for information about acknowledging service of a claim under the Part 8 procedure).

## The Form of Acknowledgment of Service

2 A defendant who wishes to acknowledge service of a claim should do so by using form N9.

## Address for Service

3.1 The defendant must include in his acknowledgment of service an address for the service of documents.[1]

3.2 Where the defendant is represented by a legal representative[2] and the legal representative has signed the acknowledgment of service form, the address must be the legal representative's business address; otherwise the address for service that is given should be as set out in rule 6.5 and the practice direction which supplements Part 6.

## Signing the Acknowledgment of Service

4.1 An acknowledgment of service must be signed by the defendant or by his legal representative.

4.2 Where the defendant is a company or other corporation, a person holding a senior position in the company or corporation may sign the acknowledgment of service on the defendant's behalf, but must state the position he holds.

4.3 Each of the following persons is a person holding a senior position:
  (1) in respect of a registered company or corporation, a director, the treasurer, secretary, chief executive, manager or other officer of the company or corporation, and
  (2) in respect of a corporation which is not a registered company, in addition to those persons set out in (1), the mayor, chairman, president, town clerk or similar officer of the corporation.

4.4 Where a cliam is brought against a partnership—
  (1) service must be acknowledged in the name of the partnership on behalf of all persons who were partners at the time when the cause of action accrued; and
  (2) the acknowledgment of service may be signed by any of those partners, or by any person authorised by any of those partners to sign it.

4.5 Children and patients may acknowledge service only by their litigation friend or his legal representative unless the court otherwise orders.[3]

## General

5.1 The defendant's name should be set out in full on the acknowledgment of service.

5.2 Where the defendant's name has been incorrectly set out in the claim form, it should be correctly set out on the acknowledgment of service followed by the words 'described as' and the incorrect name.

---

[1] See rule 6.5.

[2] See rule 2.3 for the definition of legal representative.

[3] See Part 21.

5.3 If two or more defendants to a claim acknowledge service of a claim through the same legal representative at the same time, only one acknowledgment of service need be used.

5.4 An acknowledgment of service may be amended or withdrawn only with the permission of the court.

5.5 An application for permission under paragraph 5.4 must be made in accordance with Part 23 and supported by evidence.

(Paragraph 8.3 of PD 6 (service of documents) makes provision for the service on the claimant of any notice of funding filed with an acknowledgment of service.)

# CPR Part 11 Disputing the Court's Jurisdiction



## 11 Procedure for Disputing the Court's Jurisdiction

(1) A defendant who wishes to—
(a) dispute the court's jurisdiction to try the claim; or
(b) argue that the court should not exercise its jurisdiction,
may apply to the court for an order declaring that it has no such jurisdiction or should not exercise any jurisdiction which it may have.

(2) A defendant who wishes to make such an application must first file an acknowledgment of service in accordance with Part 10.

(3) A defendant who files an acknowledgment of service does not, by doing so, lose any right that he may have to dispute the court's jurisdiction.

(4) An application under this rule must—
(a) be made within 14 days after filing an acknowledgment of service; and
(b) be supported by evidence.

(5) If the defendant—
(a) files an acknowledgment of service; and
(b) does not make such an application within the period specified in paragraph (4),
he is to be treated as having accepted that the court has jurisdiction to try the claim.

(6) An order containing a declaration that the court has no jurisdiction or will not exercise its jurisdiction may also make further provision including—
(a) setting aside the claim form;
(b) setting aside service of the claim form;
(c) discharging any order made before the claim was commenced or before the claim form was served; and
(d) staying(GL) the proceedings.

(7) If on an application under this rule the court does not make a declaration—
(a) the acknowledgment of service shall cease to have effect; and
(b) the defendant may file a further acknowledgment of service within 14 days or such other period as the court may direct; and
(c) the court shall give directions as to the filing and service of the defence in a claim under Part 7 or the filing of evidence in a claim under Part 8 in the event that a further acknowledgment of service is filed.

(8) If the defendant files a further acknowledgment of service in accordance with paragraph (7)(b) he shall be treated as having accepted that the court has jurisdiction to try the claim.

(9) If a defendant makes an application under this rule, he must file and serve his written evidence in support with the application notice, but he need not before the hearing of the application file—
(a) in a Part 7 claim, a defence; or
(b) in a Part 8 claim, any other written evidence.

# CPR Part 12 Default Judgment



## 12.1 Meaning of 'Default Judgment'

In these Rules, 'default judgment' means judgment without trial where a defendant—
(a) has failed to file an acknowledgment of service; or
(b) has failed to file a defence.

(Part 10 contains provisions about filing an acknowledgment of service and Part 15 contains provisions about filing a defence)

## 12.2 Claims in Which Default Judgment May Not be Obtained

A claimant may not obtain a default judgment—
(a) on a claim for delivery of goods subject to an agreement regulated by the Consumer Credit Act 1974;
(b) where he uses the procedure set out in Part 8 (alternative procedure for claims); or
(c) in any other case where a practice direction provides that the claimant may not obtain default judgment.

## 12.3 Conditions to be Satisfied

(1) The claimant may obtain judgment in default of an acknowledgment of service only if—
  (a) the defendant has not filed an acknowledgment of service or a defence to the claim (or any part of the claim); and
  (b) the relevant time for doing so has expired.
(2) Judgment in default of defence may be obtained only—
  (a) where an acknowledgment of service has been filed but a defence has not been filed;
  (b) in a counterclaim made under rule 20.4, where a defence has not been filed,
  and, in either case, the relevant time limit for doing so has expired.

(Rules 10.3 and 15.4 deal respectively with the period for filing an acknowledgment of service and the period for filing a defence)

(Rule 20.4 makes general provision for a defendant's counterclaim against a claimant, and rule 20.4(3) provides that Part 10 (acknowledgment of service) does not apply to a counter- claim made under that rule)

(3) The claimant may not obtain a default judgment if—
  (a) the defendant has applied—
    (i) to have the claimant's statement of case struck out under rule 3.4; or
    (ii) for summary judgment under Part 24,
  and, in either case, that application has not been disposed of;

(b) the defendant has satisfied the whole claim (including any claim for costs) on which the claimant is seeking judgment; or
(c) (i) the claimant is seeking judgment on a claim for money; and
(ii) the defendant has filed or served on the claimant an admission under rule 14.4 or 14.7 (admission of liability to pay all of the money claimed) together with a request for time to pay.

(Part 14 sets out the procedure where a defendant admits a money claim and asks for time to pay.)

(Rule 6.14 provides that, where the claim form is served by the claimant, he may not obtain default judgment unless he has filed a certificate of service.)

(Article 19(1) of Council Regulation (EC) No. 1348/2000 of 29 May 2000 on the service in the Member States of judicial and extrajudicial documents in civil or commercial matters applies in relation to judgment in default where the claim form is served in accordance with that Regulation.)

## 12.4 Procedure for Obtaining Default Judgment

(1) Subject to paragraph (2), a claimant may obtain a default judgment by filing a request in the relevant practice form where the claim is for—
(a) a specified amount of money;
(b) an amount of money to be decided by the court;
(c) delivery of goods where the claim form gives the defendant the alternative of paying their value; or
(d) any combination of these remedies.

(2) The claimant must make an application in accordance with Part 23 if he wishes to obtain a default judgment—
(a) on a claim which consists of or includes a claim for any other remedy; or
(b) where rule 12.9 or rule 12.10 so provides,
and where the defendant is an individual, the claimant must provide the defendant's date of birth (if known) in Part C of the application notice.

(3) Where a claimant—
(a) claims any other remedy in his claim form in addition to those specified in paragraph (1); but
(b) abandons that claim in his request for judgment,
he may still obtain a default judgment by filing a request under paragraph (1); and
(c) the court shall give directions as to the filing and service of the defence in a claim under Part 7 or the filing of evidence in a claim under Part 8 in the event that a further acknowledgment of service is filed.

## 12.5 Nature of Judgment Where Default Judgment Obtained by Filing a Request

(1) Where the claim is for a specified sum of money, the claimant may specify in a request filed under rule 12.4(1)—
(a) the date by which the whole of the judgment debt is to be paid; or
(b) the times and rate at which it is to be paid by instalments.

(2) Except where paragraph (4) applies, a default judgment on a claim for a specified amount of money obtained on the filing of a request, will be judgment for the amount of the claim (less any payments made) and costs—
(a) to be paid by the date or at the rate specified in the request for judgment; or
(b) if none is specified, immediately.

(Interest may be included in a default judgment obtained by filing a request if the conditions set out in Rule 12.6 are satisfied.)

(Rule 45.4 provides for fixed costs on the entry of a default judgment.)

(3) Where the claim is for an unspecified amount of money a default judgment obtained on the filing of a request will be for an amount to be decided by the court and costs.

(4) Where the claim is for delivery of goods and the claim form gives the defendant the

alternative of paying their value, a default judgment obtained on the filing of a request will be judgment requiring the defendant to—
(a) deliver the goods or (if he does not do so) pay the value of the goods as decided by the court (less any payments made); and
(b) pay costs.

(Rule 12.7 sets out the procedure for deciding the amount of a judgment or the value of the goods)

(5) The claimant's right to enter judgment requiring the defendant to deliver goods is subject to rule 40.14 (judgment in favour of certain part owners relating to the detention of goods.).

## 12.6 Interest

(1) A default judgment on a claim for a specified amount of money obtained on the filing of a request may include the amount of interest claimed to the date of judgment if—
(a) the particulars of claim include the details required by rule 16.4;
(b) where interest is claimed under section 35A of the Supreme Court Act 1981 or section 69 of the County Courts Act 1984, the rate is no higher than the rate of interest payable on judgment debts at the date when the claim form was issued; and
(c) the claimant's request for judgment includes a calculation of the interest claimed for the period from the date up to which interest was stated to be calculated in the claim form to the date of the request for judgment.

(2) In any case where paragraph (1) does not apply, judgment will be for an amount of interest to be decided by the court.

(Rule 12.7 sets out the procedure for deciding the amount of interest.)

## 12.7 Procedure for Deciding an Amount or Value

(1) This rule applies where the claimant obtains a default judgment on the filing of a request under rule 12.4(1) and judgment is for—
(a) an amount of money to be decided by the court;
(b) the value of goods to be decided by the court; or
(c) an amount of interest to be decided by the court.

(2) Where the court enters judgment it will—
(a) give any directions it considers appropriate; and
(b) if it considers it appropriate, allocate the case.

## 12.8 Claim Against More Than One Defendant

(1) A claimant may obtain a default judgment on request under this Part on a claim for money or a claim for delivery of goods against one of two or more defendants, and proceed with his claim against the other defendants.

(2) Where a claimant applies for a default judgment against one of two or more defendants—
(a) if the claim can be dealt with separately from the claim against the other defendants—
(i) the court may enter a default judgment against that defendant; and
(ii) the claimant may continue the proceedings against the other defendants;
(b) if the claim cannot be dealt with separately from the claim against the other defendants—
(i) the court will not enter default judgment against that defendant; and
(ii) the court must deal with the application at the same time as it disposes of the claim against the other defendants.

(3) A claimant may not enforce against one of two or more defendants any judgment obtained under this Part for possession of land or for delivery of goods unless—

(a) he has obtained a judgment for possession or delivery (whether or not obtained under this Part) against all the defendants to the claim; or
(b) the court gives permission.

## 12.9 Procedure for Obtaining a Default Judgment for Costs Only

(1) Where a claimant wishes to obtain a default judgment for costs only—
(a) if the claim is for fixed costs, he may obtain it by filing a request in the relevant practice form;
(b) if the claim is for any other type of costs, he must make an application in accordance with Part 23.
(2) Where an application is made under this rule for costs only, judgment shall be for an amount to be decided by the court.
(Part 45 sets out when a claimant is entitled to fixed costs.)

## 12.10 Default Judgment Obtained by Making an Application

The claimant must make an application in accordance with Part 23 where—
(a) the claim is—
(i) a claim against a child or patient; or
(ii) a claim in tort by one spouse or civil partner against the other;
(b) he wishes to obtain a default judgment where the defendant has failed to file an acknowledgment of service—
(i) against a defendant who has been served with the claim out of the jurisdiction under rule 6.19(1) or (1A) (service without leave);
(ii) against a defendant domiciled in Scotland or Northern Ireland or in any other Convention territory or Regulation State;
(iii) against a State;
(iv) against a diplomatic agent who enjoys immunity from civil jurisdiction by virtue of the Diplomatic Privileges Act 1964; or
(v) against persons or organisations who enjoy immunity from civil jurisdiction pursuant to the provisions of the International Organisations Acts 1968 and 1981.

## 12.11 Supplementary Provisions Where Applications for Default Judgment are Made

(1) Where the claimant makes an application for a default judgment, judgment shall be such judgment as it appears to the court that the claimant is entitled to on his statement of case.
(2) Any evidence relied on by the claimant in support of his application need not be served on a party who has failed to file an acknowledgment of service.
(3) An application for a default judgment on a claim against a child or patient or a claim in tort between spouses or civil partners must be supported by evidence.
(4) An application for a default judgment may be made without notice if—
(a) the claim under the Civil Jurisdiction and Judgments Act 1982 or the Judgments Regulation, was served in accordance with rules 6.19(1) or 6.19(1A) as appropriate;
(b) the defendant has failed to file an acknowledgment of service; and
(c) notice does not need to be given under any other provision of these Rules.
(5) Where an application is made against a State for a default judgment where the defendant has failed to file an acknowledgment of service—
(a) the application may be made without notice, but the court hearing the application may direct that a copy of the application notice be served on the State;
(b) if the court—
(i) grants the application; or
(ii) directs that a copy of the application notice be served on the State, the

judgment or application notice (and the evidence in support) may be served out of the jurisdiction without any further order;

(c) where paragraph (5)(b) permits a judgment or an application notice to be served out of the jurisdiction, the procedure for serving the judgment or the application notice is the same as for serving a claim form under Section III of Part 6 except where an alternative method of service has been agreed under section 12(6) of the State Immunity Act 1978.

(Rule 23.1 defines 'application notice'.)

(6) For the purposes of this rule and rule 12.10—

(a) 'domicile' is to be determined—

(i) in relation to a Convention territory, in accordance with sections 41 to 46 of the Civil Jurisdiction and Judgments Act 1982;

(ii) in relation to a Regulation State, in accordance with the Judgments Regulation and paragraphs 9 to 12 of Schedule 1 to the Civil Jurisdiction and Judgments Order 2001;

(b) 'Convention territory' means the territory or territories of any Contracting State, as defined by section 1(3) of the Civil Jurisdiction and Judgments Act 1982, to which the Brussels Conventions or Lugano Convention apply;

(c) 'State' has the meaning given by section 14 of the State Immunity Act 1978; and

(d) 'Diplomatic agent' has the meaning given by Article 1(e) of Schedule 1 to the Diplomatic Privileges Act 1964.

(e) 'the Judgments Regulation' means Council Regulation (EC) No. 44/2001 of 22nd December 2000 on jurisdiction and the recognition and enforcement of judgments in civil and commercial matters; and

(f) 'Regulation State' has the same meaning as 'Member State' in the Judgments Regulation, that is all Member States except Denmark.

# PD 12 Practice Direction — Default Judgment

This practice direction supplements CPR Part 12.

## Default Judgment

1.1 A default judgment is judgment without a trial where a defendant has failed to file either:
(1) an acknowledgment of service, or
(2) a defence.
For this purpose a defence includes any document purporting to be a defence.
(See Part 10 and PD 10 for information about the acknowledgment of service, and Parts 15 and 16, PD 15 and PD 16 for information about the defence and what it should contain.)

1.2 A claimant may not obtain a default judgment under Part 12 (notwithstanding that no acknowledgment of service or defence has been filed) if:
(1) the procedure set out in Part 8 (alternative procedure for claims) is being used, or
(2) the claim is for delivery of goods subject to an agreement regulated by the Consumer Credit Act 1974.

1.3 Other rules and practice directions provide that default judgment under Part 12 cannot be obtained in particular types of proceedings. Examples are:
(1) admiralty proceedings;
(2) arbitration proceedings;
(3) contentious probate proceedings;
(4) claims for provisional damages;
(5) possession claims.

## Obtaining Default Judgment

2.1 Rules 12.4(1) and 12.9(1) describe the claims in respect of which a default judgment may be obtained by filing a request in the appropriate practice form.

2.2 A default judgment on:
(1) the claims referred to in rules 12.9(1)(b) and 12.10, and
(2) claims other than those described in rule 12.4(1),
can only be obtained if an application for default judgment is made and cannot be obtained by filing a request.

2.3 The following are some of the types of claim which require an application for a default judgment:
(1) against children and patients,[1]
(2) for costs (other than fixed costs) only,[2]
(3) by one spouse or civil partner against the other[3] on a claim in tort,[4]
(4) for delivery up of goods where the defendant will not be allowed the alternative of paying their value; and
(5) [*Omitted*]
(6) against persons or organisations who enjoy immunity from civil jurisdiction under the provisions of the International Organisations Acts 1968 and 1981.

---

[1] See rule 12.10(a)(i).

[2] See rule 12.9(b).

[3] See rule 12.10(a)(ii).

[4] Tort may be defined as an act or a failure to do an act which causes harm or damage to another person and which gives the other person a right to claim compensation without having to rely on a contract with the person who caused the harm or damage.

## Default Judgment by Request

3.1 Requests for default judgment:
(1) in respect of a claim for a specified amount of money or for the delivery of goods where the defendant will be given the alternative of paying a specified sum representing their value, or for fixed costs only, must be in form N205A or N225, and
(2) in respect of a claim where an amount of money (including an amount representing the value of goods) is to be decided by the court, must be in form N205B or N227.

3.2 The forms require the claimant to provide the date of birth (if known) of the defendant where the defendant is an individual.

## Evidence

4.1 Both on a request and on an application for default judgment the court must be satisfied that:
(1) the particulars of claim have been served on the defendant (a certificate of service on the court file will be sufficient evidence),
(2) either the defendant has not filed an acknowledgment of service or has not filed a defence and that in either case the relevant period for doing so has expired,
(3) the defendant has not satisfied the claim, and
(4) the defendant has not returned an admission to the claimant under rule 14.4 or filed an admission with the court under rule 14.6.

4.2 On an application against a child or patient:[5]
(1) a litigation friend[6] to act on behalf of the child or patient must be appointed by the court before judgment can be obtained, and
(2) the claimant must satisfy the court by evidence that he is entitled to the judgment claimed.

4.3 On an application where the defendant was served with the claim either:
(1) outside the jurisdiction[7] without leave under the Civil Jurisdiction and Judgments Act 1982, or
(2) within the jurisdiction but when domiciled[8][E4] in Scotland or Northern Ireland or in any other Convention territory,[9] and the defendant has not acknowledged service, the evidence must establish that:
(a) the claim is one that the court has power to hear and decide,
(b) no other court has exclusive jurisdiction under the Act to hear and decide the claim, and
(c) the claim has been properly served in accordance with Article 20 of Schedule 1, or 3C to the Act, paragraph 15 of Schedule 4 to the Act, or Article 26 of the Judgements Regulation.

4.4 On an application against a State[10] the evidence must:
(1) set out the grounds of the application,
(2) establish the facts proving that the State is excepted from the immunity conferred by s. 1 of the State Immunity Act 1978,
(3) establish that the claim was sent through the Foreign and Commonwealth Office to the Ministry of Foreign Affairs of the State or, where the State has agreed to another form of service, that the claim was served in the manner agreed, and
(4) establish that the time for acknowledging service (which is extended to two

---

[5] As defined in rule 21.1(2).
[6] As defined in PD 21.
[7] As defined in rule 2.3.
[8] As determined in accordance with the provisions of ss. 41 to 46 of the Civil Jurisdiction and Judgments Act 1982.
[9] Means the territory of a Contracting State as defined in s. 1(3) of the Civil Jurisdiction and Judgments Act 1982.
[10] As defined in s. 14 of the State Immunity Act 1978.

months by s. 12(2) of the Act when the claim is sent through the Foreign and Commonwealth Office to the Ministry of Foreign Affairs of the State) has expired. (See rule [40.10*] for when default judgment against a State takes effect.)

4.5 Evidence in support of an application referred to in paragraphs 4.3 and 4.4 above must be by affidavit.

4.6 On an application for judgment for delivery up of goods where the defendant will not be given the alternative of paying their value, the evidence must identify the goods and state where the claimant believes the goods to be situated and why their specific delivery up is sought.

## General

5.1 On all applications to which this practice direction applies, other than those referred to in paragraphs 4.3 and 4.4 above,[11] notice should be given in accordance with Part 23.

5.2 Where default judgment is given on a claim for a sum of money expressed in a foreign currency, the judgment should be for the amount of the foreign currency with the addition of 'or the sterling equivalent at the time of payment'.

[* The text issued by the Department for Constitutional Affairs mistakenly refers to r. 40.8.]

[11] See rule 12.11(4) and (5).

# CPR Part 13 Setting Aside or Varying Default Judgment



## 13.1 Scope of this Part

The rules in this Part set out the procedure for setting aside or varying judgment entered under Part 12 (default judgment).

(CCR Order 22, r. 10 sets out the procedure for varying the rate at which a judgment debt must be paid.)

## 13.2 Cases Where the Court Must Set Aside Judgment Entered Under Part 12

The court must set aside(GL) a judgment entered under Part 12 if judgment was wrongly entered because—

(a) in the case of a judgment in default of an acknowledgment of service, any of the conditions in rule 12.3(1) and 12.3(3) was not satisfied;
(b) in the case of a judgment in default of a defence, any of the conditions in rule 12.3(2) and 12.3(3) was not satisfied; or
(c) the whole of the claim was satisfied before judgment was entered.

## 13.3 Cases Where the Court May Set Aside or Vary Judgment Entered Under Part 12

(1) In any other case, the court may set aside(GL) or vary a judgment entered under Part 12 if—
 (a) the defendant has a real prospect of successfully defending the claim; or
 (b) it appears to the court that there is some other good reason why—
  (i) the judgment should be set aside or varied; or
  (ii) the defendant should be allowed to defend the claim.
(2) In considering whether to set aside(GL) or vary a judgment entered under Part 12, the matters to which the court must have regard include whether the person seeking to set aside the judgment made an application to do so promptly.

(Rule 3.1(3) provides that the court may attach conditions when it makes an order.)

(Article 19(4) of Council Regulation (EC) No. 1348/2000 of 29 May 2000 on the service in the Member States of judicial and extrajudicial documents in civil or commercial matters applies to applications to appeal a judgment in default when the time limit for appealing has expired.)

## 13.4 Application to Set Aside or Vary Judgment—Procedure

(1) Where—
 (a) the claim is for a specified amount of money;
 (b) the judgment was obtained in a court which is not the defendant's home court;
 (c) the claim has not been transferred to another defendant's home court under rule 14.12 (admission—determination of rate of payment by judge) or rule 26.2 (automatic transfer); and

(d) the defendant is an individual

the court will transfer an application by a defendant under this Part to set aside(GL) or vary judgment to the defendant's home court.

(2) Paragraph (1) does not apply where the claim was commenced in a specialist list.

(3) An application under rule 13.3 (cases where the court may set aside(GL) or vary judgment) must be supported by evidence.

## 13.5 [*Revoked*]

## 13.6 Abandoned Claim Restored Where Default Judgment Set Aside

Where—

(a) the claimant claimed a remedy in addition to one specified in rule 12.4(1) (claims in respect of which the claimant may obtain default judgment by filing a request);

(b) the claimant abandoned his claim for that remedy in order to obtain default judgment on request in accordance with rule 12.4(3); and

(c) that default judgment is set aside(GL) under this Part,

the abandoned claim is restored when the default judgment is set aside.

# CPR Part 14 Admissions



### 14.1 Admissions made after commencement of proceedings

(1) A party may admit the truth of the whole or any part of another party's case.
(2) He may do this by giving notice in writing (such as in a statement of case or by letter).
(3) Where the only remedy which the claimant is seeking is the payment of money, the defendant may also make an admission in accordance with—
    (a) rule 14.4 (admission of whole claim for specified amount of money);
    (b) rule 14.5 (admission of part of claim for specified amount of money);
    (c) rule 14.6 (admission of liability to pay whole of claim for unspecified amount of money); or
    (d) rule 14.7 (admission of liability to pay claim for unspecified amount of money where defendant offers a sum in satisfaction of the claim).
(4) Where the defendant makes an admission as mentioned in paragraph (3), the claimant has a right to enter judgment except where—
    (a) the defendant is a child or patient; or
    (b) the claimant is a child or patient and the admission is made under rule 14.5 or 14.7

(Rule 21.10 provides that, where a claim is made by or on behalf of a child or patient or against a child or patient, no settlement, compromise or payment shall be valid, so far as it relates to that person's claim, without the approval of the court.)

(5) The permission of the court is required to amend or withdraw an admission.

(Rule 3.1(3) provides that the court may attach conditions when it makes an order.)

### Rule 14.1A Admissions made before commencement of proceedings*

(1) A person may, by giving notice in writing, admit the truth of the whole or any part of another party's case before commencement of proceedings (a 'pre-action admission').
(2) Paragraphs (3) to (5) of this rule apply to a pre-action admission made in the types of proceedings listed at paragraph 1.1(2) of the Practice Direction to this Part if one of the following conditions is met—
    (a) it is made after the party making it has received a letter of claim in accordance with the relevant pre-action protocol; or
    (b) it is made before such letter of claim has been received, but it is stated to be made under Part 14.

* Editorial note: Rule 14.1A will not apply to an admission made before 6th April 2007.

(3) A person may, by giving notice in writing, withdraw a pre-action admission—
 (a) before commencement of proceedings, if the person to whom the admission was made agrees;
 (b) after commencement of proceedings, if all parties to the proceedings consent or with the permission of the court.
(4) After commencement of proceedings—
 (a) any party may apply for judgment on the pre-action admission; and
 (b) the party who made the pre-action admission may apply to withdraw it.
(5) An application to withdraw a pre-action admission or to enter judgment on such an admission—
 (a) must be made in accordance with Part 23;
 (b) may be made as a cross-application.

## 14.2 Period for Making an Admission

(1) The period for returning an admission under rule 14.4 or for filing it under rules 14.5, 14.6 or 14.7 is—
 (a) where the defendant is served with a claim form which states that particulars of claim will follow, 14 days after service of the particulars; and
 (b) in any other case, 14 days after service of the claim form.
(2) Paragraph (1) is subject to the following rules—
 (a) rule 6.22 (which specifies how the period for filing or returning an admission is calculated where the claim form is served out of the jurisdiction); and
 (b) rule 6.16(4) (which requires the court to specify the period for responding to the particulars of claim when it makes an order under that rule).
(3) A defendant may return an admission under rule 14.4 or file it under rules 14.5, 14.6 or 14.7 after the end of the period for returning or filing it specified in paragraph (1) if the claimant has not obtained default judgment under Part 12.
(4) If he does so, this Part shall apply as if he had made the admission within that period.

## 14.3 Admission by Notice in Writing—Application for Judgment

(1) Where a party makes an admission under rule 14.1(2) (admission by notice in writing), any other party may apply for judgment on the admission.
(2) Judgment shall be such judgment as it appears to the court that the applicant is entitled to on the admission.

## 14.4 Admission of Whole of Claim for Specified Amount of Money

(1) This rule applies where—
 (a) the only remedy which the claimant is seeking is the payment of a specified amount of money; and
 (b) the defendant admits the whole of the claim.
(2) The defendant may admit the claim by returning to the claimant an admission in the relevant practice form.
(3) The claimant may obtain judgment by filing a request in the relevant practice form and, if he does so—
 (a) if the defendant has not requested time to pay, the procedure in paragraphs (4) to (6) will apply;
 (b) if the defendant has requested time to pay, the procedure in rule 14.9 will apply.
(4) The claimant may specify in his request for judgment—
 (a) the date by which the whole of the judgment debt is to be paid; or
 (b) the times and rate at which it is to be paid by instalments.
(5) On receipt of the request for judgment the court will enter judgment.
(6) Judgment will be for the amount of the claim (less any payments made) and costs—
 (a) to be paid by the date or at the rate specified in the request for judgment; or
 (b) if none is specified, immediately.

(Rule 14.14 deals with the circumstances in which judgment under this rule may include interest.)

## 14.5 Admission of Part of a Claim for a Specified Amount of Money

(1) This rule applies where—
 (a) the only remedy which the claimant is seeking is the payment of a specified amount of money; and
 (b) the defendant admits part of the claim.
(2) The defendant may admit part of the claim by filing an admission in the relevant practice form.
(3) On receipt of the admission, the court will serve a notice on the claimant requiring him to return the notice stating that—
 (a) he accepts the amount admitted in satisfaction of the claim;
 (b) he does not accept the amount admitted by the defendant and wishes the proceedings to continue; or
 (c) if the defendant has requested time to pay, he accepts the amount admitted in satisfaction of the claim, but not the defendant's proposals as to payment.
(4) The claimant must—
 (a) file the notice; and
 (b) serve a copy on the defendant, within 14 days after it is served on him.
(5) If the claimant does not file the notice within 14 days after it is served on him, the claim is stayed(GL) until he files the notice.
(6) If the claimant accepts the amount admitted in satisfaction of the claim, he may obtain judgment by filing a request in the relevant practice form and, if he does so—
 (a) if the defendant has not requested time to pay, the procedure in paragraphs (7) to (9) will apply;
 (b) if the defendant has requested time to pay, the procedure in rule 14.9 will apply.
(7) The claimant may specify in his request for judgment—
 (a) the date by which the whole of the judgment debt is to be paid; or
 (b) the time and rate at which it is to be paid by instalments.
(8) On receipt of the request for judgment, the court will enter judgment.
(9) Judgment will be for the amount admitted (less any payments made) and costs—
 (a) to be paid by the date or at the rate specified in the request for judgment; or
 (b) if none is specified, immediately.

(If the claimant files notice under paragraph (3) that he wishes the proceedings to continue, the procedure which then follows is set out in Part 26.)

## 14.6 Admission of Liability to Pay Whole of Claim for Unspecified Amount of Money

(1) This rule applies where—
 (a) the only remedy which the claimant is seeking is the payment of money;
 (b) the amount of the claim is not specified; and
 (c) the defendant admits liability but does not offer to pay a specified amount of money in satisfaction of the claim.
(2) The defendant may admit the claim by filing an admission in the relevant practice form.
(3) On receipt of the admission, the court will serve a copy on the claimant.
(4) The claimant may obtain judgment by filing a request in the relevant practice form.
(5) If the claimant does not file a request for judgment within 14 days after service of the admission on him, the claim is stayed (GL) until he files the request.
(6) On receipt of the request for judgment the court will enter judgment.
(7) Judgment will be for an amount to be decided by the court and costs.

## 14.7 Admission of Liability to Pay Claim for Unspecified Amount of Money Where Defendant Offers a Sum in Satisfaction of the Claim

(1) This rule applies where—
 (a) the only remedy which the claimant is seeking is the payment of money;
 (b) the amount of the claim is not specified; and
 (c) the defendant—
  (i) admits liability; and
  (ii) offers to pay a specified amount of money in satisfaction of the claim.

(2) The defendant may admit the claim by filing an admission in the relevant practice form.

(3) On receipt of the admission, the court will serve a notice on the claimant requiring him to return the notice stating whether or not he accepts the amount in satisfaction of the claim.

(4) If the claimant does not file the notice within 14 days after it is served on him, the claim is stayed(GL) until he files the notice.

(5) If the claimant accepts the offer he may obtain judgment by filing a request in the relevant practice form and if he does so—
 (a) if the defendant has not requested time to pay, the procedure in paragraphs (6) to (8) will apply;
 (b) if the defendant has requested time to pay, the procedure in rule 14.9 will apply.

(6) The claimant may specify in his request for judgment—
 (a) the date by which the whole of the judgment debt is to be paid; or
 (b) the times and rate at which it is to be paid by instalments.

(7) On receipt of the request for judgment, the court will enter judgment.

(8) Judgment will be for the amount offered by the defendant (less any payments made) and costs—
 (a) to be paid on the date or at the rate specified in the request for judgment; or
 (b) if none is specified, immediately.

(9) If the claimant does not accept the amount offered by the defendant, he may obtain judgment by filing a request in the relevant practice form.

(10) Judgment under paragraph (9) will be for an amount to be decided by the court and costs.

## 14.8 Allocation of Claims in Relation to Outstanding Matters

Where the court enters judgment under rule 14.6 or 14.7 for an amount to be decided by the court it will—
(a) give any directions it considers appropriate; and
(b) if it considers it appropriate, allocate the case.

## 14.9 Request for Time to Pay

(1) A defendant who makes an admission under rules 14.4, 14.5 or 14.7 (admission relating to a claim for a specified amount of money or offering to pay a specified amount of money) may make a request for time to pay.

(2) A request for time to pay is a proposal about the date of payment or a proposal to pay by instalments at the times and rate specified in the request.

(3) The defendant's request for time to pay must be served or filed (as the case may be) with his admission.

(4) If the claimant accepts the defendant's request, he may obtain judgment by filing a request in the relevant practice form.

(5) On receipt of the request for judgment, the court will enter judgment.

(6) Judgment will be—
 (a) where rule 14.4 applies, for the amount of the claim (less any payments made) and costs;

(b) where rule 14.5 applies, for the amount admitted (less any payments made) and costs; or
(c) where rule 14.7 applies, for the amount offered by the defendant (less any payments made) and costs; and

(in all cases) will be for payment at the time and rate specified in the defendant's request for time to pay.

(Rule 14.10 sets out the procedure to be followed if the claimant does not accept the defendant's request for time to pay.)

### 14.10 Determination of Rate of Payment

(1) This rule applies where the defendant makes a request for time to pay under rule 14.9.
(2) If the claimant does not accept the defendant's proposals for payment, he must file a notice in the relevant practice form.
(3) Where the defendant's admission was served direct on the claimant, a copy of the admission and the request for time to pay must be filed with the claimant's notice.
(4) When the court receives the claimant's notice, it will enter judgment for the amount admitted (less any payments made) to be paid at the time and rate of payment determined by the court.

### 14.11 Determination of Rate of Payment by Court Officer

(1) A court officer may exercise the powers of the court under rule 14.10(4) where the amount outstanding (including costs) is not more than £50,000.
(2) Where a court officer is to determine the time and rate of payment, he must do so without a hearing.

### 14.12 Determination of Rate of Payment by Judge

(1) Where a judge is to determine the time and rate of payment, he may do so without a hearing.
(2) Where a judge is to determine the time and rate of payment at a hearing, the proceedings must be transferred automatically to the defendant's home court if—
  (a) the only claim is for a specified amount of money;
  (b) the defendant is an individual;
  (c) the claim has not been transferred to another defendant's home court under rule 13.4 (application to set aside[GL] or vary default judgment—procedure) or rule 26.2 (automatic transfer);
  (d) the claim was not started in the defendant's home court; and
  (e) the claim was not started in a specialist list.

(Rule 2.3 explains which court is a defendant's home court.)

(3) If there is to be a hearing to determine the time and rate of payment, the court must give each party at least 7 days' notice of the hearing.

### 14.13 Right of Redetermination

(1) Where—
  (a) a court officer has determined the time and rate of payment under rule 14.11; or
  (b) a judge has determined the time and rate of payment under rule 14.12 without a hearing, either party may apply for the decision to be redetermined by a judge.
(2) An application for redetermination must be made within 14 days after service of the determination on the applicant.
(3) Where an application for redetermination is made, the proceedings must be transferred to the defendant's home court if—
  (a) the only claim (apart from a claim for interest or costs) is for a specified amount of money;
  (b) the defendant is an individual;

(c) the claim has not been transferred to another defendant's home court under rule 13.4 (application to set aside(GL) or vary default judgment—procedure) or rule 26.2 (automatic transfer);
(d) the claim was not started in the defendant's home court; and
(e) the claim was not started in a specialist list.

(Rule 2.3 explains which court is a defendant's home court.)

## 14.14 Interest

(1) Judgment under rule 14.4 (admission of whole of claim for specified amount of money) shall include the amount of interest claimed to the date of judgment if—
  (a) the particulars of claim include the details required by rule 16.4;
  (b) where interest is claimed under section 35A of the Supreme Court Act 1981 or section 69 of the County Courts Act 1984, the rate is no higher than the rate of interest payable on judgment debts at the date when the claim form was issued; and
  (c) the claimant's request for judgment includes a calculation of the interest claimed for the period from the date up to which interest was stated to be calculated in the claim form to the date of the request for judgment.
(2) In any case where judgment is entered under rule 14.4 and the conditions in paragraph (1) are not satisfied judgment shall be for an amount of interest to be decided by the court.
(3) Where judgment is entered for an amount of interest to be decided by the court, the court will give directions for the management of the case.

# PD 14 Practice Direction — Admissions

This practice direction supplements CPR Part 14.

## Admissions Generally

1.1 (1) Rules 14.1, 14.1A and 14.2 deal with the manner in which a defendant may make an admission of a claim or part of a claim.

(2) Rule 14.1A makes provision about admissions made before commencement of a claim. It applies only to admissions made after 6th April 2007, and only in proceedings to which one of the following pre-action protocols apply—

(a) the pre-action protocol for personal injury claims;

(b) the pre-action protocol for the resolution of clinical disputes; or

(c) the pre-action protocol for disease and illness claims.

(The pre-action protocol for personal injury claims states that it is primarily designed for certain types of personal injury claim with a value of less than £15,000; but paragraph 2.2 of the protocol indicates that it generally applies to all claims which include a claim for personal injury.)

1.2 Rules 14.3, 14.4, 14.5, 14.6 and 14.7 set out how judgment may be obtained on a written admission.

## Forms

2.1 When particulars of claim are served on a defendant the forms for responding to the claim that will accompany them will include a form[1] for making an admission.

2.2 If the defendant is requesting time to pay he should complete as fully as possible the statement of means contained in the admission form, or otherwise give in writing the same details of his means as could have been given in the admission form.

## Returning or Filing the Admission

3.1 If the defendant wishes to make an admission in respect of the whole of a claim for a specified amount of money, the admission form or other written notice of the admission should be completed and returned to the claimant within 14 days of service of the particulars of claim.[2]

3.2 If the defendant wishes to make an admission in respect of a part of a claim for a specified amount of money, or in respect of a claim for an unspecified amount of money, the admission form or other written notice of admission should be completed and filed with the court within 14 days of service of the particulars of claim.[3]

3.3 The defendant may also file a defence under rule 15.2.

## Request for Time to Pay

4.1 A defendant who makes an admission in respect of a claim for a specified sum of money or offers to pay a sum of money in respect of a claim for an unspecified sum may, in the admission form, make a request for time to pay.[4]

4.2 If the claimant accepts the defendant's request, he may obtain judgment by filing a request for judgment contained in form N225A;[5] the court will then enter judgment for payment at the time and rate specified in the defendant's request.[6]

---

[1] Forms N9A (specified amount) or N9C (unspecified amount).

[2] Rules 14.2 and 14.4.

[3] Rules 14.2, 14.5, 14.6 and 14.7.

[4] Rule 14.9.

[5] Rule 14.9(4).

[6] Rule 14.9(5) and (6).

4.3 If the claimant does not accept the request for time to pay, he should file notice to that effect by completing form N225A; the court will then enter judgment for the amount of the admission (less any payments made) at a time and rate of payment decided by the court (see rule 14.10).

## Determining the Rate of Payment

5.1 In deciding the time and rate of payment the court will take into account:
(1) the defendant's statement of means set out in the admission form or in any other written notice of the admission filed,
(2) the claimant's objections to the defendant's request set out in the claimant's notice,[7] and
(3) any other relevant factors.

5.2 The time and rate of payment may be decided:
(1) by a judge with or without a hearing, or
(2) by a court officer without a hearing provided that:
(a) the only claim is for a specified sum of money, and
(b) the amount outstanding is not more than £50,000 (including costs).

5.3 Where a decision has been made without a hearing whether by a court officer or by a judge, either party may apply for the decision to be redetermined by a judge.[8]

5.4 If the decision was made by a court officer the redetermination may take place without a hearing, unless a hearing is requested in the application notice.

5.5 If the decision was made by a judge the redetermination must be made at a hearing unless the parties otherwise agree.

5.6 Rule 14.13(2) describes how to apply for a redetermination.

## Varying the Rate of Payment

6.1 Either party may, on account of a change in circumstances since the date of the decision (or redetermination as the case may be) apply to vary the time and rate of payment of instalments still remaining unpaid.

6.2 An application to vary under paragraph 6.1 above should be made in accordance with Part 23.

## Withdrawing an admission

7.1 An admission made under Part 14 may be withdrawn with the court's permission.

7.2 In deciding whether to give permission for an admission to be withdrawn, the court will have regard to all the circumstances of the case, including—
(a) the grounds upon which the applicant seeks to withdraw the admission including whether or not new evidence has come to light which was not available at the time the admission was made;
(b) the conduct of the parties, including any conduct which led the party making the admission to do so;
(c) the prejudice that may be caused to any person if the admission is withdrawn;
(d) the prejudice that may be caused to any person if the application is refused;
(e) the stage in the proceedings at which the application to withdraw is made, in particular in relation to the date or period fixed for trial;
(f) the prospects of success (if the admission is withdrawn) of the claim or part of the claim in relation to which the offer was made; and
(g) the interests of the administration of justice.

[7] Form N225A.
[8] Rule 14.13(1).

# CPR Part 15 Defence and Reply



### 15.1 Part Not to Apply Where Claimant Uses Part 8 Procedure

This Part does not apply where the claimant uses the procedure set out in Part 8 (alternative procedure for claims).

### 15.2 Filing a defence

A defendant who wishes to defend all or part of a claim must file a defence.
(Part 14 contains further provisions which apply where the defendant admits a claim.)

### 15.3 Consequence of Not Filing a Defence

If a defendant fails to file a defence, the claimant may obtain default judgment if Part 12 allows it.

### 15.4 The Period for Filing a Defence

(1) The general rule is that the period for filing a defence is—
 (a) 14 days after service of the particulars of claim; or
 (b) if the defendant files an acknowledgment of service under Part 10, 28 days after service of the particulars of claim.

(Rule 7.4 provides for the particulars of claim to be contained in or served with the claim form or served within 14 days of service of the claim form.)

(2) The general rule is subject to the following rules—
 (a) rule 6.23 (which specifies how the period for filing a defence is calculated where the claim form is served out of the jurisdiction);
 (b) rule 11 (which provides that, where the defendant makes an application disputing the court's jurisdiction, he need not file a defence before the hearing);
 (c) rule 24.4(2) (which provides that, if the claimant applies for summary judgment before the defendant has filed a defence, the defendant need not file a defence before the summary judgment hearing); and
 (d) rule 6.16(4) (which requires the court to specify the period for responding to the particulars of claim when it makes an order under that rule).

### 15.5 Agreement Extending the Period for Filing a Defence

(1) The defendant and the claimant may agree that the period for filing a defence specified in rule 15.4 shall be extended by up to 28 days.
(2) Where the defendant and the claimant agree to extend the period for filing a defence, the defendant must notify the court in writing.

### 15.6 Service of Copy of Defence

A copy of the defence must be served on every other party.
(Part 16 sets out what a defence must contain.)

(The costs practice direction sets out the information about a funding arrangement to be provided with the defence where the defendant intends to seek to recover an additional liability)
('Funding arrangement' and 'additional liability' are defined in rule 43.2.)

### 15.7 Making a Counterclaim

Part 20 applies to a defendant who wishes to make a counterclaim.

### 15.8 Reply to Defence

If a claimant files a reply to the defence, he must—
(a) file his reply when he files his allocation questionnaire; and
(b) serve his reply on the other parties at the same time as he files it.
(Rule 26.3(6) requires the parties to file allocation questionnaires and specifies the period for doing so.)
(Part 22 requires a reply to be verified by a statement of truth.)

### 15.9 No Statement of Case After a Reply to be Filed Without Court's Permission

A party may not file or serve any statement of case after a reply without the permission of the court.

### 15.10 Claimant's Notice Where Defence is That Money Claimed Has Been Paid

(1) Where—
  (a) the only claim (apart from a claim for costs and interest) is for a specified amount of money; and
  (b) the defendant states in his defence that he has paid to the claimant the amount claimed,

  the court will send notice to the claimant requiring him to state in writing whether he wishes the proceedings to continue.
(2) When the claimant responds, he must serve a copy of his response on the defendant.
(3) If the claimant fails to respond under this rule within 28 days after service of the court's notice on him the claim shall be stayed(GL).
(4) Where a claim is stayed under this rule any party may apply for the stay(GL) to be lifted.

(If the claimant files notice under this rule that he wishes the proceedings to continue, the procedure which then follows is set out in Part 26.)

### 15.11 Claim Stayed if it is Not Defended or Admitted

(1) Where—
  (a) at least 6 months have expired since the end of the period for filing a defence specified in rule 15.4;
  (b) no defendant has served or filed an admission or filed a defence or counterclaim; and
  (c) the claimant has not entered or applied for judgment under Part 12 (default judgment), or Part 24 (summary judgment),

  the claim shall be stayed(GL).
(2) Where a claim is stayed(GL) under this rule any party may apply for the stay to be lifted.

# PD 15 Practice Direction — Defence and Reply

This practice direction supplements CPR Part 15.

## Defending the Claim

1.1 The provisions of Part 15 do not apply to claims in respect of which the Part 8 procedure is being used.

1.2 In relation to specialist proceedings (see Part 49) in respect of which special provisions for defence and reply are made by the rules and practice directions applicable to those claims, the provisions of Part 15 apply only to the extent that they are not inconsistent with those rules and practice directions.

1.3 Form N9B (specified amount) or N9D (unspecified amount or non-money claims) may be used for the purpose of defence and is included in the response pack served on the defendant with the particulars of claim.

1.4 Attention is drawn to r. 15.3 which sets out a possible consequence of not filing a defence.

(Part 16 (statements of case) and PD 16 contain rules and directions about the contents of a defence.)

(PD 43–48 contains details of the information required to be filed with a defence to comply with r. 44.15 (providing information about funding arrangements).)

## Statement of Truth

2.1 Part 22 requires a defence to be verified by a statement of truth.

2.2 The form of the statement of truth is as follows: '[I believe] [the defendant believes] that the facts stated in this defence are true.'

2.3 Attention is drawn to r. 32.14 which sets out the consequences of verifying a statement of case containing a false statement without an honest belief in its truth.

(For information about statements of truth see Part 22 and PD 22.)

## General

3.1 Where a defendant to a claim serves a counterclaim under Part 20, the defence and counterclaim should normally form one document with the counterclaim following on from the defence.

3.2 Where a claimant serves a reply and a defence to counterclaim, the reply and defence to counterclaim should normally form one document with the defence to counterclaim following on from the reply.

3.3 Where a claim has been stayed under r. 15.10(3) or 15.11(1) any party may apply for the stay to be lifted.[1]

3.4 The application should be made in accordance with Part 23 and should give the reason for the applicant's delay in proceeding with or responding to the claim.

(Paragraph 8.3 of PD 6 (service of documents) makes provision for the service on the claimant of any notice of funding filed with a defence.)

[1] Rules 15.10(4) and 15.11(2).

# CPR Part 16 Statements of Case



## 16.1 Part Not to Apply Where Claimant Uses Part 8 Procedure

This Part does not apply where the claimant uses the procedure set out in Part 8 (alternative procedure for claims).

## 16.2 Contents of the Claim Form

(1) The claim form must—
  (a) contain a concise statement of the nature of the claim;
  (b) specify the remedy which the claimant seeks;
  (c) where the claimant is making a claim for money, contain a statement of value in accordance with rule 16.3;
  (cc) where the claimant's only claim is for a specified sum, contain a statement of the interest accrued on that sum; and
  (d) contain such other matters as may be set out in a practice direction.

(1A) In civil proceedings against the Crown, as defined in rule 66.1(2), the claim form must also contain—
  (a) the names of the government departments and officers of the Crown concerned; and
  (b) brief details of the circumstances in which it is alleged that the liability of the Crown arose.

(2) If the particulars of claim specified in rule 16.4 are not contained in, or are not served with the claim form, the claimant must state on the claim form that the particulars of claim will follow.

(3) If the claimant is claiming in a representative capacity, the claim form must state what that capacity is.

(4) If the defendant is sued in a representative capacity, the claim form must state what that capacity is.

(5) The court may grant any remedy to which the claimant is entitled even if that remedy is not specified in the claim form.

(Part 22 requires a claim form to be verified by a statement of truth.)

(The costs practice direction [PD 43–48] sets out the information about a funding arrangement to be provided with the statement of case where the defendant intends to seek to recover an additional liability.)

(Funding arrangement' and 'additional liability' are defined in rule 43.2.)

## 16.3 Statement of Value to be Included in the Claim Form

(1) This rule applies where the claimant is making a claim for money.

(2) The claimant must, in the claim form, state—
  (a) the amount of money which he is claiming;
  (b) that he expects to recover—
    (i) not more than £5,000;

(ii) more than £5,000 but not more than £15,000; or
(iii) more than £15,000; or
(c) that he cannot say how much he expects to recover.

(3) In a claim for personal injuries, the claimant must also state in the claim form whether the amount which he expects to recover as general damages for pain, suffering and loss of amenity is—
(a) not more than £1,000; or
(b) more than £1,000.

(4) In a claim which includes a claim by a tenant of residential premises against his landlord where the tenant is seeking an order requiring the landlord to carry out repairs or other work to the premises, the claimant must also state in the claim form—
(a) whether the estimated costs of those repairs or other work is—
(i) not more than £1,000; or
(ii) more than £1,000; and
(b) whether the financial value of any other claim for damages is—
(i) not more than £1,000; or
(ii) more than £1,000.

(5) If the claim form is to be issued in the High Court it must, where this rule applies—
(a) state that the claimant expects to recover more than £15,000;
(b) state that some other enactment provides that the claim may be commenced only in the High Court and specify that enactment;
(c) if the claim is a claim for personal injuries state that the claimant expects to recover £50,000 or more; or
(d) state that the claim is to be in one of the specialist High Court lists and state which list.

(6) When calculating how much he expects to recover, the claimant must disregard any possibility—
(a) that he may recover—
(i) interest;
(ii) costs;
(b) that the court may make a finding of contributory negligence against him;
(c) that the defendant may make a counterclaim or that the defence may include a setoff; or
(d) that the defendant may be liable to pay an amount of money which the court awards to the claimant to the Secretary of State for Social Security under section 6 of the Social Security (Recovery of Benefits) Act 1997.

(7) The statement of value in the claim form does not limit the power of the court to give judgment for the amount which it finds the claimant is entitled to.

## 16.4 Contents of the Particulars of Claim

(1) Particulars of claim must include—
(a) a concise statement of the facts on which the claimant relies;
(b) if the claimant is seeking interest, a statement to that effect and the details set out in paragraph (2);
(c) if the claimant is seeking aggravated damages(GL) or exemplary damages(GL), a statement to that effect and his grounds for claiming them;
(d) if the claimant is seeking provisional damages, a statement to that effect and his grounds for claiming them; and
(e) such other matters as may be set out in a practice direction.

(2) If the claimant is seeking interest he must—
(a) state whether he is doing so—
(i) under the terms of a contract;
(ii) under an enactment and if so which; or
(iii) on some other basis and if so what that basis is; and

(b) if the claim is for a specified amount of money, state—
(i) the percentage rate at which interest is claimed;
(ii) the date from which it is claimed;
(iii) the date to which it is calculated, which must not be later than the date on which the claim form is issued;
(iv) the total amount of interest claimed to the date of calculation; and
(v) the daily rate at which interest accrues after that date.

(Part 22 requires particulars of claim to be verified by a statement of truth.)

## 16.5 Contents of Defence

(1) In his defence, the defendant must state—
(a) which of the allegations in the particulars of claim he denies;
(b) which allegations he is unable to admit or deny, but which he requires the claimant to prove; and
(c) which allegations he admits.

(2) Where the defendant denies an allegation—
(a) he must state his reasons for doing so; and
(b) if he intends to put forward a different version of events from that given by the claimant, he must state his own version.

(3) A defendant who—
(a) fails to deal with an allegation; but
(b) has set out in his defence the nature of his case in relation to the issue to which that allegation is relevant, shall be taken to require that allegation to be proved.

(4) Where the claim includes a money claim, a defendant shall be taken to require that any allegation relating to the amount of money claimed be proved unless he expressly admits the allegation.

(5) Subject to paragraphs (3) and (4), a defendant who fails to deal with an allegation shall be taken to admit that allegation.

(6) If the defendant disputes the claimant's statement of value under rule 16.3 he must—
(a) state why he disputes it; and
(b) if he is able, give his own statement of the value of the claim.

(7) If the defendant is defending in a representative capacity, he must state what that capacity is.

(8) If the defendant has not filed an acknowledgment of service under Part 10, he must give an address for service.

(Part 22 requires a defence to be verified by a statement of truth.)

(Rule 6.5 provides that an address for service must be within the jurisdiction.)

## 16.6 Defence of Set-off

Where a defendant—
(a) contends he is entitled to money from the claimant; and
(b) relies on this as a defence to the whole or part of the claim,

the contention may be included in the defence and set off against the claim, whether or not it is also a Part 20 claim.

## 16.7 Reply to Defence

(1) A claimant who does not file a reply to the defence shall not be taken to admit the matters raised in the defence.

(2) A claimant who—
(a) files a reply to a defence; but
(b) fails to deal with a matter raised in the defence,

shall be taken to require that matter to be proved.

(Part 22 requires a reply to be verified by a statement of truth.)

## 16.8 Court's Power to Dispense With Statements of Case

If a claim form has been—

(a) issued in accordance with rule 7.2; and

(b) served in accordance with rule 7.5,

the court may make an order that the claim will continue without any other statement of case.

# PD 16 Practice Direction — Statements of Case

This practice direction supplements CPR Part 16.

## General

1.1 The provisions of Part 16 do not apply to claims in respect of which the Part 8 procedure is being used.

1.2 Where special provisions about statements of case are made by the rules and practice directions applying to particular types of proceedings, the provisions of Part 16 and of this practice direction apply only to the extent that they are not inconsistent with those rules and practice directions.

1.3 Examples of types of proceedings with special provisions about statements of case include:
(1) defamation claims (Part 53);
(2) possession claims (Part 55); and
(3) probate claims (Part 57).

1.4 If exceptionally a statement of case exceeds 25 pages (excluding schedules) an appropriate short summary must also be filed and served.

## The Claim Form

2.1 Rule 16.2 refers to matters which the claim form must contain. Where the claim is for money, the claim form must also contain the statement of value referred to in r. 16.3.

2.2 The claim form must include an address at which the claimant resides or carries on business. This paragraph applies even though the claimant's address for service is the business address of his solicitor.

2.3 Where the defendant is an individual, the claimant should (if he is able to do so) include in the claim form an address at which the defendant resides or carries on business. This paragraph applies even though the defendant's solicitor have agreed to accept service on the defendant's behalf.

2.4 Any address which is provided for the purpose of these provisions must include a postcode, unless the court orders otherwise. Postcode information may be obtained from <http://www.royalmail.com> or the Royal Mail Address Management Guide.

2.5 If the claim form does not show a full address, including postcode, at which the claimant(s) and defendant(s) reside or carry on business, the claim form will be issued but will be retained by the court and will not be served until the claimant has supplied a full address, including postcode, or the court has dispensed with the requirement to do so. The court will notify the claimant.

2.6 The claim form must be headed with the title of the proceedings, including the full name of each party. The full name means, in each case where it is known:
(a) in the case of an individual, his full unabbreviated name and title by which he is known;
(b) in the case of an individual carrying on business in a name other than his own name, the full unabbreviated name of the individual, together with the title by which he is known, and the full trading name (for example, John Smith 'trading as' or 'T/as' 'JS Autos');
(c) in the case of a partnership (other than a limited liability partnership (LLP))—
(i) where partners are being sued in the name of the partnership, the full name by which the partnership is known, together with the words '(A Firm)'; or
(ii) where partners are being sued as individuals, the full unabbreviated name of each partner and the title by which he is known;
(d) in the case of a company or limited liability partnership registered in England and Wales, the full registered name, including suffix (plc, limited, LLP, etc), if any;

(e) in the case of any other company or corporation, the full name by which it is known, including suffix where appropriate.

(RSC O81 contains rules about claims made by or against partners in their firm name.)

(For information about how and where a claim may be started see Part 7 and PD 7.)

## Particulars of Claim

3.1 If practicable, the particulars of claim should be set out in the claim form.

3.2 Where the claimant does not include the particulars of claim in the claim form, particulars of claim may be served separately:

(1) either at the same time as the claim form, or

(2) within 14 days after service of the claim form[1] provided that the service of the particulars of claim is not later than four months from the date of issue of the claim form[2] (or six months where the claim form is to be served out of the jurisdiction[3]).

3.3 If the particulars of claim are not included in or have not been served with the claim form, the claim form must also contain a statement that particulars of claim will follow.[4]

3.4 Particulars of claim which are not included in the claim form must be verified by a statement of truth, the form of which is as follows:

[I believe] [the claimant believes] that the facts stated in these particulars of claim are true.

3.5 Attention is drawn to r. 32.14 which sets out the consequences of verifying a statement of case containing a false statement without an honest belief in its truth.

3.6 The full particulars of claim must include:

(1) the matters set out in r. 16.4, and

(2) where appropriate, the matters set out in practice directions relating to specific types of claims.

3.7 Attention is drawn to the provisions of r. 16.4(2) in respect of a claim for interest.

3.8 Particulars of claim served separately from the claim form must also contain:

(1) the name of the court in which the claim is proceeding,

(2) the claim number,

(3) the title of the proceedings, and

(4) the claimant's address for service.

## Matters Which Must be Included in the Particulars of Claim in Certain Types of Claim

*Personal injury claims*

4.1 The particulars of claim must contain:

(1) the claimant's date of birth, and

(2) brief details of the claimant's personal injuries.

4.2 The claimant must attach to his particulars of claim a schedule of details of any past and future expenses and losses which he claims.

4.3 Where the claimant is relying on the evidence of a medical practitioner the claimant must attach to or serve with his particulars of claim a report from a medical practitioner about the personal injuries which he alleges in his claim.

4.4 In a provisional damages claim the claimant must state in his particulars of claim:

(1) that he is seeking an award of provisional damages under either the Supreme Court Act 1981, s. 32A or the County Courts Act 1984, s. 51,

(2) that there is a chance that at some future time the claimant will develop some

[1] See r. 7.4(1)(b).

[2] See r. 7.4(2) and 7.5(2).

[3] See r. 7.5(3).

[4] See r. 16.2(2).

serious disease or suffer some serious deterioration in his physical or mental condition, and
(3) specify the disease or type of deterioration in respect of which an application may be made at a future date.

(Part 41 and PD 41 contain information about awards for provisional damages.)

*Fatal accident claims*

5.1 In a fatal accident claim the claimant must state in his particulars of claim:
(1) that it is brought under the Fatal Accidents Act 1976,
(2) the dependants on whose behalf the claim is made,
(3) the date of birth of each dependant, and
(4) details of the nature of the dependency claim.

5.2 A fatal accident claim may include a claim for damages for bereavement.

5.3 In a fatal accident claim the claimant may also bring a claim under the Law Reform (Miscellaneous Provisions) Act 1934 on behalf of the estate of the deceased.
(For information on apportionment under the Law Reform (Miscellaneous Provisions) Act 1934 and the Fatal Accidents Act 1976 or between dependants see Part 37 and PD 37.)

*Hire-purchase claims*

6.1 Where the claim is for the delivery of goods let under a hire-purchase agreement or conditional sale agreement to a person other than a company or other corporation, the claimant must state in the particulars of claim:
(1) the date of the agreement,
(2) the parties to the agreement,
(3) the number or other identification of the agreement,
(4) where the claimant was not one of the original parties to the agreement, the means by which the rights and duties of the creditor passed to him,
(5) whether the agreement is a regulated agreement, and if it is not a regulated agreement, the reason why,
(6) the place where the agreement was signed by the defendant,
(7) the goods claimed,
(8) the total price of the goods,
(9) the paid-up sum,
(10) the unpaid balance of the total price,
(11) whether a default notice or a notice under s. 76(1) or 98(1) of the Consumer Credit Act 1974 has been served on the defendant, and if it has, the date and method of service,
(12) the date when the right to demand delivery of the goods accrued,
(13) the amount (if any) claimed as an alternative to the delivery of goods, and
(14) the amount (if any) claimed in addition to:
(a) the delivery of the goods, or
(b) any claim under (13) above, with the grounds of each claim.

(If the agreement is a regulated agreement the procedure set out in PD 7B should be used.)

6.2 Where the claim is not for the delivery of goods, the claimant must state in his particulars of claim:
(1) the matters set out in para. 6.1(1) to (6) above,
(2) the goods let under the agreement,
(3) the amount of the total price,
(4) the paid-up sum,
(5) the amount (if any) claimed as being due and unpaid in respect of any instalment or instalments of the total price, and
(6) the nature and amount of any other claim and how it arises.

## Other Matters to be Included in Particulars of Claim

7.1 Where a claim is made for an injunction or declaration in respect of or relating to any land or the possession, occupation, use or enjoyment of any land the particulars of claim must:
(1) state whether or not the injunction or declaration relates to residential premises, and
(2) identify the land (by reference to a plan where necessary).

7.2 Where a claim is brought to enforce a right to recover possession of goods the particulars of claim must contain a statement showing the value of the goods.

7.3 Where a claim is based upon a written agreement:
(1) a copy of the contract or documents constituting the agreement should be attached to or served with the particulars of claim and the original(s) should be available at the hearing, and
(2) any general conditions of sale incorporated in the contract should also be attached (but where the contract is or the documents constituting the agreement are bulky this practice direction is complied with by attaching or serving only the relevant parts of the contract or documents).

7.4 Where a claim is based upon an oral agreement, the particulars of claim should set out the contractual words used and state by whom, to whom, when and where they were spoken.

7.5 Where a claim is based upon an agreement by conduct, the particulars of claim must specify the conduct relied on and state by whom, when and where the acts constituting the conduct were done.

7.6 In a claim issued in the High Court relating to a consumer credit agreement, the particulars of claim must contain a statement that the action is not one to which the Consumer Credit Act 1974, s. 141, applies.

## Matters Which Must be Specifically Set Out in the Particulars of Claim if Relied On

8.1 A claimant who wishes to rely on evidence:
(1) under the Civil Evidence Act 1968, s. 11 of a conviction of an offence, or
(2) under s. 12 of the above-mentioned Act of a finding or adjudication of adultery or paternity,
must include in his particulars of claim a statement to that effect and give the following details:
(1) the type of conviction, finding or adjudication and its date,
(2) the court or court-martial which made the conviction, finding or adjudication, and
(3) the issue in the claim to which it relates.

8.2 The claimant must specifically set out the following matters in his particulars of claim where he wishes to rely on them in support of his claim:
(1) any allegation of fraud,
(2) the fact of any illegality,
(3) details of any misrepresentation,
(4) details of all breaches of trust,
(5) notice or knowledge of a fact,
(6) details of unsoundness of mind or undue influence,
(7) details of wilful default, and
(8) any facts relating to mitigation of loss or damage.

## General

9.1 Where a claim is for a sum of money expressed in a foreign currency it must expressly state:
(1) that the claim is for payment in a specified foreign currency,
(2) why it is for payment in that currency,

(3) the sterling equivalent of the sum at the date of the claim, and
(4) the source of the exchange rate relied on to calculate the sterling equivalent.

9.2 A subsequent statement of case must not contradict or be inconsistent with an earlier one; for example a reply to a defence must not bring in a new claim. Where new matters have come to light the appropriate course may be to seek the court's permission to amend the statement of case.

9.3 In clinical negligence claims, the words 'clinical negligence' should be inserted at the top of every statement of case.

## The Defence

*General*

10.1 Rule 16.5 deals with the contents of the defence.

10.2 A defendant should deal with every allegation in accordance with r. 16.5(1) and (2).

10.3 Rule 16.5(3), (4) and (5) sets out the consequences of not dealing with an allegation.

10.4 Where the defendant is an individual, and the claim form does not contain an address at which he resides or carries on business, or contains an incorrect address, the defendant must provide such an address in the defence.

10.5 Where the defendant's address for service is not where he resides or carries on business, he must still provide the address required by [para. 10.4*].

10.6 Any address which is provided for the purpose of these provisions must include a postcode, unless the court orders otherwise. Postcode information may be obtained from <http://www.royalmail.com> or the Royal Mail Address Management Guide.

10.7 Where a defendant to a claim or counterclaim is an individual, he must provide his date of birth (if known) in the acknowledgment of service, admission, defence, defence and counterclaim, reply or other response.

*Statement of truth*

11.1 Part 22 requires a defence to be verified by a statement of truth.

11.2 The form of the statement of truth is as follows:

[I believe] [the defendant believes] that the facts stated in the defence are true.

11.3 Attention is drawn to r. 32.14 which sets out the consequences of verifying a statement of case containing a false statement without an honest belief in its truth.

## Matters Which Must be Included in the Defence

*Personal injury claims*

12.1 Where the claim is for personal injuries and the claimant has attached a medical report in respect of his alleged injuries, the defendant should:

(1) state in his defence whether he:
  (a) agrees,
  (b) disputes, or
  (c) neither agrees nor disputes but has no knowledge of,
  the matters contained in the medical report,
(2) where he disputes any part of the medical report, give in his defence his reasons for doing so, and
(3) where he has obtained his own medical report on which he intends to rely, attach it to his defence.

12.2 Where the claim is for personal injuries and the claimant has included a schedule of past and future expenses and losses, the defendant should include in or attach to his defence a counter-schedule stating:

(1) which of those items he:
  (a) agrees,

[* The text issued by the Department for Constitutional Affairs mistakenly refers to para. 11.4.]

(b) disputes, or
(c) neither agrees nor disputes but has no knowledge of, and
(2) where any items are disputed, supplying alternative figures where appropriate.
(PD 43–48 contains details of the information required to be filed with certain statements of case to comply with r. 44.15 (providing information about funding arrangements).)

*Other matters*

13.1 The defendant must give details of the expiry of any relevant limitation period relied on.

13.2 Rule 37.3 and PD 37, para. 2, contain information about a defence of tender.

13.3 A party may:
(1) refer in his statement of case to any point of law on which his claim or defence, as the case may be, is based,
(2) give in his statement of case the name of any witness he proposes to call, and
(3) attach to or serve with this statement of case a copy of any document which he considers is necessary to his claim or defence, as the case may be (including any expert's report to be filed in accordance with Part 35).

## Competition Act 1998

14 A party who wishes to rely on a finding of the Office of Fair Trading as provided by the Competition Act 1998, s. 58, must include in his statement of case a statement to that effect and identify the Office's finding on which he seeks to rely.

## Human Rights

15.1 A party who seeks to rely on any provision of or right arising under the Human Rights Act 1998 or seeks a remedy available under that Act:
(1) must state that fact in his statement of case; and
(2) must in his statement of case:
(a) give precise details of the Convention right which it is alleged has been infringed and details of the alleged infringement;
(b) specify the relief sought;
(c) state if the relief sought includes:
(i) a declaration of incompatibility in accordance with s. 4 of that Act, or
(ii) damages in respect of a judicial act to which s. 9(3) of that Act applies;
(d) where the relief sought includes a declaration of incompatibility in accordance with s. 4 of that Act, give precise details of the legislative provision alleged to be incompatible and details of the alleged incompatibility;
(e) where the claim is founded on a finding of unlawfulness by another court or tribunal, give details of the finding; and
(f) where the claim is founded on a judicial act which is alleged to have infringed a Convention right of the party as provided by the Human Rights Act 1998, s. 9, the judicial act complained of and the court or tribunal which is alleged to have made it.

(PD 19 provides for notice to be given and parties joined in the circumstances referred to in (c), (d) and (f).)

15.2 A party who seeks to amend his statement of case to include the matters referred to in para. 15.1 must, unless the court orders otherwise, do so as soon as possible.
(Part 17 provides for the amendment of a statement of case.)

# CPR Part 17 Amendments to Statements of Case



## 17.1 Amendments to Statements of Case

(1) A party may amend his statement of case at any time before it has been served on any other party.
(2) If his statement of case has been served, a party may amend it only—
  (a) with the written consent of all the other parties; or
  (b) with the permission of the court.
(3) If a statement of case has been served, an application to amend it by removing, adding or substituting a party must be made in accordance with rule 19.4.

(Part 22 requires amendments to a statement of case to be verified by a statement of truth unless the court orders otherwise.)

## 17.2 Power of Court to Disallow Amendments Made Without Permission

(1) If a party has amended his statement of case where permission of the court was not required, the court may disallow the amendment.
(2) A party may apply to the court for an order under paragraph (1) within 14 days of service of a copy of the amended statement of case on him.

## 17.3 Amendments to Statements of Case with the Permission of the Court

(1) Where the court gives permission for a party to amend his statement of case, it may give directions as to—
  (a) amendments to be made to any other statement of case; and
  (b) service of any amended statement of case.
(2) The power of the court to give permission under this rule is subject to—
  (a) rule 19.1 (change of parties—general);
  (b) rule 19.4 (special provisions about adding or substituting parties after the end of a relevant limitation period[GL]); and
  (c) rule 17.4 (amendments of statement of case after the end of a relevant limitation period).

## 17.4 Amendments to Statements of Case After the End of a Relevant Limitation Period

(1) This rule applies where—
  (a) a party applies to amend his statement of case in one of the ways mentioned in this rule; and
  (b) a period of limitation has expired under—
    (i) the Limitation Act 1980;
    (ii) the Foreign Limitation Periods Act 1984; or
    (iii) any other enactment which allows such an amendment, or under which such an amendment is allowed.
(2) The court may allow an amendment whose effect will be to add or substitute a new claim, but only if the new claim arises out of the same facts or substantially the same facts as a claim in respect of which the party applying for permission has already claimed a remedy in the proceedings.

(3) The court may allow an amendment to correct a mistake as to the name of a party, but only where the mistake was genuine and not one which would cause reasonable doubt as to the identity of the party in question.
(4) The court may allow an amendment to alter the capacity in which a party claims if the new capacity is one which that party had when the proceedings started or has since acquired.

(Rule 19.5 specifies the circumstances in which the court may allow a new party to be added or substituted after the end of a relevant limitation period(GL).)

# PD 17 Practice Direction — Amendments to Statements of Case

This practice direction supplements CPR Part 17.
A party applying for an amendment will usually be responsible for the costs of and arising from the amendment.

## Applications to Amend Where the Permission of the Court is Required

1.1 The application may be dealt with at a hearing or, if rule 23.8 applies, without a hearing.

1.2 When making an application to amend a statement of case, the applicant should file with the court:
(1) the application notice, and
(2) a copy of the statement of case with the proposed amendments.

1.3 Where permission to amend has been given, the applicant should within 14 days of the date of the order, or within such other period as the court may direct, file with the court the amended statement of case.

1.4 If the substance of the statement of case is changed by reason of the amendment, the statement of case should be re-verified by a statement of truth.[1]

1.5 A copy of the order and the amended statement of case should be served on every party to the proceedings, unless the court orders otherwise.

## General

2.1 The amended statement of case and the court copy of it should be endorsed as follows:
(1) where the court's permission was required:
'Amended [Particulars of Claim *or as may be*] by Order of [Master . . . . . . . . . .][District Judge . . . *or as may be*] dated . . . . . . . . . . .'
(2) Where the court's permission was not required:
'Amended [Particulars of Claim *or as may be*] under CPR [rule 17.1(1) or (2)(a)] dated . . . . . . . . . . . . .'

2.2 The statement of case in its amended form need not show the original text. However, where the court thinks it desirable for both the original text and the amendments to be shown, the court may direct that the amendments should be shown either:
(1) by coloured amendments, either manuscript or computer generated, or
(2) by use of a numerical code in a monochrome computer generated document.

2.3 Where colour is used, the text to be deleted should be struck through in colour and any text replacing it should be inserted or underlined in the same colour.

2.4 The order of colours to be used for successive amendments is: (1) red, (2) green, (3) violet and (4) yellow.

(For information about changes to parties see Part 19 and PD 19.)

[1] See Part 22 for information about the statement of truth.

# CPR Part 18 Further Information



## 18.1 Obtaining Further Information

(1) The court may at any time order a party to—
   (a) clarify any matter which is in dispute in the proceedings; or
   (b) give additional information in relation to any such matter, whether or not the matter is contained or referred to in a statement of case.

(2) Paragraph (1) is subject to any rule of law to the contrary.

(3) Where the court makes an order under paragraph (1), the party against whom it is made must—
   (a) file his response; and
   (b) serve it on the other parties,

   within the time specified by the court.

(Part 22 requires a response to be verified by a statement of truth.)

(Part 53 (defamation) restricts requirements for providing further information about sources of information in defamation claims.)

## 18.2 Restriction on the Use of Further Information

The court may direct that information provided by a party to another party (whether given voluntarily or following an order made under rule 18.1) must not be used for any purpose except for that of the proceedings in which it is given.

# PD 18 Practice Direction — Further Information

This practice direction supplements CPR Part 18.
Attention is also drawn to Part 22 (statements of truth).

## Preliminary Request for Further Information or Clarification

1.1 Before making an application to the court for an order under Part 18, the party seeking clarification or information (the first party) should first serve on the party from whom it is sought (the second party) a written request for that clarification or information (a Request) stating a date by which the response to the Request should be served. The date must allow the second party a reasonable time to respond.

1.2 A Request should be concise and strictly confined to matters which are reasonably necessary and proportionate to enable the first party to prepare his own case or to understand the case he has to meet.

1.3 Requests must be made as far as possible in a single comprehensive document and not piecemeal.

1.4 A Request may be made by letter if the text of the Request is brief and the reply is likely to be brief; otherwise the Request should be made in a separate document.

1.5 If a Request is made in a letter, the letter should, in order to distinguish it from any other that might routinely be written in the course of a case,
   (1) state that it contains a Request made under Part 18, and
   (2) deal with no matters other than the Request.

1.6 (1) A Request (whether made by letter or in a separate document) must—
      (a) be headed with the name of the court and the title and number of the claim,
      (b) in its heading state that it is a Request made under Part 18, identify the first party and the second party and state the date on which it is made,
      (c) set out in a separate numbered paragraph each request for information or clarification,
      (d) where a Request relates to a document, identify that document and (if relevant) the paragraph or words to which it relates,
      (e) state the date by which the first party expects a response to the Request,
   (2) (a) A Request which is not in the form of a letter may, if convenient, be prepared in such a way that the response may be given on the same document.
      (b) To do this the numbered paragraphs of the Request should appear on the left hand half of each sheet so that the paragraphs of the response may then appear on the right.
      (c) Where a Request is prepared in this form an extra copy should be served for the use of the second party.

1.7 Subject to the provisions of paragraphs 3.1 to 3.3 of the Practice Direction to Part 6, a request should be served by email if reasonably practicable.

## Responding to a Request

2.1 A response to a Request must be in writing, dated and signed by the second party or his legal representative.

2.2 (1) Where the Request is made in a letter the second party may give his response in a letter or in a formal reply.
   (2) Such a letter should identify itself as a response to the Request and deal with no other matters than the response.

2.3 (1) Unless the Request is in the format described in paragraph 1.6(2) and the second party uses the document supplied for the purpose, a response must:

(a) be headed with the name of the court and the title and number of the claim,
(b) in its heading identify itself as a response to that Request,
(c) repeat the text of each separate paragraph of the Request and set out under each paragraph the response to it,
(d) refer to and have attached to it a copy of any document not already in the possession of the first party which forms part of the response.

(2) A second or supplementary response to a Request must identify itself as such in its heading.

2.4 The second party must when he serves his response on the first party serve on every other party and file with the court a copy of the Request and of his response.

## Statements of Truth

3 Attention is drawn to Part 22 and to the definition of a statement of case in Part 2 of the rules; a response should be verified by a statement of truth.

## General Matters

4.1 (1) If the second party objects to complying with the Request or part of it or is unable to do so at all or within the time stated in the Request he must inform the first party promptly and in any event within that time.

(2) He may do so in a letter or in a separate document (a formal response), but in either case he must give reasons and, where relevant, give a date by which he expects to be able to comply.

4.2 (1) There is no need for a second party to apply to the court if he objects to a Request or is unable to comply with it at all or within the stated time. He need only comply with paragraph 4.1(1) above.

(2) Where a second party considers that a Request can only be complied with at disproportionate expense and objects to comply for that reason he should say so in his reply and explain briefly why he has taken that view.

## Applications for Orders Under Part 18

5.1 Attention is drawn to Part 23 (applications) and to PD 23.

5.2 An application notice for an order under Part 18 should set out or have attached to it the text of the order sought and in particular should specify the matter or matters in respect of which the clarification or information is sought.

5.3 (1) If a Request under paragraph 1 for the information or clarification has not been made, the application notice should, in addition, explain why not.

(2) If a Request for clarification or information has been made, the application notice or the evidence in support should describe the response, if any.

5.4 Both the first party and the second party should consider whether evidence in support of or in opposition to the application is required.

5.5 (1) Where the second party has made no response to a Request served on him, the first party need not serve the application notice on the second party, and the court may deal with the application without a hearing.

(2) Sub-paragraph (1) above only applies if at least 14 days have passed since the Request was served and the time stated in it for a response has expired.

5.6 Unless paragraph 5.5 applies the application notice must be served on the second party and on all other parties to the claim.

5.7 An order made under Part 18 must be served on all parties to the claim.

5.8 Costs:

(1) Attention is drawn to PD 43–48 and in particular the court's power to make a summary assessment of costs.

(2) Attention is also drawn to rule 44.13(1) which provides that the general rule is that if an order does not mention costs no party is entitled to costs relating to that order.

# CPR Part 19 Parties and Group Litigation



## 19.1 Parties — General

Any number of claimants or defendants may be joined as parties to a claim.

## I ADDITION AND SUBSTITUTION OF PARTIES

## 19.2 Change of Parties—General

(1) This rule applies where a party is to be added or substituted except where the case falls within rule 19.5 (special provisions about changing parties after the end of a relevant limitation period (GL)).
(2) The court may order a person to be added as a new party if—
    (a) it is desirable to add the new party so that the court can resolve all the matters in dispute in the proceedings; or
    (b) there is an issue involving the new party and an existing party which is connected to the matters in dispute in the proceedings, and it is desirable to add the new party so that the court can resolve that issue.
(3) The court may order any person to cease to be a party if it is not desirable for that person to be a party to the proceedings.
(4) The court may order a new party to be substituted for an existing one if—
    (a) the existing party's interest or liability has passed to the new party; and
    (b) it is desirable to substitute the new party so that the court can resolve the matters in dispute in the proceedings.

## 19.3 Provisions Applicable Where Two or More Persons are Jointly Entitled to a Remedy

(1) Where a claimant claims a remedy to which some other person is jointly entitled with him, all persons jointly entitled to the remedy must be parties unless the court orders otherwise.
(2) If any person does not agree to be a claimant, he must be made a defendant, unless the court orders otherwise.
(3) This rule does not apply in probate proceedings.

## 19.4 Procedure for Adding and Substituting Parties

(1) The court's permission is required to remove, add or substitute a party, unless the claim form has not been served.

(2) An application for permission under paragraph (1) may be made by—
- (a) an existing party; or
- (b) a person who wishes to become a party.

(3) An application for an order under rule 19.2(4) (substitution of a new party where existing party's interest or liability has passed)—
- (a) may be made without notice; and
- (b) must be supported by evidence.

(4) Nobody may be added or substituted as a claimant unless—
- (a) he has given his consent in writing; and
- (b) that consent has been filed with the court.

(4A) The Commissioners for HM Revenue and Customs may be added as a party to proceedings only if they consent in writing.

(5) An order for the removal, addition or substitution of a party must be served on—
- (a) all parties to the proceedings; and
- (b) any other person affected by the order.

(6) When the court makes an order for the removal, addition or substitution of a party, it may give consequential directions about—
- (a) filing and serving the claim form on any new defendant;
- (b) serving relevant documents on the new party; and
- (c) the management of the proceedings.

## 19.4A Human Rights

*Section 4 of the Human Rights Act 1998*

(1) The court may not make a declaration of incompatibility in accordance with section 4 of the Human Rights Act 1998 unless 21 days' notice, or such other period of notice as the court directs, has been given to the Crown.

(2) Where notice has been given to the Crown a Minister, or other person permitted by that Act, shall be joined as a party on giving notice to the court.

(Only courts specified in section 4 of the Human Rights Act 1998 can make a declaration of incompatibility.)

*Section 9 of the Human Rights Act 1998*

(3) Where a claim is made under that Act for damages in respect of a judicial act—
- (a) that claim must be set out in the statement of case or the appeal notice; and
- (b) notice must be given to the Crown.

(4) Where paragraph (3) applies and the appropriate person has not applied to be joined as a party within 21 days, or such other period as the court directs, after the notice is served, the court may join the appropriate person as a party.

(A practice direction makes provision for these notices.)

## 19.5 Special Provisions About Adding or Substituting Parties After the End of a Relevant Limitation Period

(1) This rule applies to a change of parties after the end of a period of limitation under—
- (a) the Limitation Act 1980;
- (b) the Foreign Limitation Periods Act 1984; or
- (c) any other enactment which allows such a change, or under which such a change is allowed.

(2) The court may add or substitute a party only if—
- (a) the relevant limitation period[GL] was current when the proceedings were started; and
- (b) the addition or substitution is necessary.

(3) The addition or substitution of a party is necessary only if the court is satisfied that—
   (a) the new party is to be substituted for a party who was named in the claim form in mistake for the new party;
   (b) the claim cannot properly be carried on by or against the original party unless the new party is added or substituted as claimant or defendant; or
   (c) the original party has died or had a bankruptcy order made against him and his interest or liability has passed to the new party.

(4) In addition, in a claim for personal injuries the court may add or substitute a party where it directs that—
   (a) (i) section 11 (special time limit for claims for personal injuries); or
      (ii) section 12 (special time limit for claims under fatal accidents legislation),
   of the Limitation Act 1980 shall not apply to the claim by or against the new party; or
   (b) the issue of whether those sections apply shall be determined at trial.

(Rule 17.4 deals with other changes after the end of a relevant limitation period(GL).)

### 19.5A Special Rules About Parties in Claims for Wrongful Interference With Goods

(1) A claimant in a claim for wrongful interference with goods must, in the particulars of claim, state the name and address of every person who, to his knowledge, has or claims an interest in the goods and who is not a party to the claim.

(2) A defendant to a claim for wrongful interference with goods may apply for a direction that another person be made a party to the claim to establish whether the other person—
   (a) has a better right to the goods than the claimant; or
   (b) has a claim which might render the defendant doubly liable under section 7 of the Torts (Interference with Goods) Act 1977.

(3) Where the person referred to in paragraph (2) fails to attend the hearing of the application, or comply with any directions, the court may order that he is deprived of any claim against the defendant in respect of the goods.

(Rule 3.1(3) provides that the court may make an order subject to conditions.)

(4) The application notice must be served on all parties and on the person referred to in paragraph (2).

## II REPRESENTATIVE PARTIES

### 19.6 Representative Parties with Same Interest

(1) Where more than one person has the same interest in a claim—
   (a) the claim may be begun; or
   (b) the court may order that the claim be continued,
   by or against one or more of the persons who have the same interest as representatives of any other persons who have that interest.

(2) The court may direct that a person may not act as a representative.

(3) Any party may apply to the court for an order under paragraph (2).

(4) Unless the court otherwise directs any judgment or order given in a claim in which a party is acting as a representative under this rule—
   (a) is binding on all persons represented in the claim; but
   (b) may only be enforced by or against a person who is not a party to the claim with the permission of the court.

(5) This rule does not apply to a claim to which rule 19.7 applies.

### 19.7 Representation of Interested Persons Who Cannot be Ascertained etc.

(1) This rule applies to claims about—
   (a) the estate of a deceased person;

(b) property subject to a trust; or
(c) the meaning of a document, including a statute.

(2) The court may make an order appointing a person to represent any other person or persons in the claim where the person or persons to be represented—
(a) are unborn;
(b) cannot be found;
(c) cannot easily be ascertained; or
(d) are a class of persons who have the same interest in a claim and—
(i) one or more members of that class are within sub-paragraphs (a), (b) or (c); or
(ii) to appoint a representative would further the overriding objective.

(3) An application for an order under paragraph (2)—
(a) may be made by—
(i) any person who seeks to be appointed under the order; or
(ii) any party to the claim; and
(b) may be made at any time before or after the claim has started.

(4) An application notice for an order under paragraph (2) must be served on—
(a) all parties to the claim, if the claim has started;
(b) the person sought to be appointed, if that person is not the applicant or a party to the claim; and
(c) any other person as directed by the court.

(5) The court's approval is required to settle a claim in which a party is acting as a representative under this rule.

(6) The court may approve a settlement where it is satisfied that the settlement is for the benefit of all the represented persons.

(7) Unless the court otherwise directs, any judgment or order given in a claim in which a party is acting as a representative under this rule—
(a) is binding on all persons represented in the claim; but
(b) may only be enforced by or against a person who is not a party to the claim with the permission of the court.

## 19.7A Representation of Beneficiaries by Trustees etc.

(1) A claim may be brought by or against trustees, executors or administrators in that capacity without adding as parties any persons who have a beneficial interest in the trust or estate ('the beneficiaries').

(2) Any judgment or order given or made in the claim is binding on the beneficiaries unless the court orders otherwise in the same or other proceedings.

## 19.7B Postal Services Act 2000 (c. 26)

(1) An application under section 92 of the Postal Services Act 2000 for permission to bring proceedings in the name of the sender or addressee of a postal packet or his personal representative is made in accordance with Part 8.

(2) A copy of the application notice must be served on the universal service provider and on the person in whose name the applicant seeks to bring the proceedings.

## 19.8 Death

(1) Where a person who had an interest in a claim has died and that person has no personal representative the court may order—
(a) the claim to proceed in the absence of a person representing the estate of the deceased; or
(b) a person to be appointed to represent the estate of the deceased.

(2) Where a defendant against whom a claim could have been brought has died and
(a) a grant of probate or administration has been made, the claim must be brought against the persons who are the personal representatives of the deceased;
(b) a grant of probate or administration has not been made—

(i) the claim must be brought against 'the estate of' the deceased; and
(ii) the claimant must apply to the court for an order appointing a person to represent the estate of the deceased in the claim.

(3) A claim shall be treated as having been brought against 'the estate of' the deceased in accordance with paragraph (2)(b)(i) where—
(a) the claim is brought against the 'personal representatives' of the deceased but a grant of probate or administration has not been made; or
(b) the person against whom the claim was brought was dead when the claim was started.

(4) Before making an order under this rule, the court may direct notice of the application to be given to any other person with an interest in the claim.

(5) Where an order has been made under paragraphs (1) or (2)(b)(ii) any judgment or order made or given in the claim is binding on the estate of the deceased.

## 19.8A Power to Make Judgments Binding on Non-parties

(1) This rule applies to any claim relating to—
(a) the estate of a deceased person;
(b) property subject to a trust; or
(c) the sale of any property.

(2) The court may at any time direct that notice of—
(a) the claim; or
(b) any judgment or order given in the claim,
be served on any person who is not a party but who is or may be affected by it.

(3) An application under this rule—
(a) may be made without notice; and
(b) must be supported by written evidence which includes the reasons why the person to be served should be bound by the judgment in the claim.

(4) Unless the court orders otherwise—
(a) a notice of a claim or of a judgment or order under this rule must be—
(i) in the form required by the practice direction;
(ii) issued by the court; and
(iii) accompanied by a form of acknowledgment of service with any necessary modifications;
(b) a notice of a claim must also be accompanied by—
(i) a copy of the claim form; and
(ii) such other statements of case, witness statements or affidavits as the court may direct; and
(c) a notice of a judgment or order must also be accompanied by a copy of the judgment or order.

(5) If a person served with notice of a claim files an acknowledgment of service of the notice within 14 days he will become a party to the claim.

(6) If a person served with notice of a claim does not acknowledge service of the notice he will be bound by any judgment given in the claim as if he were a party.

(7) If, after service of a notice of a claim on a person, the claim form is amended so as substantially to alter the remedy claimed, the court may direct that a judgment shall not bind that person unless a further notice, together with a copy of the amended claim form, is served on him.

(8) Any person served with a notice of a judgment or order under this rule—
(a) shall be bound by the judgment or order as if he had been a party to the claim; but
(b) may, provided he acknowledges service—
(i) within 28 days after the notice is served on him, apply to the court to set aside or vary the judgment or order; and
(ii) take part in any proceedings relating to the judgment or order.

(9) The following rules of Part 10 (acknowledgment of service) apply—
(a) rule 10.4; and

(b) rule 10.5, subject to the modification that references to the defendant are to be read as references to the person served with the notice.

(10) A notice under this rule is issued on the date entered on the notice by the court.

### 19.9 Derivative Claims

(1) This rule applies where a company, other incorporated body or trade union is alleged to be entitled to claim a remedy and a claim is made by one or more members of the company, body or trade union for it to be given that remedy (a 'derivative claim').

(2) The company, body or trade union for whose benefit a remedy is sought must be a defendant to the claim.

(3) After the claim form has been issued the claimant must apply to the court for permission to continue the claim and may not take any other step in the proceedings except—
- (a) as provided by paragraph (5); or
- (b) where the court gives permission.

(4) An application in accordance with paragraph (3) must be supported by written evidence.

(5) The—
- (a) claim form;
- (b) application notice; and
- (c) written evidence in support of the application,

must be served on the defendant within the period within which the claim form must be served and, in any event, at least 14 days before the court is to deal with the application.

(6) If the court gives the claimant permission to continue the claim, the time within which the defence must be filed is 14 days after the date on which the permission is given or such period as the court may specify.

(7) The court may order the company, body or trade union to indemnify the claimant against any liability in respect of costs incurred in the claim.

## III GROUP LITIGATION

### 19.10 Definition

A Group Litigation Order ('GLO') means an order made under rule 19.11 to provide for the case management of claims which give rise to common or related issues of fact or law (the 'GLO issues').

### 19.11 Group Litigation Order

(1) The court may make a GLO where there are or are likely to be a number of claims giving rise to the GLO issues.

(The practice direction provides the procedure for applying for a GLO.)

(2) A GLO must—
- (a) contain directions about the establishment of a register (the 'group register') on which the claims managed under the GLO will be entered;
- (b) specify the GLO issues which will identify the claims to be managed as a group under the GLO; and
- (c) specify the court (the 'management court') which will manage the claims on the group register.

(3) A GLO may—
- (a) in relation to claims which raise one or more of the GLO issues—
  - (i) direct their transfer to the management court;
  - (ii) order their stay (GL) until further order; and
  - (iii) direct their entry on the group register;
- (b) direct that from a specified date claims which raise one or more of the GLO issues should be started in the management court and entered on the group register; and
- (c) give directions for publicising the GLO.

## 19.12 Effect of the GLO

(1) Where a judgment or order is given or made in a claim on the group register in relation to one or more GLO issues—
  (a) that judgment or order is binding on the parties to all other claims that are on the group register at the time the judgment is given or the order is made unless the court orders otherwise; and
  (b) the court may give directions as to the extent to which that judgment or order is binding on the parties to any claim which is subsequently entered on the group register.
(2) Unless paragraph (3) applies, any party who is adversely affected by a judgment or order which is binding on him may seek permission to appeal the order.
(3) A party to a claim which was entered on the group register after a judgment or order which is binding on him was given or made may not—
  (a) apply for the judgment or order to be set aside(GL), varied or stayed(GL); or
  (b) appeal the judgment or order,
  but may apply to the court for an order that the judgment or order is not binding on him.
(4) Unless the court orders otherwise, disclosure of any document relating to the GLO issues by a party to a claim on the group register is disclosure of that document to all parties to claims—
  (a) on the group register; and
  (b) which are subsequently entered on the group register.

## 19.13 Case Management

Directions given by the management court may include directions—
(a) varying the GLO issues;
(b) providing for one or more claims on the group register to proceed as test claims;
(c) appointing the solicitor of one or more parties to be the lead solicitor for the claimants or defendants;
(d) specifying the details to be included in a statement of case in order to show that the criteria for entry of the claim on the group register have been met;
(e) specifying a date after which no claim may be added to the group register unless the court gives permission; and
(f) for the entry of any particular claim which meets one or more of the GLO issues on the group register.

(Part 3 contains general provisions about the case management powers of the court.)

## 19.14 Removal From the Register

(1) A party to a claim entered on the group register may apply to the management.
(2) If the management court orders the claim to be removed from the register it may give directions about the future management of the claim.

## 19.15 Test Claims

(1) Where a direction has been given for a claim on the group register to proceed as a test claim and that claim is settled, the management court may order that another claim on the group register be substituted as the test claim.
(2) Where an order is made under paragraph (1), any order made in the test claim before the date of substitution is binding on the substituted claim unless the court orders otherwise.

# PD 19 Practice Direction — Addition and Substitution of Parties

This practice direction supplements CPR Part 19.

*A party applying for an amendment will usually be responsible for the costs of and arising from the amendment.*

## Changes of Parties

*General*

1.1 Parties may be removed, added or substituted in existing proceedings either on the court's own initiative or on the application of either an existing party or a person who wishes to become a party.

1.2 The application may be dealt with without a hearing where all the existing parties and the proposed new party are in agreement.

1.3 The application to add or substitute a new party should be supported by evidence setting out the proposed new party's interest in or connection with the claim.

1.4 The application notice should be filed in accordance with rule 23.3 and, unless the application is made under rule 19.2(4),[1] be served in accordance with rule 23.4.

1.5 An order giving permission to amend will, unless the court orders otherwise, be drawn up. It will be served by the court unless the parties wish to serve it or the court orders them to do so.

*Addition or substitution of claimant*

2.1 Where an application is made to the court to add or to substitute a new party to the proceedings as claimant, the party applying must file:

(1) the application notice,

(2) the proposed amended claim form and particulars of claim, and

(3) the signed, written consent of the new claimant to be so added or substituted.

2.2 Where the court makes an order adding or substituting a party as claimant but the signed, written consent of the new claimant has not been filed:

(1) the order, and

(2) the addition or substitution of the new party as claimant,

will not take effect until the signed, written consent of the new claimant is filed.

2.3 Where the court has made an order adding or substituting a new claimant, the court may direct:

(1) a copy of the order to be served on every party to the proceedings and any other person affected by the order,

(2) copies of the statements of case and of documents referred to in any statement of case to be served on the new party,

(3) the party who made the application to file within 14 days an amended claim form and particulars of claim.

*Addition or substitution of defendant*

3.1 The Civil Procedure Rules apply to a new defendant who has been added or substituted as they apply to any other defendant (see in particular the provisions of Parts 9, 10, 11 and 15).

3.2 Where the court has made an order adding or substituting a defendant whether on its own initiative or on an application, the court may direct:

(1) the claimant to file with the court within 14 days (or as ordered) an amended claim form and particulars of claim for the court file,

[1] See rule 19.4(3)(a).

(2) a copy of the order to be served on all parties to the proceedings and any other person affected by it,
(3) the amended claim form and particulars of claim, forms for admitting, defending and acknowledging the claim and copies of the statements of case and any other documents referred to in any statement of case to be served on the new defendant,
(4) unless the court orders otherwise, the amended claim form and particulars of claim to be served on any other defendants.

3.3 A new defendant does not become a party to the proceedings until the amended claim form has been served on him.[2]

*Removal of party*

4 Where the court makes an order for the removal of a party from the proceedings:
(1) the claimant must file with the court an amended claim form and particulars of claim, and
(2) a copy of the order must be served on every party to the proceedings and on any other person affected by the order.

*Transfer of interest or liability*

5.1 Where the interest or liability of an existing party has passed to some other person, application should be made to the court to add or substitute that person.[3]

5.2 The application must be supported by evidence showing the stage the proceedings have reached and what change has occurred to cause the transfer of interest or liability.

(For information about making amendments generally, see PD 17.)

## Human Rights, Joining the Crown

*Section 4 of the Human Rights Act 1998*

6.1 Where a party has included in his statement of case:
(1) a claim for a declaration of incompatibility in accordance with s. 4 of the Human Rights Act 1998, or
(2) an issue for the court to decide which may lead to the court considering making a declaration,

then the court may at any time consider whether notice should be given to the Crown as required by that Act and give directions for the content and service of the notice. The rule [i.e., r. 19.4A] allows a period of 21 days before the court will make the declaration but the court may vary this period of time.

6.2 The court will normally consider the issues and give the directions referred to in para. 6.1 at the case management conference.

6.3 Where a party amends his statement of case to include any matter referred to in para. 6.1, then the court will consider whether notice should be given to the Crown and give directions for the content and service of the notice.

(PD 16 requires a party to include issues under the Human Rights Act 1998 in his statement of case.)

6.4 (1) The notice given under r. 19.4A must be served on the person named in the list published under s. 17 of the Crown Proceedings Act 1947.

(The list, made by the Minister for the Civil Service, is annexed to the practice direction to Part 66.)

(2) The notice will be in the form directed by the court but will normally include the directions given by the court and all the statements of case in the claim. The notice will also be served on all the parties.
(3) The court may require the parties to assist in the preparation of the notice.

[2] *Ketteman v Hansel Properties Ltd* [1987] AC 189, HL.

[3] See rule 19.2(4).

(4) In the circumstances described in the National Assembly for Wales (Transfer of Functions) (No. 2) Order 2000 the notice must also be served on the National Assembly for Wales.

(Section 5(3) of the Human Rights Act 1998 provides that the Crown may give notice that it intends to become a party at any stage in the proceedings once notice has been given.)

6.5 Unless the court orders otherwise, the minister or other person permitted by the Human Rights Act 1998 to be joined as a party must, if he wishes to be joined, give notice of his intention to be joined as a party to the court and every other party. Where the minister has nominated a person to be joined as a party the notice must be accompanied by the written nomination.

(Section 5(2)(a) of the Human Rights Act 1998 permits a person nominated by a minister of the Crown to be joined as a party. The nomination may be signed on behalf of the minister.)

*Section 9 of the Human Rights Act 1998*

6.6 (1) The procedure in paras 6.1 to 6.5 also applies where a claim is made under ss. 7(1)(a) and 9(3) of the Human Rights Act 1998 for damages in respect of a judicial act.

(2) Notice must be given to the Lord Chancellor and should be served on the Treasury Solicitor on his behalf, except where the judicial act is of a court martial when the appropriate person is the Secretary of State for Defence and the notice must be served on the Treasury Solicitor on his behalf.

(3) The notice will also give details of the judicial act, which is the subject of the claim for damages, and of the court or tribunal that made it.

(Section 9(4) of the Human Rights Act 1998 provides that no award of damages may be made against the Crown as provided for in s. 9(3) unless the appropriate person is joined in the proceedings. The appropriate person is the minister responsible for the court concerned or a person or department nominated by him (s. 9(5) of the Act).)

# PD 19B Practice Direction — Group Litigation

This practice direction supplements Section III of CPR Part 19.

## Introduction

1 This practice direction deals with group litigation where the multiple parties are claimants. Section III of Part 19 (group litigation orders) also applies where the multiple parties are defendants. The court will give such directions in such a case as are appropriate.

## Preliminary Steps

2.1 Before applying for a group litigation order ('GLO') the solicitor acting for the proposed applicant should consult the Law Society's Multi-Party Actions Information Service in order to obtain information about other cases giving rise to the proposed GLO issues.

2.2 It will often be convenient for the claimants' solicitors to form a solicitors' group and to choose one of their number to take the lead in applying for the GLO and in litigating the GLO issues. The lead solicitor's role and relationship with the other members of the solicitors' group should be carefully defined in writing and will be subject to any directions given by the court under r. 19.13(c).

2.3 In considering whether to apply for a GLO, the applicant should consider whether any other order would be more appropriate. In particular he should consider whether, in the circumstances of the case, it would be more appropriate for:
(1) the claims to be consolidated; or
(2) the rules in Section II of Part 19 (representative parties) to be used.

## Application for a GLO

3.1 An application for a GLO must be made in accordance with CPR, Part 23, may be made at any time before or after any relevant claims have been issued and may be made either by a claimant or by a defendant.

3.2 The following information should be included in the application notice or in written evidence filed in support of the application:
(1) a summary of the nature of the litigation;
(2) the number, and nature of claims already issued;
(3) the number of parties likely to be involved;
(4) the common issues of fact or law (the 'GLO issues') that are likely to arise in the litigation; and
(5) whether there are any matters that distinguish smaller groups of claims within the wider group.

3.3 A GLO may not be made:
(1) in the Queen's Bench Division, without the consent of the Lord Chief Justice;
(2) in the Chancery Division, without the consent of the Vice-Chancellor; or
(3) in a county court, without the consent of the Head of Civil Justice.

3.4 The court to which the application for a GLO is made will, if minded to make the GLO, send to the Lord Chief Justice, the Vice-Chancellor, or the Head of Civil Justice, as appropriate:
(1) a copy of the application notice;
(2) a copy of any relevant written evidence; and
(3) a written statement as to why a GLO is considered to be desirable.
These steps may be taken either before or after a hearing of the application.

*High Court in London*

3.5 The application for the GLO should be made to the Senior Master in the Queen's Bench Division or the Chief Chancery Master in the Chancery Division. For claims that are proceeding or are likely to proceed in a specialist list, the application should be made to the senior judge of that list.

*High Court outside London*

3.6 Outside London, the application should be made to a presiding judge or a Chancery supervising judge of the circuit in which the district registry which has issued the application notice is situated.

*County courts*

3.7 The application should be made to the designated civil judge for the area in which the county court which has issued the application notice is situated.

3.8 The applicant for a GLO should request the relevant court to refer the application notice to the judge by whom the application will be heard as soon as possible after the application notice has been issued. This is to enable the judge to consider whether to follow the practice set out in para. 3.4 above prior to the hearing of the application.

3.9 The directions under paras 3.5, 3.6 and 3.7 above do not prevent the judges referred to from making arrangements for other judges to hear applications for GLOs when they themselves are unavailable.

## GLO Made by Court of its Own Initiative

4 Subject to obtaining the appropriate consent referred to in para. 3.3 and the procedure set out in para. 3.4, the court may make a GLO of its own initiative.
(Rule 3.3 deals with the procedure that applies when a court proposes to make an order of its own initiative.)

## The GLO

5 Paragraphs 2 and (3) of r. 19.11 set out rules relating to the contents of GLOs.

## The Group Register

6.1 Once a GLO has been made a group register will be established on which will be entered such details as the court may direct of the cases which are to be subject to the GLO.

6.1A A claim must be issued before it can be entered on a group register.

6.2 An application for details of a case to be entered on a group register may be made by any party to the case.

6.3 An order for details of the case to be entered on the group register will not be made unless the case gives rise to at least one of the GLO issues.

(Rule 19.10 defines GLO issues.)

6.4 The court, if it is not satisfied that a case can be conveniently case managed with the other cases on the group register, or if it is satisfied that the entry of the case on the group register would adversely affect the case management of the other cases, may refuse to allow details of the case to be entered on the group register, or order their removal from the register if already entered, although the case gives rise to one or more of the Group issues.

6.5 The group register will normally be maintained by and kept at the court but the court may direct this to be done by the solicitor for one of the parties to a case entered on the register.

6.6 (1) Rules 5.4 (Register of Claims), 5.4B (Supply of documents from court records – a party) and 5.4C (Supply of document from court records – a non-party) apply where the register is maintained by the court. A party to a claim on the group register may request documents relating to any other claim on the group register in accordance with r. 5.4(1) as if he were a party to those proceedings.

(2) Where the register is maintained by a solicitor, any person may inspect the group register during normal business hours and upon giving reasonable notice to the solicitor; the solicitor may charge a fee not exceeding the fee prescribed for a search at the court office.

6.7 In this paragraph, 'the court' means the management court specified in the GLO.

## Allocation to Track

7 Once a GLO has been made and unless the management court directs otherwise:

(1) every claim in a case entered on the group register will be automatically allocated, or reallocated (as the case may be), to the multi-track;

(2) any case management directions that have already been given in any such case otherwise than by the management court will be set aside; and

(3) any hearing date already fixed otherwise than for the purposes of the group litigation will be vacated.

## Managing Judge

8 A judge ('the managing judge') will be appointed for the purpose of the GLO as soon as possible. He will assume overall responsibility for the management of the claims and will generally hear the GLO issues. A master or a district judge may be appointed to deal with procedural matters, which he will do in accordance with any directions given by the managing judge. A costs judge may be appointed and may be invited to attend case management hearings.

## Claims to be Started in Management Court

9.1 The management court may order that as from a specified date all claims that raise one or more of the GLO issues shall be started in the management court.

9.2 Failure to comply with an order made under para. 9.1 will not invalidate the commencement of the claim but the claim should be transferred to the management court and details entered on the group register as soon as possible. Any party to the claim may apply to the management court for an order under r. 19.14 removing the case from the register or, as the case may be, for an order that details of the case be not entered on the register.

## Transfer

10 Where the management court is a county court and a claim raising one or more of the GLO issues is proceeding in the High Court, an order transferring the case to the management court and directing the details of the case to be entered on the group register can only be made in the High Court.

## Publicising the GLO

11 After a GLO has been made, a copy of the GLO should be supplied:

(1) to the Law Society, 113 Chancery Lane, London WC2A 1PL; and

(2) to the Senior Master, Queen's Bench Division, Royal Courts of Justice, Strand, London WC2A 2LL.

## Case Management

12.1 The management court may give case management directions at the time the GLO is made or subsequently. Directions given at a case management hearing will generally be binding on all claims that are subsequently entered on the group register (see r. 19.12(1)).

12.2 Any application to vary the terms of the GLO must be made to the management court.

12.3 The management court may direct that one or more of the claims are to proceed as test claims.

12.4 The management court may give directions about how the costs of resolving common issues or the costs of claims proceeding as test claims are to be borne or shared as between the claimants on the group register.

## Cut-off Dates

13 The management court may specify a date after which no claim may be added to the group register unless the court gives permission. An early cut-off date may be appropriate in the case of 'instant disasters' (such as transport accidents). In the case of consumer claims, and particularly pharmaceutical claims, it may be necessary to delay the ordering of a cut-off date.

## Statements of Case

14.1 The management court may direct that the GLO claimants serve 'group particulars of claim' which set out the various claims of all the claimants on the group register at the time the particulars are filed. Such particulars of claim will usually contain:
(1) general allegations relating to all claims; and
(2) a schedule containing entries relating to each individual claim specifying which of the general allegations are relied on and any specific facts relevant to the claimant.

14.2 The directions given under para. 14.1 should include directions as to whether the group particulars should be verified by a statement or statements of truth and, if so, by whom.

14.3 The specific facts relating to each claimant on the group register may be obtained by the use of a questionnaire. Where this is proposed, the management court should be asked to approve the questionnaire. The management court may direct that the questionnaires completed by individual claimants take the place of the schedule referred to in para. 14.1(2).

14.4 The management court may also give directions about the form that particulars of claim relating to claims which are to be entered on the group register should take.

## The Trial

15.1 The management court may give directions:
(1) for the trial of common issues; and
(2) for the trial of individual issues.

15.2 Common issues and test claims will normally be tried at the management court. Individual issues may be directed to be tried at other courts whose locality is convenient for the parties.

## Costs

16.1 Part 48 contains rules about costs where a GLO has been made.

16.2 Where the court has made an order about costs in relation to any application or hearing which involved both:
(1) one or more of the GLO issues; and
(2) an issue or issues relevant only to individual claims;
and the court has not directed the proportion of the costs that is to relate to common costs and the proportion that is to relate to individual costs in accordance with r. 48.6A(5), the costs judge will make a decision as to the relevant proportions at or before the commencement of the detailed assessment of costs.

# CPR Part 20 Counterclaims and Other Additional Claims



## 20.1 Purpose of this Part

The purpose of this Part is to enable counterclaims and other additional claims to be managed in the most convenient and effective manner.

## 20.2 Scope and Interpretation

(1) This Part applies to—
  (a) a counterclaim by a defendant against the claimant or against the claimant and some other person;
  (b) an additional claim by a defendant against any person (whether or not already a party) for contribution or indemnity or some other remedy; and
  (c) where an additional claim has been made against a person who is not already a party, any additional claim made by that person against any other person (whether or not already a party).

(2) In these Rules—
  (a) 'additional claim' means any claim other than the claim by the claimant against the defendant; and
  (b) unless the context requires otherwise, references to a claimant or defendant include a party bringing or defending an additional claim.

## 20.3 Application of these Rules to Additional Claims

(1) An additional claim shall be treated as if it were a claim for the purposes of these Rules, except as provided by this Part.

(2) The following rules do not apply to additional claims—
  (a) rules 7.5 and 7.6 (time within which a claim form may be served);
  (b) rule 16.3(5) (statement of value where claim to be issued in the High Court); and
  (c) Part 26 (case management—preliminary stage).

(3) Part 12 (default judgment) applies to a counterclaim but not to other additional claims.

(4) Part 14 (admissions) applies to a counterclaim, but only—
  (a) rules 14.1(1) and 14.1(2) (which provide that a party may admit the truth of another party's case in writing); and
  (b) rule 14.3 (admission by notice in writing—application for judgment),

apply to other additional claims.

(Rule 12.3(2) sets out how to obtain judgment in default of defence for a counterclaim against the claimant, and rule 20.11 makes special provision for default judgment for some additional claims.)

## 20.4 Defendant's Counterclaim Against the Claimant

(1) A defendant may make a counterclaim against a claimant by filing particulars of the counterclaim.
(2) A defendant may make a counterclaim against a claimant—
  (a) without the court's permission if he files it with his defence; or
  (b) at any other time with the court's permission.

(Part 15 makes provision for a defence to a claim and applies to a defence to a counterclaim by virtue of rule 20.3.)

(3) Part 10 (acknowledgment of service) does not apply to a claimant who wishes to defend a counterclaim.

## 20.5 Counterclaim Against a Person Other Than the Claimant

(1) A defendant who wishes to counterclaim against a person other than the claimant must apply to the court for an order that that person be added as an additional party.
(2) An application for an order under paragraph (1) may be made without notice unless the court directs otherwise.
(3) Where the court makes an order under paragraph (1), it will give directions as to the management of the case.

## 20.6 Defendant's Additional Claim for Contribution or Indemnity from another Party

(1) A defendant who has filed an acknowledgment of service or a defence may make an additional claim for contribution or indemnity against a person who is already a party to the proceedings by—
  (a) filing a notice containing a statement of the nature and grounds of his additional claim; and
  (b) serving the notice on that party.
(2) A defendant may file and serve a notice under this rule—
  (a) without the court's permission, if he files and serves it—
    (i) with his defence; or
    (ii) if his additional claim for contribution or indemnity is against a party added to the claim later, within 28 days after that party files his defence; or
  (b) at any other time with the court's permission.

## 20.7 Procedure for Making any Other Additional Claim

(1) This rule applies to any additional claim except—
  (a) a counterclaim only against an existing party; and
  (b) a claim for contribution or indemnity made in accordance with rule 20.6.
(2) An additional claim is made when the court issues the appropriate claim form.

(Rule 7.2(2) provides that a claim form is issued on the date entered on the form by the court.)

(3) A defendant may make an additional claim—
  (a) without the court's permission if the additional claim is issued before or at the same time as he files his defence;
  (b) at any other time with the court's permission.

(Rule 15.4 sets out the period for filing a defence.)

(4) Particulars of an additional claim must be contained in or served with the additional claim.
(5) An application for permission to make an additional claim may be made without notice, unless the court directs otherwise.

## 20.8 Service of Claim Form

(1) Where an additional claim may be made without the court's permission, any claim form must—
  (a) in the case of a counterclaim against an additional party only, be served on every other party when a copy of the defence is served;
  (b) in the case of any other additional claim, be served on the person against whom it is made within 14 days after the date on which the additional claim is issued by the court.

(2) Paragraph (1) does not apply to a claim for contribution or indemnity made in accordance with rule 20.6.

(3) Where the court gives permission to make an additional claim it will at the same time give directions as to its service.

## 20.9 Matters Relevant to Question of Whether an Additional Claim Should be Separate from the Claim

(1) This rule applies where the court is considering whether to—
  (a) permit an additional claim to be made;
  (b) dismiss an additional claim; or
  (c) require an additional claim to be dealt with separately from the claim by the claimant against the defendant.

(Rule 3.1(2)(e) and (j) deal respectively with the court's power to order that part of proceedings be dealt with as separate proceedings and to decide the order in which issues are to be tried.)

(2) The matters to which the court may have regard include—
  (a) the connection between the additional claim and the claim made by the claimant against the defendant;
  (b) whether the additional claimant is seeking substantially the same remedy which some other party is claiming from him; and
  (c) whether the additional claimant wants the court to decide any question connected with the subject matter of the proceedings—
    (i) not only between existing parties but also between existing parties and a person not already a party; or
    (ii) against an existing party not only in a capacity in which he is already a party but also in some further capacity.

## 20.10 Effect of Service of an Additional Claim

(1) A person on whom an additional claim is served becomes a party to the proceedings if he is not a party already.

(2) When an additional claim is served on an existing party for the purpose of requiring the court to decide a question against that party in a further capacity, that party also becomes a party in the further capacity specified in the additional claim.

## 20.11 Special Provisions Relating to Default Judgment on an Additional Claim Other Than a Counterclaim or a Contribution or Indemnity Notice

(1) This rule applies if—
  (a) the additional claim is not—
    (i) a counterclaim; or
    (ii) a claim by a defendant for contribution or indemnity against another defendant under rule 20.6; and
  (b) the party against whom an additional claim is made fails to file an acknowledgment of service or defence in respect of the additional claim.

(2) The party against whom the additional claim is made—
  (a) is deemed to admit the additional claim, and is bound by any judgment or decision

in the proceedings in so far as it is relevant to any matter arising in the additional claim;

(b) subject to paragraph (3), if default judgment under Part 12 is given against the additional claimant, the additional claimant may obtain judgment in respect of the additional claim by filing a request in the relevant practice form.

(3) An additional claimant may not enter judgment under paragraph (2)(b) without the court's permission if—

(a) he has not satisfied the default judgment which has been given against him; or

(b) he wishes to obtain judgment for any remedy other than a contribution or indemnity.

(4) An application for the court's permission under paragraph (3) may be made without notice unless the court directs otherwise.

(5) The court may at any time set aside or vary a judgment entered under paragraph (2)(b).

## 20.12 Procedural Steps on Service of an Additional Claim Form on a Non-party

(1) Where an additional claim form is served on a person who is not already a party it must be accompanied by—

(a) a form for defending the claim;

(b) a form for admitting the claim;

(c) a form for acknowledging service; and

(d) a copy of—

(i) every statement of case which has already been served in the proceedings; and

(ii) such other documents as the court may direct.

(2) A copy of the additional claim form must be served on every existing party.

## 20.13 Case Management Where a Defence to an Additional Claim is Filed

(1) Where a defence is filed to an additional claim the court must consider the future conduct of the proceedings and give appropriate directions.

(2) In giving directions under paragraph (1) the court must ensure that, so far as practicable, the original claim and all additional claims are managed together.

(CCR Order 42, in Schedule 2, makes provision for an additional claim against the Crown where the Crown is not a party.)

# PD 20 Practice Direction – Counterclaims and Other Additional Claims

This Practice Direction supplements CPR Part 20.

An additional claim is any claim other than the claim by the claimant against the defendant.

Claims under this Part were formerly known as 'Part 20 claims'. As a result of the amendments to Part 20, introduced by the Civil Procedure (Amendment No. 4) Rules 2005, they are now called 'additional claims'.

However, they are described as 'Part 20 claims' on a number of court forms. For the present, some of those forms will continue to refer to Part 20 claims. These references should be construed as being additional claims under this Part. Any reference to a Part 20 claimant or a Part 20 defendant means a claimant or defendant in an additional claim under this Part.

## Cases Where Court's Permission to Make an Additional Claim is Required

1.1 Rules 20.4(2)(b), 20.5(1) and 20.7(3)(b) set out the circumstances in which the court's permission will be needed for making an additional claim.

1.2 Where an application is made for permission to make an additional claim the application notice should be filed together with a copy of the proposed additional claim.

## Applications for Permission to Issue an Additional Claim

2.1 An application for permission to make an additional claim must be supported by evidence stating:

(1) the stage which the proceedings have reached,

(2) the nature of the additional claim to be made or details of the question or issue which needs to be decided,

(3) a summary of the facts on which the additional claim is based, and

(4) the name and address of any proposed additional party.

(For further information regarding evidence see the practice direction which supplements Part 32.)

2.2 Where delay has been a factor contributing to the need to apply for permission to make an additional claim an explanation of the delay should be given in evidence.

2.3 Where possible the applicant should provide a timetable of the proceedings to date.

2.4 Rules 20.5(2) and 20.7(5) allow applications to be made to the court without notice unless the court directs otherwise.

## General

3. The Civil Procedure Rules apply generally to additional claims as if they were claims. Parties should be aware that the provisions relating to failure to respond to a claim will apply.

## Statement of Truth

4.1 The contents of an additional claim should be verified by a statement of truth. Part 22 requires a statement of case to be verified by a statement of truth.

4.2 The form of the statement of truth should be as required by paragraph 2.1 of the practice direction supplementing Part 22.

4.3 Attention is drawn to rule 32.14 which sets out the consequences of verifying a statement of case containing a false statement without an honest belief in its truth.

## Case Management Where There is a Defence to an Additional Claim

5.1 Where the defendant to an additional claim files a defence, other than to a counterclaim, the court will arrange a hearing to consider case management of the additional claim. This will normally be at the same time as a case management hearing for the original claim and any other additional claims.

5.2 The court will give notice of the hearing to each party likely to be affected by any order made at the hearing.

5.3 At the hearing the court may:
(1) treat the hearing as a summary judgment hearing,
(2) order that the additional claim be dismissed,
(3) give directions about the way any claim, question or issue set out in or arising from the additional claim should be dealt with,
(4) give directions as to the part, if any, the additional defendant will take at the trial of the claim,
(5) give directions about the extent to which the additional defendant is to be bound by any judgment or decision to be made in the claim.

5.4 The court may make any of the orders in 5.3(1) to (5) either before or after any judgment in the claim has been entered by the claimant against the defendant.

## Form of Counterclaim

6.1 Where a defendant to a claim serves a counterclaim, the defence and counterclaim should normally form one document with the counterclaim following on from the defence.

6.2 Where a claimant serves a reply and a defence to counterclaim, the reply and the defence to counterclaim should normally form one document with the defence to counterclaim following on from the reply.

## Titles of Proceedings Where There are Additional Claims

7.1 Paragraph 4 of the practice direction supplementing Part 7 contains directions regarding the title to proceedings.

7.2 Where there are additional claims which add parties, the title to the proceedings should comprise a list of all parties describing each by giving them a single identification. Subject to paragraph 7.11, this identification should be used throughout.

7.3 Claimants and defendants in the original claim should always be referred to as such in the title to the proceedings, even if they subsequently acquire an additional procedural status.

7.4 Additional parties should be referred to in the title to the proceedings in accordance with the order in which they are joined to the proceedings, for example 'Third Party' or 'Fourth Party', whatever their actual procedural status.
Examples:
(a) If the defendant makes an additional claim against a single additional party, the additional party should be referred to in the title as 'Third Party'.
(b) If the defendant makes separate additional claims against two additional parties, the additional parties should be referred to in the title as 'Third Party' and 'Fourth Party'.
(c) If the defendant makes a counterclaim against the claimant and an additional party, the claimant should remain as 'Claimant' and the additional party should be referred to in the title as 'Third Party'.
(d) If the Third Party in example (b) makes an additional claim against a further additional party, that additional party should be referred to in the title as 'Fifth Party'.

7.5 If an additional claim is brought against more than one party jointly, they should be referred to in the title to the proceedings as, for example, 'First Named Third Party' and 'Second Named Third Party'.

7.6 In group litigation, the court should give directions about the designation of parties.

7.7 All parties should co-operate to ensure that two parties each making additional claims do not attribute the same nominal status to more than one party.

7.8 In proceedings with numerous parties, the court will if necessary give directions as to the preparation and updating of a list of parties giving their roles in the claim and each additional claim.

7.9 If an additional party ceases to be a party to the proceedings, for example because the claim against that party is discontinued or dismissed, all other additional parties should retain their existing nominal status.

7.10 In proceedings where there are additional parties, the description of all statements of case or other similar documents should clearly identify the nature of the document with reference to each relevant party.
Examples:
(e) In example (a), the defendant's additional claim should be headed 'Defendant's Additional Claim against Third Party' and the Third Party's defence to it should be headed 'Third Party's Defence to Defendant's Additional Claim'.
(f) In example (c), the defendant's counterclaim should be headed 'Defendant's Counterclaim against Claimant and Third Party' and the Third Party's defence to it should be headed 'Third Party's Defence to Defendant's Counterclaim'.

7.11 In proceedings where there are Fourth or subsequent parties, additional parties should be referred to in the text of statements of case or other similar documents by name, suitably abbreviated if appropriate. If parties have similar names, suitable distinguishing abbreviations should be used.

# CPR Part 21 Children and Patients



## 21.1 Scope of this Part

(1) This Part—
 (a) contains special provisions which apply in proceedings involving children and patients; and
 (b) sets out how a person becomes a litigation friend.
(2) In this Part—
 (a) 'child' means a person under 18; and
 (b) 'patient' means a person who by reason of mental disorder within the meaning of the Mental Health Act 1983 is incapable of managing and administering his property and affairs.

(Rule 6.6 contains provisions about the service of documents on children and patients.)
(Rule 48.5 deals with costs where money is payable by or to a child or patient.)

## 21.2 Requirement for Litigation Friend in Proceedings by or Against Children and Patients

(1) A patient must have a litigation friend to conduct proceedings on his behalf.
(2) A child must have a litigation friend to conduct proceedings on his behalf unless the court makes an order under paragraph (3).
(3) The court may make an order permitting the child to conduct proceedings without a litigation friend.
(4) An application for an order under paragraph (3)—
 (a) may be made by the child;
 (b) if the child already has a litigation friend, must be made on notice to the litigation friend; and
 (c) if the child has no litigation friend, may be made without notice.
(5) Where—
 (a) the court has made an order under paragraph (3); and
 (b) it subsequently appears to the court that it is desirable for a litigation friend to conduct the proceedings on behalf of the child,

the court may appoint a person to be the child's litigation friend.

## 21.3 Stage of Proceedings at Which a Litigation Friend Becomes Necessary

(1) This rule does not apply where the court has made an order under rule 21.2(3).

(2) A person may not, without the permission of the court—
   (a) make an application against a child or patient before proceedings have started; or
   (b) take any step in proceedings except—
      (i) issuing and serving a claim form; or
      (ii) applying for the appointment of a litigation friend under rule 21.6,
   until the child or patient has a litigation friend.
(3) If a party becomes a patient during proceedings, no party may take any step in the proceedings without the permission of the court until the patient has a litigation friend.
(4) Any step taken before a child or patient has a litigation friend shall be of no effect unless the court otherwise orders.

## 21.4 Who May be a Litigation Friend Without a Court Order

(1) This rule does not apply if the court has appointed a person to be a litigation friend.
(2) A person authorised under Part VII of the Mental Health Act 1983 to conduct legal proceedings in the name of a patient or on his behalf is entitled to be the litigation friend of the patient in any proceedings to which his authority extends.
(3) If nobody has been appointed by the court or, in the case of a patient, authorised under Part VII, a person may act as a litigation friend if he—
   (a) can fairly and competently conduct proceedings on behalf of the child or patient;
   (b) has no interest adverse to that of the child or patient; and
   (c) where the child or patient is a claimant, undertakes to pay any costs which the child or patient may be ordered to pay in relation to the proceedings, subject to any right he may have to be repaid from the assets of the child or patient.

## 21.5 How a Person Becomes a Litigation Friend Without a Court Order

(1) If the court has not appointed a litigation friend, a person who wishes to act as a litigation friend must follow the procedure set out in this rule.
(2) A person authorised under Part VII of the Mental Health Act 1983 must file an official copy(GL) of the order or other document which constitutes his authorisation to act.
(3) Any other person must file a certificate of suitability stating that he satisfies the conditions specified in rule 21.4(3).
(4) A person who is to act as a litigation friend for a claimant must file—
   (a) the authorisation; or
   (b) the certificate of suitability,
   at the time when the claim is made.
(5) A person who is to act as a litigation friend for a defendant must file—
   (a) the authorisation; or
   (b) the certificate of suitability,
   at the time when he first takes a step in the proceedings on behalf of the defendant.
(6) The litigation friend must—
   (a) serve the certificate of suitability on every person on whom, in accordance with rule 6.6 (service on parent, guardian etc.), the claim form should be served; and
   (b) file a certificate of service when he files the certificate of suitability.

(Rule 6.10 sets out the details to be contained in a certificate of service.)

## 21.6 How a Person Becomes a Litigation Friend by Court Order

(1) The court may make an order appointing a litigation friend.
(2) An application for an order appointing a litigation friend may be made by—
   (a) a person who wishes to be the litigation friend; or
   (b) a party.
(3) Where—
   (a) a person makes a claim against a child or patient;
   (b) the child or patient has no litigation friend;

(c) the court has not made an order under rule 21.2(3) (order that a child can act without a litigation friend); and
(d) either—
(i) someone who is not entitled to be a litigation friend files a defence; or
(ii) the claimant wishes to take some step in the proceedings,

the claimant must apply to the court for an order appointing a litigation friend for the child or patient.

(4) An application for an order appointing a litigation friend must be supported by evidence.
(5) The court may not appoint a litigation friend under this rule unless it is satisfied that the person to be appointed complies with the conditions specified in rule 21.4(3).

### 21.7 Court's Power to Change Litigation Friend and to Prevent Person Acting as Litigation Friend

(1) The court may—
(a) direct that a person may not act as a litigation friend;
(b) terminate a litigation friend's appointment;
(c) appoint a new litigation friend in substitution for an existing one.
(2) An application for an order under paragraph (1) must be supported by evidence.
(3) The court may not appoint a litigation friend under this rule unless it is satisfied that the person to be appointed complies with the conditions specified in rule 21.4(3).

### 21.8 Appointment of Litigation Friend by Court Order—Supplementary

(1) An application for an order under rule 21.6 or 21.7 must be served on every person on whom, in accordance with rule 6.6 (service on parent, guardian etc.), the claim form should be served.
(2) Where an application for an order under rule 21.6 is in respect of a patient, the application must also be served on the patient unless the court orders otherwise.
(3) An application for an order under rule 21.7 must also be served on—
(a) the person who is the litigation friend, or who is purporting to act as the litigation friend, when the application is made; and
(b) the person who it is proposed should be the litigation friend, if he is not the applicant.
(4) On an application for an order under rule 21.6 or 21.7, the court may appoint the person proposed or any other person who complies with the conditions specified in rule 21.4(3).

### 21.9 Procedure Where Appointment of Litigation Friend Ceases

(1) When a child who is not a patient reaches the age of 18, a litigation friend's appointment ceases.
(2) When a party ceases to be a patient, the litigation friend's appointment continues until it is ended by a court order.
(3) An application for an order under paragraph (2) may be made by—
(a) the former patient;
(b) the litigation friend; or
(c) a party.
(4) The child or patient in respect of whom the appointment to act has ceased must serve notice on the other parties—
(a) stating that the appointment of his litigation friend to act has ceased;
(b) giving his address for service; and
(c) stating whether or not he intends to carry on the proceedings.
(5) If he does not do so within 28 days after the day on which the appointment of the litigation friend ceases the court may, on application, strike out(GL) any claim or defence brought by him.

(6) The liability of a litigation friend for costs continues until—
  (a) the person in respect of whom his appointment to act has ceased serves the notice referred to in paragraph (4); or
  (b) the litigation friend serves notice on the parties that his appointment to act has ceased.

## 21.10 Compromise etc. by or on Behalf of Child or Patient

(1) Where a claim is made—
  (a) by or on behalf of a child or patient; or
  (b) against a child or patient,

  no settlement, compromise or payment and no acceptance of money paid into court shall be valid, so far as it relates to the claim by, on behalf of or against the child or patient, without the approval of the court.

(2) Where—
  (a) before proceedings in which a claim is made by or on behalf of, or against a child or patient (whether alone or with any other person) are begun, an agreement is reached for the settlement of the claim; and
  (b) the sole purpose of proceedings on that claim is to obtain the approval of the court to a settlement or compromise of the claim,

  the claim must—
    (i) be made using the procedure set out in Part 8 (alternative procedure for claims); and
    (ii) include a request to the court for approval of the settlement or compromise.

(3) In proceedings to which Section II of Part 45 applies, the court shall not make an order for detailed assessment of the costs payable to the child or patient but shall assess the costs in the manner set out in that Section.

(Rule 48.5 contains provisions about costs where money is payable to a child or patient.)

## 21.11 Control of Money Recovered by or on Behalf of Child or Patient

(1) Where in any proceedings—
  (a) money is recovered by or on behalf of or for the benefit of a child or patient; or
  (b) money paid into court is accepted by or on behalf of a child or patient, the money shall be dealt with in accordance with directions given by the court under this rule and not otherwise.

(2) Directions given under this rule may provide that the money shall be wholly or partly paid into court and invested or otherwise dealt with.

## 21.11A Expenses Incurred by a Litigation Friend

(1) In proceedings to which rule 21.11 applies, a litigation friend who incurs expenses on behalf of a child or patient in any proceedings is entitled to recover the amount paid or payable out of any money recovered or paid into court to the extent that it—
  (a) has been reasonably incurred; and
  (b) is reasonable in amount.

(2) Expenses may include all or part of—
  (a) an insurance premium, as defined by rule 43.2(1)(m); or
  (b) interest on a loan taken out to pay an insurance premium or other recoverable disbursement.

(3) No application may be made under this rule for expenses that—
  (a) are of a type that may be recoverable on an assessment of costs payable by or out of money belonging to a child or patient; but
  (b) are disallowed in whole or in part on such an assessment.

(Expenses which are also 'costs' as defined in rule 43.2(1)(a) are dealt with under rule 48.5(2).)

(4) In deciding whether the expense was reasonably incurred and reasonable in amount, the

court must have regard to all the circumstances of the case including the factors set out in rule 44.5(3).

(5) When the court is considering the factors to be taken into account in assessing the reasonableness of expenses incurred by the litigation friend on behalf of a child or patient, it will have regard to the facts and circumstances as they reasonably appeared to the litigation friend or child's or patient's legal representative when the expense was incurred.

(6) Where the claim is settled or compromised, or judgment is given, on terms that an amount not exceeding £5,000 is paid to the child or patient, the total amount the litigation friend may recover under paragraph (1) of this rule shall not exceed 25% of the sum so agreed or awarded, unless the court directs otherwise. Such total amount shall not exceed 50% of the sum so agreed or awarded.

## 21.12 Appointment of Guardian of Child's Estate

(1) The court may appoint the Official Solicitor to be a guardian of a child's estate where—
  - (a) money is paid into court on behalf of the child in accordance with directions given under rule 21.11 (control of money received by a child or patient);
  - (b) the Criminal Injuries Compensation Board or the Criminal Injuries Compensation Authority notifies the court that it has made or intends to make an award to the child;
  - (c) a court or tribunal outside England and Wales notifies the court that it has ordered or intends to order that money be paid to the child;
  - (d) the child is absolutely entitled to the proceeds of a pension fund; or
  - (e) in any other case, such an appointment seems desirable to the court.

(2) The court may not appoint the Official Solicitor under this rule unless—
  - (a) the persons with parental responsibility (within the meaning of section 3 of the Children Act 1989) agree; or
  - (b) the court considers that their agreement can be dispensed with.

(3) The Official Solicitor's appointment may continue only until the child reaches 18.

# PD 21 Practice Direction — Children and Patients

This practice direction supplements CPR Part 21.

## General

1.1 In this practice direction 'child' means a person under 18 years old and 'patient' means a person who by reason of mental disorder within the meaning of the Mental Health Act 1983 is incapable of managing and administering his property and affairs.[1]

1.2 A patient must bring or defend proceedings by a litigation friend (see paragraph 2 below for the definition of a litigation friend).

1.3 In the proceedings referred to in paragraph 1.2 above the patient should be referred to in the title as 'A.B. (by C.D. his litigation friend)'.

1.4 A child must bring or defend proceedings by a litigation friend unless the court has made an order permitting the child to do so on his own behalf.[2]

1.5 Where:
(1) the child has a litigation friend, the child should be referred to in the title to proceedings as 'A.B. (a child by C.D. his litigation friend)', and
(2) the child is conducting proceedings on his own behalf, the child should be referred to in the title as 'A.B. (a child)'.

1.6 The approval of the court must be obtained if a settlement of a claim by or against a child or patient is to be valid.[3] A settlement includes an agreement on a sum to be apportioned to a dependent child under the Fatal Accidents Act 1976.

1.7 The approval of the court must also be obtained before making a voluntary interim payment to a child or patient.

(Rule 39.2(3) provides for a hearing or part of a hearing to be in private.)

## The Litigation Friend

2.1 It is the duty of a litigation friend fairly and competently to conduct proceedings on behalf of a child or patient. He must have no interest in the proceedings adverse to that of the child or patient and all steps and decisions he takes in the proceedings must be taken for the benefit of the child or patient.

2.2 A person may become a litigation friend:
(1) of a child:
(a) without a court order under the provisions of rule 21.5, or
(b) by a court order under rule 21.6, and
(2) of a patient:
(a) by authorisation under Part VII of the Mental Health Act 1983, or
(b) by a court order under rule 21.6.

2.3 In order to become a litigation friend without a court order the person who wishes to act as litigation friend must:
(1) if he wishes to act on behalf of a patient, file an official copy of the order or other document which constitutes the authorisation referred to in paragraph 2.2(2)(a) above, or
(2) if he wishes to act on behalf of a child, or on behalf of a patient without the authorisation referred to in (1) above, file a certificate of suitability:[4]
(a) stating that he consents to act,

---

[1] See rule 21.1(2).
[2] See rule 21.2(3).
[3] See rule 21.10.
[4] See rule 21.5(3).

(b) stating that he knows or believes that the [claimant] [defendant] is a [child] [patient],
(c) in the case of a patient, stating the grounds of his belief and if his belief is based upon medical opinion attaching any relevant document to the certificate,
(d) stating that he can fairly and competently conduct proceedings on behalf of the child or patient and has no interest adverse to that of the child or patient,
(e) where the child or patient is a claimant, undertaking to pay any costs which the child or patient may be ordered to pay in relation to the proceedings, subject to any right he may have to be repaid from the assets of the child or patient, and
(f) which he has signed in verification of its contents.

2.4 The litigation friend must serve a certificate of suitability:[5]
(1) in the case of a child (who is not also a patient) on one of the child's parents or guardians or if there is no parent or guardian, on the person with whom the child resides or in whose care the child is, and
(2) in the case of a patient on the person authorised under Part VII of the Mental Health Act 1983 to conduct proceedings on behalf of the patient or if there is no person so authorised, on the person with whom the patient resides or in whose care the patient is.

2.4A The litigation friend is not required to serve the documents referred to in paragraph 2.3(2)(c) when he serves a certificate of suitability on the person to be served under paragraph 2.4.

2.5 The litigation friend must file either the certificate of suitability together with a certificate of service[6] of it, or the authorisation referred to in paragraph 2.31(1) above:
(1) where the litigation friend is acting on behalf of a claimant, when the claim form is issued, and
(2) where the litigation friend is acting on behalf of a defendant, when he first takes a step in the action.

## Application for a Court Order Appointing a Litigation Friend

3.1 Rule 21.6 sets out who may apply for an order appointing a litigation friend.

3.2 An application should be made in accordance with Part 23 and must be supported by evidence.[7]

3.3 The application notice must be served:
(1) on the persons referred to in paragraph 2.4 above, and
(2) where the application is in respect of a patient, on the patient unless the court orders otherwise.

3.4 The evidence in support must satisfy the court that the proposed litigation friend:
(1) consents to act,
(2) can fairly and competently conduct proceedings on behalf of the child or patient,
(3) has no interest adverse to that of the child or patient, and
(4) where the child or patient is a claimant, undertakes to pay any costs which the child or patient may be ordered to pay in relation to the proceedings, subject to any right he may have to be repaid from the assets of the child or patient.

3.5 Where a claimant wishes to take a step in proceedings against a child or patient who does not have a litigation friend he must apply to the court for an order appointing a litigation friend.

3.6 The proposed litigation friend must satisfy the conditions in paragraph 3.4(1), (2) and

[5] See rule 21.5(6) and rule 6.9 (service).
[6] See rule 6.10 for the certificate of service.
[7] See rule 21.6(4).

(3) above and may be one of the persons referred to in paragraph 2.4 above where appropriate, or otherwise may be the Official Solicitor. Where it is sought to appoint the Official Solicitor, provision should be made for payment of his charges.

## Change of Litigation Friend and Prevention of Person Acting as Litigation Friend

4.1 Rule 21.7(1) states that the court may:
- (1) direct that a person may not act as a litigation friend,
- (2) terminate a litigation friend's appointment,
- (3) substitute a new litigation friend for an existing one.

4.2 Where an application is made for an order under rule 21.7(1), the application notice must set out the reasons for seeking it. The application must be supported by evidence.

4.3 If the order sought is the substitution of a new litigation friend for an existing one, the evidence must satisfy the court of the matters set out in paragraph 3.4 above.

4.4 The application notice must be served:
- (1) on the persons referred to in paragraph 2.4 above, and
- (2) on the litigation friend or person purporting to act as litigation friend.

## Procedure Where the Need for a Litigation Friend Has Come to an End

5.1 Rule 21.9 deals with the situation where the need for a litigation friend comes to an end during the proceedings because either:
- (1) a child who is not also a patient reaches the age of 18 (full age) during the proceedings, or
- (2) a patient ceases to be a patient (recovers).

5.2 A child on reaching full age must serve on the other parties to the proceedings and file with the court a notice:
- (1) stating that he has reached full age,
- (2) stating that his litigation friend's appointment has ceased,[8]
- (3) giving an address for service,[9] and
- (4) stating whether or not he intends to carry on with or continue to defend the proceedings.

5.3 If the notice states that the child intends to carry on with or continue to defend the proceedings he shall subsequently be described in the proceedings as:
'A.B. (formerly a child but now of full age)'

5.4 Whether or not a child having reached full age serves a notice in accordance with rule 21.9(4)(a) and paragraph 5.2(2) above, a litigation friend may at any time after the child has reached full age serve a notice on the other parties that his appointment has ceased.

5.5 The liability of a litigation friend for costs continues until a notice that his appointment to act has ceased is served on the other parties.[10]

5.6 Where a patient recovers, an application under rule 21.9(3) must be made for an order under rule 21.9(2) that the litigation friend's appointment has ceased.

5.7 The application must be supported by the following evidence:
- (1) a medical report indicating that the patient has recovered and that he is capable of managing and administering his property and affairs,
- (2) where the patient's affairs were under the control of the Court of Protection, a copy of the order or notice discharging the receiver, and
- (3) if the application is made by the patient, a statement whether or not he intends to carry on with or continue to defend the proceedings.

5.8 An order under rule 21.9(2) must be served on the other parties to the proceedings. The patient must file with the court a notice;

[8] Rule 21.9(4)(a).

[9] See rule 6.5.

[10] Rule 21.9(6).

(1) stating that his litigation friend's appointment has ceased,
(2) giving an address for service,[11] and
(3) stating whether or not he intends to carry on with or continue to defend the proceedings.

## Settlement or Compromise by or on Behalf of a Child or Patient Prior to the Start of Proceedings

6.1 Where a claim by or on behalf of a child or patient has been dealt with by agreement prior to the start of proceedings and only the approval of the court to the agreement is sought, the claim:
(1) must be made using the Part 8 procedure,
(2) must include a request for approval of the settlement or compromise, and
(3) subject to paragraph 6.4 in addition to the details of the claim, must set out the terms of the settlement or compromise or have attached to it a draft consent order in form N292.

6.2 In order to approve the settlement or compromise, the information concerning the claim that the court will require will include:
(1) whether and to what extent the defendant admits liability,
(2) the age and occupation (if any) of the child or patient,
(3) the litigation friend's approval of the proposed settlement or compromise, and
(4) in a personal injury case arising from an accident:
(a) the circumstances of the accident,
(b) any medical reports,
(c) where appropriate, a schedule of any past and future expenses and losses claimed and any other relevant information relating to personal injury as set out in PD 16, and
(d) where considerations of liability are raised:
(i) any evidence or police reports in any criminal proceedings or in an inquest, and
(ii) details of any prosecution brought.

6.3 (1) An opinion on the merits of the settlement or compromise given by counsel or solicitor acting for the child or patient should, except in very clear cases, be obtained.
(2) A copy of the opinion and, unless the instructions on which it was given are sufficiently set out in it, a copy of the instructions, must also be supplied to the court.
(3) A copy or record of any financial advice must also be supplied to the court.

6.4 Where in any personal injury case a claim for damages for future pecuniary loss is settled, the provisions in paragraphs 6.4A and 6.4B must in addition be complied with.

6.5 Applications for the approval of a settlement or compromise will normally be heard by a master or district judge.

(For information about structured settlements see PD 40C.)
(For information about provisional damages claims see Part 41 and PD 41.)

## Settlement or Compromise by or on Behalf of a Child or Patient after Proceedings have been Commenced

6.6 Where in any personal injury case a claim for damages for future pecuniary loss, by or on behalf of a child or patient, is dealt with by agreement after proceedings have been commenced, an application should be made for the court's approval of the agreement.

6.7 The court must be satisfied that the parties have considered whether the damages should wholly or partly take the form of periodical payments.

[11] See rule 6.5.

6.8 Where the settlement includes provision for periodical payments, an application under paragraph 6.6 must—
(1) set out the terms of the settlement or compromise; or
(2) have attached to it a draft consent order,
which must include the requirements of rules 41.8 and 41.9 as appropriate.

6.9 The court must be supplied with—
(1) an opinion on the merits of the settlement or compromise given by counsel or solicitor acting for the child or patient, except in very clear cases; and
(2) a copy or record of any financial advice.

## Apportionment Under the Fatal Accidents Act 1976

7.1 A judgment on or settlement in respect of a claim under the Fatal Accidents Act 1976 must be apportioned between the persons by or on whose behalf the claim has been brought.

7.2 Where a claim is brought on behalf of a dependent child or children, the money apportioned to any child must be invested on his behalf in accordance with rules 21.10 and 21.11 and paragraphs 8 and 9 below.

7.3 In order to approve an apportionment of money to a dependent child, the court will require the following information:
(1) the matters set out in paragraph 6.2(1),(2) above, and
(2) in respect of the deceased:
(a) where death was caused by an accident, the matters set out in paragraph 6.2(3)(a),(b) and (c) above, and
(b) his future loss of earnings, and
(3) the extent and nature of the dependency.

## Control of Money Recovered by or on Behalf of a Child or Patient

8.1 Money recovered or paid into court on behalf of or for the benefit of a child or patient shall be dealt with in accordance with directions of the court under rule 21.11.

8.2 The court:
(1) may direct the money to be paid into the High Court for investment,
(2) may also direct that certain sums be paid direct to the child or patient, his litigation friend or his legal representative[12] for the immediate benefit of the child or patient or for expenses incurred on his behalf, and
(3) may direct the applications in respect of the investment of the money be transferred to a local district registry.

8.3 The master or district judge will consider the general aims to be achieved for the money in court (the fund) by investment and will give directions as to the type of investment.

8.4 Where a child is also a patient, and likely to remain so on reaching full age, his fund should be administered as a patient's fund.

8.5 Where a child or patient is legally aided the fund will be subject to a first charge under s. 16 of the Legal Aid Act 1988 (the legal aid charge) and an order for the investment of money on the child or patient's behalf must contain a direction to that effect.

## Expenses Incurred by Litigation Friend

8A.1 A litigation friend may make a claim for expenses under rule 21.11A(1)—
(a) where the court has ordered an assessment of costs under rule 48.5(2), at the detailed assessment hearing;
(b) where the litigation friend's expenses are not of a type which would be recoverable as costs on an assessment of costs between the parties, to the master or district

[12] See rule 2.3 for a definition of legal representative.

judge at the hearing to approve the settlement or compromise under Part 21 (the master or district judge may adjourn the matter to the costs judge); or

(c) where an assessment of costs under Part 48.5(2) is not required, and no approval under Part 21 is necessary, by a Part 23 application supported by a witness statement to a costs judge or district judge as appropriate.

8A.2 In all circumstances, the litigation friend shall support a claim for expenses by filing a witness statement setting out—

(i) the nature and amount of the expense;

(ii) the reason the expense was incurred.

## Guardian's Accounts

9 Paragraph 8 of PD 40 deals with the approval of the accounts of a guardian of assets of a child.

## Investment on Behalf of a Child

10.1 At the hearing of the application for the approval of the agreement the litigation friend or his legal representative should provide a CFO form 320 (request for investment) for completion by the master or district judge.

10.2 On receipt of that form in the Court Funds Office the investment managers of the Public Trust Office will make the appropriate investment.

10.3 Where an award of damages for a child is made at trial the trial judge may direct:

(1) the money to be paid into court and placed in the special investment account, and

(2) the litigation friend to make an application to a master or district judge for further investment directions.

10.4 If the money to be invested is very small the court may order it to be paid direct to the litigation friend to be put into a building society account (or similar) for the child's use.

10.5 If the money is invested in court it must be paid out to the child when he reaches full age.

## Investment on Behalf of a Patient

11.1 The Court of Protection is responsible for protecting the property of patients and is given extensive powers to do so under the Mental Health Act 1983. Fees are charged for the administration of funds by the Court of Protection and these should be provided for in any settlement.

11.2 Where the sum to be administered is:

(1) over £30,000, the order approving the settlement will contain a direction to the litigation friend to apply to the Court of Protection for the appointment of a receiver, after which the fund will be transferred to the Court of Protection,

(2) under £20,000, it may be retained in court and invested in the same way as the fund of a child, or

(3) in intermediate cases the advice of the Master of the Court of Protection should be sought.

11.3 A form of order transferring the fund to the Court of Protection is set out in form N292.

11.4 In order for the Court Funds Office to release a fund which is subject to the legal aid charge to the Court of Protection the litigation friend or his legal representative should provide the appropriate area office of the Legal Aid Board with an undertaking in respect of a sum to cover their costs, following which the area office will advise the Court Funds Office in writing of that sum, enabling them to transfer the balance to the Court of Protection on receipt of a CFO form 200 payment schedule authorised by the court.

11.5 The CFO form 200 should be completed and presented to the court where the settlement or trial took place for authorisation, subject to paragraphs 11.6 and 11.7 below.

11.6 Where the settlement took place in the Royal Courts of Justice the CFO form 200 should be completed and presented for authorisation:
(1) on behalf of a child, in the Masters' Secretary's Office, Room E214, and
(2) on behalf of a patient, in the Action Department, Room E15.

11.7 Where the trial took place in the Royal Courts of Justice the CFO form 200 is completed and authorised by the court officer.

## Payment Out of Funds in Court

12.1 Applications to a master or district judge:
(1) for payment out of money from the fund for the benefit of the child, or
(2) to vary an investment strategy,
may be dealt with without a hearing unless the court directs otherwise.

12.2 When the child reaches full age, his fund in court:
(1) where it is a sum of money will be paid out to him, and
(2) where it is in the form of investments other than money (for example shares or unit trusts), will be transferred into his name.

12.3 An application for payment out of funds being administered by the Court of Protection must be made to the Court of Protection.

(For further information on payments out of court, see the Practice Direction supplementing Part 37.)

# CPR Part 22 Statements of Truth



## 22.1 Documents to be Verified by a Statement of Truth

(1) The following documents must be verified by a statement of truth—
   (a) a statement of case;
   (b) a response complying with an order under rule 18.1 to provide further information;
   (c) a witness statement;
   (d) an acknowledgment of service in a claim begun by way of the Part 8 procedure;
   (e) a certificate stating the reasons for bringing a possession claim or a landlord and tenant claim in the High Court in accordance with rules 55.3(2) and 56.2(2); and
   (f) a certificate of service; and
   (g) any other document where a rule or practice direction requires.
(2) Where a statement of case is amended, the amendments must be verified by a statement of truth unless the court orders otherwise.
(Part 17 provides for amendments to statements of case.)
(3) If an applicant wishes to rely on matters set out in his application notice as evidence, the application notice must be verified by a statement of truth.
(4) Subject to paragraph (5), a statement of truth is a statement that—
   (a) the party putting forward the document; or
   (b) in the case of a witness statement, the maker of the witness statement,
   believes the facts stated in the document are true; or
   (c) in the case of a certificate of service, the person who signs the certificate.
(5) If a party is conducting proceedings with a litigation friend, the statement of truth in—
   (a) a statement of case;
   (b) a response; or
   (c) an application notice,
   is a statement that the litigation friend believes the facts stated in the document being verified are true.
(6) The statement of truth must be signed by—
   (a) in the case of a statement of case, a response or an application—
      (i) the party or litigation friend; or
      (ii) the legal representative on behalf of the party or litigation friend; and
   (b) in the case of a witness statement, the maker of the statement.
(7) A statement of truth which is not contained in the document which it verifies, must clearly identify that document.
(8) A statement of truth in a statement of case may be made by—
   (a) a person who is not a party; or
   (b) by two parties jointly,
   where this is permitted by a relevant practice direction.

## 22.2 Failure to Verify a Statement of Case

(1) If a party fails to verify his statement of case by a statement of truth—
   (a) the statement of case shall remain effective unless struck out; but
   (b) the party may not rely on the statement of case as evidence of any of the matters set out in it.

(2) The court may strike out[(GL)] a statement of case which is not verified by a statement of truth.
(3) Any party may apply for an order under paragraph (2).

## 22.3 Failure to Verify a Witness Statement

If the maker of a witness statement fails to verify the witness statement by a statement of truth the court may direct that it shall not be admissible as evidence.

## 22.4 Power of the Court to Require a Document to be Verified

(1) The court may order a person who has failed to verify a document in accordance with rule 22.1 to verify the document.
(2) Any party may apply for an order under paragraph (1).

# PD 22 Practice Direction — Statements of Truth

This practice direction supplements CPR Part 22.

## Documents to be Verified by a Statement of Truth

1.1 Rule 22.1(1) sets out the documents which must be verified by a statement of truth. The documents include:
  (1) a statement of case,
  (2) a response complying with an order under rule 18.1 to provide further information,
  (3) a witness statement,
  (4) an acknowledgment of service in a claim begun by the Part 8 procedure,
  (5) a certificate stating the reasons for bringing a possession claim or a landlord and tenant claim in the High Court in accordance with rr. 55.3(2) and 56.2(2),
  (6) a certificate of service.

1.2 If an applicant wishes to rely on matters set out in his application notice as evidence, the application notice must be verified by a statement of truth.[1]

1.3 An expert's report should also be verified by a statement of truth. For the form of the statement of truth verifying an expert's report (which differs from that set out below) see PD 35.

1.4 In addition, the following documents must be verified by a statement of truth:
  (1) an application notice for:
    (a) a third party debt order (r. 72.3),
    (b) a hardship payment order (r. 72.7), or
    (c) a charging order (r. 73.3).
  (2) a notice of objections to an account being taken by the court, unless verified by an affidavit or witness statement;
  (3) a schedule or counter-schedule of expenses and losses in a personal injury claim, and any amendments to such a schedule or counter-schedule, whether or not they are contained in a statement of case.

1.5 The statement of truth may be contained in the document it verifies or it may be in a separate document served subsequently, in which case it must identify the document to which it relates.

1.6 Where the form to be used includes a jurat for the content to be verified by an affidavit then a statement of truth is not required in addition.

## Form of the Statement of Truth

2.1 The form of the statement of truth verifying a statement of case, a response, an application notice or a notice of objections should be as follows:
  '[I believe] [the (*claimant or as may be*) believes] that the facts stated in this [*name document being verified*] are true.'

2.2 The form of the statement of truth verifying a witness statement should be as follows:
  'I believe that the facts stated in this witness statement are true.'

2.3 Where the statement of truth is contained in a separate document, the document containing the statement of truth must be headed with the title of the proceedings and the claim number. The document being verified should be identified in the statement of truth as follows:
  (1) claim form: 'the claim form issued on [*date*]',
  (2) particulars of claim: 'the particulars of claim issued on [*date*]',
  (3) statement of case: 'the [*defence or as may be*] served on the [*name of party*] on [*date*]',

[1] See rule 22.1(3).

(4) application notice: 'the application notice issued on [*date*] for [*set out the remedy sought*]',
(5) witness statement: 'the witness statement filed on [*date*] or served on [*party*] on [*date*]'.

## Who May Sign the Statement of Truth

3.1 In a statement of case, a response or an application notice, the statement of truth must be signed by:
(1) the party or his litigation friend,[2] or
(2) the legal representative[3] of the party or litigation friend.

3.2 A statement of truth verifying a witness statement must be signed by the witness.

3.3 A statement of truth verifying a notice of objections to an account must be signed by the objecting party or his legal representative.

3.4 Where a document is to be verified on behalf of a company or other corporation, subject to paragraph 3.7 below, the statement of truth must be signed by a person holding a senior position[4] in the company or corporation. That person must state the office or position he holds.

3.5 Each of the following persons is a person holding a senior position:
(1) in respect of a registered company or corporation, a director, the treasurer, secretary, chief executive, manager or other officer of the company or corporation, and
(2) in respect of a corporation which is not a registered company, in addition to those persons set out in (1), the mayor, chairman, president or town clerk or other similar officer of the corporation.

3.6 Where the document is to be verified on behalf of a partnership, those who may sign the statement of truth are:
(1) any of the partners, or
(2) a person having the control or management of the partnership business.

3.6A An insurer or the Motor Insurers' Bureau may sign a statement of truth in a statement of case on behalf of a party where the insurer or the Motor Insurers' Bureau has a financial interest in the result of proceedings brought wholly or partially by or against that party.

3.6B If insurers are conducting proceedings on behalf of many claimants or defendants a statement of truth in a statement of case may be signed by a senior person responsible for the case at a lead insurer, but:
(1) the person signing must specify the capacity in which he signs;
(2) the statement of truth must be a statement that the lead insurer believes that the facts stated in the document are true; and
(3) the court may order that a statement of truth also be signed by one or more of the parties.

3.7 Where a party is legally represented, the legal representative may sign the statement of truth on his behalf. The statement signed by the legal representative will refer to the client's belief, not his own. In signing he must state the capacity in which he signs and the name of his firm where appropriate.

3.8 Where a legal representative has signed a statement of truth, his signature will be taken by the court as his statement:
(1) that the client on whose behalf he has signed had authorised him to do so,
(2) that before signing he had explained to the client that in signing the statement of truth he would be confirming the client's belief that the facts stated in the document were true, and

[2] See Part 21 (children and patients).
[3] See rule 2.3 for the definition of legal representative.
[4] See rule 6.4(4).

(3) that before signing he had informed the client of the possible consequences to the client if it should subsequently appear that the client did not have an honest belief in the truth of those facts (see rule 32.14).

3.9 The individual who signs a statement of truth must print his full name clearly beneath his signature.

3.10 A legal representative who signs a statement of truth must sign in his own name and not that of his firm or employer.

3.11 The following are examples of the possible application of this practice direction describing who may sign a statement of truth verifying statements in documents other than a witness statement. These are only examples and not an indication of how a court might apply the practice direction to a specific situation.

| | |
|---|---|
| Managing agent | An agent who manages property or investments for the party cannot sign a statement of truth. It must be signed by the party or by the legal representative of the party. |
| Trusts | Where some or all of the trustees comprise a single party one, some or all of the trustees comprising the party may sign a statement of truth. The legal representative of the trustees may sign it. |
| Insurers and the Motor Insurers' Bureau | If an insurer has a financial interest in a claim involving its insured then, if the insured is the party, the insurer may sign a statement of truth in a statement of case for the insured party. Paragraphs 3.4 and 3.5 apply to the insurer if it is a company. The claims manager employed by the insurer responsible for handling the insurance claim or managing the staff handling the claim may sign the statement of truth for the insurer (see next example). The position for the Motor Insurers' Bureau is similar. |
| Companies | Paragraphs 3.4 and 3.5 apply. The word manager will be construed in the context of the phrase 'a person holding a senior position' which it is used to define. The court will consider the size of the company and the size and nature of the claim. It would expect the manager signing the statement of truth to have personal knowledge of the content of the document or to be responsible for managing those who have that knowledge of the content. A small company may not have a manager, apart from the directors, who holds a senior position. A large company will have many such managers. In a larger company with specialist claims, insurance or legal departments the statement may be signed by the manager of such a department if he or she is responsible for handling the claim or managing the staff handling it. |
| In-house legal representatives | Legal representative is defined in rule 2.3(1). A legal representative employed by a party may sign a statement of truth. However a person who is not a solicitor, barrister or other authorised litigator, but who is employed by the company and is managed by such a person, is not employed by that person and so cannot sign a statement of truth. (This is unlike the employee of a solicitor in private practice who would come within the definition of legal representative.) However such a person may be a manager and able to sign the statement on behalf of the company in that capacity. |

## Inability of Persons to Read or Sign Documents to be Verified by a Statement of Truth

3A.1 Where a document containing a statement of truth is to be signed by a person who is unable to read or sign the document, it must contain a certificate made by an authorised person.

3A.2 An authorised person is a person able to administer oaths and take affidavits but need not be independent of the parties or their representatives.

3A.3 The authorised person must certify:

(1) that the document has been read to the person signing it;
(2) that that person appeared to understand it and approved its content as accurate;
(3) that the declaration of truth has been read to that person;
(4) that that person appeared to understand the declaration and the consequences of making a false declaration; and
(5) that that person signed or made his mark in the presence of the authorised person.

3A.4 The form of the certificate is set out at Annex 1 to this practice direction.

## Consequences of Failure to Verify

4.1 If a statement of case is not verified by a statement of truth, the statement of case will remain effective unless it is struck out,[5] but a party may not rely on the contents of a statement of case as evidence until it has been verified by a statement of truth.

4.2 Any party may apply to the court for an order that unless within such period as the court may specify the statement of case is verified by the service of a statement of truth, the statement of case will be struck out.

4.3 The usual order for the costs of an application referred to in paragraph 4.2 will be that the costs be paid by the party who had failed to verify in any event and forthwith.

## Penalty

5 Attention is drawn to rule 32.14 which sets out the consequences of verifying a statement of case containing a false statement without an honest belief in its truth, and to the procedures set out in PD 32, para. 28.

## Annex 1

Certificate to be used where a person is unable to read or sign a document to be verified by a statement of truth:

I certify that I [*name and address of authorised person*] have read over the contents of this document and the declaration of truth to the person signing the document [*if there are exhibits, add* 'and explained the nature and effect of the exhibits referred to in it'] who appeared to understand (a) the document and approved its content as accurate and (b) the declaration of truth and the consequences of making a false declaration, and made his mark in my presence.

[5] See rule 22.2(1).

# CPR Part 23 General Rules About Applications for Court Orders



## 23.1 Meaning of 'Application Notice' and 'Respondent'

In this Part—

'application notice' means a document in which the applicant states his intention to seek a court order; and

'respondent' means—

(a) the person against whom the order is sought; and

(b) such other person as the court may direct.

## 23.2 Where to Make an Application

(1) The general rule is that an application must be made to the court where the claim was started.

(2) If a claim has been transferred to another court since it was started, an application must be made to the court to which the claim has been transferred.

(3) If the parties have been notified of a fixed date for the trial, an application must be made to the court where the trial is to take place.

(4) If an application is made before a claim has been started, it must be made to the court where it is likely that the claim to which the application relates will be started unless there is good reason to make the application to a different court.

(5) If an application is made after proceedings to enforce judgment have begun, it must be made to any court which is dealing with the enforcement of the judgment unless any rule or practice direction provides otherwise.

## 23.3 Application Notice to be Filed

(1) The general rule is that an applicant must file an application notice.

(2) An applicant may make an application without filing an application notice if—

(a) this is permitted by a rule or practice direction; or

(b) the court dispenses with the requirement for an application notice.

## 23.4 Notice of an Application

(1) The general rule is that a copy of the application notice must be served on each respondent.

(2) An application may be made without serving a copy of the application notice if this is permitted by—

(a) a rule;

(b) a practice direction; or
(c) a court order.

(Rule 23.7 deals with service of a copy of the application notice.)

## 23.5 Time When an Application is Made

Where an application must be made within a specified time, it is so made if the application notice is received by the court within that time.

## 23.6 What an Application Notice Must Include

An application notice must state—
(a) what order the applicant is seeking; and
(b) briefly, why the applicant is seeking the order.

(Part 22 requires an application notice to be verified by a statement of truth if the applicant wishes to rely on matters set out in his application notice as evidence.)

## 23.7 Service of a Copy of an Application Notice

(1) A copy of the application notice—
  (a) must be served as soon as practicable after it is filed; and
  (b) except where another time limit is specified in these Rules or a practice direction, must in any event be served at least 3 days before the court is to deal with the application.
(2) If a copy of the application notice is to be served by the court, the applicant must, when he files the application notice, file a copy of any written evidence in support.
(3) When a copy of an application notice is served it must be accompanied by—
  (a) a copy of any written evidence in support; and
  (b) a copy of any draft order which the applicant has attached to his application.
(4) If—
  (a) an application notice is served; but
  (b) the period of notice is shorter than the period required by these Rules or a practice direction, the court may direct that, in the circumstances of the case, sufficient notice has been given and hear the application.
(5) This rule does not require written evidence—
  (a) to be filed if it has already been filed; or
  (b) to be served on a party on whom it has already been served.

(Part 6 contains the general rules about service of documents including who must serve a copy of the application notice.)

## 23.8 Applications Which May be Dealt With Without a Hearing

The court may deal with an application without a hearing if—
(a) the parties agree as to the terms of the order sought;
(b) the parties agree that the court should dispose of the application without a hearing, or
(c) the court does not consider that a hearing would be appropriate.

## 23.9 Service of Application Where Application Made Without Notice

(1) This rule applies where the court has disposed of an application which it permitted to be made without service of a copy of the application notice.
(2) Where the court makes an order, whether granting or dismissing the application, a copy of the application notice and any evidence in support must, unless the court orders otherwise, be served with the order on any party or other person—
  (a) against whom the order was made; and
  (b) against whom the order was sought.
(3) The order must contain a statement of the right to make an application to set aside[(GL)] or vary the order under rule 23.10.

## 23.10 Application to Set Aside or Vary Order Made Without Notice

(1) A person who was not served with a copy of the application notice before an order was made under rule 23.9, may apply to have the order set aside(GL) or varied.
(2) An application under this rule must be made within 7 days after the date on which the order was served on the person making the application.

## 23.11 Power of the Court to Proceed in the Absence of a Party

(1) Where the applicant or any respondent fails to attend the hearing of an application, the court may proceed in his absence.
(2) Where—
 (a) the applicant or any respondent fails to attend the hearing of an application; and
 (b) the court makes an order at the hearing,
 the court may, on application or of its own initiative, re-list the application.

(Part 40 deals with service of orders.)

## 23.12 Dismissal of Totally Without Merit Applications

If the court dismisses an application and it considers that the application (including an application for permission to appeal or for permission to apply for judicial review) is totally without merit—
(a) the court's order must record that fact; and
(b) the court must at the same time consider whether it is appropriate to make a civil restraint order.

# PD 23 Practice Direction — Applications

This practice direction supplements CPR Part 23.

## Reference to a Judge

1 A master or district judge may refer to a judge any matter which he thinks should properly be decided by a judge, and the judge may either dispose of the matter or refer it back to the master or district judge.

## Application Notices

2.1 An application notice must, in addition to the matters set out in r. 23.6, be signed and include:
(1) the title of the claim,
(2) the reference number of the claim,
(3) the full name of the applicant,
(4) where the applicant is not already a party, his address for service, including a postcode. Postcode information may be obtained from <http://www.royalmail.com> or the Royal Mail Address Management Guide, and
(5) either a request for a hearing or a request that the application be dealt with without a hearing.
(Form N244 may be used.)

2.2 On receipt of an application notice containing a request for a hearing the court will notify the applicant of the time and date for the hearing of the application.

2.3 On receipt of an application notice containing a request that the application be dealt with without a hearing, the application notice will be sent to a master or district judge so that he may decide whether the application is suitable for consideration without a hearing.

2.4 Where the master or district judge agrees that the application is suitable for consideration without a hearing, the court will so inform the applicant and the respondent and may give directions for the filing of evidence. (Rules 23.9 and 23.10 enable a party to apply for an order made without a hearing to be set aside or varied.)

2.5 Where the master or district judge does not agree that the application is suitable for consideration without a hearing, the court will notify the applicant and the respondent of the time, date and place for the hearing of the application and may at the same time give directions as to the filing of evidence.

2.6 If the application is intended to be made to a judge, the application notice should so state. In that case, paragraphs 2.3, 2.4 and 2.5 will apply as though references to the master or district judge were references to a judge.

2.7 Every application should be made as soon as it becomes apparent that it is necessary or desirable to make it.

2.8 Applications should wherever possible be made so that they can be considered at any other hearing for which a date has already been fixed or for which a date is about to be fixed. This is particularly so in relation to case management conferences, allocation and listing hearings and pre-trial reviews fixed by the court.

2.9 The parties must anticipate that at any hearing the court may wish to review the conduct of the case as a whole and give any necessary case management directions. They should be ready to assist the court in doing so and to answer questions the court may ask for this purpose.

2.10 Where a date for a hearing has been fixed and a party wishes to make an application at that hearing but he does not have sufficient time to serve an application notice he should inform the other party and the court (if possible in writing) as soon as he can of the nature of the application and the reason for it. He should then make the application orally at the hearing.

## Applications Without Service of Application Notice

3 An application may be made without serving an application notice only:
(1) where there is exceptional urgency,
(2) where the overriding objective is best furthered by doing so,
(3) by consent of all parties,
(4) with the permission of the court,
(5) where para. 2.10 above applies, or
(6) where a court order, rule or practice direction permits.

## Giving Notice of an Application

4.1 Unless the court otherwise directs or para. 3 of this practice direction applies the application notice must be served as soon as practicable after it has been issued and, if there is to be a hearing, at least three clear days before the hearing date (r. 23.7(1)(b)).

4.2 Where an application notice should be served but there is not sufficient time to do so, informal notification of the application should be given unless the circumstances of the application require secrecy.

## Pre-action Applications

5 All applications made before a claim is commenced should be made under Part 23. Attention is drawn in particular to r. 23.2(4).

## TELEPHONE HEARINGS

## Interpretation

6.1 In this paragraph—
(a) 'designated legal representative' means the applicant's legal representative (if any), or the legal representative of such other party as the court directs to arrange the telephone hearing; and
(b) 'telephone conference enabled court' means—
(i) a district registry of the High Court; or
(ii) a county court,
in which telephone conferencing facilities are available.

## When a hearing is to be conducted by telephone

6.2 Subject to paragraph 6.3, at a telephone conference enabled court the following hearings will be conducted by telephone unless the court otherwise orders—
(a) allocation hearings;
(b) listing hearings; and
(c) interim applications, case management conferences and pre-trial reviews with a time estimate of less than one hour.

6.3 Paragraph 6.2 does not apply where—
(a) the hearing is of an application made without notice to the other party;
(b) all the parties are unrepresented; or
(c) more than four parties wish to make representations at the hearing (for this purpose where two or more parties are represented by the same person, they are to be treated as one party).

6.4 A request for a direction that a hearing under paragraph 6.2 should not be conducted by telephone—
(a) must be made at least 7 days before the hearing or such shorter time as the court may permit; and
(b) may be made by letter,

and the court shall determine such request without requiring the attendance of the parties.

6.5 The court may order that an application, or part of an application, to which paragraph 6.2 does not apply be dealt with by a telephone hearing. The court may make such order—

(a) of its own initiative; or

(b) at the request of the parties.

6.6 The applicant should indicate on his application notice if he seeks a court order under paragraph 6.5. Where he has not done so but nevertheless wishes to seek an order, the request should be made as early as possible.

6.7 An order under paragraph 6.5 will not normally be made unless every party entitled to be given notice of the application and to be heard at the hearing has consented to the order.

6.8 If the court makes an order under paragraph 6.5 it will give any directions necessary for the telephone hearing.

## Conduct of the telephone hearing

6.9 No party, or representative of a party, to an application being heard by telephone may attend the judge in person while the application is being heard unless every other party to the application has agreed that he may do so.

6.10 If an application is to be heard by telephone the following directions will apply, subject to any direction to the contrary—

(1) The designated legal representative is responsible for arranging the telephone conference for precisely the time fixed by the court. The telecommunications provider used must be one on the approved panel of service providers (see Her Majesty's Courts Service website at <http://www.hmcourts-service.gov.uk>).

(2) The designated legal representative must tell the operator the telephone numbers of all those participating in the conference call and the sequence in which they are to be called.

(3) It is the responsibility of the designated legal representative to ascertain from all the other parties whether they have instructed counsel and, if so, the identity of counsel, and whether the legal representative and counsel will be on the same or different telephone numbers.

(4) The sequence in which they are to be called will be—

(a) the designated legal representative and (if on a different number) his counsel;

(b) the legal representative (and counsel) for all other parties; and

(c) the judge.

(5) Each speaker is to remain on the line after being called by the operator setting up the conference call. The call shall be connected at least ten minutes before the time fixed for the hearing.

(6) When the judge has been connected the designated legal representative (or his counsel) will introduce the parties in the usual way.

(7) If the use of a 'speakerphone' by any party causes the judge or any other party any difficulty in hearing what is said the judge may require that party to use a hand held telephone.

(8) The telephone charges debited to the account of the party initiating the conference call will be treated as part of the costs of the application.

## Documents

6.11 The designated legal representative must file and serve a case summary and draft order no later than 4 p.m. on the last working day before the hearing—

(a) if the claim has been allocated to the multi-track; and

(b) in any other case, if the court so directs.

6.12 Where a party seeks to rely on any other document at the hearing, he must file and serve the document no later than 4 p.m. on the last working day before the hearing.

## Videoconferencing

7 Where the parties to a matter wish to use videoconferencing facilities, and those facilities are available in the relevant court, they should apply to the master or district judge for directions.

(Paragraph 29 and Annex 3 of Practice Direction 32 provide guidance on the use of videoconferencing in the civil courts.)

## Note of Proceedings

8 The procedural judge should keep, either by way of a note or a tape recording, brief details of all proceedings before him, including the dates of the proceedings and a short statement of the decision taken at each hearing.

## Evidence

9.1 The requirement for evidence in certain types of applications is set out in some of the rules and practice directions. Where there is no specific requirement to provide evidence it should be borne in mind that, as a practical matter, the court will often need to be satisfied by evidence of the facts that are relied on in support of or for opposing the application.

9.2 The court may give directions for the filing of evidence in support of or opposing a particular application. The court may also give directions for the filing of evidence in relation to any hearing that it fixes on its own initiative. The directions may specify the form that evidence is to take and when it is to be served.

9.3 Where it is intended to rely on evidence which is not contained in the application itself, the evidence, if it has not already been served, should be served with the application.

9.4 Where a respondent to an application wishes to rely on evidence which has not yet been served he should serve it as soon as possible and in any event in accordance with any directions the court may have given.

9.5 If it is necessary for the applicant to serve any evidence in reply it should be served as soon as possible and in any event in accordance with any directions the court may have given.

9.6 Evidence must be filed with the court as well as served on the parties. Exhibits should not be filed unless the court otherwise directs.

9.7 The contents of an application notice may be used as evidence (otherwise than at trial) provided the contents have been verified by a statement of truth.[1]

## Consent Orders

10.1 Rule 40.6 sets out the circumstances where an agreed judgment or order may be entered and sealed.

10.2 Where all parties affected by an order have written to the court consenting to the making of the order a draft of which has been filed with the court, the court will treat the draft as having been signed in accordance with r. 40.6(7).

10.3 Where a consent order must be made by a judge (i.e. r. 40.6(2) does not apply) the order must be drawn so that the judge's name and judicial title can be inserted.

10.4 The parties to an application for a consent order must ensure that they provide the court with any material it needs to be satisfied that it is appropriate to make the order. Subject to any rule or practice direction a letter will generally be acceptable for this purpose.

10.5 Where a judgment or order has been agreed in respect of an application or claim where a hearing date has been fixed, the parties must inform the court immediately. (Note that parties are reminded that under rr. 28.4 and 29.5 the case management timetable cannot be varied by written agreement of the parties.)

[1] See Part 22.

## Other Applications Considered Without a Hearing

11.1 Where r. 23.8(b) applies the parties should so inform the court in writing and each should confirm that all evidence and other material on which he relies has been disclosed to the other parties to the application.

11.2 Where r. 23.8(c) applies the court will treat the application as if it were proposing to make an order on its own initiative.

## Applications to Stay Claim Where Related Criminal Proceedings

11A.1 An application for the stay of civil proceedings pending the determination of related criminal proceedings may be made by any party to the civil proceedings or by the prosecutor or any defendant in the criminal proceedings.

11A.2 Every party to the civil proceedings must, unless he is the applicant, be made a respondent to the application.

11A.3 The evidence in support of the application must contain an estimate of the expected duration of the stay and must identify the respects in which the continuance of the civil proceedings may prejudice the criminal trial.

11A.4 In order to make an application under para. 11A.1, it is not necessary for the prosecutor or defendant in the criminal proceedings to be joined as a party to the civil proceedings.

## Miscellaneous

12.1 Except in the most simple application the applicant should bring to any hearing a draft of the order sought. If the case is proceeding in the Royal Courts of Justice and the order is unusually long or complex it should also be supplied on disk for use by the court office.

12.2 Where r. 23.11 applies, the power to re-list the application in r. 23.11(2) is in addition to any other powers of the court with regard to the order (for example, to set aside, vary, discharge or suspend the order).

## Costs

13.1 Attention is drawn to PD 43–48 and, in particular, to the court's power to make a summary assessment of costs.

13.2 Attention is also drawn to r. 44.13(1) which provides that if an order makes no mention of costs, none are payable in respect of the proceedings to which it relates.

# PD 23B Practice Direction — Applications under Particular Statutes

## Applications under Part III of the Family Law Reform Act 1969 for use of Scientific Tests to determine Parentage

1.1 In this section—
- (1) 'the Act' means the Family Law Reform Act 1969;
- (2) 'direction' means a direction under section 20(1) of the Act made in any proceedings in which a person's parentage falls to be determined;
- (3) 'responsible adult' means a person having care and control of a person to whom paragraph 1.2 of this Practice Direction applies;
- (4) 'samples' means bodily samples within the meaning of section 25 of the Act; and
- (5) 'tests' means scientific tests within the meaning of section 25 of the Act.

1.2 Where an application is made for a direction in respect of a person who is either—
- (a) under 16; or
- (b) suffering from a mental disorder within the meaning of the Mental Heath Act 1983 and is incapable of understanding the nature and process of the tests,

the application notice must state the name and address of the responsible adult.

1.3 Unless the court orders otherwise—
- (1) the court will serve a copy of the application notice on every party to the proceedings other than the applicant; and
- (2) the applicant must serve a copy of the application notice personally on any other person who would be directed to give samples and, where paragraph 1.2 applies, on the responsible adult.

1.4 Unless the court orders otherwise, where the court gives a direction—
- (1) the court will serve a copy of the direction on every party to the proceedings;
- (2) the applicant must serve a copy of the direction personally on any other person directed to give samples and, where paragraph 1.2 applies, on the responsible adult; and
- (3) further consideration of the proceedings shall be adjourned until the court receives a report of the tests carried out or samples taken.

1.5 When the court receives the report of the tests carried out or samples taken, the court officer shall send a copy of the report to—
- (1) every party to the proceedings;
- (2) the responsible adult where paragraph 1.2 applies; and
- (3) every other person directed to give samples.

## Applications in Proceedings under Section 55 of the National Debt Act 1870

2.1 Where a claim is brought under section 55 of the National Debt Act 1870, the claimant must apply to the court for directions about giving notice of the claim.

2.2 The court may—
- (a) direct that notice of the proceedings shall be given by advertisement or by such other method as appropriate; or
- (b) dispense with notice.

# CPR Part 24 Summary Judgment



## 24.1 Scope of this Part

This Part sets out a procedure by which the court may decide a claim or a particular issue without a trial.

(Part 53 makes special provision about summary disposal of defamation claims in accordance with the Defamation Act 1996.)

## 24.2 Grounds for Summary Judgment

The court may give summary judgment against a claimant or defendant on the whole of a claim or on a particular issue if—

(a) it considers that—
 (i) that claimant has no real prospect of succeeding on the claim or issue; or
 (ii) that defendant has no real prospect of successfully defending the claim or issue; and
(b) there is no other compelling reason why the case or issue should be disposed of at a trial.

(Rule 3.4 makes provision for the court to strike out(GL) a statement of case or part of a statement of case if it appears that it discloses no reasonable grounds for bringing or defending a claim.)

## 24.3 Types of Proceedings in Which Summary Judgment is Available

(1) The court may give summary judgment against a claimant in any type of proceedings.
(2) The court may give summary judgment against a defendant in any type of proceedings except—
 (a) proceedings for possession of residential premises against—
  (i) a mortgagor; or
  (ii) a tenant or person holding over after the end of his tenancy, whose occupancy is protected within the meaning of the Rent Act 1977, or the Housing Act 1988; and
 (b) proceedings for an admiralty claim *in rem*.

## 24.4 Procedure

(1) A claimant may not apply for summary judgment until the defendant against whom the application is made has filed—
 (a) an acknowledgment of service; or
 (b) a defence,
 unless—
  (i) the court gives permission; or
  (ii) a practice direction provides otherwise.

(Rule 10.3 sets out the period for filing an acknowledgment of service and rule 15.4 the period for filing a defence.)

(1A) In civil proceedings against the Crown, as defined in rule 66.1(2), a claimant may not apply for summary judgment until after expiry of the period for filing a defence specified in rule 15.4.
(2) If a claimant applies for summary judgment before a defendant against whom the

application is made has filed a defence, that defendant need not file a defence before the hearing.

(3) Where a summary judgment hearing is fixed, the respondent (or the parties where the hearing is fixed of the court's own initiative) must be given at least 14 days' notice of—
  (a) the date fixed for the hearing; and
  (b) the issues which it is proposed that the court will decide at the hearing.

(4) A practice direction may provide for a different period of notice to be given.

(Part 23 contains the general rules about how to make an application.)
(Rule 3.3 applies where the court exercises its powers of its own initiative.)

## 24.5 Evidence for the Purposes of a Summary Judgment Hearing

(1) If the respondent to an application for summary judgment wishes to rely on written evidence at the hearing, he must—
  (a) file the written evidence; and
  (b) serve copies on every other party to the application,
  at least 7 days before the summary judgment hearing.

(2) If the applicant wishes to rely on written evidence in reply, he must—
  (a) file the written evidence; and
  (b) serve a copy on the respondent,
  at least 3 days before the summary judgment hearing.

(3) Where a summary judgment hearing is fixed by the court of its own initiative—
  (a) any party who wishes to rely on written evidence at the hearing must—
    (i) file the written evidence; and
    (ii) unless the court orders otherwise, serve copies on every other party to the proceedings,
    at least 7 days before the date of the hearing;
  (b) any party who wishes to rely on written evidence at the hearing in reply to any other party's written evidence must—
    (i) file the written evidence in reply; and
    (ii) unless the court orders otherwise serve copies on every other party to the proceedings, at least 3 days before the date of the hearing.

(4) This rule does not require written evidence—
  (a) to be filed if it has already been filed; or
  (b) to be served on a party on whom it has already been served.

## 24.6 Court's Powers When it Determines a Summary Judgment Application

When the court determines a summary judgment application it may—
(a) give directions as to the filing and service of a defence;
(b) give further directions about the management of the case.

(Rule 3.1(3) provides that the court may attach conditions when it makes an order.)

# PD 24 Practice Direction — The Summary Disposal of Claims

This practice direction supplements CPR Part 24.

## Applications for Summary Judgment Under Part 24

1.1 Attention is drawn to Part 24 itself and to:
Part 3, in particular rule 3.1(3) and (5),
Part 22,
Part 23, in particular rule 23.6,
Part 32, in particular rule 32.6(2).

1.2 In this paragraph, where the context so admits, the word 'claim' includes:
(1) a part of a claim, and
(2) an issue on which the claim in whole or part depends.

1.3 An application for summary judgment under rule 24.2 may be based on:
(1) a point of law (including a question of construction of a document),
(2) the evidence which can reasonably be expected to be available at trial or the lack of it, or
(3) a combination of these.

1.4 Rule 24.4(1) deals with the stage in the proceedings at which an application under Part 24 can be made (but see paragraph 7.1 below).

## Procedure for Making an Application

2 (1) Attention is drawn to rules 24.4(3) and 23.6.
(2) The application notice must include a statement that it is an application for summary judgment made under Part 24.
(3) The application notice or the evidence contained or referred to in it or served with it must:
(a) identify concisely any point of law or provision in a document on which the applicant relies, and/or
(b) state that it is made because the applicant believes that on the evidence the respondent has no real prospect of succeeding on the claim or issue or (as the case may be) of successfully defending the claim or issue to which the application relates,
and in either case state that the applicant knows of no other reason why the disposal of the claim or issue should await trial.
(4) Unless the application notice itself contains all the evidence (if any) on which the applicant relies, the application notice should identify the written evidence on which the applicant relies. This does not affect the applicant's right to file further evidence under rule 24.5(2).
(5) The application notice should draw the attention of the respondent to rule 24.5(1).
(6) Where the claimant has failed to comply with any relevant pre-action protocol, an action for summary judgment will not normally be entertained before the defence has been filed or, alternatively, the time for doing so has expired.

## The Hearing

3 (1) The hearing of the application will normally take place before a master or a district judge.
(2) The master or district judge may direct that the application be heard by a High Court judge (if the case is in the High Court) or a circuit judge (if the case is in a county court).

## The Court's Approach

4 Where it appears to the court possible that a claim or defence may succeed but improbable that it will do so, the court may make a conditional order, as described below.

## Orders the Court May Make

5.1 The orders the court may make on an application under Part 24 include:
(1) judgment on the claim,
(2) the striking out or dismissal of the claim,
(3) the dismissal of the application,
(4) a conditional order.

5.2 A conditional order is an order which requires a party:
(1) to pay a sum of money into court, or
(2) to take a specified step in relation to his claim or defence, as the case may be,
and provides that that party's claim will be dismissed or his statement of case will be struck out if he does not comply.
(Note—the court will not follow its former practice of granting leave to a defendant to defend a claim, whether conditionally or unconditionally.)

## Accounts and Inquiries

6 If a remedy sought by a claimant in his claim form includes, or necessarily involves, taking an account or making an inquiry, an application can be made under Part 24 by any party to the proceedings for an order directing any necessary accounts or inquiries to be taken or made.
(PD 40 contains further provisions as to orders for accounts and inquiries.)

## Specific Performance

7.1 (1) If a remedy sought by a claimant in his claim form includes a claim—
(a) for specific performance of an agreement (whether in writing or not) for the sale, purchase, exchange, mortgage or charge of any property, or for the grant or assignment of a lease or tenancy of any property, with or without an alternative claim for damages, or
(b) for rescission of such an agreement, or
(c) for the forfeiture or return of any deposit made under such an agreement,
the claimant may apply under Part 24 for judgment.
(2) The claimant may do so at any time after the claim form has been served, whether or not the defendant has acknowledged service of the claim form, whether or not the time for acknowledging service has expired and whether or not any particulars of claim have been served.

7.2 The application notice by which an application under paragraph 7.1 is made must have attached to it the text of the order sought by the claimant.

7.3 The application notice and a copy of every affidavit or witness statement in support and of any exhibit referred to therein must be served on the defendant not less than 4 days before the hearing of the application. (Note—the 4 days replaces for these applications the 14 days specified in rule 24.4(3). Rule 24.5 cannot, therefore, apply.)
(This paragraph replaces RSC, ord. 86, rr. 1 and 2, but applies to county court proceedings as well as to High Court proceedings.)

## Setting Aside Order for Summary Judgment

8.1 If an order for summary judgment is made against a respondent who does not appear at the hearing of the application, the respondent may apply for the order to be set aside or varied (see also rule 23.11).

8.2 On the hearing of an application under paragraph 8.1 the court may make such order as it thinks just.

## Costs

9.1 Attention is drawn to Part 45 (fixed costs).

9.2 Attention is drawn to PD 43–48 and in particular to the court's power to make a summary assessment of costs.

9.3 Attention is also drawn to rule 44.13(1) which provides that if an order does not mention costs no party is entitled to costs relating to that order.

## Case Management

10 Where the court dismisses the application or makes an order that does not completely dispose of the claim, the court will give case management directions as to the future conduct of the case.

# CPR Part 25 Interim Remedies and Security for Costs



## I INTERIM REMEDIES

### 25.1 Orders for Interim Remedies

(1) The court may grant the following interim remedies—
  (a) an interim injunction(GL);
  (b) an interim declaration;
  (c) an order—
    (i) for the detention, custody or preservation of relevant property;
    (ii) for the inspection of relevant property;
    (iii) for the taking of a sample of relevant property;
    (iv) for the carrying out of an experiment on or with relevant property;
    (v) for the sale of relevant property which is of a perishable nature or which for any other good reason it is desirable to sell quickly; and
    (vi) for the payment of income from relevant property until a claim is decided;
  (d) an order authorising a person to enter any land or building in the possession of a party to the proceedings for the purposes of carrying out an order under sub-paragraph (c);
  (e) an order under section 4 of the Torts (Interference with Goods) Act 1977 to deliver up goods;
  (f) an order (referred to as a 'freezing injunction(GL)')—
    (i) restraining a party from removing from the jurisdiction assets located there; or
    (ii) restraining a party from dealing with any assets whether located within the jurisdiction or not;
  (g) an order directing a party to provide information about the location of relevant property or assets or to provide information about relevant property or assets which are or may be the subject of an application for a freezing injunction(GL);
  (h) an order (referred to as a 'search order') under section 7 of the Civil Procedure Act 1997 (order requiring a party to admit another party to premises for the purpose of preserving evidence etc.);
  (i) an order under section 33 of the Supreme Court Act 1981 or section 52 of the County Courts Act 1984 (order for disclosure of documents or inspection of property before a claim has been made);
  (j) an order under section 34 of the Supreme Court Act 1981 or section 53 of the

County Courts Act 1984 (order in certain proceedings for disclosure of documents or inspection of property against a non-party);

(k) an order (referred to as an order for interim payment) under rule 25.6 for payment by a defendant on account of any damages, debt or other sum (except costs) which the court may hold the defendant liable to pay;

(l) an order for a specified fund to be paid into court or otherwise secured, where there is a dispute over a party's right to the fund;

(m) an order permitting a party seeking to recover personal property to pay money into court pending the outcome of the proceedings and directing that, if he does so, the property shall be given up to him;

(n) an order directing a party to prepare and file accounts relating to the dispute;

(o) an order directing any account to be taken or inquiry to be made by the court; and

(p) an order under Article 9 of Council Directive (EC) 2004/48 on the enforcement of intellectual property rights (order in intellectual property proceedings making the continuation of an alleged infringement subject to the lodging of guarantees).

(Rule 34.2 provides for the court to issue a witness summons requiring a witness to produce documents to the court at the hearing or on such date as the court may direct.)

(2) In paragraph (1)(c) and (g), 'relevant property' means property (including land) which is the subject of a claim or as to which any question may arise on a claim.

(3) The fact that a particular kind of interim remedy is not listed in paragraph (1) does not affect any power that the court may have to grant that remedy.

(4) The court may grant an interim remedy whether or not there has been a claim for a final remedy of that kind.

## 25.2 Time When an Order for an Interim Remedy May be Made

(1) An order for an interim remedy may be made at any time, including—

(a) before proceedings are started; and

(b) after judgment has been given.

(Rule 7.2 provides that proceedings are started when the court issues a claim form.)

(2) However—

(a) paragraph (1) is subject to any rule, practice direction or other enactment which provides otherwise;

(b) the court may grant an interim remedy before a claim has been made only if—

(i) the matter is urgent; or

(ii) it is otherwise desirable to do so in the interests of justice; and

(c) unless the court otherwise orders, a defendant may not apply for any of the orders listed in rule 25.1(1) before he has filed either an acknowledgment of service or a defence.

(Part 10 provides for filing an acknowledgment of service and Part 15 for filing a defence.)

(3) Where it grants an interim remedy before a claim has been commenced, the court should give directions requiring a claim to be commenced.

(4) In particular, the court need not direct that a claim be commenced where the application is made under section 33 of the Supreme Court Act 1981 or section 52 of the County Courts Act 1984 (order for disclosure, inspection etc. before commencement of a claim).

## 25.3 How to Apply for an Interim Remedy

(1) The court may grant an interim remedy on an application made without notice if it appears to the court that there are good reasons for not giving notice.

(2) An application for an interim remedy must be supported by evidence, unless the court orders otherwise.

(3) If the applicant makes an application without giving notice, the evidence in support of the application must state the reasons why notice has not been given.

(Part 3 lists general powers of the court.)
(Part 23 contains general rules about making an application.)

### 25.4 Application for an Interim Remedy Where There is no Related Claim

(1) This rule applies where a party wishes to apply for an interim remedy but—
  (a) the remedy is sought in relation to proceedings which are taking place, or will take place, outside the jurisdiction; or
  (b) the application is made under section 33 of the Supreme Court Act 1981 or section 52 of the County Courts Act 1984 (order for disclosure, inspection etc. before commencement) before a claim has been commenced.
(2) An application under this rule must be made in accordance with the general rules about applications contained in Part 23.

(The following provisions are also relevant—
- Rule 25.5 (inspection of property before commencement or against a non-party)
- Rule 31.16 (orders for disclosure of documents before proceedings start)
- Rule 31.17 (orders for disclosure of documents against a person not a party))

### 25.5 Inspection of Property Before Commencement or Against a Non-party

(1) This rule applies where a person makes an application under—
  (a) section 33(1) of the Supreme Court Act 1981 or section 52(1) of the County Courts Act 1984 (inspection etc. of property before commencement);
  (b) section 34(3) of the Supreme Court Act 1981 or section 53(3) of the County Courts Act 1984 (inspection etc. of property against a non-party).
(2) The evidence in support of such an application must show, if practicable by reference to any statement of case prepared in relation to the proceedings or anticipated proceedings, that the property—
  (a) is or may become the subject matter of such proceedings; or
  (b) is relevant to the issues that will arise in relation to such proceedings.
(3) A copy of the application notice and a copy of the evidence in support must be served on—
  (a) the person against whom the order is sought; and
  (b) in relation to an application under section 34(3) of the Supreme Court Act 1981 or section 53(3) of the County Courts Act 1984, every party to the proceedings other than the applicant.

### 25.6 Interim Payments—General Procedure

(1) The claimant may not apply for an order for an interim payment before the end of the period for filing an acknowledgment of service applicable to the defendant against whom the application is made.

(Rule 10.3 sets out the period for filing an acknowledgment of service.)
(Rule 25.1(1)(k) defines an interim payment.)

(2) The claimant may make more than one application for an order for an interim payment.
(3) A copy of an application notice for an order for an interim payment must—
  (a) be served at least 14 days before the hearing of the application; and
  (b) be supported by evidence.
(4) If the respondent to an application for an order for an interim payment wishes to rely on written evidence at the hearing, he must—
  (a) file the written evidence; and
  (b) serve copies on every other party to the application,
  at least 7 days before the hearing of the application.
(5) If the applicant wishes to rely on written evidence in reply, he must—
  (a) file the written evidence; and
  (b) serve a copy on the respondent,
  at least 3 days before the hearing of the application.

(6) This rule does not require written evidence—
 (a) to be filed if it has already been filed; or
 (b) to be served on a party on whom it has already been served.
(7) The court may order an interim payment in one sum or in instalments.
(Part 23 contains general rules about applications.)

## 25.7 Interim Payments — Conditions to be Satisfied and Matters to be Taken Into Account

(1) The court may only make an order for an interim payment where any of the following conditions are satisfied—
 (a) the defendant against whom the order is sought has admitted liability to pay damages or some other sum of money to the claimant;
 (b) the claimant has obtained judgment against that defendant for damages to be assessed or for a sum of money (other than costs) to be assessed;
 (c) it is satisfied that, if the claim went to trial, the claimant would obtain judgment for a substantial amount of money (other than costs) against the defendant from whom he is seeking an order for an interim payment whether or not that defendant is the only defendant or one of a number of defendants to the claim;
 (d) the following conditions are satisfied—
  (i) the claimant is seeking an order for possession of land (whether or not any other order is also sought); and
  (ii) the court is satisfied that, if the case went to trial, the defendant would be held liable (even if the claim for possession fails) to pay the claimant a sum of money for the defendant's occupation and use of the land while the claim for possession was pending; or
 (e) in a claim in which there are two or more defendants and the order is sought against any one or more of those defendants, the following conditions are satisfied—
  (i) the court is satisfied that, if the claim went to trial, the claimant would obtain judgment for a substantial amount of money (other than costs) against at least one of the defendants (but the court cannot determine which); and
  (ii) all the defendants are either—
   (a) a defendant that is insured in respect of the claim;
   (b) a defendant whose liability will be met by an insurer under section 151 of the Road Traffic Act 1988 or an insurer acting under the Motor Insurers Bureau Agreement, or the Motor Insurers Bureau where it is acting itself; or
   (c) a defendant that is a public body.
(2) *[Revoked]*
(3) *[Revoked]*
(4) The court must not order an interim payment of more than a reasonable proportion of the likely amount of the final judgment.
(5) The court must take into account—
 (a) contributory negligence; and
 (b) any relevant set-off or counterclaim.

## 25.8 Powers of Court Where it Has Made an Order for Interim Payment

(1) Where a defendant has been ordered to make an interim payment, or has in fact made an interim payment (whether voluntarily or under an order), the court may make an order to adjust the interim payment.
(2) The court may in particular—
 (a) order all or part of the interim payment to be repaid;
 (b) vary or discharge the order for the interim payment;
 (c) order a defendant to reimburse, either wholly or partly, another defendant who has made an interim payment.

(3) The court may make an order under paragraph (2)(c) only if—
(a) the defendant to be reimbursed made the interim payment in relation to a claim in respect of which he has made a claim against the other defendant for a contribution(GL), indemnity(GL) or other remedy; and
(b) where the claim or part to which the interim payment relates has not been discontinued or disposed of, the circumstances are such that the court could make an order for interim payment under rule 25.7.
(4) The court may make an order under this rule without an application by any party if it makes the order when it disposes of the claim or any part of it.
(5) Where—
(a) a defendant has made an interim payment; and
(b) the amount of the payment is more than his total liability under the final judgment or order, the court may award him interest on the overpaid amount from the date when he made the interim payment.

## 25.9 Restriction on Disclosure of an Interim Payment

The fact that a defendant has made an interim payment, whether voluntarily or by court order, shall not be disclosed to the trial judge until all questions of liability and the amount of money to be awarded have been decided unless the defendant agrees.

## 25.10 Interim Injunction to Cease if Claim is Stayed

If—
(a) the court has granted an interim injunction(GL) other than a freezing injunction; and
(b) the claim is stayed(GL) other than by agreement between the parties,
the interim injunction(GL) shall be set aside(GL) unless the court orders that it should continue to have effect even though the claim is stayed.

## 25.11 Interim Injunction to Cease After 14 Days if Claim Struck Out

(1) If—
(a) the court has granted an interim injunction(GL); and
(b) the claim is struck out under rule 3.7 (sanction for non-payment of certain fees),
the interim injunction shall cease to have effect 14 days after the date that the claim is struck out unless paragraph (2) applies.
(2) If the claimant applies to reinstate the claim before the interim injunction ceases to have effect under paragraph (1), the injunction shall continue until the hearing of the application unless the court orders otherwise.

# II SECURITY FOR COSTS

## 25.12 Security For Costs

(1) A defendant to any claim may apply under this Section of this Part for security for his costs of the proceedings.
(Part 3 provides for the court to order payment of sums into court in other circumstances. Rule 20.3 provides for this Section of this Part to apply to Part 20 claims.)
(2) An application for security for costs must be supported by written evidence.
(3) Where the court makes an order for security for costs, it will—
(a) determine the amount of security; and
(b) direct—
(i) the manner in which; and
(ii) the time within which
the security must be given.

## 25.13 Conditions to be Satisfied

(1) The court may make an order for security for costs under rule 25.12 if—

(a) it is satisfied, having regard to all the circumstances of the case, that it is just to make such an order; and
(b) (i) one or more of the conditions in paragraph (2) applies, or
(ii) an enactment permits the court to require security for costs.
(2) The conditions are—
(a) The claimant is—
(i) resident out of the jurisdiction; but
(ii) not resident in a Brussels Contracting State, a Lugano Contracting State or a Regulation State, as defined in section 1(3) of the Civil Jurisdiction and Judgments Act 1982;
(b) *[Revoked]*
(c) the claimant is a company or other body (whether incorporated inside or outside Great Britain) and there is reason to believe that it will be unable to pay the defendant's costs if ordered to do so;
(d) the claimant has changed his address since the claim was commenced with a view to evading the consequences of the litigation;
(e) the claimant failed to give his address in the claim form, or gave an incorrect address in that form;
(f) the claimant is acting as a nominal claimant, other than as a representative claimant under Part 19, and there is reason to believe that he will be unable to pay the defendant's costs if ordered to do so;
(g) the claimant has taken steps in relation to his assets that would make it difficult to enforce an order for costs against him.

(Rule 3.4 allows the court to strike out a statement of case and Part 24 for it to give summary judgment.)

## 25.14 Security for Costs Other Than from the Claimant

(1) The defendant may seek an order against someone other than the claimant, and the court may make an order for security for costs against that person if—
(a) it is satisfied, having regard to all the circumstances of the case, that it is just to make such an order; and
(b) one or more of the conditions in paragraph (2) applies.
(2) The conditions are that the person—
(a) has assigned the right to the claim to the claimant with a view to avoiding the possibility of a costs order being made against him; or
(b) has contributed or agreed to contribute to the claimant's costs in return for a share of any money or property which the claimant may recover in the proceedings; and
is a person against whom a costs order may be made.

(Rule 48.2 makes provision for costs orders against non-parties.)

## 25.15 Security for Costs of an Appeal

(1) The court may order security for costs of an appeal against—
(a) an appellant;
(b) a respondent who also appeals,
on the same grounds as it may order security for costs against a claimant under this Part.
(2) The court may also make an order under paragraph (1) where the appellant, or the respondent who also appeals, is a limited company and there is reason to believe it will be unable to pay the costs of the other parties to the appeal should its appeal be unsuccessful.

# PD 25 Practice Direction — Interim Injunctions

This practice direction supplements CPR Part 25.

## Jurisdiction

1.1 High Court judges and any other judge duly authorised may grant 'search orders'[1] and 'freezing injunctions'.[2]

1.2 In a case in the High Court, masters and district judges have the power to grant injunctions:
(1) by consent,
(2) in connection with charging orders and appointments of receivers,
(3) in aid of execution of judgments.

1.3 In any other case any judge who has jurisdiction to conduct the trial of the action has the power to grant an injunction in that action.

1.4 A master or district judge has the power to vary or discharge an injunction granted by any judge with the consent of all the parties.

## Making an Application

2.1 The application notice must state:
(1) the order sought, and
(2) the date, time and place of the hearing.

2.2 The application notice and evidence in support must be served as soon as practicable after issue and in any event not less than three days before the court is due to hear the application.[3]

2.3 Where the court is to serve, sufficient copies of the application notice and evidence in support for the court and for each respondent should be filed for issue and service.

2.4 Whenever possible a draft of the order sought should be filed with the application notice and a disk containing the draft should also be available to the court in a format compatible with the word processing software used by the court. This will enable the court officer to arrange for any amendments to be incorporated and for the speedy preparation and sealing of the order.

## Evidence

3.1 Applications for search orders and freezing injunctions must be supported by affidavit evidence.

3.2 Applications for other interim injunctions must be supported by evidence set out in either:
(1) a witness statement, or
(2) a statement of case provided that it is verified by a statement of truth,[4] or
(3) the application provided that it is verified by a statement of truth,
unless the court, an Act, a rule or a practice direction requires evidence by affidavit.

3.3 The evidence must set out the facts on which the applicant relies for the claim being made against the respondent, including all material facts of which the court should be made aware.

3.4 Where an application is made without notice to the respondent, the evidence must also set out why notice was not given.
(See Part 32 and PD 32 for information about evidence.)

---

[1] Rule 25.1(1)(h).
[2] Rule 25.1(1)(f).
[3] Rule 23.7(1) and (2) and see rule 23.7(4) (short service).
[4] See Part 22.

## Urgent Applications and Applications Without Notice

4.1 These fall into two categories:
 (1) applications where a claim form has already been issued, and
 (2) applications where a claim form has not yet been issued,
 and, in both cases, where notice of the application has not been given to the respondent.

4.2 These applications are normally dealt with at a court hearing but cases of extreme urgency may be dealt with by telephone.

4.3 Applications dealt with at a court hearing after issue of a claim form:
 (1) the application notice, evidence in support and a draft order (as in para. 2.4 above) should be filed with the court two hours before the hearing wherever possible,
 (2) if an application is made before the application notice has been issued, a draft order (as in para. 2.4 above) should be provided at the hearing, and the application notice and evidence in support must be filed with the court on the same or next working day or as ordered by the court, and
 (3) except in cases where secrecy is essential, the applicant should take steps to notify the respondent informally of the application.

4.4 Applications made before the issue of a claim form:
 (1) in addition to the provisions set out at para. 4.3 above, unless the court orders otherwise, either the applicant must undertake to the court to issue a claim form immediately or the court will give directions for the commencement of the claim,[5]
 (2) where possible the claim form should be served with the order for the injunction,
 (3) an order made before the issue of a claim form should state in the title after the names of the applicant and respondent 'the Claimant and Defendant in an Intended Action'.

4.5 Applications made by telephone:
 (1) where it is not possible to arrange a hearing, application can be made between 10.00 a.m. and 5.00 p.m. weekdays by telephoning the Royal Courts of Justice on (020) 7947 6000 and asking to be put in contact with a High Court judge of the appropriate Division available to deal with an emergency application in a High Court matter. The appropriate district registry may also be contacted by telephone. In county court proceedings, the appropriate county court should be contacted,
 (2) where an application is made outside those hours the applicant should either:
  (a) telephone the Royal Courts of Justice on (020) 7947 6000 where he will be put in contact with the clerk to the appropriate duty judge in the High Court (or the appropriate area circuit judge where known), or
  (b) the Urgent Court Business Officer of the appropriate circuit who will contact the local duty judge,
 (3) where the facility is available it is likely that the judge will require a draft order to be faxed to him,
 (4) the application notice and evidence in support must be filed with the court on the same or next working day or as ordered, together with two copies of the order for sealing,
 (5) injunctions will be heard by telephone only where the applicant is acting by counsel or solicitors.

## Orders for Injunctions

5.1 Any order for an injunction, unless the court orders otherwise, must contain:
 (1) an undertaking by the applicant to the court to pay any damages which the respondent sustains which the court considers the applicant should pay.
 (2) if made without notice to any other party, an undertaking by the applicant to the

[5] Rule 25.2(3).

court to serve on the respondent the application notice, evidence in support and any order made as soon as practicable,

(3) if made without notice to any other party, a return date for a further hearing at which the other party can be present,

(4) if made before filing the application notice, an undertaking to file and pay the appropriate fee on the same or next working day, and

(5) if made before issue of a claim form:

(a) an undertaking to issue and pay the appropriate fee on the same or next working day, or

(b) directions for the commencement of the claim.

5.1A When the court makes an order for an injunction, it should consider whether to require an undertaking by the applicant to pay any damages sustained by a person other than the respondent, including another party to the proceedings or any other person who may suffer loss as a consequence of the order.

5.2 An order for an injunction made in the presence of all parties to be bound by it or made at a hearing of which they have had notice, may state that it is effective until trial or further order.

5.3 Any order for an injunction must set out clearly what the respondent must do or not do.

## Freezing Injunctions

*Orders to restrain disposal of assets worldwide and within England and Wales*

6.1 An example of a freezing injunction is annexed to this practice direction.

6.2 This example may be modified as appropriate in any particular case. In particular, the court may if it considers it appropriate, require the applicant's solicitors, as well as the applicant, to give undertakings.

## Search Orders

7.1 The following provisions apply to search orders in addition to those listed above.

## The Supervising Solicitor

7.2 The Supervising Solicitor must be experienced in the operation of search orders. A Supervising Solicitor may be contacted either through the Law Society or, for the London area, through the London Solicitors Litigation Association.

7.3 Evidence:

(1) the affidavit must state the name, firm and its address, and experience of the Supervising Solicitor, also the address of the premises and whether it is a private or business address, and

(2) the affidavit must disclose very fully the reason the order is sought, including the probability that relevant material would disappear if the order were not made.

7.4 Service:

(1) the order must be served personally by the Supervising Solicitor, unless the court otherwise orders, and must be accompanied by the evidence in support and any documents capable of being copied,

(2) confidential exhibits need not be served but they must be made available for inspection by the respondent in the presence of the applicant's solicitors while the order is carried out and afterwards be retained by the respondent's solicitors on their undertaking not to permit the respondent:

(a) to see them or copies of them except in their presence, and

(b) to make or take away any note or record of them,

(3) the Supervising Solicitor may be accompanied only by the persons mentioned in the order,

(4) the Supervising Solicitor must explain the terms and effect of the order to the respondent in everyday language and advise him

(a) of his right to take legal advice and to apply to vary or discharge the order; and

(b) that he may be entitled to avail himself of
  (i) legal professional privilege; and
  (ii) the privilege against self-incrimination,

(5) where the Supervising Solicitor is a man and the respondent is likely to be an unaccompanied woman, at least one other person named in the order must be a woman and must accompany the Supervising Solicitor, and

(6) the order may only be served between 9.30 a.m. and 5.30 p.m. Monday to Friday unless the court otherwise orders.

7.5 Search and custody of materials:

(1) no material shall be removed unless clearly covered by the terms of the order,

(2) the premises must not be searched and no items shall be removed from them except in the presence of the respondent or a person who appears to be a responsible employee of the respondent,

(3) where copies of documents are sought, the documents should be retained for no more than two days before return to the owner,

(4) where material in dispute is removed pending trial, the applicant's solicitors should place it in the custody of the respondent's solicitors on their undertaking to retain it in safekeeping and to produce it to the court when required,

(5) in appropriate cases the applicant should insure the material retained in the respondent's solicitors' custody,

(6) the Supervising Solicitor must make a list of all material removed from the premises and supply a copy of the list to the respondent,

(7) no material shall be removed from the premises until the respondent has had reasonable time to check the list,

(8) if any of the listed items exists only in computer-readable form, the respondent must immediately give the applicant's solicitors effective access to the computers, with all necessary passwords, to enable them to be searched, and cause the listed items to be printed out,

(9) the applicant must take all reasonable steps to ensure that no damage is done to any computer or data,

(10) the applicant and his representatives may not themselves search the respondent's computers unless they have sufficient expertise to do so without damaging the respondent's system,

(11) the Supervising Solicitor shall provide a report on the carrying out of the order to the applicant's solicitors,

(12) as soon as the report is received the applicant's solicitors shall:
  (a) serve a copy of it on the respondent, and
  (b) file a copy of it with the court, and

(13) where the Supervising Solicitor is satisfied that full compliance with para. 7.5(7) and (8) above is impracticable, he may permit the search to proceed and items to be removed without compliance with the impracticable requirements.

## General

7.6 The Supervising Solicitor must not be an employee or member of the applicant's firm of solicitors.

7.7 If the court orders that the order need not be served by the Supervising Solicitor, the reason for so ordering must be set out in the order.

7.8 The search order must not be carried out at the same time as a police search warrant.

7.9 There is no privilege against self-incrimination in:

(1) intellectual property cases in respect of a 'related offence' or for the recovery of a 'related penalty' as defined in section 72 of the Supreme Court Act 1981;

(2) proceedings for the recovery or administration of any property, for the execution of a trust or for an account of any property or dealings with property, in relation to—

(a) an offence under the Theft Act 1968 (see section 31 of the Theft Act 1968);[6] or

(b) an offence under the Fraud Act 2006 (see section 13 of the Fraud Act 2006)[7] or a related offence within the meaning given by section 13(4) of that Act—that is, conspiracy to defraud or any other offence involving any form of fraudulent conduct or purpose; or

(3) proceedings in which a court is hearing an application for an order under Part IV or Part V of the Children Act 1989 (see section 98 of the Children Act 1989).

However, the privilege may still be claimed in relation to material or information required to be disclosed by an order, as regards potential criminal proceedings outside those statutory provisions.

7.10 Applications in intellectual property cases should be made in the Chancery Division.

7.11 An example of a search order is annexed to this practice direction. This example may be modified as appropriate in any particular case.

## Delivery-up Orders

8.1 The following provisions apply to orders, other than search orders, for delivery up or preservation of evidence or property where it is likely that such an order will be executed at the premises of the respondent or a third party.

8.2 In such cases the court shall consider whether to include in the order for the benefit or protection of the parties similar provisions to those specified above in relation to injunctions and search orders.

## Injunctions Against Third Parties

9.1 The following provisions apply to orders which will affect a person other than the applicant or respondent, who:

(1) did not attend the hearing at which the order was made; and

(2) is served with the order.

9.2 Where such a person served with the order requests

(1) a copy of any materials read by the judge, including material prepared after the hearing at the direction of the judge or in compliance with the order; or

(2) a note of the hearing,

the applicant, or his legal representative, must comply promptly with the request, unless the court orders otherwise.

## ANNEX

**Freezing Injunction**

**IN THE HIGH COURT OF JUSTICE**
**[ ] DIVISION**
**[ ]**

**Before The Honourable Mr Justice**

**Claim No.**
**Dated**

**Applicant**

Seal

**Respondent**

Name, address and reference of Respondent

[6] 1968 c. 60.

[7] 2006 c. 35.

**PENAL NOTICE**

**IF YOU [ ][1] DISOBEY THIS ORDER YOU MAY BE HELD TO BE IN CONTEMPT OF COURT AND MAY BE IMPRISONED, FINED OR HAVE YOUR ASSETS SEIZED.**

**ANY OTHER PERSON WHO KNOWS OF THIS ORDER AND DOES ANYTHING WHICH HELPS OR PERMITS THE RESPONDENT TO BREACH THE TERMS OF THIS ORDER MAY ALSO BE HELD TO BE IN CONTEMPT OF COURT AND MAY BE IMPRISONED, FINED OR HAVE THEIR ASSETS SEIZED.**

THIS ORDER

1. This is a Freezing Injunction made against [ ] ('the Respondent') on [ ] by Mr Justice [ ] on the application of [ ] ('the Applicant'). The Judge read the Affidavits listed in Schedule A and accepted the undertakings set out in Schedule B at the end of this Order.
2. This order was made at a hearing without notice to the Respondent. The Respondent has a right to apply to the court to vary or discharge the order—see paragraph 13 below.
3. There will be a further hearing in respect of this order on [ ] ('the return date').
4. If there is more than one Respondent:
   (a) unless otherwise stated, references in this order to 'the Respondent' mean both or all of them; and
   (b) this order is effective against any Respondent on whom it is served or who is given notice of it.

FREEZING INJUNCTION

*[For injunction limited to assets in England and Wales]*

5. Until the return date or further order of the court, the Respondent must not remove from England and Wales or in any way dispose of, deal with or diminish the value of any of his assets which are in England and Wales up to the value of £ .

*[For worldwide injunction]*

5. Until the return date or further order of the court, the Respondent must not:
   (1) remove from England and Wales any of his assets which are in England and Wales up to the value of £ ; or
   (2) in any way dispose of, deal with or diminish the value of any of his assets whether they are in or outside England and Wales up to the same value.

*[For either form of injunction]*

6. Paragraph 5 applies to all the Respondent's assets whether or not they are in his own name and whether they are solely or jointly owned. For the purpose of this order the Respondent's assets include any asset which he has the power, directly or indirectly, to dispose of or deal with as if it were his own. The Respondent is to be regarded as having such power if a third party holds or controls the asset in accordance with his direct or indirect instructions.
7. This prohibition includes the following assets in particular:
   (a) the property known as [title/address] or the net sale money after payment of any mortgages if it has been sold;
   (b) the property and assets of the Respondent's business [known as [name] ] [carried on at [address] ] or the sale money if any of them have been sold; and
   (c) any money standing to the credit of any bank account including the amount of any cheque drawn on such account which has not been cleared.

*[For injunction limited to assets in England and Wales]*

8. If the total value free of charges or other securities ('unencumbered value') of the

[1] Insert name of Respondent.

Respondent's assets in England and Wales exceeds £ , the Respondent may remove any of those assets from England and Wales or may dispose of or deal with them so long as the total unencumbered value of his assets still in England and Wales remains above £ .

*[For worldwide injunction]*

8. (1) If the total value free of charges or other securities ('unencumbered value') of the Respondent's assets in England and Wales exceeds £ , the Respondent may remove any of those assets from England and Wales or may dispose of or deal with them so long as the total unencumbered value of the Respondent's assets still in England and Wales remains above £ .
   (2) If the total unencumbered value of the Respondent's assets in England and Wales does not exceed £ , the Respondent must not remove any of those assets from England and Wales and must not dispose of or deal with any of them. If the Respondent has other assets outside England and Wales, he may dispose of or deal with those assets outside England and Wales so long as the total unencumbered value of all his assets whether in or outside England and Wales remains above £ .

PROVISION OF INFORMATION

9. (1) Unless paragraph (2) applies, the Respondent must [immediately] [within hours of service of this order] and to the best of his ability inform the Applicant's solicitors of all his assets [in England and Wales] [worldwide] [exceeding £ in value] whether in his own name or not and whether solely or jointly owned, giving the value, location and details of all such assets.
   (2) If the provision of any of this information is likely to incriminate the Respondent, he may be entitled to refuse to provide it, but is recommended to take legal advice before refusing to provide the information. Wrongful refusal to provide the information is contempt of court and may render the Respondent liable to be imprisoned, fined or have his assets seized.

10. Within [ ] working days after being served with this order, the Respondent must swear and serve on the Applicant's solicitors an affidavit setting out the above information.

EXCEPTIONS TO THIS ORDER

11. (1) This order does not prohibit the Respondent from spending £ a week towards his ordinary living expenses and also £ [or a reasonable sum] on legal advice and representation. [But before spending any money the Respondent must tell the Applicant's legal representatives where the money is to come from.]
   [(2) This order does not prohibit the Respondent from dealing with or disposing of any of his assets in the ordinary and proper course of business.]
   (3) The Respondent may agree with the Applicant's legal representatives that the above spending limits should be increased or that this order should be varied in any other respect, but any agreement must be in writing.
   (4) The order will cease to have effect if the Respondent:
      (a) provides security by paying the sum of £ into court, to be held to the order of the court; or
      (b) makes provision for security in that sum by another method agreed with the Applicant's legal representatives.

COSTS

12. The costs of this application are reserved to the judge hearing the application on the return date.

VARIATION OR DISCHARGE OF THIS ORDER

13. Anyone served with or notified of this order may apply to the court at any time to vary or discharge this order (or so much of it as affects that person), but they must first

inform the Applicant's solicitors. If any evidence is to be relied upon in support of the application, the substance of it must be communicated in writing to the Applicant's solicitors in advance.

INTERPRETATION OF THIS ORDER

14. A Respondent who is an individual who is ordered not to do something must not do it himself or in any other way. He must not do it through others acting on his behalf or on his instructions or with his encouragement.
15. A Respondent which is not an individual which is ordered not to do something must not do it itself or by its directors, officers, partners, employees or agents or in any other way.

PARTIES OTHER THAN THE APPLICANT AND RESPONDENT EFFECT OF THIS ORDER

16. It is a contempt of court for any person notified of this order knowingly to assist in or permit a breach of this order. Any person doing so may be imprisoned, fined or have their assets seized.

SET-OFF BY BANKS

17. This injunction does not prevent any bank from exercising any right of set-off it may have in respect of any facility which it gave to the respondent before it was notified of this order.

WITHDRAWALS BY THE RESPONDENT

18. No bank need enquire as to the application or proposed application of any money withdrawn by the Respondent if the withdrawal appears to be permitted by this order.

*[For worldwide injunction]*

PERSONS OUTSIDE ENGLAND AND WALES

19. (1) Except as provided in paragraph (2) below, the terms of this order do not affect or concern anyone outside the jurisdiction of this court.
    (2) The terms of this order will affect the following persons in a country or State outside the jurisdiction of this court:
        (a) the Respondent or his officer or agent appointed by power of attorney;
        (b) any person who:
            (i) is subject to the jurisdiction of this court;
            (ii) has been given written notice of this order at his residence or place of business within the jurisdiction of this court; and
            (iii) is able to prevent acts or omissions outside the jurisdiction of this court which constitute or assist in a breach of the terms of this order; and
        (c) any other person, only to the extent that this order is declared enforceable by or is enforced by a court in that country or State.

*[For worldwide injunction]*

ASSETS LOCATED OUTSIDE ENGLAND AND WALES

20. Nothing in this order shall, in respect of assets located outside England and Wales, prevent any third party from complying with:
    (1) what it reasonably believes to be its obligations, contractual or otherwise, under the laws and obligations of the country or State in which those assets are situated or under the proper law of any contract between itself and the Respondent; and
    (2) any orders of the courts of that country or State, provided that reasonable notice of any application for such an order is given to the Applicant's solicitors.

COMMUNICATIONS WITH THE COURT

All communications to the court about this order should be sent to:

[Insert the address and telephone number of the appropriate court office]

If the order is made at the Royal Courts of Justice, communications should be addressed as follows:

Where the order is made in the Chancery Division:
Room TM 505, Royal Courts of Justice, Strand, London WC2A 2LL quoting the case number. The telephone number is (020) 7947 6754.

*Where the order is made in the Queen's Bench Division*
Room WG08, Royal Courts of Justice, Strand, London WC2A 2LL quoting the case number. The telephone number is (020) 7947 6010.

*Where the order is made in the Commercial Court*
Room EB09, Royal Courts of Justice, Strand, London WC2A 2LL quoting the case number. The telephone number is (020) 7947 6826.

The offices are open between 10 a.m. and 4.30 p.m. Monday to Friday.

SCHEDULE A AFFIDAVITS

The Applicant relied on the following affidavits:
[name] [number of affidavit] [date sworn]
[filed on behalf of]
(1)
(2)

SCHEDULE B UNDERTAKINGS GIVEN TO THE COURT BY THE APPLICANT

(1) If the court later finds that this order has caused loss to the Respondent, and decides that the Respondent should be compensated for that loss, the Applicant will comply with any order the court may make.

[(2) The Applicant will:
  (a) on or before [date] cause a written guarantee in the sum of £ to be issued from a bank with a place of business within England or Wales, in respect of any order the court may make pursuant to paragraph (1) above; and
  (b) immediately upon issue of the guarantee, cause a copy of it to be served on the Respondent.]

(3) As soon as practicable the Applicant will issue and serve a claim form [in the form of the draft produced to the court] [claiming the appropriate relief].

(4) The Applicant will [swear and file an affidavit] [cause an affidavit to be sworn and filed] [substantially in the terms of the draft affidavit produced to the court] [confirming the substance of what was said to the court by the Applicant's counsel/solicitors].

(5) The Applicant will serve upon the Respondent [together with this order] [as soon as practicable]:
  (i) copies of the affidavits and exhibits containing the evidence relied upon by the Applicant, and any other documents provided to the court on the making of the application;
  (ii) the claim form; and
  (iii) an application notice for continuation of the order.

[(6) Anyone notified of this order will be given a copy of it by the Applicant's legal representatives.]

(7) The Applicant will pay the reasonable costs of anyone other than the Respondent which have been incurred as a result of this order including the costs of finding out whether that person holds any of the Respondent's assets and if the court later finds that this order has caused such person loss, and decides that such person should be compensated for that loss, the Applicant will comply with any order the court may make.

(8) If this order ceases to have effect (for example, if the Respondent provides security or the Applicant does not provide a bank guarantee as provided for above) the Applicant

will immediately take all reasonable steps to inform in writing anyone to whom he has given notice of this order, or who he has reasonable grounds for supposing may act upon this order, that it has ceased to have effect.

[(9) The Applicant will not without the permission of the court use any information obtained as a result of this order for the purpose of any civil or criminal proceedings, either in England and Wales or in any other jurisdiction, other than this claim.]

[(10) The Applicant will not without the permission of the court seek to enforce this order in any country outside England and Wales [or seek an order of a similar nature including orders conferring a charge or other security against the Respondent or the Respondent's assets].]

NAME AND ADDRESS OF APPLICANT'S LEGAL REPRESENTATIVES

The Applicant's legal representatives are:

[Name, address, reference, fax and telephone numbers both in and out of office hours and email]

**Search Order**

**IN THE HIGH COURT OF JUSTICE**

**[ ] DIVISION**

**[ ]**

**Before The Honourable Mr Justice**

**Claim No.**

**Dated**

**Applicant**

Seal

**Respondent**

Name, address and reference of Respondent

**PENAL NOTICE**

**IF YOU [ ][1] DISOBEY THIS ORDER YOU MAY BE HELD TO BE IN CONTEMPT OF COURT AND LIABLE TO IMPRISONMENT OR FINED OR HAVE OR YOUR ASSETS SEIZED.**

**ANY OTHER PERSON WHO KNOWS OF THIS ORDER AND DOES ANYTHING WHICH HELPS OR PERMITS THE RESPONDENT TO BREACH THE TERMS OF THIS ORDER MAY ALSO BE HELD TO BE IN CONTEMPT OF COURT AND MAY BE IMPRISONED, FINED OR HAVE THEIR ASSETS SEIZED.**

THIS ORDER

1. This is a Search Order made against [ ] ('the Respondent') on [ ] by Mr Justice [ ] on the application of [ ] ('the Applicant'). The Judge read the Affidavits listed in Schedule F and accepted the undertakings set out in Schedules C, D and E at the end of this order.
2. This order was made at a hearing without notice to the Respondent. The Respondent has a right to apply to the court to vary or discharge the order—see paragraph 27 below.
3. There will be a further hearing in respect of this order on [ ] ('the return date').
4. If there is more than one Respondent:
   (a) unless otherwise stated, references in this order to 'the Respondent' mean both or all of them; and
   (b) this order is effective against any Respondent on whom it is served or who is given notice of it.

[1] Insert name of Respondent.

5. This order must be complied with by:
(a) the Respondent;
(b) any director, officer, partner or responsible employee of the Respondent; and
(c) if the Respondent is an individual, any other person having responsible control of the premises to be searched.

THE SEARCH

6. The Respondent must permit the following persons:[8]
(a) [ ] ('the Supervising Solicitor');
(b) [ ], a solicitor in the firm of [ ], the Applicant's solicitors; and
(c) up to [ ] other persons[9] being [their identity or capacity] accompanying them, (together 'the search party'), to enter the premises mentioned in Schedule A to this order and any other premises of the Respondent disclosed under paragraph 18 below and any vehicles under the Respondent's control on or around the premises ('the premises') so that they can search for, inspect, photograph or photocopy, and deliver into the safe keeping of the Applicant's solicitors all the documents and articles which are listed in Schedule B to this order ('the listed items').

7. Having permitted the search party to enter the premises, the Respondent must allow the search party to remain on the premises until the search is complete. In the event that it becomes necessary for any of those persons to leave the premises before the search is complete, the Respondent must allow them to re-enter the premises immediately upon their seeking re-entry on the same or the following day in order to complete the search.

RESTRICTIONS ON SEARCH

8. This order may not be carried out at the same time as a police search warrant.

9. Before the Respondent allows anybody on to the premises to carry out this order, he is entitled to have the Supervising Solicitor explain to him what it means in everyday language.

10. The Respondent is entitled to seek legal advice and to ask the court to vary or discharge this order. Whilst doing so, he may ask the Supervising Solicitor to delay starting the search for up to 2 hours or such other longer period as the Supervising Solicitor may permit. However, the Respondent must:
(a) comply with the terms of paragraph 27 below;
(b) not disturb or remove any listed items; and
(c) permit the Supervising Solicitor to enter, but not start to search.

11. (1) Before permitting entry to the premises by any person other than the Supervising Solicitor, the Respondent may, for a short time (not to exceed two hours, unless the Supervising Solicitor agrees to a longer period)—
(a) gather together any documents he believes may be incriminating or privileged; and
(b) hand them to the Supervising Solicitor for him to assess whether they are incriminating or privileged as claimed.
(2) If the Supervising Solicitor decides that the Respondent is entitled to withhold production of any of the documents on the ground that they are privileged or incriminating, he will exclude them from the search, record them in a list for inclusion in his report and return them to the Respondent.
(3) If the Supervising Solicitor believes that the Respondent may be entitled to withhold production of the whole or any part of a document on the ground that it or part of it may be privileged or incriminating, or if the Respondent claims to be

[8] Where the premises are likely to be occupied by an unaccompanied woman and the Supervising Solicitor is a man, at least one of the persons accompanying him should be a woman.

[9] None of these persons should be people who could gain personally or commercially from anything they might read or see on the premises, unless their presence is essential.

entitled to withhold production on those grounds, the Supervising Solicitor will exclude it from the search and retain it in his possession pending further order of the court.

12. If the Respondent wishes to take legal advice and gather documents as permitted, he must first inform the Supervising Solicitor and keep him informed of the steps being taken.
13. No item may be removed from the premises until a list of the items to be removed has been prepared, and a copy of the list has been supplied to the Respondent, and he has been given a reasonable opportunity to check the list.
14. The premises must not be searched, and items must not be removed from them, except in the presence of the Respondent.
15. If the Supervising Solicitor is satisfied that full compliance with paragraphs 13 or 14 is not practicable, he may permit the search to proceed and items to be removed without fully complying with them.

DELIVERY UP OF ARTICLES/DOCUMENTS

16. The Respondent must immediately hand over to the Applicant's solicitors any of the listed items, which are in his possession or under his control, save for any computer or hard disk integral to any computer. Any items the subject of a dispute as to whether they are listed items must immediately be handed over to the Supervising Solicitor for safe keeping pending resolution of the dispute or further order of the court.
17. The Respondent must immediately give the search party effective access to the computers on the premises, with all necessary passwords, to enable the computers to be searched. If they contain any listed items the Respondent must cause the listed items to be displayed so that they can be read and copied.[10] The Respondent must provide the Applicant's Solicitors with copies of all listed items contained in the computers. All reasonable steps shall be taken by the Applicant and the Applicant's solicitors to ensure that no damage is done to any computer or data. The Applicant and his representatives may not themselves search the Respondent's computers unless they have sufficient expertise to do so without damaging the Respondent's system.

PROVISION OF INFORMATION

18. The Respondent must immediately inform the Applicant's Solicitors (in the presence of the Supervising Solicitor) so far as he is aware:
    (a) where all the listed items are;
    (b) the name and address of everyone who has supplied him, or offered to supply him, with listed items;
    (c) the name and address of everyone to whom he has supplied, or offered to supply, listed items; and
    (d) full details of the dates and quantities of every such supply and offer.
19. Within [ ] working days after being served with this order the Respondent must swear and serve an affidavit setting out the above information.[11]

PROHIBITED ACTS

20. Except for the purpose of obtaining legal advice, the Respondent must not directly or indirectly inform anyone of these proceedings or of the contents of this order, or warn anyone that proceedings have been or may be brought against him by the Applicant until 4.30 p.m. on the return date or further order of the court.

[10] If it is envisaged that the Respondent's computers are to be imaged (i.e. the hard drives are to be copied wholesale, thereby reproducing listed items and other items indiscriminately), special provision needs to be made and independent computer specialists need to be appointed, who should be required to give undertakings to the court.

[11] The period should ordinarily be longer than the period in paragraph (2) of Schedule D, if any of the information is likely to be included in listed items taken away of which the Respondent does not have copies.

21. Until 4.30 p.m. on the return date the Respondent must not destroy, tamper with, cancel or part with possession, power, custody or control of the listed items otherwise than in accordance with the terms of this order.
22. [Insert any negative injunctions.]
23. [Insert any further order]

COSTS

24. The costs of this application are reserved to the judge hearing the application on the return date.

RESTRICTIONS ON SERVICE

25. This order may only be served between [ ] a.m./p.m. and [ ] a.m./p.m. [and on a weekday].[12]
26. This order must be served by the Supervising Solicitor, and paragraph 6 of the order must be carried out in his presence and under his supervision.

VARIATION AND DISCHARGE OF THIS ORDER

27. Anyone served with or notified of this order may apply to the court at any time to vary or discharge this order (or so much of it as affects that person), but they must first inform the Applicant's solicitors. If any evidence is to be relied upon in support of the application, the substance of it must be communicated in writing to the Applicant's solicitors in advance.

INTERPRETATION OF THIS ORDER

28. Any requirement that something shall be done to or in the presence of the Respondent means:
    (a) if there is more than one Respondent, to or in the presence of any one of them; and
    (b) if a Respondent is not an individual, to or in the presence of a director, officer, partner or responsible employee.
29. A Respondent who is an individual who is ordered not to do something must not do it himself or in any other way. He must not do it through others acting on his behalf or on his instructions or with his encouragement.
30. A Respondent which is not an individual which is ordered not to do something must not do it itself or by its directors, officers, partners, employees or agents or in any other way.

COMMUNICATIONS WITH THE COURT

All communications to the court about this order should be sent to:

[Insert the address and telephone number of the appropriate court office]

If the order is made at the Royal Courts of Justice, communications should be addressed as follows:

*Where the order is made in the Chancery Division:*
Room TM 505, Royal Courts of Justice, Strand, London WC2A 2LL quoting the case number. The telephone number is (020) 7947 6754.

*Where the order is made in the Queen's Bench Division*
Room WG08, Royal Courts of Justice, Strand, London WC2A 2LL quoting the case number. The telephone number is (020) 7947 6010.

*Where the order is made in the Commercial Court*
Room EB09, Royal Courts of Justice, Strand, London WC2A 2LL quoting the case number. The telephone number is (020) 7947 6826.

[12] Normally, the order should be served in the morning (not before 9.30 a.m.) and on a weekday to enable the Respondent more readily to obtain legal advice.

SCHEDULE A THE PREMISES

SCHEDULE B THE LISTED ITEMS

SCHEDULE C UNDERTAKINGS GIVEN TO THE COURT BY THE APPLICANT

(1) If the court later finds that this order or carrying it out has caused loss to the Respondent, and decides that the Respondent should be compensated for that loss, the Applicant will comply with any order the court may make. Further if the carrying out of this order has been in breach of the terms of this order or otherwise in a manner inconsistent with the Applicant's solicitors' duties as officers of the court, the Applicant will comply with any order for damages the court may make.

[(2) As soon as practicable the Applicant will issue a claim form [in the form of the draft produced to the court] [claiming the appropriate relief].]

(3) The Applicant will [swear and file an affidavit] [cause an affidavit to be sworn and filed] [substantially in the terms of the draft affidavit produced to the court] [confirming the substance of what was said to the court by the Applicant's counsel/solicitors].

(4) The Applicant will not, without the permission of the court, use any information or documents obtained as a result of carrying out this order nor inform anyone else of these proceedings except for the purposes of these proceedings (including adding further Respondents) or commencing civil proceedings in relation to the same or related subject matter to these proceedings until after the return date.

[(5) The Applicant will maintain pending further order the sum of £ in an account controlled by the Applicant's solicitors.]

[(6) The Applicant will insure the items removed from the premises.]

SCHEDULE D UNDERTAKINGS GIVEN BY THE APPLICANT'S SOLICITORS

(1) The Applicant's solicitors will provide to the Supervising Solicitor for service on the Respondent:
   (i) a service copy of this order;
   (ii) the claim form (with defendant's response pack) or, if not issued, the draft produced to the court;
   (iii) an application for hearing on the return date;
   (iv) copies of the affidavits [or draft affidavits] and exhibits capable of being copied containing the evidence relied upon by the applicant;
   (v) a note of any allegation of fact made orally to the court where such allegation is not contained in the affidavits or draft affidavits read by the judge; and
   (vi) a copy of the skeleton argument produced to the court by the Applicant's [counsel/solicitors].

(2) The Applicant's solicitors will answer at once to the best of their ability any question whether a particular item is a listed item.

(3) Subject as provided below the Applicant's solicitors will retain in their own safe keeping all items obtained as a result of this order until the court directs otherwise.

(4) The Applicant's solicitors will return the originals of all documents obtained as a result of this order (except original documents which belong to the Applicant) as soon as possible and in any event within [2] working days of their removal.

SCHEDULE E UNDERTAKINGS GIVEN BY THE SUPERVISING SOLICITOR

(1) The Supervising Solicitor will use his best endeavours to serve this order upon the Respondent and at the same time to serve upon the Respondent the other documents required to be served and referred to in paragraph (1) of Schedule D.

(2) The Supervising Solicitor will offer to explain to the person served with the order its meaning and effect fairly and in everyday language, and to inform him of his right to take legal advice (including an explanation that the Respondent may be entitled to avail himself of the privilege against self-incrimination and legal professional privilege) and to apply to vary or discharge this order as mentioned in paragraph 27 above.

(3) The Supervising Solicitor will retain in the safe keeping of his firm all items retained by him as a result of this order until the court directs otherwise.
(4) Unless and until the court otherwise orders, or unless otherwise necessary to comply with any duty to the court pursuant to this order, the Supervising Solicitor shall not disclose to any person any information relating to those items, and shall keep the existence of such items confidential.
(5) Within [48] hours of completion of the search the Supervising Solicitor will make and provide to the Applicant's solicitors, the Respondent or his solicitors and to the judge who made this order (for the purposes of the court file) a written report on the carrying out of the order.

SCHEDULE F AFFIDAVITS

The Applicant relied on the following affidavits:

[name] [number of affidavit] [date sworn] [filed on behalf of]
(1)
(2)

NAME AND ADDRESS OF APPLICANT'S SOLICITORS

The Applicant's solicitors are:

[Name, address, reference, fax and telephone numbers both in and out of office hours.]

# PD 25B Practice Direction — Interim Payments

This practice direction supplements CPR Part 25.

## General

1.1 Rule 25.7 sets out the conditions to be satisfied and matters to be taken into account before the court will make an order for an interim payment.

1.2 The permission of the court must be obtained before making a voluntary interim payment in respect of a claim by a child or patient.

## Evidence

2.1 An application for an interim payment of damages must be supported by evidence dealing with the following:
- (1) the sum of money sought by way of an interim payment,
- (2) the items or matters in respect of which the interim payment is sought,
- (3) the sum of money for which final judgment is likely to be given,
- (4) the reasons for believing that the conditions set out in rule 25.7 are satisfied,
- (5) any other relevant matters,
- (6) in claims for personal injuries, details of special damages and past and future loss, and
- (7) in a claim under the Fatal Accidents Act 1976, details of the person(s) on whose behalf the claim is made and the nature of the claim.

2.2 Any documents in support of the application should be exhibited, including, in personal injuries claims, the medical report(s).

2.3 If a respondent to an application for an interim payment wishes to rely on written evidence at the hearing he must comply with the provisions of rule 25.6(4).

2.4 If the applicant wishes to rely on written evidence in reply he must comply with the provisions of rule 25.6(5).

## Interim Payment Where Account to be Taken

2A.1 This section of this practice direction applies if a party seeks an interim payment under r. 25.7(b) where the court has ordered an account to be taken.

2A.2 If the evidence on the application for interim payment shows that the account is bound to result in a payment to the applicant the court will, before making an order for interim payment, order that the liable party pay to the applicant 'the amount shown by the account to be due'.

## Instalments

3 Where an interim payment is to be paid in instalments the order should set out:
- (1) the total amount of the payment,
- (2) the amount of each instalment,
- (3) the number of instalments and the date on which each is to be paid, and
- (4) to whom the payment should be made.

## Compensation Recovery Payments

4.1 Where in a claim for personal injuries there is an application for an interim payment of damages:
- (1) which is other than by consent,
- (2) which fails under the heads of damage set out in column 1 of sch. 2 to the Social Security (Recovery of Benefits) Act 1997 in respect of recoverable benefits received by the claimant set out in column 2 of that schedule, and
- (3) where the defendant is liable to pay recoverable benefits to the Secretary of State,

the defendant should obtain from the Secretary of State a certificate of recoverable benefits.

4.2 A copy of the certificate should be filed at the hearing of the application for an interim payment.

4.3 The order will set out the amount by which the payment to be made to the claimant has been reduced according to the Act and the Social Security (Recovery of Benefits) Regulations 1997.

4.4 The payment made to the claimant will be the net amount but the interim payment for the purposes of paragraph 5 below will be the gross amount.

## Adjustment of Final Judgment Figure

5.1 In this paragraph 'judgment' means:
(1) any order to pay a sum of money,
(2) a final award of damages,
(3) an assessment of damages.

5.2 In a final judgment where an interim payment has previously been made which is less than the total amount awarded by the judge, the order should set out in a preamble:
(1) the total amount awarded by the judge, and
(2) the amounts and dates of the interim payment(s).

5.3 The total amount awarded by the judge should then be reduced by the total amount of any interim payments, and an order made for entry of judgment and payment of the balance.

5.4 In a final judgment where an interim payment has previously been made which is more than the total amount awarded by the judge, the order should set out in a preamble:
(1) the total amount awarded by the judge, and
(2) the amounts and dates of the interim payment(s).

5.5 An order should then be made for repayment, reimbursement, variation or discharge under rule 25.8(2) and for interest on an overpayment under rule 25.8(5).

5.6 PD 40B provides further information concerning adjustment of the final judgment sum.

# CPR Part 26 Case Management — Preliminary Stage



## 26.1 Scope of this Part

(1) This Part provides for—
  (a) the automatic transfer of some defended cases between courts; and
  (b) the allocation of defended cases to case management tracks.
(2) There are three tracks—
  (a) the small claims track;
  (b) the fast track; and
  (c) the multi-track.

(Rule 26.6 sets out the normal scope of each track. Part 27 makes provision for the small claims track. Part 28 makes provision for the fast track. Part 29 makes provision for the multi-track.)

## 26.2 Automatic Transfer

(1) This rule applies to proceedings where—
  (a) the claim is for a specified amount of money;
  (b) the claim was commenced in a court which is not the defendant's home court;
  (c) the claim has not been transferred to another defendant's home court under rule 13.4 (application to set aside(GL) or vary default judgment—procedure) or rule 14.12 (admission—determination of rate of payment by judge); and
  (d) the defendant is an individual.
(2) This rule does not apply where the claim was commenced in a specialist list(GL).
(3) Where this rule applies, the court will transfer the proceedings to the defendant's home court when a defence is filed, unless paragraph (4) applies.

(Rule 2.3 defines 'defendant's home court'.)

(4) Where the claimant notifies the court under rule 15.10 or rule 14.5 that he wishes the proceedings to continue, the court will transfer the proceedings to the defendant's home court when it receives that notification from the claimant.

(Rule 15.10 deals with a claimant's notice where the defence is that money claimed has been paid.)

(Rule 14.5 sets out the procedure where the defendant admits part of a claim for a specified amount of money.)

(5) Where—
  (a) the claim is against two or more defendants with different home courts; and
  (b) the defendant whose defence is filed first is an individual,

  proceedings are to be transferred under this rule to the home court of that defendant.
(6) The time when a claim is automatically transferred under this rule may be varied by a practice direction in respect of claims issued by the Production Centre.

(Rule 7.10 makes provision for the Production Centre.)

## 26.3 Allocation Questionnaire

(1) When a defendant files a defence the court will serve an allocation questionnaire on each party unless—
(a) rule 15.10 or rule 14.5 applies; or
(b) the court dispenses with the need for a questionnaire.

(2) Where there are two or more defendants and at least one of them files a defence, the court will serve the allocation questionnaire under paragraph (1)—
(a) when all the defendants have filed a defence; or
(b) when the period for the filing of the last defence has expired, whichever is the sooner.

(Rule 15.4 specifies the period for filing a defence.)

(3) Where proceedings are automatically transferred to the defendant's home court under rule 26.2, the court in which the proceedings have been commenced will serve an allocation questionnaire before the proceedings are transferred.

(4) Where—
(a) rule 15.10 or 14.5 applies; and
(b) the proceedings are not automatically transferred to the defendant's home court under rule 26.2,

the court will serve an allocation questionnaire on each party when the claimant files a notice indicating that he wishes the proceedings to continue.

(5) The court may, on the application of the claimant, serve an allocation questionnaire earlier than it would otherwise serve it under this rule.

(6) Each party must file the completed allocation questionnaire no later than the date specified in it, which shall be at least 14 days after the date when it is deemed to be served on the party in question.

(6A) The date for filing the completed allocation questionnaire may not be varied by agreement between the parties.

(7) The time when the court serves an allocation questionnaire under this rule may be varied by a practice direction in respect of claims issued by the Production Centre.

(Rule 7.10 makes provision for the Production Centre.)
(Rule 6.7 specifies when a document is deemed to be served.)

## 26.4 Stay to Allow for Settlement of the Case

(1) A party may, when filing the completed allocation questionnaire, make a written request for the proceedings to be stayed(GL) while the parties try to settle the case by alternative dispute resolution(GL) or other means.

(2) Where—
(a) all parties request a stay(GL) under paragraph (1); or
(b) the court, of its own initiative, considers that such a stay would be appropriate,

the court will direct that the proceedings, either in whole or in part, be stayed for one month, or for such specified period as it considers appropriate.

(3) The court may extend the stays(GL) until such date or for such specified period as it considers appropriate.

(4) Where the court stays(GL) the proceedings under this rule, the claimant must tell the court if a settlement is reached.

(5) If the claimant does not tell the court by the end of the period of the stay(GL) that a settlement has been reached, the court will give such directions as to the management of the case as it considers appropriate.

## 26.5 Allocation

(1) The court will allocate the claim to a track—
(a) when every defendant has filed an allocation questionnaire, or
(b) when the period for filing the allocation questionnaires has expired,

whichever is the sooner, unless it has—
(i) stayed(GL) the proceedings under rule 26.4; or
(ii) dispensed with the need for allocation questionnaires.

(Rules 12.7 and 14.8 provide for the court to allocate a claim to a track where the claimant obtains default judgment on request or judgment on admission for an amount to be decided by the court.)

(2) If the court has stayed(GL) the proceedings under rule 26.4, it will allocate the claim to a track at the end of the period of the stay.
(3) Before deciding the track to which to allocate proceedings or deciding whether to give directions for an allocation hearing to be fixed, the court may order a party to provide further information about his case.
(4) The court may hold an allocation hearing if it thinks it is necessary.
(5) If a party fails to file an allocation questionnaire, the court may give any direction it considers appropriate.

## 26.6 Scope of Each Track

(1) The small claims track is the normal track for—
(a) any claim for personal injuries where—
(i) the financial value of the claim is not more than £5,000; and
(ii) the financial value of any claim for damages for personal injuries is not more than £1,000;
(b) any claim which includes a claim by a tenant of residential premises against his landlord where—
(i) the tenant is seeking an order requiring the landlord to carry out repairs or other work to the premises (whether or not the tenant is also seeking some other remedy);
(ii) the cost of the repairs or other work to the premises is estimated to be not more than £1,000; and
(iii) the financial value of any other claim for damages is not more than £1,000.

(Rule 2.3 defines 'claim for personal injuries' as proceedings in which there is a claim for damages in respect of personal injuries to the claimant or any other person or in respect of a person's death.)

(2) For the purposes of paragraph (1) 'damages for personal injuries' means damages claimed as compensation for pain, suffering and loss of amenity and does not include any other damages which are claimed.
(3) Subject to paragraph (1), the small claims track is the normal track for any claim which has a financial value of not more than £5,000.

(Rule 26.7(4) provides that the court will not allocate to the small claims track certain claims in respect of harassment or unlawful eviction.)

(4) Subject to paragraph (5), the fast track is the normal track for any claim—
(a) for which the small claims track is not the normal track; and
(b) which has a financial value of not more than £15,000.
(5) The fast track is the normal track for the claims referred to in paragraph (4) only if the court considers that—
(a) the trial is likely to last for no longer than one day; and
(b) oral expert evidence at trial will be limited to—
(i) one expert per party in relation to any expert field; and
(ii) expert evidence in two expert fields.
(6) The multi-track is the normal track for any claim for which the small claims track or the fast track is not the normal track.

## 26.7 General Rule for Allocation

(1) In considering whether to allocate a claim to the normal track for that claim under rule 26.6, the court will have regard to the matters mentioned in rule 26.8(1).

(2) The court will allocate a claim which has no financial value to the track which it considers most suitable having regard to the matters mentioned in rule 26.8(1).
(3) The court will not allocate proceedings to a track if the financial value of the claim, assessed by the court under rule 26.8, exceeds the limit for that track unless all the parties consent to the allocation of the claim to that track.
(4) The court will not allocate a claim to the small claims track, if it includes a claim by a tenant of residential premises against his landlord for a remedy in respect of harassment or unlawful eviction.

## 26.8 Matters Relevant to Allocation to a Track

(1) When deciding the track for a claim, the matters to which the court shall have regard include—
 (a) the financial value, if any, of the claim;
 (b) the nature of the remedy sought;
 (c) the likely complexity of the facts, law or evidence;
 (d) the number of parties or likely parties;
 (e) the value of any counterclaim or other Part 20 claim and the complexity of any matters relating to it;
 (f) the amount of oral evidence which may be required;
 (g) the importance of the claim to persons who are not parties to the proceedings;
 (h) the views expressed by the parties; and
 (i) the circumstances of the parties.
(2) It is for the court to assess the financial value of a claim and in doing so it will disregard—
 (a) any amount not in dispute;
 (b) any claim for interest;
 (c) costs; and
 (d) any contributory negligence.
(3) Where—
 (a) two or more claimants have started a claim against the same defendant using the same claim form; and
 (b) each claimant has a claim against the defendant separate from the other claimants,
 the court will consider the claim of each claimant separately when it assesses financial value under paragraph (1).

## 26.9 Notice of Allocation

(1) When it has allocated a claim to a track, the court will serve notice of allocation on every party.
(2) When the court serves notice of allocation on a party, it will also serve—
 (a) a copy of the allocation questionnaires filed by the other parties; and
 (b) a copy of any further information provided by another party about his case (whether by order or not).

(Rule 26.5 provides that the court may, before allocating proceedings, order a party to provide further information about his case.)

## 26.10 Reallocation

The court may subsequently reallocate a claim to a different track.

## 26.11 Trial with a Jury

An application for a claim to be tried with a jury must be made within 28 days of service of the defence.

(Section 69 of the Supreme Court Act 1981 and section 66 of the County Courts Act 1984 specify when a claim may be tried with a jury.)

# PD 26 Practice Direction — Case Management — Preliminary Stage: Allocation and Reallocation

This practice direction supplements CPR Part 26.

## Reminders of Important Rule Provisions other than Parts 26–29

Attention is drawn in particular to the following provisions of the Civil Procedure Rules:

**Part 1** The Overriding Objective (defined in rule 1.1).
The duty of the court to further that objective by actively managing cases (set out in rule 1.4).
The requirement that the parties help the court to further that objective (set out in rule 1.3).

**Part 3** The court's case management powers (which may be exercised on application or on its own initiative) and the sanctions which it may impose.

**Part 24** The court's power to grant summary judgment.

**Parts 32–35** Evidence, especially the court's power to control evidence.
Attention is also drawn to the practice directions which supplement those Parts and Parts 27–29, and to those which relate to the various specialist jurisdictions.

## The Allocation Questionnaire

*Form*

2.1 (1) The allocation questionnaire referred to in Part 26 will be in Form N149 or Form N150.

(2) (a) Attention is drawn to Section 6 of PD 43–48, which requires an estimate of costs to be filed and served when an allocation questionnaire is filed by a party to a claim which is outside the limits of the small claims track.

(b) A party will comply with that obligation if the costs estimate he files and serves states the figures for the base costs, incurred and to be incurred, which he expects, if he is successful, to recover from the other party. The estimate should show an itemised breakdown of how it is calculated, showing separately the amounts included for profit costs, disbursements and VAT. It should be substantially in the form illustrated in precedent H in the schedule to PD 43–48.
(Paragraph 2.2 of PD 43–48 defines 'base costs'.)

(c) Any party who has entered into a funding arrangement need not reveal the amount of any additional liability.
(Rule 43.2 defines 'funding arrangement' and 'additional liability'.)

(d) No later than when he files the estimate the solicitor acting for that party must deliver a copy to his client.

*Provision of extra information*

2.2 (1) This paragraph sets out what a party should do when he files his allocation questionnaire if he wishes to give the court information about matters which he believes may affect its decision about allocation or case management.

(2) The general rule is that the court will not take such information into account unless the document containing it either:

(a) confirms that all parties have agreed that the information is correct and that it should be put before the court, or

(b) confirms that the party who has sent the document to the court has delivered a copy to all the other parties.

(3) The following are examples of information which will be likely to help the court:

(a) a party's intention to apply for summary judgment or some other order that may dispose of the case or reduce the amount in dispute or the number of issues remaining to be decided,
(b) a party's intention to issue a Part 20 claim or to add another party,
(c) the steps the parties have taken in the preparation of evidence (in particular expert evidence), the steps they intend to take and whether those steps are to be taken in cooperation with any other party,
(d) the directions the party believes will be appropriate to be given for the management of the case,
(e) about any particular facts that may affect the timetable the court will set,
(f) any facts which may make it desirable for the court to fix an allocation hearing or a hearing at which case management directions will be given.

*Consultation*

2.3 (1) The parties should consult one another and cooperate in completing the allocation questionnaires and giving other information to the court.
(2) They should try to agree the case management directions which they will invite the court to make. Further details appear in the PD 28 and PD 29.
(3) The process of consultation must not delay the filing of the allocation questionnaires.

*Hearings before allocation*

2.4 Where a court hearing takes place (for example on an application for an interim injunction or for summary judgment under Part 24) before the claim is allocated to a track, the court may at that hearing:
(1) dispense with the need for the parties to file allocation questionnaires, treat the hearing as an allocation hearing, make an order for allocation and give directions for case management, or
(2) fix a date for allocation questionnaires to be filed and give other directions.

*Consequences of failure to file an allocation questionnaire*

2.5 (1) If no party files an allocation questionnaire within the time specified by Form N152, the court will order that unless an allocation questionnaire is filed within 7 days from service of that order, the claim, defence and any counterclaim will be struck out without further order of the court.
(2) Where a party files an allocation questionnaire but another party does not, the file will be referred to a judge for his directions and the court may:
(a) allocate the claim to a track if it considers that it has enough information to do so, or
(b) order that an allocation hearing is listed and that all or any parties must attend.

## Stay to Allow for Settlement of the Case

*Procedure for the parties to apply to extend the stay*

3.1 (1) (a) The court will generally accept a letter from any party or from the solicitor for any party as an application to extend the stay under rule 26.4.
(b) The letter should—
(i) confirm that the application is made with the agreement of all parties, and
(ii) explain the steps being taken and identify any mediator or expert assisting with the process.
(2) (a) An order extending the stay must be made by a judge.
(b) The extension will generally be for no more than 4 weeks unless clear reasons are given to justify a longer time.
(3) More than one extension of the stay may be granted.

3.2 Position at the end of the stay if no settlement is reached
(1) At the end of the stay the file will be referred to a judge for his directions.
(2) He will consider whether to allocate the claim to a track and what other directions

to give, or may require any party to give further information or fix an allocation hearing.

3.3 Any party may apply for a stay to be lifted.

*Position where settlement is reached during a stay*

3.4 Where the whole of the proceedings are settled during a stay, the taking of any of the following steps will be treated as an application for the stay to be lifted:

(1) an application for a consent order (in any form) to give effect to the settlement,

(2) an application for the approval of a settlement where a party is a person under a disability,

(3) giving notice of acceptance of money paid into court in satisfaction of the claim or applying for money in court to be paid out.

## Allocation, Reallocation and Case Management

*The court's general approach*

4.1 The Civil Procedure Rules lay down the overriding objective, the powers and duties of the court and the factors to which it must have regard in exercising them. The court will expect to exercise its powers as far as possible in cooperation with the parties and their legal representatives so as to deal with the case justly in accordance with that objective.

*Allocation to track*

4.2 (1) In most cases the court will expect to have enough information from the statements of case and allocation questionnaires to be able to allocate the claim to a track and to give case management directions.

(2) If the court does not have enough information to allocate the claim it will generally make an order under rule 26.5(3) requiring one or more parties to provide further information within 14 days.

(3) Where there has been no allocation hearing the notice of allocation will be in forms N154 (fast track), N155 (multi-track) or N157, N158, N159 or N160 (small claims).

(4) (a) The general rule is that the court will give brief reasons for its allocation decision, and these will be set out in the notice of allocation.

(b) The general rule does not apply where all the allocation questionnaires which have been filed have expressed the wish for the claim to be allocated to the track to which the court has allocated it.

(5) Paragraph 6 of this practice direction deals with allocation hearings and paragraph 7 deals with allocation principles.

(6) Paragraph 11 of this practice direction deals with reallocation.

4.3 PD 27, PD 28 and PD 29 contain further information about the giving of case management directions at the allocation stage.

## Summary Judgment or Other Early Termination

5.1 Part of the court's duty of active case management is the summary disposal of issues which do not need full investigation and trial (rule 1.4(2)(c)).

5.2 The court's powers to make orders to dispose of issues in that way include:

(a) under rule 3.4, striking out a statement of case, or part of a statement of case, and

(b) under Part 24, giving summary judgment where a claimant or a defendant has no reasonable prospect of success.

The court may use these powers on an application or on its own initiative. PD 24 contains further information.

5.3 (1) A party intending to make such an application should do so before or when filing his allocation questionnaire.

(2) Where a party makes an application for such an order before a claim has been allocated to a track the court will not normally allocate the claim before the hearing of the application.

(3) Where a party files an allocation questionnaire stating that he intends to make such an application but has not done so, the judge will usually direct that an allocation hearing is listed.

(4) The application may be heard at that allocation hearing if the application notice has been issued and served in sufficient time.

5.4 (1) This paragraph applies where the court proposes to make such an order of its own initiative.

(2) The court will not allocate the claim to a track but instead it will either:

(a) fix a hearing, giving the parties at least 14 days notice of the date of the hearing and of the issues which it is proposed that the court will decide, or

(b) make an order directing a party to take the steps described in the order within a stated time and specifying the consequence of not taking those steps.

5.5 Where the court decides at the hearing of an application or a hearing fixed under paragraph 5.4(2)(a) that the claim (or part of the claim) is to continue it may:

(1) treat that hearing as an allocation hearing, allocate the claim and give case management directions, or

(2) give other directions.

## Allocation Hearings

*General principle*

6.1 The court will only hold an allocation hearing on its own initiative if it considers that it is necessary to do so.

*Procedure*

6.2 Where the court orders an allocation hearing to take place:

(1) it will give the parties at least seven days' notice of the hearing in form N153, and

(2) form N153 will give a brief explanation of the decision to order the hearing.

6.3 Power to treat another hearing as an allocation hearing

Where the court may treat another hearing as an allocation hearing it does not need to give notice to any party that it proposes to do so.

6.4 The notice of allocation after an allocation hearing will be in forms N154, N155 or N157.

*Representation*

6.5 A legal representative who attends an allocation hearing should, if possible, be the person responsible for the case and must in any event be familiar with the case, be able to provide the court with the information it is likely to need to take its decisions about allocation and case management, and have sufficient authority to deal with any issues that are likely to arise.

*Sanctions*

6.6 (1) This paragraph sets out the sanctions that the court will usually impose for default in connection with the allocation procedure, but the court may make a different order.

(2) (a) Where an allocation hearing takes place because a party has failed to file an allocation questionnaire or to provide further information which the court has ordered, the court will usually order that party to pay on the indemnity basis the costs of any other party who has attended the hearing, summarily assess the amount of those costs, and order them to be paid forthwith or within a stated period.

(b) The court may order that if the party does not pay those costs within the time stated his statement of case will be struck out.

(3) Where a party whose default has led to a fixing of an allocation hearing is still in default and does not attend the hearing the court will usually make an order specifying the steps he is required to take and providing that unless he takes them within a stated time his statement of case will be struck out.

## Allocation Principles

*Rules 26.6, 26.7 and 26.8*

7.1 (1) Rule 26.6 sets out the scope of each track,
(2) Rule 26.7 states the general rule for allocation, and
(3) Rule 26.8 sets out the matters relevant to allocation to a track.

*Objective of this paragraph*

7.2 The object of this paragraph is to explain what will be the court's general approach to some of the matters set out in rule 26.8.

*'the financial value of the claim'*

7.3 (1) Rule 26.8(2) provides that it is for the court to assess the financial value of a claim.
(2) Where the court believes that the amount the claimant is seeking exceeds what he may reasonably be expected to recover it may make an order under rule 26.5(3) directing the claimant to justify the amount.

*'any amount not in dispute'*

7.4 In deciding, for the purposes of rule 26.8(2), whether an amount is in dispute the court will apply the following general principles:
(1) Any amount for which the defendant does not admit liability is in dispute,
(2) Any sum in respect of an item forming part of the claim for which judgment has been entered (for example a summary judgment) is not in dispute,
(3) Any specific sum claimed as a distinct item and which the defendant admits he is liable to pay is not in dispute,
(4) Any sum offered by the defendant which has been accepted by the claimant in satisfaction of any item which forms a distinct part of the claim is not in dispute.

It follows from these provisions that if, in relation to a claim the value of which is above the small claims track limit of £5,000, the defendant makes, before allocation, an admission that reduces the amount in dispute to a figure below £5,000 (see CPR Part 14), the normal track for the claim will be the small claims track. As to recovery of pre-allocation costs, the claimant can, before allocation, apply for judgment with costs on the amount of the claim that has been admitted (see CPR rule 14.3 but see also PD 43–48, para. 15.1(3), under which the court has a discretion to allow pre-allocation costs).

*'the views expressed by the parties'*

7.5 The court will treat these views as an important factor, but the allocation decision is one for the court, to be taken in the light of all the circumstances, and the court will not be bound by any agreement or common view of the parties.

*'the circumstances of the parties'*

7.6 See paragraph 8.

*'the value of any counterclaim or other Part 20 claim'*

7.7 Where the case involves more than one money claim (for example where there is a Part 20 claim or there is more than one claimant each making separate claims) the court will not generally aggregate the claims. Instead it will generally regard the largest of them as determining the financial value of the claims.

## The Small Claims Track—Allocation and Case Management

*Allocation*

8.1 (1) (a) The small claims track is intended to provide a proportionate procedure by which most straightforward claims with a financial value of not more than £5,000 can be decided, without the need for substantial pre-hearing preparation and the formalities of a traditional trial, and without incurring large legal costs. (Rule 26.6 provides for a lower financial value in certain types of case.)
(b) The procedure laid down in Part 27 for the preparation of the case and the

conduct of the hearing are designed to make it possible for a litigant to conduct his own case without legal representation if he wishes.

(c) Cases generally suitable for the small claims track will include consumer disputes, accident claims, disputes about the ownership of goods and most disputes between a landlord and tenant other than opposed claims under Part 56, disputed claims for possession under Part 55 and demotion claims whether in the alternative to possession claims or under Part 65.

(d) A case involving a disputed allegation of dishonesty will not usually be suitable for the small claims track.

(2) Rule 26.7(3) and rule 27.14(5)

(a) These rules allow the parties to consent to the allocation to the small claims track of a claim the value of which is above the limits mentioned in rule 26.6(2) and, in that event, the rules make provision about costs.

(b) The court will not allocate such a claim to the small claims track, notwithstanding that the parties have consented to the allocation, unless it is satisfied that it is suitable for that track.

(c) The court will not normally allow more than one day for the hearing of such a claim.

(d) The court will give case management directions to ensure that the case is dealt with in as short a time as possible. These may include directions of a kind that are not usually given in small claim cases, for example, for Scott Schedules.

*Case management*

8.2 (1) Directions for case management of claims allocated to the small claims track will generally be given by the court on allocation.

(2) Rule 27.4 contains further provisions about directions and PD 27 sets out the standard directions which the court will usually give.

## The Fast Track

*Allocation*

9.1 (1) Where the court is to decide whether to allocate to the fast track or the multi-track a claim for which the normal track is the fast track, it will allocate the claim to the fast track unless it believes that it cannot be dealt with justly on that track.

(2) The court will, in particular, take into account the limits likely to be placed on disclosure, the extent to which expert evidence may be necessary and whether the trial is likely to last more than a day.

(3) (a) When it is considering the likely length of the trial the court will regard a day as being a period of 5 hours, and will consider whether that is likely to be sufficient time for the case to be heard.

(b) The court will also take into account the case management directions (including the fixing of a trial timetable) that are likely to be given and the court's powers to control evidence and to limit cross-examination.

(c) The possibility that a trial might last longer than one day is not necessarily a conclusive reason for the court to allocate or to reallocate a claim to the multi-track.

(d) A claim may be allocated to the fast track or ordered to remain on that track although there is to be a split trial.

(e) Where the case involves a counterclaim or other Part 20 claim that will be tried with the claim and as a result the trial will last more than a day, the court may not allocate it to the fast track.

*Case management*

9.2 (1) Directions for the case management of claims which have been allocated to the fast track will be given at the allocation stage or at the listing stage (in either case with or without a hearing) or at both, and if necessary at other times. The trial judge may, at or before the trial, give directions for its conduct.

(2) PD 28 contains further provisions and contains standard directions which the court may give.

## The Multi-track

10.1 Paragraph 10.2 does not apply to:

(1) a claim for possession of land in the county court or a demotion claim whether in the alternative to possession or under Part 65;

(2) any claim which is being dealt with at the Royal Courts of Justice.

*Venue for allocation and case management*

10.2 (1) The case management of a claim which is allocated to the multi-track will normally be dealt with at a Civil Trial Centre.

(2) In the case of a claim to which any of Parts 49 or 58 to 62 apply, case management must be dealt with at a Civil Trial Centre. Sub-paragraphs (4) to (10) do not apply to such a claim. The claim will be allocated to the multi-track irrespective of its value, and must be transferred to a Civil Trial Centre for allocation and case management if not already there.

(3) Where a claim is issued in or automatically transferred to a Civil Trial Centre it will be allocated and managed at that court.

(4) The following sub-paragraphs apply to a claim which is issued in or automatically transferred to a court which is not a Civil Trial Centre. Such a court is referred to as a 'feeder court'.

(5) Where a judge sitting at a feeder court decides, on the basis of the allocation questionnaires and any other documents filed by the parties, that the claim should be dealt with on the multi-track he will normally make an order:

(a) allocating the claim to that track,

(b) giving case management directions, and

(c) transferring the claim to a Civil Trial Centre.

(6) If he decides that an allocation hearing or some pre-allocation hearing is to take place (for example to strike out a statement of case under Part 3 of the Rules) that hearing will take place at the feeder court.

(7) If, before allocation, a hearing takes place at a feeder court and in exercising his powers under paragraph 2.4(1) above the judge allocates the claim to the multi-track, he will also normally make an order transferring the claim to a Civil Trial Centre.

(8) A judge sitting at a feeder court may, rather than making an allocation order himself, transfer the claim to a Civil Trial Centre for the decision about allocation to be taken there.

(9) When, following an order for transfer, the file is received at the Civil Trial Centre, a judge sitting at that Centre will consider it and give any further directions that appear necessary or desirable.

(10) Where there is reason to believe that more than one case management conference may be needed and the parties or their legal advisers are located inconveniently far from the Civil Trial Centre, a judge sitting at a feeder court may, with the agreement of the Designated Civil Judge and notwithstanding the allocation of the case to the multi-track, decide that in the particular circumstances of the case it should not be transferred to a Civil Trial Centre, but should be case managed for the time being at the feeder court.

(11) A Designated Civil Judge may at any time make an order transferring a claim from a feeder court to a Civil Trial Centre and he may do so irrespective of the track, if any, to which it has been allocated. He may also permit a feeder court to keep for trial a claim or (subject to review from time to time) a category of claims.

Any such permission should take into account the ability of the feeder court in relation to the Civil Trial Centre to provide suitable and effective trial within an appropriate trial period.

(12) No order will be made by a feeder court fixing a date for a hearing at a Civil Trial Centre unless that date has been given or confirmed by a judge or listing officer of that Centre.

*Case management*

10.3 Part 29 of the Rules and PD 29 set out the procedure to be adopted.

## Reallocation of Claims and the Variation of Directions

11.1 (1) Where a party is dissatisfied with an order made allocating the claim to a track he may appeal or apply to the court to reallocate the claim.

(2) He should appeal if the order was made at a hearing at which he was present or represented, or of which he was given due notice.

(3) In any other case he should apply to the court to reallocate the claim.

11.2 Where there has been a change in the circumstances since an order was made allocating the claim to a track the court may reallocate the claim. It may do so on application or on its own initiative.

(PD 28 and PD 29 contain provisions about the variation of case management directions.)

## Determining the Amount to be Paid Under a Judgment or Order

*Scope*

12.1 (1) In the following paragraphs:

(a) a 'relevant order' means a judgment or order of the court which requires the amount of money to be paid by one party to another to be decided by the court; and

(b) a 'disposal hearing' means a hearing in accordance with para. 12.4.

(2) A relevant order may have been obtained:

(a) by a judgment in default under Part 12;

(b) by a judgment on an admission under Part 14;

(c) on the striking out of a statement of case under Part 3;

(d) on a summary judgment application under Part 24;

(e) on the determination of a preliminary issue or on a trial as to liability; or

(f) at trial.

(3) A relevant order includes any order for the amount of a debt, damages or interest to be decided by the court (including an order for the taking of an account or the making of an inquiry as to any sum due, and any similar order), but does not include an order for the assessment of costs.

*Directions*

12.2 (1) When the court makes a relevant order it will give directions, which may include:

(a) listing the claim for a disposal hearing;

(b) allocating or reallocating the claim (but see para. 12.3);

(c) directing the parties to file allocation questionnaires by a specified date; and

(d) staying the claim while the parties try to settle the case by alternative dispute resolution or other means.

(2) Directions may specify the level or type of judge before whom a hearing or a further hearing will take place and the nature and purpose of that hearing.

(3) Where the parties apply for a relevant order by consent, they should if possible file with their draft consent order agreed directions for the court's approval.

*Allocation*

12.3 (1) If, when the court makes a relevant order:

(a) the claim has not previously been allocated to a track; and
(b) the financial value of the claim (determined in accordance with Part 26) is such that the claim would, if defended be allocated to the small claims track,

the court will normally allocate it to that track.

(2) Where para. (1)(b) does not apply, the court will not normally allocate the claim to a track (other than the small claims track) unless:
(a) the amount payable appears to be genuinely disputed on substantial grounds; or
(b) the dispute is not suitable to be dealt with at a disposal hearing.

*Disposal hearings*

12.4 (1) A disposal hearing is a hearing:
(a) which will not normally last longer than 30 minutes, and
(b) at which the court will not normally hear oral evidence.

(2) At a disposal hearing the court may:
(a) decide the amount payable under or in consequence of the relevant order and give judgment for that amount; or
(b) give directions as to the future conduct of the proceedings.

(3) If the claim has been allocated to the small claims track, or the court decides at the disposal hearing to allocate it to that track, the court may treat the disposal hearing as a final hearing in accordance with Part 27.

(4) Rule 32.6 applies to evidence at a disposal hearing unless the court directs otherwise.

(5) Except where the claim has been allocated to the small claims track, the court will not exercise its power under sub-paragraph (2)(a) unless any written evidence on which the claimant relies has been served on the defendant at least three days before the disposal hearing.

*Costs*

12.5 (1) Attention is drawn to:
(a) PD 43–48 and in particular to the court's power to make a summary assessment of costs;
(b) r. 44.13(1) which provides that if an order makes no mention of costs, none are payable in respect of the proceedings to which it relates; and
(c) r. 27.14 (special rules about costs in cases allocated to the small claims track).

(2) Part 46 (fast track trial costs) will not apply to a case dealt with at a disposal hearing whatever the financial value of the claim. So the costs of a disposal hearing will be in the discretion of the court.

*Jurisdiction of masters and district judges*

12.6 Unless the court otherwise directs, a master or a district judge may decide the amount payable under a relevant order irrespective of the financial value of the claim and of the track to which the claim may have been allocated.

# PD 26B Practice Direction — Pilot Scheme for Mediation in Central London County Court

This Practice Direction Supplements CPR Part 26.

## General

1.1 This practice direction provides for a pilot scheme to operate from 1st April 2004 to 31st March 2005 in relation to claims in the Central London County Court.

1.2 This practice direction enables the Central London County Court to—

(1) require the parties to certain types of claims either to attend a mediation appointment or to give reasons for objecting to doing so; and

(2) stay the claim until such an appointment takes place.

1.3 Cases in which a notice of referral to mediation has been served under paragraph 3.1 prior to 31st March 2005 shall remain subject to this practice direction until either—

(1) a mediation appointment has taken place; or

(2) any stay of execution imposed under paragraph 5 has expired or been lifted by the court,

whichever shall be the sooner.

## Types of claims to which this practice direction applies

2 This practice direction applies to a claim if it meets all the following conditions—

(1) the small claims track is not the normal track for the claim;

(2) no party to the claim is—

(a) a child or patient; or

(b) exempt from payment of court fees; and

(3) the court has not granted an interim injunction in the proceedings.

## Service of mediation notice

3.1 The court may, when it serves the allocation questionnaire under rule 26.3, serve a notice of referral to mediation on each party—

(1) notifying them that the claim is to be referred to mediation; and

(2) requiring them, within 14 days after service of the notice on them, to file and serve a reply to the notice in which they must—

(a) state whether they agree or object to mediation;

(b) specify any dates within three months of the date of filing the response on which they would not be able to attend a mediation appointment; and

(c) if they object to mediation, set out their reasons for doing so.

3.2 The cases where a notice of referral to mediation is served on the parties will be chosen at random from those that meet the criteria set out in paragraph 2.

3.3 A party who receives a notice of referral to mediation need not complete and file an allocation questionnaire unless or until directed to do so by the court.

## Objection to mediation

4.1 If one or more of the parties states in his reply that he objects to mediation, the case will be referred to a district judge who may—

(1) direct the case to be listed for a hearing of the objections to mediation;

(2) direct that a mediation appointment should proceed;

(3) order the parties to file and serve completed allocation questionnaires; or

(4) give such directions as to the management of the case as he considers appropriate.

4.2 If a party does not file a reply within the time specified in the notice of referral to mediation, the court and all other parties may proceed as if that party has no objection to the use of mediation in the case.

## Mediation appointment

5.1 If no party objects to mediation, or the court directs that mediation should proceed, the court will direct that the proceedings be stayed for an initial period of two months.

5.2 In accordance with the existing Central London County Court Mediation Scheme, the court will fix a date, time and place for the mediation appointment and notify the parties accordingly once all the parties have paid the mediator's charges.

5.3 When the court fixes a mediation appointment it will if necessary extend the stay of proceedings until the date of the appointment.

## Mediator's charges

6.1 A mediator's charge is payable by each party who is to attend a mediation appointment. The court will notify each party of the amount of the charge and request payment of that amount in the notice of referral to mediation.

6.2 A party must pay the mediator's charge to the court within 14 days of being requested to do so or such other period as the court may direct. Any request for further time in which to pay the mediator's charge may be made by letter.

6.3 If any party fails to pay the mediator's charge the court will refer the case to a district judge for directions.

## Unsuccessful mediation

7. If the mediation does not proceed or does not fully resolve the dispute, the mediator will notify the court and the court will—
   (1) either—
      (a) allocate the claim to a track; or
      (b) order the parties to file and serve completed allocation questionnaires (if not already filed); and
   (2) give such directions for the further management of the case as it considers appropriate.

# CPR Part 27 The Small Claims Track



## 27.1 Scope of this Part

(1) This Part—
- (a) sets out the special procedure for dealing with claims which have been allocated to the small claims track under Part 26; and
- (b) limits the amount of costs that can be recovered in respect of a claim which has been allocated to the small claims track.

(Rule 27.14 deals with costs on the small claims track.)

(2) A claim being dealt with under this Part is called a small claim.

(Rule 26.6 provides for the scope of the small claims track. A claim for a remedy for harassment or unlawful eviction relating, in either case, to residential premises shall not be allocated to the small claims track whatever the financial value of the claim. Otherwise, the small claims track will be the normal track for—
- any claim which has a financial value of not more than £5,000 subject to the special provisions about claims for personal injuries and housing disrepair claims;
- any claim for personal injuries which has a financial value of not more than £5,000 where the claim for damages for personal injuries is not more than £1,000; and
- any claim which includes a claim by a tenant of residential premises against his landlord for repairs or other work to the premises where the estimated cost of the repairs or other work is not more than £1,000 and the financial value of any other claim for damages in respect of those repairs or other work is not more than £1,000.)

## 27.2 Extent to Which Other Parts Apply

(1) The following Parts of these Rules do not apply to small claims—
- (a) Part 25 (interim remedies) except as it relates to interim injunctions(GL);
- (b) Part 31 (disclosure and inspection);
- (c) Part 32 (evidence) except rule 32.1 (power of court to control evidence);
- (d) Part 33 (miscellaneous rules about evidence);
- (e) Part 35 (experts and assessors) except rules 35.1 (duty to restrict expert evidence), 35.3 (experts—overriding duty to the court), 35.7 (court's power to direct that evidence is to be given by single joint expert) and 35.8 (instructions to a single joint expert);
- (f) Subject to paragraph (3), Part 18 (further information);
- (g) Part 36 (offers to settle); and
- (h) Part 39 (hearings) except rule 39.2 (general rule—hearing to be in public).

(2) The other Parts of these Rules apply to small claims except to the extent that a rule limits such application.

(3) The court of its own initiative may order a party to provide further information if it considers it appropriate to do so.

## 27.3 Court's Power to Grant a Final Remedy

The court may grant any final remedy in relation to a small claim which it could grant if the proceedings were on the fast track or the multi-track.

## 27.4 Preparation for the Hearing

(1) After allocation the court will—
  (a) give standard directions and fix a date for the final hearing;
  (b) give special directions and fix a date for the final hearing;
  (c) give special directions and direct that the court will consider what further directions are to be given no later than 28 days after the date the special directions were given;
  (d) fix a date for a preliminary hearing under rule 27.6; or
  (e) give notice that it proposes to deal with the claim without a hearing under rule 27.10 and invite the parties to notify the court by a specified date if they agree the proposal.
(2) The court will—
  (a) give the parties at least 21 days' notice of the date fixed for the final hearing, unless the parties agree to accept less notice; and
  (b) inform them of the amount of time allowed for the final hearing.
(3) In this rule—
  (a) 'standard directions' means—
    (i) a direction that each party shall, at least 14 days before the date fixed for the final hearing, file and serve on every other party copies of all documents (including any expert's report) on which he intends to rely at the hearing; and
    (ii) any other standard directions set out in the relevant practice direction; and
  (b) 'special directions' means directions given in addition to or instead of the standard directions.

## 27.5 Experts

No expert may give evidence, whether written or oral, at a hearing without the permission of the court.

(Rule 27.14(3)(d) provides for the payment of an expert's fees.)

## 27.6 Preliminary Hearing

(1) The court may hold a preliminary hearing for the consideration of the claim, but only—
  (a) where—
    (i) it considers that special directions, as defined in rule 27.4, are needed to ensure a fair hearing; and
    (ii) it appears necessary for a party to attend at court to ensure that he understands what he must do to comply with the special directions; or
  (b) to enable it to dispose of the claim on the basis that one or other of the parties has no real prospect of success at a final hearing; or
  (c) to enable it to strike out(GL) a statement of case or part of a statement of case on the basis that the statement of case, or the part to be struck out, discloses no reasonable grounds for bringing or defending the claim.
(2) When considering whether or not to hold a preliminary hearing, the court must have regard to the desirability of limiting the expense to the parties of attending court.
(3) Where the court decides to hold a preliminary hearing, it will give the parties at least 14 days' notice of the date of the hearing.
(4) The court may treat the preliminary hearing as the final hearing of the claim if all the parties agree.
(5) At or after the preliminary hearing the court will—
  (a) fix the date of the final hearing (if it has not been fixed already) and give the parties at least 21 days' notice of the date fixed unless the parties agree to accept less notice;

(b) inform them of the amount of time allowed for the final hearing; and
(c) give any appropriate directions.

## 27.7 Power of Court to Add to, Vary or Revoke Directions

The court may add to, vary or revoke directions.

## 27.8 Conduct of the Hearing

(1) The court may adopt any method of proceeding at a hearing that it considers to be fair.
(2) Hearings will be informal.
(3) The strict rules of evidence do not apply.
(4) The court need not take evidence on oath.
(5) The court may limit cross-examination(GL).
(6) The court must give reasons for its decision.

## 27.9 Non-attendance of Parties at a Final Hearing

(1) If a party who does not attend a final hearing—
(a) has given written notice to the court and the other party at least 7 days before the hearing date that he will not attend;
(b) has served on the other party at least 7 days before the hearing date any other documents which he has filed with the court; and
(c) has, in his written notice, requested the court to decide the claim in his absence and has confirmed his compliance with paragraphs (a) and (b) above,
the court will take into account that party's statement of case and any other documents he has filed and served when it decides the claim.
(2) If a claimant does not—
(a) attend the hearing; and
(b) give the notice referred to in paragraph (1),
the court may strike out(GL) the claim.
(3) If—
(a) a defendant does not—
(i) attend the hearing; or
(ii) give the notice referred to in paragraph (1); and
(b) the claimant either—
(i) does attend the hearing; or
(ii) gives the notice referred to in paragraph (1),
the court may decide the claim on the basis of the evidence of the claimant alone.
(4) If neither party attends or gives the notice referred to in paragraph (1), the court may strike out(GL) the claim and any defence and counterclaim.

## 27.10 Disposal Without a Hearing

The court may, if all parties agree, deal with the claim without a hearing.

## 27.11 Setting Judgment Aside and Rehearing

(1) A party—
(a) who was neither present nor represented at the hearing of the claim; and
(b) who has not given written notice to the court under rule 27.9(1),
may apply for an order that a judgment under this Part shall be set aside(GL) and the claim reheard.
(2) A party who applies for an order setting aside a judgment under this rule must make the application not more than 14 days after the day on which notice of the judgment was served on him.
(3) The court may grant an application under paragraph (2) only if the applicant—
(a) had a good reason for not attending or being represented at the hearing or giving written notice to the court under rule 27.9(1); and

(b) has a reasonable prospect of success at the hearing.
(4) If a judgment is set aside[(GL)]—
(a) the court must fix a new hearing for the claim; and
(b) the hearing may take place immediately after the hearing of the application to set the judgment aside and may be dealt with by the judge who set aside[(GL)] the judgment.
(5) A party may not apply to set aside[(GL)] a judgment under this rule if the court dealt with the claim without a hearing under rule 27.10.

**27.12** [*Revoked*]

**27.13** [*Revoked*]

## 27.14 Costs on the Small Claims Track

(1) This rule applies to any case which has been allocated to the small claims track unless paragraph (5) applies.

(Rules 44.9 and 44.11 make provision in relation to orders for costs made before a claim has been allocated to the small claims track.)

(2) The court may not order a party to pay a sum to another party in respect of that other party's costs, fees and expenses, including those relating to an appeal, except—
(a) the fixed costs attributable to issuing the claim which—
(i) are payable under Part 45; or
(ii) would be payable under Part 45 if that Part applied to the claim;
(b) in proceedings which included a claim for an injunction or an order for specific performance a sum not exceeding the amount specified in the relevant practice direction for legal advice and assistance relating to that claim;
(c) any court fees paid by that other party;
(d) expenses which a party or witness has reasonably incurred in travelling to and from a hearing or in staying away from home for the purposes of attending a hearing;
(e) a sum not exceeding the amount specified in the relevant practice direction for any loss of earnings or loss of leave by a party or witness due to attending a hearing or to staying away from home for the purposes of attending a hearing;
(f) a sum not exceeding the amount specified in the relevant practice direction for an expert's fees; and
(g) such further costs as the court may assess by the summary procedure and order to be paid by a party who has behaved unreasonably.
(3) A party's rejection of an offer in settlement will not of itself constitute unreasonable behaviour under paragraph (2)(g) but the court may take it into consideration when it is applying the unreasonableness test.
(4) The limits on costs imposed by this rule also apply to any fee or reward for acting on behalf of a party to the proceedings charged by a person exercising a right of audience by virtue of an order under section 11 of the Courts and Legal Services Act 1990[1] (a lay representative).
(5) Where—
(a) the financial value of a claim exceeds the limit for the small claims track; but
(b) the claim has been allocated to the small claims track in accordance with rule 26.7(3),

the small claims track costs provisions will apply unless the parties agree that the fast track costs provisions are to apply.
(6) Where the parties agree that the fast track costs provisions are to apply, the claim and any appeal will be treated for the purposes of costs as if it were proceeding on the fast

[1] 1990 c.41.

track except that trial costs will be in the discretion of the court and will not exceed the amount set out for the value of claim in rule 46.2 (amount of fast track trial costs).

## 27.15 Claim Reallocated from the Small Claims Track to Another Track

Where a claim is allocated to the small claims track and subsequently reallocated to another track, rule 27.14 (costs on the small claims track) will cease to apply after the claim has been reallocated and the fast track or multi-track costs rules will apply from the date of reallocation.

# PD 27 Practice Direction — Small Claims Track

This practice direction supplements CPR Part 27.

## Judges

1 The functions of the court described in Part 27 which are to be carried out by a judge will generally be carried out by a district judge but may be carried out by a circuit judge.

## Case Management Directions

2.1 Rule 27.4 explains how directions will be given, and r. 27.6 contains provisions about the holding of a preliminary hearing and the court's powers at such a hearing.

2.2 Appendix A sets out details of the case that the court usually needs in the type of case described. Appendix B sets out the standard directions that the court may give. Appendix C sets out special directions that the court may give.

2.3 Before allocating the claim to the small claims track and giving directions for a hearing the court may require a party to give further information about that party's case.

2.4 A party may ask the court to give particular directions about the conduct of the case.

2.5 In deciding whether to make an order for exchange of witness statements the court will have regard to the following—

(a) whether either or both the parties are represented;
(b) the amount in dispute in the proceedings;
(c) the nature of the matters in dispute;
(d) whether the need for any party to clarify his case can better be dealt with by an order under paragraph 2.3;
(e) the need for the parties to have access to justice without undue formality, cost or delay.

## Representation at a Hearing

3.1 In this paragraph:

(1) a lawyer means a barrister, a solicitor or a legal executive employed by a solicitor, and
(2) a lay representative means any other person.

3.2 (1) A party may present his own case at a hearing or a lawyer or lay representative may present it for him.

(2) The Lay Representatives (Rights of Audience) Order 1999 (SI 1999/1225) provides that a lay representative may not exercise any right of audience:

(a) where his client does not attend the hearing,
(b) at any stage after judgment, or
(c) on any appeal brought against any decision made by the district judge in the proceedings.

(3) However the court, exercising its general discretion to hear anybody, may hear a lay representative even in circumstances excluded by the Order.

(4) Any of its officers or employees may represent a corporate party.

## Small Claim Hearing

4.1 (1) The general rule is that a small claim hearing will be in public.

(2) The judge may decide to hold it in private if:

(a) the parties agree, or
(b) a ground mentioned in r. 39.2(3) applies.

(3) A hearing or part of a hearing which takes place other than at the court, for example at the home or business premises of a party, will not be in public.

4.2 A hearing that takes place at the court will generally be in the judge's room but it may take place in a courtroom.

4.3 Rule 27.8 allows the court to adopt any method of proceeding that it considers to be fair and to limit cross-examination. The judge may in particular:
(1) ask questions of any witness himself before allowing any other person to do so,
(2) ask questions of all or any of the witnesses himself before allowing any other person to ask questions of any witnesses,
(3) refuse to allow cross-examination of any witness until all the witnesses have given evidence in chief,
(4) limit cross-examination of a witness to a fixed time or to a particular subject or issue, or both.

## Recording Evidence and the Giving of Reasons

5.1 A hearing that takes place at the court will be tape-recorded by the court. A party may obtain a transcript of such a recording on payment of the proper transcriber's charges.
5.2 Attention is drawn to the Contempt of Court Act 1981, s. 9 (which deals with the unauthorised use of tape recorders in court), and to Practice Direction (Tape Recorders) [1981] 1 WLR 1526 which relates to it.
5.3 (1) The judge may give reasons for his judgment as briefly and simply as the nature of the case allows.
(2) He will normally do so orally at the hearing, but he may give them later at a hearing either orally or in writing.
5.4 Where the judge decides the case without a hearing under r. 27.10 or a party who has given notice under r. 27.9(1) does not attend the hearing, the judge will prepare a note of his reasons and the court will send a copy to each party.
5.5 Nothing in this practice direction affects the duty of a judge at the request of a party to make a note of the matters referred to in the County Courts Act 1984, s. 80.

## Non-attendance of a Party at a Hearing

6.1 Attention is drawn to r. 27.9 (which enables a party to give notice that he will not attend a final hearing and sets out the effect of his giving such notice and of not doing so), and to para. 3 above.
6.2 Nothing in those provisions affects the general power of the court to adjourn a hearing, for example where a party who wishes to attend a hearing on the date fixed cannot do so for a good reason.

## Costs

7.1 Attention is drawn to r. 27.14 which contains provisions about the costs which may be ordered to be paid by one party to another.
7.2 The amount which a party may be ordered to pay under r. 27.14(2)(b) (for legal advice and assistance in claims including an injunction or specific performance) is a sum not exceeding £260.
7.3 The amounts which a party may be ordered to pay under r. 27.14(3)(c) (loss of earnings) and (d) (experts' fees) are:
(1) for the loss of earnings or loss of leave of each party or witness due to attending a hearing or staying away from home for the purpose of attending a hearing, a sum not exceeding £50 per day for each person, and
(2) for expert's fees, a sum not exceeding £200 for each expert.
(As to recovery of pre-allocation costs in a case in which an admission by the defendant has reduced the amount in dispute to a figure below £5,000, reference should be made to PD 26, para. 7.4 and to [PD 43–48, para. 15.1(3)*].)

[* The text issued by the Department for Constitutional Affairs refers to an earlier version of this practice direction.]

## Appeals

8.1 Part 52 deals with appeals and attention is drawn to that Part and the accompanying practice direction.

8A An appellant's notice in small claims must be filed and served in Form N164.

8.2 Where the court dealt with the claim to which the appellant is a party:

(1) under r. 27.10 without a hearing; or

(2) in his absence because he gave notice under r. 27.9 requesting the court to decide the claim in his absence,

an application for permission to appeal must be made to the appeal court.

8.3 Where an appeal is allowed the court will if possible, dispose of the case at the same time without referring the claim to the lower court or ordering a new hearing. It may do so without hearing further evidence.

8.7 The circuit judge will give any necessary directions:

(1) about the filing of any evidence concerning any allegation of serious irregularity, and

(2) about the supply to the parties of copies of any document (including any note made by the judge who heard the case) which he has taken or may have taken into account in dealing with the appeal.

8.8 Where the circuit judge dismisses the appeal without a hearing his order will contain brief reasons for his decision.

8.9 Where the circuit judge directs that the appeal is to be listed for hearing the court will give at least seven days' notice of the hearing to all parties.

8.10 If the appeal is allowed, the circuit judge will if possible dispose of the case at the same time without ordering the claim to be reheard. He may do so without hearing further evidence.

# APPENDIX A

# INFORMATION AND DOCUMENTATION THE COURT USUALLY NEEDS IN PARTICULAR TYPES OF CASE

## ROAD ACCIDENT CASES (where the information or documentation is available)

- witness statements (including statements from the parties themselves);
- invoices and estimates for repairs;
- agreements and invoices for any car hire costs;
- the police accident report;
- sketch plan which should wherever possible be agreed;
- photographs of the scene of the accident and of the damage.

## BUILDING DISPUTES, REPAIRS, GOODS SOLD AND SIMILAR CONTRACTUAL CLAIMS (where the information or documentation is available)

- any written contract;
- photographs;
- any plans;
- a list of works complained of;
- a list of any outstanding works;
- any relevant estimate, invoice or receipt including any relating to repairs to each of the defects;
- invoices for work done or goods supplied;
- estimates for work to be completed;
- a valuation of work done to date.

### LANDLORD AND TENANT CLAIMS (where the information or documentation is available)

- a calculation of the amount of any rent alleged to be owing, showing amounts received;
- details of breaches of an agreement which are said to justify withholding any deposit itemised showing how the total is made up and with invoices and estimates to support them.

### BREACH OF DUTY CASES (negligence, deficient professional services and the like)

Details of the following:

- what it is said by the claimant was done negligently by the defendant;
- why it is said that the negligence is the fault of the defendant;
- what damage is said to have been caused;
- what injury or losses have been suffered and how any (and each) sum claimed has been calculated;
- the response of the defendant to each of the above.

## APPENDIX B

## STANDARD DIRECTIONS

(For use where the district judge specifies no other directions.)

### THE COURT DIRECTS:

1 Each party must deliver to every other party and to the court office copies of all documents on which he intends to rely at the hearing no later than [ ] [14 days before the hearing]. (These should include the letter making the claim and the reply.)

2 The original documents must be brought to the hearing.

3 [Notice of hearing date and time allowed.]

4 The parties are encouraged to contact each other with a view to trying to settle the case or narrow the issues. However the court must be informed immediately if the case is settled by agreement before the hearing date.

5 No party may rely at the hearing on any report from an expert unless express permission has been granted by the court beforehand. Anyone wishing to rely on an expert must write to the court immediately on receipt of this order and seek permission, giving an explanation why the assistance of an expert is necessary.

NOTE: Failure to comply with the directions may result in the case being adjourned and in the party at fault having to pay costs. The parties are encouraged always to try to settle the case by negotiating with each other. The court must be informed immediately if the case is settled before the hearing.

## APPENDIX C

## SPECIAL DIRECTIONS

The must clarify his case.

He must do this by delivering to the court office and to the no later than

[a list of ]

[details of ]

The must allow the to inspect by appointment within days of receiving a request to do so.

The hearing will not take place at the court but at .

The must bring to court at the hearing the .

Signed statements setting out the evidence of all witnesses on whom each party intends to rely must be prepared and copies included in the documents mentioned in paragraph 1. This includes the evidence of the parties themselves and of any other witness, whether or not he is going to come to court to give evidence.

The court may decide not to take into account a document [or video] or the evidence of a witness if these directions have not been complied with.

If he does not [do so] [          ] his [Claim][Defence] [and Counterclaim] will be struck out and (specify consequence).

It appears to the court that expert evidence is necessary on the issue of           and that that evidence should be given by a single expert to be instructed by the parties jointly. If the parties cannot agree about who to choose and what arrangements to make about paying his fee, either party MUST apply to the court for further directions. The evidence is to be given in the form of a written report. Either party may ask the expert questions and must then send copies of the questions and replies to the other party and to the court. Oral expert evidence may be allowed in exceptional circumstances but only after a further order of the court. Attention is drawn to the limit of £200 on experts' fees that may be recovered.

If either party intends to show a video as evidence he must—

(a) contact the court at once to make arrangements for him to do so, because the court may not have the necessary equipment, and
(b) provide the other party with a copy of the video or the opportunity to see it at least           days before the hearing.

# CPR Part 28 The Fast Track



## 28.1 Scope of this Part

This Part contains general provisions about management of cases allocated to the fast track and applies only to cases allocated to that track.

(Part 27 sets out the procedure for claims allocated to the small claims track.)

(Part 29 sets out the procedure for claims allocated to the multi-track.)

## 28.2 General Provisions

(1) When it allocates a case to the fast track, the court will give directions for the management of the case and set a timetable for the steps to be taken between the giving of the directions and the trial.

(2) When it gives directions, the court will—
  (a) fix the trial date; or
  (b) fix a period, not exceeding 3 weeks, within which the trial is to take place.

(3) The trial date or trial period will be specified in the notice of allocation.

(4) The standard period between the giving of directions and the trial will be not more than 30 weeks.

(5) The court's power to award trial costs is limited in accordance with Part 46.

## 28.3 Directions

(1) The matters to be dealt with by directions under rule 28.2(1) include—
  (a) disclosure of documents;
  (b) service of witness statements; and
  (c) expert evidence.

(2) If the court decides not to direct standard disclosure, it may—
  (a) direct that no disclosure take place; or
  (b) specify the documents or the classes of documents which the parties must disclose.

(Rule 31.6 explains what is meant by standard disclosure.)

(Rule 26.6(5) deals with limitations in relation to expert evidence and the likely length of trial in fast track cases.)

## 28.4 Variation of Case Management Timetable

(1) A party must apply to the court if he wishes to vary the date which the court has fixed for—
  (a) the return of a pre-trial checklist under rule 28.5;
  (b) the trial; or
  (c) the trial period.

(2) Any date set by the court or these Rules for doing any act may not be varied by the parties if the variation would make it necessary to vary any of the dates mentioned in paragraph (1).

(Rule 2.11 allows the parties to vary a date by written agreement except where the rules provide otherwise or the court orders otherwise.)

## 28.5 Pre-trial Checklist (Listing Questionnaire)

(1) The court will send the parties a pre-trial checklist (listing questionnaire) for completion and return by the date specified in the notice of allocation unless it considers that the claim can proceed to trial without the need for a pre-trial checklist.

(2) The date specified for filing a pre-trial checklist will not be more than 8 weeks before the trial date or the beginning of the trial period.

(3) If no party files the completed pre-trial checklist by the date specified, the court will order that unless a completed pre-trial checklist is filed within 7 days from service of that order, the claim, defence and any counterclaim will be struck out without further order of the court.

(4) If—
  (a) a party files a completed pre-trial checklist but another party does not;
  (b) a party has failed to give all the information requested by the pre-trial checklist; or
  (c) the court considers that a hearing is necessary to enable it to decide what directions to give in order to complete preparation of the case for trial,

the court may give such directions as it thinks appropriate.

## 28.6 Fixing or Confirming the Trial Date and Giving Directions

(1) As soon as practicable after the date specified for filing a completed pre-trial checklist the court will—
  (a) fix the date for the trial (or, if it has already done so, confirm that date);
  (b) give any directions for the trial, including a trial timetable, which it considers appropriate; and
  (c) specify any further steps that need to be taken before trial.

(2) The court will give the parties at least 3 weeks' notice of the date of the trial unless, in exceptional circumstances, the court directs that shorter notice will be given.

## 28.7 Conduct of Trial

Unless the trial judge otherwise directs, the trial will be conducted in accordance with any order previously made.

# PD 28 Practice Direction — The Fast Track

This practice direction supplements CPR Part 28.

## General

1.1 Attention is drawn in particular to the following Parts of the Civil Procedure Rules:

| | |
|---|---|
| Part 1 | The overriding objective |
| Part 3 | The court's case management powers |
| Part 26 | Case management—preliminary stage |
| Part 31 | Disclosure and inspection of documents |
| Parts 32–34 | Evidence |
| Part 35 | Experts and assessors |

and to the practice directions which relate to those Parts.

1.2 Attention is also drawn to:
Rule 26.6(5)—which makes provision about limitations on expert evidence and the length of trial in fast track cases.
Part 46—Fast Track Trial Costs
Rule 19.4A and PD 19, para. 6, on joining the Crown in certain cases raising Convention rights issues.

## Case Management

2.1 Case management of cases allocated to the fast track will generally be by directions given at two stages in the case:
(1) at allocation to the track, and
(2) on the filing of pre-trial checklists (listing questionnaires).

2.2 The court will seek whenever possible to give directions at those stages only and to do so without the need for a hearing to take place. It will expect to do so with the cooperation of the parties.

2.3 The court will however hold a hearing to give directions whenever it appears necessary or desirable to do so, and where this happens because of the default of a party or his legal representative it will usually impose a sanction.

2.4 The court may give directions at any hearing on the application of a party or on its own initiative.

2.5 When any hearing has been fixed it is the duty of the parties to consider what directions the court should be asked to give and to make any application that may be appropriate to be dealt with at that hearing.

2.6 When the court fixes a hearing to give directions it will give the parties at least 3 days' notice of the hearing.

2.7 Appendix A contains forms of directions. When making an order the court will as far as possible base its order on those forms. Agreed directions which the parties file and invite the court to make should also be based on those forms.

2.8 Where a party needs to apply for a direction of a kind not included in the case management timetable which has been set (for example to amend his statement of case or for further information to be given by another party) he must do so as soon as possible so as to minimise the need to change that timetable.

2.9 Courts will make arrangements to ensure that applications and other hearings are listed promptly to avoid delay in the conduct of cases.

## Directions on Allocation

3.1 Attention is drawn to the court's duty under rule 28.2(2) to set a case management timetable and to fix a trial date or a trial period, and to the matters which are to be dealt with by directions under rule 28.3(1).

3.2 The court will seek to tailor its directions to the needs of the case and the steps of which it is aware that the parties have already taken to prepare the case. In particular it will have regard to the extent to which any pre-action protocol has or (as the case may be) has not been complied with.

3.3 At this stage the court's first concern will be to ensure that the issues between the parties be identified and that the necessary evidence is prepared and disclosed.

3.4 The court may have regard to any document filed by a party with his allocation questionnaire containing further information provided that the document states either that its contents have been agreed with every other party or that it has been served on every other party and when it was served.

3.5 If:
(1) the parties have filed agreed directions for the management of the case, and
(2) the court considers that the proposals are suitable, it may approve them and give directions in the terms proposed.

3.6 (1) To obtain the court's approval the agreed directions must:
(a) set out a timetable by reference to calendar dates for the taking of steps for the preparation of the case,
(b) include a date or a period (the trial period) when it is proposed that the trial will take place,
(c) include provision about disclosure of documents, and
(d) include provision about both factual and expert evidence.
(2) The latest proposed date for the trial or the end of the trial period must be not later than 30 weeks from the date the directions order is made.
(3) The trial period must not be longer than 3 weeks.
(4) The provision in (1)(c) above may:
(a) limit disclosure to standard disclosure between all parties or to less than that, and/or
(b) direct that disclosure will take place by the supply of copy documents without a list, but it must in that case either direct that the parties must serve a disclosure statement with the copies or record that they have agreed to disclose in that way without such a statement.
(5) The provision in (1)(d) may be to the effect that no expert evidence is required.

3.7 Directions agreed by the parties should also where appropriate contain provisions about:
(1) the filing of any reply or amended statement of case that may be required,
(2) dates for the service of requests for further information under the practice direction supplementing Part 18 and questions to experts under rule 35.6 and when they are to be dealt with,
(3) the disclosure of evidence,
(4) the use of a single joint expert, or in cases where the use of a single expert has not been agreed the exchange and agreement of expert evidence (including whether exchange is to be simultaneous or sequential) and without-prejudice discussions of the experts.

3.8 If the court does not approve the agreed directions filed by the parties but decides that it will give directions on its own initiative without a hearing, it will take them into account in deciding what directions to give.

3.9 Where the court is to give directions on its own initiative and it is not aware of any steps taken by the parties other than the service of statements of case, its general approach will be:
(1) to give directions for the filing and service of any further information required to clarify either party's case,
(2) to direct standard disclosure between the parties,
(3) to direct the disclosure of witness statements by way of simultaneous exchange,

(4) to give directions for a single joint expert unless there is good reason not to do so,
(5) in cases where directions for a single expert are not given:
(a) to direct disclosure of experts' reports by way of simultaneous exchange, and
(b) if experts' reports are not agreed, to direct a discussion between the experts for the purpose set out in rule 35.12(1) and the preparation of a report under rule 35.12(3).

3.10 (1) If it appears to the court that the claim is one which will be allocated to the fast track but that it cannot properly give directions on its own initiative or approve agreed directions that have been filed, the court may either:
(a) allocate the claim to the fast track, fix a trial date or trial period and direct that a case management hearing is to be listed and give directions at that hearing, or
(b) direct that an allocation hearing is to be listed and give directions at that hearing.
(2) In either case the hearing will be listed as promptly as possible.

3.11 Where the court is proposing on its own initiative to make an order under rule 35.15 (which gives the court power to appoint an assessor), the court must, unless the parties have consented in writing to the order, list a directions hearing.

3.12 The table set out below contains a typical timetable the court may give for the preparation of the case.

| | |
|---|---|
| Disclosure | 4 weeks |
| Exchange of witness statements | 10 weeks |
| Exchange of experts' reports | 14 weeks |
| Sending of pre-trial checklists (listing questionnaires) by the court | 20 weeks |
| Filing of completed pre-trial checklists | 22 weeks |
| Hearing | 30 weeks |

These periods will run from the date of the notice of allocation.

3.13 (1) Where it considers that some or all of the steps in that timetable are not necessary the court may omit them and direct an earlier trial.
(2) This may happen where the court is informed that a pre-action protocol has been complied with or that steps which it would otherwise order to be taken have already been taken.
(3) It may also happen where an application (for example for summary judgment or for an injunction) has been heard before allocation and little or no further preparation is required. In such a case the court may dispense with the need for a pretrial checklist.

## Variation of Directions

4.1 This paragraph deals with the procedure to be adopted:
(1) where a party is dissatisfied with a direction given by the court,
(2) where the parties agree about changes they wish made to the directions given, or
(3) where a party wishes to apply to vary a direction.

4.2 (1) It is essential that any party who wishes to have a direction varied takes steps to do so as soon as possible.
(2) The court will assume for the purposes of any later application that a party who did not appeal and who made no application to vary within 14 days of service of the order containing the directions was content that they were correct in the circumstances then existing.

4.3 (1) Where a party is dissatisfied with a direction given or other order made by the court he may appeal or apply to the court for it to reconsider its decision.
(2) He should appeal if the direction was given or the order was made at a hearing at which he was present or represented, or of which he had due notice.
(3) In any other case he should apply to the court to reconsider its decision.
(4) If an application is made for the court to reconsider its decision:

(a) it will usually be heard by the judge who gave the directions or another judge of the same level,
(b) the court will give all parties at least 3 days' notice of the hearing, and
(c) the court may confirm its decision or make a different order.

4.4 Where there has been a change in the circumstances since the order was made the court may set aside or vary any direction it has given. It may do so on application or on its own initiative.

4.5 Where the parties agree about changes to be made to the directions given:
(1) If rule 2.11 (variation by agreement of a date set by the court for doing any act other than those stated in the note to that rule) or rule 31.5, 31.10(8) or 31.13 (agreements about disclosure) applied the parties need not file the written agreement.
(2) (a) In any other case the parties must apply for an order by consent.
(b) The parties must file a draft of the order sought and an agreed statement of the reasons why the variation is sought.
(c) The court may make an order in the agreed terms or in other terms without a hearing, but it may direct that a hearing is to be listed.

## Failure to Comply with Case Management Directions

5.1 Where a party has failed to comply with a direction given by the court any other party may apply for an order to enforce compliance or for a sanction to be imposed or both of these.

5.2 The party entitled to apply for such an order must do so without delay but should first warn the other party of his intention to do so.

5.3 The court may take any such delay into account when it decides whether to make an order imposing a sanction or whether to grant relief from a sanction imposed by the rules or any practice direction.

5.4 (1) The court will not allow a failure to comply with directions to lead to the postponement of the trial unless the circumstances of the case are exceptional.
(2) If it is practicable to do so the court will exercise its powers in a manner that enables the case to come on for trial on the date or within the period previously set.
(3) In particular the court will assess what steps each party should take to prepare the case for trial, direct that those steps are taken in the shortest possible time and impose a sanction for non-compliance. Such a sanction may, for example, deprive a party of the right to raise or contest an issue or to rely on evidence to which the direction relates.
(4) Where it appears that one or more issues are or can be made ready for trial at the time fixed while others cannot, the court may direct that the trial will proceed on the issues which are or will then be ready, and order that no costs will be allowed for any later trial of the remaining issues or that those costs will be paid by the party in default.
(5) Where the court has no option but to postpone the trial it will do so for the shortest possible time and will give directions for the taking of the necessary steps in the meantime as rapidly as possible.
(6) Litigants and lawyers must be in no doubt that the court will regard the postponement of a trial as an order of last resort. The court may exercise its power to require a party as well as his legal representative to attend court at a hearing where such an order is to be sought.

## Pre-trial Checklists (Listing Questionnaires)

6.1 (1) The pre-trial checklist (listing questionnaire) will be in form N170.
(2) Unless it has dispensed with listing questionnaires, the court will send forms N170 and N171 (notice of date for return of the listing questionnaire) to each party no later than two weeks before the date specified in the notice of allocation or in any later direction of the court for the return of the completed questionnaires.

(3) When all the pre-trial checklists have been filed or when the time for filing them has expired and where a party has filed a pre-trial checklist but another party has not done so, the file will be placed before a judge for his directions.

(4) Although the Rules do not require the parties to exchange copies of the checklists before they are filed they are encouraged to do so to avoid the court being given conflicting or incomplete information.

Attention is drawn to PD 43–48, Section 6, which requires a costs estimate to be filed and served at the same time as the pre-trial checklist is filed.

6.2 Attention is drawn to rule 28.6(1) (which sets out the court's duty at the pre-trial checklist stage) and to rule 28.5(4) (which sets out circumstances in which the court may decide to hold a hearing).

6.3 Where the judge decides to hold a hearing under rule 28.5(4) the court will fix a date which is as early as possible and the parties will be given at least 3 days' notice of the date.

The notice of such a hearing will be in form N153.

6.4 The court's general approach will be as set out in the following paragraphs. The court may however decide to make other orders, and in particular the court will take into account the steps, if any, which the parties have taken to prepare the case for trial.

6.5 (1) Where no party files a pre-trial checklist the court will order that unless a completed pre-trial checklist is filed within 7 days from service of that order, the claim, defence and any counterclaim will be struck out without further order of the court.

(2) Where a party files a pre-trial checklist but another party does not do so, the court normally will give directions. These will usually fix or confirm the trial date and provide for steps to be taken to prepare the case for trial.

## Directions the Court Will Give on Listing

7.1 Directions the court must give:

(1) The court must confirm or fix the trial date, specify the place of trial and give a time estimate. The trial date must be fixed and the case listed on the footing that the hearing will end on the same calendar day as that on which it commenced.

(2) The court will serve a notice of hearing on the parties at least 3 weeks before the hearing unless they agree to accept shorter notice or the court authorises shorter service under rule 28.6(2), and

(3) The notice of hearing will be in form N172.

7.2 Other directions:

(1) The parties should seek to agree directions and may file the proposed order. The court may make an order in those terms or it may make a different order.

(2) Agreed directions should include provision about:

(a) evidence,

(b) a trial timetable and time estimate,

(c) the preparation of a trial bundle,

(d) any other matter needed to prepare the case for trial.

(3) The court will include such of these provisions as are appropriate in any order that it may make, whether or not the parties have filed agreed directions.

(4) (a) A direction giving permission to use expert evidence will say whether it gives permission for oral evidence or reports or both and will name the experts concerned.

(b) The court will not make a direction giving permission for an expert to give oral evidence unless it believes it is necessary in the interests of justice to do so.

(c) Where no 'without prejudice' meeting or other discussion between experts has taken place the court may grant that permission conditionally on such a discussion taking place and a report being filed before the trial.

7.3 The principles set out in paragraph 4 of this practice direction about the variation of directions apply also to directions given at this stage.

## The Trial

8.1 The trial will normally take place at the court where the case is being managed, but it may be at another court if it is appropriate having regard to the needs of the parties and the availability of court resources.

8.2 The judge will generally have read the papers in the trial bundle and may dispense with an opening address.

8.3 The judge may confirm or vary any timetable given previously, or if none has been given set his own.

8.4 Attention is drawn to the provisions in Part 32 and the following parts of the Rules about evidence, and in particular—

(1) to rule 32.1 (court's power to control evidence and to restrict cross-examination), and

(2) to rule 32.5(2) (witness statements to stand as evidence in chief).

8.5 At the conclusion of the trial the judge will normally summarily assess the costs of the claim in accordance with rule 44.7 and Part 46 (fast track trial costs). Attention is drawn to the steps the practice directions about costs require the parties to take.

8.6 Where a trial is not finished on the day for which it is listed the judge will normally sit on the next court day to complete it.

# APPENDIX

# FAST TRACK STANDARD DIRECTIONS

## Further Statements of Case

The must file a and serve a copy on no later than .

## Requests for Further Information

Any request for clarification or further information based on another party's statement of case shall be served no later than .
[Any such request shall be dealt with no later than ].

## Disclosure of Documents

[No disclosure of documents is required].
[[Each party] [The ]
shall give [to the ]
[to every other party] standard disclosure of documents
[relating to ]
by serving copies together with a disclosure statement no later than ].
[Disclosure shall take place as follows:
[Each party shall give standard discovery to every other party by list]
[Disclosure is limited to [standard] [disclosure by the to the ]
[of documents relating to damage]
[the following documents ]
[The latest date for delivery of the lists is ]
[The latest date for service of any request to inspect or for a copy of a document is ]].

## Witnesses of Fact

Each party shall serve on every other party the witness statements of all witnesses of fact on whom he intends to rely.
There shall be simultaneous exchange of such statements no later than

## Expert Evidence

[No expert evidence being necessary, no party has permission to call or rely on expert evidence].
[On it appearing to the court that expert evidence is necessary on the issue of
[ ]
and that that evidence should be given by the report of a single expert instructed jointly by the parties, the shall no later than
inform the court whether or not such an expert has been instructed].
[The expert evidence on the issue of
shall be limited to a single expert
jointly instructed by the parties.
If the parties cannot agree by who that expert is to be and about the payment of his fees either party may apply for further directions.
Unless the parties agree in writing or the court orders otherwise, the fees and expenses of such an expert shall be paid to him [by the parties equally]
[ ] and be limited to £ .
[The report of the expert shall be filed at the court no later than ].
[No party shall be entitled to recover by way of costs from any other party more than £ for the fees or expenses of an expert].
The parties shall exchange reports setting out the substance of any expert evidence on which they intend to rely.
The exchange shall take place simultaneously no later than ].
[The shall serve his report(s) no later than the and the shall serve his reports no later than the ].
[The exchange of reports relating to [causation] [ ]
shall take place simultaneously no later than .
The shall serve his report(s) relating to [damage] [ ] no later than
and the shall serve his reports relating to it no later than ].
Reports shall be agreed if possible no later than [ days after service] [ ].
[If the reports are not agreed within that time there shall be a without prejudice discussion between the relevant experts no later than
to identify the issues between them and to reach agreement if possible.
The experts shall prepare for the court a statement of the issues on which they agree and on which they disagree with a summary of their reasons, and that statement shall be filed with the court [no later than ]
[with] [no later than the date for filing] [the listing questionnaire].
[Each party has permission to use [ ] as expert witness(es) to give [oral] evidence [in the form of a report] at the trial in the field of provided that the substance of the evidence to be given has been disclosed as above and has not been agreed].
[Each party has permission to use in evidence experts' report(s) [and the court will consider when the claim is listed for trial whether expert oral evidence will be allowed].]

## Questions to Experts

The time for service on another party of any question addressed to an expert instructed by that party is not later than days after service of that expert's report.
Any such question shall be answered within days of service.

## Requests for Information etc.

Each party shall serve any request for clarification or further information based on any document disclosed or statement served by another party no later than days after disclosure or service.

Any such request shall be dealt with within days of service.

## Documents to be Filed With Pre-trial Checklists

The parties must file with their listing questionnaires* copies of [their experts' reports] [witness statements] [replies to requests for further information].

## Dates for Filing Pre-trial Checklists and the Trial

Each party must file a completed pre-trial checklist no later than .

The trial of this case will take place [on ][on a date to be fixed between and ].

## Directions Following Filing of Pre-trial Checklist

*Expert evidence*

The parties have permission to rely at the trial on expert evidence as follows:

| | |
|---|---|
| The claimant: | Oral evidence— |
| | Written evidence— |
| The defendant: | Oral evidence— |
| | Written evidence— |

*Trial timetable*

The time allowed for the trial is

[The timetable for the trial may be agreed by the parties, subject to the approval of the trial judge].

[The timetable for the trial (subject to the approval of the trial judge) will be that ].

[The evidence in chief for each party will be contained in witness statements and reports, the time allowed for cross-examination by the defendant is limited to and the time allowed for cross-examination by the claimant is limited to ].

[The time allowed for the claimant's evidence is . The time allowed for the defendant's evidence is ].

The time allowed for the submissions on behalf of each party is .

The remainder of the time allowed for the trial (being ) is reserved for the judge to consider and give the judgment and to deal with costs].

*Trial bundle etc.*

The claimant shall lodge an indexed bundle of documents contained in a ring binder and with each page clearly numbered at the court not more than 7 days and not less than 3 days before the start of the trial.

[A case summary (which should not exceed 250 words) outlining the matters still in issue, and referring where appropriate to the relevant documents shall be included in the bundle for the assistance of the judge in reading the papers before the trial].

[The parties shall seek to agree the contents of the trial bundle and the case summary].

*Settlement*

Each party must inform the court immediately if the claim is settled whether or not it is then possible to file a draft consent order to give effect to their agreement.

[* In the text issued by the Department for Constitutional Affairs the old term 'listing questionnaires' has not been changed to 'pre-trial checklists'.]

# CPR Part 29 The Multi-track



## 29.1 Scope of this Part

This Part contains general provisions about management of cases allocated to the multi-track and applies only to cases allocated to that track.

(Part 27 sets out the procedure for claims allocated to the small claims track.)

(Part 28 sets out the procedure for claims allocated to the fast track.)

## 29.2 Case Management

(1) When it allocates a case to the multi-track, the court will—
- (a) give directions for the management of the case and set a timetable for the steps to be taken between the giving of directions and the trial; or
- (b) fix—
  - (i) a case management conference; or
  - (ii) a pre-trial review,

  or both, and give such other directions relating to the management of the case as it sees fit.

(2) The court will fix the trial date or the period in which the trial is to take place as soon as practicable.

(3) When the court fixes the trial date or the trial period under paragraph (2), it will—
- (a) give notice to the parties of the date or period; and
- (b) specify the date by which the parties must file a pre-trial checklist.

## 29.3 Case Management Conference and Pre-trial Review

(1) The court may fix—
- (a) a case management conference; or
- (b) a pre-trial review, at any time after the claim has been allocated.

(2) If a party has a legal representative, a representative—
- (a) familiar with the case; and
- (b) with sufficient authority to deal with any issues that are likely to arise, must attend case management conferences and pre-trial reviews.

(Rule 3.1(2)(c) provides that the court may require a party to attend the court.)

## 29.4 Steps Taken by the Parties

If—

(a) the parties agree proposals for the management of the proceedings (including a proposed trial date or period in which the trial is to take place); and

(b) the court considers that the proposals are suitable,

it may approve them without a hearing and give directions in the terms proposed.

## 29.5 Variation of Case Management Timetable

(1) A party must apply to the court if he wishes to vary the date which the court has fixed for—
  (a) a case management conference;
  (b) a pre-trial review;
  (c) the return of a pre-trial checklist under rule 29.6;
  (d) the trial; or
  (e) the trial period.
(2) Any date set by the court or these Rules for doing any act may not be varied by the parties if the variation would make it necessary to vary any of the dates mentioned in paragraph (1).

(Rule 2.11 allows the parties to vary a date by written agreement except where the rules provide otherwise or the court orders otherwise.)

## 29.6 Pre-trial Checklist (Listing Questionnaire)

(1) The court will send the parties a pre-trial checklist (listing questionnaire) for completion and return by the date specified in directions given under rule 29.2(3) unless it considers that the claim can proceed to trial without the need for a pre-trial checklist.
(2) Each party must file the completed pre-trial checklist by the date specified by the court.
(3) If no party files the completed pre-trial checklist by the date specified, the court will order that unless a completed pre-trial checklist is filed within 7 days from service of that order, the claim, defence and any counterclaim will be struck out without further order of the court.
(4) If—
  (a) a party files a completed pre-trial checklist but another party does not;
  (b) a party has failed to give all the information requested by the pre-trial checklist; or
  (c) the court considers that a hearing is necessary to enable it to decide what directions to give in order to complete preparation of the case for trial,

  the court may give such directions as it thinks appropriate.

## 29.7 Pre-trial Review

If, on receipt of the parties' pre-trial checklists, the court decides—
(a) to hold a pre-trial review; or
(b) to cancel a pre-trial review which has already been fixed,

it will serve notice of its decision at least 7 days before the date fixed for the hearing or, as the case may be, the cancelled hearing.

## 29.8 Setting a Trial Timetable and Fixing or Confirming the Trial Date or Week

As soon as practicable after—
(a) each party has filed a completed pre-trial checklist;
(b) the court has held a listing hearing under rule 29.6(3); or
(c) the court has held a pre-trial review under rule 29.7

the court will—
  (i) set a timetable for the trial unless a timetable has already been fixed, or the court considers that it would be inappropriate to do so;
  (ii) fix the date for the trial or the week within which the trial is to begin (or, if it has already done so, confirm that date); and
  (iii) notify the parties of the trial timetable (where one is fixed under this rule) and the date or trial period.

## 29.9 Conduct of Trial

Unless the trial judge otherwise directs, the trial will be conducted in accordance with any order previously made.

# PD 29 Practice Direction — The Multi-track

This practice direction supplements CPR Part 29.

## General

1.1 Attention is drawn in particular to the following Parts of the Civil Procedure Rules

| | |
|---|---|
| Part 1 | The overriding objective |
| Part 3 | The court's case management powers |
| Part 26 | Case management—preliminary stage |
| Part 31 | Disclosure and inspection of documents |
| Parts 32 to 34 | Evidence |
| Part 35 | Experts and assessors |

and to the practice directions which relate to those Parts.

## Case Management in the Royal Courts of Justice

2.1 This part of the practice direction applies to claims begun by claim form issued in the Central Office or Chancery Chambers in the Royal Courts of Justice.

2.2 A claim with an estimated value of less than £50,000 will generally, unless:

(a) it is required by an enactment to be tried in the High Court,
(b) it falls within a specialist list, or
(c) it falls within one of the categories specified in 2.6 below or is otherwise within the criteria of article 7(5) of the High Court and County Courts Jurisdiction Order 1991,

be transferred to a county court.

2.3 Paragraph 2.2 is without prejudice to the power of the court in accordance with Part 30 to transfer to a county court a claim with an estimated value that exceeds £50,000.

2.4 The decision to transfer may be made at any stage in the proceedings but should, subject to paragraph 2.5, be made as soon as possible and in any event not later than the date for the filing of pre-trial checklists (listing questionnaires).

2.5 If an application is made under rule 3.4 (striking out) or under Part 24 (summary judgment) or under Part 25 (interim remedies), it will usually be convenient for the application to be dealt with before a decision to transfer is taken.

2.6 Each party should state in his allocation questionnaire whether he considers the claim should be managed and tried at the Royal Courts of Justice and, if so, why. Claims suitable for trial in the Royal Courts of Justice include:

(1) professional negligence claims,
(2) Fatal Accident Act claims,
(3) fraud or undue influence claims,
(4) defamation claims,
(5) claims for malicious prosecution or false imprisonment,
(6) claims against the police,
(7) contentious probate claims.

Such claims may fall within the criteria of article 7(5) of the High Court and County Courts Jurisdiction Order 1991.

2.7 Attention is drawn to PD 30.

## Case Management—General Provisions

3.1 (1) Case management of a claim which is proceeding at the Royal Courts of Justice will be undertaken there.

(2) (a) Case management of any other claim which has been allocated to the multi-track will normally be undertaken at a Civil Trial Centre.

(b) The practice direction supplementing Part 26 provides for what will happen in the case of a claim which is issued in or transferred to a court which is not a Civil Trial Centre.

3.2 The hallmarks of the multi-track are:
(1) the ability of the court to deal with cases of widely differing values and complexity, and
(2) the flexibility given to the court in the way it will manage a case in a way appropriate to its particular needs.

3.3 (1) On allocating a claim to the multi-track the court may give directions without a hearing, including fixing a trial date or a period in which the trial will take place,
(2) Alternatively, whether or not it fixes a trial date or period, it may either—
(a) give directions for certain steps to be taken and fix a date for a case management conference or a pre-trial review to take place after they have been taken, or
(b) fix a date for a case management conference.
(3) Attention is drawn to rule 29.2(2) which requires the court to fix a trial date or period as soon as practicable.

3.4 The court may give or vary directions at any hearing which may take place on the application of a party or of its own initiative.

3.5 When any hearing has been fixed it is the duty of the parties to consider what directions the court should be asked to give and to make any application that may be appropriate to be dealt with then.

3.6 The court will hold a hearing to give directions whenever it appears necessary or desirable to do so, and where this happens because of the default of a party or his legal representative it will usually impose a sanction.

3.7 When the court fixes a hearing to give directions it will give the parties at least 3 days' notice of the hearing unless rule 29.7 applies (7 days' notice to be given in the case of a pre-trial review).

3.8 Where a party needs to apply for a direction of a kind not included in the case management timetable which has been set (for example to amend his statement of case or for further information to be given by another party) he must do so as soon as possible so as to minimise the need to change that timetable.

3.9 Courts will make arrangements to ensure that applications and other hearings are listed promptly to avoid delay in the conduct of cases.

3.10 (1) Case management will generally be dealt with by:
(a) a master in cases proceeding in the Royal Courts of Justice,
(b) a district judge in cases proceeding in a district registry of the High Court, and
(c) a district judge or a circuit judge in cases proceeding in a county court.
(2) A master or a district judge may consult and seek the directions of a judge of a higher level about any aspect of case management.
(3) A member of the court staff who is dealing with the listing of a hearing may seek the directions of any judge about any aspect of that listing.

## Case Management—Consideration of Periodical Payments

3A Attention is drawn to Practice Direction 41B supplementing Part 41 and in particular to the direction that in a personal injury claim the court should consider and indicate to the parties as soon as practicable whether periodical payments or a lump sum is likely to be the more appropriate form for all or part of an award of damages for future pecuniary loss.

## Directions on Allocation

4.1 Attention is drawn to the court's duties under rule 29.2.

4.2 The court will seek to tailor its directions to the needs of the case and the steps which the parties have already taken to prepare the case of which it is aware. In particular it will have regard to the extent to which any pre-action protocol has or (as the case may be) has not been complied with.

4.3 At this stage the court's first concern will be to ensure that the issues between the parties are identified and that the necessary evidence is prepared and disclosed.

4.4 The court may have regard to any document filed by a party with his allocation questionnaire containing further information, provided that the document states either that its contents has been agreed with every other party or that it has been served on every other party, and when it was served.

4.5 On the allocation of a claim to the multi-track the court will consider whether it is desirable or necessary to hold a case management conference straight away, or whether it is appropriate instead to give directions on its own initiative.

4.6 The parties and their advisers are encouraged to try to agree directions and to take advantage of rule 29.4 which provides that if:

(1) the parties agree proposals for the management of the proceedings (including a proposed trial date or period in which the trial is to take place), and
(2) the court considers that the proposals are suitable,

it may approve them without a hearing and give directions in the terms proposed.

4.7 (1) To obtain the court's approval the agreed directions must:

(a) set out a timetable by reference to calendar dates for the taking of steps for the preparation of the case,
(b) include a date or a period (the trial period) when it is proposed that the trial will take place,
(c) include provision about disclosure of documents, and
(d) include provision about both factual and expert evidence.

(2) The court will scrutinise the timetable carefully and in particular will be concerned to see that any proposed date or period for the trial and (if provided for) for a case management conference is no later than is reasonably necessary.

(3) The provision in (1)(c) above may:

(a) limit disclosure to standard disclosure or less than that, and/or
(b) direct that disclosure will take place by the supply of copy documents without a list, but it must in that case say either that the parties must serve a disclosure statement with the copies or that they have agreed to disclose in that way without such a statement.

(4) The provision in (1)(d) about expert evidence may be to the effect that none is required.

4.8 Directions agreed by the parties should also where appropriate contain provisions about:

(1) the filing of any reply or amended statement of case that may be required,
(2) dates for the service of requests for further information under the practice direction supplementing Part 18 and of questions to experts under rule 35.6 and by when they are to be dealt with,
(3) the disclosure of evidence,
(4) the use of a single joint expert, or in cases where it is not agreed, the exchange of expert evidence (including whether exchange is to be simultaneous or sequential) and without prejudice discussions between experts.

4.9 If the court does not approve the agreed directions filed by the parties but decides that it will give directions of its own initiative without fixing a case management conference, it will take them into account in deciding what directions to give.

4.10 Where the court is to give directions on its own initiative without holding a case management conference and it is not aware of any steps taken by the parties other than the exchange of statements of case, its general approach will be:

(1) to give directions for the filing and service of any further information required to clarify either party's case,
(2) to direct standard disclosure between the parties,
(3) to direct the disclosure of witness statements by way of simultaneous exchange,

(4) to give directions for a single joint expert on any appropriate issue unless there is a good reason not to do so,
(5) unless paragraph 4.11 (below) applies, to direct disclosure of experts' reports by way of simultaneous exchange on those issues where a single joint expert is not directed,
(6) if experts' reports are not agreed, to direct a discussion between experts for the purpose set out in rule 35.12(1) and the preparation of a statement under rule 35.12(3),
(7) to list a case management conference to take place after the date for compliance with those directions,
(8) to specify a trial period; and
(9) in such cases as the court thinks appropriate, the court may give directions requiring the parties to consider ADR. Such directions may be, for example, in the following terms:

'The parties shall by [date] consider whether the case is capable of resolution by ADR. If any party considers that the case is unsuitable for resolution by ADR, that party shall be prepared to justify that decision at the conclusion of the trial, should the judge consider that such means of resolution were appropriate, when he is considering the appropriate costs order to make.

The party considering the case unsuitable for ADR shall, not less than 28 days before the commencement of the trial, file with the court a witness statement without prejudice save as to costs, giving reasons upon which they rely for saying that the case was unsuitable.'

4.11 If it appears that expert evidence will be required both on issues of liability and on the amount of damages, the court may direct that the exchange of those reports that relate to liability will be exchanged simultaneously but that those relating to the amount of damages will be exchanged sequentially.

4.12 (1) If it appears to the court that it cannot properly give directions on its own initiative and no agreed directions have been filed which it can approve, the court will direct a case management conference to be listed.
(2) The conference will be listed as promptly as possible.

4.13 Where the court is proposing on its own initiative to make an order under rule 35.7 (which gives the court power to direct that evidence on a particular issue is to be given by a single expert) or under rule 35.15 (which gives the court power to appoint an assessor), the court must, unless the parties have consented in writing to the order, list a case management conference.

## Case Management Conferences

5.1 The court will at any case management conference:
(1) review the steps which the parties have taken in the preparation of the case, and in particular their compliance with any directions that the court may have given,
(2) decide and give directions about the steps which are to be taken to secure the progress of the claim in accordance with the overriding objective, and
(3) ensure as far as it can that all agreements that can be reached between the parties about the matters in issue and the conduct of the claim are made and recorded.

5.2 (1) Rule 29.3(2) provides that where a party has a legal representative, a representative familiar with the case and with sufficient authority to deal with any issues that are likely to arise must attend case management conferences and pre-trial reviews.
(2) That person should be someone who is personally involved in the conduct of the case, and who has the authority and information to deal with any matter which may reasonably be expected to be dealt with at such a hearing, including the fixing of the timetable, the identification of issues and matters of evidence.
(3) Where the inadequacy of the person attending or of his instructions leads to the adjournment of a hearing, the court will expect to make a wasted costs order.

5.3 The topics the court will consider at a case management conference are likely to include
(1) whether the claimant has made clear the claim he is bringing, in particular the amount he is claiming, so that the other party can understand the case he has to meet,
(2) whether any amendments are required to the claim, a statement of case or any other document,
(3) what disclosure of documents, if any, is necessary,
(4) what expert evidence is reasonably required in accordance with rule 35.1 and how and when that evidence should be obtained and disclosed,
(5) what factual evidence should be disclosed,
(6) what arrangements should be made about the giving of clarification or further information and the putting of questions to experts, and
(7) whether it will be just and will save costs to order a split trial or the trial of one or more preliminary issues.

5.4 In all cases the court will set a timetable for the steps it decides are necessary to be taken. These steps may include the holding of a case management conference or a pre-trial review, and the court will be alert to perform its duty to fix a trial date or period as soon as it can.

5.5 (1) The court will not at this stage give permission to use expert evidence unless it can identify each expert by name or field in its order and say whether his evidence is to be given orally or by the use of his report.
(2) A party who obtains expert evidence before obtaining a direction about it does so at his own risk as to costs, except where he obtained the evidence in compliance with a pre-action protocol.

5.6 To assist the court, the parties and their legal advisers should:
(1) ensure that all documents that the court is likely to ask to see (including witness statements and experts' reports) are brought to the hearing,
(2) consider whether the parties should attend,
(3) consider whether a case summary will be useful, and
(4) consider what orders each wishes to be made and give notice of them to the other parties.

5.7 (1) A case summary:
(a) should be designed to assist the court to understand and deal with the questions before it,
(b) should set out a brief chronology of the claim, the issues of fact which are agreed or in dispute and the evidence needed to decide them,
(c) should not normally exceed 500 words in length, and
(d) should be prepared by the claimant and agreed with the other parties if possible.

5.8 (1) Where a party wishes to obtain an order not routinely made at a case management conference and believes that his application will be opposed, he should issue and serve the application in time for it to be heard at the case management conference.
(2) If the time allowed for the case management conference is likely to be insufficient for the application to be heard he should inform the court at once so that a fresh date can be fixed.
(3) A costs sanction may be imposed on a party who fails to comply with sub-paragraph (1) or (2).

5.9 At a case management conference the court may also consider whether the case ought to be tried by a High Court judge or by a judge who specialises in that type of claim and how that question will be decided. In that case the claim may need to be transferred to another court.

## Variation of Directions

6.1 This paragraph deals with the procedure to be adopted:
(1) where a party is dissatisfied with a direction given by the court,

(2) where the parties have agreed about changes they wish made to the directions given, or
(3) where a party wishes to apply to vary a direction.

6.2 (1) It is essential that any party who wishes to have a direction varied takes steps to do so as soon as possible.
(2) The court will assume for the purposes of any later application that a party who did not appeal, and who made no application to vary within 14 days of service of the order containing the directions, was content that they were correct in the circumstances then existing.

6.3 (1) Where a party is dissatisfied with a direction given or other order made by the court he may appeal or apply to the court for it to reconsider its decision.
(2) Unless paragraph 6.4 applies, a party should appeal if the direction was given or the order was made at a hearing at which he was present, or of which he had due notice.
(3) In any other case he should apply to the court to reconsider its decision.
(4) If an application is made for the court to reconsider its decision:
(a) it will usually be heard by the judge who gave the directions or another judge of the same level,
(b) the court will give all parties at least 3 days' notice of the hearing, and
(c) the court may confirm its directions or make a different order.

6.4 Where there has been a change in the circumstances since the order was made the court may set aside or vary a direction it has given. It may do so on application or on its own initiative.

6.5 Where the parties agree about changes they wish made to the directions given:
(1) If rule 2.11 (variation by agreement of a date set by the court for doing any act other than those stated in the note to that rule) or rule 31.5, 31.10(8) or 31.13 (agreements about disclosure) applies the parties need not file the written agreement.
(2) (a) In any other case the parties must apply for an order by consent.
(b) The parties must file a draft of the order sought and an agreed statement of the reasons why the variation is sought.
(c) The court may make an order in the agreed terms or in other terms without a hearing, but it may direct that a hearing is to be listed.

## Failure to Comply with Case Management Directions

7.1 Where a party fails to comply with a direction given by the court any other party may apply for an order that he must do so or for a sanction to be imposed or both of these.

7.2 The party entitled to apply for such an order must do so without delay but should first warn the other party of his intention to do so.

7.3 The court may take any such delay into account when it decides whether to make an order imposing a sanction or to grant relief from a sanction imposed by the rules or any other practice direction.

7.4 (1) The court will not allow a failure to comply with directions to lead to the postponement of the trial unless the circumstances are exceptional.
(2) If it is practical to do so the court will exercise its powers in a manner that enables the case to come on for trial on the date or within the period previously set.
(3) In particular the court will assess what steps each party should take to prepare the case for trial, direct that those steps are taken in the shortest possible time and impose a sanction for non-compliance. Such a sanction may, for example, deprive a party of the right to raise or contest an issue or to rely on evidence to which the direction relates.
(4) Where it appears that one or more issues are or can be made ready for trial at the time fixed while others cannot, the court may direct that the trial will proceed on the issues which are then ready, and direct that no costs will be allowed for any later trial of the remaining issues or that those costs will be paid by the party in default.

(5) Where the court has no option but to postpone the trial it will do so for the shortest possible time and will give directions for the taking of the necessary steps in the meantime as rapidly as possible.

(6) Litigants and lawyers must be in no doubt that the court will regard the postponement of a trial as an order of last resort. Where it appears inevitable the court may exercise its power to require a party as well as his legal representative to attend court at the hearing where such an order is to be sought.

(7) The court will not postpone any other hearing without a very good reason, and for that purpose the failure of a party to comply on time with directions previously given will not be treated as a good reason.

## Pre-trial Checklists (Listing Questionnaires)

8.1 (1) The pre-trial checklist (listing questionnaire) will be in form N170.

(2) Unless it dispenses with pre-trial checklist and orders an early trial on a fixed date, the court will specify the date for filing completed pre-trial checklist when it fixes the trial date or trial period under rule 29.2(2).

(3) The date for filing the completed pre-trial checklist will be not later than eight weeks before the trial date or the start of the trial period.

(4) The court will serve the pre-trial checklist on the parties at least 14 days before that date.

(5) Although the rules do not require the parties to exchange copies of the checklists before they are filed they are encouraged to do so to avoid the court being given conflicting or incomplete information.

(6) The file will be placed before a judge for his directions when all the checklists have been filed or when the time for filing them has expired and where a party has filed a checklist but another party has not done so.

8.2 The court's general approach will be as set out in the following paragraphs. The court may however decide to make other orders, and in particular the court will take into account the steps, if any, of which it is aware which the parties have taken to prepare the case for trial.

8.3 (1) Where no party files a pre-trial checklist the court will order that unless a completed pre-trial checklist is filed within 7 days from service of that order, the claim, defence and any counterclaim will be struck out without further order of the court.

(2) Where a party files a pre-trial checklist but another party (the defaulting party) does not do so, the court will fix a hearing under rule 29.6(4). Whether or not the defaulting party attends the hearing, the court will normally fix or confirm the trial date and make other orders about the steps to be taken to prepare the case for trial.

8.4 Where the court decides to hold a hearing under rule 29.6(4) the court will fix a date which is as early as possible and the parties will be given at least three days' notice of the date.

8.5 Where the court decides to hold a pre-trial review (whether or not this is in addition to a hearing under rule 29.6(4)) the court will give the parties at least 7 days' notice of the date.

## Directions the Court Will Give on Listing

*Directions the court must give*

9.1 The court must fix the trial date or week, give a time estimate and fix the place of trial.

*Other directions*

9.2 (1) The parties should seek to agree directions and may file an agreed order. The court may make an order in those terms or it may make a different order.

(2) Agreed directions should include provision about:

(a) evidence especially expert evidence,

(b) a trial timetable and time estimate,
(c) the preparation of a trial bundle, and
(d) any other matter needed to prepare the case for trial.

(3) The court will include such of these provisions as are appropriate in any order that it may make, whether or not the parties have filed agreed directions.

(4) Unless a direction doing so has been given before, a direction giving permission to use expert evidence will say whether it gives permission to use oral evidence or reports or both and will name the experts concerned.

9.3 The principles set out in paragraph 6 of this practice direction about variation of directions applies equally to directions given at this stage.

## The Trial

10.1 The trial will normally take place at a Civil Trial Centre but it may be at another court if it is appropriate having regard to the needs of the parties and the availability of court resources.

10.2 The judge will generally have read the papers in the trial bundle and may dispense with an opening address.

10.3 The judge may confirm or vary any timetable given previously, or if none has been given set his own.

10.4 Attention is drawn to the provisions in Part 32 and the following parts of the Rules about evidence, and in particular:

(1) to rule 32.1 (court's power to control evidence and to restrict cross-examination), and

(2) to rule 32.5(2) (statements and reports to stand as evidence in chief).

10.5 In an appropriate case the judge may summarily assess costs in accordance with rule 44.7. Attention is drawn to the practice directions about costs and the steps the parties are required to take.

10.6 Once the trial of a multi-track claim has begun, the judge will normally sit on consecutive court days until it has been concluded.

# CPR Part 30 Transfer



## 30.1 Scope of this Part

(1) This Part deals with the transfer of proceedings between county courts, between the High Court and the county courts and within the High Court.

(2) The practice direction may make provision about the transfer of proceedings between the court and a tribunal.

(Rule 26.2 provides for automatic transfer in certain cases.)

## 30.2 Transfer Between County Courts and Within the High Court

(1) A county court may order proceedings before that court, or any part of them (such as a counterclaim or an application made in the proceedings), to be transferred to another county court if it is satisfied that—
   (a) an order should be made having regard to the criteria in rule 30.3; or
   (b) proceedings for—
      (i) the detailed assessment of costs; or
      (ii) the enforcement of a judgment or order, could be more conveniently or fairly taken in that other county court.

(2) If proceedings have been started in the wrong county court, a judge of the county court may order that the proceedings—
   (a) be transferred to the county court in which they ought to have been started;
   (b) continue in the county court in which they have been started; or
   (c) be struck out.

(3) An application for an order under paragraph (1) or (2) must be made to the county court where the claim is proceeding.

(4) The High Court may, having regard to the criteria in rule 30.3, order proceedings in the Royal Courts of Justice or a district registry, or any part of such proceedings (such as a counterclaim or an application made in the proceedings), to be transferred—
   (a) from the Royal Courts of Justice to a district registry; or
   (b) from a district registry to the Royal Courts of Justice or to another district registry.

(5) A district registry may order proceedings before it for the detailed assessment of costs to be transferred to another district registry if it is satisfied that the proceedings could be more conveniently or fairly taken in that other district registry.

(6) An application for an order under paragraph (4) or (5) must, if the claim is proceeding in a district registry, be made to that registry.

(7) Where some enactment, other than these Rules, requires proceedings to be started in a particular county court, neither paragraphs (1) nor (2) give the court power to order proceedings to be transferred to a county court which is not the court in which they should have been started or to order them to continue in the wrong court.

(8) Probate proceedings may only be transferred under paragraph (4) to the Chancery Division at the Royal Courts of Justice or to one of the Chancery district registries.

### 30.3 Criteria for a Transfer Order

(1) Paragraph (2) sets out the matters to which the court must have regard when considering whether to make an order under—
  (a) section 40(2), 41(1) or 42(2) of the County Courts Act 1984 (transfer between the High Court and a county court);
  (b) rule 30.2(1) (transfer between county courts); or
  (c) rule 30.2(4) (transfer between the Royal Courts of Justice and the district registries).

(2) The matters to which the court must have regard include—
  (a) the financial value of the claim and the amount in dispute, if different;
  (b) whether it would be more convenient or fair for hearings (including the trial) to be held in some other court;
  (c) the availability of a judge specialising in the type of claim in question;
  (d) whether the facts, legal issues, remedies or procedures involved are simple or complex;
  (e) the importance of the outcome of the claim to the public in general;
  (f) the facilities available at the court where the claim is being dealt with and whether they may be inadequate because of any disabilities of a party or potential witness;
  (g) whether the making of a declaration of incompatibility under section 4 of the Human Rights Act 1998 has arisen or may arise;
  (h) in the case of civil proceedings by or against the Crown, as defined in rule 66.1(2), the location of the relevant government department or officers of the Crown and, where appropriate, any relevant public interest that the matter should be tried in London.

### 30.4 Procedure

(1) Where the court orders proceedings to be transferred, the court from which they are to be transferred must give notice of the transfer to all the parties.

(2) An order made before the transfer of the proceedings shall not be affected by the order to transfer.

### 30.5 Transfer Between Divisions and to and from a Specialist List

(1) The High Court may order proceedings in any Division of the High Court to be transferred to another Division.

(2) A judge dealing with claims in a specialist list may order proceedings to be transferred to or from that list.

(3) An application for the transfer of proceedings to or from a specialist list must be made to a judge dealing with claims in that list.

### 30.6 Power to Specify Place Where Hearings are to be Held

The court may specify the place (for instance, a particular county court) where the trial or some other hearing in any proceedings is to be held and may do so without ordering the proceedings to be transferred.

### 30.7 Transfer of Control of Money in Court

The court may order that control of any money held by it under rule 21.11 (control of money recovered by or on behalf of a child or patient) be transferred to another court if that court would be more convenient.

### 30.8 Transfer of Competition Law Claims

(1) This rule applies if, in any proceedings in the Queen's Bench Division (other than proceedings in the Commercial or Admiralty Courts), a district registry of the High Court or a county court, a party's statement of case raises an issue relating to the application of—

(a) Article 81 or Article 82 of the Treaty establishing the European Community; or
(b) Chapter I or II of Part I of the Competition Act 1998.

(2) Rules 30.2 and 30.3 do not apply.

(3) The court must transfer the proceedings to the Chancery Division of the High Court at the Royal Courts of Justice.

(4) If any such proceedings which have been commenced in the Queen's Bench Division or a Mercantile Court fall within the scope of rule 58.1(2), any party to those proceedings may apply for the transfer of the proceedings to the Commercial Court, in accordance with rules 58.4(2) and 30.5(3). If the application is refused, the proceedings must be transferred to the Chancery Division of the High Court at the Royal Courts of Justice.

# PD 30 Practice Direction — Transfer

This practice direction supplements CPR Part 30.

## Value of a Case and Transfer

1 In addition to the criteria set out in r. 30.3(2) attention is drawn to the financial limits set out in the High Court and County Courts Jurisdiction Order 1991, as amended.

2 Attention is also drawn to PD 29, para. 2.

## Date of Transfer

3 Where the court orders proceedings to be transferred, the order will take effect from the date it is made by the court.

## Procedure on Transfer

4.1 Where an order for transfer has been made the transferring court will immediately send notice of the transfer to the receiving court. The notice will contain:
 (1) the name of the case, and
 (2) the number of the case.

4.2 At the same time as the transferring court notifies the receiving court it will also notify the parties of the transfer under r. 30.4(1).

## Procedure for an Appeal Against Order of Transfer

5.1 Where a district judge orders proceedings to be transferred and both the transferring and receiving courts are county courts, any appeal against that order should be made in the receiving court.

5.2 The receiving court may, if it is more convenient for the parties, remit the appeal to the transferring court to be dealt with there.

## Applications to Set Aside

6.1 Where a party may apply to set aside an order for transfer (e.g. under r. 23.10) the application should be made to the court which made the order.

6.2 Such application should be made in accordance with Part 23 of the Rules and PD 23.

## Transfer on the Criterion in Rule 30.3(2)(g)

7 A transfer should only be made on the basis of the criterion in r. 30.3(2)(g) where there is a real prospect that a declaration of incompatibility will be made.

## Enterprise Act 2002

8.1 In this paragraph:
 (1) 'the 1998 Act' means the Competition Act 1998;
 (2) 'the 2002 Act' means the Enterprise Act 2002; and
 (3) 'the CAT' means the Competition Appeal Tribunal.

8.2 Rules 30.1, 30.4 and 30.5 and paras 3 and 6 apply.

*Transfer from the High Court or a county court to the Competition Appeal Tribunal under the Enterprise Act 2002, s. 16(4)*

8.3 The High Court or a county court may pursuant to s. 16(4) of the 2002 Act, on its own initiative or on application by the claimant or defendant, order the transfer of any part of the proceedings before it, which relates to a claim to which s. 47A of the 1998 Act applies, to the CAT.

8.4 When considering whether to make an order under para. 8.3 the court shall take into account whether:

(1) there is a similar claim under s. 47A of the 1998 Act based on the same infringement currently before the CAT;
(2) the CAT has previously made a decision on a similar claim under s. 47A of the 1998 Act based on the same infringement; or
(3) the CAT has developed considerable expertise by previously dealing with a significant number of cases arising from the same or similar infringements.

8.5 Where the court orders a transfer under para. 8.3 it will immediately:
(1) send to the CAT:
(a) a notice of the transfer containing the name of the case; and
(b) all papers relating to the case; and
(2) notify the parties of the transfer.

8.6 An appeal against a transfer order made under para. 8.3 must be brought in the court which made the transfer order.

*Transfer from the Competition Appeal Tribunal to the High Court under the Enterprise Act 2002, s. 16(5)*

8.7 Where the CAT pursuant to s. 16(5) of the 2002 Act directs transfer of a claim made in proceedings under s. 47A of the 1998 Act to the High Court, the claim should be transferred to the Chancery Division of the High Court at the Royal Courts of Justice.

8.8 As soon as a claim has been transferred under para. 8.7, the High Court must:
(1) allocate a case number; and
(2) list the case for a case management hearing before a judge.

8.9 A party to a claim which has been transferred under para. 8.7 may apply to transfer it to the Commercial Court if it otherwise falls within the scope of r. 58.2(1), in accordance with the procedure set out in rr. 58.4(2) and 30.5(3).

# CPR Part 31 Disclosure and Inspection of Documents



## 31.1 Scope of this Part

(1) This Part sets out rules about the disclosure and inspection of documents.
(2) This Part applies to all claims except a claim on the small claims track.

## 31.2 Meaning of Disclosure

A party discloses a document by stating that the document exists or has existed.

## 31.3 Right of Inspection of a Disclosed Document

(1) A party to whom a document has been disclosed has a right to inspect that document except where—
  (a) the document is no longer in the control of the party who disclosed it;
  (b) the party disclosing the document has a right or a duty to withhold inspection of it; or
  (c) paragraph (2) applies.

(Rule 31.8 sets out when a document is in the control of a party.)

(Rule 31.19 sets out the procedure for claiming a right or duty to withhold inspection.)

(2) Where a party considers that it would be disproportionate to the issues in the case to permit inspection of documents within a category or class of document disclosed under rule 31.6(b)—
  (a) he is not required to permit inspection of documents within that category or class; but
  (b) he must state in his disclosure statement that inspection of those documents will not be permitted on the grounds that to do so would be disproportionate.

(Rule 31.6 provides for standard disclosure.)

(Rule 31.10 makes provision for a disclosure statement.)

(Rule 31.12 provides for a party to apply for an order for specific inspection of documents.)

## 31.4 Meaning of Document

In this Part—

'document' means anything in which information of any description is recorded; and

'copy', in relation to a document, means anything onto which information recorded in the document has been copied, by whatever means and whether directly or indirectly.

## 31.5 Disclosure Limited to Standard Disclosure

(1) An order to give disclosure is an order to give standard disclosure unless the court directs otherwise.

(2) The court may dispense with or limit standard disclosure.

(3) The parties may agree in writing to dispense with or to limit standard disclosure.

(The court may make an order requiring standard disclosure under rule 28.3 which deals with directions in relation to cases on the fast track and under rule 29.2 which deals with case management in relation to cases on the multi-track.)

## 31.6 Standard Disclosure—What Documents Are to be Disclosed

Standard disclosure requires a party to disclose only—

(a) the documents on which he relies; and

(b) the documents which—

  (i) adversely affect his own case;

  (ii) adversely affect another party's case; or

  (iii) support another party's case; and

(c) the documents which he is required to disclose by a relevant practice direction.

## 31.7 Duty of Search

(1) When giving standard disclosure, a party is required to make a reasonable search for documents falling within rule 31.6(b) or (c).

(2) The factors relevant in deciding the reasonableness of a search include the following—

  (a) the number of documents involved;

  (b) the nature and complexity of the proceedings;

  (c) the ease and expense of retrieval of any particular document; and

  (d) the significance of any document which is likely to be located during the search.

(3) Where a party has not searched for a category or class of document on the grounds that to do so would be unreasonable, he must state this in his disclosure statement and identify the category or class of document.

(Rule 31.10 makes provision for a disclosure statement.)

## 31.8 Duty of Disclosure Limited to Documents Which Are or Have Been in a Party's Control

(1) A party's duty to disclose documents is limited to documents which are or have been in his control.

(2) For this purpose a party has or has had a document in his control if—

  (a) it is or was in his physical possession;

  (b) he has or has had a right to possession of it; or

  (c) he has or has had a right to inspect or take copies of it.

## 31.9 Disclosure of Copies

(1) A party need not disclose more than one copy of a document.

(2) A copy of a document that contains a modification, obliteration or other marking or feature—

  (a) on which a party intends to rely; or

(b) which adversely affects his own case or another party's case or supports another party's case;

shall be treated as a separate document.

(Rule 31.4 sets out the meaning of a copy of a document.)

## 31.10 Procedure for Standard Disclosure

(1) The procedure for standard disclosure is as follows.
(2) Each party must make and serve on every other party, a list of documents in the relevant practice form.
(3) The list must identify the documents in a convenient order and manner and as concisely as possible.
(4) The list must indicate—
  (a) those documents in respect of which the party claims a right or duty to withhold inspection; and
  (b) (i) those documents which are no longer in the party's control; and
    (ii) what has happened to those documents.

(Rule 31.19(3) and (4) require a statement in the list of documents relating to any documents inspection of which a person claims he has a right or duty to withhold.)

(5) The list must include a disclosure statement.
(6) A disclosure statement is a statement made by the party disclosing the documents—
  (a) setting out the extent of the search that has been made to locate documents which he is required to disclose;
  (b) certifying that he understands the duty to disclose documents; and
  (c) certifying that to the best of his knowledge he has carried out that duty.
(7) Where the party making the disclosure statement is a company, firm, association or other organisation, the statement must also—
  (a) identify the person making the statement; and
  (b) explain why he is considered an appropriate person to make the statement.
(8) The parties may agree in writing—
  (a) to disclose documents without making a list; and
  (b) to disclose documents without the disclosing party making a disclosure statement.
(9) A disclosure statement may be made by a person who is not a party where this is permitted by a relevant practice direction.

## 31.11 Duty of Disclosure Continues During Proceedings

(1) Any duty of disclosure continues until the proceedings are concluded.
(2) If documents to which that duty extends come to a party's notice at any time during the proceedings, he must immediately notify every other party.

## 31.12 Specific Disclosure or Inspection

(1) The court may make an order for specific disclosure or specific inspection.
(2) An order for specific disclosure is an order that a party must do one or more of the following things—
  (a) disclose documents or classes of documents specified in the order;
  (b) carry out a search to the extent stated in the order;
  (c) disclose any documents located as a result of that search.
(3) An order for specific inspection is an order that a party permit inspection of a document referred to in rule 31.3(2).

(Rule 31.3(2) allows a party to state in his disclosure statement that he will not permit inspection of a document on the grounds that it would be disproportionate to do so.)

## 31.13 Disclosure in Stages

The parties may agree in writing, or the court may direct, that disclosure or inspection or both shall take place in stages.

### 31.14 Documents Referred to in Statements of Case etc.

(1) A party may inspect a document mentioned in—
  (a) a statement of case;
  (b) a witness statement;
  (c) a witness summary; or
  (d) an affidavit(GL).
(2) Subject to rule 35.10(4), a party may apply for an order for inspection of any document mentioned in an expert's report which has not already been disclosed in the proceedings.

(Rule 35.10(4) makes provision in relation to instructions referred to in an expert's report.)

### 31.15 Inspection and Copying of Documents

Where a party has a right to inspect a document—
(a) that party must give the party who disclosed the document written notice of his wish to inspect it;
(b) the party who disclosed the document must permit inspection not more than 7 days after the date on which he received the notice; and
(c) that party may request a copy of the document and, if he also undertakes to pay reasonable copying costs, the party who disclosed the document must supply him with a copy not more than 7 days after the date on which he received the request.

(Rule[s] 31.3 and 31.14 deal with the right of a party to inspect a document.)

### 31.16 Disclosure Before Proceedings Start

(1) This rule applies where an application is made to the court under any Act for disclosure before proceedings have started.
(2) The application must be supported by evidence.
(3) The court may make an order under this rule only where—
  (a) the respondent is likely to be a party to subsequent proceedings;
  (b) the applicant is also likely to be a party to those proceedings;
  (c) if proceedings had started, the respondent's duty by way of standard disclosure, set out in rule 31.6, would extend to the documents or classes of documents of which the applicant seeks disclosure; and
  (d) disclosure before proceedings have started is desirable in order to—
    (i) dispose fairly of the anticipated proceedings;
    (ii) assist the dispute to be resolved without proceedings; or
    (iii) save costs.
(4) An order under this rule must—
  (a) specify the documents or the classes of documents which the respondent must disclose; and
  (b) require him, when making disclosure, to specify any of those documents—
    (i) which are no longer in his control; or
    (ii) in respect of which he claims a right or duty to withhold inspection.
(5) Such an order may—
  (a) require the respondent to indicate what has happened to any documents which are no longer in his control; and
  (b) specify the time and place for disclosure and inspection.

### 31.17 Orders for Disclosure Against a Person Not a Party

(1) This rule applies where an application is made to the court under any Act for disclosure by a person who is not a party to the proceedings.
(2) The application must be supported by evidence.
(3) The court may make an order under this rule only where—
  (a) the documents of which disclosure is sought are likely to support the case of the applicant or adversely affect the case of one of the other parties to the proceedings; and
  (b) disclosure is necessary in order to dispose fairly of the claim or to save costs.

(4) An order under this rule must—
 (a) specify the documents or the classes of documents which the respondent must disclose; and
 (b) require the respondent, when making disclosure, to specify any of those documents—
  (i) which are no longer in his control; or
  (ii) in respect of which he claims a right or duty to withhold inspection.
(5) Such an order may—
 (a) require the respondent to indicate what has happened to any documents which are no longer in his control; and
 (b) specify the time and place for disclosure and inspection.

## 31.18 Rules Not to Limit Other Powers of the Court to Order Disclosure

Rules 31.16 and 31.17 do not limit any other power which the court may have to order—
(a) disclosure before proceedings have started; and
(b) disclosure against a person who is not a party to proceedings.

## 31.19 Claim to Withhold Inspection or Disclosure of a Document

(1) A person may apply, without notice, for an order permitting him to withhold disclosure of a document on the ground that disclosure would damage the public interest.
(2) Unless the court orders otherwise, an order of the court under paragraph (1)—
 (a) must not be served on any other person; and
 (b) must not be open to inspection by any person.
(3) A person who wishes to claim that he has a right or a duty to withhold inspection of a document, or part of a document, must state in writing—
 (a) that he has such a right or duty; and
 (b) the grounds on which he claims that right or duty.
(4) The statement referred to in paragraph (3) must be made—
 (a) in the list in which the document is disclosed; or
 (b) if there is no list, to the person wishing to inspect the document.
(5) A party may apply to the court to decide whether a claim made under paragraph (3) should be upheld.
(6) For the purpose of deciding an application under paragraph (1) (application to withhold disclosure) or paragraph (3) (claim to withhold inspection) the court may—
 (a) require the person seeking to withhold disclosure or inspection of a document to produce that document to the court; and
 (b) invite any person, whether or not a party, to make representations.
(7) An application under paragraph (1) or paragraph (5) must be supported by evidence.
(8) This Part does not affect any rule of law which permits or requires a document to be withheld from disclosure or inspection on the ground that its disclosure or inspection would damage the public interest.

## 31.20 Restriction on Use of a Privileged Document Inspection of Which Has Been Inadvertently Allowed

Where a party inadvertently allows a privileged document to be inspected, the party who has inspected the document may use it or its contents only with the permission of the court.

## 31.21 Consequence of Failure to Disclose Documents or Permit Inspection

A party may not rely on any document which he fails to disclose or in respect of which he fails to permit inspection unless the court gives permission.

## 31.22 Subsequent Use of Disclosed Documents

(1) A party to whom a document has been disclosed may use the document only for the purpose of the proceedings in which it is disclosed, except where—
   (a) the document has been read to or by the court, or referred to, at a hearing which has been held in public;
   (b) the court gives permission; or
   (c) the party who disclosed the document and the person to whom the document belongs agree.

(2) The court may make an order restricting or prohibiting the use of a document which has been disclosed, even where the document has been read to or by the court, or referred to, at a hearing which has been held in public.

(3) An application for such an order may be made—
   (a) by a party; or
   (b) by any person to whom the document belongs.

## 31.23 False Disclosure Statements

(1) Proceedings for contempt of court may be brought against a person if he makes, or causes to be made, a false disclosure statement, without an honest belief in its truth.

(2) Proceedings under this rule may be brought only—
   (a) by the Attorney General; or
   (b) with the permission of the court.

# PD 31 Practice Direction — Disclosure and Inspection

This practice direction supplements CPR Part 31.

## General

1.1 The normal order for disclosure will be an order that the parties give standard disclosure.

1.2 In order to give standard disclosure the disclosing party must make a reasonable search for documents falling within the paragraphs of rule 31.6.

1.3 Having made the search the disclosing party must (unless rule 31.10(8) applies) make a list of the documents of whose existence the party is aware that fall within those paragraphs and which are or have been in the party's control (see rule 31.8).

1.4 The obligations imposed by an order for standard disclosure may be dispensed with or limited either by the court or by written agreement between the parties. Any such written agreement should be lodged with the court.

## The Search

2 The extent of the search which must be made will depend upon the circumstances of the case including, in particular, the factors referred to in rule 31.7(2). The parties should bear in mind the overriding principle of proportionality (see rule 1.1(2)(c)). It may, for example, be reasonable to decide not to search for documents coming into existence before some particular date, or to limit the search to documents in some particular place or places, or to documents falling into particular categories.

## Electronic Disclosure

2A.1 Rule 31.4 contains a broad definition of a document. This extends to electronic documents, including e-mail and other electronic communications, word processed documents and databases. In addition to documents that are readily accessible from computer systems and other electronic devices and media, the definition covers those documents that are stored on servers and back-up systems and electronic documents that have been 'deleted'. It also extends to additional information stored and associated with electronic documents known as metadata.

2A.2 The parties should, prior to the first case management conference, discuss any issues that may arise regarding searches for and the preservation of electronic documents. This may involve the parties providing information about the categories of electronic documents within their control, the computer systems, electronic devices and media on which any relevant documents may be held, the storage systems maintained by the parties and their document retention policies. In the case of difficulty or disagreement, the matter should be referred to a judge for directions at the earliest practical date, if possible at the first case management conference.

2A.3 The parties should cooperate at an early stage as to the format in which electronic copy documents are to be provided on inspection. In the case of difficulty or disagreement, the matter should be referred to a judge for directions at the earliest practical date, if possible at the first case management conference.

2A.4 The existence of electronic documents impacts upon the extent of the reasonable search required by rule 31.7 for the purposes of standard disclosure. The factors that may be relevant in deciding the reasonableness of a search for electronic documents include (but are not limited to) the following—

(a) the number of documents involved;

(b) the nature and complexity of the proceedings;

(c) the ease and expense of retrieval of any particular document. This includes:

(i) the accessibility of electronic documents or data including e-mail communications on computer systems, servers, back-up systems and other electronic devices or media that may contain such documents taking into account alterations or developments in hardware or software systems used by the disclosing party and/or available to enable access to such documents;

(ii) the location of relevant electronic documents, data, computer systems, servers, back-up systems and other electronic devices or media that may contain such documents;

(iii) the likelihood of locating relevant data;

(iv) the cost of recovering any electronic documents;

(v) the cost of disclosing and providing inspection of any relevant electronic documents;

(vi) the likelihood that electronic documents will be materially altered in the course of recovery, disclosure or inspection;

(d) the significance of any document which is likely to be located during the search.

2A.5 It may be reasonable to search some or all of the parties' electronic storage systems. In some circumstances, it may be reasonable to search for electronic documents by means of keyword searches (agreed as far as possible between the parties) even where a full review of each and every document would be unreasonable. There may be other forms of electronic search that may be appropriate in particular circumstances.

## The List

3.1 The list should be in form N265.

3.2 In order to comply with rule 31.10(3) it will normally be necessary to list the documents in date order, to number them consecutively and to give each a concise description (e.g. letter, claimant to defendant). Where there is a large number of documents all falling into a particular category the disclosing party may list those documents as a category rather than individually e.g. 50 bank statements relating to account number _ at _ Bank, _ 20 _ to _ 20 _; or, 35 letters passing between _ and _ between _ 20 _ and _ 20 _.

3.3 The obligations imposed by an order for disclosure will continue until the proceedings come to an end. If, after a list of documents has been prepared and served, the existence of further documents to which the order applies comes to the attention of the disclosing party, the party must prepare and serve a supplemental list.

## Disclosure Statement

4.1 A list of documents must (unless rule 31.10(8)(b) applies) contain a disclosure statement complying with rule 31.10. The form of disclosure statement is set out in the Annex to this practice direction.

4.2 The disclosure statement should:

(1) expressly state that the disclosing party believes the extent of the search to have been reasonable in all the circumstances, and

(2) in setting out the extent of the search (see rule 31.10(6)) draw attention to any particular limitations on the extent of the search which were adopted for proportionality reasons and give the reasons why the limitations were adopted, e.g. the difficulty or expense that a search not subject to those limitations would have entailed or the marginal relevance of categories of documents omitted from the search.

4.3 Where rule 31.10(7) applies, the details given in the disclosure statement about the person making the statement must include his name and address and the office or position he holds in the disclosing party or the basis upon which he makes the statement on behalf of the party.

4.4 If the disclosing party has a legal representative acting for him, the legal representative must endeavour to ensure that the person making the disclosure statement (whether the disclosing party or, in a case to which rule 31.10(7) applies, some other person) understands the duty of disclosure under Part 31.

4.5 If the disclosing party wishes to claim that he has a right or duty to withhold a document, or part of a document, in his list of documents from inspection (see rule 31.19(3)), he must state in writing:
(1) that he has such a right or duty, and
(2) the grounds on which he claims that right or duty.

4.6 The statement referred to in paragraph 4.5 above should normally be included in the disclosure statement and must identify the document, or part of a document, to which the claim relates.

4.7 An insurer or the Motor Insurers' Bureau may sign a disclosure statement on behalf of a party where the insurer or the Motor Insurers' Bureau has a financial interest in the result of proceedings brought wholly or partially by or against that party. Rule 31.10(7) and paragraph 4.3 above shall apply to the insurer or the Motor Insurers' Bureau making such a statement.

## Specific Disclosure

5.1 If a party believes that the disclosure of documents given by a disclosing party is inadequate he may make an application for an order for specific disclosure (see rule 31.12).

5.2 The application notice must specify the order that the applicant intends to ask the court to make and must be supported by evidence (see rule 31.12(2) which describes the orders the court may make).

5.3 The grounds on which the order is sought may be set out in the application notice itself but if not there set out must be set out in the evidence filed in support of the application.

5.4 In deciding whether or not to make an order for specific disclosure the court will take into account all the circumstances of the case and, in particular, the overriding objective described in Part 1. But if the court concludes that the party from whom specific disclosure is sought has failed adequately to comply with the obligations imposed by an order for disclosure (whether by failing to make a sufficient search for documents or otherwise) the court will usually make such order as is necessary to ensure that those obligations are properly complied with.

5.5 An order for specific disclosure may in an appropriate case direct a party to:
(1) carry out a search for any documents which it is reasonable to suppose may contain information which may:
(a) enable the party applying for disclosure either to advance his own case or to damage that of the party giving disclosure; or
(b) lead to a train of enquiry which has either of those consequences; and
(2) disclose any documents found as a result of that search.

## Claims to Withhold Disclosure or Inspection of a Document

6.1 A claim to withhold inspection of a document, or part of a document, disclosed in a list of documents does not require an application to the court. Where such a claim has been made, a party who wishes to challenge it must apply to the court (see rule 31.19(5)).

6.2 Rule 31.19(1) and (6) provide a procedure enabling a party to apply for an order permitting disclosure of the existence of a document to be withheld.

## Inspection of Documents Mentioned in Expert's Report (Rule 31.14(2))

7.1 If a party wishes to inspect documents referred to in the expert report of another party, before issuing an application he should request inspection of the documents informally, and inspection should be provided by agreement unless the request is unreasonable.

7.2 Where an expert report refers to a large number or volume of documents and it would be burdensome to copy or collate them, the court will only order inspection of such documents if it is satisfied that it is necessary for the just disposal of the proceedings and the party cannot reasonably obtain the documents from another source.

8 Attention is drawn to r. 31.23 which sets out the consequences of making a false disclosure statement without an honest belief in its truth, and to the procedures set out in PD 32, paras 28.1 to 28.3.

## ANNEX DISCLOSURE STATEMENT

I, the above-named claimant [or defendant] [if party making disclosure is a company, firm or other organisation identify here who the person making the disclosure statement is and why he is the appropriate person to make it] state that I have carried out a reasonable and proportionate search to locate all the documents which I am required to disclose under the order made by the court on day of . I did not search:
(1) for documents predating ............................................
(2) for documents located elsewhere than............................................
(3) for documents in categories other than............................................
(4) for electronic documents.

I carried out a search for electronic documents contained on or created by the following:

[list what was searched and extent of search]

I did not search for the following:

(1) documents created before ............................................,

(2) documents contained on or created by the Claimant's/Defendant's PCs/portable data storage media/databases/servers/back-up tapes/off-site storage/mobile phones/laptops/ notebooks/handheld devices/PDA devices (delete as appropriate),

(3) documents contained on or created by the Claimant's/Defendant's mail files/ document files/calendar files/spreadsheet files/graphic and presentation files/web-based applications (delete as appropriate),

(4) documents other than by reference to the following keyword(s)/concepts (delete if your search was not confined to specific keywords or concepts).

I certify that I understand the duty of disclosure and to the best of my knowledge I have carried out that duty. I certify that the list above is a complete list of all documents which are or have been in my control and which I am obliged under the said order to disclose.

# CPR Part 32 Evidence



## 32.1 Power of Court to Control Evidence

(1) The court may control the evidence by giving directions as to—
   (a) the issues on which it requires evidence;
   (b) the nature of the evidence which it requires to decide those issues; and
   (c) the way in which the evidence is to be placed before the court.
(2) The court may use its power under this rule to exclude evidence that would otherwise be admissible.
(3) The court may limit cross-examination[(GL)].

## 32.2 Evidence of Witnesses—General Rule

(1) The general rule is that any fact which needs to be proved by the evidence of witnesses is to be proved—
   (a) at trial, by their oral evidence given in public; and
   (b) at any other hearing, by their evidence in writing.
(2) This is subject—
   (a) to any provision to the contrary contained in these Rules or elsewhere; or
   (b) to any order of the court.

## 32.3 Evidence by Video Link or Other Means

The court may allow a witness to give evidence through a video link or by other means.

## 32.4 Requirement to Serve Witness Statements for Use at Trial

(1) A witness statement is a written statement signed by a person which contains the evidence which that person would be allowed to give orally.
(2) The court will order a party to serve on the other parties any witness statement of the oral evidence which the party serving the statement intends to rely on in relation to any issues of fact to be decided at the trial.
(3) The court may give directions as to—
   (a) the order in which witness statements are to be served; and
   (b) whether or not the witness statements are to be filed.

### 32.5 Use at Trial of Witness Statements Which Have Been Served

(1) If—
 (a) a party has served a witness statement; and
 (b) he wishes to rely at trial on the evidence of the witness who made the statement, he must call the witness to give oral evidence unless the court orders otherwise or he puts the statement in as hearsay evidence.

(Part 33 contains provisions about hearsay evidence.)

(2) Where a witness is called to give oral evidence under paragraph (1), his witness statement shall stand as his evidence in chief(GL) unless the court orders otherwise.
(3) A witness giving oral evidence at trial may with the permission of the court—
 (a) amplify his witness statement; and
 (b) give evidence in relation to new matters which have arisen since the witness statement was served on the other parties.
(4) The court will give permission under paragraph (3) only if it considers that there is good reason not to confine the evidence of the witness to the contents of his witness statement.
(5) If a party who has served a witness statement does not—
 (a) call the witness to give evidence at trial; or
 (b) put the witness statement in as hearsay evidence,
 any other party may put the witness statement in as hearsay evidence.

### 32.6 Evidence in Proceedings Other than at Trial

(1) Subject to paragraph (2), the general rule is that evidence at hearings other than the trial is to be by witness statement unless the court, a practice direction or any other enactment requires otherwise.
(2) At hearings other than the trial, a party may rely on the matters set out in—
 (a) his statement of case; or
 (b) his application notice,
 if the statement of case or application notice is verified by a statement of truth.

### 32.7 Order for Cross-examination

(1) Where, at a hearing other than the trial, evidence is given in writing, any party may apply to the court for permission to cross-examine the person giving the evidence.
(2) If the court gives permission under paragraph (1) but the person in question does not attend as required by the order, his evidence may not be used unless the court gives permission.

### 32.8 Form of Witness Statement

A witness statement must comply with the requirements set out in the relevant practice direction.

(Part 22 requires a witness statement to be verified by a statement of truth.)

### 32.9 Witness Summaries

(1) A party who—
 (a) is required to serve a witness statement for use at trial; but
 (b) is unable to obtain one,
 may apply, without notice, for permission to serve a witness summary instead.
(2) A witness summary is a summary of—
 (a) the evidence, if known, which would otherwise be included in a witness statement; or
 (b) if the evidence is not known, the matters about which the party serving the witness summary proposes to question the witness.
(3) Unless the court orders otherwise, a witness summary must include the name and address of the intended witness.

(4) Unless the court orders otherwise, a witness summary must be served within the period in which a witness statement would have had to be served.
(5) Where a party serves a witness summary, so far as practicable rules 32.4 (requirement to serve witness statements for use at trial), 32.5(3) (amplifying witness statements), and 32.8 (form of witness statement) shall apply to the summary.

### 32.10 Consequence of Failure to Serve Witness Statement or Summary

If a witness statement or a witness summary for use at trial is not served in respect of an intended witness within the time specified by the court, then the witness may not be called to give oral evidence unless the court gives permission.

### 32.11 Cross-examination on a Witness Statement

Where a witness is called to give evidence at trial, he may be cross-examined on his witness statement whether or not the statement or any part of it was referred to during the witness's evidence in chief(GL).

### 32.12 Use of Witness Statements For Other Purposes

(1) Except as provided by this rule, a witness statement may be used only for the purpose of the proceedings in which it is served.
(2) Paragraph (1) does not apply if and to the extent that—
    (a) the witness gives consent in writing to some other use of it;
    (b) the court gives permission for some other use; or
    (c) the witness statement has been put in evidence at a hearing held in public.

### 32.13 Availability of Witness Statements For Inspection

(1) A witness statement which stands as evidence in chief(GL) is open to inspection during the course of the trial unless the court otherwise directs.
(2) Any person may ask for a direction that a witness statement is not open to inspection.
(3) The court will not make a direction under paragraph (2) unless it is satisfied that a witness statement should not be open to inspection because of—
    (a) the interests of justice;
    (b) the public interest;
    (c) the nature of any expert medical evidence in the statement;
    (d) the nature of any confidential information (including information relating to personal financial matters) in the statement; or
    (e) the need to protect the interests of any child or patient.
(4) The court may exclude from inspection words or passages in the statement.

### 32.14 False Statements

(1) Proceedings for contempt of court may be brought against a person if he makes, or causes to be made, a false statement in a document verified by a statement of truth without an honest belief in its truth.

(Part 22 makes provision for a statement of truth.)

(2) Proceedings under this rule may be brought only—
    (a) by the Attorney General; or
    (b) with the permission of the court.

### 32.15 Affidavit Evidence

(1) Evidence must be given by affidavit(GL) instead of or in addition to a witness statement if this is required by the court, a provision contained in any other rule, a practice direction or any other enactment.
(2) Nothing in these Rules prevents a witness giving evidence by affidavit(GL) at a hearing other than the trial if he chooses to do so in a case where paragraph (1) does not apply,

but the party putting forward the affidavit(GL) may not recover the additional cost of making it from any other party unless the court orders otherwise.

## 32.16 Form of Affidavit

An affidavit(GL) must comply with the requirements set out in the relevant practice direction.

## 32.17 Affidavit Made Outside the Jurisdiction

A person may make an affidavit(GL) outside the jurisdiction in accordance with—
(a) this Part; or
(b) the law of the place where he makes the affidavit(GL).

## 32.18 Notice to Admit Facts

(1) A party may serve notice on another party requiring him to admit the facts, or the part of the case of the serving party, specified in the notice.
(2) A notice to admit facts must be served no later than 21 days before the trial.
(3) Where the other party makes any admission in response to the notice, the admission may be used against him only—
  (a) in the proceedings in which the notice to admit is served; and
  (b) by the party who served the notice.
(4) The court may allow a party to amend or withdraw any admission made by him on such terms as it thinks just.

## 32.19 Notice to Admit or Produce Documents

(1) A party shall be deemed to admit the authenticity of a document disclosed to him under Part 31 (disclosure and inspection of documents) unless he serves notice that he wishes the document to be proved at trial.
(2) A notice to prove a document must be served—
  (a) by the latest date for serving witness statements; or
  (b) within 7 days of disclosure of the document,
  whichever is later.

## 32.20 Notarial acts and instruments

A notarial act or instrument may be received in evidence without further proof as duly authenticated in accordance with the requirements of law unless the contrary is proved.

# PD 32 Practice Direction — Evidence

This practice direction supplements CPR Part 32.

## Evidence in General

1.1 Rule 32.2 sets out how evidence is to be given and facts are to be proved.

1.2 Evidence at a hearing other than the trial should normally be given by witness statement* (see para. 17 onwards). However, a witness may give evidence by affidavit if he wishes to do so[1] (and see para. 1.4 below).

1.3 Statements of case (see para. 26 onwards) and application notices[2] may also be used as evidence provided that their contents have been verified by a statement of truth.[3]
(For information regarding evidence by deposition see Part 34 and PD 34.)

1.4 Affidavits must be used as evidence in the following instances:
(1) where sworn evidence is required by an enactment,[4] rule, order or practice direction,
(2) in any application for a search order, a freezing injunction, or an order requiring an occupier to permit another to enter his land, and
(3) in any application for an order against anyone for alleged contempt of court.

1.5 If a party believes that sworn evidence is required by a court in another jurisdiction for any purpose connected with the proceedings, he may apply to the court for a direction that evidence shall be given only by affidavit on any pre-trial applications.

1.6 The court may give a direction under r. 32.15 that evidence shall be given by affidavit instead of or in addition to a witness statement or statement of case:
(1) on its own initiative, or
(2) after any party has applied to the court for such a direction.

1.7 An affidavit, where referred to in the Civil Procedure Rules or a practice direction, also means an affirmation unless the context requires otherwise.

## Affidavits

*Deponent*

2 A deponent is a person who gives evidence by affidavit or affirmation.

*Heading*

3.1 The affidavit should be headed with the title of the proceedings (see PD 7, para. 4, and PD 20, para. 7); where the proceedings are between several parties with the same status it is sufficient to identify the parties as follows:

| | |
|---|---|
| | Number: |
| A.B. (and others) | Claimants/Applicants |
| C.D. (and others) | Defendants/Respondents |
| (as appropriate) | |

3.2 At the top right-hand corner of the first page (and on the backsheet) there should be clearly written:
(1) the party on whose behalf it is made,
(2) the initials and surname of the deponent,
(3) the number of the affidavit in relation to that deponent,

[* In fact no practice direction supplementing Part 9 has been issued. See rule 32.6(1).]

1 See Rule 32.15(2).

2 See Part 23 for information about making an application.

3 Rule 32.6(2) and see Part 22 for information about the statement of truth.

4 See, e.g., s. 3(5)(a) of the Protection from Harassment Act 1997.

(4) the identifying initials and number of each exhibit referred to, and
(5) the date sworn.

*Body of affidavit*

4.1 The affidavit must, if practicable, be in the deponent's own words, the affidavit should be expressed in the first person and the deponent should:
(1) commence 'I (*full name*) of (*address*) state on oath . . .',
(2) if giving evidence in his professional, business or other occupational capacity, give the address at which he works in (1) above, the position he holds and the name of his firm or employer,
(3) give his occupation or, if he has none, his description, and
(4) state if he is a party to the proceedings or employed by a party to the proceedings, if it be the case.

4.2 An affidavit must indicate:
(1) which of the statements in it are made from the deponent's own knowledge and which are matters of information or belief, and
(2) the source for any matters of information or belief.

4.3 Where a deponent:
(1) refers to an exhibit or exhibits, he should state 'there is now shown to me marked ". . ." the (*description of exhibit*)', and
(2) makes more than one affidavit (to which there are exhibits) in the same proceedings, the numbering of the exhibits should run consecutively throughout and not start again with each affidavit.

*Jurat*

5.1 The jurat of an affidavit is a statement set out at the end of the document which authenticates the affidavit.

5.2 It must:
(1) be signed by all deponents,
(2) be completed and signed by the person before whom the affidavit was sworn whose name and qualification must be printed beneath his signature,
(3) contain the full address of the person before whom the affidavit was sworn, and
(4) follow immediately on from the text and not be put on a separate page.

*Format of affidavits*

6.1 An affidavit should:
(1) be produced on durable quality A4 paper with a 3.5 cm margin,
(2) be fully legible and should normally be typed on one side of the paper only,
(3) where possible, be bound securely in a manner which would not hamper filing, or otherwise each page should be endorsed with the case number and should bear the initials of the deponent and of the person before whom it was sworn,
(4) have the pages numbered consecutively as a separate document (or as one of several documents contained in a file),
(5) be divided into numbered paragraphs,
(6) have all numbers, including dates, expressed in figures, and
(7) give the reference to any document or documents mentioned either in the margin or in bold text in the body of the affidavit.

6.2 It is usually convenient for an affidavit to follow the chronological sequence of events or matters dealt with; each paragraph of an affidavit should as far as possible be confined to a distinct portion of the subject.

*Inability of deponent to read or sign affidavit*

7.1 Where an affidavit is sworn by a person who is unable to read or sign it, the person before whom the affidavit is sworn must certify in the jurat that:
(1) he read the affidavit to the deponent,

(2) the deponent appeared to understand it, and
(3) the deponent signed or made his mark, in his presence.

7.2 If that certificate is not included in the jurat, the affidavit may not be used in evidence unless the court is satisfied that it was read to the deponent and that he appeared to understand it. Two versions of the form of jurat with the certificate are set out at Annex 1 to this practice direction.

*Alterations to affidavits*

8.1 Any alteration to an affidavit must be initialled by both the deponent and the person before whom the affidavit was sworn.

8.2 An affidavit which contains an alteration that has not been initialled may be filed or used in evidence only with the permission of the court.

*Who may administer oaths and take affidavits*

9.1 Only the following may administer oaths and take affidavits:
(1) commissioners for oaths,[5]
(2) practising solicitors,[6]
(3) other persons specified by statute,[7]
(4) certain officials of the Supreme Court,[8]
(5) a circuit judge or district judge,[9]
(6) any justice of the peace,[10] and
(7) certain officials of any county court appointed by the judge of that court for the purpose.[11]

9.2 An affidavit must be sworn before a person independent of the parties or their representatives.

*Filing of affidavits*

10.1 If the court directs that an affidavit is to be filed,[12] it must be filed in the court or Division, or office or registry of the court or Division where the action in which it was or is to be used, is proceeding or will proceed.

10.2 Where an affidavit is in a foreign language:
(1) the party wishing to rely on it:
(a) must have it translated, and
(b) must file the foreign-language affidavit with the court, and
(2) the translator must make and file with the court an affidavit verifying the translation and exhibiting both the translation and a copy of the foreign-language affidavit.

## Exhibits

*Manner of exhibiting documents*

11.1 A document used in conjunction with an affidavit should be:
(1) produced to and verified by the deponent, and remain separate from the affidavit, and
(2) identified by a declaration of the person before whom the affidavit was sworn.

11.2 The declaration should be headed with the name of the proceedings in the same way as the affidavit.

11.3 The first page of each exhibit should be marked:

---

[5] Commissioners for Oaths Acts 1889 and 1891.
[6] Section 81 of the Solicitors Act 1974.
[7] Section 65 of the Administration of Justice Act 1985, s. 113 of the Courts and Legal Services Act 1990 and the Commissioners for Oaths (Prescribed Bodies) Regulations 1994 and 1995.
[8] Section 2 of the Commissioners for Oaths Act 1889.
[9] Section 58 of the County Courts Act 1984.
[10] Section 58 as above.
[11] Section 58 as above.
[12] Rules 32.1(3) and 32.4(3)(b).

(1) as in para. 3.2 above, and
(2) with the exhibit mark referred to in the affidavit.

*Letters*

12.1 Copies of individual letters should be collected together and exhibited in a bundle or bundles. They should be arranged in chronological order with the earliest at the top, and firmly secured.

12.2 When a bundle of correspondence is exhibited, the exhibit should have a front page attached stating that the bundle consists of original letters and copies. They should be arranged and secured as above and numbered consecutively.

*Other documents*

13.1 Photocopies instead of original documents may be exhibited provided the originals are made available for inspection by the other parties before the hearing and by the judge at the hearing.

13.2 Court documents must not be exhibited (official copies of such documents prove themselves).

13.3 Where an exhibit contains more than one document, a front page should be attached setting out a list of the documents contained in the exhibit; the list should contain the dates of the documents.

*Exhibits other than documents*

14.1 Items other than documents should be clearly marked with an exhibit number or letter in such a manner that the mark cannot become detached from the exhibit.

14.2 Small items may be placed in a container and the container appropriately marked.

*General provisions*

15.1 Where an exhibit contains more than one document:
(1) the bundle should not be stapled but should be securely fastened in a way that does not hinder the reading of the documents, and
(2) the pages should be numbered consecutively at bottom centre.

15.2 Every page of an exhibit should be clearly legible; typed copies of illegible documents should be included, paginated with 'a' numbers.

15.3 Where affidavits and exhibits have become numerous, they should be put into separate bundles and the pages numbered consecutively throughout.

15.4 Where on account of their bulk the service of exhibits or copies of exhibits on the other parties would be difficult or impracticable, the directions of the court should be sought as to arrangements for bringing the exhibits to the attention of the other parties and as to their custody pending trial.

*Affirmations*

16 All provisions in this or any other practice direction relating to affidavits apply to affirmations with the following exceptions:
(1) the deponent should commence 'I (*name*) of (*address*) do solemnly and sincerely affirm . . .', and
(2) in the jurat the word 'sworn' is replaced by the word 'affirmed'.

## Witness Statements

*Heading*

17.1 The witness statement should be headed with the title of the proceedings (see PD 7, para. 4, and PD 20, para. 7); where the proceedings are between several parties with the same status it is sufficient to identify the parties as follows:

| | Number: |
|---|---|
| A.B. (and others) | Claimants/Applicants |
| C.D. (and others) | Defendants/Respondents (as appropriate) |

17.2 At the top right-hand corner of the first page there should be clearly written:
(1) the party on whose behalf it is made,
(2) the initials and surname of the witness,
(3) the number of the statement in relation to that witness,
(4) the identifying initials and number of each exhibit referred to, and
(5) the date the statement was made.

*Body of witness statement*

18.1 The witness statement must, if practicable, be in the intended witness's own words, the statement should be expressed in the first person and should also state:
(1) the full name of the witness,
(2) his place of residence or, if he is making the statement in his professional, business or other occupational capacity, the address at which he works, the position he holds and the name of his firm or employer,
(3) his occupation, or if he has none, his description, and
(4) the fact that he is a party to the proceedings or is the employee of such a party if it be the case.

18.2 A witness statement must indicate:
(1) which of the statements in it are made from the witness's own knowledge and which are matters of information or belief, and
(2) the source for any matters of information or belief.

18.3 An exhibit used in conjunction with a witness statement should be verified and identified by the witness and remain separate from the witness statement.

18.4 Where a witness refers to an exhibit or exhibits, he should state 'I refer to the (*description of exhibit*) marked "..." '.

18.5 The provisions of paras 11.3 to 15.4 (exhibits) apply similarly to witness statements as they do to affidavits.

18.6 Where a witness makes more than one witness statement to which there are exhibits, in the same proceedings, the numbering of the exhibits should run consecutively throughout and not start again with each witness statement.

*Format of witness statement*

19.1 A witness statement should:
(1) be produced on durable quality A4 paper with a 3.5 cm margin,
(2) be fully legible and should normally be typed on one side of the paper only,
(3) where possible, be bound securely in a manner which would not hamper filing, or otherwise each page should be endorsed with the case number and should bear the initials of the witness,
(4) have the pages numbered consecutively as a separate statement (or as one of several statements contained in a file),
(5) be divided into numbered paragraphs,
(6) have all numbers, including dates, expressed in figures, and
(7) give the reference to any document or documents mentioned either in the margin or in bold text in the body of the statement.

19.2 It is usually convenient for a witness statement to follow the chronological sequence of the events or matters dealt with, each paragraph of a witness statement should as far as possible be confined to a distinct portion of the subject.

*Statement of truth*

20.1 A witness statement is the equivalent of the oral evidence which that witness would, if called, give in evidence; it must include a statement by the intended witness that he believes the facts in it are true.[13]

[13] See Part 22 for information about the statement of truth.

20.2 To verify a witness statement the statement of truth is as follows:
'I believe that the facts stated in this witness statement are true'

20.3 Attention is drawn to r. 32.14 which sets out the consequences of verifying a witness statement containing a false statement without an honest belief in its truth.

(Paragraph 3A of the practice direction to Part 22 sets out the procedure to be followed where the person who should sign a document which is verified by a statement of truth is unable to read or sign the document.)

21. *[21 is omitted as a result of Update 41 to the CPR]*

*Alterations to witness statements*

22.1 Any alteration to a witness statement must be initialled by the person making the statement or by the authorised person where appropriate (see para. 21).

22.2 A witness statement which contains an alteration that has not been initialled may be used in evidence only with the permission of the court.

*Filing of witness statements*

23.1 If the court directs that a witness statement is to be filed,[14] it must be filed in the court or Division, or office or registry of the court or Division where the action in which it was or is to be used, is proceeding or will proceed.

23.2 Where the court has directed that a witness statement in a foreign language is to be filed:
(1) the party wishing to rely on it must:
(a) have it translated, and
(b) file the foreign-language witness statement with the court, and
(2) the translator must make and file with the court an affidavit verifying the translation and exhibiting both the translation and a copy of the foreign-language witness statement.

*Certificate of court officer*

24.1 Where the court has ordered that a witness statement is not to be open to inspection by the public[15] or that words or passages in the statement are not to be open to inspection[16] the court officer will so certify on the statement and make any deletions directed by the court under r. 32.13(4).

*Defects in affidavits, witness statements and exhibits*

25.1 Where:
(1) an affidavit,
(2) a witness statement, or
(3) an exhibit to either an affidavit or a witness statement
does not comply with Part 32 or this practice direction in relation to its form, the court may refuse to admit it as evidence and may refuse to allow the costs arising from its preparation.

25.2 Permission to file a defective affidavit or witness statement or to use a defective exhibit may be obtained from a judge[17] in the court where the case is proceeding.

## Statements of Case

26.1 A statement of case may be used as evidence in an interim application provided it is verified by a statement of truth.[18]

26.2 To verify a statement of case the statement of truth should be set out as follows:
'[I believe] [the (*party on whose behalf the statement of case is being signed*) believes] that the facts stated in the statement of case are true'.

---

14 Rule 32.4(3)(b).
15 Rule 32.13(2).
16 Rule 32.13(4).
17 Rule 2.3(1); definition of judge.
18 See rule 32.6(2)(a).

26.3 Attention is drawn to rule 32.14 which sets out the consequences of verifying a witness statement containing a false statement without an honest belief in its truth.
(For information regarding statements of truth see Part 22 and PD 22.)
(Practice directions supplementing Parts 7, 9 and 17 provide further information concerning statements of case.*)

## Agreed Bundles for Hearings

27.1 The court may give directions requiring the parties to use their best endeavours to agree a bundle or bundles of documents for use at any hearing.

27.2 All documents contained in bundles which have been agreed for use at a hearing shall be admissible at that hearing as evidence of their contents, unless:
(1) the court orders otherwise; or
(2) a party gives written notice of objection to the admissibility of particular documents.

## Penalty

28.1 (1) Where a party alleges that a statement of truth or a disclosure statement is false the party shall refer that allegation to the court dealing with the claim in which the statement of truth or disclosure statement has been made.
(2) The court may:
(a) exercise any of its powers under the CPR;
(b) initiate steps to consider if there is a contempt of court and, where there is, to punish it;
(PD RSC Ord. 52 makes provision where committal to prison is a possibility if contempt is proved.)
(c) direct the party making the allegation to refer the matter to the Attorney-General with a request to him to consider whether he wishes to bring proceedings for contempt of court.

28.2 (1) An application to the Attorney-General should be made to his chambers at 9 Buckingham Gate, London SW1E 6JP in writing. The Attorney-General will initially require a copy of the order recording the direction of the judge referring the matter to him and information which:
(a) identifies the statement said to be false; and
(b) explains:
(i) why it is false, and
(ii) why the maker knew it to be false at the time he made it; and
(c) explains why contempt proceedings would be appropriate in the light of the overriding objective in CPR, Part 1.
(2) The practice of the Attorney-General is to prefer an application that comes from the court, and so has received preliminary consideration by a judge, to one made direct to him by a party to the claim in which the alleged contempt occurred without prior consideration by the court. An application to the Attorney-General is not a way of appealing against, or reviewing, the decision of the judge.

28.3 Where a party makes an application to the court for permission for that party to commence proceedings for contempt of court, it must be supported by written evidence containing the information specified in para. 28.2(1) and the result of the application to the Attorney-General made by the applicant.

28.4 The rules do not change the law of contempt or introduce new categories of contempt. A person applying to commence such proceedings should consider whether the incident complained of does amount to contempt of court and whether such proceedings would further the overriding objective in CPR, Part 1.

[* In fact no practice direction supplementing Part 9 has been issued.]

## Videoconferencing

29.1 Guidance on the use of videoconferencing in the civil courts is set out at Annex 3 to this practice direction.

A list of the sites which are available for video conferencing can be found on Her Majesty's Courts Service website at http://www.hmcourts-service.gov.uk.

## ANNEX 1

### Certificate to be Used Where a Deponent to an Affidavit is Unable to Read or Sign it

Sworn at . . . . . this . . . . . day of . . . . . Before me, I having first read over the contents of this affidavit to the deponent [*if there are exhibits, add* 'and explained the nature and effect of the exhibits referred to in it'] who appeared to understand it and approved its content as accurate, and made his mark on the affidavit in my presence.

*Or,* (after, *Before me*) the witness to the mark of the deponent having been first sworn that he had read over etc. (*as above*) and that he saw him make his mark on the affidavit. (*Witness must sign*).

### Certificate to be Used Where a Deponent to an Affirmation is Unable to Read or Sign it

Affirmed at . . . . . this . . . . . day of . . . . . Before me, I having first read over the contents of this affirmation to the deponent [*if there are exhibits, add* 'and explained the nature and effect of the exhibits referred to in it'] who appeared to understand it and approved its content as accurate, and made his mark on the affirmation in my presence.

*Or,* (after, *Before me*) the witness to the mark of the deponent having been first sworn that he had read over etc. (*as above*) and that he saw him make his mark on the affirmation. (*Witness must sign*).

## ANNEX 2

*[Omitted as a result of Update 41 to the CPR]*

## ANNEX 3

### Videoconferencing Guidance

This guidance is for the use of videoconferencing (VCF) in civil proceedings. It is in part based, with permission, upon the protocol of the Federal Court of Australia. It is intended to provide a guide to all persons involved in the use of VCF, although it does not attempt to cover all the practical questions which might arise.

### Videoconferencing Generally

1. The guidance covers the use of VCF equipment both (a) in a courtroom, whether via equipment which is permanently placed there or via a mobile unit, and (b) in a separate studio or conference room. In either case, the location at which the judge sits is referred to as the 'local site'. The other site or sites to and from which transmission is made are referred to as the 'remote site' and in any particular case any such site may be another courtroom. The guidance applies to cases where VCF is used for the taking of evidence and also to its use for other parts of any legal proceedings (for example, interim applications, case management conferences, pre-trial reviews).
2. VCF may be a convenient way of dealing with any part of proceedings: it can involve considerable savings in time and cost. Its use for the taking of evidence from overseas witnesses will, in particular, be likely to achieve a material saving of costs, and such savings may also be achieved by its use for taking domestic evidence. It is, however, inevitably not as ideal as having the witness physically present in court. Its convenience

should not therefore be allowed to dictate its use. A judgment must be made in every case in which the use of VCF is being considered not only as to whether it will achieve an overall cost saving but as to whether its use will be likely to be beneficial to the efficient, fair and economic disposal of the litigation. In particular, it needs to be recognised that the degree of control a court can exercise over a witness at the remote site is or may be more limited than it can exercise over a witness physically before it.

3. When used for the taking of evidence, the objective should be to make the VCF session as close as possible to the usual practice in a trial court where evidence is taken in open court. To gain the maximum benefit, several differences have to be taken into account. Some matters, which are taken for granted when evidence is taken in the conventional way, take on a different dimension when it is taken by VCF: for example, the administration of the oath, ensuring that the witness understands who is at the local site and what their various roles are, the raising of any objections to the evidence and the use of documents.
4. It should not be presumed that all foreign governments are willing to allow their nationals or others within their jurisdiction to be examined before a court in England or Wales by means of VCF. If there is any doubt about this, enquiries should be directed to the Foreign and Commonwealth Office (International Legal Matters Unit, Consular Division) with a view to ensuring that the country from which the evidence is to be taken raises no objection to it at diplomatic level. The party who is directed to be responsible for arranging the VCF (see para. 8 below) will be required to make all necessary inquiries about this well in advance of the VCF and must be able to inform the court what those inquiries were and of their outcome.
5. Time zone differences need to be considered when a witness abroad is to be examined in England or Wales by VCF. The convenience of the witness, the parties, their representatives and the court must all be taken into account. The cost of the use of a commercial studio is usually greater outside normal business hours.
6. Those involved with VCF need to be aware that, even with the most advanced systems currently available, there are the briefest of delays between the receipt of the picture and that of the accompanying sound. If due allowance is not made for this, there will be a tendency to 'speak over' the witness, whose voice will continue to be heard for a millisecond or so after he or she appears on the screen to have finished speaking.
7. With current technology, picture quality is good, but not as good as a television picture. The quality of the picture is enhanced if those appearing on VCF monitors keep their movements to a minimum.

## Preliminary Arrangements

8. The court's permission is required for any part of any proceedings to be dealt with by means of VCF. Before seeking a direction, the applicant should notify the listing officer, diary manager or other appropriate court officer of the intention to seek it, and should enquire as to the availability of court VCF equipment for the day or days of the proposed VCF. The application for a direction should be made to the master, district judge or judge, as may be appropriate. If all parties consent to a direction, permission can be sought by letter, fax or email, although the court may still require an oral hearing. All parties are entitled to be heard on whether or not such a direction should be given and as to its terms. If a witness at a remote site is to give evidence by an interpreter, consideration should be given at this stage as to whether the interpreter should be at the local site or the remote site. If a VCF direction is given, arrangements for the transmission will then need to be made. The court will ordinarily direct that the party seeking permission to use VCF is to be responsible for this. That party is hereafter referred to as the 'VCF arranging party'.
9. Subject to any order to the contrary, all costs of the transmission, including the costs of hiring equipment and technical personnel to operate it, will initially be the responsibility of, and must be met by, the VCF arranging party. All reasonable efforts should be

made to keep the transmission to a minimum and so keep the costs down. All such costs will be considered to be part of the costs of the proceedings and the court will determine at such subsequent time as is convenient or appropriate who, as between the parties, should be responsible for them and (if appropriate) in what proportions.

10. The local site will, if practicable, be a courtroom but it may instead be an appropriate studio or conference room. The VCF arranging party must contact the listing officer, diary manager or other appropriate officer of the court which made the VCF direction and make arrangements for the VCF transmission. Details of the remote site, and of the equipment to be used both at the local site (if not being supplied by the court) and the remote site (including the number of ISDN lines and connection speed), together with all necessary contact names and telephone numbers, will have to be provided to the listing officer, diary manager or other court officer. The court will need to be satisfied that any equipment provided by the parties for use at the local site and also that at the remote site is of sufficient quality for a satisfactory transmission. The VCF arranging party must ensure that an appropriate person will be present at the local site to supervise the operation of the VCF throughout the transmission in order to deal with any technical problems. That party must also arrange for a technical assistant to be similarly present at the remote site for like purposes.
11. It is recommended that the judge, practitioners and witness should arrive at their respective VCF sites about 20 minutes prior to the scheduled commencement of the transmission.
12. If the local site is not a courtroom, but a conference room or studio, the judge will need to determine who is to sit where. The VCF arranging party must take care to ensure that the number of microphones is adequate for the speakers and that the panning of the camera for the practitioners' table encompasses all legal representatives so that the viewer can see everyone seated there.
13. The proceedings, wherever they may take place, form part of a trial to which the public is entitled to have access (unless the court has determined that they should be heard in private). If the local site is to be a studio or conference room, the VCF arranging party must ensure that it provides sufficient accommodation to enable a reasonable number of members of the public to attend.
14. In cases where the local site is a studio or conference room, the VCF arranging party should make arrangements, if practicable, for the royal coat of arms to be placed above the judge's seat.
15. In cases in which the VCF is to be used for the taking of evidence, the VCF arranging party must arrange for recording equipment to be provided by the court which made the VCF direction so that the evidence can be recorded. An associate will normally be present to operate the recording equipment when the local site is a courtroom. The VCF arranging party should take steps to ensure that an associate is present to do likewise when it is a studio or conference room. The equipment should be set up and tested before the VCF transmission. It will often be a valuable safeguard for the VCF arranging party also to arrange for the provision of recording equipment at the remote site. This will provide a useful back-up if there is any reduction in sound quality during the transmission. A direction from the court for the making of such a back-up recording must, however, be obtained first. This is because the proceedings are court proceedings and, save as directed by the court, no other recording of them must be made. The court will direct what is to happen to the back-up recording.
16. Some countries may require that any oath or affirmation to be taken by a witness accord with local custom rather than the usual form of oath or affirmation used in England and Wales. The VCF arranging party must make all appropriate prior inquiries and put in place all arrangements necessary to enable the oath or affirmation to be taken in accordance with any local custom. That party must be in a position to inform the court what those inquiries were, what their outcome was and what arrangements have been made. If the oath or affirmation can be administered in the manner normal in England and

Wales, the VCF arranging party must arrange in advance to have the appropriate holy book at the remote site. The associate will normally administer the oath.

17. Consideration will need to be given in advance to the documents to which the witness is likely to be referred. The parties should endeavour to agree on this. It will usually be most convenient for a bundle of the copy documents to be prepared in advance, which the VCF arranging party should then send to the remote site.
18. Additional documents are sometimes quite properly introduced during the course of a witness's evidence. To cater for this, the VCF arranging party should ensure that equipment is available to enable documents to be transmitted between sites during the course of the VCF transmission. Consideration should be given to whether to use a document camera. If it is decided to use one, arrangements for its use will need to be established in advance. The panel operator will need to know the number and size of documents or objects if their images are to be sent by document camera. In many cases, a simpler and sufficient alternative will be to ensure that there are fax transmission and reception facilities at the participating sites.

## The Hearing

19. The procedure for conducting the transmission will be determined by the judge. He will determine who is to control the cameras. In cases where the VCF is being used for an application in the course of the proceedings, the judge will ordinarily not enter the local site until both sites are on line. Similarly, at the conclusion of the hearing, he will ordinarily leave the local site while both sites are still on line. The following paragraphs apply primarily to cases where the VCF is being used for the taking of the evidence of a witness at a remote site. In all cases, the judge will need to decide whether court dress is appropriate when using VCF facilities. It might be appropriate when transmitting from courtroom to courtroom. It might not be when a commercial facility is being used.
20. At the beginning of the transmission, the judge will probably wish to introduce himself and the advocates to the witness. He will probably want to know who is at the remote site and will invite the witness to introduce himself and anyone else who is with him. He may wish to give directions as to the seating arrangements at the remote site so that those present are visible at the local site during the taking of the evidence. He will probably wish to explain to the witness the method of taking the oath or of affirming, the manner in which the evidence will be taken, and who will be conducting the examination and cross-examination. He will probably also wish to inform the witness of the matters referred to in paras 6 and 7 above (coordination of picture with sound, and picture quality).
21. The examination of the witness at the remote site should follow as closely as possible the practice adopted when a witness is in the courtroom. During examination, cross-examination and re-examination, the witness must be able to see the legal representative asking the question and also any other person (whether another legal representative or the judge) making any statements in regard to the witness's evidence. It will in practice be most convenient if everyone remains seated throughout the transmission.

# CPR Part 33 Miscellaneous Rules About Evidence



## 33.1 Introductory

In this Part—

(a) 'hearsay' means a statement made, otherwise than by a person while giving oral evidence in proceedings, which is tendered as evidence of the matters stated; and

(b) references to hearsay include hearsay of whatever degree.

## 33.2 Notice of Intention to Rely on Hearsay Evidence

(1) Where a party intends to rely on hearsay evidence at trial and either—

  (a) that evidence is to be given by a witness giving oral evidence; or

  (b) that evidence is contained in a witness statement of a person who is not being called to give oral evidence;

that party complies with section 2(1)(a) of the Civil Evidence Act 1995 by serving a witness statement on the other parties in accordance with the court's order.

(2) Where paragraph (1)(b) applies, the party intending to rely on the hearsay evidence must, when he serves the witness statement—

  (a) inform the other parties that the witness is not being called to give oral evidence; and

  (b) give the reason why the witness will not be called.

(3) In all other cases where a party intends to rely on hearsay evidence at trial, that party complies with section 2(1)(a) of the Civil Evidence Act 1995 by serving a notice on the other parties which—

  (a) identifies the hearsay evidence;

  (b) states that the party serving the notice proposes to rely on the hearsay evidence at trial; and

  (c) gives the reason why the witness will not be called.

(4) The party proposing to rely on the hearsay evidence must—

  (a) serve the notice no later than the latest date for serving witness statements; and

  (b) if the hearsay evidence is to be in a document, supply a copy to any party who requests him to do so.

## 33.3 Circumstances in Which Notice of Intention to Rely on Hearsay Evidence is Not Required

Section 2(1) of the Civil Evidence Act 1995 (duty to give notice of intention to rely on hearsay evidence) does not apply—

(a) to evidence at hearings other than trials;

(aa) to an affidavit or witness statement which is to be used at trial but which does not contain hearsay evidence;

(b) to a statement which a party to a probate action wishes to put in evidence and which is alleged to have been made by the person whose estate is the subject of the proceedings; or
(c) where the requirement is excluded by a practice direction.

## 33.4 Power to Call Witness for Cross-examination on Hearsay Evidence

(1) Where a party—
  (a) proposes to rely on hearsay evidence; and
  (b) does not propose to call the person who made the original statement to give oral evidence,

  the court may, on the application of any other party, permit that party to call the maker of the statement to be cross-examined on the contents of the statement.
(2) An application for permission to cross-examine under this rule must be made not more than 14 days after the day on which a notice of intention to rely on the hearsay evidence was served on the applicant.

## 33.5 Credibility

(1) Where a party—
  (a) proposes to rely on hearsay evidence; but
  (b) does not propose to call the person who made the original statement to give oral evidence; and
  (c) another party wishes to call evidence to attack the credibility of the person who made the statement,

  the party who so wishes must give notice of his intention to the party who proposes to give the hearsay statement in evidence.
(2) A party must give notice under paragraph (1) not more than 14 days after the day on which a hearsay notice relating to the hearsay evidence was served on him.

## 33.6 Use of Plans, Photographs and Models as Evidence

(1) This rule applies to evidence (such as a plan, photograph or model) which is not—
  (a) contained in a witness statement, affidavit(GL) or expert's report;
  (b) to be given orally at trial; or
  (c) evidence of which prior notice must be given under rule 33.2.
(2) This rule includes documents which may be received in evidence without further proof under section 9 of the Civil Evidence Act 1995.
(3) Unless the court orders otherwise the evidence shall not be receivable at a trial unless the party intending to put it in evidence has given notice to the other parties in accordance with this rule.
(4) Where the party intends to use the evidence as evidence of any fact then, except where paragraph (6) applies, he must give notice not later than the latest date for serving witness statements.
(5) He must give notice at least 21 days before the hearing at which he proposes to put in the evidence, if—
  (a) there are not to be witness statements; or
  (b) he intends to put in the evidence solely in order to disprove an allegation made in a witness statement.
(6) Where the evidence forms part of expert evidence, he must give notice when the expert's report is served on the other party.
(7) Where the evidence is being produced to the court for any reason other than as part of factual or expert evidence, he must give notice at least 21 days before the hearing at which he proposes to put in the evidence.
(8) Where a party has given notice that he intends to put in the evidence, he must give every other party an opportunity to inspect it and to agree to its admission without further proof.

## 33.7 Evidence of Finding on Question of Foreign Law

(1) This rule sets out the procedure which must be followed by a party who intends to put in evidence a finding on a question of foreign law by virtue of section 4(2) of the Civil Evidence Act 1972.
(2) He must give any other party notice of his intention.
(3) He must give the notice—
  (a) if there are to be witness statements, not later than the latest date for serving them; or
  (b) otherwise, not less than 21 days before the hearing at which he proposes to put the finding in evidence.
(4) The notice must—
  (a) specify the question on which the finding was made; and
  (b) enclose a copy of a document where it is reported or recorded.

## 33.8 Evidence of Consent of Trustee to Act

A document purporting to contain the written consent of a person to act as trustee and to bear his signature verified by some other person is evidence of such consent.

## 33.9 Human Rights

(1) This rule applies where a claim is—
  (a) for a remedy under section 7 of the Human Rights Act 1998 in respect of a judicial act which is alleged to have infringed the claimant's Article 5 Convention rights; and
  (b) based on a finding by a court or tribunal that the claimant's Convention rights have been infringed.
(2) The court hearing the claim—
  (a) may proceed on the basis of the finding of that other court or tribunal that there has been an infringement but it is not required to do so; and
  (b) may reach its own conclusion in the light of that finding and of the evidence heard by that other court or tribunal.

# PD 33 Practice Direction — Civil Evidence Act 1995

This practice direction supplements CPR Part 33.

1. Section 16(3A) of the Civil Evidence Act 1995 (as amended) provides that transitional provisions for the application of the provisions of the Civil Evidence Act 1995 to proceedings begun before 31 January 1997 may be made by practice direction.
2. Except as provided for by para. 3, the provisions of the Civil Evidence Act 1995 apply to claims commenced before 31 January 1997.
3. The provisions of the Civil Evidence Act 1995 do not apply to claims commenced before 31 January 1997 if, before 26 April 1999:
   (a) directions were given, or orders were made, as to the evidence to be given at the trial or hearing; or
   (b) the trial or hearing had begun.

# CPR Part 34 Witnesses, Depositions and Evidence for Foreign Courts



## I WITNESSES AND DEPOSITIONS

### 34.1 Scope of this Section

(1) This Section of this Part provides—
   (a) for the circumstances in which a person may be required to attend court to give evidence or to produce a document; and
   (b) for a party to obtain evidence before a hearing to be used at the hearing.
(2) In this Section, reference to a hearing includes a reference to the trial.

### 34.2 Witness Summonses

(1) A witness summons is a document issued by the court requiring a witness to—
   (a) attend court to give evidence; or
   (b) produce documents to the court.
(2) A witness summons must be in the relevant practice form.
(3) There must be a separate witness summons for each witness.
(4) A witness summons may require a witness to produce documents to the court either—
   (a) on the date fixed for a hearing; or
   (b) on such date as the court may direct.
(5) The only documents that a summons under this rule can require a person to produce before a hearing are documents which that person could be required to produce at the hearing.

### 34.3 Issue of a Witness Summons

(1) A witness summons is issued on the date entered on the summons by the court.
(2) A party must obtain permission from the court where he wishes to—
   (a) have a summons issued less than 7 days before the date of the trial;

(b) have a summons issued for a witness to attend court to give evidence or to produce documents on any date except the date fixed for the trial; or
(c) have a summons issued for a witness to attend court to give evidence or to produce documents at any hearing except the trial.

(3) A witness summons must be issued by—
(a) the court where the case is proceeding; or
(b) the court where the hearing in question will be held.

(4) The court may set aside(GL) or vary a witness summons issued under this rule.

## 34.4 Witness Summons in Aid of Inferior Court or of Tribunal

(1) The court may issue a witness summons in aid of an inferior court or of a tribunal.
(2) The court which issued the witness summons under this rule may set it aside.
(3) In this rule, 'inferior court or tribunal' means any court or tribunal that does not have power to issue a witness summons in relation to proceedings before it.

## 34.5 Time for Serving a Witness Summons

(1) The general rule is that a witness summons is binding if it is served at least 7 days before the date on which the witness is required to attend before the court or tribunal.
(2) The court may direct that a witness summons shall be binding although it will be served less than 7 days before the date on which the witness is required to attend before the court or tribunal.
(3) A witness summons which is—
(a) served in accordance with this rule; and
(b) requires the witness to attend court to give evidence,
is binding until the conclusion of the hearing at which the attendance of the witness is required.

## 34.6 Who is to Serve a Witness Summons

(1) A witness summons is to be served by the court unless the party on whose behalf it is issued indicates in writing, when he asks the court to issue the summons, that he wishes to serve it himself.
(2) Where the court is to serve the witness summons, the party on whose behalf it is issued must deposit, in the court office, the money to be paid or offered to the witness under rule 34.7.

## 34.7 Right of Witness to Travelling Expenses and Compensation for Loss of Time

At the time of service of a witness summons the witness must be offered or paid—
(a) a sum reasonably sufficient to cover his expenses in travelling to and from the court; and
(b) such sum by way of compensation for loss of time as may be specified in the relevant practice direction.

## 34.8 Evidence by Deposition

(1) A party may apply for an order for a person to be examined before the hearing takes place.
(2) A person from whom evidence is to be obtained following an order under this rule is referred to as a 'deponent' and the evidence is referred to as a 'deposition'.
(3) An order under this rule shall be for a deponent to be examined on oath before—
(a) a judge;
(b) an examiner of the court; or
(c) such other person as the court appoints.

(Rule 34.15 makes provision for the appointment of examiners of the court.)

(4) The order may require the production of any document which the court considers is necessary for the purposes of the examination.
(5) The order must state the date, time and place of the examination.

(6) At the time of service of the order the deponent must be offered or paid—
(a) a sum reasonably sufficient to cover his expenses in travelling to and from the place of examination; and
(b) such sum by way of compensation for loss of time as may be specified in the relevant practice direction.
(7) Where the court makes an order for a deposition to be taken, it may also order the party who obtained the order to serve a witness statement or witness summary in relation to the evidence to be given by the person to be examined.
(Part 32 contains the general rules about witness statements and witness summaries.)

### 34.9 Conduct of Examination

(1) Subject to any directions contained in the order for examination, the examination must be conducted in the same way as if the witness were giving evidence at a trial.
(2) If all the parties are present, the examiner may conduct the examination of a person not named in the order for examination if all the parties and the person to be examined consent.
(3) The examiner may conduct the examination in private if he considers it appropriate to do so.
(4) The examiner must ensure that the evidence given by the witness is recorded in full.
(5) The examiner must send a copy of the deposition—
(a) to the person who obtained the order for the examination of the witness; and
(b) to the court where the case is proceeding.
(6) The party who obtained the order must send each of the other parties a copy of the deposition which he receives from the examiner.

### 34.10 Enforcing Attendance of Witness

(1) If a person served with an order to attend before an examiner—
(a) fails to attend; or
(b) refuses to be sworn for the purpose of the examination or to answer any lawful question or produce any document at the examination,
a certificate of his failure or refusal, signed by the examiner, must be filed by the party requiring the deposition.
(2) On the certificate being filed, the party requiring the deposition may apply to the court for an order requiring that person to attend or to be sworn or to answer any question or produce any document, as the case may be.
(3) An application for an order under this rule may be made without notice.
(4) The court may order the person against whom an order is made under this rule to pay any costs resulting from his failure or refusal.

### 34.11 Use of Deposition at a Hearing

(1) A deposition ordered under rule 34.8 may be given in evidence at a hearing unless the court orders otherwise.
(2) A party intending to put in evidence a deposition at a hearing must serve notice of his intention to do so on every other party.
(3) He must serve the notice at least 21 days before the day fixed for the hearing.
(4) The court may require a deponent to attend the hearing and give evidence orally.
(5) Where a deposition is given in evidence at trial, it shall be treated as if it were a witness statement for the purposes of rule 32.13 (availability of witness statements for inspection).

### 34.12 Restrictions on Subsequent Use of Deposition Taken for the Purpose of Any Hearing Except the Trial

(1) Where the court orders a party to be examined about his or any other assets for the purpose of any hearing except the trial, the deposition may be used only for the purpose of the proceedings in which the order was made.

(2) However, it may be used for some other purpose—
  (a) by the party who was examined;
  (b) if the party who was examined agrees; or
  (c) if the court gives permission.

### 34.13 Where a Person to be Examined is Out of the Jurisdiction—Letter of Request

(1) This rule applies where a party wishes to take a deposition from a person who is—
  (a) out of the jurisdiction; and
  (b) not in a Regulation State within the meaning of Section III of this Part.

(1A) The High Court may order the issue of a letter of request to the judicial authorities of the country in which the proposed deponent is.

(2) A letter of request is a request to a judicial authority to take the evidence of that person, or arrange for it to be taken.

(3) The High Court may make an order under this rule in relation to county court proceedings.

(4) If the government of a country allows a person appointed by the High Court to examine a person in that country, the High Court may make an order appointing a special examiner for that purpose.

(5) A person may be examined under this rule on oath or affirmation or in accordance with any procedure permitted in the country in which the examination is to take place.

(6) If the High Court makes an order for the issue of a letter of request, the party who sought the order must file—
  (a) the following documents and, except where paragraph (7) applies, a translation of them—
    (i) a draft letter of request;
    (ii) a statement of the issues relevant to the proceedings;
    (iii) a list of questions or the subject matter of questions to be put to the person to be examined; and
  (b) an undertaking to be responsible for the Secretary of State's expenses.

(7) There is no need to file a translation if—
  (a) English is one of the official languages of the country where the examination is to take place; or
  (b) practice direction has specified that country as a country where no translation is necessary.

### 34.13A Letter of Request—Proceeds of Crime Act 2002

(1) This rule applies where a party to existing or contemplated proceedings in—
  (a) the High Court; or
  (b) a magistrates' court,

under Part 5 of the Proceeds of Crime Act 2002 (civil recovery of the proceeds etc. of unlawful conduct) wishes to take a deposition from a person who is out of the jurisdiction.

(2) The High Court may, on the application of such a party, order the issue of a letter of request to the judicial authorities of the country in which the proposed deponent is.

(3) Paragraphs (4) to (7) of rule 34.13 shall apply irrespective of where the proposed deponent is, and rule 34.23 shall not apply in cases where the proposed deponent is in a Regulation State within the meaning of Section III of this Part.

### 34.14 Fees and Expenses of Examiner of the Court

(1) An examiner of the court may charge a fee for the examination.

(2) He need not send the deposition to the court unless the fee is paid.

(3) The examiner's fees and expenses must be paid by the party who obtained the order for examination.

(4) If the fees and expenses due to an examiner are not paid within a reasonable time, he may report that fact to the court.
(5) The court may order the party who obtained the order for examination to deposit in the court office a specified sum in respect of the examiner's fees and, where it does so, the examiner will not be asked to act until the sum has been deposited.
(6) An order under this rule does not affect any decision as to the party who is ultimately to bear the costs of the examination.

### 34.15 Examiners of the Court

(1) The Lord Chancellor shall appoint persons to be examiners of the court.
(2) The persons appointed shall be barristers or solicitor-advocates who have been practising for a period of not less than three years.
(3) The Lord Chancellor may revoke an appointment at any time.

## II EVIDENCE FOR FOREIGN COURTS

### 34.16 Scope and Interpretation

(1) This Section applies to an application for an order under the 1975 Act for evidence to be obtained, other than an application made as a result of a request by a court in another Regulation State.
(2) In this Section—
 (a) 'the 1975 Act' means the Evidence (Proceedings in Other Jurisdictions) Act 1975; and
 (b) 'Regulation State' has the same meaning as in Section III of this Part.

### 34.17 Application for Order

An application for an order under the 1975 Act for evidence to be obtained—
(a) must be—
 (i) made to the High Court;
 (ii) supported by written evidence; and
 (iii) accompanied by the request as a result of which the application is made, and where appropriate, a translation of the request into English; and
(b) may be made without notice.

### 34.18 Examination

(1) The court may order an examination to be taken before—
 (a) any fit and proper person nominated by the person applying for the order;
 (b) an examiner of the court; or
 (c) any other person whom the court considers suitable.
(2) Unless the court orders otherwise—
 (a) the examination will be taken as provided by rule 34.9; and
 (b) rule 34.10 applies.
(3) The court may make an order under rule 34.14 for payment of the fees and expenses of the examination.

### 34.19 Dealing with Deposition

(1) The examiner must send the deposition of the witness to the Senior Master unless the court orders otherwise.
(2) The Senior Master will—
 (a) give a certificate sealed with the seal of the Supreme Court for use out of the jurisdiction identifying the following documents—
  (i) the request;
  (ii) the order of the court for examination; and
  (iii) the deposition of the witness; and

(b) send the certificate and the documents referred to in paragraph (a) to—
    (i) the Secretary of State; or
    (ii) where the request was sent to the Senior Master by another person in accordance with a Civil Procedure Convention, to that other person,

for transmission to the court or tribunal requesting the examination.

### 34.20 Claim to Privilege

(1) This rule applies where—
    (a) a witness claims to be exempt from giving evidence on the ground specified in section 3(1)(b) of the 1975 Act; and
    (b) that claim is not supported or conceded as referred to in section 3(2) of that Act.

(2) The examiner may require the witness to give the evidence which he claims to be exempt from giving.

(3) Where the examiner does not require the witness to give that evidence, the court may order the witness to do so.

(4) An application for an order under paragraph (3) may be made by the person who obtained the order under section 2 of the 1975 Act.

(5) Where such evidence is taken—
    (a) it must be contained in a document separate from the remainder of the deposition;
    (b) the examiner will send to the Senior Master—
        (i) the deposition; and
        (ii) a signed statement setting out the claim to be exempt and the ground on which it was made.

(6) On receipt of the statement referred to in paragraph (5)(b)(ii), the Senior Master will—
    (a) retain the document containing the part of the witness's evidence to which the claim to be exempt relates; and
    (b) send the statement and a request to determine that claim to the foreign court or tribunal together with the documents referred to in rule 34.17.

(7) The Senior Master will—
    (a) if the claim to be exempt is rejected by the foreign court or tribunal, send the document referred to in paragraph (5)(a) to that court or tribunal;
    (b) if the claim is upheld, send the document to the witness; and
    (c) in either case, notify the witness and person who obtained the order under section 2 of the foreign court or tribunal's decision.

### 34.21 Order Under 1975 Act as Applied by Patents Act 1977

Where an order is made for the examination of witnesses under section 1 of the 1975 Act as applied by section 92 of the Patents Act 1977 the court may permit an officer of the European Patent Office to—
    (a) attend the examination and examine the witnesses; or
    (b) request the court or the examiner before whom the examination takes place to put specified questions to them.

## III TAKING OF EVIDENCE — MEMBER STATES OF THE EUROPEAN UNION

### 34.22 Interpretation

In this Section—

(a) 'designated court' has the meaning given in the relevant practice direction;

(b) 'Regulation State' has the same meaning as 'Member State' in the Taking of Evidence Regulation, that is all Member States except Denmark;

(c) 'the Taking of Evidence Regulation' means Council Regulation (EC) No. 1206/2001 of 28 May 2001 on cooperation between the courts of the Member States in the taking of evidence in civil and commercial matters.

(The Taking of Evidence Regulation is annexed to the relevant practice direction.)

## 34.23 Where a Person to be Examined is in Another Regulation State

(1) Subject to rule 34.13A, this rule applies where a party wishes to take a deposition from a person who is in another Regulation State—
  (a) outside the jurisdiction; and
  (b) in a Regulation State.*
(2) The court may order the issue of a request to a designated court ('the requested court') in the Regulation State in which the proposed deponent is.
(3) If the court makes an order for the issue of a request, the party who sought the order must file—
  (a) a draft Form A as set out in the annex to the Taking of Evidence Regulation (request for the taking of evidence);
  (b) except where paragraph (4) applies, a translation of the form;
  (c) an undertaking to be responsible for costs sought by the requested court in relation to—
    (i) fees paid to experts and interpreters; and
    (ii) where requested by that party, the use of special procedures or communications technology; and
  (d) an undertaking to be responsible for the court's expenses.
(4) There is no need to file a translation if—
  (a) English is one of the official languages of the Regulation State where the examination is to take place; or
  (b) the Regulation State has indicated, in accordance with the Taking of Evidence Regulation, that English is a language which it will accept.
(5) Where article 17 of the Taking of Evidence Regulation (direct taking of evidence by the requested court) allows evidence to be taken directly in another Regulation State, the court may make an order for the submission of a request in accordance with that article.
(6) If the court makes an order for the submission of a request under paragraph (5), the party who sought the order must file—
  (a) a draft Form I as set out in the annex to the Taking of Evidence Regulation (request for direct taking of evidence);
  (b) except where paragraph (4) applies, a translation of the form; and
  (c) an undertaking to be responsible for the court's expenses.

## 34.24 Evidence for Courts of Other Regulation States

(1) This rule applies where a court in another Regulation State ('the requesting court') issues a request for evidence to be taken from a person who is in the jurisdiction.
(2) An application for an order for evidence to be taken—
  (b) must be accompanied by—
    (i) the form of request for the taking of evidence as a result of which the application is made; and
    (ii) where appropriate, a translation of the form of request; and
  (c) may be made without notice.
(3) Rule 34.18(1) and (2) apply.
(4) The examiner must send—
  (a) the deposition to the court for transmission to the requesting court; and
  (b) a copy of the deposition to the person who obtained the order for evidence to be taken.

[* The text related by the DCA appears to mistakenly fail to delete (a) and (b).]

# PD 34 Practice Direction — Depositions and Court Attendance by Witnesses

This practice direction supplements CPR Part 34.

## WITNESS SUMMONSES

### Issue of Witness Summons

1.1 A witness summons may require a witness to:
(1) attend court to give evidence,
(2) produce documents to the court, or
(3) both,
on either a date fixed for the hearing or such date as the court may direct.*

1.2 Two copies of the witness summons[1] should be filed with the court for sealing, one of which will be retained on the court file.

1.3 A mistake in the name or address of a person named in a witness summons may be corrected if the summons has not been served.

1.4 The corrected summons must be resealed by the court and marked 'Amended and Resealed'.

### Witness Summons Issued in Aid of an Inferior Court or Tribunal

2.1 A witness summons may be issued in the High Court or a county court in aid of a court or tribunal which does not have the power to issue a witness summons in relation to the proceedings before it.[2]

2.2 A witness summons referred to in paragraph 2.1 may be set aside by the court which issued it.[3]

2.3 An application to set aside a witness summons referred to in paragraph 2.1 will be heard:
(1) in the High Court by a master at the Royal Courts of Justice or by a district judge in a District Registry, and
(2) in a county court by a district judge.

2.4 Unless the court otherwise directs, the applicant must give at least 2 days' notice to the party who issued the witness summons of the application, which will normally be dealt with at a hearing.

### Travelling Expenses and Compensation for Loss of Time

3.1 When a witness is served with a witness summons he must be offered a sum to cover his travelling expenses to and from the court and compensation for his loss of time.[4]

3.2 If the witness summons is to be served by the court, the party issuing the summons must deposit with the court:
(1) a sum sufficient to pay for the witness's expenses in travelling to the court and in returning to his home or place of work, and
(2) a sum in respect of the period during which earnings or benefit are lost, or such lesser sum as it may be proved that the witness will lose as a result of his attendance at court in answer to the witness summons.

[* Not reproduced in this work. Rule 34.2(4).]
[1] In form N20.
[2] Rule 34.4(1).
[3] Rule 34.4(2).
[4] Rule 34.7.

3.3 The sum referred to in 3.2(2) is to be based on the sums payable to witnesses attending the Crown Court.[5]

3.4 Where the party issuing the witness summons wishes to serve it himself,[6] he must:
(1) notify the court in writing that he wishes to do so, and
(2) at the time of service offer the witness the sums mentioned in paragraph 3.2 above.

## DEPOSITIONS

### To be Taken in England and Wales for Use as Evidence in Proceedings in Courts in England and Wales

4.1 A party may apply for an order for a person to be examined on oath before:
(1) a judge,
(2) an examiner of the court, or
(3) such other person as the court may appoint.[7]

4.2 The party who obtains an order for the examination of a deponent[8] before an examiner of the court[9] must:
(1) apply to the Foreign Process Section of the Masters' Secretary's Department at the Royal Courts of Justice for the allocation of an examiner,
(2) when allocated, provide the examiner with copies of all documents in the proceedings necessary to inform the examiner of the issues, and
(3) pay the deponent a sum to cover his travelling expenses to and from the examination and compensation for his loss of time.[10]

4.3 In ensuring that the deponent's evidence is recorded in full, the court or the examiner may permit it to be recorded on audiotape or videotape, but the deposition[11] must always be recorded in writing by him or by a competent shorthand writer or stenographer.

4.4 If the deposition is not recorded word for word, it must contain, as nearly as may be, the statement of the deponent; the examiner may record word for word any particular questions and answers which appear to him to have special importance.

4.5 If a deponent objects to answering any question or where any objection is taken to any question, the examiner must:
(1) record in the deposition or a document attached to it:
(a) the question,
(b) the nature of and grounds for the objection, and
(c) any answer given, and
(2) give his opinion as to the validity of the objection and must record it in the deposition or a document attached to it.

The court will decide as to the validity of the objection and any question of costs arising from it.

4.6 Documents and exhibits must:
(1) have an identifying number or letter marked on them by the examiner, and
(2) be preserved by the party or his legal representative[12] who obtained the order for the examination, or as the court or the examiner may direct.

4.7 The examiner may put any question to the deponent as to:

---

[5] Fixed pursuant to the Prosecution of Offences Act 1985 and the Costs in Criminal Cases (General) Regulations 1986 (SI 1986/1335).

[6] Rule 34.6(1).

[7] Rule 34.8(3).

[8] See rule 34.8(2) for explanation of 'deponent' and 'deposition'.

[9] For the appointment of examiners of the court see rule 34.15.

[10] Rule 34.8(6).

[11] See rule 34.8(2) for explanation of 'deponent' and 'deposition'.

[12] For the definition of legal representative see rule 2.3.

(1) the meaning of any of his answers, or
(2) any matter arising in the course of the examination.

4.8 Where a deponent:
(1) fails to attend the examination, or
(2) refuses to:
(a) be sworn, or
(b) answer any lawful question, or
(c) produce any document,

the examiner will sign a certificate[13] of such failure or refusal and may include in his certificate any comment as to the conduct of the deponent or of any person attending the examination.

4.9 The party who obtained the order for the examination must file the certificate with the court and may apply for an order that the deponent attend for examination or as may be.[14] The application may be made without notice.[15]

4.10 The court will make such order on the application as it thinks fit including an order for the deponent to pay any costs resulting from his failure or refusal.[16]

4.11 A deponent who wilfully refuses to obey an order made against him under Part 34 may be proceeded against for contempt of court.

4.12 A deposition must:
(1) be signed by the examiner,
(2) have any amendments to it initialled by the examiner and the deponent,
(3) be endorsed by the examiner with:
(a) a statement of the time occupied by the examination, and
(b) a record of any refusal by the deponent to sign the deposition and of his reasons for not doing so, and
(4) be sent by the examiner to the court where the proceedings are taking place for filing on the court file.

4.13 Rule 34.14 deals with the fees and expenses of an examiner.

## Depositions to be Taken Abroad for Use as Evidence in Proceedings Before Courts in England and Wales Where the Taking of Evidence Regulation Does Not Apply

5.1 Where a party wishes to take a deposition from a person outside the jurisdiction, the High Court may order the issue of a letter of request to the judicial authorities of the country in which the proposed deponent is.[17]

5.2 An application for an order referred to in paragraph 5.1 should be made by application notice in accordance with Part 23.

5.3 The documents which a party applying for an order for the issue of a letter of request must file with his application notice are set out in rule 34.13(6). They are as follows:
(1) a draft letter of request is set out in Annex A to this practice direction,
(2) a statement of the issues relevant to the proceedings,
(3) a list of questions or the subject matter of questions to be put to the proposed deponent,
(4) a translation of the documents in (1), (2) and (3) above unless the proposed deponent is in a country of which English is an official language, and
(5) an undertaking to be responsible for the expenses of the Secretary of State.

---

13 Rule 34.10.
14 Rule 34.10(2) and (3).
15 Rule 34.10(3).
16 Rule 34.10(4).
17 Rule 34.13(1).

In addition to the documents listed above the party applying for the order must file a draft order.

5.4 The above documents should be filed with the Masters' Secretary in Room E214, Royal Courts of Justice, Strand, London WC2A 2LL.

5.5 The application will be dealt with by the Senior Master of the Queen's Bench Division of the High Court who will, if appropriate, sign the letter of request.

5.6 Attention is drawn to the provisions of rule 23.10 (application to vary or discharge an order made without notice).

5.7 If parties are in doubt as to whether a translation under paragraph 5.3(4) above is required, they should seek guidance from the Foreign Process Section of the Masters' Secretary's Department.

5.8 A special examiner appointed under rule 34.13(4) may be the British consul or the consul-general or his deputy in the country where the evidence is to be taken if:
- (1) there is in respect of that country a Civil Procedure Convention providing for the taking of evidence in that country for the assistance of proceedings in the High Court or other court in this country, or
- (2) with the consent of the Secretary of State.

5.9 The provisions of paragraphs 4.1 to 4.12 above apply to the depositions referred to in this paragraph.

## Depositions to be Taken in England and Wales for Use as Evidence in Proceedings Before Courts Abroad Pursuant to Letters of Request Where the Taking of Evidence Regulation Does Not Apply

6.1 Section II of Part 34 relating to obtaining evidence for foreign courts and should be read in conjunction with this part of the practice direction.

6.2 The Evidence (Proceedings in Other Jurisdictions) Act 1975 applies to these depositions.

6.3 The written evidence supporting an application under r. 34.17 (which should be made by application notice: see Part 23) must include or exhibit:
- (1) a statement of the issues relevant to the proceedings;
- (2) a list of questions or the subject matter of questions to be put to the proposed deponent;
- (3) a draft order; and
- (4) a translation of the documents in (1) and (2) into English, if necessary.

6.4 (1) The Senior Master will send to the Treasury Solicitor any request:
- (a) forwarded by the Secretary of State with a recommendation that effect should be given to the request without requiring an application to be made; or
- (b) received by him in pursuance of a civil procedure convention providing for the taking of evidence of any person in England and Wales to assist a court or tribunal in a foreign country where no person is named in the document as the applicant.

(2) In relation to such a request, the Treasury Solicitor may, with the consent of the Treasury:
- (a) apply for an order under the 1975 Act; and
- (b) take such other steps as are necessary to give effect to the request.

6.5 The order for the deponent to attend and be examined together with the evidence upon which the order was made must be served on the deponent.

6.6 Attention is drawn to the provisions of r. 23.10 (application to vary or discharge an order made without notice).

6.7 Arrangements for the examination to take place at a specified time and place before an examiner of the court or such other person as the court may appoint shall be made by the applicant for the order and approved by the Senior Master.

6.8 The provisions of paragraphs 4.2 to 4.12 apply to the depositions referred to in this paragraph, except that the examiner must send the deposition to the Senior Master.

(For further information about evidence see Part 32 and PD 32.)

## TAKING OF EVIDENCE BETWEEN EU MEMBER STATES

### Taking of Evidence Regulation

7.1 Where evidence is to be taken:

(a) from a person in another Member State of the European Union for use as evidence in proceedings before courts in England and Wales; or

(b) from a person in England and Wales for use as evidence in proceedings before a court in another Member State,

Council Regulation (EC) No. 1206/2001 of 28 May 2001 on cooperation between the courts of the Member States in the taking of evidence in civil or commercial matters ('the Taking of Evidence Regulation') applies.

7.2 The Taking of Evidence Regulation is [on the CD-ROM version of *Blackstone's Civil Practice*].

7.3 The Taking of Evidence Regulation does not apply to Denmark. In relation to Denmark, therefore, r. 34.13 and Section II of Part 34 will continue to apply.

(Article 21(1) of the Taking of Evidence Regulation provides that the Regulation prevails over other provisions contained in bilateral or multilateral agreements or arrangements concluded by the Member States and in particular the Hague Convention of 1 March 1954 on Civil Procedure and the Hague Convention of 18 March 1970 on the Taking of Evidence Abroad in Civil or Commercial Matters.)

### Meaning of 'Designated Court'

8.1 In accordance with the Taking of Evidence Regulation, each Regulation State has prepared a list of courts competent to take evidence in accordance with the Regulation indicating the territorial and, where appropriate, special jurisdiction of those courts.

8.2 Where Part 34, Section III, refers to a 'designated court' in relation to another Regulation State, the reference is to the court, referred to in the list of competent courts of that State, which is appropriate to the application in hand.

8.3 Where the reference is to the 'designated court' in England and Wales, the reference is to the appropriate competent court in the jurisdiction. The designated courts for England and Wales are listed in Annex C to this practice direction.

### Central Body

9.1 The Taking of Evidence Regulation stipulates that each Regulation State must nominate a Central Body responsible for:

(a) supplying information to courts;

(b) seeking solutions to any difficulties which may arise in respect of a request; and

(c) forwarding, in exceptional cases, at the request of a requesting court, a request to the competent court.

9.2 The United Kingdom has nominated the Senior Master, Queen's Bench Division, to be the Central Body for England and Wales.

9.3 The Senior Master, as Central Body, has been designated responsible for taking decisions on requests pursuant to art. 17 of the Regulation. Article 17 allows a court to submit a request to the Central Body or a designated competent authority in another Regulation State to take evidence directly in that State.

### Evidence to be Taken in Another Regulation State for Use in England and Wales

10.1 Where a person wishes to take a deposition from a person in another Regulation State, the court where the proceedings are taking place may order the issue of a request to the designated court in the Regulation State (r. 34.23(2)). The form of request is prescribed as form A in the Taking of Evidence Regulation.

10.2 An application to the court for an order under r. 34.23(2) should be made by application notice in accordance with Part 23.

10.3 Rule 34.23(3) provides that the party applying for the order must file a draft form of request in the prescribed form. Where completion of the form requires attachments or documents to accompany the form, these must also be filed.

10.4 If the court grants an order under r. 34.23(2), it will send the form of request directly to the designated court.

10.5 Where the taking of evidence requires the use of an expert, the designated court may require a deposit in advance towards the costs of that expert. The party who obtained the order is responsible for the payment of any such deposit which should be deposited with the court for onward transmission. Under the provisions of the Taking of Evidence Regulation, the designated court is not required to execute the request until such payment is received.

10.6 Article 17 permits the court where proceedings are taking place to take evidence directly from a deponent in another Regulation State if the conditions of the article are satisfied. Direct taking of evidence can only take place if evidence is given voluntarily without the need for coercive measures. Rule 34.23(5) provides for the court to make an order for the submission of a request to take evidence directly. The form of request is form I annexed to the Taking of Evidence Regulation and r. 34.23(6) makes provision for a draft of this form to be filed by the party seeking the order. An application for an order under r. 34.23(5) should be by application notice in accordance with Part 23.

10.7 Attention is drawn to the provisions of r. 23.10 (application to vary or discharge an order made without notice).

## Evidence to be Taken in England and Wales for Use in Another Regulation State

11.1 Where a designated court in England and Wales receives a request to take evidence from a court in a Regulation State, the court will send the request to the Treasury Solicitor.

11.2 On receipt of the request, the Treasury Solicitor may, with the consent of the Treasury, apply for an order under r. 34.24.

11.3 An application to the court for an order must be accompanied by the form of request to take evidence and any accompanying documents, translated if required under para. 11.4

11.4 The United Kingdom has indicated that, in addition to English, it will accept French as a language in which documents may be submitted. Where the form or request and any accompanying documents are received in French they will be translated into English by the Treasury Solicitor.

11.5 The order for the deponent to attend and be examined together with the evidence on which the order was made must be served on the deponent.

11.6 Arrangements for the examination to take place at a specified time and place shall be made by the Treasury Solicitor and approved by the court.

11.7 The court shall send details of the arrangements for the examination to such of:

(a) the parties and, if any, their representatives; or

(b) the representatives of the foreign court,

who have indicated, in accordance with the Taking of Evidence Regulation, that they wish to be present at the examination.

11.8 The provisions of para. 4.3 to 4.12 apply to the depositions referred to in this paragraph.

## ANNEX A

### Draft Letter of Request (Where the Taking of Evidence Regulation Does Not Apply)

To the Competent Judicial Authority of
in the of

I [name] Senior Master of the Queen's Bench Division of the Supreme Court of England and Wales respectfully request the assistance of your court with regard to the following matters.

1. A claim is now pending in the Division of the High Court of Justice in England and Wales entitled as follows
   [*set out full title and claim number*]
   in which [*name*] of [*address*] is the claimant and [*name*] of [*address*] is the defendant.
2. The names and addresses of the representatives or agents of [*set out names and addresses of representatives of the parties*].
3. The claim by the claimant is for:—
   (a) [*set out the nature of the claim*]
   (b) [*the relief sought, and*]
   (c) [*a summary of the facts.*]
4. It is necessary for the purposes of justice and for the due determination of the matters in dispute between the parties that you cause the following witnesses, who are resident within your jurisdiction, to be examined. The names and addresses of the witnesses are as follows:—
5. The witnesses should be examined on oath or if that is not possible within your laws or is impossible of performance by reason of the internal practice and procedure of your court or by reason of practical difficulties, they should be examined in accordance with whatever procedure your laws provide for in these matters.
6. Either/
   The witnesses should be examined in accordance with the list of questions annexed hereto.
   Or/
   The witnesses should be examined regarding [*set out full details of evidence sought*]
   N.B. Where the witness is required to produce documents, these should be clearly identified.
7. I would ask that you cause me, or the agents of the parties (if appointed), to be informed of the date and place where the examination is to take place.
8. Finally, I request that you will cause the evidence of the said witnesses to be reduced into writing and all documents produced on such examinations to be duly marked for identification and that you will further be pleased to authenticate such examinations by the seal of your court or in such other way as is in accordance with your procedure and return the written evidence and documents produced to me addressed as follows:—
   Senior Master of the Queen's Bench Division
   Royal Courts of Justice
   Strand
   London WC2A 2LL
   England

## ANNEX B

**Council Regulation (EC) No. 1206/2001***

## ANNEX C

Designated courts in England and Wales under the Taking of Evidence Regulation (see para. 8 above)

| Area | Designated court |
|---|---|
| London and South Eastern Circuit | Royal Courts of Justice (Queen's Bench Division) |
| Midland Circuit | Birmingham Civil Justice Centre |
| Western Circuit | Bristol County Court |
| Wales Circuit | Cardiff Civil Justice Centre |
| Northern Circuit | Manchester County Court |
| North Eastern Circuit | Leeds County Court |

[* Not reproduced in this work. Rule 34.2(4).]

# PD 34B Practice Direction — Fees for Examiners of the Court

This practice direction supplements CPR Part 34.

## Scope

1.1 This practice direction sets out:

(1) how to calculate the fees an examiner of the court ('an examiner') may charge; and

(2) the expenses he may recover.

(Rule 34.8(3)(b) provides that the court may make an order for evidence to be obtained by the examination of a witness before an examiner of the court.)

1.2 The party who obtained the order for the examination must pay the fees and expenses of the examiner.

(Rule 34.14 permits an examiner to charge a fee for the examination and contains other provisions about his fees and expenses, and r. 34.15 provides who may be appointed as an examiner of the court.)

## The Examination Fee

2.1 An examiner may charge an hourly rate for each hour (or part of an hour) that he is engaged in examining the witness.

2.2 The hourly rate is to be calculated by reference to the formula set out in para. 3.

2.3 The examination fee will be the hourly rate multiplied by the number of hours the examination has taken. For example:

Examination fee = hourly rate × number of hours.

## How to Calculate the Hourly Rate—The Formula

3.1 Divide the amount of the minimum annual salary of a post within Group 7 of the judicial salary structure as designated by the Review Body on Senior Salaries,[1] by 220 to give '**x**'; and then divide '**x**' by **6** to give **the hourly rate**.

For example:

$$\frac{\text{minimum annual salary}}{220} = x$$

$$\frac{x}{6} = \text{hourly rate}$$

## Single Fee Chargeable on Making the Appointment for Examination

4.1 An examiner of court is also entitled to charge a single fee of twice the hourly rate (calculated in accordance with para. 3 above) as 'the appointment fee' when the appointment for the examination is made.

4.2 The examiner is entitled to retain the appointment fee where the witness fails to attend on the date and time arranged.

4.3 Where the examiner fails to attend on the date and time arranged he may not charge a further appointment fee for arranging a subsequent appointment.

(The examiner need not send the deposition to the court until his fees are paid—see r. 34.14(2).)

---

[1] The Report of the Review Body on Senior Salaries is published annually by the Stationery Office.

## Examiners' Expenses

5.1 The examiner of court is also entitled to recover the following expenses:
(1) all reasonable travelling expenses;
(2) any other expenses reasonably incurred; and
(3) subject to para. 5.2, any reasonable charge for the room where the examination takes place.

5.2 No expenses may be recovered under para. 5.1(3) above if the examination takes place at the examiner's usual business address.
(If the examiner's fees and expenses are not paid within a reasonable time he may report the fact to the court, see r. 34.14(4) and (5).)

# CPR Part 35 Experts and Assessors



## 35.1 Duty to Restrict Expert Evidence

Expert evidence shall be restricted to that which is reasonably required to resolve the proceedings.

## 35.2 Interpretation

A reference to an 'expert' in this Part is a reference to an expert who has been instructed to give or prepare evidence for the purpose of court proceedings.

## 35.3 Experts—Overriding Duty to the Court

(1) It is the duty of an expert to help the court on the matters within his expertise.
(2) This duty overrides any obligation to the person from whom he has received instructions or by whom he is paid.

## 35.4 Court's Power to Restrict Expert Evidence

(1) No party may call an expert or put in evidence an expert's report without the court's permission.
(2) When a party applies for permission under this rule he must identify—
    (a) the field in which he wishes to rely on expert evidence; and
    (b) where practicable the expert in that field on whose evidence he wishes to rely.
(3) If permission is granted under this rule it shall be in relation only to the expert named or the field identified under paragraph (2).
(4) The court may limit the amount of the expert's fees and expenses that the party who wishes to rely on the expert may recover from any other party.

## 35.5 General Requirement for Expert Evidence to be Given in a Written Report

(1) Expert evidence is to be given in a written report unless the court directs otherwise.
(2) If a claim is on the fast track, the court will not direct an expert to attend a hearing unless it is necessary to do so in the interests of justice.

## 35.6 Written Questions to Experts

(1) A party may put to—
    (a) an expert instructed by another party; or
    (b) a single joint expert appointed under rule 35.7,

    written questions about his report.
(2) Written questions under paragraph (1)—

(a) may be put once only;
(b) must be put within 28 days of service of the expert's report; and
(c) must be for the purpose only of clarification of the report,

unless in any case—

(i) the court gives permission; or
(ii) the other party agrees.

(3) An expert's answers to questions put in accordance with paragraph (1) shall be treated as part of the expert's report.

(4) Where—

(a) a party has put a written question to an expert instructed by another party in accordance with this rule; and
(b) the expert does not answer that question,

the court may make one or both of the following orders in relation to the party who instructed the expert—

(i) that the party may not rely on the evidence of that expert; or
(ii) that the party may not recover the fees and expenses of that expert from any other party.

### 35.7 Court's Power to Direct that Evidence is to be Given by a Single Joint Expert

(1) Where two or more parties wish to submit expert evidence on a particular issue, the court may direct that the evidence on that issue is to given [*sic*] by one expert only.
(2) The parties wishing to submit the expert evidence are called 'the instructing parties'.
(3) Where the instructing parties cannot agree who should be the expert, the court may—

(a) select the expert from a list prepared or identified by the instructing parties; or
(b) direct that the expert be selected in such other manner as the court may direct.

### 35.8 Instructions to a Single Joint Expert

(1) Where the court gives a direction under rule 35.7 for a single joint expert to be used, each instructing party may give instructions to the expert.
(2) When an instructing party gives instructions to the expert he must, at the same time, send a copy of the instructions to the other instructing parties.
(3) The court may give directions about—

(a) the payment of the expert's fees and expenses; and
(b) any inspection, examination or experiments which the expert wishes to carry out.

(4) The court may, before an expert is instructed—

(a) limit the amount that can be paid by way of fees and expenses to the expert; and
(b) direct that the instructing parties pay that amount into court.

(5) Unless the court otherwise directs, the instructing parties are jointly and severally liable(GL) for the payment of the expert's fees and expenses.

### 35.9 Power of Court to Direct a Party to Provide Information

Where a party has access to information which is not reasonably available to the other party, the court may direct the party who has access to the information to—

(a) prepare and file a document recording the information; and
(b) serve a copy of that document on the other party.

### 35.10 Contents of Report

(1) An expert's report must comply with the requirements set out in the relevant practice direction.
(2) At the end of an expert's report there must be a statement that—

(a) the expert understands his duty to the court; and
(b) he has complied with that duty.

(3) The expert's report must state the substance of all material instructions, whether written or oral, on the basis of which the report was written.

(4) The instructions referred to in paragraph (3) shall not be privileged(GL) against disclosure but the court will not, in relation to those instructions—
 (a) order disclosure of any specific document; or
 (b) permit any questioning in court, other than by the party who instructed the expert, unless it is satisfied that there are reasonable grounds to consider the statement of instructions given under paragraph (3) to be inaccurate or incomplete.

## 35.11 Use by One Party of Expert's Report Disclosed by Another

Where a party has disclosed an expert's report, any party may use that expert's report as evidence at the trial.

## 35.12 Discussions Between Experts

(1) The court may, at any stage, direct a discussion between experts for the purpose of requiring the experts to—
 (a) identify and discuss the expert issues in the proceedings; and
 (b) where possible, reach an agreed opinion on those issues.
(2) The court may specify the issues which the experts must discuss.
(3) The court may direct that following a discussion between the experts they must prepare a statement for the court showing—
 (a) those issues on which they agree; and
 (b) those issues on which they disagree and a summary of their reasons for disagreeing.
(4) The content of the discussion between the experts shall not be referred to at the trial unless the parties agree.
(5) Where experts reach agreement on an issue during their discussions, the agreement shall not bind the parties unless the parties expressly agree to be bound by the agreement.

## 35.13 Consequence of Failure to Disclose Expert's Report

A party who fails to disclose an expert's report may not use the report at the trial or call the expert to give evidence orally unless the court gives permission.

## 35.14 Expert's Right to Ask Court for Directions

(1) An expert may file a written request for directions to assist him in carrying out his function as an expert.
(2) An expert must, unless the court orders otherwise, provide a copy of any proposed request for directions under paragraph (1)—
 (a) to the party instructing him, at least 7 days before he files the request; and
 (b) to all other parties, at least 4 days before he files it.
(3) The court, when it gives directions, may also direct that a party be served with a copy of the directions.

## 35.15 Assessors

(1) This rule applies where the court appoints one or more persons (an 'assessor') under section 70 of the Supreme Court Act 1981 or section 63 of the County Courts Act 1984.
(2) The assessor shall assist the court in dealing with a matter in which the assessor has skill and experience.
(3) An assessor shall take such part in the proceedings as the court may direct and in particular the court may—
 (a) direct the assessor to prepare a report for the court on any matter at issue in the proceedings; and
 (b) direct the assessor to attend the whole or any part of the trial to advise the court on any such matter.

(4) If the assessor prepares a report for the court before the trial has begun—
   (a) the court will send a copy to each of the parties; and
   (b) the parties may use it at trial.
(5) The remuneration to be paid to the assessor for his services shall be determined by the court and shall form part of the costs of the proceedings.
(6) The court may order any party to deposit in the court office a specified sum in respect of the assessor's fees and, where it does so, the assessor will not be asked to act until the sum has been deposited.
(7) Paragraphs (5) and (6) do not apply where the remuneration of the assessor is to be paid out of money provided by Parliament.

# PD 35 Practice Direction — Experts and Assessors

This practice direction supplements CPR Part 35.

Part 35 is intended to limit the use of oral expert evidence to that which is reasonably required. In addition, where possible, matters requiring expert evidence should be dealt with by a single expert. Permission of the court is always required either to call an expert or to put an expert's report in evidence. There is annexed to this practice direction a protocol for the instruction of experts to give evidence in civil claims. Experts and those instructing them are expected to have regard to the guidance contained in the protocol.

## Expert Evidence—General Requirements

1.1 It is the duty of an expert to help the court on matters within his own expertise (r. 35.3(1)). This duty is paramount and overrides any obligation to the person from whom the expert has received instructions or by whom he is paid (r. 35.3(2)).

1.2 Expert evidence should be the independent product of the expert uninfluenced by the pressures of litigation.

1.3 An expert should assist the court by providing objective, unbiased opinion on matters within his expertise, and should not assume the role of an advocate.

1.4 An expert should consider all material facts, including those which might detract from his opinion.

1.5 An expert should make it clear:

(a) when a question or issue falls outside his expertise; and

(b) when he is not able to reach a definite opinion, for example because he has insufficient information.

1.6 If, after producing a report, an expert changes his view on any material matter, such change of view should be communicated to all the parties without delay, and when appropriate to the court.

## Form and Content of Experts' Reports

2.1 An expert's report should be addressed to the court and not to the party from whom the expert has received his instructions.

2.2 An expert's report must:

(1) give details of the expert's qualifications;

(2) give details of any literature or other material which the expert has relied on in making the report;

(3) contain a statement setting out the substance of all facts and instructions given to the expert which are material to the opinions expressed in the report or upon which those opinions are based;

(4) make clear which of the facts stated in the report are within the expert's own knowledge;

(5) say who carried out any examination, measurement, test or experiment which the expert has used for the report, give the qualifications of that person, and say whether or not the test or experiment has been carried out under the expert's supervision;

(6) where there is a range of opinion on the matters dealt with in the report:

(a) summarise the range of opinion, and

(b) give reasons for his own opinion;

(7) contain a summary of the conclusions reached;

(8) if the expert is not able to give his opinion without qualification, state the qualification; and

(9) contain a statement that the expert understands his duty to the court, and has complied and will continue to comply with that duty.

2.3 An expert's report must be verified by a statement of truth as well as containing the statements required in para. 2.2(8) and (9) above.

2.4 The form of the statement of truth is as follows:
I confirm that in so far as the facts stated in my report are within my own knowledge I have made clear which they are and I believe them to be true, and that the opinions I have expressed represent my true and complete professional opinion.

2.5 Attention is drawn to r. 32.14 which sets out the consequences of verifying a document containing a false statement without an honest belief in its truth.
(For information about statements of truth see Part 22 and PD 22.)

## Information

3 Under r. 35.9 the court may direct a party with access to information which is not reasonably available to another party to serve on that other party a document which records the information. The document served must include sufficient details of all the facts, tests, experiments and assumptions which underlie any part of the information to enable the party on whom it is served to make, or to obtain, a proper interpretation of the information and an assessment of its significance.

## Instructions

4 The instructions referred to in para. 2.2(3) will not be protected by privilege (see r. 35.10(4)). But cross-examination of the expert on the contents of his instructions will not be allowed unless the court permits it (or unless the party who gave the instructions consents to it). Before it gives permission the court must be satisfied that there are reasonable grounds to consider that the statement in the report of the substance of the instructions is inaccurate or incomplete. If the court is so satisfied, it will allow the cross-examination where it appears to be in the interests of justice to do so.

## Questions to Experts

5.1 Questions asked for the purpose of clarifying the expert's report (see r. 35.6) should be put, in writing, to the expert not later than 28 days after receipt of the expert's report (see paras [2.3 to 2.5*] above as to verification).

5.2 Where a party sends a written question or questions direct to an expert, a copy of the questions should, at the same time, be sent to the other party or parties.

5.3 The party or parties instructing the expert must pay any fees charged by that expert for answering questions put under r. 35.6. This does not affect any decision of the court as to the party who is ultimately to bear the expert's costs.

## Single Expert

6 Where the court has directed that the evidence on a particular issue is to be given by one expert only (r. 35.7) but there are a number of disciplines relevant to that issue, a leading expert in the dominant discipline should be identified as the single expert. He should prepare the general part of the report and be responsible for annexing or incorporating the contents of any reports from experts in other disciplines.

## Orders

6A Where an order requires an act to be done by an expert, or otherwise affects an expert, the party instructing that expert must serve a copy of the order on the expert instructed by him. In the case of a jointly instructed expert, the claimant must serve the order.

[* In the text issued by the Department for Constitutional Affairs this cross-reference was not updated when the paragraphs of the practice direction were renumbered.]

## Assessors

7.1 An assessor may be appointed to assist the court under r. 35.15. Not less than 21 days before making any such appointment, the court will notify each party in writing of the name of the proposed assessor, of the matter in respect of which the assistance of the assessor will be sought and of the qualifications of the assessor to give that assistance.

7.2 Where any person has been proposed for appointment as an assessor, objection to him, either personally or in respect of his qualification, may be taken by any party.

7.3 Any such objection must be made in writing and filed with the court within seven days of receipt of the notification referred to in para. [7.1*] and will be taken into account by the court in deciding whether or not to make the appointment (County Courts Act 1984, s. 63(5)).

7.4 Copies of any report prepared by the assessor will be sent to each of the parties but the assessor will not give oral evidence or be open to cross-examination or questioning.

# ANNEX

## Protocol for the Instruction of Experts to give Evidence in Civil Claims†

## CONTENTS



## 1 Introduction

Expert witnesses perform a vital role in civil litigation. It is essential that both those who instruct experts and experts themselves are given clear guidance as to what they are expected to do in civil proceedings. The purpose of this Protocol is to provide such guidance. It has been drafted by the Civil Justice Council and reflects the rules and practice directions current [in June 2005], replacing the Code of Guidance on Expert Evidence. The authors of the

[* In the text issued by the Department for Constitutional Affairs this cross-reference was not updated when the paragraphs of the practice direction were renumbered.]

† We are grateful to the Civil Justice Council for granting permission to reproduce this Protocol. Readers' attentions are also drawn to the Code of Practice for Experts, which was jointly agreed by the Experts Witness Institute and the Academy of Experts, and which can be obtained from either of these organisations or downloaded from their websites.

Protocol wish to acknowledge the valuable assistance they obtained by drawing on earlier documents produced by the Academy of Experts and the Expert Witness Institute, as well as suggestions made by the Clinical Dispute Forum. The Protocol has been approved by the Master of the Rolls.

## 2 Aims of Protocol

2.1 This Protocol offers guidance to experts and to those instructing them in the interpretation of and compliance with Part 35 of the Civil Procedure Rules (CPR 35) and its associated Practice Direction (PD 35) and to further the objectives of the Civil Procedure Rules in general. It is intended to assist in the interpretation of those provisions in the interests of good practice but it does not replace them. It sets out standards for the use of experts and the conduct of experts and those who instruct them. The existence of this Protocol does not remove the need for experts and those who instruct them to be familiar with CPR 35 and PD 35.

2.2 Experts and those who instruct them should also bear in mind paragraph 1.4 of the Practice Direction on Protocols which contains the following objectives, namely to:

(a) encourage the exchange of early and full information about the expert issues involved in a prospective legal claim;

(b) enable the parties to avoid or reduce the scope of litigation by agreeing the whole or part of an expert issue before commencement of proceedings; and

(c) support the efficient management of proceedings where litigation cannot be avoided.

## 3 Application

3.1 This Protocol applies to any steps taken for the purpose of civil proceedings by experts or those who instruct them on or after 5 September 2005.

3.2 It applies to all experts who are, or who may be, governed by CPR Part 35 and to those who instruct them. Experts are governed by Part 35 if they are or have been instructed to give or prepare evidence for the purpose of civil proceedings in a court in England and Wales (CPR 35.2).

3.3 Experts, and those instructing them, should be aware that some cases may be 'specialist proceedings' (CPR 49) where there are modifications to the Civil Procedure Rules. Proceedings may also be governed by other Protocols. Further, some courts have published their own Guides which supplement the Civil Procedure Rules for proceedings in those courts. They contain provisions affecting expert evidence. Expert witnesses and those instructing them should be familiar with them when they are relevant.

3.4 Courts may take into account any failure to comply with this Protocol when making orders in relation to costs, interest, time limits, the stay of proceedings and whether to order a party to pay a sum of money into court.

*Limitation*

3.5 If, as a result of complying with any part of this Protocol, claims would or might be time barred under any provision in the Limitation Act 1980, or any other legislation that imposes a time limit for the bringing an action, claimants may commence proceedings without complying with this Protocol. In such circumstances, claimants who commence proceedings without complying with all, or any part, of this Protocol must apply, giving notice to all other parties, to the court for directions as to the timetable and form of procedure to be adopted, at the same time as they request the court to issue proceedings. The court may consider whether to order a stay of the whole or part of the proceedings pending compliance with this Protocol and may make orders in relation to costs.

## 4 Duties of Experts

4.1 Experts always owe a duty to exercise reasonable skill and care to those instructing them, and to comply with any relevant professional code of ethics. However when they are instructed to give or prepare evidence for the purpose of civil proceedings in England and Wales they have an overriding duty to help the court on matters within their expertise (CPR 35.3). This duty overrides any obligation to the person instructing or paying them. Experts must not serve the exclusive interest of those who retain them.

4.2 Experts should be aware of the overriding objective that courts deal with cases justly. This includes dealing with cases proportionately, expeditiously and fairly (CPR 1.1). Experts are under an obligation to assist the court so as to enable them to deal with cases in accordance with the overriding objective. However the overriding objective does not impose on experts any duty to act as mediators between the parties or require them to trespass on the role of the court in deciding facts.

4.3 Experts should provide opinions which are independent, regardless of the pressures of litigation. In this context, a useful test of 'independence' is that the expert would express the same opinion if given the same instructions by an opposing party. Experts should not take it upon themselves to promote the point of view of the party instructing them or engage in the role of advocates.

4.4 Experts should confine their opinions to matters which are material to the disputes between the parties and provide opinions only in relation to matters which lie within their expertise. Experts should indicate without delay where particular questions or issues fall outside their expertise.

4.5 Experts should take into account all material facts before them at the time that they give their opinion. Their reports should set out those facts and any literature or any other material on which they have relied in forming their opinions. They should indicate if an opinion is provisional, or qualified, or where they consider that further information is required or if, for any other reason, they are not satisfied that an opinion can be expressed finally and without qualification.

4.6 Experts should inform those instructing them without delay of any change in their opinions on any material matter and the reason for it.

4.7 Experts should be aware that any failure by them to comply with the Civil Procedure Rules or court orders or any excessive delay for which they are responsible may result in the parties who instructed them being penalized in costs and even, in extreme cases, being debarred from placing the experts' evidence before the court. In *Phillips v Symes*[1] Peter Smith J held that courts may also make orders for costs (under section 51 of the Supreme Court Act 1981) directly against expert witnesses who by their evidence cause significant expense to be incurred, and do so in flagrant and reckless disregard of their duties to the court.

## 5 Conduct of Experts Instructed Only to Advise

5.1 Part 35 only applies where experts are instructed to give opinions which are relied on for the purposes of court proceedings. Advice which the parties do not intend to adduce in litigation is likely to be confidential; the Protocol does not apply in these circumstances.[2,3]

5.2 The same applies where, after the commencement of proceedings, experts are instructed only to advise (eg to comment upon a single joint expert's report) and not to give or prepare evidence for use in the proceedings.

[1] *Phillips v Symes* [2004] EWHC 2330 (Ch).

[2] *Carlson v Townsend* [2001] 1 WLR 2415.

[3] *Jackson v Marley Davenport* [2004] 1 WLR 2926.

5.3 However this Protocol does apply if experts who were formerly instructed only to advise are later instructed to give or prepare evidence for the purpose of civil proceedings.

## 6 The Need for Experts

6.1 Those intending to instruct experts to give or prepare evidence for the purpose of civil proceedings should consider whether expert evidence is appropriate, taking account of the principles set out in CPR Parts 1 and 35, and in particular whether:
- (a) it is relevant to a matter which is in dispute between the parties;
- (b) it is reasonably required to resolve the proceedings (CPR 35.1);
- (c) the expert has expertise relevant to the issue on which an opinion is sought;
- (d) the expert has the experience, expertise and training appropriate to the value, complexity and importance of the case; and whether
- (e) these objects can be achieved by the appointment of a single joint expert (see section 17 below).

6.2 Although the court's permission is not generally required to instruct an expert, the court's permission is required before experts can be called to give evidence or their evidence can be put in (CPR 35.4).

## 7 The Appointment of Experts

7.1 Before experts are formally instructed or the court's permission to appoint named experts is sought, the following should be established:
- (a) that they have the appropriate expertise and experience;
- (b) that they are familiar with the general duties of an expert;
- (c) that they can produce a report, deal with questions and have discussions with other experts within a reasonable time and at a cost proportionate to the matters in issue;
- (d) a description of the work required;
- (e) whether they are available to attend the trial, if attendance is required; and
- (f) there is no potential conflict of interest.

7.2 Terms of appointment should be agreed at the outset and should normally include:
- (a) the capacity in which the expert is to be appointed (eg party appointed expert, single joint expert or expert advisor);
- (b) the services required of the expert (eg provision of expert's report, answering questions in writing, attendance at meetings and attendance at court);
- (c) time for delivery of the report;
- (d) the basis of the expert's charges (either daily or hourly rates and an estimate of the time likely to be required, or a total fee for the services);
- (e) travelling expenses and disbursements;
- (f) cancellation charges;
- (g) any fees for attending court;
- (h) time for making the payment;
- (i) whether fees are to be paid by a third party; and
- (j) if a party is publicly funded, whether or not the expert's charges will be subject to assessment by a costs officer.

7.3 As to the appointment of single joint experts, see section 17 below.

7.4 When necessary, arrangements should be made for dealing with questions to experts and discussions between experts, including any directions given by the court, and provision should be made for the cost of this work.

7.5 Experts should be informed regularly about deadlines for all matters concerning them. Those instructing experts should promptly send them copies of all court orders and directions which may affect the preparation of their reports or any other matters concerning their obligations.

*Conditional and Contingency Fees*

7.6 Payments contingent upon the nature of the expert evidence given in legal proceedings, or upon the outcome of a case, must not be offered or accepted. To do so would contravene experts' overriding duty to the court and compromise their duty of independence.

7.7 Agreement to delay payment of experts' fees until after the conclusion of cases is permissible as long as the amount of the fee does not depend on the outcome of the case.

## 8 Instructions

8.1 Those instructing experts should ensure that they give clear instructions, including the following:

(a) basic information, such as names, addresses, telephone numbers, dates of birth and dates of incidents;
(b) the nature and extent of the expertise which is called for;
(c) the purpose of requesting the advice or report, a description of the matter(s) to be investigated, the principal known issues and the identity of all parties;
(d) the statement(s) of case (if any), those documents which form part of standard disclosure and witness statements which are relevant to the advice or report;
(e) where proceedings have not been started, whether proceedings are being contemplated and, if so, whether the expert is asked only for advice;
(f) an outline programme, consistent with good case management and the expert's availability, for the completion and delivery of each stage of the expert's work; and
(g) where proceedings have been started, the dates of any hearings (including any case management conferences and/or pre-trial reviews), the name of the court, the claim number and the track to which the claim has been allocated.

8.2 Experts who do not receive clear instructions should request clarification and may indicate that they are not prepared to act unless and until such clear instructions are received.

8.3 As to the instruction of single joint experts, see section 17 below.

## 9 Experts' Acceptance of Instructions

9.1 Experts should confirm without delay whether or not they accept instructions. They should also inform those instructing them (whether on initial instruction or at any later stage) without delay if:

(a) instructions are not acceptable because, for example, they require work that falls outside their expertise, impose unrealistic deadlines, or are insufficiently clear;
(b) they consider that instructions are or have become insufficient to complete the work;
(c) they become aware that they may not be able to fulfil any of the terms of appointment;
(d) the instructions and/or work have, for any reason, placed them in conflict with their duties as an expert; or
(e) they are not satisfied that they can comply with any orders that have been made.

9.2 Experts must neither express an opinion outside the scope of their field of expertise, nor accept any instructions to do so.

## 10 Withdrawal

10.1 Where experts' instructions remain incompatible with their duties, whether through incompleteness, a conflict between their duty to the court and their instructions, or for any other substantial and significant reason, they may consider withdrawing from the case. However, experts should not withdraw without first discussing the position fully with those who instruct them and considering carefully whether it would be more appropriate to make a written request for directions from the court. If experts do withdraw, they must give formal written notice to those instructing them.

## 11 Experts' Right to ask Court for Directions

11.1 Experts may request directions from the court to assist them in carrying out their functions as experts. Experts should normally discuss such matters with those who instruct them before making any such request. Unless the court otherwise orders, any proposed request for directions should be copied to the party instructing the expert at least 7 days before filing any request to the court, and to all other parties at least 4 days before filing it (CPR 35.14).

11.2 Requests to the court for directions should be made by letter, containing:
(a) the title of the claim;
(b) the claim number of the case;
(c) the name of the expert;
(d) full details of why directions are sought; and
(e) copies of any relevant documentation.

## 12 Power of the Court to Direct a Party to Provide Information

12.1 If experts consider that those instructing them have not provided information which they require, they may, after discussion with those instructing them and giving notice, write to the court to seek directions (CPR 35.14).

12.2 Experts and those who instruct them should also be aware of CPR 35.9. This provides that where one party has access to information which is not readily available to the other party, the court may direct the party who has access to the information to prepare, file and copy to the other party a document recording the information. If experts require such information which has not been disclosed, they should discuss the position with those instructing them without delay, so that a request for the information can be made, and, if not forthcoming, an application can be made to the court. Unless a document appears to be essential, experts should assess the cost and time involved in the production of a document and whether its provision would be proportionate in the context of the case.

## 13 Contents of Experts' Reports

13.1 The content and extent of experts' reports should be governed by the scope of their instructions and general obligations, the contents of CPR 35 and PD 35 and their overriding duty to the court.

13.2 In preparing reports, experts should maintain professional objectivity and impartiality at all times.

13.3 PD 35, paragraph 2 provides that experts' reports should be addressed to the court and gives detailed directions about the form and content of such reports. All experts and those who instruct them should ensure that they are familiar with these requirements.

13.4 Model forms of Experts' Reports are available from bodies such as the Academy of Experts or the Expert Witness Institute.

13.5 Experts' reports must contain statements that they understand their duty to the court and have complied and will continue to comply with that duty (PD 35 paragraph 2.2(9)). They must also be verified by a statement of truth. The form of the statement of truth is as follows:

> I confirm that insofar as the facts stated in my report are within my own knowledge I have made clear which they are and I believe them to be true, and that the opinions I have expressed represent my true and complete professional opinion.

This wording is mandatory and must not be modified.

*Qualifications*

13.6 The details of experts' qualifications to be given in reports should be commensurate with the nature and complexity of the case. It may be sufficient merely to state academic and professional qualifications. However, where highly specialized expertise is called for, experts should include the detail of particular training and/or experience that qualifies them to provide that highly specialized evidence.

*Tests*

13.7 Where tests of a scientific or technical nature have been carried out, experts should state:

(a) the methodology used; and
(b) by whom the tests were undertaken and under whose supervision, summarizing their respective qualifications and experience.

*Reliance on the work of others*

13.8 Where experts rely in their reports on literature or other material and cite the opinions of others without having verified them, they must give details of those opinions relied on. It is likely to assist the court if the qualifications of the originator(s) are also stated.

*Facts*

13.9 When addressing questions of fact and opinion, experts should keep the two separate and discrete.

13.10 Experts must state those facts (whether assumed or otherwise) upon which their opinions are based. They must distinguish clearly between those facts which experts know to be true and those facts which they assume.

13.11 Where there are material facts in dispute experts should express separate opinions on each hypothesis put forward. They should not express a view in favour of one or other disputed version of the facts unless, as a result of particular expertise and experience, they consider one set of facts as being improbable or less probable, in which case they may express that view, and should give reasons for holding it.

*Range of opinion*

13.12 If the mandatory summary of the range of opinion is based on published sources, experts should explain those sources and, where appropriate, state the qualifications of the originator(s) of the opinions from which they differ, particularly if such opinions represent a well-established school of thought.

13.13 Where there is no available source for the range of opinion, experts may need to express opinions on what they believe to be the range which other experts would arrive at if asked. In those circumstances, experts should make it clear that the range that they summarize is based on their own judgement and explain the basis of that judgement.

*Conclusions*

13.14 A summary of conclusions is mandatory. The summary should be at the end of the report after all the reasoning. There may be cases, however, where the benefit to the court is heightened by placing a short summary at the beginning of the report whilst giving the full conclusions at the end. For example, it can assist with the comprehension of the analysis and with the absorption of the detailed facts if the court is told at the outset of the direction in which the report's logic will flow in cases involving highly complex matters which fall outside the general knowledge of the court.

*Basis of report: material instructions*

13.15 The mandatory statement of the substance of all material instructions should not be incomplete or otherwise tend to mislead. The imperative is transparency. The term 'instructions' includes all material which solicitors place in front of experts in order to gain advice. The omission from the statement of 'off-the-record' oral instructions is not permitted. Courts may allow cross-examination about the instructions if there are reasonable grounds to consider that the statement may be inaccurate or incomplete.

## 14 After Receipt of Experts' Reports

14.1 Following the receipt of experts' reports, those instructing them should advise the experts as soon as reasonably practicable whether, and if so when, the report will be disclosed to other parties; and, if so disclosed, the date of actual disclosure.

14.2 If experts' reports are to be relied upon, and if experts are to give oral evidence, those instructing them should give the experts the opportunity to consider and comment upon other reports within their area of expertise and which deal with relevant issues at the earliest opportunity.

14.3 Those instructing experts should keep experts informed of the progress of cases, including amendments to statements of case relevant to experts' opinion.

14.4 If those instructing experts become aware of material changes in circumstances or that relevant information within their control was not previously provided to experts, they should without delay instruct experts to review, and if necessary, update the contents of their reports.

## 15 Amendment of Reports

15.1 It may become necessary for experts to amend their reports:
(a) as a result of an exchange of questions and answers;
(b) following agreements reached at meetings between experts; or
(c) where further evidence or documentation is disclosed.

15.2 Experts should not be asked to, and should not, amend, expand or alter any parts of reports in a manner which distorts their true opinion, but may be invited to amend or expand reports to ensure accuracy, internal consistency, completeness and relevance to the issues and clarity. Although experts should generally follow the recommendations of solicitors with regard to the form of reports, they should form their own independent views as to the opinions and contents expressed in their reports and exclude any suggestions which do not accord with their views.

15.3 Where experts change their opinion following a meeting of experts, a simple signed and dated addendum or memorandum to that effect is generally sufficient. In some cases, however, the benefit to the court of having an amended report may justify the cost of making the amendment.

15.4 Where experts significantly alter their opinion, as a result of new evidence or because evidence on which they relied has become unreliable, or for any other reason, they should amend their reports to reflect that fact. Amended reports should include reasons for amendments. In such circumstances those instructing experts should inform other parties as soon as possible of any change of opinion.

15.5 When experts intend to amend their reports, they should inform those instructing them without delay and give reasons. They should provide the amended version (or an addendum or memorandum) clearly marked as such as quickly as possible.

## 16 Written Questions to Experts

16.1 The procedure for putting written questions to experts (CPR 35.6) is intended to facilitate the clarification of opinions and issues after experts' reports have been served. Experts have a duty to provide answers to questions properly put. Where they fail to do so, the court may impose sanctions against the party instructing the expert, and, if there is continued non-compliance, debar a party from relying on the report. Experts should copy their answers to those instructing them.

16.2 Experts' answers to questions automatically become part of their reports. They are covered by the statement of truth and form part of the expert evidence.

16.3 Where experts believe that questions put are not properly directed to the clarification of the report, or are disproportionate, or have been asked out of time, they should discuss the questions with those instructing them and, if appropriate, those asking the questions. Attempts should be made to resolve such problems without the need for an application to the court for directions.

*Written requests for directions in relation to questions*

16.4 If those instructing experts do not apply to the court in respect of questions, but experts still believe that questions are improper or out of time, experts may file written requests with the court for directions to assist in carrying out their functions as experts (CPR 35.14). See section 11 above.

## 17 Single Joint Experts

17.1 CPR 35 and PD 35 deal extensively with the instruction and use of joint experts by the parties and the powers of the court to order their use (see CPR 35.7 and 35.8, PD 35, paragraph 5).

17.2 The Civil Procedure Rules encourage the use of joint experts. Wherever possible a joint report should be obtained. Consideration should therefore be given by all parties to the appointment of single joint experts in all cases where a court might direct such an appointment. Single joint experts are the norm in cases allocated to the small claims track and the fast track.

17.3 Where, in the early stages of a dispute, examinations, investigations, tests, site inspections, experiments, preparation of photographs, plans or other similar preliminary expert tasks are necessary, consideration should be given to the instruction of a single joint expert, especially where such matters are not, at that stage, expected to be contentious as between the parties. The objective of such an appointment should be to agree or to narrow issues.

17.4 Experts who have previously advised a party (whether in the same case or otherwise) should only be proposed as single joint experts if other parties are given all relevant information about the previous involvement.

17.5 The appointment of a single joint expert does not prevent parties from instructing their own experts to advise (but the costs of such expert advisers may not be recoverable in the case).

*Joint instructions*

17.6 The parties should try to agree joint instructions to single joint experts, but, in default of agreement, each party may give instructions. In particular, all parties should try to agree what documents should be included with instructions and what assumptions single joint experts should make.

17.7 Where the parties fail to agree joint instructions, they should try to agree where the areas of disagreement lie and their instructions should make this clear. If separate instructions are given, they should be copied at the same time to the other instructing parties.

17.8 Where experts are instructed by two or more parties, the terms of appointment should, unless the court has directed otherwise, or the parties have agreed otherwise, include:

(a) a statement that all the instructing parties are jointly and severally liable to pay the experts' fees and, accordingly, that experts' invoices should be sent simultaneously to all instructing parties or their solicitors (as appropriate); and

(b) a statement as to whether any order has been made limiting the amount of experts' fees and expenses (CPR 35.8(4)(a)).

17.9 Where instructions have not been received by the expert from one or more of the instructing parties the expert should give notice (normally at least 7 days) of a deadline to all instructing parties for the receipt by the expert of such instructions. Unless the instructions are received within the deadline the expert may begin work. In the event that instructions are received after the deadline but before the signing off of the report the expert should consider whether it is practicable to comply with those instructions without adversely affecting the timetable set for delivery of the report and in such a manner as to comply with the proportionality principle. An expert who decides to issue a report without taking into account instructions received after the deadline should inform the parties who may apply to the court for directions. In either event the report must show clearly that the expert did not receive instructions within the deadline, or, as the case may be, at all.

*Conduct of the single joint expert*

17.10 Single joint experts should keep all instructing parties informed of any material steps that they may be taking by, for example, copying all correspondence to those instructing them.

17.11 Single joint experts are Part 35 experts and so have an overriding duty to the court. They are the parties' appointed experts and therefore owe an equal duty to all parties. They should maintain independence, impartiality and transparency at all times.

17.12 Single joint experts should not attend any meeting or conference which is not a joint one, unless all the parties have agreed in writing or the court has directed that such a meeting may be held[4] and who is to pay the experts' fees for the meeting.

17.13 Single joint experts may request directions from the court—see section 11 above.

17.14 Single joint experts should serve their reports simultaneously on all instructing parties. They should provide a single report even though they may have received instructions which contain areas of conflicting fact or allegation. If conflicting instructions lead to different opinions (for example, because the instructions require experts to make different assumptions of fact), reports may need to contain more than one set of opinions on any issue. It is for the court to determine the facts.

*Cross-examination*

17.15 Single joint experts do not normally give oral evidence at trial but if they do, all parties may cross-examine them. In general written questions (CPR 35.6) should be put to single joint experts before requests are made for them to attend court for the purpose of cross-examination.[5]

## 18 Discussions between Experts

18.1 The court has powers to direct discussions between experts for the purposes set out in the Rules (CPR 35.12). Parties may also agree that discussions take place between their experts.

18.2 Where single joint experts have been instructed but parties have, with the permission of the court, instructed their own additional Part 35 experts, there may, if the court so orders or the parties agree, be discussions between the single joint experts and the additional Part 35 experts. Such discussions should be confined to those matters within the remit of the additional Part 35 experts or as ordered by the court.

18.3 The purpose of discussions between experts should be, wherever possible, to:
- (a) identify and discuss the expert issues in the proceedings;
- (b) reach agreed opinions on those issues, and, if that is not possible, to narrow the issues in the case;
- (c) identify those issues on which they agree and disagree and summarize their reasons for disagreement on any issue; and
- (d) identify what action, if any, may be taken to resolve any of the outstanding issues between the parties.

[4] *Peet v Mid Kent Area Healthcare NHS Trust* [2002] 1 WLR 210.

[5] *Daniels v Walker* [2000] 1 WLR 1382.

*Arrangements for discussions between experts*

18.4 Arrangements for discussions between experts should be proportionate to the value of cases. In small claims and fast-track cases there should not normally be meetings between experts. Where discussion is justified in such cases, telephone discussion or an exchange of letters should, in the interests of proportionality, usually suffice. In multi-track cases, discussion may be face to face, but the practicalities or the proportionality principle may require discussions to be by telephone or video conference.

18.5 The parties, their lawyers and experts should co-operate to produce the agenda for any discussion between experts, although primary responsibility for preparation of the agenda should normally lie with the parties' solicitors.

18.6 The agenda should indicate what matters have been agreed and summarise concisely those which are in issue. It is often helpful for it to include questions to be answered by the experts. If agreement cannot be reached promptly or a party is unrepresented, the court may give directions for the drawing up of the agenda. The agenda should be circulated to experts and those instructing them to allow sufficient time for the experts to prepare for the discussion.

18.7 Those instructing experts must not instruct experts to avoid reaching agreement (or to defer doing so) on any matter within the experts' competence. Experts are not permitted to accept such instructions.

18.8 The parties' lawyers may only be present at discussions between experts if all the parties agree or the court so orders. If lawyers do attend, they should not normally intervene except to answer questions put to them by the experts or to advise about the law.[6]

18.9 The content of discussions between experts should not be referred to at trial unless the parties agree (CPR 35.12(4)). It is good practice for any such agreement to be in writing.

18.10 At the conclusion of any discussion between experts, a statement should be prepared setting out:
(a) a list of issues that have been agreed, including, in each instance, the basis of agreement;
(b) a list of issues that have not been agreed, including, in each instance, the basis of disagreement;
(c) a list of any further issues that have arisen that were not included in the original agenda for discussion;
(d) a record of further action, if any, to be taken or recommended, including as appropriate the holding of further discussions between experts.

18.11 The statement should be agreed and signed by all the parties to the discussion as soon as may be practicable.

18.12 Agreements between experts during discussions do not bind the parties unless the parties expressly agree to be bound by the agreement (CPR 35.12(5)). However, in view of the overriding objective, parties should give careful consideration before refusing to be bound by such an agreement and be able to explain their refusal should it become relevant to the issue of costs.

## 19 Attendance of Experts at Court

19.1 Experts instructed in cases have an obligation to attend court if called upon to do so and accordingly should ensure that those instructing them are always aware of their dates to be avoided and take all reasonable steps to be available.

19.2 Those instructing experts should:
(a) ascertain the availability of experts before trial dates are fixed;

[6] *Hubbard v Lambeth, Southwark and Lewisham HA* [2001] EWCA 1455.

(b) keep experts updated with timetables (including the dates and times experts are to attend) and the location of the court;
(c) give consideration, where appropriate, to experts giving evidence via a video-link;
(d) inform experts immediately if trial dates are vacated.

19.3 Experts should normally attend court without the need for the service of witness summonses, but on occasion they may be served to require attendance (CPR 34). The use of witness summonses does not affect the contractual or other obligations of the parties to pay experts' fees.

# CPR Part 36 Offers to Settle*



## 36.1 Scope of this Part

(1) This Part contains rules about—
   (a) offers to settle; and
   (b) the consequences where an offer to settle is made in accordance with this Part.

(2) Nothing in this Part prevents a party making an offer to settle in whatever way he chooses, but if the offer is not made in accordance with rule 36.2, it will not have the consequences specified in rules 36.10, 36.11 and 36.14.

(Rule 44.3 requires the court to consider an offer to settle that does not have the costs consequences set out in this Part in deciding what order to make about costs.)

## 36.2 Form and Content of a Part 36 Offer

(1) An offer to settle which is made in accordance with this rule is called a Part 36 offer.

(2) A Part 36 offer must—
   (a) be in writing;
   (b) state on its face that it is intended to have the consequences of Part 36;

---

* Editorial Note: **Transitional provisions.** This version of Part 36 wholly replaced the previous version with effect from Update 44 (for the previous version of Part 36 please see Civil Procedure Handbook 3rd edition, 2006). By reg. 7(2)–(7) of The Civil Procedure (Amendment No. 3) Rules 2006:

'(2) Where a Part 36 offer or Part 36 payment was made before 6th April 2007, if it would have had the consequences set out in the rules of court contained in Part 36 as it was in force immediately before 6th April 2007, it will have the consequences set out in rules 36.10, 36.11 and 36.14 after that date.

(3) Where a Part 36 offer or Part 36 payment was made before 6th April 2007, the permission of the court is required to accept that offer or payment, if permission would have been required under the rules of court contained in Part 36 as it was in force immediately before 6th April 2007.

(4) Rule 37.3 will apply to a Part 36 payment made before 6th April 2007 as if that payment into court had been made under a court order.

(5) Subject to paragraph (6), where a person has made a Part 36 offer or Part 36 payment less than 21 days before 6th April 2007—
   (a) paragraphs (1) to (4) of this Rule shall not apply to the offer or payment; and
   (b) the rules of court contained in Part 36 as it was in force immediately before 6th April 2007 shall continue to apply to that offer or payment as if they had not been revoked.

(6) Paragraph (5) ceases to apply to a Part 36 offer or Part 36 payment made less than 21 days before 6th April 2007 at the expiry of 21 days from the date that offer or payment was made unless the trial has started within that period.

(7) Where, before 6th April 2007, a person has made an offer to settle before commencement of proceedings which complied with rule 36.10 as it was in force immediately before 6th April 2007—
   (a) the court will take that offer into account when making any order as to costs; and
   (b) the permission of the court will be required to accept the offer after proceedings have been commenced.'

(c) specify a period of not less than 21 days within which the defendant will be liable for the claimant's costs in accordance with rule 36.10 if the offer is accepted;
(d) state whether it relates to the whole of the claim or to part of it or to an issue that arises in it and if so to which part or issue; and
(e) state whether it takes into account any counterclaim.

(Rule 36.7 makes provision for when a Part 36 offer is made.)

(3) Rule 36.2(2)(c) does not apply if the offer is made less than 21 days before the start of the trial.
(4) In appropriate cases, a Part 36 offer must contain such further information as is required by rule 36.5 (Personal injury claims for future pecuniary loss), rule 36.6 (Offer to settle a claim for provisional damages), and rule 36.15 (Deduction of benefits).
(5) An offeror may make a Part 36 offer solely in relation to liability.

### 36.3 Part 36 Offers—General Provisions

(1) In this Part—
(a) the party who makes an offer is the 'offeror';
(b) the party to whom an offer is made is the 'offeree'; and
(c) 'the relevant period' means—
(i) in the case of an offer made not less than 21 days before trial, the period stated under rule 36.2(2)(c) or such longer period as the parties agree;
(ii) otherwise, the period up to end of the trial or such other period as the court has determined.
(2) A Part 36 offer—
(a) may be made at any time, including before the commencement of proceedings; and
(b) may be made in appeal proceedings.
(3) A Part 36 offer which offers to pay or offers to accept a sum of money will be treated as inclusive of all interest until—
(a) the date on which the period stated under rule 36.2(2)(c) expires; or
(b) if rule 36.2(3) applies, a date 21 days after the date the offer was made.
(4) A Part 36 offer shall have the consequences set out in this Part only in relation to the costs of the proceedings in respect of which it is made, and not in relation to the costs of any appeal from the final decision in those proceedings.
(5) Before expiry of the relevant period, a Part 36 offer may be withdrawn or its terms changed to be less advantageous to the offeree, only if the court gives permission.
(6) After expiry of the relevant period and provided that the offeree has not previously served notice of acceptance, the offeror may withdraw the offer or change its terms to be less advantageous to the offeree without the permission of the court.
(7) The offeror does so by serving written notice of the withdrawal or change of terms on the offeree.

(Rule 36.14(6) deals with the costs consequences following judgment of an offer that is withdrawn.)

### 36.4 Part 36 Offers—Defendants' Offers

(1) Subject to rule 36.5(3) and rule 36.6(1), a Part 36 offer by a defendant to pay a sum of money in settlement of a claim must be an offer to pay a single sum of money.
(2) But, an offer that includes an offer to pay all or part of the sum, if accepted, at a date later than 14 days following the date of acceptance will not be treated as a Part 36 offer unless the offeree accepts the offer.

### 36.5 Personal Injury Claims for Future Pecuniary Loss

(1) This rule applies to a claim for damages for personal injury which is or includes a claim for future pecuniary loss.
(2) An offer to settle such a claim will not have the consequences set out in rules 36.10, 36.11 and 36.14 unless it is made by way of a Part 36 offer under this rule.

(3) A Part 36 offer to which this rule applies may contain an offer to pay, or an offer to accept—
(a) the whole or part of the damages for future pecuniary loss in the form of—
(i) a lump sum; or
(ii) periodical payments; or
(iii) both a lump sum and periodical payments;
(b) the whole or part of any other damages in the form of a lump sum.
(4) A Part 36 offer to which this rule applies—
(a) must state the amount of any offer to pay the whole or part of any damages in the form of a lump sum;
(b) may state—
(i) what part of the lump sum, if any, relates to damages for future pecuniary loss; and
(ii) what part relates to other damages to be accepted in the form of a lump sum;
(c) must state what part of the offer relates to damages for future pecuniary loss to be paid or accepted in the form of periodical payments and must specify—
(i) the amount and duration of the periodical payments;
(ii) the amount of any payments for substantial capital purchases and when they are to be made; and
(iii) that each amount is to vary by reference to the retail prices index (or to some other named index, or that it is not to vary by reference to any index); and
(d) must state either that any damages which take the form of periodical payments will be funded in a way which ensures that the continuity of payment is reasonably secure in accordance with section 2(4) of the Damages Act 1996 or how such damages are to be paid and how the continuity of their payment is to be secured.
(5) Rule 36.4 applies to the extent that a Part 36 offer by a defendant under this rule includes an offer to pay all or part of any damages in the form of a lump sum.
(6) Where the offeror makes a Part 36 offer to which this rule applies and which offers to pay or to accept damages in the form of both a lump sum and periodical payments, the offeree may only give notice of acceptance of the offer as a whole.
(7) If the offeree accepts a Part 36 offer which includes payment of any part of the damages in the form of periodical payments, the claimant must, within 7 days of the date of acceptance, apply to the court for an order for an award of damages in the form of periodical payments under rule 41.8.

(A practice direction supplementing Part 41 contains information about periodical payments under the Damages Act 1996.)

## 36.6 Offer to Settle a Claim for Provisional Damages

(1) An offeror may make a Part 36 offer in respect of a claim which includes a claim for provisional damages.
(2) Where he does so, the Part 36 offer must specify whether or not the offeror is proposing that the settlement shall include an award of provisional damages.
(3) Where the offeror is offering to agree to the making of an award of provisional damages the Part 36 offer must also state—
(a) that the sum offered is in satisfaction of the claim for damages on the assumption that the injured person will not develop the disease or suffer the type of deterioration specified in the offer;
(b) that the offer is subject to the condition that the claimant must make any claim for further damages within a limited period; and
(c) what that period is.
(4) Rule 36.4 applies to the extent that a Part 36 offer by a defendant includes an offer to agree to the making of an award of provisional damages.
(5) If the offeree accepts the Part 36 offer, the claimant must, within 7 days of the date of

acceptance, apply to the court for an order for an award of provisional damages under rule 41.2.

### 36.7 Time when a Part 36 Offer is Made

(1) A Part 36 offer is made when it is served on the offeree.
(2) A change in the terms of a Part 36 offer will be effective when notice of the change is served on the offeree.

(Rule 36.3 makes provision about when permission is required to change the terms of an offer to make it less advantageous to the offeree.)

### 36.8 Clarification of a Part 36 Offer

(1) The offeree may, within 7 days of a Part 36 offer being made, request the offeror to clarify the offer.
(2) If the offeror does not give the clarification requested under paragraph (1) within 7 days of receiving the request, the offeree may, unless the trial has started, apply for an order that he does so.

(Part 23 contains provisions about making an application to the court.)

(3) If the court makes an order under paragraph (2), it must specify the date when the Part 36 offer is to be treated as having been made.

### 36.9 Acceptance of a Part 36 Offer

(1) A Part 36 offer is accepted by serving written notice of the acceptance on the offeror.
(2) Subject to rule 36.9(3), a Part 36 offer may be accepted at any time (whether or not the offeree has subsequently made a different offer) unless the offeror serves notice of withdrawal on the offeree.

(Rule 21.10 provides that acceptance on behalf of a child or patient shall not be valid unless the court has approved the settlement.)

(3) The court's permission is required to accept a Part 36 offer where—
    (a) rule 36.12(4) applies;
    (b) rule 36.15(3)(b) applies, the relevant period has expired and further deductible benefits have been paid to the claimant since the date of the offer;
    (c) an apportionment is required under rule 41.3A; or
    (d) the trial has started.

(Rule 36.12 deals with offers by some but not all of multiple defendants.)

(Rule 36.15 deals with recoverable benefits and deductible benefits.)

(Rule 41.3A requires an apportionment in proceedings under the Fatal Accidents Act 1976 and Law Reform (Miscellaneous Provisions) Act 1934.)

(4) Where the court gives permission under paragraph (3), unless all the parties have agreed costs, the court will make an order dealing with costs, and may order that the costs consequences set out in rule 36.10 will apply.
(5) Unless the parties agree, a Part 36 offer may not be accepted after the end of the trial but before judgment is handed down.

### 36.10 Costs Consequences of Acceptance of a Part 36 Offer

(1) Subject to paragraph (2) and paragraph (4)(a), where a Part 36 offer is accepted within the relevant period the claimant will be entitled to his costs of the proceedings up to the date on which notice of acceptance was served on the offeror.
(2) Where—
    (a) a defendant's Part 36 offer relates to part only of the claim; and
    (b) at the time of serving notice of acceptance within the relevant period the claimant abandons the balance of the claim,

    the claimant will be entitled to his costs of the proceedings up to the date of serving notice of acceptance unless the court orders otherwise.

(3) Costs under paragraphs (1) and (2) of this rule will be assessed on the standard basis if the amount of costs is not agreed.

(Rule 44.4(2) explains the standard basis for assessment of costs.)

(4) Where—
  (a) a Part 36 offer that was made less than 21 days before the start of trial is accepted; or
  (b) a Part 36 offer is accepted after expiry of the relevant period,

  if the parties do not agree the liability for costs, the court will make an order as to costs.

(5) Where paragraph (4)(b) applies, unless the court orders otherwise—
  (a) the claimant will be entitled to his costs of the proceedings up to the date on which the relevant period expired; and
  (b) the offeree will be liable for the offeror's costs for the period from the date of expiry of the relevant period to the date of acceptance.

(6) The claimant's costs include any costs incurred in dealing with the defendant's counterclaim if the Part 36 offer states that it takes into account the counterclaim.

## 36.11 The Effect of Acceptance of a Part 36 Offer

(1) If a Part 36 offer is accepted, the claim will be stayed (GL).

(2) In the case of acceptance of a Part 36 offer which relates to the whole claim the stay (GL) will be upon the terms of the offer.

(3) If a Part 36 offer which relates to part only of the claim is accepted—
  (a) the claim will be stayed (GL) as to that part upon the terms of the offer; and
  (b) subject to rule 36.10(2), unless the parties have agreed costs, the liability for costs shall be decided by the court.

(4) If the approval of the court is required before a settlement can be binding, any stay (GL) which would otherwise arise on the acceptance of a Part 36 offer will take effect only when that approval has been given.

(5) Any stay (GL) arising under this rule will not affect the power of the court—
  (a) to enforce the terms of a Part 36 offer;
  (b) to deal with any question of costs (including interest on costs) relating to the proceedings.

(6) Unless the parties agree otherwise in writing, where a Part 36 offer by a defendant that is or that includes an offer to pay a single sum of money is accepted, that sum must be paid to the offeree within 14 days of the date of—
  (a) acceptance; or
  (b) the order when the court makes an order under rule 41.2 (order for an award of provisional damages) or rule 41.8 (order for an award of periodical payments), unless the court orders otherwise.

(7) If the accepted sum is not paid within 14 days or such other period as has been agreed the offeree may enter judgment for the unpaid sum.

(8) Where—
  (a) a Part 36 offer (or part of a Part 36 offer) which is not an offer to which paragraph (6) applies is accepted; and
  (b) a party alleges that the other party has not honoured the terms of the offer,

  that party may apply to enforce the terms of the offer without the need for a new claim.

## 36.12 Acceptance of a Part 36 Offer Made by one or more, but not all, Defendants

(1) This rule applies where the claimant wishes to accept a Part 36 offer made by one or more, but not all, of a number of defendants.

(2) If the defendants are sued jointly or in the alternative, the claimant may accept the offer if—
  (a) he discontinues his claim against those defendants who have not made the offer; and
  (b) those defendants give written consent to the acceptance of the offer.

(3) If the claimant alleges that the defendants have a several liability (GL) to him, the claimant may—
 (a) accept the offer; and
 (b) continue with his claims against the other defendants if he is entitled to do so.
(4) In all other cases the claimant must apply to the court for an order permitting him to accept the Part 36 offer.

## 36.13 Restriction on Disclosure of a Part 36 Offer

(1) A Part 36 offer will be treated as 'without prejudice (GL) except as to costs'.
(2) The fact that a Part 36 offer has been made must not be communicated to the trial judge or to the judge (if any) allocated in advance to conduct the trial until the case has been decided.
(3) Paragraph (2) does not apply—
 (a) where the defence of tender before claim (GL) has been raised;
 (b) where the proceedings have been stayed (GL) under rule 36.11 following acceptance of a Part 36 offer; or
 (c) where the offeror and the offeree agree in writing that it should not apply.

## 36.14 Costs Consequences following Judgment

(1) This rule applies where upon judgment being entered—
 (a) a claimant fails to obtain a judgment more advantageous than a defendant's Part 36 offer; or
 (b) judgment against the defendant is at least as advantageous to the claimant as the proposals contained in a claimant's Part 36 offer.
(2) Subject to paragraph (6), where rule 36.14(1)(a) applies, the court will, unless it considers it unjust to do so, order that the defendant is entitled to—
 (a) his costs from the date on which the relevant period expired; and
 (b) interest on those costs.
(3) Subject to paragraph (6), where rule 36.14(1)(b) applies, the court will, unless it considers it unjust to do so, order that the claimant is entitled to—
 (a) interest on the whole or part of any sum of money (excluding interest) awarded at a rate not exceeding 10% above base rate (GL) for some or all of the period starting with the date on which the relevant period expired;
 (b) his costs on the indemnity basis from the date on which the relevant period expired; and
 (c) interest on those costs at a rate not exceeding 10% above base rate (GL).
(4) In considering whether it would be unjust to make the orders referred to in paragraphs (2) and (3) above, the court will take into account all the circumstances of the case including—
 (a) the terms of any Part 36 offer;
 (b) the stage in the proceedings when any Part 36 offer was made, including in particular how long before the trial started the offer was made;
 (c) the information available to the parties at the time when the Part 36 offer was made; and
 (d) the conduct of the parties with regard to the giving or refusing to give information for the purposes of enabling the offer to be made or evaluated.
(5) Where the court awards interest under this rule and also awards interest on the same sum and for the same period under any other power, the total rate of interest may not exceed 10% above base rate (GL).
(6) Paragraphs (2) and (3) of this rule do not apply to a Part 36 offer—
 (a) that has been withdrawn;
 (b) that has been changed so that its terms are less advantageous to the offeree, and the offeree has beaten the less advantageous offer;

(c) made less than 21 days before trial, unless the court has abridged the relevant period.

(Rule 44.3 requires the court to consider an offer to settle that does not have the costs consequences set out in this Part in deciding what order to make about costs.)

### 36.15 Deduction of Benefits

(1) This rule applies where a payment to a claimant following acceptance of a Part 36 offer would be a compensation payment as defined in section 1 of the Social Security (Recovery of Benefits) Act 1997.

(2) In this rule, and in rule 36.9—
(a) 'recoverable benefits' means any of the benefits referred to in section 1, subsection (1)(b) of the 1997 Act; and
(b) 'deductible benefits' means any benefits by the amount of which damages are to be reduced in accordance with section 8 and Schedule 2 to the 1997 Act.

(3) A defendant who makes a Part 36 offer should state either—
(a) that the offer is made without regard to any liability for recoverable benefits; or
(b) that it is intended to include any deductible benefits.

# PD 36 Practice Direction—Offers to Settle

This Practice Direction supplements CPR Part 36.

## Formalities of Part 36 Offers and other Notices under this Part

1.1 A Part 36 offer may be made using Form N242A.

1.2 Where a Part 36 offer, notice of acceptance or notice of withdrawal or change of terms is to be served on a party who is legally represented, the document to be served must be served on the legal representative.

## Application for Permission to Withdraw a Part 36 Offer

2.1 Rule 36.3(4) provides that before expiry of the relevant period a Part 36 offer may only be withdrawn or its terms changed to be less advantageous to the offeree with the permission of the court.

2.2 The permission of the court must be sought—

(1) by making an application under Part 23, which must be dealt with by a judge other than the judge (if any) allocated in advance to conduct the trial, unless the parties agree that such judge may hear the application;

(2) at a trial or other hearing, provided that it is not to the trial judge or to the judge (if any) allocated in advance to conduct the trial, unless the parties agree that such judge may hear the application.

## Acceptance of a Part 36 Offer

3.1 Where a Part 36 offer is accepted in accordance with rule 36.9(1) the notice of acceptance must be served on the offeror and filed with the court where the case is proceeding.

3.2 Where the court's permission is required to accept a Part 36 offer, the permission of the court must be sought—

(1) by making an application under Part 23, which must be dealt with by a judge other than the judge (if any) allocated in advance to conduct the trial, unless the parties agree that such judge may hear the application;

(2) at a trial or other hearing, provided that it is not to the trial judge or to the judge (if any) allocated in advance to conduct the trial, unless the parties agree that such judge may hear the application.

3.3 Where rule 36.9(3)(b) applies, the application for permission to accept the offer must—

(1) state—

(a) the net amount offered in the Part 36 offer;

(b) the deductible benefits that had accrued at the date the offer was made;

(c) the deductible benefits that have subsequently accrued; and

(2) be accompanied by a copy of the current certificate of recoverable benefits.

# PD 36B Practice Direction

From 6th April 2007, new rules came into force concerning offers to settle, and Part 36, as it was in force immediately before 6th April 2007, was substituted by a new Part 36.
Rule 7 of the Civil Procedure (Amendment No. 3) Rules 2006 that brought those new rules into force and replaced the previous rules contained some provisions that dealt with how the rules are to apply to offers and payments into court made before 6th April 2007.

This Practice Direction explains how those provisions will operate.

## Offers and Payments Made before 6th April 2007

1.1 Paragraph (2) of rule 7 provides that where a Part 36 offer or Part 36 payment was made before 6th April 2007, if it would have had the consequences set out in the rules of court contained in Part 36 as it was in force immediately before 6th April 2007, it will have the consequences set out in rules 36.10, 36.11 and 36.14 after that date.

1.2 This provision makes clear that a Part 36 offer or Part 36 payment that was valid before 6th April 2007 will continue to be a valid Part 36 offer under the rules in force from 6th April 2007, and will have the consequences set out in those rules, specifically in relation to costs and the effect of acceptance.

## Permission of the Court

2.1 Paragraph (3) of rule 7 provides that where a Part 36 offer or Part 36 payment was made before 6th April 2007, the permission of the court is required to accept that offer or payment, if permission would have been required under the rules of court contained in Part 36 as it was in force immediately before 6th April 2007.

2.2 This provision preserves the requirement to obtain the permission of the court to accept an offer as it existed under the rules in force immediately before 6th April 2007. Therefore, if permission would have been required before 6th April 2007, it will be required after that date. But, if permission would not have been required because the parties have been able to agree liability for costs, or if a further offer has been made triggering a new period for acceptance, permission will not be required after 6th April 2007.

## Payments into Court Made before 6th April 2007

3.1 Paragraph (4) of rule 7 provides that rule 37.3 will apply to a Part 36 payment made before 6th April 2007 as if that payment into court had been made under a court order.

3.2 Rule 37.3 applies to all payments under Part 37, including payments into court under order, and permission is required to take the money out of court.

3.3 By applying rule 37.3 to payments into court made before 6th April 2007, this provision preserves in particular the requirement that permission be obtained to withdraw such payment.

3.4 But, rule 37.3 also provides that money may be taken out of court without the court's permission where a Part 36 offer (including an offer underlying a Part 36 payment) is accepted without needing the permission of the court and the defendant agrees that the sum may be paid out in satisfaction of the offer. Paragraph 3.4 of the Practice Direction to Part 37 makes provision about how to take money out of court.

3.5 This exception to the permission requirement preserves the right under rule 37.2, as it was in force immediately before 6th April 2007, to treat a payment into court made under order or by way of a defence of tender before claim as a Part 36 payment.

3.6 This provision has the effect that a Part 36 payment made before 6th April 2007 may be taken out of court simply by filing a request for payment if the offer underlying the Part 36 payment is accepted without needing permission. In those circumstances, it may be assumed that the defendant agrees to the money being used in satisfaction of the sum offered, and the requirement in paragraph 3.4 of the Practice Direction to Part 37 to file a Form 202 will not apply.

### Offers Remaining open for Acceptance

4.1 Paragraph (5) of rule 7 provides that the rules of court contained in Part 36 as it was in force immediately before 6th April 2007 shall continue to apply to a Part 36 offer or Part 36 payment made less than 21 days before 6th April 2007.

4.2 This provision preserves those rules in their entirety in relation to offers and payments made less than 21 days before 6th April 2007 for the period that they are expressed to remain open for acceptance.

4.3 Paragraph (6) of rule 7 provides that paragraph (5) ceases to apply at the expiry of 21 days from the date that the offer or payment was made, unless the trial has started within that period.

4.4 This provision has the effect that once the 21 day period has expired, the new regime (including the modifications at paragraphs (2), (3) and (4) of rule 7) will apply to the offer or payment.

4.5 If the trial has started within the 21 day period, the rules that were in force before 6th April 2007 will continue to apply to the offer or payment.

### Offers Made before Commencement of Proceedings

5.1 Paragraph (7) of rule 7 deals with the position where, before 6th April 2007, a person made an offer to settle before commencement of proceedings which complied with the provisions of rule 36.10 as it was in force immediately before 6th April 2007.

5.2 The court will take that offer into account when making any order as to costs. This preserves the discretion of the court to take into account an offer made before commencement of proceedings as it existed before 6th April 2007.

5.3 The permission of the court will be required to accept such an offer after proceedings have been commenced. This preserves the position under rule 36.10(4) as it was in force immediately before 6th April 2007.

5.4 If proceedings are commenced after 6th April 2007, the requirement to pay money into court in respect of a defendant's money offer under rule 36.10(3)(a) (as it was in force before 6th April 2007) will not apply to a defendant's money offer made before the proceedings were commenced.

# CPR Part 37 Miscellaneous Provisions About Payments Into Court



### 37.1 Money Paid into Court under a Court Order

A party who makes a payment into court under a court order must—

(a) serve notice of the payment on every other party; and
(b) in relation to each such notice, file a certificate of service.

### 37.2 Money Paid into Court where Defendant Wishes to Rely on a Defence of Tender before Claim

(1) Where a defendant wishes to rely on a defence of tender before claim (GL) he must make a payment into court of the amount he says was tendered.
(2) If the defendant does not make a payment in accordance with paragraph (1), the defence of tender before claim will not be available to him until he does so.

### 37.3 Payment out of Money Paid into Court

Money paid into court under a court order or in support of a defence of tender before claim (GL) may not be paid out without the court's permission except where—

(a) a Part 36 offer is accepted without needing the permission of the court; and
(b) the defendant agrees that a sum paid into court by him should be used to satisfy the offer (in whole or in part).

(Rule 36.9 sets out when the court's permission is required to accept a Part 36 offer.)

### 37.4 Payment into Court under Enactments

A practice direction may set out special provisions with regard to payments into court under various enactments.

# PD 37 Practice Direction—Miscellaneous Provisions About Payments Into Court

This practice direction supplements CPR Part 37.

## Payment into Court under an Order, etc

1.1 Except where paragraph 1.2 applies, a party paying money into court under an order or in support of a defence of tender before claim must—
- (1) send to the Court Funds Office—
  - (a) the payment, usually a cheque made payable to the Accountant General of the Supreme Court;
  - (b) a sealed copy of the order or a copy of the defence; and
  - (c) Court Funds Office form 100;
- (2) serve notice of payment on the other parties; and
- (3) file at the court—
  - (a) a copy of the notice of payment; and
  - (b) a certificate of service confirming service of the notice on each party served.

1.2 Instead of complying with paragraph 1.1(1), a litigant in person without a current account may, in a claim proceeding in a county court or District Registry, make a payment into court by—
- (1) lodging the payment in cash with the court; and
- (2) giving the court a completed Court Funds Office form 100.

## Applications Relating to Funds in Court

2.1 This paragraph applies to an application relating to money or securities which have been paid into court other than an application for the payment out of the money or securities (for example, an application for money to be invested, or for payment of interest to any person).

2.2 An application—
- (1) must be made in accordance with Part 23; and
- (2) may be made without notice, but the court may direct notice to be served on any person.

(Where money paid into court is accepted by or on behalf of a child or patient, rule 21.11(1)(b) provides that the money shall be dealt with in accordance with directions given by the court under that rule and not otherwise. Paragraphs 8 to 12 of the practice direction supplementing Part 21 make further provision about how the money may be dealt with.)

## Payment out of Court

3.1 Rule 37.3 provides that the court's permission is required to take money out of court except where the defendant agrees that the money which has been paid into court should be used to satisfy a Part 36 offer.

3.2 Permission may be obtained by making an application in accordance with Part 23. The application notice must state the grounds on which the order for payment out is sought. Evidence of any facts on which the applicant relies may also be necessary.

3.3 Where the court gives permission under rule 37.3, it will include a direction for the payment out of any money in court, including any interest accrued.

3.4 Where permission is not required to take money out of court, the requesting party should file a request for payment in Court Funds Office form 201 with the Court Funds Office, accompanied by a statement that the defendant agrees that the money should be used to satisfy the Part 36 offer in Court Funds Office form 202.

(Paragraph 3.6 of Practice Direction B supplementing Part 36 provides that a defendant who made a Part 36 payment before 6th April 2007, and whose Part 36 offer underlying the payment is accepted without requiring the permission of the court, is not required to file form 202.)

3.5 The request for payment should contain the following details—
   (1) where the party receiving the payment is legally represented—
      (a) the name, business address and reference of the legal representative; and
      (b) the name of the bank and the sort code number, the title of the account and the account number where the payment is to be transmitted;
   (2) where the party is acting in person—
      (a) his name and address; and
      (b) his bank account details as in paragraph (1)(b) above; and
   (3) whether the party receiving the payment is, or has been, in receipt of services funded by the Legal Services Commission as part of the Community Legal Service.

3.6 Where paragraph 3.4 applies, interest accruing up to the date of acceptance will be paid to the defendant.

(Rule 20.2 provides that in these Rules references to a claimant or defendant include a party bringing or defending an additional claim.)

3.7 Subject to paragraph 3.8, if a party does not wish the payment to be transmitted into his bank account or if he does not have a bank account, he may send a written request to the Accountant-General for the payment to be made to him by cheque.

3.8 Where a party seeking payment out of court has provided the necessary information, the payment—
   (1) where a party is legally represented, must be made to the legal representative;
   (2) if the party is not legally represented but has given notice under paragraph 3.5(3), must be made to the Legal Services Commission.

## Payment into Court by Life Assurance Company

4.1 A company wishing to make a payment into court under the Life Assurance Companies (Payment into Court) Act 1896 ('the 1896 Act') must file a witness statement or an affidavit setting out—
   (1) a short description of the policy under which money is payable;
   (2) a statement of the persons entitled under the policy, including their names and addresses so far as known to the company;
   (3) a short statement of—
      (a) the notices received by the company making any claim to the money assured, or withdrawing any such claim;
      (b) the dates of receipt of such notices; and
      (c) the names and addresses of the persons by whom they were given;
   (4) a statement that, in the opinion of the board of directors of the company, no sufficient discharge can be obtained for the money which is payable, other than by paying it into court under the 1896 Act;
   (5) a statement that the company agrees to comply with any order or direction the court may make—
      (a) to pay any further sum into court; or
      (b) to pay any costs;
   (6) an undertaking by the company to immediately send to the Accountant General at the Court Funds Office any notice of claim received by the company after the witness statement or affidavit has been filed, together with a letter referring to the Court Funds Office reference number; and
   (7) the company's address for service.

4.2 The witness statement or affidavit must be filed at—
   (1) Chancery Chambers at the Royal Courts of Justice, or
   (2) a Chancery district registry of the High Court.

4.3 The company must not deduct from the money payable by it under the policy any costs of the payment into court, except for any court fee.

4.4 If the company is a party to any proceedings issued in relation to the policy or the money assured by it, it may not make a payment into court under the 1896 Act without the permission of the court in those proceedings.

4.5 If a company pays money into court under the 1896 Act, unless the court orders otherwise it must immediately serve notice of the payment on every person who is entitled under the policy or has made a claim to the money assured.

## Application for Payment out of Money Paid into Court by Life Assurance Company

5.1 Any application for the payment out of money which has been paid into court under the 1896 Act must be made in accordance with paragraph 3 of this practice direction.

5.2 The application must be served on—
- (1) every person stated in the written evidence of the company which made the payment to be entitled to or to have an interest in the money;
- (2) any other person who has given notice of a claim to the money; and
- (3) the company which made the payment, if an application is being made for costs against it, but not otherwise.

## Payment into Court under Trustee Act 1925

6.1 A trustee wishing to make a payment into court under section 63 of the Trustee Act 1925 must file a witness statement or an affidavit setting out—
- (1) a short description of—
  - (a) the trust; and
  - (b) the instrument creating the trust, or the circumstances in which the trust arose;
- (2) the names of the persons interested in or entitled to the money or securities to be paid into court, with their address so far as known to him;
- (3) a statement that he agrees to answer any inquiries which the court may make or direct relating to the application of the money or securities; and
- (4) his address for service.

6.2 The witness statement or affidavit must be filed at—
- (1) Chancery Chambers at the Royal Courts of Justice;
- (2) a Chancery district registry of the High Court; or
- (3) a county court.

6.3 If a trustee pays money or securities into court, unless the court orders otherwise he must immediately serve notice of the payment into court on every person interested in or entitled to the money or securities.

## Application for Payment out of Funds Paid into Court by Trustee

7.1 An application for the payment out of any money or securities paid into court under section 63 of the Trustee Act 1925 must be made in accordance with paragraph 3 of this practice direction.

7.2 The application may be made without notice, but the court may direct notice to be served on any person.

## Payment into Court under Vehicular Access Across Common and Other Land (England) Regulations 2002

8.1 In this section of this Practice Direction—
- (1) expressions used have the meanings given by the Vehicular Access Across Common and Other Land (England) Regulations 2002; and
- (2) a regulation referred to by number alone means the regulation so numbered in those Regulations.

8.2 Where the applicant wishes to pay money into a county court under regulation 14 he must file a witness statement or an affidavit when he lodges the money.

8.3 The witness statement or affidavit must—

(1) state briefly why the applicant is making the payment into court; and

(2) be accompanied by copies of—

(a) the notice served under regulation 6;

(b) any counter-notice served under regulation 8;

(c) any amended notice or counter-notice served under regulation 9;

(d) any determination of the Lands Tribunal of a matter referred to it under regulation 10; and

(e) any determination of the value of the premises by a chartered surveyor following the service of a valuation notice under regulation 12.

8.4 If an applicant pays money into court under regulation 14, he must immediately serve notice of the payment and a copy of the witness statement or affidavit on the land owner.

8.5 An application for payment out of the money must be made in accordance with paragraph 3 of this practice direction.

# CPR Part 38 Discontinuance



### 38.1 Scope of this Part

(1) The rules in this Part set out the procedure by which a claimant may discontinue all or part of a claim.

(2) A claimant who—
   (a) claims more than one remedy; and
   (b) subsequently abandons his claim to one or more of the remedies but continues with his claim for the other remedies,

   is not treated as discontinuing all or part of a claim for the purposes of this Part.

(The procedure for amending a statement of case, set out in Part 17, applies where a claimant abandons a claim for a particular remedy but wishes to continue with his claim for other remedies.)

### 38.2 Right to Discontinue Claim

(1) A claimant may discontinue all or part of a claim at any time.

(2) However—
   (a) a claimant must obtain the permission of the court if he wishes to discontinue all or part of a claim in relation to which—
      (i) the court has granted an interim injunction(GL); or
      (ii) any party has given an undertaking to the court;
   (b) where the claimant has received an interim payment in relation to a claim (whether voluntarily or pursuant to an order under Part 25), he may discontinue that claim only if—
      (i) the defendant who made the interim payment consents in writing; or
      (ii) the court gives permission;
   (c) where there is more than one claimant, a claimant may not discontinue unless—
      (i) every other claimant consents in writing; or
      (ii) the court gives permission.

(3) Where there is more than one defendant, the claimant may discontinue all or part of a claim against all or any of the defendants.

### 38.3 Procedure for Discontinuing

(1) To discontinue a claim or part of a claim, a claimant must—
   (a) file a notice of discontinuance; and
   (b) serve a copy of it on every other party to the proceedings.

(2) The claimant must state in the notice of discontinuance which he files that he has served notice of discontinuance on every other party to the proceedings.

(3) Where the claimant needs the consent of some other party, a copy of the necessary consent must be attached to the notice of discontinuance.

(4) Where there is more than one defendant, the notice of discontinuance must specify against which defendants the claim is discontinued.

## 38.4 Right to Apply to Have Notice of Discontinuance Set Aside

(1) Where the claimant discontinues under rule 38.2(1) the defendant may apply to have the notice of discontinuance set aside(GL).

(2) The defendant may not make an application under this rule more than 28 days after the date when the notice of discontinuance was served on him.

## 38.5 When Discontinuance Takes Effect Where Permission of the Court is Not Needed

(1) Discontinuance against any defendant takes effect on the date when notice of discontinuance is served on him under rule 38.3(1).

(2) Subject to rule 38.4, the proceedings are brought to an end as against him on that date.

(3) However, this does not affect proceedings to deal with any question of costs.

## 38.6 Liability for Costs

(1) Unless the court orders otherwise, a claimant who discontinues is liable for the costs which a defendant against whom he discontinues incurred on or before the date on which notice of discontinuance was served on him.

(2) If proceedings are only partly discontinued—

(a) the claimant is liable under paragraph (1) for costs relating only to the part of the proceedings which he is discontinuing; and

(b) unless the court orders otherwise, the costs which the claimant is liable to pay must not be assessed until the conclusion of the rest of the proceedings.

(3) This rule does not apply to claims allocated to the small claims track.

(Rule 44.12 provides for the basis of assessment where right to costs arises on discontinuance.)

## 38.7 Discontinuance and Subsequent Proceedings

A claimant who discontinues a claim needs the permission of the court to make another claim against the same defendant if—

(a) he discontinued the claim after the defendant filed a defence; and

(b) the other claim arises out of facts which are the same or substantially the same as those relating to the discontinued claim.

## 38.8 Stay of Remainder of Partly Discontinued Proceedings Where Costs Not Paid

(1) This rule applies where—

(a) proceedings are partly discontinued;

(b) a claimant is liable to pay costs under rule 38.6; and

(c) the claimant fails to pay those costs within 14 days of—

(i) the date on which the parties agreed the sum payable by the claimant; or

(ii) the date on which the court ordered the costs to be paid.

(2) Where this rule applies, the court may stay(GL) the remainder of the proceedings until the claimant pays the whole of the costs which he is liable to pay under rule 38.6.

# CPR Part 39 Miscellaneous Provisions Relating to Hearings



## 39.1 Interpretation

In this Part, reference to a hearing includes a reference to the trial.

## 39.2 General Rule—Hearing to be in Public

(1) The general rule is that a hearing is to be in public.
(2) The requirement for a hearing to be in public does not require the court to make special arrangements for accommodating members of the public.
(3) A hearing, or any part of it, may be in private if—
    (a) publicity would defeat the object of the hearing;
    (b) it involves matters relating to national security;
    (c) it involves confidential information (including information relating to personal financial matters) and publicity would damage that confidentiality;
    (d) a private hearing is necessary to protect the interests of any child or patient;
    (e) it is a hearing of an application made without notice and it would be unjust to any respondent for there to be a public hearing;
    (f) it involves uncontentious matters arising in the administration of trusts or in the administration of a deceased person's estate; or
    (g) the court considers this to be necessary, in the interests of justice.
(4) The court may order that the identity of any party or witness must not be disclosed if it considers non-disclosure necessary in order to protect the interests of that party or witness.

## 39.3 Failure to Attend the Trial

(1) The court may proceed with a trial in the absence of a party but—
    (a) if no party attends the trial, it may strike out(GL) the whole of the proceedings;
    (b) if the claimant does not attend, it may strike out his claim and any defence to counterclaim; and
    (c) if a defendant does not attend, it may strike out his defence or counterclaim (or both).
(2) Where the court strikes out proceedings, or any part of them, under this rule, it may subsequently restore the proceedings, or that part.
(3) Where a party does not attend and the court gives judgment or makes an order against him, the party who failed to attend may apply for the judgment or order to be set aside(GL).
(4) An application under paragraph (2) or paragraph (3) must be supported by evidence.
(5) Where an application is made under paragraph (2) or (3) by a party who failed to attend the trial, the court may grant the application only if the applicant—
    (a) acted promptly when he found out that the court had exercised its power to strike out(GL) or to enter judgment or make an order against him;

(b) had a good reason for not attending the trial; and
(c) has a reasonable prospect of success at the trial.

### 39.4 Timetable for Trial

When the court sets a timetable for a trial in accordance with rule 28.6 (fixing or confirming the trial date and giving directions—fast track) or rule 29.8 (setting a trial timetable and fixing or confirming the trial date or week—multi-track) it will do so in consultation with the parties.

### 39.5 Trial Bundles

(1) Unless the court orders otherwise, the claimant must file a trial bundle containing documents required by—
 (a) a relevant practice direction; and
 (b) any court order.
(2) The claimant must file the trial bundle not more than 7 days and not less than 3 days before the start of the trial.

### 39.6 Representation at Trial of Companies or Other Corporations

A company or other corporation may be represented at trial by an employee if—
(a) the employee has been authorised by the company or corporation to appear at trial on its behalf; and
(b) the court gives permission.

### 39.7 Impounded Documents

(1) Documents impounded by order of the court must not be released from the custody of the court except in compliance—
 (a) with a court order; or
 (b) with a written request made by a Law Officer or the Director of Public Prosecutions.
(2) A document released from the custody of the court under paragraph (1)(b) must be released into the custody of the person who requested it.
(3) Documents impounded by order of the court, while in the custody of the court, may not be inspected except by a person authorised to do so by a court order.

### 39.8 Claims Under the Race Relations Act 1976

*Omitted*

# PD 39 Practice Direction — Miscellaneous Provisions Relating to Hearings

This practice direction supplements CPR Part 39.

## Hearings

1.1 In Part 39, reference to a hearing includes reference to the trial.[1]

1.2 The general rule is that a hearing is to be in public.[2]

1.3 Rule 39.2(3) sets out the type of proceedings which may be dealt with in private.

1.4 The decision as to whether to hold a hearing in public or in private must be made by the judge conducting the hearing having regard to any representations which may have been made to him.

1.4A The judge should also have regard to Article 6(1) of the European Convention on Human Rights. This requires that, in general, court hearings are to be held in public, but the press and public may be excluded in the circumstances specified in that Article. Article 6(1) will usually be relevant, for example, where a party applies for a hearing which would normally be held in public to be held in private as well as where a hearing would normally be held in private. The judge may need to consider whether the case is within any of the exceptions permitted by Article 6(1).

1.5 The hearings set out below shall in the first instance be listed by the court as hearings in private under rule 39.2(3)(c), namely:

(1) a claim by a mortgagee against one or more individuals for an order for possession of land,

(2) a claim by a landlord against one or more tenants or former tenants for the repossession of a dwelling house based on the non-payment of rent,

(3) an application to suspend a warrant of execution or a warrant of possession or to stay execution where the court is being invited to consider the ability of a party to make payments to another party,

(4) a redetermination under rule 14.13 or an application to vary or suspend the payment of a judgment debt by instalments,

(5) an application for a charging order (including an application to enforce a charging order), third party debt order, attachment of earnings order, administration order, or the appointment of a receiver,

(6) an order to attend court for questioning,

(7) the determination of an LSC funded client under regulations 9 and 10 of the Community Legal Service (Costs) Regulations 2000, or of an assisted person's liability for costs under regulation 127 of the Civil Legal Aid (General) Regulations 1989,

(8) an application for security for costs under section 726(1) of the Companies Act 1985, and

(9) proceedings brought under the Consumer Credit Act 1974, the Inheritance (Provision for Family and Dependants) Act 1975 or the Protection from Harassment Act 1997,

(10) an application by a trustee or personal representative for directions as to bringing or defending legal proceedings.

1.6 Rule 39.2(3)(d) states that a hearing may be in private where it involves the interests of a child or patient. This includes the approval of a compromise or settlement on behalf

---

[1] Rule 39.1.

[2] Rule 39.2(1).

of a child or patient or an application for the payment of money out of court to such a person.

1.7 Attention is drawn to paragraph 5.1 of the Practice Direction which supplements Part 27 (relating to the hearing of claims in the small claims track), which provides that the judge may decide to hold a small claim hearing in private if the parties agree or if a ground mentioned in rule 39.2(3) applies. A hearing of a small claim in premises other than the court will not be a hearing in public.

1.8 Nothing in this practice direction prevents a judge ordering that a hearing taking place in public shall continue in private, or vice versa.

1.9 If the court or judge's room in which the proceedings are taking place has a sign on the door indicating that the proceedings are private, members of the public who are not parties to the proceedings will not be admitted unless the court permits.

1.10 Where there is no such sign on the door of the court or judge's room, members of the public will be admitted where practicable. The judge may, if he thinks it appropriate, adjourn the proceedings to a larger room or court.

1.11 When a hearing takes place in public, members of the public may obtain a transcript of any judgment given or a copy of any order made, subject to payment of the appropriate fee.

1.12 When a judgment is given or an order is made in private, if any member of the public who is not a party to the proceedings seeks a transcript of the judgment or a copy of the order, he must seek the leave of the judge who gave the judgment or made the order.

1.13 A judgment or order given or made in private, when drawn up, must have clearly marked in the title:
'Before [*title and name of judge*] sitting in Private'

1.14 References to hearings being in public or private or in a judge's room contained in the Civil Procedure Rules (including the Rules of the Supreme Court and the County Court Rules scheduled to Part 50) and the practice directions which supplement them do not restrict any existing rights of audience or confer any new rights of audience in respect of applications or proceedings which under the rules previously in force would have been heard in court or in chambers respectively.

1.15 Where the court lists a hearing of a claim by a mortgagee for an order for possession of land under para. 1.5(1) above to be in private, any fact which needs to be proved by the evidence of witnesses may be proved by evidence in writing.
(CPR, r. 32.2, sets out the general rule as to how evidence is to be given and facts are to be proved.)

## Failure to Attend the Trial

2.1 Rule 39.3 sets out the consequences of a party's failure to attend the trial.

2.2 The court may proceed with a trial in the absence of a party.[3] In the absence of:
- (1) the defendant, the claimant may:
  - (a) prove his claim at trial and obtain judgment on his claim and for costs, and
  - (b) seek the striking out of any counterclaim,
- (2) the claimant, the defendant may:
  - (a) prove any counterclaim at trial and obtain judgment on his counterclaim and for costs, and
  - (b) seek the striking out of the claim, or
- (3) both parties, the court may strike out the whole of the proceedings.

2.3 Where the court has struck out proceedings, or any part of them, on the failure of a party to attend, that party may apply in accordance with Part 23 for the proceedings,

[3] Rule 39.3(1).

or that part of them, to be restored and for any judgment given against that party to be set aside.[4]

2.4 The application referred to in paragraph 2.3 above must be supported by evidence giving reasons for the failure to attend court and stating when the applicant found out about the order against him.

## Bundles of Documents for Hearings or Trial

3.1 Unless the court orders otherwise, the claimant must file the trial bundle not more than seven days and not less than three days before the start of the trial.

3.2 Unless the court orders otherwise, the trial bundle should include a copy of:
(1) the claim form and all statements of case,
(2) a case summary and/or chronology where appropriate,
(3) requests for further information and responses to the requests,
(4) all witness statements to be relied on as evidence,
(5) any witness summaries,
(6) any notices of intention to rely on hearsay evidence under rule [33.2*],
(7) any notices of intention to rely on evidence (such as a plan, photograph etc.) under rule 33.6 which is not:
(a) contained in a witness statement, affidavit or expert's report,
(b) being given orally at trial,
(c) hearsay evidence under rule 33.2,
(8) any medical reports and responses to them,
(9) any experts' reports and responses to them,
(10) any order giving directions as to the conduct of the trial, and
(11) any other necessary documents.

3.3 The originals of the documents contained in the trial bundle, together with copies of any other court orders should be available at the trial.

3.4 The preparation and production of the trial bundle, even where it is delegated to another person, is the responsibility of the legal representative[5] who has conduct of the claim on behalf of the claimant.

3.5 The trial bundle should be paginated (continuously) throughout, and indexed with a description of each document and the page number. Where the total number of pages is more than 100, numbered dividers should be placed at intervals between groups of documents.

3.6 The bundle should normally be contained in a ring binder or lever arch file. Where more than one bundle is supplied, they should be clearly distinguishable, for example, by different colours or letters. If there are numerous bundles, a core bundle should be prepared containing the core documents essential to the proceedings, with references to the supplementary documents in the other bundles.

3.7 For convenience, experts' reports may be contained in a separate bundle and cross referenced in the main bundle.

3.8 If a document to be included in the trial bundle is illegible, a typed copy should be included in the bundle next to it, suitably cross-referenced.

3.9 The contents of the trial bundle should be agreed where possible. The parties should also agree where possible:
(1) that the documents contained in the bundle are authentic even if not disclosed under Part 31, and
(2) that documents in the bundle may be treated as evidence of the facts stated in them even if a notice under the Civil Evidence Act 1995 has not been served.

[4] Rule 39.3(2) and (3).
[* The text issued by the Department for Constitutional Affairs refers, mistakenly, to rule 32.2.]
[5] For the definition of legal representative see rule 2.3.

Where it is not possible to agree the contents of the bundle, a summary of the points on which the parties are unable to agree should be included.

3.10 The party filing the trial bundle should supply identical bundles to all the parties to the proceedings and for the use of the witnesses.

## Settlement or Discontinuance After the Trial Date is Fixed

4.1 Where:

(1) an offer to settle a claim is accepted,
(2) or a settlement is reached, or
(3) a claim is discontinued,

which disposes of the whole of a claim for which a date or 'window' has been fixed for the trial, the parties must ensure that the listing officer for the trial court is notified immediately.

4.2 If an order is drawn up giving effect to the settlement or discontinuance, a copy of the sealed order should be filed with the listing officer.

## Representation at Hearings

5.1 At any hearing, a written statement containing the following information should be provided for the court:

(1) the name and address of each advocate,
(2) his qualification or entitlement to act as an advocate, and
(3) the party for whom he so acts.

5.2 Where a party is a company or other corporation and is to be represented at a hearing by an employee the written statement should contain the following additional information:

(1) The full name of the company or corporation as stated in its certificate of registration.
(2) The registered number of the company or corporation.
(3) The position or office in the company or corporation held by the representative.
(4) The date on which and manner in which the representative was authorised to act for the company or corporation, eg —— 20 —— : written authority from managing director; or —— 20 —— : Board resolution dated —— 20 ——.

5.3 Rule 39.6 is intended to enable a company or other corporation to represent itself as a litigant in person. Permission under rule 39.6(b) should therefore be given by the court unless there is some particular and sufficient reason why it should be withheld. In considering whether to grant permission the matters to be taken into account include the complexity of the issues and the experience and position in the company or corporation of the proposed representative.

5.4 Permission under rule 39.6(b) should be obtained in advance of the hearing from, preferably, the judge who is to hear the case, but may, if it is for any reason impracticable or inconvenient to do so, be obtained from any judge by whom the case could be heard.

5.5 The permission may be obtained informally and without notice to the other parties. The judge who gives the permission should record in writing that he has done so and supply a copy to the company or corporation in question and to any other party who asks for one.

5.6 Permission should not normally be granted under Rule 39.6:

(a) in jury trials;
(b) in contempt proceedings.

## Recording of Proceedings

6.1 At any hearing, whether in the High Court or a county court, the proceedings will be tape-recorded unless the judge directs otherwise.

6.2 No party or member of the public may use unofficial recording equipment in any court or judge's room without the permission of the court. To do so without permission constitutes a contempt of court.[6]

6.3 Any party or person may require a transcript or transcripts of the recording of any hearing to be supplied to him, upon payment of the charges authorised by any scheme in force for the making of the recording or the transcript.

6.4 Where the person requiring the transcript or transcripts is not a party to the proceedings and the hearing or any part of it was held in private under CPR rule 39.2, paragraph 6.3 does not apply unless the court so orders.

6.5 Attention is drawn to [PD 52, paras 5.17 and 5.18* which deal] with the provision of transcripts for use in the Court of Appeal at public expense.

## Exhibits at Trial

7 Exhibits which are handed in and proved during the course of the trial should be recorded on an exhibit list and kept in the custody of the court until the conclusion of the trial, unless the judge directs otherwise. At the conclusion of the trial it is the parties' responsibility to obtain the return of those exhibits which they handed in and to preserve them for the period in which any appeal may take place.

## Citation of Authorities

*Human rights*

8.1 If it is necessary for a party to give evidence at a hearing of an authority referred to in s. 2 of the Human Rights Act 1998:

(1) the authority to be cited should be an authoritative and complete report; and

(2) the party must give to the court and any other party a list of the authorities he intends to cite and copies of the reports not less than three days before the hearing. (Section 2(1) of the Human Rights Act 1998 requires the court to take into account the authorities listed there.)

(3) Copies of the complete original texts issued by the European Court and Commission either paper based or from the Court's judgment database (HUDOC), which is available on the Internet, may be used.

[6] Section 9 of the Contempt of Court Act 1981.

[* The text issued by the Department for Constitutional Affairs refers to an earlier practice direction.]

# PD 39B Practice Direction — Court Sittings

This practice direction supplements CPR Part 39.

## Court Sittings

1.1 (1) The sittings of the Court of Appeal and of the High Court shall be four in every year, that is to say:
(a) the Michaelmas sittings which shall begin on 1 October and end on 21 December;
(b) the Hilary sittings which shall begin on 11 January and end on the Wednesday before Easter Sunday;
(c) the Easter sittings which shall begin on the second Tuesday after Easter Sunday and end on the Friday before the spring holiday; and
(d) the Trinity sittings which shall begin on the second Tuesday after the spring holiday and end on 31 July.

(2) In the above paragraph 'spring holiday' means the bank holiday falling on the last Monday in May or any day appointed instead of that day under the Banking and Financial Dealings Act 1971, s. 1(2).

## Vacations: The High Court

2.1 (1) One or more judges of each Division of the High Court shall sit in vacation on such days as the senior judge of that Division may from time to time direct, to hear such cases, claims, matters or applications as require to be immediately or promptly heard and to hear other cases, claims, matters or applications if the senior judge of that Division determines that sittings are necessary for that purpose.

(2) Any party to a claim or matter may at any time apply to the court for an order that such claim or matter be heard in vacation and, if the court is satisfied that the claim or matter requires to be immediately or promptly heard, it may make an order accordingly and fix a date for the hearing.

(3) Any judge of the High Court may hear such other cases, claims, matters or applications in vacation as the court may direct.

2.2 The directions in para. [2.1]* shall not apply in relation to the trial or hearing of cases, claims, matters or applications outside the Royal Courts of Justice but the senior presiding judge of each circuit, with the concurrence of the senior presiding judge, and the Vice-Chancellor of the County Palatine of Lancaster and the Chancery supervising judge for Birmingham, Bristol and Cardiff, with the concurrence of the Vice-Chancellor, may make such arrangements for vacation sittings in the courts for which they are respectively responsible as they think desirable.

2.3 (1) Subject to the discretion of the judge, any appeal and any application normally made to a judge may be made in the month of September.

(2) In the month of August, save with the permission of a judge or under arrangements for vacation sittings in courts outside the Royal Courts of Justice, appeals to a judge will be limited to the matters set out in para. [2.5]† below, and only applications of real urgency will be dealt with, for example, urgent applications in respect of injunctions or for possession under RSC, ord. 113 in CPR, sch. 1.

(3) It is desirable, where this is practical, that applications or appeals are submitted to a master, district judge or judge prior to the hearing of the application or appeal so that they can be marked 'fit for August' or 'fit for vacation'. If they are so marked,

[* The text issued by the Department for Constitutional Affairs mistakenly refers to para. 3.1.]

[† The text issued by the Department for Constitutional Affairs mistakenly refers to para. 3.5.]

then normally the judge will be prepared to hear the application or appeal in August, if marked 'fit for August' or in September if marked 'fit for vacation'. A request to have the papers so marked should normally be made in writing, shortly setting out the nature of the application or appeal and the reasons why it should be dealt with in August or in September, as the case may be.

*Chancery masters*

2.4 There is no distinction between term time and vacation so far as business before the Chancery masters is concerned. The masters will deal with all types of business throughout the year, and when a master is on holiday his list will normally be taken by a deputy master.

*Queen's Bench masters*

2.5 (1) An application notice may, without permission, be issued returnable before a master in the month of August for any of the following purposes:
to set aside a claim form or particulars of claim, or service of a claim form or particulars of claim;
to set aside judgment; for stay of execution;
for any order by consent;
for judgment or permission to enter judgment;
for approval of settlements or for interim payment;
for relief from forfeiture; for charging order; for garnishee order;
for appointment or discharge of a receiver;
for relief by way of interpleader by a sheriff or High Court enforcement officer;
for transfer to a county court or for trial by master;
for time where time is running in the month of August;

(2) In any case of urgency any other type of application notice (that is, other than those for the purposes in (1) above), may, with the permission of a master be issued returnable before a master during the month of August.

# CPR Part 40 Judgments, Orders, Sale of Land etc.



## I JUDGMENTS AND ORDERS

### 40.1 Scope of this Section

This Section sets out rules about judgments and orders which apply except where any other of these Rules or a practice direction makes a different provision in relation to the judgment or order in question.

### 40.2 Standard Requirements

(1) Every judgment or order must state the name and judicial title of the person who made it, unless it is—
   (a) default judgment entered under rule 12.4(1) (entry of default judgment where judgment is entered by a court officer) or a default costs certificate obtained under rule 47.11;
   (b) judgment entered under rule 14.4, 14.5, 14.6, 14.7 and 14.9 (entry of judgment on admission where judgment is entered by a court officer);
   (c) a consent order under rule 40.6(2) (consent orders made by court officers);
   (d) an order made by a court officer under rule 70.5 (orders to enforce awards as if payable under a court order); or
   (e) an order made by a court officer under rule 71.2 (orders to obtain information from judgment debtors).
(2) Every judgment or order must—
   (a) bear the date on which it is given or made; and
   (b) be sealed(GL) by the court.
(3) Paragraph (4) applies where a party applies for permission to appeal against a judgment or order at the hearing at which the judgment or order was made.
(4) Where this paragraph applies, the judgment or order shall state—
   (a) whether or not the judgment or order is final;
   (b) whether an appeal lies from the judgment or order and, if so, to which appeal court;
   (c) whether the court gives permission to appeal; and

(d) if not, the appropriate appeal court to which any further application for permission may be made.

(Paragraph 4.3B of the practice direction supplementing Part 52 deals with the court's power to adjourn a hearing where a judgment or order is handed down and no application for permission to appeal is made at that hearing.)

## 40.3 Drawing Up and Filing of Judgments and Orders

(1) Except as is provided at paragraph (4) below or by any practice direction, every judgment or order will be drawn up by the court unless—
  (a) the court orders a party to draw it up;
  (b) a party, with the permission of the court, agrees to draw it up;
  (c) the court dispenses with the need to draw it up; or
  (d) it is a consent order under rule 40.6.

(2) The court may direct that—
  (a) a judgment or an order drawn up by a party must be checked by the court before it is sealed(GL); or
  (b) before a judgment or an order is drawn up by the court, the parties must file an agreed statement of its terms.

(3) Where a judgment or an order is to be drawn up by a party—
  (a) he must file it no later than 7 days after the date on which the court ordered or permitted him to draw it up so that it can be sealed(GL) by the court; and
  (b) if he fails to file it within that period, any other party may draw it up and file it.

(4) Except for orders made by the court of its own initiative and unless the court otherwise orders, every judgment or order made in claims proceeding in the Queen's Bench Division at the Royal Courts of Justice, other than in the Administrative Court, will be drawn up by the parties, and rule 40.3 is modified accordingly.

## 40.4 Service of Judgments and Orders

(1) Where a judgment or an order has been drawn up by a party and is to be served by the court—
  (a) the party who drew it up must file a copy to be retained at court and sufficient copies for service on him and on the other parties; and
  (b) once it has been sealed(GL), the court must serve a copy of it on each party to the proceedings.

(2) Unless the court directs otherwise, any order made otherwise than at trial must be served on—
  (a) the applicant and the respondent; and
  (b) any other person on whom the court orders it to be served.

(Rule 6.3 specifies who must serve judgments and orders.)

## 40.5 Power to Require Judgment or Order to be Served on a Party as Well as His Solicitor

Where the party on whom a judgment or order is to be served is acting by a solicitor, the court may order the judgment or order to be served on the party as well as on his solicitor.

## 40.6 Consent Judgments and Orders

(1) This rule applies where all the parties agree the terms in which a judgment should be given or an order should be made.

(2) A court officer may enter and seal(GL) an agreed judgment or order if—
  (a) the judgment or order is listed in paragraph (3);
  (b) none of the parties is a litigant in person; and
  (c) the approval of the court is not required by these Rules, a practice direction or any enactment before an agreed order can be made.

(3) The judgments and orders referred to in paragraph (2) are—
  (a) a judgment or order for—
    (i) the payment of an amount of money (including a judgment or order for damages or the value of goods to be decided by the court); or
    (ii) the delivery up of goods with or without the option of paying the value of the goods or the agreed value.
  (b) an order for—
    (i) the dismissal of any proceedings, wholly or in part;
    (ii) the stay(GL) of proceedings on agreed terms, disposing of the proceedings, whether those terms are recorded in a schedule to the order or elsewhere;
    (iii) the stay(GL) of enforcement of a judgment, either unconditionally or on condition that the money due under the judgment is paid by instalments specified in the order;
    (iv) the setting aside under Part 13 of a default judgment which has not been satisfied;
    (v) the payment out of money which has been paid into court;
    (vi) the discharge from liability of any party;
    (vii) the payment, assessment or waiver of costs, or such other provision for costs as may be agreed.

(4) Rule 40.3 (drawing up and filing of judgments and orders) applies to judgments and orders entered and sealed(GL) by a court officer under paragraph (2) as it applies to other judgments and orders.

(5) Where paragraph (2) does not apply, any party may apply for a judgment or order in the terms agreed.

(6) The court may deal with an application under paragraph (5) without a hearing.

(7) Where this rule applies—
  (a) the order which is agreed by the parties must be drawn up in the terms agreed;
  (b) it must be expressed as being 'By Consent';
  (c) it must be signed by the legal representative acting for each of the parties to whom the order relates or, where paragraph (5) applies, by the party if he is a litigant in person.

## 40.7 When Judgment or Order Takes Effect

(1) A judgment or order takes effect from the day when it is given or made, or such later date as the court may specify.

(2) This rule applies to all judgments and orders except those to which rule 40.10 (judgment against a State) applies.

## 40.8 Time From Which Interest Begins to Run

(1) Where interest is payable on a judgment pursuant to section 17 of the Judgments Act 1838 or section 74 of the County Courts Act 1984, the interest shall begin to run from the date that judgment is given unless—
  (a) a rule in another Part or a practice direction makes different provision; or
  (b) the court orders otherwise.

(2) The court may order that interest shall begin to run from a date before the date that judgment is given.

## 40.9 Who May Apply to Set Aside or Vary a Judgment or Order

A person who is not a party but who is directly affected by a judgment or order may apply to have the judgment or order set aside or varied.

## 40.10 Judgment Against a State in Default of Acknowledgment of Service

(1) Where the claimant obtains default judgment under Part 12 on a claim against a State where the defendant has failed to file an acknowledgment of service, the judgment does not take effect until 2 months after service on the State of—

(a) a copy of the judgment; and
(b) a copy of the evidence in support of the application for permission to enter default judgment (unless the evidence has already been served on the State in accordance with an order made under Part 12).

(2) In this rule, 'State' has the meaning given by section 14 of the State Immunity Act 1978.

## 40.11 Time for Complying With a Judgment or Order

A party must comply with a judgment or order for the payment of an amount of money (including costs) within 14 days of the date of the judgment or order, unless—
(a) the judgment or order specifies a different date for compliance (including specifying payment by instalments);
(b) any of these Rules specifies a different date for compliance; or
(c) the court has stayed the proceedings or judgment.

(Parts 12 and 14 specify different dates for complying with certain default judgments and judgments on admissions.)

## 40.12 Correction of Errors in Judgments and Orders

(1) The court may at any time correct an accidental slip or omission in a judgment or order.
(2) A party may apply for a correction without notice.

## 40.13 Cases Where Court Gives Judgment Both on Claim and Counterclaim

(1) This rule applies where the court gives judgment for specified amounts both for the claimant on his claim and against the claimant on a counterclaim.
(2) If there is a balance in favour of one of the parties, it may order the party whose judgment is for the lesser amount to pay the balance.
(3) In a case to which this rule applies, the court may make a separate order as to costs against each party.

## 40.14 Judgment in Favour of Certain Part Owners Relating to the Detention of Goods

(1) In this rule 'part owner' means one of two or more persons who have an interest in the same goods.
(2) Where—
  (a) a part owner makes a claim relating to the detention of the goods; and
  (b) the claim is not based on a right to possession,

  any judgment or order given or made in respect of the claim is to be for the payment of damages only, unless the claimant had the written authority of every other part owner of the goods to make the claim on his behalf as well as for himself.
(3) This rule applies notwithstanding anything in subsection (3) of section 3 of the Torts (Interference with Goods) Act 1977, but does not affect the remedies and jurisdiction mentioned in subsection (8) of that section.

# II SALE OF LAND ETC. AND CONVEYANCING COUNSEL

## 40.15 Scope of this Section

(1) This Section—
  (a) deals with the court's power to order the sale, mortgage, partition or exchange of land; and
  (b) contains provisions about conveyancing counsel.

(Section 131 of the Supreme Court Act 1981 provides for the appointment of the conveyancing counsel of the Supreme Court.)

(2) In this Section 'land' includes any interest in, or right over, land.

### 40.16 Power to Order Sale etc

In any proceedings relating to land, the court may order the land, or part of it, to be—
(a) sold;
(b) mortgaged;
(c) exchanged; or
(d) partitioned.

### 40.17 Power to Order Delivery Up of Possession etc

Where the court has made an order under rule 40.16, it may order any party to deliver up to the purchaser or any other person—
(a) possession of the land;
(b) receipt of rents or profits relating to it; or
(c) both.

### 40.18 Reference to Conveyancing Counsel

(1) The court may direct conveyancing counsel to investigate and prepare a report on the title of any land or to draft any document.
(2) The court may take the report on title into account when it decides the issue in question.

(Provisions dealing with the fees payable to conveyancing counsel are set out in the practice direction relating to Part 44 [PD 43–48, para. 8.8].)

### 40.19 Party May Object to Report

(1) Any party to the proceedings may object to the report on title prepared by conveyancing counsel.
(2) Where there is an objection, the issue will be referred to a judge for determination.

(Part 23 contains general rules about making an application.)

## III DECLARATORY JUDGMENTS

### 40.20 Declaratory judgments

The court may make binding declarations whether or not any other remedy is claimed.

# PD 40 Practice Direction — Accounts, Inquiries etc.

This practice direction supplements CPR Part 40.

## Accounts and Inquiries: General

1.1 Where the court orders any account to be taken or any inquiry to be made, it may, by the same or a subsequent order, give directions as to the manner in which the account is to be taken and verified or the inquiry is to be conducted.

1.2 In particular, the court may direct that in taking an account, the relevant books of account shall be evidence of their contents but that any party may take such objections to the contents as he may think fit.

1.3 Any party may apply to the court in accordance with CPR Part 23 for directions as to the taking of an account or the conduct of an inquiry or for the variation of directions already made.

1.4 Every direction for the taking of an account or the making of an inquiry shall be numbered in the order so that, as far as possible, each distinct account and inquiry is given its own separate number.

## Verifying the Account

2 Subject to any order to the contrary:

(1) the accounting party must make out his account and verify it by an affidavit or witness statement to which the account is exhibited,

(2) the accounting party must file the account with the court and at the same time notify the other parties that he has done so and of the filing of any affidavit or witness statement verifying or supporting the account.

## Objections

3.1 Any party who wishes to contend:

(a) that an accounting party has received more than the amount shown by the account to have been received, or

(b) that the accounting party should be treated as having received more than he has actually received, or

(c) that any item in the account is erroneous in respect of amount, or

(d) that in any other respect the account is inaccurate,

must, unless the court directs otherwise, give written notice to the accounting party of his objections.

3.2 The written notice referred to in paragraph 3.1 must, so far as the objecting party is able to do so:

(a) state the amount by which it is contended that the account understates the amount received by the accounting party,

(b) state the amount which it is contended that the accounting party should be treated as having received in addition to the amount he actually received,

(c) specify the respects in which it is contended that the account is inaccurate, and

(d) in each case, give the grounds on which the contention is made.

3.3 The contents of the written notice must, unless the notice contains a statement of truth, be verified by either an affidavit or a witness statement to which the notice is an exhibit. (Part 22 and PD 22 contain provisions about statements of truth.)

## Allowances

4 In taking any account all just allowances shall be made without any express direction to that effect.

## Management of Proceedings

5 The court may at any stage in the taking of an account or in the course of an inquiry direct a hearing in order to resolve an issue that has arisen and for that purpose may order that points of claim and points of defence be served and give any necessary directions.

## Delay

6.1 If it appears to the court that there is undue delay in the taking of any account or the progress of any inquiry the court may require the accounting party or the party with the conduct of the inquiry, as the case may be, to explain the delay and may then make such order for the management of the proceedings (including a stay) and for costs as the circumstances may require.

6.2 The directions the court may give under para. 6.1 include a direction that the Official Solicitor take over the conduct of the proceedings and directions providing for the payment of the Official Solicitor's costs.

## Distribution

7 Where some of the persons entitled to share in a fund are known but there is, or is likely to be, difficulty or delay in ascertaining other persons so entitled, the court may direct, or allow, immediate payment of their shares to the known persons without reserving any part of those shares to meet the subsequent costs of ascertaining the other persons.

## Guardian's Accounts

8 The accounts of a person appointed guardian of the property of a child (defined in CPR, r. 21.1(2)) must be verified and approved in such manner as the court may direct.

## Accounts and Inquiries to be Conducted Before Master or District Judge

9 Unless the court orders otherwise, an account or inquiry will be taken or made:
(1) by a master or district judge, if the proceedings are in the High Court; and
(2) by a district judge, if the proceedings are in a county court.

## Advertisements

10 The court may:
(1) direct any necessary advertisement; and
(2) fix the time within which the advertisement should require a reply.

## Examination of Claims

11.1 Where the court orders an account of debts or other liabilities to be taken, it may direct any party, within a specified time, to:
(1) examine the claims of persons claiming to be owed money out of the estate or fund in question.
(2) determine, so far as he is able, which of them are valid; and
(3) file written evidence:
(a) stating his findings and his reasons for them; and
(b) listing any other debts which are or may be owed out of the estate or fund.

11.2 Where the court orders an inquiry for next of kin or other unascertained claimants to an estate or fund, it may direct any party, within a specified time, to:
(1) examine the claims that are made;
(2) determine, so far as he is able, which of them are valid; and
(3) file written evidence stating his findings and his reasons for them.

11.3 If the personal representatives or trustees concerned are not the parties directed by the court to examine claims, the court may direct them to join with the party directed to examine claims in producing the written evidence required by this rule.

## Consideration of Claims by the Court

12 For the purpose of considering a claim the court may:
(1) direct it to be investigated in any manner;
(2) direct the person making the claim to give further details of it; and
(3) direct that person to:
(a) file written evidence; or
(b) attend court to give evidence,
to support his claim.

## Notice of Decision

13 If:
(1) the court has allowed or disallowed any claim or part of a claim; and
(2) the person making the claim was not present when the decision was made,
the court will serve on that person a notice informing him of its decision.

## Interest on Debts

14 (1) Where an account of the debts of a deceased person is directed by any judgment, unless the deceased's estate is insolvent or the court orders otherwise, interest shall be allowed:
(a) on any debt which carries interest, at the rate it carries, and
(b) on any other debt, from the date of the judgment, at the rate payable on judgment debts at that date.
(2) Where interest on a debt is allowed under para. (1)(b), it shall be paid out of any assets of the estate which remain after payment of:
(a) any costs of the proceedings directed to be paid out of the estate;
(b) all the debts which have been established; and
(c) the interest on such of those debts as by law carry interest.
(3) For the purpose of this rule:
(a) 'debt' includes funeral, testamentary or administration expenses; and
(b) in relation to any expenses incurred after the judgment, para. (1)(b) applies as if, instead of the date of the judgment, it referred to the date when the expenses became payable.

## Interest on Legacies

15 Where an account of legacies is directed by any judgment, then, subject to:
(a) any directions contained in the will or codicil in question; and
(b) any order made by the court,
interest shall be allowed on each legacy at the basic rate payable for the time being on funds in court or at such other rate as the court shall direct, beginning one year after the testator's death.

# PD 40B Practice Direction — Judgments and Orders

This practice direction supplements CPR Part 40.

## Drawing up and Filing of Judgments and Orders

1.1 Rule 40.2 sets out the standard requirements for judgments and orders and rule 40.3 deals with how judgments and orders should be drawn up.

1.2 A party who has been ordered or given permission to draw up an order must file it for sealing within seven days of being ordered or permitted to do so.[1] If he falls to do so, any other party may draw it up and file it.[2]

1.3 If the court directs that a judgment or order which is being drawn up by a party must be checked by the court before it is sealed, the party responsible must file the draft within seven days of the date the order was made with a request that the draft be checked before it is sealed.

1.4 If the court directs the parties to file an agreed statement of terms of an order which the court is to draw up,[3] the parties must do so no later than seven days from the date the order was made, unless the court directs otherwise.

1.5 If the court requires the terms of an order which is being drawn up by the court to be agreed by the parties the court may direct that a copy of the draft order is to be sent to all the parties:

(1) for their agreement to be endorsed on it and returned to the court before the order is sealed, or

(2) with notice of an appointment to attend before the court to agree the terms of the order.

## Preparation of Deeds or Documents Under an Order

2.1 Where a judgment or order directs any deed or document to be prepared, executed or signed, the order will state:

(1) the person who is to prepare the deed or document, and

(2) if the deed or document is to be approved, the person who is to approve it.

2.2 If the parties are unable to agree the form of the deed or document, any party may apply in accordance with Part 23 for the form of the deed or document to be settled.

2.3 In such case the judge may:

(1) settle the deed or document himself, or

(2) refer it to

(a) a master, or

(b) a district judge, or

(c) a conveyancing counsel of the Supreme Court to settle.

(See also PD 40D.)

## Consent Orders

3.1 Rule 40.6(3) sets out the types of consent judgments and orders which may be entered and sealed by a court officer. The court officer may do so in those cases provided that:

(1) none of the parties is a litigant in person, and

(2) the approval of the court is not required by the Rules, a practice direction or any enactment.[4]

---

[1] Rule 40.3(3)(a).

[2] Rule 40.3(3)(b).

[3] Rule 40.3(2)(b).

[4] Rule 40.6(2).

3.2 If a consent order filed for sealing appears to be unclear or incorrect the court officer may refer it to a judge for consideration.[5]

3.3 Where a consent judgment or order does not come within the provisions of rule 40.6(2):
(1) an application notice requesting a judgment or order in the agreed terms should be filed with the draft judgment or order to be entered or sealed, and
(2) the draft judgment or order must be drawn so that the judge's name and judicial title can be inserted.

3.4 A consent judgment or order must:
(1) be drawn up in the terms agreed,
(2) bear on it the words 'By Consent', and
(3) be signed by
(a) solicitors or counsel acting for each of the parties to the order, or
(b) where a party is a litigant in person, the litigant.[6]

3.5 Where the parties draw up a consent order in the form of a stay of proceedings on agreed terms, disposing of the proceedings,[7] and where the terms are recorded in a schedule to the order, any direction for:
(1) payment of money out of court, or
(2) payment and assessment of costs
should be contained in the body of the order and not in the schedule.

## Correction of Errors in Judgments and Orders

4.1 Where a judgment or order contains an accidental slip or omission a party may apply for it to be corrected.[8]

4.2 The application notice (which may be an informal document such as a letter) should describe the error and set out the correction required. An application may be dealt with without a hearing:
(1) where the applicant so requests,
(2) with the consent of the parties, or
(3) where the court does not consider that a hearing would be appropriate.

4.3 The judge may deal with the application without notice if the slip or omission is obvious or may direct notice of the application to be given to the other party or parties.

4.4 If the application is opposed it should, if practicable, be listed for hearing before the judge who gave the judgment or made the order.

4.5 The court has an inherent power to vary its own orders to make the meaning and intention of the court clear.

## Adjustment of Final Judgment Figure in Respect of Compensation Recovery Payments

5.1 In a final judgment[9] where some or all of the damages awarded:
(2) fall under the heads of damage set out in column 1 of sch. 2 to the Social Security (Recovery of Benefits) Act 1997 in respect of recoverable benefits received by the claimant set out in column 2 of that schedule and
(3) where the defendant has paid to the Secretary of State the recoverable benefits in accordance with the certificate of recoverable benefits,

---

[5] Rule 3.2.

[6] Rule 40.6(7).

[7] Rule 40.6(3)(b)(ii).

[8] Rule [40.12]. [The text issued by the Department for Constitutional Affairs mistakenly refers to r. 40.10.]

[9] In this paragraph final 'judgment' includes any order to pay a sum of money, a final award of damages and an assessment of damages.

there should be stated in a preamble to the judgment or order the amount awarded under each head of damage and the amount by which it has been reduced in accordance with s. 8 of and sch. 2 to the Social Security (Recovery of Benefits) Act 1997.

5.2 The judgment or order should then provide for entry of judgment and payment of the balance.

## Adjustment of Final Judgment Figure in Respect of an Interim Payment

6.1 In a final judgment[10] where an interim payment has previously been made which is less than the total amount awarded by the judge, the judgment or order should set out in a preamble:
(1) the total amount awarded by the judge, and
(2) the amount and date of the interim payment(s).

6.2 The total amount awarded by the judge should then be reduced by the total amount of any interim payments, and the judgment or order should then provide for entry of judgment and payment of the balance.

6.3 In a final judgment where an interim payment has previously been made which is more than the total amount awarded by the judge, the judgment or order should set out in a preamble:
(1) the total amount awarded by the judge, and
(2) the amount and date of the interim payment(s).

6.4 An order should then be made for repayment, reimbursement, variation or discharge under rule 25.8(2) and for interest on an overpayment under rule 25.8(5).

## Statement as to Service of a Claim Form

7.1 Where a party to proceedings which have gone to trial requires a statement to be included in the judgment as to where, and by what means the claim form issued in those proceedings was served, application should made to the trial judge when judgment is given.

7.2 If the judge so orders, the statement will be included in a preamble to the judgment as entered.

## Orders Requiring an Act to be Done

8.1 An order which requires an act to be done (other than a judgment or order for the payment of an amount of money) must specify the time within which the act should be done.

8.2 The consequences of failure to do an act within the time specified may be set out in the order. In this case the wording of the following examples suitably adapted must be used:
(1) Unless the [claimant] [defendant] serves his list of documents by 4.00 p.m. on Friday, January 22, 1999 his [claim] [defence] will be struck out and judgment entered for the [defendant] [claimant], or
(2) Unless the [claimant] [defendant] serves his list of documents within 14 days of service of this order his [claim] [defence] will be struck out and judgment entered for the [defendant] [claimant].

Example (1) should be used wherever possible.

## Non-compliance with a Judgment or Order

9.1 An order which restrains a party from doing an act or requires an act to be done should, if disobedience is to be dealt with by an application to bring contempt of court proceedings, have a penal notice endorsed on it as follows:

'If you the within-named [          ] do not comply with this order you may be held to be in contempt of court and imprisoned or fined, or [in the case of a company or corporation] your assets may be seized.'

[10] As in note 9 above.

9.2 The provisions of paragraph [9.1*] above also apply to an order which contains an undertaking by a party to do or not do an act, subject to paragraph 9.3 below.

9.3 The court has the power to decline to:

(1) accept an undertaking, and

(2) deal with disobedience in respect of an undertaking by contempt of court proceedings,

unless the party giving the undertaking has made a signed statement to the effect that he understands the terms of his undertaking and the consequences of failure to comply with it.

9.4 The statement may be endorsed on the [court copy of the] order containing the undertaking or may be filed in a separate document such as a letter.

## Foreign Currency

10 Where judgment is ordered to be entered in a foreign currency, the order should be in the following form:

'It is ordered that the defendant pay the claimant (state the sum in the foreign currency) or the sterling equivalent at the time of payment.'

## Costs

11.1 Attention is drawn to the costs practice direction and, in particular, to the court's power to make a summary assessment of costs and the provisions relating to interest in detailed assessment proceedings.

11.2 Attention is also drawn to r. 44.13(1) which provides that if an order makes no mention of costs, none are payable in respect of the proceedings to which it relates.

## Judgments Paid by Instalments

12 Where a judgment is to be paid by instalments, the judgment should set out:

(1) the total amount of the judgment,

(2) the amount of each instalment,

(3) the number of instalments and the date on which each is to be paid, and

(4) to whom the instalments should be paid.

## Order to Make an Order of The House of Lords an Order of The High Court

13.1 Application may be made in accordance with Part 23 for an order to make an order of the House of Lords an order of the High Court. The application should be made to the procedural judge of the Division, District Registry or court in which the proceedings are taking place and may be made without notice unless the court directs otherwise.

13.2 The application must be supported by the following evidence:

(1) details of the order which was the subject of the appeal to the House of Lords,

(2) details of the order of the House of Lords, with a copy annexed, and

(3) a copy annexed of the certificate of the Clerk of Parliaments of the assessment of the costs of the appeal to the House of Lords in the sum of £ . . .

13.3 The order to make an order of the House of Lords an order of the High Court should be in form PF 68.

## Examples of Forms of Trial Judgment

14.1 The following general forms may be used:

(1) judgment after trial before judge without jury—form No. 45,

(2) judgment after trial before judge with jury—form No. 46,

[* The text issued by the Departent for Constitutional Affairs mistakenly refers to para. 8.1.]

(3) judgment after trial before a Master or district judge—form No. 47,
(4) judgment after trial before a judge of the Technology and Construction court—form No. 47 but with any necessary modifications.

14.2 A trial judgment should, in addition to the matters set out in paragraphs 5, 6 and 7 above, have the following matters set out in a preamble:
(1) the questions put to a jury and their answers to those questions,
(2) the findings of a jury and whether unanimous or by a majority,
(3) any order made during the course of the trial concerning the use of evidence,
(4) any matters that were agreed between the parties prior to or during the course of the trial in respect of
  (a) liability,
  (b) contribution,
  (c) the amount of the damages or part of the damages, and
(5) the findings of the judge in respect of each head of damage in a personal injury case.

14.3 Form No. 49 should be used for a trial judgment against an estate.
The forms referred to in this practice direction are listed in PD 4.

14.4 On any application or appeal concerning:
(i) a committal order;
(ii) a refusal to grant habeas corpus; or
(iii) a secure accommodation order made under s. 25 of the Children Act 1998,
if the court ordering the release of the person concludes that his Convention rights have been infringed by the making of the order to which the application or appeal relates, the judgment or order should so state. If the court does not do so, that failure will not prevent another court from deciding the matter.

## For Information About

(1) Orders for provisional damages: see Part 41 and PD 41.
(2) Orders in respect of children and patients: see Part [21 and the Practice Direction which supplements it*].
(3) Orders containing directions for payment of money out of court: see Parts 36 and 37 and PD 36 and 37.
(4) Structured settlement orders: see the separate practice direction supplementing Part 40.
(5) Taking accounts and conducting inquiries under a judgment or order: see the separate practice direction supplementing Part 40.

[* The text issued by the Department for Constitutional Affairs mistakenly refers to Part 22.]

# PD 40D Practice Direction
# 1 Court's Powers in Relation to Land
# 2 Conveyancing Counsel of the Court

This practice direction supplements CPR Part 40.

## PART 1 COURT'S POWERS IN RELATION TO LAND

### Application to the Court Where Land Subject to an Encumbrance

1.1 In this paragraph 'encumbrance' has the same meaning as it has in s. 205(1) of the Law of Property Act 1925.

1.2 Where land subject to any encumbrance is sold or exchanged any party to the sale or exchange may apply to the court for a direction under s. 50 of the Law of Property Act 1925 (discharge of encumbrances by the court on sales or exchanges).

1.3 The directions a court may give on such an application include a direction for the payment into court of a sum of money that the court considers sufficient to meet:
(1) the value of the encumbrance; and
(2) further costs, expenses and interest that may become due on or in respect of the encumbrance.
(Section 50(1) of the Law of Property Act 1925 contains provisions relating to the calculation of these amounts.)

1.4 Where a payment into court has been made in accordance with a direction under s. 50(1) the court may:
(1) declare the land to be freed from the encumbrance; and
(2) make any order it considers appropriate for giving effect to an order made under r. 40.16 or relating to the money in court and the income thereof.

1.5 An application under s. 50 should:
(1) if made in existing proceedings, be made in accordance with CPR, Part 23;
(2) otherwise, be made by claim form under CPR, Part 8.

### Directions About the Sale etc.

2 Where the court has made an order under r. 40.16 it may give any other directions it considers appropriate for giving effect to the order. In particular the court may give directions:
(1) appointing a party or other person to conduct the sale;
(2) for obtaining evidence of the value of the land;
(3) as to the manner of sale;
(4) settling the particulars and conditions of the sale;
(5) fixing a minimum or reserve price;
(6) as to the fees and expenses to be allowed to an auctioneer or estate agent;
(7) for the purchase money to be paid
(a) into court;
(b) to trustees; or
(c) to any other person;
(8) for the result of a sale to be certified;
(9) under r. 40.18.

### Application for Permission to Bid

3.1 Where:
(1) the court has made an order under r. 40.16 for land to be sold; and

(2) a party wishes to bid for land,
he should apply to the court for permission to do so.

3.2 An application for permission to bid must be made before the sale takes place.

3.3 If the court gives permission to all the parties to bid, it may appoint an independent person to conduct the sale.

3.4 'Bid' in this paragraph includes submitting a tender or other offer to buy.

## Certifying Sale Result

4.1 If:
(1) the court has directed the purchase money to be paid into court; or
(2) the court has directed that the result of the sale be certified,
the result of the sale must be certified by the person having conduct of the sale.

4.2 Unless the court directs otherwise, the certificate must give details of:
(1) the amount of the purchase price;
(2) the amount of the fees and expenses payable to any auctioneer or estate agent;
(3) the amount of any other expenses of the sale;
(4) the net amount received in respect of the sale;
and must be verified by a statement of truth.
(Part 22 sets out requirements about statements of truth.)

4.3 The certificate must be filed:
(1) if the proceedings are being dealt with in the Royal Courts of Justice, in Chancery Chambers;
(2) if the proceedings are being dealt with anywhere else, in the court where the proceedings are being dealt with.

## Fees and Expenses of Auctioneers and Estate Agents

5.1 (1) Where the court has ordered the sale of land under r. 40.16, auctioneer's and estate agent's charges may, unless the court orders otherwise, include:
(a) commission;
(b) fees for valuation of the land;
(c) charges for advertising the land;
(2) The court's authorisation is required for charges relating to surveys.

5.2 If the total amount of the auctioneer's and estate agent's charges authorised under para. 5.1(1):
(1) does not exceed 2.5 per cent of the sale price; and
(2) does not exceed the rate of commission that that agent would normally charge on a sole agency basis,
the charges may, unless the court orders otherwise and subject to para. 5.3(3) and (4), be met by deduction of the amount of the charges from the proceeds of sale without the need for any further authorisation from the court.

5.3 If:
(1) a charge made by an auctioneer or estate agent (whether in respect of fees or expenses or both) is not authorised under para. 5.1(1);
(2) the total amount of the charges so authorised exceeds the limits set out in para. 5.2;
(3) the land is sold in lots or by valuation; or
(4) the sale is of investment property, business property or farm property,
an application must be made to the court for approval of the fees and expenses to be allowed.

5.4 An application under para. 5.3 may be made by any party or, if he is not a party, by the person having conduct of the sale, and may be made either before or after the sale has taken place.

## PART 2 CONVEYANCING COUNSEL OF THE COURT

### Reference to Conveyancing Counsel

6.1 When the court refers a matter under r. 40.18, the court may specify a particular conveyancing counsel.

6.2 If the court does not specify a particular conveyancing counsel, references will be distributed among conveyancing counsel in accordance with arrangements made by the Chief Chancery Master.

6.3 Notice of every reference under r. 40.18 must be given to the Chief Chancery Master.

6.4 The court will send a copy of the order, together with all other necessary documents, to conveyancing counsel.

6.5 A court order sent to conveyancing counsel under para. 6.4 will be sufficient authority for him to prepare his report or draft the document.

6.6 (1) An objection under r. 40.19 to a report on title prepared by conveyancing counsel must be made by application notice.

(2) The application notice must state:

(a) the matters the applicant objects to; and

(b) the reason for the objection.

# PD 40E Practice Direction — Reserved Judgments

This practice direction supplements Part 40.

## Scope and Interpretation

1.1 This practice direction applies to all judgments given in—
  (a) the Court of Appeal (Civil Division); and
  (b) the Queen's Bench Division and Chancery Division of the High Court at the Royal Courts of Justice,
  including judgments given by Masters, Registrars and Costs Judges.

1.2 In this practice direction—
  (a) 'relevant court office' means the office of the court in which judgment is to be given; and
  (b) 'working day' means any day on which the relevant court office is open.

## Availability of Reserved Judgments before Handing Down

2.1 Where judgment is to be reserved the judge (or presiding judge) may, at the conclusion of the hearing, invite the views of the parties' legal representatives as to the arrangements to be made for the handing down of the judgment.

2.2 Unless the court directs otherwise, the following provisions of this paragraph apply where the judge or presiding judge is satisfied that the judgment will attract no special degree of confidentiality or sensitivity.

2.3 The court will provide a copy of the draft judgment to the parties' legal representatives by 4 p.m. on the second working day before handing down, or at such other time as the court may direct.

2.4 A copy of the draft judgment may be shown, in confidence, to the parties provided that:
  (a) neither the judgment nor its substance is disclosed to any other person or used in the public domain; and
  (b) no action is taken (other than internally) in response to the judgment, before the judgment is handed down.

2.5 Any breach of the obligation of confidentiality prescribed by paragraph 2.4 may be treated as contempt of court.

2.6 The case will be listed for judgment, and the judgment handed down at the appropriate time.

## Attendance at Handing Down

3.1 Where any consequential orders are agreed, the parties' advocates need not attend on the handing down.

3.2 Where an advocate does attend the court may, if it considers such attendance was unnecessary, disallow the costs of the attendance.

3.3 If the parties do not indicate that they intend to attend, the judgment may be handed down by a single member of the court.

## Agreed Orders Following Judgment

4.1 Unless the parties or their legal representatives are told otherwise when the draft judgment is circulated, the parties must, in respect of any draft agreed order—
  (a) fax or e-mail a copy to the clerk to the judge or presiding judge (together with any proposed corrections or amendments to the draft judgment); and
  (b) file four copies (with completed backsheets) in the relevant court office, by 12 noon on the working day before handing down.

4.2 A copy of a draft order must bear the case reference, the date of handing down and the name of the judge or presiding judge.

### Corrections to the Draft Judgment

5. Unless the parties or their legal representatives are told otherwise when the draft judgment is circulated, any proposed corrections to the draft judgment should be sent to the clerk to the judge who prepared the draft with a copy to any other party.

(Paragraphs 15.12 to 15.21 of the practice direction supplementing Part 52 contain provision about the handing down of reserved judgments in appeals.)

# CPR Part 41 Damages



## I PROCEEDINGS TO WHICH SECTION 32A OF THE SUPREME COURT ACT 1981 OR SECTION 51 OF THE COUNTY COURTS ACT 1984 APPLIES

### 41.1 Application and Definitions

(1) This Section of this Part applies to proceedings to which SCA s. 32A or CCA s. 51 applies.
(2) In this Part—
  (a) 'SCA s. 32A' means section 32A of the Supreme Court Act 1981;[1]
  (b) 'CCA s. 51' means section 51 of the County Courts Act 1984;[2] and
  (c) 'award of provisional damages' means an award of damages for personal injuries under which
    (i) damages are assessed on the assumption referred to in SCA s. 32A or CCA s. 51 that the injured person will not develop the disease or suffer the deterioration; and
    (ii) the injured person is entitled to apply for further damages at a future date if he develops the disease or suffers the deterioration.

### 41.2 Order for an Award of Provisional Damages

(1) The court may make an order for an award of provisional damages if—
  (a) the particulars of claim include a claim for provisional damages; and
  (b) the court is satisfied that SCA s. 32A or CCA s. 51 applies.

(Rule 16.4(1)(d) sets out what must be included in the particulars of claim where the claimant is claiming provisional damages.)

(2) An order for an award of provisional damages—
  (a) must specify the disease or type of deterioration in respect of which an application may be made at a future date;
  (b) must specify the period within which such an application may be made; and
  (c) may be made in respect of more than one disease or type of deterioration and may, in respect of each disease or type of deterioration, specify a different period within which a subsequent application may be made.
(3) The claimant may make more than one application to extend the period specified under paragraph (2)(b) or (2)(c).

### 41.3 Application for Further Damages

(1) The claimant may not make an application for further damages after the end of the period specified under rule 41.2(2), or such period as extended by the court.

[1] 1981 c.54. Section 32A was inserted by section 6(1) of the Administration of Justice Act 1982 (c.53).
[2] 1984 c.28.

(2) Only one application for further damages may be made in respect of each disease or type of deterioration specified in the award of provisional damages.
(3) The claimant must give at least 28 days' written notice to the defendant of his intention to apply for further damages.
(4) If the claimant knows—
(a) that the defendant is insured in respect of the claim; and
(b) the identity of the defendant's insurers,
he must also give at least 28 days' written notice to the insurers.
(5) Within 21 days after the end of the 28 day notice period referred to in paragraphs (3) and (4), the claimant must apply for directions.
(6) [*Revoked*]

41.3A—(1) Where—
(a) a claim includes claims arising under–
(i) the Fatal Accidents Act 1976; and
(ii) the Law Reform (Miscellaneous Provisions) Act 1934; and
(b) a single sum of money is ordered or agreed to be paid in satisfaction of the claims, the court will apportion the money between the different claims.
(2) Where, in an action in which a claim under the Fatal Accidents Act 1976 is made by or on behalf of more than one person, a single sum of money is ordered or agreed to be paid in satisfaction of the claim, the court will apportion it between the persons entitled to it.
(3) Unless it has already been apportioned by the court, a jury or agreement between the parties, the court will apportion money under paragraphs (1) and (2)–
(a) when it gives directions under rule 21.11 (control of money received by a child or patient); or
(b) if rule 21.11 does not apply, on application by one of the parties in accordance with Part 23.

## II PERIODICAL PAYMENTS UNDER THE DAMAGES ACT 1996

### 41.4 Scope and Interpretation

(1) This Section of this Part contains rules about the exercise of the court's powers under section 2(1) of the 1996 Act to order that all or part of an award of damages in respect of personal injury is to take the form of periodical payments.
(2) In this Section—
(a) 'the 1996 Act' means the Damages Act 1996;[3]
(b) 'damages' means damages for future pecuniary loss; and
(c) 'periodical payments' means periodical payments under section 2(1) of the 1996 Act.[4]

### 41.5 Statement of Case

(1) In a claim for damages for personal injury, each party in its statement of case may state whether it considers periodical payments or a lump sum is the more appropriate form for all or part of an award of damages and where such statement is given must provide relevant particulars of the circumstances which are relied on.
(2) Where a statement under paragraph (1) is not given, the court may order a party to make such a statement.
(3) Where the court considers that a statement of case contains insufficient particulars

[3] 1996 c.48.
[4] Section 21 is substituted by section 100 of the Courts Act 2003 (c. 39).

under paragraph (1), the court may order a party to provide such further particulars as it considers appropriate.

### 41.6 Court's Indication to Parties

The court shall consider and indicate to the parties as soon as practicable whether periodical payments or a lump sum is likely to be the more appropriate form for all or part of an award of damages.

### 41.7 Factors to be Taken into Account

When considering—
(a) its indication as to whether periodical payments or a lump sum is likely to be the more appropriate form for all or part of an award of damages under rule 41.6; or
(b) whether to make an order under section 2(1)(a) of the 1996 Act,

the court shall have regard to all the circumstances of the case and in particular the form of award which best meets the claimant's needs, having regard to the factors set out in the practice direction.

### 41.8 The Award

(1) Where the court awards damages in the form of periodical payments, the order must specify—
   (a) the annual amount awarded, how each payment is to be made during the year and at what intervals;
   (b) the amount awarded for future—
      (i) loss of earnings and other income; and
      (ii) care and medical costs and other recurring or capital costs;
   (c) that the claimant's annual future pecuniary losses, as assessed by the court, are to be paid for the duration of the claimant's life, or such other period as the court orders; and
   (d) that the amount of the payments shall vary annually by reference to the retail prices index, unless the court orders otherwise under section 2(9) of the 1996 Act.

(2) Where the court orders that any part of the award shall continue after the claimant's death, for the benefit of the claimant's dependants, the order must also specify the relevant amount and duration of the payments and how each payment is to be made during the year and at what intervals.

(3) Where an amount awarded under paragraph (1)(b) is to increase or decrease on a certain date, the order must also specify—
   (a) the date on which the increase or decrease will take effect; and
   (b) the amount of the increase or decrease at current value.

(4) Where damages for substantial capital purchases are awarded under paragraph (1)(b)(ii), the order must also specify—
   (a) the amount of the payments at current value;
   (b) when the payments are to be made; and
   (c) that the amount of the payments shall be adjusted by reference to the retail prices index, unless the court orders otherwise under section 2(9) of the 1996 Act.

### 41.9 Continuity of Payment

(1) An order for periodical payments shall specify that the payments must be funded in accordance with section 2(4) of the 1996 Act, unless the court orders an alternative method of funding.

(2) Before ordering an alternative method of funding, the court must be satisfied that—
   (a) the continuity of payment under the order is reasonably secure; and
   (b) the criteria set out in the practice direction are met.

(3) An order under paragraph (2) must specify the alternative method of funding.

### 41.10 Assignment or Charge

Where the court under section 2(6)(a) of the 1996 Act is satisfied that special circumstances make an assignment or charge of periodical payments necessary, it shall, in deciding whether or not to approve the assignment or charge, also have regard to the factors set out in the practice direction.

# PD 41 Practice Direction — Provisional Damages

This practice direction supplements CPR Part 41.

## Claims for Provisional Damages

1.1 CPR Part 16 and PD 16 set out information which must be included in the particulars of claim if a claim for provisional damages is made

## Judgment for an Award of Provisional Damages

2.1 When giving judgment at trial the judge will:
  (1) specify the disease or type of deterioration, or diseases or types of deterioration, which
    (a) for the purpose of the award of immediate damages it has been assumed will not occur, and
    (b) will entitle the claimant to further damages if it or they do occur at a future date,
  (2) give an award of immediate damages,
  (3) specify the period or periods within which an application for further damages may be made in respect of each disease or type of deterioration, and
  (4) direct what documents are to be filed and preserved as the case file in support of any application for further damages.

2.2 The claimant may make an application or applications to extend the periods referred to in paragraph 2.1(3) above.[1]

2.3 A period specified under paragraph 2.1(3) may be expressed as being for the duration of the life of the claimant.

2.4 The documents to be preserved as the case file ('the case file documents') referred to in paragraph 2.1(4) will be set out in a schedule to the judgment as entered.

2.5 Causation of any further damages within the scope of the order shall be determined when any application for further damages is made.

2.6 A form for a provisional damages judgment is set out in the Annex to this practice direction.

## The Case File

3.1 The case file documents must be preserved until the expiry of the period or periods specified or of any extension of them.

3.2 The case file documents will normally include:
  (1) the judgment as entered,
  (2) the statements of case,
  (3) a transcript of the judge's oral judgment,
  (4) all medical reports relied on, and
  (5) a transcript of any parts of the claimant's own evidence which the judge considers necessary.

3.3 The associate/court clerk will:
  (1) ensure that the case file documents are provided by the parties where necessary and filed on the court file,
  (2) endorse the court file
    (a) to the effect that it contains the case file documents, and
    (b) with the period during which the case file documents must be preserved, and
  (3) preserve the case file documents in the court office where the proceedings took place.

[1] See CPR rule 41.2(3).

3.4 Any subsequent order:

(1) extending the period within which an application for further damages may be made, or

(2) of the Court of Appeal discharging or varying the provisions of the original judgment or of any subsequent order under sub-paragraph (1) above,

will become one of the case file documents and must be preserved accordingly and any variation of the period within which an application for further damages may be made should be endorsed on the court file containing the case file documents.

3.5 On an application to extend the periods referred to in paragraph 2.1(3) above a current medical report should be filed.

3.6 Legal representatives are reminded that it is their duty to preserve their own case file.

## Consent Orders

4.1 An application to give effect to a consent order for provisional damages should be made in accordance with CPR Part 23. If the claimant is a child or patient[2] the approval of the court must also be sought and the application for approval will normally be dealt with at a hearing.

4.2 The order should be in the form of a consent judgment and should contain;

(1) the matters set out in paragraph 2.1(1) to (3) above, and

(2) a direction as to the documents to be preserved as the case file documents, which will normally be

(a) the consent judgment,

(b) any statements of case,

(c) an agreed statement of facts, and

(d) any agreed medical report(s).

4.3 The claimant or his legal representative must lodge the case file documents in the court office where the proceedings are taking place for inclusion in the court file. The court file should be endorsed as in paragraph 3.3(2) above, and the case file documents preserved as in paragraph 13(3) above.

## Default Judgment

5.1 Where a defendant:

(1) fails to file an acknowledgment of service in accordance with CPR Part 10, and

(2) fails to file a defence in accordance with CPR Part 15,

within the time specified for doing so, the claimant may not, unless he abandons his claim for provisional damages, enter judgment in default but should make an application in accordance with CPR Part 23 for directions.

5.2 The Master or district judge will normally direct the following issues to be decided:

(1) whether the claim is an appropriate one for an award of provisional damages and if so, on what terms, and

(2) the amount of immediate damages.

5.3 If the judge makes an award of provisional damages, the provisions of paragraph 3 above apply.

## ANNEX

## Example of an Award of Provisional Damages After Trial

*Title of proceedings*

THIS CLAIM having been tried before [*title and name of judge*] without a jury at [the Royal Courts of Justice *or as may be*] and [*title and name of judge*] having ordered that judgment as set out below be entered for the claimant.

[2] See CPR Part 21 for the definitions of child and patient.

IT IS ORDERED:

(1) that the defendant pay the claimant by way of immediate damages the sum of £................ (being (i) £................ for special damages and £................ [agreed interest] [interest at the rate of ................. from ................. to .................] (ii) £................ for general damages and £................ [agreed interest] [interest at the rate of 2% from ................ to ................ ] and (iii) £................ for loss of future earnings and/or earning capacity) on the assumption that the claimant would not at a future date as a result of the act or omission giving rise to the claim develop the following disease/type of deterioration namely [*set out disease or type of deterioration*]

(2) that if the claimant at a further date does develop that [disease] [type of deterioration] he should be entitled to apply for further damages provided that the application is made on or before [*set out period*]

(3) that the documents set out in the schedule to this order be filed on the court file and preserved as the case file until the expiry of the period set out in paragraph (2) above or of any extension of that period which has been ordered

(4) (costs)

## Schedule

(*list documents referred to in paragraph (3)*)

# PD 41B Practice Direction — Periodical Payments Under the Damages Act 1996

This practice direction supplements CPR Part 41.

## Factors to be taken into Account (Rule 41.7)

1. The factors which the court shall have regard to under rule 41.7 include—
   (1) the scale of the annual payments taking into account any deduction for contributory negligence;
   (2) the form of award preferred by the claimant including—
      (a) the reasons for the claimant's preference; and
      (b) the nature of any financial advice received by the claimant when considering the form of award; and
   (3) the form of award preferred by the defendant including the reasons for the defendant's preference.

## The Award (Rule 41.8)

2.1 An order may be made under rule 41.8(2) where a dependant would have had a claim under section 1 of the Fatal Accidents Act 1976 if the claimant had died at the time of the accident.

2.2 Examples of circumstances which might lead the court to order an increase or decrease under rule 41.8(3) are where the court determines that—
   (1) the claimant's condition will change leading to an increase or reduction in his or her need to incur care, medical or other recurring or capital costs;
   (2) gratuitous carers will no longer continue to provide care;
   (3) the claimant's educational circumstances will change;
   (4) the claimant would have received a promotional increase in pay;
   (5) the claimant will cease earning.

## Continuity of Payment (Rule 41.9)

3. Before ordering an alternative method of funding under rule 41.9(1), the court must be satisfied that the following criteria are met—
   (1) that a method of funding provided for under section 2(4) of the 1996 Act is not possible or there are good reasons to justify an alternative method of funding;
   (2) that the proposed method of funding can be maintained for the duration of the award or for the proposed duration of the method of funding; and
   (3) that the proposed method of funding will meet the level of payment ordered by the court.

## Assignment or Charge (Rule 41.10)

4. The factors which the court shall have regard to under rule 41.10 include—
   (1) whether the capitalised value of the assignment or charge represents value for money;
   (2) whether the assignment or charge is in the claimant's best interests, taking into account whether these interests can be met in some other way; and
   (3) how the claimant will be financially supported following the assignment or charge.

## Variation

5. The Damages (Variation of Periodical Payments) Order 2004 sets out provisions which enable the court in certain circumstances to provide in an order for periodical payments that it may be varied.

## Settlement

6. Where the parties settle a claim to which rule 36.5 applies, any consent order, whether made under rule 40.6 or on an application under Part 23, must satisfy the requirements of rules 41.8 and 41.9.

## Settlement or Compromise on Behalf of Child or Patient

7. Where a claim for damages for personal injury is made by or on behalf of a child or patient and is settled prior to the start of proceedings or before trial, the provisions of the Practice Direction which supplements Part 21 must be complied with.

# CPR Part 42 Change of Solicitor



## 42.1 Solicitor Acting for a Party

Where the address for service of a party is the business address of his solicitor, the solicitor will be considered to be acting for that party until the provisions of this Part have been complied with.

(Part 6 contains provisions about the address for service.)

## 42.2 Change of Solicitor—Duty to Give Notice

(1) This rule applies where—
 (a) a party for whom a solicitor is acting wants to change his solicitor;
 (b) a party, after having conducted the claim in person, appoints a solicitor to act on his behalf (except where the solicitor is appointed only to act as an advocate for a hearing); or
 (c) a party, after having conducted the claim by a solicitor, intends to act in person.

(2) Where this rule applies, the party or his solicitor (where one is acting) must—
 (a) file notice of the change; and
 (b) serve notice of the change on every other party and, where paragraph (1)(a) or (c) applies, on the former solicitor.

(3) The notice must state the party's new address for service.

(4) The notice filed at court must state that notice has been served as required by paragraph (2)(b).

(5) Subject to paragraph (6), where a party has changed his solicitor or intends to act in person, the former solicitor will be considered to be the party's solicitor unless and until—
 (a) notice is filed and served in accordance with paragraph (2); or
 (b) the court makes an order under rule 42.3 and the order is served as required by paragraph (3) of that rule.

(6) Where the certificate of a LSC funded client or an assisted person is revoked or discharged—
 (a) the solicitor who acted for that person will cease to be the solicitor acting in the case as soon as his retainer is determined—
  (i) under regulation 4 of the Community Legal Service (Costs) Regulations 2000; or
  (ii) under regulation 83 of the Civil Legal Aid (General) Regulations 1989; and
 (b) if that person wishes to continue—
  (i) where he appoints a solicitor to act on his behalf, paragraph (2) will apply as if he had previously conducted the claim in person; and
  (ii) where he wants to act in person, he must give an address for service.

(Rule 6.5 deals with a party's address for service.)

('LSC funded client' and 'assisted person' are defined in rule 43.2.)

(7) 'Certificate' in paragraph (6) means—
 (a) in the case of a LSC funded client, a certificate issued under the Funding Code (approved under section 9 of the Access to Justice Act 1999), or
 (b) in the case of an assisted person, a certificate within the meaning of the Civil Legal Aid (General) Regulations 1989.

## 42.3 Order That a Solicitor Has Ceased to Act

(1) A solicitor may apply for an order declaring that he has ceased to be the solicitor acting for a party.
(2) Where an application is made under this rule—
   (a) notice of the application must be given to the party for whom the solicitor is acting, unless the court directs otherwise; and
   (b) the application must be supported by evidence.
(3) Where the court makes an order that a solicitor has ceased to act—
   (a) a copy of the order must be served on every party to the proceedings; and
   (b) if it is served by a party or the solicitor, the party or the solicitor (as the case may be) must file a certificate of service.

## 42.4 Removal of Solicitor Who Has Ceased to Act on Application of Another Party

(1) Where—
   (a) a solicitor who has acted for a party—
      (i) has died;
      (ii) has become bankrupt;
      (iii) has ceased to practise; or
      (iv) cannot be found; and
   (b) the party has not given notice of a change of solicitor or notice of intention to act in person as required by rule 42.2(2),

   any other party may apply for an order declaring that the solicitor has ceased to be the solicitor acting for the other party in the case.
(2) Where an application is made under this rule, notice of the application must be given to the party to whose solicitor the application relates unless the court directs otherwise.
(3) Were the court makes an order made under this rule—
   (a) a copy of the order must be served on every other party to the proceedings; and
   (b) where it is served by a party, that party must file a certificate of service.

# PD 42 Practice Direction — Change of Solicitor

This practice direction supplements CPR Part 42.

## Solicitor Acting for a Party

1.1 Rule 42.1 states that where the address for service of a party is the business address[1] of his solicitor, the solicitor will be considered to be acting for that party until the provisions of Part 42 have been complied with.

1.2 Subject to r. 42.2(6) (where the certificate of a LSC funded client or assisted person is revoked or discharged), where a party has changed his solicitor or intends to act in person, the former solicitor will be considered to be the party's solicitor unless or until:

(1) a notice of the change is
 (a) filed with the court,[2] and
 (b) served on every other party,[3] or

(2) the court makes an order under r. 42.3 and the order is served on every other party.[4]

The notice should not be filed until every other party has been served.

1.3 A solicitor appointed to represent a party only as an advocate at a hearing will not be considered to be acting for that party within the meaning of Part 42.

## Notice of Change of Solicitor

2.1 Rule 42.2(1) sets out the circumstances following which a notice of the change must be filed and served.

2.2 A notice of the change giving the last known address of the former assisted person must also be filed and served on every party where, under r. 42.2(6):

(1) the certificate of a LSC funded client or assisted person is revoked or discharged,

(2) the solicitor who acted for that person has ceased to act on determination of his retainer under reg. 83 of [the Civil Legal Aid (General) Regulations 1989], and

(3) the assisted person wishes either to act in person or appoint another solicitor to act on his behalf.

2.3 In addition, where a party or solicitor changes his address for service, a notice of that change should be filed and served on every party.

2.4 A party who, having conducted a claim by a solicitor, intends to act in person must give in his notice an address for service that is within the jurisdiction.[5]

2.5 Form N434 should be used to give notice of any change. The notice should be filed in the court office in which the claim is proceeding.

2.6 Where the claim is proceeding in the High Court the notice should be filed either in the appropriate district registry or if the claim is proceeding in the Royal Courts of Justice, as follows:

(1) a claim proceeding in the Queen's Bench Division—in the Action Department of the Central Office,

(2) a claim proceeding in the Chancery Division—in Chancery Chambers,

(3) a claim proceeding in the Administrative Court—in the Administrative Court Office,

(4) a claim proceeding in the Admiralty and Commercial Registry—in the Admiralty and Commercial Registry, and

---

[1] Rule 6.5 and PD 6 contain information about the business address.

[2] Rule 42.2(2)(a).

[3] Rule 42.2(2)(b).

[4] Rule 42.2(5).

[5] See r. 6.5(3).

(5) a claim proceeding in the Technology and Construction Court—in the Registry of the Technology and Construction Court.

2.7 Where the claim is the subject of an appeal to the Court of Appeal, the notice should also be filed in the Civil Appeals Office.
(PD 43–48 contains details of the information required to be included when the funding arrangements for the claim change.)

## Application for an Order That a Solicitor Has Ceased to Act

3.1 A solicitor may apply under r. 42.3 for an order declaring that he has ceased to be the solicitor acting for a party.

3.2 The application should be made in accordance with Part 23[6] and must be supported by evidence.[7] Unless the court directs otherwise the application notice must be served on the party.[8]

3.3 An order made under r. 42.3 must be served on every party and takes effect when it is served. Where the order is not served by the court, the person serving must file a certificate of service in form N215.

## Application by Another Party to Remove a Solicitor

4.1 Rule 42.4 sets out circumstances in which any other party may apply for an order declaring that a solicitor has ceased to be the solicitor acting for another party in the proceedings.

4.2 The application should be made in accordance with Part 23 and must be supported by evidence. Unless the court directs otherwise the application notice must be served on the party to whose solicitor the application relates.

4.3 An order made under r. 42.4 must be served on every other party to the proceedings. Where the order is not served by the court, the person serving must file a certificate of service in form N215.

## New Address for Service Where Order Made Under Rules 42.3 or 42.4

5.1 Where the court has made an order under r. 42.3 that a solicitor has ceased to act or under r. 42.4 declaring that a solicitor has ceased to be the solicitor for a party, the party for whom the solicitor was acting must give a new address for service to comply with r. 6.5(2).

(Rule 6.5(2) provides that a party must give an address for service within the jurisdiction.)
(Until such time as a new address for service is given r. 6.5(6) will apply.)

---

[6] See Part 23 and PD 23.
[7] See Part 32 and PD 32 for information about evidence.
[8] Rule 42.3(2).

# CPR Part 43 Scope of Cost Rules and Definitions



## 43.1 Scope of this Part

This Part contains definitions and interpretation of certain matters set out in the rules about costs contained in Parts 44 to 48.

(Part 44 contains general rules about costs; Part 45 deals with fixed costs; Part 46 deals with fast track trial costs; Part 47 deals with the detailed assessment of costs and related appeals and Part 48 deals with costs payable in special cases.)

## 43.2 Definitions and Application

(1) In Parts 44 to 48, unless the context otherwise requires—

(a) 'costs' includes fees, charges, disbursements, expenses, remuneration, reimbursement allowed to a litigant in person under rule 48.6, any additional liability incurred under a funding arrangement and any fee or reward charged by a lay representative for acting on behalf of a party in proceedings allocated to the small claims track;

(b) 'costs judge' means a taxing master of the Supreme Court;

(c) 'costs officer' means—

(i) a costs judge;

(ii) a district judge; and

(iii) an authorised court officer;

(d) 'authorised court officer' means any officer of—

(i) a county court;

(ii) a district registry;

(iii) the Principal Registry of the Family Division; or

(iv) the Supreme Court Costs Office, whom the Lord Chancellor has authorised to assess costs.

(e) 'fund' includes any estate or property held for the benefit of any person or class of person and any fund to which a trustee or personal representative is entitled in his capacity as such;

(f) 'receiving party' means a party entitled to be paid costs;

(g) 'paying party' means a party liable to pay costs;

(h) 'assisted person' means an assisted person within the statutory provisions relating to legal aid;

(i) 'LSC funding client' means an individual who receives services funded by the Legal Service Commission as part of the Community Legal Service within the meaning of Part I of the Access to Justice Act 1999;

(j) 'fixed costs' means the amounts which are to be allowed in respect of solicitors' charges in the circumstances set out in section I of Part 45.

(k) 'funding arrangement' means an arrangement where a person has—

(i) entered into a conditional fee agreement or a collective conditional fee agreement which provides for a success fee within the meaning of section 58(2) of the Courts and Legal Services Act 1990;

(ii) taken out an insurance policy to which section 29 of the Access to Justice Act 1999 (recovery of insurance premiums by way of costs) applies; or

(iii) made an agreement with a membership organisation to meet his legal costs;

(l) 'percentage increase' means the percentage by which the amount of a legal representative's fee can be increased in accordance with a conditional fee agreement which provides for a success fee;
(m) 'insurance premium' means a sum of money paid or payable for insurance against the risk of incurring a costs liability in the proceedings, taken out after the event that is the subject matter of the claim;
(n) 'membership organisation' means a body prescribed for the purposes of section 30 of the Access to Justice Act 1999 (recovery where body undertakes to meet costs liabilities); and
(o) 'additional liability' means the percentage increase, the insurance premium, or the additional amount in respect of provision made by a membership organisation, as the case may be.

(2) The costs to which Parts 44 to 48 apply include—
(a) the following costs where those costs may be assessed by the court—
(i) costs of proceedings before an arbitrator or umpire;
(ii) costs of proceedings before a tribunal or other statutory body; and
(iii) costs payable by a client to his solicitor; and
(b) costs which are payable by one party to another party under the terms of a contract, where the court makes an order for an assessment of those costs.

(3) Where advocacy or litigation services are provided to a client under a conditional fee agreement, costs are recoverable under Parts 44 to 48 notwithstanding that the client is liable to pay his legal representative's fees and expenses only to the extent that sums are recovered in respect of the proceedings, whether by way of costs or otherwise.

(4) In paragraph (3), the reference to a conditional fee agreement is to an agreement which satisfies all the conditions applicable to it by virtue of section 58 of the Courts and Legal Services Act 1990.

## 43.3 Meaning of Summary Assessment

'Summary assessment' means the procedure by which the court, when making an order about costs, orders payment of a sum of money instead of fixed costs or 'detailed assessment'.

## 43.4 Meaning of Detailed Assessment

'Detailed assessment' means the procedure by which the amount of costs is decided by a costs officer in accordance with Part 47.

**[PD 43–48 is positioned after CPR 48.]**

# CPR Part 44 General Rules About Costs



## 44.1 Scope of this Part

This Part contains general rules about costs and entitlement to costs.
(The definitions contained in Part 43 are relevant to this Part.)

## 44.2 Solicitor's Duty to Notify Client

Where—
(a) the court makes a costs order against a legally represented party; and
(b) the party is not present when the order is made,
the party's solicitor must notify his client in writing of the costs order no later than 7 days after the solicitor receives notice of the order.

## 44.3 Court's Discretion and Circumstances to be Taken Into Account When Exercising its Discretion as to Costs

(1) The court has discretion as to—
  (a) whether costs are payable by one party to another;
  (b) the amount of those costs; and
  (c) when they are to be paid.
(2) If the court decides to make an order about costs—
  (a) the general rule is that the unsuccessful party will be ordered to pay the costs of the successful party; but
  (b) the court may make a different order.
(3) The general rule does not apply to the following proceedings—
  (a) proceedings in the Court of Appeal on an application or appeal made in connection with proceedings in the Family Division; or
  (b) proceedings in the Court of Appeal from a judgment, direction, decision or order given or made in probate proceedings or family proceedings.
(4) In deciding what order (if any) to make about costs, the court must have regard to all the circumstances, including—
  (a) the conduct of all the parties;

(b) whether a party has succeeded on part of his case, even if he has not been wholly successful; and
(c) any payment into court or admissible offer to settle made by a party which is drawn to the court's attention, and which is not an offer to which costs consequences under Part 36 apply.

(5) The conduct of the parties includes—
(a) conduct before, as well as during, the proceedings and in particular the extent to which the parties followed any relevant pre-action protocol;
(b) whether it was reasonable for a party to raise, pursue or contest a particular allegation or issue;
(c) the manner in which a party has pursued or defended his case or a particular allegation or issue; and
(d) whether a claimant who has succeeded in his claim, in whole or in part, exaggerated his claim.

(6) The orders which the court may make under this rule include an order that a party must pay—
(a) a proportion of another party's costs;
(b) a stated amount in respect of another party's costs;
(c) costs from or until a certain date only;
(d) costs incurred before proceedings have begun;
(e) costs relating to particular steps taken in the proceedings;
(f) costs relating only to a distinct part of the proceedings; and
(g) interest on costs from or until a certain date, including a date before judgment.

(7) Where the court would otherwise consider making an order under paragraph (6)(f), it must instead, if practicable, make an order under paragraph (6)(a) or (c).

(8) Where the court has ordered a party to pay costs, it may order an amount to be paid on account before the costs are assessed.

(9) Where a party entitled to costs is also liable to pay costs the court may assess the costs which that party is liable to pay and either—
(a) set off the amount assessed against the amount the party is entitled to be paid and direct him to pay any balance; or
(b) delay the issue of a certificate for the costs to which the party is entitled until he has paid the amount which he is liable to pay.

## 44.3A Costs Orders Relating to Funding Arrangements

(1) The court will not access any additional liability until the conclusion of the proceedings, or the part of the proceedings, to which the funding arrangement relates.
('Funding arrangement' and 'additional liability' are defined in rule 43.2.)

(2) At the conclusion of the proceedings, or the part of the proceedings, to which the funding arrangement relates the court may—
(a) make a summary assessment of all the costs, including any additional liability;
(b) make an order for detailed assessment of the additional liability but make a summary assessment of the other costs; or
(c) make an order for detailed assessment of all the costs.

(Part 47 sets out the procedure for the detailed assessment of costs.)

## 44.3B Limits on Recovery Under Funding Arrangements

(1) A party may not recover as an additional liability—
(a) any proportion of the percentage increase relating to the cost to the legal representative of the postponement of the payment of his fees and expenses;
(b) any provision made by a membership organisation which exceeds the likely cost to that party of the premium of an insurance policy against the risk of incurring a liability to pay the costs of other parties to the proceedings;

(c) any additional liability for any period in the proceedings during which he failed to provide information about a funding arrangement in accordance with a rule, practice direction or court order;
(d) any percentage increase where a party has failed to comply with—
(i) a requirement in the costs practice direction; or
(ii) a court order,
to disclose in any assessment proceedings the reasons for setting the percentage increase at the level stated in the conditional fee agreement.

(2) This rule does not apply in an assessment under rule 48.9 (assessment of a solicitor's bill to his client).

(Rule 3.9 sets out the circumstances the court will consider on an application for relief from a sanction for failure to comply with any rule, practice direction or court order.)

## 44.4 Basis of Assessment

(1) Where the court is to assess the amount of costs (whether by summary or detailed assessment) it will assess those costs—
(a) on the standard basis; or
(b) on the indemnity basis,
but the court will not in either case allow costs which have been unreasonably incurred or are unreasonable in amount.

(Rule 48.3 sets out how the court decides the amount of costs payable under a contract.)

(2) Where the amount of costs is to be assessed on the standard basis, the court will—
(a) only allow costs which are proportionate to the matters in issue; and
(b) resolve any doubt which it may have as to whether costs were reasonably incurred or reasonable and proportionate in amount in favour of the paying party.

(Factors which the court may take into account are set out in rule 44.5.)

(3) Where the amount of costs is to be assessed on the indemnity basis, the court will resolve any doubt which it may have as to whether costs were reasonably incurred or were reasonable in amount in favour of the receiving party.

(4) Where—
(a) the court makes an order about costs without indicating the basis on which the costs are to be assessed; or
(b) the court makes an order for costs to be assessed on a basis other than the standard basis or the indemnity basis,
the costs will be assessed on the standard basis.

(5) [*Revoked*]

(6) Where the amount of a solicitor's remuneration in respect of non-contentious business is regulated by any general orders made under the Solicitors Act 1974, the amount of the costs to be allowed in respect of any such business which falls to be assessed by the court will be decided in accordance with those general orders rather than this rule and rule 44.5.

## 44.5 Factors to be Taken Into Account in Deciding the Amount of Costs

(1) The court is to have regard to all the circumstances in deciding whether costs were—
(a) if it is assessing costs on the standard basis—
(i) proportionately and reasonably incurred; or
(ii) were proportionate and reasonable in amount, or
(b) if it is assessing costs on the indemnity basis—
(i) unreasonably incurred; or
(ii) unreasonable in amount.

(2) In particular the court must give effect to any orders which have already been made.

(3) The court must also have regard to—
(a) the conduct of all the parties, including in particular—
(i) conduct before, as well as during, the proceedings; and

(ii) the efforts made, if any, before and during the proceedings in order to try to resolve the dispute;
(b) the amount or value of any money or property involved;
(c) the importance of the matter to all the parties;
(d) the particular complexity of the matter or the difficulty or novelty of the questions raised;
(e) the skill, effort, specialised knowledge and responsibility involved;
(f) the time spent on the case; and
(g) the place where and the circumstances in which work or any part of it was done.

(Rule 35.4(4) gives the court power to limit the amount that a party may recover with regard to the fees and expenses of an expert.)

## 44.6 Fixed Costs

A party may recover the fixed costs specified in Part 45 in accordance with that Part.

## 44.7 Procedure for Assessing Costs

Where the court orders a party to pay costs to another party (other than fixed costs) it may either—
(a) make a summary assessment of the costs; or
(b) order detailed assessment of the costs by a costs officer,

unless any rule, practice direction or other enactment provides otherwise.

(The costs practice direction [PD 43–48] sets out the factors which will affect the court's decision under this rule.)

## 44.8 Time for Complying with an Order for Costs

A party must comply with an order for the payment of costs within 14 days of—
(a) the date of the judgment or order if it states the amount of those costs;
(b) if the amount of those costs (or part of them) is decided later in accordance with Part 47, the date of the certificate which states the amount; or
(c) in either case, such later date as the court may specify.

(Part 47 sets out the procedure for detailed assessment of costs.)

## 44.9 Costs on the Small Claims Track and Fast Track

(1) Part 27 (small claims) and Part 46 (fast track trial costs) contain special rules about—
(a) liability for costs;
(b) the amount of costs which the court may award; and
(c) the procedure for assessing costs.

(2) Once a claim is allocated to a particular track, those special rules shall apply to the period before, as well as after, allocation except where the court or a practice direction provides otherwise.

## 44.10 Limitation on Amount Court May Allow Where a Claim Allocated to the Fast Track Settles Before Trial

(1) Where the court—
(a) assesses costs in relation to a claim which—
(i) has been allocated to the fast track; and
(ii) settles before the start of the trial; and
(b) is considering the amount of costs to be allowed in respect of a party's advocate for preparing for the trial,

it may not allow, in respect of those advocate's costs, an amount that exceeds the amount of fast track trial costs which would have been payable in relation to the claim had the trial taken place.

(2) When deciding the amount to be allowed in respect of the advocate's costs, the court shall have regard to—

(a) when the claim was settled; and
(b) when the court was notified that the claim had settled.

(3) In this rule, 'advocate' and 'fast track trial costs' have the meanings given to them by Part 46.

(Part 46 sets out the amount of fast track trial costs which may be awarded.)

## 44.11 Costs Following Allocation and Reallocation

(1) Any costs orders made before a claim is allocated will not be affected by allocation.

(2) Where—
(a) a claim is allocated to a track; and
(b) the court subsequently reallocates that claim to a different track,
then unless the court orders otherwise, any special rules about costs applying—
(i) to the first track, will apply to the claim up to the date of reallocation; and
(ii) to the second track, will apply from the date of reallocation.

(Part 26 deals with the allocation and reallocation of claims between tracks.)

## 44.12 Cases Where Costs Orders Deemed to Have Been Made

(1) Where a right to costs arises under—
(a) rule 3.7 (defendant's right to costs where claim struck out for non-payment of fees);
(b) rule 36.10(1) or (2) (claimant's entitlement to costs where a Part 36 offer is accepted);
(c) *Omitted*
(d) rule 38.6 (defendant's right to costs where claimant discontinues),
a costs order will be deemed to have been made on the standard basis.

(2) Interest payable pursuant to section 17 of the Judgments Act 1838 or section 74 of the County Courts Act 1984 on the costs deemed to have been ordered under paragraph (1) shall begin to run from the date on which the event which gave rise to the entitlement to costs occurred.

## 44.12A Costs-only Proceedings

(1) This rule sets out a procedure which may be followed where—
(a) the parties to a dispute have reached an agreement on all issues (including which party is to pay the costs) which is made or confirmed in writing; but
(b) they have failed to agree the amount of those costs; and
(c) no proceedings have been started.

(2) Either party to the agreement may start proceedings under this rule by issuing a claim form in accordance with Part 8.

(3) The claim form must contain or be accompanied by the agreement or confirmation.

(4) Except as provided in paragraph (4A), in proceedings to which this rule applies the court—
(a) may—
(i) make an order for costs to be determined by detailed assessment; or
(ii) dismiss the claim; and
(b) must dismiss the claim if it is opposed.

(4A) In proceedings to which Section II of Part 45 applies, the court shall assess the costs in the manner set out in that Section.

(5) Rule 48.3 (amount of costs where costs are payable pursuant to a contract) does not apply to claims started under the procedure in this rule.

(Rule 7.2 provides that proceedings are started when the court issues a claim form at the request of the claimant.)

(Rule 8.1(6) provides that a practice direction may modify the Part 8 procedure.)

## 44.13 Special Situations

(1) Where the court makes an order which does not mention costs—

(a) subject to paragraphs (1A) and (1B), the general rule is that no party is entitled to costs in relation to that order; but
(b) this does not affect any entitlement of a party to recover costs out of a fund held by him as trustee or personal representative, or pursuant to any lease, mortgage or other security.

(1A) Where the court makes—
(a) an order granting permission to appeal;
(b) an order granting permission to apply for judicial review; or
(c) any other order or direction sought by a party on an application without notice,
and its order does not mention costs, it will be deemed to include an order for an applicant's costs in the case.

(1B) Any party affected by a deemed order for costs under paragraph (1A) may apply at any time to vary the order.

(2) The court hearing an appeal may, unless it dismisses the appeal, make orders about the costs of the proceedings giving rise to the appeal as well as the costs of the appeal.

(3) Where proceedings are transferred from one court to another, the court to which they are transferred may deal with all the costs, including the costs before the transfer.

(4) Paragraph (3) is subject to any order of the court which ordered the transfer.

## 44.14 Court's Powers in Relation to Misconduct

(1) The court may make an order under this rule where—
(a) a party or his legal representative in connection with a summary or detailed assessment, fails to comply with a rule, practice direction or court order; or
(b) it appears to the court that the conduct of a party or his legal representative, before or during the proceedings which gave rise to the assessment proceedings, was unreasonable or improper.

(2) Where paragraph (1) applies, the court may—
(a) allow all or part of the costs which are being assessed; or
(b) order the party at fault or his legal representative to pay costs which he has caused any other party to incur.

(3) Where—
(a) the court makes an order under paragraph (2) against a legally represented party; and
(b) the party is not present when the order is made,
the party's solicitor must notify his client in writing of the order no later than 7 days after the solicitor receives notice of the order.

## 44.15 Providing Information About Funding Arrangements

(1) A party who seeks to recover an additional liability must provide information about the funding arrangement to the court and to other parties as required by a rule, practice direction or court order.

(2) Where the funding arrangement has changed, and the information a party has previously provided in accordance with paragraph (1) is no longer accurate, that party must file notice of the change and serve it on all other parties within 7 days.

(3) Where paragraph (2) applies, and a party has already filed—
(a) an allocation questionnaire; or
(b) a pre-trial checklist (listing questionnaire),
he must file and serve a new estimate of costs with the notice.

(The costs practice direction [PD 43–48] sets out—
- the information to be provided when a party issues or responds to a claim form, files an allocation questionnaire, a pre-trial checklist, and a claim for costs;
- the meaning of estimate of costs and the information required in it)

(Rule 44.3B sets out situations where a party will not recover a sum representing any additional liability.)

### 44.16 Adjournment Where Legal Representative Seeks to Challenge Disallowance of any Amount of Percentage Increase

(1) This rule applies where the Conditional Fee Agreements Regulations 2000 or the Collective Conditional Fee Agreements Regulations 2000 continue to apply to an agreement which provides for a success fee.

(2) Where—

(a) the court disallows any amount of a legal representative's percentage increase in summary or detailed assessment proceedings; and

(b) the legal representative applies for an order that the disallowed amount should continue to be payable by his client,

the court may adjourn the hearing to allow the client to be—

(i) notified of the order sought; and

(ii) separately represented.

(Regulation 3(2)(b) of the Conditional Fee Agreements Regulations 2000, which applies to Conditional Fee Agreements entered into before 1 November 2005, provides that a conditional fee agreement which provides for a success fee must state that any amount of a percentage increase disallowed on assessment ceases to be payable unless the court is satisfied that it should continue to be so payable. Regulation 5(2)(b) of the Collective Conditional Fee Agreements Regulations 2000, which applies to Collective Conditional Fee Agreements entered into before 1 November 2005, makes similar provision in relation to collective conditional fee agreements.)

### 44.17 Application of Costs Rules

This Part and Part 45 (fixed costs), Part 46 (fast track trial costs), Part 47 (procedure for detailed assessment of costs and default provisions) and Part 48 (special cases), do not apply to the assessment of costs in proceedings to the extent that—

(a) section 11 of the Access to Justice Act 1999, and provisions made under that Act, or

(b) regulations made under the Legal Aid Act 1988,

make different provision.

(The costs practice direction [PD 43–48] sets out the procedure to be followed where a party was wholly or partially funded by the Legal Services Commission.)

**[PD 43–48 is positioned after CPR 48.]**

# CPR Part 45 Fixed Costs



## I FIXED COSTS

### 45.1 Scope of this Section

(1) This Section sets out the amounts which, unless the court orders otherwise, are to be allowed in respect of solicitors' charges in the cases to which this Section applies.
(2) This Section applies where—
  (a) the only claim is a claim for a specified sum of money where the value of the claim exceeds £25 and—
    (i) judgment in default is obtained under rule 12.4(1);
    (ii) judgment on admission is obtained under rule 14.4(3);
    (iii) judgment on admission on part of the claim is obtained under rule 14.5(6);
    (iv) summary judgment is given under Part 24;
    (v) the court has made an order to strike out(GL) a defence under rule 3.4(2)(a) as disclosing no reasonable grounds for defending the claim; or
    (vi) rule 45.3 applies;
  (b) the only claim is a claim where the court gave a fixed date for the hearing when it issued the claim and judgment is given for the delivery of goods, and the value of the claim exceeds £25;
  (c) the claim is for the recovery of land, including a possession claim under Part 55, whether or not the claim includes a claim for a sum of money and the defendant gives up possession, pays the amount claimed, if any, and the fixed commencement costs stated in the claim form;
  (d) the claim is for the recovery of land, including a possession claim under Part 55,

where one of the grounds for possession is arrears of rent, for which the court gave a fixed date for the hearing when it issued the claim and judgment is given for the possession of land (whether or not the order for possession is suspended on terms) and the defendant—
(i) has neither delivered a defence, or counterclaim, nor otherwise denied liability; or
(ii) has delivered a defence which is limited to specifying his proposals for the payment of arrears of rent;
(e) the claim is a possession claim under Section II of Part 55 (accelerated possession claims of land let on an assured shorthold tenancy) and a possession order is made where the defendant has neither delivered a defence, or counterclaim, nor otherwise denied liability;
(f) the claim is a demotion claim under Section III of Part 65 or a demotion claim is made in the same claim form in which a claim for possession is made under Part 55 and that demotion claim is successful; or
(g) a judgment creditor has taken steps under Parts 70 to 73 to enforce a judgment or order.

(The practice direction supplementing rule 7.9 sets out the types of case where a court will give a fixed date for a hearing when it issues a claim.)
(3) Any appropriate court fee will be allowed in addition to the costs set out in this Section.
(4) The claim form may include a claim for fixed commencement costs.

## 45.2 Amount of Fixed Commencement Costs in a Claim for the Recovery of Money or Goods

(1) The amount of fixed commencement costs in a claim to which rule 45.1(2)(a) or (b) applies—
(a) shall be calculated by reference to Table 1; and

**Table 1** Fixed costs on commencement of a claim for the recovery of money or goods

| Relevant band | Where the claim form is served by the court or by any method other than personal service by the claimant | Where— • the claim form is served personally by the claimant; and • there is only one defendant | Where there is more than one defendant, for each additional defendant personally served at separate addresses by the claimant |
|---|---|---|---|
| Where— • the value of the claim exceeds £25 but does not exceed £500 | £50 | £60 | £15 |
| Where— • the value of the claim exceeds £500 but does not exceed £1,000 | £70 | £80 | £15 |
| Where— • the value of the claim exceeds £1,000 but does not exceed £5,000; or | £80 | £90 | £15 |
| • the only claim is for delivery of goods and no value is specified or stated on the claim form | £80 | £90 | £15 |
| Where— • the value of the claim exceeds £5,000 | £100 | £110 | £15 |

(b) the amount claimed, or the value of the goods claimed if specified, in the claim form is to be used for determining the band in Table 1 that applies to the claim.

(2) The amounts shown in Table 4 are to be allowed in addition, if applicable.

### 45.2A Amount of Fixed Commencement Costs in a Claim for the Recovery of Land or a Demotion Claim

(1) The amount of fixed commencement costs in a claim to which rule 45.1(2)(c), (d) or (f) applies shall be calculated by reference to Table 2.

(2) The amounts shown in Table 4 are to be allowed in addition, if applicable.

**Table 2** Fixed costs on commencement of a claim for the recovery of land or a demotion claim

| Where the claim form is served by the court or by any method other than personal service by the claimant | Where<br>• the claim form is served personally by the claimant; and<br>• there is only one defendant | Where there is more than one defendant, for each additional defendant personally served at separate addresses by the claimant |
|---|---|---|
| £69.50 | £77.00 | £15.00 |

### 45.3 When Defendant Only Liable for Fixed Commencement Costs

(1) Where—

(a) the only claim is for a specified sum of money; and

(b) the defendant pays the money claimed within 14 days after service of particulars of claim on him, together with the fixed commencement costs stated in the claim form,

the defendant is not liable for any further costs unless the court orders otherwise.

(2) *Omitted*

### 45.4 Costs on Entry of Judgment in a Claim for the Recovery of Money or Goods

Where—

(a) the claimant has claimed fixed commencement costs under rule 45.2; and

(b) judgment is entered in a claim to which rule 45.1(2)(a) or (b) applies in the circumstances specified in Table 3, the amount to be included in the judgment for the claimant's solicitor's charges is the total of—

(i) the fixed commencement costs; and

(ii) the relevant amount shown in Table 3.

**Table 3** Fixed Costs on Entry of Judgment in a claim for the recovery of money or goods

| | **Where the amount of the judgment exceeds £25 but does not exceed £5,000** | **Where the amount of the judgment exceeds £5,000** |
|---|---|---|
| Where judgment in default of an acknowledgment of service is entered under rule 12.4(1) (entry of judgment by request on claim for money only) | £22 | £30 |
| Where judgment in default of a defence is entered under rule 12.4(1) (entry of judgment by request on claim for money only) | £25 | £35 |
| Where judgment is entered under rule 14.4 (judgment on admission), or rule 14.5 (judgment on admission of part of claim) and claimant accepts the defendant's proposal as to the manner of payment | £40 | £55 |
| Where judgment is entered under rule 14.4 (judgment on admission), or rule 14.5 (judgment on admission of part of claim) and court decides the date or time of payment | £55 | £70 |
| Where summary judgment is given under Part 24 or the court strikes out a defence under rule 3.4(2)(a), in either case, on application by a party | £175 | £210 |
| Where judgment is given on a claim for delivery of goods under a regulated agreement within the meaning of the Consumer Credit Act 1974 and no other entry in this table applies | £60 | £85 |

## 45.4A Costs on Entry of Judgment in a Claim for the Recovery of Land or a Demotion Claim

(1) Where—
   (a) the claimant has claimed fixed commencement costs under rule 45.2A; and
   (b) judgment is entered in a claim to which rule 45.1(2)(d) or (f) applies, the amount to be included in the judgment for the claimant's solicitor's charges is the total of—
      (i) the fixed commencement costs; and
      (ii) the sum of £57.25.

(2) Where an order for possession is made in a claim to which rule 45.1(2)(e) applies, the amount allowed for the claimant's solicitor's charges for preparing and filing—
   (a) the claim form;
   (b) the documents that accompany the claim form; and
   (c) the request for possession,
   is £79.50.

## 45.5 Miscellaneous Fixed Costs

Table 4 Miscellaneous Fixed Costs

| | |
|---|---|
| For service by a party of any document required to be served personally including preparing and copying a certificate of service for each individual served | £15.00 |
| Where service by an alternative method is permitted by an order under rule 6.8 for each individual served | £53.25 |
| Where a document is served out of the jurisdiction— | |
| (a) in Scotland, Northern Ireland, the Isle of Man or the Channel Islands; | £68.25 |
| (b) in any other place | £77.00 |

## 45.6 Fixed Enforcement Costs

Table 5 shows the amount to be allowed in respect of solicitors' costs in the circumstances mentioned. The amounts shown in Table 4 are to be allowed in addition, if applicable.

Table 5 Fixed Enforcement Costs

| | |
|---|---|
| For an application under rule 70.5(4) that an award may be enforced as if payable under a court order, where the amount outstanding under the award: | |
| exceeds £25 but does not exceed £250 | £30.75 |
| exceeds £250 but does not exceed £600 | £41.00 |
| exceeds £600 but does not exceed £2,000 | £69.50 |
| exceeds £2,000 | £75.50 |
| On attendance to question a judgment debtor (or officer of a company or other corporation) who has been ordered to attend court under rule 71.2 where the questioning takes place before a court officer, including attendance by a responsible representative of the solicitor | for each half hour or part, £15.00 (When the questioning takes place before a judge, he may summarily assess any costs allowed.) |
| On the making of a final third party debt order under rule 72.8(6)(a) or an order for the payment to the judgment creditor of money in court under rule 72.10(1)(b): | |
| if the amount recovered is less than £150 | one-half of the amount recovered |
| otherwise | £98.50 |
| On the making of a final charging order under rule 73.8(2)(a): | £110.00 The court may also allow reasonable disbursements in respect of search fees and the registration of the order. |
| Where a certificate is issued and registered under Schedule 6 to the Civil Jurisdiction and Judgments Act 1982, the costs of registration | £39.00 |
| Where permission is given under RSC Order 45, rule 3 to enforce a judgment or order giving possession of land and costs are allowed on the judgment or order, the amount to be added to the judgment or order for costs— | |
| (a) basic costs | £42.50 |
| (b) where notice of the proceedings is to be to more than one person, for each additional person | £2.75 |
| Where a writ of execution as defined in the RSC Order 46, rule 1, is issued against any party | £51.75 |

| | |
|---|---|
| Where a request is filed for the issue of a warrant of execution under CCR Order 26, rule 1, for a sum exceeding £25 | £2.25 |
| Where an application for an attachment of earnings order is made and costs are allowed under CCR Order 27, rule 9 or CCR Order 28, rule 10, for each attendance on the hearing of the application | £8.50 |

## II ROAD TRAFFIC ACCIDENTS — FIXED RECOVERABLE COSTS

### 45.7 Scope and Interpretation

(1) This Section sets out the costs which are to be allowed in—
 (a) costs-only proceedings under the procedure set out in rule 44.12A; or
 (b) proceedings for approval of a settlement or compromise under rule 21.10(2),
 in cases to which this Section applies.
(2) This Section applies where—
 (a) the dispute arises from a road traffic accident;
 (b) the agreed damages include damages in respect of personal injury, damage to property, or both;
 (c) the total value of the agreed damages does not exceed £10,000; and
 (d) if a claim had been issued for the amount of the agreed damages, the small claims track would not have been the normal track for that claim.
(3) This Section does not apply where the claimant is a litigant in person.
(Rule 2.3 defines 'personal injuries' as including any disease and any impairment of a person's physical or mental condition.)
(Rule 26.6 provides for when the small claims track is the normal track.)
(4) In this Section—
 (a) 'road traffic accident' means an accident resulting in bodily injury to any person or damage to property caused by, or arising out of, the use of a motor vehicle on a road or other public place in England and Wales;
 (b) 'motor vehicle' means a mechanically propelled vehicle intended for use on roads; and
 (c) 'road' means any highway and any other road to which the public has access and includes bridges over which a road passes.

### 45.8 Application of Fixed Recoverable Costs

Subject to rule 45.12, the only costs which are to be allowed are—
(a) fixed recoverable costs calculated in accordance with rule 45.9;
(b) disbursements allowed in accordance with rule 45.10; and
(c) a success fee allowed in accordance with rule 45.11.
(Rule 45.12 provides for where a party issues a claim for more than the fixed recoverable costs.)

### 45.9 Amount of Fixed Recoverable Costs

(1) Subject to paragraphs (2) and (3), the amount of fixed recoverable costs is the total of—
 (a) £800;
 (b) 20% of the damages agreed up to £5,000; and
 (c) 15% of the damages agreed between £5,000 and £10,000.
(2) Where the claimant—
 (a) lives or works in an area set out in the relevant practice direction; and
 (b) instructs a solicitor or firm of solicitors who practise in that area,
 the fixed recoverable costs shall include, in addition to the costs specified in paragraph (1), an amount equal to 12.5% of the costs allowable under that paragraph.

(3) Where appropriate, value added tax (VAT) may be recovered in addition to the amount of fixed recoverable costs and any reference in this Section to fixed recoverable costs is a reference to those costs net of any such VAT.

## 45.10 Disbursements

(1) The court—
- (a) may allow a claim for a disbursement of a type mentioned in paragraph (2); but
- (b) must not allow a claim for any other type of disbursement.

(2) The disbursements referred to in paragraph (1) are—
- (a) the cost of obtaining—
  - (i) medical records;
  - (ii) a medical report;
  - (iii) a police report;
  - (iv) an engineer's report; or
  - (v) a search of the records of the Driver Vehicle Licensing Authority;
- (b) the amount of an insurance premium or, where a membership organisation undertakes to meet liabilities incurred to pay the costs of other parties to proceedings, a sum not exceeding such additional amount of costs as would be allowed under section 30 in respect of provision made against the risk of having to meet such liabilities;

('membership organisation' is defined in rule 43.2(1)(n).)
- (c) where they are necessarily incurred by reason of one or more of the claimants being a child or patient as defined in Part 21—
  - (i) fees payable for instructing counsel; or
  - (ii) court fees payable on an application to the court;
- (d) any other disbursement that has arisen due to a particular feature of the dispute.

('insurance premium' is defined in rule 43.2).

## 45.11 Success Fee

(1) A claimant may recover a success fee if he has entered into a funding arrangement of a type specified in rule 43.2(k)(i).

(2) The amount of the success fee shall be 12.5% of the fixed recoverable costs calculated in accordance with rule 45.9(1), disregarding any additional amount which may be included in the fixed recoverable costs by virtue of rule 45.9(2).

(Rule 43.2(k)(i) defines [a] funding arrangement as including a conditional fee agreement or collective conditional fee agreement which provides for a success fee.)

## 45.12 Claims for an Amount of Costs Exceeding Fixed Recoverable Costs

(1) The court will entertain a claim for an amount of costs (excluding any success fee or disbursements) greater than the fixed recoverable costs but only if it considers that there are exceptional circumstances making it appropriate to do so.

(2) If the court considers such a claim appropriate, it may—
- (a) assess the costs; or
- (b) make an order for the costs to be assessed.

(3) If the court does not consider the claim appropriate, it must make an order for fixed recoverable costs only.

## 45.13 Failure to Achieve Costs Greater Than Fixed Recoverable Costs

(1) This rule applies where—
- (a) costs are assessed in accordance with rule 45.12(2); and
- (b) the court assesses the costs (excluding any VAT) as being an amount which is less than 20% greater than the amount of the fixed recoverable costs.

(2) The court must order the defendant to pay to the claimant the lesser of—
- (a) the fixed recoverable costs; and
- (b) the assessed costs.

### 45.14 Costs of the Costs-only Proceedings or the Detailed Assessment

Where—
(a) the court makes an order for fixed recoverable costs in accordance with rule 45.12(3); or
(b) rule 45.13 applies,
the court must—
(i) make no award for the payment of the claimant's costs in bringing the proceedings under rule 44.12A; and
(ii) order that the claimant pay the defendant's costs of defending those proceedings.

## III FIXED PERCENTAGE INCREASE IN ROAD TRAFFIC ACCIDENT CLAIMS

### 45.15 Scope and Interpretation

(1) This Section sets out the percentage increase which is to be allowed in the cases to which this Section applies.
(Rule 43.2(1)(l) defines 'percentage increase' as the percentage by which the amount of a legal representative's fee can be increased in accordance with a conditional fee agreement which provides for a success fee.)
(2) This Section applies where—
(a) the dispute arises from a road traffic accident; and
(b) the claimant has entered into a funding arrangement of a type specified in rule 43.2(k)(i).
(Rule 43.2(k)(i) defines a funding arrangement as including an arrangement where a person has entered into a conditional fee agreement or collective conditional fee agreement which provides for a success fee.)
(3) This Section does not apply if the proceedings are costs only proceedings to which Section II of this Part applies.
(4) This Section does not apply—
(a) to a claim which has been allocated to the small claims track;
(b) to a claim not allocated to a track, but for which the small claims track is the normal track; or
(c) where the road traffic accident which gave rise to the dispute occurred before 6th October 2003.
(5) The definitions in rule 45.7(4) apply to this Section as they apply to Section II.
(6) In this Section—
(a) a reference to 'fees' is a reference to fees for work done under a conditional fee agreement or collective conditional fee agreement;
(b) a reference to 'trial' is a reference to the final contested hearing or to the contested hearing of any issue ordered to be tried separately;
(c) a reference to a claim concluding at trial is a reference to a claim concluding by settlement after the trial has commenced or by judgment; and
(d) 'trial period' means a period of time fixed by the court within which the trial is to take place and where the court fixes more than one such period in relation to a claim, means the most recent period to be fixed.

### 45.16 Percentage Increase of Solicitors' Fees

Subject to rule 45.18, the percentage increase which is to be allowed in relation to solicitors' fees is—
(a) 100% where the claim concludes at trial; or
(b) 12.5% where—
(i) the claim concludes before a trial has commenced; or
(ii) the dispute is settled before a claim is issued.

## 45.17 Percentage Increase of Counsel's Fees

(1) Subject to rule 45.18, the percentage increase which is to be allowed in relation to counsel's fees is—
    (a) 100% where the claim concludes at trial;
    (b) if the claim has been allocated to the fast track—
        (i) 50% if the claim concludes 14 days or less before the date fixed for the commencement of the trial; or
        (ii) 12.5% if the claim concludes more than 14 days before the date fixed for the commencement of the trial or before any such date has been fixed;
    (c) if the claim has been allocated to the multi-track—
        (i) 75% if the claim concludes 21 days or less before the date fixed for the commencement of the trial; or
        (ii) 12.5% if the claim concludes more than 21 days before the date fixed for the commencement of the trial or before any such date has been fixed;
    (d) 12.5% where—
        (i) the claim has been issued but concludes before it has been allocated to a track; or
        (ii) in relation to costs-only proceedings, the dispute is settled before a claim is issued.

(2) Where a trial period has been fixed, if—
    (a) the claim concludes before the first day of that period; and
    (b) no trial date has been fixed within that period before the claim concludes,
    the first day of that period is treated as the date fixed for the commencement of the trial for the purposes of paragraph (1).

(3) Where a trial period has been fixed, if
    (a) the claim concludes before the first day of that period; but
    (b) before the claim concludes, a trial date had been fixed within that period,
    the trial date is the date fixed for the commencement of the trial for the purposes of paragraph (1).

(4) Where a trial period has been fixed and the claim concludes—
    (a) on or after the first day of that period; but
    (b) before commencement of the trial,
    the percentage increase in paragraph (1)(b)(i) or (1)(c)(i) shall apply as appropriate, whether or not a trial date has been fixed within that period.

(5) For the purposes of this rule, in calculating the periods of time, the day fixed for the commencement of the trial (or the first day of the trial period, where appropriate) is not included.

## 45.18 Application for an Alternative Percentage Increase where the Fixed Increase is 12.5%

(1) This rule applies where the percentage increase to be allowed—
    (a) in relation to solicitors' fees under the provisions of rule 45.16; or
    (b) in relation to counsel's fees under rule 45.17,
    is 12.5%.

(2) A party may apply for a percentage increase greater or less than that amount if—
    (a) the parties agree damages of an amount greater than £500,000 or the court awards damages of an amount greater than £500,000; or
    (b) the court awards damages of £500,000 or less but would have awarded damages greater than £500,000 if it had not made a finding of contributory negligence; or
    (c) the parties agree damages of £500,000 or less and it is reasonable to expect that if the court had made an award of damages, it would have awarded damages greater than £500,000, disregarding any reduction the court may have made in respect of contributory negligence.

(3) In paragraph (2), a reference to a lump sum of damages includes a reference to periodical payments of equivalent value.
(4) If the court is satisfied that the circumstances set out in paragraph (2) apply it must—
(a) assess the percentage increase; or
(b) make an order for the percentage increase to be assessed.

### 45.19 Assessment of Alternative Percentage Increase

(1) This rule applies where the percentage increase of fees is assessed under rule 45.18(4).
(2) If the percentage increase is assessed as greater than 20% or less than 7.5%, the percentage increase to be allowed shall be that assessed by the court.
(3) If the percentage increase is assessed as no greater than 20% and no less than 7.5%—
(a) the percentage increase to be allowed shall be 12.5%; and
(b) the costs of the application and assessment shall be paid by the applicant.

## IV FIXED PERCENTAGE INCREASE IN EMPLOYERS LIABILITY CLAIMS

### 45.20 Scope and Interpretation

(1) Subject to paragraph (2), this Section applies where—
(a) the dispute is between an employee and his employer arising from a bodily injury sustained by the employee in the course of his employment; and
(b) the claimant has entered into a funding arrangement of a type specified in rule 43.2(1)(k)(i).
(2) This Section does not apply—
(a) where the dispute—
(i) relates to a disease; or
(ii) relates to an injury sustained before 1st October 2004; or
(iii) arises from a road traffic accident (as defined in rule 45.7(4)(a)); or
(iv) relates to an injury to which Section V of this Part applies; or
(b) to a claim—
(i) which has been allocated to the small claims track; or
(ii) not allocated to a track, but for which the small claims track is the normal track.
(3) For the purposes of this Section—
(a) 'employee' has the meaning given to it by section 2(1) of the Employers' Liability (Compulsory Insurance) Act 1969[3]; and
(b) a reference to 'fees' is a reference to fees for work done under a conditional fee agreement or collective conditional fee agreement.

### 45.21 Percentage Increase of Solicitors' and Counsel's Fees

In the cases to which this Section applies, subject to rule 45.22 the percentage increase which is to be allowed in relation to solicitors' and counsel's fees is to be determined in accordance with rules 45.16 and 45.17, subject to the modifications that—
(a) the percentage increase which is to be allowed in relation to solicitors' fees under rule 45.16(b) is—
(i) 27.5% if a membership organisation has undertaken to meet the claimant's liabilities for legal costs in accordance with section 30 of the Access to Justice Act 1999; and
(ii) 25% in any other case; and
(b) the percentage increase which is to be allowed in relation to counsel's fees under rule 45.17(1)(b)(ii), (1)(c)(ii) or (1)(d) is 25%.
('membership organisation' is defined in rule 43.2(1)(n).)

### 45.22 Alternative Percentage Increase

(1) In the cases to which this Section applies, rule 45.18(2)–(4) applies where—
(a) the percentage increase of solicitors' fees to be allowed in accordance with rule 45.21 is 25% or 27.5%; or
(b) the percentage increase of counsel's fees to be allowed is 25%.

(2) Where the percentage increase of fees is assessed by the court under rule 45.18(4) as applied by paragraph (1) above—
 (a) if the percentage increase is assessed as greater than 40% or less than 15%, the percentage increase to be allowed shall be that assessed by the court; and
 (b) if the percentage increase is assessed as no greater than 40% and no less than 15%—
  (i) the percentage increase to be allowed shall be 25% or 27.5% (as the case may be); and
  (ii) the costs of the application and assessment shall be paid by the applicant.

## V FIXED RECOVERABLE SUCCESS FEES IN EMPLOYERS LIABILITY DISEASE CLAIMS

### 45.23 Scope and Interpretation

(1) Subject to paragraph (2), this Section applies where—
 (a) the dispute is between an employee (or, if the employee is deceased, the employee's estate or dependants) and his employer (or a person alleged to be liable for the employer's alleged breach of statutory or common law duties of care); and
 (b) the dispute relates to a disease with which the employee is diagnosed that is alleged to have been contracted as a consequence of the employer's alleged breach of statutory or common law duties of care in the course of the employee's employment; and
 (c) the claimant has entered into a funding arrangement of a type specified in rule 43.2(1)(k)(i).
(2) This Section does not apply where—
 (a) the claimant sent a letter of claim to the defendant containing a summary of the facts on which the claim is based and main allegations of fault before 1 October 2005; or
 (b) rule 45.20(2)(b) applies.
(3) For the purposes of this Section—
 (a) rule 45.15(6) applies;
 (b) 'employee' has the meaning given to it by section 2(1) of the Employers' Liability (Compulsory Insurance) Act 1969;
 (c) 'Type A claim' means a claim relating to a disease or physical injury alleged to have been caused by exposure to asbestos;
 (d) 'Type B claim' means a claim relating to—
  (i) a psychiatric injury alleged to have been caused by work-related psychological stress;
  (ii) a work-related upper limb disorder which is alleged to have been caused by physical stress or strain, excluding hand/arm vibration injuries; and
 (e) 'Type C claim' means a claim relating to a disease not falling within either type A or type B.

(The Table annexed to the practice direction supplementing Part 45 contains a non-exclusive list of diseases within Type A and Type B:)

### 45.24 Percentage Increase of Solicitors' Fees

(1) In the cases to which this Section applies, subject to rule 45.26, the percentage increase which is to be allowed in relation to solicitors' fees is—
 (a) 100% if the claim concludes at trial; or
 (b) where—
  (i) the claim concludes before a trial has commenced; or
  (ii) the dispute is settled before a claim is issued,
 to be determined by rule 45.24(2).
(2) Where rule 45.24(1)(b) applies, the percentage increase which is to be allowed in relation to solicitors' fees is—
 (a) in type A claims—

(i) 30% if a membership organisation has undertaken to meet the claimant's liabilities for legal costs in accordance with section 30 of the Access to Justice Act 1999; and
(ii) 27.5% in any other case;
(b) in type B claims, 100%; and
(c) in type C claims—
(i) 70% if a membership organisation has undertaken to meet the claimant's liabilities for legal costs in accordance with section 30 of the Access to Justice Act 1999; and
(ii) 62.5% in any other case.
('Membership organisation' is defined in rule 43.2(1)(n).)

## 45.25 Percentage Increase of Counsel's Fees

(1) In the cases to which this Section applies, subject to rule 45.26, the percentage increase which is to be allowed in relation to counsel's fees is—
(a) 100% if the claim concludes at trial; or
(b) where—
(i) the claim concludes before a trial has commenced; or
(ii) the dispute is settled before a claim is issued,
to be determined by rule 45.25(2).
(2) Where rule 45.25(1)(b) applies, the percentage increase which is to be allowed in relation to counsel's fees is—
(a) if the claim has been allocated to the fast track, the amount shown in Table 6; and
(b) if the claim has been allocated to the multi-track, the amount shown in Table 7.
(3) Where a trial period has been fixed, rules 45.17(2) to 45.17(5) apply for the purposes of determining the date fixed for the commencement of the trial.

**Table 6** Claims allocated to the fast track

| | **If the claim concludes 14 days or less before the date fixed for commencement of the trial** | **If the claim concludes more than 14 days before the date fixed for commencement of the trial or before any such date has been fixed** |
|---|---|---|
| Type A claim | 50% | 27.5% |
| Type B claim | 100% | 100% |
| Type C claim | 62.5% | 62.5% |

**Table 7** Claims allocated to the multi-track

| | **If the claim concludes 21 days or less before the date fixed for commencement of the trial** | **If the claim concludes more than 21 days before the date fixed for commencement of the trial or before any such date has been fixed** |
|---|---|---|
| Type A claim | 75% | 27.5% |
| Type B claim | 100% | 100% |
| Type C claim | 75% | 62.5% |

## 45.26 Alternative Percentage Increase

(1) In cases to which this Section applies and subject to paragraph (2) below, rules 45.18(2) to (4) apply where the percentage increase is the amount allowed under rules 45.24 and 45.25.

(2) For the purposes of this Section, the sum of £250,000 shall be substituted for the sum of £500,000 in rules 45.18(2)(a) to (c).
(3) Where the percentage increase of fees is assessed by the court under rule 45.18(4), as applied by paragraph 1 above, the percentage increase to be allowed shall be the amount shown in Table 8.
(4) The percentage increase cannot be varied where the case concludes at trial.

**Table 8**

| Type of claim | Amount Allowed |
|---|---|
| A If the percentage increase is assessed as greater than 40% or less than 15%, the percentage increase that is assessed by the court. | If the percentage increase is assessed as no greater than 40% and no less than 15%<br>(i) 27.5%; and<br>(ii) the costs of the application and assessment shall be paid by the applicant. |
| B If the percentage increase is assessed as less than 75%, the percentage increase that is assessed by the court. | If the percentage increase is assessed as no less than 75%<br>(i) 100%; and<br>(ii) the costs of the application and assessment shall be paid by the applicant. |
| C If the percentage increase is assessed as greater than 75% or less than 50%, the percentage increase that is assessed by the court. | If the percentage increase is assessed as no greater than 75% and no less than 50%<br>(i) 62.5%; and<br>(ii) the costs of the application and assessment shall be paid by the applicant. |

**[PD 43–48 is positioned after CPR 48.]**

# CPR Part 46 Fast Track Trial Costs



## 46.1 Scope of this Part

(1) This Part deals with the amount of costs which the court may award as the costs of an advocate for preparing for and appearing at the trial of a claim in the fast track (referred to in this rule as 'fast track trial costs').

(2) For the purposes of this Part—
  (a) 'advocate' means a person exercising a right of audience as a representative of, or on behalf of, a party;
  (b) 'fast track trial costs' means the costs of a party's advocate for preparing for and appearing at the trial, but does not include—
    (i) any other disbursements; or
    (ii) any value added tax payable on the fees of a party's advocate; and
  (c) 'trial' includes a hearing where the court decides an amount of money or the value of goods following a judgment under Part 12 (default judgment) or Part 14 (admissions) but does not include—
    (i) the hearing of an application for summary judgment under Part 24; or
    (ii) the court's approval of a settlement or other compromise under rule 21.10.

(Part 21 deals with claims made by or on behalf of, or gainst, children and patients.)

## 46.2 Amount of Fast Track Trial Costs

(1) The following table shows the amount of fast track trial costs which the court may award (whether by summary or detailed assessment).

| Value of the claim | Amount of fast track trial costs which the court may award |
|---|---|
| Up to £3,000 | £350 |
| More than £3,000 but not more than £10,000 | £500 |
| More than £10,000 | £750 |

(2) The court may not award more or less than the amount shown in the table except where—
  (a) it decides not to award any fast track trial costs; or
  (b) rule 46.3 applies,

  but the court may apportion the amount awarded between the parties to reflect their respective degrees of success on the issues at trial.

(3) Where the only claim is for the payment of money—
  (a) for the purpose of quantifying fast track trial costs awarded to a claimant, the value of the claim is the total amount of the judgment excluding—
    (i) interest and costs; and
    (ii) any reduction made for contributory negligence.
  (b) for the purpose of the quantifying fast track trial costs awarded to a defendant, the value of the claim is—
    (i) the amount specified in the claim form (excluding interest and costs);

(ii) if no amount is specified, the maximum amount which the claimant reasonably expected to recover according to the statement of value included in the claim form under rule 16.3; or

(iii) more than £10,000, if the claim form states that the claimant cannot reasonably say how much he expects to recover.

(4) Where the claim is only for a remedy other than the payment of money the value of the claim is deemed to be more than £3,000 but not more than £10,000, unless the court orders otherwise.

(5) Where the claim includes both a claim for the payment of money and for a remedy other than the payment of money, the value of the claim is deemed to be the higher of—

(a) the value of the money claim decided in accordance with paragraph (3); or

(b) the deemed value of the other remedy decided in accordance with paragraph (4), unless the court orders otherwise.

(6) Where—

(a) a defendant has made a counterclaim against the claimant;

(b) the counterclaim has a higher value than the claim; and

(c) the claimant succeeds at trial both on his claim and the counterclaim,

for the purpose of quantifying fast track trial costs awarded to the claimant, the value of the claim is the value of the defendant's counterclaim calculated in accordance with this rule.

(Rule 20.4 sets out how a defendant may make a counterclaim.)

## 46.3 Power to Award More or Less Than the Amount of Fast Track Trial Costs

(1) This rule sets out when a court may award—

(a) an additional amount to the amount of fast track trial costs shown in the table in rule 46.2(1); and

(b) less than those amounts.

(2) If—

(a) in addition to the advocate, a party's legal representative attends the trial;

(b) the court considers that it was necessary for a legal representative to attend to assist the advocate; and

(c) the court awards fast track trial costs to that party,

the court may award an additional £250 in respect of the legal representative's attendance at the trial.

(Legal representative is defined in rule 2.3.)

(2A) The court may in addition award a sum representing an additional liability.

(The requirements to provide information about a funding arrangement where a party wishes to recover any additional liability under a funding arrangement are set out in the costs practice direction.)

('Additional liability' is defined in rule 43.2.)

(3) If the court considers that it is necessary to direct a separate trial of an issue then the court may award an additional amount in respect of the separate trial but that amount is limited in accordance with paragraph (4) of this rule.

(4) The additional amount the court may award under paragraph 3 must not exceed two-thirds of the amount payable for that claim, subject to a minimum award of £350.

(5) Where the party to whom fast track trial costs are to be awarded is a litigant in person, the court will award—

(a) if the litigant in person can prove financial loss, two-thirds of the amount that would otherwise be awarded; or

(b) if the litigant in person fails to prove financial loss, an amount in respect of the time spent reasonably doing the work at the rate specified in the costs practice direction.

(6) Where a defendant has made a counterclaim against the claimant, and—

(a) the claimant has succeeded on his claim; and
(b) the defendant has succeeded on his counterclaim,

the court will quantify the amount of the award of fast track trial costs to which—

(i) but for the counterclaim, the claimant would be entitled for succeeding on his claim; and
(ii) but for the claim, the defendant would be entitled for succeeding on his counterclaim,

and make one award of the difference, if any, to the party entitled to the higher award of costs.

(7) Where the court considers that the party to whom fast track trial costs are to be awarded has behaved unreasonably or improperly during the trial, it may award that party an amount less than would otherwise be payable for that claim, as it considers appropriate.

(8) Where the court considers that the party who is to pay the fast track trial costs has behaved improperly during the trial the court may award such additional amount to the other party as it considers appropriate.

## 46.4 Fast Track Trial Costs Where There is More Than One Claimant or Defendant

(1) Where the same advocate is acting for more than one party—

(a) the court may make only one award in respect of fast track trial costs payable to that advocate; and
(b) the parties for whom the advocate is acting are jointly entitled to any fast track trial costs awarded by the court.

(2) Where—

(a) the same advocate is acting for more than one claimant; and
(b) each claimant has a separate claim against the defendant,

the value of the claim, for the purpose of quantifying the award in respect of fast track trial costs is to be ascertained in accordance with paragraph (3).

(3) The value of the claim in the circumstances mentioned in paragraph (2) is—

(a) where the only claim of each claimant is for the payment of money—

(i) if the award of fast track trial costs is in favour of the claimants, the total amount of the judgment made in favour of all the claimants jointly represented; or
(ii) if the award is in favour of the defendant, the total amount claimed by the claimants,

and in either case, quantified in accordance with rule 46.2(3);

(b) where the only claim of each claimant is for a remedy other than the payment of money, deemed to be more than £3,000 but not more than £10,000; and
(c) where claims of the claimants include both a claim for the payment of money and for a remedy other than the payment of money, deemed to be—

(i) more than £3,000 but not more than £10,000; or
(ii) if greater, the value of the money claims calculated in accordance with sub-paragraph (a) above.

(4) Where—

(a) there is more than one defendant; and
(b) any or all of the defendants are separately represented,

the court may award fast track trial costs to each party who is separately represented.

(5) Where—

(a) there is more than one claimant; and
(b) a single defendant,

the court may make only one award to the defendant of fast track trial costs, for which the claimants are jointly and severally liable[(GL)].

(6) For the purpose of quantifying the fast track trial costs awarded to the single defendant under paragraph (5), the value of the claim is to be calculated in accordance with paragraph (3) of this rule.

**[PD 43–48 is positioned after CPR 48.]**

# CPR Part 47 Procedure for Detailed Assessment of Costs and Default Provisions



(The definitions contained in Part 43 are relevant to this Part.)

## I GENERAL RULES ABOUT DETAILED ASSESSMENT

### 47.1 Time When Detailed Assessment May be Carried Out

The general rule is that the costs of any proceedings or any part of the proceedings are not to be assessed by the detailed procedure until the conclusion of the proceedings but the court may order them to be assessed immediately.
(The costs practice direction [PD 43–48] gives further guidance about when proceedings are concluded for the purpose of this rule.)

### 47.2 No Stay of Detailed Assessment Where There is an Appeal

Detailed assessment is not stayed pending an appeal unless the court so orders.

### 47.3 Powers of an Authorised Court Officer

(1) An authorised court officer has all the powers of the court when making a detailed assessment, except—

(a) power to make a wasted costs order as defined in rule 48.7;
(b) power to make an order under—
  (i) rule 44.14 (powers in relation to misconduct);
  (ii) rule 47.8 (sanction for delay in commencing detailed assessment proceedings);
  (iii) paragraph (2) (objection to detailed assessment by authorised court officer); and
(c) power to make a detailed assessment of costs payable to a solicitor by his client, unless the costs are being assessed under rule 48.5 (costs where money is payable to a child or patient).

(2) Where a party objects to the detailed assessment of costs being made by an authorised court officer, the court may order it to be made by a costs judge or a district judge.

(The costs practice direction [PD 43–48] sets out the relevant procedure.)

### 47.4 Venue for Detailed Assessment Proceedings

(1) All applications and requests in detailed assessment proceedings must be made to or filed at the appropriate office.
(The costs practice direction sets out the meaning of 'appropriate office' in any particular case.)
(2) The court may direct that the appropriate office is to be the Supreme Court Costs Office.
(3) A county court may direct that another county court is to be the appropriate office.
(4) A direction under paragraph (3) may be made without proceedings being transferred to that court.

(Rule 30.2 makes provision for any county court to transfer the proceedings to another county court for detailed assessment of costs.)

## II COSTS PAYABLE BY ONE PARTY TO ANOTHER — COMMENCEMENT OF DETAILED ASSESSMENT PROCEEDINGS

### 47.5 Application of this Section

This section of Part 47 applies where a costs officer is to make a detailed assessment of costs which are payable by one party to another.

### 47.6 Commencement of Detailed Assessment Proceedings

(1) Detailed assessment proceedings are commenced by the receiving party serving on the paying party—
  (a) notice of commencement in the relevant practice form; and
  (b) a copy of the bill of costs.

(Rule 47.7 sets out the period for commencing detailed assessment proceedings.)

(2) The receiving party must also serve a copy of the notice of commencement and the bill on any other relevant persons specified in the costs practice direction.
(3) A person on whom a copy of the notice of commencement is served under paragraph (2) is a party to the detailed assessment proceedings (in addition to the paying party and the receiving party).

(The costs practice direction [PD 43–48] deals with—
- other documents which the party must file when he requests detailed assessment;
- the court's powers where it considers that a hearing may be necessary;
- the form of a bill; and
- the length of notice which will be given if a hearing date is fixed.)

### 47.7 Period for Commencing Detailed Assessment Proceedings

The following table shows the period for commencing detailed assessment proceedings.

| Source of right to detailed assessment | Time by which detailed assessment proceedings must be commenced |
|---|---|
| Judgment, direction, order, award or other determination | 3 months after the date of the judgment etc. Where detailed assessment is stayed pending an appeal, 3 months after the date of the order lifting the stay |
| Discontinuance under Part 38 | 3 months after the date of service of notice of discontinuance under rule 38.3; or 3 months after the date of the dismissal of application to set the notice of discontinuance aside under rule 38.4 |
| Acceptance of an offer to settle under Part 36 | 3 months after the date when the right to costs arose |

## 47.8 Sanction for Delay in Commencing Detailed Assessment Proceedings

(1) Where the receiving party fails to commence detailed assessment proceedings within the period specified—
   (a) in rule 47.7; or
   (b) by any direction of the court,

   the paying party may apply for an order requiring the receiving party to commence detailed assessment proceedings within such time as the court may specify.

(2) On an application under paragraph (1), the court may direct that, unless the receiving party commences detailed assessment proceedings within the time specified by the court, all or part of the costs to which the receiving party would otherwise be entitled will be disallowed.

(3) If—
   (a) the paying party has not made an application in accordance with paragraph (1); and
   (b) the receiving party commences the proceedings later than the period specified in rule 47.7,

   the court may disallow all or part of the interest otherwise payable to the receiving party under—
      (i) section 17 of the Judgments Act 1838; or
      (ii) section 74 of the County Courts Act 1984,

   but must not impose any other sanction except in accordance with rule 44.14 (powers in relation to misconduct).

(4) Where the costs to be assessed in a detailed assessment are payable out of the Community Legal Service Fund, this rule applies as if the receiving party were the solicitor to whom the costs are payable and the paying party were the Legal Services Commission.

## 47.9 Points of Dispute and Consequence of Not Serving

(1) The paying party and any other party to the detailed assessment proceedings may dispute any item in the bill of costs by serving points of dispute on—
   (a) the receiving party; and
   (b) every other party to the detailed assessment proceedings.

(2) The period for serving points of dispute is 21 days after the date of service of the notice of commencement.

(3) If a party serves points of dispute after the period set out in paragraph (2), he may not be heard further in the detailed assessment proceedings unless the court gives permission.

(The costs practice direction [PD 43–48] sets out requirements about the form of points of dispute.)

(4) The receiving party may file a request for a default costs certificate if—

(a) the period set out in rule 47.9(2) for serving points of dispute has expired; and
(b) he has not been served with any points of dispute.

(5) If any party (including the paying party) serves points of dispute before the issue of a default costs certificate the court may not issue the default costs certificate.

(Section IV of this Part sets out the procedure to be followed after points of dispute have been filed.)

### 47.10 Procedure Where Costs are Agreed

(1) If the paying party and the receiving party agree the amount of costs, either party may apply for a costs certificate (either interim or final) in the amount agreed.

(Rule 47.15 and rule 47.16 contain further provisions about interim and final costs certificates respectively.)

(2) An application for a certificate under paragraph (1) must be made to the court which would be the venue for detailed assessment proceedings under rule 47.4.

## III COSTS PAYABLE BY ONE PARTY TO ANOTHER — DEFAULT PROVISIONS

### 47.11 Default Costs Certificate

(1) Where the receiving party is permitted by rule 47.9 to obtain a default costs certificate, he does so by filing a request in the relevant practice form.

(The costs practice direction [PD 43–48] deals with the procedure by which the receiving party may obtain a default costs certificate.)

(2) A default costs certificate will include an order to pay the costs to which it relates.

(3) Where a receiving party obtains a default costs certificate, the costs payable to him for the commencement of detailed assessment proceedings shall be the sum set out in the costs practice direction.

### 47.12 Setting Aside Default Costs Certificate

(1) The court must set aside a default costs certificate if the receiving party was not entitled to it.

(2) In any other case, the court may set aside or vary a default costs certificate if it appears to the court that there is some good reason why the detailed assessment proceedings should continue.

(3) Where—
(a) the receiving party has purported to serve the notice of commencement on the paying party;
(b) a default costs certificate has been issued; and
(c) the receiving party subsequently discovers that the notice of commencement did not reach the paying party at least 21 days before the default costs certificate was issued,

the receiving party must—
(i) file a request for the default costs certificate to be set aside; or
(ii) apply to the court for directions.

(4) Where paragraph (3) applies, the receiving party may take no further step in—
(a) the detailed assessment proceedings; or
(b) the enforcement of the default costs certificate,

until the certificate has been set aside or the court has given directions.

(The costs practice direction [PD 43–48] contains further details about the procedure for setting aside a default costs certificate and the matters which the court must take into account.)

## IV COSTS PAYABLE BY ONE PARTY TO ANOTHER — PROCEDURE WHERE POINTS OF DISPUTE ARE SERVED

### 47.13 Optional Reply

(1) Where any party to the detailed assessment proceedings serves points of dispute, the receiving party may serve a reply on the other parties to the assessment proceedings.
(2) He may do so within 21 days after service on him of the points of dispute to which his reply relates.

(The costs practice direction [PD 43–48] sets out the meaning of reply.)

### 47.14 Detailed Assessment Hearing

(1) Where points of dispute are served in accordance with this Part, the receiving party must file a request for a detailed assessment hearing.
(2) He must file the request within 3 months of the expiry of the period for commencing detailed assessment proceedings as specified—
  (a) in rule 47.7; or
  (b) by any direction of the court.
(3) Where the receiving party fails to file a request in accordance with paragraph (2), the paying party may apply for an order requiring the receiving party to file the request within such time as the court may specify.
(4) On an application under paragraph (3), the court may direct that, unless the receiving party requests a detailed assessment hearing within the time specified by the court, all or part of the costs to which the receiving party would otherwise be entitled will be disallowed.
(5) If—
  (a) the paying party has not made an application in accordance with paragraph (3); and
  (b) the receiving party files a request for a detailed assessment hearing later than the period specified in paragraph (2),

  the court may disallow all or part of the interest otherwise payable to the receiving party under—
    (i) section 17 of the Judgments Act 1838; or
    (ii) section 74 of the County Courts Act 1984,

  but must not impose any other sanction except in accordance with rule 44.14 (powers in relation to misconduct).
(6) No party other than—
  (a) the receiving party;
  (b) the paying party; and
  (c) any party who has served points of dispute under rule 47.9,

  may be heard at the detailed assessment hearing unless the court gives permission.
(7) Only items specified in the points of dispute may be raised at the hearing, unless the court gives permission.

(The costs practice direction [PD 43–48] specifies other documents which must be filed with the request for hearing and the length of notice which the court will give when it fixes a hearing date.)

## V INTERIM COSTS CERTIFICATE AND FINAL COSTS CERTIFICATE

### 47.15 Power to Issue an Interim Certificate

(1) The court may at any time after the receiving party has filed a request for a detailed assessment hearing—
  (a) issue an interim costs certificate for such sum as it considers appropriate;
  (b) amend or cancel an interim certificate.
(2) An interim certificate will include an order to pay the costs to which it relates, unless the court orders otherwise.

(3) The court may order the costs certified in an interim certificate to be paid into court.

### 47.16 Final Costs Certificate

(1) In this rule a completed bill means a bill calculated to show the amount due following the detailed assessment of the costs.
(2) The period for filing the completed bill is 14 days after the end of the detailed assessment hearing.
(3) When a completed bill is filed the court will issue a final costs certificate and serve it on the parties to the detailed assessment proceedings.
(4) Paragraph (3) is subject to any order made by the court that a certificate is not to be issued until other costs have been paid.
(5) A final costs certificate will include an order to pay the costs to which it relates, unless the court orders otherwise.

(The costs practice direction [PD 43–48] deals with the form of a final costs certificate.)

## VI DETAILED ASSESSMENT PROCEDURE FOR COSTS OF A LSC FUNDED CLIENT OR AN ASSISTED PERSON WHERE COSTS ARE PAYABLE OUT OF THE COMMUNITY LEGAL SERVICE FUND

### 47.17 Detailed Assessment Procedure for Costs of a LSC Funded Client or an Assisted Person Where Costs are Payable Out of the Community Legal Service Fund

(1) Where the court is to assess costs of a LSC funded client or an assisted person which are payable out of the Community Legal Service Fund, that person's solicitor may commence detailed assessment proceedings by filing a request in the relevant practice form.
(2) A request under paragraph (1) must be filed within 3 months after the date when the right to detailed assessment arose.
(3) The solicitor must also serve a copy of the request for detailed assessment on the LSC funded client or the assisted person, if notice of that person's interest has been given to the court in accordance with community legal service or legal aid regulations.
(4) Where the solicitor has certified that the LSC funded client or the assisted person wishes to attend an assessment hearing, the court will, on receipt of the request for assessment, fix a date for the assessment hearing.
(5) Where paragraph (3) does not apply, the court will, on receipt of the request for assessment provisionally assess the costs without the attendance of the solicitor, unless it considers that a hearing is necessary.
(6) After the court has provisionally assessed the bill, it will return the bill to the solicitor.
(7) The court will fix a date for an assessment hearing if the solicitor informs the court, within 14 days after he receives the provisionally assessed bill, that he wants the court to hold such a hearing.

### 47.17A Detailed Assessment Procedure Where Costs are Payable Out of a Fund Other Than the Community Legal Service Fund

(1) Where the court is to assess costs which are payable out of a fund other than the Community Legal Service Fund, the receiving party may commence detailed assessment proceedings by filing a request in the relevant practice form.
(2) A request under paragraph (1) must be filed within 3 months after the date when the right to detailed assessment arose.
(3) The court may direct that the party seeking assessment serve a copy of the request on any person who has a financial interest in the outcome of the assessment.

(4) The court will, on receipt of the request for assessment, provisionally assess the costs without the attendance of the receiving party, unless it considers that a hearing is necessary.
(5) After the court has provisionally assessed the bill, it will return the bill to the receiving party.
(6) The court will fix a date for an assessment hearing if the party informs the court, within 14 days after he receives the provisionally assessed bill, that he wants the court to hold such a hearing.

## VII COSTS OF DETAILED ASSESSMENT PROCEEDINGS

### 47.18 Liability for Costs of Detailed Assessment Proceedings

(1) The receiving party is entitled to his costs of the detailed assessment proceedings except where—
  (a) the provisions of any Act, any of these Rules or any relevant practice direction provide otherwise; or
  (b) the court makes some other order in relation to all or part of the costs of the detailed assessment proceedings.
(2) In deciding whether to make some other order, the court must have regard to all the circumstances, including—
  (a) the conduct of all the parties;
  (b) the amount, if any, by which the bill of costs has been reduced; and
  (c) whether it was reasonable for a party to claim the costs of a particular item or to dispute that item.

### 47.19 Offers to Settle Without Prejudice Save as to Costs of the Detailed Assessment Proceedings

(1) Where—
  (a) a party (whether the paying party or the receiving party) makes a written offer to settle the costs of the proceedings which gave rise to the assessment proceedings; and
  (b) the offer is expressed to be without prejudice(GL) save as to the costs of the detailed assessment proceedings,

  the court will take the offer into account in deciding who should pay the costs of those proceedings.
(2) The fact of the offer must not be communicated to the costs officer until the question of costs of the detailed assessment proceedings falls to be decided.

(The costs practice direction [PD 43–48] provides that rule 47.19 does not apply where the receiving party is a LSC funded client or an assisted person, unless the court orders otherwise.)

## VIII APPEALS FROM AUTHORISED COURT OFFICERS IN DETAILED ASSESSMENT PROCEEDINGS

### 47.20 Right to Appeal

(1) Any party to detailed assessment proceedings may appeal against a decision of an authorised court officer in those proceedings.
(2) For the purposes of this Section, a LSC funded client or an assisted person is not a party to detailed assessment proceedings.

(Part 52 sets out general rules about appeals.)

### 47.21 Court to Hear Appeal

An appeal against a decision of an authorised court officer is to a costs judge or a district judge of the High Court.

### 47.22 Appeal Procedure

(1) The appellant must file an appeal notice within 14 days after the date of the decision he wishes to appeal against.
(2) On receipt of the appeal notice, the court will—
  (a) serve a copy of the notice on the parties to the detailed assessment proceedings; and
  (b) give notice of the appeal hearing to those parties.

### 47.23 Powers of the Court on Appeal

On an appeal from an authorised court officer the court will—
(a) rehear the proceedings which gave rise to the decision appealed against; and
(b) make any order and give any directions as it considers appropriate.

**[PD 43–48 is positioned after CPR 48.]**

# CPR Part 48 Costs — Special Cases



(The definitions contained in Part 43 are relevant to this Part.)

## I COSTS PAYABLE BY OR TO PARTICULAR PERSONS

### 48.1 Pre-commencement Disclosure and Orders for Disclosure Against a Person Who is Not a Party

(1) This paragraph applies where a person applies—
 (a) for an order under—
  (i) section 33 of the Supreme Court Act 1981;[1] or
  (ii) section 52 of the County Courts Act 1984,[2]
 (which give the court powers exercisable before commencement of proceedings); or
 (b) for an order under—
  (i) section 34 of the Supreme Court Act 1981;[3] or
  (ii) section 53 of the County Courts Act 1984,[4]
 (which give the court power to make an order against a non-party for disclosure of documents, inspection of property etc.).
(2) The general rule is that the court will award the person against whom the order is sought his costs—
 (a) of the application; and
 (b) of complying with any order made on the application.
(3) The court may however make a different order, having regard to all the circumstances, including—
 (a) the extent to which it was reasonable for the person against whom the order was sought to oppose the application; and
 (b) whether the parties to the application have complied with any relevant pre-action protocol.

[1] 1981 c. 54. Section 33 was amended by SI 1998/2940.
[2] 1984 c. 28. Section 52 was amended by the Courts and Legal Services Act 1990 (c. 41), Sch. 18 para. 43 and by SI 1998/2940.
[3] 1981 c. 54. Section 34 was amended by SI 1998/2940.
[4] 1984 c. 28. Section 53 was amended by the Courts and Legal Services Act 1990 (c. 41), Sch. 18 para. 44 and by SI 1998/2940.

## 48.2 Costs Orders in Favour of or Against Non-parties

(1) Where the court is considering whether to exercise its power under section 51 of the Supreme Court Act 1981[5] (costs are in the discretion of the court) to make a costs order in favour of or against a person who is not a party to proceedings—
   (a) that person must be added as a party to the proceedings for the purposes of costs only; and
   (b) he must be given a reasonable opportunity to attend a hearing at which the court will consider the matter further.
(2) This rule does not apply—
   (a) where the court is considering whether to—
      (i) make an order against the Legal Services Commission;
      (ii) make a wasted costs order (as defined in 48.7); and
   (b) in proceedings to which rule 48.1 applies (pre-commencement disclosure and orders for disclosure against a person who is not a party).

## 48.3 Amount of Costs Where Costs Are Payable Pursuant to a Contract

(1) Where the court assesses (whether by the summary or detailed procedure) costs which are payable by the paying party to the receiving party under the terms of a contract, the costs payable under those terms are, unless the contract expressly provides otherwise, to be presumed to be costs which—
   (a) have been reasonably incurred; and
   (b) are reasonable in amount,
   and the court will assess them accordingly.
(The costs practice direction [PD 43–48] sets out circumstances where the court may order otherwise.)
(2) This rule does not apply where the contract is between a solicitor and his client.

## 48.4 Limitations on Court's Power to Award Costs in Favour of Trustee or Personal Representative

(1) This rule applies where—
   (a) a person is or has been a party to any proceedings in the capacity of trustee or personal representative; and
   (b) rule 48.3 does not apply.
(2) The general rule is that he is entitled to be paid the costs of those proceedings, in so far as they are not recovered from or paid by any other person, out of the relevant trust fund or estate.
(3) Where he is entitled to be paid any of those costs out of the fund or estate, those costs will be assessed on the indemnity basis.

## 48.5 Costs Where Money is Payable by or to a Child or Patient

(1) This rule applies to any proceedings where a party is a child or patient and—
   (a) money is ordered or agreed to be paid to, or for the benefit of, that party; or
   (b) money is ordered to be paid by him or on his behalf.
('Child' and 'patient' are defined in rule 2.3.)
(2) The general rule is that—
   (a) the court must order a detailed assessment of the costs payable by, or out of money belonging to, any party who is a child or patient; and
   (b) on an assessment under paragraph (a), the court must also assess any costs payable to that party in the proceedings, unless—

[5] 1981 c. 54. Section 51 was replaced by s. 4(1) of the Courts and Legal Services Act 1990 (c. 41).

(i) the court has issued a default costs certificate in relation to those costs under rule 47.11; or
(ii) the costs are payable in proceedings to which Section II of Part 45 applies.

(3) The court need not order detailed assessment of costs in the circumstances set out in the costs practice direction.

(4) Where—
(a) a claimant is a child or patient; and
(b) a detailed assessment has taken place under paragraph (2)(a),
the only amount payable by the child or patient is the amount which the court certifies as payable.

(This rule applies to a counterclaim by or on behalf of a child or patient by virtue of rule 20.3.)

## 48.6 Litigants in Person

(1) This rule applies where the court orders (whether by summary assessment or detailed assessment) that the costs of a litigant in person are to be paid by any other person.

(2) The costs allowed under this rule must not exceed, except in the case of a disbursement, two-thirds of the amount which would have been allowed if the litigant in person had been represented by a legal representative.

(3) The litigant in person shall be allowed—
(a) costs for the same categories of—
(i) work; and
(ii) disbursements,
which would have been allowed if the work had been done or the disbursements had been made by a legal representative on the litigant in person's behalf;
(b) the payments reasonably made by him for legal services relating to the conduct of the proceedings; and
(c) the costs of obtaining expert assistance in assessing the costs claim.

(4) The amount of costs to be allowed to the litigant in person for any item of work claimed shall be—
(a) where the litigant can prove financial loss, the amount that he can prove he has lost for time reasonably spent on doing the work; or
(b) where the litigant cannot prove financial loss, an amount for the time reasonably spent on doing the work at the rate set out in the practice direction.

(5) A litigant who is allowed costs for attending at court to conduct his case is not entitled to a witness allowance in respect of such attendance in addition to those costs.

(6) For the purposes of this rule, a litigant in person includes—
(a) a company or other corporation which is acting without a legal representative; and
(b) a barrister, solicitor, solicitor's employee or other authorised litigator (as defined in the Courts and Legal Services Act 1990)[6] who is acting for himself.

## 48.6A Costs Where the Court Has Made a Group Litigation Order

(1) This rule applies where the court has made a Group Litigation Order (GLO).

(2) In this rule—
(a) 'individual costs' means costs incurred in relation to an individual claim on the group register;
(b) 'common costs' means—
(i) costs incurred in relation to the GLO issues;
(ii) individual costs incurred in a claim while it is proceeding as a test claim, and
(iii) costs incurred by the lead solicitor in administering the group litigation; and
(c) 'group litigant' means a claimant or defendant, as the case may be, whose claim is entered on the group register.

[6] 1990 c. 41.

(3) Unless the court orders otherwise, any order for common costs against group litigants imposes on each group litigant several liability(GL) for an equal proportion of those common costs.
(4) The general rule is that where a group litigant is the paying party, he will, in addition to any costs he is liable to pay to the receiving party, be liable for—
 (a) the individual costs of his claim; and
 (b) an equal proportion, together with all the other group litigants, of the common costs.
(5) Where the court makes an order about costs in relation to any application or hearing which involved—
 (a) one or more GLO issues; and
 (b) issues relevant only to individual claims,
 the court will direct the proportion of the costs that is to relate to common costs and the proportion that is to relate to individual costs.
(6) Where common costs have been incurred before a claim is entered on the group register, the court may order the group litigant to be liable for a proportion of those costs.
(7) Where a claim is removed from the group register, the court may make an order for costs in that claim which includes a proportion of the common costs incurred up to the date on which the claim is removed from the group register.

(Part 19 sets out rules about group litigation)

## II COSTS RELATING TO SOLICITORS AND OTHER LEGAL REPRESENTATIVES

### 48.7 Personal Liability of Legal Representative For Costs—Wasted Costs Orders

(1) This rule applies where the court is considering whether to make an order under section 51(6) of the Supreme Court Act 1981[7] (court's power to disallow or (as the case may be) order a legal representative to meet, 'wasted costs').
(2) The court must give the legal representative a reasonable opportunity to attend a hearing to give reasons why it should not make such an order.
(3) [*Revoked*]
(4) When the court makes a wasted costs order, it must—
 (a) specify the amount to be disallowed or paid; or
 (b) direct a costs judge or a district judge to decide the amount of costs to be disallowed or paid.
(5) The court may direct that notice must be given to the legal representative's client, in such manner as the court may direct—
 (a) of any proceedings under this rule; or
 (b) of any order made under it against his legal representative.
(6) Before making a wasted costs order, the court may direct a costs judge or a district judge to inquire into the matter and report to the court.
(7) The court may refer the question of wasted costs to a costs judge or a district judge, instead of making a wasted costs order.

### 48.8 Basis of Detailed Assessment of Solicitor and Client Costs

(1) This rule applies to every assessment of a solicitor's bill to his client except a bill which is to be paid out of the Community Legal Service Fund under the Legal Aid Act 1988[8] or the Access to Justice Act 1999.[9]
(1A) Section 74(3) of the Solicitors Act 1974[10] applies unless the solicitor and client have

[7] 1981 c. 54. Section 51 was replaced by s. 4(1) of the Courts and Legal Services Act 1990 (c. 41).
[8] 1988 c. 34.
[9] 1999 c. 22.
[10] 1974 c. 47.

entered into a written agreement which expressly permits payment to the solicitor of an amount of costs greater than that which the client could have recovered from another party to the proceedings.

(2) Subject to paragraph (1A), costs are to be assessed on the indemnity basis but are to be presumed—
  (a) to have been reasonably incurred if they were incurred with the express or implied approval of the client;
  (b) to be reasonable in amount if their amount was expressly or impliedly approved by the client;
  (c) to have been unreasonably incurred if—
    (i) they are of an unusual nature or amount; and
    (ii) the solicitor did not tell his client that as a result he might not recover all of them from the other party.

(3) Where the court is considering a percentage increase, whether on the application of the legal representative under rule 44.16 or on the application of the client, the court will have regard to all the relevant factors as they reasonably appeared to the solicitor or counsel when the conditional fee agreement was entered into or varied.

(4) In paragraph (3), 'conditional fee agreement' means an agreement enforceable under section 58 of the Courts and Legal Services Act 1990 at the date on which that agreement was entered into or varied.

**48.9** [*Revoked*]

## 48.10 Assessment Procedure

(1) This rule sets out the procedure to be followed where the court has made an order under Part III of the Solicitors Act 1974 for the assessment of costs payable to a solicitor by his client.

(2) The solicitor must serve a breakdown of costs within 28 days of the order for costs to be assessed.

(3) The client must serve points of dispute within 14 days after service on him of the breakdown of costs.

(4) If the solicitor wishes to serve a reply, he must do so within 14 days of service on him of the points of dispute.

(5) Either party may file a request for a hearing date—
  (a) after points of dispute have been served; but
  (b) no later than 3 months after the date of the order for the costs to be assessed.

(6) This procedure applies subject to any contrary order made by the court.

# PD 43–48 Practice Direction About Costs

This practice direction supplements CPR Parts 43 to 48.

## Section 1 Introduction

1.1 This practice direction supplements Parts 43 to 48 of the Civil Procedure Rules. It applies to all proceedings to which those Parts apply.

1.2 Paragraphs 57.1 to 57.9 of this practice direction deal with various transitional provisions affecting proceedings about costs.

1.3 Attention is drawn to the powers to make orders about costs conferred on the Supreme Court and any county court by the Supreme Court Act 1981, s. 51.

1.4 In these directions:

'counsel' means a barrister or other person with a right of audience in relation to proceedings in the High Court or in the county courts in which he is instructed to act;

'LSC' means Legal Services Commission;

'solicitor' means a solicitor of the Supreme Court or other person with a right of audience in relation to proceedings, who is conducting the claim or defence (as the case may be) on behalf of a party to the proceedings and, where the context admits, includes a patent agent.

1.5 In respect of any document which is required by these directions to be signed by a party or his legal representative PD 22 will apply as if the document in question was a statement of truth. (PD 22 makes provision for cases in which a party is a child, a patient or a company or other corporation and cases in which a document is signed on behalf of a partnership.)

## Section 2 Scope of Costs Rules and Definitions

*Rule 43.2 definitions and application*

2.1 Where the court makes an order for costs and the receiving party has entered into a funding arrangement as defined in r. 43.2, the costs payable by the paying party include any additional liability (also defined in r. 43.2) unless the court orders otherwise.

2.2 In the following paragraphs—

'funding arrangement', 'percentage increase', 'insurance premium', 'membership organisation' and 'additional liability' have the meanings given to them by r. 43.2; a 'conditional fee agreement' is an agreement with a person providing advocacy or litigation services which provides for his fees and expenses, or part of them, to be payable only in specified circumstances, whether or not it provides for a success fee as mentioned in the Courts and Legal Services Act 1990, s. 58(2)(b);

'base costs' means costs other than the amount of any additional liability.

2.3 Rule 44.3A(1) provides that the court will not assess any additional liability until the conclusion of the proceedings or the part of the proceedings to which the funding arrangement relates. (As to the time when detailed assessment may be carried out see para. 27.1 below.)

2.4 For the purposes of the following paragraphs of this practice direction and r. 44.3A proceedings are concluded when the court has finally determined the matters in issue in the claim, whether or not there is an appeal. The making of an award of provisional damages under Part 41 will also be treated as a final determination of the matters in issue.

2.5 The court may order or the parties may agree in writing that, although the proceedings are continuing, they will nevertheless be treated as concluded.

## Section 3 Model Forms for Claims for Costs

*Rule 43.3 meaning of summary assessment*

3.1 Rule 43.3 defines summary assessment. When carrying out a summary assessment of costs where there is an additional liability the court may assess the base costs alone, or the base costs and the additional liability.

3.2 Form N260 is a model form of statement of costs to be used for summary assessments.

3.3 Further details about statements of costs are given in para. 13.5 below.

*Rule 43.4 meaning of detailed assessment*

3.4 Rule 43.4 defines detailed assessment. When carrying out a detailed assessment of costs where there is an additional liability the court will assess both the base costs and the additional liability, or, if the base costs have already been assessed, the additional liability alone.

3.5 Precedents A, B, C and D in the Schedule of Costs Precedents annexed to this practice direction are model forms of bills of costs to be used for detailed assessments.

3.6 Further details about bills of costs are given in the next section of these directions and in para. 28.1 to 49.1 below.

3.7 Precedents A, B, C and D in the Schedule of Costs Precedents and the next section of this practice direction all refer to a model form of bill of costs. The use of a model form is not compulsory, but is encouraged. A party wishing to rely upon a bill which departs from the model forms should include in the background information of the bill an explanation for that departure.

3.8 In any order of the court (whether made before or after 26 April 1999) the word 'taxation' will be taken to mean 'detailed assessment' and the words 'to be taxed' will be taken to mean 'to be decided by detailed assessment' unless in either case the context otherwise requires.

## Section 4 Form and Contents of Bills of Costs

4.1 A bill of costs may consist of such of the following sections as may be appropriate:

(1) title page;
(2) background information;
(3) items of costs claimed under the headings specified in para. 4.6;
(4) summary showing the total costs claimed on each page of the bill;
(5) schedules of time spent on non-routine attendances; and
(6) the certificates referred to in para. 4.15.

4.2 Where it is necessary or convenient to do so, a bill of costs may be divided into two or more parts, each part containing sections (2), (3) and (4) above. A division into parts will be necessary or convenient in the following circumstances:

(1) Where the receiving party acted in person during the course of the proceedings

(whether or not he also had a legal representative at that time) the bill should be divided into different parts so as to distinguish between;
(a) the costs claimed for work done by the legal representative; and
(b) the costs claimed for work done by the receiving party in person.
(2) Where the receiving party was represented by different solicitors during the course of the proceedings, the bill should be divided into different parts so as to distinguish between the costs payable in respect of each solicitor.
(3) Where the receiving party obtained legal aid or LSC funding in respect of all or part of the proceedings the bill should be divided into separate parts so as to distinguish between:
(a) costs claimed before legal aid or LSC funding was granted;
(b) costs claimed after legal aid or LSC funding was granted; and
(c) any costs claimed after legal aid or LSC funding ceased.
(4) Where value added tax (VAT) is claimed and there was a change in the rate of VAT during the course of the proceedings, the bill should be divided into separate parts so as to distinguish between:
(a) costs claimed at the old rate of VAT; and
(b) costs claimed at the new rate of VAT.
(5) Where the bill covers costs payable under an order or orders under which there are different paying parties the bill should be divided into parts so as to deal separately with the costs payable by each paying party.
(6) Where the bill covers costs payable under an order or orders, in respect of which the receiving party wishes to claim interest from different dates, the bill should be divided to enable such interest to be calculated.

4.3 Where a party claims costs against another party and also claims costs against the LSC only for work done in the same period, the costs claimed against the LSC only can be claimed either in a separate part of the bill or in additional columns in the same part of the bill. Precedents C and D in the Schedule of Costs Precedents annexed to this practice direction show how bills should be drafted when costs are claimed against the LSC only.

4.4 The title page of the bill of costs must set out:
(1) the full title of the proceedings;
(2) the name of the party whose bill it is and a description of the document showing the right to assessment (as to which see para. 40.4 below);
(3) if VAT is included as part of the claim for costs, the VAT number of the legal representative or other person in respect of whom VAT is claimed;
(4) details of all legal aid certificates, LSC certificates and relevant amendment certificates in respect of which claims for costs are included in the bill.

4.5 The background information included in the bill of costs should set out:
(1) a brief description of the proceedings up to the date of the notice of commencement;
(2) a statement of the status of the solicitor or solicitor's employee in respect of whom costs are claimed and (if those costs are calculated on the basis of hourly rates) the hourly rates claimed for each such person.
It should be noted that 'legal executive' means a Fellow of the Institute of Legal Executives.
Other clerks, who are fee earners of equivalent experience, may be entitled to similar rates. It should be borne in mind that Fellows of the Institute of Legal Executives will have spent approximately six years in practice, and taken both general and specialist examinations. The Fellows have therefore acquired considerable practical and academic experience. Clerks without the equivalent experience of legal executives will normally be treated as being the equivalent of trainee solicitors and paralegals.
(3) a brief explanation of any agreement or arrangement between the receiving party and his solicitors, which affects the costs claimed in the bill.

4.6 The bill of costs may consist of items under such of the following heads as may be appropriate:

(1) attendance on the court and counsel up to the date of the notice of commencement;
(2) attendances on and communications with the receiving party;
(3) attendances on and communications with witnesses including any expert witness;
(4) attendances to inspect any property or place for the purposes of the proceedings;
(5) attendances on and communications with other persons, including offices of public records;
(6) communications with the court and with counsel;
(7) work done on documents: preparing and considering documentation, including documentation relating to pre-action protocols where appropriate, work done in connection with arithmetical calculations of compensation and/or interest and time spent collating documents;
(8) work done in connection with negotiations with a view to settlement if not already covered in the heads listed above;
(9) attendances on and communications with London and other agents and work done by them;
(10) other work done which was of or incidental to the proceedings and which is not already covered in the heads listed above.

4.7 In respect of each of the heads of costs:

(1) 'communications' means letters out and telephone calls;
(2) communications, which are not routine communications, must be set out in chronological order;
(3) routine communications should be set out as a single item at the end of each head.

4.8 Routine communications are letters out, emails out and telephone calls which because of their simplicity should not be regarded as letters or emails of substance or telephone calls which properly amount to an attendance.

4.9 Each item claimed in the bill of costs must be consecutively numbered.

4.10 In each part of the bill of costs which claims items under head (1) (attendances on court and counsel) a note should be made of:

(1) all relevant events, including events which do not constitute chargeable items;
(2) any orders for costs which the court made (whether or not a claim is made in respect of those costs in this bill of costs).

4.11 The numbered items of costs may be set out on paper divided into columns. Precedents A, B, C and D in the Schedule of Costs precedents annexed to this practice direction illustrate various model forms of bills of costs.

4.12 In respect of heads (2) to (10) in para. 4.6 above, if the number of attendances and communications other than routine communications is 20 or more, the claim for the costs of those items in that section of the bill of costs should be for the total only and should refer to a schedule in which the full record of dates and details is set out. If the bill of costs contains more than one schedule each schedule should be numbered consecutively.

4.13 The bill of costs must not contain any claims in respect of costs or court fees which relate solely to the detailed assessment proceedings other than costs claimed for preparing and checking the bill.

4.14 The summary must show the total profit costs and disbursements claimed separately from the total VAT claimed. Where the bill of costs is divided into parts the summary must also give totals for each part. If each page of the bill gives a page total the summary must also set out the page totals for each page.

4.15 The bill of costs must contain such of the certificates, the texts of which are set out in Precedent F of the Schedule of Costs Precedents annexed to this practice direction, as are appropriate.

4.16 The following provisions relate to work done by solicitors:

(1) Routine letters out and routine telephone calls will in general be allowed on a unit basis of 6 minutes each, the charge being calculated by reference to the appropriate hourly rate. The unit charge for letters out will include perusing and considering the relevant letters in and no separate charge should be made for incoming letters.

(2) Emails received by solicitors will not normally be allowed. The court may, in its discretion, allow an actual time charge for preparation of emails sent by solicitors, which properly amount to attendances provided that the time taken has been recorded. The court may also, in its discretion allow a sum in respect of routine emails sent to the client or others on a unit basis of 6 minutes each, the charge being calculated by reference to the appropriate hourly rate.

(3) Local travelling expenses incurred by solicitors will not be allowed. The definition of 'local' is a matter for the discretion of the court. While no absolute rule can be laid down, as a matter of guidance, 'local' will, in general, be taken to mean within a radius of 10 miles from the court dealing with the case at the relevant time. Where travelling and waiting time is claimed, this should be allowed at the rate agreed with the client unless this is more than the hourly rate on the assessment.

(4) The cast of postage, couriers, outgoing telephone calls, fax and telex messages will in general not be allowed but the court may exceptionally in its discretion allow such expenses in unusual circumstances or where the cost is unusually heavy.

(5) The cost of making copies of documents will not in general be allowed but the court may exceptionally in its discretion make an allowance for copying in unusual circumstances or where the documents copied are unusually numerous in relation to the nature of the case. Where this discretion is invoked the number of copies made, their purpose and the costs claimed for them must be set out in the bill.

(6) Agency charges as between a principal solicitor and his agent will be dealt with on the principle that such charges, where appropriate, form part of the principal solicitor's charges. Where these charges relate to head (1) in para. 4.6 (attendances at court and on counsel) they should be included in their chronological order in that head. In other cases they should be included in head (9) (attendances on London and other agents).

4.17 (1) Where a claim is made for a percentage increase in addition to an hourly rate or base fee, the amount of the increase must be shown separately, either in the appropriate arithmetic column or in the narrative column. (For an example see Precedent A or Precedent B.)

(2) Where a claim is made against the LSC only and includes enhancement and where a claim is made in family proceedings and includes a claim for uplift or general care and conduct, the amount of enhancement uplift and general care and conduct must be shown, in respect of each item upon which it is claimed, as a separate amount either in the appropriate arithmetic column or in the narrative column. (For an example, see Precedent C.)

'Enhancement' means the increase in prescribed rates which may be allowed by a costs officer in accordance with the Legal Aid in Civil Proceedings (Remuneration) Regulations 1994 or the Legal Aid in Family Proceedings Regulations 1991.

*Costs of preparing the bill*

4.18 A claim may be made for the reasonable costs of preparing and checking the bill of costs.

## Section 5 Special Provisions Relating to VAT

5.1 This section deals with claims for value added tax (VAT) which are made in respect of costs being dealt with by way of summary assessment or detailed assessment.

*VAT registration number*

5.2 The number allocated by HM Revenue and Customs to every person registered under the Value Added Tax Act 1994* (except a government department) must appear in a prominent place at the head of every statement, bill of costs, fee sheet, account or voucher on which VAT is being included as part of a claim for costs.

*Entitlement to VAT on costs*

5.3 VAT should not be included in a claim for costs if the receiving party is able to recover the VAT as input tax. Where the receiving party is able to obtain credit from HM Revenue and Customs for a proportion of the VAT as input tax, only that proportion which is not eligible for credit should be included in the claim for costs.

5.4 The receiving party has responsibility for ensuring that VAT is claimed only when the receiving party is unable to recover the VAT or a proportion thereof as input tax.

5.5 Where there is a dispute as to whether VAT is properly claimed the receiving party must provide a certificate signed by the solicitors or the auditors of the receiving party substantially in the form illustrated in precedent F in the Schedule of Costs Precedents annexed to this practice direction. Where the receiving party is a litigant in person who is claiming VAT, reference should be made by him to HM Revenue and Customs and wherever possible a statement to similar effect produced at the hearing at which the costs are assessed.

5.6 Where there is a dispute as to whether any service in respect of which a charge is proposed to be made in the bill is zero rated or exempt, reference should be made to HM Revenue and Customs and wherever possible the view of HM Revenue and Customs obtained and made known at the hearing at which the costs are assessed. Such application should be made by the receiving party. In the case of a bill from a solicitor to his own client, such application should be made by the client.

*Form of bill of costs where VAT rate changes*

5.7 Where there is a change in the rate of VAT, suppliers of goods and services are entitled ss. 88(1) and (2) of the Value Added Tax Act 1994 in most circumstances to elect whether the new or the old rate of VAT should apply to a supply where the basic and actual tax points span a period during which there has been a change in VAT rates.

5.8 It will be assumed, unless a contrary indication is given in writing, that an election to take advantage of the provisions mentioned in para. 5.7 above and to charge VAT at the lower rate has been made. In any case in which an election to charge at the lower rate is not made, such a decision must be justified to the court assessing the costs.

*Apportionment*

5.9 All bills of costs, fees and disbursements on which VAT is included must be divided into separate parts so as to show work done before, on and after the date or dates from which any change in the rate of VAT takes effect. Where, however, a lump-sum charge is made for work which spans a period during which there has been a change in VAT rates, and paras 5.7 and 5.8 above do not apply, reference should be made to paras 8 and 9 of Appendix F of Customs and Excise Notice 700 (or any revised edition of that notice),† a copy of which should be in the possession of every registered trader. If necessary, the lump sum should be apportioned. The totals of profit costs and disbursements in each part must be carried separately to the summary.

5.10 Should there be a change in the rate between the conclusion of a detailed assessment and the issue of the final costs certificate, any interested party may apply for the detailed assessment to be varied so as to take account of any increase or reduction in

[* The text issued by the Department for Constitutional Affairs mistakenly refers to the Value Added Tax Act 1983.]

[† A revised version of Notice 700 was issued in April 2002. In the revised version, changes in VAT rates are dealt with in section 30.]

the amount of tax payable. Once the final costs certificate has been issued, no variation under this paragraph will be permitted.

*Disbursements*

5.11 Petty (or general) disbursements such as postage, fares etc. which are normally treated as part of a solicitor's overheads and included in his profit costs should be charged with VAT even though they bear no tax when the solicitor incurs them. The cost of travel by public transport on a specific journey for a particular client where it forms part of the service rendered by a solicitor to his client and is charged in his bill of costs, attracts VAT.

5.12 Reference is made to the criteria set out in the VAT Guide (Customs and Excise Notice 700, 1 August 1991 ed., para. 83, or any revised edition of that notice)* as to expenses which are not subject to VAT. Charges for the cost of travel by public transport, postage, telephone calls and telegraphic transfers where these form part of the service rendered by the solicitor to his client are examples of charges which do not satisfy these criteria and are thus liable to VAT at the standard rate.

*Legal aid/LSC funding*

5.13 (1) VAT will be payable in respect of every supply made pursuant to a legal aid/LSC certificate where:
- (a) the person making the supply is a taxable person; and
- (b) the assisted person/LSC funded client:
  - (i) belongs in the United Kingdom or another member State of the European Union; and
  - (ii) is a private individual or receives the supply for non-business purposes.

(2) Where the assisted person/LSC funded client belongs outside the European Union, VAT is generally not payable unless the supply relates to land in the United Kingdom.

(3) For the purpose of sub-paragraphs (1) and (2), the place where a person belongs is determined by the Value Added Tax Act 1994, s. 9.

(4) Where the assisted person/LSC funded client is registered for VAT and the legal services paid for by the LSC are in connection with that person's business, the VAT on those services will be payable by the LSC only.

5.14 Any summary of costs payable by the LSC must be drawn so as to show the total VAT on counsel's fees as a separate item from the VAT on other disbursements and the VAT on profit costs.

*Tax invoice*

5.15 A bill of costs filed for detailed assessment is always retained by the court. Accordingly if a solicitor waives his solicitor and client costs and accepts the costs certified by the court as payable by the unsuccessful party in settlement, it will be necessary for a short statement as to the amount of the certified costs and the VAT thereon to be prepared for use as the tax invoice.

*Vouchers*

5.16 Where receipted accounts for disbursements made by the solicitor or his client are retained as tax invoices a photostat copy of any such receipted account may be produced and will be accepted as sufficient evidence of payment when disbursements are vouched.

*Certificates*

5.17 In a costs certificate payable by the LSC, the VAT on solicitor's costs, counsel's fees and disbursements will be shown separately.

[* A revised version of Notice 700 was issued in April 2002.]

*Litigants acting in person*

5.18 Where a litigant acts in litigation on his own behalf he is not treated for the purposes of VAT as having supplied services and therefore no VAT is chargeable in respect of work done by that litigant (even where, for example, that litigant is a solicitor or other legal representative).

5.19 Consequently in the circumstances described in the preceding paragraph, a bill of costs presented for agreement or assessment should not claim any VAT which will not be allowed on assessment.

*Government departments*

5.20 On an assessment between parties, where costs are being paid to a government department in respect of services rendered by its legal staff, VAT should not be added.

## Section 6 Estimates of Costs

6.1 This section sets out certain steps which parties and their legal representatives must take in order to keep the parties informed about their potential liability in respect of costs and in order to assist the court to decide what, if any, order to make about costs and about case management.

6.2 (1) In this section an 'estimate of costs' means—

(a) an estimate of base costs (including disbursements) already incurred; and

(b) an estimate of base costs (including disbursements) to be incurred,

which a party intends to seek to recover from any other party under an order for costs if he is successful in the case.

('Base costs' are defined in paragraph 2.2 of this practice direction.)

(2) A party who intends to recover an additional liability (defined in rule 43.2) need not reveal the amount of that liability in the estimate.

6.3 The court may at any stage in a case order any party to file an estimate of costs and to serve copies of the estimate on all other parties. The court may direct that the estimate be prepared in such a way as to demonstrate the likely effects of giving or not giving a particular case management direction which the court is considering, for example a direction for a split trial or for the trial of a preliminary issue. The court may specify a time limit for filing and serving the estimate. However, if no time limit is specified the estimate should be filed and served within 28 days of the date of the order.

6.4 (1) When—

(a) a party to a claim which is outside the financial scope of the small claims track files an allocation questionnaire; or

(b) a party to a claim which is being dealt with on the fast track or the multi-track, or under Part 8, files a pre-trial check list (listing questionnaire),

he must also file an estimate of costs and serve a copy of it on every other party, unless the court otherwise directs. Where a party is represented, the legal representative must in addition serve an estimate on the party he represents.

(2) Where a party is required to file and serve a new estimate of costs in accordance with rule 44.15(3), if that party is represented the legal representative must in addition serve the new estimate on the party he represents.

(3) This paragraph does not apply to litigants in person.

6.5 An estimate of costs should be substantially in the form illustrated in Precedent H in the Schedule of Costs Precedents annexed to the practice direction.

6.5A (1) If there is a difference of 20% or more between the base costs claimed by a receiving party on detailed assessment and the costs shown in an estimate of costs filed by that party, the receiving party must provide a statement of the reasons for the difference with his bill of costs.

(2) If a paying party—

(a) claims that he reasonably relied on an estimate of costs filed by a receiving party; or

(b) wishes to rely upon the costs shown in the estimate in order to dispute the reasonableness or proportionality of the costs claimed,

the paying party must serve a statement setting out his case in this regard in his points of dispute.

('Relevant person' is defined in paragraph 32.10(1) of the Costs Practice Direction)

6.6 (1) On an assessment of the costs of a party, the court may have regard to any estimate previously filed by that party, or by any other party in the same proceedings. Such an estimate may be taken into account as a factor among others, when assessing the reasonableness and proportionality of any costs claimed.

(2) In particular, where—

(a) there is a difference of 20% or more between the base costs claimed by a receiving party and the costs shown in an estimate of costs filed by that party; and

(b) it appears to the court that—

(i) the receiving party has not provided a satisfactory explanation for that difference; or

(ii) the paying party reasonably relied on the estimate of costs;

the court may regard the difference between the costs claimed and the costs shown in the estimate as evidence that the costs claimed are unreasonable or disproportionate.

## DIRECTIONS RELATING TO PART 44 GENERAL RULES ABOUT COSTS

### Section 7 Solicitor's Duty to Notify Client: Rule 44.2

7.1 For the purposes of r. 44.2 'client' includes a party for whom a solicitor is acting and any other person (for example, an insurer, a trade union or the LSC) who has instructed the solicitor to act or who is liable to pay his fees.

7.2 Where a solicitor notifies a client of an order under that rule, he must also explain why the order came to be made.

7.3 Although r. 44.2 does not specify any sanction for breach of the rule the court may, either in the order for costs itself or in a subsequent order, require the solicitor to produce to the court evidence showing that he took reasonable steps to comply with the rule.

### Section 8 Court's Discretion and Circumstances to be Taken into Account When Exercising its Discretion as to Costs: Rule 44.3

8.1 Attention is drawn to the factors set out in this rule which may lead the court to depart from the general rule stated in r. 44.3(2) and to make a different order about costs.

8.2 In a probate claim where a defendant has in his defence given notice that he requires the will to be proved in solemn form (see [r. 57.7(5)*]), the court will not make an order for costs against the defendant unless it appears that there was no reasonable ground for opposing the will. The term 'probate claim' is defined in r. 57.1(2).

8.3 (1) The court may make an order about costs at any stage in a case.

(2) In particular the court may make an order about costs when it deals with any application, makes any order or holds any hearing and that order about costs may relate to the costs of that application, order or hearing.

(3) Rule 44.3A(1) provides that the court will not assess any additional liability until the conclusion of the proceedings or the part of the proceedings to which the funding arrangement relates. (Paragraphs 2.4 and 2.5 above explain when proceedings are concluded. As to the time when detailed assessment may be carried out see para. 28.1, below.)

[* The text issued by the Department for Constitutional Affairs mistakenly refers to PD 57, para. 8.3.]

8.4 In deciding what order to make about costs the court is required to have regard to all the circumstances including any payment into court or admissible offer to settle made by a party which is drawn to the court's attention, and which is not an offer to which costs consequences under Part 36 apply.

8.5 There are certain costs orders which the court will commonly make in proceedings before trial. The following table sets out the general effect of these orders. The table is not an exhaustive list of the orders which the court may make.

| Term | Effect |
|---|---|
| • Costs<br>• Costs in any event | The party in whose favour the order is made is entitled to the costs in respect of the part of the proceedings to which the order relates, whatever other costs orders are made in the proceedings. |
| • Costs in the case<br>• Costs in the application | The party in whose favour the court makes an order for costs at the end of the proceedings is entitled to his costs of the part of the proceedings to which the order relates. |
| • Costs reserved | The decision about costs is deferred to a later occasion, but if no later order is made the costs will be costs in the case. |
| • Claimant's/Defendant's costs in the case/ application | If the party in whose favour the costs order is made is awarded costs at the end of the proceedings, that party is entitled to his costs of the part of the proceedings to which the order relates.<br>If any other party is awarded costs at the end of the proceedings, the party in whose favour the final costs order is made is not liable to pay the costs of any other party in respect of the part of the proceedings to which the order relates. |
| • Costs thrown away | Where, for example, a judgment or order is set aside, the party in whose favour the costs order is made is entitled to the costs which have been incurred as a consequence. This includes the costs of:<br>(a) preparing for and attending any hearing at which the judgment or order which has been set aside was made;<br>(b) preparing for and attending any hearing to set aside the judgment or order in question;<br>(c) preparing for and attending any hearing at which the court orders the proceedings or the part in question to be adjourned;<br>(d) any steps taken to enforce a judgment or order which has subsequently been set aside. |
| • Costs of and caused by | Where, for example, the court makes this order on an application to amend a statement of case, the party in whose favour the costs order is made is entitled to the costs of preparing for and attending the application and the costs of any consequential amendment to his own statement of case. |
| • Costs here and below | The party in whose favour the costs order is made is entitled not only to his costs in respect of the proceedings in which the court makes the order but also to his costs of the proceedings in any lower court. In the case of an appeal from a Divisional Court the party is not entitled to any costs incurred in any court below the Divisional Court. |
| • No order as to costs<br>• Each party to pay his own costs | Each party is to bear his own costs of the part of the proceedings to which the order relates whatever costs order the court makes at the end of the proceedings. |

8.6 Where, under r. 44.3(8), the court orders an amount to be paid before costs are assessed:
(1) the order will state that amount, and
(2) if no other date for payment is specified in the order r. 44.8 (time for complying with an order for costs) will apply.

*Fees of counsel*

8.7 (1) This paragraph applies where the court orders the detailed assessment of the costs of a hearing at which one or more counsel appeared for a party.
(2) Where an order for costs states the opinion of the court as to whether or not the hearing was fit for the attendance of one or more counsel, a costs officer conducting a detailed assessment of costs to which that order relates will have regard to the opinion stated.
(3) The court will generally express an opinion only where:
(a) the paying party asks it to do so;
(b) more than one counsel appeared for a party; or
(c) the court wishes to record its opinion that the case was not fit for the attendance of counsel.

*Fees payable to conveyancing counsel appointed by the court to assist it*

8.8 (1) Where the court refers any matter to the conveyancing counsel of the court the fees payable to counsel in respect of the work done or to be done will be assessed by the court in accordance with r. 44.3.
(2) An appeal from a decision of the court in respect of the fees of such counsel will be dealt with under the general rules as to appeals set out in Part 52. If the appeal is against the decision of an authorised court officer, it will be dealt with in accordance with rr. 47.20 to 47.23.

## Section 9 Costs Orders Relating to Funding Arrangements: Rule 44.3A

9.1 Under an order for payment of 'costs' the costs payable will include an additional liability incurred under a funding arrangement.

9.2 (1) If before the conclusion of the proceedings the court carries out a summary assessment of the base costs it may identify separately the amount allowed in respect of: solicitor's charges; counsel's fees; other disbursements; and any value added tax (VAT). (Sections 13 and 14 of this practice direction deal with summary assessment.)
(2) If an order for the base costs of a previous application or hearing did not identify separately the amounts allowed for solicitor's charges, counsel's fees and other disbursements, a court which later makes an assessment of an additional liability may apportion the base costs previously ordered.

## Section 10 Limits on Recovery Under Funding Arrangements: Rule 44.3B

10.1 In a case to which r. 44.3B(1)(c) or (d) applies the party in default may apply for relief from the sanction. He should do so as quickly as possible after he becomes aware of the default. An application, supported by evidence, should be made under Part 23 to a costs judge or district judge of the court which is dealing with the case. (Attention is drawn to rr. 3.8 and 3.9 which deal with sanctions and relief from sanctions.)

10.2 Where the amount of any percentage increase recoverable by counsel may be affected by the outcome of the application, the solicitor issuing the application must serve on counsel a copy of the application notice and notice of the hearing as soon as practicable and in any event at least two days before the hearing. Counsel may make written submissions or may attend and make oral submissions at the hearing. (Paragraph 1.4 contains definitions of the terms 'counsel' and 'solicitor'.)

## Section 11 Factors to be Taken into Account in Deciding the Amount of Costs: Rule 44.5

11.1 In applying the test of proportionality the court will have regard to r. 1.1(2)(c). The relationship between the total of the costs incurred and the financial value of the claim may not be a reliable guide. A fixed percentage cannot be applied in all cases to the value of the claim in order to ascertain whether or not the costs are proportionate.

11.2 In any proceedings there will be costs which will inevitably be incurred and which are necessary for the successful conduct of the case. Solicitors are not required to conduct litigation at rates which are uneconomic. Thus in a modest claim the proportion of costs is likely to be higher than in a large claim, and may even equal or possibly exceed the amount in dispute.

11.3 Where a trial takes place, the time taken by the court in dealing with a particular issue may not be an accurate guide to the amount of time properly spent by the legal or other representatives in preparation for the trial of that issue.

11.4 Where a party has entered into a funding arrangement the costs claimed may, subject to r. 44.3B include an additional liability.

11.5 In deciding whether the costs claimed are reasonable and (on a standard basis assessment) proportionate, the court will consider the amount of any additional liability separately from the base costs.

11.6 In deciding whether the base costs are reasonable and (if relevant) proportionate the court will consider the factors set out in r. 44.5.

11.7 Subject to para. 17.8(2), when the court is considering the factors to be taken into account in assessing an additional liability, it will have regard to the facts and circumstances as they reasonably appeared to the solicitor or counsel when the funding arrangement was entered into and at the time of any variation of the arrangement.

11.8 (1) In deciding whether a percentage increase is reasonable relevant factors to be taken into account may include:
 (a) the risk that the circumstances in which the costs, fees or expenses would be payable might or might not occur;
 (b) the legal representative's liability for any disbursements;
 (c) what other methods of financing the costs were available to the receiving party.
(2) [*Omitted*]

11.9 A percentage increase will not be reduced simply on the ground that, when added to base costs which are reasonable and (where relevant) proportionate, the total appears disproportionate.

11.10 In deciding whether the cost of insurance cover is reasonable, relevant factors to be taken into account include:
(1) where the insurance cover is not purchased in support of a conditional fee agreement with a success fee, how its cost compares with the likely cost of funding the case with a conditional fee agreement with a success fee and supporting insurance cover;
(2) the level and extent of the cover provided;
(3) the availability of any pre-existing insurance cover;
(4) whether any part of the premium would be rebated in the event of early settlement;
(5) the amount of commission payable to the receiving party or his legal representatives or other agents.

11.11 Where the court is considering a provision made by a membership organisation, r. 44.3B(1)(b) provides that any such provision which exceeds the likely cost to the receiving party of the premium of an insurance policy against the risk of incurring a liability to pay the costs of other parties to the proceedings is not recoverable.

In such circumstances the court will, when assessing the additional liability, have regard to the factors set out in para. 11.10 above, in addition to the factors set out in r. 44.5.

## Section 12 Procedure for Assessing Costs: Rule 44.7

12.1 Where the court does not order fixed costs (or no fixed costs are provided for) the amount of costs payable will be assessed by the court. This rule allows the court making an order about costs either:
(a) to make a summary assessment of the amount of the costs, or
(b) to order the amount to be decided in accordance with Part 47 (a detailed assessment).

12.2 An order for costs will be treated as an order for the amount of costs to be decided by a detailed assessment unless the order otherwise provides.

12.3 Whenever the court awards costs to be assessed by way of detailed assessment it should consider whether to exercise the power in r. 44.3(8) (court's discretion as to costs) to order the paying party to pay such sum of money as it thinks just on account of those costs.

## Section 13 Summary Assessment: General Provisions

13.1 Whenever a court makes an order about costs which does not provide for fixed costs to be paid the court should consider whether to make a summary assessment of costs.

13.2 The general rule is that the court should make a summary assessment of the costs:
(1) at the conclusion of the trial of a case which has been dealt with on the fast track, in which case the order will deal with the costs of the whole claim, and
(2) at the conclusion of any other hearing, which has lasted not more than one day, in which case the order will deal with the costs of the application or matter to which the hearing related. If this hearing disposes of the claim, the order may deal with the costs of the whole claim;
(3) in hearings in the Court of Appeal to which PD 52, para. 14, applies, unless there is good reason not to do, for example, where the paying party shows substantial grounds for disputing the sum claimed for costs that cannot be dealt with summarily or there is insufficient time to carry out a summary assessment.

13.3 The general rule in para. 13.2 does not apply to a mortgagee's costs incurred in mortgage possession proceedings or other proceedings relating to a mortgage unless the mortgagee asks the court to make an order for his costs to be paid by another party. Paragraphs 50.3 and 50.4 deal in more detail with costs relating to mortgages.

13.4 Where an application has been made and the parties to the application agree an order by consent without any party attending, the parties should agree a figure for costs to be inserted in the consent order or agree that there should be no order for costs. If the parties cannot agree the costs position, attendance on the appointment will be necessary but, unless good reason can be shown for the failure to deal with costs as set out above, no costs will be allowed for that attendance.

13.5 (1) It is the duty of the parties and their legal representatives to assist the judge in making a summary assessment of costs in any case to which para. 13.2 above applies, in accordance with the following paragraphs.
(2) Each party who intends to claim costs must prepare a written statement of the costs he intends to claim showing separately in the form of a schedule:
(a) the number of hours to be claimed,
(b) the hourly rate to be claimed,
(c) the grade of fee earner,
(d) the amount and nature of any disbursement to be claimed, other than counsel's fee for appearing at the hearing,

(e) the amount of solicitor's costs to be claimed for attending or appearing at the hearing,
(f) the fees of counsel to be claimed in respect of the hearing, and
(g) any value added tax (VAT) to be claimed on these amounts.

(3) The statement of costs should follow as closely as possible form N260 and must be signed by the party or his legal representative. Where a litigant is an assisted person or is a LSC funded client or is represented by a solicitor in the litigant's employment the statement of costs need not include the certificate appended at the end of form N260.

(4) The statement of costs must be filed at court and copies of it must be served on any party against whom an order for payment of those costs is intended to be sought. The statement of costs should be filed and the copies of it should be served as soon as possible and in any event not less than 24 hours before the date fixed for the hearing.

(5) Where the litigant is or may be entitled to claim an additional liability the statement filed and served need not reveal the amount of that liability.

13.6 The failure by a party, without reasonable excuse, to comply with the foregoing paragraphs will be taken into account by the court in deciding what order to make about the costs of the claim, hearing or application, and about the costs of any further hearing or detailed assessment hearing that may be necessary as a result of that failure.

13.7 If the court makes a summary assessment of costs at the conclusion of proceedings the court will specify separately:

(1) the base costs, and if appropriate, the additional liability allowed as solicitor's charges, counsel's fees, other disbursements and any VAT; and
(2) the amount which is awarded under Part 46 (fast track trial costs).

13.8 The court awarding costs cannot make an order for a summary assessment of costs by a costs officer. If a summary assessment of costs is appropriate but the court awarding costs is unable to do so on the day, the court must give directions as to a further hearing before the same judge.

13.9 The court will not make a summary assessment of the costs of a receiving party who is an assisted person or LSC funded client.

13.10 A summary assessment of costs payable by an assisted person or LSC funded client is not by itself a determination of that person's liability to pay those costs (as to which see r. 44.17 and paras 21.1 to 23.17 of this practice direction).

13.11 (1) The court will not make a summary assessment of the costs of a receiving party who is a child or patient within the meaning of Part 21 unless the solicitor acting for the child or patient has waived the right to further costs (see para. 51.1 below).

(2) The court may make a summary assessment of costs payable by a child or patient.

13.12 (1) Attention is drawn to r. 44.3A which prevents the court from making a summary assessment of an additional liability before the conclusion of the proceedings or the part of the proceedings to which the funding arrangement relates. Where this applies, the court should nonetheless make a summary assessment of the base costs of the hearing or application unless there is a good reason not to do so.

(2) Where the court makes a summary assessment of the base costs all statements of costs and costs estimates put before the judge will be retained on the court file.

13.13 The court will not give its approval to disproportionate and unreasonable costs. Accordingly:

(a) When the amount of the costs to be paid has been agreed between the parties the order for costs must state that the order is by consent.
(b) If the judge is to make an order which is not by consent, the judge will, so far as possible, ensure that the final figure is not disproportionate and/or unreasonable having regard to Part 1 of the CPR. The judge will retain this responsibility

notwithstanding the absence of challenge to individual items in the make-up of the figure sought. The fact that the paying party is not disputing the amount of costs can however be taken as some indication that the amount is proportionate and reasonable. The judge will therefore intervene only if satisfied that the costs are so disproportionate that it is right to do so.

## Section 14 Summary Assessment Where Costs Claimed Include an Additional Liability

*Orders made before the conclusion of the proceedings*

14.1 The existence of a conditional fee agreement or other funding arrangement within the meaning of r. 43.2 is not by itself a sufficient reason for not carrying out a summary assessment.

14.2 Where a legal representative acting for the receiving party has entered into a conditional fee agreement the court may summarily assess all the costs (other than any additional liability).

14.3 Where costs have been summarily assessed an order for payment will not be made unless the court has been satisfied that in respect of the costs claimed, the receiving party is at the time liable to pay to his legal representative an amount equal to or greater than the costs claimed. A statement in the form of the certificate appended at the end of form N260 may be sufficient proof of liability. The giving of information under r. 44.15 (where that rule applies) is not sufficient.

14.4 The court may direct that any costs, for which the receiving party may not in the event be liable, shall be paid into court to await the outcome of the case, or shall not be enforceable until further order, or it may postpone the receiving party's right to receive payment in some other way.

*Orders made at the conclusion of the proceedings*

14.5 Where there has been a trial of one or more issues separately from other issues, the court will not normally order detailed assessment of the additional liability until all issues have been tried unless the parties agree.

14.6 Rule 44.3A(2) sets out the ways in which the court may deal with the assessment of the costs where there is a funding arrangement. Where the court makes a summary assessment of the base costs:

(1) The order may state separately the base costs allowed as (a) solicitor's charges, (b) counsel's fees, (c) any other disbursements and (d) any VAT;

(2) the statements of costs upon which the judge based his summary assessment will be retained on the court file.

14.7 Where the court makes a summary assessment of an additional liability at the conclusion of proceedings, that assessment must relate to the whole of the proceedings; this will include any additional liability relating to base costs allowed by the court when making a summary assessment on a previous application or hearing.

14.8 Paragraph 13.13 applies where the parties are agreed about the total amount to be paid by way of costs, or are agreed about the amount of the base costs that will be paid. Where they disagree about the additional liability the court may summarily assess that liability or make an order for a detailed assessment.

14.9 In order to facilitate the court in making a summary assessment of any additional liability at the conclusion of the proceedings the party seeking such costs must prepare and have available for the court a bundle of documents which must include:

(1) a copy of every notice of funding arrangement (form N251) which has been filed by him;

(2) a copy of every estimate and statement of costs filed by him;

(3) a copy of the risk assessment prepared at the time any relevant funding arrangement was entered into and on the basis of which the amount of the additional liability was fixed.

## Section 15 Costs on the Small Claims Track and Fast Track: Rule 44.9

15.1 (1) Before a claim is allocated to one of those tracks the court is not restricted by any of the special rules that apply to that track.

(2) Where a claim has been allocated to one of those tracks, the special rules which relate to that track will apply to work done before as well as after allocation save to the extent (if any) that an order for costs in respect of that work was made before allocation.

(3) (i) This paragraph applies where a claim, issued for a sum in excess of the normal financial scope of the small claims track, is allocated to that track only because an admission of part of the claim by the defendant reduces the amount in dispute to a sum within the normal scope of that track.
(See also PD 26, para. 7.4)

(ii) On entering judgment for the admitted part before allocation of the balance of the claim the court may allow costs in respect of the proceedings down to that date.

## Section 16 Costs Following Allocation and Reallocation: Rule 44.11

16.1 This paragraph applies where the court is about to make an order to reallocate a claim from the small claims track to another track.

16.2 Before making the order to reallocate the claim, the court must decide whether any party is to pay costs to any other party down to the date of the order to reallocate in accordance with the rules about costs contained in Part 27 (the small claims track).

16.3 If it decides to make such an order about costs, the court will make a summary assessment of those costs in accordance with that Part.

## Section 17 Costs-only Proceedings: Rule 44.12A

17.1 A claim form under this rule should not be issued in the High Court unless the dispute to which the agreement relates was of such a value or type that had proceedings been begun they would have been commenced in the High Court.

17.2 A claim form which is to be issued in the High Court at the Royal Courts of Justice will be issued in the Supreme Court Costs Office.

17.3 Attention is drawn to r. 8.2 (in particular to para. (b)(ii)) and to r. 44.12A(3). The claim form must:

(1) identify the claim or dispute to which the agreement to pay costs relates;
(2) state the date and terms of the agreement on which the claimant relies;
(3) set out or have attached to it a draft of the order which the claimant seeks;
(4) state the amount of the costs claimed; and,
(5) state whether the costs are claimed on the standard or indemnity basis. If no basis is specified the costs will be treated as being claimed on the standard basis.

17.4 The evidence to be filed and served with the claim form under r. 8.5 must include copies of the documents on which the claimant relies to prove the defendant's agreement to pay costs.

17.5 A costs judge or a district judge has jurisdiction to hear and decide any issue which may arise in a claim issued under this rule irrespective of the amount of the costs claimed or of the value of the claim to which the agreement to pay costs relates. A costs officer may make an order by consent under para. 17.7, or an order dismissing a claim under para. 17.9 below.

17.6 When the time for filing the defendant's acknowledgment of service has expired, the claimant may by letter request the court to make an order in the terms of his claim, unless the defendant has filed an acknowledgment of service stating that he intends to contest the claim or to seek a different order.

17.7 Rule 40.6 applies where an order is to be made by consent. An order may be made by consent in terms which differ from those set out in the claim form.

17.8 (1) An order for costs made under this rule will be treated as an order for the amount of costs to be decided by a detailed assessment to which Part 47 and the practice directions relating to it apply. Rule 44.4(4) (determination of basis of assessment) also applies to the order.

(2) In cases in which an additional liability is claimed, the costs judge or district judge should have regard to the time when and the extent to which the claim has been settled and to the fact that the claim has been settled without the need to commence proceedings.

17.9 (1) For the purposes of r. 44.12A(4)(b):

(a) a claim will be treated as opposed if the defendant files an acknowledgment of service stating that he intends to contest the making of an order for costs or to seek a different remedy; and

(b) a claim will not be treated as opposed if the defendant files an acknowledgment of service stating that he disputes the amount of the claim for costs.

(2) An order dismissing the claim will be made as soon as an acknowledgment of service opposing the claim is filed. The dismissal of a claim under r. 44.12A(4) does not prevent the claimant from issuing another claim form under Part 7 or Part 8 based on the agreement or alleged agreement to which the proceedings under this rule related.

17.10 (1) Rule 8.9 (which provides that claims issued under Part 8 shall be treated as allocated to the multi-track) shall not apply to claims issued under this rule. A claim issued under this rule may be dealt with without being allocated to a track.

(2) Rule 8.1(3) and Part 24 do not apply to proceedings brought under r. 44.12A.

17.11 Nothing in this rule prevents a person from issuing a claim form under Part 7 or Part 8 to sue on an agreement made in settlement of a dispute where that agreement makes provision for costs, nor from claiming in that case an order for costs or a specified sum in respect of costs.

## Section 18 Court's Powers in Relation to Misconduct: Rule 44.14

18.1 Before making an order under r. 44.14 the court must give the party or legal representative in question a reasonable opportunity to attend a hearing to give reasons why it should not make such an order.

18.2 Conduct before or during the proceedings which gave rise to the assessment which is unreasonable or improper includes steps which are calculated to prevent or inhibit the court from furthering the overriding objective.

18.3 Although r. 44.14(3) does not specify any sanction for breach of the obligation imposed by the rule the court may, either in the order under paragraph (2) or in a subsequent order, require the solicitor to produce to the court evidence that he took reasonable steps to comply with the obligation.

## Section 19 Providing Information About Funding Arrangements: Rule 44.15

19.1 (1) A party who wishes to claim an additional liability in respect of a funding arrangement must give any other party information about that claim if he is to recover the additional liability. There is no requirement to specify the amount of the additional liability separately nor to state how it is calculated until it falls to be assessed. That principle is reflected in rr. 44.3A and 44.15, in the following paragraphs and in sections 6, 13, 14 and 31 of this practice direction. Section 6 deals with estimates of costs, sections 13 and 14 deal with summary assessment and section 31 deals with detailed assessment.

(2) In the following paragraphs a party who has entered into a funding arrangement is treated as a person who intends to recover a sum representing an additional liability by way of costs.

(3) Attention is drawn to para. 57.9 of this practice direction which sets out time limits for the provision of information where a funding arrangement is entered

into between 31 March and 2 July 2000 and proceedings relevant to that arrangement are commenced before 3 July 2000.

*Method of giving information*

19.2 (1) In this paragraph, 'claim form' includes petition and application notice, and the notice of funding to be filed or served is a notice containing the information set out in form N251.

(2) (a) A claimant who has entered into a funding arrangement before starting the proceedings to which it relates must provide information to the court by filing the notice when he issues the claim form.

(b) He must provide information to every other party by serving the notice. If he serves the claim form himself he must serve the notice with the claim form. If the court is to serve the claim form, the court will also serve the notice if the claimant provides it with sufficient copies for service.

(3) A defendant who has entered into a funding arrangement before filing any document:

(a) must provide information to the court by filing notice with his first document. A 'first document' may be an acknowledgment of service, a defence, or any other document, such as an application to set aside a default judgment.

(b) must provide information to every party by serving notice. If he serves his first document himself he must serve the notice with that document. If the court is to serve his first document the court will also serve the notice if the defendant provides it with sufficient copies for service.

(4) In all other circumstances a party must file and serve notice within seven days of entering into the funding arrangement concerned.

(5) There is no requirement in this practice direction for the provision of information about funding arrangements before the commencement of proceedings. Such provision is however recommended and may be required by a pre-action protocol.

*Notice of change of information*

19.3 (1) Rule 44.15 imposes a duty on a party to give notice of change if the information he has previously provided is no longer accurate. To comply he must file and serve notice containing the information set out in form N251. Rule 44.15(3) may impose other duties in relation to new estimates of costs.

(2) Further notification need not be provided where a party has already given notice:

(a) that he has entered into a conditional fee agreement with a legal representative and during the currency of that agreement either of them enters into another such agreement with an additional legal representative; or

(b) of some insurance cover, unless that cover is cancelled or unless new cover is taken out with a different insurer.

(3) Part 6 applies to the service of notices.

(4) The notice must be signed by the party or by his legal representative.

*Information which must be provided*

19.4 (1) Unless the court otherwise orders, a party who is required to supply information about a funding arrangement must state whether he has:

(a) entered into a conditional fee agreement which provides for a success fee within the meaning of section 58(2) of the Courts and Legal Services Act 1990;

(b) taken out an insurance policy to which section 29 of the Access to Justice Act 1999 applies;

(c) made an arrangement with a body which is prescribed for the purpose of section 30 of that Act;

or more than one of these.

(2) Where the funding arrangement is a conditional fee agreement, the party must

state the date of the agreement and identify the claim or claims to which it relates (including Part 20 claims if any).

(3) Where the funding arrangement is an insurance policy, the party must state the name of the insurer, the policy number and the date of the policy, and must identify the claim or claims to which it relates (including Part 20 claims if any).

(4) Where the funding arrangement is by way of an arrangement with a relevant body the party must state the name of the body and set out the date and terms of the undertaking it has given and must identify the claim or claims to which it relates (including Part 20 claims if any).

(5) Where a party has entered into more than one funding arrangement in respect of a claim, for example, a conditional fee agreement and an insurance policy, a single notice containing the information set out in form N251 may contain the required information about both or all of them.

19.5 Where the court makes a Group Litigation Order, the court may give directions as to the extent to which individual parties should provide information in accordance with r. 44.15. (Part 19 deals with Group Litigation Orders.)

## Section 20 Procedure Where Legal Representative Wishes to Recover from His Client an Agreed Percentage Increase Which Has Been Disallowed or Reduced on Assessment: Rule 44.16

20.1 (1) Attention is drawn to the Conditional Fee Agreements Regulations 2000, reg. 3(2)(b), and to the Collective Conditional Fee Agreements Regulations 2000, reg. 5(2)(b), which provide that some or all of a success fee ceases to be payable in certain circumstances. [Both sets of regulations were revoked by the Conditional Fee Agreements (Revocation) Regulations 2005 but continue to have effect in relation to conditional fee agreements and collective conditional fee agreements entered into before 1 November 2005.]

(2) Rule 44.16 allows the court to adjourn a hearing at which the legal representative acting for the receiving party applies for an order that a disallowed amount should continue to be payable under the agreement.

20.2 In the following paragraphs 'counsel' means counsel who has acted in the case under a conditional fee agreement which provides for a success fee. A reference to counsel includes a reference to any person who appeared as an advocate in the case and who is not a partner or employee of the solicitor or firm which is conducting the claim or defence (as the case may be) on behalf of the receiving party.

*Procedure following summary assessment*

20.3 (1) If the court disallows any amount of a legal representative's percentage increase, the court will, unless sub-para. (2) applies, give directions to enable an application to be made by the legal representative for the disallowed amount to be payable by his client, including, if appropriate, a direction that the application will be determined by a costs judge or district judge of the court dealing with the case.

(2) The court that has made the summary assessment may then and there decide the issue whether the disallowed amount should continue to be payable, if:

(a) the receiving party and all parties to the relevant agreement consent to the court doing so;

(b) the receiving party (or, if corporate, an officer) is present in court; and

(c) the court is satisfied that the issue can be fairly decided then and there.

*Procedure following detailed assessment*

20.4 (1) Where detailed assessment proceedings have been commenced, and the paying party serves points of dispute (as to which see section 34 of this practice direction), which show that he is seeking a reduction in any percentage increase charged by counsel on his fees, the solicitor acting for the receiving party must within three days of service deliver to counsel a copy of the relevant points of dispute and the bill of costs or the relevant parts of the bill.

(2) Counsel must within 10 days thereafter inform the solicitor in writing whether or not he will accept the reduction sought or some other reduction. Counsel may state any points he wishes to have made in a reply to the points of dispute, and the solicitor must serve them on the paying party as or as part of a reply.

(3) Counsel who fails to inform the solicitor within the time limits set out above will be taken to accept the reduction unless the court otherwise orders.

20.5 Where the paying party serves points of dispute seeking a reduction in any percentage increase charged by a legal representative acting for the receiving party, and that legal representative intends, if necessary, to apply for an order that any amount of the percentage disallowed as against the paying party shall continue to be payable by his client, the solicitor acting for the receiving party must, within 14 days of service of the points of dispute, give to his client a clear written explanation of the nature of the relevant point of dispute and the effect it will have if it is upheld in whole or in part by the court, and of the client's right to attend any subsequent hearings at court when the matter is raised.

20.6 Where the solicitor acting for a receiving party files a request for a detailed assessment hearing it must if appropriate, be accompanied by a certificate signed by him stating:

(1) that the amount of the percentage increase in respect of counsel's fees or solicitor's charges is disputed;

(2) whether an application will be made for an order that any amount of that increase which is disallowed should continue to be payable by his client;

(3) that he has given his client an explanation in accordance with para. 20.5; and

(4) whether his client wishes to attend court when the amount of any relevant percentage increase may be decided.

20.7 (1) The solicitor acting for the receiving party must within seven days of receiving from the court notice of the date of the assessment hearing, notify his client, and if appropriate, counsel in writing of the date, time and place of the hearing.

(2) Counsel may attend or be represented at the detailed assessment hearing and may make oral or written submissions.

20.8 (1) At the detailed assessment hearing, the court will deal with the assessment of the costs payable by one party to another, including the amount of the percentage increase, and give a certificate accordingly.

(2) The court may decide the issue whether the disallowed amount should continue to be payable under the relevant conditional fee agreement without an adjournment if:

(a) the receiving party and all parties to the relevant agreement consent to the court deciding the issue without an adjournment,

(b) the receiving party (or, if corporate, an officer or employee who has authority to consent on behalf of the receiving party) is present in court, and

(c) the court is satisfied that the issue can be fairly decided without an adjournment.

(3) In any other case the court will give directions and fix a date for the hearing of the application.

## Section 21 Application of Costs Rules: Rule 44.17

21.1 Rule 44.17(b) excludes the costs rules to the extent that regulations under the Legal Aid Act 1988 make different provision. The primary examples of such regulations are the regulations providing prescribed rates (with or without enhancement).

21.2 Rule 44.17(a) provides that the procedure for detailed assessment does not apply to the extent that section 11 of the Access to Justice Act 1999 and provisions made under that Act make different provision.

21.3 Section 11 of the Access to Justice Act 1999 provides special protection against

liability for costs for litigants who receive funding by the LSC (Legal Services Commission) as part of the Community Legal Service. Any costs ordered to be paid by a LSC funded client must not exceed the amount which is reasonable for him to pay having regard to all the circumstances including:
(a) the financial resources of all the parties to the proceedings, and
(b) their conduct in connection with the dispute to which the proceedings relate.

21.4 In this practice direction:
'cost protection' means the limit on costs awarded against a LSC funded client set out in s. 11(1) of the Access to Justice Act 1999;
'partner' has the meaning given by the Community Legal Service (Costs) Regulations 2000 (SI 2000/441).

21.5 Whether or not cost protection applies depends upon the 'level of service' for which funding was provided by the LSC in accordance with the Funding Code approved under s. 9 of the Access to Justice Act 1999. The levels of service referred to are:
(1) Legal Help—advice and assistance about a legal problem, not including representation or advocacy in proceedings.
(2) Help at Court—advocacy at a specific hearing, where the advocate is not formally representing the client in the proceedings.
(3) Family Mediation.
(4) Legal Representation—representation in actual or contemplated proceedings. Legal Representation can take the form of Investigative Help (limited to investigating the merits of a potential claim) or Full Representation.
(5) General Family Help and Help with Mediation.
(6) *[Omitted]*

21.6 Levels of service (4) and (5) are provided under a certificate (similar to a legal aid certificate). The certificate will state which level of service is covered. Where there are proceedings, a copy of the certificate will be lodged with the court.

21.7 Cost protection does not apply where—
(1) the LSC funded client receives Help at Court;
(2) the LSC funded client receives Legal Help only i.e. where the solicitor is advising, but not representing a litigant in person. However, where the LSC funded client receives Legal Help e.g. to write a letter before action, but later receives Legal Representation or General Family Help or Help with Mediation in respect of the same dispute, other than in family proceedings, cost protection does apply to all costs incurred by the receiving party in the funded proceedings or prospective proceedings;
(3) the LSC funded client receives General Family Help or Help with Mediation in family proceedings;
(4) the LSC funded client receives Legal Representation in family proceedings.

21.8 Where cost protection does not apply, the court may award costs in the normal way.

21.9 Where work is done before the issue of a certificate, cost protection does not apply to those costs, except where:
(1) pre-action Legal Help is given and the LSC funded client subsequently receives Legal Representation or General Family Help or Help with Mediation in respect of the same dispute, other than in family proceedings; or
(2) where urgent work is undertaken immediately before the grant of an emergency certificate, other than in family proceedings, when no emergency application could be made as the LSC's offices were closed, provided that the solicitor seeks an emergency certificate at the first available opportunity and the certificate is granted.

21.10 If a LSC funded client's certificate is revoked, costs protection does not apply to work done before or after revocation.

21.11 If a LSC funded client's certificate is discharged, costs protection only applies to costs incurred before the date on which funded services ceased to be provided under the certificate. This may be a date before the date on which the certificate is formally discharged by the LSC (*Burridge v Stafford* [2000] 1 WLR 927, [1999] 4 All ER 660, CA).

21.11A Where an LSC funded client has cost protection, the procedure described in sections 22 and 23 of this practice direction applies. However that procedure does not apply in relation to costs claimed during any periods in the proceedings when the LSC funded client did not have cost protection, and the procedure set out in CPR Parts 45 to 47 will apply (as appropriate) in relation to those periods.

*Assessing a LSC funded client's resources*

21.12 The first £100,000 of the value of the LSC funded client's interest in the main or only home is disregarded when assessing his or her financial resources for the purposes of s. 11 and cannot be the subject of any enforcement process by the receiving party. The receiving party cannot apply for an order to sell the LSC funded client's home, but could secure the debt against any value exceeding £100,000 by way of a charging order.

21.13 The court may only take into account the value of the LSC funded client's clothes, household furniture, tools and implements of trade to the extent that it considers that having regard to the quantity or value of the items, the circumstances are exceptional.

21.14 The LSC funded client's resources include the resources of his partner, unless the partner has a contrary interest in the dispute in respect of which funded services are provided.

*Party acting in a representative, fiduciary or official capacity*

21.15 (1) Where a LSC funded client is acting in a representative, fiduciary or official capacity, the court shall not take the personal resources of the party into account for the purposes of either a s. 11 order or costs against the Commission, but shall have regard to the value of any property or estate or the amount of any fund out of which the party is entitled to be indemnified, and may also have regard to the resources of any persons who are beneficially interested in the property, estate or fund.

(2) Similarly, where a party is acting as a litigation friend to a client who is a child or a patient, the court shall not take the personal resources of the litigation friend into account in assessing the resources of the client.

(3) The purpose of this provision is to ensure that any liability is determined with reference to the value of the property or fund being used to pay for the litigation, and the financial position of those who may benefit from or rely on it.

*Costs against the LSC*

21.16 Regulation 5 of the Community Legal Service (Cost Protection) Regulations 2000 (SI 2000/824) governs when costs can be awarded against the LSC. This provision only applies where cost protection applies and the costs ordered to be paid by the LSC funded client do not fully meet the costs that would have been ordered to be paid by him if cost protection did not apply.

21.17 In this section and the following two sections of this practice direction 'non-funded party' means a party to proceedings who has not received LSC funded services in relation to these proceedings under a legal aid certificate or a certificate issued under the LSC Funding Code other than a certificate which has been revoked.

21.18 The following criteria set out in reg. 5 must be satisfied before the LSC can be ordered to pay the whole or any part of the costs incurred by a non-funded party:

(1) the proceedings are finally decided in favour of a non-funded party;

(2) unless there is good reason for delay the non-funded party provides written notice of intention to seek an order against the LSC within three months of the making of the s. 11(1) costs order;

(3) the court is satisfied that it is just and equitable in the circumstances that provision for the costs should be made out of public funds; and

(4) where costs are incurred in a court of first instance, the following additional criteria must also be met:
(i) the proceedings were instituted by the LSC funded client;
(ii) the non-funded party is an individual; and
(iii) the non-funded party will suffer financial hardship unless the order is made.

('Section 11(1) costs order' is defined in para. 22.1 below)

21.19 In determining whether conditions (3) and (4) are satisfied, the court shall take into account the resources of the non-funded party and his partner, unless the partner has a contrary interest.

21.19A An order under reg. 5 may be made in relation to proceedings in the Court of Appeal, High Court or a County Court, by a costs judge or a district judge.

*Effect of appeals*

21.20 (1) An order for costs can only be made against the LSC when the proceedings (including any appeal) are finally decided. Therefore, where a court of first instance decides in favour of a non-funded party and an appeal lies, any order made against the LSC shall not take effect unless:
(a) where permission to appeal is required, the time limit for permission to appeal expires, without permission being granted;
(b) where permission to appeal is granted or is not required, the time limit for appeal expires without an appeal being brought.

(2) Accordingly, if the LSC funded client appeals, any earlier order against the LSC can never take effect. If the appeal is unsuccessful, an application can be made to the appeal court for a fresh order.

## Section 22 Orders for Costs to Which Section 11 of the Access to Justice Act 1999 Applies

22.1 In this practice direction:

'order for costs to be determined' means an order for costs to which s. 11 of the Access to Justice Act 1999 applies under which the amount of costs payable by the LSC funded client is to be determined by a costs judge or district judge under section 23 of this practice direction.

'order specifying the costs payable' means an order for costs to which s. 11 of the Act applies and which specifies the amount which the LSC funded client is to pay.

'full costs' means, where an order to which s. 11 of the Act applies is made against an LSC funded client, the amount of costs which that person would, had cost protection not applied, have been ordered to pay.

'determination proceedings' means proceedings to which paras 22.1 to 22.10 apply.

's. 11(1) costs order' means an order for costs to be determined or an order specifying the costs payable other than an order specifying the costs payable which was made in determination proceedings.

'statement of resources' means:

(1) a statement, verified by a statement of truth, made by a party to proceedings setting out:
(a) his income and capital and financial commitments during the previous year and, if applicable, those of his partner;
(b) his estimated future financial resources and expectations and, if applicable, those of his partner ('partner' is defined in para. 21.4, above);
(c) a declaration that he and, if applicable, his partner, has not deliberately forgone or deprived himself of any resources or expectations;
(d) particulars of any application for funding made by him in connection with the proceedings; and
(e) any other facts relevant to the determination of his resources; or

(2) a statement, verified by a statement of truth, made by a client receiving funded services, setting out the information provided by the client under reg. 6 of the Community Legal Service (Financial) Regulations 2000 (SI 2000/516), and stating that there has been no significant change in the client's financial circumstances since the date on which the information was provided or, as the case may be, details of any such change.

'regional director' means any regional director appointed by the LSC and any member of his staff authorised to act on his behalf.

22.2 Regulations 8 to 13 of the Community Legal Service (Costs) Regulations 2000 as amended set out the procedure for seeking costs against a funded client and the LSC. The effect of these Regulations is set out in this section and the next section of this practice direction.

22.3 As from 5 June 2000, regs 9 to 13 of the Community Legal Service (Costs) Regulations 2000 as amended also apply to certificates issued under the Legal Aid Act 1988 where costs against the assisted person fall to be assessed under reg. 124 of the Civil Legal Aid (General) Regulations 1989. In this section and the next section of this practice direction the expression 'LSC funded client' includes an assisted person (defined in r. 43.2).

22.4 Regulation 8 of the Community Legal Service (Costs) Regulations 2000 as amended provides that a party intending to seek an order for costs against a LSC funded client may at any time file and serve on the LSC funded client a statement of resources. If that statement is served seven or more days before a date fixed for a hearing at which an order for costs may be made, the LSC funded client must also make a statement of resources and produce it at the hearing.

22.5 If the court decides to make an order for costs against an LSC funded client to whom cost protection applies it may either:

(1) make an order for costs to be determined, or

(2) make an order specifying the costs payable.

22.6 If the court makes an order for costs to be determined it may also:

(1) state the amount of full costs, or

(2) make findings of facts, eg, concerning the conduct of all the parties which are to be taken into account by the court in the subsequent determination proceedings.

22.7 The court will not make an order specifying the costs payable unless:

(1) it considers that it has sufficient information before it to decide what amount is a reasonable amount for the LSC funded client to pay in accordance with s. 11 of the Act, and

(2) either:

(a) the order also states the amount of full costs, or

(b) the court considers that it has sufficient information before it to decide what amount is a reasonable amount for the LSC funded client to pay in accordance with s. 11 of the Act and is satisfied that, if it were to determine the full costs at that time, they would exceed the amounts specified in the order.

22.8 Where an order specifying the costs payable is made and the LSC funded client does not have cost protection in respect of all of the costs awarded in that order, the order must identify the sum payable (if any) in respect of which the LSC funded client has cost protection and the sum payable (if any) in respect of which he does not have cost protection.

22.9 The court cannot make an order under regs 8 to 13 of the Community Legal Service (Costs) Regulations 2000 as amended except in proceedings to which the next section of this practice direction applies.

## Section 23 Determination Proceedings and Similar Proceedings Under the Community Legal Service (Costs) Regulations 2000

23.1 This section of this practice direction deals with:

(1) proceedings subsequent to the making of an order for costs to be determined,

(2) variations in the amount stated in an order specifying the amount of costs payable,
(3) the late determination of costs under an order for costs to be determined, and
(4) appeals in respect of determination.

23.2 In this section of this practice direction 'appropriate court office' means:
(1) the district registry or county court in which the case was being dealt with when the s. 11(1) order was made, or to which it has subsequently been transferred; or
(2) in all other cases, the Supreme Court Costs Office.

23.2A (1) This paragraph applies where the appropriate office is any of the following county courts:
Barnet, Bow, Brentford, Bromley, Central London, Clerkenwell, Croydon, Edmonton, Ilford, Kingston, Lambeth, Mayors and City of London, Romford, Shoreditch, Uxbridge, Wandsworth, West London, Willesden and Woolwich.
(2) Where this paragraph applies—
(i) a receiving party seeking an order specifying costs payable by an LSC funded client and/or by the Legal Services Commission under this section must file his application in the Supreme Court Costs Office and, for all purposes relating to that application, the Supreme Court Costs Office will be treated as the appropriate office in that case; and
(ii) unless an order is made transferring the application to the Supreme Court Costs Office as part of the High Court, an appeal from any decision made by a costs judge shall lie to the designated civil judge for the London Group of County Courts or such judge as he shall nominate. The appeal notice and any other relevant papers should be lodged at the Central London Civil Justice Centre.

23.3 (1) A receiving party seeking an order specifying costs payable by an LSC funded client and/or by the LSC may within three months of an order for costs to be determined, file in the appropriate court office an application in form N244 accompanied by:
(a) the receiving party's bill of costs (unless the full costs have already been determined);
(b) the receiving party's statement of resources (unless the court is determining an application against a costs order against the LSC and the costs were not incurred in the court of first instance); and
(c) if the receiving party intends to seek costs against the LSC, written notice to that effect.
(2) If the LSC funded client's liability has already been determined and is less than the full costs, the application will be for costs against the LSC only. If the LSC funded client's liability has not yet been determined, the receiving party must indicate if costs will be sought against the LSC if the funded client's liability is determined as less than the full costs.
(The LSC funded client's certificate will contain the addresses of the LSC funded client, his solicitor, and the relevant regional office of the LSC.)

23.4 The receiving party must file the above documents in the appropriate court office and (where relevant) serve copies on the LSC funded client and the Regional Director. In respect of applications for funded services made before 3 December 2001 a failure to file a request within the 3-month time limit specified in regulation 10(2) is an absolute bar to the making of a costs order against the LSC. Where the application for funded services was made on or after 3 December 2001 the court does have power to extend the 3-month time limit, but only if the applicant can show good reason for the delay.

23.5 On being served with the application, the LSC funded client must respond by filing a statement of resources and serving a copy of it on the receiving party (and the regional director where relevant) within 21 days. The LSC funded client may also file and serve written points disputing the bill within the same time limit. (Under r. 3.1 the court may extend or shorten this time limit.)

23.6 If the LSC funded client fails to file a statement of resources without good reason, the court will determine his liability (and the amount of full costs if relevant) and need not hold an oral hearing for such determination.

23.7 When the LSC funded client files a statement or the 21 day period for doing so expires, the court will fix a hearing date and give the relevant parties at least 14 days' notice. The court may fix a hearing without waiting for the expiry of the 21-day period if the application is made only against the LSC.

23.8 Determination proceedings will be listed for hearing before a costs judge or district judge. The determination of the liability on the LSC funded client will be listed as a private hearing.

23.9 Where the LSC funded client does not have cost protection in respect of all of the costs awarded, the order made by the costs judge or district judge must in addition to specifying the costs payable, identify the full costs in respect of which cost protection applies and the full costs in respect of which cost protection does not apply.

23.10 The regional director may appear at any hearing at which a costs order may be made against the LSC. Instead of appearing, he may file a written statement at court and serve a copy on the receiving party. The written statement should be filed and a copy served, not less than seven days before the hearing.

*Variation of an order specifying the costs payable*

23.11 (1) This paragraph applies where the amount stated in an order specifying the costs payable plus the amount ordered to be paid by the LSC is less than the full costs to which cost protection applies.

(2) The receiving party may apply to the court for a variation of the amount which the LSC funded client is required to pay on the ground that there has been a significant change in the client's circumstances since the date of the order.

23.12 On an application under para. 23.11, where the order specifying the costs payable does not state the full costs:

(1) the receiving party must file with his application the receiving party's statement of resources and bill of costs and copies of these documents should be served with the application.

(2) The LSC funded client must respond to the application by making a statement of resources which must be filed at court and served on the receiving party within 21 days thereafter. The LSC funded client may also file and serve written points disputing the bill within the same time limit.

(3) The court will, when determining the application assess the full costs identifying any part of them to which cost protection does apply and any part of them to which cost protection does not apply.

23.13 On an application under para. 23.11 the order specifying the costs payable may be varied as the court thinks fit. That variation must not increase:

(1) the amount of any costs ordered to be paid by the LSC, and

(2) the amount payable by the LSC funded client, to a sum which is greater than the amount of the full costs plus the costs of the application.

23.14 (1) Where an order for costs to be determined has been made but the receiving party has not applied, within the three-month time limit under para. 23.2, the receiving party may apply on any of the following grounds for a determination of the amount which the funded client is required to pay:

(a) there has been a significant change in the funded client's circumstances since the date of the order for costs to be determined; or

(b) material additional information about the funded client's financial resources

is available which could not with reasonable diligence have been obtained by the receiving party at the relevant time; or
(c) there were other good reasons for the failure by the receiving party to make an application within the time limit.
(2) An application for costs payable by the LSC cannot be made under this paragraph.

23.15 (1) Where the receiving party has received funded services in relation to the proceedings, the LSC may make an application under paras 23.11 and 23.14 above.
(2) In respect of an application under para. 23.11 made by the LSC, the LSC must file and serve copies of the documents described in para. 23.12(1).

23.16 An application under para. 23.11, 23.14 and 23.15 must be commenced before the expiration of 6 years from the date on which the court made the order specifying the costs payable, or (as the case may be) the order for costs to be determined.

23.17 Applications under para. 23.11, 23.14 and 23.15 should be made in the appropriate court office and should be made in form N244 to be listed for a hearing before a costs judge or district judge.

*Appeals*

23.18 (1) Save as mentioned above any determination made under regulation 9 or 10 of the Costs Regulations is final (regulation 11(1)). Any party with a financial interest in the assessment of the full costs, other than a funded party, may appeal against that assessment in accordance with CPR Part 52 (regulation 11(2) and rule 47.20).
(2) The receiving party or the Commission may appeal on a point of law against the making of a costs order against the Commission, against the amount of costs the Commission is required to pay or against the court's refusal to make such an order (regulation 11(4)).

## DIRECTIONS RELATING TO PART 45 FIXED COSTS

### Section 24 Fixed Costs in Small Claims

24.1 Under r. 27.14 the costs which can be awarded to a claimant in a small claims track case include the fixed costs payable under Part 45 attributable to issuing the claim.

24.2 Those fixed costs shall be the sum of:
(a) the fixed commencement costs calculated in accordance with Table 1 of r. 45.2; and
(b) the appropriate court fee or fees paid by the claimant.

### Section 24A Claims to which Part 45 does not Apply

24A In a claim to which Part 45 does not apply, no amount shall be entered on the claim form for the charges of the claimant's solicitor, but the words 'to be assessed' shall be inserted.

### Section 25 Fixed Costs on the Issue of a Default Costs Certificate

25.1 Unless [para. 25.2*] applies or unless the court orders otherwise, the fixed costs to be included in a default costs certificate are £80 plus a sum equal to any appropriate court fee payable on the issue of the certificate.

25.2 The fixed costs included in a certificate must not exceed the maximum sum specified for costs and court fee in the notice of commencement.

* [The text issued by the Department for Constitutional Affairs mistakenly refers to para. 24.2.]

## Section 25A Road Traffic Accidents: Fixed Recoverable Costs in Costs-only Proceedings

*Scope*

25A.1 Section II of Part 45 ('the Section') provides for certain fixed costs to be recoverable between parties in respect of costs incurred in disputes which are settled prior to proceedings being issued. The Section applies to road traffic accident disputes as defined in r. 45.7(4)(a), where the accident which gave rise to the dispute occurred on or after 6 October 2003.

25A.2 The Section does not apply to disputes where the total agreed value of the damages is within the small claims limit or exceeds £10,000. Rule 26.8(2) sets out how the financial value of a claim is assessed for the purposes of allocation to track.

25A.3 Fixed recoverable costs are to be calculated by reference to the amount of agreed damages which are payable to the receiving party. In calculating the amount of these damages:

(a) account must be taken of both general and special damages and interest;
(b) any interim payments made must be included;
(c) where the parties have agreed an element of contributory negligence, the amount of damages attributed to that negligence must be deducted;
(d) any amount required by statute to be paid by the compensating party directly to a third party (such as sums paid by way of compensation recovery payments and National Health Service expenses) must not be included.

25A.4 The Section applies to cases which fall within the scope of the Uninsured Drivers Agreement dated 13 August 1999. The Section does not apply to cases which fall within the scope of the Untraced Drivers Agreement dated 14 February 2003.

*Fixed recoverable costs formula*

25A.5 The amount of fixed costs recoverable is calculated by totalling the following:

(a) £800;
(b) 20% of the agreed damages up to £5,000; and
(c) 15% of the agreed damages between £5,000 and £10,000.

For example, agreed damages of £7,523 would result in recoverable costs of £2,178.45, i.e.: £800 + (20% of £5,000) + (15% of £2,523).

*Additional costs for work in specified areas*

25A.6 The area referred to in r. 45.9(2) consists of (within London) the county court districts of Barnet, Bow, Brentford, Central London, Clerkenwell, Edmonton, Ilford, Lambeth, Mayor's and City of London, Romford, Shoreditch, Wandsworth, West London, Willesden and Woolwich and (outside London) the county court districts of Bromley, Croydon, Dartford, Gravesend and Uxbridge.

*Multiple claimants*

25A.7 Where there is more than one potential claimant in relation to a dispute and two or more claimants instruct the same solicitor or firm of solicitors, the provisions of the section apply in respect of each claimant.

*Information to be included in the claim form*

25A.8 Costs only proceedings are commenced using the procedure set out in r. 44.12A. A claim form should be issued in accordance with Part 8. Where the claimant is claiming an amount of costs which exceed the amount of the fixed recoverable costs he must include on the claim form details of the exceptional circumstances which he considers justifies the additional costs.

25A.9 The claimant must also include on the claim form details of any disbursements or success fee he wishes to claim. The disbursements that may be claimed are set out in r. 45.10(1). If the disbursement falls within r. 45.10(2)(d) (disbursements that have arisen due to a particular feature of the dispute) the claimant must give details of the particular feature of the dispute and why he considers the disbursement to be necessary.

*Disbursements and success fee*

25A.10 If the parties agree the amount of the fixed recoverable costs and the only dispute is as to the payment of, or amount of, a disbursement or as to the amount of a success fee, then proceedings should be issued under r. 44.12A in the normal way and not by reference to Section II of Part 45.

## Section 25b Fixed Recoverable Success Fees In Employers' Liability Disease Claims

25B.1 The following table is a non-exclusive list of the conditions that will fall within Type A and Type B claims for the purposes of rule 45.23.

| Claim type | Description |
|---|---|
| A | Asbestosis |
| | Mesothelioma |
| | Bilateral Pleural Thickening |
| | Pleural Plaques |
| B | Repetitive Strain Injury/WRULD |
| | Carpal Tunnel Syndrome caused by Repetitive Strain Injury |
| | Occupational Stress |

# DIRECTIONS RELATING TO PART 46 FAST TRACK TRIAL COSTS

## Section 26 Scope of Part 46: Rule 46.1

26.1 Part 46 applies to the costs of an advocate for preparing for and appearing at the trial of a claim in the fast track.

26.2 It applies only where, at the date of the trial, the claim is allocated to the fast track. It does not apply in any other case, irrespective of the final value of the claim.

26.3 In particular it does not apply to:

(a) the hearing of a claim which is allocated to the small claims track with the consent of the parties given under r. 26.7(3); or

(b) a disposal hearing at which the amount to be paid under a judgment or order is decided by the court (see PD 26, para. 12.8).

*Cases which settle before trial*

26.4 Attention is drawn to r. 44.10 (limitation on amount court may award where a claim allocated to the fast track settles before trial).

## Section 27 Power to Award More or Less than the Amount of Fast Track Trial Costs: Rule 46.3

27.1 Rule 44.15 (providing information about funding arrangements) sets out the requirement to provide information about funding arrangements to the court and other parties. Section 19 of this practice direction sets out the information to be provided and when this is to be done.

27.2 Section 11 of this practice direction explains how the court will approach the question of what sum to allow in respect of additional liability.

27.3 The court has the power, when considering whether a percentage increase is reasonable, to allow different percentages for different items of costs or for different periods during which costs were incurred.

# DIRECTIONS RELATING TO PART 47 PROCEDURE FOR DETAILED ASSESSMENT OF COSTS AND DEFAULT PROVISIONS

## Section 28 Time When Assessment May be Carried Out: Rule 47.1

28.1 (1) For the purposes of r. 47.1, proceedings are concluded when the court has finally determined the matters in issue in the claim, whether or not there is an appeal.

(2) For the purposes of this rule, the making of an award of provisional damages under Part 41 will be treated as a final determination of the matters in issue.

(3) The court may order or the parties may agree in writing that, although the proceedings are continuing, they will nevertheless be treated as concluded.

(4) (a) A party who is served with a notice of commencement (see para. 32.3 below) may apply to a costs judge or a district judge to determine whether the party who served it is entitled to commence detailed assessment proceedings.

(b) On hearing such an application the orders which the court may make include: an order allowing the detailed assessment proceedings to continue, or an order setting aside the notice of commencement.

(5) A costs judge or a district judge may make an order allowing detailed assessment proceedings to be commenced where there is no realistic prospect of the claim continuing.

## Section 29 No Stay of Detailed Assessment Where There is an Appeal: Rule 47.2

29.1 (1) Rule 47.2 provides that detailed assessment is not stayed pending an appeal unless the court so orders.

(2) An application to stay the detailed assessment of costs pending an appeal may be made to the court whose order is being appealed or to the court who will hear the appeal.

## Section 30 Powers of an Authorised Court Officer: Rule 47.3

30.1 (1) The court officers authorised by the Lord Chancellor to assess costs in the Supreme Court Costs Office and the Principal Registry of the Family Division are authorised to deal with claims for costs not exceeding £30,000 (excluding VAT) in the case of senior executive officers, or their equivalent, and £75,000 (excluding VAT) in the case of principal officers.

(2) In calculating whether or not a bill of costs is within the authorised amounts, the figure to be taken into account is the total claim for costs including any additional liability.

(3) Where the receiving party, paying party and any other party to the detailed assessment proceedings who has served points of dispute are agreed that the assessment should not be made by an authorised court officer, the receiving party should so inform the court when requesting a hearing date. The court will then list the hearing before a costs judge or a district judge.

(4) In any other case a party who objects to the assessment being made by an authorised court officer must make an application to the costs judge or district judge under Part 23 setting out the reasons for the objection and if sufficient reason is shown the court will direct that the bill be assessed by a costs judge or district judge.

## Section 31 Venue for Detailed Assessment Proceedings: Rule 47.4

31.1 For the purposes of r. 47.4(1) the 'appropriate office' means:

(1) the district registry or county court in which the case was being dealt with when the judgment or order was made or the event occurred which gave rise to the right to assessment, or to which it has subsequently been transferred; or

(2) in all other cases, including Court of Appeal cases, the Supreme Court Costs Office.

31.1A (1) This paragraph applies where the appropriate office is any of the following county courts:
Barnet, Bow, Brentford, Bromley, Central London, Clerkenwell, Croydon, Edmonton, Ilford, Kingston, Lambeth, Mayors and City of London, Romford, Shoreditch, Uxbridge, Wandsworth, West London, Willesden and Woolwich.
(2) Where this paragraph applies—
(i) the receiving party must file any request for a detailed assessment hearing in the Supreme Court Costs Office and, for all purposes relating to that detailed assessment, the Supreme Court Costs Office will be treated as the appropriate office in that case; and
(ii) unless an order is made under rule 47.4(2) directing that the Supreme Court Costs Office as part of the High Court shall be the appropriate office, an appeal from any decision made by a costs judge shall lie to the designated civil judge for the London Group of County Courts or such judge as he shall nominate. The appeal notice and any other relevant papers should be lodged at the Central London Civil Justice Centre.

31.2 (1) A direction under r. 47.4(2) or (3) specifying a particular court, registry or office as the appropriate office may be given on application or on the court's own initiative.
(2) Before making such a direction on its own initiative the court will give the parties the opportunity to make representations.
(3) Unless the Supreme Court Costs Office is the appropriate office for the purposes of r. 47.4(1) an order directing that an assessment is to take place at the Supreme Court Costs Office will be made only if it is appropriate to do so having regard to the size of the bill of costs, the difficulty of the issues involved, the likely length of the hearing, the cost to the parties and any other relevant matter.

## Section 32 Commencement of Detailed Assessment Proceedings: Rule 47.6

32.1 Precedents A, B, C and D in the Schedule of Costs Precedents annexed to this practice direction are model forms of bills of costs for detailed assessment. Further information about bills of costs is set out in section 4.

32.2 A detailed assessment may be in respect of:
(1) base costs, where a claim for additional liability has not been made or has been agreed;
(2) a claim for additional liability only, base costs having been summarily assessed or agreed; or
(3) both base costs and additional liability.

32.3 If the detailed assessment is in respect of costs without any additional liability, the receiving party must serve on the paying party and all the other relevant persons the following documents:
(a) a notice of commencement;
(b) a copy of the bill of costs;
(c) copies of the fee notes of counsel and of any expert in respect of fees claimed in the bill;
(d) written evidence as to any other disbursement which is claimed and which exceeds £250;
(e) a statement giving the name and address for service of any person upon whom the receiving party intends to serve the notice of commencement.

32.4 If the detailed assessment is in respect of an additional liability only, the receiving party must serve on the paying party and all other relevant persons the following documents:
(a) a notice of commencement;
(b) a copy of the bill of costs;
(c) the relevant details of the additional liability;
(d) a statement giving the name and address of any person upon whom the receiving party intends to serve the notice of commencement.

32.5 The relevant details of an additional liability are as follows:

(1) In the case of a conditional fee agreement with a success fee:

(a) a statement showing the amount of costs which have been summarily assessed or agreed, and the percentage increase which has been claimed in respect of those costs;

(b) a statement of the reasons for the percentage increase given in accordance with regulation 3(1)(a) of the Conditional Fee Agreements Regulations or regulation 5(1)(c) of the Collective Conditional Fee Agreements Regulations 2000. [Both sets of regulations were revoked by the Conditional Fee Agreements (Revocation) Regulations 2005 but continue to have effect in relation to conditional fee agreements and collective conditional fee agreements entered into before 1 November 2005.]

(2) If the additional liability is an insurance premium: a copy of the insurance certificate showing whether the policy covers the receiving party's own costs; his opponent's costs; or his own costs and his opponent's costs; and the maximum extent of that cover, and the amount of the premium paid or payable.

(3) If the receiving party claims an additional amount under s. 30 of the Access to Justice Act 1999: a statement setting out the basis upon which the receiving party's liability for the additional amount is calculated.

32.6 Attention is drawn to the fact that the additional amount recoverable pursuant to s. 30 of the Access to Justice Act 1999 in respect of a membership organisation must not exceed the likely cost of the premium of an insurance policy against the risk of incurring a liability to pay the costs of other parties to the proceedings as provided by the Access to Justice (Membership Organisations) Regulations 2000 (SI 2000/693), reg. 4. (for the purposes of arrangements entered into before 1 November 2005) and The Access to Justice (Membership Organisation) Regulations 2005, regulation 5 (for the purposes of arrangements entered into on or after 1 November 2005).

32.7 If a detailed assessment is in respect of both base costs and an additional liability, the receiving party must serve on the paying party and all other relevant persons the documents listed in para. 32.3 and the documents giving relevant details of an additional liability listed in para. 32.5.

32.8 (1) The notice of commencement should be in form N252.

(2) Before it is served, it must be completed to show as separate items:

(a) the total amount of the costs claimed in the bill;

(b) the extra sum which will be payable by way of fixed costs and court fees if a default costs certificate is obtained.

32.9 (1) This paragraph applies where the notice of commencement is to be served outside England and Wales.

(2) The date to be inserted in the notice of commencement for the paying party to send points of dispute is a date (not less than 21 days from the date of service of the notice) which must be calculated by reference to Part 6, Section III, as if the notice were a claim form and as if the date to be inserted was the date for the filing of a defence.

32.10 (1) For the purposes of r. 47.6(2) a 'relevant person' means:

(a) any person who has taken part in the proceedings which gave rise to the assessment and who is directly liable under an order for costs made against him;

(b) any person who has given to the receiving party notice in writing that he has a financial interest in the outcome of the assessment and wishes to be a party accordingly;

(c) any other person whom the court orders to be treated as such.

(2) Where a party is unsure whether a person is or is not a relevant person, that party may apply to the appropriate office for directions.

(3) The court will generally not make an order that the person in respect of whom

the application is made will be treated as a relevant person, unless within a specified time he applies to the court to be joined as a party to the assessment proceedings in accordance with Part 19 (parties and group litigation).

32.11 (1) This paragraph applies in cases in which the bill of costs is capable of being copied on to a computer disk.

(2) If, before the detailed assessment hearing, a paying party requests a disk copy of a bill to which this paragraph applies, the receiving party must supply him with a copy free of charge not more than seven days after the date on which he received the request.

## Section 33 Period for Commencing Detailed Assessment Proceedings: Rule 47.7

33.1 The parties may agree under r. 2.11 (time limits may be varied by parties) to extend or shorten the time specified by r. 47.7 for commencing the detailed assessment proceedings.

33.2 A party may apply to the appropriate office for an order under r. 3.1(2)(a) to extend or shorten that time.

33.3 Attention is drawn to r. 47.6(1). The detailed assessment proceedings are commenced by service of the documents referred to.

33.4 Permission to commence assessment proceedings out of time is not required.

## Section 34 Sanction for Delay in Commencing Detailed Assessment Proceedings: Rule 47.8

34.1 (1) An application for an order under r. 47.8 must be made in writing and be issued in the appropriate office.

(2) The application notice must be served at least seven days before the hearing.

## Section 35 Points of Dispute and Consequences of Not Serving: Rule 47.9

35.1 The parties may agree under r. 2.11 (time limits may be varied by parties) to extend or shorten the time specified by r. 47.9 for service of points of dispute. A party may apply to the appropriate office for an order under r. 3.1(2)(a) to extend or shorten that time.

35.2 Points of dispute should be short and to the point and should follow as closely as possible Precedent G of the Schedule of Costs Precedents annexed to this practice direction.

35.3 Points of dispute must:

(1) identify each item in the bill of costs which is disputed,

(2) in each case, state concisely the nature and grounds of dispute,

(3) where practicable suggest a figure to be allowed for each item in respect of which a reduction is sought, and

(4) be signed by the party serving them or his solicitor.

35.4 (1) The normal period for serving points of dispute is 21 days after the date of service of the notice of commencement.

(2) Where a notice of commencement is served on a party outside England and Wales the period within which that party should serve points of dispute is to be calculated by reference to Part 6, Section III, as if the notice of commencement was a claim form and as if the period for serving points of dispute were the period for filing a defence.

35.5 A party who serves points of dispute on the receiving party must at the same time serve a copy on every other party to the detailed assessment proceedings, whose name and address for service appears on the statement served by the receiving party in accordance with para. 32.3 or 32.4 above.

35.6 (1) This paragraph applies in cases in which points of dispute are capable of being copied on to a computer disk.

(2) If, within 14 days of the receipt of the points of dispute, the receiving party requests a disk copy of them, the paying party must supply him with a copy free of charge not more than seven days after the date on which he received the request.

35.7 (1) Where the receiving party claims an additional liability, a party who serves points of dispute on the receiving party may include a request for information about other methods of financing costs which were available to the receiving party.

(2) Part 18 (further information) and PD 18 apply to such a request.

## Section 36 Procedure Where Costs Are Agreed: Rule 47.10

36.1 Where the parties have agreed terms as to the issue of a costs certificate (either interim or final) they should apply under r. 40.6 (consent judgments and orders) for an order that a certificate be issued in terms set out in the application. Such an application may be dealt with by a court officer, who may issue the certificate.

36.2 Where in the course of proceedings the receiving party claims that the paying party has agreed to pay costs but that he will neither pay those costs nor join in a consent application under para. 36.1, the receiving party may apply under Part 23 (general rules about applications for court orders) for a certificate either interim or final to be issued.

36.3 An application under para. 36.2 must be supported by evidence and will be heard by a costs judge or a district judge. The respondent to the application must file and serve any evidence he relies on at least two days before the hearing date.

36.4 Nothing in r. 47.10 prevents parties who seek a judgment or order by consent from including in the draft a term that a party shall pay to another party a specified sum in respect of costs.

36.5 (1) The receiving party may discontinue the detailed assessment proceedings in accordance with Part 38 (discontinuance).

(2) Where the receiving party discontinues the detailed assessment proceedings before a detailed assessment hearing has been requested, the paying party may apply to the appropriate office for an order about the costs of the detailed assessment proceedings.

(3) Where a detailed assessment hearing has been requested the receiving party may not discontinue unless the court gives permission.

(4) A bill of costs may be withdrawn by consent whether or not a detailed assessment hearing has been requested.

## Section 37 Default Costs Certificate: Rule 47.11

37.1 (1) A request for the issue of a default costs certificate must be made in form N254 and must be signed by the receiving party or his solicitor.

(2) The request must be accompanied by a copy of the document giving the right to detailed assessment. (Paragraph 40.4 identifies the appropriate documents.)

37.2 The request must be filed at the appropriate office.

37.3 A default costs certificate will be in form N255.

37.4 Attention is drawn to r. 40.3 (drawing up and filing of judgments and orders) and r. 40.4 (service of judgments and orders) which apply to the preparation and service of a default costs certificate. The receiving party will be treated as having permission to draw up a default costs certificate by virtue of this practice direction.

37.5 The issue of a default costs certificate does not prohibit, govern or affect any detailed assessment of the same costs which are payable out of the Community Legal Service Fund.

37.6 An application for an order staying enforcement of a default costs certificate may be made either:

(1) to a costs judge or district judge of the court office which issued the certificate; or

(2) to the court (if different) which has general jurisdiction to enforce the certificate.

37.7 Proceedings for enforcement of default costs certificates may not be issued in the Supreme Court Costs Office.

37.8 The fixed costs payable in respect of solicitor's charges on the issue of the default costs certificate are £80.

## Section 38 Setting Aside Default Costs Certificate: Rule 47.12

38.1 (1) A court officer may set aside a default costs certificate at the request of the receiving party under r. 47.12(3).

(2) A costs judge or a district judge will make any other order or give any directions under this rule.

38.2 (1) An application for an order under r. 47.12(2) to set aside or vary a default costs certificate must be supported by evidence.

(2) In deciding whether to set aside or vary a certificate under r. 47.12(2) the matters to which the court must have regard include whether the party seeking the order made the application promptly.

(3) As a general rule a default costs certificate will be set aside under r. 47.12(2) only if the applicant shows a good reason for the court to do so and if he files with his application a copy of the bill and a copy of the default costs certificate, and a draft of the points of dispute he proposes to serve if his application is granted.

38.3 (1) Attention is drawn to r. 3.1(3) (which enables the court when making an order to make it subject to conditions) and to r. 44.3(8) (which enables the court to order a party whom it has ordered to pay costs to pay an amount on account before the costs are assessed).

(2) A costs judge or a district judge may exercise the power of the court to make an order under r. 44.3(8) although he did not make the order about costs which led to the issue of the default costs certificate.

38.4 If a default costs certificate is set aside the court will give directions for the management of the detailed assessment proceedings.

## Section 39 Optional Reply: Rule 47.13

39.1 (1) Where the receiving party wishes to serve a reply, he must also serve a copy on every other party to the detailed assessment proceedings. The time for doing so is within 21 days after service of the points of dispute.

(2) A reply means:

(i) a separate document prepared by the receiving party; or

(ii) his written comments added to the points of dispute.

(3) A reply must be signed by the party serving it or his solicitor.

## Section 40 Detailed Assessment Hearing: Rule 47.14

40.1 The time for requesting a detailed assessment hearing is within three months of the expiry of the period for commencing detailed assessment proceedings.

40.2 The request for a detailed assessment hearing must be in form N258. The request must be accompanied by:

(a) a copy of the notice of commencement of detailed assessment proceedings;

(b) a copy of the bill of costs,

(c) the document giving the right to detailed assessment (see para. 40.4 below);

(d) a copy of the points of dispute, annotated as necessary in order to show which items have been agreed and their value and to show which items remain in dispute and their value;

(e) as many copies of the points of dispute so annotated as there are persons who have served points of dispute;

(f) a copy of any replies served;

(g) a copy of all orders made by the court relating to the costs which are to be assessed;

(h) copies of the fee notes and other written evidence as served on the paying party in accordance with para. 32.3 above;

(i) where there is a dispute as to the receiving party's liability to pay costs to the solicitors who acted for the receiving party, any agreement, letter or other written information provided by the solicitor to his client explaining how the solicitor's charges are to be calculated;

(j) a statement signed by the receiving party or his solicitor giving the name, address for service, reference and telephone number and fax number, if any, of:
  (i) the receiving party;
  (ii) the paying party;
  (iii) any other person who has served points of dispute or who has given notice to the receiving party under para. 32.10(1)(b) above;

  and giving an estimate of the length of time the detailed assessment hearing will take;

(k) where the application for a detailed assessment hearing is made by a party other than the receiving party, such of the documents set out in this paragraph as are in the possession of that party;

(l) where the court is to assess the costs of an assisted person or LSC funded client:
  (i) the legal aid certificate, LSC certificate and relevant amendment certificates, any authorities and any certificates of discharge or revocation;
  (ii) a certificate, in Precedent F(3) of the Schedule of Costs Precedents;
  (iii) if the assisted person has a financial interest in the detailed assessment hearing and wishes to attend, the postal address of that person to which the court will send notice of any hearing;
  (iv) if the rates payable out of the LSC fund are prescribed rates, a schedule to the bill of costs setting out all the items in the bill which are claimed against other parties calculated at the legal aid prescribed rates with or without any claim for enhancement (further information as to this schedule is set out in section 48 of this practice direction);
  (v) a copy of any default costs certificate in respect of costs claimed in the bill of costs.

40.3 (1) This paragraph applies to any document described in para. 40.2(i) above which the receiving party has filed in the appropriate office. The document must be the latest relevant version and in any event have been filed not more than two years before filing the request for a detailed assessment hearing.

(2) In respect of any documents to which this paragraph applies, the receiving party may, instead of filing a copy of it, specify in the request for a detailed assessment hearing the case number under which a copy of the document was previously filed.

40.4 'The document giving the right to detailed assessment' means such one or more of the following documents as are appropriate to the detailed assessment proceedings:

(a) a copy of the judgment or order of the court giving the right to detailed assessment;
(b) a copy of the notice served under r. 3.7 (sanctions for non-payment of certain fees) where a claim is struck out under that rule;
(c) a copy of the notice of acceptance where an offer to settle is accepted under Part 36 (Offers to settle);
(d) a copy of the notice of discontinuance in a case which is discontinued under Part 38 (discontinuance);
(e) a copy of the award made on an arbitration under any Act or pursuant to an agreement, where no court has made an order for the enforcement of the award;
(f) a copy of the order, award or determination of a statutorily constituted tribunal or body;
(g) in a case under the Sheriffs Act 1887, the sheriff's bill of fees and charges, unless a court order giving the right to detailed assessment has been made;
(h) a notice of revocation or discharge under reg. 82 of the Civil Legal Aid (General) Regulations 1989;

(j) in the county courts certain Acts and Regulations provide for costs incurred in proceedings under those Acts and Regulations to be assessed in the county court if so ordered on application. Where such an application is made, a copy of the order.

40.5 On receipt of the request for a detailed assessment hearing the court will fix a date for the hearing, or, if the costs officer so decides, will give directions or fix a date for a preliminary appointment.

40.6 (1) The court will give at least 14 days' notice of the time and place of the detailed assessment hearing to every person named in the statement referred to in para. 40.2(j) above.

(2) The court will when giving notice, give each person who has served points of dispute a copy of the points of dispute annotated by the receiving party in compliance with para. 40.2(d) above.

(3) Attention is drawn to r. 47.14(6) and (7): apart from the receiving party, only those who have served points of dispute may be heard on the detailed assessment unless the court gives permission, and only items specified in the points of dispute may be raised unless the court gives permission.

40.7 (1) If the receiving party does not file a request for a detailed assessment hearing within the prescribed time, the paying party may apply to the court to fix a time within which the receiving party must do so. The sanction, for failure to commence detailed assessment proceedings within the time specified by the court, is that all or part of the costs may be disallowed (see r. 47.8(2)).

(2) Where the receiving party commences detailed assessment proceedings after the time specified in the rules but before the paying party has made an application to the court to specify a time, the only sanction which the court may impose is to disallow all or part of the interest which would otherwise be payable for the period of delay, unless the court exercises its powers under r. 44.14 (court's powers in relation to misconduct).

40.8 If either party wishes to make an application in the detailed assessment proceedings the provisions of Part 23 (general rules about applications for court orders) apply.

40.9 (1) This paragraph deals with the procedure to be adopted where a date has been given by the court for a detailed assessment hearing and:

(a) the detailed assessment proceedings are settled; or

(b) a party to the detailed assessment proceedings wishes to apply to vary the date which the court has fixed; or

(c) the parties to the detailed assessment proceedings agree about changes they wish to make to any direction given for the management of the detailed assessment proceedings.

(2) If detailed assessment proceedings are settled, the receiving party must give notice of that fact to the court immediately, preferably by fax.

(3) A party who wishes to apply to vary a direction must do so in accordance with Part 23 (general rules about applications for court orders).

(4) If the parties agree about changes they wish to make to any direction given for the management of the detailed assessment proceedings:

(a) they must apply to the court for an order by consent; and

(b) they must file a draft of the directions sought and an agreed statement of the reasons why the variation is sought; and

(c) the court may make an order in the agreed terms or in other terms without a hearing, but it may direct that a hearing is to be listed.

40.10 (1) If a party wishes to vary his bill of costs, points of dispute or a reply, an amended or supplementary document must be filed with the court and copies of it must be served on all other relevant parties.

(2) Permission is not required to vary a bill of costs, points of dispute or a reply but the court may disallow the variation or permit it only upon conditions, including conditions as to payment of any costs caused or wasted by the variation.

40.11 Unless the court directs otherwise the receiving party must file with the court the papers in support of the bill not less than seven days before the date for the detailed assessment hearing and not more than 14 days before that date.

40.12 The following provisions apply in respect of the papers to be filed in support of the bill:

(a) If the claim is for costs only without any additional liability the papers to be filed, and the order in which they are to be arranged are as follows:

(i) instructions and briefs to counsel arranged in chronological order together with all advices, opinions and drafts received and response to such instructions;

(ii) reports and opinions of medical and other experts;

(iii) any other relevant papers;

(iv) a full set of any relevant pleadings to the extent that they have not already been filed in court.

(v) correspondence, files and attendance notes;

(b) where the claim is in respect of an additional liability only, such of the papers listed at (a) above, as are relevant to the issues raised by the claim for additional liability.

(c) where the claim is for both base costs and an additional liability, the papers listed at (a) above, together with any papers relevant to the issues raised by the claim for additional liability.

40.13 The provisions set out in section 20 of this practice direction apply where the court disallows any amount of a legal representative's percentage increase, and the legal representative applies for an order that the disallowed amount should continue to be payable by the client in accordance with r. 44.16.

40.14 The court may direct the receiving party to produce any document which in the opinion of the court is necessary to enable it to reach its decision. These documents will in the first instance be produced to the court, but the court may ask the receiving party to elect whether to disclose the particular document to the paying party in order to rely on the contents of the document, or whether to decline disclosure and instead rely on other evidence.

40.15 Costs assessed at a detailed assessment at the conclusion of proceedings may include an assessment of any additional liability in respect of the costs of a previous application or hearing.

40.16 Once the detailed assessment hearing has ended it is the responsibility of the legal representative appearing for the receiving party or, as the case may be, the receiving party in person to remove the papers filed in support of the bill.

## Section 41 Power to Issue an Interim Certificate: Rule 47.15

41.1 (1) A party wishing to apply for an interim certificate may do so by making an application in accordance with Part 23 (general rules about applications for court orders).

(2) Attention is drawn to the fact that the court's power to issue an interim certificate arises only after the receiving party has filed a request for a detailed assessment hearing.

## Section 42 Final Costs Certificate: Rule 47.16

42.1 At the detailed assessment hearing the court will indicate any disallowance or reduction in the sums claimed in the bill of costs by making an appropriate note on the bill.

42.2 The receiving party must, in order to complete the bill after the detailed assessment hearing make clear the correct figures agreed or allowed in respect of each item and must recalculate the summary of the bill appropriately.

42.3 The completed bill of costs must be filed with the court no later than 14 days after the detailed assessment hearing.

42.4 At the same time as filing the completed bill of costs, the party whose bill it is must also produce receipted fee notes and receipted accounts in respect of all disbursements except those covered by a certificate in Precedent F(5) in the Schedule of Costs Precedents annexed to this practice direction.

42.5 No final costs certificate will be issued until all relevant court fees payable on the assessment of costs have been paid.

42.6 If the receiving party fails to file a completed bill in accordance with r. 47.16 the paying party may make an application under Part 23 (general rules about applications for court orders) seeking an appropriate order under r. 3.1 (the court's general powers of management).

42.7 A final costs certificate will show:

(a) the amount of any costs which have been agreed between the parties or which have been allowed on detailed assessment;

(b) where applicable the amount agreed or allowed in respect of VAT on the costs agreed or allowed.

This provision is subject to any contrary provision made by the statutory provisions relating to costs payable out of the Community Legal Service Fund.

42.8 A final costs certificate will include disbursements in respect of the fees of counsel only if receipted fee notes or accounts in respect of those disbursements have been produced to the court and only to the extent indicated by those receipts.

42.9 Where the certificate relates to costs payable between parties a separate certificate will be issued for each party entitled to costs.

42.10 Form N257 is a model form of interim costs certificate and forms N256 and N256HC are model forms of final costs certificate.

42.11 An application for an order staying enforcement of an interim costs certificate or final costs certificate may be made either:

(1) to a costs judge or district judge of the court office which issued the certificate; or

(2) to the court (if different) which has general jurisdiction to enforce the certificate.

42.12 Proceedings for enforcement of interim costs certificates or final costs certificates may not be issued in the Supreme Court Costs Office.

## Section 43 Detailed Assessment Procedure Where Costs are Payable Out of the Community Legal Service Fund: Rule 47.17

43.1 The provisions of this section apply where the court is to assess costs which are payable only out of the community legal service fund. Paragraphs 39.1 to 40.16 and 49.1 to 49.8 apply in cases involving costs payable by another person as well as costs payable only out of the community legal service fund.

43.2 The time for requesting a detailed assessment under r. 47.17 is within 3 months after the date when the right to detailed assessment arose.

43.3 The request for a detailed assessment of costs must be in form N258A. The request must be accompanied by:

(a) a copy of the bill of costs;

(b) the document giving the right to detailed assessment (for further information as to this document, see para. 40.4 above);

(c) a copy of all orders made by the court relating to the costs which are to be assessed;

(d) copies of any fee notes of counsel and any expert in respect of fees claimed in the bill;

(e) written evidence as to any other disbursement which is claimed and which exceeds £250;

(f) the legal aid certificates, LSC certificates, any relevant amendment certificates, any authorities and any certificates of discharge or revocation;

(g) in the Supreme Court Costs Office the relevant papers in support of the bill as described in para. 40.12 above; in cases proceeding in district registries and county courts this provision does not apply and the papers should only be lodged if requested by the costs officer;

(h) a statement signed by the solicitor giving his name, address for service, reference, telephone number, fax number and, if the assisted person has a financial interest in the detailed assessment and wishes to attend, giving the postal address of that person, to which the court will send notice of any hearing.

43.4 Rule 47.17 provides that the court will hold a detailed assessment hearing if the assisted person has a financial interest in the detailed assessment and wishes to attend. The court may also hold a detailed assessment hearing in any other case, instead of provisionally assessing a bill of costs, where it considers that a hearing is necessary. Before deciding whether a hearing is necessary under this rule, the court may require the solicitor whose bill it is, to provide further information relating to the bill.

43.5 Where the court has provisionally assessed a bill of costs it will send to the solicitor a notice, in form N253 annexed to this practice direction, of the amount of costs which the court proposed to allow together with the bill itself. The legal representative should, if the provisional assessment is to be accepted, then complete the bill.

43.6 The court will fix a date for a detailed assessment hearing if the solicitor informs the court within 14 days after he receives the notice of the amount allowed on the provisional assessment that he wants the court to hold such a hearing.

43.7 The court will give at least 14 days' notice of the time and place of the detailed assessment hearing to the solicitor and, if the assisted person has a financial interest in the detailed assessment and wishes to attend, to the assisted person.

43.8 If the solicitor whose bill it is, or any other party wishes to make an application in the detailed assessment proceedings, the provisions of Part 23 (general rules about applications for court orders) applies.

43.9 It is the responsibility of the legal representative to complete the bill by entering in the bill the correct figures allowed in respect of each item, recalculating the summary of the bill appropriately and completing the Community Legal Service assessment certificate (form EX80A).

## Section 44 Costs of Detailed Assessment Proceedings Where Costs are Payable Out of a Fund Other Than the Community Legal Service Fund: Rule 47.17A

44.1 Rule 47.17A provides that the court will make a provisional assessment of a bill of costs payable out of a fund (other than the Community Legal Service Fund) unless it considers that a hearing is necessary. It also enables the court to direct under r. 47.17A(3) that the receiving party must serve a copy of the request for assessment and copies of the documents which accompany it, on any person who has a financial interest in the outcome of the assessment.

44.2 (a) A person has a financial interest in the outcome of the assessment if the assessment will or may affect the amount of money or property to which he is or may become entitled out of the fund.

(b) Where an interest in the fund is itself held by a trustee for the benefit of some other person, that trustee will be treated as the person having such a financial interest.

(c) 'Trustee' includes a personal representative, receiver or any other person acting in a fiduciary capacity.

44.3 The request for a detailed assessment of costs out of the fund should be in form N258B, be accompanied by the documents set out at para. 43.3(a) to (e) and (g) above and the following:

(a) a statement signed by the receiving party giving his name, address for service, reference, telephone number, fax number; and

(b) a statement of the postal address of any person who has a financial interest in the outcome of the assessment, to which the court may send notice of any hearing; and

(c) in respect of each person stated to have such an interest if such person is a child or patient, a statement to that effect.

44.4 The court will decide, having regard to the amount of the bill, the size of the fund and the number of persons who have a financial interest, which of those persons should be served. The court may dispense with service on all or some of them.

44.5 Where the court makes an order dispensing with service on all such persons it may proceed at once to make a provisional assessment, or, if it decides that a hearing is necessary, give appropriate directions. Before deciding whether a hearing is necessary under this rule, the court may require the receiving party to provide further information relating to the bill.

44.6 (1) Where the court has provisionally assessed a bill of costs, it will send to the receiving party, a notice in form N253 of the amount of costs which the court proposes to allow together with the bill itself. If the receiving party is legally represented the legal representative should, if the provisional assessment is to be accepted, then complete the bill.

(2) The court will fix a date for a detailed assessment hearing, if the receiving party informs the court within 14 days after he receives the notice in form N253 of the amount allowed on the provisional assessment, that he wants the court to hold such a hearing.

44.7 Where the court makes an order that a person who has a financial interest is to be served with a copy of the request for assessment, it may give directions about service and about the hearing.

44.8 The court will give at least 14 days' notice of the time and place of the detailed assessment hearing to the receiving party and to any person who has a financial interest in the outcome of the assessment and has been served with a copy of the request for assessment.

44.9 If the receiving party, or any other party or any person who has a financial interest in the outcome of assessment, wishes to make an application in the detailed assessment proceedings, the provisions of Part 23 (general rules about applications for court orders) applies.

44.10 If the receiving party is legally represented the legal representative must in order to complete the bill after the assessment make clear the correct figures allowed in respect of each item and must recalculate the summary of the bill if appropriate.

## Section 45 Liability for Costs of Detailed Assessment Proceedings: Rule 47.18

45.1 As a general rule the court will assess the receiving party's costs of the detailed assessment proceedings and add them to the bill of costs.

45.2 If the costs of the detailed assessment proceedings are awarded to the paying party, the court will either assess those costs by summary assessment or make an order for them to be decided by detailed assessment.

45.3 No party should file or serve a statement of costs of the detailed assessment proceedings unless the court orders him to do so.

45.4 Attention is drawn to the fact that in deciding what order to make about the costs of detailed assessment proceedings the court must have regard to the conduct of all parties, the amount by which the bill of costs has been reduced and whether it was reasonable for a party to claim the costs of a particular item or to dispute that item.

45.5 (1) In respect of interest on the costs of detailed assessment proceedings, the interest shall begin to run from the date of the default, interim or final costs certificate as the case may be.

(2) This provision applies only to the costs of the detailed assessment proceedings themselves. The costs of the substantive proceedings are governed by r. 40.8(1).

## Section 46 Offers to Settle Without Prejudice Save as to the Costs of the Detailed Assessment Proceedings: Rule 47.19

46.1 Rule 47.19 allows the court to take into account offers to settle, without prejudice save as to the costs of detailed assessment proceedings, when deciding who is liable for the costs of those proceedings. The rule does not specify a time within which such an offer should be made. An offer made by the paying party should usually be made within 14 days after service of the notice of commencement on that party. If the offer is made by the receiving party, it should normally be made within 14 days after the service of points of dispute by the paying party. Offers made after these periods are likely to be given less weight by the court in deciding what order as to costs to make unless there is good reason for the offer not being made until the later time.

46.2 Where an offer to settle is made it should specify whether or not it is intended to be inclusive of the cost of preparation of the bill, interest and value added tax (VAT). The offer may include or exclude some or all of these items but the position must be made clear on the face of the offer so that the offeree is clear about the terms of the offer when it is being considered. Unless the offer states otherwise, the offer will be treated as being inclusive of all these items.

46.3 Where an offer to settle is accepted, an application may be made for a certificate in agreed terms, or the bill of costs may be withdrawn, in accordance with r. 47.10 (procedure where costs are agreed).

46.4 Where the receiving party is an assisted person or a LSC funded client, an offer to settle without prejudice save as to the costs of the detailed assessment proceedings will not have the consequences specified under r. 47.19 unless the court so orders.

## Section 47 Appeals from Authorised Court Officers in Detailed Assessment Proceedings: Right to Appeal: Rule 47.20

47.1 This section and the next section of this practice direction relate only to appeals from authorised court officers in detailed assessment proceedings. All other appeals arising out of detailed assessment proceedings (and arising out of summary assessments) are dealt with in accordance with Part 52 and PD 52. The destination of appeals is dealt with in accordance with the Access to Justice Act 1999 (Destination of Appeals) Order 2000.

47.2 In respect of appeals from authorised court officers, there is no requirement to obtain permission, or to seek written reasons.

## Section 48 Procedure on Appeal from Authorised Court Officers: Rule 47.22

48.1 The appellant must file a notice which should be in form N161 (an appellant's notice).

48.2 The appeal will be heard by a costs judge or a district judge of the High Court, and is a rehearing.

48.3 The appellant's notice should, if possible, be accompanied by a suitable record of the judgment appealed against. Where reasons given for the decision have been officially recorded by the court an approved transcript of that record should accompany the notice. Photocopies will not be accepted for this purpose. Where there is no official record the following documents will be acceptable:

(1) The officers' comments written on the bill.

(2) Advocates' notes of the reasons agreed by the respondent if possible and approved by the authorised court officer.

When the appellant was unrepresented before the authorised court officer, it is the duty of any advocate for the respondent to make his own note of the reasons promptly available, free of charge to the appellant where there is no official record or if the court so directs. Where the appellant was represented before the authorised court officer, it is the duty of his/her own former advocate to make his/her notes available. The appellant should submit the note of the reasons to the costs judge or district judge hearing the appeal.

48.4 The appellant may not be able to obtain a suitable record of the authorised court officers decision within the time in which the appellant's notice must be filed. In such cases, the appellant's notice must still be completed to the best of the appellant's ability. It may however be amended subsequently with the permission of the costs judge or district judge hearing the appeal.

## Section 49 Costs Payable by the LSC at Prescribed Rates

49.1 This section applies to a bill of costs of an assisted person or LSC funded client which is payable by another person where the costs which can be claimed against the LSC are restricted to prescribed rates (with or without enhancement).

49.2 Where this section applies, the solicitor of the assisted person or LSC funded client must file a legal aid/LSC schedule in accordance with para. 40.2(l) above. The schedule should follow as closely as possible Precedent E of the Schedule of Costs Precedents annexed to this practice direction.

49.3 The schedule must set out by reference to the item numbers in the bill of costs, all the costs claimed as payable by another person, but the arithmetic in the schedule should claim those items at prescribed rates only (with or without any claim for enhancement).

49.4 Where there has been a change in the prescribed rates during the period covered by the bill of costs, the schedule (as opposed to the bill) should be divided into separate parts, so as to deal separately with each change of rate. The schedule must also be divided so as to correspond with any divisions in the bill of costs.

49.5 If the bill of costs contains additional columns setting out costs claimed against the LSC only, the schedule may be set out in a separate document or, alternatively, may be included in the additional columns of the bill.

49.6 The detailed assessment of the legal aid/LSC schedule will take place immediately after the detailed assessment of the bill of costs.

49.7 Attention is drawn to the possibility that, on occasions, the court may decide to conduct the detailed assessment of the legal aid/LSC schedule separately from any detailed assessment of the bill of costs. This will occur, for example, where a default costs certificate is obtained as between the parties but that certificate is not set aside at the time of the detailed assessment pursuant to the Legal Aid Act 1988 or regulations thereunder.

49.8 Where costs have been assessed at prescribed rates it is the responsibility of the legal representative to enter the correct figures allowed in respect of each item and to recalculate the summary of the legal aid/LSC schedule.

## Section 49A Costs Payable by the Trustee for Civil Recovery under a Recovery Order

49A.1 In this section—

'the Act' means the Proceeds of Crime Act 2002;

'the Order in Council' means the Proceeds of Crime Act 2002 (External Requests and Orders) Order 2005; and

'the Regulations' means the Proceeds of Crime Act 2002 (Legal Expenses in Civil Recovery Proceedings) Regulations 2005.

49A.2 This section applies to the assessment of costs where the court has made a recovery order which provides for the payment by the trustee for civil recovery of a person's reasonable legal costs in respect of civil recovery proceedings. Such an order may be made under section 266(8A) of the Act or article 177(10) of the Order in Council. The procedure for obtaining a recovery order is set out in the Act and Order in Council, together with the Civil Recovery Proceedings Practice Direction.

49A.3 Where this section applies, costs are to be assessed in accordance with the procedure for detailed assessment under Part 47, subject to the modifications set out in Parts 4 and 5 of the Regulations.

49A.4 The detailed assessment will normally be made by a costs judge, even if the costs are within the authorised amounts specified in paragraph 30.1(1). The appropriate office for the purpose of rule 47.4(1) is the Supreme Court Costs Office.

49A.5 In detailed assessment proceedings to which this section applies—
(1) the paying party is the trustee for civil recovery;
(2) the receiving party is the person whose reasonable legal costs are payable pursuant to provision made in the recovery order under section 266(8A) of the Act or article 177(10) of the Order in Council; and
(3) the relevant persons for the purpose of rule 47.6(2) include the Director of the Assets Recovery Agency in addition to the persons referred to in paragraph 32.10.

49A.6 On commencing detailed assessment proceedings, the receiving party must, in addition to serving the documents listed in paragraph 32.3 on the paying party and all other relevant persons, serve a statement giving the date, amount and source of all interim payments which have been released in respect of any of those costs under Part 3 of the Regulations.

49A.7 By virtue of regulation 13(2) of the Regulations, detailed assessment proceedings must be commenced not later than 2 months after the date of the recovery order, and a request for a detailed assessment hearing must be filed not later than 2 months after the expiry of the period for commencing the detailed assessment proceedings.

49A.8 The documents which must accompany the request for a detailed assessment hearing shall include copies of all exclusions from property freezing orders or interim receiving orders made by the court for the purpose of enabling the receiving party to meet the costs which are to be assessed, and of every estimate of costs filed by the receiving party in support of an application for such an exclusion.

49A.9 The receiving party's costs will be assessed on the standard basis, subject to Part 5 of the Regulations (and in particular regulation 17, which specifies the hourly rates which may be allowed). Attention is also drawn to regulation 14, which provides that the amounts of any interim payments released in respect of the receiving party's costs will be deducted from the costs allowed in accordance with Part 5 of the Regulations.

## DIRECTIONS RELATING TO PART 48 COSTS — SPECIAL CASES

### Section 50 Amount of Costs Where Costs Are Payable Pursuant to Contract: Rule 48.3

50.1 Where the court is assessing costs payable under a contract, it may make an order that all or part of the costs payable under the contract shall be disallowed if it is satisfied by the paying party that costs have been unreasonably incurred or are unreasonable in amount.

50.2 Rule 48.3 only applies if the court is assessing costs payable under a contract. It does not:
(1) require the court to make an assessment of such costs; or
(2) require a mortgagee to apply for an order for those costs that he has a contractual right to recover out of the mortgage funds.

50.3 The following principles apply to costs relating to a mortgage:
(1) An order for the payment of costs of proceedings by one party to another is always a discretionary order (Supreme Court Act 1981, s. 51).
(2) Where there is a contractual right to the costs the discretion should ordinarily be exercised so as to reflect that contractual right.
(3) The power of the court to disallow a mortgagee's costs sought to be added to the mortgage security is a power that does not derive from s. 51, but from the power of the courts of equity to fix the terms on which redemption will be allowed.

(4) A decision by a court to refuse costs in whole or in part to a mortgagee litigant may be:
(a) a decision in the exercise of the s. 51 discretion;
(b) a decision in the exercise of the power to fix the terms on which redemption will be allowed;
(c) a decision as to the extent of a mortgagee's contractual right to add his costs to the security; or
(d) a combination of two or more of these things.
The statements of case in the proceedings or the submissions made to the court may indicate which of the decisions has been made.
(5) A mortgagee is not to be deprived of a contractual or equitable right to add costs to the security merely by reason of an order for payment of costs made without reference to the mortgagee's contractual or equitable rights, and without any adjudication as to whether or not the mortgagee should be deprived of those costs.

50.4 (1) Where the contract entitles a mortgagee to:
(a) add the costs of litigation relating to the mortgage to the sum secured by it;
(b) require a mortgagor to pay those costs; or
(c) both,
the mortgagor may make an application for the court to direct that an account of the mortgagee's costs be taken.
(Rule 25.1(1)(n) provides that the court may direct that a party file an account.)
(2) The mortgagor may then dispute an amount in the mortgagee's account on the basis that is has been unreasonably incurred or is unreasonable in amount.
(3) Where a mortgagor disputes an amount, the court may make an order that the disputed costs are assessed under r. 48.3.

## Section 50A Limitation on Court's Power to Award Costs in Favour of Trustee or Personal Representative: Rule 48.4

50A.1 A trustee or personal representative is entitled to an indemnity out of the relevant trust fund or estate for costs properly incurred, which may include costs awarded against the trustee or personal representative in favour of another party.

50A.2 Whether costs were properly incurred depends on all the circumstances of the case, and may, for example, depend on:
(1) whether the trustee or personal representative obtained directions from the court before bringing or defending the proceedings;
(2) whether the trustee or personal representative acted in the interests of the fund or estate or in substance for a benefit other than that of the estate, including his own; and
(3) whether the trustee or personal representative acted in some way unreasonably in bringing or defending, or in the conduct of, the proceedings.

50A.3 The trustee or personal representative is not to be taken to have acted in substance for a benefit other than that of the fund by reason only that he has defended a claim in which relief is sought against him personally.

## Section 51 Costs Where Money is Payable by or to a Child or Patient: Rule 48.5

51.1 The circumstances in which the court need not order the assessment of costs under r. 48.5(3) are as follows:
(a) where there is no need to do so to protect the interests of the child or patient or his estate;
(b) where another party has agreed to pay a specified sum in respect of the costs of the child or patient and the solicitor acting for the child or patient has waived the right to claim further costs;

(c) where the court has decided the costs payable to the child or patient by way of summary assessment and the solicitor acting for the child or patient has waived the right to claim further costs;
(d) where an insurer or other person is liable to discharge the costs which the child or patient would otherwise be liable to pay to his solicitor and the court is satisfied that the insurer or other person is financially able to discharge those costs.

## Section 52 Litigants in Person: Rule 48.6

52.1 In order to qualify as an expert for the purpose of r. 48.6(3)(c) (expert assistance in connection with assessing the claim for costs), the person in question must be a:
(1) barrister,
(2) solicitor,
(3) Fellow of the Institute of Legal Executives,
(4) Fellow of the Association of Law Costs Draftsmen,
(5) law costs draftsman who is a member of the Academy of Experts,
(6) law costs draftsman who is a member of the Expert Witness Institute.

52.2 Where a litigant in person wishes to prove that he has suffered financial loss he should produce to the court any written evidence he relies on to support that claim, and serve a copy of that evidence on any party against whom he seeks costs at least 24 hours before the hearing at which the question may be decided.

52.3 Where a litigant in person commences detailed assessment proceedings under r. 47.6 he should serve copies of that written evidence with the notice of commencement.

52.4 The amount, which may be allowed to a litigant in person under r. 46.3(5)(b) and r. 48.6(4), is £9.25 per hour.

52.5 Attention is drawn to r. 48.6(6)(b). A solicitor who, instead of acting for himself, is represented in the proceedings by his firm or by himself in his firm name, is not, for the purpose of the Civil Procedure Rules, a litigant in person.

## Section 53 Personal Liability of Legal Representative for Costs—Wasted Costs Orders: Rule 48.7

53.1 Rule 48.7 deals with wasted costs orders against legal representatives. Such orders can be made at any stage in the proceedings up to and including the proceedings relating to the detailed assessment of costs. In general, applications for wasted costs are best left until after the end of the trial.

53.2 The court may make a wasted costs order against a legal representative on its own initiative.

53.3 A party may apply for a wasted costs order:
(1) by filing an application notice in accordance with Part 23; or
(2) by making an application orally in the course of any hearing.

53.4 It is appropriate for the court to make a wasted costs order against a legal representative, only if:
(1) the legal representative has acted improperly, unreasonably or negligently;
(2) his conduct has caused a party to incur unnecessary costs; and
(3) it is just in all the circumstances to order him to compensate that party for the whole or part of those costs.

53.5 The court will give directions about the procedure that will be followed in each case in order to ensure that the issues are dealt with in a way which is fair and as simple and summary as the circumstances permit.

53.6 As a general rule the court will consider whether to make a wasted costs order in two stages:
(1) in the first stage, the court must be satisfied:
(a) that it has before it evidence or other material which, if unanswered, would be likely to lead to a wasted costs order being made; and

(b) the wasted costs proceedings are justified notwithstanding the likely costs involved.

(2) at the second stage (even if the court is satisfied under sub-para. (1)) the court will consider, after giving the legal representative an opportunity to give reasons why the court should not make a wasted costs order, whether it is appropriate to make a wasted costs order in accordance with para. 53.4 above.

53.7 On an application for a wasted costs order under Part 23 the court may proceed to the second stage described in para. 53.6 without first adjourning the hearing if it is satisfied that the legal representative has already had a reasonable opportunity to give reasons why the court should not make a wasted costs order. In other cases the court will adjourn the hearing before proceeding to the second stage.

53.8 On an application for a wasted costs order under Part 23 the application notice and any evidence in support must identify:

(1) what the legal representative is alleged to have done or failed to do; and

(2) the costs that he may be ordered to pay or which are sought against him.

53.9 A wasted costs order is an order:

(1) that the legal representative pay a specified sum in respect of costs to a party; or

(2) for costs relating to a specified sum or items of work to be disallowed.

53.10 Attention is drawn to r. 44.3A(1) and (2) which respectively prevent the court from assessing any additional liability until the conclusion of the proceedings (or the part of the proceedings) to which the funding arrangement relates, and set out the orders the court may make at the conclusion of the proceedings.

## Section 54 Basis of Detailed Assessment of Solicitor and Client Costs: Rule 48.8

54.1 A client and his solicitor may agree whatever terms they consider appropriate about the payment of the solicitor's charges for his services. If however, the costs are of an unusual nature (either in amount or in the type of costs incurred) those costs will be presumed to have been unreasonably incurred unless the solicitor satisfies the court that he informed the client that they were unusual and, where the costs relate to litigation, that he informed the client they might not be allowed on an assessment of costs between the parties. That information must have been given to the client before the costs were incurred.

54.2 (1) Costs as between a solicitor and client are assessed on the indemnity basis as defined by r. 44.4.

(2) Attention is drawn to the presumptions set out in r. 48.8(2). These presumptions may be rebutted by evidence to the contrary.

54.3 Rule 48.10 and section 56 of this practice direction deal with the procedure to be followed for obtaining the assessment of a solicitor's bill pursuant to an order under Part III of the Solicitors Act 1974.

54.4 If a party fails to comply with the requirements of r. 48.10 concerning the service of a breakdown of costs or points of dispute, any other party may apply to the court in which the detailed assessment hearing should take place for an order requiring compliance with r. 48.10. If the court makes such an order, it may:

(a) make it subject to conditions including a condition to pay a sum of money into court; and

(b) specify the consequence of failure to comply with the order or a condition.

54.5 (1) A client who has entered into a conditional fee agreement with a solicitor may apply for assessment of the base costs (which is carried out in accordance with r. 48.8(2) as if there were no conditional fee agreement) or for assessment of the percentage increase (success fee) or both.

(2) Where the court is to assess the percentage increase the court will have regard to all the relevant factors as they appeared to the solicitor or counsel when the conditional fee agreement was entered into.

54.6 Where the client applies to the court to reduce the percentage increase which the solicitor has charged the client under the conditional fee agreement, the client must set out in his application notice:

(a) the reasons why the percentage increase should be reduced; and
(b) what the percentage increase should be.

54.7 The factors relevant to assessing the percentage increase include:

(a) the risk that the circumstances in which the fees or expenses would be payable might not occur;
(b) the disadvantages relating to the absence of payment on account;
(c) whether there is a conditional fee agreement between the solicitor and counsel;
(d) the solicitor's liability for any disbursements.

54.8 When the court is considering the factors to be taken into account, it will have regard to the circumstances as they reasonably appeared to the solicitor or counsel when the conditional fee agreement was entered into.

## Section 56 Procedure on Assessment of Solicitor and Client Costs: Rule 48.10

56.1 The paragraphs in this section apply to orders made under Part III of the Solicitors Act 1974 for the assessment of costs. In these paragraphs 'client' includes any person entitled to make an application under Part III of that Act.

56.2 The procedure for obtaining an order under Part III of the Solicitors Act 1974 is by the alternative procedure for claims under Part 8, as modified by rule 67.3 and the Practice Direction supplementing Part 67. Precedent J of the Schedule of Costs Precedents annexed to this practice direction is a model form of claim form. The application must be accompanied by the bill or bills in respect of which assessment is sought, and, if the claim concerns a conditional fee agreement, a copy of that agreement. If the original bill is not available a copy will suffice.

56.3 Model forms of order, which the court may make, are set out in Precedents K, L and M of the Schedule of Costs Precedents annexed to this practice direction.

56.4 Attention is drawn to the time limits within which the required steps must be taken: i.e. the solicitor must serve a breakdown of costs within 28 days of the order for costs to be assessed, the client must serve points of dispute within 14 days after service on him of the breakdown, and any reply must be served within 14 days of service of the points of dispute.

56.5 The breakdown of costs referred to in r. 48.10 is a document which contains the following information:

(a) details of the work done under each of the bills sent for assessment; and
(b) in applications under the Solicitors Act 1974, s. 70, an account showing money received by the solicitor to the credit of the client and sums paid out of that money on behalf of the client but not payments out which were made in satisfaction of the bill or of any items which are claimed in the bill.

56.6 Precedent P of the Schedule of Costs Precedents annexed to this practice direction is a model form of breakdown of costs. A party who is required to serve a breakdown of costs must also serve:

(1) copies of the fee notes of counsel and of any expert in respect of fees claimed in the breakdown, and
(2) written evidence as to any other disbursement which is claimed in the breakdown and which exceeds £250.

56.7 The provisions relating to default costs certificates (r. 47.11) do not apply to cases to which r. 48.10 applies.

56.8 Points of dispute should, as far as practicable, be in the form complying with paras 35.1 to 35.7.

56.9 The time for requesting a detailed assessment hearing is within three months after the date of the order for the costs to be assessed.

56.10 The form of request for a hearing date must be in form N258C. The request must be accompanied by copies of:

(a) the order sending the bill or bills for assessment;
(b) the bill or bills sent for assessment;
(c) the solicitor's breakdown of costs and any invoices or accounts served with that breakdown;
(d) a copy of the points of dispute, annotated as necessary in order to show which items have been agreed and their value and to show which items remain in dispute;
(e) as many copies of the points of dispute so annotated as there are other parties to the proceedings to whom the court should give details of the assessment hearing requested;
(f) a copy of any replies served;
(g) a statement signed by the party filing the request or his legal representative giving the names and addresses for service of all parties to the proceedings.

56.11 The request must include an estimate of the length of time the detailed assessment hearing will take.

56.12 On receipt of the request for a detailed assessment hearing the court will fix a date for the hearing or if the costs judge or district judge so decides, will give directions or fix a date for a preliminary appointment.

56.13 (1) The court will give at least 14 days' notice of the time and place of the detailed assessment hearing to every person named in the statement referred to in para. 56.10(g) above.
(2) The court will when giving notice, give all parties other than the party who requested the hearing a copy of the points of dispute annotated by the party requesting the hearing in compliance with para. 56.10(e) above.
(3) Attention is drawn to r. 47.14(6) and (7): apart from the solicitor whose bill it is, only those parties who have served points of dispute may be heard on the detailed assessment unless the court gives permission, and only items specified in the points of dispute may be raised unless the court gives permission.

56.14 (1) If a party wishes to vary his breakdown of costs, points of dispute or reply, an amended or supplementary document must be filed with the court and copies of it must be served on all other relevant parties.
(2) Permission is not required to vary a breakdown of costs, points of dispute or a reply but the court may disallow the variation or permit it only upon conditions, including conditions as to the payment of any costs caused or wasted by the variation.

56.15 Unless the court directs otherwise the solicitor must file with the court the papers in support of the bill not less than seven days before the date for the detailed assessment hearing and not more than 14 days before that date.

56.16 Once the detailed assessment hearing has ended it is the responsibility of the legal representative appearing for the solicitor or, as the case may be, the solicitor in person to remove the papers filed in support of the bill.

56.17 (1) Attention is drawn to r. 47.15 (power to issue an interim certificate).
(2) If, in the course of a detailed assessment hearing of a solicitor's bill to his client, it appears to the costs judge or district judge that in any event the solicitor will be liable in connection with that bill to pay money to the client, he may issue an interim certificate specifying an amount which in his opinion is payable by the solicitor to his client. Such a certificate will include an order to pay the sum it certifies unless the court orders otherwise.

56.18 (1) Attention is drawn to r. 47.16 which requires the solicitor to file a completed bill within 14 days after the end of the detailed assessment hearing. The court may dispense with the requirement to file a completed bill.
(2) After the detailed assessment hearing is concluded the court will:
(a) complete the court copy of the bill so as to show the amount allowed;
(b) determine the result of the cash account;

(c) award the costs of the detailed assessment hearing in accordance with the Solicitors Act 1974, s. 70(8); and
(d) issue a final costs certificate showing the amount due following the detailed assessment hearing.

56.19 A final costs certificate will include an order to pay the sum it certifies unless the court orders otherwise.

## Section 57 Transitional Arrangements

57.1 In this section 'the previous rules' means the Rules of the Supreme Court 1965 ('RSC') or County Court Rules 1981 ('CCR'), as appropriate.

*General scheme of transitional arrangements concerning costs proceedings*

57.2 (1) Paragraph 18 of PD 51 (transitional arrangements) provides that the CPR govern any assessments of costs which take place on or after 26 April 1999 and states a presumption to be applied in respect of costs for work undertaken before 26 April 1999.
(2) The following paragraphs provide five further transitional arrangements:
(a) to provide an additional presumption to be applied when assessing costs which were awarded by an order made in a county court before 26 April 1999 which allowed costs 'on Scale 1' to be determined in accordance with CCR, Appendix A, or 'on the lower scale' to be determined in accordance with CCR, Appendix C.
(b) to preserve the effect of CCR, Appendix B, Part III, para. 2.
(c) to clarify the approach to be taken where a bill of costs was provisionally taxed before 26 April 1999 and the receiving party is unwilling to accept the result of the provisional taxation.
(d) to preserve the right to carry in objections or apply for a reconsideration in all taxation proceedings commenced before 26 April 1999.
(e) to deal with funding arrangements made before 3 July 2000.

*Scale 1 or lower scale costs*

57.3 Where an order was made in county court proceedings before 26 April 1999 under which the costs were allowed on Scale 1 or the lower scale, the general presumption is that no costs will be allowed under that order which would not have been allowed in a taxation before 26 April 1999.

*Fixed costs on the lower scale*

57.4 The amount to be allowed as fixed costs for making or opposing an application for a rehearing to set aside a judgment given before 26 April 1999 where the costs are on lower scale is £11.25.

*Bills provisionally taxed before 26 April 1999*

57.5 In respect of bills of costs provisionally taxed before 26 April 1999:
(1) the previous rules apply on the question who can request a hearing and the time limits for doing so; and
(2) the CPR govern any subsequent hearing in that case.

*Bills taxed before 26 April 1999*

57.6 Where a bill of costs was taxed before 26 April 1999, the previous rules govern the steps which can be taken to challenge that taxation.

*Other taxation proceedings*

57.7 (1) This paragraph applies to taxation proceedings which were commenced before 26 April 1999, were assigned for taxation to a taxing master or district judge, and which were still pending on 26 April 1999.
(2) Any assessment of costs that takes place in cases to which this paragraph applies

which is conducted on or after 26 April 1999, will be conducted in accordance with the CPR.

(3) In addition to the possibility of appeal under rr. 47.20 to 47.23 and Part 52 any party to a detailed assessment who is dissatisfied with any decision on a detailed assessment made by a costs judge or district judge may apply to that costs judge or district judge for a review of the decision. The review shall, for procedural purposes, be treated as if it were an appeal from an authorised court officer.

(4) The right of review provided by sub-para. (3) above, will not apply in cases in which, at least 28 days before the date of the assessment hearing, all parties were served with notice that the rights of appeal in respect of that hearing would be governed by Part 47, Section VIII (appeals from authorised court officers in detailed assessment proceedings) and Part 52 (appeals).

(5) An order for the service of notice under sub-para. (4) above may be made on the application of any party to the detailed assessment proceedings or may be made by the court of its own initiative.

*Transitional provisions concerning the Access to Justice Act 1999, sections 28 to 31*

57.8 (1) Sections 28 to 31 of the Access to Justice Act 1999, the Conditional Fee Agreements Regulations 2000 (SI 2000/692), the Access to Justice (Membership Organisations) Regulations 2000 (SI 2000/693), and the Access to Justice Act 1999 (Transitional Provisions) Order 2000 (SI 2000/900) came into force on 1 April 2000. The Civil Procedure (Amendment No. 3) Rules 2000 (SI 2000/1317) came into force on 3 July 2000. [The Conditional Fee Agreements Regulations 2000 were revoked by the Conditional Fee Agreements (Revocation) Regulations 2005 but continue to have effect in relation to conditional fee agreements entered into before 1 November 2005. The Access to Justice (Membership Organisation) Regulations 2000 were revoked by the Access to Justice (Membership Organisation) Regulations 2005 but continue to have effect in relation to arrangements entered into before 1 November 2005.]

(2) The Access to Justice Act 1999 (Transitional Provisions) Order 2000 provides that no conditional fee agreement or other arrangement about costs entered into before 1 April 2000 can be a funding arrangement, as defined in r. 43.2. The order also has the effect that where a conditional fee agreement or other funding arrangement has been entered into before 1 April 2000 and a second or subsequent funding arrangement of the same type is entered into on or after 1 April 2000, the second or subsequent funding arrangement does not give rise to a liability which is recoverable from a paying party.

(3) The Collective Conditional Fee Agreements Regulations 2000 came into force on 30 November 2000. The Regulations apply to agreements entered into between 30 November 2000 and 31 October 2005. Agreements entered into before 30 November 2000 are treated as if the Regulations had not come into force. The Regulations do not apply to collective conditional fee agreements entered into on or after 1 November 2005.

57.9 (1) Rule 39 of the Civil Procedure (Amendment No. 3) Rules 2000 applies where between 1 April and 2 July 2000 (including both dates):

(a) a funding arrangement is entered into, and

(b) proceedings are started in respect of a claim which is the subject of that agreement.

(2) Attention is drawn to the need to act promptly so as to comply with the requirements of the rules and the practice directions by 31 July 2000 (ie within the 28 days from 3 July 2000 permitted by r. 39) if that compliance is to be treated as compliance with the relevant provision. Attention is drawn in particular to r. 44.15 (providing information about funding arrangements) and section 19 of this practice direction.

(3) Nothing in the legislation referred to above makes provision for a party who has entered into a funding arrangement to recover from another party any amount of an additional liability which relates to anything done or any costs incurred before the arrangement was entered into.

## SCHEDULE OF COSTS PRECEDENTS

The following precedents are not reproduced in this work but may be accessed via the DCA website at <http://www.dca.gov.uk>:

A: Model form of bill of costs (receiving party's solicitor and counsel on CPA terms)
B: Model form of bill of costs (detailed assessment of additional liability only)
C: Model form of bill of costs (payable by defendant and the LSC)
D: Model form of bill of costs (alternative form, single column for amounts claimed, separate parts for costs payable by the LSC only)
E: Legal Aid/LSC schedule of costs
F: Certificates for inclusion in bill of costs
G: Points of dispute
H: Estimate of costs served on other parties
J: Solicitors Act 1974: Part 8 claim form under Part III of the Act
K: Solicitors Act 1974: order for delivery of bill
L: Solicitors Act 1974: order for detailed assessment (client)
M: Solicitors Act 1974: order for detailed assessment (solicitors)
P: Solicitors Act 1974: breakdown of costs

# CPR Part 49 Specialist Proceedings

**49**

(1) These Rules shall apply to the proceedings listed in paragraph (2) subject to the provisions of the relevant practice direction which applies to those proceedings.

(2) The proceedings referred to in paragraph (1) are—

(a) [*Revoked.*]

(b) [*Revoked.*]

(c) [*Revoked.*]

(f) proceedings under the Companies Act 1985[1] and the Companies Act 1989.[2]

---

[1] 1985 c. 6.

[2] 1989 c. 40.

# PD 49B Practice Direction — Applications under the Companies Act 1985 and other Legislation Relating to Companies

This practice direction supplements CPR Part 49 and replaces, with modifications, RSC Order 102 and CCR Order 49 rule 3.

## General

1 (1) In this practice direction:
'the Act' means the Companies Act 1985 and includes the Act as applied to limited liability partnerships by the Limited Liability Partnerships Regulations 2001 (SI 2001/1090);
'the CJPA' means the Criminal Justice and Police Act 2001;
'the Companies Court registrar' means any officer of the High Court who is a registrar within the meaning of any rules for the time being in force relating to the winding-up of companies;
'the court' includes the Companies Court registrar;
'the EC Regulation' means Council Regulation (EC) No 2157/2001 of 8 October 2001 on the Statute for a European company (SE);
'the ICA' means the Insurance Companies Act 1982;
'Part VII FISMA' means Part VII of the Financial Services and Markets 2000;
'the Rules' means the Civil Procedure Rules 1998.
'SE' means a European public limited-liability company (Societas Europaea) within the meaning of Article 1 of the EC Regulation.

(2) Applications under the Act may be made in the county court if the county court would have jurisdiction to wind up the company in question (see the definition of 'the court' in section 744 of the Act). A company can be wound up in the county court if its paid-up capital is not more than £120,000 (Insolvency Act 1986, s. 117(2)).

(3) Every claim form or petition by which an application under the Act, Part VII FISMA or the ICA is begun and all affidavits, witness statements, notices and other documents in those proceedings must be entitled in the matter of the company in question and in the matter of the Act, Part VII FISMA or the ICA as the case may be.

## Commencement of Proceedings

2 (1) Except in the case of the applications mentioned in sub-paragraph (4) below:
(a) every application under the Act, whether made in the High Court or in the county court; and
(b) every application under Part VII FISMA,
(c) every application under Articles 25 and 26 of the EC Regulation; and
(d) every application under section 59 of the CJPA,
must be made by the issue of a claim form and the use of the procedure set out in CPR, Part 8, subject to any modification of that procedure under this practice direction or any other practice direction relating to applications under the Act.

(2) Notice of an application under section 721 of the Act need not be given to the respondent and the claim form need not be served on him.

(3) A claim form issued under this paragraph must, in the High Court, be issued out of the office of the companies court registrar or a chancery district registry or, in the county court, out of a county court office.

(4) This paragraph does not apply to applications under sections 459 or 460 of the Act or to any of the applications specified in paragraph 4(1) of this practice direction.

3 All High Court applications to which this practice direction applies shall be assigned to the Chancery Division.

3A (1) From 1 December 2001 applications to sanction insurance business transfer schemes or banking business transfer schemes must be made under Part VII FISMA. Schedule 2C to the ICA, subject to minor modifications, will continue to apply to applications to sanction or approve transfers of insurance business which are made up to and including 30 November 2001 (see the Financial Services and Markets Act 2000 (Transitional Provisions and Savings) (Business Transfers) Order 2001 (SI 2001/3639)).

(2) Any application under Part VII FISMA must comply with the requirements of the Control of Business Transfers (Requirements on Applicants) Regulations 2001.

(3) In relation to insurance business transfer schemes, the Supervision Manual of the Financial Services Authority (FSA), available on the FSA's website (<http:// www.fsa.gov.uk>), contains rules and guidance with regard to the operation of Part VII FISMA and the FSA's role thereunder which should be referred to before any application under Part VII FISMA is made.

(4) Paragraphs 10 to 13 of this practice direction apply to applications under Part VII FISMA.

## Applications under the EC Regulation

3B. (1) An application for a certificate under Article 25(2) of the EC Regulation must—

(a) be issued in the Chancery Division of the High Court;

(b) identify the pre-merger acts and formalities applicable to the applicant company, and be accompanied by evidence that those acts and formalities have been completed;

(c) be accompanied by copies of:

(i) the draft terms of merger as provided for in Article 20 of the EC Regulation;

(ii) the entry in the Gazette containing the particulars specified in Article 21 of the EC Regulation;

(iii) a report drawn up and adopted by the directors of the applicant company containing the same information as would be required by paragraph 4 of Schedule 15B to the Act if there were to be a scheme of arrangement under sections 425 and 427A of the Act;

(iv) the expert's report to the members of the applicant company drawn up in accordance with paragraph 5 of Schedule 15B to the Act or Article 22 of the EC Regulation; and

(v) the resolution of the applicant company approving the draft terms of merger in accordance with Article 23 of the EC Regulation.

(2) Attention is drawn to Article 26(2) of the EC Regulation. Where it is proposed that the registered office of an SE should be in England or Wales, each of the merging companies is required, within 6 months after a certificate is issued in respect of that company under Article 25(2), to submit the certificate to the High Court in order that it may scrutinise the legality of the merger.

(3) Where a merging company is required to submit a certificate to the High Court under Article 26(2) of the EC Regulation, if no other merging company has commenced proceedings under Article 26, that company shall commence such proceedings by issuing a claim form in the Chancery Division.

(4) The claim form must—

(a) identify the SE and all of the merging companies;

(b) be accompanied by the documents referred to in paragraph 3B(6); and

(c) be served on each of the other merging companies.

(5) Where a merging company is required to submit a certificate to the High Court under Article 26(2) of the EC Regulation and proceedings under Article 26 have already been commenced, that company shall—
   (a) file an acknowledgment of service not more than 14 days after service of the claim form, and serve the acknowledgment of service on each of the other merging companies; and
   (b) file the documents referred to in paragraph 3B(6) within the time limit specified in Article 26(2), and serve copies of those documents on each of the other merging companies.

(6) Each merging company must file and serve the following documents in proceedings under Article 26 of the EC Regulation—
   (a) the certificate issued under Article 25(2) in respect of that company;
   (b) a copy of the draft terms of merger approved by that company;
   (c) evidence that arrangements for employee involvement have been determined by that company pursuant to Council Directive 2001/86/EC of 8 October 2001 supplementing the Statute for a European company with regard to the involvement of employees; and
   (d) evidence that the SE has been formed in accordance with the requirements of Article 26(4) of the EC Regulation.

(7) Proceedings under Article 25 and Article 26 of the EC Regulation will be heard by a High Court judge.

(8) Paragraphs 10 to 13 of this practice direction apply to proceedings under Article 25 and 26 of the EC Regulation.

## Applications Made by Petition

4 (1) The following applications under the Act in addition to applications under sections 459 and 460 of the Act and applications under the ICA must be made by petition, namely, applications:
   (a) under section 5 to cancel the alteration of a company's objects,
   (b) under section 17 to cancel the alteration of a condition contained in a company's memorandum,
   (c) under section 130 to confirm a reduction of the share premium account of a company,
   (d) under section 136 to confirm a reduction of the share capital of a company,
   (e) under section 127 to cancel any variation or abrogation of the rights attached to any class of shares in a company,
   (f) under section 425 to sanction a compromise or arrangement between a company and its creditors or any class of them or between a company and its members or any class of them,
   (g) under section 653 for an order restoring the name of a company to the register, where the application is made in conjunction with an application for the winding up of the company,
   (h) under section 690 to cancel the alteration of the form of a company's constitution,
   (i) under section 727 for relief from liability of an officer of a company or a person employed by a company as auditor,
   (j) under section 54(1) to cancel a special resolution to which that section applies,
   (k) under sections 157(2) or 176(1) to cancel a special resolution to which either of those sections applies, and
   (l) under section 170 in relation to the reduction of capital redemption reserve.

(2) Paragraphs 5 to 14 of this practice direction apply to the applications specified in sub-paragraph (1).

5 (1) After the presentation of a petition by which any application mentioned in paragraph 4 is made, the petitioner, except where his application is one of those

mentioned in sub-paragraph (2), must apply for directions by filing an application notice.

(2) The exceptions referred to in sub-paragraph (1) are:

(a) an application under section 425 of the Act to sanction a compromise or arrangement unless there is included in the petition for such sanction an application for an order under section 427 of the Act,

(b) an application under section 653 of the Act for an order restoring the name of a company to the register,

(c) an application under section 54(1) of the Act for an order cancelling a special resolution to which that section applies, and

(d) an application under section 157(2) or 176(1) of the Act for an order cancelling a special resolution to which those sections apply.

(3) At the directions hearing the court may by order give such directions for the hearing of the application as it thinks fit including, in particular, directions for the publication of notices and the making of any inquiry.

(4) Where the application made by the petition is to confirm a reduction of the share capital, the share premium account, or the capital redemption reserve, of a company the court may give directions:

(a) for an inquiry to be made as to the debts of, and claims against, the company or as to any class or classes of such debts or claims,

(b) as to the proceedings to be taken for settling the list of creditors entitled to object to the reduction and fixing the date by reference to which the list is to be made,

and the power of the court under section 136(6) of the Act to direct that section 136(3) to (5) thereof shall not apply as regards any class of creditors may be exercised at any directions hearing.

## Reduction of Capital and Schemes of Arrangement

6 (1) The consent of a creditor to such reduction as is mentioned in paragraph 5(4) may be proved in such manner as the court thinks sufficient.

(2) The evidence in support of a petition to confirm a reduction of capital need not show as regards any issue of shares made since 1900 for a consideration other than cash that the statutory requirements as to registration were complied with. It is sufficient to state in the petition the extent to which any issued shares (other than shares issued otherwise than for cash before 1901) are or are deemed to be paid up.

(3) The existing practice will remain unaltered in respect of issues of shares otherwise than for cash made before 1901 whilst s. 25 of the Companies Act 1867 remained in operation.

7 (1) This paragraph applies to:

(a) schemes of arrangement under ss. 425 to 427A of the Companies Act 1985, whether made with creditors or members,

(b) schemes for the transfer of the whole or part of the long-term business of an insurance company to which sch. 2C to the ICA applies, and

(c) reductions of capital, share premium account or capital redemption reserve.

References in this and subsequent paragraphs to 'schemes' are to schemes failing within (a) or (b) above, and references to 'reductions' are to reductions failing within (c) above.

(2) Petitions to sanction schemes will be heard by the Companies Court judge.

(3) Petitions to confirm reductions will be heard by the Companies Court Registrar unless otherwise ordered. The Registrar will hear petitions to confirm reductions in open court on a Wednesday each week after completion of the list of winding-up petitions.

## Schemes and Reductions in the Long Vacation

8 (1) The following requirements must be satisfied for a hearing to be fixed to sanction a scheme and/or confirm a reduction in the Long Vacation:

(a) The application is one in which for financial, commercial or economic reasons a hearing before the end of the Long Vacation is desirable. This category will include cases of mergers and takeovers which arise in the summer and are likely to be affected by market fluctuations.

(b) The application is one which could not with reasonable diligence have been made and prosecuted in time to be heard before the Long Vacation begins.

(2) An informal application in chambers, to the Court Manager, accompanied by an advocate's certificate that requirements (a) and (b) are satisfied, must be made as soon as possible so that a suitable timetable may be settled, including a date for hearing.

(3) In the case of reductions to be heard by the Registrar, certain applications which do not fall within the above categories will be heard provided (i) that there is an urgent need for a hearing or (ii) that there is sufficient time available after the Registrar has disposed of the urgent applications.

(4) Applications to the Registrar in chambers for orders convening meetings to consider schemes and for directions on reduction applications will continue to be heard during the Long Vacation. Provided notice is given to the court before the Long Vacation begins, a timetable will be fixed which will enable any necessary documents to be settled in chambers and enable the Registrar to hear the application.

(5) The Vacation Judge will be available to hear petitions to sanction schemes and any petitions to confirm reductions which require to be heard by a judge on one Wednesday in August and two Wednesdays in September on dates to be arranged and subsequently notified in the Long Vacation Notice which is printed in the Daily Cause List.

(6) The Vacation Judge may also hear petitions to sanction schemes or confirm reductions on other days if he thinks fit.

9 (1) Attention is drawn to the undesirability of asking as a matter of course for a winding-up order as an alternative to an order under s. 459 of the Companies Act 1985. The petition should not ask for a winding up order unless that is the relief which the petitioner prefers or it is thought that it may be the only relief to which the petitioner is entitled.

(2) Whenever a winding-up order is asked for in a contributory's petition, the petition must state whether the petitioner consents or objects to an order under s. 127 of the Act in the standard form. If he objects, the written evidence in support must contain a short statement of his reasons.

(3) If the petitioner objects to a s. 127 order in the standard form but consents to such an order in a modified form, the petition must set out the form of order to which he consents, and the written evidence in support must contain a short statement of his reasons for seeking the modification.

(4) If the petition contains a statement that the petitioner consents to a s. 127 order, whether in the standard or a modified form, but the petitioner changes his mind before the first hearing of the petition, he must notify the respondents and may apply on notice to a judge for an order directing that no s. 127 order or a modified order only (as the case may be) shall be made by the Registrar, but validating dispositions made without notice of the order made by the judge.

(5) If the petition contains a statement that the petitioner consents to a s. 127 order, whether in the standard or a modified form, the Registrar shall without further enquiry make an order in such form at the first hearing unless an order to the contrary has been made by the judge in the meantime.

(6) If the petition contains a statement that the petitioner objects to a s. 127 order in the standard form, the company may apply (in the case of urgency, without notice) to the judge for an order.

(7) Section 127 Order—Standard Form:
(Title etc.)
ORDER that notwithstanding the presentation of the said Petition
(1) payments made into or out of the bank accounts of the Company in the ordinary course of the business of the Company and
(2) dispositions of the property of the Company made in the ordinary course of its business for proper value
between the date of presentation of the Petition and the date of judgment on the Petition or further order in the meantime shall not be void by virtue of the provisions of section 127 of the Insolvency Act 1986 in the event of an Order for the winding up of the Company being made on the said Petition Provided that (the relevant bank) shall be under no obligation to verify for itself whether any transaction through the company's bank accounts is in the ordinary course of business, or that it represents full market value for the relevant transaction.
This form of Order may be departed from where the circumstances of the case require.

## Case Management

10 Every application to which this practice direction applies shall be allocated to the multi-track and the CPR relating to allocation questionnaires and track allocation will not apply.

## Service

11 Service of documents in proceedings in the High Court to which this practice direction applies will be the responsibility of the parties and will not be undertaken by the court. Subject to that CPR Part 6 applies.

## Filing of Documents

12 (1) Where an application to which this practice direction relates is proceeding in any Chancery district registry, all affidavits and witness statements made in connection with the application must be filed in that registry.

(2) Where an application to which this practice direction relates is proceeding in any county court, all affidavits and witness statements made in connection with the application must be filed in the office of that county court.

## Drawing up of Orders

13 The court will draw up all orders with the following exceptions:
(a) orders by the Registrar on the application of the Official Receiver or for which the Treasury Solicitor is responsible under the existing practice,
(b) orders by the court in relation to reductions or schemes.

## Applications under Section 59 of the CJPA

14 (1) This paragraph applies to applications under section 59 of the CJPA in respect of property seized in the exercise of the power conferred by section 448(3) of the Act (including any additional powers of seizure conferred by section 50 of the CJPA which are exercisable by reference to that power).

(2) An application to which this paragraph applies should be made to a judge of the Chancery Division.

(3) The defendant to an application under section 59(2) or 59(5)(c) of the CJPA shall be the person for the time being having possession of the property to which the application relates.

(4) On an application under section 59(2) or 59(5)(c) of the CJPA, the claim form and the claimant's evidence must be served on—
  (a) the person for the time being having possession of the property to which the application relates;
  (b) in the case of an application under section 59(2) for the return of seized property, the person specified as the person to whom notice of such an application should be given by any notice served under section 52 of the CJPA when the property was seized;
  (c) in the case of an application under section 59(5)(c), the person from whom the property was seized (if not the claimant); and
  (d) in all cases, any other person appearing to have a relevant interest in the property within the meaning of section 59(11) of the CJPA.

(5) An application under section 59(2) or 59(5)(c) of the CJPA must be supported by evidence—
  (a) that the claimant has a relevant interest in the property to which the application relates within the meaning of section 59(11) of the CJPA; and
  (b) in the case of an application under section 59(2), that one or more of the grounds set out in section 59(3) of the CJPA is satisfied in relation to the property.

(6) The defendants to an application under section 59(5)(b) of the CJPA by a person for the time being in possession of seized property shall be—
  (a) the person from whom the property was seized; and
  (b) any other person appearing to have a relevant interest in the property to which the application relates within the meaning of section 59(11) of the CJPA.

(7) If an application to which this paragraph applies would not otherwise be served on the person who seized the property, and the identity of that person is known to the applicant, notice of the application shall be given to the person who seized the property.

(8) In all applications to which this paragraph applies, when the court issues the claim form it will fix a date for the hearing.

# CPR Part 50 Application of the Schedules

**50**

(1) The Schedules to these Rules set out, with modifications, certain provisions previously contained in the Rules of the Supreme Court 1965 and the County Court Rules 1981.

(2) These Rules apply in relation to the proceedings to which the Schedules apply subject to the provisions in the Schedules and the relevant practice directions.

(3) A provision previously contained in the Rules of the Supreme Court 1965—
  (a) is headed 'RSC';
  (b) is numbered with the Order and rule numbers it bore as part of the RSC; and
  (c) unless otherwise stated in the Schedules or the relevant practice direction, applies only to proceedings in the High Court.

(4) A provision previously contained in the County Court Rules 1981—
  (a) is headed 'CCR';
  (b) is numbered with the Order and rule numbers it bore as part of the CCR; and
  (c) unless otherwise stated in the Schedules or the relevant practice direction, applies only to proceedings in the county court.

(5) A reference in a Schedule to a rule by number alone is a reference to the rule so numbered in the Order in which the reference occurs.

(6) A reference in a Schedule to a rule by number prefixed by 'CPR' is a reference to the rule with that number in these Rules.

(7) In the Schedules, unless otherwise stated, 'the Act' means—
  (a) in a provision headed 'RSC', the Supreme Court Act 1981; and
  (b) in a provision headed 'CCR', the County Courts Act 1984.

# CPR Part 51 Transitional Arrangements and Pilot Schemes

## 51.1

A practice direction shall make provision for the extent to which these Rules shall apply to proceedings issued before 26 April 1999.

## 51.2

Practice directions may modify or disapply any provision of these Rules—
(a) for specified periods; and
(b) in relation to proceedings in specified courts,
during the operation of pilot schemes for assessing the use of new practices and procedures in connection with proceedings.

# PD 51 Practice Direction — Transitional Arrangements

This practice direction supplements CPR Part 51.

## Contents of this Practice Direction

1 (1) This Practice Direction deals with the application of the Civil Procedure Rules ('CPR') to proceedings issued before 26 April 1999 ('existing proceedings').
(2) In this Practice Direction 'the previous rules' means, as appropriate the Rules of the Supreme Court 1965 ('RSC') or County Court Rules 1981 ('CCR') in force immediately before 26 April 1999.

## General Scheme of Transitional Arrangements

2 The general scheme is:
(a) to apply the previous rules to undefended cases, allowing them to progress to their disposal, but
(b) to apply the CPR to defended cases so far as is practicable.

## Where the Previous Rules Will Normally Apply

*General principle*

3 Where an initiating step has been taken in a case before 26 April 1999, in particular one that uses forms or other documentation required by the previous rules, the case will proceed in the first instance under the previous rules. Any step which a party must take in response to something done by another party in accordance with the previous rules must also be in accordance with those rules.

*Responding to old process*

4 A party who is served with an old type of originating process (writ, summons etc.) on or after 26 April 1999 is required to respond in accordance with the previous rules and the instructions on any forms received with the originating process.

*Filing and service of pleadings where old process served*

5 Where a case has been begun by an old type of originating process (whether served before or after 26 April 1999), filing and service of pleadings will continue according to the previous rules.

## Automatic Directions/Discovery

*High Court*

6 (1) Where the timetable for automatic directions under RSC Order 25, rule 8 or automatic discovery under RSC Order 24 has begun to apply to proceedings before 26 April 1999, those directions will continue to have effect on or after 26 April 1999.

*County court*

(2) Where automatic directions under CCR Order 17, rule 11 have begun to apply to existing proceedings before 26 April 1999 or the court has sent out notice that automatic directions under CCR Order 17, rule 11 (Form N.450) will apply (even if the timetable will not begin until 26 April 1999 or after), those directions will continue to have effect on or after 26 April 1999.
(3) However CCR Order 17, rule 11(9) will not apply and therefore proceedings will not be struck out where there has been no request for a hearing to be fixed within 15 months of the date when pleadings were deemed to close. (But see paragraph 19.)

*High Court and county court*

(4) However, if the case comes before the court on or after 26 April 1999, the new rules may apply. (See paragraph 15.)

*Default judgment*

7 (1) If a party wishes default judgment to be entered in existing proceedings, he must do so in accordance with the previous rules.

(2) Where default judgment has been entered and there are outstanding issues to be resolved (e.g. damages to be assessed), the court officer may refer the proceedings to the judge, so that case management decisions about the proceedings and the conduct of the hearing can be made in accordance with the practice set out in paragraph 15.

(3) If a party needs to apply for permission to enter default judgment, he must make that application under CPR Part 23 (general rules about applications for court orders).

(4) An application to set aside judgment entered in default must be made under CPR Part 23 (general rules about applications for court orders) and CPR Part 13 (setting aside or varying default judgment) will apply to the proceedings as it would apply to default judgment entered under the CPR.

(5) CPR rule 15.11 (claims stayed if it is not defended or admitted) applies to these proceedings.

*Judgment on admission in the county court*

8 (1) If a party to existing proceedings in the county court wishes to request judgment to be entered on an admission, he must do so in accordance with the previous rules.

(2) Where judgment has been entered and there are outstanding issues to be resolved (e.g. damages to be assessed), the court officer may refer the proceedings to the judge, so that case management decisions about the proceedings and the conduct of the hearing can be made in accordance with the practice set out in paragraph 15.

(3) If a party needs to apply for permission to enter judgment, he must make that application under CPR Part 23 (general rules about applications for court orders).

*Order inconsistent with CPR*

9 Where a court order has been made before 26 April 1999, that order must still be complied with on or after 26 April 1999.

*Steps taken before 26 April 1999*

10 (1) Where a party has taken any step in the proceedings in accordance with the previous rules that step will remain valid on or after 26 April 1999.

(2) A party will not normally be required to take any action that would amount to taking that step again under the CPR. For example if discovery has been given, a party will not normally be required to provide disclosure under CPR Part 31.

## Where the CPR Will Normally Apply

*General principle*

11 Where a new step is to be taken in any existing proceedings on or after 26 April 1999, it is to be taken under the CPR.

*Part 1 (overriding objective) to apply*

12 Part 1 (overriding objective) will apply to all existing proceedings from 26 April 1999 onwards.

*Originating process*

13 (1) Only claim forms under the CPR will be issued by the court on or after 26 April 1999.

(2) If a request to issue an old type of originating process (writ, summons etc.) is received at the court on or after 26 April 1999 it will be returned unissued.

(3) An application made on or after 26 April 1999 to extend the validity of originating process issued before 26 April 1999 must be made in accordance with CPR Part 23 (general rules about applications for court orders), but the court will decide whether to allow the application in accordance with the previous law.

*Application to the court*

14 (1) Any application to the court made on or after 26 April 1999 must be made in accordance with CPR Part 23 (general rules about applications for court orders).

(2) Any other relevant CPR will apply to the substance of the application, unless this practice direction provides otherwise. (See paragraphs 13(3) (application to extend the validity of originating process) and 18(2) (costs)).

(3) For example, a party wishing to apply for summary judgment must do so having regard to the test in CPR Part 24. A party wishing to apply for an interim remedy must do so under CPR Part 25 etc.

(4) Any other CPR will apply as necessary. For example, CPR Part 4 will apply as to forms and CPR Part 6 will apply to service of documents.

(5) If the pleadings have not been filed at court, the applicant must file all pleadings served when he files his application notice.

*First time before a judge on or after 26 April 1999*

15 (1) When proceedings come before a judge (whether at a hearing or on paper) for the first time on or after 26 April 1999, he may direct how the CPR are to apply to the proceedings and may disapply certain provisions of the CPR. He may also give case management directions (which may include allocating the proceedings to a case management track).

(2) The general presumption will be that the CPR will apply to the proceedings from then on unless the judge directs or this practice direction provides otherwise. (See paragraphs 13(3) (application to extend the validity of originating process) and 18(2) (costs).)

(3) If an application has been issued before 26 April 1999 and the hearing of the application has been set for a date on or after 26 April 1999, the general presumption is that the application will be decided having regard to the CPR. (For example an application for summary judgment issued before 26 April 1999, with a hearing date set for 1 May 1999, will be decided having regard to the test in CPR Part 24 (summary judgment).)

(4) When the first occasion on which existing proceedings are before a judge on or after 26 April 1999 is a trial or hearing of a substantive issue, the general presumption is that the trial or hearing will be conducted having regard to the CPR.

*Where pleadings deemed to close on or after 26 April 1999*

16 (1) This paragraph applies to existing proceedings where pleadings are deemed to close on or after 26 April 1999. However, this paragraph does not apply to those county court proceedings where notice that automatic directions apply (Form N.450) has been sent (in which case the automatic directions will apply—see paragraph 6).

(2) CPR Part 26 (case management—preliminary stage) applies to these proceedings.

(3) If a defence is filed at court on or after 26 April 1999, the court will serve an allocation questionnaire where CPR rule 26.3 would apply, unless it dispenses with the need for one.

(4) If pleadings have not been filed at court (this will normally be the case in the Queen's Bench Division) the claimant must file copies of all the pleadings served within 14 days of the date that pleadings are deemed to close.

(5) Unless it dispenses with the need for one, the court will then serve an allocation questionnaire.

(6) In the previous rules pleadings are deemed to close:
(a) High court:
(i) 14 days after service of any reply, or
(ii) if there is no reply, 14 days after service of the defence to counterclaim, or
(iii) if there is no reply or defence to counterclaim, 14 days after the service of the defence.
(b) County court:
14 days after the delivery of a defence or, where a counterclaim is served with the defence, 28 days after the delivery of the defence.
(7) Where there are 2 or more defendants the court will normally wait until the claimant has filed copies of all the pleadings before serving an allocation questionnaire. However, the court may (in cases where there is a delay) serve allocation questionnaires despite the fact that pleadings have not closed in respect of any other defendant.
(8) The court will then allocate the proceedings in accordance with CPR rule 26.5.
(9) The CPR will then apply generally to the proceedings.

*Agreement to apply the CPR*

17 The parties may agree in writing that the CPR will apply to any proceedings from the date of the agreement. When they do so:
(a) all those who are parties at that time must agree,
(b) the CPR must apply in their entirety,
(c) the agreement is revocable,
(d) the claimant must file a copy of the agreement at court.

*Costs*

18 (1) Any assessment of costs that takes place on or after 26 April 1999 will be in accordance with CPR Parts 43 to 48.
(2) However, the general presumption is that no costs for work undertaken before 26 April 1999 will be disallowed if those costs would have been allowed in a costs taxation before 26 April 1999.
(3) The decision as to whether to allow costs for work undertaken on or after 26 April will generally be taken in accordance with CPR Parts 43 to 48.
(PD 43–48 contains more information on the operation of the transitional arrangements in relation to costs.)

*Existing proceedings after one year*

19 (1) If any existing proceedings have not come before a judge, at a hearing or on paper, between 26 April 1999 and 25 April 2000, those proceedings shall be stayed.
(2) Any party to those proceedings may apply for the stay to be lifted.
(3) Proceedings of the following types will not be stayed as a result of this provision:
(a) where the case has been given a fixed trial date which is after 25 April 2000,
(b) personal injury cases where there is no issue on liability but the proceedings have been adjourned by court order to determine the prognosis,
(c) where the court is dealing with the continuing administration of an estate or a trust or a receivership,
(d) applications relating to funds in court.
(4) For the purposes of this paragraph proceedings will not be 'existing proceedings' once final judgment has been given.

# CPR Part 52 Appeals



## I GENERAL RULES ABOUT APPEALS

### 52.1 Scope and Interpretation

(1) The rules in this Part apply to appeals to—
   (a) the civil division of the Court of Appeal;
   (b) the High Court; and
   (c) a county court.
(2) This Part does not apply to an appeal in detailed assessment proceedings against a decision of an authorised court officer.

(Rules [47.20 to 47.23] deal with appeals against a decision of an authorised court officer in detailed assessment proceedings.)

(3) In this Part—
   (a) 'appeal' includes an appeal by way of case stated;
   (b) 'appeal court' means the court to which an appeal is made;
   (c) 'lower court' means the court, tribunal or other person or body from whose decision an appeal is brought;
   (d) 'appellant' means a person who brings or seeks to bring an appeal;
   (e) 'respondent' means—
      (i) a person other than the appellant who was a party to the proceedings in the lower court and who is affected by the appeal; and
      (ii) a person who is permitted by the appeal court to be a party to the appeal; and
   (f) 'appeal notice' means an appellant's or respondent's notice.
(4) This Part is subject to any rule, enactment or practice direction which sets out special provisions with regard to any particular category of appeal.

### 52.2 Parties to Comply with the Practice Direction

All parties to an appeal must comply with the relevant practice direction.

### 52.3 Permission

(1) An appellant or respondent requires permission to appeal—
   (a) where the appeal is from a decision of a judge in a county court or the High Court, except where the appeal is against—
      (i) a committal order;

(ii) a refusal to grant habeas corpus; or
(iii) a secure accommodation order made under section 25 of the Children Act 1989; or
(b) as provided by the relevant practice direction.

(Other enactments may provide that permission is required for particular appeals.)

(2) An application for permission to appeal may be made—
(a) to the lower court at the hearing at which the decision to be appealed was made; or
(b) to the appeal court in an appeal notice.

(Rule 52.4 sets out the time limits for filing an appellant's notice at the appeal court. Rule 52.5 sets out the time limits for filing a respondent's notice at the appeal court. Any application for permission to appeal to the appeal court must be made in the appeal notice (see rules 52.4(1) and 52.5(3).)

(Rule 52.13(1) provides that permission is required from the Court of Appeal for all appeals to that court from a decision of a county court or the High Court which was itself made on appeal.)

(3) Where the lower court refuses an application for permission to appeal, a further application for permission to appeal may be made to the appeal court.

(4) Subject to paragraph (4A), where the appeal court, without a hearing, refuses permission to appeal, the person seeking permission may request the decision to be reconsidered at a hearing.

(4A) Where the Court of Appeal refuses permission to appeal without a hearing, it may, if it considers that the application is totally without merit, make an order that the person seeking permission may not request the decision to be reconsidered at a hearing. The court may not make such an order in family proceedings.

('Family proceedings' is defined by section 32 of the Matrimonial and Family Proceedings Act 1984.)

(4B) Rule 3.3(5) will not apply to an order that the person seeking permission may not request the decision to be reconsidered at a hearing made under paragraph (4A).

(5) A request under paragraph (4) must be filed within 7 days after service of the notice that permission has been refused.

(6) Permission to appeal may be given only where—
(a) the court considers that the appeal would have a real prospect of success; or
(b) there is some other compelling reason why the appeal should be heard.

(7) An order giving permission may—
(a) limit the issues to be heard; and
(b) be made subject to conditions.

(Rule 3.1(3) also provides that the court may make an order subject to conditions.)

(Rule 25.15 provides for the court to order security for costs of an appeal.)

## 52.4 Appellant's Notice

(1) Where the appellant seeks permission from the appeal court it must be requested in the appellant's notice.

(2) The appellant must file the appellant's notice at the appeal court within—
(a) such period as may be directed by the lower court (which may be longer or shorter than the period referred to in sub-paragraph (b)); or
(b) where the court makes no such direction, 21 days after the date of the decision of the lower court that the appellant wishes to appeal.

(3) Unless the appeal court orders otherwise, an appellant's notice must be served on each respondent—
(a) as soon as practicable; and
(b) in any event not later than 7 days,
after it is filed.

## 52.5 Respondent's Notice

(1) A respondent may file and serve a respondent's notice.
(2) A respondent who—
  (a) is seeking permission to appeal from the appeal court; or
  (b) wishes to ask the appeal court to uphold the order of the lower court for reasons different from or additional to those given by the lower court,
 must file a respondent's notice.
(3) Where the respondent seeks permission from the appeal court it must be requested in the respondent's notice.
(4) A respondent's notice must be filed within—
  (a) such period as may be directed by the lower court; or
  (b) where the court makes no such direction, 14 days, after the date in paragraph (5).
(5) The date referred to in paragraph (4) is—
  (a) the date the respondent is served with the appellant's notice where—
    (i) permission to appeal was given by the lower court; or
    (ii) permission to appeal is not required;
  (b) the date the respondent is served with notification that the appeal court has given the appellant permission to appeal; or
  (c) the date the respondent is served with notification that the application for permission to appeal and the appeal itself are to be heard together.
(6) Unless the appeal court orders otherwise a respondent's notice must be served on the appellant and any other respondent—
  (a) as soon as practicable; and
  (b) in any event not later than 7 days,
 after it is filed.

## 52.6 Variation of Time

(1) An application to vary the time limit for filing an appeal notice must be made to the appeal court.
(2) The parties may not agree to extend any date or time limit set by—
  (a) these Rules;
  (b) the relevant practice direction; or
  (c) an order of the appeal court or the lower court.

(Rule 3.1(2)(a) provides that the court may extend or shorten the time for compliance with any rule, practice direction or court order (even if an application for extension is made after the time for compliance has expired).)

(Rule 3.1(2)(b) provides that the court may adjourn or bring forward a hearing.)

## 52.7 Stay(GL)

Unless—
(a) the appeal court or the lower court orders otherwise; or
(b) the appeal is from the Asylum and Immigration Tribunal,
an appeal shall not operate as a stay of any order or decision of the lower court.

## 52.8 Amendment of Appeal Notice

An appeal notice may not be amended without the permission of the appeal court.

## 52.9 Striking Out(GL) Appeal Notices and Setting Aside or Imposing Conditions on Permission to Appeal

(1) The appeal court may—
  (a) strike out the whole or part of an appeal notice;
  (b) set aside(GL) permission to appeal in whole or in part;
  (c) impose or vary conditions upon which an appeal may be brought.

(2) The court will only exercise its powers under paragraph (1) where there is a compelling reason for doing so.
(3) Where a party was present at the hearing at which permission was given he may not subsequently apply for an order that the court exercise its powers under sub-paragraphs (1)(b) or (1)(c).

## 52.10 Appeal Court's Powers

(1) In relation to an appeal the appeal court has all the powers of the lower court.
(Rule 52.1(4) provides that this Part is subject to any enactment that sets out special provisions with regard to any particular category of appeal—where such an enactment gives a statutory power to a tribunal, person or other body it may be the case that the appeal court may not exercise that power on an appeal.)
(2) The appeal court has power to—
(a) affirm, set aside or vary any order or judgment made or given by the lower court;
(b) refer any claim or issue for determination by the lower court;
(c) order a new trial or hearing;
(d) make orders for the payment of interest;
(e) make a costs order.
(3) In an appeal from a claim tried with a jury the Court of Appeal may, instead of ordering a new trial—
(a) make an order for damages(GL); or
(b) vary an award of damages made by the jury.
(4) The appeal court may exercise its powers in relation to the whole or part of an order of the lower court.
(5) If the appeal court—
(a) refuses an application for permission to appeal;
(b) strikes out an appellant's notice; or
(c) dismisses an appeal,
and it considers that the application, the appellant's notice or the appeal is totally without merit, the provisions of paragraph (6) must be complied with.
(6) Where paragraph (5) applies—
(a) the court's order must record the fact that it considers the application, the appellant's notice or the appeal to be totally without merit; and
(b) the court must at the same time consider whether it is appropriate to make a civil restraint order.
(Part 3 contains general rules about the court's case management powers.)

## 52.11 Hearing of Appeals

(1) Every appeal will be limited to a review of the decision of the lower court unless—
(a) a practice direction makes different provision for a particular category of appeal; or
(b) the court considers that in the circumstances of an individual appeal it would be in the interests of justice to hold a rehearing.
(2) Unless it orders otherwise, the appeal court will not receive—
(a) oral evidence; or
(b) evidence which was not before the lower court.
(3) The appeal court will allow an appeal where the decision of the lower court was—
(a) wrong; or
(b) unjust because of a serious procedural or other irregularity in the proceedings in the lower court.
(4) The appeal court may draw any inference of fact which it considers justified on the evidence.
(5) At the hearing of the appeal a party may not rely on a matter not contained in his appeal notice unless the appeal court gives permission.

### 52.12 Non-disclosure of Part 36 Offers and Payments

(1) The fact that a Part 36 offer or payment into court has been made must not be disclosed to any judge of the appeal court who is to hear or determine—
   (a) an application for permission to appeal; or
   (b) an appeal,
   until all questions (other than costs) have been determined.
(2) Paragraph (1) does not apply if the Part 36 offer or payment into court is relevant to the substance of the appeal.
(3) Paragraph (1) does not prevent disclosure in any application in the appeal proceedings if disclosure of the fact that a Part 36 offer or payment into court has been made is properly relevant to the matter to be decided.

(Rule 36.3 has the effect that a Part 36 offer made in proceedings at first instance will not have consequences in any appeal proceedings. Therefore, a fresh Part 36 offer needs to be made in appeal proceedings. However, rule 52.12 applies to a Part 36 offer whether made in the original proceedings or in the appeal.)

## II SPECIAL PROVISIONS APPLYING TO THE COURT OF APPEAL

### 52.13 Second Appeals to the Court

(1) Permission is required from the Court of Appeal for any appeal to that court from a decision of a county court or the High Court which was itself made on appeal.
(2) The Court of Appeal will not give permission unless it considers that—
   (a) the appeal would raise an important point of principle or practice; or
   (b) there is some other compelling reason for the Court of Appeal to hear it.

### 52.14 Assignment of Appeals to the Court of Appeal

(1) Where the court from or to which an appeal is made or from which permission to appeal is sought ('the relevant court') considers that—
   (a) an appeal which is to be heard by a county court or the High Court would raise an important point of principle or practice; or
   (b) there is some other compelling reason for the Court of Appeal to hear it,
   the relevant court may order the appeal to be transferred to the Court of Appeal.

(The Master of the Rolls has the power to direct that an appeal which would be heard by a county court or the High Court should be heard instead by the Court of Appeal—see section 57 of the Access to Justice Act 1999.)

(2) The Master of the Rolls or the Court of Appeal may remit an appeal to the court in which the original appeal was or would have been brought.

### 52.15 Judicial Review Appeals

(1) Where permission to apply for judicial review has been refused at a hearing in the High Court, the person seeking that permission may apply to the Court of Appeal for permission to appeal.
(2) An application in accordance with paragraph (1)must be made within 7 days of the decision of the High Court to refuse to give permission to apply for judicial review.
(3) On an application under paragraph (1), the Court of Appeal may, instead of giving permission to appeal, give permission to apply for judicial review.
(4) Where the Court of Appeal gives permission to apply for judicial review in accordance with paragraph (3), the case will proceed in the High Court unless the Court of Appeal orders otherwise.

### 52.16 Who May Exercise the Powers of the Court of Appeal

(1) A court officer assigned to the Civil Appeals Office who is—
   (a) a barrister; or

(b) a solicitor

may exercise the jurisdiction of the Court of Appeal with regard to the matters set out in paragraph (2) with the consent of the Master of the Rolls.

(2) The matters referred to in paragraph (1) are—
   (a) any matter incidental to any proceedings in the Court of Appeal;
   (b) any other matter where there is no substantial dispute between the parties; and
   (c) the dismissal of an appeal or application where a party has failed to comply with any order, rule or practice direction.

(3) A court officer may not decide an application for—
   (a) permission to appeal;
   (b) bail pending an appeal;
   (c) an injunction(GL);
   (d) a stay(GL) of any proceedings, other than a temporary stay of any order or decision of the lower court over a period when the Court of Appeal is not sitting or cannot conveniently be convened.

(4) Decisions of a court officer may be made without a hearing.

(5) A party may request any decision of a court officer to be reviewed by the Court of Appeal.

(6) At the request of a party, a hearing will be held to reconsider a decision of—
   (a) a single judge; or
   (b) a court officer,

made without a hearing.

(6A) A request under paragraph (5) or (6) must be filed within 7 days after the party is served with notice of the decision.

(7) A single judge may refer any matter for a decision by a court consisting of two or more judges.

(Section 54(6) of the Supreme Court Act 1981 provides that there is no appeal from the decision of a single judge on an application for permission to appeal.)

(Section 58(2) of the Supreme Court Act 1981 provides that there is no appeal to the House of Lords from decisions of the Court of Appeal that—
   (a) are taken by a single judge or any officer or member of staff of that court in proceedings incidental to any cause or matter pending before the civil division of that court; and
   (b) do not involve the determination of an appeal or of an application for permission to appeal, and which may be called into question by rules of court. Rules 52.16(5) and (6) provide the procedure for the calling into question of such decisions.)

## III PROVISIONS ABOUT REOPENING APPEALS

### 52.17 Reopening of Final Appeals

(1) The Court of Appeal or the High Court will not reopen a final determination of any appeal unless—
   (a) it is necessary to do so in order to avoid real injustice;
   (b) the circumstances are exceptional and make it appropriate to reopen the appeal; and
   (c) there is no alternative effective remedy.

(2) In paragraphs (1), (3), (4) and (6), 'appeal' includes an application for permission to appeal.

(3) This rule does not apply to appeals to a county court.

(4) Permission is needed to make an application under this rule to reopen a final determination of an appeal even in cases where under rule 52.3(1) permission was not needed for the original appeal.

(5) There is no right to an oral hearing of an application for permission unless, exceptionally, the judge so directs.

(6) The judge will not grant permission without directing the application to be served

on the other party to the original appeal and giving him an opportunity to make representations.

(7) There is no right of appeal or review from the decision of the judge on the application for permission, which is final.

(8) The procedure for making an application for permission is set out in the practice direction.

# PD 52 Practice Direction — Appeals

This practice direction supplements CPR Part 52.

## Contents of this Practice Direction

1.1 This practice direction is divided into four Sections:

- Section I—General provisions about appeals.
- Section II—General provisions about statutory appeals and appeals by way of case stated.
- Section III—Provisions about specific appeals.
- Section IV—Provisions about reopening appeals.

## SECTION I — GENERAL PROVISIONS ABOUT APPEALS

2.1 This practice direction applies to all appeals to which Part 52 applies except where specific provision is made for appeals to the Court of Appeal.

2.2 For the purpose only of appeals to the Court of Appeal from cases in family proceedings this Practice Direction will apply with such modifications as may be required.

### Routes of Appeal

2A.1 The court or judge to which an appeal is to be made (subject to obtaining any necessary permission) is set out in the tables below:

Table 1[1] addresses appeals in cases other than insolvency proceedings and those cases to which Table 3 applies;

Table 2 addresses insolvency proceedings; and

Table 3 addresses certain family cases to which CPR Part 52 may apply.

The tables do not include so-called 'leap frog' appeals either to the Court of Appeal pursuant to s. 57 of the Access to Justice Act 1999 or to the House of Lords pursuant to s. 13 of the Administration of Justice Act 1969.

(An interactive routes of appeal guide can be found on the Court of Appeal's website at <http://www.hmcourts-service.gov.uk/infoabout/coa_civil/routes_app/index.htm>.)

2A.2 A 'final decision' is a decision of a court that would finally determine (subject to any possible appeal or detailed assessment of costs) the entire proceedings whichever way the court decided the issues before it. Decisions made on an application to strike out or for summary judgment are not final decisions for the purpose of determining the appropriate route of appeal (Article 1 of the Access to Justice Act 1999 (Destination of Appeals) Order 2000). Accordingly:

(1) a case management decision;
(2) the grant or refusal of interim relief;
(3) a summary judgment;
(4) a striking out,

are not final decisions for this purpose.

2A.3 A decision of a court is to be treated as a final decision for routes of appeal purposes where it:

(1) is made at the conclusion of part of a hearing or trial which has been split into parts; and
(2) would, if it had been made at the conclusion of that hearing or trial, have been a final decision.

[1] Reproduced with the kind permission of Tottel Publishing, publisher of *Manual of Civil Appeals*.

**Table 1** Appeals other than insolvency

In this Table references to a 'circuit judge' include a recorder or a district judge who is exercising the jurisdiction of a circuit judge with the permission of the designated civil judge in respect of that case (see: Practice Direction 2B, paragraph 11.1(d)).

For the meaning of 'final decision' for the purposes of this table see paragraphs 2A.2 and 2A.3 above.

| Court | Track/nature of claim | Judge who made decision | Nature of decision under appeal | Appeal Court |
|---|---|---|---|---|
| County | Unallocated<br>Small<br>Fast | District judge | Any | Circuit judge in county court |
| County | CPR Pt 8 (if not allocated to any track or if simply treated as allocated to the multi-track under CPR 8.9(c)) | District judge | Final | Circuit judge in county court |
| County | Multi-track | District judge | Any decision other than a final decision | Circuit judge in county court |
| County | Multi-track | District judge | Final decision | Court of Appeal |
| County | Specialist proceedings (under the Companies Acts 1985 or 1989 or to which sections I, II or III of Part 57 or any of Parts 59, 60, 62 or 63 apply) | District judge | Any decision other than a final decision | Circuit judge in county court |
| County | Specialist proceedings (under the Companies Acts 1985 or 1989 or to which sections I, II or III Part 57 or any of Parts 59, 60, 62 or 63 apply) | District judge | Final decision | Court of Appeal |
| County | Unallocated<br>Small<br>Fast | Circuit judge | Any (except final decision in specialist proceedings; see below) | Single judge of the High Court |
| County | Multi-track | Circuit judge | Any decision other than a final decision | Single judge of the High Court |
| County | CPR Pt 8 (if not allocated to any track or if simply treated as allocated to the multi-track under CPR 8.9(c)) | Circuit judge | Final | Single judge of the High Court |

| | | | | |
|---|---|---|---|---|
| County | Specialist proceedings (under the Companies Acts 1985 or 1989 or to which sections I, II or III of Part 57 or any of Parts 59, 60, 62 or 63 apply) | Circuit judge | Final | Court of Appeal |
| County | Multi-track | Circuit judge | Final decision | Court of Appeal |
| High Court | Multi-track | Master or district judge sitting in a District Registry | Any decision other than a final decision | Single judge of the High Court |
| High Court | CPR Pt 8 (if not allocated to any track or if simply treated as allocated to the multi-track under CPR 8.9(c)) | Master or district judge sitting in a District Registry | Final | Single judge of the High Court |
| High Court | Multi-track | Master or district judge sitting in a District Registry | Final | Court of Appeal |
| High Court | Specialist proceedings (under the Companies Acts 1985 or 1989 or to which sections I, II or III of Part 57 or any of Parts 58 to 63 apply) | Master or district judge sitting in a District Registry | Any decision other than a final decision | High Court |
| High Court | Specialist proceedings (under the Companies Acts 1985 or 1989 or to which sections I, II or III of Part 57 or any of Parts 58 to 63 apply) | Master or district judge sitting in a District Registry | Final decision | Court of Appeal |
| High Court | Any | High Court judge | Any | Court of Appeal |

**Table 2** Insolvency proceedings

In this Table references to a 'circuit judge' include a recorder or a district judge who is exercising the jurisdiction of a circuit judge with the permission of the designated civil judge in respect of that case (see: Practice Direction 2B, paragraph 11.1(d)).

| Court | Track/nature of claim | Judge who made decision | Nature of decision under appeal | Appeal Court |
|---|---|---|---|---|
| County | Insolvency | District judge or circuit judge | Any | Single judge of the High Court |
| High Court | Insolvency | Registrar | Any | Single judge of the High Court |
| High Court | Insolvency | High Court judge | Any | Court of Appeal |

**Table 3** Proceedings which may be heard in the Family Division of the High Court and to which the CPR may apply

The proceedings to which this table will apply include proceedings under the Inheritance (Provision for Family and Dependants) Act 1975 and proceedings under the Trusts of Land and Appointment of Trustees Act 1996.
For the meaning of 'final decision' for the purposes of this table see paragraphs 2A.2 and 2A.3 above.

| Court | Judge who made decision | Track/ nature of claim | Nature of decision under appeal | Appeal Court |
|---|---|---|---|---|
| High Court Principal Registry of the Family Division | District judge | Proceedings under CPR Pt 8 (if not allocated to any track or if simply treated as allocated to the multi-track under CPR 8.9(c)) | Any decision | High Court judge of the Family Division |
| High Court Principal Registry of the Family Division | District judge | Proceedings under CPR Pt 8 specifically allocated to the multi-track by an order of the court | Any decision | High Court judge of the Family Division |
| High Court Principal Registry of the Family Division | District judge | Proceedings under CPR Pt 7 | Any decision other than a final decision | High Court judge of the Family Division |
| High Court Principal Registry of the Family Division | District judge | Proceedings under CPR Pt 7 and allocated to the multi-track | Final decision | Court of Appeal |
| High Court Family Division | High Court Judge | Proceedings under CPR Pt 7 or 8 | Any | Court of Appeal |

Accordingly, a judgment on liability at the end of a split trial is a 'final decision' for this purpose and the judgment at the conclusion of the assessment of damages following a judgment on liability is also a 'final decision' for this purpose.

2A.4 An order made:

(1) on a summary or detailed assessment of costs; or

(2) on an application to enforce a final decision,

is not a 'final decision' and any appeal from such an order will follow the routes of appeal set out in the tables above.

(Section 16(1) of the Supreme Court Act 1981 (as amended); section 77(1) of the County Courts Act 1984 (as amended); and the Access to Justice Act 1999 (Destination of Appeals) Order 2000 set out the provisions governing routes of appeal.)

2A.5 (1)Where an applicant attempts to file an appellant's notice and the appeal court does not have jurisdiction to issue the notice, a court officer may notify the applicant in writing that the appeal court does not have jurisdiction in respect of the notice.

(2) Before notifying a person under paragraph (1) the court officer must confer—
(a) with a judge of the appeal court; or,
(b) where the Court of Appeal, Civil Division is the appeal court, with a court officer who exercises the jurisdiction of that Court under rule 52.16.
(3) Where a court officer in the Court of Appeal, Civil Division notifies a person under paragraph (1), rule 52.16(5) shall not apply.

## Grounds for Appeal

3.1 Rule 52.11(3) (a) and (b) sets out the circumstances in which the appeal court will allow an appeal.
3.2 The grounds of appeal should—
(1) set out clearly the reasons why rule 52.11(3)(a) or (b) is said to apply; and
(2) specify, in respect of each ground, whether the ground raises an appeal on a point of law or is an appeal against a finding of fact.

## Permission to Appeal

4.1 Rule 52.3 sets out the circumstances when permission to appeal is required.
4.2 The permission of—
(1) the Court of Appeal; or
(2) where the lower court's rules allow, the lower court,
is required for all appeals to the Court of Appeal except as provided for by statute or rule 52.3.
(The requirement of permission to appeal may be imposed by a practice direction—see rule 52.3(b).)
4.3 Where the lower court is not required to give permission to appeal, it may give an indication of its opinion as to whether permission should be given.
(Rule 52.1(3)(c) defines 'lower court'.)
4.3A (1) This paragraph applies where a party applies for permission to appeal against a decision at the hearing at which the decision was made.
(2) Where this paragraph applies, the judge making the decision shall state—
(a) whether or not the judgment or order is final;
(b) whether an appeal lies from the judgment or order and, if so, to which appeal court;
(c) whether the court gives permission to appeal; and
(d) if not, the appropriate appeal court to which any further application for permission may be made.
(Rule 40.2(4) contains requirements as to the contents of the judgment or order in these circumstances.)
4.3B Where no application for permission to appeal has been made in accordance with rule 52.3(2)(a) but a party requests further time to make such an application, the court may adjourn the hearing to give that party the opportunity to do so.

## Appeals from Case Management Decisions

4.4 Case management decisions include decisions made under rule 3.1(2) and decisions about:
(1) disclosure;
(2) filing of witness statements or experts reports;
(3) directions about the timetable of the claim;
(4) adding a party to a claim;
(5) security for costs.
4.5 Where the application is for permission to appeal from a case management decision, the court dealing with the application may take into account whether:
(1) the issue is of sufficient significance to justify the costs of an appeal;

(2) the procedural consequences of an appeal (e.g. loss of trial date) outweigh the significance of the case management decision;
(3) it would be more convenient to determine the issue at or after trial.

## Court to which Permission to Appeal Application Should be Made

4.6 An application for permission should be made orally at the hearing at which the decision to be appealed against is made.

4.7 Where:
(a) no application for permission to appeal is made at the hearing; or
(b) the lower court refuses permission to appeal,
an application for permission to appeal may be made to the appeal court in accordance with rules 52.3(2) and (3).

4.8 There is no appeal from a decision of the appeal court to allow or refuse permission to appeal to that court (although where the appeal court, without a hearing, refuses permission to appeal, the person seeking permission may request that decision to be reconsidered at a hearing). See section 54(4) of the Access to Justice Act and rule 52.3(2), (3), (4) and (5).

## Second Appeals

4.9 An application for permission to appeal from a decision of the High Court or a county court which was itself made on appeal must be made to the Court of Appeal.

4.10 If permission to appeal is granted the appeal will be heard by the Court of Appeal.

## Consideration of Permission without a Hearing

4.11 Applications for permission to appeal may be considered by the appeal court without a hearing.

4.12 If permission is granted without a hearing the parties will be notified of that decision and the procedure in paragraphs 6.1 to 6.6 will then apply.

4.13 If permission is refused without a hearing the parties will be notified of that decision with the reasons for it. The decision is subject to the appellant's right to have it reconsidered at an oral hearing. This may be before the same judge.

4.14 A request for the decision to be reconsidered at an oral hearing must be filed at the appeal court within 7 days after service of the notice that permission has been refused. A copy of the request must be served by the appellant on the respondent at the same time.

## Permission Hearing

4.14A (1) This paragraph applies where an appellant, who is represented, makes a request for a decision to be reconsidered at an oral hearing.
(2) The appellant's advocate must, at least 4 days before the hearing, in a brief written statement—
(a) inform the court and the respondent of the points which he proposes to raise at the hearing;
(b) set out his reasons why permission should be granted notwithstanding the reasons given for the refusal of permission; and
(c) confirm, where applicable, that the requirements of paragraph 4.17 have been complied with (appellant in receipt of services funded by the Legal Services Commission).

4.15 Notice of a permission hearing will be given to the respondent but he is not required to attend unless the court requests him to do so.

4.16 If the court requests the respondent's attendance at the permission hearing, the appellant must supply the respondent with a copy of the appeal bundle (see paragraph 5.6A) within 7 days of being notified of the request, or such other period as the court may direct. The costs of providing that bundle shall be borne by the appellant initially, but will form part of the costs of the permission application.

## Appellants in Receipt of Services Funded by the Legal Services Commission Applying for Permission to Appeal

4.17 Where the appellant is in receipt of services funded by the Legal Services Commission (or legally aided) and permission to appeal has been refused by the appeal court without a hearing, the appellant must send a copy of the reasons the appeal court gave for refusing permission to the relevant office of the Legal Services Commission as soon as it has been received from the court. The court will require confirmation that this has been done if a hearing is requested to reconsider the question of permission.

## Limited Permission

4.18 Where a court under rule 52.3(7) gives permission to appeal on some issues only, it will—

(1) refuse permission on any remaining issues; or

(2) reserve the question of permission to appeal on any remaining issues to the court hearing the appeal.

4.19 If the court reserves the question of permission under paragraph 4.18(2), the appellant must, within 14 days after service of the court's order, inform the appeal court and the respondent in writing whether he intends to pursue the reserved issues. If the appellant does intend to pursue the reserved issues, the parties must include in any time estimate for the appeal hearing, their time estimate for the reserved issues.

4.20 If the appeal court refuses permission to appeal on the remaining issues without a hearing and the applicant wishes to have that decision reconsidered at an oral hearing, the time limit in rule 52.3(5) shall apply. Any application for an extension of this time limit should be made promptly. The court hearing the appeal on the issues for which permission has been granted will not normally grant, at the appeal hearing, an application to extend the time limit in rule 52.3(5) for the remaining issues.

4.21 If the appeal court refuses permission to appeal on remaining issues at or after an oral hearing, the application for permission to appeal on those issues cannot be renewed at the appeal hearing. See section 54(4) of the Access to Justice Act 1999.

## Respondents' Costs of Permission Applications

4.22 In most cases, applications for permission to appeal will be determined without the court requesting—

(1) submissions from, or

(2) if there is an oral hearing, attendance by the respondent.

4.23 Where the court does not request submissions from or attendance by the respondent, costs will not normally be allowed to a respondent who volunteers submissions or attendance.

4.24 Where the court does request—

(1) submissions from; or

(2) attendance by the respondent,

the court will normally allow the respondent his costs if permission is refused.

# APPELLANT'S NOTICE

5.1 An appellant's notice must be filed and served in all cases. Where an application for permission to appeal is made to the appeal court it must be applied for in the appellant's notice.

## Human Rights

5.1A (1) This paragraph applies where the appellant seeks—

(a) to rely on any issue under the Human Rights Act 1998; or

(b) a remedy available under that Act,

for the first time in an appeal.

(2) The appellant must include in his appeal notice the information required by paragraph 15.1 of the practice direction supplementing Part 16.

(3) Paragraph 15.2 of the practice direction supplementing Part 16 applies as if references to a statement of case were to the appeal notice.

5.1B CPR rule 19.4A and the practice direction supplementing it shall apply as if references to the case management conference were to the application for permission to appeal.

(The practice direction to Part 19 provides for notice to be given and parties joined in certain circumstances to which this paragraph applies.)

## EXTENSION OF TIME FOR FILING APPELLANT'S NOTICE

5.2 Where the time for filing an appellant's notice has expired, the appellant must—

(a) file the appellant's notice; and

(b) include in that appellant's notice an application for an extension of time.

The appellant's notice should state the reason for the delay and the steps taken prior to the application being made.

5.3 Where the appellant's notice includes an application for an extension of time and permission to appeal has been given or is not required the respondent has the right to be heard on that application. He must be served with a copy of the appeal bundle (see paragraph 5.6A). However, a respondent who unreasonably opposes an extension of time runs the risk of being ordered to pay the appellant's costs of that application.

5.4 If an extension of time is given following such an application the procedure at paragraphs 6.1 to 6.6 applies.

### Applications

5.5 Notice of an application to be made to the appeal court for a remedy incidental to the appeal (e.g. an interim remedy under rule 25.1 or an order for security for costs) may be included in the appeal notice or in a Part 23 application notice.

(Rule 25.15 deals with security for costs of an appeal.)

(Paragraph 11 of this practice direction contains other provisions relating to applications.)

### Documents

5.6 (1) This paragraph applies to every case except where the appeal—

(a) relates to a claim allocated to the small claims track; and

(b) is being heard in a county court or the High Court.

(Paragraph 5.8 applies where this paragraph does not apply.)

(2) The appellant must file the following documents together with an appeal bundle (see paragraph 5.6A) with his appellant's notice—

(a) two additional copies of the appellant's notice for the appeal court; and

(b) one copy of the appellant's notice for each of the respondents;

(c) one copy of his skeleton argument for each copy of the appellant's notice that is filed (see paragraph 5.9);

(d) a sealed copy of the order being appealed;

(e) a copy of any order giving or refusing permission to appeal, together with a copy of the judge's reasons for allowing or refusing permission to appeal;

(f) any witness statements or affidavits in support of any application included in the appellant's notice;

(g) a copy of the order allocating a case to a track (if any).

5.6A (1) An appellant must include in his appeal bundle the following documents:

(a) a sealed copy of the appellant's notice;

(b) a sealed copy of the order being appealed;

(c) a copy of any order giving or refusing permission to appeal, together with a copy of the judge's reasons for allowing or refusing permission to appeal;

(d) any affidavit or witness statement filed in support of any application included in the appellant's notice;
(e) a copy of his skeleton argument;
(f) a transcript or note of judgment (see paragraph 5.12), and in cases where permission to appeal was given by the lower court or is not required those parts of any transcript of evidence which are directly relevant to any question at issue on the appeal;
(g) the claim form and statements of case (where relevant to the subject of the appeal);
(h) any application notice (or case management documentation) relevant to the subject of the appeal;
(i) in cases where the decision appealed was itself made on appeal (eg from district judge to circuit judge), the first order, the reasons given and the appellant's notice used to appeal from that order;
(j) in the case of judicial review or a statutory appeal, the original decision which was the subject of the application to the lower court;
(k) in cases where the appeal is from a Tribunal, a copy of the Tribunal's reasons for the decision, a copy of the decision reviewed by the Tribunal and the reasons for the original decision and any document filed with the Tribunal setting out the grounds of appeal from that decision;
(l) any other documents which the appellant reasonably considers necessary to enable the appeal court to reach its decision on the hearing of the application or appeal; and
(m) such other documents as the court may direct.

(2) All documents that are extraneous to the issues to be considered on the application or the appeal must be excluded. The appeal bundle may include affidavits, witness statements, summaries, experts' reports and exhibits but only where these are directly relevant to the subject matter of the appeal.

(3) Where the appellant is represented, the appeal bundle must contain a certificate signed by his solicitor, counsel or other representative to the effect that he has read and understood paragraph (2) above and that the composition of the appeal bundle complies with it.

5.7 Where it is not possible to file all the above documents, the appellant must indicate which documents have not yet been filed and the reasons why they are not currently available. The appellant must then provide a reasonable estimate of when the missing document or documents can be filed and file them as soon as reasonably practicable.

## Small Claims

5.8 (1) This paragraph applies where—
(a) the appeal relates to a claim allocated to the small claims track; and
(b) the appeal is being heard in a county court or the High Court.

(1A) An appellant's notice must be filed and served in Form N164.

(2) The appellant must file the following documents with his appellant's notice—
(a) a sealed copy of the order being appealed; and
(b) any order giving or refusing permission to appeal, together with a copy of the reasons for that decision.

(3) The appellant may, if relevant to the issues to be determined on the appeal, file any other document listed in paragraph 5.6 or 5.6A in addition to the documents referred to in sub-paragraph (2).

(4) The appellant need not file a record of the reasons for judgment of the lower court with his appellant's notice unless sub-paragraph (5) applies.

(5) The court may order a suitable record of the reasons for judgment of the lower court (see paragraph 5.12) to be filed—

(a) to enable it to decide if permission should be granted; or
(b) if permission is granted to enable it to decide the appeal.

## Skeleton Arguments

5.9 (1) The appellant's notice must, subject to (2) and (3) below, be accompanied by a skeleton argument. Alternatively the skeleton argument may be included in the appellant's notice. Where the skeleton argument is so included it will not form part of the notice for the purposes of rule 52.8.
(2) Where it is impracticable for the appellant's skeleton argument to accompany the appellant's notice it must be filed and served on all respondents within 14 days of filing the notice.
(3) An appellant who is not represented need not file a skeleton argument but is encouraged to do so since this will be helpful to the court.

*Content of skeleton arguments*

5.10 (1) A skeleton argument must contain a numbered list of the points which the party wishes to make. These should both define and confine the areas of controversy. Each point should be stated as concisely as the nature of the case allows.
(2) A numbered point must be followed by a reference to any document on which the party wishes to rely.
(3) A skeleton argument must state, in respect of each authority cited—
(a) the proposition of law that the authority demonstrates; and
(b) the parts of the authority (identified by page or paragraph references) that support the proposition.
(4) If more than one authority is cited in support of a given proposition, the skeleton argument must briefly state the reason for taking that course.
(5) The statement referred to in sub-paragraph (4) should not materially add to the length of the skeleton argument but should be sufficient to demonstrate, in the context of the argument—
(a) the relevance of the authority or authorities to that argument; and
(b) that the citation is necessary for a proper presentation of that argument.
(6) The cost of preparing a skeleton argument which—
(a) does not comply with the requirements set out in this paragraph; or
(b) was not filed within the time limits provided by this Practice Direction (or any further time granted by the court),
will not be allowed on assessment except to the extent that the court otherwise directs.
(7) A skeleton argument filed in the Court of Appeal, Civil Division on behalf of the appellant should contain in paragraph 1 the advocate's time estimate for the hearing of the appeal.

5.11 The appellant should consider what other information the appeal court will need. This may include a list of persons who feature in the case or glossaries of technical terms. A chronology of relevant events will be necessary in most appeals.

## Suitable Record of the Judgment

5.12 Where the judgment to be appealed has been officially recorded by the court, an approved transcript of that record should accompany the appellant's notice. Photocopies will not be accepted for this purpose. However, where there is no officially recorded judgment, the following documents will be acceptable:

*Written judgments*

(1) Where the judgment was made in writing a copy of that judgment endorsed with the judge's signature.

*Note of judgment*

(2) When judgment was not officially recorded or made in writing a note of the

judgment (agreed between the appellant's and respondent's advocates) should be submitted for approval to the judge whose decision is being appealed. If the parties cannot agree on a single note of the judgment, both versions should be provided to that judge with an explanatory letter. For the purpose of an application for permission to appeal the note need not be approved by the respondent or the lower court judge.

*Advocates' notes of judgments where the appellant is unrepresented*

(3) When the appellant was unrepresented in the lower court it is the duty of any advocate for the respondent to make his/her note of judgment promptly available, free of charge to the appellant where there is no officially recorded judgment or if the court so directs. Where the appellant was represented in the lower court it is the duty of his/her own former advocate to make his/her note available in these circumstances. The appellant should submit the note of judgment to the appeal court.

*Reasons for judgment in Tribunal cases*

(4) A sealed copy of the Tribunal's reasons for the decision.

5.13 An appellant may not be able to obtain an official transcript or other suitable record of the lower court's decision within the time within which the appellant's notice must be filed. In such cases the appellant's notice must still be completed to the best of the appellant's ability on the basis of the documentation available. However it may be amended subsequently with the permission of the appeal court.

## Advocates' Notes of Judgments

5.14 Advocates' brief (or, where appropriate, refresher) fee includes:

(1) remuneration for taking a note of the judgment of the court;
(2) having the note transcribed accurately;
(3) attempting to agree the note with the other side if represented;
(4) submitting the note to the judge for approval where appropriate;
(5) revising it if so requested by the judge,
(6) providing any copies required for the appeal court, instructing solicitors and lay client; and
(7) providing a copy of his note to an unrepresented appellant.

## Transcripts or Notes of Evidence

5.15 When the evidence is relevant to the appeal an official transcript of the relevant evidence must be obtained. Transcripts or notes of evidence are generally not needed for the purpose of determining an application for permission to appeal.

## Notes of Evidence

5.16 If evidence relevant to the appeal was not officially recorded, a typed version of the judge's notes of evidence must be obtained.

## Transcripts at Public Expense

5.17 Where the lower court or the appeal court is satisfied that:

(1) an unrepresented appellant; or
(2) an appellant whose legal representation is provided free of charge to the appellant and not funded by the Community Legal Service;

is in such poor financial circumstances that the cost of a transcript would be an excessive burden the court may certify that the cost of obtaining one official transcript should be borne at public expense.

5.18 In the case of a request for an official transcript of evidence or proceedings to be paid for at public expense, the court must also be satisfied that there are reasonable grounds for appeal. Whenever possible a request for a transcript at public expense should be made to the lower court when asking for permission to appeal.

## Filing and Service of Appellant's Notice

5.19 Rule 52.4 sets out the procedure and time limits for filing and serving an appellant's notice. The appellant must file the appellant's notice at the appeal court within such period as may be directed by the lower court which should not normally exceed 35 days or, where the lower court directs no such period, within 21 days of the date of the decision that the appellant wishes to appeal.

(Rule 52.15 sets out the time limit for filing an application for permission to appeal against the refusal of the High Court to grant permission to apply for judicial review.)

5.20 Where the lower court judge announces his decision and reserves the reasons for his judgment or order until a later date, he should, in the exercise of powers under rule 52.4(2)(a), fix a period for filing the appellant's notice at the appeal court that takes this into account.

5.21 (1) Except where the appeal court orders otherwise a sealed copy of the appellant's notice, including any skeleton arguments must be served on all respondents in accordance with the timetable prescribed by rule 52.4(3) except where this requirement is modified by paragraph 5.9(2) in which case the skeleton argument should be served as soon as it is filed.

(2) The appellant must, as soon as practicable, file a certificate of service of the documents referred to in paragraph (1).

5.22 Unless the court otherwise directs a respondent need not take any action when served with an appellant's notice until such time as notification is given to him that permission to appeal has been given.

5.23 The court may dispense with the requirement for service of the notice on a respondent. Any application notice seeking an order under rule 6.9 to dispense with service should set out the reasons relied on and be verified by a statement of truth.

5.24 (1) Where the appellant is applying for permission to appeal in his appellant's notice, he must serve on the respondents his appellant's notice and skeleton argument (but not the appeal bundle), unless the appeal court directs otherwise.

(2) Where permission to appeal—

(a) has been given by the lower court; or

(b) is not required,

the appellant must serve the appeal bundle on the respondents with the appellant's notice.

## Amendment of Appeal Notice

5.25 An appeal notice may be amended with permission. Such an application to amend and any application in opposition will normally be dealt with at the hearing unless that course would cause unnecessary expense or delay in which case a request should be made for the application to amend to be heard in advance.

## PROCEDURE AFTER PERMISSION IS OBTAINED

6.1 This paragraph sets out the procedure where:

(1) permission to appeal is given by the appeal court; or

(2) the appellant's notice is filed in the appeal court and—

(a) permission was given by the lower court; or

(b) permission is not required.

6.2 If the appeal court gives permission to appeal, the appeal bundle must be served on each of the respondents within 7 days of receiving the order giving permission to appeal.

(Part 6 (service of documents) provides rules on service.)

6.3 The appeal court will send the parties—

(1) notification of—

(a) the date of the hearing or the period of time (the 'listing window') during which the appeal is likely to be heard; and

(b) in the Court of Appeal, the date by which the appeal will be heard (the 'hear by date');
(2) where permission is granted by the appeal court a copy of the order giving permission to appeal; and
(3) any other directions given by the court.

6.3A (1) Where the appeal court grants permission to appeal, the appellant must add the following documents to the appeal bundle—
(a) the respondent's notice and skeleton argument (if any);
(b) those parts of the transcripts of evidence which are directly relevant to any question at issue on the appeal;
(c) the order granting permission to appeal and, where permission to appeal was granted at an oral hearing, the transcript (or note) of any judgment which was given; and
(d) any document which the appellant and respondent have agreed to add to the appeal bundle in accordance with paragraph 7.11.
(2) Where permission to appeal has been refused on a particular issue, the appellant must remove from the appeal bundle all documents that are relevant only to that issue.

## Appeal Questionnaire in the Court of Appeal

6.4 The Court of Appeal will send an Appeal Questionnaire to the appellant when it notifies him of the matters referred to in paragraph 6.3.

6.5 The appellant must complete and file the Appeal Questionnaire within 14 days of the date of the letter of notification of the matters in paragraph 6.3. The Appeal Questionnaire must contain:
(1) if the appellant is legally represented, the advocate's time estimate for the hearing of the appeal;
(2) where a transcript of evidence is relevant to the appeal, confirmation as to what parts of a transcript of evidence have been ordered where this is not already in the bundle of documents;
(3) confirmation that copies of the appeal bundle are being prepared and will be held ready for the use of the Court of Appeal and an undertaking that they will be supplied to the court on request. For the purpose of these bundles photocopies of the transcripts will be accepted;
(4) confirmation that copies of the Appeal Questionnaire and the appeal bundle have been served on the respondents and the date of that service.

## Time Estimates

6.6 The time estimate included in an Appeal Questionnaire must be that of the advocate who will argue the appeal. It should exclude the time required by the court to give judgment. If the respondent disagrees with the time estimate, the respondent must inform the court within 7 days of receipt of the Appeal Questionnaire. In the absence of such notification the respondent will be deemed to have accepted the estimate proposed on behalf of the appellant.

## RESPONDENT

7.1 A respondent who wishes to ask the appeal court to vary the order of the lower court in any way must appeal and permission will be required on the same basis as for an appellant.

(Paragraph 3.2 applies to grounds of appeal by a respondent.)

7.2 A respondent who wishes only to request that the appeal court upholds the judgment or order of the lower court whether for the reasons given in the lower court or otherwise does not make an appeal and does not therefore require permission to appeal in accordance with rule 52.3(1).

(Paragraph 7.6 requires a respondent to file a skeleton argument where he wishes to address the appeal court.)

7.3 (1) A respondent who wishes to appeal or who wishes to ask the appeal court to uphold the order of the lower court for reasons different from or additional to those given by the lower court must file a respondent's notice.

(2) If the respondent does not file a respondent's notice, he will not be entitled, except with the permission of the court, to rely on any reason not relied on in the lower court.

7.3A Paragraphs 5.1A, 5.1B and 5.2 of this practice direction (Human Rights and extension for time for filing appellant's notice) also apply to a respondent and a respondent's notice.

## Time Limits

7.4 The time limits for filing a respondent's notice are set out in rule 52.5 (4) and (5).

7.5 Where an extension of time is required the extension must be requested in the respondent's notice and the reasons why the respondent failed to act within the specified time must be included.

7.6 Except where paragraph 7.7A applies, the respondent must file a skeleton argument for the court in all cases where he proposes to address arguments to the court. The respondent's skeleton argument may be included within a respondent's notice. Where a skeleton argument is included within a respondent's notice it will not form part of the notice for the purposes of rule 52.8.

7.7 (1) A respondent who—

(a) files a respondent's notice; but

(b) does not include his skeleton argument within that notice, must file and serve his skeleton argument within 14 days of filing the notice.

(2) A respondent who does not file a respondent's notice but who files a skeleton argument must file and serve that skeleton argument at least 7 days before the appeal hearing.

(Rule 52.5(4) sets out the period for filing and serving a respondent's notice.)

7.7A (1) Where the appeal relates to a claim allocated to the small claims track and is being heard in a county court or the High Court, the respondent may file a skeleton argument but is not required to do so.

(2) A respondent who is not represented need not file a skeleton argument but is encouraged to do so in order to assist the court.

7.7B The respondent must—

(1) serve his skeleton argument on—

(a) the appellant; and

(b) any other respondent,

at the same time as he files it at the court; and

(2) file a certificate of service.

## Content of Skeleton Arguments

7.8 A respondent's skeleton argument must conform to the directions at paragraphs 5.10 and 5.11 with any necessary modifications. It should, where appropriate, answer the arguments set out in the appellant's skeleton argument.

## Applications Within Respondent's Notices

7.9 A respondent may include an application within a respondent's notice in accordance with paragraph 5.5 above.

## Filing Respondent's Notices and Skeleton Arguments

7.10 (1) The respondent must file the following documents with his respondent's notice in every case:

(a) two additional copies of the respondent's notice for the appeal court; and
(b) one copy each for the appellant and any other respondents.
(2) The respondent may file a skeleton argument with his respondent's notice and—
(a) where he does so he must file two copies; and
(b) where he does not do so he must comply with paragraph 7.7.

7.11 If the respondent wishes to rely on any documents which he reasonably considers necessary to enable the appeal court to reach its decision on the appeal in addition to those filed by the appellant, he must make every effort to agree amendments to the appeal bundle with the appellant.

7.12 (1) If the representatives for the parties are unable to reach agreement, the respondent may prepare a supplemental bundle.
(2) If the respondent prepares a supplemental bundle he must file it, together with the requisite number of copies for the appeal court, at the appeal court—
(a) with the respondent's notice; or
(b) if a respondent's notice is not filed, within 21 days after he is served with the appeal bundle.

7.13 The respondent must serve—
(1) the respondent's notice;
(2) his skeleton argument (if any); and
(3) the supplemental bundle (if any),
on—
(a) the appellant; and
(b) any other respondent,
at the same time as he files them at the court.

## APPEALS TO THE HIGH COURT

### Application

8.1 This paragraph applies where an appeal lies to a High Court judge from the decision of a county court or a district judge of the High Court.

8.2 The following table sets out the following venues for each circuit—
(a) Appeal centres—court centres where appeals to which this paragraph applies may be filed, managed and heard. Paragraphs 8.6 to 8.8 provide for special arrangements in relation to the South Eastern Circuit.
(b) Hearing only centres—court centres where appeals to which this paragraph applies may be heard by order made at an appeal centre (see paragraph 8.10).

| Circuit | Appeal Centres | Hearing Only Centres |
|---|---|---|
| **Midland Circuit** | Birmingham<br>Nottingham | Lincoln<br>Leicester<br>Northampton<br>Stafford |
| **North Eastern Circuit** | Leeds<br>Newcastle<br>Sheffield | Teesside |
| **Northern Circuit** | Manchester<br>Liverpool<br>Preston<br>Chester | Carlisle |
| **Wales Circuit** | Cardiff<br>Swansea | |
| **Western Circuit** | Bristol<br>Exeter<br>Winchester | Truro<br>Plymouth |

| | |
|---|---|
| **South Eastern Circuit** | Royal Courts of Justice<br>Lewes<br>Luton<br>Norwich<br>Reading<br>Chelmsford<br>St Albans<br>Maidstone<br>Oxford |

## Venue for Appeals and Filing of Notices on Circuits Other Than the South Eastern Circuit

8.3 Paragraphs 8.4 and 8.5 apply where the lower court is situated on a circuit other than the South Eastern Circuit.

8.4 The appellant's notice must be filed at an appeal centre on the circuit in which the lower court is situated. The appeal will be managed and heard at that appeal centre unless the appeal court orders otherwise.

8.5 A respondent's notice must be filed at the appeal centre where the appellant's notice was filed unless the appeal has been transferred to another appeal centre, in which case it must be filed at that appeal centre.

## Venue for Appeals and Filing of Notices on the South Eastern Circuit

8.6 Paragraphs 8.7 and 8.8 apply where the lower court is situated on the South Eastern Circuit.

8.7 The appellant's notice must be filed at an appeal centre on the South Eastern Circuit. The appeal will be managed and heard at the Royal Courts of Justice unless the appeal court orders otherwise. An order that an appeal is to be managed or heard at another appeal centre may not be made unless the consent of the Presiding Judge of the circuit in charge of civil matters has been obtained.

8.8 A respondent's notice must be filed at the Royal Courts of Justice unless the appeal has been transferred to another appeal centre, in which case it must be filed at that appeal centre.

## General Provisions

8.9 The appeal court may transfer an appeal to another appeal centre (whether or not on the same circuit). In deciding whether to do so the court will have regard to the criteria in rule 30.3 (criteria for a transfer order). The appeal court may do so either on application by a party or of its own initiative. Where an appeal is transferred under this paragraph, notice of transfer must be served on every person on whom the appellant's notice has been served. An appeal may not be transferred to an appeal centre on another circuit, either for management or hearing, unless the consent of the Presiding Judge of that circuit in charge of civil matters has been obtained.

8.10 Directions may be given for—

(a) an appeal to be heard at a hearing only centre; or

(b) an application in an appeal to be heard at any other venue,

instead of at the appeal centre managing the appeal.

8.11 Unless a direction has been made under 8.10, any application in the appeal must be made at the appeal centre where the appeal is being managed.

8.12 The appeal court may adopt all or any part of the procedure set out in paragraphs 6.4 to 6.6.

8.13 Where the lower court is a county court:

(1) subject to paragraph (1A), appeals and applications for permission to appeal will be heard by a High Court Judge or by a person authorized under paragraphs (1),

(2) or (4) of the Table in section 9(1) of the Supreme Court Act 1981 to act as a judge of the High Court;

(1A) an appeal or application for permission to appeal from the decision of a recorder in the county court may be heard by a designated civil judge who is authorized under paragraph (5) of the Table in section 9(1) of the Supreme Court Act 1981 to act as a judge of the High Court; and

(2) other applications in the appeal may be heard and directions in the appeal may be given either by a High Court Judge or by any person authorised under section 9 of the Supreme Court Act 1981 to act as a judge of the High Court.

8.14 In the case of appeals from Masters or district judges of the High Court, appeals, applications for permission and any other applications in the appeal may be heard and directions in the appeal may be given by a High Court Judge or by any person authorised under section 9 of the Supreme Court Act 1981 to act as a judge of the High Court.

## APPEALS TO A JUDGE OF A COUNTY COURT FROM A DISTRICT JUDGE

8A.1 The Designated Civil Judge in consultation with his Presiding Judges has responsibility for allocating appeals from decisions of district judges to circuit judges.

### Re-hearings

9.1 The hearing of an appeal will be a re-hearing (as opposed to a review of the decision of the lower court) if the appeal is from the decision of a minister, person or other body and the minister, person or other body—

(1) did not hold a hearing to come to that decision; or

(2) held a hearing to come to that decision, but the procedure adopted did not provide for the consideration of evidence.

## APPEALS TRANSFERRED TO THE COURT OF APPEAL

10.1 Where an appeal is transferred to the Court of Appeal under rule 52.14 the Court of Appeal may give such additional directions as are considered appropriate.

## APPLICATIONS

11.1 Where a party to an appeal makes an application whether in an appeal notice or by Part 23 application notice, the provisions of Part 23 will apply.

11.2 The applicant must file the following documents with the notice

(1) one additional copy of the application notice for the appeal court and one copy for each of the respondents;

(2) where applicable a sealed copy of the order which is the subject of the main appeal;

(3) a bundle of documents in support which should include:

(a) the Part 23 application notice; and

(b) any witness statements and affidavits filed in support of the application notice.

## DISPOSING OF APPLICATIONS OR APPEALS BY CONSENT

### Dismissal of Applications or Appeals by Consent

12.1 These paragraphs do not apply where any party to the proceedings is a child or patient.

12.2 Where an appellant does not wish to pursue an application or an appeal, he may request the appeal court for an order that his application or appeal be dismissed. Such a request must contain a statement that the appellant is not a child or patient. If such a request is granted it will usually be on the basis that the appellant pays the costs of the application or appeal.

12.3 If the appellant wishes to have the application or appeal dismissed without costs, his request must be accompanied by a consent signed by the respondent or his legal representative stating that the respondent is not a child or patient and consents to the dismissal of the application or appeal without costs.

12.4 Where a settlement has been reached disposing of the application or appeal, the parties may make a joint request to the court stating that none of them is a child or patient, and asking that the application or appeal be dismissed by consent. If the request is granted the application or appeal will be dismissed.

### Allowing Unopposed Appeals or Applications on Paper

13.1 The appeal court will not normally make an order allowing an appeal unless satisfied that the decision of the lower court was wrong, but the appeal court may set aside or vary the order of the lower court with consent and without determining the merits of the appeal, if it is satisfied that there are good and sufficient reasons for doing so. Where the appeal court is requested by all parties to allow an application or an appeal the court may consider the request on the papers. The request should state that none of the parties is a child or patient and set out the relevant history of the proceedings and the matters relied on as justifying the proposed order and be accompanied by a copy of the proposed order.

### Procedure for Consent Orders and Agreements to Pay Periodical Payments Involving a Child or Patient

13.2 Where one of the parties is a child or patient—

(1) a settlement relating to an appeal or application; or

(2) in a personal injury claim for damages for future pecuniary loss, an agreement reached at the appeal stage to pay periodical payments,

requires the court's approval.

### Child

13.3 In cases involving a child a copy of the proposed order signed by the parties' solicitors should be sent to the appeal court, together with an opinion from the advocate acting on behalf of the child.

### Patient

13.4 Where a party is a patient the same procedure will be adopted, but the documents filed should also include any relevant reports prepared for the Court of Protection and a document evidencing formal approval by that court where required.

### Periodical Payments

13.5 Where periodical payments for future pecuniary loss have been negotiated in a personal injury case which is under appeal, the documents filed should include those which would be required in the case of a personal injury claim for damages for future pecuniary loss dealt with at first instance. Details can be found in the Practice Direction which supplements Part 21.

## SUMMARY ASSESSMENT OF COSTS

14.1 Costs are likely to be assessed by way of summary assessment at the following hearings:

(1) contested directions hearings;

(2) applications for permission to appeal at which the respondent is present;

(3) dismissal list hearings in the Court of Appeal at which the respondent is present;

(4) appeals from case management decisions; and

(5) appeals listed for one day or less.

14.2 Parties attending any of the hearings referred to in paragraph 14.1 should be prepared to deal with the summary assessment.

## OTHER SPECIAL PROVISIONS REGARDING THE COURT OF APPEAL

### Filing of Documents

15.1 (1) The documents relevant to proceedings in the Court of Appeal, Civil Division must be filed in the Civil Appeals Office Registry, Room E307, Royal Courts of Justice, Strand, London, WC2A 2LL.

(2) The Civil Appeals Office will not serve documents and where service is required by the CPR or this practice direction it must be effected by the parties.

15.1A (1) A party may file by e-mail—

(a) an appellant's notice;

(b) a respondent's notice;

(c) an application notice,

in the Court of Appeal, Civil Division, using the e-mail account specified in the 'Guidelines for filing by E-mail' which appear on the Court of Appeal, Civil Division website at <http://www.civilappeals.gov.uk>.

(2) A party may only file a notice in accordance with paragraph (1) where he is permitted to do so by the 'Guidelines for filing by E-mail'.

15.1B (1) A party to an appeal in the Court of Appeal, Civil Division may file—

(a) an appellant's notice;

(b) a respondent's notice; or

(c) an application notice,

electronically using the online forms service on the Court of Appeal, Civil Division website at <http://www.civilappeals.gov.uk>.

(2) A party may only file a notice in accordance with paragraph (1) where he is permitted to so do by the 'Guidelines for filing electronically'. The Guidelines for filing electronically may be found on the Court of Appeal, Civil Division website.

(3) The online forms service will assist the user in completing a document accurately but the user is responsible for ensuring that the rules and practice directions relating to the document have been complied with. Transmission by the service does not guarantee that the document will be accepted by the Court of Appeal, Civil Division.

(4) A party using the online forms service in accordance with this paragraph is responsible for ensuring that the transmission or any document attached to it is filed within any relevant time limits.

(5) Parties are advised not to transmit electronically any correspondence or documents of a confidential or sensitive nature, as security cannot be guaranteed.

(6) Where a party wishes to file a document containing a statement of truth electronically, that party should retain the document containing the original signature and file with the court a version of the document on which the name of the person who has signed the statement of truth is typed underneath the statement.

### Core Bundles

15.2 In cases where the appeal bundle comprises more than 500 pages, exclusive of transcripts, the appellant's solicitors must, after consultation with the respondent's solicitors, also prepare and file with the court, in addition to copies of the appeal bundle (as amended in accordance with paragraph 7.11) the requisite number of copies of a core bundle.

15.3 (1) The core bundle must be filed within 28 days of receipt of the order giving permission to appeal or, where permission to appeal was granted by the lower court or is not required, within 28 days of the date of service of the appellant's notice on the respondent.

(2) The core bundle—

(a) must contain the documents which are central to the appeal; and
(b) must not exceed 150 pages.

## Preparation of Bundles

15.4 The provisions of this paragraph apply to the preparation of appeal bundles, supplemental respondents' bundles where the parties are unable to agree amendments to the appeal bundle, and core bundles.

(1) **Rejection of bundles.** Where documents are copied unnecessarily or bundled incompletely, costs may be disallowed. Where the provisions of this Practice Direction as to the preparation or delivery of bundles are not followed the bundle may be rejected by the court or be made the subject of a special costs order.

(2) **Avoidance of duplication.** No more than one copy of any document should be included unless there is a good reason for doing otherwise (such as the use of a separate core bundle—see paragraph 15.2).

(3) **Pagination**

(a) Bundles must be paginated, each page being numbered individually and consecutively. The pagination used at trial must also be indicated. Letters and other documents should normally be included in chronological order. (An exception to consecutive page numbering arises in the case of core bundles where it may be preferable to retain the original numbering).

(b) Page numbers should be inserted in bold figures at the bottom of the page and in a form that can be clearly distinguished from any other pagination on the document.

(4) **Format and presentation**

(a) Where possible the documents should be in A4 format. Where a document has to be read across rather than down the page, it should be so placed in the bundle as to ensure that the text starts nearest the spine.

(b) Where any marking or writing in colour on a document is important, the document must be copied in colour or marked up correctly in colour.

(c) Documents which are not easily legible should be transcribed and the transcription marked and placed adjacent to the document transcribed.

(d) Documents in a foreign language should be translated and the translation marked and placed adjacent to the document translated. The translation should be agreed or, if it cannot be agreed, each party's proposed translation should be included.

(e) The size of any bundle should be tailored to its contents. A large lever arch file should not be used for just a few pages nor should files of whatever size be overloaded.

(f) Where it will assist the Court of Appeal, different sections of the file may be separated by cardboard or other tabbed dividers so long as these are clearly indexed. Where, for example, a document is awaited when the appeal bundle is filed, a single sheet of paper can be inserted after a divider, indicating the nature of the document awaited. For example, 'Transcript of evidence of Mr J Smith (to follow)'.

(5) **Binding**

(a) All documents, with the exception of transcripts, must be bound together. This may be in a lever arch file, ring binder or plastic folder. Plastic sleeves containing loose documents must not be used. Binders and files must be strong enough to withstand heavy use.

(b) Large documents such as plans should be placed in an easily accessible file. Large documents which will need to be opened up frequently should be inserted in a file larger than A4 size.

(6) **Indices and labels**

(a) An index must be included at the front of the bundle listing all the documents and providing the page references for each. In the case of documents such as letters, invoices or bank statements, they may be given a general description.

(b) Where the bundles consist of more than one file, an index to all the files should be included in the first file and an index included for each file. Indices should, if possible, be on a single sheet. The full name of the case should not be inserted on the index if this would waste space. Documents should be identified briefly but properly.

(7) **Identification**

(a) Every bundle must be clearly identified, on the spine and on the front cover, with the name of the case and the Court of Appeal's reference. Where the bundle consists of more than one file, each file must be numbered on the spine, the front cover and the inside of the front cover.

(b) Outer labels should use large lettering eg ' Appeal Bundle A' or 'Core Bundle'. The full title of the appeal and solicitors' names and addresses should be omitted. A label should be used on the front as well as on the spine.

(8) **Staples etc.** All staples, heavy metal clips etc, must be removed.

(9) **Statements of case**

(a) Statements of case should be assembled in 'chapter' form—i.e claim followed by particulars of claim, followed by further information, irrespective of date.

(b) Redundant documents, eg particulars of claim overtaken by amendments, requests for further information recited in the answers given, should generally be excluded.

(10) **New Documents**

(a) Before a new document is introduced into bundles which have already been delivered to the court, steps should be taken to ensure that it carries an appropriate bundle/page number so that it can be added to the court documents. It should not be stapled and it should be prepared with punch holes for immediate inclusion in the binders in use.

(b) If it is expected that a large number of miscellaneous new documents will from time to time be introduced, there should be a special tabbed empty loose-leaf file for that purpose. An index should be produced for this file, updated as necessary.

(11) **Inter-solicitor correspondence.** Since inter-solicitor correspondence is unlikely to be required for the purposes of an appeal, only those letters which will need to be referred to should be copied.

(12) **Sanctions for non-compliance.** If the appellant fails to comply with the requirements as to the provision of bundles of documents, the application or appeal will be referred for consideration to be given as to why it should not be dismissed for failure to so comply.

## Master in the Court of Appeal, Civil Division

15.5 When the Head of the Civil Appeals Office acts in a judicial capacity pursuant to rule 52.16, he shall be known as Master. Other eligible officers may also be designated by the Master of the Rolls to exercise judicial authority under rule 52.16 and shall then be known as Deputy Masters.

## Respondent to Notify Civil Appeals Office whether He Intends to File Respondent's Notice

15.6 A respondent must, no later than 21 days after the date he is served with notification that—

(1) permission to appeal has been granted; or

(2) the application for permission to appeal and the appeal are to be heard together,

inform the Civil Appeals Office and the appellant in writing whether—

(a) he proposes to file a respondent's notice appealing the order or seeking to uphold the order for reasons different from, or additional to, those given by the lower court; or

(b) he proposes to rely on the reasons given by the lower court for its decision.

(Paragraph 15.11B requires all documents needed for an appeal hearing, including a respondent's skeleton argument, to be filed at least 7 days before the hearing.)

## Listing and Hear-by Dates

15.7 The management of the list will be dealt with by the listing officer under the direction of the Master.

15.8 The Civil Appeals List of the Court of Appeal is divided as follows:

*The applications list*—applications for permission to appeal and other applications.

*The appeals list*—appeals where permission to appeal has been given or where an appeal lies without permission being required where a hearing date is fixed in advance. (Appeals in this list which require special listing arrangements will be assigned to the special fixtures list)

*The expedited list*—appeals or applications where the Court of Appeal has directed an expedited hearing. The current practice of the Court of Appeal is summarised in *Unilever plc. v. Chefaro Proprietaries Ltd. (Practice Note)* [1995]1 W.L.R. 243.

*The stand-out list*—appeals or applications which, for good reason, are not at present ready to proceed and have been stood out by judicial direction.

*The second fixtures list*—[see paragraph 15.9A(1) below].

*The second fixtures list*—if an appeal is designated as a 'second fixture' it means that a hearing date is arranged in advance on the express basis that the list is fully booked for the period in question and therefore the case will be heard only if a suitable gap occurs in the list.

*The short-warned list*—appeals which the court considers may be prepared for the hearing by an advocate other than the one originally instructed with a half day's notice, or such other period as the court may direct.

## Special Provisions Relating to the Short-warned List

15.9 (1) Where an appeal is assigned to the short-warned list, the Civil Appeals Office will notify the parties' solicitors in writing. The court may abridge the time for filing any outstanding bundles in an appeal assigned to this list.

(2) The solicitors for the parties must notify their advocate and their client as soon as the Civil Appeals Office notifies them that the appeal has been assigned to the short-warned list.

(3) The appellant may apply in writing for the appeal to be removed from the short-warned list within 14 days of notification of its assignment. The application will be decided by a Lord Justice, or the Master, and will only be granted for the most compelling reasons.

(4) The Civil Appeals Listing Officer may place an appeal from the short-warned list 'on call' from a given date and will inform the parties' advocates accordingly.

(5) An appeal which is 'on call' may be listed for hearing on half a day's notice or such longer period as the court may direct.

(6) Once an appeal is listed for hearing from the short-warned list it becomes the immediate professional duty of the advocate instructed in the appeal, if he is unable to appear at the hearing, to take all practicable measures to ensure that his lay client is represented at the hearing by an advocate who is fully instructed and able to argue the appeal.

## Special Provisions Relating to the Special Fixtures List

15.9A (1) The special fixtures list is a sub-division of the appeals list and is used to deal with appeals that may require special listing arrangements, such as the need to list a number of cases before the same constitution, in a particular order, during a particular period or at a given location.

(2) The Civil Appeals Office will notify the parties' representatives, or the parties if acting in person, of the particular arrangements that will apply. The notice—

(a) will give details of the specific period during which a case is scheduled to be heard; and

(b) may give directions in relation to the filing of any outstanding documents.

(3) The listing officer will notify the parties' representatives of the precise hearing date as soon as practicable. While every effort will be made to accommodate the availability of counsel, the requirements of the court will prevail.

## Requests for Directions

15.10 To ensure that all requests for directions are centrally monitored and correctly allocated, all requests for directions or rulings (whether relating to listing or any other matters) should be made to the Civil Appeals Office. Those seeking directions or rulings must not approach the supervising Lord Justice either directly, or via his or her clerk.

## Bundles of Authorities

15.11 (1) Once the parties have been notified of the date fixed for the hearing, the appellant's advocate must, after consultation with his opponent, file a bundle containing photocopies of the authorities upon which each side will rely at the hearing.

(2) The bundle of authorities should, in general—

(a) have the relevant passages of the authorities marked;

(b) not include authorities for propositions not in dispute; and

(c) not contain more than 10 authorities unless the scale of the appeal warrants more extensive citation.

(3) The bundle of authorities must be filed—

(a) at least 7 days before the hearing; or

(b) where the period of notice of the hearing is less than 7 days, immediately.

(4) If, through some oversight, a party intends, during the hearing, to refer to other authorities the parties may agree a second agreed bundle. The appellant's advocate must file this bundle at least 48 hours before the hearing commences.

(5) A bundle of authorities must bear a certification by the advocates responsible for arguing the case that the requirements of sub-paragraphs (3) to (5) of paragraph 5.10 have been complied with in respect of each authority included.

## Supplementary Skeleton Arguments

15.11A (1) A supplementary skeleton argument on which the appellant wishes to rely must be filed at least 14 days before the hearing.

(2) A supplementary skeleton argument on which the respondent wishes to rely must be filed at least 7 days before the hearing.

(3) All supplementary skeleton arguments must comply with the requirements set out in paragraph 5.10.

(4) At the hearing the court may refuse to hear argument from a party not contained in a skeleton argument filed within the relevant time limit set out in this paragraph.

## Papers for the Appeal Hearing

15.11B (1) All the documents which are needed for the appeal hearing must be filed at least 7 days before the hearing. Where a document has not been filed 10 days before the hearing a reminder will be sent by the Civil Appeals Office.

(2) Any party who fails to comply with the provisions of paragraph (1) may be required to attend before the Presiding Lord Justice to seek permission to proceed with, or to oppose, the appeal.

## Disposal of Bundles of Documents

15.11C (1) Where the court has determined a case, the official transcriber will retain one set of papers. The Civil Appeals Office will destroy any remaining sets of papers not collected within 21 days of—
(a) where one or more parties attend the hearing, the date of the court's decision;
(b) where there is no attendance, the date of the notification of court's decision.
(2) The parties should ensure that bundles of papers supplied to the court do not contain original documents (other than transcripts). The parties must ensure that they—
(a) bring any necessary original documents to the hearing; and
(b) retrieve any original documents handed up to the court before leaving the court.
(3) The court will retain application bundles where permission to appeal has been granted. Where permission is refused the arrangements in sub-paragraph (1) will apply.
(4) Where a single Lord Justice has refused permission to appeal on paper, application bundles will not be destroyed until after the time limit for seeking a hearing has expired.

## Availability of Reserved Judgments Before Hand Down

15.12 This section applies where the presiding Lord Justice is satisfied that the result of the appeal will attract no special degree of confidentiality or sensitivity.

15.13 A copy of the written judgment will be made available to the parties' legal advisers by 4 p.m. on the second working day before judgment is due to be pronounced or such other period as the court may direct. This can be shown, in confidence, to the parties but only for the purpose of obtaining instructions and on the strict understanding that the judgment, or its effect, is not to be disclosed to any other person. A working day is any day on which the Civil Appeals Office is open for business.

15.14 The appeal will be listed for judgment in the cause list and the judgment handed down at the appropriate time.

## Attendance of Advocates on the Handing Down of a Reserved Judgment

15.15 Where any consequential orders are agreed, the parties' advocates need not attend on the handing down of a reserved judgment. Where an advocate does attend the court may, if it considers such attendance unnecessary, disallow the costs of the attendance. If the parties do not indicate that they intend to attend, the judgment may be handed down by a single member of the court.

## Agreed Orders Following Judgment

15.16 The parties must, in respect of any draft agreed orders—
(a) fax a copy to the clerk to the presiding Lord Justice; and
(b) file four copies in the Civil Appeals Office,
no later than 12 noon on the working day before the judgment is handed down.

15.17 A copy of a draft order must bear the Court of Appeal case reference, the date the judgment is to be handed down and the name of the presiding Lord Justice.

## Corrections to the Draft Judgment

15.18 Any proposed correction to the draft judgment should be sent to the clerk to the judge who prepared the draft with a copy to any other party.

## Application for Leave to Appeal

15.19 Where a party wishes to apply for leave to appeal to the House of Lords under section 1 of the Administration of Justice (Appeals) Act 1934 the court may deal with the application on the basis of written submissions.

15.20 A party must, in relation to his submission—
(a) fax a copy to the clerk to the presiding Lord Justice; and
(b) file four copies in the Civil Appeals Office,
no later than 12 noon on the working day before the judgment is handed down.

15.21 A copy of a submission must bear the Court of Appeal case reference, the date the judgment is to be handed down and the name of the presiding Lord Justice.

## SECTION II—GENERAL PROVISIONS ABOUT STATUTORY APPEALS AND APPEALS BY WAY OF CASE STATED

16.1 This Section of this practice direction contains general provisions about statutory appeals (paras 17.1–17.6) and appeals by way of case stated (paras 18.1–18.20).

16.2 Where any of the provisions in this section provide for documents to be filed at the appeal court, these documents are in addition to any documents required under Part 52 or Section I of this practice direction.

### Statutory Appeals

17.1 This part of this section:
(1) applies where under any enactment an appeal (other than by way of case stated) lies to the court from a minister of State, government department, tribunal or other person ('statutory appeals'); and
(2) is subject to any provision about a specific category of appeal in any enactment or Section III of this practice direction.

*Part 52*

17.2 Part 52 applies to statutory appeals with the following amendments.

*Filing of appellant's notice*

17.3 The appellant must file the appellant's notice at the appeal court within 28 days after the date of the decision of the lower court he wishes to appeal.

17.4 Where a statement of the reasons for a decision is given later than the notice of that decision, the period for filing the appellant's notice is calculated from the date on which the statement is received by the appellant.

*Service of appellant's notice*

17.5 In addition to the respondents to the appeal, the appellant must serve the appellant's notice in accordance with r. 52.4(3) on the chairman of the tribunal, minister of State, government department or other person from whose decision the appeal is brought.

*Right of minister etc. to be heard on the appeal*

17.6 Where the appeal is from an order or decision of a minister of State or government department, the minister or department, as the case may be, is entitled to attend the hearing and to make representations to the court.

### Appeals by Way of Case Stated

18.1 This part of this Section:
(1) applies where under any enactment:
(a) an appeal lies to the court by way of case stated; or
(b) a question of law may be referred to the court by way of case stated; and
(2) is subject to any provision about to a specific category of appeal in any enactment or Section III of this practice direction.

*Part 52*

18.2 Part 52 applies to appeals by way of case stated subject to the following amendments.

**Case stated by Crown Court or magistrates' court**

*Application to state a case*

18.3 The procedure for applying to the Crown Court or a magistrates' court to have a case stated for the opinion of the High Court is set out in the Crown Court Rules 1982 and the Magistrates' Courts Rules 1981 respectively.

*Filing of appellant's notice*

18.4 The appellant must file the appellant's notice at the appeal court within 10 days after he receives the stated case.

*Documents to be lodged*

18.5 The appellant must lodge the following documents with his appellant's notice:
(1) the stated case;
(2) a copy of the judgment, order or decision in respect of which the case has been stated; and
(3) where the judgment, order or decision in respect of which the case has been stated was itself given or made on appeal, a copy of the judgment, order or decision appealed from.

*Service of appellant's notice*

18.6 The appellant must serve the appellant's notice and accompanying documents on all respondents within four days after they are filed or lodged at the appeal court.

**Case stated by minister, government department, tribunal or other person**

*Application to state a case*

18.7 The procedure for applying to a minister, government department, tribunal or other person ('minister or tribunal etc.') to have a case stated for the opinion of the court may be set out in:
(1) the enactment which provides for the right of appeal; or
(2) any rules of procedure relating to the minister or tribunal etc.

*Signing of stated case by minister or tribunal etc.*

18.8 A case stated by a tribunal must be signed by the chairman or president of the tribunal. A case stated by any other person must be signed by that person or by a person authorised to do so.

*Service of stated case by minister or tribunal etc.*

18.9 The minister or tribunal etc. must serve the stated case on:
(1) the party who requests the case to be stated; or
(2) the party as a result of whose application to the court, the case was stated.

18.10 Where an enactment provides that a minister or tribunal etc. may state a case or refer a question of law to the court by way of case stated without a request being made, the minister or tribunal etc. must:
(1) serve the stated case on those parties that the minister or tribunal etc. considers appropriate; and
(2) give notice to every other party to the proceedings that the stated case has been served on the party named and on the date specified in the notice.

*Filing and service of appellant's notice*

18.11 The party on whom the stated case was served must file the appellant's notice and the stated case at the appeal court and serve copies of the notice and stated case on:
(1) the minister or tribunal etc. who stated the case; and
(2) every party to the proceedings to which the stated case relates,
within 14 days after the stated case was served on him.

18.12 Where para. 18.10 applies the minister or tribunal etc. must:
(1) file an appellant's notice and the stated case at the appeal court; and

(2) serve copies of those documents on the persons served under para. 18.10,
within 14 days after stating the case.

18.13 Where:
(1) a stated case has been served by the minister or tribunal etc. in accordance with para. 18.9; and
(2) the party on whom the stated case was served does not file an appellant's notice in accordance with para. 18.11,
any other party may file an appellant's notice with the stated case at the appeal court and serve a copy of the notice and the case on the persons listed in para. 18.11 within the period of time set out in para. 18.14.

18.14 The period of time referred to in para. 18.13 is 14 days from the last day on which the party on whom the stated case was served may file an appellant's notice in accordance with para. 18.11.

*Amendment of stated case*

18.15 The court may amend the stated case or order it to be returned to the minister or tribunal etc. for amendment and may draw inferences of fact from the facts stated in the case.

*Right of minister etc. to be heard on the appeal*

18.16 Where the case is stated by a minister or government department, that minister or department, as the case may be, is entitled to appear on the appeal and to make representations to the court.

*Application for order to state a case*

18.17 An application to the court for an order requiring a minister or tribunal etc. to state a case for the decision of the court, or to refer a question of law to the court by way of case stated must be made to the court which would be the appeal court if the case were stated.

18.18 An application to the court for an order directing a minister or tribunal etc. to:
(1) state a case for determination by the court; or
(2) refer a question of law to the court by way of case stated,
must be made in accordance with CPR, Part 23.

18.19 The application notice must contain:
(1) the grounds of the application;
(2) the question of law on which it is sought to have the case stated; and
(3) any reasons given by the minister or tribunal etc. for his or its refusal to state a case.

18.20 The application notice must be filed at the appeal court and served on:
(1) the minister, department, secretary of the tribunal or other person as the case may be; and
(2) every party to the proceedings to which the application relates,
within 14 days after the appellant receives notice of the refusal of his request to state a case.

## SECTION III—PROVISIONS ABOUT SPECIFIC APPEALS

20.1 This section of this practice direction provides special provisions about the appeals to which the following table refers. This Section is not exhaustive and does not create, amend or remove any right of appeal.

20.2 Part 52 applies to all appeals to which this Section applies subject to any special provisions set out in this Section.

20.3 Where any of the provisions in this Section provide for documents to be filed at the appeal court, these documents are in addition to any documents required under Part 52 or Sections I or II of this practice direction.

| | Paragraph |
|---|---|
| **Appeals to the Court of Appeal** | |
| Articles 81 and 82 of the EC Treaty and Chapters I and II of Part I of the Competition Act 1998 | 21.10A |
| Civil partnership–conditional order for dissolution or nullity | 21.1 |
| Competition Appeal Tribunal | 21.10 |
| Contempt of court | 21.4 |
| Decree nisi of divorce | 21.1 |
| Asylum and Immigration Tribunal | 21.7 |
| Lands Tribunal | 21.9 |
| Nullity of marriage | 21.1 |
| Patents Court on appeal from Comptroller | 21.3 |
| Revocation of patent | 21.2 |
| Social Security Commissioners | 21.5 |
| Special commissioner (where the appeal is direct to the Court of Appeal) | 21.8 |
| Value added tax and duties tribunals (where the appeal is direct to the Court of Appeal) | 21.6 |
| **Appeals to the High Court** | |
| Agricultural Land Tribunal | 22.7 |
| Architects Act 1997, s. 22 | 22.3 |
| Charities Act 1993 | 23.8A |
| Chiropractors Act 1994, s. 31 | 22.3 |
| Clergy Pensions Measure 1961, s. 38(3) | 23.2 |
| Commons Registration Act 1965 | 23.9 |
| Consumer Credit Act 1974 | 22.4 |
| Dentists Act 1984, s. 20 or s. 44 | 22.3 |
| Extradition Act 2003 | 22.6A |
| Friendly Societies Act 1974 | 23.7 |
| Friendly Societies Act 1992 | 23.7 |
| Industrial and Provident Societies Act 1965 | 23.2, 23.7 |
| Industrial Assurance Act 1923 | 23.2, 23.7 |
| Industrial Assurance Act 1923, s. 17 | 23.6 |
| Inheritance Tax Act 1984, s. 222 | 23.3 |
| Inheritance Tax Act 1984, s. 225 | 23.5 |
| Inheritance Tax Act 1984, ss. 249(3) and 251 | 23.4 |
| Land Registration Act 1925 | 23.2 |
| Land Registration Act 2002 | 23.2, 23.8B |
| Law of Property Act 1922, sch. 15, para. 16 | 23.2 |
| Medical Act 1983, s. 40 | 22.3 |
| Medicines Act 1968, ss. 82(3) and 83(2) | 22.3 |
| Mental Health Review Tribunal | 22.8 |
| Merchant Shipping Act 1995 | 22.2 |
| Nurses, Midwives and Health Visitors Act 1997, s. 12 | 22.3 |
| Nursing and Midwifery Order 2001 (SI 2002/253), art. 38 | 22.3 |
| Opticians Act 1989, s. 23 | 22.3 |
| Osteopaths Act 1993, s. 31 | 22.3 |
| Pension Schemes Act 1993, ss. 151 and 173 | 22.2 |
| Pensions Act 1995, s. 97 | 23.2 |
| Pensions Appeal Tribunals Act 1943 | 22.5 |
| Pharmacy Act 1954 | 22.3 |
| Social Security Administration Act 1992 | 22.6 |
| Stamp Duty Reserve Tax Regulations 1986, reg. 10 | 23.5 |
| Taxes Management Act 1970, ss. 53 and 100C(4) | 23.4 |
| Taxes Management Act 1970, s. 56A | 23.5 |
| Value added tax and duties tribunal | 23.8 |

| | |
|---|---|
| Water Resources Act 1991, s. 205(4) | 23.2 |
| **Appeals to County Court** | |
| Local Government (Miscellaneous Provisions) Act 1976 | 24.1 |
| Housing Act 1996, ss. 204 and 204A | 24.2 |
| Immigration and Asylum Act 1999, part II | 24.3 |

## Appeals to the Court of Appeal

*Appeal against decree nisi of divorce or nullity of marriage or conditional dissolution or nullity order in relation to civil partnership*

21.1 (1) The appellant must file the appellant's notice at the Court of Appeal within 28 days after the date on which the decree was pronounced or conditional order made.

(2) The appellant must file the following documents with the appellant's notice:

(a) the decree or conditional order; and

(b) a certificate of service of the appellant's notice.

(3) The appellant's notice must be served on the appropriate district judge (see sub-para. (6)) in addition to the persons to be served under r. 52.4(3) and in accordance with that rule.

(4) The lower court may not alter the time limits for filing of the appeal notices.

(5) Where an appellant intends to apply to the Court of Appeal for an extension of time for serving or filing the appellant's notice he must give notice of that intention to the appropriate district judge (see sub-para. (6)) before the application is made.

(6) In this paragraph 'the appropriate district judge' means where the lower court is:

(a) a county court, the district judge of that court;

(b) a district registry, the district judge of that registry;

(c) the Principal Registry of the Family Division, the senior district judge of that division.

*Appeal against order for revocation of patent*

21.2 (1) This paragraph applies where an appeal lies to the Court of Appeal from an order for the revocation of a patent.

(2) The appellant must serve the appellant's notice on the Comptroller-General of Patents, Designs and Trade Marks (the 'Comptroller' in addition to the persons to be served under r. 52.4(3) and in accordance with that rule.

(3) Where, before the appeal hearing, the respondent decides not to oppose the appeal or not to attend the appeal hearing, he must immediately serve notice of that decision on:

(a) the Comptroller; and

(b) the appellant

(4) Where the respondent serves a notice in accordance with sub-para. (3), he must also serve copies of the following documents on the Comptroller with that notice:

(a) the petition;

(b) any statements of claim;

(c) any written evidence filed in the claim.

(5) Within 14 days after receiving the notice in accordance with sub-para. (3), the Comptroller must serve on the appellant a notice stating whether or not he intends to attend the appeal hearing.

(6) The Comptroller may attend the appeal hearing and oppose the appeal:

(a) in any case where he has given notice under sub-para. (5) of his intention to attend; and

(b) in any other case (including, in particular, a case where the respondent withdraws his opposition to the appeal during the hearing) if the Court of Appeal so directs or permits.

*Appeal from Patents Court on appeal from Comptroller*

21.3 Where the appeal is from a decision of the Patents Court which was itself made on an appeal from a decision of the Comptroller-General of Patents, Designs and Trade Marks, the appellant must serve the appellant's notice on the Comptroller in addition to the persons to be served under r. 52.4(3) and in accordance with that rule.

*Appeals in cases of contempt of court*

21.4 In an appeal under section 13 of the Administration of Justice Act 1960 (appeals in cases of contempt of court), the appellant must serve the appellant's notice on the court from whose order or decision the appeal is brought in addition to the persons to be served under r. 52.4(3) and in accordance with that rule.

*Appeals from Social Security or Child Support Commissioners*

21.5 (1) This paragraph applies to appeals under the following provisions (appeals from the decision of a Social Security Commissioner or a Child Support Commissioner on a question of law)—

(a) section 6C of the Pensions Appeal Tribunals Act 1943;
(b) section 25 of the Child Support Act 1991;
(c) section 15 of the Social Security Act 1998;
(d) paragraph 9 of Schedule 7 to the Child Support, Pensions and Social Security Act 2000.

(2) The appellant must file the appellant's notice within 6 weeks after the date on which the Commissioner's decision on permission to appeal to the Court of Appeal was given in writing to the appellant.

(3) In an appeal brought under paragraph 9 of Schedule 7 to the Child Support, Pensions and Social Security Act 2000 by a party other than the Secretary of State, the appellant must serve the appellant's notice on the Secretary of State in addition to the persons to be served under rule 52.4(3) and in accordance with that rule.

(4) Where, after a Commissioner has given a decision, responsibility for the subject matter of the appeal has been transferred from a government department or the Commissioners for HM Revenue and Customs or a local authority ('the first body') to another such body ('the second body') and an appeal is brought by a party other than the second body—

(a) the second body shall be a respondent in place of the first body and the second body shall notify the court accordingly;
(b) if the appellant serves the appellant's notice or any other document on the first body, or if the court sends to the first body any communication in relation to the appeal, the first body shall forthwith send the notice, document or communication to the second body and the date on which the appellant's notice or other document was served on the first body shall be treated as the date on which it was served on the second body.

(5) This sub-paragraph applies where the appellant is the Secretary of State, the Commissioners for HM Revenue and Customs or a local authority. The appellant must serve the appellant's notice on any person appointed by the appellant to proceed with a claim, or an appeal arising out of a claim, in addition to the persons to be served under rule 52.4(3) and in accordance with that rule.

(Sub-paragraph (5) applies where the Secretary of State, the Commissioners for HM Revenue and Customs or a local authority is the appellant and that appellant appoints a person to proceed, in effect, on behalf of a respondent who is not himself able to proceed. An example is regulation 33 of the Social Security (Claims and Payments) Regulations 1987 which authorises the Secretary of State to appoint a person to proceed with the claim of another person who is unable for the time being to act.)

*Appeals from value added tax and duties tribunals*

21.6 (1) An application to the Court of Appeal for permission to appeal from a value added tax and duties tribunal direct to that court must be made within 28 days after the date on which the tribunal certifies that its decision involves a point of law relating wholly or mainly to the construction of:

(a) an enactment or of a statutory instrument; or

(b) any of the Community treaties or any Community instrument,

which has been fully argued before and fully considered by it.

(2) The application must be made by the parties jointly filing at the Court of Appeal an appellant's notice that:

(a) contains a statement of the grounds for the application; and

(b) is accompanied by a copy of the decision to be appealed, endorsed with the certificate of the tribunal.

(3) The court will notify the appellant of its decision and:

(a) where permission to appeal to the Court of Appeal is given, the appellant must serve the appellant's notice on the chairman of the tribunal in addition to the persons to be served under r. 52.4(3) within 14 days after that notification.

(b) where permission to appeal to the Court of Appeal is refused, the period for appealing to the High Court is to be calculated from the date of the notification of that refusal.

*Asylum and Immigration Appeals*

21.7 (1) This paragraph applies to appeals—

(a) from the Immigration Appeal Tribunal under section 103 of the Nationality, Immigration and Asylum Act 2002 ('the 2002 Act'); and

(b) from the Asylum and Immigration Tribunal under the following provisions of the 2002 Act—

(i) section 103B (appeal from the Tribunal following reconsideration); and

(ii) section 103E (appeal from the Tribunal sitting as a panel).

(2) The appellant is not required to file an appeal bundle in accordance with paragraph 5.6A of this practice direction, but must file the documents specified in paragraphs 5.6(2)(a) to (f) together with a copy of the Tribunal's determination.

(3) The appellant's notice must be filed at the Court of Appeal within 14 days after the appellant is served with written notice of the decision of the Tribunal to grant or refuse permission to appeal.

(4) The appellant must serve the appellant's notice in accordance with rule 52.4(3) on—

(a) the persons to be served under that rule; and

(b) the Asylum and Immigration Tribunal.

(5) On being served with the appellant's notice, the Asylum and Immigration Tribunal must send to the Court of Appeal copies of the documents which were before the relevant Tribunal when it considered the appeal.

21.7A (1) This paragraph applies to appeals from the Asylum and Immigration Tribunal referred to the Court of Appeal under section 103C of the Nationality, Immigration and Asylum Act 2002.

(2) On making an order referring an appeal to the Court of Appeal, the High Court shall send to the Court of Appeal copies of—

(a) that order and any other order made in relation to the application for reconsideration; and

(b) the application notice, written submissions and other documents filed under rule 54.29.

(3) Unless the court directs otherwise, the application notice filed under rule 54.29 shall be treated as the appellant's notice.

(4) The respondent may file a respondent's notice within 14 days after the date on which the respondent is served with the order of the High Court referring the appeal to the Court of Appeal.

(5) The Court of Appeal may give such additional directions as are appropriate.

21.7B (1) This paragraph applies to appeals from the Asylum and Immigration Tribunal which—

(a) would otherwise be treated as abandoned under section 104(4A) of the Nationality, Immigration and Asylum Act 2002 (the '2002 Act'); but

(b) meet the conditions set out in section 104(4B) or section 104(4C) of the 2002 Act.

(2) Where section 104(4A) of the 2002 Act applies and the appellant wishes to pursue his appeal, the appellant must file a notice at the Court of Appeal—

(a) where section 104(4B) of the 2002 Act applies, within 28 days of the date on which the appellant received notice of the grant of leave to enter or remain in the United Kingdom for a period exceeding 12 months; or

(b) where section 104(4C) of the 2002 Act applies, within 28 days of the date on which the appellant received notice of the grant of leave to enter or remain in the United Kingdom.

(3) Where the appellant does not comply with the time limits specified in paragraph (2) the appeal will be treated as abandoned in accordance with section 104(4) of the 2002 Act.

(4) The appellant must serve the notice filed under paragraph (2) on the respondent.

(5) Where section 104(4B) of the 2002 Act applies, the notice filed under paragraph (2) must state—

(a) the appellant's full name and date of birth;

(b) the Court of Appeal reference number;

(c) the Home Office reference number, if applicable;

(d) the date on which the appellant was granted leave to enter or remain in the United Kingdom for a period exceeding 12 months; and

(e) that the appellant wishes to pursue the appeal in so far as it is brought on the ground relating to the Refugee Convention specified in section 84(1)(g) of the 2002 Act.

(6) Where section 104(4C) of the 2002 Act applies, the notice filed under paragraph (2) must state—

(a) the appellant's full name and date of birth;

(b) the Court of Appeal reference number;

(c) the Home Office reference number, if applicable;

(d) the date on which the appellant was granted leave to enter or remain in the United Kingdom; and

(e) that the appellant wishes to pursue the appeal in so far as it is brought on the ground relating to section 19B of the Race Relations Act 1976 specified in section 84(1)(b) of the 2002 Act.

(7) Where an appellant has filed a notice under paragraph (2) the Court of Appeal will notify the appellant of the date on which it received the notice.

(8) The Court of Appeal will send a copy of the notice issued under paragraph (7) to the respondent.

*Appeal from special commissioners*

21.8 (1) An application to the Court of Appeal for permission to appeal from the special commissioners direct to that court under s. 56A of the Taxes Management Act 1970 must be made within 28 days after the date on which the special commissioners certify that their decision involves a point of law relating wholly or mainly to the construction of an enactment which has been fully argued before and fully considered before them.

(2) The application must be made by the parties jointly filing at the Court of Appeal an appellant's notice that:
   (a) contains a statement of the grounds for the application; and
   (b) is accompanied by a copy of the decision to be appealed, endorsed with the certificate of the tribunal.
(3) The court will notify the parties of its decision and:
   (a) where permission to appeal to the Court of Appeal is given, the appellant must serve the appellant's notice on the Clerk to the Special Commissioners in addition to the persons to be served under r. 52.4(3) within 14 days after that notification.
   (b) where permission to appeal to the Court of Appeal is refused, the period for appealing to the High Court is to be calculated from the date of the notification of that refusal.

*Appeal from Lands Tribunal*

21.9 The appellant must file the appellant's notice at the Court of Appeal within 28 days after the date of the decision of the tribunal.

*Appeal from Competition Appeal Tribunal*

21.10 (1) Where the appellant applies for permission to appeal at the hearing at which the decision is delivered by the tribunal and:
   (a) permission is given; or
   (b) permission is refused and the appellant wishes to make an application to the Court of Appeal for permission to appeal,

   the appellant's notice must be filed at the Court of Appeal within 14 days after the date of that hearing.
(2) Where the appellant applies in writing to the registrar of the tribunal for permission to appeal and:
   (a) permission is given; or
   (b) permission is refused and the appellant wishes to make an application to the Court of Appeal for permission to appeal,

   the appellant's notice must be filed at the Court of Appeal within 14 days after the date of receipt of the tribunal's decision on permission.
(3) Where the appellant does not make an application to the tribunal for permission to appeal, but wishes to make an application to the Court of Appeal for permission, the appellant's notice must be filed at the Court of Appeal within 14 days after the end of the period within which he may make a written application to the registrar of the tribunal.

## Appeals Relating to the Application of Articles 81 and 82 of the EC Treaty and Chapters I and II of Part I of the Competition Act 1998

21.10A (1) This paragraph applies to any appeal to the Court of Appeal relating to the application of—
   (a) Article 81 or Article 82 of the Treaty establishing the European Community; or
   (b) Chapter I or Chapter II of Part I of the Competition Act 1998.
(2) In this paragraph—
   (a) 'the Act' means the Competition Act 1998;
   (b) 'the Commission' means the European Commission;
   (c) 'the Competition Regulation' means Council Regulation (EC) No. 1/2003 of 16 December 2002 on the implementation of the rules on competition laid down in Articles 81 and 82 of the Treaty;
   (d) 'national competition authority' means—
      (i) the Office of Fair Trading; and

(ii) any other person or body designated pursuant to Article 35 of the Competition Regulation as a national competition authority of the United Kingdom;

(e) 'the Treaty' means the Treaty establishing the European Community.

(3) Any party whose appeal notice raises an issue relating to the application of Article 81 or 82 of the Treaty, or Chapter I or II of Part I of the Act, must—

(a) state that fact in his appeal notice; and

(b) serve a copy of the appeal notice on the Office of Fair Trading at the same time as it is served on the other party to the appeal (addressed to the Director of Competition Policy Co-ordination, Office of Fair Trading, Fleetbank House, 2–6 Salisbury Square, London EC4Y 8JX).

(4) Attention is drawn to the provisions of article 15.3 of the Competition Regulation, which entitles competition authorities and the Commission to submit written observations to national courts on issues relating to the application of Article 81 or 82 and, with the permission of the court in question, to submit oral observations to the court.

(5) A national competition authority may also make written observations to the Court of Appeal, or apply for permission to make oral observations, on issues relating to the application of Chapter I or II.

(6) If a national competition authority or the Commission intends to make written observations to the Court of Appeal, it must give notice of its intention to do so by letter to the Civil Appeals Office at the earliest opportunity.

(7) An application by a national competition authority or the Commission for permission to make oral representations at the hearing of an appeal must be made by letter to the Civil Appeals Office at the earliest opportunity, identifying the appeal and indicating why the applicant wishes to make oral representations.

(8) If a national competition authority or the Commission files a notice under sub-paragraph (6) or an application under sub-paragraph (7), it must at the same time serve a copy of the notice or application on every party to the appeal.

(9) Any request by a national competition authority or the Commission for the court to send it any documents relating to an appeal should be made at the same time as filing a notice under sub-paragraph (6) or an application under sub-paragraph (7).

(10) When the Court of Appeal receives a notice under sub-paragraph (6) it may give case management directions to the national competition authority or the Commission, including directions about the date by which any written observations are to be filed.

(11) The Court of Appeal will serve on every party to the appeal a copy of any directions given or order made—

(a) on an application under sub-paragraph (7); or

(b) under sub-paragraph (10).

(12) Every party to an appeal which raises an issue relating to the application of Article 81 or 82, and any national competition authority which has been served with a copy of a party's appeal notice, is under a duty to notify the Court of Appeal at any stage of the appeal if they are aware that—

(a) the Commission has adopted, or is contemplating adopting, a decision in relation to proceedings which it has initiated; and

(b) the decision referred to in (a) above has or would have legal effects in relation to the particular agreement, decision or practice in issue before the court.

(13) Where the Court of Appeal is aware that the Commission is contemplating adopting a decision as mentioned in sub-paragraph (12)(a), it shall consider whether to stay the appeal pending the Commission's decision.

(14) Where any judgment is given which decides on the application of Article 81 or 82, the court shall direct that a copy of the transcript of the judgment shall be sent to the Commission.

Judgments may be sent to the Commission electronically to comp-amicus@cec.eu.int or by post to the European Commission—DG Competition, B-1049, Brussels.

*Appeal from Proscribed Organisations Appeal Commission*

21.11 (1) The appellant's notice must be filed at the Court of Appeal within 14 days after the date when the Proscribed Organisations Appeal Commission:
(a) granted; or
(b) where the Terrorism Act 2000, s. 6(2)(b), applies, refused permission to appeal.

## Appeals to the High Court—Queen's Bench Division

22.1 The following appeals are to be heard in the Queen's Bench Division.

## Statutory appeals

*Appeals under the Merchant Shipping Act 1995*

22.2 (1) This paragraph applies to appeals under the Merchant Shipping Act 1995 and for this purpose a rehearing and an application under s. 61 of the Merchant Shipping Act 1995 are treated as appeals.
(2) The appellant must file any report to the Secretary of State containing the decision from which the appeal is brought with the appellant's notice.
(3) Where a rehearing by the High Court is ordered under ss. 64 or 269 of the Merchant Shipping Act 1995, the Secretary of State must give reasonable notice to the parties whom he considers to be affected by the rehearing.

*Appeal where court's decision is final*

22.3 (1) This paragraph applies to an appeal to the High Court under:
(a) the Architects Act 1997, s. 22;
(b) the Medicines Act 1968, s. 82(3) and 83(2);
(c) the Nurses, Midwives and Health Visitors Act 1997, s. 12;
(cc) the Nursing and Midwifery Order 2001 (SI 2002/253), arti. 38;
(d) the Pharmacy Act 1954, s. 10;
(e) the Medical Act 1983, s. 40;
(f) the Dentists Act 1984, s. 29 or s. 44;
(g) the Opticians Act 1989, s. 23;
(h) the Osteopaths Act 1993, s. 31; and
(i) the Chiropractors Act 1994, s. 31.
(2) Every appeal to which this paragraph applies must be supported by written evidence and, if the court so orders, oral evidence and will be by way of rehearing.
(3) The appellant must file the appellant's notice within 28 days after the decision that the appellant wishes to appeal.
(4) In the case of an appeal under an enactment specified in column 1 of the following table, the persons to be made respondents are the persons specified in relation to that enactment in column 2 of the table and the person to be served with the appellant's notice is the person so specified in column 3.

| 1<br>Enactment | 2<br>Respondent | 3<br>Person to be served |
|---|---|---|
| Architects Act 1997, s. 22 | The Architects' Registration Council of the United Kingdom | The Registrar of the Council |
| Chiropractors Act 1994, s. 31 | The General Chiropractic Council | The Registrar of the Council |
| Dentists Act 1984, s. 29 or s. 44 | The General Dental Council | The Registrar of the Council |
| Medical Act 1983, s. 40 | The General Medical Council | The Registrar of the Council |
| Medicines Act 1968, s. 82(3) and s. 83(2) | The Pharmaceutical Society of Great Britain | The Registrar of the Society |
| Nurses, Midwives and Health Visitors Act 1997, s. 12; Nursing and Midwifery Order 2001 (SI 2002/253), art. 38 | The United Kingdom Central Council for Nursing, Midwifery and Health Visiting | The Registrar of the Council |
| Opticians Act 1989, s. 23 | The General Optical Council | The Registrar of the Council |
| Osteopaths Act 1993, s. 31 | The General Osteopathic Council | The Registrar of the Council |
| Pharmacy Act 1954, s. 10 | The Pharmaceutical Society of Great Britain | The Registrar of the Society |

*Consumer Credit Act 1974: appeal from Secretary of State*

22.4 (1) A person dissatisfied in point of law with a decision of the Secretary of State on an appeal under s. 41 of the Consumer Credit Act 1974 from a determination of the Office of Fair Trading who had a right to appeal to the Secretary of State, whether or not he exercised that right, may appeal to the High Court.

(2) The appellant must serve the appellant's notice on:
(a) the Secretary of State;
(b) the original applicant if any, where the appeal is by a licensee under a group licence against compulsory variation, suspension or revocation of that licence; and
(c) any other person as directed by the court.

(3) The appeal court may remit the matter to the Secretary of State to the extent necessary to enable him to provide the court with such further information as the court may direct.

(4) If the appeal court allows the appeal, it shall not set aside or vary the decision but shall remit the matter to the Secretary of State with the opinion of the court for hearing and determination by him.

*The Pensions Appeal Tribunals Act 1943*

22.5 (1) In this paragraph 'the judge' means the judge nominated by the Lord Chancellor under s. 6(2)of the Pensions Appeal Tribunals Act 1943 ('the Act').

(2) An application to the judge for permission to appeal against a decision of a Pensions Appeal Tribunal:
(a) may not be made unless an application was made to the tribunal and was refused; and
(b) must be made within 28 days after the date of the tribunal's refusal.

(3) The appellant's notice seeking permission to appeal from the judge must contain:
(a) the point of law as respects which the appellant alleges that the tribunal's decision was wrong; and
(b) the date of the tribunal's decision refusing permission to appeal.

(4) The court officer shall request the chairman of the tribunal to give the judge a written statement of the reasons for the tribunal's decision to refuse permission to appeal, and within seven days after receiving the request, the chairman must give the judge such a statement.

(5) Where permission to appeal was given by:

(a) the tribunal, the appellant must file and serve the appellant's notice;

(b) the judge, the appellant must serve the appellant's notice,

within 28 days after permission to appeal was given.

(6) Within 28 days after service of the notice of appeal on him, the chairman of the tribunal must:

(a) state a case selling out the facts on which the decision appealed against was based;

(b) file the case stated at the court; and

(c) serve a copy of the case stated on the appellant and the respondent.

(7) A copy of the judge's order on the appeal must be sent by the court officer to the appellant, the respondent and the chairman of the tribunal.

*The Social Security Administration Act 1992*

22.6 (1) Any person who by virtue of s. 18 or 58(8) of the Social Security Administration Act 1992 ('the Act') is entitled and wishes to appeal against a decision of the Secretary of State on a question of law must within the prescribed period, or within such further time as the Secretary of State may allow, serve on the Secretary of State a notice requiring him to state a case setting out:

(a) his decision; and

(b) the facts on which his decision was based.

(2) Unless paragraph (3) applies the prescribed period is 28 days after receipt of the notice of the decision.

(3) Where, within 28 days after receipt of notice of the decision, a request is made to the Secretary of State in accordance with regulations made under the Act to furnish a statement of the grounds of the decision, the prescribed period is 28 days after receipt of that statement.

(4) Where under s. 18 or s. 58(8) of the Act the Secretary of State refers a question of law to the court, he must state that question together with the relevant facts in a case.

(5) The appellant's notice and the case stated must be filed at the appeal court and a copy of the notice and the case stated served on:

(a) the Secretary of State; and

(b) every person as between whom and the Secretary of State the question has arisen,

within 28 days after the case stated was served on the party at whose request, or as a result of whose application to the court, the case was stated.

(6) Unless the appeal court otherwise orders, the appeal or reference shall not be heard sooner than 28 days after service of the appellant's notice.

(7) The appeal court may order the case stated by the Secretary of State to be returned to the Secretary of State for him to hear further evidence.

*Appeals under the Extradition Act 2003*

22.6A (1) In this paragraph, 'the Act' means the Extradition Act 2003.

(2) Appeals to the High Court under the Act must be brought in the Administrative Court of the Queen's Bench Division.

(3) Where an appeal is brought under section 26 or 28 of the Act:

(a) the appellant's notice must be filed and served before the expiry of seven days, starting with the day on which the order is made;

(b) the appellant must endorse the appellant's notice with the date of the person's arrest;

(c) the High Court must begin to hear the substantive appeal within 40 days of the person's arrest; and
(d) the appellant must serve a copy of the appellant's notice on the Crown Prosecution Service, if they are not a party to the appeal, in addition to the persons to be served under rule 52.4(3) and in accordance with that rule.

(4) The High Court may extend the period of 40 days under paragraph (3)(c) if it believes it to be in the interests of justice to do so.

(5) Where an appeal is brought under section 103 of the Act, the appellant's notice must be filed and served before the expiry of 14 days, starting with the day on which the Secretary of State informs the person under section 100(1) or (4) of the Act of the order he has made in respect of the person.

(6) Where an appeal is brought under section 105 of the Act, the appellant's notice must be filed and served before the expiry of 14 days, starting with the day on which the order for discharge is made.

(7) Where an appeal is brought under section 108 of the Act the appellant's notice must be filed and served before the expiry of 14 days, starting with the day on which the Secretary of State informs the person that he has ordered his extradition.

(8) Where an appeal is brought under section 110 of the Act the appellant's notice must be filed and served before the expiry of 14 days, starting with the day on which the Secretary of State informs the person acting on behalf of a category 2 territory, as defined in section 69 of the Act, of the order for discharge. (Section 69 of the Act provides that a category 2 territory is that designated for the purposes of Part 2 of the Act.)

(9) Subject to paragraph (10), where an appeal is brought under section 103, 105, 108 or 110 of the Act, the High Court must begin to hear the substantive appeal within 76 days of the appellant's notice being filed.

(10) Where an appeal is brought under section 103 of the Act before the Secretary of State has decided whether the person is to be extradited:
(a) the period of 76 days does not start until the day on which the Secretary of State informs the person of his decision; and
(b) the Secretary of State must, as soon as practicable after he informs the person of his decision, inform the High Court:
(i) of his decision; and
(ii) of the date on which he informs the person of his decision.

(11) The High Court may extend the period of 76 days if it believes it to be in the interests of justice to do so.

(12) Where an appeal is brought under section 103, 105, 108 or 110 of the Act, the appellant must serve a copy of the appellant's notice on:
(a) the Crown Prosecution Service; and
(b) the Home Office,
if they are not a party to the appeal, in addition to the persons to be served under rule 52.4(3) and in accordance with that rule.

*Appeals under section 49 of the Solicitors Act 1974*

22.6B (1) This paragraph applies to appeals from the Solicitors Disciplinary Tribunal ('the Tribunal') to the High Court under section 49(1)(b) of the Solicitors Act 1974 ('the Act'). The procedure for appeals to the Master of the Rolls under section 49(1)(a) of the Act is set out in the Master of the Rolls (Appeals and Applications) Regulations 2001.

(2) Appeals to the High Court under section 49(1)(b) of the Act must be brought in the Administrative Court of the Queen's Bench Division.

(3) The appellant's notice—

(a) must state in the heading that the appeal relates to a solicitor, or a solicitor's clerk, and is made under section 49 of the Act;
(b) must be filed within 14 days after the date on which the Tribunal's statement of its findings was filed with the Law Society in accordance with section 48(1) of the Act; and
(c) must be accompanied by copies of the order appealed against and the statement of the Tribunal's findings required by section 48(1) of the Act; and
(d) unless the court orders otherwise, must be served by the appellant on—
(i) every party to the proceedings before the Tribunal; and
(ii) the Law Society.

(4) The court—
(a) may order an appellant to give security for the costs of an appeal only if he was the applicant in the proceedings before the tribunal;
and
(b) may not order any other party to give security for costs.

(5) The court may direct the Tribunal to provide it with a written statement of their opinion on the case, or on any question arising in it. If the court gives such a direction, the clerk to the Tribunal must as soon as possible—
(a) file the statement; and
(b) serve a copy on each party to the appeal.

(6) The court may give permission for any person to intervene to be heard in opposition to the appeal.

(7) An appellant may at any time discontinue his appeal by—
(a) serving notice of discontinuance on the clerk to the Tribunal and every other party to the appeal; and
(b) filing a copy of the notice.

(8) Unless the court orders otherwise, an appellant who discontinues is liable for the costs of every other party to the appeal.

**Appeals by way of case stated**

*Reference of question of law by Agricultural Land Tribunal*

22.7 (1) A question of law referred to the High Court by an Agricultural Land Tribunal under s. 6 of the Agriculture (Miscellaneous Provisions) Act 1954 shall be referred by way of case stated by the tribunal.

(2) Where the proceedings before the tribunal arose on an application under s. 11 of the Agricultural Holdings Act 1986, an:
(a) application notice for an order under s. 6 that the tribunal refers a question of law to the court; and
(b) appellant's notice by which an appellant seeks the court's determination on a question of law,

must be served on the authority having power to enforce the statutory requirement specified in the notice in addition to every other party to those proceedings and on the secretary of the tribunal.

(3) Where, in accordance with paragraph (2), a notice is served on the authority mentioned in that paragraph, that authority may attend the appeal hearing and make representations to the court.

*Case stated by Mental Health Review Tribunal*

22.8 (1) In this paragraph 'the Act' means the Mental Health Act 1983 and 'party to proceedings' means:
(a) the person who initiated the proceedings; and
(b) any person to whom, in accordance with rules made under s. 78 of the Act, the tribunal sent notice of the application or reference or a request instead notice of reference.

(2) A party to proceedings shall not be entitled to apply to the High Court for an order under s. 78(8) of the Act directing the tribunal to state a case for determination by court unless:
(a) within 21 days after the decision of the tribunal was communicated to him in accordance with rules made under s. 78 of the Act he made a written request to the tribunal to state a case; and
(b) either the tribunal:
(i) failed to comply with that request within 21 days after it was made; or
(ii) refused to comply with it.
(3) The period for filing the application notice for an order under s. 78(8) of the Act is:
(a) where the tribunal failed to comply with the applicant's request to state a case within the period mentioned in sub-para. (2)(b)(i), 14 days after the expiration of that period;
(b) where the tribunal refused that request, 14 days after receipt by the applicant of notice of the refusal of his request.
(4) A Mental Health Review Tribunal by whom a case is stated shall be entitled to attend the proceedings for the determination of the case and make representations to the court.
(5) If the court allows the appeal, it may give any direction which the tribunal ought to have given under Part V of the Act.

## Appeals to the High Court—Chancery Division

23.1 The following appeals are to be heard in the Chancery Division.

*Determination of appeal or case stated under various Acts*

23.2 Any appeal to the High Court, and any case stated or question referred for the opinion of that court under any of the following enactments shall be heard in the Chancery Division:
(1) the Law of Property Act 1922, sch. 15, para. 16;
(2) the Industrial Assurance Act 1923;
(3) the Land Registration Act 1925;
(4) the Water Resources Act 1991, s. 205(4);
(5) the Clergy Pensions Measure 1961, s. 38(3);
(6) the Industrial and Provident Societies Act 1965;
(7) the Pension Schemes Act 1993, s. 151;
(8) the Pension Schemes Act 1993, s. 173;
(9) the Pensions Act 1995, s. 97;
(10) the Charities Act 1993;
(11) the Stamp Act 1891, ss. 13 and 13B;
(12) the Income and Corporation Taxes Act 1988, s. 705A;
(13) the General Commissioners (Jurisdiction and Procedure) Regulations 1994, reg. 22;
(14) the Taxes Management Act 1970, ss. 53, 56A or 100C(4);
(15) the Inheritance Tax Act 1984, ss. 222(3), 225, 249(3) or 251;
(16) the Stamp Duty Reserve Tax Regulations 1986, regs 8(3) or 10;
(17) the Land Registration Act 2002;
(18) regulation 74 of the European Public Limited-Liability Company Regulations 2004.
(This list is not exhaustive.)

## Statutory appeals

*Appeal under s. 222 of the Inheritance Tax Act 1984*

23.3 (1) This paragraph applies to appeals to the High Court under s. 222(3) of the Inheritance Tax Act 1984 (the '1984 Act') and reg. 8(3) of the Stamp Duty Reserve Tax Regulations 1986 (the '1986 Regulations').

(2) The appellant's notice must:
(a) state the date on which the Commissioners for HM Revenue and Customs (the 'Board') gave notice to the appellant under s. 221 of the 1984 Act or reg. 6 of the 1986 Regulations of the determination that is the subject of the appeal;
(b) state the date on which the appellant gave to the Board notice of appeal under s. 222(1) of the 1984 Act or reg. 8(1) of the 1986 Regulations and, if notice was not given within the time permitted, whether the Board or the Special Commissioners have given their consent to the appeal being brought out of time, and, if they have, the date they gave their consent; and
(c) either state that the appellant and the Board have agreed that the appeal may be to the High Court or contain an application for permission to appeal to the High Court.

(3) The appellant must file the following documents with the appellant's notice:
(a) two copies of the notice referred to in sub-para. 2(a);
(b) two copies of the notice of appeal (under s. 222(1) of the 1984 Act or reg. 8(1) of the 1986 Regulations) referred to in sub-para. 2(b); and
(c) where the appellant's notice contains an application for permission to appeal, written evidence setting out the grounds on which it is alleged that he matters to be decided on the appeal are likely to be substantially confined to questions of law.

(4) The appellant must:
(a) file the appellant's notice at the court; and
(b) serve the appellant's notice on the Board,

within 30 days of the date on which the appellant gave to the Board notice of appeal under s. 222(1) of the 1984 Act or reg. 8(1) of the 1986 Regulations or, if the Board or the Special Commissioners have given consent to the appeal being brought out of time, within 30 days of the date on which such consent was given.

(5) The court will set a date for the hearing of not less than 40 days from the date that the appellant's notice was filed.

(6) Where the appellant's notice contains an application for permission to appeal:
(a) a copy of the written evidence filed in accordance with para. (3)(c) must be served on the Board with the appellant's notice; and
(b) the Board:
(i) may file written evidence; and
(ii) if it does so, must serve a copy of that evidence on the appellant,

within 30 days after service of the written evidence under para. (6)(a).

(7) The appellant may not rely on any grounds of appeal not specified in the notice referred to in para. (2)(b) on the hearing of the appeal without the permission of the court.

*Appeals under s. 53 and 100C(4) of the Taxes Management Act 1970 and s. 249(3) or 251 of the Inheritance Tax Act 1984*

23.4 (1) The appellant must serve the appellant's notice on:
(a) the General or Special Commissioners against whose decision, award or determination the appeal is brought; and
(b) (i) in the case of an appeal brought under s. 100C(4) of the Taxes Management Act 1970 or s. 249(3) of the Inheritance Tax Act 1984 by any party other than the defendant in the proceedings before the Commissioners, that defendant; or
(ii) in any other case, the Commissioners for HM Revenue and Customs.

(2) The appellant must file the appellant's notice at the court within 30 days after the date of the decision, award or determination against which the appeal is brought.

(3) Within 30 days of the service on them of the appellant's notice, the general or special commissioners, as the case may be, must:

(a) file two copies of a note of their findings and of the reasons for their decision, award or determination at the court; and
(b) serve a copy of the note on every other party to the appeal.
(4) Any document to be served on the general or special commissioners may be served by delivering or sending it to their clerk.

*Appeals under s. 56A of the Taxes Management Act 1970, s. 225 of the Inheritance Tax Act 1984 and reg. 10 of the Stamp Duty Reserve Tax Regulations 1986*

23.5 (1) The appellant must file the appellant's notice:
(a) where the appeal is made following the refusal of the special commissioners to issue a certificate under s. 56A(2)(b) of the Taxes Management Act 1970, within 28 days from the date of the release of the decision of the special commissioners containing the refusal;
(b) where the appeal is made following the refusal of permission to appeal to the Court of Appeal under s. 56A(2)(c) of that Act, within 28 days from the date when permission is refused; or
(c) in all other cases within 56 days after the date of the decision or determination that the appellant wishes to appeal.

*Appeal under s. 17 of the Industrial Assurance Act 1923*

23.6 The appellant must file the appellant's notice within 21 days after the date of the Commissioner's refusal or direction under s. 17(3) of the Industrial Assurance Act 1923.

*Appeals affecting industrial and provident societies etc.*

23.7 (1) This paragraph applies to all appeals under:
(a) the Friendly Societies Act 1974;
(b) the Friendly Societies Act 1992;
(c) the Industrial Assurance Act 1923; and
(d) the Industrial and Provident Societies Act 1965.
(2) At any stage on an appeal, the court may:
(a) direct that the appellant's notice be served on any person;
(b) direct that notice be given by advertisement or otherwise of:
(i) the bringing of the appeal;
(ii) the nature of the appeal; and
(iii) the time when the appeal will or is likely to be heard; or
(c) give such other directions as it thinks proper to enable any person interested in:
(i) the society, trade union, alleged trade union or industrial assurance company; or
(ii) the subject matter of the appeal,
to appear and be heard at the appeal hearing.

*Appeal from value added tax and duties tribunal*

23.8 (1) A party to proceedings before a value added tax and duties tribunal who is dissatisfied in point of law with a decision of the tribunal may appeal under s. 11(1) of the Tribunals and Inquiries Act 1992 to the High Court.
(2) The appellant must file the appellant's notice:
(a) where the appeal is made following the refusal of the value added tax and duties tribunal to grant a certificate under art. 2(b) of the Value Added Tax and Duties Tribunal Appeals Order 1986, within 28 days from the date of the release of the decision containing the refusal;
(b) in all other cases within 56 days after the date of the decision or determination that the appellant wishes to appeal.

*Appeal against an order or decision of the Charity Commissioners*

23.8A (1) In this paragraph:

'the Act' means the Charities Act 1993; and
'the Commissioners' means the Charity Commissioners for England and Wales

(2) The Attorney-General, unless he is the appellant, must be made a respondent to the appeal.

(3) The appellant's notice must state the grounds of the appeal, and the appellant may not rely on any other grounds without the permission of the court.

(4) Sub-paragraphs (5) and (6) apply, in addition to the above provisions, where the appeal is made under s. 16(12) of the Act.

(5) If the Commissioners have granted a certificate that it is a proper case for an appeal, a copy of the certificate must be filed with the appellant's notice.

(6) If the appellant applies in the appellant's notice for permission to appeal under s. 16(13) of the Act:
   (a) the appellant's notice must state:
      (i) that the appellant has requested the Commissioners to grant a certificate that it is a proper case for an appeal, and they have refused to do so;
      (ii) the date of such refusal;
      (iii) the grounds on which the appellant alleges that it is a proper case for an appeal; and
      (iv) if the application for permission to appeal is made with the consent of any other party to the proposed appeal, that fact;
   (b) if the Commissioners have given reasons for refusing a certificate, a copy of the reasons must be attached to the appellant's notice;
   (c) the court may, before determining the application, direct the Commissioners to file a written statement of their reasons for refusing a certificate;
   (d) the court will serve on the appellant a copy of any statement filed under sub-paragraph (c).

*Appeal against a decision of the adjudicator under the Land Registration Act 2002, s. 111*

23.8B (1) A person who is aggrieved by a decision of the adjudicator and who wishes to appeal that decision must obtain permission to appeal.

(2) The appellant must serve on the adjudicator a copy of the appeal court's decision on a request for permission to appeal as soon as reasonably practicable and in any event within 14 days of receipt by the appellant of the decision on permission.

(3) The appellant must serve on the adjudicator and the Chief Land Registrar a copy of any order by the appeal court to stay a decision of the adjudicator pending the outcome of the appeal as soon as reasonably practicable and in any event within 14 days of receipt by the appellant of the appeal court's order to stay.

(4) The appellant must serve on the adjudicator and the Chief Land Registrar a copy of the appeal court's decision on the appeal as soon as reasonably practicable and in any event within 14 days of receipt by the appellant of the appeal court's decision.

*Appeals under regulation 74 of the European Public Limited-Liability Company Regulations 2004*

23.8C (1) In this paragraph—
   (a) 'the 2004 Regulations' means the European Public Limited-Liability Company Regulations 2004;
   (b) 'the EC Regulation' means Council Regulation (EC) No 2157/2001 of 8 October 2001 on the Statute for a European company (SE);
   (c) 'SE' means a European public limited-liability company (Societas Europaea) within the meaning of Article 1 of the EC Regulation.

(2) This paragraph applies to appeals under regulation 74 of the 2004 Regulations against the opposition—

(a) of the Secretary of State or national financial supervisory authority to the transfer of the registered office of an SE under Article 8(14) of the EC Regulation; and
(b) of the Secretary of State to the participation by a company in the formation of an SE by merger under Article 19 of the EC Regulation.

(3) Where an SE seeks to appeal against the opposition of the national financial supervisory authority to the transfer of its registered office under Article 8(14) of the EC Regulation, it must serve the appellant's notice on both the national financial supervisory authority and the Secretary of State.
(4) The appellant's notice must contain an application for permission to appeal.
(5) The appeal will be a review of the decision of the Secretary of State and not a re-hearing. The grounds of review are set out in regulation 74(2) of the 2004 Regulations.
(6) The appeal will be heard by a High Court judge.

## Appeals by way of case stated

*Proceedings under the Commons Registration Act 1965*

23.9 A person aggrieved by the decision of a Commons Commissioner who requires the Commissioner to state a case for the opinion of the High Court under s. 18 of the Commons Registration Act 1965 must file the appellant's notice within 42 days from the date on which notice of the decision was sent to the aggrieved person.

## Appeals to a County Court

*Local Government (Miscellaneous Provisions) Act 1976*

24.1 Where one of the grounds upon which an appeal against a notice under ss. 21, 23 or 35 of the Local Government (Miscellaneous Provisions) Act 1976 is brought is that:
(a) it would have been fairer to serve the notice on another person; or
(b) that it would be reasonable for the whole or part of the expenses to which the appeal relates to be paid by some other person,

that person must be made a respondent to the appeal, unless the court, on application of the appellant made without notice, otherwise directs.

*Appeals under sections 204 and 204A of the Housing Act 1996*

24.2 (1) An appellant should include appeals under s. 204 and s. 204A of the Housing Act 1996 in one appellant's notice.
(2) If it is not possible to do so (for example because an urgent application under s. 204A is required) the appeals may be included in separate appellant's notices.
(3) An appeal under s. 204A may include an application for an order under s. 204A(4)(a) requiring the authority to secure that accommodation is available for the applicant's occupation.
(4) If, exceptionally, the court makes an order under s. 204A(4)(a) without notice, the appellant's notice must be served on the authority together with the order. Such an order will normally require the authority to secure that accommodation is available until a hearing date when the authority can make representations as to whether the order under s. 204A(4)(a) should be continued.

*Appeal under part II of the Immigration and Asylum Act 1999 (carriers' liability)*

24.3 (1) A person appealing to a county court under s. 35A or s. 40B of the Immigration and Asylum Act 1999 ('the Act') against a decision by the Secretary of State to impose a penalty under s. 32 or a charge under s. 40 of the Act must, subject to sub-paragraph (2), file the appellant's notice within 28 days after receiving the penalty notice or charge notice.
(2) Where the appellant has given notice of objection to the Secretary of State under s. 35(4) or s. 40A(3) of the Act within the time prescribed for doing so, he must

file the appellant's notice within 28 days after receiving notice of the Secretary of State's decision in response to the notice of objection.

(3) Sections 35A and 40B of the Act provide that any appeal under those sections shall be a rehearing of the Secretary of State's decision to impose a penalty or charge, and therefore r. 52.11(1) does not apply.

## SECTION IV—PROVISIONS ABOUT REOPENING APPEALS

### Reopening of Final Appeals

25.1 This paragraph applies to applications under r. 52.17 for permission to reopen a final determination of an appeal.

25.2 In this paragraph, 'appeal' includes an application for permission to appeal.

25.3 Permission must be sought from the court whose decision the applicant wishes to reopen.

25.4 The application for permission must be made by application notice and supported by written evidence, verified by a statement of truth.

25.5 A copy of the application for permission must not be served on any other party to the original appeal unless the court so directs.

25.6 Where the court directs that the application for permission is to be served on another party, that party may within 14 days of the service on him of the copy of the application file and serve a written statement either supporting or opposing the application.

25.7 The application for permission, and any written statements supporting or opposing it, will be considered on paper by a single judge, and will be allowed to proceed only if the judge so directs.

# CPR Part 53 Defamation Claims



## 53.1 Scope of this Part

This Part contains rules about defamation claims.

## 53.2 Summary Disposal Under the Defamation Act 1996

(1) This rule provides for summary disposal in accordance with the Defamation Act 1996 ('the Act').
(2) In proceedings for summary disposal under sections 8 and 9 of the Act, rules 24.4 (procedure), 24.5 (evidence) and 24.6 (directions) apply.
(3) An application for summary judgment under Part 24 may not be made if—
  (a) an application has been made for summary disposal in accordance with the Act, and that application has not been disposed of; or
  (b) summary relief has been granted on an application for summary disposal under the Act.
(4) The court may on any application for summary disposal direct the defendant to elect whether or not to make an offer to make amends under section 2 of the Act.
(5) When it makes a direction under paragraph (4), the court will specify the time by which and the manner in which—
  (a) the election is to be made; and
  (b) notification of it is to be given to the court and the other parties.

## 53.3 Sources of Information

Unless the court orders otherwise, a party will not be required to provide further information about the identity of the defendant's sources of information.
(Part 18 provides for requests for further information.)

# PD 53 Practice Direction — Defamation Claims

This practice direction supplements CPR Part 53.

## General

1 This practice direction applies to defamation claims.

## Statements of Case

2.1 Statements of case should be confined to the information necessary to inform the other party of the nature of the case he has to meet. Such information should be set out concisely and in a manner proportionate to the subject matter of the claim.

2.2 (1) In a claim for libel the publication the subject of the claim must be identified in the claim form.

(2) In a claim for slander the claim form must so far as possible contain the words complained of, and identify the person to whom they were spoken and when.

2.3 (1) The claimant must specify in the particulars of claim the defamatory meaning which he alleges that the words or matters complained of conveyed, both:

(a) as to their natural and ordinary meaning; and

(b) as to any innuendo meaning (that is a meaning alleged to be conveyed to some person by reason of knowing facts extraneous to the words complained of).

(2) In the case of an innuendo meaning, the claimant must also identify the relevant extraneous facts.

2.4 In a claim for slander the precise words used and the names of the persons to whom they were spoken and when must, so far as possible, be set out in the particulars of claim, if not already contained in the claim form.

2.5 Where a defendant alleges that the words complained of are true he must:

(1) specify the defamatory meanings he seeks to justify; and

(2) give details of the matters on which he relies in support of that allegation.

2.6 Where a defendant alleges that the words complained of are fair comment on a matter of public interest he must:

(1) specify the defamatory meaning he seeks to defend as fair comment on a matter of public interest; and

(2) give details of the matters on which he relies in support of that allegation.

2.7 Where a defendant alleges that the words complained of were published on a privileged occasion he must specify the circumstances he relies on in support of that contention.

2.8 Where a defendant alleges that the words complained of are true, or are fair comment on a matter of public interest, the claimant must serve a reply specifically admitting or denying the allegation and giving the facts on which he relies.

2.9 If the defendant contends that any of the words or matters are fair comment on a matter of public interest, or were published on a privileged occasion, and the claimant intends to allege that the defendant acted with malice, the claimant must serve a reply giving details of the facts or matters relied on.

2.10 (1) A claimant must give full details of the facts and matters on which he relies in support of his claim for damages.

(2) Where a claimant seeks aggravated or exemplary damages he must provide the information specified in r. 16.4(1)(c).

2.11 A defendant who relies on an offer to make amends under s. 2 of the Defamation Act 1996, as his defence must:

(1) state in his defence:

(a) that he is relying on the offer in accordance with s. 4(2) of the Defamation Act 1996; and
(b) that it has not been withdrawn by him or been accepted, and
(2) attach a copy of the offer he made with his defence.

## Court's Powers in Connection with an Offer of Amends

3.1 Sections 2 to 4 of the Defamation Act 1996 make provision for a person who has made a statement which is alleged to be defamatory to make an offer to make amends. Section 3 provides for the court to assist in the process of making amends.

3.2 A claim under s. 3 of the Defamation Act 1996 made other than in existing proceedings may be made under CPR Part 8:
(1) where the parties agree on the steps to make amends, and the sole purpose of the claim is for the court to make an order under s. 3(3) for an order that the offer be fulfilled; or
(2) where the parties do not agree:
(a) on the steps to be taken by way of correction, apology and publication (see s. 3(4));
(b) on the amount to be paid by way of compensation (see s. 3(5)); or
(c) on the amount to be paid by way of costs (see s. 3(6)).

(Applications in existing proceedings made under s. 3 of the Defamation Act 1996 must be made in accordance with CPR Part 23.)

3.3 (1) A claim or application under s. 3 of the Defamation Act 1996 must be supported by written evidence.
(2) The evidence referred to in para. (1) must include:
(a) a copy of the offer of amends;
(b) details of the steps taken to fulfil the offer of amends;
(c) a copy of the text of any correction and apology;
(d) details of the publication of the correction and apology;
(e) a statement of the amount of any sum paid as compensation;
(f) a statement of the amount of any sum paid for costs;
(g) why the offer is unsatisfactory.
(3) Where any step specified in s. 2(4) of the Defamation Act 1996 has not been taken, then the evidence referred to in sub-para. (2)(c) to (f) must state what steps are proposed by the party to fulfil the offer of amends and the date or dates on which each step will be fulfilled and, if none, that no proposal has been made to take that step.

## Ruling on Meaning

4.1 At any time the court may decide:
(1) whether a statement complained of is capable of having any meaning attributed to it in a statement of case;
(2) whether the statement is capable of being defamatory of the claimant;
(3) whether the statement is capable of bearing any other meaning defamatory of the claimant.

4.2 An application for a ruling on meaning may be made at any time after the service of particulars of claim. Such an application should be made promptly.

(This provision disapplies for these applications the usual time restriction on making applications in r. 24.4(1).)

4.3 Where an application is made for a ruling on meaning, the application notice must state that it is an application for a ruling on meaning made in accordance with this practice direction.

4.4 The application notice or the evidence contained or referred to in it, or served with it, must identify precisely the statement, and the meaning attributed to it, that the court is being asked to consider.

(Rule 3.3 applies where the court exercises its powers of its own initiative.)

(Following a ruling on meaning the court may exercise its power under r. 3.4.)
(Section 7 of the Defamation Act 1996 applies to rulings on meaning.)

## Summary Disposal

5.1 Where an application is made for summary disposal, the application notice must state:
  (1) that it is an application for summary disposal made in accordance with s. 8 of the Defamation Act 1996.
  (2) the matters set out in para. 2(3) of PD 24; and
  (3) whether or not the defendant has made an offer to make amends under s. 2 of the Act and whether or not it has been withdrawn.

5.2 An application for summary disposal may be made at any time after the service of particulars of claim.

(This provision disapplies for these applications the usual time restriction on making applications in r. 24.4(1).)

5.3 (1) This paragraph applies where:
    (a) the court has ordered the defendant in defamation proceedings to agree and publish a correction and apology as summary relief under s. 8(2) of the Defamation Act 1996; and
    (b) the parties are unable to agree its content within the time specified in the order.
  (2) Where the court grants this type of summary relief under the Act, the order will specify the date by which the parties should reach agreement about the content, time, manner, form and place of publication of the correction and apology.
  (3) Where the parties cannot agree the content of the correction and apology by the date specified in the order, then the claimant must prepare a summary of the judgment given by the court and serve it on all the other parties within three days following the date specified in the order.
  (4) Where the parties cannot agree the summary of the judgment prepared by the claimant they must within three days of receiving the summary:
    (a) file with the court and serve on all the other parties a copy of the summary showing the revisions they wish to make to it; and
    (b) apply to the court for the court to settle the summary.
  (5) The court will then itself settle the summary and the judge who delivered the judgment being summarised will normally do this.

## Statements in Open Court

6.1 This paragraph only applies where a party wishes to accept a Part 36 offer or other offer of settlement in relation to a claim for:
  (1) libel;
  (2) slander.

6.2 A party may apply for permission to make a statement in open court before or after he accepts the Part 36 offer in accordance with r. 36.9(1) or other offer to settle the claim.

6.3 The statement that the applicant wishes to make must be submitted for the approval of the court and must accompany the notice of application.

6.4 The court may postpone the time for making the statement if other claims relating to the subject matter of the statement are still proceeding.

(Applications must be made in accordance with Part 23.)

## Transitional Provision Relating to Section 4 of The Defamation Act 1952

7 Paragraph 3 of this practice direction applies, with any necessary modifications to an application to the court to determine any question as to the steps to be taken to fulfil an offer made under s. 4 of the Defamation Act 1952.

(Section 4 of the Defamation Act 1952 is repealed by the Defamation Act 1996. The commencement order bringing in the repeal makes transitional provision for offers which have been made at the date the repeal came into force.)

# CPR Part 54 Judicial Review and Statutory Review



## I JUDICIAL REVIEW

### 54.1 Scope and Interpretation

(1) This Section of this Part contains rules about judicial review.
(2) In this Section—
  (a) a 'claim for judicial review' means a claim to review the lawfulness of—
    (i) an enactment; or
    (ii) a decision, action or failure to act in relation to the exercise of a public function.

. . .

  (e) 'the judicial review procedure' means the Part 8 procedure as modified by this Section;
  (f) 'interested party' means any person (other than the claimant and defendant) who is directly affected by the claim; and
  (g) 'court' means the High Court, unless otherwise stated.

(Rule 8.1(6)(b) provides that a rule or practice direction may, in relation to a specified type of proceedings, disapply or modify any of the rules set out in Part 8 as they apply to those proceedings.)

### 54.2 When this Section Must be Used

The judicial review procedure must be used in a claim for judicial review where the claimant is seeking—

(a) a mandatory order;
(b) a prohibiting order;
(c) a quashing order; or
(d) an injunction under section 30 of the Supreme Court Act 1981[1] (restraining a person from acting in any office in which he is not entitled to act).

### 54.3 When this Section May be Used

(1) The judicial review procedure may be used in a claim for judicial review where the claimant is seeking—
 (a) a declaration; or
 (b) an injunction(GL).

(Section 31(2) of the Supreme Court Act 1981 sets out the circumstances in which the court may grant a declaration or injunction in a claim for judicial review.)

(Where the claimant is seeking a declaration or injunction in addition to one of the remedies listed in rule 54.2, the judicial review procedure must be used.)

(2) A claim for judicial review may include a claim for damages, restitution or the recovery of a sum due but may not seek such a remedy alone.

(Section 31(2) of the Supreme Court Act sets out the circumstances in which the court may award damages, restitution or the recovery of a sum due on a claim for judicial review.)

### 54.4 Permission Required

The court's permission to proceed is required in a claim for judicial review whether started under this Section or transferred to the Administrative Court.

### 54.5 Time Limit for Filing Claim Form

(1) The claim form must be filed—
 (a) promptly; and
 (b) in any event not later than 3 months after the grounds to make the claim first arose.
(2) The time limit in this rule may not be extended by agreement between the parties.
(3) This rule does not apply when any other enactment specifies a shorter time limit for making the claim for judicial review.

### 54.6 Claim Form

(1) In addition to the matters set out in rule 8.2 (contents of the claim form) the claimant must also state—
 (a) the name and address of any person he considers to be an interested party;
 (b) that he is requesting permission to proceed with a claim for judicial review; and
 (c) any remedy (including any interim remedy) he is claiming.

(Part 25 sets out how to apply for an interim remedy.)

(2) The claim form must be accompanied by the documents required by the relevant practice direction.

### 54.7 Service of Claim Form

The claim form must be served on—
(a) the defendant; and
(b) unless the court otherwise directs, any person the claimant considers to be an interested party,

within 7 days after the date of issue.

### 54.8 Acknowledgment of Service

(1) Any person served with the claim form who wishes to take part in the judicial review

[1] 1981 c.54.

must file an acknowledgment of service in the relevant practice form in accordance with the following provisions of this rule.

(2) Any acknowledgment of service must be—
  (a) filed not more than 21 days after service of the claim form; and
  (b) served on—
    (i) the claimant; and
    (ii) subject to any direction under rule 54.7(b), any other person named in the claim form,

as soon as practicable and, in any event, not later than 7 days after it is filed.

(3) The time limits under this rule may not be extended by agreement between the parties.

(4) The acknowledgment of service—
  (a) must—
    (i) where the person filing it intends to contest the claim, set out a summary of his grounds for doing so; and
    (ii) state the name and address of any person the person filing it considers to be an interested party; and
  (b) may include or be accompanied by an application for directions.

(5) Rule 10.3(2) does not apply.

## 54.9 Failure to File Acknowledgment of Service

(1) Where a person served with the claim form has failed to file an acknowledgment of service in accordance with rule 54.8, he—
  (a) may not take part in a hearing to decide whether permission should be given unless the court allows him to do so; but
  (b) provided he complies with rule 54.14 or any other direction of the court regarding the filing and service of—
    (i) detailed grounds for contesting the claim or supporting it on additional grounds; and
    (ii) any written evidence,

may take part in the hearing of the judicial review.

(2) Where that person takes part in the hearing of the judicial review, the court may take his failure to file an acknowledgment of service into account when deciding what order to make about costs.

(3) Rule 8.4 does not apply.

## 54.10 Permission Given

(1) Where permission to proceed is given the court may also give directions.

(2) Directions under paragraph (1) may include a stay[(GL)] of proceedings to which the claim relates.

(Rule 3.7 provides a sanction for the non-payment of the fee payable when permission to proceed has been given.)

## 54.11 Service of Order Giving or Refusing Permission

The court will serve—

(a) the order giving or refusing permission; and
(b) any directions, on—
  (i) the claimant;
  (ii) the defendant; and
  (iii) any other person who filed an acknowledgment of service.

## 54.12 Permission Decision Without a Hearing

(1) This rule applies where the court, without a hearing—
  (a) refuses permission to proceed; or
  (b) gives permission to proceed—

(i) subject to conditions; or
(ii) on certain grounds only.

(2) The court will serve its reasons for making the decision when it serves the order giving or refusing permission in accordance with rule 54.11.
(3) The claimant may not appeal but may request the decision to be reconsidered at a hearing.
(4) A request under paragraph (3) must be filed within 7 days after service of the reasons under paragraph (2).
(5) The claimant, defendant and any other person who has filed an acknowledgment of service will be given at least 2 days' notice of the hearing date.

### 54.13 Defendant etc. May Not Apply to Set Aside(GL)

Neither the defendant nor any other person served with the claim form may apply to set aside(GL) an order giving permission to proceed.

### 54.14 Response

(1) A defendant and any other person served with the claim form who wishes to contest the claim or support it on additional grounds must file and serve—
(a) detailed grounds for contesting the claim or supporting it on additional grounds; and
(b) any written evidence,
within 35 days after service of the order giving permission.
(2) The following rules do not apply—
(a) rule 8.5(3) and 8.5(4) (defendant to file and serve written evidence at the same time as acknowledgment of service); and
(b) rule 8.5(5) and 8.5(6) (claimant to file and serve any reply within 14 days).

### 54.15 Where Claimant Seeks to Rely on Additional Grounds

The court's permission is required if a claimant seeks to rely on grounds other than those for which he has been given permission to proceed.

### 54.16 Evidence

(1) Rule 8.6(1) does not apply.
(2) No written evidence may be relied on unless—
(a) it has been served in accordance with any—
(i) rule under this Section; or
(ii) direction of the court; or
(b) the court gives permission.

### 54.17 Court's Powers to Hear Any Person

(1) Any person may apply for permission—
(a) to file evidence; or
(b) make representations at the hearing of the judicial review.
(2) An application under paragraph (1) should be made promptly.

### 54.18 Judicial Review May be Decided Without a Hearing

The court may decide the claim for judicial review without a hearing where all the parties agree.

### 54.19 Court's Powers in Respect of Quashing Orders

(1) This rule applies where the court makes a quashing order in respect of the decision to which the claim relates.
(2) The court may—
(a) remit the matter to the decision-maker; and
(b) direct it to reconsider the matter and reach a decision in accordance with the judgment of the court.

(3) Where the court considers that there is no purpose to be served in remitting the matter to the decision-maker it may, subject to any statutory provision, take the decision itself.

(Where a statutory power is given to a tribunal, person or other body it may be the case that the court cannot take the decision itself.)

### 54.20 Transfer

The court may—

(a) order a claim to continue as if it had not been started under this Section; and

(b) where it does so, give directions about the future management of the claim.

(Part 30 (transfer) applies to transfers to and from the Administrative Court.)

## II STATUTORY REVIEW UNDER THE NATIONALITY, IMMIGRATION AND ASYLUM ACT 2002

### 54.21 Scope and Interpretation

(1) This Section of this Part contains rules about applications to the High Court under section 101(2) of the Nationality, Immigration and Asylum Act 2002[2] for a review of a decision of the Immigration Appeal Tribunal on an application for permission to appeal from an adjudicator.

(2) In this Section—

- (a) 'the Act' means the Nationality, Immigration and Asylum Act 2002;
- (b) 'adjudicator' means an adjudicator appointed for the purposes of Part 5 of the Act;
- (c) 'applicant' means a person applying to the High Court under section 101(2) of the Act;
- (d) 'other party' means the other party to the proceedings before the Tribunal; and
- (e) 'Tribunal' means the Immigration Appeal Tribunal.

### 54.22 Application for Review

(1) An application under section 101(2) of the Act must be made to the Administrative Court.

(2) The application must be made by filing an application notice.

(3) The applicant must file with the application notice—

- (a) the immigration or asylum decision to which the proceedings relate, and any document giving reasons for that decision;
- (b) the grounds of appeal to the adjudicator;
- (c) the adjudicator's determination;
- (d) the grounds of appeal to the Tribunal together with any documents sent with them;
- (e) the Tribunal's determination on the application for permission to appeal; and
- (f) any other documents material to the application which were before the adjudicator.

(4) The applicant must also file with the application notice written submissions setting out—

- (a) the grounds upon which it is contended that the Tribunal made an error of law; and
- (b) reasons in support of those grounds.

### 54.23 Time Limit for Application

(1) The application notice must be filed not later than 14 days after the applicant is deemed to have received notice of the Tribunal's decision in accordance with rules made under section 106 of the Act.

(2) The court may extend the time limit in paragraph (1) in exceptional circumstances.

(3) An application to extend the time limit must be made in the application notice and supported by written evidence verified by a statement of truth.

---

[2] 2002 c.41.

## 54.24 Service of Application

(1) The applicant must serve on the Asylum and Immigration Tribunal copies of the application notice and written submissions.
(2) Where an application is for review of a decision by the Tribunal to grant permission to appeal, the applicant must serve on the other party copies of—
 (a) the application notice;
 (b) the written submissions; and
 (c) all the documents filed in support of the application, except for documents which come from or have already been served on that party.
(3) Where documents are required to be served under paragraphs (1) and (2), they must be served as soon as practicable after they are filed.

## 54.25 Determining the Application

(1) The application will be determined by a single judge without a hearing, and by reference only to the written submissions and the documents filed with them.
(2) If the applicant relies on evidence which was not submitted to the adjudicator or the Tribunal, the court will not consider that evidence unless it is satisfied that there were good reasons why it was not submitted to the adjudicator or the Tribunal.
(3) The court may—
 (a) affirm the Tribunal's decision to refuse permission to appeal;
 (b) reverse the Tribunal's decision to grant permission to appeal; or
 (c) order the Asylum and Immigration Tribunal to reconsider the adjudicator's decision on the appeal.
(4) Where the Tribunal refused permission to appeal, the court will order the Asylum and Immigration Tribunal to reconsider the adjudicator's decision on the appeal only if it is satisfied that—
 (a) the Tribunal may have made an error of law; and
 (b) there is a real possibility that the Asylum and Immigration Tribunal would make a different decision from the adjudicator on reconsidering the appeal (which may include making a different direction under section 87 of the 2002 Act).
(5) Where the Tribunal granted permission to appeal, the court will reverse the Tribunal's decision only if it is satisfied that there is no real possibility that the Asylum and Immigration Tribunal, on reconsidering the adjudicator's decision on the appeal, would make a different decision from the adjudicator.
(6) The court's decision shall be final and there shall be no appeal from that decision or renewal of the application.

## 54.26 Service of Order

(1) The court will send copies of its order to—
 (a) the applicant, except where paragraph (2) applies;
 (b) the other party; and
 (c) the Asylum and Immigration Tribunal.
(2) Where—
 (a) the application relates, in whole or in part, to a claim for asylum;
 (b) the Tribunal refused permission to appeal; and
 (c) the court affirms the Tribunal's decision,
 the court will send a copy of its order to the Secretary of State, who must serve the order on the applicant.
(3) Where the Secretary of State has served an order in accordance with paragraph (2), he must notify the court on what date and by what method the order was served.
(4) If the court issues a certificate under section 101(3)(d) of the Act, it will send a copy of the certificate together with the order to—
 (a) the persons to whom it sends the order under paragraphs (1) and (2); and
 (b) if the applicant is in receipt of public funding, the Legal Services Commission.

### 54.27 Costs

The court may reserve the costs of the application to be determined by the Asylum and Immigration Tribunal.

## III APPLICATIONS FOR STATUTORY REVIEW UNDER SECTION 103A OF THE NATIONALITY, IMMIGRATION AND ASYLUM ACT 2002

### 54.28 Scope and Interpretation

(1) This Section of this Part contains rules about applications to the High Court under section 103A of the Nationality, Immigration and Asylum Act 2002[3] for an order requiring the Asylum and Immigration Tribunal to reconsider its decision on an appeal.

(2) In this Section—
  (a) 'the 2002 Act' means the Nationality, Immigration and Asylum Act 2002;
  (b) 'the 2004 Act' means the Asylum and Immigration (Treatment of Claimants, etc.) Act 2004;[4]
  (c) 'appellant' means the appellant in the proceedings before the Tribunal;
  (d) 'applicant' means a person applying to the High Court under section 103A;
  (e) 'asylum claim' has the meaning given in section 113(1) of the 2002 Act;
  (ea) 'fast track case' means any case in relation to which an order made under section 26(8) of the 2004 Act provides that the time period for making an application under section 103A(1) of the 2002 Act or giving notification under paragraph 30(5) of Schedule 2 to the 2004 Act is less than 5 days;
  (f) 'filter provision' means paragraph 30 of Schedule 2 to the 2004 Act;
  (g) 'order for reconsideration' means an order under section 103A(1) requiring the Tribunal to reconsider its decision on an appeal;
  (h) 'section 103A' means section 103A of the 2002 Act;
  (i) 'Tribunal' means the Asylum and Immigration Tribunal.

(3) Any reference in this Section to a period of time specified in—
  (a) section 103A(3) for making an application for an order under section 103A(1); or
  (b) paragraph 30(5)(b) of Schedule 2 to the 2004 Act for giving notice under that paragraph, includes a reference to that period as varied by any order under section 26(8) of the 2004 Act.

(4) Rule 2.8 applies to the calculation of the periods of time specified in—
  (a) section 103A(3); and
  (b) paragraph 30(5)(b) of Schedule 2 to the 2004 Act.

(5) Save as provided otherwise, the provisions of this Section apply to an application under section 103A regardless of whether the filter provision has effect in relation to that application.

### 54.28A Representation of Applicants while Filter Provision has Effect

(1) This rule applies during any period in which the filter provision has effect.

(2) An applicant may, for the purpose of taking any step under rule 54.29 or 54.30, be represented by any person permitted to provide him with immigration advice or immigration services under section 84 of the Immigration and Asylum Act 1999.

(3) A representative acting for an applicant under paragraph (2) shall be regarded as the applicant's legal representative for the purpose of rule 22.1 (documents to be verified by a statement of truth) regardless of whether he would otherwise be so regarded.

[3] 2002 c.41.

[4] 2004 c.19.

## 54.28B Service of Documents on Appellants within the Jurisdiction

(1) In proceedings under this Section, rules 6.4(2) and 6.5(5) do not apply to the service of documents on an appellant who is within the jurisdiction.

(2) Where a representative is acting for an appellant who is within the jurisdiction, a document must be served on the appellant by—
- (a) serving it on his representative; or
- (b) serving it on the appellant personally or sending it to his address by first class post (or an alternative service which provides for delivery on the next working day),

but if the document is served on the appellant under sub-paragraph (b), a copy must also at the same time be sent to his representative.

## 54.29 Application for Review

(1) Subject to paragraph (5), an application for an order for reconsideration must be made by filing an application notice—
- (a) during a period in which the filter provision has effect, with the Tribunal at the address specified in the relevant practice direction; and
- (b) at any other time, at the Administrative Court Office.

(2) During any period in which the filter provision does not have effect, the applicant must file with the application notice—
- (a) the notice of the immigration, asylum or nationality decision to which the appeal related;
- (b) any other document which was served on the appellant giving reasons for that decision;
- (c) the grounds of appeal to the Tribunal;
- (d) the Tribunal's determination on the appeal; and
- (e) any other documents material to the application which were before the Tribunal.

(2A) During any period in which the filter provision has effect, the applicant must file with the application notice a list of the documents referred to in paragraph (2)(a) to (e).

(3) The applicant must also file with the application notice written submissions setting out—
- (a) the grounds upon which it is contended that the Tribunal made an error of law which may have affected its decision; and
- (b) reasons in support of those grounds.

(4) Where the applicant—
- (a) was the respondent to the appeal; and
- (b) was required to serve the Tribunal's determination on the appellant,

the application notice must contain a statement of the date on which, and the means by which, the determination was served.

(5) Where the applicant is in detention under the Immigration Acts, the application may be made either—
- (a) in accordance with paragraphs (1) to (3); or
- (b) by serving the documents specified in paragraphs (1) to (3) on the person having custody of him.

(6) Where an application is made in accordance with paragraph (5)(b), the person on whom the application notice is served must—
- (a) endorse on the notice the date that it is served on him;
- (b) give the applicant an acknowledgment in writing of receipt of the notice; and
- (c) forward the notice and documents within 2 days
  - (i) during a period in which the filter provision has effect, to the Tribunal; and
  - (ii) at any other time, to the Administrative Court Office.

## 54.30 Application to Extend Time Limit

An application to extend the time limit for making an application under section 103A(1) must—

(a) be made in the application notice;
(b) set out the grounds on which it is contended that the application notice could not reasonably practicably have been filed within the time limit; and
(c) be supported by written evidence verified by a statement of truth.

## 54.31 Procedure while Filter Provision has Effect

(1) This rule applies during any period in which the filter provision has effect.
(2) Where the applicant receives notice from the Tribunal that it—
(a) does not propose to make an order for reconsideration; or
(b) does not propose to grant permission for the application to be made outside the relevant time limit,
and the applicant wishes the court to consider the application, the applicant must file a notice in writing at the Administrative Court Office in accordance with paragraph 30(5)(b) of Schedule 2 to the 2004 Act.
(2A) The applicant must file with the notice—
(a) a copy of the Tribunal's notification that it does not propose to make an order for reconsideration or does not propose to grant permission for the application to be made outside the relevant time limit (referred to in CPR rule 54.31(2));
(b) any other document which was served on the applicant by the Tribunal giving reasons for its decision in paragraph (a);
(c) written evidence in support of any application by the applicant seeking permission to make the application outside the relevant time limit, if applicable;
(d) a copy of the application for reconsideration under section 103A of the 2002 Act (Form AIT/103A), as submitted to the Tribunal (referred to in Rule 54.29(1)(a).
1(3) Where the applicant—
(a) was the respondent to the appeal; and
(b) was required to serve the notice from the Tribunal mentioned in paragraph (2) on the appellant,
the notice filed in accordance with paragraph 30(5)(b) of Schedule 2 to the 2004 Act must contain a statement of the date on which, and the means by which, the notice from the Tribunal was served.
(4) A notice which is filed outside the period specified in paragraph 30(5)(b) must—
(a) set out the grounds on which it is contended that the notice could not reasonably practicably have been filed within that period; and
(b) be supported by written evidence verified by a statement of truth.
(5) If the applicant wishes to respond to the reasons given by the Tribunal for its decision that it—
(a) does not propose to make an order for reconsideration; or
(b) does not propose to grant permission for the application to be made outside the relevant time limit,
the notice filed in accordance with paragraph 30(5)(b) of Schedule 2 to the 2004 Act must be accompanied by written submissions setting out the grounds upon which the applicant disputes any of the reasons given by the Tribunal and giving reasons in support of those grounds.

## 54.32 Procedure in Fast Track Cases while Filter Provision does not have Effect

(1) This rule applies only during a period in which the filter provision does not have effect.
(2) Where a party applies for an order for reconsideration in a fast track case—
(a) the court will serve copies of the application notice and written submissions on the other party to the appeal; and
(b) the other party to the appeal may file submissions in response to the application not later than 2 days after being served with the application.

## 54.33 Determination of the Application by the Administrative Court

(1) This rule, and rules 54.34 and 54.35, apply to applications under section 103A which are determined by the Administrative Court.

(2) The application will be considered by a single judge without a hearing.

(3) Unless it orders otherwise, the court will not receive evidence which was not submitted to the Tribunal.

(4) Subject to paragraph (5), where the court determines an application for an order for reconsideration, it may—

(a) dismiss the application;

(b) make an order requiring the Tribunal to reconsider its decision on the appeal under section 103A(1) of the 2002 Act; or

(c) refer the appeal to the Court of Appeal under section 103C of the 2002 Act.

(5) The court will only make an order requiring the Tribunal to reconsider its decision on an appeal if it thinks that—

(a) the Tribunal may have made an error of law; and

(b) there is a real possibility that the Tribunal would make a different decision on reconsidering the appeal (which may include making a different direction under section 87 of the 2002 Act).

(6) Where the Court of Appeal has restored the application to the court under section 103C(2)(g) of the 2002 Act, the court may not refer the appeal to the Court of Appeal.

(7) The court's decision shall be final and there shall be no appeal from that decision or renewal of the application.

## 54.34 Service of Order

(1) The court will send copies of its order to—

(a) the applicant and the other party to the appeal, except where paragraph (2) applies; and

(b) the Tribunal.

(2) Where the appellant is within the jurisdiction and the application relates, in whole or in part, to an asylum claim, the court will send a copy of its order to the Secretary of State.

(2A) Paragraph (2) does not apply in a fast track case.

(3) Where the court sends an order to the Secretary of State under paragraph (2), the Secretary of State must—

(a) serve the order on the appellant; and

(b) immediately after serving the order, notify—

(i) the court; and

(ii) where the order requires the Tribunal to reconsider its decision on the appeal, the Tribunal,

on what date and by what method the order was served.

(4) The Secretary of State must provide the notification required by paragraph (3)(b) no later than 28 days after the date on which the court sends him a copy of its order.

(5) If, 28 days after the date on which the court sends a copy of its order to the Secretary of State in accordance with paragraph (2), the Secretary of State has not provided the notification required by paragraph (3)(b)(i), the court may serve the order on the appellant.

(5A) Where the court serves an order for reconsideration under paragraph (5), it will notify the Tribunal of the date on which the order was served.

(6) If the court makes an order under section 103D(1) of the 2002 Act, it will send copies of that order to—

(a) the appellant's legal representative; and

(b) the Legal Services Commission.

(7) Where paragraph (2) applies, the court will not serve copies of an order under section 103D(1) of the 2002 Act until either—
   (a) the Secretary of State has provided the notification required by paragraph (3)(b); or
   (b) 28 days after the date on which the court sent a copy of its order to the Secretary of State,

whichever is the earlier.

### 54.35 Costs

The court shall make no order as to the costs of an application under this Section except, where appropriate, an order under section 103D(1) of the 2002 Act.

### 54.36 Continuing an application in circumstances in which it would otherwise be treated as abandoned

(1) This rule applies to an application under section 103A of the 2002 Act which—
   (a) would otherwise be treated as abandoned under section 104(4A) of the 2002 Act; but
   (b) meets the conditions set out in section 104(4B) or section 104(4C) of the 2002 Act.

(2) Where section 104(4A) of the 2002 Act applies and the applicant wishes to pursue the application, the applicant must file a notice at the Administrative Court Office—
   (a) where section 104(4B) of the 2002 Act applies, within 28 days of the date on which the applicant received notice of the grant of leave to enter or remain in the United Kingdom for a period exceeding 12 months; or
   (b) where section 104(4C) of the 2002 Act applies, within 28 days of the date on which the applicant received notice of the grant of leave to enter or remain in the United Kingdom.

(3) Where the applicant does not comply with the time limits specified in paragraph (2), the application will be treated as abandoned in accordance with section 104(4) of the 2002 Act.

(4) The applicant must serve the notice filed under paragraph (2) on the other party to the appeal.

(5) Where section 104(4B) of the 2002 Act applies, the notice filed under paragraph (2) must state—
   (a) the applicant's full name and date of birth;
   (b) the Administrative Court reference number;
   (c) the Home Office reference number, if applicable;
   (d) the date on which the applicant was granted leave to enter or remain in the United Kingdom for a period exceeding 12 months; and
   (e) that the applicant wishes to pursue the application insofar as it is brought on grounds relating to the Refugee Convention specified in section 84(1)(g) of the 2002 Act.

(6) Where section 104(4C) of the 2002 Act applies, the notice filed under paragraph (2) must state—
   (a) the applicant's full name and date of birth;
   (b) the Administrative Court reference number;
   (c) the Home Office reference number, if applicable;
   (d) the date on which the applicant was granted leave to enter or remain in the United Kingdom; and
   (e) that the applicant wishes to pursue the application insofar as it is brought on grounds relating to section 19B of the Race Relations Act 1976 specified in section 84(1)(b) of the 2002 Act.

(7) Where an applicant has filed a notice under paragraph (2) the court will notify the applicant of the date on which it received the notice.

(8) The court will send a copy of the notice issued under paragraph (7) to the other party to the appeal.

# PD 54 Practice Direction — Judicial Review

This practice direction supplements CPR Part 54.

## SECTION I—GENERAL PROVISIONS RELATING TO JUDICIAL REVIEW

1.1 In addition to Part 54 and this practice direction attention is drawn to:
- s. 31 of the Supreme Court Act 1981; and
- the Human Rights Act 1998.

### The Court

2.1 Part 54 claims for judicial review are dealt with in the Administrative Court.

2.2 Where the claim is proceeding in the Administrative Court in London, documents must be filed at the Administrative Court Office, the Royal Courts of Justice, Strand, London WC2A 2LL.

2.3 Where the claim is proceeding in the Administrative Court in Wales (see para. 3.1), documents must be filed at the Civil Justice Centre, 2 Park Street, Cardiff CF10 1ET.

*Urgent applications*

2.4 Where urgency makes it necessary for the claim for judicial review to be made outside London or Cardiff, the Administrative Court Office in London should be consulted (if necessary, by telephone) prior to filing the claim form.

### Judicial Review Claims in Wales

3.1 A claim for judicial review may be brought in the Administrative Court in Wales where the claim or any remedy sought involves:
(1) a devolution issue arising out of the Government of Wales Act 1998; or
(2) an issue concerning the National Assembly for Wales, the Welsh executive, or any Welsh public body (including a Welsh local authority) (whether or not it involves a devolution issue).

3.2 Such claims may also be brought in the Administrative Court at the Royal Courts of Justice.

### Time Limit for Filing Claim Form: Rule 54.5

4.1 Where the claim is for a quashing order in respect of a judgment, order or conviction, the date when the grounds to make the claim first arise, for the purposes of r. 54.5(1)(b), is the date of that judgment, order or conviction.

### Claim Form: Rule 54.6

*Interested parties*

5.1 Where the claim for judicial review relates to proceedings in a court or tribunal, any other parties to those proceedings must be named in the claim form as interested parties under r. 54.6(1)(a) (and therefore served with the claim form under r. 54.7(b)).

5.2 For example, in a claim by a defendant in a criminal case in the magistrates' or Crown Court for judicial review of a decision in that case, the prosecution must always be named as an interested party.

*Human rights*

5.3 Where the claimant is seeking to raise any issue under the Human Rights Act 1998, or seeks a remedy available under that Act, the claim form must include the information required by PD 16, para. 15.

*Devolution issues*

5.4 Where the claimant intends to raise a devolution issue, the claim form must:

(1) specify that the applicant wishes to raise a devolution issue and identify the relevant provisions of the Government of Wales Act 1998, the Northern Ireland Act 1998 or the Scotland Act 1998; and
(2) contain a summary of the facts, circumstances and points of law on the basis of which it is alleged that a devolution issue arises.

5.5 In this practice direction 'devolution issue' has the same meaning as in the Government of Wales Act 1998, sch. 8, para. 1; the Northern Ireland Act 1998, sch. 10, para. 1; and the Scotland Act 1998, sch. 6, para. 1.

*Claim form*

5.6 The claim form must include or be accompanied by:
(1) a detailed statement of the claimant's grounds for bringing the claim for judicial review;
(2) a statement of the facts relied on;
(3) any application to extend the time limit for filing the claim form;
(4) any application for directions.

5.7 In addition, the claim form must be accompanied by:
(1) any written evidence in support of the claim or application to extend time;
(2) a copy of any order that the claimant seeks to have quashed;
(3) where the claim for judicial review relates to a decision of a court or tribunal, an approved copy of the reasons for reaching that decision;
(4) copies of any documents on which the claimant proposes to rely;
(5) copies of any relevant statutory material;
(6) a list of essential documents for advance reading by the court (with page references to the passages relied on); and

5.8 Where it is not possible to file all the above documents, the claimant must indicate which documents have not been filed and the reasons why they are not currently available.

*Bundle of documents*

5.9 The claimant must file two copies of a paginated and indexed bundle containing all the documents referred to in paras 5.6 and 5.7.

5.10 Attention is drawn to r. 8.5(1) and (7).

## Service of Claim Form: Rule 54.7

6.1 Except as required by r. 54.11 or 54.12(2), the Administrative Court will not serve documents and service must be effected by the parties.

## Acknowledgment of Service: Rule 54.8

7.1 Attention is drawn to r. 8.3(2) and PD 8 and to r. 10.5.

## Permission Given: Rule 54.10

*Directions*

8.1 Case management directions under r. 54.10(1) may include directions about serving the claim form and any evidence on other persons.

8.2 Where a claim is made under the Human Rights Act 1998, a direction may be made for giving notice to the Crown or joining the Crown as a party. Attention is drawn to r. 19.4A and PD 19, para. 6.

8.3 A direction may be made for the hearing of the claim for judicial review to be held outside London or Cardiff. Before making any such direction the judge will consult the judge in charge of the Administrative Court as to its feasibility.

*Permission without a hearing*

8.4 The court will generally, in the first instance, consider the question of permission without a hearing.

*Permission hearing*

8.5 Neither the defendant nor any other interested party need attend a hearing on the question of permission unless the court directs otherwise.

8.6 Where the defendant or any party does attend a hearing, the court will not generally make an order for costs against the claimant.

## Service of Order Giving or Refusing Permission: Rule 54.11

9.1 An order refusing permission or giving it subject to conditions or on certain grounds only must set out or be accompanied by the court's reasons for coming to that decision.

## Response: Rule 54.14

10.1 Where the party filing the detailed grounds intends to rely on documents not already filed, he must file a paginated bundle of those documents when he files the detailed grounds.

## Where Claimant Seeks to Rely on Additional Grounds: Rule 54.15

11.1 Where the claimant intends to apply to rely on additional grounds at the hearing of the claim for judicial review, he must give notice to the court and to any other person served with the claim form no later than seven clear days before the hearing (or the warned date where appropriate).

## Evidence: Rule 54.16

12.1 Disclosure is not required unless the court orders otherwise.

## Court's Powers to Hear Any Person: Rule 54.17

13.1 Where all the parties consent, the court may deal with an application under r. 54.17 without a hearing.

13.2 Where the court gives permission for a person to file evidence or make representations at the hearing of the claim for judicial review, it may do so on conditions and may give case management directions.

13.3 An application for permission should be made by letter to the Administrative Court office, identifying the claim, explaining who the applicant is and indicating why and in what form the applicant wants to participate in the hearing.

13.4 If the applicant is seeking a prospective order as to costs, the letter should say what kind of order and on what grounds.

13.5 Applications to intervene must be made at the earliest reasonable opportunity, since it will usually be essential not to delay the hearing.

## Transfer: Rule 54.20

14.1 Attention is drawn to r. 30.5.

14.2 In deciding whether a claim is suitable for transfer to the Administrative Court, the court will consider whether it raises issues of public law to which Part 54 should apply.

*Skeleton arguments*

15.1 The claimant must file and serve a skeleton argument not less than 21 working days before the date of the hearing of the judicial review (or the warned date).

15.2 The defendant and any other party wishing to make representations at the hearing of the judicial review must file and serve a skeleton argument not less than 14 working days before the date of the hearing of the judicial review (or the warned date).

15.3 Skeleton arguments must contain:

(1) a time estimate for the complete hearing, including delivery of judgment;

(2) a list of issues;

(3) a list of the legal points to be taken (together with any relevant authorities with page references to the passages relied on);

(4) a chronology of events (with page references to the bundle of documents (see para. 16.1);
(5) a list of essential documents for the advance reading of the court (with page references to the passages relied on) (if different from that filed with the claim form) and a time estimate for that reading; and
(6) a list of persons referred to.

### Bundle of Documents to be Filed

16.1 The claimant must file a paginated and indexed bundle of all relevant documents required for the hearing of the judicial review when he files his skeleton argument.
16.2 The bundle must also include those documents required by the defendant and any other party who is to make representations at the hearing.

### Agreed Final Order

17.1 If the parties agree about the final order to be made in a claim for judicial review, the claimant must file at the court a document (with two copies) signed by all the parties setting out the terms of the proposed agreed order together with a short statement of the matters relied on as justifying the proposed agreed order and copies of any authorities or statutory provisions relied on.
17.2 The court will consider the documents referred to in para. 17.1 and will make the order if satisfied that the order should be made.
17.3 If the court is not satisfied that the order should be made, a hearing date will be set.
17.4 Where the agreement relates to an order for costs only, the parties need only file a document signed by all the parties setting out the terms of the proposed order.

## SECTION II—APPLICATIONS FOR PERMISSION TO APPLY FOR JUDICIAL REVIEW IN IMMIGRATION AND ASYLUM CASES—CHALLENGING REMOVAL

18.1 (1) This Section applies where—
(a) a person has been served with a copy of directions for his removal from the United Kingdom by the Immigration and Nationality Directorate of the Home Office and notified that this Section applies; and
(b) that person makes an application for permission to apply for judicial review before his removal takes effect.
(2) This Section does not prevent a person from applying for judicial review after he has been removed.
(3) The requirements contained in this Section of this Practice Direction are additional to those contained elsewhere in the Practice Direction.
18.2 (1) A person who makes an application for permission to apply for judicial review must file a claim form and a copy at court, and the claim form must—
(a) indicate on its face that this Section of the Practice Direction applies; and
(b) be accompanied by—
(i) a copy of the removal directions and the decision to which the application relates; and
(ii) any document served with the removal directions including any document which contains the Immigration and Nationality Directorate's factual summary of the case; and
(c) contain or be accompanied by the detailed statement of the claimant's grounds for bringing the claim for judicial review; or
(d) if the claimant is unable to comply with paragraph (b) or (c), contain or be accompanied by a statement of the reasons why.
(2) The claimant must, immediately upon issue of the claim, send copies of the issued

claim form and accompanying documents to the address specified by the Immigration and Nationality Directorate.

(Rule 54.7 also requires the defendant to be served with the claim form within 7 days of the date of issue. Rule 6.5(8) provides that service on a Government Department must be effected on the solicitor acting for that Department, which in the case of the Immigration and Nationality Directorate is the Treasury Solicitor. The address for the Treasury Solicitor may be found in the Annex to Part 66 of these Rules.)

18.3 Where the claimant has not complied with paragraph 18.2(1)(b) or (c) and has provided reasons why he is unable to comply, and the court has issued the claim form, the Administrative Court—

(a) will refer the matter to a Judge for consideration as soon as practicable; and

(b) will notify the parties that it has done so.

18.4 If, upon a refusal to grant permission to apply for judicial review, the Court indicates that the application is clearly without merit, that indication will be included in the order refusing permission.

# PD 54B Practice Direction — Applications for Statutory Review under Section 103A of The Nationality, Immigration and Asylum Act 2002

This practice direction supplements Section III of CPR Part 54.

1 Attention is drawn to:
- Sections 103A, 103C and 103D of the Nationality, Immigration and Asylum Act 2002 (inserted by section 26(6) of the Asylum and Immigration (Treatment of Claimants, etc.) Act 2004); and
- (2) Paragraph 30 of Schedule 2 to the 2004 Act.

## The Court

2.1 Applications for review under section 103A(1) of the 2002 Act are dealt with in the Administrative Court, subject to the transitional filter provision in paragraph 30 of Schedule 2 of the 2004 Act which provides that they shall initially be considered by a member of the Tribunal.

2.2 During any period in which the filter provision has effect, the address for filing section 103A applications shall be the Asylum and Immigration Tribunal, P.O. Box 6987, Leicester LE1 6ZX.

2.3 Where a fast track order within the meaning of Rule 54.32(3) applies to a section 103A application, paragraph 2.2 shall not apply and the address for filing the application shall be the address specified in the Tribunal's determination of the appeal.

## Access to Court Orders served on the Appellant by the Secretary of State

3.1 Where the court sends a copy of its order on a section 103A application to the Secretary of State but not the appellant in accordance with rule 54.34(2), then rules 5.4(3)(b) and 5.4(5)(a)(ii) are modified as follows.

3.2 Neither the appellant nor any other person may obtain from the records of the court a copy of the court's order on the section 103A application, or of any order made under section 103D(1) of the 2002 Act in relation to that application, until either the Secretary of State has given the court the notification required by rule 54.34(3)(b) or 28 days after the date on which the court sent a copy of the order to the Secretary of State, whichever is the earlier.

## Referral to Court of Appeal

4.1 Where the court refers an appeal to the Court of Appeal, its order will set out the question of law raised by the appeal which is of such importance that it should be decided by the Court of Appeal.

4.2 Paragraph 21.7A of the practice direction supplementing Part 52 makes provision about appeals which are referred to the Court of Appeal.

# PD 54C Practice Direction — References by the Legal Services Commission

## References by the Legal Services Commission

1.1 This Practice Direction applies where the Legal Services Commission ('the Commission') refers to the High Court a question that arises on a review of a decision about an individual's financial eligibility for a representation order in criminal proceedings under the Criminal Defence Service (Financial Eligibility) Regulations 2006.

1.2 A reference of a question by the Legal Services Commission must be made to the Administrative Court.

1.3 Part 52 does not apply to a review under this paragraph.

1.4 The Commission must—

(a) file at the court—

(i) the individual's applications for a representation order and for a review, and any supporting documents;

(ii) a copy of the question on which the court's decision is sought; and

(iii) a statement of the Commission's observations on the question; and

(b) serve a copy of the question and the statement on the individual.

1.5 The individual may file representations on the question at the court within 7 days after service on him of the copy of the question and the statement.

1.6 The question will be decided without a hearing unless the court directs otherwise.

# CPR Part 55 Possession Claims



## 55.1 Interpretation

In this Part—

(a) 'a possession claim' means a claim for the recovery of possession of land (including buildings or parts of buildings);
(b) 'a possession claim against trespassers' means a claim for the recovery of land which the claimant alleges is occupied only by a person or persons who entered or remained on the land without the consent of a person entitled to possession of that land but does not include a claim against a tenant or sub-tenant whether his tenancy has been terminated or not;
(c) 'mortgage' includes a legal or equitable mortgage and a legal or equitable charge and 'mortgagee' is to be interpreted accordingly;
(d) 'the 1985 Act' means the Housing Act 1985;[1]
(e) 'the 1988 Act' means the Housing Act 1988;[2]
(f) 'a demotion claim' means a claim made by a landlord for an order under section 82A of the 1985 Act or section 6A of the 1988 Act ('a demotion order');
(g) 'a demoted tenancy' means a tenancy created by virtue of a demotion order; and
(h) 'a suspension claim' means a claim made by a landlord for an order under section 121A of the 1985 Act.

## I GENERAL RULES

## 55.2 Scope

(1) The procedure set out in this Section of this Part must be used where the claim includes—
    (a) a possession claim brought by a—
        (i) landlord (or former landlord);
        (ii) mortgagee; or
        (iii) licensor (or former licensor);

---

[1] 1985 c.68.
[2] 1988 c.50.

(b) a possession claim against trespassers; or
(c) a claim by a tenant seeking relief from forfeiture.

(Where a demotion claim or a suspension claim (or both) is made in the same claim form in which a possession claim is started, this Section of this Part applies as modified by rule 65.12. Where the claim is a demotion claim or a suspension claim only, or a suspension claim made in addition to a demotion claim, Section III of Part 65 applies.)

(2) This Section of this Part—
(a) is subject to any enactment or practice direction which sets out special provisions with regard to any particular category of claim;
(b) does not apply where the claimant uses the procedure set out in Section II of this Part; and
(c) does not apply where the claimant seeks an interim possession order under Section III of this Part except where the court orders otherwise or that Section so provides.

## 55.3 Starting the Claim

(1) The claim must be started in the county court for the district in which the land is situated unless paragraph (2) applies or an enactment provides otherwise.
(2) The claim may be started in the High Court if the claimant files with his claim form a certificate stating the reasons for bringing the claim in that court verified by a statement of truth in accordance with rule 22.1(1).
(3) The practice direction refers to circumstances which may justify starting the claim in the High Court.
(4) Where, in a possession claim against trespassers, the claimant does not know the name of a person in occupation or possession of the land, the claim must be brought against 'persons unknown' in addition to any named defendants.
(5) The claim form and form of defence sent with it must be in the forms set out in the relevant practice direction.

## 55.4 Particulars of Claim

The particulars of claim must be filed and served with the claim form.

(The relevant practice direction and Part 16 provide details about the contents of the particulars of claim.)

## 55.5 Hearing Date

(1) The court will fix a date for the hearing when it issues the claim form.
(2) In a possession claim against trespassers the defendant must be served with the claim form, particulars of claim and any witness statements—
(a) in the case of residential property, not less than 5 days; and
(b) in the case of other land, not less than 2 days,
before the hearing date.
(3) In all other possession claims—
(a) the hearing date will be not less than 28 days from the date of issue of the claim form;
(b) the standard period between the issue of the claim form and the hearing will be not more than 8 weeks; and
(c) the defendant must be served with the claim form and particulars of claim not less than 21 days before the hearing date.

(Rule 3.1(2)(a) provides that the court may extend or shorten the time for compliance with any rule.)

## 55.6 Service of Claims Against Trespassers

Where, in a possession claim against trespassers, the claim has been issued against 'persons unknown', the claim form, particulars of claim and any witness statements must be served on those persons by—

(a) (i) attaching copies of the claim form, particulars of claim and any witness statements to the main door or some other part of the land so that they are clearly visible; and
(ii) if practicable, inserting copies of those documents in a sealed transparent envelope addressed to 'the occupiers' through the letter box; or

(b) placing stakes in the land in places where they are clearly visible and attaching to each stake copies of the claim form, particulars of claim and any witness statements in a sealed transparent envelope addressed to 'the occupiers'.

## 55.7 Defendant's Response

(1) An acknowledgment of service is not required and Part 10 does not apply.
(2) In a possession claim against trespassers rule 15.2 does not apply and the defendant need not file a defence.
(3) Where, in any other possession claim, the defendant does not file a defence within the time specified in rule 15.4, he may take part in any hearing but the court may take his failure to do so into account when deciding what order to make about costs.
(4) Part 12 (default judgment) does not apply in a claim to which this Part applies.

## 55.8 The Hearing

(1) At the hearing fixed in accordance with rule 55.5(1) or at any adjournment of that hearing, the court may—
(a) decide the claim; or
(b) give case management directions.
(2) Where the claim is genuinely disputed on grounds which appear to be substantial, case management directions given under paragraph (1)(b) will include the allocation of the claim to a track or directions to enable it to be allocated.
(3) Except where—
(a) the claim is allocated to the fast track or the multi-track; or
(b) the court orders otherwise,
any fact that needs to be proved by the evidence of witnesses at a hearing referred to in paragraph (1) may be proved by evidence in writing.

(Rule 32.2(1) sets out the general rule about evidence. Rule 32.2(2) provides that rule 32.2(1) is subject to any provision to the contrary.)

(4) Subject to paragraph (5), all witness statements must be filed and served at least 2 days before the hearing.
(5) In a possession claim against trespassers all witness statements on which the claimant intends to rely must be filed and served with the claim form.
(6) Where the claimant serves the claim form and particulars of claim, he must produce at the hearing a certificate of service of those documents and rule 6.14(2)(a) does not apply.

## 55.9 Allocation

(1) When the court decides the track for a possession claim, the matters to which it shall have regard include—
(a) the matters set out in rule 26.8 as modified by the relevant practice direction;
(b) the amount of any arrears of rent or mortgage instalments;
(c) the importance to the defendant of retaining possession of the land; and
(d) the importance of vacant possession to the claimant; and
(e) if applicable, the alleged conduct of the defendant.
(2) The court will only allocate possession claims to the small claims track if all the parties agree.
(3) Where a possession claim has been allocated to the small claims track the claim shall be treated, for the purposes of costs, as if it were proceeding on the fast track except that trial costs shall be in the discretion of the court and shall not exceed the amount that

would be recoverable under rule 46.2 (amount of fast track costs) if the value of the claim were up to £3,000.

(4) Where all the parties agree the court may, when it allocates the claim, order that rule 27.14 (costs on the small claims track) applies and, where it does so, paragraph (3) does not apply.

### 55.10 Possession Claims Relating to Mortgaged Residential Property

(1) This rule applies where a mortgagee seeks possession of land which consists of or includes residential property.

(2) Not less than 14 days before the hearing the claimant must send a notice to the property addressed to 'the occupiers'.

(3) The notice referred to in paragraph (2) must—
  (a) state that a possession claim for the property has started;
  (b) show the name and address of the claimant, the defendant and the court which issued the claim form; and
  (c) give details of the hearing.

(4) The claimant must produce at the hearing—
  (a) copy of the notice; and
  (b) evidence that he has served it.

## II ACCELERATED POSSESSION CLAIMS OF PROPERTY LET ON AN ASSURED SHORTHOLD TENANCY

### 55.11 When this Section May be Used

(1) The claimant may bring a possession claim under this Section of this Part where—
  (a) the claim is brought under section 21 of the 1988 Act to recover possession of residential property let under an assured shorthold tenancy; and
  (b) subject to rule 55.12(2), all the conditions listed in rule 55.12(1) are satisfied.

(2) The claim must be started in the county court for the district in which the property is situated.

(3) In this Section of this Part, a 'demoted assured shorthold tenancy' means a demoted tenancy where the landlord is a registered social landlord. (By virtue of section 20B of the 1988 Act, a demoted assured shorthold tenancy is an assured shorthold tenancy.)

### 55.12 Conditions

(1) The conditions referred to in rule 55.11(1)(b) are that—
  (a) the tenancy and any agreement for the tenancy were entered into on or after 15 January 1989;
  (b) the only purpose of the claim is to recover possession of the property and no other claim is made;
  (c) the tenancy did not immediately follow an assured tenancy which was not an assured shorthold tenancy;
  (d) the tenancy fulfilled the conditions provided by section 19A or 20(1)(a) to (c) of the 1988 Act;
  (e) the tenancy—
    (i) was the subject of a written agreement;
    (ii) arises by virtue of section 5 of the 1988 Act but follows a tenancy that was the subject of a written agreement; or
    (iii) relates to the same or substantially the same property let to the same tenant and on the same terms (though not necessarily as to rent or duration) as a tenancy which was the subject of a written agreement; and
  (f) a notice in accordance with sections 21(1) or 21(4) of the 1988 Act was given to the tenant in writing.

(2) If the tenancy is a demoted assured shorthold tenancy, only the conditions in paragraphs (1)(b) and (f) need be satisfied.

## 55.13 Claim Form

(1) The claim form must—
  (a) be in the form set out in the relevant practice direction; and
  (b) (i) contain such information; and
    (ii) be accompanied by such documents, as are required by that form.
(2) All relevant sections of the form must be completed.
(3) The court will serve the claim form by first class post (or an alternative service which provides for delivery on the next working day).

## 55.14 Defence

(1) A defendant who wishes to—
  (a) oppose the claim; or
  (b) seek a postponement of possession in accordance with rule 55.18,
  must file his defence within 14 days after service of the claim form.
(2) The defence should be in the form set out in the relevant practice direction.

## 55.15 Claim Referred to Judge

(1) On receipt of the defence the court will—
  (a) send a copy to the claimant; and
  (b) refer the claim and defence to a judge.
(2) Where the period set out in rule 55.14 has expired without the defendant filing a defence—
  (a) the claimant may file a written request for an order for possession; and
  (b) the court will refer that request to a judge.
(3) Where the defence is received after the period set out in rule 55.14 has expired but before a request is filed in accordance with paragraph (2), paragraph (1) will still apply.
(4) Where—
  (a) the period set out in rule 55.14 has expired without the defendant filing a defence; and
  (b) the claimant has not made a request for an order for possession under paragraph (2) within 3 months after the expiry of the period set out in rule 55.14,
  the claim will be stayed.

## 55.16 Consideration of the Claim

(1) After considering the claim and any defence, the judge will—
  (a) make an order for possession under rule 55.17;
  (b) where he is not satisfied as to any of the matters set out in paragraph (2)—
    (i) direct that a date be fixed for a hearing; and
    (ii) give any appropriate case management directions; or
  (c) strike out the claim if the claim form discloses no reasonable grounds for bringing the claim.
(2) The matters referred to in paragraph (1)(b) are that—
  (a) the claim form was served; and
  (b) the claimant has established that he is entitled to recover possession under section 21 of the 1988 Act against the defendant.
(3) The court will give all parties not less than 14 days' notice of a hearing fixed under paragraph (1)(b)(i).
(4) Where a claim is struck out under paragraph (1)(c)—
  (a) the court will serve its reasons for striking out the claim with the order; and
  (b) the claimant may apply to restore the claim within 28 days after the date the order was served on him.

### 55.17 Possession Order

Except where rules 55.16(1)(b) or (c) apply, the judge will make an order for possession without requiring the attendance of the parties.

### 55.18 Postponement of Possession

(1) Where the defendant seeks postponement of possession on the ground of exceptional hardship under section 89 of the Housing Act 1980, the judge may direct a hearing of that issue.
(2) Where the judge directs a hearing under paragraph (1)—
  (a) the hearing must be held before the date on which possession is to be given up; and
  (b) the judge will direct how many days' notice the parties must be given of that hearing.
(3) Where the judge is satisfied, on a hearing directed under paragraph (1), that exceptional hardship would be caused by requiring possession to be given up by the date in the order of possession, he may vary the date on which possession must be given up.

### 55.19 Application to Set Aside or Vary

The court may—
(a) on application by a party within 14 days of service of the order; or
(b) of its own initiative,
set aside or vary any order made under rule 55.17.

## III INTERIM POSSESSION ORDERS

### 55.20 When this Section May be Used

(1) This Section of this Part applies where the claimant seeks an Interim Possession Order.
(2) In this Section—
  (a) 'IPO' means Interim Possession Order; and
  (b) 'premises' has the same meaning as in section 12 of the Criminal Law Act 1977.
(3) Where this Section requires an act to be done within a specified number of hours, rule 2.8(4) does not apply.

### 55.21 Conditions for IPO Application

(1) An application for an IPO may be made where the following conditions are satisfied—
  (a) the only claim made is a possession claim against trespassers for the recovery of premises;
  (b) the claimant—
    (i) has an immediate right to possession of the premises; and
    (ii) has had such a right throughout the period of alleged unlawful occupation; and
  (c) the claim is made within 28 days of the date on which the claimant first knew, or ought reasonably to have known, that the defendant (or any of the defendants), was in occupation.
(2) An application for an IPO may not be made against a defendant who entered or remained on the premises with the consent of a person who, at the time consent was given, had an immediate right to possession of the premises.

### 55.22 The Application

(1) Rules 55.3(1) and (4) apply to the claim.
(2) The claim form and the defendant's form of witness statement must be in the form set out in the relevant practice direction.
(3) When he files his claim form, the claimant must also file—
  (a) an application notice in the form set out in the relevant practice direction; and
  (b) written evidence.

(4) The written evidence must be given—
  (a) by the claimant personally; or
  (b) where the claimant is a body corporate, by a duly authorised officer.

(Rule 22.1(6)(b) provides that the statement of truth must be signed by the maker of the witness statement.)

(5) The court will—
  (a) issue—
    (i) the claim form; and
    (ii) the application for the IPO; and
  (b) set a date for the hearing of the application.

(6) The hearing of the application will be as soon as practicable but not less than 3 days after the date of issue.

## 55.23 Service

(1) Within 24 hours of the issue of the application, the claimant must serve on the defendant—
  (a) the claim form;
  (b) the application notice together with the written evidence in support; and
  (c) a blank form for the defendant's witness statement (as set out in the relevant practice direction) which must be attached to the application notice.

(2) The claimant must serve the documents listed in paragraph (1) in accordance with rule 55.6(a).

(3) At or before the hearing the claimant must file a certificate of service in relation to the documents listed in paragraph (1) and rule 6.14(2)(a) does not apply.

## 55.24 Defendant's Response

(1) At any time before the hearing the defendant may file a witness statement in response to the application.

(2) The witness statement should be in the form set out in the relevant practice direction.

## 55.25 Hearing of the Application

(1) In deciding whether to grant an IPO, the court will have regard to whether the claimant has given, or is prepared to give, the following undertakings in support of his application—
  (a) if, after an IPO is made, the court decides that the claimant was not entitled to the order to—
    (i) reinstate the defendant if so ordered by the court; and
    (ii) pay such damages as the court may order; and
  (b) before the claim for possession is finally decided, not to—
    (i) damage the premises;
    (ii) grant a right of occupation to any other person; and
    (iii) damage or dispose of any of the defendant's property.

(2) The court will make an IPO if—
  (a) the claimant has—
    (i) filed a certificate of service of the documents referred to in rule 55.23(1); or
    (ii) proved service of those documents to the satisfaction of the court; and
  (b) the court considers that—
    (i) the conditions set out in rule 55.21(1) are satisfied; and
    (ii) any undertakings given by the claimant as a condition of making the order are adequate.

(3) An IPO will be in the form set out in the relevant practice direction and will require the defendant to vacate the premises specified in the claim form within 24 hours of the service of the order.

(4) On making an IPO the court will set a date for the hearing of the claim for possession which will be not less than 7 days after the date on which the IPO is made.
(5) Where the court does not make an IPO—
  (a) the court will set a date for the hearing of the claim;
  (b) the court may give directions for the future conduct of the claim; and
  (c) subject to such directions, the claim shall proceed in accordance with Section I of this Part.

### 55.26 Service and Enforcement of the IPO

(1) An IPO must be served within 48 hours after it is sealed.
(2) The claimant must serve the IPO on the defendant together with copies of—
  (a) the claim form; and
  (b) the written evidence in support,
  in accordance with rule 55.6(a).
(3) CCR Order 26, rule 17 does not apply to the enforcement of an IPO.
(4) If an IPO is not served within the time limit specified by this rule, the claimant may apply to the court for directions for the claim for possession to continue under Section I of this Part.

### 55.27 After IPO Made

(1) Before the date for the hearing of the claim, the claimant must file a certificate of service in relation to the documents specified in rule 55.26(2).
(2) The IPO will expire on the date of the hearing of the claim.
(3) At the hearing the court may make any order it considers appropriate and may, in particular—
  (a) make a final order for possession;
  (b) dismiss the claim for possession;
  (c) give directions for the claim for possession to continue under Section I of this Part; or
  (d) enforce any of the claimant's undertakings.
(4) Unless the court directs otherwise, the claimant must serve any order or directions in accordance with rule 55.6(a).
(5) CCR Order 24, rule 6 applies to the enforcement of a final order for possession.

### 55.28 Application to Set Aside IPO

(1) If the defendant has left the premises, he may apply on grounds of urgency for the IPO to be set aside before the date of the hearing of the claim.
(2) An application under paragraph (1) must be supported by a witness statement.
(3) On receipt of the application, the court will give directions as to—
  (a) the date for the hearing; and
  (b) the period of notice, if any, to be given to the claimant and the method of service of any such notice.
(4) No application to set aside an IPO may be made under rule 39.3.
(5) Where no notice is required under paragraph (3)(b), the only matters to be dealt with at the hearing of the application to set aside are whether—
  (a) the IPO should be set aside; and
  (b) any undertaking to reinstate the defendant should be enforced,
  and all other matters will be dealt with at the hearing of the claim.
(6) The court will serve on all the parties—
  (a) a copy of the order made under paragraph (5); and
  (b) where no notice was required under paragraph (3)(b), a copy of the defendant's application to set aside and the witness statement in support.
(7) Where notice is required under paragraph (3)(b), the court may treat the hearing of the application to set aside as the hearing of the claim.

# PD 55 Practice Direction — Possession Claims

This practice direction supplements CPR Part 55.

## SECTION I GENERAL RULES

### Starting the Claim: Rule 55.3

1.1 Except where the county court does not have jurisdiction, possession claims should normally be brought in the county court. Only exceptional circumstances justify starting a claim in the High Court.

1.2 If a claimant starts a claim in the High Court and the court decides that it should have been started in the county court, the court will normally either strike the claim out or transfer it to the county court on its own initiative. This is likely to result in delay and the court will normally disallow the costs of starting the claim in the High Court and of any transfer.

1.3 Circumstances which may, in an appropriate case, justify starting a claim in the High Court are if:

(1) there are complicated disputes of fact;
(2) there are points of law of general importance; or
(3) the claim is against trespassers and there is a substantial risk of public disturbance or of serious harm to persons or property which properly require immediate determination.

1.4 The value of the property and the amount of any financial claim may be relevant circumstances, but these factors alone will not normally justify starting the claim in the High Court.

1.5 The claimant must use the appropriate claim form and particulars of claim form set out in Table 1 to PD 4. The defence must be in form N11, N11B, N11M or N11R, as appropriate.

1.6 High Court claims for the possession of land subject to a mortgage will be assigned to the Chancery Division.

1.7 A claim which is not a possession claim may be brought under the procedure set out in Section I of Part 55 if it is started in the same claim form as a possession claim which, by virtue of r. 55.2(1) must be brought in accordance with that Section.

(Rule 7.3 provides that a claimant may use a single claim form to start all claims which can be conveniently disposed of in the same proceedings.)

1.8 For example a claim under the Mobile Homes Act 1983, sch. 1, part 1, paras 4, 5 or 6, may be brought using the procedure set out in Section I of CPR, Part 55, if the claim is started in the same claim form as a claim enforcing the rights referred to in the Caravan Sites Act 1968, s. 3(1)(b) (which, by virtue of CPR, r. 55.2(1), must be brought under Section I of Part 55).

1.9 Where the claim form includes a demotion claim, the claim must be started in the county court for the district in which the land is situated.

### Particulars of Claim: Rule 55.4

2.1 In a possession claim the particulars of claim must:

(1) identify the land to which the claim relates;
(2) state whether the claim relates to residential property;
(3) state the ground on which possession is claimed;
(4) give full details about any mortgage or tenancy agreement; and
(5) give details of every person who, to the best of the claimant's knowledge, is in possession of the property.

*Residential property let on a tenancy*

2.2 Paragraphs 2.3, 2.4 and 2.4A apply if the claim relates to residential property let on a tenancy.

2.3 If the claim includes a claim for non-payment of rent the particulars of claim must set out:

(1) the amount due at the start of the proceedings;

(2) in schedule form, the dates and amounts of all payments due and payments made under the tenancy agreement for a period of 2 years immediately preceding the date of issue, or if the first date of default occurred less than 2 years before the date of issue from the first date of default and a running total of the arrears;

(3) the daily rate of any rent and interest;

(4) any previous steps taken to recover the arrears of rent with full details of any court proceedings; and

(5) any relevant information about the defendant's circumstances, in particular:

(a) whether the defendant is in receipt of social security benefits; and

(b) whether any payments are made on his behalf directly to the claimant under the Social Security Contributions and Benefits Act 1992.

2.3A If the claimant wishes to rely on a history of arrears which is longer than 2 years, he should state this in his particulars and exhibit a full (or longer) schedule to a witness statement.

2.4 If the claimant knows of any person (including a mortgagee) entitled to claim relief against forfeiture as underlessee under s. 146(4) of the Law of Property Act 1925 (or in accordance with s. 38 of the Supreme Court Act 1981, or s. 138(9C) of the County Courts Act 1984):

(1) the particulars of claim must state the name and address of that person; and

(2) the claimant must file a copy of the particulars of claim for service on him.

2.4A If the possession claim relates to the conduct of the tenant, the particulars of claim must state details of the conduct alleged.

*Land subject to a mortgage*

2.5 If the claim is a possession claim by a mortgagee, the particulars of claim must also set out:

(1) if the claim relates to residential property whether:

(a) a land charge of Class F has been registered under s. 2(7) of the Matrimonial Homes Act 1967;

(b) notice registered under s. 2(8) or 8(3) of the Matrimonial Homes Act 1983 has been entered and on whose behalf; or

(c) a notice under s. 31(10) of the Family Law Act 1996 has been registered and on whose behalf; and

if so, that the claimant will serve notice of the claim on the persons on whose behalf the land charge is registered or the notice or caution entered;

(2) the state of the mortgage account by including:

(a) the amount of:

(i) the advance;

(ii) any periodic repayment; and

(iii) any payment of interest required to be made;

(b) the amount which would have to be paid (after taking into account any adjustment for early settlement) in order to redeem the mortgage at a stated date not more than 14 days after the claim started specifying the amount of solicitor's costs and administration charges which would be payable;

(c) if the loan which is secured by the mortgage is a regulated consumer credit agreement, the total amount outstanding under the terms of the mortgage; and

(d) the rate of interest payable:

(i) at the commencement of the mortgage;

(ii) immediately before any arrears referred to in sub-paragraph (3) accrued;
(iii) at the commencement of the proceedings;

(3) if the claim is brought because of failure to pay the periodic payments when due:
(a) in schedule form, the dates and amounts of all payments due and payments made under the mortgage agreement or mortgage deed for a period of 2 years immediately preceding the date of issue, or if the first date of default occurred less than 2 years before the date of issue from the first date of default and a running total of the arrears;
(b) give details of:
(i) any other payments required to be made as a term of the mortgage (such as for insurance premiums, legal costs, default interest, penalties, administrative or other charges);
(ii) any other sums claimed and stating the nature and amount of each such charge; and
(iii) whether any of these payments is in arrears and whether or not it is included in the amount of any periodic payment;

(4) whether or not the loan which is secured by the mortgage is a regulated consumer credit agreement and, if so, specify the date on which any notice required by s. 76 or 87 of the Consumer Credit Act 1974 was given;

(5) if appropriate details that show the property is not one to which s. 141 of the Consumer Credit Act 1974 applies;

(6) any relevant information about the defendant's circumstances, in particular:
(a) whether the defendant is in receipt of social security benefits; and
(b) whether any payments are made on his behalf directly to the claimant under the Social Security Contributions and Benefits Act 1992;

(7) give details of any tenancy entered into between the mortgagor and mortgagee (including any notices served); and

(8) state any previous steps which the claimant has taken to recover the money secured by the mortgage or the mortgaged property and, in the case of court proceedings, state:
(a) the dates when the claim started and concluded; and
(b) the dates and terms of any orders made.

2.5A If the claimant wishes to rely on a history of arrears which is longer than 2 years, he should state this in his particulars and exhibit a full (or longer) schedule to a witness statement.

*Possession claim against trespassers*

2.6 If the claim is a possession claim against trespassers, the particulars of claim must state the claimant's interest in the land or the basis of his right to claim possession and the circumstances in which it has been occupied without licence or consent.

*Possession claim in relation to a demoted tenancy by a housing action trust or a local housing authority*

2.7 If the claim is a possession claim under section 143D of the Housing Act 1996 (possession claim in relation to a demoted tenancy where the landlord is a housing action trust or a local housing authority), the particulars of claim must have attached to them a copy of the notice to the tenant served under section 143E of the 1996 Act.

## Hearing Date: Rule 55.5

3.1 The court may exercise its powers under r. 3.1(2)(a) and (b) to shorten the time periods set out in r. 55.5(2) and (3).

3.2 Particular consideration should be given to the exercise of this power if:
(1) the defendant, or a person for whom the defendant is responsible, has assaulted or threatened to assault:
(a) the claimant;

(b) a member of the claimant's staff; or
(c) another resident in the locality;
(2) there are reasonable grounds for fearing such an assault; or
(3) the defendant, or a person for whom the defendant is responsible, has caused serious damage or threatened to cause serious damage to the property or to the home or property of another resident in the locality.

3.3 Where para. 3.2 applies but the case cannot be determined at the first hearing fixed under r. 55.5, the court will consider what steps are needed to finally determine the case as quickly as reasonably practicable.

### Service in Claims Against Trespassers: Rule 55.6

4.1 If the claim form is to be served by the court and in accordance with r. 55.6(b) the claimant must provide sufficient stakes and transparent envelopes.

### The Hearing: Rule 55.8

5.1 Attention is drawn to r. 55.8(3). Each party should wherever possible include all the evidence he wishes to present in his statement of case, verified by a statement of truth.

5.2 If relevant the claimant's evidence should include the amount of any rent or mortgage arrears and interest on those arrears. These amounts should, if possible, be up to date to the date of the hearing (if necessary by specifying a daily rate of arrears and interest). However, r. 55.8(4) does not prevent such evidence being brought up to date orally or in writing on the day of the hearing if necessary.

5.3 If relevant the defendant should give evidence of:
(1) the amount of any outstanding social security or housing benefit payments relevant to rent or mortgage arrears; and
(2) the status of:
(a) any claims for social security or housing benefit about which a decision has not yet been made; and
(b) any applications to appeal or review a social security or housing benefit decision where that appeal or review has not yet concluded.

5.4 If:
(1) the maker of a witness statement does not attend a hearing; and
(2) the other party disputes material evidence contained in his statement,
the court will normally adjourn the hearing so that oral evidence can be given.

6.1 [*Revoked*]

### Consumer Credit Act Claims Relating to the Recovery Of Land

7.1 Any application by the defendant for a time order under s. 129 of the Consumer Credit Act 1974 may be made:
(1) in his defence; or
(2) by application notice in the proceedings.

### Enforcement of Charging Order by Sale

7.2 A party seeking to enforce a charging order by sale should follow the procedure set out in r. 73.10 and the Part 55 procedure should not be used.

## SECTION II ACCELERATED POSSESSION CLAIMS OF PROPERTY LET ON AN ASSURED SHORTHOLD TENANCY

### Postponement of Possession: Rule 55.18

8.1 If the judge is satisfied as to the matters set out in r. 55.16(2), he will make an order for possession in accordance with r. 55.17, whether or not the defendant seeks a postponement of possession on the ground of exceptional hardship under s. 89 of the Housing Act 1980.

8.2 In a claim in which the judge is satisfied that the defendant has shown exceptional hardship, he will only postpone possession without directing a hearing under r. 55.18(1) if:

(1) he considers that possession should be given up six weeks after the date of the order or, if the defendant has requested postponement to an earlier date, on that date; and

(2) the claimant indicated on his claim form that he would be content for the court to make such an order without a hearing.

8.3 In all other cases if the defendant seeks a postponement of possession under s. 89 of the Housing Act 1980, the judge will direct a hearing under r. 55.18(1).

8.4 If, at that hearing, the judge is satisfied that exceptional hardship would be caused by requiring possession to be given up by the date in the order of possession, he may vary that order under r. 55.18(3) so that possession is to be given up at a later date. That later date may be no later than six weeks after the making of the order for possession on the papers (see s. 89 of the Housing Act 1980).

## SECTION III INTERIM POSSESSION ORDERS

9.1 The claim form must be in form N5, the application notice seeking the interim possession order must be in form N130 and the defendant's witness statement must be in form N133.

9.2 The IPO will be in form N134.

## SECTION IV ORDERS FIXING A DATE FOR POSSESSION

10.1 This paragraph applies where the court has made an order postponing the date for possession under section 85(2)(b) of the Housing Act 1985 (secure tenancies).

10.2 If the defendant fails to comply with any of the terms of the order which relate to payment, the claimant, after following the procedure set out in paragraph 10.3, may apply for an order fixing the date upon which the defendant has to give up possession of the property. Unless the court further postpones the date for possession, the defendant will be required to give up possession on that date.

10.3 At least 14 days and not more than 3 months before applying for an order under paragraph 10.2, the claimant must give written notice to the defendant in accordance with paragraph 10.4.

10.4 The notice referred to in paragraph 10.3 must—

(1) state that the claimant intends to apply for an order fixing the date upon which the defendant is to give up possession of the property;

(2) record the current arrears and state how the defendant has failed to comply with the order referred to in paragraph 10.1 (by reference to a statement of the rent account enclosed with the notice);

(3) request that the defendant reply to the claimant within 7 days, agreeing or disputing the stated arrears; and

(4) inform the defendant of his right to apply to the court—

(a) for a further postponement of the date for possession; or

(b) to stay or suspend enforcement.

10.5 In his reply to the notice, the defendant must—

(1) where he disputes the stated arrears, provide details of payments or credits made;

(2) where he agrees the stated arrears, explain why payments have not been made.

10.6 An application for an order under paragraph 10.2 must be made by filing an application notice in accordance with Part 23. The application notice must state whether or not there is any outstanding claim by the defendant for housing benefit.

10.7 The claimant must file the following documents with the application notice—

(1) a copy of the notice referred to in paragraph 10.3;

(2) a copy of the defendant's reply, if any, to the notice and any relevant subsequent correspondence between the claimant and the defendant;

(3) a statement of the rent account showing—

(a) the arrears that have accrued since the first failure to pay in accordance with the order referred to in paragraph 10.2; or

(b) the arrears that have accrued during the period of two years immediately preceding the date of the application notice, where the first such failure to pay occurs more than two years before that date.

10.8 Rules 23.2.3, 23.2.4 and 23.2.5 (dealing with applications without a hearing), 23.7 (service of a copy of an application notice), and 23.10 (right to set aside or vary an order made without service of the application notice) do not apply to an application under this section.

10.9 On being filed, the application will be referred to the District Judge who—

(1) will normally determine the application without a hearing by fixing the date for possession as the next working day; but

(2) if he considers that a hearing is necessary—

(a) will fix a date for the application to be heard; and

(b) direct service of the application notice and supporting evidence on the defendant.

10.10 The court does not have jurisdiction to review a decision that it was reasonable to make an order for possession.

## 55.10A Electronic issue of certain possession claims

(1) A practice direction may make provision for a claimant to start certain types of possession claim in certain courts by requesting the issue of a claim form electronically.

(2) The practice direction may, in particular—

(a) provide that only particular provisions apply in specific courts;

(b) specify—

(i) the type of possession claim which may be issued electronically;

(ii) the conditions that a claim must meet before it may be issued electronically;

(c) specify the court where the claim may be issued;

(d) enable the parties to make certain applications or take further steps in relation to the claim electronically;

(e) specify the requirements that must be fulfilled in relation to such applications or steps;

(f) enable the parties to correspond electronically with the court about the claim;

(g) specify the requirements that must be fulfilled in relation to electronic correspondence;

(h) provide how any fee payable on the filing of any document is to be paid where the document is filed electronically.

(3) The Practice Direction may disapply or modify these Rules as appropriate in relation to possession claims started electronically.

# PD 55B Practice Direction — Possession Claims Online

This practice direction supplements CPR Rule 55.10A.

## Scope of this Practice Direction

1.1 This practice direction provides for a scheme ('Possession Claims Online') to operate in specified county courts—
(1) enabling claimants and their representatives to start certain possession claims under CPR Part 55 by requesting the issue of a claim form electronically via the PCOL website; and
(2) where a claim has been started electronically, enabling the claimant or defendant and their representatives to take further steps in the claim electronically as specified below.

1.2 In this practice direction—
(1) 'PCOL website' means the website <http://www.possessionclaim.gov.uk> which may be accessed via Her Majesty's Courts Service website (<http://www.hmcourts-service.gov.uk>) and through which Possession Claims Online will operate; and
(2) 'specified court' means a county court specified on the PCOL website as one in which Possession Claims Online is available.

## Information on the PCOL Website

2.1 The PCOL website contains further details and guidance about the operation of Possession Claims Online.

2.2 In particular the PCOL website sets out—
(1) the specified courts; and
(2) the dates from which Possession Claims Online will be available in each specified court.

2.3 The operation of Possession Claims Online in any specified court may be restricted to taking certain of the steps specified in this practice direction, and in such cases the PCOL website will set out the steps which may be taken using Possession Claims Online in that specified court.

## Security

3.1 Her Majesty's Courts Service will take such measures as it thinks fit to ensure the security of steps taken or information stored electronically. These may include requiring users of Possession Claims Online—
(1) to enter a customer identification number or password;
(2) to provide personal information for identification purposes; and
(3) to comply with any other security measures,
before taking any step online.

## Fees

4.1 A step may only be taken using Possession Claims Online on payment of the prescribed fee where a fee is payable. Where this practice direction provides for a fee to be paid electronically, it may be paid by—
(1) credit card;
(2) debit card; or
(3) any other method which Her Majesty's Courts Service may permit.

4.2 A defendant who wishes to claim exemption from payment of fees must do so through an organization approved by Her Majesty's Courts Service before taking any step using PCOL which attracts a fee. If satisfied that the defendant is entitled to fee exemption, the organization will submit the fee exemption form through the PCOL website to Her

Majesty's Courts Service. The defendant may then use PCOL to take such a step.
(Her Majesty's Courts Service website contains guidance as to when the entitlement to claim an exemption from payment of fees arises. The PCOL website will contain a list of organizations through which the defendant may claim an exemption from fees.)

## Claims which may be Started Using Possession Claims Online

5.1 A claim may be started online if—
- (1) it is brought under Section I of Part 55;
- (2) it includes a possession claim for residential property by—
  - (a) a landlord against a tenant, solely on the ground of arrears of rent (but not a claim for forfeiture of a lease); or
  - (b) a mortgagee against a mortgagor, solely on the ground of default in the payment of sums due under a mortgage,

  relating to land within the district of a specified court;
- (3) it does not include a claim for any other remedy except for payment of arrears of rent or money due under a mortgage, interest and costs;
- (4) the defendant has an address for service in England and Wales; and
- (5) the claimant is able to provide a postcode for the property.

5.2 A claim must not be started online if a defendant is known to be a child or patient.

## Starting a Claim

6.1 A claimant may request the issue of a claim form by—
- (1) completing an online claim form at the PCOL website;
- (2) paying the appropriate issue fee electronically at the PCOL website or by some other means approved by Her Majesty's Courts Service.

6.2 The particulars of claim must be included in the online claim form and may not be filed separately. It is not necessary to file a copy of the tenancy agreement, mortgage deed or mortgage agreement with the particulars of claim.

6.3 Subject to paragraphs 6.3A and 6.3B, the particulars of claim must include a history of the rent or mortgage account, in schedule form setting out—
- (1) the dates and amounts of all payments due and payments made under the tenancy agreement, mortgage deed or mortgage agreement either from the first date of default if that date occurred less than 2 years before the date of issue or for a period of 2 years immediately preceding the date of issue; and
- (2) a running total of the arrears.

6.3A Paragraph 6.3B applies where the claimant has provided the defendant with—
- (1) the information required by MCOB 13.4.1 and MCOB 13.4.4 of the Mortgages: Conduct of Business Rules issued by the Financial Services Authority; or
- (2) in schedule form, the dates and amounts of all payments due and payments made under the tenancy agreement for a period of two years immediately preceding the date of issue, or if the first date of default occurred less than two years before the date of issue, from the first date of default and a running total of the arrears.

(MCOB 13.4.1 and MCOB 13.4.4 may be found at <http://fsahandbook.info/FSA/html/handbook/MCOB/13>.)

6.3B Where this paragraph applies the claimant may, in place of the information required by paragraph 6.3, include in his particulars of claim a summary only of the arrears containing at least the following information—
- (1) The amount of arrears as stated in the notice of seeking possession served under either section 83 of the Housing Act 1985 or section 8 of the Housing Act 1988, or at the date of the claimant's letter before action, as appropriate;
- (2) the dates and amounts of the last three payments in cleared funds made by the defendant or, if less than three payments have been made, the dates and amounts of all payments made;

(3) the arrears at the date of issue, assuming that no further payments are made by the defendant.

6.3C Where the particulars of claim include a summary only of the arrears the claimant must—

(1) serve on the defendant not more than 7 days after the date of issue, a full arrears history containing at least the information required by paragraph 6.3; and

(2) either—

(a) make a witness statement confirming that he has complied with sub-paragraph (1) or (2) of paragraph 6.3A as appropriate, and including or exhibiting the full arrears history; or

(b) verify by way of oral evidence at the hearing that he has complied with sub-paragraph (1) or (2) of paragraph 6.3A as appropriate and also produce and verify the full arrears history.

(Rule 55.8(4) requires all witness statements to be filed and served at least 2 days before the hearing.)

6.4 If the claimant wishes to rely on a history of arrears which is longer than 2 years, he should state this in his particulars and exhibit a full (or longer) schedule to a witness statement.

6.5 When an online claim form is received, an acknowledgment of receipt will automatically be sent to the claimant. The acknowledgment does not constitute notice that the claim form has been issued or served.

6.6 When the court issues a claim form following the submission of an online claim form, the claim is 'brought' for the purposes of the Limitation Act 1980 and any other enactment on the date on which the online claim form is received by the court's computer system. The court will keep a record, by electronic or other means, of when online claim forms are received.

6.7 When the court issues a claim form it will—

(1) serve a printed version of the claim form and a defence form on the defendant; and

(2) send the claimant notice of issue by post or, where the claimant has supplied an e-mail address, by electronic means.

6.8 The claim shall be deemed to be served on the fifth day after the claim was issued irrespective of whether that day is a business day or not.

6.9 Where the period of time within which a defence must be filed ends on a day when the court is closed, the defendant may file his defence on the next day that the court is open.

6.10 The claim form shall have printed on it a unique customer identification number or a password by which the defendant may access the claim on the PCOL website.

6.11 PCOL will issue the proceedings in the appropriate county court by reference to the post code provided by the claimant and that court shall have jurisdiction to hear and determine the claim and to carry out enforcement of any judgment irrespective of whether the property is within or outside the jurisdiction of that court.

(CPR 30.2(1) authorises proceedings to be transferred from one county court to another.)

## Defence

7.1 A defendant wishing to file—

(1) a defence; or

(2) a counterclaim (to be filed together with a defence) to a claim which has been issued through the PCOL system,

may, instead of filing a written form, do so by—

(a) completing the relevant online form at the PCOL website; and

(b) if the defendant is making a counterclaim, paying the appropriate fee electronically at the PCOL website or by some other means approved by Her Majesty's Courts Service.

7.2 Where a defendant files a defence by completing the relevant online form, he must not send the court a hard copy.

7.3 When an online defence form is received, an acknowledgment of receipt will automatically be sent to the defendant. The acknowledgment does not constitute notice that the defence has been served.

7.4 The online defence form will be treated as being filed—
(1) on the day the court receives it, if it receives it before 4 p.m. on a working day; and
(2) otherwise, on the next working day after the court receives the online defence form.

7.5 A defence is filed when the online defence form is received by the court's computer system. The court will keep a record, by electronic or other means, of when online defence forms are received.

## Statement of Truth

8.1 CPR Part 22 requires any statement of case to be verified by a statement of truth. This applies to any online claims and defences and application notices.

8.2 CPR Part 22 also requires that if an applicant wishes to rely on matters set out in his application notice as evidence, the application notice must be verified by a statement of truth. This applies to any application notice completed online that contains matters on which the applicant wishes to rely as evidence.

8.3 Attention is drawn to—
(1) paragraph 2 of the practice direction supplementing CPR Part 22, which stipulates the form of the statement of truth; and
(2) paragraph 3 of the practice direction supplementing CPR Part 22, which provides who may sign a statement of truth; and
(3) CPR 32.14, which sets out the consequences of making, or causing to be made, a false statement in a document verified by a statement of truth, without an honest belief in its truth.

## Signature

9.1 Any provision of the CPR which requires a document to be signed by any person is satisfied by that person entering his name on an online form.

## Communication with the Court Electronically by the Messaging Service

10.1 If the PCOL website specifies that a court accepts electronic communications relating to claims brought using Possession Claims Online the parties may communicate with the court using the messaging service facility, available on the PCOL website ('the messaging service').

10.2 The messaging service is for brief and straightforward communications only. The PCOL website contains a list of examples of when it will not be appropriate to use the messaging service.

10.3 Parties must not send to the court forms or attachments via the messaging service.

10.4 The court shall treat any forms or attachments sent via the messaging service as not having been filed or received.

10.5 The court will normally reply via the messaging service where—
(1) the response is to a message transmitted via the messaging service; and
(2) the sender has provided an e-mail address.

## Electronic Applications

11.1 Certain applications in relation to a possession claim started online may be made electronically ('online applications'). An online application may be made if a form for that application is published on the PCOL website ('online application form') and the application is made at least 5 clear days before the hearing.

11.2 If a claim for possession has been started online and a party wishes to make an online application, he may do so by—
(1) completing the appropriate online application form at the PCOL website; and

(2) paying the appropriate fee electronically at the PCOL website or by some other means approved by Her Majesty's Courts Service.

11.3 When an online application form is received, an acknowledgment of receipt will automatically be sent to the applicant. The acknowledgment does not constitute a notice that the online application form has been issued or served.

11.4 Where an application must be made within a specified time, it is so made if the online application form is received by the court's computer system within that time. The court will keep a record, by electronic or other means, of when online application forms are received.

11.5 When the court receives an online application form it shall—

(1) serve a copy of the online application endorsed with the date of the hearing by post on the claimant at least 2 clear days before the hearing; and

(2) send the defendant notice of service and confirmation of the date of the hearing by post; provided that

(3) where either party has provided the court with an e-mail address for service, service of the application and/or the notice of service and confirmation of the hearing date may be effected by electronic means.

## Request for Issue of Warrant

12.1 Where—

(1) the court has made an order for possession in a claim started online; and

(2) the claimant is entitled to the issue of a warrant of possession without requiring the permission of the court

the claimant may request the issue of a warrant by completing an online request form at the PCOL website and paying the appropriate fee electronically at the PCOL website or by some other means approved by Her Majesty's Courts Service.

12.2 A request under paragraph 12.1 will be treated as being filed—

(1) on the day the court receives the request, if it receives it before 4 p.m. on a working day; and

(2) otherwise, on the next working day after the court receives the request.

(CCR Order 26 rule 5 sets out certain circumstances in which a warrant of execution may not be issued without the permission of the court. CCR Order 26 rule 17(6) applies rule 5 of that Order with necessary modifications to a warrant of possession.)

## Application to Suspend Warrant of Possession

13.1 Where the court has issued a warrant of possession, the defendant may apply electronically for the suspension of the warrant, provided that:

(1) the application is made at least 5 clear days before the appointment for possession; and

(2) the defendant is not prevented from making such an application without the permission of the court.

13.2 The defendant may apply electronically for the suspension of the warrant, by—

(1) completing an online application for suspension at the PCOL website; and

(2) paying the appropriate fee electronically at the PCOL website or by some other means approved by Her Majesty's Courts Service.

13.3 When an online application for suspension is received, an acknowledgment of receipt will automatically be sent to the defendant. The acknowledgment does not constitute a notice that the online application for suspension has been served.

13.4 Where an application must be made within a specified time, it is so made if the online application for suspension is received by the court's computer system within that time. The court will keep a record, by electronic or other means, of when online applications for suspension are received.

13.5 When the court receives an online application for suspension it shall—

(1) serve a copy of the online application for suspension endorsed with the date

of the hearing by post on the claimant at least 2 clear days before the hearing; and

(2) send the defendant notice of service and confirmation of the date of the hearing by post; provided that

(3) where either party has provided the court with an e-mail address for service, service of the application and/or the notice of service and confirmation of the hearing date may be effected by electronic means.

## Viewing the Case Record

14.1 A facility will be provided on the PCOL website for parties or their representatives to view—

(1) an electronic record of the status of claims started online, which will be reviewed and, if necessary, updated at least once each day; and

(2) all information relating to the case that has been filed by the parties electronically.

14.2 In addition, where the PCOL website specifies that the court has the facility to provide viewing of such information by electronic means, the parties or their representatives may view the following information electronically—

(1) court orders made in relation to the case; and

(2) details of progress on enforcement and subsequent orders made.

# CPR Part 56 Landlord and Tenant Claims and Miscellaneous Provisions About Land



## I LANDLORD AND TENANT CLAIMS

### 56.1 Scope and Interpretation

(1) In this Section of this Part 'landlord and tenant claim' means a claim under—
   (a) the Landlord and Tenant Act 1927;
   (b) the Leasehold Property (Repairs) Act 1938;
   (c) the Landlord and Tenant Act 1954;
   (d) the Landlord and Tenant Act 1985; or
   (e) the Landlord and Tenant Act 1987.

(2) A practice direction may set out special provisions with regard to any particular category of landlord and tenant claim.

### 56.2 Starting the Claim

(1) The claim must be started in the county court for the district in which the land is situated unless paragraph (2) applies or an enactment provides otherwise.

(2) The claim may be started in the High Court if the claimant files with his claim form a certificate stating the reasons for bringing the claim in that court verified by a statement of truth in accordance with rule 22.1(1).

(3) The practice direction refers to circumstances which may justify starting the claim in the High Court.

### 56.3 Claims for a New Tenancy under Section 24 and for the Termination of a Tenancy under Section 29(2) of the Landlord and Tenant Act 1954

(1) This rule applies to a claim for a new tenancy under section 24 and to a claim for the termination of a tenancy under section 29(2) of the 1954 Act.

(2) In this rule—
   (a) 'the 1954 Act' means the Landlord and Tenant Act 1954;
   (b) 'an unopposed claim' means a claim for a new tenancy under section 24 of the 1954 Act in circumstances where the grant of a new tenancy is not opposed;
   (c) 'an opposed claim' means a claim for—
      (i) a new tenancy under section 24 of the 1954 Act in circumstances where the grant of a new tenancy is opposed; or
      (ii) the termination of a tenancy under section 29(2) of the 1954 Act.

(3) Where the claim is an unopposed claim—
   (a) the claimant must use the Part 8 procedure, but the following rules do not apply—
      (i) rule 8.5; and
      (ii) rule 8.6;
   (b) the claim form must be served within 2 months after the date of issue and rules 7.5 and 7.6 are modified accordingly; and

(c) the court will give directions about the future management of the claim following receipt of the acknowledgment of service.

(4) Where the claim is an opposed claim—

(a) the claimant must use the Part 7 procedure; but

(b) the claim form must be served within 2 months after the date of issue, and rules 7.5 and 7.6 are modified accordingly.

(The practice direction to this Part contains provisions about evidence, including expert evidence in opposed claims.)

## II MISCELLANEOUS PROVISIONS ABOUT LAND

### 56.4 Scope

A practice direction may set out special provisions with regard to claims under the following enactments—

(a) the Chancel Repairs Act 1932;
(b) the Leasehold Reform Act 1967;
(c) the Access to Neighbouring Land Act 1992;
(d) the Leasehold Reform, Housing and Urban Development Act 1993; and
(e) the Commonhold and Leasehold Reform Act 2002.

# PD 56 Practice Direction — Landlord and Tenant Claims and Miscellaneous Provisions About Land

This practice direction supplements CPR Part 56.

## SECTION I LANDLORD AND TENANT CLAIMS

1.1 In this section of this practice direction:
'the 1927 Act' means the Landlord and Tenant Act 1927;
'the 1954 Act' means the Landlord and Tenant Act 1954;
'the 1985 Act' means the Landlord and Tenant Act 1985; and
'the 1987 Act' means the Landlord and Tenant Act 1987.

### Starting the Claim: Rule 56.2

2.1 Subject to paragraph 2.1A, the claimant in a landlord and tenant claim must use the Part 8 procedure as modified by Part 56 and this practice direction.

2.1A Where the landlord and tenant claim is a claim for—

(1) a new tenancy under section 24 of the 1954 Act in circumstances where the grant of a new tenancy is opposed; or

(2) the termination of a tenancy under section 29(2) of the 1954 Act,

the claimant must use the Part 7 procedure as modified by Part 56 and this practice direction.

2.2 Except where the county court does not have jurisdiction, landlord and tenant claims should normally be brought in the county court. Only exceptional circumstances justify starting a claim in the High Court.

2.3 If a claimant starts a claim in the High Court and the court decides that it should have been started in the county court, the court will normally either strike the claim out or transfer it to the county court on its own initiative. This is likely to result in delay and the court will normally disallow the costs of starting the claim in the High Court and of any transfer.

2.4 Circumstances which may, in an appropriate case, justify starting a claim in the High Court are if:

(1) there are complicated disputes of fact; or

(2) there are points of law of general importance.

2.5 The value of the property and the amount of any financial claim may be relevant circumstances, but these factors alone will not normally justify starting the claim in the High Court.

2.6 A landlord and tenant claim started in the High Court must be brought in the Chancery Division.

### Claims for a New Tenancy under Section 24 and Termination of a Tenancy under Section 29(2) of the 1954 Act

3.1 This paragraph applies to a claim for a new tenancy under section 24 and termination of a tenancy under section 29(2) of the 1954 Act where rule 56.3 applies and in this paragraph—

(1) 'an unopposed claim' means a claim for a new tenancy under section 24 of the 1954 Act in circumstances where the grant of a new tenancy is not opposed;

(2) 'an opposed claim' means a claim for—

(a) a new tenancy under section 24 of the 1954 Act in circumstances where the grant of a new tenancy is opposed; or

(b) the termination of a tenancy under section 29(2) of the 1954 Act; and

(3) 'grounds of opposition' means—
(a) the grounds specified in section 30(1) of the 1954 Act on which a landlord may oppose an application for a new tenancy under section 24(1) of the 1954 Act or make an application under section 29(2) of the 1954 Act; or
(b) any other basis on which the landlord asserts that a new tenancy ought not to be granted.

*Precedence of claim forms where there is more than one application to the court under section 24(1) or section 29(2) of the 1954 Act*

3.2 Where more than one application to the court under section 24(1) or section 29(2) of the 1954 Act is made, the following provisions shall apply—
(1) once an application to the court under section 24(1) of the 1954 Act has been served on a defendant, no further application to the court in respect of the same tenancy whether under section 24(1) or section 29(2) of the 1954 Act may be served by that defendant without the permission of the court;
(2) if more than one application to the court under section 24(1) of the 1954 Act in respect of the same tenancy is served on the same day, any landlord's application shall stand stayed until further order of the court;
(3) if applications to the court under both section 24(1) and section 29(2) of the 1954 Act in respect of the same tenancy are served on the same day, any tenant's application shall stand stayed until further order of the court; and
(4) if a defendant is served with an application under section 29(2) of the 1954 Act ('the section 29(2) application') which was issued at a time when an application to the court had already been made by that defendant in respect of the same tenancy under section 24(1) of the 1954 Act ('the section 24(1) application'), the service of the section 29(2) application shall be deemed to be a notice under rule 7.7 requiring service or discontinuance of the section 24(1) application within a period of 14 days after the service of the section 29(2) application.

*Defendant where the claimant is the tenant making a claim for a new tenancy under section 24 of the 1954 Act*

3.3 Where a claim for a new tenancy under section 24 of the 1954 Act is made by a tenant, the person who, in relation to the claimant's current tenancy, is the landlord as defined in section 44 of the 1954 Act must be a defendant.

*Contents of the claim form in all cases*

3.4 The claim form must contain details of—
(1) the property to which the claim relates;
(2) the particulars of the current tenancy (including date, parties and duration), the current rent (if not the original rent) and the date and method of termination;
(3) every notice or request given or made under sections 25 or 26 of the 1954 Act; and
(4) the expiry date of—
(a) the statutory period under section 29A(2) of the 1954 Act; or
(b) any agreed extended period made under section 29B(1) or 29B(2) of the 1954 Act.

*Claim form where the claimant is the tenant making a claim for a new tenancy under section 24 of the 1954 Act*

3.5 Where the claimant is the tenant making a claim for a new tenancy under section 24 of the 1954 Act, in addition to the details specified in paragraph 3.4, the claim form must contain details of—
(1) the nature of the business carried on at the property;
(2) whether the claimant relies on section 23(1A), 41 or 42 of the 1954 Act and, if so, the basis on which he does so;
(3) whether the claimant relies on section 31A of the 1954 Act and, if so, the basis on which he does so;

(4) whether any, and if so what part, of the property comprised in the tenancy is occupied neither by the claimant nor by a person employed by the claimant for the purpose of the claimant's business;
(5) the claimant's proposed terms of the new tenancy; and
(6) the name and address of—
(a) anyone known to the claimant who has an interest in the reversion in the property (whether immediate or in not more than 15 years) on the termination of the claimant's current tenancy and who is likely to be affected by the grant of a new tenancy; or
(b) if the claimant does not know of anyone specified by sub-paragraph (6)(a), anyone who has a freehold interest in the property.

3.6 The claim form must be served on the persons referred to in paragraph 3.5(6)(a) or (b) as appropriate.

*Claim form where the claimant is the landlord making a claim for a new tenancy under section 24 of the 1954 Act*

3.7 Where the claimant is the landlord making a claim for a new tenancy under section 24 of the 1954 Act, in addition to the details specified in paragraph 3.4, the claim form must contain details of—
(1) the claimant's proposed terms of the new tenancy;
(2) whether the claimant is aware that the defendant's tenancy is one to which section 32(2) of the 1954 Act applies and, if so, whether the claimant requires that any new tenancy shall be a tenancy of the whole of the property comprised in the defendant's current tenancy or just of the holding as defined by section 23(3) of the 1954 Act; and
(3) the name and address of—
(a) anyone known to the claimant who has an interest in the reversion in the property (whether immediate or in not more than 15 years) on the termination of the claimant's current tenancy and who is likely to be affected by the grant of a new tenancy; or
(b) if the claimant does not know of anyone specified by sub-paragraph (3)(a), anyone who has a freehold interest in the property.

3.8 The claim form must be served on the persons referred to in paragraph 3.7(3)(a) or (b) as appropriate.

*Claim form where the claimant is the landlord making an application for the termination of a tenancy under section 29(2) of the 1954 Act*

3.9 Where the claimant is the landlord making an application for the termination of a tenancy under section 29(2) of the 1954 Act, in addition to the details specified in paragraph 3.4, the claim form must contain—
(1) the claimant's grounds of opposition;
(2) full details of those grounds of opposition; and
(3) the terms of a new tenancy that the claimant proposes in the event that his claim fails.

*Acknowledgment of service where the claim is an unopposed claim and where the claimant is the tenant*

3.10 Where the claim is an unopposed claim and the claimant is the tenant, the acknowledgment of service is to be in form N210 and must state with particulars—
(1) whether, if a new tenancy is granted, the defendant objects to any of the terms proposed by the claimant and if so—
(a) the terms to which he objects; and
[(b)]* the terms that he proposes in so far as they differ from those proposed by the claimant;

[* The text released by the DCA mistakenly uses two subparagraphs (a).]

(2) whether the defendant is a tenant under a lease having less than 15 years unexpired at the date of the termination of the claimant's current tenancy and, if so, the name and address of any person who, to the knowledge of the defendant, has an interest in the reversion in the property expectant (whether immediate or in not more than 15 years from that date) on the termination of the defendant's tenancy;
(3) the name and address of any person having an interest in the property who is likely to be affected by the grant of a new tenancy; and
(4) if the claimant's current tenancy is one to which section 32(2) of the 1954 Act applies, whether the defendant requires that any new tenancy shall be a tenancy of the whole of the property comprised in the claimant's current tenancy.

*Acknowledgment of service where the claim is an unopposed claim and the claimant is the landlord*

3.11 Where the claim is an unopposed claim and the claimant is the landlord, the acknowledgment of service is to be in form N210 and must state with particulars—
(1) the nature of the business carried on at the property;
(2) if the defendant relies on section 23(1A), 41 or 42 of the 1954 Act, the basis on which he does so;
(3) whether any, and if so what part, of the property comprised in the tenancy is occupied neither by the defendant nor by a person employed by the defendant for the purpose of the defendant's business;
(4) the name and address of—
(a) anyone known to the defendant who has an interest in the reversion in the property (whether immediate or in not more than 15 years) on the termination of the defendant's current tenancy and who is likely to be affected by the grant of a new tenancy; or
(b) if the defendant does not know of anyone specified by sub-paragraph (4)(a), anyone who has a freehold interest in the property; and
(5) whether, if a new tenancy is granted, the defendant objects to any of the terms proposed by the claimant and, if so—
(a) the terms to which he objects; and
(b) the terms that he proposes in so far as they differ from those proposed by the claimant.

*Acknowledgment of service and defence where the claim is an opposed claim and where the claimant is the tenant*

3.12 Where the claim is an opposed claim and the claimant is the tenant—
(1) the acknowledgment of service is to be in form N9; and
(2) in his defence the defendant must state with particulars—
(a) the defendant's grounds of opposition;
(b) full details of those grounds of opposition;
(c) whether, if a new tenancy is granted, the defendant objects to any of the terms proposed by the claimant and if so—
(i) the terms to which he objects; and
(ii) the terms that he proposes in so far as they differ from those proposed by the claimant;
(d) whether the defendant is a tenant under a lease having less than 15 years unexpired at the date of the termination of the claimant's current tenancy and, if so, the name and address of any person who, to the knowledge of the defendant, has an interest in the reversion in the property expectant (whether immediately or in not more than 15 years from that date) on the termination of the defendant's tenancy;
(e) the name and address of any person having an interest in the property who is likely to be affected by the grant of a new tenancy; and

(f) if the claimant's current tenancy is one to which section 32(2) of the 1954 Act applies, whether the defendant requires that any new tenancy shall be a tenancy of the whole of the property comprised in the claimant's current tenancy.

*Acknowledgment of service and defence where the claimant is the landlord making an application for the termination of a tenancy under section 29(2) of the 1954 Act*

3.13 Where the claim is an opposed claim and the claimant is the landlord—
(1) the acknowledgment of service is to be in form N9; and
(2) in his defence the defendant must state with particulars—
(a) whether the defendant relies on section 23(1A), 41 or 42 of the 1954 Act and, if so, the basis on which he does so;
(b) whether the defendant relies on section 31A of the 1954 Act and, if so, the basis on which he does so; and
(c) the terms of the new tenancy that the defendant would propose in the event that the claimant's claim to terminate the current tenancy fails.

*Evidence in an unopposed claim*

3.14 Where the claim is an unopposed claim, no evidence need be filed unless and until the court directs it to be filed.

*Evidence in an opposed claim*

3.15 Where the claim is an opposed claim, evidence (including expert evidence) must be filed by the parties as the court directs and the landlord shall be required to file his evidence first.

*Grounds of opposition to be tried as a preliminary issue*

3.16 Unless in the circumstances of the case it is unreasonable to do so, any grounds of opposition shall be tried as a preliminary issue.

*Applications for interim rent under section 24A to 24D of the 1954 Act*

3.17 Where proceedings have already been commenced for the grant of a new tenancy or the termination of an existing tenancy, the claim for interim rent under section 24A of the 1954 Act shall be made in those proceedings by—
(1) the claim form;
(2) the acknowledgment of service or defence; or
(3) an application on notice under Part 23.

3.18 Any application under section 24D(3) of the 1954 Act shall be made by an application on notice under Part 23 in the original proceedings.

3.19 Where no other proceedings have been commenced for the grant of a new tenancy or termination of an existing tenancy or where such proceedings have been disposed of, an application for interim rent under section 24A of the 1954 Act shall be made under the procedure in Part 8 and the claim form shall include details of—
(1) the property to which the claim relates;
(2) the particulars of the relevant tenancy (including date, parties and duration) and the current rent (if not the original rent);
(3) every notice or request given or made under sections 25 or 26 of the 1954 Act;
(4) if the relevant tenancy has terminated, the date and mode of termination; and
(5) if the relevant tenancy has been terminated and the landlord has granted a new tenancy of the property to the tenant—
(a) particulars of the new tenancy (including date, parties and duration) and the rent; and
(b) in a case where section 24C(2) of the 1954 Act applies but the claimant seeks a different rent under section 24C(3) of that Act, particulars and matters on which the claimant relies as satisfying section 24C(3).

## Other Claims Under Part II of the 1954 Act

4.1 The mesne landlord to whose consent a claim for the determination of any question arising under para. 4(3) of sch. 6 to the 1954 Act shall be made a defendant to the claim.

4.2 If any dispute as to the rateable value of any holding has been referred under s. 37(5) of the 1954 Act to the Commissioners for HM Revenue and Customs for decision by a valuation officer, any document purporting to be a statement of the valuation officer of his decision is admissible as evidence of the matters contained in it.

## Claim for Compensation for Improvements Under Part I of the 1927 Act

5.1 This paragraph applies to a claim under Part I of the 1927 Act.

*The claim form*

5.2 The claim form must include details of:
- (1) the nature of the claim or the matter to be determined;
- (2) the property to which the claim relates;
- (3) the nature of the business carried on at the property;
- (4) particulars of the lease or agreement for the tenancy including:
  - (a) the names and addresses of the parties to the lease or agreement;
  - (b) its duration;
  - (c) the rent payable;
  - (d) details of any assignment or other devolution of the lease or agreement;
- (5) the date and mode of termination of the tenancy;
- (6) if the claimant has left the property, the date on which he did so;
- (7) particulars of the improvement or proposed improvement to which the claim relates; and
- (8) if the claim is for payment of compensation, the amount claimed;

5.3 The court will fix a date for a hearing when it issues the claim form.

*Defendant*

5.4 The claimant's immediate landlord must be a defendant to the claim.

5.5 The defendant must immediately serve a copy of the claim form and any document served with it and of his acknowledgment of service on his immediate landlord. If the person so served is not the freeholder, he must serve a copy of these documents on his landlord and so on from landlord to landlord.

*Evidence*

5.6 Evidence need not be filed—with the claim form or acknowledgment of service.

*Certification under section 3 of the 1927 Act*

5.7 If the court intends to certify under s. 3 of the 1927 Act that an improvement is a proper improvement or has been duly executed, it shall do so by way of an order.

*Compensation under section 1 or 8 of the 1927 Act*

5.8 A claim under s. 1(1) or 8(1) of the 1927 Act must be in writing, signed by the claimant, his solicitor or agent and include details of:
- (1) the name and address of the claimant and of the landlord against whom the claim is made;
- (2) the property to which the claim relates;
- (3) the nature of the business carried on at the property;
- (4) a concise statement of the nature of the claim;
- (5) particulars of the improvement, including the date when it was completed and costs; and
- (6) the amount claimed.

5.9 A mesne landlord must immediately serve a copy of the claim on his immediate superior landlord. If the person so served is not the freeholder, he must serve a copy of the document on his landlord and so on from landlord to landlord.

(Paragraphs 5.8 and 5.9 provide the procedure for making claims under s. 1(1) and 8(1) of the 1927 Act—these 'claims' do not, at this stage, relate to proceedings before the court.)

## Transfer to Leasehold Valuation Tribunal Under 1985 Act

6.1 If a question is ordered to be transferred to a leasehold valuation tribunal for determination under s. 31C of the 1985 Act the court will:

(1) send notice of the transfer to all parties to the claim; and

(2) send to the leasehold valuation tribunal:

(a) copies certified by the district judge of all entries in the records of the court relating to the question;

(b) the order of transfer; and

(c) all documents filed in the claim relating to the question.

(Paragraph 6.1 no longer applies to proceedings in England but continues to apply to proceedings in Wales.)

## Claim to Enforce Obligation Under Part I of the 1987 Act

7.1 A copy of the notice served under s. 19(2)(a) of the 1987 Act must accompany the claim form seeking an order under s. 19(1) of that Act.

## Claim for Acquisition Order Under Section 28 of the 1987 Act

8.1 This paragraph applies to a claim for an acquisition order under s. 28 of the 1987 Act.

*Claim form*

8.2 The claim form must:

(1) identify the property to which the claim relates and give details to show that s. 25 of the 1987 Act applies;

(2) give details of the claimants to show that they constitute the requisite majority of qualifying tenants;

(3) state the names and addresses of the claimants and of the landlord of the property, or, if the landlord cannot be found or his identity ascertained, the steps taken to find him or ascertain his identity;

(4) state the name and address of:

(a) the person nominated by the claimants for the purposes of part III of the 1987 Act; and

(b) every person known to the claimants who is likely to be affected by the application, including (but not limited to), the other tenants of flats contained in the property (whether or not they could have made a claim), any mortgagee or superior landlord of the landlord, and any tenants' association (within the meaning of s. 29 of the 1985 Act); and

(5) state the grounds of the claim.

*Notice under section 27*

8.3 A copy of the notice served on the landlord under s. 27 of the 1987 Act must accompany the claim form unless the court has dispensed with the requirement to serve a notice under s. 27(3) of the 1987 Act.

*Defendants*

8.4 The landlord of the property (and the nominated person, if he is not a claimant) must be defendants.

*Service*

8.5 A copy of the claim form must be served on each of the persons named by the claimant under para. 8.2(4)(b) together with a notice that he may apply to be made a party.

*Payment into court by nominated person*

8.6 If the nominated person pays money into court in accordance with an order under s. 33(1) of the 1987 Act, he must file a copy of the certificate of the surveyor selected under s. 33(2)(a) of that Act.

## Claim for an Order Varying Leases Under the 1987 Act

9.1 This paragraph applies to a claim for an order under s. 38 or s. 40 of the 1987 Act.

*Claim form*

9.2 The claim form must state:

(1) the name and address of the claimant and of the other current parties to the lease or leases to which the claim relates;

(2) the date of the lease or leases, the property to which they relate, any relevant terms and the variation sought;

(3) the name and address of every person known to the claimant who is likely to be affected by the claim, including (but not limited to), the other tenants of flats contained in premises of which the relevant property forms a part, any previous parties to the lease, any mortgagee or superior landlord of the landlord, any mortgagee of the claimant and any tenants' association (within the meaning of s. 29 of the 1985 Act); and

(4) the grounds of the claim.

*Defendants*

9.3 The other current parties to the lease must be defendants.

*Service*

9.4 A copy of the claim form must be served on each of the persons named under para. 9.2(3).

9.5 If the defendant knows of or has reason to believe that another person or persons are likely to be affected by the variation, he must serve a copy of the claim form on those persons, together with a notice that they may apply to be made a party.

*Defendant's application to vary other leases*

9.6 If a defendant wishes to apply to vary other leases under s. 36 of the 1987 Act:

(1) he must make the application in his acknowledgment of service;

(2) paras 9.2 to 9.5 apply as if the defendant were the claimant; and

(3) Part 20 does not apply.

(Paragraphs 9.1 to 9.6 no longer apply to proceedings in England but continue to apply to proceedings in Wales.)

## Service of Documents in Claims Under the 1987 Act

10.1 All documents must be served by the parties.

10.2 If a notice is to be served in or before a claim under the 1987 Act, it must be served:

(1) in accordance with s. 54, and

(2) in the case of service on a landlord, at the address given under s. 48(1).

# SECTION II MISCELLANEOUS PROVISIONS ABOUT LAND

## Access to Neighbouring Land Act 1992

11.1 The claimant must use the Part 8 procedure.

11.2 The claim form must set out:

(1) details of the dominant and servient land involved and whether the dominant land includes or consists of residential property;

(2) the work required;

(3) why entry to the servient land is required with plans (if applicable);

(4) the names and addresses of the persons who will carry out the work;

(5) the proposed date when the work will be carried out; and
(6) what (if any) provision has been made by way of insurance in the event of possible injury to persons or damage to property arising out of the proposed work.

11.3 The owner and occupier of the servient land must be defendants to the claim.

## Chancel Repairs Act 1932

12.1 The claimant in a claim to recover the sum required to put a chancel in proper repair must use the Part 8 procedure.

12.2 A notice to repair under s. 2 of the Chancel Repairs Act 1932 must:
(1) state:
(a) the responsible authority by whom the notice is given;
(b) the chancel alleged to be in need of repair;
(c) the repairs alleged to be necessary; and
(d) the grounds on which the person to whom the notice is addressed is alleged to be liable to repair the chancel; and
(2) call upon the person to whom the notice is addressed to put the chancel in proper repair.

12.3 The notice must be served in accordance with Part 6.

## Leasehold Reform Act 1967

13.1 In this paragraph a section or schedule referred to by number means the section or schedule so numbered in the Leasehold Reform Act 1967.

13.2 If a tenant of a house and premises wishes to pay money into court under ss. 11(4), 13(1) or 13(3):
(1) he must file in the office of the appropriate court an application notice containing or accompanied by evidence stating:
(a) the reasons for the payment into court,
(b) the house and premises to which the payment relates;
(c) the name and address of the landlord; and
(d) so far as they are known to the tenant, the name and address of every person who is or may be interested in or entitled to the money;
(2) on the filing of the witness statement the tenant must pay the money into court and the court will send notice of the payment to the landlord and every person whose name and address are given in the witness statement;
(3) any subsequent payment into court by the landlord under s. 11(4) must be made to the credit of the same account as the payment into court by the tenant and sub-paras (1) and (2) will apply to the landlord as if he were a tenant;
(4) the appropriate court for the purposes of sub-para. (1)(a) is the county court for the district in which the property is situated or, if the payment into court is made by reason of a notice under s. 13(3), any other county court as specified in the notice.

13.3 If an order is made transferring an application to a leasehold valuation tribunal under s. 21(3), the court will:
(1) send notice of the transfer to all parties to the application; and
(2) send to the tribunal copies of the order of transfer and all documents filed in the proceedings.
(Paragraph 13.3 no longer applies to proceedings in England but continues to apply to proceedings in Wales.)

13.4 A claim under s. 17 or 18 for an order for possession of a house and premises must be made in accordance with Part 55.

13.5 In a claim under s. 17 or 18, the defendant must:
(1) immediately after being served with the claim form, serve on every person in occupation of the property or part of it under an immediate or derivative sub-tenancy, a notice informing him of the claim and of his right under para. 3(4) of

sch. 2 [to] take part in the hearing of the claim with the permission of the court; and

(2) within 14 days after being served with the claim form, file a defence stating the ground, if any, on which he intends to oppose the claim and giving particulars of every such sub-tenancy.

13.6 An application made to the High Court under s. 19 or 27 shall be assigned to the Chancery Division.

## Leasehold Reform, Housing and Urban Development Act 1993

14.1 In this paragraph:

(1) 'the 1993 Act' means the Leasehold Reform, Housing and Urban Development Act 1993; and

(2) a section or schedule referred to by number means the section or schedule so numbered in the 1993 Act.

14.2 If a claim is made under s. 23(1) by a person other than the reversioner:

(1) on the issue of the claim form in accordance with Part 8, the claimant must send a copy to the reversioner; and

(2) the claimant must promptly inform the reversioner either:

(a) of the court's decision; or

(b) that the claim has been withdrawn.

14.3 Where an application is made under s. 26(1) or (2) or s. 50(1) or (2):

(1) it must be made by the issue of a claim form in accordance with the Part 8 procedure which need not be served on any other party; and

(2) the court may grant or refuse the application or give directions for its future conduct, including the addition as defendants of such persons as appear to have an interest in it.

14.4 An application under s. 26(3) must be made by the issue of a claim form in accordance with the Part 8 procedure and:

(1) the claimants must serve the claim form on any person who they know or have reason to believe is a relevant landlord, giving particulars of the claim and the hearing date and informing that person of his right to be joined as a party to the claim;

(2) the landlord whom it is sought to appoint as the reversioner must be a defendant, and must file an acknowledgment of service;

(3) a person on whom notice is served under sub-para. (1) must be joined as a defendant to the claim if he gives notice in writing to the court of his wish to be added as a party, and the court will notify all other parties of the addition.

14.5 If a person wishes to pay money into court under s. 27(3), s. 51(3) or para. 4 of sch. 8:

(1) he must file in the office of the appropriate court an application notice containing or accompanied by evidence stating:

(a) the reasons for the payment into court,

(b) the interest or interests in the property to which the payment relates or where the payment into court is made under s. 51(3), the flat to which it relates;

(c) details of any vesting order;

(d) the name and address of the landlord; and

(e) so far as they are known to the tenant, the name and address of every person who is or may be interested in or entitled to the money;

(2) on the filing of the witness statement the money must be paid into court and the court will send notice of the payment to the landlord and every person whose name and address are given in the witness statement;

(3) any subsequent payment into court by the landlord must be made to the credit of the same account as the earlier payment into court;

(4) the appropriate court for the purposes of sub-para. (1) is:

(a) where a vesting order has been made, the county court that made the order; or
(b) where no such order has been made, the county court in whose district the property is situated.

14.6 If an order is made transferring an application to a leasehold valuation tribunal under s. 91(4), the court will:
(1) send notice of the transfer to all parties to the application; and
(2) send to the tribunal copies of the order of transfer and all documents filed in the proceedings.

(Paragraph 14.6 no longer applies to proceedings in England but continues to apply to proceedings in Wales.)

14.7 If a relevant landlord acts independently under sch. 1, para. 7, he is entitled to require any party to claims under the 1993 Act (as described in para. 7(1)(b) of sch. 1) to supply him, on payment of the reasonable costs of copying, with copies of all documents which that party has served on the other parties to the claim.

## Transfer to Leasehold Valuation Tribunal Under the Commonhold and Leasehold Reform Act 2002

15.1 If a question is ordered to be transferred to a leasehold valuation tribunal for determination under the Commonhold and Leasehold Reform Act 2002, sch. 12, para. 3, the court will:
(1) send notice of the transfer to all parties to the claim; and
(2) send to the leasehold valuation tribunal:
(a) the order of transfer; and
(b) all documents filed in the claim relating to the question.

(Paragraph 15.1 applies to proceedings in England but does not apply to proceedings in Wales.)

# CPR Part 57 Probate and Inheritance



## 57.1 Scope of this Part and Definitions

(1) This Part contains rules about—
- (a) probate claims;
- (b) claims for the rectification of wills;
- (c) claims and applications to—
  - (i) substitute another person for a personal representative; or
  - (ii) remove a personal representative; and
- (d) claims under the Inheritance (Provision for Family and Dependants) Act 1975.

(2) In this Part:
- (a) 'probate claim' means a claim for—
  - (i) the grant of probate of the will, or letters of administration of the estate, of a deceased person;
  - (ii) the revocation of such a grant; or
  - (iii) a decree pronouncing for or against the validity of an alleged will; not being a claim which is non-contentious (or common form) probate business;

(Section 128 of the Supreme Court Act 1981 defines non-contentious (or common form) probate business.)

- (b) 'relevant office' means—
  - (i) in the case of High Court proceedings in a Chancery district registry, that registry;
  - (ii) in the case of any other High Court proceedings, Chancery Chambers at the Royal Courts of Justice, Strand, London, WC2A 2LL; and
  - (iii) in the case of county court proceedings, the office of the county court in question;
- (c) 'testamentary document' means a will, a draft of a will, written instructions for a will made by or at the request of, or under the instructions of, the testator, and any document purporting to be evidence of the contents, or to be a copy, of a will which is alleged to have been lost or destroyed;
- (d) 'will' includes a codicil.

### I PROBATE CLAIMS

## 57.2 General

(1) This Section contains rules about probate claims.

(2) Probate claims in the High Court are assigned to the Chancery Division.
(3) Probate claims in the county court must only be brought in—
 (a) a county court where there is also a Chancery district registry; or
 (b) the Central London County Court.
(4) All probate claims are allocated to the multi-track.

### 57.3 How to Start a Probate Claim

A probate claim must be commenced—
(a) in the relevant office; and
(b) using the procedure in Part 7.

### 57.4 Acknowledgment of Service and Defence

(1) A defendant who is served with a claim form must file an acknowledgment of service.
(2) Subject to paragraph (3), the period for filing an acknowledgment of service is—
 (a) if the defendant is served with a claim form which states that particulars of claim are to follow, 28 days after service of the particulars of claim; and
 (b) in any other case, 28 days after service of the claim form.
(3) If the claim form is served out of the jurisdiction under rule 6.19, the period for filing an acknowledgment of service is 14 days longer than the relevant period specified in rule 6.22 or the practice direction supplementing Section 3 of Part 6.
(4) Rule 15.4 (which provides the period for filing a defence) applies as if the words 'under Part 10' were omitted from rule 15.4(1)(b).

### 57.5 Lodging of Testamentary Documents and Filing of Evidence About Testamentary Documents

(1) Any testamentary document of the deceased person in the possession or control of any party must be lodged with the court.
(2) Unless the court directs otherwise, the testamentary documents must be lodged in the relevant office—
 (a) by the claimant when the claim form is issued; and
 (b) by a defendant when he acknowledges service.
(3) The claimant and every defendant who acknowledges service of the claim form must in written evidence—
 (a) describe any testamentary document of the deceased of which he has any knowledge or, if he does not know of any such testamentary document, state that fact, and
 (b) if any testamentary document of which he has knowledge is not in his possession or under his control, give the name and address of the person in whose possession or under whose control it is or, if he does not know the name or address of that person, state that fact.

(A specimen form for the written evidence about testamentary documents is annexed to the practice direction.)

(4) Unless the court directs otherwise, the written evidence required by paragraph (3) must be filed in the relevant office—
 (a) by the claimant, when the claim form is issued; and
 (b) by a defendant when he acknowledges service.
(5) Except with the permission of the court, a party shall not be allowed to inspect the testamentary documents or written evidence lodged or filed by any other party until he himself has lodged his testamentary documents and filed his evidence.
(6) The provisions of paragraphs (2) and (4) may be modified by a practice direction under this Part.

## 57.6 Revocation of Existing Grant

(1) In a probate claim which seeks the revocation of a grant of probate or letters of administration every person who is entitled, or claims to be entitled, to administer the estate under that grant must be made a party to the claim.
(2) If the claimant is the person to whom the grant was made, he must lodge the probate or letters of administration in the relevant office when the claim form is issued.
(3) If a defendant has the probate or letters of administration under his control, he must lodge it in the relevant office when he acknowledges service.
(4) Paragraphs (2) and (3) do not apply where the grant has already been lodged at the court, which in this paragraph includes the Principal Registry of the Family Division or a district probate registry.

## 57.7 Contents of Statements of Case

(1) The claim form must contain a statement of the nature of the interest of the claimant and of each defendant in the estate.
(2) If a party disputes another party's interest in the estate he must state this in his statement of case and set out his reasons.
(3) Any party who contends that at the time when a will was executed the testator did not know of and approve its contents must give particulars of the facts and matters relied on.
(4) Any party who wishes to contend that—
  (a) a will was not duly executed;
  (b) at the time of the execution of a will the testator was not of sound mind, memory and understanding; or
  (c) the execution of a will was obtained by undue influence or fraud,
  must set out the contention specifically and give particulars of the facts and matters relied on.
(5) (a) A defendant may give notice in his defence that he does not raise any positive case, but insists on the will being proved in solemn form and, for that purpose, will cross-examine the witnesses who attested the will.
  (b) If a defendant gives such a notice, the court will not make an order for costs against him unless it considers that there was no reasonable ground for opposing the will.

## 57.8 Counterclaim

(1) A defendant who contends that he has any claim or is entitled to any remedy relating to the grant of probate of the will, or letters of administration of the estate, of the deceased person must serve a counterclaim making that contention.
(2) If the claimant fails to serve particulars of claim within the time allowed, the defendant may, with the permission of the court, serve a counterclaim and the probate claim shall then proceed as if the counterclaim were the particulars of claim.

## 57.9 Probate Counterclaim in Other Proceedings

(1) In this rule 'probate counterclaim' means a counterclaim in any claim other than a probate claim by which the defendant claims any such remedy as is mentioned in rule 57.1(2)(a).
(2) Subject to the following paragraphs of this rule, this Part shall apply with the necessary modifications to a probate counterclaim as it applies to a probate claim.
(3) A probate counterclaim must contain a statement of the nature of the interest of each of the parties in the estate of the deceased to which the probate counterclaim relates.
(4) Unless an application notice is issued within 7 days after the service of a probate counterclaim for an order under rule 3.1(2)(e) or 3.4 for the probate counterclaim to be dealt with in separate proceedings or to be struck out, and the application is granted, the court shall order the transfer of the proceedings to either—

(a) the Chancery Division (if it is not already assigned to that Division) and to either the Royal Courts of Justice or a Chancery district registry (if it is not already proceeding in one of those places); or
(b) if the county court has jurisdiction, to a county court where there is also a Chancery district registry or the Central London County Court.

(5) If an order is made that a probate counterclaim be dealt with in separate proceedings, the order shall order the transfer of the probate counterclaim as required under paragraph (4).

### 57.10 Failure to Acknowledge Service or to File a Defence

(1) A default judgment cannot be obtained in a probate claim and rule 10.2 and Part 12 do not apply.

(2) If any of several defendants fails to acknowledge service the claimant may—
(a) after the time for acknowledging service has expired; and
(b) upon filing written evidence of service of the claim form and (if no particulars of claim were contained in or served with the claim form) the particulars of claim on that defendant;

proceed with the probate claim as if that defendant had acknowledged service.

(3) If no defendant acknowledges service or files a defence then, unless on the application of the claimant the court orders the claim to be discontinued, the claimant may, after the time for acknowledging service or for filing a defence (as the case may be) has expired, apply to the court for an order that the claim is to proceed to trial.

(4) When making an application under paragraph (3) the claimant must file written evidence of service of the claim form and (if no particulars of claim were contained in or served with the claim form) the particulars of claim on each of the defendants.

(5) Where the court makes an order under paragraph (3), it may direct that the claim be tried on written evidence.

### 57.11 Discontinuance and Dismissal

(1) Part 38 does not apply to probate claims.

(2) At any stage of a probate claim the court, on the application of the claimant or of any defendant who has acknowledged service, may order that—
(a) the claim be discontinued or dismissed on such terms as to costs or otherwise as it thinks just; and
(b) a grant of probate of the will, or letters of administration of the estate, of the deceased person be made to the person entitled to the grant.

## II RECTIFICATION OF WILLS

### 57.12

(1) This Section contains rules about claims for the rectification of a will.

(Section 20 of the Administration of Justice Act 1982 provides for rectification of a will. Additional provisions are contained in rule 55 of the Non-Contentious Probate Rules 1987.)

(2) Every personal representative of the estate shall be joined as a party.

(3) The practice direction makes provision for lodging the grant of probate or letters of administration with the will annexed in a claim under this Section.

## III SUBSTITUTION AND REMOVAL OF PERSONAL REPRESENTATIVES

### 57.13

(1) This Section contains rules about claims and applications for substitution or removal of a personal representative.

(2) Claims under this Section must be brought in the High Court and are assigned to the Chancery Division.

(Section 50 of the Administration of Justice Act 1985 gives the High Court power to appoint a substitute for, or to remove, a personal representative.)

(3) Every personal representative of the estate shall be joined as a party.

(4) The practice direction makes provision for lodging the grant of probate or letters of administration in a claim under this Section.

(5) If substitution or removal of a personal representative is sought by application in existing proceedings, this rule shall apply with references to claims being read as if they referred to applications.

## IV CLAIMS UNDER THE INHERITANCE (PROVISION FOR FAMILY AND DEPENDANTS) ACT 1975

### 57.14 Scope of this Section

This Section contains rules about claims under the Inheritance (Provision for Family and Dependants) Act 1975 ('the Act').

### 57.15 Proceedings in the High Court

(1) Proceedings in the High Court under the Act shall be issued in either—
  (a) the Chancery Division; or
  (b) the Family Division.

(2) The Civil Procedure Rules apply to proceedings under the Act which are brought in the Family Division, except that the provisions of the Family Proceedings Rules 1991 relating to the drawing up and service of orders apply instead of the provisions in Part 40 and its practice direction.

### 57.16 Procedure for Claims Under Section 1 of the Act

(1) A claim under section 1 of the Act must be made by issuing a claim form in accordance with Part 8.

(2) Rule 8.3 (acknowledgment of service) and rule 8.5 (filing and serving written evidence) apply as modified by paragraphs (3) to (5) of this rule.

(3) The written evidence filed and served by the claimant with the claim form must have exhibited to it an official copy of—
  (a) the grant of probate or letters of administration in respect of the deceased's estate; and
  (b) every testamentary document in respect of which probate or letters of administration were granted.

(4) Subject to paragraph 4(A), the time within which a defendant must file and serve—
  (a) an acknowledgment of service; and
  (b) any written evidence,
  is not more than 21 days after service of the claim form on him.

(4A) If the claim form is served out of the jurisdiction under rule 6.19, the period for filing as acknowledgment of service and any written evidence is 7 days longer than the relevant period specified in rule 6.22 or the practice direction supplementing Section III of Part 6.

(5) A defendant who is a personal representative of the deceased must file and serve written evidence, which must include the information required by the practice direction.

# PD 57 Practice Direction — Probate

This practice direction supplements CPR Part 57.

## I PROBATE CLAIMS

### General

1.1 This Section of this practice direction applies to contentious probate claims.

1.2 The rules and procedure relating to non-contentious probate proceedings (also known as 'common form') are the Non-Contentious Probate Rules 1987 (SI 1987/2024) as amended.

### How to Start a Probate Claim

2.1 A claim form and all subsequent court documents relating to a probate claim must be marked at the top 'In the estate of [name] deceased (Probate)'.

2.2 The claim form must be issued out of:
   (1) Chancery Chambers at the Royal Courts of Justice; or
   (2) one of the Chancery district registries; or
   (3) if the claim is suitable to be heard in the county court:
      (a) a county court in a place where there is also a Chancery district registry; or
      (b) the Central London County Court.

   There are Chancery district registries at Birmingham, Bristol, Cardiff, Leeds, Liverpool, Manchester, Newcastle upon Tyne and Preston.

   (Section 32 of the County Courts Act 1984 identifies which probate claims may be heard in a county court.)

2.3 When the claim form is issued, the relevant office will send a notice to Leeds District Probate Registry, Coronet House, Queen Street, Leeds LS1 2BA, DX 26451 Leeds (Park Square), telephone (0113) 243 1505, requesting that all testamentary documents, grants of representation and other relevant documents currently held at any probate registry are sent to the relevant office.

2.4 The commencement of a probate claim will, unless a court otherwise directs, prevent any grant of probate or letters of administration being made until the probate claim has been disposed of.

   (Rule 45 of the Non-Contentious Probate Rules 1987 makes provision for notice of the probate claim to be given, and s. 117 of the Supreme Court Act 1981 for the grant of letters of administration pending the determination of a probate claim. Paragraph 8 of this practice direction makes provision about an application for such a grant.)

### Testamentary Documents and Evidence About Testamentary Documents

3.1 Unless the court orders otherwise, if a testamentary document is held by the court (whether it was lodged by a party or it was previously held at a probate registry) when the claim has been disposed of the court will send it to the Leeds District Probate Registry.

3.2 The written evidence about testamentary documents required by this Part:
   (1) should be in the form annexed to this practice direction; and
   (2) must be signed by the party personally and not by his solicitor or other representative (except that if the party is a child or patient the written evidence must be signed by his litigation friend).

3.3 In a case in which there is urgent need to commence a probate claim (for example, in order to be able to apply immediately for the appointment of an administrator pending the determination of the claim) and it is not possible for the claimant to lodge the testamentary documents or to file the evidence about testamentary documents in the relevant office at the same time as the claim form is to be issued, the court may direct that the claimant shall be allowed to issue the claim form upon his giving an undertaking to the court to lodge the documents and file the evidence within such time as the court shall specify.

## Case Management

4 In giving case management directions in a probate claim the court will give consideration to the questions:

(1) whether any person who may be affected by the claim and who is not joined as a party should be joined as a party or given notice of the claim, whether under r. 19.8A or otherwise; and

(2) whether to make a representation order under r. 19.6 or r. 19.7.

## Summary Judgment

5.1 If an order pronouncing for a will in solemn form is sought on an application for summary judgment, the evidence in support of the application must include written evidence proving due execution of the will.

5.2 If a defendant has given notice in his defence under r. 57.7(5) that he raises no positive case but:

(1) he insists that the will be proved in solemn form; and

(2) for that purpose he will cross-examine the witnesses who attested the will,

any application by the claimant for summary judgment is subject to the right of that defendant to require those witnesses to attend court for cross-examination.

## Settlement of a Probate Claim

6.1 If at any time the parties agree to settle a probate claim, the court may:

(1) order the trial of the claim on written evidence, which will lead to a grant in solemn form;

(2) order that the claim be discontinued or dismissed under r. 57.11, which will lead to a grant in common form; or

(3) pronounce for or against the validity of one or more wills under s. 49 of the Administration of Justice Act 1985.

(For a form of order which is also applicable to discontinuance and which may be adapted as appropriate, see PF 38 CH.)

(Section 49 of the Administration of Justice Act 1985 permits a probate claim to be compromised without a trial if every 'relevant beneficiary', as defined in that section, has consented to the proposed order. It is only available in the High Court.)

6.2 Applications under s. 49 of the Administration of Justice Act 1985 may be heard by a master or district judge and must be supported by written evidence identifying the relevant beneficiaries and exhibiting the written consent of each of them. The written evidence of testamentary documents required by r. 57.5 will still be necessary.

## Application for an Order to Bring in a Will, etc.

7.1 Any party applying for an order under s. 122 of the Supreme Court Act 1981 ('the 1981 Act') must serve the application notice on the person against whom the order is sought. (Section 122 of the 1981 Act empowers the court to order a person to attend court for examination, and to answer questions and bring in documents, if there are reasonable grounds for believing that such person has knowledge of a testamentary document. Rule 50(1) of the Non-Contentious Probate Rules 1987 makes similar provision where a probate claim has not been commenced.)

7.2 An application for the issue of a witness summons under s. 123 of the 1981 Act:

(1) may be made without notice; and

(2) must be supported by written evidence setting out the grounds of the application.

(Section 123 of the 1981 Act empowers the court, where it appears that any person has in his possession, custody or power a testamentary document, to issue a witness summons ordering such person to bring in that document. Rule 50(2) of the Non-Contentious Probate Rules makes similar provision where a probate claim has not been commenced.)

7.3 An application under s. 122 or 123 of the 1981 Act should be made to a master or district judge.

7.4 A person against whom a witness summons is issued under s. 123 of the 1981 Act who denies that the testamentary document referred to in the witness summons is in his possession or under his control may file written evidence to that effect.

### Administration Pending the Determination of a Probate Claim

8.1 An application under s. 117 of the Supreme Court Act 1981 for an order for the grant of administration pending the determination of a probate claim should be made by application notice in the probate claim.

8.2 If an order for a grant of administration is made under s. 117 of the 1981 Act:

(1) Rules 69.4 to 69.7 shall apply as if the administrator were a receiver appointed by the court;

(2) if the court allows the administrator remuneration under r. 69.7, it may make an order under s. 117(3) of the 1981 Act assigning the remuneration out of the estate of the deceased; and

(3) every application relating to the conduct of the administration shall be made by application notice in the probate claim.

8.3 An order under s. 117 may be made by a master or district judge.

8.4 If an order is made under s. 117 an application for the grant of letters of administration should be made to the Principal Registry of the Family Division, First Avenue House, 42–49 High Holborn, London WC1V 6NP.

8.5 The appointment of an administrator to whom letters of administration are granted following an order under s. 117 will cease automatically when a final order in the probate claim is made but will continue pending any appeal.

## II RECTIFICATION OF WILLS

### Scope of this Section

9 This Section of this practice direction applies to claims for the rectification of a will.

### Lodging the Grant

10.1 If the claimant is the person to whom the grant was made in respect of the will of which rectification is sought, he must, unless the court orders otherwise, lodge the probate or letters of administration with the will annexed with the court when the claim form is issued.

10.2 If a defendant has the probate or letters of administration in his possession or under his control, he must, unless the court orders otherwise, lodge it in the relevant office within 14 days after the service of the claim form on him.

### Orders

11 A copy of every order made for the rectification of a will shall be sent to the Principal Registry of the Family Division for filing, and a memorandum of the order shall be endorsed on, or permanently annexed to, the grant under which the estate is administered.

## III SUBSTITUTION AND REMOVAL OF PERSONAL REPRESENTATIVES

### Scope of this Section

12 This Section of this practice direction applies to claims and applications for substitution or removal of a personal representative. If substitution or removal of a personal representative is sought by application in existing proceedings, this Section shall apply with references to the claim, claim form and claimant being read as if they referred to the application, application notice and applicant respectively.

### Starting the Claim

13.1 The claim form must be accompanied by:
- (1) a sealed or certified copy of the grant of probate or letters of administration; and
- (2) written evidence containing the grounds of the claim and the following information so far as it is known to the claimant:
  - (a) brief details of the property comprised in the estate, with an approximate estimate of its capital value and any income that is received from it;
  - (b) brief details of the liabilities of the estate;
  - (c) the names and addresses of the persons who are in possession of the documents relating to the estate;
  - (d) the names of the beneficiaries and their respective interests in the estate; and
  - (e) the name, address and occupation of any proposed substituted personal representative;

13.2 If the claim is for the appointment of a substituted personal representative, the claim form must be accompanied by:
- (1) a signed or (in the case of the Public Trustee or a corporation) sealed consent to act; and
- (2) written evidence as to the fitness of the proposed substituted personal representative, if an individual, to act.

### Production of the Grant

14.1 On the hearing of the claim the personal representative must produce to the court the grant of representation to the deceased's estate.

14.2 If an order is made substituting or removing the personal representative, the grant (together with a sealed copy of the order) must be sent to and remain in the custody of the Principal Registry of the Family Division until a memorandum of the order has been endorsed on or permanently annexed to the grant.

## IV CLAIMS UNDER THE INHERITANCE (PROVISION FOR FAMILY AND DEPENDANTS) ACT 1975

### Acknowledgment of Service by Personal Representatives—Rule 57.16(4)

15 Where a defendant who is a personal representative wishes to remain neutral in relation to the claim, and agrees to abide by any decision which the court may make, he should state this in Section A of the acknowledgment of service form.

### Written Evidence of Personal Representative—Rule 57.16(5)

16 The written evidence filed by a defendant who is a personal representative must state to the best of that person's ability:
- (1) full details of the value of the deceased's net estate, as defined in s. 25(1) of the Act;
- (2) the person or classes of persons beneficially interested in the estate, and:
  - (a) the names and (unless they are parties to the claim) addresses of all living beneficiaries; and
  - (b) the value of their interests in the estate so far as they are known.

(3) whether any living beneficiary (and if so, naming him) is a child or patient within the meaning of r. 21.1(2); and
(4) any facts which might affect the exercise of the court's powers under the Act.

## Separate Representation of Claimants

17 If a claim is made jointly by two or more claimants, and it later appears that any of the claimants have a conflict of interests:
(1) any claimant may choose to be represented at any hearing by separate solicitors or counsel, or may appear in person; and
(2) if the court considers that claimants who are represented by the same solicitors or counsel ought to be separately represented, it may adjourn the application until they are.

## Production of the Grant

18.1 On the hearing of a claim the personal representative must produce to the court the original grant of representation to the deceased's estate.
18.2 If the court makes an order under the Act, the original grant (together with a sealed copy of the order) must be sent to the Principal Registry of the Family Division for a memorandum of the order to be endorsed on or permanently annexed to the grant in accordance with s. 19(3) of the Act.
18.3 Every final order embodying terms of compromise made in proceedings under the Act, whether made with or without a hearing, must contain a direction that a memorandum of the order shall be endorsed on or permanently annexed to the probate or letters of administration and a copy of the order shall be sent to the Principal Registry of the Family Division with the relevant grant of probate or letters of administration for endorsement.

# ANNEX

# A FORM OF WITNESS STATEMENT OR AFFIDAVIT ABOUT TESTAMENTARY DOCUMENTS (CPR, RULE 57.5)

*[Title of the claim]*

I [*name and address*] the claimant/defendant in this claim state [on oath] that I have no knowledge of any document:
(1) being or purported to be or having the form or effect of a will or codicil of [*name of deceased*] whose estate is the subject of this claim;
(2) being or purporting to be a draft or written instructions for any such will or codicil made by or at the request of or under the instructions of the deceased;
(3) being or purporting to be evidence of the contents or a copy of any such will or codicil which is alleged to have been lost or destroyed, except [*describe any testamentary document of the deceased, and if any such document is not in your control, give the name and address of the person who you believe has possession or control of it, or state that you do not know the name and address of that person*].

[I believe that the facts stated in this witness statement are true] [*or jurat for affidavit*]
[*NOTE: 'testamentary document' is defined in CPR, r. 57.1.*]

# CPR Part 58 Commercial Court



## 58.1 Scope of this Part and Interpretation

(1) This Part applies to claims in the Commercial Court of the Queen's Bench Division.
(2) In this Part and its practice direction, 'commercial claim' means any claim arising out of the transaction of trade and commerce and includes any claim relating to—
  (a) a business document or contract;
  (b) the export or import of goods;
  (c) the carriage of goods by land, sea, air or pipeline;
  (d) the exploitation of oil and gas reserves or other natural resources;
  (e) insurance and re-insurance;
  (f) banking and financial services;
  (g) the operation of markets and exchanges;
  (h) the purchase and sale of commodities;
  (i) the construction of ships;
  (j) business agency; and
  (k) arbitration.

## 58.2 Specialist List

(1) The commercial list is a specialist list for claims proceeding in the Commercial Court.
(2) One of the judges of the Commercial Court shall be in charge of the commercial list.

## 58.3 Application of the Civil Procedure Rules

These rules and their practice directions apply to claims in the commercial list unless this Part or a practice direction provides otherwise.

## 58.4 Proceedings in the Commercial List

(1) A commercial claim may be started in the commercial list.
(2) Rule 30.5 applies to claims in the commercial list, except that a Commercial Court judge may order a claim to be transferred to any other specialist list.

(Rule 30.5(3) provides that an application for the transfer of proceedings to or from a specialist list must be made to a judge dealing with claims in that list.)

## 58.5 Claim Form and Particulars of Claim

(1) If, in a Part 7 claim, particulars of claim are not contained in or served with the claim form—
  (a) the claim form must state that, if an acknowledgment of service is filed which indicates an intention to defend the claim, particulars of claim will follow;
  (b) when the claim form is served, it must be accompanied by the documents specified in rule 7.8(1);

(c) the claimant must serve particulars of claim within 28 days of the filing of an acknowledgment of service which indicates an intention to defend; and
(d) rule 7.4(2) does not apply.

(2) A statement of value is not required to be included in the claim form.
(3) If the claimant is claiming interest, he must—
(a) include a statement to that effect; and
(b) give the details set out in rule 16.4(2),
in both the claim form and the particulars of claim.

## 58.6 Acknowledgment of Service

(1) A defendant must file an acknowledgment of service in every case.
(2) Unless paragraph (3) applies, the period for filing an acknowledgment of service is 14 days after service of the claim form.
(3) Where the claim form is served out of the jurisdiction, or on the agent of a defendant who is overseas, the time periods provided by rules 6.16(4), 6.21(4) and 6.22 apply after service of the claim form.

## 58.7 Disputing the Court's Jurisdiction

(1) Part 11 applies to claims in the commercial list with the modifications set out in this rule.
(2) An application under rule 11(1) must be made within 28 days after filing an acknowledgment of service.
(3) If the defendant files an acknowledgment of service indicating an intention to dispute the court's jurisdiction, the claimant need not serve particulars of claim before the hearing of the application.

## 58.8 Default Judgment

(1) If, in a Part 7 claim in the commercial list, a defendant fails to file an acknowledgment of service, the claimant need not serve particulars of claim before he may obtain or apply for default judgment in accordance with Part 12.
(2) Rule 12.6(1) applies with the modification that paragraph (a) shall be read as if it referred to the claim form instead of the particulars of claim.

## 58.9 Admissions

(1) Rule 14.5 does not apply to claims in the commercial list.
(2) If the defendant admits part of a claim for a specified amount of money, the claimant may apply under rule 14.3 for judgment on the admission.
(3) Rule 14.14(1) applies with the modification that paragraph (a) shall be read as if it referred to the claim form instead of the particulars of claim.

## 58.10 Defence and Reply

(1) Part 15 (defence and reply) applies to claims in the commercial list with the modification to rule 15.8 that the claimant must—
(a) file any reply to a defence; and
(b) serve it on all other parties,
within 21 days after service of the defence.

(2) Rule 6.23 (period for filing a defence where the claim form is served out of the jurisdiction) applies to claims in the commercial list, except that if the particulars of claim are served after the defendant has filed an acknowledgment of service the period for filing a defence is 28 days from service of the particulars of claim.

## 58.11 Statements of Case

The court may at any time before or after the issue of the claim form order a claim in the commercial list to proceed without the filing or service of statements of case.

## 58.12 Part 8 Claims

Part 8 applies to claims in the commercial list, with the modification that a defendant to a Part 8 claim who wishes to rely on written evidence must file and serve it within 28 days after filing an acknowledgment of service.

## 58.13 Case Management

(1) All proceedings in the commercial list are treated as being allocated to the multi-track and Part 26 does not apply.
(2) The following parts only of Part 29 apply—
  (a) rule 29.3(2) (legal representative to attend case management conferences and pre-trial reviews);
  (b) rule 29.5 (variation of case management timetable) with the exception of rule 29.5(1)(c).
(3) As soon as practicable the court will hold a case management conference which must be fixed in accordance with the practice direction.
(4) At the case management conference or at any hearing at which the parties are represented the court may give such directions for the management of the case as it considers appropriate.

## 58.14 Disclosure—Ships Papers

(1) If, in proceedings relating to a marine insurance policy, the underwriters apply for specific disclosure under rule 31.12, the court may—
  (a) order a party to produce all the ship's papers; and
  (b) require that party to use his best endeavours to obtain and disclose documents which are not or have not been in his control.
(2) An order under this rule may be made at any stage of the proceedings and on such terms, if any, as to staying the proceedings or otherwise, as the court thinks fit.

## 58.15 Judgments and Orders

(1) Except for orders made by the court on its own initiative and unless the court orders otherwise, every judgment or order will be drawn up by the parties, and rule 40.3 is modified accordingly.
(2) An application for a consent order must include a draft of the proposed order signed on behalf of all the parties to whom it relates.
(3) Rule 40.6 (consent judgments and orders) does not apply.

# PD 58 Practice Direction — Commercial Court

This practice direction supplements CPR Part 58.

## General

1.1 This practice direction applies to commercial claims proceeding in the commercial list of the Queen's Bench Division. It supersedes all previous practice directions and practice statements in the Commercial Court.

1.2 All proceedings in the commercial list, including any appeal from a judgment, order or decision of a master or district judge before the proceedings were transferred to the Commercial Court, will be heard or determined by a Commercial Court judge, except that:

(1) another judge of the Queen's Bench Division or Chancery Division may hear urgent applications if no Commercial Court judge is available; and

(2) unless the court otherwise orders, any application relating to the enforcement of a Commercial Court judgment or order for the payment of money will be dealt with by a master of the Queen's Bench Division or a district judge.

1.3 Provisions in other practice directions which refer to a master or district judge are to be read, in relation to claims in the commercial list, as if they referred to a Commercial Court judge.

1.4 The Admiralty and Commercial Registry in the Royal Courts of Justice is the administrative office of the court for all proceedings in the commercial list.

## Starting Proceedings in the Commercial Court

2.1 Claims in the Commercial Court must be issued in the Admiralty and Commercial Registry.

2.2 When the Registry is closed, a request to issue a claim form may be made by fax, using the procedure set out in Appendix A to this practice direction. If a request is made which complies with that procedure, the claim form is issued when the fax is received by the Registry.

2.3 The claim form must be marked in the top right hand corner 'Queen's Bench Division, Commercial Court'.

2.4 A claimant starting proceedings in the commercial list, other than an arbitration claim, must use form N1(CC) for Part 7 claims or form N208(CC) for Part 8 claims.

## Applications Before Proceedings Are Issued

3.1 A party who intends to bring a claim in the commercial list must make any application before the claim form is issued to a Commercial Court judge.

3.2 The written evidence in support of such an application must state that the claimant intends to bring proceedings in the commercial list.

3.3 If the Commercial Court judge hearing the application considers that the proceedings should not be brought in the commercial list, he may adjourn the application to be heard by a master or by a judge who is not a Commercial Court judge.

## Transferring Proceedings to or from the Commercial Court

4.1 If an application is made to a court other than the Commercial Court to transfer proceedings to the commercial list, the other court may:

(1) adjourn the application to be heard by a Commercial Court judge; or

(2) dismiss the application.

4.2 If the Commercial Court orders proceedings to be transferred to the commercial list:

(1) it will order them to be transferred to the Royal Courts of Justice; and

(2) it may give case management directions.

4.3 An application by a defendant, including a Part 20 defendant, for an order transferring proceedings from the commercial list should be made promptly and normally not later than the first case management conference.

4.4 A party applying to the Commercial Court to transfer a claim to the commercial list must give notice of the application to the court in which the claim is proceeding, and the Commercial Court will not make an order for transfer until it is satisfied that such notice has been given.

## Acknowledgment of Service

5.1 For Part 7 claims, a defendant must file an acknowledgment of service using form N9 (CC).

5.2 For Part 8 claims, a defendant must file an acknowledgment of service using form N210 (CC).

## Default Judgment and Admissions

6 PD 12 and PD 14 apply with the following modifications:

(1) PD 12, para. 4.1(1), is to be read as referring to the service of the claim form; and

(2) the references to 'particulars of claim' in PD 14, paras 2.1, 3.1 and 3.2, are to be read as referring to the claim form.

## Variation of Time Limits

7.1 If the parties, in accordance with r. 2.11, agree in writing to vary a time limit, the claimant must notify the court in writing, giving brief written reasons for the agreed variation.

7.2 The court may make an order overriding an agreement by the parties varying a time limit.

## Amendments

8 PD 17, para. 2.2, is modified so that amendments to a statement of case must show the original text, unless the court orders otherwise.

## Service of Documents

9 Unless the court orders otherwise, the Commercial Court will not serve documents or orders and service must be effected by the parties.

## Case Management

10.1 The following parts only of PD 29 apply:

(1) para. 5 (case management conferences), excluding para. 5.9 and modified so far as is made necessary by other specific provisions of this practice direction; and

(2) para. 7 (failure to comply with case management directions).

10.2 If the proceedings are started in the commercial list, the claimant must apply for a case management conference:

(a) for a Part 7 claim, within 14 days of the date when all defendants who intend to file and serve a defence have done so; and

(b) for a Part 8 claim, within 14 days of the date when all defendants who intend to serve evidence have done so.

10.3 If the proceedings are transferred to the commercial list, the claimant must apply for a case management conference within 14 days of the date of the order transferring them, unless the judge held, or gave directions for, a case management conference when he made the order transferring the proceedings.

10.4 Any party may, at a time earlier than that provided in paras 10.2 or 10.3, apply in writing to the court to fix a case management conference.

10.5 If the claimant does not make an application in accordance with paras 10.2 or 10.3, any other party may apply for a case management conference.

10.6 The court may fix a case management conference at any time on its own initiative. If it does so, the court will give at least seven days' notice to the parties, unless there are compelling reasons for a shorter period of notice.

10.7 Not less than seven days before a case management conference, each party must file and serve:

(1) a completed case management information sheet; and

(2) an application notice for any order which that party intends to seek at the case management conference, other than directions referred to in the case management information sheet.

10.8 Unless the court orders otherwise, the claimant, in consultation with the other parties, must prepare:

(1) a case memorandum, containing a short and uncontroversial summary of what the case is about and of its material case history;

(2) a list of issues, with a section listing important matters which are not in dispute; and

(3) a case management bundle containing:

(a) the claim form;

(b) all statements of case (excluding schedules), except that, if a summary of a statement of case has been filed, the bundle should contain the summary, and not the full statement of case;

(c) the case memorandum;

(d) the list of issues;

(e) the case management information sheets and, if a pre-trial timetable has been agreed or ordered, that timetable;

(f) the principal orders of the court; and

(g) any agreement in writing made by the parties as to disclosure,

and provide copies of the case management bundle for the court and the other parties at least seven days before the first case management conference or any earlier hearing at which the court may give case management directions.

10.9 The claimant, in consultation with the other parties, must revise and update the documents referred to in para. 10.8 appropriately as the case proceeds. This must include making all necessary revisions and additions at least seven days before any subsequent hearing at which the court may give case management directions.

## Pre-trial Review

11.1 At any pre-trial review or case management hearing, the court will ensure that case management directions have been complied with and give any further directions for the trial that are necessary.

11.2 Advocates who are to represent the parties at the trial should represent them at the pre-trial review and any case management hearing at which arrangements for the trial are to be discussed.

11.3 Before the pre-trial review, the parties must discuss and, if possible, agree a draft written timetable for the trial.

11.4 The claimant must file a copy of the draft timetable for the trial at least two days before the hearing of the pre-trial review. Any parts of the timetable which are not agreed must be identified and short explanations of the disagreement must be given.

11.5 At the pre-trial review, the court will set a timetable for the trial, unless a timetable has already been fixed or the court considers that it would be inappropriate to do so or appropriate to do so at a later time.

## Case Management Where There is a Part 20 Claim

12 PD 20, para. 5, applies, except that, unless the court otherwise orders, the court will give case management directions for Part 20 claims at the same case management conferences as it gives directions for the main claim.

## Evidence for Applications

13.1 The general requirement is that, unless the court orders otherwise:
(1) evidence in support of an application must be filed and served with the application (see r. 23.7(3));
(2) evidence in answer must be filed and served within 14 days after the application is served; and
(3) evidence in reply must be filed and served within seven days of the service of evidence in answer.

13.2 In any case in which the application is likely to require an oral hearing of more than half a day the periods set out in paras 13.1(2) and (3) will be 28 days and 14 days respectively.

13.3 If the date fixed for the hearing of an application means that the times in paras 13.1(2) and (3) cannot both be achieved, the evidence must be filed and served:
(1) as soon as possible; and
(2) in sufficient time to ensure that the application may fairly proceed on the date fixed.

13.4 The parties may, in accordance with r. 2.11, agree different periods from those in paras 13.1(2) and (3) provided that the agreement does not affect the date fixed for the hearing of the application.

## Judgments and Orders

14.1 An application for a consent order must include a draft of the proposed order signed on behalf of all parties to whom it relates (see PD 23, para. 10.4).

14.2 Judgments and orders are generally drawn up by the parties (see r. 58.15). The parties are not therefore required to supply draft orders on disk (see PD 23, para. 12.1).

# APPENDIX A
# PROCEDURE FOR ISSUE OF CLAIM FORM WHEN REGISTRY IS CLOSED — PARAGRAPH 2.2

1 A request to issue a claim form may be made by fax when the Registry is closed, provided that:
(a) the claim form is signed by a solicitor acting on behalf of the claimant; and
(b) it does not require the permission of the court for its issue (unless such permission has already been given).

2 The solicitor requesting the issue of the claim form ('the issuing solicitor') must:
(a) endorse on the claim form and sign the endorsement set out below;
(b) send a copy of the claim form so endorsed to the Registry by fax for issue under para. 2.2 of this practice direction; and
(c) complete and sign a certificate in the form set out below, certifying that he has received a transmission report confirming that the fax has been transmitted in full, and stating the time and date of transmission.

3 When the Registry is next open to the public after the issue of a claim form in accordance with this procedure, the issuing solicitor or his agent must attend and deliver to the Registry:
(a) the original of the claim form which was sent by fax (including the endorsement and the certificate) or, if the claim form has been served, a true and certified copy of it;
(b) as many copies of the claim form as the Registry requires; and
(c) the transmission report.

4 When a court officer at the Registry has checked that:
(a) the claim form delivered under para. 3 matches the claim form received by fax; and
(b) the correct issue fee has been paid,

he will allocate a number to the case, and seal, mark as 'original' and date the claim form with the date of issue (being the date when the fax is recorded at the Registry as having been received).

5 If the issuing solicitor has served the unsealed claim form on any person, he must as soon as practicable:
   (a) inform that person of the case number; and
   (b) if requested, serve him with a copy of the sealed and dated claim form at any address in England and Wales.

6 Any person served with a claim form issued under this procedure may, without paying a fee, inspect and take copies of the documents lodged at the Registry under paras 2 and 3 above.

7 The issue of a claim form in accordance with this procedure takes place when the fax is recorded at the Registry as having been received, and the claim form has the same effect for all purposes as a claim form issued under Part 7 or 8. Unless the court otherwise orders, the sealed version of the claim form retained by the Registry is conclusive proof that the claim form was issued at the time and on the date stated.

8 If the procedure set out in this Appendix is not complied with, the court may declare that a claim form shall be treated as not having been issued.

## Endorsement

A claim form issued pursuant to a request by fax must be endorsed as follows:

(1) This claim form is issued under paragraph 2.2 of the Commercial Court practice direction and may be served notwithstanding that it does not bear the seal of the Court.

(2) A true copy of this claim form and endorsement has been sent to the Admiralty and Commercial Registry, Royal Courts of Justice, Strand, London WC2A 2LL, at the time and date certified below by the solicitor whose name appears below ('the issuing solicitor').

(3) It is the duty of the issuing solicitor or his agent to attend at the Registry when it is next open to the public for the claim form to be sealed.

(4) Any person served with this unsealed claim form:
   (a) will be notified by the issuing solicitor of the case number;
   (b) may require the issuing solicitor to serve him with a copy of the sealed claim form at an address in England and Wales; and
   (c) may inspect without charge the documents lodged at the Registry by the issuing solicitor.

(5) I, the issuing solicitor, undertake [to the Court, to the defendants named in this claim form, and to any other person served with this claim form]:
   (a) that the statement in paragraph 2 above is correct;
   (b) that the time and date given in the certificate with this endorsement are correct;
   (c) that this claim form is a claim form which may be issued under paragraph 2.2 of and Appendix A to the Commercial Court practice direction;
   (d) that I will comply in all respects with the requirements of Appendix A of the Commercial Court practice direction; and
   (e) that I will indemnify any person served with the claim form before it is sealed against any loss suffered as a result of the claim form being or becoming invalid as a result of any failure to comply with Appendix A of the Commercial Court practice direction.

(Signed)
Solicitor for the claimant

Note: the endorsement may be signed in the name of the firm of solicitors rather than an individual solicitor, or by solicitors' agents in their capacity as agents acting on behalf of their professional clients.

## Certificate

The issuing solicitor must sign a certificate in the following form:

I certify that I have received a transmission report confirming that the transmission of a copy of this claim form to the Registry by fax was fully completed and that the time and date of transmission to the Registry were [enter the time and date shown on the transmission report].

Dated

(Signed)
Solicitor for the claimant

Note: the certificate must be signed in the name of the firm of solicitors rather than an individual solicitor, or by solicitors' agents in their capacity as agents acting on behalf of their professional clients.

[The following forms are annexed to PD 58:

| | |
|---|---|
| N1(CC) | Claim form (CPR, Part 7) |
| N1C(CC) | Notes for defendant on replying to the Part 7 claim form (Commercial Court) |
| N9(CC) | Acknowledgment of service |
| N208(CC) | Claim form (CPR, Part 8) |
| N208C(CC) | Notes for defendant on replying to the Part 8 claim form |
| N210(CC) | Acknowledgment of service (Part 8) claim |
| N211(CC) | Claim form (additional claims—CPR, Part 20) |
| N211C(CC) | Notes for Part 20 defendant on replying to the Part 20 claim form (Commercial Court) |
| N213(CC) | Acknowledgment of service (Part 20 claim) |

These forms are not reproduced in this work but may be accessed via the DCA website at <http://www.dca.gov.uk>.]

# CPR Part 59 Mercantile Courts



## 59.1 Scope of this Part and Interpretation

(1) This Part applies to claims in Mercantile Courts.
(2) A claim may only be started in a Mercantile Court if it—
   (a) relates to a commercial or business matter in a broad sense; and
   (b) is not required to proceed in the Chancery Division or in another specialist list.
(3) In this Part and its practice direction—
   (a) 'Mercantile Court' means a specialist list established within the courts listed in the Practice Direction;
   (b) 'mercantile claim' means a claim proceeding in a Mercantile Court; and
   (c) 'Mercantile judge' means a judge authorised to sit in a Mercantile Court.

## 59.2 Application of the Civil Procedure Rules

These Rules and their practice directions apply to mercantile claims unless this Part or a practice direction provides otherwise.

## 59.3 Transfer of Proceedings

Rule 30.5 applies with the modifications that—
(a) a Mercantile judge may transfer a mercantile claim to another Mercantile Court; and
(b) a Commercial Court judge may transfer a claim from the Commercial Court to a Mercantile Court.

(Rule 30.5(3) provides that an application for the transfer of proceedings to or from a specialist list must be made to a judge dealing with claims in that list.)

## 59.4 Claim Form and Particulars of Claim

(1) If particulars of claim are not contained in or served with the claim form—
   (a) the claim form must state that, if an acknowledgment of service is filed which indicates an intention to defend the claim, particulars of claim will follow;
   (b) when the claim form is served, it must be accompanied by the documents specified in rule 7.8(1);
   (c) the claimant must serve particulars of claim within 28 days of the filing of an acknowledgment of service which indicates an intention to defend; and
   (d) rule 7.4(2) does not apply.
(2) If the claimant is claiming interest, he must—
   (a) include a statement to that effect; and
   (b) give the details set out in rule 16.4(2),

   in both the claim form and the particulars of claim.
(3) Rules 12.6(1)(a) and 14.14(1)(a) apply with the modification that references to the particulars of claim shall be read as if they referred to the claim form.

## 59.5 Acknowledgment of Service

(1) A defendant must file an acknowledgment of service in every case.

(2) Unless paragraph (3) applies, the period for filing an acknowledgment of service is 14 days after service of the claim form.
(3) Where the claim form is served out of the jurisdiction, or on the agent of a defendant who is overseas, the time periods provided by rules 6.16(4), 6.21(4) and 6.22 apply after service of the claim form.

## 59.6 Disputing the Court's Jurisdiction

(1) Part 11 applies to mercantile claims with the modifications set out in this rule.
(2) An application under rule 11(1) must be made within 28 days after filing an acknowledgment of service.
(3) If the defendant files an acknowledgment of service indicating an intention to dispute the court's jurisdiction, the claimant need not serve particulars of claim before the hearing of the application.

## 59.7 Default Judgment

(1) Part 12 applies to mercantile claims, except that rules 12.10 and 12.11 apply as modified by paragraphs (2) and (3) of this rule.
(2) If, in a Part 7 claim—
 (a) the claim form has been served but no particulars of claim have been served; and
 (b) the defendant has failed to file an acknowledgment of service,
 the claimant must make an application if he wishes to obtain a default judgment.
(3) The application may be made without notice, but the court may direct it to be served on the defendant.

## 59.8 Admissions

(1) Rule 14.5 does not apply to mercantile claims.
(2) If the defendant admits part of a claim for a specified amount of money, the claimant may apply under rule 14.3 for judgment on the admission.

## 59.9 Defence and Reply

(1) Part 15 (defence and reply) applies to mercantile claims with the modification to rule 15.8 that the claimant must—
 (a) file any reply to a defence; and
 (b) serve it on all other parties,
 within 21 days after service of the defence.
(2) Rule 6.23 (period for filing a defence where the claim form is served out of the jurisdiction) applies to mercantile claims, except that if the particulars of claim are served after the defendant has filed an acknowledgment of service the period for filing a defence is 28 days from service of the particulars of claim.

## 59.10 Statements of Case

The court may at any time before or after issue of the claim form order a mercantile claim to proceed without the filing or service of statements of case.

## 59.11 Case Management

(1) All mercantile claims are treated as being allocated to the multi-track, and Part 26 does not apply.
(2) The following parts only of Part 29 apply—
 (a) rule 29.3(2) (appropriate legal representative to attend case management conferences and pre-trial reviews); and
 (b) rule 29.5 (variation of case management timetable) with the exception of rule 29.5(1)(c).
(3) As soon as practicable the court will hold a case management conference which must be fixed in accordance with the practice direction.

(4) At the case management conference or at any hearing at which the parties are represented the court may give such directions for the management of the case as it considers appropriate.

## 59.12 Judgments and Orders

(1) Except for orders made by the court of its own initiative and unless the court otherwise orders every judgment or order will be drawn up by the parties, and rule 40.3 is modified accordingly.
(2) An application for a consent order must include a draft of the proposed order signed on behalf of all the parties to whom it relates.
(3) Rule 40.6 (consent judgments and orders) does not apply.

# PD 59 Practice Direction — Mercantile Courts

This practice direction supplements CPR Part 59.

## General

1.1 This practice direction applies to mercantile claims.

1.2 Mercantile Courts are established in:
(1) the following district registries of the High Court: Birmingham, Bristol, Cardiff, Chester, Leeds, Liverpool, Manchester and Newcastle; and
(2) the Commercial Court of the Queen's Bench Division at the Royal Courts of Justice (called 'The London Mercantile Court').

1.3 All mercantile claims will be heard or determined by a mercantile judge, except that:
(1) an application may be heard and determined by any other judge who, if the claim were not a mercantile claim, would have jurisdiction to determine it, if:
(a) the application is urgent and no mercantile judge is available to hear it; or
(b) a mercantile judge directs it to be heard by another judge; and
(2) unless the court otherwise orders, all proceedings for the enforcement of a Mercantile Court judgment or order for the payment of money will be dealt with by a district judge.

1.4 Provisions in other practice directions which refer to a master or district judge are to be read, in relation to mercantile claims, as if they referred to a mercantile judge.

## Starting Proceedings in a Mercantile Court

2.1 A claim should only be started in a Mercantile Court if it will benefit from the expertise of a mercantile judge.

2.2 The claim form must be marked in the top right hand corner 'Queen's Bench Division, _______________ District Registry, Mercantile Court' or 'Queen's Bench Division, The London Mercantile Court' as appropriate.

2.3 *Omitted*

2.4 *Omitted*

## Applications Before Proceedings Are Issued

3.1 A party who intends to bring a claim in a Mercantile Court must make any application before the claim form is issued to a judge of that court.

3.2 The written evidence in support of such an application should show why the claim is suitable to proceed as a mercantile claim.

## Transfer of Proceedings to or from a Mercantile Court

4.1 If a claim which has not been issued in a Mercantile Court is suitable to continue as a mercantile claim:
(1) any party wishing the claim to be transferred to a Mercantile Court may make an application for transfer to the court to which transfer is sought;
(2) if all parties consent to the transfer, the application may be made by letter to the mercantile listing officer of the court to which transfer is sought, stating why the case is suitable to be transferred to that court and enclosing the written consents of the parties, the claim form and statements of case.

4.2 If an application for transfer is made to a court which does not have power to make the order, that court may:
(1) adjourn the application to be heard by a mercantile judge; or
(2) dismiss the application.

4.3 A mercantile judge may make an order under r. 59.3 of his own initiative.

## Default Judgment and Admissions

5 PD 12 and PD 14 apply with the following modifications:
(1) PD 12, para. 4.1(1), is to be read as referring to the service of the claim form; and
(2) the references to 'particulars of claim' in PD 14, paras 2.1, 3.1 and 3.2, are to be read as referring to the claim form.

## Variation of Time Limits by Agreement

6.1 If the parties, in accordance with r. 2.11, agree in writing to vary a time limit, the claimant must notify the court in writing, giving brief written reasons for the agreed variation.

6.2 The court may make an order overriding an agreement by the parties varying a time limit.

## Case Management

7.1 The following parts only of PD 29 apply:
(1) para. 5 (case management conferences), excluding para. 5.9 and modified so far as is made necessary by other specific provisions of this practice direction; and
(2) para. 7 (failure to comply with case management directions).

7.2 If proceedings are started in a Mercantile Court, the claimant must apply for a case management conference:
(1) for a Part 7 claim, within 14 days of the date when all defendants who intend to file and serve a defence have done so; and
(2) for a Part 8 claim, within 14 days of the date when all defendants who intend to serve evidence have done so.

7.3 If proceedings are transferred to a Mercantile Court, the claimant must apply for a case management conference within 14 days of receiving an acknowledgment of the transfer from the receiving court, unless the judge held, or gave directions for, a case management conference when he made the order transferring the proceedings.

7.4 Any party may, at a time earlier than that provided in paras 7.2 or 7.3, apply in writing to the court to fix a case management conference.

7.5 If the claimant does not make an application in accordance with paras 7.2 or 7.3, any other party may apply for a case management conference.

7.6 The court may fix a case management conference at any time on its own initiative. If it does so, the court will give at least 7 days' notice to the parties, unless there are comelling reasons for a shorter period of notice.

7.7 Not less than 7 days before a case management conference:
(1) each party shall file and serve:
(a) a case management information sheet substantially in the form set out at Appendix A to this practice direction; and
(b) an application notice for any order which that party intends to seek at the case management conference, other than directions referred to in the case management information sheet; and
(2) the claimant (or other party applying for the conference) shall in addition file and serve:
(a) a case management file containing:
— the claim form;
— the statements of case (excluding schedules of more than 15 pages);
— any orders already made;
— the case management information sheets; and
— a short list of the principal issues to be prepared by the claimant; and
(b) a draft order substantially in the form set out at Appendix B to this practice direction, setting out the directions which that party thinks appropriate.

7.8 In appropriate cases:

(1) the parties may, not less than 7 days before the date fixed for the case management conference, submit agreed directions for the approval of the judge;
(2) the judge will then either:
(a) make the directions proposed; or
(b) make them with alterations; or
(c) require the case management conference to proceed; but
(3) the parties must assume that the conference will proceed until informed to the contrary.

7.9 If the parties submit agreed directions and the judge makes them with alterations, any party objecting to the alterations may, within seven days of receiving the order containing the directions, apply to the court for the directions to be varied.

7.10 The directions given at the case management conference:
(1) will normally cover all steps in the case through to trial, including the fixing of a trial date or window, or directions for the taking of steps to fix the trial date or window; and
(2) may include the fixing of a progress monitoring date or dates, and make provision for the court to be informed as to the progress of the case at the date or dates fixed.

7.11 If the court fixes a progress monitoring date, it may after that date fix a further case management conference or a pre-trial review on its own initiative if:
(1) no or insufficient information is provided by the parties; or
(2) it is appropriate in view of the information provided.

## Pre-trial Review and Questionnaire

8.1 The court may order a pre-trial review at any time.

8.2 Each party must file and serve a completed pre-trial checklist substantially in the form set out in Appendix C to this practice direction:
(1) if a pre-trial review has been ordered, not less than seven days before the date of the review; or
(2) if no pre-trial review has been ordered, not less than six weeks before the trial date.

8.3 When pre-trial checklists are filed under para. 8.2(2):
(1) the judge will consider them and decide whether to order a pre-trial review; and
(2) if he does not order a pre-trial review, he may on his own initiative give directions for the further preparation of the case or as to the conduct of the trial.

8.4 At a pre-trial review:
(1) the parties should if possible be represented by the advocates who will be appearing at the trial;
(2) any representatives appearing must be fully informed and authorised for the purposes of the review; and
(3) the court will give such directions for the conduct of the trial as it sees fit.

## Evidence for Applications

9.1 The general requirement is that, unless the court orders otherwise:
(1) evidence in support of an application must be filed and served with the application: see r. 23.7(3);
(2) evidence in answer must be filed and served within 14 days after the application is served;
(3) evidence in reply must be filed and served within seven days of the service of the evidence in answer.

9.2 In any case in which the application is likely to require an oral hearing of more than half a day the periods set out in paras 9.1(2) and (3) will be 28 days and 14 days respectively.

9.3 If the date fixed for the hearing of the application means that the times in paras 9.1(2) and (3) cannot both be achieved, the evidence must be filed and served:
(1) as soon as possible; and

(2) in sufficient time to ensure that the application may fairly proceed on the date fixed.

9.4 The parties may, in accordance with r. 2.11, agree different periods from those provided above, provided that the agreement does not affect the ability to proceed on the date fixed for the hearing of the application.

## Files for Applications

10 Before the hearing of any application, the applicant must:

(1) provide to the court and each other party an appropriate indexed file for the application with consecutively numbered pages; and

(2) attach to the file an estimate of the reading time required by the judge.

## Judgments and Orders

11.1 After any hearing the claimant must draw up a draft order, unless the decision was made on the application of another party in which case that party must do so.

11.2 A draft order must be submitted by the party responsible for drawing it up within three clear days of the decision, with sufficient copies for each party and for one to be retained by the court.

11.3 The sealed orders will be returned to the party submitting them, who will be responsible for serving the order on the other parties.

11.4 Orders must be dated with the date of the decision, except for consent orders submitted for approval, which must be left undated.

## ANNEX A

## CASE MANAGEMENT INFORMATION SHEET — MERCANTILE COURTS

[Title of case]

This information sheet must be filed with Mercantile Listing at least 7 days before the case management conference, and copies served on all other parties: see PD 59, para. 7.7.

Party filing:
Solicitors:
Advocate(s) for trial:
Date:

*Substance of case*

1. What in about 20 words maximum is the case about? Please provide a separate concise list of issues in a complex case.

*Parties*

2. Are all parties still effective?
3. Do you intend to add any further party?

*Statements of case*

4. Do you intend to amend your statement of case?
5. Do you require any 'further information': see CPR, Part 18?

*Disclosure*

6. By what date can you give standard disclosure?
7. Do you contend that to search for any type of document falling within r. 31.6(b) would be unreasonable within r. 31.7(2); if so, what type and on what grounds?
8. Is any specific disclosure required (r. 31.12)?
9. Is a full disclosure order appropriate?
10. By what dates could you give:
    (i) any specific disclosure referred to at 8; and
    (ii) full disclosure?

*Admissions*

11. Can you make any additional admissions?

*Preliminary issues*

12. Are any issues suitable for trial as preliminary issues? If yes, which?

*Witnesses of fact*

13. On how many witnesses of fact do you intend to rely at the trial (subject to the court's direction)?
14. Please name them, or explain why you do not.
15. Which of them will be called to give oral evidence?
16. When can you serve their witness statements?
17. Will any require an interpreter?

*Expert evidence*

18. Are there issues requiring expert evidence?
19. If yes, what issues?
20. Might a single joint expert be suitable on any issues (see r. 35.7)?
21. What experts do you intend (subject to the court's direction) to call? Please give the number, their names and expertise.
22. By what date can you serve signed expert reports?
23. Should there be meetings of experts of like disciplines, of all disciplines? By when?
24. Which experts, if any, do you intend not to call at the trial?
25. Will any require an interpreter?

*Trial*

26. What are the advocates' present estimates of the length of the trial?
27. What is the earliest date that you think the case can be ready for trial?
28. Where should the trial be held?
29. Is a pre-trial review advisable?

*ADR*

30. Might some form of alternative dispute resolution assist to resolve the dispute or some part of it?
31. Has this been considered with the client?
32. Has this been considered with the other parties?
33. Do you want the case to be stayed pending ADR or other means of settlement (r. 26.4); or any other directions relating to ADR?

*Other applications*

34. What applications, if any, not covered above, will you be making at the conference?

*Costs*

35. What, do you estimate, are your costs to date?
36. What, do you estimate, will be your costs to end of trial?

[Signature of party/solicitor]

## ANNEX B

## STANDARD DIRECTIONS IN MERCANTILE COURTS

[Title of case with judge's name]

Order for directions

made on [ ]

1. Standard disclosure is to be made by [ ]. Inspection on 48 hours' notice to be completed by [ ].
2. Signed statements of witnesses of fact, and hearsay notices when required by r. 33.2, are

to be exchanged not later than [ ]. Unless otherwise ordered, the witness statements are to stand as the evidence-in-chief of the witnesses at trial.

3. Each party has permission to call at the trial expert witnesses as follows:

*Number Expertise Issue(s) to be covered*

whose reports are to be exchanged by [ ].

4. Experts of like disciplines are to:
   (i) meet without prejudice by [ ] to identify the issues between them and to attempt to reach agreement on such issues, and
   (ii) prepare a joint statement pursuant to r. 35.12(3), by [ ].

or

3. Expert evidence in the following field(s) of expertise is limited to a written report by a single expert jointly instructed by the parties:

*Expertise Issue(s) to be covered*

4. (i) The report of the single joint expert is to be produced by [ ].
   (ii) Any questions to the expert are to be presented to him by [ ] and answered by [ ].
   (iii) Any party may apply not later than [ ] for an order that the expert witness shall give oral evidence at the trial.
5. The case will be tried in [ ] by judge alone, estimated length of trial [ ] days, [commencing on ] [not before ]. [The claimant is to apply to the mercantile listing officer to fix a date for the trial, not later than [ ], specifying dates which any party wishes to avoid.]
[6. The progress monitoring date is [ ]. Each party is to notify the court in writing by that date (with a copy to all other parties) of the progress of the case, including:
   (i) whether the directions have been complied with in all respects;
   (ii) if any directions are outstanding, which of them and why; and
   (iii) whether a further case management conference or a pre-trial review is required.]
7. There will be a pre-trial review on [ ]. [In the event of both parties notifying the court in writing not less than [ ] days before the pre-trial review that it is not required, then it will be vacated.]
8. Signed pre-trial checklists are to be filed and served by [ ] [not less than seven days before the pre-trial review] [not less than six weeks before the trial date].
9. Trial bundles must be agreed, prepared and delivered to counsel not less than [ ] days before the trial date, and to the court not less than [ ] days before the trial date.
10. Costs in the case.

DATED

## ANNEX C

## PRE-TRIAL CHECKLIST — MERCANTILE COURTS

[Title of case]

Where a pre-trial review has been ordered, this checklist must be filed with Mercantile Listing not less than seven days before the pre-trial review, and copies served on all other parties. Where a pre-trial review has not been ordered, it must be filed and served not less than six weeks before the trial date. See PD 59, para. 8.2.

a. Trial date:
b. Whether pre-trial review ordered:
c. Date of review:
d. Party lodging:
e. Solicitors:

f. Advocate(s) for trial:

g. Date lodged:

[Note: this checklist should normally be completed with the involvement of the advocate(s) instructed for trial.]

1. Have all the directions made to date been carried out?
2. If not, what remains to be carried out? When will it be carried out?
3. Do you intend to take any further steps regarding:
   (i) statements of case?
   (ii) disclosure?
   (iii) witnesses and witness statements?
   (iv) experts and expert reports?
   If yes in any case, what and by when?
4. Will the preparation of trial bundles be completed not later than three weeks before the date fixed for trial? If not, what is the position?
5. What witnesses of fact do you intend to call?
6. (Where directions for expert evidence have been given) what experts do you intend to call?
7. Is any interpreter needed: for whom?
8. If a pre-trial review has not been ordered, do you think one would be useful?
9. What are the advocate(s)' confirmed estimates of the minimum and maximum lengths of the trial? A confirmed estimate signed by the advocate(s) and dated must be attached.
10. (i) Might some form of alternative dispute resolution now assist?
    (ii) Has the question been considered with the client?
    (iii) Has the question been explored with the other parties to the case?

[Signature of party/solicitor]

# CPR Part 60 Technology and Construction Court Claims



## 60.1 General

(1) This Part applies to Technology and Construction Court claims ('TCC claims').
(2) In this Part and its practice direction—
   (a) 'TCC claim' means a claim which—
      (i) satisfies the requirements of paragraph (3); and
      (ii) has been issued in or transferred into the specialist list for such claims;
   (b) 'Technology and Construction Court' means any court in which TCC claims are dealt with in accordance with this Part or its practice direction; and
   (c) 'TCC judge' means any judge authorised to hear TCC claims.
(3) A claim may be brought as a TCC claim if—
   (a) it involves issues or questions which are technically complex; or
   (b) a trial by a TCC judge is desirable.

(The practice direction gives examples of types of claims which it may be appropriate to bring as TCC claims.)

(4) TCC claims include all official referees' business referred to in section 68(1)(a) of the Supreme Court Act 1981.
(5) TCC claims will be dealt with—
   (a) in a Technology and Construction Court; and
   (b) by a TCC judge, unless—
      (i) this Part or its practice direction permits otherwise; or
      (ii) a TCC judge directs otherwise.

## 60.2 Specialist List

(1) TCC claims form a specialist list.
(2) A judge will be appointed to be the judge in charge of the TCC specialist list.

## 60.3 Application of the Civil Procedure Rules

These Rules and their practice directions apply to TCC claims unless this Part or a practice direction provides otherwise.

## 60.4 Issuing a TCC Claim

A TCC claim must be issued in—
(a) the High Court in London;
(b) a district registry of the High Court; or
(c) a county court specified in the practice direction.

## 60.5 Reply

Part 15 (defence and reply) applies to TCC claims with the modification to rule 15.8 that the claimant must—
(a) file any reply to a defence; and
(b) serve it on all other parties,
within 21 days after service of the defence.

## 60.6 Case Management

(1) All TCC claims are treated as being allocated to the multi-track and Part 26 does not apply.
(2) Part 29 and its practice direction apply to the case management of TCC claims, except where they are varied by or inconsistent with the practice direction to this Part.

## 60.7 Judgments and Orders

(1) Except for orders made by the court of its own initiative and unless the court otherwise orders, every judgment or order made in claims proceeding in the Technology and Construction Court will be drawn up by the parties, and rule 40.3 is modified accordingly.
(2) An application for a consent order must include a draft of the proposed order signed on behalf of all the parties to whom it relates.
(3) Rule 40.6 (consent judgments and orders) does not apply.

# PD 60 Practice Direction — Technology and Construction Court Claims

This practice direction supplements CPR Part 60.

## General

1 This practice direction applies to Technology and Construction Court claims ('TCC claims').

## TCC Claims

2.1 The following are examples of the types of claim which it may be appropriate to bring as TCC claims:

(a) building or other construction disputes, including claims for the enforcement of the decisions of adjudicators under the Housing Grants, Construction and Regeneration Act 1996;
(b) engineering disputes;
(c) claims by and against engineers, architects, surveyors, accountants and other specialised advisers relating to the services they provide;
(d) claims by and against local authorities relating to their statutory duties concerning the development of land or the construction of buildings;
(e) claims relating to the design, supply and installation of computers, computer software and related network systems;
(f) claims relating to the quality of goods sold or hired, and work done, materials supplied or services rendered;
(g) claims between landlord and tenant for breach of a repairing covenant;
(h) claims between neighbours, owners and occupiers of land in trespass, nuisance etc.;
(i) claims relating to the environment (for example, pollution cases);
(j) claims arising out of fires;
(k) claims involving taking of accounts where these are complicated; and
(l) challenges to decisions of arbitrators in construction and engineering disputes including applications for permission to appeal and appeals.

2.2 A claim given as an example in para. 2.1 will not be suitable for this specialist list unless it demonstrates the characteristics in r. 60.1(3). Similarly, the examples are not exhaustive and other types of claim may be appropriate to this specialist list.

## How to Start a TCC Claim

3.1 TCC claims must be issued in the High Court or in a county court specified in this practice direction.

3.2 The claim form must be marked in the top right-hand corner 'Technology and Construction Court' below the words 'The High Court, Queen's Bench Division' or 'The__________County Court'.

3.3 TCC claims brought in the High Court outside London may be issued in any District Registry, but it is preferable that wherever possible they should be issued in one of the following district registries, in which a TCC judge will usually be available: Birmingham, Bristol, Cardiff, Chester, Exeter, Leeds, Liverpool, Newcastle, Nottingham and Salford.

3.4 The county courts in which a TCC claim may be issued are the following: Birmingham, Bristol, Cardiff, Central London, Chester, Exeter, Leeds, Liverpool, Newcastle, Nottingham and Salford.

## Applications Before Proceedings Are Issued

4.1 A party who intends to issue a TCC claim must make any application before the claim form is issued to a TCC judge.

4.2 The written evidence in support of such an application must state that the proposed claim is a TCC claim.

## Transfer of Proceedings

5.1 Where no TCC judge is available to deal with a claim which has been issued in a High Court District Registry or one of the county courts listed in para. 3.4 above, the claim may be transferred:

(1) if it has been issued in a district registry, to another district registry or to the High Court in London; or

(2) if it has been issued in a county court, to another county court where a TCC judge would be available.

5.2 Paragraph 5.1 is without prejudice to the court's general powers to transfer proceedings under Part 30.

(Rule 30.5(3) provides that an application for the transfer of proceedings to or from a specialist list must be made to a judge dealing with claims in that list)

5.3 A party applying to a TCC judge to transfer a claim to the TCC specialist list must give notice of the application to the court in which the claim is proceeding, and a TCC judge will not make an order for transfer until he is satisfied that such notice has been given.

## Assignment of Claim to a TCC Judge

6.1 When a TCC claim is issued or an order is made transferring a claim to the TCC specialist list, the court will assign the claim to a named TCC judge ('the assigned TCC judge') who will have the primary responsibility for the case management of that claim.

6.2 All documents relating to the claim must be marked in similar manner to the claim form with the words 'Technology and Construction Court' and the name of the assigned TCC judge.

## Applications

7.1 An application should normally be made to the assigned TCC judge. If the assigned TCC judge is not available, or the court gives permission, the application may be made to another TCC judge.

7.2 If an application is urgent and there is no TCC judge available to deal with it, the application may be made to any judge who, if the claim were not a TCC claim, would be authorised to deal with the application.

## Case Management Conference

8.1 The court will fix a case management conference within 14 days of the earliest of these events:

(1) the filing of an acknowledgment of service;

(2) the filing of a defence; or

(3) the date of an order transferring the claim to a TCC.

8.2 When the court notifies the parties of the date and time of the case management conference, it will at the same time send each party a case management information sheet and a case management directions form.

(The case management information sheet and the case management directions form are in the form set out in Appendices A and B to this practice direction.)

8.3 Not less than two days before the case management conference, each party must file and serve on all other parties:

(1) completed copies of the case management information sheet and case management directions form; and

(2) an application notice for any order which that party intends to seek at the case

management conference, other than directions referred to in the case management directions form.

8.4 The parties are encouraged to agree directions to propose to the court by reference to the case management directions form.

8.5 If any party fails to file or serve the case management information sheet and the case management directions form by the date specified, the court may:

(1) impose such sanction as it sees fit; and

(2) either proceed with or adjourn the case management conference.

8.6 The directions given at the case management conference will normally include the fixing of dates for:

(1) any further case management conferences;

(2) a pre-trial review;

(3) the trial of any preliminary issues that it orders to be tried; and

(4) the trial.

## Pre-trial Review

9.1 When the court fixes the date for a pre-trial review it will send each party a pre-trial review questionnaire.

(The pre-trial review questionnaire is in the form set out in Appendix C to this practice direction.)

9.2 Each party must file and serve on all other parties completed copies of the questionnaire not less than two days before the date fixed for the pre-trial review.

9.3 The parties are encouraged to agree directions to propose to the court.

9.4 If any party fails to return or exchange the questionnaire by the date specified the court may:

(1) impose such sanction as it sees fit; and

(2) either proceed with or adjourn the pre-trial review.

9.5 At the pre-trial review, the court will give such directions for the conduct of the trial as it sees fit.

## Listing

10 The provisions about listing questionnaires and listing in Part 29 and PD 29 do not apply to TCC claims.

## Trial

11.1 Whenever possible the trial of a claim will be heard by the assigned TCC judge.

11.2 A TCC claim may be tried at any place where there is a TCC judge available to try the claim.

[The following forms are appended to PD 60:

Appendix A/TCC/CM1 Case management information sheet
Appendix B/TCC/CMD Case management directions form (Appendix B)
Appendix C/TCC/PTR1 Pre-trial review questionnaire

These forms are not reproduced in this work but may be accessed via the DCA website at <http://www.dca.gov.uk>.

# CPR Part 61 Admiralty Claims



## 61.1 Scope and Interpretation

(1) This Part applies to admiralty claims.
(2) In this Part—
- (a) 'admiralty claim' means a claim within the Admiralty jurisdiction of the High Court as set out in section 20 of the Supreme Court Act 1981;
- (b) 'the Admiralty Court' means the Admiralty Court of the Queen's Bench Division of the High Court of Justice;
- (c) 'claim in rem' means a claim in an admiralty action in rem;
- (d) 'collision claim' means a claim within section 20(3)(b) of the Supreme Court Act 1981;
- (e) 'limitation claim' means a claim under the Merchant Shipping Act 1995 for the limitation of liability in connection with a ship or other property;
- (f) 'salvage claim' means a claim—
  - (i) for or in the nature of salvage;
  - (ii) for special compensation under Article 14 of Schedule 11 to the Merchant Shipping Act 1995;
  - (iii) for the apportionment of salvage; and
  - (iv) arising out of or connected with any contract for salvage services;
- (g) 'caution against arrest' means a caution entered in the Register under rule 61.7;
- (h) 'caution against release' means a caution entered in the Register under rule 61.8;
- (i) 'the Register' means the Register of cautions against arrest and release which is open to inspection as provided by the practice direction;
- (j) 'the Marshal' means the Admiralty Marshal;
- (k) 'ship' includes any vessel used in navigation; and
- (l) 'the Registrar' means the Queen's Bench Master with responsibility for Admiralty claims.

(3) Part 58 (Commercial Court) applies to claims in the Admiralty Court except where this Part provides otherwise.
(4) The Registrar has all the powers of the Admiralty judge except where a rule or practice direction provides otherwise.

## 61.2 Admiralty Claims

(1) The following claims must be started in the Admiralty Court—
- (a) a claim—
  - (i) in rem;
  - (ii) for damage done by a ship;
  - (iii) concerning the ownership of a ship;
  - (iv) under the Merchant Shipping Act 1995;

(v) for loss of life or personal injury specified in section 20(2)(f) of the Supreme Court Act 1981;
(vi) by a master or member of a crew for wages;
(vii) in the nature of towage; or
(viii) in the nature of pilotage;

(b) a collision claim;
(c) a limitation claim; or
(d) a salvage claim.

(2) Any other admiralty claim may be started in the Admiralty Court.
(3) Rule 30.5 applies to claims in the Admiralty Court except that the Admiralty Court may order the transfer of a claim to—
(a) the Commercial list;
(b) a Mercantile Court;
(c) the Mercantile list at the Central London County Court; or
(d) any other appropriate court.

### 61.3 Claims In Rem

(1) This rule applies to claims in rem.
(2) A claim in rem is started by the issue of an in rem claim form as set out in the practice direction.
(3) Subject to rule 61.4, the particulars of claim must—
(a) be contained in or served with the claim form; or
(b) be served on the defendant by the claimant within 75 days after service of the claim form.
(4) An acknowledgment of service must be filed within 14 days after service of the claim form.
(5) The claim form must be served—
(a) in accordance with the practice direction; and
(b) within 12 months after the date of issue and rules 7.5 and 7.6 are modified accordingly.
(6) If a claim form has been issued (whether served or not), any person who wishes to defend the claim may file an acknowledgment of service.

### 61.4 Special Provisions Relating to Collision Claims

(1) This rule applies to collision claims.
(2) A claim form need not contain or be followed by particulars of claim and rule 7.4 does not apply.
(3) An acknowledgment of service must be filed.
(4) A party who wishes to dispute the court's jurisdiction must make an application under Part 11 within 2 months after filing his acknowledgment of service.
(5) Every party must—
(a) within 2 months after the defendant files the acknowledgment of service; or
(b) where the defendant applies under Part 11, within 2 months after the defendant files the further acknowledgment of service,

file at the court a completed collision statement of case in the form specified in the practice direction.
(6) A collision statement of case must be—
(a) in the form set out in the practice direction; and
(b) verified by a statement of truth.
(7) A claim form in a collision claim may not be served out of the jurisdiction unless—
(a) the case falls within section 22(2)(a), (b) or (c) of the Supreme Court Act 1981; or
(b) the defendant has submitted to or agreed to submit to the jurisdiction; and the court gives permission in accordance with Section III of Part 6.

(8) Where permission to serve a claim form out of the jurisdiction is given, the court will specify the period within which the defendant may file an acknowledgment of service and, where appropriate, a collision statement of case.

(9) Where, in a collision claim in rem ('the original claim')—
 (a) (i) a Part 20 claim; or
  (ii) a cross-claim in rem
 arising out of the same collision or occurrence is made; and
 (b) (i) the party bringing the original claim has caused the arrest of a ship or has obtained security in order to prevent such arrest; and
  (ii) the party bringing the Part 20 claim or cross-claim is unable to arrest a ship or otherwise obtain security,

the party bringing the Part 20 claim or cross-claim may apply to the court to stay the original claim until sufficient security is given to satisfy any judgment that may be given in favour of that party.

(10) The consequences set out in paragraph (11) apply where a party to a claim to establish liability for a collision claim (other than a claim for loss of life or personal injury)—
 (a) makes an offer to settle in the form set out in paragraph (12) not less than 21 days before the start of the trial;
 (b) that offer is not accepted; and
 (c) the maker of the offer obtains at trial an apportionment equal to or more favourable than his offer.

(11) Where paragraph (10) applies the parties will, unless the court considers it unjust, be entitled to the following costs—
 (a) the maker of the offer will be entitled to—
  (i) all his costs from 21 days after the offer was made; and
  (ii) his costs before then in the percentage to which he would have been entitled had the offer been accepted; and
 (b) all other parties to whom the offer was made—
  (i) will be entitled to their costs up to 21 days after the offer was made in the percentage to which they would have been entitled had the offer been accepted; but
  (ii) will not be entitled to their costs thereafter.

(12) An offer under paragraph (10) must be in writing and must contain—
 (a) an offer to settle liability at stated percentages;
 (b) an offer to pay costs in accordance with the same percentages;
 (c) a term that the offer remain open for 21 days after the date it is made; and
 (d) a term that, unless the court orders otherwise, on expiry of that period the offer remains open on the same terms except that the offeree should pay all the costs from that date until acceptance.

## 61.5 Arrest

(1) In a claim in rem—
 (a) a claimant; and
 (b) a judgment creditor

may apply to have the property proceeded against arrested.

(2) The practice direction sets out the procedure for applying for arrest.

(3) A party making an application for arrest must—
 (a) request a search to be made in the Register before the warrant is issued to determine whether there is a caution against arrest in force with respect to that property; and
 (b) file a declaration in the form set out in the practice direction.

(4) A warrant of arrest may not be issued as of right in the case of property in respect of which the beneficial ownership, as a result of a sale or disposal by any court in any jurisdiction exercising admiralty jurisdiction in rem, has changed since the claim form was issued.

(5) A warrant of arrest may not be issued against a ship owned by a State where by any convention or treaty, the United Kingdom has undertaken to minimise the possibility of arrest of ships of that State until—
  (a) notice in the form set out in the practice direction has been served on a consular officer at the consular office of that State in London or the port at which it is intended to arrest the ship; and
  (b) a copy of that notice is attached to any declaration under paragraph (3)(b).

(6) Except—
  (a) with the permission of the court; or
  (b) where notice has been given under paragraph (5),

a warrant of arrest may not be issued in a claim in rem against a foreign ship belonging to a port of a State in respect of which an order in council has been made under section 4 of the Consular Relations Act 1968, until the expiration of 2 weeks from appropriate notice to the consul.

(7) A warrant of arrest is valid for 12 months but may only be executed if the claim form—
  (a) has been served; or
  (b) remains valid for service at the date of execution.

(8) Property may only be arrested by the Marshal or his substitute.

(9) Property under arrest—
  (a) may not be moved unless the court orders otherwise; and
  (b) may be immobilised or prevented from sailing in such manner as the Marshal may consider appropriate.

(10) Where an in rem claim form has been issued and security sought, any person who has filed an acknowledgment of service may apply for an order specifying the amount and form of security to be provided.

## 61.6 Security Claim In Rem

(1) This rule applies if, in a claim in rem, security has been given to—
  (a) obtain the release of property under arrest; or
  (b) prevent the arrest of property.

(2) The court may order that the—
  (a) amount of security be reduced and may stay the claim until the order is complied with; or
  (b) claimant may arrest or re-arrest the property proceeded against to obtain further security.

(3) The court may not make an order under paragraph (2)(b) if the total security to be provided would exceed the value of the property at the time—
  (a) of the original arrest; or
  (b) security was first given (if the property was not arrested).

## 61.7 Cautions Against Arrest

(1) Any person may file a request for a caution against arrest.

(2) When a request under paragraph (1) is filed the court will enter the caution in the Register if the request is in the form set out in the practice direction and—
  (a) the person filing the request undertakes—
    (i) to file an acknowledgment of service; and
    (ii) to give sufficient security to satisfy the claim with interest and costs; or
  (b) where the person filing the request has constituted a limitation fund in accordance with Article 11 of the Convention on Limitation of Liability for Maritime Claims 1976 he—
    (i) states that such a fund has been constituted; and
    (ii) undertakes that the claimant will acknowledge service of the claim form by which any claim may be begun against the property described in the request.

(3) A caution against arrest—
 (a) is valid for 12 months after the date it is entered in the Register; but
 (b) may be renewed for a further 12 months by filing a further request.
(4) Paragraphs (1) and (2) apply to a further request under paragraph (3)(b).
(5) Property may be arrested if a caution against arrest has been entered in the Register but the court may order that—
 (a) the arrest be discharged; and
 (b) the party procuring the arrest pays compensation to the owner of or other persons interested in the arrested property.

## 61.8 Release and Cautions Against Release

(1) Where property is under arrest—
 (a) an in rem claim form may be served upon it; and
 (b) it may be arrested by any other person claiming to have an in rem claim against it.
(2) Any person who—
 (a) claims to have an in rem right against any property under arrest; and
 (b) wishes to be given notice of any application in respect of that property or its proceeds of sale,

 may file a request for a caution against release in the form set out in the practice direction.
(3) When a request under paragraph (2) is filed, a caution against release will be entered in the Register.
(4) Property will be released from arrest if—
 (a) it is sold by the court;
 (b) the court orders release on an application made by any party;
 (c) (i) the arresting party; and
  (ii) all persons who have entered cautions against release

  file a request for release in the form set out in the practice direction; or
 (d) any party files—
  (i) a request for release in the form set out in the practice direction (containing an undertaking); and
  (ii) consents to the release of the arresting party and all persons who have entered cautions against release.
(5) Where the release of any property is delayed by the entry of a caution against release under this rule any person who has an interest in the property may apply for an order that the person who entered the caution pay damages for losses suffered by the applicant because of the delay.
(6) The court may not make an order under paragraph (5) if satisfied that there was good reason to—
 (a) request the entry of; and
 (b) maintain

 the caution.
(7) Any person—
 (a) interested in property under arrest or in the proceeds of sale of such property; or
 (b) whose interests are affected by any order sought or made,

 may be made a party to any claim in rem against the property or proceeds of sale.
(8) Where—
 (a) (i) a ship is not under arrest but cargo on board her is; or
  (ii) a ship is under arrest but cargo on board her is not; and
 (b) persons interested in the ship or cargo wish to discharge the cargo,

 they may, without being made parties, request the Marshal to authorise steps to discharge the cargo.

(9) If—
(a) the Marshal considers a request under paragraph (8) reasonable; and
(b) the applicant gives an undertaking in writing acceptable to the Marshal to pay—
(i) his fees; and
(ii) all expenses to be incurred by him or on his behalf
on demand,
the Marshal will apply to the court for an order to permit the discharge of the cargo.
(10) Where persons interested in the ship or cargo are unable or unwilling to give an undertaking as referred to in paragraph (9)(b), they may—
(a) be made parties to the claim; and
(b) apply to the court for an order for—
(i) discharge of the cargo; and
(ii) directions as to the fees and expenses of the Marshal with regard to the discharge and storage of the cargo.

## 61.9 Judgment in Default

(1) In a claim in rem (other than a collision claim) the claimant may obtain judgment in default of—
(a) an acknowledgment of service only if—
(i) the defendant has not filed an acknowledgment of service; and
(ii) the time for doing so set out in rule 61.3(4) has expired; and
(b) defence only if—
(i) a defence has not been filed; and
(ii) the relevant time limit for doing so has expired.
(2) In a collision claim, a party who has filed a collision statement of case within the time specified by rule 61.4(5) may obtain judgment in default of a collision statement of case only if—
(a) the party against whom judgment is sought has not filed a collision statement of case; and
(b) the time for doing so set out in rule 61.4(5) has expired.
(3) An application for judgment in default—
(a) under paragraph (1) or paragraph (2) in an in rem claim must be made by filing—
(i) an application notice as set out in the practice direction;
(ii) a certificate proving service of the claim form; and
(iii) evidence proving the claim to the satisfaction of the court; and
(b) under paragraph (2) in any other claim must be made in accordance with Part 12 with any necessary modifications.
(4) An application notice seeking judgment in default and, unless the court orders otherwise, all evidence in support, must be served on all persons who have entered cautions against release on the Register.
(5) The court may set aside or vary any judgment in default entered under this rule.
(6) The claimant may apply to the court for judgment against a party at whose instance a notice against arrest was entered where—
(a) the claim form has been served on that party;
(b) the sum claimed in the claim form does not exceed the amount specified in the undertaking given by that party in accordance with rule 61.7(2)(a)(ii); and
(c) that party has not fulfilled that undertaking within 14 days after service on him of the claim form.

## 61.10 Sale by the Court, Priorities and Payment Out

(1) An application for an order for the survey, appraisement or sale of a ship may be made in a claim in rem at any stage by any party.
(2) If the court makes an order for sale, it may—

(a) set a time within which notice of claims against the proceeds of sale must be filed; and
(b) the time and manner in which such notice must be advertised.
(3) Any party with a judgment against the property or proceeds of sale may at any time after the time referred to in paragraph (2) apply to the court for the determination of priorities.
(4) An application notice under paragraph (3) must be served on all persons who have filed a claim against the property.
(5) Payment out of the proceeds of sale will be made only to judgment creditors and—
(a) in accordance with the determination of priorities; or
(b) as the court orders.

## 61.11 Limitation Claims

(1) This rule applies to limitation claims.
(2) A claim is started by the issue of a limitation claim form as set out in the practice direction.
(3) The—
(a) claimant; and
(b) at least one defendant
must be named in the claim form, but all other defendants may be described.
(4) The claim form—
(a) must be served on all named defendants and any other defendant who requests service upon him; and
(b) may be served on any other defendant.
(5) The claim form may not be served out of the jurisdiction unless—
(a) the claim falls within section 22(2)(a), (b) or (c) of the Supreme Court Act 1981;
(b) the defendant has submitted to or agreed to submit to the jurisdiction of the court; or
(c) the Admiralty Court has jurisdiction over the claim under any applicable Convention; and
the court grants permission in accordance with Section III of Part 6.
(6) An acknowledgment of service is not required.
(7) Every defendant upon whom a claim form is served must—
(a) within 28 days of service file—
(i) a defence; or
(ii) a notice that he admits the right of the claimant to limit liability; or
(b) if he wishes to—
(i) dispute the jurisdiction of the court; or
(ii) argue that the court should not exercise its jurisdiction,
file within 14 days of service (or where the claim form is served out of the jurisdiction, within the time specified in rule 6.22) an acknowledgment of service as set out in the practice direction.
(8) If a defendant files an acknowledgment of service under paragraph (7)(b) he will be treated as having accepted that the court has jurisdiction to hear the claim unless he applies under Part 11 within 14 days after filing the acknowledgment of service.
(9) Where one or more named defendants admits the right to limit—
(a) the claimant may apply for a restricted limitation decree in the form set out in the practice direction; and
(b) the court will issue a decree in the form set out in the practice direction limiting liability only against those named defendants who have admitted the claimant's right to limit liability.
(10) A restricted limitation decree—
(a) may be obtained against any named defendant who fails to file a defence within the time specified for doing so; and

(b) need not be advertised, but a copy must be served on the defendants to whom it applies.

(11) Where all the defendants upon whom the claim form has been served admit the claimant's right to limit liability—
  (a) the claimant may apply to the Admiralty Registrar for a general limitation decree in the form set out in the practice direction; and
  (b) the court will issue a limitation decree.

(12) Where one or more of the defendants upon whom the claim form has been served do not admit the claimant's right to limit, the claimant may apply for a general limitation decree in the form set out in the practice direction.

(13) When a limitation decree is granted the court—
  (a) may—
    (i) order that any proceedings relating to any claim arising out of the occurrence be stayed;
    (ii) order the claimant to establish a limitation fund if one has not been established or make such other arrangements for payment of claims against which liability is limited; or
    (iii) if the decree is a restricted limitation decree, distribute the limitation fund; and
  (b) will, if the decree is a general limitation decree, give directions as to advertisement of the decree and set a time within which notice of claims against the fund must be filed or an application made to set aside the decree.

(14) When the court grants a general limitation decree the claimant must—
  (a) advertise it in such manner and within such time as the court directs; and
  (b) file—
    (i) a declaration that the decree has been advertised in accordance with paragraph (a); and
    (ii) copies of the advertisements.

(15) No later than the time set in the decree for filing claims, each of the defendants who wishes to assert a claim must file and serve his statement of case on—
  (a) the limiting party; and
  (b) all other defendants except where the court orders otherwise.

(16) Any person other than a defendant upon whom the claim form has been served may apply to the court within the time fixed in the decree to have a general limitation decree set aside.

(17) An application under paragraph (16) must be supported by a declaration—
  (a) stating that the applicant has a claim against the claimant arising out of the occurrence; and
  (b) setting out grounds for contending that the claimant is not entitled to the decree, either in the amount of limitation or at all.

(18) The claimant may constitute a limitation fund by making a payment into court.

(19) A limitation fund may be established before or after a limitation claim has been started.

(20) If a limitation claim is not commenced within 75 days after the date the fund was established—
  (a) the fund will lapse; and
  (b) all money in court (including interest) will be repaid to the person who made the payment into court.

(21) Money paid into court under paragraph (18) will not be paid out except under an order of the court.

(22) A limitation claim for—
  (a) a restricted decree may be brought by counterclaim; and
  (b) a general decree may only be brought by counterclaim with the permission of the court.

## 61.12 Stay of Proceedings

Where the court orders a stay of any claim in rem—
(a) any property under arrest in the claim remains under arrest; and
(b) any security representing the property remains in force,
unless the court orders otherwise.

## 61.13 Assessors

The court may sit with assessors when hearing—
(a) collision claims; or
(b) other claims involving issues of navigation or seamanship, and
the parties will not be permitted to call expert witnesses unless the court orders otherwise.

# PD 61 Practice Direction — Admiralty Claims

This practice direction supplements CPR Part 61.

## Scope: Rule 61.1

1.1 PD 58 (commercial claims) also applies to Admiralty claims except where it is inconsistent with Part 61 or this practice direction.

## Case Management

2.1 After a claim form is issued the Registrar will issue a direction in writing stating:
- (1) whether the claim will remain in the Admiralty Court or be transferred to another court; and
- (2) if the claim remains in the Admiralty Court:
  - (a) whether it will be dealt with by:
    - (i) the Admiralty judge; or
    - (ii) the Registrar; and
  - (b) whether the trial will be in London or elsewhere.

2.2 In making these directions the Registrar will have regard to:
- (1) the nature of the issues and the sums in dispute; and
- (2) the criteria set in r. 26.8 so far as they are applicable.

2.3 Where the Registrar directs that the claim will be dealt with by the Admiralty judge, case management directions will be given and any case management conference or pre-trial review will be heard by the Admiralty judge.

## Claims *In Rem*: Rule 61.3

3.1 A claim form *in rem* must be in form ADM1.

3.2 The claimant in a claim *in rem* may be named or may be described, but if not named in the claim form must identify himself by name if requested to do so by any other party.

3.3 The defendant must be described in the claim form.

3.4 The acknowledgment of service must be in form ADM2. The person who acknowledges service must identify himself by name.

3.5 The period for acknowledging service under r. 61.3(4) applies irrespective of whether the claim form contains particulars of claim.

3.6 A claim form *in rem* may be served in the following ways:
- (1) on the property against which the claim is brought by fixing a copy of the claim form:
  - (a) on the outside of the property in a position which may reasonably be expected to be seen; or
  - (b) where the property is freight, either:
    - (i) on the cargo in respect of which the freight was earned; or
    - (ii) on the ship on which the cargo was carried;
- (2) if the property to be served is in the custody of a person who will not permit access to it, by leaving a copy of the claim form with that person;
- (3) where the property has been sold by the Marshal, by filing the claim form at the court;
- (4) where there is a notice against arrest, on the person named in the notice as being authorised to accept service;
- (5) on any solicitor authorised to accept service;
- (6) in accordance with any agreement providing for service of proceedings; or
- (7) in any other manner as the court may direct under r. 6.8 provided that the property against which the claim is brought or part of it is within the jurisdiction of the court.

3.7 In claims where the property:
 (1) is to be arrested; or
 (2) is already under arrest in current proceedings,
 the Marshal will serve the *in rem* claim form if the claimant requests the court to do so.

3.8 In all other cases *in rem* claim forms must be served by the claimant.

3.9 Where the defendants are described and not named on the claim form (for example as 'the Owners of the Ship X'), any acknowledgment of service in addition to stating that description must also state the full names of the persons acknowledging service and the nature of their ownership.

3.10 After the acknowledgment of service has been filed, the claim will follow the procedure applicable to a claim proceeding in the Commercial list except that the claimant is allowed 75 days to serve the particulars of claim.

3.11 A defendant who files an acknowledgment of service to an *in rem* claim does not lose any right he may have to dispute the jurisdiction of the court (see r. 10.1(3)(b) and Part 11).

3.12 Any person who pays the prescribed fee may, during office hours, search for, inspect and take a copy of any claim form *in rem* whether or not it has been served.

## Collision Claims: Rule 61.4

4.1 A collision statement of case must be in form ADM3.

4.2 A collision statement of case must contain:
 (1) in part 1 of the form, answers to the questions set out in that part; and
 (2) in part 2 of the form, a statement:
  (a) of any other facts and matters on which the party filing the collision statement of case relies;
  (b) of all allegations of negligence or other fault which the party filing the collision statement of case makes; and
  (c) of the remedy which the party filing the collision statement of case claims.

4.3 When he files his collision statement of case each party must give notice to every other party that he has done so.

4.4 Within 14 days after the last collision statement of case is filed each party must serve a copy of his collision statement of case on every other party.

4.5 Before the coming into force of Part 61, a collision statement of case was known as a preliminary act and the law relating to preliminary acts will continue to apply to collision statements of case.

## Arrest: Rule 61.5

5.1 An application for arrest must be:
 (1) in form ADM4 (which must also contain an undertaking); and
 (2) accompanied by a declaration in form ADM5.

5.2 When it receives an application for arrest that complies with the rules and the practice direction the court will issue an arrest warrant.

5.3 The declaration required by r. 61.5(3)(b) must be verified by a statement of truth and must state:
 (1) in every claim:
  (a) the nature of the claim or counterclaim and that it has not been satisfied and if it arises in connection with a ship, the name of that ship;
  (b) the nature of the property to be arrested and, if the property is a ship, the name of the ship and her port of registry; and
  (c) the amount of the security sought, if any;
 (2) in a claim against a ship by virtue of the Supreme Court Act 1981, s. 21(4):
  (a) the name of the person who would be liable on the claim if it were not commenced *in rem*;
  (b) that the person referred to in sub-paragraph (a) was, when the right to bring the claim arose:

(i) the owner or charterer of; or
(ii) in possession or in control of,
the ship in connection with which the claim arose; and
(c) that at the time the claim form was issued the person referred to in sub-paragraph (a) was either:
(i) the beneficial owner of all the shares in the ship in respect of which the warrant is required; or
(ii) the charterer of it under a charter by demise;
(3) in the cases set out in rr. 61.5(5) and (6) that the relevant notice has been sent or served, as appropriate; and
(4) in the case of a claim in respect of liability incurred under the Merchant Shipping Act 1995, s. 153, the facts relied on as establishing that the court is not prevented from considering the claim by reason of s. 166(2) of that Act.

5.4 The notice required by r. 61.5(5)(a) must be in form ADM6.

5.5 Property is arrested:
(1) by service on it of an arrest warrant in form ADM9 in the manner set out at para. 3.6(1); or
(2) where it is not reasonably practicable to serve the warrant, by service of a notice of the issue of the warrant:
(a) in the manner set out in para. 3.6(1) on the property; or
(b) by giving notice to those in charge of the property.

5.6 When property is arrested the Registrar will issue standard directions in form ADM10.

5.7 The Marshal does not insure property under arrest.

## Cautions Against Arrest: Rule 61.7

6.1 The entry of a caution against arrest is not treated as a submission to the jurisdiction of the court.

6.2 The request for a caution against arrest must be in form ADM7.

6.3 On the filing of such a request, a caution against arrest will be entered in the Register.

6.4 The Register is open for inspection when the Admiralty and Commercial Registry is open.

## Release and Cautions Against Release: Rule 61.8

7.1 The request for a caution against release must be in form ADM11.

7.2 On the filing of such a request, a caution against release will be entered in the Register.

7.3 The Register is open for inspection when the Admiralty and Commercial Registry is open.

7.4 A request for release under r. 61.8(4)(c) and (d) must be in form ADM12.

7.5 A withdrawal of a caution against release must be in form ADM12A.

## Judgment in Default: Rule 61.9

8.1 An application notice for judgment in default must be in form ADM13.

## Sale by the Court and Priorities: Rule 61.10

9.1 Any application to the court concerning:
(1) the sale of the property under arrest; or
(2) the proceeds of sale of property sold by the court
will be heard in public and the application notice served on:
(a) all parties to the claim;
(b) all persons who have requested cautions against release with regard to the property or the proceeds of sale; and
(c) the Marshal.

9.2 Unless the court orders otherwise an order for sale will be in form ADM14.

9.3 An order for sale before judgment may only be made by the Admiralty judge.

9.4 Unless the Admiralty judge orders otherwise, a determination of priorities may only be made by the Admiralty judge.

9.5 When:

(1) proceeds of sale are paid into court by the Marshal; and

(2) such proceeds are in a foreign currency,

the funds will be placed on one-day-call interest-bearing account unless the court orders otherwise.

9.6 Unless made at the same time as an application for sale, or other prior application, an application to place foreign currency on longer-term deposit may be made to the Registrar.

9.7 Notice of the placement of foreign currency in an interest-bearing account must be given to all parties interested in the fund by the party who made the application under para. 9.6.

9.8 Any interested party who wishes to object to the mode of investment of foreign currency paid into court may apply to the Registrar for directions.

## Limitation Claims: Rule 61.11

10.1 The claim form in a limitation claim must be:

(1) in form ADM15; and

(2) accompanied by a declaration:

(a) setting out the facts upon which the claimant relies; and

(b) stating the names and addresses (if known) of all persons who, to the knowledge of the claimant, have claims against him in respect of the occurrence to which the claim relates (other than named defendants),

verified by a statement of truth.

10.2 A defence to a limitation claim must be in form ADM16A.

10.3 A notice admitting the right of the claimant to limit liability in a limitation claim must be in form ADM16.

10.4 An acknowledgment of service in a limitation claim must be in form ADM16B.

10.5 An application for a restricted limitation decree must be in form ADM17 and the decree issued by the court on such an application must be in form ADM18.

10.6 An application for a general limitation decree must be in form ADM17A.

10.7 Where:

(1) the right to limit is not admitted; and

(2) the claimant seeks a general limitation decree in form ADM17A,

the claimant must, within seven days after the date of the filing of the defence of the defendant last served or the expiry of the time for doing so, apply for an appointment before the Registrar for a case management conference.

10.8 On an application under r. 61.11(12) the Registrar may:

(1) grant a general limitation decree; or

(2) if he does not grant a decree:

(a) order service of a defence;

(b) order disclosure by the claimant; or

(c) make such other case management directions as may be appropriate.

10.9 The fact that a limitation fund has lapsed under r. 61.11(20)(a) does not prevent the establishment of a new fund.

10.10 Where a limitation fund is established, it must be:

(1) the sterling equivalent of the number of special drawing rights to which the claimant claims to be entitled to limit his liability under the Merchant Shipping Act 1995; together with

(2) interest from the date of the occurrence giving rise to his liability to the date of payment into court.

10.11 Where the claimant does not know the sterling equivalent referred to in para. 10.10(1) on the date of payment into court he may:

(1) calculate it on the basis of the latest available published sterling equivalent of a special drawing right as fixed by the International Monetary Fund; and
(2) in the event of the sterling equivalent of a special drawing right on the date of payment into court being different from that used for calculating the amount of that payment into court the claimant may:
(a) make up any deficiency by making a further payment into court which, if made within 14 days after the payment into court, will be treated, except for the purpose of the rules relating to the accrual of interest on money paid into court, as if made on the date of that payment into court; or
(b) apply to the court for payment out of any excess amount (together with any interest accrued) paid into court.

10.12 An application under para. 10.11(2)(b):
(1) may be made without notice to any party; and
(2) must be supported by evidence proving, to the satisfaction of the court, the sterling equivalent of the appropriate number of special drawing rights on the date of payment into court.

10.13 The claimant must give notice in writing to every named defendant of:
(1) any payment into court specifying:
(a) the date of the payment in;
(b) the amount paid in;
(c) the amount and rate of interest included; and
(d) the period to which it relates; and
(2) any excess amount (and interest) paid out to him under para. 10.11(2)(b).

10.14 A claim against the fund must be in form ADM20.

10.15 A defendant's statement of case filed and served in accordance with r. 61.11(15) must contain particulars of the defendant's claim.

10.16 Any defendant who is unable to file and serve a statement of case in accordance with r. 61.11(15) and para. 10.15 must file a declaration, verified by a statement of truth, in form ADM21 stating the reason for his inability.

10.17 No later than 7 days after the time for filing claims or declarations, the Registrar will fix a date for a case management conference at which directions will be given for the further conduct of the proceedings.

10.18 Nothing in r. 61.11 prevents limitation being relied on by way of defence.

## Proceeding Against or Concerning the International Oil Pollution Compensation Fund 1992 and the International Oil Pollution Supplementary Fund

11.1 For the purposes of section 177 of the Merchant Shipping Act 1995 ('the Act'), the Fund may be given notice of proceedings by any party to a claim against an owner or guarantor in respect of liability under section 153 of the Act by that person serving a notice in writing on the Fund together with copies of the claim form and any statements of case served in the claim.

11.2 Notice given to the Fund under paragraph 11.1 shall be deemed to have been given to the Supplementary Fund.

11.3 The Fund or the Supplementary Fund may intervene in any claim to which paragraph 11.1 applies, (whether or not served with the notice), by serving notice of intervention on the—
(1) owner;
(2) guarantor; and
(3) court.

11.4 Where a judgment is given against—
(1) the Fund in any claim under section 175 of the Act;
(2) the Supplementary Fund in any claim under section 176A of the Act, the Registrar will arrange for a stamped copy of the judgment to be sent by post to—

(a) the Fund (where paragraph (1) applies);
(b) the Supplementary Fund (where paragraph (2) applies).

11.5 Notice to the Registrar of the matters set out in—
(1) section 176(3)(b) of the Act in proceedings under section 175; or
(2) section 176B(2)(b) of the Act in proceedings under section 176A, must be given in writing and sent to the court by—
(a) the Fund (where paragraph (1) applies);
(b) the Supplementary Fund (where paragraph (2) applies).

## Other Claims

12.1 This section applies to Admiralty claims which, before the coming into force of Part 61, would have been called claims *in personam*. Subject to the provisions of Part 61 and this practice direction relating to limitation claims and to collision claims, the following provisions apply to such claims.

12.2 All such claims will proceed in accordance with Part 58 (Commercial Court).

12.3 The claim form must be in form ADM1A and must be served by the claimant.

12.4 The claimant may be named or may be described, but if not named in the claim form must identify himself by name if requested to do so by any other party.

12.5 The defendant must be named in the claim form.

12.6 Any person who files a defence must identify himself by name in the defence.

## References to the Registrar

13.1 The court may at any stage in the claim refer any question or issue for determination by the Registrar (a 'reference').

13.2 Unless the court orders otherwise, where a reference has been ordered:
(1) if particulars of claim have not already been served, the claimant must file and serve particulars of claim on all other parties within 14 days after the date of the order; and
(2) any party opposing the claim must file a defence to the claim within 14 days after service of the particulars of claim on him.

13.3 Within 7 days after the defence is filed, the claimant must apply for an appointment before the Registrar for a case management conference.

## Undertakings

14.1 Where, in Part 61 or this practice direction, any undertaking to the Marshal is required it must be given:
(1) in writing and to his satisfaction; or
(2) in accordance with such other arrangements as he may require.

14.2 Where any party is dissatisfied with a direction given by the Marshal in this respect he may apply to the Registrar for a ruling.

[The following forms are annexed to PD 61:

| | |
|---|---|
| ADM1 | Claim form (Admiralty claim *in rem*) |
| ADM1A | Claim form (Admiralty claim) |
| ADM1C | Notes for defendant |
| ADM2 | Acknowledgment of service |
| ADM3 | Collision statement of case |
| ADM4 | Application and undertaking for arrest and custody |
| ADM5 | Declaration in support of application for warrant of arrest |
| ADM6 | Notice to consular officer of intention to apply for warrant of arrest |
| ADM7 | Request for caution against arrest |
| ADM9 | Warrant of arrest |
| ADM10 | Standard directions to the Admiralty Marshal |
| ADM11 | Request for caution against release |

| | |
|---|---|
| ADM12 | Request and undertaking for release |
| ADM12A | Request for withdrawal of caution against release |
| ADM 3 | Application for judgment in default of filing an acknowledgment of service and/or defence or collision statement of case |
| ADM14 | Order for sale of a ship |
| ADM15 | Claim form (Admiralty limitation claim) |
| ADM15B | Notes for defendant (Admiralty limitation claim) |
| ADM16 | Notice of admission of right of claimant to limit liability |
| ADM16A | Defence to Admiralty limitation claim |
| ADM16B | Acknowledgment of service (Admiralty limitation claim) |
| ADM17 | Application for restricted limitation decree |
| ADM17A | Application for general limitation decree |
| ADM18 | Restricted limitation decree |
| ADM19 | General limitation decree |
| ADM20 | Defendant's claim in a limitation claim |
| ADM21 | Declaration as to inability of a defendant to file and serve statement of case under a decree of limitation |

These forms are not reproduced in this work but may be accessed via the DCA website at <http://www.dca.gov.uk>]

# CPR Part 62 Arbitration Claims



## 62.1 Scope of this Part and Interpretation

(1) This Part contains rules about arbitration claims.
(2) In this Part—
  (a) 'the 1950 Act' means the Arbitration Act 1950;
  (b) 'the 1975 Act' means the Arbitration Act 1975;
  (c) 'the 1979 Act' means the Arbitration Act 1979;
  (d) 'the 1996 Act' means the Arbitration Act 1996;
  (e) references to—
    (i) the 1996 Act; or
    (ii) any particular section of that Act
  include references to that Act or to the particular section of that Act as applied with modifications by the ACAS Arbitration Scheme (England and Wales) Order 2001; and
  (f) 'arbitration claim form' means a claim form in the form set out in the practice direction.
(3) Part 58 (Commercial Court) applies to arbitration claims in the Commercial Court, Part 59 (Mercantile Court) applies to arbitration claims in the Mercantile Court and Part 60 (Technology and Construction Court claims) applies to arbitration claims in the Technology and Construction Court, except where this Part provides otherwise.

## I CLAIMS UNDER THE 1996 ACT

## 62.2 Interpretation

(1) In this Section of this Part 'arbitration claim' means—
  (a) any application to the court under the 1996 Act;
  (b) a claim to determine—
    (i) whether there is a valid arbitration agreement;
    (ii) whether an arbitration tribunal is properly constituted; or
  what matters have been submitted to arbitration in accordance with an arbitration agreement;
  (c) a claim to declare that an award by an arbitral tribunal is not binding on a party; and
  (d) any other application affecting—

(i) arbitration proceedings (whether started or not); or
(ii) an arbitration agreement.

(2) This Section of this Part does not apply to an arbitration claim to which Sections II or III of this Part apply.

## 62.3 Starting the Claim

(1) Except where paragraph (2) applies an arbitration claim must be started by the issue of an arbitration claim form in accordance with the Part 8 procedure.

(2) An application under section 9 of the 1996 Act to stay legal proceedings must be made by application notice to the court dealing with those proceedings.

(3) The courts in which an arbitration claim may be started are set out in the practice direction.

(4) Rule 30.5 applies with the modification that a judge of the Technology and Construction Court may transfer the claim to any other court or specialist list.

## 62.4 Arbitration Claim Form

(1) An arbitration claim form must—
  (a) include a concise statement of—
    (i) the remedy claimed; and
    (ii) any questions on which the claimant seeks the decision of the court;
  (b) give details of any arbitration award challenged by the claimant, identifying which part or parts of the award are challenged and specifying the grounds for the challenge;
  (c) show that any statutory requirements have been met;
  (d) specify under which section of the 1996 Act the claim is made;
  (e) identify against which (if any) defendants a costs order is sought; and
  (f) specify either—
    (i) the persons on whom the arbitration claim form is to be served, stating their role in the arbitration and whether they are defendants; or
    (ii) that the claim is made without notice under section 44(3) of the 1996 Act and the grounds relied on.

(2) Unless the court orders otherwise an arbitration claim form must be served on the defendant within 1 month from the date of issue and rules 7.5 and 7.6 are modified accordingly.

(3) Where the claimant applies for an order under section 12 of the 1996 Act (extension of time for beginning arbitral proceedings or other dispute resolution procedures), he may include in his arbitration claim form an alternative application for a declaration that such an order is not needed.

## 62.5 Service Out of the Jurisdiction

(1) The court may give permission to serve an arbitration claim form out of the jurisdiction if—
  (a) the claimant seeks to—
    (i) challenge; or
    (ii) appeal on a question of law arising out of,
    an arbitration award made within the jurisdiction;

(The place where an award is treated as made is determined by section 53 of the 1996 Act.)
  (b) the claim is for an order under section 44 of the 1996 Act; or
  (c) the claimant—
    (i) seeks some other remedy or requires a question to be decided by the court affecting an arbitration (whether started or not), an arbitration agreement or an arbitration award; and
    (ii) the seat of the arbitration is or will be within the jurisdiction or the conditions in section 2(4) of the 1996 Act are satisfied.

(2) An application for permission under paragraph (1) must be supported by written evidence—
   (a) stating the grounds on which the application is made; and
   (b) showing in what place or country the person to be served is, or probably may be found.
(3) Rules 6.24 to 6.29 apply to the service of an arbitration claim form under paragraph (1).
(4) An order giving permission to serve an arbitration claim form out of the jurisdiction must specify the period within which the defendant may file an acknowledgment of service.

## 62.6 Notice

(1) Where an arbitration claim is made under section 24, 28 or 56 of the 1996 Act, each arbitrator must be a defendant.
(2) Where notice must be given to an arbitrator or any other person it may be given by sending him a copy of—
   (a) the arbitration claim form; and
   (b) any written evidence in support.
(3) Where the 1996 Act requires an application to the court to be made on notice to any other party to the arbitration, that notice must be given by making that party a defendant.

## 62.7 Case Management

(1) Part 26 and any other rule that requires a party to file an allocation questionnaire does not apply.
(2) Arbitration claims are allocated to the multi-track.
(3) Part 29 does not apply.
(4) The automatic directions set out in the practice direction apply unless the court orders otherwise.

## 62.8 Stay of Legal Proceedings

(1) An application notice seeking a stay of legal proceedings under section 9 of the 1996 Act must be served on all parties to those proceedings who have given an address for service.
(2) A copy of an application notice under paragraph (1) must be served on any other party to the legal proceedings (whether or not he is within the jurisdiction) who has not given an address for service, at—
   (a) his last known address; or
   (b) a place where it is likely to come to his attention.
(3) Where a question arises as to whether—
   (a) an arbitration agreement has been concluded; or
   (b) the dispute which is the subject-matter of the proceedings falls within the terms of such an agreement,

   the court may decide that question or give directions to enable it to be decided and may order the proceedings to be stayed pending its decision.

## 62.9 Variation of Time

(1) The court may vary the period of 28 days fixed by section 70(3) of the 1996 Act for—
   (a) challenging the award under section 67 or 68 of the Act; and
   (b) appealing against an award under section 69 of the Act.
(2) An application for an order under paragraph (1) may be made without notice being served on any other party before the period of 28 days expires.
(3) After the period of 28 days has expired—
   (a) an application for an order extending time under paragraph (1) must—
      (i) be made in the arbitration claim form; and
      (ii) state the grounds on which the application is made;

(b) any defendant may file written evidence opposing the extension of time within 7 days after service of the arbitration claim form; and
(c) if the court extends the period of 28 days, each defendant's time for acknowledging service and serving evidence shall start to run as if the arbitration claim form had been served on the date when the court's order is served on that defendant.

### 62.10 Hearings

(1) The court may order that an arbitration claim be heard either in public or in private.
(2) Rule 39.2 does not apply.
(3) Subject to any order made under paragraph (1)—
  (a) the determination of—
    (i) a preliminary point of law under section 45 of the 1996 Act; or
    (ii) an appeal under section 69 of the 1996 Act on a question of law arising out of an award,
  will be heard in public; and
  (b) all other arbitration claims will be heard in private.
(4) Paragraph (3)(a) does not apply to—
  (a) the preliminary question of whether the court is satisfied of the matters set out in section 45(2)(b); or
  (b) an application for permission to appeal under section 69(2)(b).

## II OTHER ARBITRATION CLAIMS

### 62.11 Scope of this Section

(1) This Section of this Part contains rules about arbitration claims to which the old law applies.
(2) In this Section—
  (a) 'the old law' means the enactments specified in Schedules 3 and 4 of the 1996 Act as they were in force before their amendment or repeal by that Act; and
  (b) 'arbitration claim' means any application to the court under the old law and includes an appeal (or application for permission to appeal) to the High Court under section 1(2) of the 1979 Act.
(3) This Section does not apply to—
  (a) a claim to which Section III of this Part applies; or
  (b) a claim on the award.

### 62.12 Applications to Judge

A claim—
(a) seeking permission to appeal under section 1(2) of the 1979 Act;
(b) under section 1(5) of that Act (including any claim seeking permission); or
(c) under section 5 of that Act,
must be made in the High Court and will be heard by a judge of the Commercial Court unless any such judge directs otherwise.

### 62.13 Starting the Claim

(1) Except where paragraph (2) applies an arbitration claim must be started by the issue of an arbitration claim form in accordance with the Part 8 procedure.
(2) Where an arbitration claim is to be made in existing proceedings—
  (a) it must be made by way of application notice; and
  (b) any reference in this Section of this Part to an arbitration claim form includes a reference to an application notice.
(3) The arbitration claim form in an arbitration claim under section 1(5) of the 1979 Act (including any claim seeking permission) must be served on—

(a) the arbitrator or umpire; and
(b) any other party to the reference.

## 62.14 Claims in District Registries

If—

(a) a claim is to be made under section 12(4) of the 1950 Act for an order for the issue of a witness summons to compel the attendance of the witness before an arbitrator or umpire; and
(b) the attendance of the witness is required within the district of a District Registry,

the claim may be started in that Registry.

## 62.15 Time Limits and Other Special Provisions About Arbitration Claims

(1) An arbitration claim to—
   (a) remit an award under section 22 of the 1950 Act;
   (b) set aside an award under section 23(2) of that Act or otherwise; or
   (c) direct an arbitrator or umpire to state the reasons for an award under section 1(5) of the 1979 Act,

   must be made, and the arbitration claim form served, within 21 days after the award has been made and published to the parties.
(2) An arbitration claim to determine any question of law arising in the course of a reference under section 2(1) of the Arbitration Act 1979 must be made, and the arbitration claim form served, within 14 days after—
   (a) the arbitrator or umpire gave his consent in writing to the claim being made; or
   (b) the other parties so consented.
(3) An appeal under section 1(2) of the 1979 Act must be filed, and the arbitration claim form served, within 21 days after the award has been made and published to the parties.
(4) Where reasons material to an appeal under section 1(2) of the 1979 Act are given on a date subsequent to the publication of the award, the period of 21 days referred to in paragraph (3) will run from the date on which reasons are given.
(5) In every arbitration claim to which this rule applies—
   (a) the arbitration claim form must state the grounds of the claim or appeal;
   (b) where the claim or appeal is based on written evidence, a copy of that evidence must be served with the arbitration claim form; and
   (c) where the claim or appeal is made with the consent of the arbitrator, the umpire or the other parties, a copy of every written consent must be served with the arbitration claim form.
(6) In an appeal under section 1(2) of the 1979 Act—
   (a) a statement of the grounds for the appeal specifying the relevant parts of the award and reasons; and
   (b) where permission is required, any written evidence in support of the contention that the question of law concerns—
      (i) a term of a contract; or
      (ii) an event,

      which is not a 'one-off' term or event,

   must be filed and served with the arbitration claim form.
(7) Any written evidence in reply to written evidence under paragraph (6)(b) must be filed and served on the claimant not less than 2 days before the hearing.
(8) A party to a claim seeking permission to appeal under section 1(2) of the 1979 Act who wishes to contend that the award should be upheld for reasons not expressed or fully expressed in the award and reasons must file and serve on the claimant, a notice specifying the grounds of his contention not less than 2 days before the hearing.

## 62.16 Service Out of the Jurisdiction

(1) Subject to paragraph (2)—

(a) any arbitration claim form in an arbitration claim under the 1950 Act or the 1979 Act; or
(b) any order made in such a claim,
may be served out of the jurisdiction with the permission of the court if the arbitration to which the claim relates—
(i) is governed by the law of England and Wales; or
(ii) has been, is being, or will be, held within the jurisdiction.
(2) An arbitration claim form seeking permission to enforce an award may be served out of the jurisdiction with the permission of the court whether or not the arbitration is governed by the law of England and Wales.
(3) An application for permission to serve an arbitration claim form out of the jurisdiction must be supported by written evidence—
(a) stating the grounds on which the application is made; and
(b) showing in what place or country the person to be served is, or probably may be found.
(4) Rules 6.24 to 6.29 apply to the service of an arbitration claim form under paragraph (1).
(5) An order giving permission to serve an arbitration claim form out of the jurisdiction must specify the period within which the defendant may file an acknowledgment of service.

## III ENFORCEMENT

### 62.17 Scope of this Section

This Section of this Part applies to all arbitration enforcement proceedings other than by a claim on the award.

### 62.18 Enforcement of Awards

(1) An application for permission under—
(a) section 66 of the 1996 Act;
(b) section 101 of the 1996 Act;
(c) section 26 of the 1950 Act; or
(d) section 3(1)(a) of the 1975 Act,
to enforce an award in the same manner as a judgment or order may be made without notice in an arbitration claim form.
(2) The court may specify parties to the arbitration on whom the arbitration claim form must be served.
(3) The parties on whom the arbitration claim form is served must acknowledge service and the enforcement proceedings will continue as if they were an arbitration claim under Section I of this Part.
(4) With the permission of the court the arbitration claim form may be served out of the jurisdiction irrespective of where the award is, or is treated as, made.
(5) Where the applicant applies to enforce an agreed award within the meaning of section 51(2) of the 1996 Act—
(a) the arbitration claim form must state that the award is an agreed award; and
(b) any order made by the court must also contain such a statement.
(6) An application for permission must be supported by written evidence—
(a) exhibiting—
(i) where the application is made under section 66 of the 1996 Act or under section 26 of the 1950 Act, the arbitration agreement and the original award (or copies);
(ii) where the application is under section 101 of the 1996 Act, the documents required to be produced by section 102 of that Act; or
(iii) where the application is under section 3(1)(a) of the 1975 Act, the documents required to be produced by section 4 of that Act;

(b) stating the name and the usual or last known place of residence or business of the claimant and of the person against whom it is sought to enforce the award; and
(c) stating either—
(i) that the award has not been complied with; or
(ii) the extent to which it has not been complied with at the date of the application.

(7) An order giving permission must—
(a) be drawn up by the claimant; and
(b) be served on the defendant by—
(i) delivering a copy to him personally; or
(ii) sending a copy to him at his usual or last known place of residence or business.

(8) An order giving permission may be served out of the jurisdiction—
(a) without permission; and
(b) in accordance with rules 6.24 to 6.29 as if the order were an arbitration claim form.

(9) Within 14 days after service of the order or, if the order is to be served out of the jurisdiction, within such other period as the court may set—
(a) the defendant may apply to set aside the order; and
(b) the award must not be enforced until after—
(i) the end of that period; or
(ii) any application made by the defendant within that period has been finally disposed of.

(10) The order must contain a statement of—
(a) the right to make an application to set the order aside; and
(b) the restrictions on enforcement under rule 62.18(9)(b).

(11) Where a body corporate is a party any reference in this rule to place of residence or business shall have effect as if the reference were to the registered or principal address of the body corporate.

## 62.19 Interest on Awards

(1) Where an applicant seeks to enforce an award of interest the whole or any part of which relates to a period after the date of the award, he must file a statement giving the following particulars—
(a) whether simple or compound interest was awarded;
(b) the date from which interest was awarded;
(c) where rests were provided for, specifying them;
(d) the rate of interest awarded; and
(e) a calculation showing—
(i) the total amount claimed up to the date of the statement; and
(ii) any sum which will become due on a daily basis.

(2) A statement under paragraph (1) must be filed whenever the amount of interest has to be quantified for the purpose of—
(a) obtaining a judgment or order under section 66 of the 1996 Act (enforcement of the award); or
(b) enforcing such a judgment or order.

## 62.20 Registration in High Court of Foreign Awards

(1) Where—
(a) an award is made in proceedings on an arbitration in any part of a United Kingdom Overseas Territory (within the meaning of rule 6.18(f)) or other territory to which Part I of the Foreign Judgments (Reciprocal Enforcement) Act 1933 ('the 1933 Act') extends;
(b) Part II of the Administration of Justice Act 1920 extended to that part immediately before Part I of the 1933 Act was extended to that part; and

(c) an award has, under the law in force in the place where it was made, become enforceable in the same manner as a judgment given by a court in that place, rules 74.1 to 74.7 and 74.9 apply in relation to the award as they apply in relation to a judgment given by the court subject to the modifications in paragraph (2).

(2) The modifications referred to in paragraph (1) are as follows—

(a) for references to the State of origin are substituted references to the place where the award was made; and

(b) the written evidence required by rule 74.4 must state (in addition to the matters required by that rule) that to the best of the information or belief of the maker of the statement the award has, under the law in force in the place where it was made, become enforceable in the same manner as a judgment given by a court in that place.

## 62.21 Registration of Awards Under the Arbitration (International Investment Disputes) Act 1966

(1) In this rule—

(a) 'the 1966 Act' means the Arbitration (International Investment Disputes) Act 1966;

(b) 'award' means an award under the Convention;

(c) 'the Convention' means the Convention on the settlement of investment disputes between States and nationals of other States which was opened for signature in Washington on 18th March 1965;

(d) 'judgment creditor' means the person seeking recognition or enforcement of an award; and

(e) 'judgment debtor' means the other party to the award.

(2) Subject to the provisions of this rule, the following provisions of RSC Order 71 apply with such modifications as may be necessary in relation to an award as they apply in relation to a judgment to which Part II of the Foreign Judgments (Reciprocal Enforcement) Act 1933 applies—

(a) rule 74.1;

(b) rule 74.3;

(c) rule 74.4(1), (2)(a) to (d), and (4);

(d) rule 74.6 (except paragraph (3)(c) to (e)); and

(e) rule 74.9(2).

(3) An application to have an award registered in the High Court under section 1 of the 1966 Act must be made in accordance with the Part 8 procedure.

(4) The written evidence required by rule 74.4 in support of an application for registration must—

(a) exhibit the award certified under the Convention instead of the judgment (or a copy of it); and

(b) in addition to stating the matters referred to in rule 74.4(2)(a) to (d), state whether—

(i) at the date of the application the enforcement of the award has been stayed (provisionally or otherwise) under the Convention; and

(ii) any, and if so what, application has been made under the Convention, which, if granted, might result in a stay of the enforcement of the award.

(5) Where, on granting permission to register an award or an application made by the judgment debtor after an award has been registered, the court considers—

(a) that the enforcement of the award has been stayed (whether provisionally or otherwise) under the Convention; or

(b) that an application has been made under the Convention which, if granted, might result in a stay of the enforcement of the award,

the court may stay the enforcement of the award for such time as it considers appropriate.

# PD 62 Practice Direction — Arbitration

This practice direction supplements CPR Part 62.

## SECTION I

1.1 This Section of this practice direction applies to arbitration claims to which Section I of Part 62 applies.
1.2 In this Section 'the 1996 Act' means the Arbitration Act 1996.
1.3 Where a rule provides for a document to be sent, it may be sent:
(1) by first-class post;
(2) through a document exchange; or
(3) by fax, electronic mail or other means of electronic communication.

### Starting the Claim: Rule 62.3

2.1 An arbitration claim under the 1996 Act (other than under s. 9) must be started in accordance with the High Court and County Courts (Allocation of Arbitration Proceedings) Order 1996 (SI 1996/3215) by the issue of an arbitration claim form.
2.2 An arbitration claim form must be substantially in [form N8].
2.3 Subject to para. 2.1, an arbitration claim form:
(1) may be issued at the courts set out in column 1 of the table below and will be entered in the list set out against that court in column 2;
(2) relating to a landlord and tenant or partnership dispute must be issued in the Chancery Division of the High Court.

| Court | List |
|---|---|
| Admiralty and Commercial Registry at the Royal Courts of Justice, London | Commercial list |
| Technology and Construction Court Registry, St. Dunstan's House, London | TCC list |
| District Registry of the High Court (where mercantile court established) | Mercantile list |
| District Registry of the High Court (where arbitration claim form marked 'Technology and Construction Court' in top right-hand corner) | TCC list |

2.3A An arbitration claim form must, in the case of an appeal, or application for permission to appeal, from a judge-arbitrator, be issued in the Civil Division of the Court of Appeal. The judge hearing the application may adjourn the matter for oral argument before two judges of that court.

### Arbitration Claim Form: Rule 62.4

Service

3.1 The court may exercise its powers under r. 6.8 to permit service of an arbitration claim form at the address of a party's solicitor or representative acting for him in the arbitration.
3.2 Where the arbitration claim form is served by the claimant he must file a certificate of service within 7 days of service of the arbitration claim form.
(Rule 6.10 specifies what a certificate of service must show.)

### Acknowledgment of Service or Making Representations by Arbitrator or ACAS

4.1 Where:
(1) an arbitrator; or
(2) ACAS (in a claim under the 1996 Act as applied with modifications by the ACAS Arbitration Scheme (England and Wales) Order 2001 (SI 2001/1185)),

is sent a copy of an arbitration claim form (including an arbitration claim form sent under r. 62.6(2)), that arbitrator or ACAS (as the case may be) may:
(a) apply to be made a defendant; or
(b) make representations to the court under para. 4.3.

4.2 An application under para. 4.1(2)(a) to be made a defendant:
(1) must be served on the claimant; but
(2) need not be served on any other party.

4.3 An arbitrator or ACAS may make representations by filing written evidence or in writing to the court.

## Supply of Documents from Court Records

5.1 An arbitration claim form may only be inspected with the permission of the court.

## Case Management: Rule 62.7

6.1 The following directions apply unless the court orders otherwise.

6.2 A defendant who wishes to rely on evidence before the court must file and serve his written evidence:
(1) within 21 days after the date by which he was required to acknowledge service; or,
(2) where a defendant is not required to file an acknowledgment of service, within 21 days after service of the arbitration claim form.

6.3 A claimant who wishes to rely on evidence in reply to written evidence filed under para. 6.2 must file and serve his written evidence within 7 days after service of the defendant's evidence.

6.4 Agreed indexed and paginated bundles of all the evidence and other documents to be used at the hearing must be prepared by the claimant.

6.5 Not later than 5 days before the hearing date estimates for the length of the hearing must be filed together with a complete set of the documents to be used.

6.6 Not later than 2 days before the hearing date the claimant must file and serve:
(1) a chronology of the relevant events cross-referenced to the bundle of documents;
(2) (where necessary) a list of the persons involved; and
(3) a skeleton argument which lists succinctly:
(a) the issues which arise for decision;
(b) the grounds of relief (or opposing relief) to be relied upon;
(c) the submissions of fact to be made with the references to the evidence; and
(d) the submissions of law with references to the relevant authorities.

6.7 Not later than the day before the hearing date the defendant must file and serve a skeleton argument which lists succinctly:
(1) the issues which arise for decision;
(2) the grounds of relief (or opposing relief) to be relied upon;
(3) the submissions of fact to be made with the references to the evidence; and
(4) the submissions of law with references to the relevant authorities.

## Securing the Attendance of Witnesses

7.1 A party to arbitral proceedings being conducted in England or Wales who wishes to rely on s. 43 of the 1996 Act to secure the attendance of a witness must apply for a witness summons in accordance with Part 34.

7.2 If the attendance of the witness is required within the district of a district registry, the application may be made at that registry.

7.3 A witness summons will not be issued until the applicant files written evidence showing that the application is made with:
(1) the permission of the tribunal; or
(2) the agreement of the other parties.

## Interim Remedies

8.1 An application for an interim remedy under s. 44 of the 1996 Act must be made in an arbitration claim form.

## Applications Under Sections 32 and 45 of the 1996 Act

9.1 This paragraph applies to arbitration claims for the determination of:

(1) a question as to the substantive jurisdiction of the arbitral tribunal under s. 32 of the 1996 Act; and

(2) a preliminary point of law under s. 45 of the 1996 Act.

9.2 Where an arbitration claim is made without the agreement in writing of all the other parties to the arbitral proceedings but with the permission of the arbitral tribunal, the written evidence or witness statements filed by the parties must set out any evidence relied on by the parties in support of their contention that the court should, or should not, consider the claim.

9.3 As soon as practicable after the written evidence is filed, the court will decide whether or not it should consider the claim and, unless the court otherwise directs, will so decide without a hearing.

## Decisions Without a Hearing

10.1 Having regard to the overriding objective the court may decide particular issues without a hearing. For example, as set out in para. 9.3, the question whether the court is satisfied as to the matters set out in s. 32(2)(b) or s. 45(2)(b) of the 1996 Act.

10.2 The court will generally decide whether to extend the time limit under s. 70(3) of the 1996 Act without a hearing. Where the court makes an order extending the time limit, the defendant must file his written evidence within 21 days from service of the order.

## Variation of Time: Rule 62.9

11.1 An application for an order under r. 62.9(1):

(1) before the period of 28 days has expired, must be made in a Part 23 application notice; and

(2) after the period of 28 days has expired, must be set out in a separately identified part in the arbitration claim form.

## Applications for Permission to Appeal

12.1 Where a party seeks permission to appeal to the court on a question of law arising out of an arbitration award, the arbitration claim form must:

(1) identify the question of law; and

(2) state the grounds on which the party alleges that permission should be given.

12.2 The written evidence in support of the application must set out any evidence relied on by the party for the purpose of satisfying the court:

(1) of the matters referred to in s. 69(3) of the 1996 Act; and

(2) that permission should be given.

12.3 The written evidence filed by the respondent to the application must:

(1) state the grounds on which the respondent opposes the grant of permission;

(2) set out any evidence relied on by him relating to the matters mentioned in s. 69(3) of the 1996 Act; and

(3) specify whether the respondent wishes to contend that the award should be upheld for reasons not expressed (or not fully expressed) in the award and, if so, state those reasons.

12.4 The court will normally determine applications for permission to appeal without an oral hearing.

12.5 Where the court refuses an application for permission to appeal without an oral hearing, it must provide brief reasons.

12.6 Where the court considers that an oral hearing is required, it may give such further directions as are necessary.

## SECTION II

13.1 This Section of this practice direction applies to arbitration claims to which Section II of Part 62 applies.

### Starting the Claim: Rule 62.13

14.1 An arbitration claim must be started in the Commercial Court and, where required to be heard by a judge, be heard by a judge of that court unless he otherwise directs.

## SECTION III

15.1 This Section of this practice direction applies to enforcement proceedings to which Section III of Part 62 applies.

### Registration of Awards Under the Arbitration (International Investment Disputes) Act 1966: Rule 62.21

16.1 Awards ordered to be registered under the 1966 Act and particulars will be entered in the Register kept for that purpose at the Admiralty and Commercial Registry.

[The following forms are annexed to PD 62:

| | |
|---|---|
| N8 | Claim form (arbitration) |
| N8A | Arbitration claim—notes for the claimant |
| N8B | Arbitration claim—notes for the defendant |
| N15 | Acknowledgment of service (arbitration claim) |

These forms are not reproduced in this work but may be accessed via the DCA website at <http://www.dca.gov.uk>]

# CPR Part 63 Patents and Other Intellectual Property Claims



## 63.1 Scope of this Part and Interpretation

(1) This Part applies to all intellectual property claims including—
- (a) registered intellectual property rights such as—
  - (i) patents;
  - (ii) registered designs; and
  - (iii) registered trade marks; and
- (b) unregistered intellectual property rights such as—
  - (i) copyright;
  - (ii) design right;
  - (iii) the right to prevent passing off; and
  - (iv) the other rights set out in the practice direction.

(2) In this Part—
- (a) 'the 1977 Act' means the Patents Act 1977;
- (b) 'the 1988 Act' means the Copyright, Designs and Patents Act 1988;
- (c) 'the 1994 Act' means the Trade Marks Act 1994;
- (d) 'the Comptroller' means the Comptroller General of Patents, Designs and Trade Marks;
- (e) 'patent' means a patent under the 1977 Act and includes any application for a patent or supplementary protection certificate granted under—
  - (i) the Patents (Supplementary Protection Certificates) Rules 1997;
  - (ii) the Patents (Supplementary Protection Certificate for Medicinal Products) Regulations 1992; and
  - (iii) the Patents (Supplementary Protection Certificate for Plant Protection Products) Regulations 1996;
- (f) 'Patents Court' means the Patents Court of the High Court constituted as part of the Chancery Division by section 6(1) of the Supreme Court Act 1981;
- (g) 'Patents County Court' means a county court designated as a Patents County Court under section 287(1) of the 1988 Act;
- (gg) 'patents judge' means a person nominated under section 291(1) of the 1988 Act as the patents judge of a patents county court;
- (h) 'the register' means whichever of the following registers is appropriate—

(i) patents maintained by the Comptroller under section 32 of the 1977 Act;
(ii) designs maintained by the registrar under section 17 of the Registered Designs Act 1949;
(iii) trade marks maintained by the registrar under section 63 of the 1994 Act;
(iv) Community trade marks maintained by the Office for Harmonisation in the Internal Market under Article 83 of Council Regulation (EC) 40/94; and
(v) Community designs maintained by the Office for Harmonisation in the Internal Market under Article 72 of Council Regulation (EC) 6/2002; and

(i) 'the registrar' means—
(i) the registrar of trade marks; or
(ii) the registrar of registered designs,
whichever is appropriate.

(3) Claims to which this Part applies are allocated to the multi-track.

### 63.2 Application of the Civil Procedure Rules

These Rules and their practice directions apply to intellectual property claims unless this Part or a practice direction provides otherwise.

## I PATENTS AND REGISTERED DESIGNS

### 63.3 Scope of Section I

(1) This Section of this Part applies to claims in—
(a) the Patents Court; and
(b) a Patents County Court.
(2) Claims in the court include any claim relating to matters arising out of—
(a) the 1977 Act;
(b) the Registered Designs Act 1949; and
(c) the Defence Contracts Act 1958.

### 63.4 Specialist List

Claims in the Patents Court and a Patents County Court form specialist lists for the purpose of rule 30.5.

### 63.4A Patents Judge

(1) Subject to paragraph (2), proceedings in the patents county court shall be dealt with by the patents judge.
(2) When a matter needs to be dealt with urgently and it is not practicable or appropriate for the patents judge to deal with such matter, the matter may be dealt with by another judge with appropriate specialist experience who shall be nominated by the Vice-Chancellor.

### 63.5 Starting the Claim

Claims to which this Section of this Part applies must be started—
(a) by issuing a Part 7 claim form; or
(b) in existing proceedings under Part 20.

### 63.6 Defence and Reply

Part 15 applies with the modification—
(a) to rule 15.4 that in a claim for infringement under rule 63.9, the defence must be filed within 42 days of service of the claim form; and
(b) to rule 15.8 that the claimant must—
(i) file any reply to a defence; and
(ii) serve it on all other parties,
within 21 days of service of the defence.

### 63.7 Case Management

(1) [*Omitted*]
(2) Part 26 and any other rule that requires a party to file an allocation questionnaire do not apply.
(3) The following provisions only of Part 29 apply—
 (a) rule 29.3(2) (legal representatives to attend case management conferences);
 (b) rule 29.4 (the court's approval of agreed proposals for the management of proceedings); and
 (c) rule 29.5 (variation of case management timetable) with the exception of paragraph (1)(b) and (c).
(4) As soon as practicable the court will hold a case management conference which must be fixed in accordance with the practice direction.

### 63.8 Disclosure and Inspection

Part 31 is modified to the extent set out in the practice direction.

### 63.9 Claim for Infringement and Challenge to Validity

(1) In a claim for infringement or an application in which the validity of a patent or registered design is challenged, the statement of case must contain particulars as set out in the practice direction.
(2) In a claim for infringement, the period for service of the defence or Part 20 claim is 42 days after service of the claim form.

### 63.10 Application to Amend a Patent Specification in Existing Proceedings

(1) An application under section 75 of the 1977 Act for permission to amend the specification of a patent by the proprietor of the patent must be made by application notice.
(2) The application notice must—
 (a) give particulars of—
  (i) the proposed amendment sought; and
  (ii) the grounds upon which the amendment is sought;
 (b) state whether the applicant will contend that the claims prior to amendment are valid; and
 (c) be served by the applicant on all parties and the Comptroller within 7 days of its issue.
(3) The application notice must, if it is reasonably possible, be served on the Comptroller electronically.
(4) Unless the court otherwise orders, the Comptroller will forthwith advertise the application to amend in the journal.
(5) The advertisement will state that any person may apply to the Comptroller for a copy of the application notice.
(6) Within 14 days of the first appearance of the advertisement any person who wishes to oppose the application must file and serve on all parties and the Comptroller a notice opposing the application which must include the grounds relied on.
(7) Within 28 days of the first appearance of the advertisement the applicant must apply to the court for directions.
(8) Unless the court otherwise orders, the applicant must within 7 days serve on the Comptroller any order of the court on the application.
(9) In this rule, 'the journal' means the journal published pursuant to rules made under section 123(6) of the 1977 Act.

### 63.11 Court's Determination of Question or Application

Where the Comptroller—
(a) declines to deal with a question under section 8(7), 12(2), 37(8) or 61(5) of the 1977 Act;

(b) declines to deal with an application under section 40(5) of the 1977 Act; or
(c) certifies under section 72(7)(b) of the 1977 Act that the court should determine the question whether a patent should be revoked,

any person seeking the court's determination of that question or application must issue a claim form within 14 days of the Comptroller's decision.

### 63.12 Application by Employee for Compensation

(1) An application by an employee for compensation under section 40(1) or (2) of the 1977 Act must be made—
  (a) in a claim form; and
  (b) within the period prescribed by paragraphs (2) and (3).
(2) The prescribed period begins on the date of the grant of the patent and ends one year after the patent has ceased to have effect.
(3) Where a patent has ceased to have effect as a result of failure to pay the renewal fees within the period prescribed under rule 39 of the Patents Rules 1995, and an application for restoration is made to the Comptroller under section 28 of the 1977 Act, the period prescribed under paragraph (2)—
  (a) if restoration is ordered, continues as if the patent had remained continuously in effect; or
  (b) if restoration is refused, is treated as expiring one year after the patent ceased to have effect, or six months after the refusal, whichever is the later.

## II REGISTERED TRADE MARKS AND OTHER INTELLECTUAL PROPERTY RIGHTS

### 63.13 Allocation

(1) This Section of this Part applies to—
  (a) claims relating to matters arising out of the 1994 Act; and
  (b) other intellectual property rights as set out in the practice direction.
(2) [*Omitted*]
(3) Claims to which this Section of this Part applies must be brought in—
  (a) the Chancery Division;
  (b) a Patents County Court; or
  (c) a county court where there is also a Chancery district registry.

### 63.14 Claims Under the 1994 Act

In a claim under the 1994 Act, the claim form or application notice must be served on the registrar where the relief sought would, if granted, affect an entry in the United Kingdom register.

### 63.15 Claim for Infringement of Registered Trade Mark

(1) In a claim for infringement of a registered trade mark the defendant may—
  (a) in his defence, challenge the validity of the registration of the trade mark; and
  (b) apply by Part 20 claim for—
    (i) revocation of the registration;
    (ii) a declaration that the registration is invalid; or
    (iii) rectification of the register.
(2) Where a defendant applies under paragraph (1)(b) and the relief sought would, if granted, affect an entry in the United Kingdom register, he must serve on the registrar a copy of his claim form.

## III SERVICE

### 63.16 Service

(1) Subject to paragraph (2), Part 6 applies to service of a claim form and any document under this Part.
(2) A claim form relating to a registered right may be served—
   (a) on a party who has registered the right at the address for service given for that right in the United Kingdom Patent Office register, provided the address is within the jurisdiction; or
   (b) in accordance with rule 6.19(1) or (1A) on a party who has registered the right at the address for service given for that right in the appropriate register at—
      (i) the United Kingdom Patent Office; or
      (ii) the Office for Harmonisation in the Internal Market.

## IV APPEALS

### 63.17 Appeals from the Comptroller

(1) Part 52 applies to appeals from the Comptroller.
(2) Patent appeals are to be made to the Patents Court, and other appeals to the Chancery Division.
(3) Where Part 52 requires a document to be served, it must also be served on the Comptroller or registrar, as appropriate.

# PD 63 Practice Direction — Patents and Other Intellectual Property Claims

This practice direction supplements CPR, Part 63.

## Contents of this Practice Direction

1.1 This practice direction is divided into four sections:
Section I—Provisions about patents and registered designs
Section II—Provisions about registered trade marks and other intellectual property rights
Section III—Provisions about appeals
Section IV—Provisions about final orders

## I PROVISIONS ABOUT PATENTS AND REGISTERED DESIGNS

2.1 This Section of this practice direction applies to claims in the Patents Court and a Patents County Court.

2.2 The following claims must be dealt with in the court:
(1) any matter arising out of the 1977 Act, including:
(a) infringement actions;
(b) revocation actions;
(c) threats under s. 70 of the 1977 Act; and
(d) disputes as to ownership;
(2) registered designs;
(3) Community registered designs; and
(4) semiconductor topography rights.

### Starting the Claim (Rule 63.5)

3.1 A claim form to which this Section of this practice direction applies must be marked in the top right-hand corner 'Patents Court' below the title of the court in which it is issued.

### Case Management (Rule 63.7)

4.1 The following parts only of PD 29 apply:
(1) para. 5 (case management conferences):
(a) excluding para. 5.9; and
(b) modified so far as is made necessary by other specific provisions of this practice direction; and
(2) para. 7 (failure to comply with case management directions).

4.2 Case management shall be dealt with by:
(1) a judge of the court; or
(2) a master or district judge where a judge of the court so directs.

4.3 The claimant must apply for a case management conference within 14 days of the date when all defendants who intend to file and serve a defence have done so.

4.4 Where the claim has been transferred, the claimant must apply for a case management conference within 14 days of the date of the order transferring the claim, unless the court:
(1) held; or
(2) gave directions for
a case management conference, when it made the order transferring the claim.

4.5 Any party may, at a time earlier than that provided in paras 4.3 and 4.4, apply in writing to the court to fix a case management conference.

4.6 If the claimant does not make an application in accordance with paras 4.3 and 4.4, any other party may apply for a case management conference.

4.7 The court may fix a case management conference at any time on its own initiative.

4.8 Not less than four days before a case management conference, each party must file and serve an application notice for any order which that party intends to seek at the case management conference.

4.9 Unless the court orders otherwise, the claimant, or the party who makes an application under para. 4.6, in consultation with the other parties, must prepare a case management bundle containing:

(1) the claim form;

(2) all statements of case (excluding schedules), except that, if a summary of a statement of case has been filed, the bundle should contain the summary, and not the full statement of case;

(3) a pre-trial timetable, if one has been agreed or ordered;

(4) the principal orders of the court; and

(5) any agreement in writing made by the parties as to disclosure,

and provide copies of the case management bundle for the court and the other parties at least four days before the first case management conference or any earlier hearing at which the court may give case management directions.

4.10 At the case management conference the court may direct that:

(1) a scientific adviser under the Supreme Court Act 1981, s. 70(3), be appointed; and

(2) a document setting out basic undisputed technology should be prepared.

(Rule 35.15 applies to scientific advisers.)

4.11 Where a trial date has not been fixed by the court, a party may apply for a trial date by filing a certificate which must:

(1) state the estimated length of the trial, agreed if possible by all parties;

(2) detail the time required for the judge to consider the documents;

(3) identify the area of technology; and

(4) assess the complexity of the technical issues involved by indicating the complexity on a scale of 1 to 5 (with 1 being the least and 5 the most complex).

4.12 The claimant, in consultation with the other parties, must revise and update the documents referred to in para. 4.9 appropriately as the case proceeds. This must include making all necessary revisions and additions at least 7 days before any subsequent hearing at which the court may give case management directions.

## Disclosure and Inspection (Rule 63.8)

5.1 Standard disclosure does not require the disclosure of documents where the documents relate to:

(1) the infringement of a patent by a product or process if, before or at the same time as serving a list of documents, the defendant has served on the claimant and any other party:

(a) full particulars of the product or process alleged to infringe; and

(b) drawings or other illustrations, if necessary;

(2) any ground on which the validity of a patent is put in issue, except documents which came into existence within the period:

(a) beginning two years before the earliest claimed priority date; and

(b) ending two years after that date; and

(3) the issue of commercial success.

5.2 Where the issue of commercial success arises, the patentee must, within such time limit as the court may direct, serve a schedule containing:

(1) where the commercial success relates to an article or product:

(a) an identification of the article or product (for example by product code number) which the patentee asserts has been made in accordance with the claims of the patent;

(b) a summary by convenient periods of sales of any such article or product;
(c) a summary for the equivalent periods of sales, if any, of any equivalent prior article or product marketed before the article or product in sub-paragraph (a); and
(d) a summary by convenient periods of any expenditure on advertising and promotion which supported the marketing of the articles or products in sub-paragraphs (a) and (c); or

(2) where the commercial success relates to the use of a process:
(a) an identification of the process which the patentee asserts has been used in accordance with the claims of the patent;
(b) a summary by convenient periods of the revenue received from the use of such process;
(c) a summary for the equivalent periods of the revenues, if any, received from the use of any equivalent prior art process; and
(d) a summary by convenient periods of any expenditure which supported the use of the process in sub-paragraphs (a) and (c).

## Short Applications

6.1 Where any application is listed for a short hearing, the parties must file all necessary documents, skeleton arguments and drafts of any orders sought, by no later than 3.00 p.m. on the preceding working day.

6.2 A short hearing is any hearing which is listed for no more than one hour.

## Timetable for a Trial

7.1 Not less than one week before the beginning of the trial, each party must inform the court in writing of the estimated length of its:
(1) oral submissions;
(2) examination in chief, if any, of its own witnesses; and
(3) cross-examination of witnesses of any other party.

7.2 At least four days before the date fixed for the trial, the claimant must file:
(1) the trial bundle; and
(2) a reading guide for the judge.

7.3 The reading guide filed under para. 7.2 must:
(1) be short and, if possible, agreed;
(2) set out the issues, the parts of the documents that need to be read on each issue and the most convenient order that they should be read;
(3) identify the relevant passages in textbooks and cases, if appropriate; and
(4) not contain argument.

## Jurisdiction of Masters

8.1 A master may deal with:
(1) orders by way of settlement, except settlement of procedural disputes;
(2) orders on applications for extension of time;
(3) applications for leave to serve out of the jurisdiction;
(4) applications for security for costs;
(5) other matters as directed by a judge of the court; and
(6) enforcement of money judgments.

## Experiments

9.1 Where a party seeks to establish any fact by experimental proof conducted for the purpose of litigation he must, at least 21 days before service of the application notice for directions under para. 9.3, or within such other time as the court may direct, serve on all parties a notice:
(1) stating the facts which he seeks to establish; and

(2) giving full particulars of the experiments proposed to establish them.

9.2 A party served with notice under para. 9.1:

(1) must within 21 days after such service, serve on the other party a notice stating whether or not he admits each fact; and

(2) may request the opportunity to inspect a repetition of all or a number of the experiments identified in the notice served under para. 9.1.

9.3 Where any fact which a party seeks to establish by experimental proof is not admitted, he must apply to the court for permission and directions by application notice.

## Use of Models or Apparatus

10.1 Where a party intends to rely on any model or apparatus, he must apply to the court for directions at the first case management conference.

## Claim for Infringement and Challenge to Validity (Rule 63.9)

11.1 In a claim for infringement of a patent:

(1) the statement of case must:

(a) show which of the claims in the specification of the patent are alleged to be infringed; and

(b) give at least one example of each type of infringement alleged; and

(2) a copy of each document referred to in the statement of case, and where necessary a translation of the document, must be served with the statement of case.

11.2 Where the validity of a patent or registered design is challenged:

(1) the statement of case must contain particulars of:

(a) the relief sought; and

(b) the issues except those relating to validity of the patent or registered design;

(2) the statement of case must have a separate document annexed to it headed 'Grounds of Invalidity' specifying the grounds on which validity of the patent is challenged;

(3) a copy of each document referred to in the grounds of invalidity, and where necessary a translation of the document, must be served with the grounds of invalidity; and

(4) the Comptroller must be sent a copy of the grounds of invalidity and where any such grounds of invalidity are amended, a copy of the amended document, at the same time as the grounds of invalidity are served or amended.

11.3 Where, in an application in which validity of a patent or a registered design is challenged, the grounds of invalidity include an allegation:

(1) that the invention is not a patentable invention because it is not new or does not involve an inventive step, the particulars must specify such details of the matter in the state of art relied on, as set out in para. 11.4;

(2) that the specification of the patent does not disclose the invention clearly enough and completely enough for it to be performed by a person skilled in the art, the particulars must state, if appropriate, which examples of the invention cannot be made to work and in which respects they do not work or do not work as described in the specification; or

(3) that the registered design is not new, the particulars must specify such details of the matter in the state of art relied on, as set out in para. 11.4.

11.4 The details required under para. 11.3(1) and (3) are:

(1) in the case of matter or a design made available to the public by written description the date on which and the means by which it was so made available, unless this is clear from the face of the matter; and

(2) in the case of matter or a design made available to the public by use:

(a) the date or dates of such use;

(b) the name of all persons making such use;

(c) any written material which identifies such use;

(d) the existence and location of any apparatus employed in such use; and
(e) all facts and matters relied on to establish that such matter was made available to the public.

11.5 In any proceedings in which the validity of a patent is challenged:
(1) on the ground that the invention did not involve an inventive step, a party who wishes to rely on the commercial success of the patent must state the grounds on which he so relies in his statement of case; and
(2) the court may order inspection of machinery or apparatus where a party alleges such machinery or apparatus was used before the priority date of the claim.

## Application to Amend a Patent Specification in Existing Proceedings (Rule 63.10)

12.1 Not later than two days before the first hearing date the applicant, the Comptroller if he wishes to be heard, the parties to the proceedings and any other opponent, must file and serve a document stating the directions sought.

12.2 Where the application notice is served on the Comptroller electronically under r. 63.10(3), it must comply with any requirements for the sending of electronic communications to the Comptroller.

## Application by Employee for Compensation (Rule 63.12)

13.1 Where an employee applies for compensation under s. 40(1) or (2) of the 1977 Act, the court must at the case management conference give directions as to:
(1) the manner in which the evidence, including any accounts of expenditure and receipts relating to the claim, is to be given at the hearing of the claim and if written evidence is to be given, specify the period within which witness statements or affidavits must be filed; and
(2) the provision to the claimant by the defendant or a person deputed by him, of reasonable facilities for inspecting and taking extracts from the accounts by which the defendant proposes to verify the accounts in sub-paragraph (1) or from which those accounts have been derived.

## Communication of Information to the European Patent Office

14.1 The court may authorise the communication of any such information in the court files as the court thinks fit to:
(1) the European Patent Office; or
(2) the competent authority of any country which is a party to the European Patent Convention.

14.2 Before authorising the disclosure of information under para. 14.1, the court shall permit any party who may be affected by the disclosure to make representations, in writing or otherwise, on the question of whether the information should be disclosed.

## Order Affecting Entry in the Register of Patents or Designs

15.1 Where any order of the court affects the validity of an entry in the register, the court and the party in whose favour the order is made, must serve a copy of such order on the Comptroller within 14 days.

15.2 Where the order is in favour of more than one party, a copy of the order must be served by such party as the court directs.

## Claim for Rectification of the Register of Patents or Designs

16.1 Where a claim is made for the rectification of the register of patents or designs, the claimant must at the same time as serving the other parties, serve a copy of:
(1) the claim form; and
(2) accompanying documents on the Comptroller or registrar, as appropriate.

16.2 Where documents under para. 16.1 are served on the Comptroller or registrar, he shall be entitled to take part in the proceedings.

## European Community Designs

17.1 The Patents Court and the Central London County Court are the designated Community design courts under Council Regulation (EC) 6/2002, art. 80(5).

17.2 Where a counterclaim is filed at the Community design court, for a declaration of invalidity of a registered Community design, the Community design court shall inform the Office for Harmonisation in the Internal Market of the date on which the counterclaim was filed, in accordance with Council Regulation (EC) 6/2002, art. 86(2).

17.3 On filing a counterclaim under para. 17.2, the party filing it must inform the Community design court in writing that it is a counterclaim to which para. 17.2 applies and that the Office for Harmonisation in the Internal Market needs to be informed of the date on which the counterclaim was filed.

17.4 Where a Community design court has given a judgment which has become final on a counterclaim for a declaration of invalidity of a registered Community design, the Community design court shall send a copy of the judgment to the Office for Harmonisation in the Internal Market, in accordance with Council Regulation (EC) 6/2002, art. 86(4).

17.5 The party in whose favour judgment is given under para. 17.4 must inform the Community design court at the time of judgment that para. 17.4 applies and that the Office for Harmonisation in the Internal Market needs to be sent a copy of the judgment.

# II PROVISIONS ABOUT REGISTERED TRADE MARKS AND OTHER INTELLECTUAL PROPERTY RIGHTS

## Allocation (Rule 63.13)

18.1 Any of the following claims must be brought in the Chancery Division, a Patents County Court or a county court where there is also a Chancery district registry:
(1) copyright;
(2) rights in performances;
(3) rights conferred under part VII of the 1988 Act;
(4) design right;
(5) Community design right;
(6) Olympic symbols;
(7) plant varieties;
(8) moral rights;
(9) database rights;
(10) unauthorised decryption rights;
(11) hallmarks;
(12) technical trade secrets litigation;
(13) passing off;
(14) geographical indications;
(15) registered trade marks; and
(16) Community registered trade marks.

18.2 There are Chancery district registries at Birmingham, Bristol, Cardiff, Leeds, Liverpool, Manchester and Newcastle upon Tyne.

## Starting the Claim

19.1 A claim form to which this Section of this practice direction applies must be marked in the top right-hand corner 'Chancery Division, Intellectual Property' below the title of the court in which it is issued.

## Claims Under the 1994 Act (Rule 63.14)

20.1 Where the registrar refers to the court an application made to him under the 1994 Act, then unless within one month of receiving notification of the decision to refer, the applicant makes the application to the court, he shall be deemed to have abandoned it.

20.2 The period prescribed under para. 20.1 may be extended by:
(1) the registrar; or
(2) the court,
where a party so applies, even if such application is not made until after the expiration of the period prescribed.

20.3 Where an application is made under s. 19 of the 1994 Act, the applicant must serve his claim form or application notice on all identifiable persons having an interest in the goods, materials or articles within the meaning of s. 19 of the 1994 Act.

## Claim for Infringement of Registered Trade Mark (Rule 63.15)

21.1 Where a document under r. 63.15(2) is served on the registrar, he:
(1) may take part in the proceedings; and
(2) need not serve a defence or other statement of case, unless the court otherwise orders.

## Order Affecting Entry in the Register of Trade Marks

22.1 Where any order of the court affects the validity of an entry in the register, the provisions of paras 15.1 and 15.2 shall apply.

## Claim for Rectification of the Register of Trade Marks

23.1 Where a claim is made for the rectification of the register of trade marks, the provisions of paras 16.1 and 16.2 shall apply.

## European Community Trade Marks

24.1 The Chancery Division of the High Court, a Patents County Court or a county court where there is also a Chancery district registry are designated Community trade mark courts under Council Regulation (EC) 40/94, art. 91(1).

24.2 Where a counterclaim is filed at the Community trade mark court, for revocation or for a declaration of invalidity of a Community trade mark, the Community trade mark court shall inform the Office for Harmonisation in the Internal Market of the date on which the counterclaim was filed, in accordance with Council Regulation (EC) 40/94, art. 96(4).

24.3 On filing a counterclaim under para. 24.2, the party filing it must inform the Community trade mark court in writing that it is a counterclaim to which para. 24.2 applies and that the Office for Harmonisation in the Internal Market needs to be informed of the date on which the counterclaim was filed.

24.4 Where the Community trade mark court has given a judgment which has become final on a counterclaim for revocation or for a declaration of invalidity of a Community trade mark, the Community trade mark court shall send a copy of the judgment to the Office for Harmonisation in the Internal Market, in accordance with Council Regulation (EC) 40/94, art. 96(6).

24.5 The party in whose favour judgment is given under para. 24.4 must inform the Community trade mark court at the time of judgment that para. 24.4 applies and that the Office for Harmonisation in the Internal Market needs to be sent a copy of the judgment.

## Claim for Additional Damages Under Section 97(2) or Section 229(3) of the 1988 Act

25.1 Where a claimant seeks to recover additional damages under s. 97(2) or s. 229(3) of the 1988 Act, the particulars of claim must include:
(1) a statement to that effect; and
(2) the grounds for claiming them.

## Application for Delivery Up or Forfeiture Under the 1988 Act

26.1 Where a claimant applies under ss. 99, 114, 195, 204, 230 or 231 of the 1988 Act for delivery up or forfeiture he must serve:
(1) the claim form; or
(2) application notice, where appropriate,
on all identifiable persons who have an interest in the goods, material or articles within the meaning of ss. 114 or 204 of the 1988 Act.

## Olympic Symbols

27.1 In this practice direction 'the Olympic Symbol Regulations' means the Olympics Association Right (Infringement Proceedings) Regulations 1995 (SI 1995/3325).

27.2 Where an application is made under reg. 5 of the Olympic Symbol Regulations, the applicant must serve his claim form or application notice on all identifiable persons having an interest in the goods, materials or articles within the meaning of reg. 5 of the Olympic Symbol Regulations.

# III PROVISIONS ABOUT APPEALS

## Appeals and References from the Comptroller (Rule 63.17)

28.1 Where:
(1) a person appointed by the Lord Chancellor to hear and decide appeals under s. 77 of the 1994 Act, refers an appeal to the Chancery Division of the High Court under s. 76(3) of the 1994 Act; or
(2) the Comptroller refers the whole proceedings or a question or issue to the Chancery Division of the High Court under s. 251(1) of the 1988 Act,
the appeal or reference must be brought within 14 days of the reference.

# IV PROVISIONS ABOUT FINAL ORDERS

29.1 Where the court makes an order for delivery up or destruction of infringing goods, or articles designed or adapted to make such goods, the defendant will pay the costs of complying with that order unless the court orders otherwise.

29.2 Where the court finds that an intellectual property right has been infringed, the court may, at the request of the applicant, order appropriate measures for the dissemination and publication of the judgment to be taken at the defendant's expense.

# CPR Part 64 Estates, Trusts and Charities



## 64.1 General

(1) This Part contains rules—
  (a) in Section I, about claims relating to—
    (i) the administration of estates of deceased persons, and
    (ii) trusts; and
  (b) in Section II, about charity proceedings.
(2) In this Part and its practice directions, where appropriate, references to trustees include executors and administrators.
(3) All proceedings in the High Court to which this Part applies must be brought in the Chancery Division.

## I CLAIMS RELATING TO THE ADMINISTRATION OF ESTATES AND TRUSTS

## 64.2 Scope of this Section

This Section of this Part applies to claims—
(a) for the court to determine any question arising in—
  (i) the administration of the estate of a deceased person; or
  (ii) the execution of a trust;
(b) for an order for the administration of the estate of a deceased person, or the execution of a trust, to be carried out under the direction of the court ('an administration order');
(c) under the Variation of Trusts Act 1958; or
(d) under section 48 of the Administration of Justice Act 1985.

## 64.3 Claim Form

A claim to which this Section applies must be made by issuing a Part 8 claim form.

## 64.4 Parties

(1) In a claim to which this Section applies, other than an application under section 48 of the Administration of Justice Act 1985—
  (a) all the trustees must be parties;
  (b) if the claim is made by trustees, any of them who does not consent to being a claimant must be made a defendant; and
  (c) the claimant may make parties to the claim any persons with an interest in or claim against the estate, or an interest under the trust, who it is appropriate to make parties having regard to the nature of the order sought.
(2) In addition, in a claim under the Variation of Trusts Act 1958, unless the court directs otherwise any person who—
  (a) created the trust; or
  (b) provided property for the purposes of the trust,
  must, if still alive, be made a party to the claim.

(The court may, under rule 19.2, order additional persons to be made parties to a claim.)

## II CHARITY PROCEEDINGS

### 64.5 Scope of this Section and Interpretation

(1) This Section applies to charity proceedings.
(2) In this Section—
 (a) 'the Act' means the Charities Act 1993;
 (b) 'charity proceedings' has the same meaning as in section 33(8) of the Act; and
 (c) 'the Commissioners' means the Charity Commissioners for England and Wales.

### 64.6 Application for Permission to Take Charity Proceedings

(1) An application to the High Court under section 33(5) of the Act for permission to start charity proceedings must be made within 21 days after the refusal by the Commissioners of an order authorising proceedings.
(2) The application must be made by issuing a Part 8 claim form, which must contain the information specified in the practice direction.
(3) The Commissioners must be made defendants to the claim, but the claim form need not be served on them or on any other person.
(4) The judge considering the application may direct the Commissioners to file a written statement of their reasons for their decision.
(5) The court will serve on the applicant a copy of any statement filed under paragraph (4).
(6) The judge may either—
 (a) give permission without a hearing; or
 (b) fix a hearing.

# PD 64 Practice Direction — Estates, Trusts and Charities

This practice direction supplements CPR Part 64.

## I CLAIMS RELATING TO THE ADMINISTRATION OF ESTATES AND TRUSTS

### Examples of Claims Under Rule 64.2(a)

1 The following are examples of the types of claims which may be made under r. 64.2(a):
- (1) a claim for the determination of any of the following questions:
  - (a) any question as to who is included in any class of persons having:
    - (i) a claim against the estate of a deceased person;
    - (ii) a beneficial interest in the estate of such a person; or
    - (iii) a beneficial interest in any property subject to a trust;
  - (b) any question as to the rights or interests of any person claiming:
    - (i) to be a creditor of the estate of a deceased person;
    - (ii) to be entitled under a will or on the intestacy of a deceased person; or
    - (iii) to be beneficially entitled under a trust;
- (2) a claim for any of the following remedies:
  - (a) an order requiring a trustee:
    - (i) to provide and, if necessary, verify accounts;
    - (ii) to pay into court money which he holds in that capacity; or
    - (iii) to do or not to do any particular act;
  - (b) an order approving any sale, purchase, compromise or other transaction by a trustee; or
  - (c) an order directing any act to be done which the court could order to be done if the estate or trust in question were being administered or executed under the direction of the court.

### Applications by Trustees for Directions

2 A separate practice direction (PD 64B) contains guidance about applications by trustees for directions.

### Administration Orders: Rule 64.2(b)

3.1 The court will only make an administration order if it considers that the issues between the parties cannot properly be resolved in any other way.

3.2 If, in a claim for an administration order, the claimant alleges that the trustees have not provided proper accounts, the court may:
- (1) stay the proceedings for a specified period, and order them to file and serve proper accounts within that period; or
- (2) if necessary to prevent proceedings by other creditors or persons claiming to be entitled to the estate or fund, make an administration order and include in it an order that no such proceedings are to be taken without the court's permission.

3.3 Where an administration order has been made in relation to the estate of a deceased person, and a claim is made against the estate by any person who is not a party to the proceedings:
- (1) no party other than the executors or administrators of the estate may take part in any proceedings relating to the claim without the permission of the court; and
- (2) the court may direct or permit any other party to take part in the proceedings, on such terms as to costs or otherwise as it thinks fit.

3.4 Where an order is made for the sale of any property vested in trustees, those persons shall have the conduct of the sale unless the court directs otherwise.

## Applications Under the Variation of Trusts Act 1958: Rule 64.2(c)

4.1 Where children or unborn beneficiaries will be affected by a proposed arrangement under the Act, the evidence filed in support of the application must:

(1) show that their litigation friends or the trustees support the arrangements as being in the interests of the children or unborn beneficiaries; and

(2) unless para. 4.3 applies or the court orders otherwise, be accompanied by a written opinion to this effect by the advocate who will appear on the hearing of the application.

4.2 A written opinion filed under para. 4.1(2) must:

(1) if it is given on formal instructions, be accompanied by a copy of those instructions; or

(2) otherwise, state fully the basis on which it is given.

4.3 No written opinion needs to be filed in support of an application to approve an arrangement under s. 1(1)(d) of the Act (discretionary interests under protective trusts).

4.4 Where the interests of two or more children, or two or more of the children and unborn beneficiaries, are similar, only a single written opinion needs to be filed.

## Applications Under Section 48 of the Administration of Justice Act 1985: Rule 64.2(d)

5 A Part 8 claim form for an application by trustees under s. 48 of the Administration of Justice Act 1985 (power of High Court to authorise action to be taken in reliance on legal opinion) may be issued without naming a defendant, under r. 8.2A. No separate application for permission under r. 8.2A need be made.

## Prospective Costs Orders

6.1 These paragraphs are about the costs of applications under r. 64.2(a).

6.2 Where trustees have power to agree to pay the costs of a party to such an application, and exercise such a power, r. 48.3 applies. In such a case, an order is not required and the trustees are entitled to recover out of the trust fund any costs which they pay pursuant to the agreement made in the exercise of such power.

6.3 Where the trustees do not have, or decide not to exercise, a power to make such an agreement, the trustees or the party concerned may apply to the court at any stage of proceedings for an order that the costs of any party (including the costs of the trustees) shall be paid out of the fund (a 'prospective costs order').

6.4 The court, on an application for a prospective costs order, may:

(a) in the case of the trustees' costs, authorise the trustees to raise and meet such costs out of the fund;

(b) in the case of the costs of any other party, authorise or direct the trustees to pay such costs (or any part of them, or the costs incurred up to a particular time) out of the trust fund to be assessed, if not agreed by the trustees, on the indemnity basis or, if the court directs, on the standard basis, and to make payments from time to time on account of such costs. A model form of order is annexed to this practice direction.

6.5 The court will always consider whether it is possible to deal with the application for a prospective costs order on paper without a hearing and in an ordinary case would expect to be able to do so. The trustees must consider whether a hearing is needed for any reason. If they consider that it is they should say so and explain why in their evidence. If any party to the application referred to in para. 6.1 above (or any other person interested in the trust fund) considers that a hearing is necessary (for instance because he wishes to oppose the making of a prospective costs order) this should be stated, and the reasons explained, in his evidence, if any, or otherwise in a letter to the court.

6.6 If the court would be minded to refuse the application on a consideration of the papers alone, the parties will be notified and given the opportunity, within a stated time, to ask for a hearing.

6.7 The evidence in support of an application for a prospective costs order should be given by witness statement. The trustees and the applicant (if different) must ensure full disclosure of the relevant matters to show that the case is one which falls within the category of case where a prospective costs order can properly be made.

6.8 The model form of order is designed for use in the more straightforward cases, where a question needs to be determined which has arisen in the administration of the trust, whether the claimants are the trustees or a beneficiary. The form may be adapted for use in less straightforward cases, in particular where the proceedings are hostile, but special factors may also have to be reflected in the terms of the order in such a case.

## II CHARITY PROCEEDINGS

### Role of Attorney-General

7 The Attorney-General is a necessary party to all charity proceedings, other than any commenced by the Charity Commissioners, and must be joined as a defendant if he is not a claimant.

### Service on Charity Commissioners or Attorney-General

8 Any document required or authorised to be served on the Commissioners or the Attorney-General must be served on the Treasury Solicitor in accordance with paragraph 2.1 of the Practice Direction supplementing Part 66.

### Applications For Permission to Take Charity Proceedings: Rule 64.6

9.1 The claim form for an application under s. 33(5) of the Act must state:
  (1) the name, address and description of the applicant;
  (2) details of the proceedings which he wishes to take;
  (3) the date of the Commissioners' refusal to grant an order authorising the taking of proceedings;
  (4) the grounds on which the applicant alleges that it is a proper case for taking proceedings; and
  (5) if the application is made with the consent of any other party to the proposed proceedings, that fact.

9.2 If the Commissioners have given reasons for refusing to grant an order, a copy of their reasons must be filed with the claim form.

### Appeals Against Orders of the Charity Commissioners

10 Part 52 applies to any appeal against an order of the Charity Commissioners. Section III of PD 52 contains special provisions about such appeals.

**Model form of prospective costs order**

UPON THE APPLICATION etc.
AND UPON HEARING etc.
AND UPON READING etc.
AND UPON the Solicitors for the . . . . . . . . . . . . . . . . Defendant undertaking to make the repayments mentioned in paragraph 2 below in the circumstances there mentioned

IT IS [BY CONSENT] ORDERED THAT:

1. The Claimants as trustees of . . . . . . . . . . . . . . . ('the [Settlement/Scheme]') do—
  (a) pay from the assets of the [Settlement/Scheme] the costs of and incidental to these proceedings incurred by the . . . . . . . . . . . . . . Defendant such costs to be subject to a detailed assessment on the indemnity basis if not agreed and (for the avoidance of doubt) to—

(i) include costs incurred by the. . . . . . . . . . Defendant from and after [*date*] in anticipation of being appointed to represent any class of persons presently or formerly beneficially interested under the trusts of the [Settlement/Scheme] irrespective of whether [he/she] is in fact so appointed; and

(ii) exclude (in the absence of any further order) costs incurred in prosecuting any Part 20 claim or any appeal;

(b) indemnify the . . . . . . . . . . . . . Defendant in respect of any costs which he may be ordered to pay to any other party to these proceedings in connection therewith.

2. Until the outcome of the detailed assessment (or the agreement regarding costs) contemplated in paragraph 1 above, the Claimants as trustees do pay from the assets of the [Settlement/Scheme] to the Solicitors for the . . . . . . . . . Defendant monthly (or at such other intervals as may be agreed) such sums on account of the costs referred to in paragraph 1(a) of this Order as the Solicitors for the . . . . . . . . . . . . Defendant shall certify—

(i) to have been reasonably and property incurred and not to exceed such amount as is likely in their opinion to be allowed on a detailed assessment on the indemnity basis; and

(ii) to have accrued on account of the present proceedings in the period prior to the date of such certificate and not to have been previously provided for under this Order.

PROVIDED ALWAYS that the Solicitors for the . . . . . . . . . . . . . . . Defendant shall repay such sums (if any) as, having been paid to them on account, are disallowed on a detailed assessment or are otherwise agreed to be repaid and any such sums shall be repaid together with interest at 1% above the base rate for the time being of [Barclays] Bank plc from and including the date of payment to those Solicitors up to and including the date of repayment, such interest to accrue daily.

3. Any party may apply to vary or discharge paragraphs 1 and 2 of this Order but only in respect of costs to be incurred after the date of such application.

*Note: this form of order assumes that the trustees are the claimants. If the claimant is a beneficiary and the trustees are defendants, references to the parties need to be adapted accordingly.*

# PD 64B Practice Direction — Applications to the Court for Directions by Trustees in Relation to the Administration of the Trust

This practice direction supplements Section I of CPR Part 64.

1 This practice direction is about applications to the court for directions by trustees in relation to the administration of the trust.

## Contents of the Claim Form

2 If confidentiality of the directions sought is important (for example, where the directions relate to actual or proposed litigation with a third party who could find out what directions the trustees are seeking through access to the claim form under r. 5.4) the statement of the remedy sought, for the purposes of r. 8.2(b), may be expressed in general terms. The trustees must, in that case, state specifically in the evidence what it is that they seek to be allowed to do.

## Proceedings in Private

3 The proceedings will in the first instance be listed in private (see PD 39, para. 1.5, and r. 39.2(3)(f)). Accordingly the order made, as well as the other documents among the court records (apart from a claim form which has been served), will not be open to inspection by third parties without the court's permission (r. 5.4(2)). If the matter is disposed of without a hearing, the order made will be expressed to have been made in private.

## Joining Defendants or Giving Notice to Those Interested

4.1 Rule 64.4(1)(c) deals with the joining of beneficiaries as defendants. Often, especially in the case of a private trust, it will be clear that some, and which, beneficiaries need to be joined as defendants. Sometimes, if there are only two views of the appropriate course, and one is advocated by one beneficiary who will be joined, it may not be necessary for other beneficiaries to be joined since the trustees may be able to present the other arguments. Equally, in the case of a pension trust, it may not be necessary for a member of every possible different class of beneficiaries to be joined.

4.2 In some cases the court may be able to assess whether or not to give the directions sought, or what directions to give, without hearing from any party other than the trustees. If the trustees consider that their case is in that category they may apply to the court to issue the claim form without naming any defendants under r. 8.2A. They must apply to the court before the claim form is issued (r. 8.2A(2)) and include a copy of the claim form that they propose to issue (r. 8.2A(3)(b)).

4.3 In other cases the trustees may know that beneficiaries need to be joined as defendants, or to be given notice, but may be in doubt as to which. Examples could include a case concerning a pension scheme with many beneficiaries and a number of different categories of interest, especially if they may be differently affected by the action for which directions are sought, or a private trust with a large class of discretionary beneficiaries. In those cases the trustees may apply to issue the claim form without naming any defendants under r. 8.2A. The application may be combined with an application to the court for directions as to which persons to join as parties or to give notice to under r. 19.8A.

4.4 In the case of a charitable trust the Attorney-General is always the appropriate defendant, and almost always the only one.

## Case Management Directions

5.1 The claim will be referred to the master or district judge once a defendant has acknowledged service, or otherwise on expiry of the period for acknowledgment of service (or, if no defendant is named, as soon as the claimants' evidence has been filed), to consider directions for the management of the case. Such directions may be given without a hearing in some cases; these might include directions as to parties or as to notice of proceedings, as mentioned in para. 4 above.

## Proceeding Without a Hearing

6.1 The court will always consider whether it is possible to deal with the application on paper without a hearing. The trustees must always consider whether a hearing is needed for any reason. If they consider that it is they should say so and explain why in their evidence. If a defendant considers that a hearing is needed, this should be stated, and the reasons explained, in his evidence, if any, or otherwise in a letter to the court.

6.2 If the court would be minded to refuse to give the directions asked for on a consideration of the papers alone, the parties will be notified and given the opportunity, within a stated time, to ask for a hearing.

6.3 In charity cases, the master or district judge may deal with the case without a hearing on the basis of a letter by or on behalf of the Attorney-General that sets out his attitude to the application.

## Evidence

7.1 The trustees' evidence should be given by witness statement. In order to ensure that, if directions are given, the trustees are properly protected by the order, they must ensure full disclosure of relevant matters, even if the case is to proceed with the participation of beneficiaries as defendants.

7.2 Applications for directions whether or not to take or defend or pursue litigation should be supported by evidence including the advice of an appropriately qualified lawyer as to the prospects of success and other matters relevant to be taken into account, including a cost estimate for the proceedings and any known facts concerning the means of the opposite party to the proceedings, and a draft of any proposed statement of case. There are cases in which it is likely to be so clear that the trustees ought to proceed as they wish that the costs of making the application, even on a simplified procedure without a hearing and perhaps without defendants, are not justified in comparison with the size of the fund or the matters at issue.

7.3 References in this practice direction to an appropriately qualified lawyer mean one whose qualifications and experience are appropriate to the circumstances of the case. The qualifications should be stated. If the advice is given on formal instructions, the instructions should always be put in evidence as well, so that the court can see the basis on which the advice was given. If it is not, the advice must state fully the basis on which it is given.

7.4 All applications for directions should be supported by evidence showing the value of the trust assets, the significance of the proposed litigation or other course of action for the trust, and why the court's directions are needed. In the case of a pension trust the evidence should include the latest actuarial valuation, and should describe the membership profile and, if a deficit on winding up is likely, the priority provisions and their likely effect.

7.5 On an application for directions about actual or possible litigation the evidence should also state whether (i) any relevant pre-action protocol has been followed; and (ii) the trustees have proposed or undertaken, or intend to propose, mediation by ADR, and (in each case) if not why not.

7.6 If a beneficiary of the trust is a party to the litigation about which directions are sought, with an interest opposed to that of the trustees, that beneficiary should be a defendant to the trustees' application, but any material which would be privileged as regards that beneficiary in the litigation should be put in evidence as exhibits to the trustees' witness statement, and should not be served on the beneficiary. However if the trustees' representatives consider that no harm would be done by the disclosure of all or some part of the material, then that material should be served on that defendant. That defendant may also be excluded from part of the hearing, including that which is devoted to discussion of the material withheld.

*Consultation with beneficiaries*

7.7 The evidence must explain what, if any, consultation there has been with beneficiaries, and with what result. In preparation for an application for directions in respect of litigation, the following guidance is to be followed:

(1) If the trust is a private trust where the beneficiaries principally concerned are not numerous and are all or mainly adult, identified and traceable, the trustees will be expected to have canvassed with all the adult beneficiaries the proposed or possible courses of action before applying for directions.

(2) If it is a private trust with a larger number of beneficiaries, including those not yet born or identified, or children, it is likely that there will nevertheless be some adult beneficiaries principally concerned, with whom the trustees must consult.

(3) In relation to a charitable trust the trustees must have consulted the Attorney-General, through the Treasury Solicitor, as well as the Charity Commissioners whose consent to the application will have been needed under the Charities Act 1993, s. 33.

(4) In relation to a pension trust, unless the members are very few in number, no particular steps by way of consultation with beneficiaries (including, where relevant, employers) or their representatives are required in preparation for the application, though the trustees' evidence should describe any consultation that has in fact taken place. If no consultation has taken place, the court could in some cases direct that meetings of one or more classes of beneficiaries be held to consider the subject matter of the application, possibly as a preliminary to deciding whether a member of a particular class ought to be joined as a defendant, though in a case concerning actual or proposed litigation, steps would need to be considered to protect privileged material from too wide disclosure.

7.8 (1) If the court gives directions allowing the trustees to take, defend or pursue litigation it may do so up to a particular stage in the litigation, requiring the trustees, before they carry on beyond that point, to renew their application to the court. What stage that should be will depend on the likely management of the litigation under the CPR. If the application is to be renewed after disclosure of documents, and disclosed documents need to be shown to the court, it may be necessary to obtain permission to do this from the court in which the other litigation is proceeding.

(2) In such a case the court may sometimes direct that the case be dealt with at that stage without a hearing if the beneficiaries obtain and lodge the written advice of an appropriately qualified lawyer stating that he or they support the continuation of the directions. Any such advice will be considered by the court and, if thought fit, the trustees will be given a direction allowing them to continue pursuing the proceedings without a hearing.

7.9 In a case of urgency, such as where a limitation period or period for service of proceedings is about to expire, the court may be able to give directions on a summary consideration of the evidence to cover the steps which need to be taken urgently, but limiting those directions so that the application needs to be renewed on fuller consideration at an early stage.

7.10 In any application for directions where a child is a defendant, the court will expect to have put before it the instructions to and advice of an appropriately qualified lawyer as to the benefits and disadvantages of the proposed, and any other relevant, course of action from the point of view of the child beneficiary.

7.11 The master or district judge may give the directions sought though, if the directions relate to actual or proposed litigation, only if it is a plain case, and therefore the master or district judge may think it appropriate to give the directions without a hearing: see PD 2B, paras 4.1 and 5.1(e), and see also para. 6 above. Otherwise the case will be referred to the judge.

7.12 Where a hearing takes place, if the advice of a lawyer has been put in evidence in accordance with para. 7.2 or 7.10, that lawyer should if possible appear on the hearing.

# CPR Part 65 Proceedings Relating to Anti-Social Behaviour and Harassment



## 65.1 Scope of this Part

This Part contains rules—

(a) in Section I, about injunctions under the Housing Act 1996;[1]

(b) in Section II, about applications by local authorities under section 91(3) of the Anti-social Behaviour Act 2003[2] for a power of arrest to be attached to an injunction;

(c) in Section III, about claims for demotion orders under the Housing Act 1985[3] and Housing Act 1988[4] and proceedings relating to demoted tenancies;

---

[1] 1996 c.52.

[2] 2003 c.38.

[3] 1985 c.68.

[4] 1988 c.50.

(d) in Section IV, about anti-social behaviour orders under the Crime and Disorder Act 1998;[5]
(e) in Section V, about claims under section 3 of the Protection from Harassment Act 1997.[6]

## I HOUSING ACT 1996 INJUNCTIONS

### 65.2 Scope of this Section and Interpretation

(1) This Section applies to applications for an injunction and other related proceedings under Chapter III of Part V of the Housing Act 1996 (injunctions against anti-social behaviour).
(2) In this Section 'the 1996 Act' means the Housing Act 1996.

### 65.3 Applications for an Injunction

(1) An application for an injunction under Chapter III of Part V of the 1996 Act shall be subject to the Part 8 procedure as modified by this rule and the relevant practice direction.
(2) The application must be—
  (a) made by a claim form in accordance with the relevant practice direction;
  (b) commenced in the court for the district in which the defendant resides or the conduct complained of occurred; and
  (c) supported by a witness statement which must be filed with the claim form.
(3) The claim form must state—
  (a) the matters required by rule 8.2; and
  (b) the terms of the injunction applied for.
(4) An application under this rule may be made without notice and where such an application without notice is made—
  (a) the witness statement in support of the application must state the reasons why notice has not been given; and
  (b) the following rules do not apply—
    (i) 8.3;
    (ii) 8.4;
    (iii) 8.5(2) to (6);
    (iv) 8.6(1);
    (v) 8.7; and
    (vi) 8.8.
(5) In every application made on notice, the application notice must be served, together with a copy of the witness statement, by the claimant on the defendant personally.
(6) An application made on notice may be listed for hearing before the expiry of the time for the defendant to file an acknowledgement of service under rule 8.3, and in such a case—
  (a) the claimant must serve the application notice and witness statement on the defendant not less than two days before the hearing; and
  (b) the defendant may take part in the hearing whether or not he has filed an acknowledgment of service.

### 65.4 Injunction Containing Provisions to which a Power of Arrest is Attached

(1) In this rule 'relevant provision' means a provision of an injunction to which a power of arrest is attached.

(Sections 153C(3) and 153D(4) of the 1996 Act[7] confer powers to attach a power of arrest to an injunction.)

(2) Where an injunction contains one or more relevant provisions—

[5] 1998 c.37.
[6] 1997 c.40.
[7] 1996 c.52. These sections were inserted by section 13 of the Anti-social Behaviour Act 2003.

(a) each relevant provision must be set out in a separate paragraph of the injunction; and
(b) subject to paragraph (3), the claimant must deliver a copy of the relevant provisions to any police station for the area where the conduct occurred.

(3) Where the injunction has been granted without notice, the claimant must not deliver a copy of the relevant provisions to any police station for the area where the conduct occurred before the defendant has been served with the injunction containing the relevant provisions.

(4) Where an order is made varying or discharging any relevant provision, the claimant must—
(a) immediately inform the police station to which a copy of the relevant provisions was delivered under paragraph (2)(b); and
(b) deliver a copy of the order to any police station so informed.

## 65.5 Application for Warrant of Arrest under Section 155(3) of the 1996 Act[8]

(1) An application for a warrant of arrest under section 155(3) of the 1996 Act must be made in accordance with Part 23 and may be made without notice.

(2) An applicant for a warrant of arrest under section 155(3) of the 1996 Act must—
(a) file an affidavit setting out grounds for the application with the application notice; or
(b) give oral evidence as to the grounds for the application at the hearing.

## 65.6 Proceedings Following Arrest

(1) This rule applies where a person is arrested pursuant to—
(a) a power of arrest attached to a provision of an injunction; or
(b) a warrant of arrest.

(2) The judge before whom a person is brought following his arrest may—
(a) deal with the matter; or
(b) adjourn the proceedings.

(3) Where the proceedings are adjourned the judge may remand the arrested person in accordance with section 155(2)(b) or (5) of the 1996 Act.

(4) Where the proceedings are adjourned and the arrested person is released—
(a) the matter must be dealt with (whether by the same or another judge) within 28 days of the date on which the arrested person appears in court; and
(b) the arrested person must be given not less than 2 days' notice of the hearing.

(5) An application notice seeking the committal for contempt of court of the arrested person may be issued even if the arrested person is not dealt with within the period mentioned in paragraph (4)(a).

(6) CCR Order 29, rule 1 shall apply where an application is made in a county court to commit a person for breach of an injunction, as if references in that rule to the judge included references to a district judge.

(For applications in the High Court for the discharge of a person committed to prison for contempt of court see RSC Order 52, rule 8. For such applications in the county court see CCR Order 29, rule 3.)

## 65.7 Recognisance

(1) Where, in accordance with paragraph 2(2)(b) of Schedule 15 to the 1996 Act, the court fixes the amount of any recognisance with a view to it being taken subsequently, the recognizance may be taken by—
(a) a judge;
(b) a justice of the peace;
(c) a justices' clerk;
(d) a police officer of the rank of inspector or above or in charge of a police station; or
(e) where the arrested person is in his custody, the governor or keeper of a prison,
with the same consequences as if it had been entered into before the court.

[8] 1996 c.52. This section was amended by section 13 of the Anti-social Behaviour Act 2003.

(2) The person having custody of an applicant for bail must release him if satisfied that the required recognisances have been taken.

## II APPLICATIONS BY LOCAL AUTHORITIES FOR POWER OF ARREST TO BE ATTACHED TO AN INJUNCTION

### 65.8 Scope of this Section and Interpretation

(1) This Section applies to applications by local authorities under section 91(3) of the Anti-social Behaviour Act 2003[9] for a power of arrest to be attached to an injunction.

(Section 91 of the 2003 Act applies to proceedings in which a local authority is a party by virtue of section 222 of the Local Government Act 1972[10] (power of local authority to bring, defend or appear in proceedings for the promotion or protection of the interests of inhabitants in their area.)

(2) In this Section 'the 2003 Act' means the Anti-social Behaviour Act 2003.

### 65.9 Applications under Section 91(3) of the 2003 Act for a Power of Arrest to be Attached to any Provision of an Injunction

(1) An application under section 91(3) of the 2003 Act for a power of arrest to be attached to any provision of an injunction must be made in the proceedings seeking the injunction by—
  (a) the claim form;
  (b) the acknowledgment of service;
  (c) the defence or counterclaim in a Part 7 claim; or
  (d) application under Part 23.

(2) Every application must be supported by written evidence.

(3) Every application made on notice must be served personally, together with a copy of the written evidence, by the local authority on the person against whom the injunction is sought not less than 2 days before the hearing.

(Attention is drawn to rule 25.3(3)—applications without notice.)

### 65.10 Injunction Containing Provisions to which a Power of Arrest is Attached

(1) Where a power of arrest is attached to a provision of an injunction on the application of a local authority under section 91(3) of the 2003 Act, the following rules in Section I of this Part shall apply—
  (a) rule 65.4; and
  (b) paragraphs (1), (2), (4) and (5) of rule 65.6.

(2) CCR Order 29, rule 1 shall apply where an application is made in a county court to commit a person for breach of an injunction.

## III DEMOTION CLAIMS, PROCEEDINGS RELATED TO DEMOTED TENANCIES AND APPLICATIONS TO SUSPEND THE RIGHT TO BUY

### 65.11 Scope of this Section and Interpretation

(1) This Section applies to—
  (a) claims by a landlord for an order under section 82A of the Housing Act 1985[11] or under section 6A of the Housing Act 1988[12] ('a demotion order');
  (aa) claims by a landlord for an order under section 121A of the Housing Act 1985 ('a suspension order'); and
  (b) proceedings relating to a tenancy created by virtue of a demotion order.

[9] 2003 c.38.

[10] 1972 c.70.

[11] 1985 c.68. This section was inserted by section 14 of the Anti-social Behaviour Act 2003.

[12] 1988 c.50. This section was inserted by section 14 of the Anti-social Behaviour Act 2003.

(2) In this Section—
(a) 'a demotion claim' means a claim made by a landlord for a demotion order;
(b) 'a demoted tenancy' means a tenancy created by virtue of a demotion order;
(c) 'suspension claim' means a claim made by a landlord for a suspension order; and
(d) 'suspension period' means the period during which the suspension order suspends the right to buy in relation to the dwelling house.

### 65.12 Demotion Claims or Suspension Claims made in the Alternative to Possession Claims

Where a demotion order or suspension order (or both) is claimed in the alternative to a possession order, the claimant must use the Part 55 procedure and Section I of Part 55 applies, except that the claim must be made in the county court for the district in which the property to which the claim relates is situated.

### 65.13 Other Demotion or Suspension Claims

Where a demotion claim or suspension claim (or both) is made other than in a possession claim, rules 65.14 to 65.19 apply.

### 65.14 Starting a Demotion or Suspension Claim

(1) The claim must be made in the county court for the district in which the property to which the claim relates is situated.
(2) The claim form and form of defence sent with it must be in the forms set out in the relevant practice direction.

(The relevant practice direction and Part 16 provide details about the contents of the particulars of claim.)

### 65.15 Particulars of Claim

The particulars of claim must be filed and served with the claim form.

### 65.16 Hearing Date

(1) The court will fix a date for the hearing when it issues the claim form.
(2) The hearing date will be not less than 28 days from the date of issue of the claim form.
(3) The standard period between the issue of the claim form and the hearing will be not more than 8 weeks.
(4) The defendant must be served with the claim form and the particulars of claim not less than 21 days before the hearing date.

(Rule 3.1(2)(a) provides that the court may extend or shorten the time for compliance with any rule and rule 3.1(2)(b) provides that the court may adjourn or bring forward a hearing.)

### 65.17 Defendant's Response

(1) An acknowledgement of service is not required and Part 10 does not apply.
(2) Where the defendant does not file a defence within the time specified in rule 15.4 he may take part in any hearing but the court may take his failure to do so into account when deciding what order to make about costs.
(3) Part 12 (default judgment) does not apply.

### 65.18 The Hearing

(1) At the hearing fixed in accordance with rule 65.16(1) or at any adjournment of that hearing the court may—
(a) decide the claim; or
(b) give case management directions.

(2) Where the claim is genuinely disputed on grounds which appear to be substantial, case management directions given under paragraph (1)(b) will include the allocation of the claim to a track or directions to enable it to be allocated.
(3) Except where—
  (a) the claim is allocated to the fast track or the multi-track; or
  (b) the court directs otherwise,

  any fact that needs to be proved by the evidence of witnesses at a hearing referred to in paragraph (1) may be proved by evidence in writing.

(Rule 32.2(1) sets out the general rule about evidence. Rule 32.2(2) provides that rule 32.2(1) is subject to any provision to the contrary.)

(4) All witness statements must be filed and served at least two days before the hearing.
(5) Where the claimant serves the claim form and particulars of claim, he must produce at the hearing a certificate of service of those documents and rule 6.14(2)(a) does not apply.

### 65.19 Allocation

When the court decides the track for the claim, the matters to which it shall have regard include—

(a) the matters set out in rule 26.8; and
(b) the nature and extent of the conduct alleged.

### 65.20 Proceedings Relating to Demoted Tenancies

A practice direction may make provision about proceedings relating to demoted tenancies.

## IV ANTI-SOCIAL BEHAVIOUR ORDERS UNDER THE CRIME AND DISORDER ACT 1998

### 65.21 Scope of this Section and Interpretation

(1) This Section applies to applications in proceedings in a county court under sub-sections (2), (3) or (3B) of section 1B of the Crime and Disorder Act 1998[13] by a relevant authority, and to applications for interim orders under section 1D of that Act.
(2) In this Section—
  (a) 'the 1998 Act' means the Crime and Disorder Act 1998;
  (b) 'relevant authority' has the same meaning as in section 1(1A) of the 1998 Act; and
  (c) 'the principal proceedings' means any proceedings in a county court.

### 65.22 Application where the Relevant Authority is a Party in Principal Proceedings

(1) Subject to paragraph (2)—
  (a) where the relevant authority is the claimant in the principal proceedings, an application under section 1B(2) of the 1998 Act for an order under section 1B(4) of the 1998 Act must be made in the claim form; and
  (b) where the relevant authority is a defendant in the principal proceedings, an application for an order must be made by application notice which must be filed with the defence.
(2) Where the relevant authority becomes aware of the circumstances that lead it to apply for an order after its claim is issued or its defence filed, the application must be made by application notice as soon as possible thereafter.
(3) Where the application is made by application notice, it should normally be made on notice to the person against whom the order is sought.

[13] 1998 c.37. Sections 1(1A) and 1B were amended by section 85 of the Anti-social Behaviour Act 2003 (c.38).

### 65.23 Application by a Relevant Authority to Join a Person to the Principal Proceedings

(1) An application under section 1B(3B) of the 1998 Act by a relevant authority which is a party to the principal proceedings to join a person to the principal proceedings must be made—
  (a) in accordance with Section I of Part 19;
  (b) in the same application notice as the application for an order under section 1B(4) of the 1998 Act against the person; and
  (c) as soon as possible after the relevant authority considers that the criteria in section 1B(3A) of the 1998 Act are met.
(2) The application notice must contain—
  (a) the relevant authority's reasons for claiming that the person's anti-social acts are material in relation to the principal proceedings; and
  (b) details of the anti-social acts alleged.
(3) The application should normally be made on notice to the person against whom the order is sought.

### 65.24 Application where the Relevant Authority is not Party in Principal Proceedings

(1) Where the relevant authority is not a party to the principal proceedings—
  (a) an application under section 1B(3) of the 1998 Act to be made a party must be made in accordance with Section I of Part 19; and
  (b) the application to be made a party and the application for an order under section 1B(4) of the 1998 Act must be made in the same application notice.
(2) The applications—
  (a) must be made as soon as possible after the authority becomes aware of the principal proceedings; and
  (b) should normally be made on notice to the person against whom the order is sought.

### 65.25 Evidence

An application for an order under section 1B(4) of the 1998 Act must be accompanied by written evidence, which must include evidence that section 1E of the 1998 Act has been complied with.

### 65.26 Application for an Interim Order

(1) An application for an interim order under section 1D of the 1998 Act must be made in accordance with Part 25.
(2) The application should normally be made—
  (a) in the claim form or application notice seeking the order; and
  (b) on notice to the person against whom the order is sought.

## V PROCEEDINGS UNDER THE PROTECTION FROM HARASSMENT ACT 1997

### 65.27 Scope of this Section

This Section applies to proceedings under section 3 of the Protection from Harassment Act 1997[14] ('the 1997 Act').

### 65.28 Claims under Section 3 of the 1997 Act

A claim under section 3 of the 1997 Act—

[14] 1997 c.40.

(a) shall be subject to the Part 8 procedure; and
(b) must be commenced—
(i) if in the High Court, in the Queen's Bench Division;
(ii) if in the county court, in the court for the district in which the defendant resides or carries on business or the court for the district in which the claimant resides or carries on business.

### 65.29 Applications for Issue of a Warrant of Arrest under Section 3(3) of the 1997 Act

(1) An application for a warrant of arrest under section 3(3) of the 1997 Act—
(a) must be made in accordance with Part 23; and
[(b)]*may be made without notice.
(2) The application notice must be supported by affidavit evidence which must—
(a) set out the grounds for the application;
(b) state whether the claimant has informed the police of the conduct of the defendant as described in the affidavit; and
(c) state whether, to the claimant's knowledge, criminal proceedings are being pursued.

### 65.30 Proceedings Following Arrest

(1) The judge before whom a person is brought following his arrest may—
(a) deal with the matter; or
(b) adjourn the proceedings.
(2) Where the proceedings are adjourned and the arrested person is released—
(a) the matter must be dealt with (whether by the same or another judge) within 28 days of the date on which the arrested person appears in court; and
(b) the arrested person must be given not less than 2 days' notice of the hearing.

## VI DRINKING BANNING ORDERS UNDER THE VIOLENT CRIME REDUCTION ACT 2006

### 65.31 Scope of this Section and Interpretation

(1) This Section applies to applications in proceedings in a county court under sub-sections (2), (3) or (5) of section 4 of the Violent Crime Reduction Act 2006 by a relevant authority, and to applications for interim orders under section 9 of that Act.
(1†) In this Section—
(a) 'the 2006 Act' means the Violent Crime Reduction Act 2006;
(b) 'relevant authority' has the same meaning as in section 14(1) of the 2006 Act; and
(c) 'the principal proceedings' means any proceedings in a county court.

### 65.32 Application where the Relevant Authority is a Party in Principal Proceedings

(1) Subject to paragraph (2)—
(a) where the relevant authority is the claimant in the principal proceedings, an application under section 4(2) of the 2006 Act for an order under section 4(7) of the 2006 Act must be made in the claim form; and
(b) where the relevant authority is a defendant in the principal proceedings, an application for an order must be made by application notice which must be filed with the defence.
(2) Where the relevant authority becomes aware of the circumstances that lead it to apply

[* The text published by the DCA mistakenly includes two sub-paragraphs (a).]

† Editorial note: the Civil Procedure (Amendment No. 3) Rules 2006 schedule 3 which introduced this rule includes two sub-paragraphs (1) as shown here. Presumably the second (1) should read (2).

for an order after its claim is issued or its defence filed, the application must be made by application notice as soon as possible thereafter.

(3) Where the application is made by application notice, it should normally be made on notice to the person against whom the order is sought.

## 65.33 Application where the Relevant Authority is not a Party in Principal Proceedings

(1) Where the relevant authority is not a party to the principal proceedings—
   (a) an application under section 4(3) of the 2006 Act to be made a party must be made in accordance with Section I of Part 19; and
   (b) the application to be made a party and the application for an order under section 4(7) of the 2006 Act must be made in the same application notice.

(2) The applications—
   (a) must be made as soon as possible after the authority becomes aware of the principal proceedings; and
   (b) should normally be made on notice to the person against whom the order is sought.

## 65.34 Application by a Relevant Authority to join a Person to the Principal Proceedings

(1) An application under section 4(5) of the 2006 Act by a relevant authority which is a party to the principal proceedings to join a person to the principal proceedings must be made—
   (a) in accordance with Section I of Part 19;
   (b) in the same application notice as the application for an order under section 4(7) of the 2006 Act against the person; and
   (c) as soon as possible after the relevant authority considers that the criteria in section 4(4) of the 2006 Act are met.

(2) The application notice must contain—
   (a) the relevant authority's reasons for claiming that the person's conduct is material in relation to the principal proceedings; and
   (b) details of the conduct alleged.

(3) The application should normally be made on notice to the person against whom the order is sought.

## 65.35 Evidence

An application for an order under section 4(7) of the 2006 Act must be accompanied by written evidence, which must include evidence that section 4(6) of the 2006 Act has been complied with.

## 65.36 Application for an Interim Order

(1) An application for an interim order under section 9 of the 2006 Act must be made in accordance with Part 25.

(2) The application should normally be made—
   (a) in the claim form or application notice seeking the order; and
   (b) on notice to the person against whom the order is sought.

(3) An application for an interim order may be—
   (a) made without a copy of the application notice being served on the person against whom the order is sought;
   (b) heard in the absence of the person against whom the order is sought, with the permission of the court.

# PD 65 Practice Direction — Anti-Social Behaviour and Harassment

This practice direction supplements CPR Part 65.

## SECTION I — HOUSING ACT 1996 INJUNCTIONS

### Issuing the Claim

1.1 An application for an injunction under Chapter III of Part V of the 1996 Act must be made by form N16A and for the purposes of applying the practice direction that supplements Part 8 to applications under Section I of Part 65, form N16A shall be treated as the Part 8 claim form.

### Warrant of Arrest on an Application under Section 155(3) of the 1996 Act

2.1 In accordance with section 155(4) of the 1996 Act, a warrant of arrest on an application under section 155(3) of that Act shall not be issued unless—
(1) the application is substantiated on oath; and
(2) the judge has reasonable grounds for believing that the defendant has failed to comply with the injunction.

### Application for Bail

3.1 An application for bail by a person arrested under—
(1) a power of arrest attached to an injunction under Chapter III of Part V of the 1996 Act; or
(2) a warrant of arrest issued on an application under section 155(3) of that Act, may be made either orally or in an application notice.

3.2 An application notice seeking bail must contain—
(1) the full name of the person making the application;
(2) the address of the place where the person making the application is detained at the time when the application is made;
(3) the address where the person making the application would reside if he were to be granted bail;
(4) the amount of the recognizance in which he would agree to be bound; and
(5) the grounds on which the application is made and, where previous application has been refused, full details of any change in circumstances which has occurred since that refusal.

3.3 A copy of the application notice must be served on the person who obtained the injunction.

### Remand for Medical Examination and Report

4.1 Section 156(4) of the 1996 Act provides that the judge has power to make an order under section 35 of the Mental Health Act 1983 in certain circumstances. If he does so attention is drawn to section 35(8) of that Act, which provides that a person remanded to hospital under that section may obtain at his own expense an independent report on his mental condition from a registered medical practitioner chosen by him and apply to the court on the basis of it for his remand to be terminated under section 35(7).

## SECTION II — DEMOTION OR SUSPENSION CLAIMS

(Suspension claims may be made in England, but may not be made in Wales.)

### Demotion Claims made in the Alternative to Possession Claims

5.1 If the claim relates to residential property let on a tenancy and if the claim includes a demotion claim, the particulars of claim must—
- (1) state whether the demotion claim is a claim under section 82A(2) of the 1985 Act or under section 6A(2) of the 1988 Act;
- (2) state whether the claimant is a local housing authority, a housing action trust or a registered social landlord;
- (3) provide details of any statement of express terms of the tenancy served on the tenant under section 82A(7) of the 1985 Act or under section 6A(10) of the 1988 Act, as applicable; and
- (4) state details of the conduct alleged.

### Suspension Claims made in the Alternative to Possession Claims

5A.1 If the claim relates to a residential property let on a tenancy and if the claim includes a suspension claim, the particulars of claim must—
- (1) state that the suspension claim is a claim under section 121A of the 1985 Act;
- (2) state which of the bodies the claimant's interest belongs to in order to comply with the landlord condition under section 80 of the 1985 Act;
- (3) state details of the conduct alleged; and
- (4) explain why it is reasonable to make the suspension order, having regard in particular to the factors set out in section 121A(4) of the 1985 Act.

### Other Demotion or Suspension Claims

6.1 Demotion or suspension claims, other than those made in the alternative to possession claims, must be made in the county court for the district in which the property to which the claim relates is situated.

6.2 The claimant must use the appropriate claim form and particulars of claim form set out in Table 1 to the Part 4 practice direction. The defence must be in form N11D as appropriate.

6.3 The claimant's evidence should include details of the conduct alleged, and any other matters relied upon.

### Particulars of Claim

7.1 In a demotion claim the particulars of claim must—
- (1) state whether the demotion claim is a claim in a claim under section 82A(2) of the 1985 Act or under section 6A(2) of the 1988 Act;
- (2) state whether the claimant is a local housing authority, a housing action trust or a registered social landlord;
- (3) identify the property to which the claim relates;
- (4) provide the following details about the tenancy to which the demotion claim relates—
  - (a) the parties to the tenancy;
  - (b) the period of the tenancy;
  - (c) the amount of the rent;
  - (d) the dates on which the rent is payable; and
  - (e) any statement of express terms of the tenancy served on the tenant under section 82A(7) of the 1985 Act or under section 6A(10) of the 1988 Act, as applicable; and
- (5) state details of the conduct alleged.

7.2 In a suspension claim, the particulars of claim must—

(1) state that the suspension claim is a claim under section 121A of the 1985 Act;
(2) state which of the bodies the claimant's interest belongs to in order to comply with the landlord condition under section 80 of the 1985 Act;
(3) identify the property to which the claim relates;
(4) state details of the conduct alleged; and
(5) explain why it is reasonable to make the order, having regard in particular to the factors set out in section 121A(4) of the 1985 Act.

### Hearing Date

8.1 The court may use its powers under rules 3.1(2)(a) and (b) to shorten the time periods set out in rules 65.16(2), (3) and (4).

8.2 Particular consideration should be given to the exercise of this power if—
(1) the defendant, or a person for whom the defendant is responsible, has assaulted or threatened to assault—
(a) the claimant;
(b) a member of the claimant's staff; or
(c) another resident in the locality;
(2) there are reasonable grounds for fearing such an assault; or
(3) the defendant, or a person for whom the defendant is responsible, has caused serious damage or threatened to cause serious damage to the property or to the home or property of another resident in the locality.

8.3 Where paragraph 8.2 applies but the case cannot be determined at the first hearing fixed under rule 65.16, the court will consider what steps are needed to finally determine the case as quickly as reasonably practicable.

### The Hearing

9.1 Attention is drawn to rule 65.18(3). Each party should wherever possible include all the evidence he wishes to present in his statement of case, verified by a statement of truth.

9.2 The claimant's evidence should include details of the conduct to which section 153A or 153B of the 1996 Act applies and in respect of which the claim is made.

9.3 If—
(1) the maker of a witness statement does not attend a hearing; and
(2) the other party disputes material evidence contained in the statement, the court will normally adjourn the hearing so that oral evidence can be given.

## SECTION III — PROCEEDINGS RELATING TO DEMOTED TENANCIES

### Proceedings for the Possession of a Demoted Tenancy

10.1 Proceedings against a tenant of a demoted tenancy for possession must be brought under the procedure in Part 55 (Possession Claims).

### Proceedings in Relation to a Written Statement of Demoted Tenancy Terms

11.1 Proceedings as to whether a statement supplied in pursuance to section 143M(4)(b) of the 1996 Act (written statement of certain terms of tenancy) is accurate must be brought under the procedure in Part 8.

### Recovery of Costs

12.1 Attention is drawn to section 143N(4) of the 1996 Act which provides that if a person takes proceedings under Chapter 1A of the 1996 Act in the High Court which he could have taken in the county court, he is not entitled to recover any costs.

## SECTION IV — ANTI-SOCIAL BEHAVIOUR ORDERS UNDER THE CRIME AND DISORDER ACT 1998

### Service of an Order under Sections 1b(4) or 1d of the 1998 Act

13.1 An order under section 1B(4) or an interim order under section 1D of the 1998 Act must be served personally on the defendant.

### Application to Join a Person to the Principal Proceedings

13.2 Except as provided in paragraph 13.3, an application by a relevant authority under section 1B(3B) of the 1998 Act to join a person to the principal proceedings may only be made against a person aged 18 or over.

### Pilot Scheme: Application to Join a Child to the Principal Proceedings

13.3 (1) A pilot scheme shall operate from 1 October 2004 to 30 September 2006 in the county courts specified below, under which a relevant authority may—
(a) apply under section 1B(3B) of the 1998 Act to join a child to the principal proceedings; and
(b) if that child is so joined, apply for an order under section 1B(4) of the 1998 Act against him.
(2) In this paragraph, 'child' means a person aged under 18.
(3) The county courts in which the pilot scheme shall operate are Bristol, Central London, Clerkenwell, Dewsbury, Huddersfield, Leicester, Manchester, Oxford, Tameside, Wigan and Wrexham.
(4) Attention is drawn to the provisions of Part 21 and its practice direction: in particular as to the requirement for a child to have a litigation friend unless the court makes an order under rule 21.2(3), and as to the procedure for appointment of a litigation friend. The Official Solicitor may be invited to act as litigation friend where there is no other willing and suitable person.
(5) Rule 21.3(2)(b) shall not apply to an application under the pilot scheme, and sub-paragraph (6) shall apply instead.
(6) A relevant authority may not, without the permission of the court, take any step in an application to join a child to the principal proceedings, except—
(a) filing and serving its application notice; and
(b) applying for the appointment of a litigation friend under rule 21.6,
unless the child has a litigation friend.

## SECTION V — PROCEEDINGS UNDER THE PROTECTION FROM HARASSMENT ACT 1997

### Warrant of Arrest on an Application under Section 3(3) of the 1997 Act

14.1 In accordance with section 3(5) of the 1997 Act, a warrant of arrest on an application under section 3(3) of that Act may only be issued if—
(1) the application is substantiated on oath; and
(2) the judge has reasonable grounds for believing that the defendant has done anything which he is prohibited from doing by the injunction.

## SECTION VI — DRINKING BANNING ORDERS UNDER THE VIOLENT CRIME REDUCTION ACT 2006

### Service of an Order under Sections 4(7) or 9 of the 2006 Act

15.1 An order under section 4(7) or an interim order under section 9 of the 2006 Act must be served personally on the defendant.

## Application to join a Person to the Principal Proceedings

15.2 An application by a relevant authority under section 4(5) of the 2006 Act to join a person to the principal proceedings may only be made against a person aged 18 or over.

# CPR Part 66 Crown Proceedings



## 66.1 Scope of this Part and Interpretation

(1) This Part contains rules for civil proceedings by or against the Crown, and other civil proceedings to which the Crown is a party.

(2) In this Part—
  - (a) 'the Act' means the Crown Proceedings Act 1947;
  - (b) 'civil proceedings by the Crown' means the civil proceedings described in section 23(1) of the Act, but excluding the proceedings described in section 23(3);
  - (c) 'civil proceedings against the Crown' means the civil proceedings described in section 23(2) of the Act, but excluding the proceedings described in section 23(3);
  - (d) 'civil proceedings to which the Crown is a party' has the same meaning as it has for the purposes of Parts III and IV of the Act by virtue of section 38(4).

## 66.2 Application of the Civil Procedure Rules

These Rules and their practice directions apply to civil proceedings by or against the Crown and to other civil proceedings to which the Crown is a party unless this Part, a practice direction or any other enactment provides otherwise.

## 66.3 Action on Behalf of the Crown

(1) Where by reason of a rule, practice direction or court order the Crown is permitted or required—
  - (a) to make a witness statement;
  - (b) to swear an affidavit;
  - (c) to verify a document by a statement of truth;
  - (d) to make a disclosure statement; or
  - (e) to discharge any other procedural obligation,

  that function shall be performed by an appropriate officer acting on behalf of the Crown.

(2) The court may if necessary nominate an appropriate officer.

## 66.4 Counterclaims, other Part 20 Claims, and Set-off

(1) In a claim by the Crown for taxes, duties or penalties, the defendant cannot make a counterclaim or other Part 20 claim or raise a defence of set-off.

(2) In any other claim by the Crown, the defendant cannot make a counterclaim or other Part 20 claim or raise a defence of set-off which is based on a claim for repayment of taxes, duties or penalties.

(3) In proceedings by or against the Crown in the name of the Attorney-General, no counterclaim or other Part 20 claim can be made or defence of set-off raised without the permission of the court.

(4) In proceedings by or against the Crown in the name of a government department, no counterclaim or other Part 20 claim can be made or defence of set-off raised without

the permission of the court unless the subject-matter relates to that government department.

### 66.5 Applications in Revenue Matters

(1) This rule sets out the procedure under section 14 of the Act, which allows the Crown to make summary applications in the High Court in certain revenue matters.
(2) The application must be made in the High Court using the Part 8 procedure.
(3) The title of the claim form must clearly identify the matters which give rise to the application.

### 66.6 Enforcement Against the Crown

(1) The following rules do not apply to any order against the Crown—
    (a) Parts 69 to 73;
    (b) RSC Orders 45 to 47 and 52; and
    (c) CCR Orders 25 to 29.
(2) In paragraph (1), 'order against the Crown' means any judgment or order against the Crown, a government department, or an officer of the Crown as such, made—
    (a) in civil proceedings by or against the Crown;
    (b) in proceedings in the Administrative Court;
    (c) in connection with an arbitration to which the Crown is a party; or
    (d) in other civil proceedings to which the Crown is a party.
(3) An application under section 25(1) of the Act for a separate certificate of costs payable to the applicant may be made without notice.

### 66.7 Money Due from the Crown

(1) None of the following orders—
    (a) a third party debt order under Part 72;
    (b) an order for the appointment of a receiver under Part 69; or
    (c) an order for the appointment of a sequestrator under RSC Order 45,
    may be made or have effect in respect of any money due from the Crown.
(2) In paragraph (1), 'money due from the Crown' includes money accruing due, and money alleged to be due or accruing due.
(3) An application for an order under section 27 of the Act—
    (a) restraining a person from receiving money payable to him by the Crown; and
    (b) directing payment of the money to the applicant or another person,
    may be made under Part 23.
(4) The application must be supported by written evidence setting out the facts on which it is based, and in particular identifying the debt from the Crown.
(5) Where the debt from the Crown is money in a National Savings Bank account, the witness must if possible identify the number of the account and the name and address of the branch where it is held.
(6) Notice of the application, with a copy of the written evidence, must be served—
    (a) on the Crown, and
    (b) on the person to be restrained,
    at least 7 days before the hearing.
(7) Rule 72.8 applies to an application under this rule as it applies to an application under rule 72.2 for a third party debt order, except that the court will not have the power to order enforcement to issue against the Crown.

# PD 66 Practice Direction — Crown Proceedings

This practice direction supplements CPR Part 66.

## Transfer

1.1 Rule 30.3(2) sets out the circumstances to which the court must have regard when considering whether to make an order under section 40(2), 41(1) or 42(2) of the County Courts Act 1984 (transfer between the High Court and County Court), rule 30.2(1) (transfer between county courts) or rule 30.2(4) (transfer between the Royal Courts of Justice and the district registries).

1.2 From time to time the Attorney General will publish a note concerning the organization of the Government Legal Service and matters relevant to the venue of Crown proceedings, for the assistance of practitioners and judges. When considering questions of venue under rule 30.3(2), the court should have regard to the Attorney General's note in addition to all the other circumstances of the case.

## Service of Documents

2.1 In civil proceedings by or against the Crown, documents required to be served on the Crown must be served in accordance with rule 6.5(8).

(The list published under section 17 of the Crown Proceedings Act 1947 of the solicitors acting for the different government departments on whom service is to be effected, and of their addresses is annexed to this practice direction.)

## ANNEX 1

## DISPUTES AS TO VENUE — FACTORS TO BE TAKEN INTO CONSIDERATION

## ATTORNEY-GENERAL'S NOTE TO SUPPLEMENT THE PRACTICE DIRECTION

### Introduction

Until the recent rule changes, the Crown was entitled in High Court matters to insist that venue was the Royal Courts of Justice in London (RCJ) (RSC O77, rule 2). This rule has now been revoked. A new rule 30.3(2)(h) provides that in cases involving civil proceedings by or against the Crown, when considering whether to order a transfer of those proceedings, the court must have regard to 'the location of the relevant government department or officers of the Crown and, where appropriate, any relevant public interest that the matter should be tried in London'.

The practice direction to Part 66, at paragraph 2, provides that the Attorney-General will publish a note concerning the organisation of the Government Legal Service and matters relevant to the venue of Crown Proceedings, for the assistance of practitioners and judges. When considering questions of venue under rule 30.3(2), the court should have regard to the Attorney-General's note in addition to all the other circumstances of the case.

This note sets out the further factors to be taken into consideration where there is a dispute as to venue between a claimant and a government department. Where there is such a dispute, it should be dealt with at a case management conference.

### Organisation of the Government Legal Service

The Government Legal Service (GLS) has the responsibility for advising the government about its legal affairs and has the conduct of civil litigation on its behalf. The Treasury

Solicitor conducts this litigation for the majority of government departments but lawyers in HM Revenue and Customs, the Department for the Environment, Food and Rural Affairs and the Department for Work and Pensions (which also acts for the Department of Health and the Food Standards Agency) have the conduct of litigation for their Departments. All government litigation lawyers are based in the London with the exception of HM Revenue and Customs, whose personal injury lawyers are in Manchester. A full list of addresses for service is annexed to the practice direction accompanying Part 66 of the CPR.

## Factors be taken into account generally

*Location*
Whilst a number of government departments have offices outside London, central government bodies are based in London and the GLS is geared towards processing claims in the RCJ (see above). Where there is a High Court claim, many witnesses as well as lawyers and officials are London based and there may be a disproportionate cost in transferring them to a venue outside London. That is not to say, bearing in mind the overriding objective, that the Crown would oppose transfer away from the RCJ where it was appropriate, for example in personal injury disputes.

*Precedent value*
Some cases have important precedent value or are of general importance to the public, which may make them more suitable for being heard in the RCJ.

## Special Considerations in relation to HM Revenue and Customs

HM Revenue and Customs has no lawyers outside London, except for those personal injury lawyers based in Manchester.

The work of HM Revenue and Customs is very specialised, needing in many cases to be dealt with by specialist judges in the Chancery Division familiar, for example, with tax work.

There is also the public interest to consider. All revenue cases (including those of HM Revenue and Customs) have important precedent value that applies across the entire tax system, with implications for the Exchequer.

## ANNEX 2

**LIST OF AUTHORISED GOVERNMENT DEPARTMENTS AND THE NAMES AND ADDRESSES FOR SERVICE OF THE PERSON WHO IS, OR IS ACTING FOR THE PURPOSES OF THE ACT AS, SOLICITOR FOR SUCH DEPARTMENTS, PUBLISHED BY THE MINISTER FOR THE CIVIL SERVICE IN PURSUANCE OF SECTION 17 OF THE CROWN PROCEEDINGS ACT 1947**

This list supersedes the list published on 6 January 2004.

| AUTHORISED GOVERNMENT DEPARTMENTS | SOLICITOR AND ADDRESSES FOR SERVICE |
| --- | --- |
| Advisory, Conciliation and Arbitration Service<br>Assets Recovery Agency<br>Board of Trade<br>Cabinet Office<br>Central Office of Information<br>Crown Prosecution Service<br>Department for Constitutional Affairs (see Note (3))<br>Department for Culture, Media and Sport<br>Department for Education and Skills<br>Department for International Development | The Treasury Solicitor<br>One Kemble Street<br>London<br>WC2B 4TS<br>(see Notes (1) and (2)) |

| AUTHORISED GOVERNMENT DEPARTMENTS | SOLICITOR AND ADDRESSES FOR SERVICE |
|---|---|
| Department for Transport<br>Department of Trade and Industry<br>Export Credits Guarantee Department<br>Foreign and Commonwealth Office<br>Government Actuary's Department<br>Health and Safety Executive<br>Her Majesty's Chief Inspector of Schools in England<br>Her Majesty's Chief Inspector of Schools in Wales<br>Her Majesty's Treasury<br>Home Office<br>The International Rail Regulator<br>Ministry of Defence<br>National Savings and Investments<br>Northern Ireland Office<br>Office of the Deputy Prime Minister<br>Office of Rail Regulation<br>Ordnance Survey<br>Privy Council Office<br>Public Record Office<br>Public Works Loan Board<br>Royal Mint<br>Serious Fraud Office<br>Wales Office (Office of the Secretary of State for Wales) (see Note (4)) | The Treasury Solicitor<br>One Kemble Street<br>London<br>WC2B 4TS<br>(see Notes (1) and (2)) |
| Crown Estate Commissioners | Head of Legal<br>The Crown Estate<br>16 Carlton House Terrace<br>London SW1Y 5AH |
| Department for Environment, Food and Rural Affairs<br>(see Note (4))<br>Forestry Commissioners | The Solicitor to the Department for Environment, Food and Rural Affairs<br>Nobel House<br>17 Smith Square<br>London SW1P 3JR |
| Department of Health<br>Department for Work and Pensions<br>Food Standards Agency<br>Office for National Statistics | The Solicitor to the Department for Work and Pensions and the Department of Health<br>New Court<br>48 Carey Street<br>London WC2A 2LS |
| Director General of Water Services | Head of Legal Services<br>The Office of Water Services<br>Centre City Tower<br>7 Hill Street<br>Birmingham B5 4UA |

| | |
|---|---|
| Gas and Electricity Markets Authority | General Counsel<br>Office of Gas and Electricity Markets<br>9 Millbank<br>London SW1P 3GE |
| Her Majesty's Revenue and Customs | The Solicitor to Her Majesty's Revenue and Customs<br>Somerset House<br>The Strand<br>London WC2R 1LB |
| National Assembly for Wales | The Director of Legal Services to the Welsh Assembly Government<br>Cathays Park<br>Cardiff CF10 3NQ |
| Office of Fair Trading | The Solicitor to the Office of Fair Trading<br>Fleetbank House<br>2–6 Salisbury Square<br>London EC4Y 8JX |
| Postal Services Commission | The Chief Legal Adviser<br>Postal Services Commission<br>Hercules House<br>6 Hercules Road<br>London SE1 7DB |

*Notes*

(1) Section 17(3) and section 18 of the Crown Proceedings Act 1947 provide as follows:

17(3) Civil proceedings against the Crown shall be instituted against the appropriate authorised Government department, or, if none of the authorised Government departments is appropriate or the person instituting the proceedings has any reasonable doubt whether any and if so which of those departments is appropriate, against the Attorney General.

18 All documents required to be served on the Crown for the purpose of or in connection with any civil proceedings by or against the Crown shall, if those proceedings are by or against an authorised Government department, be served on the solicitor, if any, for that department, or the person, if any, acting for the purposes of this Act as solicitor for that department, or if there is no such solicitor and no person so acting, or if the proceedings are brought by or against the Attorney General, on the Solicitor for the affairs of His Majesty's Treasury.

(2) The above-mentioned provisions do not apply to Scotland, where in accordance with the Crown Suits (Scotland) Act 1857, as amended by the Scotland Act 1998, civil proceedings against the Crown (other than the Scottish Administration) or any Government Department (other than the Scottish Executive) may be directed against the Advocate General for Scotland. The Advocate General's address for service is the Office of the Solicitor to the Advocate General for Scotland, Victoria Quay, Edinburgh EH6 6QQ. Civil proceedings against the Scottish Administration may be directed against the Scottish Ministers at St.Andrew's House, Edinburgh EH1 3DG, or against the Lord Advocate for and on behalf of the Scottish Executive. The Lord Advocate's address for service is 25 Chambers Street, Edinburgh, EH1 1LA.

(3) The reference to the Department for Constitutional Affairs includes a reference to the Lord Chancellor's Department.

(4) The Solicitor and address for service for the purposes of or in connection with civil proceedings brought by or against the Crown which relate to those matters for which

the Secretary of State is responsible in Wales and for which the Secretary of State for Environment, Food and Rural Affairs is responsible is the Solicitor to the Department for Environment, Food and Rural Affairs, Nobel House, 17 Smith Square, London, SW1P 3JR. The Treasury Solicitor is the Solicitor acting for the Wales Office (Office of the Secretary of State for Wales) in all other civil proceedings affecting that Office.

CABINET OFFICE
WHITEHALL
LONDON SW1

(Signed) SIR GUS O'DONNELL

*31 August 2005*

# CPR Part 67 Proceedings Relating to Solicitors



## 67.1 Scope and Interpretation

(1) This Part contains rules about the following types of proceedings relating to solicitors—
  (a) proceedings to obtain an order for a solicitor to deliver a bill or cash account and proceedings in relation to money or papers received by a solicitor (rule 67.2);
  (b) proceedings under Part III of the Solicitors Act 1974[1] relating to the remuneration of solicitors (rule 67.3); and
  (c) proceedings under Schedule 1 to the Solicitors Act 1974[2] arising out of the Law Society's intervention in a solicitor's practice (rule 67.4).

(2) In this Part—
  'the Act' means the Solicitors Act 1974; and
  'LLP' means limited liability partnership.

(Part 48 and Section 56 of the Costs Practice Direction contain provisions about the procedure and basis for the detailed assessment of solicitor and client costs under Part III of the Act.)

(The practice direction supplementing Part 52 contains provisions about appeals to the High Court from the Solicitors Disciplinary Tribunal under section 49 of the Act.)

## 67.2 Power to Order Solicitor to Deliver Cash Account etc.

(1) Where the relationship of solicitor and client exists or has existed, the orders which the court may make against the solicitor, on the application of the client or his personal representatives, include any of the following—
  (a) to deliver a bill or cash account;
  (b) to pay or deliver up any money or securities;
  (c) to deliver a list of the moneys or securities which the solicitor has in his possession or control on behalf of the applicant;
  (d) to pay into or lodge in court any such money or securities.

(2) An application for an order under this rule must be made—
  (a) by Part 8 claim form; or
  (b) if the application is made in existing proceedings, by application notice in accordance with Part 23.

(3) If the solicitor alleges that he has a claim for costs against the applicant, the court may make an order for—
  (a) the detailed assessment and payment of those costs; and
  (b) securing the payment of the costs, or protecting any solicitor's lien.

## 67.3 Proceedings under Part III of the Act

(1) A claim for an order under Part III of the Act for the assessment of costs payable to a solicitor by his client—

---

[1] 1974 c.47.

[2] 1974 c.47. The relevant provisions of Schedule 1 to the Solicitors Act 1974 were amended by the Criminal Justice Act 1982 (c.48), sections 37, 38 and 46; the Administration of Justice Act 1985 (c.61), section 8 and paragraph 13 of Schedule 1; and the Postal Service Act 2000 (Consequential Modifications No.1) Order 2001 (S.I. 2001/1149), article 3 and paragraph 39 of Schedule 1.

(a) which—
(i) relates to contentious business done in a county court; and
(ii) is within the financial limit of the county court's jurisdiction specified in section 69(3) of the Act,[3]
may be made in that county court;
(b) in every other case, must be made in the High Court.

(Rule 30.2 makes provision for any county court to transfer the proceedings to another county court for detailed assessment of costs.)

(Provisions about the venue for detailed assessment proceedings are contained in rule 47.4, Section 31 of the Costs Practice Direction and the Costs Pilot Scheme Practice Direction supplementing Part 47.)

(2) A claim for an order under Part III of the Act must be made—
(a) by Part 8 claim form; or
(b) if the claim is made in existing proceedings, by application notice in accordance with Part 23.

(A model form of claim form is annexed to the Costs Practice Direction)

(3) A claim in the High Court under Part III of the Act may be determined by—
(a) a High Court judge;
(b) a Master, a costs judge or a district judge of the Principal Registry of the Family Division; or
(c) a district judge, if the costs are for—
(i) contentious business done in proceedings in the district registry of which he is the district judge;
(ii) contentious business done in proceedings in a county court within the district of that district registry; or
(iii) non-contentious business.

## 67.4 Proceedings under Schedule 1 to the Act

(1) Proceedings in the High Court under Schedule 1 to the Act must be brought—
(a) in the Chancery Division; and
(b) by Part 8 claim form, unless paragraph (4) below applies.

(2) The heading of the claim form must state that the claim relates to a solicitor and is made under Schedule 1 to the Act.

(3) Where proceedings are brought under paragraph 6(4) or 9(8) of Schedule 1 to the Act, the court will give directions and fix a date for the hearing immediately upon issuing the claim form.

(4) If the court has made an order under Schedule 1 to the Act, any subsequent application for an order under that Schedule which has the same parties may be made by a Part 23 application in the same proceedings.

(5) The table below sets out who must be made a defendant to each type of application under Schedule 1.

## Defendants to applications under Schedule 1 to the Act

| *Paragraph of Schedule 1 under which the application is made* | *Defendant to application* |
|---|---|
| Paragraph 5 | if the application relates to money held on behalf of an individual solicitor, the solicitor |
| | if the application relates to money held on behalf of a firm, every partner in the firm |

[3] The limit in section 69(3) of the Act was amended by the High Court and County Courts Jurisdiction Order 1991 (S.I. 1991/724), article 2(7) and (8) and Part 1 of the Schedule.

| *Paragraph of Schedule 1 under which the application is made* | *Defendant to application* |
|---|---|
| Paragraph 5 | if the application relates to money held on behalf of a LLP or other corporation, the LLP or other corporation |
| Paragraph 6(4) or 9(8) | the Law Society |
| Paragraph 8, 9(4), 9(5) or 9(6) | the person against whom the Law Society is seeking an order |
| Paragraph 9(10) | the person from whom the Law Society took possession of the documents which it wishes to dispose of or destroy |
| | if the application relates to postal packets addressed to an individual solicitor, the solicitor |
| Paragraph 10 | if the application relates to postal packets addressed to a firm, every partner in the firm |
| | if the application relates to postal packets addressed to a LLP or other corporation, the LLP or other corporation |
| Paragraph 11 | the trustee whom the Law Society is seeking to replace and, if he is a co-trustee, the other trustees of the trust |

(6) At any time after the Law Society has issued an application for an order under paragraph 5 of Schedule 1 to the Act, the court may, on an application by the Society—
- (a) make an interim order under that paragraph to have effect until the hearing of the application; and
- (b) order the defendant, if he objects to the order being continued at the hearing, to file and serve written evidence showing cause why the order should not be continued.

# PD 67 Practice Direction — Proceedings Relating to Solicitors

This practice direction supplements CPR Part 67.

## General

1 This Practice Direction applies to proceedings under rule 67.2 and to the following types of claim under Rule 67.3 and Part III of the Solicitors Act 1974 ('the Act'):

(1) an application under section 57(5) of the Act for a costs officer to enquire into the facts and certify whether a non-contentious business agreement should be set aside or the amount payable under it reduced;

(2) a claim under section 61(1) of the Act for the court to enforce or set aside a contentious business agreement and determine questions as to its validity and effect;

(3) a claim by a client under section 61(3) of the Act for a costs officer to examine a contentious business agreement as to its fairness and reasonableness;

(4) where the amount agreed under a contentious business agreement has been paid, a claim under section 61(5) of the Act for the agreement to be re-opened and the costs assessed;

(5) proceedings under section 62 of the Act for the examination of a contentious business agreement, where the client makes the agreement as a representative of a person whose property will be chargeable with the amount payable;

(6) proceedings under section 63 of the Act where, after some business has been done under a contentious business agreement, but before the solicitor has wholly performed it:

(a) the solicitor dies or becomes incapable of acting; or

(b) the client changes solicitor;

(7) where an action is commenced on a gross sum bill, an application under section 64(3) of the Act for an order that the bill be assessed;

(8) a claim under section 68 of the Act for the delivery by a solicitor of a bill of costs and for the delivery up of, or otherwise in relation to, any documents;

(9) an application under section 69 of the Act for an order that the solicitor be at liberty to commence an action to recover his costs within one month of delivery of the bill;

(10) a claim under section 70(1) of the Act, by the party chargeable with the solicitor's bill, for an order that the bill be assessed and that no action be taken on the bill until the assessment is completed;

(11) a claim under section 70(2) of the Act, by either party, for an order that the bill be assessed and that no action be commenced or continued on the bill until the assessment is completed;

(12) a claim under section 70(3) of the Act, by the party chargeable with the bill, for detailed assessment showing special circumstances;

(13) a claim under section 71(1) of the Act, by a person other than the party chargeable with the bill, for detailed assessment;

(14) a claim under section 71(3) of the Act, by any person interested in any property out of which a trustee, executor or administrator has paid or is entitled to pay a solicitor's bill, for detailed assessment; and

(15) a claim by a solicitor under section 73 of the Act for a charging order.

## Proceedings in the Supreme Court Costs Office

2.1 Where a claim to which this practice direction applies is made by Part 8 claim form in the High Court in London—

(1) if the claim is of a type referred to in paragraphs 1(1) to (5), it must be issued in the Supreme Court Costs Office;

(2) in any other case, the claim may be issued in the Supreme Court Costs Office.

2.2 A claim which is made by Part 8 claim form in a district registry or by Part 23 application notice in existing High Court proceedings may be referred to the Supreme Court Costs Office.

## Jurisdiction and Allocation of Claims between Judiciary

3.1 Rule 67.3(3) makes provision about jurisdiction to determine claims under Part III of the Act.

3.2 Claims for any of the orders listed in paragraph 1 should normally be made to a master, costs judge or district judge. Only exceptional circumstances will justify making the claim directly to a High Court Judge.

3.3 Paragraph 1 of the practice direction supplementing Part 23 sets out the circumstances in which a matter may be referred to a judge.

## Evidence in Proceedings for Order for Detailed Assessment

4 Where a Part 8 claim is brought for an order for the detailed assessment of a solicitor's bill of costs, the parties are not required to comply with rule 8.5 unless:

(1) the claim will be contested; or

(2) the court directs that the parties should comply with rule 8.5.

## Drawing up and Service of Orders

5 Unless the court orders otherwise, an order in proceedings in the Supreme Court Costs Office to which this practice direction applies shall be drawn up and served by the party who made the relevant claim or application.

# CPR Part 68 References to the European Court



## 68.1 Interpretation

In this Part—

(a) 'the court' means the court making the order;

(b) 'the European Court' means the Court of Justice of the European Communities;

(c) 'order' means an order referring a question to the European Court for a preliminary ruling under—

  (i) article 234 of the Treaty establishing the European Community;

  (ii) article 150 of the Euratom Treaty;

  (iii) article 41 of the ECSC Treaty;

  (iv) the Protocol of 3 June 1971 on the interpretation by the European Court of the Convention of 27 September 1968 on Jurisdiction and the Enforcement of Judgments in Civil and Commercial Matters; or

  (v) the Protocol of 19 December 1988 on the interpretation by the European Court of the Convention of 19 June 1980 on the Law applicable to Contractual Obligations.

## 68.2 Making Order of Reference

(1) An order may be made at any stage of the proceedings—

  (a) by the court of its own initiative; or

  (b) on an application by a party in accordance with Part 23.

(2) An order may not be made—

  (a) in the High Court, by a Master or district judge;

  (b) in a county court, by a district judge.

(3) The request to the European Court for a preliminary ruling must be set out in a schedule to the order, and the court may give directions on the preparation of the schedule.

## 68.3 Transmission to the European Court

(1) The Senior Master will send a copy of the order to the Registrar of the European Court.

(2) Where an order is made by a county court, the proper officer will send a copy of it to the Senior Master for onward transmission to the European Court.

(3) Unless the court orders otherwise, the Senior Master will not send a copy of the order to the European Court until—

  (a) the time for appealing against the order has expired; or

  (b) any application for permission to appeal has been refused, or any appeal has been determined.

## 68.4 Stay of Proceedings

Where an order is made, unless the court orders otherwise the proceedings will be stayed until the European Court has given a preliminary ruling on the question referred to it.

# PD 68 Practice Direction — References to the European Court

This practice direction supplements CPR Part 68.

## Wording of References

1.1 Where the court intends to refer a question to the European Court it will welcome suggestions from the parties for the wording of the reference. However the responsibility for settling the terms of the reference lies with the English court and not with the parties.

1.2 The reference should identify as clearly and succinctly as possible the question on which the court seeks the ruling of the European Court. In choosing the wording of the reference, it should be remembered that it will need to be translated into many other languages.

1.3 The court will incorporate the reference in its order. Scheduled to the order should be a document:

(1) giving the full name of the referring court;
(2) identifying the parties;
(3) summarising the nature and history of the proceedings, including the salient facts, indicating whether these are proved or admitted or assumed;
(4) setting out the relevant rules of national law;
(5) summarising the relevant contentions of the parties;
(6) explaining why a ruling of the European Court is sought; and
(7) identifying the provisions of Community law which it is being requested to interpret.

1.4 Where, as will often be convenient, some of these matters are in the form of a judgment, passages of the judgment not relevant to the reference should be omitted.

## Transmission to the European Court

2.1 The order containing the reference, and the document scheduled to it, should be sent to The Senior Master, Room E115, Queen's Bench Division, Royal Courts of Justice, Strand, London WC2A 2LL, for onward transmission to the European Court.

2.2 The relevant court file should also be sent to the Senior Master at the above address.

## European Court Information Note

3 There is annexed to this practice direction an Information Note issued by the European Court. The reference in the opening passage to Article 177 of the EC Treaty should now be read as a reference to Article 234.

## ANNEX
## INFORMATION NOTE ON REFERENCES FROM NATIONAL COURTS FOR A PRELIMINARY RULING*

1. The preliminary ruling system is a fundamental mechanism of European Union law aimed at enabling national courts to ensure uniform interpretation and application of that law in all the Member States.

---

* This Note is reproduced with the kind permission of the European Court of Justice from their website. Disclaimer: The texts of the judgments, orders, opinions and notices present on the site are subject to amendment; only the versions published in the Reports of Cases before the Court of Justice and the Court of First Instance or the Official Journal of the European Union are authentic.

2. The Court of Justice of the European Communities has jurisdiction to give preliminary rulings on the interpretation of the law of the European Union and on the validity of acts of secondary legislation. That general jurisdiction is conferred on it by Article 234 of the EC Treaty and, in certain specific cases, by other provisions.
3. The preliminary ruling procedure being based on cooperation between the Court and national courts, it may be helpful, in order to ensure that that cooperation is effective, to provide the national courts with the following information.
4. This practical information, which is in no way binding, is intended to provide guidance to national courts as to whether it is appropriate to make a reference for a preliminary ruling and, should they proceed, to help them formulate and submit questions to the Court.

## The role of the Court in the preliminary ruling procedure

5. Under the preliminary ruling procedure, the Court's role is to give an interpretation of Community law or to rule on its validity, not to apply that law to the factual situation underlying the main proceedings, which is the task of the national court. It is not for the Court to decide issues of fact raised in the main proceedings or to resolve differences of opinion on the interpretation or application of rules of national law.
6. In ruling on the interpretation or validity of Community law, the Court makes every effort to give a reply which will be of assistance in resolving the dispute, but it is for the referring court to draw the appropriate conclusions from that reply, if necessary by disapplying the rule of national law in question.

## The decision to submit a question to the Court

*The originator of the question*

7. Under Article 234 of the EC Treaty and Article 150 of the EAEC Treaty, any court or tribunal of a Member State, in so far as it is called upon to give a ruling in proceedings intended to arrive at a decision of a judicial nature, may as a rule refer a question to the Court for a preliminary ruling. The status of that court or tribunal is interpreted by the Court as a self-standing concept of Community law.
8. However, in the specific sphere of acts of the institutions in Title IV of Part Three of the EC Treaty on visa, asylum, immigration and other policies related to free movement of persons—in particular jurisdiction and the recognition and enforcement of judicial decisions—a reference may be made only by courts or tribunals against the decisions of which there is no appeal, in accordance with Article 68 of the EC Treaty.
9. Likewise, under Article 35 of the Treaty on European Union, acts of the institutions in the area of police and judicial cooperation in criminal matters may be the subject of a reference for a preliminary ruling only from courts in the Member States which have accepted the jurisdiction of the Court, each Member State specifying whether that right of referral to the Court applies to any court or tribunal of that State or only to those against the decisions of which there is no appeal.
10. It is not necessary for the parties in the case to raise the question; the national court may do so of its own motion.

*References on interpretation*

11. Any court or tribunal **may** refer a question to the Court on the interpretation of a rule of Community law if it considers it necessary to do so in order to resolve a dispute brought before it.
12. However, courts or tribunals against whose decisions there is no judicial remedy under national law **must**, as a rule, refer such a question to the Court, unless the Court has already ruled on the point (and there is no new context that raises any serious doubt as to whether that case-law may be applied), or unless the correct interpretation of the rule of Community law is obvious.

13. Thus, a court or tribunal against whose decisions there is a judicial remedy may, in particular when it considers that sufficient clarification is given by the case-law of the Court, itself decide on the correct interpretation of Community law and its application to the factual situation before it. However, a reference for a preliminary ruling may prove particularly useful, at an appropriate stage of the proceedings, when there is a new question of interpretation of general interest for the uniform application of Community law throughout the Union, or where the existing case-law does not appear to be applicable to a new set of facts.
14. It is for the national court to explain why the interpretation sought is necessary to enable it to give judgment.

*References on determination of validity*

15. Although national courts may reject pleas raised before them challenging the validity of Community acts, the Court has exclusive jurisdiction to declare such acts invalid.
16. All national courts **must** therefore refer a question to the Court when they have doubts about the validity of a Community act, stating the reasons for which they consider that the Community act may be invalid.
17. If a national court has serious doubts about the validity of a Community act on which a national measure is based, it may exceptionally suspend application of that measure temporarily or grant other interim relief with respect to it. It must then refer the question of validity to the Court of Justice, stating the reasons for which it considers the Community act to be invalid.

## The stage at which to submit a question for a preliminary ruling

18. A national court or tribunal may refer a question to the Court of Justice for a preliminary ruling as soon as it finds that a ruling on the point or points of interpretation or validity is necessary to enable it to give judgment; it is the national court which is in the best position to decide at what stage of the proceedings such a question should be referred.
19. It is, however, desirable that a decision to seek a preliminary ruling should be taken when the proceedings have reached a stage at which the national court is able to define the factual and legal context of the question, so that the Court has available to it all the information necessary to check, where appropriate, that Community law applies to the main proceedings. It may also be in the interests of justice to refer a question for a preliminary ruling only after both sides have been heard.

## The form of the reference for a preliminary ruling

20. The decision by which a national court or tribunal refers a question to the Court of Justice for a preliminary ruling may be in any form allowed by national law as regards procedural steps. It must however be borne in mind that it is that document which serves as the basis of the proceedings before the Court and that it must therefore contain such information as will enable the latter to give a reply which is of assistance to the national court. Moreover, it is only the actual reference for a preliminary ruling which is notified to the parties entitled to submit observations to the Court, in particular the Member States and the institutions, and which is translated.
21. Owing to the need to translate the reference, it should be drafted simply, clearly and precisely, avoiding superfluous detail.
22. A maximum of about ten pages is often sufficient to set out in a proper manner the context of a reference for a preliminary ruling. The order for reference must be succinct but sufficiently complete and must contain all the relevant information to give the Court and the parties entitled to submit observations a clear understanding of the factual and legal context of the main proceedings. In particular, the order for reference must:

- include a brief account of the subject-matter of the dispute and the relevant findings of fact, or, at least, set out the factual situation on which the question referred is based;
- set out the tenor of any applicable national provisions and identify, where necessary, the relevant national case-law, giving in each case precise references (e.g. page of an official journal or specific law report, with any internet reference);
- identify the Community provisions relevant to the case as accurately as possible;
- explain the reasons which prompted the national court to raise the question of the interpretation or validity of the Community provisions, and the relationship between those provisions and the national provisions applicable to the main proceedings;
- include, where appropriate, a summary of the main arguments of the parties.

In order to make it easier to read and refer to the document, it is helpful if the different points or paragraphs of the order for reference are numbered.

23. Finally, the referring court may, if it considers itself to be in a position to do so, briefly state its view on the answer to be given to the questions referred for a preliminary ruling.
24. The question or questions themselves should appear in a separate and clearly identified section of the order for reference, generally at the beginning or the end. It must be possible to understand them without referring to the statement of the grounds for the reference, which however provides the necessary background for a proper assessment.

## The effects of the reference for a preliminary ruling on the national proceedings

25. A reference for a preliminary ruling in general calls for the national proceedings to be stayed until the Court has given its ruling.
26. However, the national court may still order protective measures, particularly in a reference on determination of validity (see point 17 above).

## Costs and legal aid

27. Proceedings for a preliminary ruling before the Court are free of charge and the Court does not rule on the costs of the parties to the main proceedings; it is for the national court to rule on those costs.
28. If a party has insufficient means and where possible under national rules, the national court may grant that party legal aid to cover the costs, including those of lawyers' fees, which it incurs before the Court. The Court itself may also grant legal aid.

## Communication between the national court and the Court of Justice

29. The order for reference and the relevant documents (including, where applicable, the case file or a copy of the case file) are to be sent by the national court directly to the Court of Justice, by registered post (addressed to the Registry of the Court of Justice of the European Communities, L-2925 Luxembourg, telephone + 352–4303–1).
30. The Court Registry will stay in contact with the national court until a ruling is given, and will send it copies of the procedural documents.
31. The Court will send its ruling to the national court. It would welcome information from the national court on the action taken upon its ruling in the national proceedings and, where appropriate, a copy of the national court's final decision.

# CPR Part 69 Court's Power to Appoint a Receiver



## 69.1 Scope of this Part

(1) This Part contains provisions about the court's power to appoint a receiver.
(2) In this Part 'receiver' includes a manager.

## 69.2 Court's Power to Appoint Receiver

(1) The court may appoint a receiver—
  (a) before proceedings have started;
  (b) in existing proceedings; or
  (c) on or after judgment.
(2) A receiver must be an individual.
(3) The court may at any time—
  (a) terminate the appointment of a receiver; and
  (b) appoint another receiver in his place.

(The practice direction describes the powers for the court to appoint a receiver.)

## 69.3 How to Apply for the Appointment of a Receiver

An application for the appointment of a receiver—
(a) may be made without notice; and
(b) must be supported by written evidence.

## 69.4 Service of Order Appointing Receiver

An order appointing a receiver must be served by the party who applied for it on—
(a) the person appointed as receiver;
(b) unless the court orders otherwise, every other party to the proceedings; and
(c) such other persons as the court may direct.

## 69.5 Security

(1) The court may direct that before a receiver begins to act or within a specified time he must either—
  (a) give such security as the court may determine; or
  (b) file and serve on all parties to the proceedings evidence that he already has in force sufficient security,

  to cover his liability for his acts and omissions as a receiver.
(2) The court may terminate the appointment of the receiver if he fails to—
  (a) give the security; or
  (b) satisfy the court as to the security he has in force,

  by the date specified.

### 69.6 Receiver's Application for Directions

(1) The receiver may apply to the court at any time for directions to assist him in carrying out his function as a receiver.
(2) The court, when it gives directions, may also direct the receiver to serve on any person—
 (a) the directions; and
 (b) the application for directions.

(The practice direction makes provision for the form of applications by, and directions to, a receiver.)

### 69.7 Receiver's Remuneration

(1) A receiver may only charge for his services if the court—
 (a) so directs; and
 (b) specifies the basis on which the receiver is to be remunerated.
(2) The court may specify—
 (a) who is to be responsible for paying the receiver; and
 (b) the fund or property from which the receiver is to recover his remuneration.
(3) If the court directs that the amount of a receiver's remuneration is to be determined by the court—
 (a) the receiver may not recover any remuneration for his services without a determination by the court; and
 (b) the receiver or any party may apply at any time for such a determination to take place.
(4) Unless the court orders otherwise, in determining the remuneration of a receiver the court shall award such sum as is reasonable and proportionate in all the circumstances and which takes into account—
 (a) the time properly given by him and his staff to the receivership;
 (b) the complexity of the receivership;
 (c) any responsibility of an exceptional kind or degree which falls on the receiver in consequence of the receivership;
 (d) the effectiveness with which the receiver appears to be carrying out, or to have carried out, his duties; and
 (e) the value and nature of the subject matter of the receivership.
(5) The court may refer the determination of a receiver's remuneration to a costs judge.

### 69.8 Accounts

(1) The court may order a receiver to prepare and serve accounts.

(The practice direction contains provisions about directions for the preparation and service of accounts.)

(2) A party served with such accounts may apply for an order permitting him to inspect any document in the possession of the receiver relevant to those accounts.
(3) Any party may, within 14 days of being served with the accounts, serve notice on the receiver—
 (a) specifying any item in the accounts to which he objects;
 (b) giving the reason for such objection; and
 (c) requiring the receiver, within 14 days of receipt of the notice, either—
  (i) to notify all the parties who were served with the accounts that he accepts the objection; or
  (ii) if he does not accept the objection, to apply for an examination of the accounts in relation to the contested item.
(4) When the receiver applies for the examination of the accounts he must at the same time file—
 (a) the accounts; and
 (b) a copy of the notice served on him under this rule.

(5) If the receiver fails to comply with paragraph (3)(c) of this rule, any party may apply to the court for an examination of the accounts in relation to the contested item.
(6) At the conclusion of its examination of the accounts the court will certify the result.
(The practice direction supplementing Part 40 provides for inquiries into accounts.)

## 69.9 Non-compliance by Receiver

(1) If a receiver fails to comply with any rule, practice direction or direction of the court the court may order him to attend a hearing to explain his non-compliance.
(2) At the hearing the court may make any order it considers appropriate, including—
 (a) terminating the appointment of the receiver;
 (b) reducing the receiver's remuneration or disallowing it altogether; and
 (c) ordering the receiver to pay the costs of any party.
(3) Where—
 (a) the court has ordered a receiver to pay a sum of money into court; and
 (b) the receiver has failed to do so,
 the court may order him to pay interest on that sum for the time he is in default at such rate as it considers appropriate.

## 69.10 Application for Discharge of Receiver

(1) A receiver or any party may apply for the receiver to be discharged on completion of his duties.
(2) The application notice must be served on the persons who were required under rule 69.4 to be served with the order appointing the receiver.

## 69.11 Order Discharging or Terminating Appointment of Receiver

(1) An order discharging or terminating the appointment of a receiver may—
 (a) require him to pay into court any money held by him; or
 (b) specify the person to whom he must pay any money or transfer any assets still in his possession; and
 (c) make provision for the discharge or cancellation of any guarantee given by the receiver as security.
(2) The order must be served on the persons who were required under rule 69.4 to be served with the order appointing the receiver.

# PD 69 Practice Direction — Court's Power to Appoint a Receiver

This practice direction supplements CPR Part 69.

## Court's Power to Appoint Receiver

1.1 The court's powers to appoint a receiver are set out in:
- (1) the Supreme Court Act 1981, s. 37 (powers of the High Court with respect to injunctions and receivers);
- (2) the County Courts Act 1984, s. 38 (remedies available in county courts); and
- (3) the County Courts Act 1984, s. 107 (receivers by way of equitable execution).

## Applications Before Proceedings Are Started—Rule 69.2(1)(a)

2.1 The court will normally only consider an application for the appointment of a receiver before proceedings are started after notice of the application has been served.

2.2 Rule 25.2(2) contains provisions about the grant of an order before proceedings are started.

## Related Injunctions

3.1 If a person applies at the same time for:
- (1) the appointment of a receiver; and
- (2) a related injunction,

he must use the same claim form or application notice for both applications.

3.2 PD 2B sets out who may grant injunctions. Among other things, it provides that a master or a district judge may grant an injunction related to an order appointing a receiver by way of equitable execution.

## Evidence in Support of an Application—Rule 69.3

4.1 The written evidence in support of an application for the appointment of a receiver must:
- (1) explain the reasons why the appointment is required;
- (2) give details of the property which it is proposed that the receiver should get in or manage, including estimates of:
  - (a) the value of the property; and
  - (b) the amount of income it is likely to produce;
- (3) if the application is to appoint a receiver by way of equitable execution, give details of:
  - (a) the judgment which the applicant is seeking to enforce;
  - (b) the extent to which the debtor has failed to comply with the judgment;
  - (c) the result of any steps already taken to enforce the judgment; and
  - (d) why the judgment cannot be enforced by any other method; and
- (4) if the applicant is asking the court to allow the receiver to act:
  - (a) without giving security; or
  - (b) before he has given security or satisfied the court that he has security in place,

  explain the reasons why that is necessary.

4.2 In addition, the written evidence should normally identify an individual whom the court is to be asked to appoint as receiver ('the nominee'), and should:
- (1) state the name, address and position of the nominee;
- (2) include written evidence by a person who knows the nominee, stating that he believes the nominee is a suitable person to be appointed as receiver, and the basis of that belief; and

(3) be accompanied by written consent, signed by the nominee, to act as receiver if appointed.

4.3 If the applicant does not nominate a person to be appointed as receiver, or if the court decides not to appoint the nominee, the court may:
(1) order that a suitable person be appointed as receiver; and
(2) direct any party to nominate a suitable individual to be appointed.

4.4 A party directed to nominate a person to be appointed as receiver must file written evidence containing the information required by para. 4.2 and accompanied by the written consent of the nominee.

## Appointment of Receiver to Enforce a Judgment

5 Where a judgment creditor applies for the appointment of a receiver as a method of enforcing a judgment, in considering whether to make the appointment the court will have regard to:
(1) the amount claimed by the judgment creditor;
(2) the amount likely to be obtained by the receiver; and
(3) the probable costs of his appointment.

## Court's Directions

6.1 The court may give directions to the receiver when it appoints him or at any time afterwards.

6.2 The court will normally, when it appoints a receiver, give directions in relation to security—see para. 7 below.

6.3 Other matters about which the court may give directions include:
(1) whether, and on what basis, the receiver is to be remunerated for carrying out his functions;
(2) the preparation and service of accounts—see r. 69.8(1) and para. 10 below;
(3) the payment of money into court; and
(4) authorising the receiver to carry on an activity or incur an expense.

## Directions Relating to Security—Rule 69.5

7.1 An order appointing a receiver will normally specify the date by which the receiver must:
(1) give security; or
(2) file and serve evidence to satisfy the court that he already has security in force.

7.2 Unless the court directs otherwise, security will be given:
(1) if the receiver is a licensed insolvency practitioner, by the bond provided by him under the Insolvency Practitioners Regulations 1990 (SI 1990/439) extended to cover appointment as a court-appointed receiver; or
(2) in any other case, by a guarantee.

7.3 Where the court has given directions about giving security, then either:
(1) written evidence of the bond, the sufficiency of its cover and that it includes appointment as a court-appointed receiver must be filed at court; or
(2) a guarantee should be prepared in a form, and entered into with a clearing bank or insurance company, approved by the court.

## Receiver's Application for Directions—Rule 69.6

8.1 An application by a receiver for directions may be made by filing an application notice in accordance with Part 23.

8.2 If the directions sought by the receiver are unlikely to be contentious or important to the parties, he may make the application by letter, and the court may reply by letter. In such cases the receiver need not serve his letter or the court's reply on the parties, unless the court orders him to do so.

8.3 Where a receiver applies for directions by letter, the court may direct him to file and serve an application notice.

## Receiver's Remuneration—Rule 69.7

9.1 A receiver may only charge for his services if the court gives directions permitting it and specifying how the remuneration is to be determined.

9.2 The court will normally determine the amount of the receiver's remuneration on the basis of the criteria in r. 69.7(4). Parts 43 to 48 (costs) do not apply to the determination of the remuneration of a receiver.

9.3 Unless the court orders otherwise, the receiver will only be paid or be able to recover his remuneration after the amount of it has been determined.

9.4 An application by a receiver for the amount of his remuneration to be determined must be supported by:

(1) written evidence showing:

(a) on what basis the remuneration is claimed; and

(b) that it is justified and in accordance with Part 69; and

(2) a certificate signed by the receiver that he considers that the remuneration he claims is reasonable and proportionate.

9.5 The court may, before determining the amount of a receiver's remuneration:

(1) require the receiver to provide further information in support of his claim; and

(2) appoint an assessor under r. 35.15 to assist the court.

9.6 Paragraphs 9.1 to 9.5 do not apply to expenses incurred by a receiver in carrying out his functions. These are accounted for as part of his account for the assets he has recovered, and not dealt with as part of the determination of his remuneration.

## Accounts—Rule 69.8

10.1 When the court gives directions under r. 69.8(1) for the receiver to prepare and serve accounts, it may:

(1) direct the receiver to prepare and serve accounts either by a specified date or at specified intervals; and

(2) specify the persons on whom he must serve the accounts.

10.2 A party should not apply for an order under r. 69.8(2) permitting him to inspect documents in the possession of the receiver, without first asking the receiver to permit such inspection without an order.

10.3 Where the court makes an order under r. 69.8(2), it will normally direct that the receiver must:

(1) permit inspection within seven days after being served with the order; and

(2) provide a copy of any documents the subject of the order within seven days after receiving a request for a copy from the party permitted to inspect them, provided that party has undertaken to pay the reasonable cost of making and providing the copy.

# CPR Part 70 General Rules About Enforcement of Judgments and Orders



## 70.1 Scope of this Part and Interpretation

(1) This Part contains general rules about enforcement of judgments and orders.

(Rules about specific methods of enforcement are contained in Parts 71 to 73, Schedule 1 RSC Orders 45 to 47 and 52 and Schedule 2 CCR Orders 25 to 29.)

(2) In this Part and in Parts 71 to 73—

(a) 'judgment creditor' means a person who has obtained or is entitled to enforce a judgment or order;

(b) 'judgment debtor' means a person against whom a judgment or order was given or made;

(c) 'judgment or order' includes an award which the court has—

(i) registered for enforcement;

(ii) ordered to be enforced; or

(iii) given permission to enforce

as if it were a judgment or order of the court, and in relation to such an award, 'the court which made the judgment or order' means the court which registered the award or made such an order; and

(d) 'judgment or order for the payment of money' includes a judgment or order for the payment of costs, but does not include a judgment or order for the payment of money into court.

## 70.2 Methods of Enforcing Judgments or Orders

(1) The relevant practice direction sets out methods of enforcing judgments or orders for the payment of money.

(2) A judgment creditor may, except where an enactment, rule or practice direction provides otherwise—

(a) use any method of enforcement which is available; and

(b) use more than one method of enforcement, either at the same time or one after another.

## 70.3 Transfer of Proceedings for Enforcement

(1) A judgment creditor wishing to enforce a High Court judgment or order in a county court must apply to the High Court for an order transferring the proceedings to that county court.

(2) A practice direction may make provisions about the transfer of proceedings for enforcement.

(CCR Order 25 rule 13 contains provisions about the transfer of county court proceedings to the High Court for enforcement.)

## 70.4 Enforcement of Judgment or Order by or Against Non-party

If a judgment or order is given or made in favour of or against a person who is not a party to proceedings, it may be enforced by or against that person by the same methods as if he were a party.

## 70.5 Enforcement of Awards of Bodies Other Than the High Court and County Courts

(1) This rule applies, subject to paragraph (2), if—
    (a) an award of a sum of money or other decision is made by any court, tribunal, body or person other than the High Court or a county court; and
    (b) an enactment provides that the award may be enforced as if payable under a court order, or that the decision may be enforced as if it were a court order.
(2) This rule does not apply to—
    (a) any judgment to which Part 74 applies;
    (b) arbitration awards; or
    (c) any order to which RSC Order 115 applies.

(Part 74 provides for the registration in the High Court for the purposes of enforcement of judgments from other jurisdictions and European Community judgments.)
(RSC Order 115 provides for the registration in the High Court for the purposes of enforcement of certain orders made in connection with criminal proceedings and investigations.)

(3) If the enactment provides that an award of a sum of money is enforceable if a court so orders, an application for such an order must be made in accordance with paragraphs (4) to (7) of this rule.
(4) An application for an order that an award may be enforced as if payable under a court order—
    (a) may be made without notice; and
    (b) must be made to the court for the district where the person against whom the award was made resides or carries on business, unless the court otherwise orders.
(5) The application notice must—
    (a) be in the form; and
    (b) contain the information
    required by the relevant practice direction.
(6) A copy of the award must be filed with the application notice.
(7) The application may be dealt with by a court officer without a hearing.
(8) If an enactment provides that an award or decision may be enforced in the same manner as an order of the High Court if it is registered, any application to the High Court for registration must be made in accordance with the relevant practice direction.

## 70.6 Effect of Setting Aside Judgment or Order

If a judgment or order is set aside, any enforcement of the judgment or order shall cease to have effect unless the court otherwise orders.

# PD 70 Practice Direction — Enforcement of Judgments and Orders

This practice direction supplements CPR Part 70.

## Methods of Enforcing Money Judgments—Rule 70.2

1.1 A judgment creditor may enforce a judgment or order for the payment of money by any of the following methods:
  (1) a writ of fieri facias or warrant of execution (see RSC, ord. 46 and ord. 47 in CPR, sch. 1; CCR, ord. 26 in CPR, sch. 2);
  (2) a third party debt order (see Part 72);
  (3) a charging order, stop order or stop notice (see Part 73);
  (4) in a county court, an attachment of earnings order (see CCR, ord. 27 in CPR, sch.2);
  (5) the appointment of a receiver (see Part 69).

1.2 In addition the court may make the following orders against a judgment debtor:
  (1) an order of committal, but only if permitted by:
    (a) a rule; and
    (b) the Debtors Acts 1869 and 1878 (See RSC, ord. 45, r. 5 in CPR, sch. 1, and CCR, ord. 28 in CPR, sch. 2. PD RSC Ord. 52 applies to an application for committal of a judgment debtor.), and
  (2) in the High Court, a writ of sequestration, but only if permitted by RSC, ord. 45, r. 5 in CPR, sch. 1.

1.3 The enforcement of a judgment or order may be affected by:
  (1) the enactments relating to insolvency; and
  (2) county court administration orders.

## Transfer of County Court Proceedings to Another County Court for Enforcement—Rule 70.3

2.1 If a judgment creditor is required by a rule or practice direction to enforce a judgment or order of one county court in a different county court, he must first make a request in writing to the court in which the case is proceeding to transfer the proceedings to that other court.

2.2 On receipt of such a request, a court officer will transfer the proceedings to the other court unless a judge orders otherwise.

2.3 The court will give notice of the transfer to all the parties.

2.4 When the proceedings have been transferred, the parties must take any further steps in the proceedings in the court to which they have been transferred, unless a rule or practice direction provides otherwise.

(Part 52 and PD 52 provide to which court or judge an appeal against the judgment or order, or an application for permission to appeal, must be made.)

## Enforcement of High Court Judgment or Order in a County Court—Rule 70.3

3.1 If a judgment creditor wishes to enforce a High Court judgment or order in a county court, he must file the following documents in the county court with his application notice or request for enforcement:
  (1) a copy of the judgment or order;
  (2) a certificate verifying the amount due under the judgment or order;
  (3) if a writ of execution has previously been issued in the High Court to enforce the judgment or order, a copy of the relevant enforcement officer's return to the writ; and

(4) a copy of the order transferring the proceedings to the county court.

3.2 In this paragraph and paragraph 7—

(1) 'enforcement officer' means an individual who is authorised to act as an enforcement officer under the Courts Act 2003; and

(2) 'relevant enforcement officer' means—

(a) in relation to a writ of execution which is directed to a single enforcement officer, that officer;

(b) in relation to a writ of execution which is directed to two or more enforcement officers, the officer to whom the writ is allocated.

## Enforcement of Awards of Bodies Other Than the High Court or a County Court—Rule 70.5

4.1 An application under r. 70.5 for an order to enforce an award as if payable under a court order must be made by filing an application notice in form N322A.

4.2 The application notice must state:

(1) the name and address of the person against whom it is sought to enforce the award; and

(2) how much of the award remains unpaid.

4.3 Rule 70.5(6) provides that a copy of the award must be filed with the application notice.

## Registration of Awards and Decisions in the High Court For Enforcement—Rule 70.5(8)

5.1 An application to the High Court under an enactment to register a decision for enforcement must be made in writing to the head clerk of the Action Department at the Royal Courts of Justice, Strand, London WC2A 2LL.

5.2 The application must:

(1) specify the statutory provision under which the application is made;

(2) state the name and address of the person against whom it is sought to enforce the decision;

(3) if the decision requires that person to pay a sum of money, state the amount which remains unpaid.

## Interest on Judgment Debts

6 If a judgment creditor is claiming interest on a judgment debt, he must include in his application or request to issue enforcement proceedings in relation to that judgment details of:

(1) the amount of interest claimed and the sum on which it is claimed;

(2) the dates from and to which interest has accrued; and

(3) the rate of interest which has been applied and, where more than one rate of interest has been applied, the relevant dates and rates.

(Interest may be claimed on High Court judgment debts under the Judgments Act 1838, s. 17. The County Courts (Interest on Judgment Debts) Order 1991 specifies when interest may be claimed on county court judgment debts.)

## Enforcing a judgment or order against a partnership

6A.1 A judgment or order made against a partnership may be enforced against any property of the partnership within the jurisdiction.

6A.2 Subject to paragraph 6A.3, a judgment or order made against a partnership may be enforced against any person who is not a limited partner and who—

(1) acknowledged service of the claim form as a partner;

(2) having been served as a partner with the claim form, failed to acknowledge service of it;

(3) admitted in his statement of case that he is or was a partner at a material time; or
(4) was found by the court to have been a partner at a material time.

6A.3 A judgment or order made against a partnership may not be enforced against a limited partner or a member of the partnership who was ordinarily resident outside the jurisdiction when the claim form was issued unless he—
(1) acknowledged service of the claim form as a partner;
(2) was served within the jurisdiction with the claim form as a partner; or
(3) was served out of the jurisdiction with the claim form, as a partner, with the permission of the court given under Section III of Part 6.

6A.4 A judgment creditor wishing to enforce a judgment or order against a person in circumstances not set out in paragraphs 6A.2 or 6A.3 must apply to the court for permission to enforce the judgment or order.

## Payment of Debt After Issue of Enforcement Proceedings

7.1 If a judgment debt or part of it is paid:
(1) after the judgment creditor has issued any application or request to enforce it; but
(2) before:
(a) any writ or warrant has been executed; or
(b) in any other case, the date fixed for the hearing of the application,
the judgment creditor must, unless para. 7.2 applies, immediately notify the court in writing.

7.2 If a judgment debt or part of it is paid after the judgment creditor has applied to the High Court for a writ of execution, para. 7.1 does not apply, and the judgment creditor must instead immediately notify the relevant enforcement officer in writing.

# CPR Part 71 Orders to Obtain Information from Judgment Debtors



## 71.1 Scope of this Part

This Part contains rules which provide for a judgment debtor to be required to attend court to provide information, for the purpose of enabling a judgment creditor to enforce a judgment or order against him.

## 71.2 Order to Attend Court

(1) A judgment creditor may apply for an order requiring—
  (a) a judgment debtor; or
  (b) if a judgment debtor is a company or other corporation, an officer of that body, to attend court to provide information about—
    (i) the judgment debtor's means; or
    (ii) any other matter about which information is needed to enforce a judgment or order.

(2) An application under paragraph (1)—
  (a) may be made without notice; and
  (b) (i) must be issued in the court which made the judgment or order which it is sought to enforce, except that
    (ii) if the proceedings have since been transferred to a different court, it must be issued in that court.

(3) The application notice must—
  (a) be in the form; and
  (b) contain the information
  required by the relevant practice direction.

(4) An application under paragraph (1) may be dealt with by a court officer without a hearing.

(5) If the application notice complies with paragraph (3), an order to attend court will be issued in the terms of paragraph (6).

(6) A person served with an order issued under this rule must—
  (a) attend court at the time and place specified in the order;
  (b) when he does so, produce at court documents in his control which are described in the order; and
  (c) answer on oath such questions as the court may require.

(7) An order under this rule will contain a notice in the following terms—
  'You must obey this order. If you do not, you may be sent to prison for contempt of court.'

## 71.3 Service of Order

(1) An order to attend court must, unless the court otherwise orders, be served personally on the person ordered to attend court not less than 14 days before the hearing.

(2) If the order is to be served by the judgment creditor, he must inform the court not less than 7 days before the date of the hearing if he has been unable to serve it.

## 71.4 Travelling Expenses

(1) A person ordered to attend court may, within 7 days of being served with the order, ask the judgment creditor to pay him a sum reasonably sufficient to cover his travelling expenses to and from court.
(2) The judgment creditor must pay such a sum if requested.

## 71.5 Judgment Creditor's Affidavit

(1) The judgment creditor must file an affidavit(GL) or affidavits—
  (a) by the person who served the order (unless it was served by the court) giving details of how and when it was served;
  (b) stating either that—
    (i) the person ordered to attend court has not requested payment of his travelling expenses; or
    (ii) the judgment creditor has paid a sum in accordance with such a request; and
  (c) stating how much of the judgment debt remains unpaid.
(2) The judgment creditor must either—
  (a) file the affidavit(GL) or affidavits not less than 2 days before the hearing; or
  (b) produce it or them at the hearing.

## 71.6 Conduct of the Hearing

(1) The person ordered to attend court will be questioned on oath.
(2) The questioning will be carried out by a court officer unless the court has ordered that the hearing shall be before a judge.
(3) The judgment creditor or his representative—
  (a) may attend and ask questions where the questioning takes place before a court officer; and
  (b) must attend and conduct the questioning if the hearing is before a judge.

## 71.7 Adjournment of the Hearing

If the hearing is adjourned, the court will give directions as to the manner in which notice of the new hearing is to be served on the judgment debtor.

## 71.8 Failure to Comply With Order

(1) If a person against whom an order has been made under rule 71.2—
  (a) fails to attend court;
  (b) refuses at the hearing to take the oath or to answer any question; or
  (c) otherwise fails to comply with the order,
  the court will refer the matter to a High Court judge or circuit judge.
(2) That judge may, subject to paragraphs (3) and (4), make a committal order against the person.
(3) A committal order for failing to attend court may not be made unless the judgment creditor has complied with rules 71.4 and 71.5.
(4) If a committal order is made, the judge will direct that—
  (a) the order shall be suspended provided that the person—
    (i) attends court at a time and place specified in the order; and
    (ii) complies with all the terms of that order and the original order; and
  (b) if the person fails to comply with any term on which the committal order is suspended, he shall be brought before a judge to consider whether the committal order should be discharged.

# PD 71 Practice Direction — Orders to Obtain Information from Judgment Debtors

This practice direction supplements CPR Part 71.

## Application Notice—Rule 71.2

1.1 An application by a judgment creditor under r. 71.2(1) must be made by filing an application notice in form N316 if the application is to question an individual judgment debtor, or N316A if the application is to question an officer of a company or other corporation.

1.2 The application notice must:
- (1) state the name and address of the judgment debtor;
- (2) identify the judgment or order which the judgment creditor is seeking to enforce;
- (3) if the application is to enforce a judgment or order for the payment of money, state the amount presently owed by the judgment debtor under the judgment or order;
- (4) if the judgment debtor is a company or other corporation, state:
  - (a) the name and address of the officer of that body whom the judgment creditor wishes to be ordered to attend court; and
  - (b) his position in the company;
- (5) if the judgment creditor wishes the questioning to be conducted before a judge, state this and give his reasons;
- (6) if the judgment creditor wishes the judgment debtor (or other person to be questioned) to be ordered to produce specific documents at court, identify those documents; and
- (7) if the application is to enforce a judgment or order which is not for the payment of money, identify the matters about which the judgment creditor wishes the judgment debtor (or officer of the judgment debtor) to be questioned.

1.3 The court officer considering the application notice:
- (1) may, in any appropriate case, refer it to a judge (r. 3.2); and
- (2) will refer it to a judge for consideration, if the judgment creditor requests the judgment debtor (or officer of the judgment debtor) to be questioned before a judge.

## Order to Attend Court—Rule 71.2

2.1 The order will provide for the judgment debtor (or other person to be questioned) to attend the county court for the district in which he resides or carries on business, unless a judge decides otherwise.

2.2 The order will provide for questioning to take place before a judge only if the judge considering the request decides that there are compelling reasons to make such an order.

## Service of Order to Attend Court—Rule 71.3

3 Service of an order to attend court for questioning must be carried out by the judgment creditor (or someone acting on his behalf), except that in county court proceedings if the judgment creditor is an individual litigant in person the order will be served by the court bailiff.

## Attendance at Court: Normal Procedure—Rule 71.6

4.1 The court officer will ask a standard series of questions, as set out in the forms in Appendices A and B to this practice direction. The form in Appendix A will be used if the person being questioned is the judgment debtor, and the form in Appendix B will be used if the person is an officer of a company or other corporation.

4.2 The judgment creditor or his representative may either:
(1) attend court and ask questions himself; or
(2) request the court officer to ask additional questions, by attaching a list of proposed additional questions to his application notice.

4.3 The court officer will:
(1) make a written record of the evidence given, unless the proceedings are tape-recorded;
(2) at the end of the questioning, read the record of evidence to the person being questioned and ask him to sign it; and
(3) if the person refuses to sign it, note that refusal on the record of evidence.

### Attendance at Court: Procedure Where the Order is to Attend Before a Judge—Rule 71.6

5.1 Where the hearing takes places before a judge, the questioning will be conducted by the judgment creditor or his representative, and the standard questions in the forms in Appendices A and B will not be used.

5.2 The proceedings will be tape-recorded and the court will not make a written record of the evidence.

### Failure to Comply with Order: Reference to Judge—Rule 71.8(1)

6 If a judge or court officer refers to a High Court judge or circuit judge the failure of a judgment debtor to comply with an order under r. 71.2, he shall certify in writing the respect in which the judgment debtor failed to comply with the order.

### Suspended Committal Order—Rule 71.8(2) And (4)(a)

7.1 A committal order will be suspended provided that the person attends court at a time and place specified in the order (r. 71.8(4)(a)(i)). The appointment specified will be:
(1) before a judge, if:
  (a) the original order under r. 71.2 was to attend before a judge; or
  (b) the judge making the suspended committal order so directs; and
(2) otherwise, before a court officer.

7.2 Rule 71.3 and para. 3 of this practice direction (service of order), and r. 71.5(1)(a) and (2) (affidavit of service), apply with the necessary changes to a suspended committal order as they do to an order to attend court.

### Breach of Terms on Which Committal Order is Suspended—Rule 71.8(4)(B)

8.1 If:
(1) the judgment debtor fails to attend court at the time and place specified in the suspended committal order; and
(2) it appears to the judge or court officer that the judgment debtor has been duly served with the order,

the judge or court officer will certify in writing the debtor's failure to attend.

8.2 If the judgment debtor fails to comply with any other term on which the committal order was suspended, the judge or court officer will certify in writing the non-compliance and set out details of it.

8.3 A warrant to bring the judgment debtor before a judge may be issued on the basis of a certificate under para. 8.1 or 8.2.

8.4 The hearing under r. 71.8(4)(b) may take place before a master or district judge.

8.5 At the hearing the judge will discharge the committal order unless he is satisfied beyond reasonable doubt that:
(1) the judgment debtor has failed to comply with:
  (a) the original order to attend court; and
  (b) the terms on which the committal order was suspended; and
(2) both orders have been duly served on the judgment debtor.

8.6 If the judge decides that the committal order should not be discharged, a warrant of committal shall be issued immediately.

[The following forms are appended to PD 71:
Appendix AEX140 Record of examination (individual)
Appendix BEX141 Record of examination (officer of company or corporation)

These forms are not reproduced in this work but may be accessed via the DCA website at <http://www.dca.gov.uk>.]

# CPR Part 72 Third Party Debt Orders



## 72.1 Scope of this Part and Interpretation

(1) This Part contains rules which provide for a judgment creditor to obtain an order for the payment to him of money which a third party who is within the jurisdiction owes to the judgment debtor.

(2) In this Part, 'bank or building society' includes any person carrying on a business in the course of which he lawfully accepts deposits in the United Kingdom.

## 72.2 Third Party Debt Order

(1) Upon the application of a judgment creditor, the court may make an order (a 'final third party debt order') requiring a third party to pay to the judgment creditor—
   (a) the amount of any debt due or accruing due to the judgment debtor from the third party; or
   (b) so much of that debt as is sufficient to satisfy the judgment debt and the judgment creditor's costs of the application.

(2) The court will not make an order under paragraph 1 without first making an order (an 'interim third party debt order') as provided by rule 72.4(2).

(3) In deciding whether money standing to the credit of the judgment debtor in an account to which section 40 of the Supreme Court Act 1981 or section 108 of the County Courts Act 1984 relates may be made the subject of a third party debt order, any condition applying to the account that a receipt for money deposited in the account must be produced before any money is withdrawn will be disregarded.

(Section 40(3) of the Supreme Court Act 1981 and section 108(3) of the County Courts Act 1984 contain a list of other conditions applying to accounts that will also be disregarded.)

## 72.3 Application for Third Party Debt Order

(1) An application for a third party debt order—
   (a) may be made without notice; and
   (b) (i) must be issued in the court which made the judgment or order which it is sought to enforce; except that
       (ii) if the proceedings have since been transferred to a different court, it must be issued in that court.

(2) The application notice must—
   (a) (i) be in the form; and
       (ii) contain the information
   required by the relevant practice direction; and
   (b) be verified by a statement of truth.

## 72.4 Interim Third Party Debt Order

(1) An application for a third party debt order will initially be dealt with by a judge without a hearing.

(2) The judge may make an interim third party debt order—
(a) fixing a hearing to consider whether to make a final third party debt order; and
(b) directing that until that hearing the third party must not make any payment which reduces the amount he owes the judgment debtor to less than the amount specified in the order.
(3) An interim third party debt order will specify the amount of money which the third party must retain, which will be the total of—
(a) the amount of money remaining due to the judgment creditor under the judgment or order; and
(b) an amount for the judgment creditor's fixed costs of the application, as specified in the relevant practice direction.
(4) An interim third party debt order becomes binding on a third party when it is served on him.
(5) The date of the hearing to consider the application shall be not less than 28 days after the interim third party debt order is made.

### 72.5 Service of Interim Order

(1) Copies of an interim third party debt order, the application notice and any documents filed in support of it must be served—
(a) on the third party, not less than 21 days before the date fixed for the hearing; and
(b) on the judgment debtor not less than—
(i) 7 days after a copy has been served on the third party; and
(ii) 7 days before the date fixed for the hearing.
(2) If the judgment creditor serves the order, he must either—
(a) file a certificate of service not less than 2 days before the hearing; or
(b) produce a certificate of service at the hearing.

### 72.6 Obligations of Third Parties Served with Interim Order

(1) A bank or building society served with an interim third party debt order must carry out a search to identify all accounts held with it by the judgment debtor.
(2) The bank or building society must disclose to the court and the creditor within seven days of being served with the order, in respect of each account held by the judgment debtor—
(a) the number of the account;
(b) whether the account is in credit; and
(c) if the account is in credit—
(i) whether the balance of the account is sufficient to cover the amount specified in the order;
(ii) the amount of the balance at the date it was served with the order, if it is less than the amount specified in the order; and
(iii) whether the bank or building society asserts any right to the money in the account, whether pursuant to a right of set-off or otherwise, and if so giving details of the grounds for that assertion.
(3) If—
(a) the judgment debtor does not hold an account with the bank or building society; or
(b) the bank or building society is unable to comply with the order for any other reason (for example, because it has more than one account holder whose details match the information contained in the order, and cannot identify which account the order applies to),
the bank or building society must inform the court and the judgment creditor of that fact within 7 days of being served with the order.
(4) Any third party other than a bank or building society served with an interim third party debt order must notify the court and the judgment creditor in writing within 7 days of being served with the order, if he claims—

(a) not to owe any money to the judgment debtor; or
(b) to owe less than the amount specified in the order.

## 72.7 Arrangements for Debtors in Hardship

(1) If—
(a) a judgment debtor is an individual;
(b) he is prevented from withdrawing money from his account with a bank or building society as a result of an interim third party debt order; and
(c) he or his family is suffering hardship in meeting ordinary living expenses as a result,
the court may, on an application by the judgment debtor, make an order permitting the bank or building society to make a payment or payments out of the account ('a hardship payment order').
(2) An application for a hardship payment order may be made—
(a) in High Court proceedings, at the Royal Courts of Justice or to any district registry; and
(b) in county court proceedings, to any county court.
(3) A judgment debtor may only apply to one court for a hardship payment order.
(4) An application notice seeking a hardship payment order must—
(a) include detailed evidence explaining why the judgment debtor needs a payment of the amount requested; and
(b) be verified by a statement of truth.
(5) Unless the court orders otherwise, the application notice—
(a) must be served on the judgment creditor at least 2 days before the hearing; but
(b) does not need to be served on the third party.
(6) A hardship payment order may—
(a) permit the third party to make one or more payments out of the account; and
(b) specify to whom the payments may be made.

## 72.8 Further Consideration of the Application

(1) If the judgment debtor or the third party objects to the court making a final third party debt order, he must file and serve written evidence stating the grounds for his objections.
(2) If the judgment debtor or the third party knows or believes that a person other than the judgment debtor has any claim to the money specified in the interim order, he must file and serve written evidence stating his knowledge of that matter.
(3) If—
(a) the third party has given notice under rule 72.6 that he does not owe any money to the judgment debtor, or that the amount which he owes is less than the amount specified in the interim order; and
(b) the judgment creditor wishes to dispute this,
the judgment creditor must file and serve written evidence setting out the grounds on which he disputes the third party's case.
(4) Written evidence under paragraphs (1), (2) or (3) must be filed and served on each other party as soon as possible, and in any event not less than 3 days before the hearing.
(5) If the court is notified that some person other than the judgment debtor may have a claim to the money specified in the interim order, it will serve on that person notice of the application and the hearing.
(6) At the hearing the court may—
(a) make a final third party debt order;
(b) discharge the interim third party debt order and dismiss the application;
(c) decide any issues in dispute between the parties, or between any of the parties and any other person who has a claim to the money specified in the interim order; or
(d) direct a trial of any such issues, and if necessary give directions.

### 72.9 Effect of Final Third Party Order

(1) A final third party debt order shall be enforceable as an order to pay money.
(2) If—
   (a) the third party pays money to the judgment creditor in compliance with a third party debt order; or
   (b) the order is enforced against him,
   the third party shall, to the extent of the amount paid by him or realised by enforcement against him, be discharged from his debt to the judgment debtor.
(3) Paragraph (2) applies even if the third party debt order, or the original judgment or order against the judgment debtor, is later set aside.

### 72.10 Money in Court

(1) If money is standing to the credit of the judgment debtor in court—
   (a) the judgment creditor may not apply for a third party debt order in respect of that money; but
   (b) he may apply for an order that the money in court, or so much of it as is sufficient to satisfy the judgment or order and the costs of the application, be paid to him.
(2) An application notice seeking an order under this rule must be served on—
   (a) the judgment debtor; and
   (b) the Accountant General at the Court Funds Office.
(3) If an application notice has been issued under this rule, the money in court must not be paid out until the application has been disposed of.

### 72.11 Costs

If the judgment creditor is awarded costs on an application for an order under rule 72.2 or 72.10—
(a) he shall, unless the court otherwise directs, retain those costs out of the money recovered by him under the order; and
(b) the costs shall be deemed to be paid first out of the money he recovers, in priority to the judgment debt.

# PD 72 Practice Direction — Third Party Debt Orders

This practice direction supplements CPR Part 72.

## Application Notice—Rule 72.3

1.1 An application for a third party debt order must be made by filing an application notice in form N349.

1.2 The application notice must contain the following information:
(1) the name and address of the judgment debtor;
(2) details of the judgment or order sought to be enforced;
(3) the amount of money remaining due under the judgment or order;
(4) if the judgment debt is payable by instalments, the amount of any instalments which have fallen due and remain unpaid;
(5) the name and address of the third party;
(6) if the third party is a bank or building society:
(a) its name and the address of the branch at which the judgment debtor's account is believed to be held; and
(b) the account number;
or, if the judgment creditor does not know all or part of this information, that fact;
(7) confirmation that to the best of the judgment creditor's knowledge or belief the third party:
(a) is within the jurisdiction; and
(b) owes money to or holds money to the credit of the judgment debtor;
(8) if the judgment creditor knows or believes that any person other than the judgment debtor has any claim to the money owed by the third party:
(a) his name and (if known) his address; and
(b) such information as is known to the judgment creditor about his claim;
(9) details of any other applications for third party debt orders issued by the judgment creditor in respect of the same judgment debt; and
(10) the sources or grounds of the judgment creditor's knowledge or belief of the matters referred to in (7), (8) and (9).

1.3 The court will not grant speculative applications for third party debt orders, and will only make an interim third party debt order against a bank or building society if the judgment creditor's application notice contains evidence to substantiate his belief that the judgment debtor has an account with the bank or building society in question.

## Interim Third Party Debt Order—Rule 72.4

2 An interim third party debt order will specify the amount of money which the third party must retain (r. 72.4(3)). This will include, in respect of the judgment creditor's fixed costs of the application, the amount which would be allowed to the judgment creditor under r. 45.6 if the whole balance of the judgment debt were recovered.

## Interim Orders Relating to Bank or Building Society Accounts—Rule 72.6(1)–(3)

3.1 A bank or building society served with an interim third party debt order is only required by r. 72.6, unless the order states otherwise:
(1) to retain money in accounts held solely by the judgment debtor (or, if there are joint judgment debtors, accounts held jointly by them or solely by either or any of them); and
(2) to search for and disclose information about such accounts.

3.2 The bank or building society is not required, for example, to retain money in, or disclose information about:

(1) accounts in the joint names of the judgment debtor and another person; or
(2) if the interim order has been made against a firm, accounts in the names of individual members of that firm.

## Attachment of debts owed by a partnership

3A.1 This paragraph relates to debts due or accruing due to a judgment creditor from a partnership.

3A.2 An interim third party debt order under rule 72.4(2) relating to such debts must be served on—
(1) a member of the partnership within the jurisdiction;
(2) a person authorised by a partner; or
(3) some other person having the control or management of the partnership business.

3A.3 Where an order made under rule 72.4(2) requires a partnership to appear before the court, it will be sufficient for a partner to appear before the court.

## Transfer

4 The court may, on an application by a judgment debtor who wishes to oppose an application for a third party debt order, transfer it to the court for the district where the judgment debtor resides or carries on business, or to another court.

## Applications for Hardship Payment Orders—Rule 72.7

5.1 The court will treat an application for a hardship payment order as being made:
(1) in the proceedings in which the interim third party debt order was made; and
(2) under the same claim number,
regardless of where the judgment debtor makes the application.

5.2 An application for a hardship payment order will be dealt with by the court to which it is made.

(Rule 72.7(2) provides that an application may be made:
- in High Court proceedings, in the Royal Courts of Justice or to any district registry; and
- in county court proceedings, to any county court.)

5.3 If the application is made to a different court from that dealing with the application for a third party debt order:
(1) the application for a third party debt order will not be transferred; but
(2) the court dealing with that application will send copies of:
(a) the application notice; and
(b) the interim third party debt order
to the court hearing the application for a hardship payment order

5.4 Rule 72.7(3) requires an application for a hardship payment order to be served on the judgment creditor at least two days before the court is to deal with the application, unless the court orders otherwise. In cases of exceptional urgency the judgment debtor may apply for a hardship payment order without notice to the judgment creditor and a judge will decide whether to:
(1) deal with the application without it being served on the judgment creditor; or
(2) direct it to be served.

5.5 If the judge decides to deal with the application without it being served on the judgment creditor, where possible he will normally:
(1) direct that the judgment creditor be informed of the application; and
(2) give him the opportunity to make representations,
by telephone, fax or other appropriate method of communication.

5.6 The evidence filed by a judgment debtor in support of an application for a hardship payment order should include documentary evidence, for example (if appropriate) bank statements, wage slips and mortgage statements, to prove his financial position and need for the payment.

### Final Orders Relating to Building Society Accounts

6 A final third party debt order will not require a payment which would reduce to less than £1 the amount in a judgment debtor's account with a building society or credit union.

# CPR Part 73 Charging Orders, Stop Orders and Stop Notices



### 73.1 Scope of this Part and Interpretation

(1) This Part contains rules which provide for a judgment creditor to enforce a judgment by obtaining—
  (a) a charging order (Section I);
  (b) a stop order (Section II); or
  (c) a stop notice (Section III),

  over or against the judgment debtor's interest in an asset.

(2) In this Part—
  (a) 'the 1979 Act' means the Charging Orders Act 1979;
  (b) 'the 1992 Regulations' means the Council Tax (Administration & Enforcement) Regulations 1992;
  (c) 'funds in court' includes securities held in court;
  (d) 'securities' means securities of any of the kinds specified in section 2(2)(b) of the 1979 Act.

## SECTION I — CHARGING ORDERS

### 73.2 Scope of this Section

This Section applies to an application by a judgment creditor for a charging order under—
(a) section 1 of the 1979 Act; or
(b) regulation 50 of the 1992 Regulations.

### 73.3 Application for Charging Order

(1) An application for a charging order may be made without notice.

(2) An application for a charging order must be issued in the court which made the judgment or order which it is sought to enforce, unless—
  (a) the proceedings have since been transferred to a different court, in which case the application must be issued in that court;
  (b) the application is made under the 1992 Regulations, in which case it must be issued in the county court for the district in which the relevant dwelling (as defined in regulation 50(3)(b) of those Regulations) is situated;

(c) the application is for a charging order over an interest in a fund in court, in which case it must be issued in the court in which the claim relating to that fund is or was proceeding; or
(d) the application is to enforce a judgment or order of the High Court and it is required by section 1(2) of the 1979 Act to be made to a county court.

(3) Subject to paragraph (2), a judgment creditor may apply for a single charging order in respect of more than one judgment or order against the same debtor.

(4) The application notice must—
(a) (i) be in the form; and
(ii) contain the information,
required by the relevant practice direction; and
(b) be verified by a statement of truth.

## 73.4 Interim Charging Order

(1) An application for a charging order will initially be dealt with by a judge without a hearing.

(2) The judge may make an order (an 'interim charging order')—
(a) imposing a charge over the judgment debtor's interest in the asset to which the application relates; and
(b) fixing a hearing to consider whether to make a final charging order as provided by rule 73.8(2)(a).

## 73.5 Service of Interim Order

(1) Copies of the interim charging order, the application notice and any documents filed in support of it must, not less than 21 days before the hearing, be served on the following persons—
(a) the judgment debtor;
(b) such other creditors as the court directs;
(c) if the order relates to an interest under a trust, on such of the trustees as the court directs;
(d) if the interest charged is in securities other than securities held in court, then—
(i) in the case of stock for which the Bank of England keeps the register, the Bank of England;
(ii) in the case of government stock to which (i) does not apply, the keeper of the register;
(iii) in the case of stock of any body incorporated within England and Wales, that body;
(iv) in the case of stock of any body incorporated outside England and Wales or of any state or territory outside the United Kingdom, which is registered in a register kept in England and Wales, the keeper of that register;
(v) in the case of units of any unit trust in respect of which a register of the unit holders is kept in England and Wales, the keeper of that register; and
(e) if the interest charged is in funds in court, the Accountant General at the Court Funds Office.

(2) If the judgment creditor serves the order, he must either—
(a) file a certificate of service not less than 2 days before the hearing; or
(b) produce a certificate of service at the hearing.

## 73.6 Effect of Interim Order in Relation to Securities

(1) If a judgment debtor disposes of his interest in any securities, while they are subject to an interim charging order which has been served on him, that disposition shall not, so long as that order remains in force, be valid as against the judgment creditor.

(2) A person served under rule 73.5(1)(d) with an interim charging order relating to securities must not, unless the court gives permission—

(a) permit any transfer of any of the securities; or
(b) pay any dividend, interest or redemption payment relating to them.

(3) If a person acts in breach of paragraph (2), he will be liable to pay to the judgment creditor—
(a) the value of the securities transferred or the amount of the payment made (as the case may be); or
(b) if less, the amount necessary to satisfy the debt in relation to which the interim charging order was made.

### 73.7 Effect of Interim Order in Relation to Funds in Court

If a judgment debtor disposes of his interest in funds in court while they are subject to an interim charging order which has been served on him and on the Accountant General in accordance with rule 73.5(1), that disposition shall not, so long as that order remains in force, be valid as against the judgment creditor.

### 73.8 Further Consideration of the Application

(1) If any person objects to the court making a final charging order, he must—
(a) file; and
(b) serve on the applicant;
written evidence stating the grounds of his objections, not less than 7 days before the hearing.

(2) At the hearing the court may—
(a) make a final charging order confirming that the charge imposed by the interim charging order shall continue, with or without modification;
(b) discharge the interim charging order and dismiss the application;
(c) decide any issues in dispute between the parties, or between any of the parties and any other person who objects to the court making a final charging order; or
(d) direct a trial of any such issues, and if necessary give directions.

(3) If the court makes a final charging order which charges securities other than securities held in court, the order will include a stop notice unless the court otherwise orders.

(Section III of this Part contains provisions about stop notices.)

(4) Any order made at the hearing must be served on all the persons on whom the interim charging order was required to be served.

### 73.9 Discharge or Variation of Order

(1) Any application to discharge or vary a charging order must be made to the court which made the charging order.

(Section 3(5) of the 1979 Act and regulation 51(4) of the 1992 Regulations provide that the court may at any time, on the application of the debtor, or of any person interested in any property to which the order relates, or (where the 1992 Regulations apply) of the authority, make an order discharging or varying the charging order.)

(2) The court may direct that—
(a) any interested person should be joined as a party to such an application; or
(b) the application should be served on any such person.

(3) An order discharging or varying a charging order must be served on all the persons on whom the charging order was required to be served.

### 73.10 Enforcement of Charging Order by Sale

(1) Subject to the provisions of any enactment, the court may, upon a claim by a person who has obtained a charging order over an interest in property, order the sale of the property to enforce the charging order.

(2) A claim for an order for sale under this rule should be made to the court which made the charging order, unless that court does not have jurisdiction to make an order for sale.

(A claim under this rule is a proceeding for the enforcement of a charge, and section 23(c) of

the County Courts Act 1984 provides the extent of the county court's jurisdiction to hear and determine such proceedings.)
(3) The claimant must use the Part 8 procedure.
(4) A copy of the charging order must be filed with the claim form.
(5) The claimant's written evidence must include the information required by the relevant practice direction.

## SECTION II — STOP ORDERS

### 73.11 Interpretation

In this Section, 'stop order' means an order of the High Court not to take, in relation to funds in court or securities specified in the order, any of the steps listed in section 5(5) of the 1979 Act.

### 73.12 Application for Stop Order

(1) The High Court may make—
  (a) a stop order relating to funds in court, on the application of any person—
    (i) who has a mortgage or charge on the interest of any person in the funds; or
    (ii) to whom that interest has been assigned; or
    (iii) who is a judgment creditor of the person entitled to that interest; or
  (b) a stop order relating to securities other than securities held in court, on the application of any person claiming to be beneficially entitled to an interest in the securities.
(2) An application for a stop order must be made—
  (a) by application notice in existing proceedings; or
  (b) by Part 8 claim form if there are no existing proceedings in the High Court.
(3) The application notice or claim form must be served on—
  (a) every person whose interest may be affected by the order applied for; and
  (b) either—
    (i) the Accountant General at the Court Funds Office, if the application relates to funds in court; or
    (ii) the person specified in rule 73.5(1)(d), if the application relates to securities other than securities held in court.

### 73.13 Stop Order Relating to Funds in Court

A stop order relating to funds in court shall prohibit the transfer, sale, delivery out, payment or other dealing with—
(a) the funds or any part of them; or
(b) any income on the funds.

### 73.14 Stop Order Relating to Securities

(1) A stop order relating to securities other than securities held in court may prohibit all or any of the following steps—
  (a) the registration of any transfer of the securities;
  (b) the making of any payment by way of dividend, interest or otherwise in respect of the securities; and
  (c) in the case of units of a unit trust, any acquisition of or other dealing with the units by any person or body exercising functions under the trust.
(2) The order shall specify—
  (a) the securities to which it relates;
  (b) the name in which the securities stand;
  (c) the steps which may not be taken; and
  (d) whether the prohibition applies to the securities only or to the dividends or interest as well.

### 73.15 Variation or Discharge of Order

(1) The court may, on the application of any person claiming to have a beneficial interest in the funds or securities to which a stop order relates, make an order discharging or varying the order.

(2) An application notice seeking the variation or discharge of a stop order must be served on the person who obtained the order.

## SECTION III — STOP NOTICES

### 73.16 General

In this Section—

(a) 'stop notice' means a notice issued by the court which requires a person or body not to take, in relation to securities specified in the notice, any of the steps listed in section 5(5) of the 1979 Act, without first giving notice to the person who obtained the notice; and

(b) 'securities' does not include securities held in court.

### 73.17 Request for Stop Notice

(1) The High Court may, on the request of any person claiming to be beneficially entitled to an interest in securities, issue a stop notice.

(A stop notice may also be included in a final charging order, by either the High Court or a county court, under rule 73.8(3).)

(2) A request for a stop notice must be made by filing—
   (a) a draft stop notice; and
   (b) written evidence which—
      (i) identifies the securities in question;
      (ii) describes the applicant's interest in the securities; and
      (iii) gives an address for service for the applicant.

(A sample form of stop notice is annexed to the relevant practice direction.)

(3) If a court officer considers that the request complies with paragraph (2), he will issue a stop notice.

(4) The applicant must serve copies of the stop notice and his written evidence on the person to whom the stop notice is addressed.

### 73.18 Effect of Stop Notice

(1) A stop notice—
   (a) takes effect when it is served in accordance with rule 73.17(4); and
   (b) remains in force unless it is withdrawn or discharged in accordance with rule 73.20 or 73.21.

(2) While a stop notice is in force, the person on whom it is served—
   (a) must not—
      (i) register a transfer of the securities described in the notice; or
      (ii) take any other step restrained by the notice,
   without first giving 14 days' notice to the person who obtained the stop notice; but
   (b) must not, by reason only of the notice, refuse to register a transfer or to take any other step, after he has given 14 days' notice under paragraph (2)(a) and that period has expired.

### 73.19 Amendment of Stop Notice

(1) If any securities are incorrectly described in a stop notice which has been obtained and served in accordance with rule 73.17, the applicant may request an amended stop notice in accordance with that rule.

(2) The amended stop notice takes effect when it is served.

## 73.20 Withdrawal of Stop Notice

(1) A person who has obtained a stop notice may withdraw it by serving a request for its withdrawal on—
  (a) the person or body on whom the stop notice was served; and
  (b) the court which issued the stop notice.

(2) The request must be signed by the person who obtained the stop notice, and his signature must be witnessed by a practising solicitor.

## 73.21 Discharge or Variation of Stop Notice

(1) The court may, on the application of any person claiming to be beneficially entitled to an interest in the securities to which a stop notice relates, make an order discharging or varying the notice.

(2) An application to discharge or vary a stop notice must be made to the court which issued the notice.

(3) The application notice must be served on the person who obtained the stop notice.

## 73.22 Rule 73.22

The practice direction supplementing this Part makes provision for the procedure to be followed when applying for an order under section 23 of the Partnership Act 1890.

# PD 73 Practice Direction — Charging Orders, Stop Orders and Stop Notices

This practice direction supplements CPR Part 73.

## SECTION I — CHARGING ORDERS

### Application Notice—Rule 73.3

1.1 An application for a charging order must be made by filing an application notice in form N379 if the application relates to land, or N380 if the application relates to securities.

1.2 The application notice must contain the following information:
(1) the name and address of the judgment debtor;
(2) details of the judgment or order sought to be enforced;
(3) the amount of money remaining due under the judgment or order;
(4) if the judgment debt is payable by instalments, the amount of any instalments which have fallen due and remain unpaid;
(5) if the judgment creditor knows of the existence of any other creditors of the judgment debtor, their names and (if known) their addresses;
(6) identification of the asset or assets which it is intended to charge;
(7) details of the judgment debtor's interest in the asset; and
(8) the names and addresses of the persons on whom an interim charging order must be served under r. 73.5(1).

1.3 A judgment creditor may apply in a single application notice for charging orders over more than one asset, but if the court makes interim charging orders over more than one asset, it will draw up a separate order relating to each asset.

### High Court and County Court Jurisdiction

2 The jurisdiction of the High Court and the county court to make charging orders is set out in the Charging Orders Act 1979, s. 1(2).

### Transfer

3 The court may, on an application by a judgment debtor who wishes to oppose an application for a charging order, transfer it to the court for the district where the judgment debtor resides or carries on business, or to another court.

### Enforcement of Charging Orders by Sale—Rule 73.10

4.1 A county court has jurisdiction to determine a claim under r. 73.10 for the enforcement of a charging order if the amount owing under the charge does not exceed the county court limit.

4.2 A claim in the High Court for an order for sale of land to enforce a charging order must be started in Chancery Chambers at the Royal Courts of Justice, or a Chancery district registry.

(There are Chancery district registries at Birmingham, Bristol, Cardiff, Leeds, Liverpool, Manchester, Newcastle upon Tyne and Preston.)

4.3 The written evidence in support of a claim under r. 73.10 must:
(1) identify the charging order and the property sought to be sold;
(2) state the amount in respect of which the charge was imposed and the amount due at the date of issue of the claim;
(3) verify, so far as known, the debtor's title to the property charged;
(4) state, so far as the claimant is able to identify:

(a) the names and addresses of any other creditors who have a prior charge or other security over the property; and
(b) the amount owed to each such creditor; and
(5) give an estimate of the price which would be obtained on sale of the property;
(6) if the claim relates to land, give details of every person who to the best of the claimant's knowledge is in possession of the property; and
(7) if the claim relates to residential property:
(a) state whether:
(i) a land charge of Class F; or
(ii) a notice under the Family Law Act 1996, s. 31(10), or under any provision of an Act which preceded that section,
has been registered; and
(b) if so, state:
(i) on whose behalf the land charge or notice has been registered; and
(ii) that the claimant will serve notice of the claim on that person.

4.4 The claimant must take all reasonable steps to obtain the information required by para. 4.3(4) before issuing the claim.

4.5 Sample forms of orders for sale are set out in Appendix A to this practice direction for guidance. These are not prescribed forms of order and they may be adapted or varied by the court to meet the requirements of individual cases.

4A.1 A charging order or interim charging order may be made against any property, within the jurisdiction, belonging to a judgment debtor that is a partnership.

4A.2 For the purposes of rule 73.5(1)(a) (service of the interim order), the specified documents must be served on—
(1) a member of the partnership within the jurisdiction;
(2) a person authorised by a partner; or
(3) some other person having the control or management of the partnership business.

4A.3 Where an order requires a partnership to appear before the court, it will be sufficient for a partner to appear before the court.

## SECTION II — STOP NOTICES

5 A sample form of stop notice is set out in Appendix B to this practice direction.

[PD 73 has the following appendices:
Appendix A Sample forms of order for sale following a charging order
Appendix B Sample form of stop notice

These appendices are not reproduced in this work but may be accessed via the DCA website at <http://www.dca.gov.uk>.]

## SECTION III — APPLICATIONS FOR ORDERS MADE UNDER SECTION 23 OF THE PARTNERSHIP ACT 1890

6.1 This paragraph relates to orders made under section 23 of the Partnership Act 1890 ('Section 23').

6.2 The following applications must be made in accordance with Part 23—
(1) an application for an order under Section 23 of the 1890 Act made by a judgment creditor of a partner;
(2) an application for any order by a partner of the judgment debtor in consequence of any application made by the judgment creditor under Section 23.

6.3 The powers conferred on a judge by Section 23 may be exercised by—
(1) a Master;
(2) the Admiralty Registrar; or
(3) a district judge.

6.4 Every application notice filed under this paragraph by a judgment creditor, and every order made following such an application, must be served on the judgment debtor and on any of the other partners that are within the jurisdiction.

6.5 Every application notice filed under this paragraph by a partner of a judgment debtor, and every order made following such an application, must be served—

(1) on the judgment creditor and the judgment debtor; and

(2) on the other partners of the judgment debtor who are not joined in the application and who are within the jurisdiction.

6.6 An application notice or order served under this paragraph on one or more, but not all, of the partners of a partnership shall be deemed to have been served on all the partners of that partnership.

# CPR Part 74 Enforcement of Judgments in Different Jurisdictions



## 74.1 Scope of this Part and Interpretation

(1) Section I of this Part applies to the enforcement in England and Wales of judgments of foreign courts.

(2) Section II applies to the enforcement in foreign countries of judgments of the High Court and of county courts.

(3) Section III applies to the enforcement of United Kingdom judgments in other parts of the United Kingdom.

(4) Section IV applies to the enforcement in England and Wales of European Community judgments and Euratom inspection orders.

(4A) Section V applies to—

(a) the certification of judgments and court settlements in England and Wales as European Enforcement Orders; and

(b) the enforcement in England and Wales of judgments, court settlements and authentic instruments certified as European Enforcement Orders by other Member States.

(5) In this Part:

(a) 'the 1920 Act' means the Administration of Justice Act 1920;

(b) 'the 1933 Act' means the Foreign Judgments (Reciprocal Enforcement) Act 1933;
(c) 'the 1982 Act' means the Civil Jurisdiction and Judgments Act 1982;
(d) 'the Judgments Regulation' means Council Regulation (EC) No. 44/2001 of 22nd December 2000 on jurisdiction and the recognition and enforcement of judgments in civil and commercial matters;
(e) 'the EEO Regulation' means Council Regulation (EC) No 805/2004 creating a European Enforcement Order for uncontested claims.

(A copy of the EEO Regulation is annexed to practice direction 74B European Enforcement Orders and can be found at <http://europa.eu.int/eur-lex/pri/en/oj/dat/2004/l_143/l_14320040430en00150039.pdf>)

## I ENFORCEMENT IN ENGLAND AND WALES OF JUDGMENTS OF FOREIGN COURTS

### 74.2 Interpretation

(1) In this Section:
(a) 'Contracting State' has the meaning given in section 1(3) of the 1982 Act;
(b) 'Regulation State' has the same meaning as 'Member State' in the Judgments Regulation, that is all Member States except Denmark;
(c) 'judgment' means, subject to any other enactment, any judgment given by a foreign court or tribunal, whatever the judgment may be called, and includes—
(i) a decree;
(ii) an order;
(iii) a decision;
(iv) a writ of execution; and
(v) the determination of costs by an officer of the court;
(d) 'State of origin', in relation to any judgment, means the State in which that judgment was given.

(2) For the purposes of this Section, 'domicile' is to be determined—
(a) in an application under the 1982 Act, in accordance with sections 41 to 46 that Act;
(b) in an application under the Judgments Regulation, in accordance with paragraphs 9 to 12 of Schedule 1 to the Civil Jurisdiction and Judgments Order 2001.

### 74.3 Applications for Registration

(1) This Section provides rules about applications under—
(a) section 9 of the 1920 Act, in respect of judgments to which Part II of that Act applies;
(b) section 2 of the 1933 Act, in respect of judgments to which Part I of that Act applies;
(c) section 4 of the 1982 Act; and
(d) the Judgments Regulation,
for the registration of foreign judgments for enforcement in England and Wales.

(2) Applications—
(a) must be made to the High Court; and
(b) may be made without notice.

### 74.4 Evidence in Support

(1) An application for registration of a judgment under the 1920, 1933 or 1982 Act must be supported by written evidence exhibiting—
(a) the judgment or a verified or certified or otherwise authenticated copy of it; and
(b) where the judgment is not in English, a translation of it into English—
(i) certified by a notary public or other qualified person; or
(ii) accompanied by written evidence confirming that the translation is accurate.

(2) The written evidence in support of the application must state—
  (a) the name of the judgment creditor and his address for service within the jurisdiction;
  (b) the name of the judgment debtor and his address or place of business, if known;
  (c) the grounds on which the judgment creditor is entitled to enforce the judgment;
  (d) in the case of a money judgment, the amount in respect of which it remains unsatisfied; and
  (e) where interest is recoverable on the judgment under the law of the State of origin—
    (i) the amount of interest which has accrued up to the date of the application, or
    (ii) the rate of interest, the date from which it is recoverable, and the date on which it ceases to accrue.

(3) Written evidence in support of an application under the 1920 Act must also state that the judgment is not a judgment—
  (a) which under section 9 of that Act may not be ordered to be registered; or
  (b) to which section 5 of the Protection of Trading Interests Act 1980 applies.

(4) Written evidence in support of an application under the 1933 Act must also—
  (a) state that the judgment is a money judgment;
  (b) confirm that it can be enforced by execution in the State of origin;
  (c) confirm that the registration could not be set aside under section 4 of that Act;
  (d) confirm that the judgment is not a judgment to which section 5 of the Protection of Trading Interests Act 1980 applies;
  (e) where the judgment contains different provisions, some but not all of which can be registered for enforcement, set out those provisions in respect of which it is sought to register the judgment; and
  (f) be accompanied by any further evidence as to—
    (i) the enforceability of the judgment in the State of origin, and
    (ii) the law of that State under which any interest has become due under the judgment,

  which may be required under the relevant Order in Council extending Part I of the 1933 Act to that State.

(5) Written evidence in support of an application under the 1982 Act must also exhibit—
  (a) documents which show that, under the law of the State of origin, the judgment is enforceable on the judgment debtor and has been served;
  (b) in the case of a judgment in default, a document which establishes that the party in default was served with the document instituting the proceedings or with an equivalent document; and
  (c) where appropriate, a document showing that the judgment creditor is in receipt of legal aid in the State of origin.

(6) An application for registration under the Judgments Regulation must, in addition to the evidence required by that Regulation, be supported by the evidence required by paragraphs (1)(b) and (2)(e) of this rule.

## 74.5 Security for Costs

(1) Subject to paragraphs (2) and (3), section II of Part 25 applies to an application for security for the costs of—
  (a) the application for registration;
  (b) any proceedings brought to set aside the registration; and
  (c) any appeal against the granting of the registration,

as if the judgment creditor were a claimant.

(2) A judgment creditor making an application under the 1982 Act or the Judgments Regulation may not be required to give security solely on the ground that he is resident out of the jurisdiction.

(3) Paragraph (1) does not apply to an application under the 1933 Act where the relevant Order in Council otherwise provides.

### 74.6 Registration Orders

(1) An order granting permission to register a judgment ('registration order') must be drawn up by the judgment creditor and served on the judgment debtor—
  (a) by delivering it to him personally;
  (b) as provided by section 725 of the Companies Act 1985; or
  (c) in such other manner as the court may direct.

(2) Permission is not required to serve a registration order out of the jurisdiction, and rules 6.24, 6.25, 6.26 and 6.29 apply to such an order as they apply to a claim form.

(3) A registration order must state—
  (a) full particulars of the judgment registered;
  (b) the name of the judgment creditor and his address for service within the jurisdiction;
  (c) the right of the judgment debtor—
    (i) in the case of registration following an application under the 1920 or the 1933 Act, to apply to have the registration set aside;
    (ii) in the case of registration following an application under the 1982 Act or under the Judgments Regulation, to appeal against the registration order;
  (d) the period within which such an application or appeal may be made; and
  (e) that no measures of enforcement will be taken before the end of that period, other than measures ordered by the court to preserve the property of the judgment debtor.

### 74.7 Applications to Set Aside Registration

(1) An application to set aside registration under the 1920 or the 1933 Act must be made within the period set out in the registration order.

(2) The court may extend that period; but an application for such an extension must be made before the end of the period as originally fixed or as subsequently extended.

(3) The court hearing the application may order any issue between the judgment creditor and the judgment debtor to be tried.

### 74.8 Appeals

(1) An appeal against the granting or the refusal of registration under the 1982 Act or the Judgments Regulation must be made in accordance with Part 52, subject to the following provisions of this rule.

(2) Permission is not required—
  (a) to appeal; or
  (b) to put in evidence.

(3) If—
  (a) the judgment debtor is not domiciled within a Contracting State or a Regulation State, as the case may be, and
  (b) an application to extend the time for appealing is made within two months of service of the registration order,

  the court may extend the period for filing an appellant's notice against the order granting registration, but not on grounds of distance.

(4) The appellant's notice must be served—
  (a) where the appeal is against the granting of registration, within—
    (i) one month; or
    (ii) where service is to be effected on a party not domiciled within the jurisdiction, two months, of service of the registration order;
  (b) where the appeal is against the refusal of registration, within one month of the decision on the application for registration.

### 74.9 Enforcement

(1) No steps may be taken to enforce a judgment—

(a) before the end of the period specified in accordance with rule 74.6(3)(d), or that period as extended by the court; or
(b) where there is an application under rule 74.7 or an appeal under rule 74.8, until the application or appeal has been determined.

(2) Any party wishing to enforce a judgment must file evidence of the service on the judgment debtor of—
(a) the registration order; and
(b) any other relevant order of the court.

(3) Nothing in this rule prevents the court from making orders to preserve the property of the judgment debtor pending final determination of any issue relating to the enforcement of the judgment.

## 74.10 Recognition

(1) Registration of a judgment serves as a decision that the judgment is recognised for the purposes of the 1982 Act and the Judgments Regulation.

(2) An application for recognition of a judgment is governed by the same rules as an application for registration of a judgment under the 1982 Act or under the Judgments Regulation, except that rule 74.4(5)(a) and (c) does not apply.

## 74.11 Authentic Instruments and Court Settlements

The rules governing the registration of judgments under the 1982 Act or under the Judgments Regulation apply as appropriate and with any necessary modifications for the enforcement of—
(a) authentic instruments which are subject to—
(i) article 50 of Schedule 1 to the 1982 Act;
(ii) article 50 of Schedule 3C to the 1982 Act; and
(iii) article 57 of the Judgments Regulation; and
(b) court settlements which are subject to—
(i) article 51 of Schedule 1 to the 1982 Act;
(ii) article 51 of Schedule 3C to the 1982 Act; and
(iii) article 58 of the Judgments Regulation.

# II ENFORCEMENT IN FOREIGN COUNTRIES OF JUDGMENTS OF THE HIGH COURT AND COUNTY COURTS

## 74.12 Application for a Certified Copy of a Judgment

(1) This Section applies to applications—
(a) to the High Court under section 10 of the 1920 Act;
(b) to the High Court or to a county court under section 10 of the 1933 Act;
(c) to the High Court or to a county court under section 12 of the 1982 Act; or
(d) to the High Court or to a county court under article 54 of the Judgments Regulation.

(2) A judgment creditor who wishes to enforce in a foreign country a judgment obtained in the High Court or in a county court must apply for a certified copy of the judgment.

(3) The application may be made without notice.

## 74.13 Evidence in Support

(1) The application must be supported by written evidence exhibiting copies of—
(a) the claim form in the proceedings in which judgment was given;
(b) evidence that it was served on the defendant;
(c) the statements of case; and
(d) where relevant, a document showing that for those proceedings the applicant was an assisted person or an LSC funded client, as defined in rule 43.2(1)(h) and (i).

(2) The written evidence must—

(a) identify the grounds on which the judgment was obtained;
(b) state whether the defendant objected to the jurisdiction and, if he did, the grounds of his objection;
(c) show that the judgment—
 (i) has been served in accordance with Part 6 and rule 40.4, and
 (ii) is not subject to a stay of execution;
(d) state—
 (i) the date on which the time for appealing expired or will expire;
 (ii) whether an appeal notice has been filed;
 (iii) the status of any application for permission to appeal; and
 (iv) whether an appeal is pending;
(e) state whether the judgment provides for the payment of a sum of money, and if so, the amount in respect of which it remains unsatisfied;
(f) state whether interest is recoverable on the judgment, and if so, either—
 (i) the amount of interest which has accrued up to the date of the application, or
 (ii) the rate of interest, the date from which it is recoverable, and the date on which it ceases to accrue.

## III ENFORCEMENT OF UNITED KINGDOM JUDGMENTS IN OTHER PARTS OF THE UNITED KINGDOM

### 74.14 Interpretation

In this Section—
(a) 'money provision' means a provision for the payment of one or more sums of money in a judgment whose enforcement is governed by section 18 of, and Schedule 6 to, the 1982 Act; and
(b) 'non-money provision' means a provision for any relief or remedy not requiring payment of a sum of money in a judgment whose enforcement is governed by section 18 of, and Schedule 7 to, the 1982 Act.

### 74.15 Registration of Money Judgments in the High Court

(1) This rule applies to applications to the High Court under paragraph 5 of Schedule 6 to the 1982 Act for the registration of a certificate for the enforcement of the money provisions of a judgment—
 (a) which has been given by a court in another part of the United Kingdom, and
 (b) to which section 18 of that Act applies.
(2) The certificate must within six months of the date of its issue be filed in the Central Office of the Supreme Court, together with a copy certified by written evidence to be a true copy.

### 74.16 Registration of Non-money Judgments in the High Court

(1) This rule applies to applications to the High Court under paragraph 5 of Schedule 7 to the 1982 Act for the registration for enforcement of the non-money provisions of a judgment—
 (a) which has been given by a court in another part of the United Kingdom, and
 (b) to which section 18 of that Act applies.
(2) An application under paragraph (1) may be made without notice.
(3) An application under paragraph (1) must be accompanied—
 (a) by a certified copy of the judgment issued under Schedule 7 to the 1982 Act; and
 (b) by a certificate, issued not more than six months before the date of the application, stating that the conditions set out in paragraph 3 of Schedule 7 are satisfied in relation to the judgment.
(4) Rule 74.6 applies to judgments registered under Schedule 7 to the 1982 Act as it applies to judgments registered under section 4 of that Act.

(5) Rule 74.7 applies to applications to set aside the registration of a judgment under paragraph 9 of Schedule 7 to the 1982 Act as it applies to applications to set aside registrations under the 1920 and 1933 Acts.

### 74.17 Certificates of High Court and County Court Money Judgments

(1) This rule applies to applications under paragraph 2 of Schedule 6 to the 1982 Act for a certificate to enable the money provisions of a judgment of the High Court or of a county court to be enforced in another part of the United Kingdom.
(2) The judgment creditor may apply for a certificate by filing at the court where the judgment was given or has been entered written evidence stating—
   (a) the name and address of the judgment creditor and, if known, of the judgment debtor;
   (b) the sums payable and unsatisfied under the money provisions of the judgment;
   (c) where interest is recoverable on the judgment, either—
      (i) the amount of interest which has accrued up to the date of the application, or
      (ii) the rate of interest, the date from which it is recoverable, and the date on which it ceases to accrue;
   (d) that the judgment is not stayed;
   (e) the date on which the time for appealing expired or will expire;
   (f) whether an appeal notice has been filed;
   (g) the status of any application for permission to appeal; and
   (h) whether an appeal is pending.

### 74.18 Certified Copies of High Court and County Court Non-money Judgments

(1) This rule applies to applications under paragraph 2 of Schedule 7 to the 1982 Act for a certified copy of a judgment of the High Court or of a county court to which section 18 of the Act applies and which contains non-money provisions for enforcement in another part of the United Kingdom.
(2) An application under paragraph (1) may be made without notice.
(3) The applicant may apply for a certified copy of a judgment by filing at the court where the judgment was given or has been entered written evidence stating—
   (a) full particulars of the judgment;
   (b) the name and address of the judgment creditor and, if known, of the judgment debtor;
   (c) that the judgment is not stayed;
   (d) the date on which the time for appealing expired or will expire;
   (e) whether an appeal notice has been filed;
   (f) the status of any application for permission to appeal; and
   (g) whether an appeal is pending.

## IV ENFORCEMENT IN ENGLAND AND WALES OF EUROPEAN COMMUNITY JUDGMENTS

### 74.19 Interpretation

In this Section—
(a) 'Community judgment' means any judgment, decision or order which is enforceable under—
   (i) article 244 or 256 of the Treaty establishing the European Community;
   (ii) article 18, 159 or 164 of the Euratom Treaty;
   (iii) article 44 or 92 of the ECSC Treaty;
   (iv) article 82 of Council Regulation (EC) 40/94 of 20 December 1993 on the Community trade mark; or
   (v) article 71 of Council Regulation (EC) 6/2002 of 12 December 2001 on Community designs;

(b) 'Euratom inspection order' means an order made by the President of the European Court, or a decision of the Commission of the European Communities, under article 81 of the Euratom Treaty;
(c) 'European Court' means the Court of Justice of the European Communities;
(d) 'order for enforcement' means an order under the authority of the Secretary of State that the Community judgment to which it is appended is to be registered for enforcement in the United Kingdom.

### 74.20 Application for Registration of a Community Judgment

An application to the High Court for the registration of a Community judgment may be made without notice.

### 74.21 Evidence in Support

(1) An application for registration must be supported by written evidence exhibiting—
   (a) the Community judgment and the order for its enforcement, or an authenticated copy; and
   (b) where the judgment is not in English, a translation of it into English—
      (i) certified by a notary public or other qualified person; or
      (ii) accompanied by written evidence confirming that the translation is accurate.
(2) Where the application is for registration of a Community judgment which is a money judgment, the evidence must state—
   (a) the name of the judgment creditor and his address for service within the jurisdiction;
   (b) the name of the judgment debtor and his address or place of business, if known;
   (c) the amount in respect of which the judgment is unsatisfied; and
   (d) that the European Court has not suspended enforcement of the judgment.

### 74.22 Registration Orders

(1) A copy of the order granting permission to register a Community judgment ('the registration order') must be served on every person against whom the judgment was given.
(2) The registration order must state the name and address for service of the person who applied for registration, and must exhibit—
   (a) a copy of the registered Community judgment; and
   (b) a copy of the order for its enforcement.
(3) In the case of a Community judgment which is a money judgment, the registration order must also state the right of the judgment debtor to apply within 28 days for the variation or cancellation of the registration under rule 74.23.

### 74.23 Application to Vary or Cancel Registration

(1) An application to vary or cancel the registration of a Community judgment which is a money judgment on the ground that at the date of registration the judgment had been partly or wholly satisfied must be made within 28 days of the date on which the registration order was served on the judgment debtor.
(2) The application must be supported by written evidence.

### 74.24 Enforcement

No steps may be taken to enforce a Community judgment which is a money judgment—
(a) before the end of the period specified in accordance with rule 74.23(1); or
(b) where an application is made under that rule, until it has been determined.

### 74.25 Application for Registration of Suspension Order

(1) Where the European Court has made an order that the enforcement of a registered Community judgment should be suspended, an application for the registration of that

order in the High Court is made by filing a copy of the order in the Central Office of the Supreme Court.

(2) The application may be made without notice.

### 74.26 Registration and Enforcement of a Euratom Inspection Order

(1) Rules 74.20, 74.21(1), and 74.22(1) and (2), which apply to the registration of a Community judgment, also apply to the registration of a Euratom inspection order but with the necessary modifications.

(2) An application under article 6 of the European Communities (Enforcement of Community Judgments) Order 1972 to give effect to a Euratom inspection order may be made on written evidence, and—

(a) where the matter is urgent, without notice;

(b) otherwise, by claim form.

## V EUROPEAN ENFORCEMENT ORDERS

### 74.27 Interpretation

(1) In this Section—

(a) 'European Enforcement Order' has the meaning given in the EEO Regulation;

(b) 'EEO' means European Enforcement Order;

(c) 'judgment', 'authentic instrument', 'member state of origin', 'member state of enforcement', and 'court of origin' have the meanings given by Article 4 of the EEO Regulation; and

(d) 'Regulation State' has the same meaning as 'Member State' in the EEO Regulation, that is all Member States except Denmark.

### 74.28 Certification of Judgments of the Courts of England and Wales

An application for an EEO certificate must be made by filing the relevant practice form in accordance with article 6 of the EEO Regulation.

### 74.29 Applications for a Certificate of Lack or Limitation of Enforceability

An application under article 6(2) of the EEO Regulation for a certificate indicating the lack or limitation of enforceability of an EEO certificate must be made to the court of origin by application in accordance with Part 23.

### 74.30 Applications for Rectification or Withdrawal

An application under article 10 of the EEO Regulation for rectification or withdrawal of an EEO certificate must be made to the court of origin and may be made by application in accordance with Part 23.

### 74.31 Enforcement of European Enforcement Orders in England and Wales

(1) A person seeking to enforce an EEO in England and Wales must lodge at the court in which enforcement proceedings are to be brought the documents required by article 20 of the EEO Regulation.

(2) Where a person applies—

(a) to the High Court for a charging order, a writ of fieri facias or an attachment of earnings order; or

(b) to the county court for a warrant of execution or an attachment of earnings order,

to enforce an EEO expressed in a foreign currency, the application must contain a certificate of the sterling equivalent of the judgment sum at the close of business on the date nearest preceding the date of issue of the application.

(Section 1 of the Charging Orders Act 1979 provides that the High Court only has jurisdiction to make a charging order where the amount of the original judgment exceeds the county court limit.)

(Article 8 of the High Court and County Courts Jurisdiction Order 1991 provides that (1) judgments in excess of £5,000 shall only be enforced by execution against goods in the High Court; (2) those in excess of £600 may be enforced in the High Court, and (3) those for less than £600 shall only be enforced in the county court.)

## 74.32 Refusal of Enforcement

(1) An application under article 21 of the EEO Regulation that the court should refuse to enforce an EEO must be made by application in accordance with Part 23 to the court in which the EEO is being enforced.

(2) The judgment debtor must, as soon as practicable, serve copies of any order made under article 21(1) on—
  (a) all other parties to the proceedings and any other person affected by the order; and
  (b) any court in which enforcement proceedings are pending in England and Wales.

(3) Upon service of the order on those persons all enforcement proceedings in England and Wales under the EEO, in respect of those persons upon whom, and those courts at which, the order has been served in accordance with paragraph (2), will cease.

## 74.33 Stay or Limitation of Enforcement

(1) Where an EEO certificate has been lodged and the judgment debtor applies to stay or limit the enforcement proceedings under article 23 of the EEO Regulation, such application must be made by application in accordance with Part 23 to the court in which the EEO is being enforced.

(2) The judgment debtor shall, as soon as practicable, serve a copy of any order made under the article on—
  (a) all other parties to the proceedings and any other person affected by the order; and
  (b) any court in which enforcement proceedings are pending in England and Wales

  and the order will not have effect on any person until it has been served in accordance with this rule and they have received it.

# PD 74 Practice Direction — Enforcement of Judgments in Different Jurisdictions

This practice direction supplements CPR Part 74.

1 This practice direction is divided into two sections:
  (1) Section I—Provisions about the enforcement of judgments
  (2) Section I I—The Merchant Shipping (Liner Conferences) Act 1982

## SECTION I ENFORCEMENT OF JUDGMENTS

### Meaning of 'Judgment'

2 In r. 74.2(1)(c), the definition of 'judgment' is 'subject to any other enactment'. Such provisions include:
  (1) s. 9(1) of the 1920 Act, which limits enforcement under that Act to judgments of superior courts;
  (2) s. 1(1) of the 1933 Act, which limits enforcement under that Act to judgments of those courts specified in the relevant Order in Council;
  (3) s. 1(2) of the 1933 Act, which limits enforcement under that Act to money judgments.

### Registers

3 There will be kept in the Central Office of the Supreme Court at the Royal Courts of Justice, under the direction of the Senior Master:
  (1) registers of foreign judgments ordered by the High Court to be enforced following applications under:
    (a) s. 9 of the 1920 Act;
    (b) s. 2 of the 1933 Act;
    (c) s. 4 of the 1982 Act; or
    (d) the Judgments Regulation;
  (2) registers of certificates issued for the enforcement in foreign countries of High Court judgments under the 1920, 1933 and 1982 Acts, and under art. 54 of the Judgments Regulation;
  (3) a register of certificates filed in the Central Office of the High Court under r. 74.15(2) for the enforcement of money judgments given by the courts of Scotland or Northern Ireland;
  (4) a register of certificates issued under r. 74.16(3) for the enforcement of non-money judgments given by the courts of Scotland or Northern Ireland;
  (5) registers of certificates issued under rr. 74.17 and 74.18 for the enforcement of High Court judgments in Scotland or Northern Ireland under sch. 6 or sch. 7 to the 1982 Act; and
  (6) a register of Community judgments and Euratom inspection orders ordered to be registered under art. 3 of the European Communities (Enforcement of Community Judgments) Order 1972 (SI 1972/1590).

### Making an Application

4.1 Applications for the registration for enforcement in England and Wales of:
  (1) foreign judgments under r. 74.3;
  (2) judgments of courts in Scotland or Northern Ireland under r. 74.15 or 74.16; and
  (3) European Community judgments under r. 74.20,

are assigned to the Queen's Bench Division and may be heard by a master.

4.2 An application under r. 74.12 for a certified copy of a High Court or county court judgment for enforcement abroad must be made:
(1) in the case of a judgment given in the Chancery Division or the Queen's Bench Division of the High Court, to a master or district judge;
(2) in the case of a judgment given in the Family Division of the High Court, to a district judge of that Division;
(3) in the case of a county court judgment, to a district judge.

4.3 An application under r. 74.17 or 74.18 for a certificate or a certified copy of a High Court or county court judgment for enforcement in Scotland or Northern Ireland must be made:
(1) in the case of a judgment given in the Chancery Division or the Queen's Bench Division of the High Court, to a master or district judge;
(2) in the case of a judgment given in the Family Division of the High Court, to a district judge of that Division;
(3) in the case of a county court judgment, to a district judge.

4.4 The following applications must be made under Part 23:
(1) applications under r. 74.3 for the registration of a judgment;
(2) applications under r. 74.7 to set aside the registration of a judgment;
(3) applications under r. 74.12 for a certified copy of a judgment;
(4) applications under section III for a certificate for enforcement of a judgment;
(5) applications under r. 74.20 for the registration of a Community judgment;
(6) applications under r. 74.23 to vary or cancel the registration of a Community judgment; and
(7) applications under r. 74.25 for the registration of an order of the European Court that the enforcement of a registered Community judgment should be suspended.

## Applications Under the 1933 Act

5 Foreign judgments are enforceable in England and Wales under the 1933 Act where there is an agreement on the reciprocal enforcement of judgments between the United Kingdom and the country in which the judgment was given. Such an agreement may contain particular provisions governing the enforcement of judgments (for example limiting the categories of judgments which are enforceable, or the courts whose judgments are enforceable). Any such specific limitations will be listed in the Order in Council giving effect in the United Kingdom to the agreement in question, and the rules in Section I of Part 74 will take effect subject to such limitations.

## Evidence in Support of an Application Under the Judgments Regulation—Rule 74.4(6)

6.1 Where a judgment is to be recognised or enforced in a Regulation State, Council Regulation (EC) No. 44/2001 of 22 December 2000 on jurisdiction and the recognition and enforcement of judgments in civil and commercial matters applies.

6.2 As a consequence of art. 38(2) of the Judgments Regulation, the provisions in Chapter III of that Regulation relating to declaring judgments enforceable are the equivalent, in the United Kingdom, of provisions relating to registering judgments for enforcement.

6.3 Chapter III of, and Annex V to, the Judgments Regulation are annexed to this practice direction. They were originally published in the official languages of the European Community in the *Official Journal of the European Communities* by the Office for Official Publications of the European Communities.

6.4 Sections 2 and 3 of Chapter III of the Judgments Regulation (in particular articles 40, 53, 54 and 55, and Annex V) set out the evidence needed in support of an application.

6.5 The Judgments Regulation is supplemented by the Civil Jurisdiction and Judgments Order 2001 (SI 2001/3929). The Order also makes amendments, in respect of that Regulation, to the Civil Jurisdiction and Judgments Act 1982.

### Certified Copies of Judgments Issued Under Rule 74.12

7.1 In an application by a judgment creditor under r. 74.12 for the enforcement abroad of a High Court judgment, the certified copy of the judgment will be an office copy, and will be accompanied by a certificate signed by a judge. The judgment and certificate will be sealed with the seal of the Supreme Court.

7.2 In an application by a judgment creditor under r. 74.12 for the enforcement abroad of a county court judgment, the certified copy will be a sealed copy, and will be accompanied by a certificate signed by a judge.

7.3 In applications under the 1920, 1933 or 1982 Acts, the certificate will be in form No. 110, and will have annexed to it a copy of the claim form by which the proceedings were begun.

7.4 In an application under the Judgments Regulation, the certificate will be in the form of Annex V to the Regulation.

### Certificates Under Section III of Part 74

8.1 A certificate of a money judgment of a court in Scotland or Northern Ireland must be filed for enforcement under r. 74.15(2) in the Action Department of the Central Office of the Supreme Court, Royal Courts of Justice, Strand, London WC2A 2LL. The copy will be sealed by a court officer before being returned to the applicant.

8.2 A certificate issued under r. 74.17 for the enforcement in Scotland or Northern Ireland of a money judgment of the High Court or of a county court will be in form No. 111.

8.3 In an application by a judgment creditor under r. 74.18 for the enforcement in Scotland or Northern Ireland of a non-money judgment of the High Court or of a county court, the certified copy of the judgment will be a sealed copy to which will be annexed a certificate in form No. 112.

### Material Additional to Section IV of Part 74

9.1 Enforcement of Community judgments and of Euratom inspection orders is governed by the European Communities (Enforcement of Community Judgments) Order 1972 (SI 1972/1590).

9.2 The Treaty establishing the European Community is the Treaty establishing the European Economic Community (Rome, 1957); relevant amendments are made by the Treaty of Amsterdam (1997, Cm 3780).

9.3 The text of the Protocol of 3 June 1971 on the interpretation by the European Court of the Convention of 27 September 1968 on Jurisdiction and the Enforcement of Judgments in Civil and Commercial Matters is set out in the Civil Jurisdiction and Judgments Act 1982, sch. 2.

9.4 The text of the Protocol of 19 December 1988 on the interpretation by the European Court of the Convention of 19 June 1980 on the Law applicable to Contractual Obligations is set out in the Contracts (Applicable Law) Act 1990, sch. 3.

## SECTION II THE MERCHANT SHIPPING (LINER CONFERENCES) ACT 1982

### Content of this Section

10 The Merchant Shipping (Liner Conferences) Act 1982 ('the Act') contains provisions for the settlement of disputes between liner conferences, shipping lines and shippers. This Section of this practice direction deals with the enforcement by the High Court under s. 9 of the Act of recommendations of conciliators, and determinations and awards of costs.

### Exercise of Powers Under the Act

11 The powers of the High Court under the Act are exercised by the Commercial Court.

## Applications for Registration

12.1 An application under s. 9 of the Act for the registration of a recommendation, determination or award is made under Part 23.

12.2 An application for the registration of a recommendation must be supported by written evidence exhibiting:

(1) a verified or certified or otherwise authenticated copy of:
  (a) the recommendation;
  (b) the reasons for it; and
  (c) the record of settlement;

(2) where any of those documents is not in English, a translation of it into English:
  (a) certified by a notary public or other qualified person; or
  (b) accompanied by written evidence confirming that the translation is accurate; and

(3) copies of the acceptance of the recommendation by the parties on whom it is binding, or otherwise verifying the acceptance where it is not in writing.

12.3 The evidence in support of the application must:

(1) give particulars of the failure to implement the recommendation; and
(2) confirm that none of the grounds which would render it unenforceable is applicable.

12.4 An application for the registration of a determination of costs or an award of costs must be supported by written evidence:

(1) exhibiting a verified or certified or otherwise authenticated copy of the recommendation or other document containing the determination or award; and
(2) stating that the costs have not been paid.

## Order for Registration

13.1 The applicant must draw up the order giving permission to register the recommendation, determination or award.

13.2 The order must include a provision that the reasonable costs of the registration should be assessed.

## Register of Recommendations

14 There will be kept in the Admiralty and Commercial Registry at the Royal Courts of Justice, under the direction of the Senior Master, a register of the recommendations, determinations and awards ordered to be registered under s. 9 of the Act, with particulars of enforcement.

## APPENDIX

[The appendix is not reproduced here but may be accessed via the DCA website at <http://www.dca.gov.uk>.]

# PD 74B Practice Direction — European Enforcement Orders

This practice direction supplements section V of Part 74.

## COUNCIL REGULATION

1.1 Certification and enforcement of European Enforcement Orders is governed by Council Regulation (EC) No 805/2004 creating a European Enforcement Order for uncontested claims.

1.2 The EEO Regulation is annexed to this practice direction and can be found at <http://europa.eu.int/eur-lex/pri/en/oj/dat/2004/l_143/l_14320040430en00150039.pdf>. It was originally published in the official languages of the European Community in the *Official Journal of the European Communities* by the Office for Official Publications of the European Communities.

1.3 Section V of Part 74 sets out the procedure for enforcement under the EEO Regulation. A claim that does not meet the requirements of the EEO Regulation, or which the judgment creditor does not wish to enforce using the EEO Regulation, may be enforceable using another method of enforcement.

### Rule 74.28—Certification of Judgments of the Courts of England and Wales

2.1 An application under rule 74.28 for a certificate of a High Court or county court judgment for enforcement in another Regulation State must be made using Form N219 or Form N219A—

(1) in the case of a judgment given in the Chancery or Queen's Bench Division of the High Court, or in a district registry, to a master or district judge; or

(2) in the case of a county court judgment, to a district judge.

2.2 Where the application is granted, the court will send the EEO certificate and a sealed copy of the judgment to the person making the application. Where the court refuses the application, the court will give reasons for the refusal and may give further directions.

### Rule 74.29—Applications for a certificate of lack of enforceability

3.1 An application must be supported by written evidence in support of the grounds on which the judgment has ceased to be enforceable or its enforceability has been suspended or limited.

### Rule 74.30—Application for rectification or withdrawal

4.1 An application must be supported by written evidence in support of the grounds on which it is contended that the EEO should be rectified or withdrawn.

### Rule 74.31—Enforcement of European Enforcement Orders in England and Wales

5.1 When an EEO is lodged at the court in which enforcement proceedings are to be brought, it will be assigned a case number.

5.2 A copy of a document will satisfy the conditions necessary to establish its authenticity if it is an official copy of the courts of the member state of origin.

5.3 The judgment creditor must notify all courts in which enforcement proceedings are pending in England and Wales under the EEO if judgment is set aside in the court of origin, as soon as reasonably practicable after the order is served on the judgment creditor. Notification may be by any means available including fax, e-mail, post or telephone.

## Rule 74.32—Refusal of Enforcement

6.1 An application must be accompanied by an official copy of the earlier judgment, any other documents relied upon and any translations required by the EEO Regulation and supported by written evidence stating—
(1) why the earlier judgment is irreconcilable; and
(2) why the irreconcilability was not, and could not have been, raised as an objection in the proceedings in the court of origin.

## Rule 74.33—Stay or limitation of enforcement

7.1 An application must, unless the court orders otherwise, be accompanied by evidence of the application in the court of origin, including—
(1) the application (or equivalent foreign process) or a copy of the application (or equivalent foreign process) certified by an appropriate officer of the court of origin; and
(2) where that document is not in English, a translation of it into English—
(a) certified by a notary public or person qualified to certify a translation in the member state of the court of origin under Article 20(2)(c) of the EEO Regulation; or
(b) accompanied by written evidence confirming that the translation is accurate.

7.2 The written evidence in support of the application must state—
(1) that an application has been brought in the member state of origin;
(2) the nature of that application, including the grounds on which the application is made and the order sought; and
(3) the date on which the application was filed, the state of the proceedings and the date by which it is believed that the application will be determined.

7.3 If on the application of a debtor under rule 74.32 the court makes a conditional order under article 23(b), the order shall be effective to bar enforcement until the creditor has lodged evidence at court that he has complied with such conditions. In cases other than where the order is conditional upon the creditor making a payment into court, the evidence lodged should be referred to the master or district judge.

# ANNEX

# REGULATION (EC) No 805/2004 OF THE EUROPEAN PARLIAMENT AND OF THE COUNCIL*

## of 21 April 2004

## creating a European Enforcement Order for uncontested claims

THE EUROPEAN PARLIAMENT AND THE COUNCIL
OF THE EUROPEAN UNION,

Having regard to the Treaty establishing the European Community, and in particular Articles 61(c) and the second indent of Article 67(5) thereof,

Having regard to the proposal from the Commission.[1]

Having regard to the Opinion of the European Economic and Social Committee.[2]

* This Regulation is reproduced with the kind permission of Europa and the European Communities from their website. Disclaimer: Only European Community Legislation printed in the paper edition of the Official Journal of the European Union is deemed authentic.

[1] OJ C 203 E, 27.8.2002, p 86.

[2] OJ C 85, 8.4.2003, p 1.

Acting in accordance with the procedure laid down in Article 251 of the Treaty,[3]

Whereas:

(1) The Community has set itself the objective of maintaining and developing an area of freedom, security and justice, in which the free movement of persons is ensured. To this end, the Community is to adopt, inter alia, measures in the field of judicial cooperation in civil matters that are necessary for the proper functioning of the internal market.

(2) On 3 December 1998, the Council adopted an Action Plan of the Council and the Commission on how best to implement the provisions of the Treaty of Amsterdam on an area of freedom, security and justice[4] (the Vienna Action Plan).

(3) The European Council meeting in Tampere on 15 and 16 October 1999 endorsed the principle of mutual recognition of judicial decisions as the cornerstone for the creation of a genuine judicial area.

(4) On 30 November 2000, the Council adopted a programme of measures for implementation of the principle of mutual recognition of decisions in civil and commercial matters.[5] This programme includes in its first stage the abolition of exequatur, that is to say, the creation of a European Enforcement Order for uncontested claims.

(5) The concept of 'uncontested claims' should cover all situations in which a creditor, given the verified absence of any dispute by the debtor as to the nature or extent of a pecuniary claim, has obtained either a court decision against that debtor or an enforceable document that requires the debtor's express consent, be it a court settlement or an authentic instrument.

(6) The absence of objections from the debtor as stipulated in Article 3(1)(b) can take the shape of default of appearance at a court hearing or of failure to comply with an invitation by the court to give written notice of an intention to defend the case.

(7) This Regulation should apply to judgments, court settlements and authentic instruments on uncontested claims and to decisions delivered following challenges to judgments, court settlements and authentic instruments certified as European Enforcement Orders.

(8) In its Tampere conclusions, the European Council considered that access to enforcement in a Member State other than that in which the judgment has been given should be accelerated and simplified by dispensing with any intermediate measures to be taken prior to enforcement in the Member State in which enforcement is sought. A judgment that has been certified as a European Enforcement Order by the court of origin should, for enforcement purposes, be treated as if it had been delivered in the Member State in which enforcement is sought. In the United Kingdom, for example, the registration of a certified foreign judgment will therefore follow the same rules as the registration of a judgment from another part of the United Kingdom and is not to imply a review as to the substance of the foreign judgment. Arrangements for the enforcement of judgments should continue to be governed by national law.

(9) Such a procedure should offer significant advantages as compared with the exequatur procedure provided for in Council Regulation (EC) No 44/2001 of 22 December 2000 on jurisdiction and the recognition and enforcement of judgments in civil and commercial matters,[6] in that there is no need for approval by the judiciary in a second Member State with the delays and expenses that this entails.

---

[3] Opinion of the European Parliament of 8 April 2003 (OJ C 64 E, 12.3.2004, p. 79), Council Common Position of 6.2.2004 (not yet published in the Official Journal) and Position of the European Parliament of 30.3.2004 (not yet published in the Official Journal).

[4] OJ C 19, 23.1.1999, p 1.

[5] OJ C 12, 15.1.2001, p 1.

[6] OJ L 12, 16.1.2001, p 1. Regulation as last amended by Commission Regulation (EC) No 1496/2002 (OJ L 225, 22.8.2002, p 13).

(10) Where a court in a Member State has given judgment on an uncontested claim in the absence of participation of the debtor in the proceedings, the abolition of any checks in the Member State of enforcement is inextricably linked to and dependent upon the existence of a sufficient guarantee of observance of the rights of the defence.

(11) This Regulation seeks to promote the fundamental rights and takes into account the principles recognized in particular by the Charter of Fundamental Rights of the European Union. In particular, it seeks to ensure full respect for the right to a fair trial as recognized in Article 47 of the Charter.

(12) Minimum standards should be established for the proceedings leading to the judgment in order to ensure that the debtor is informed about the court action against him, the requirements for his active participation in the proceedings to contest the claim and the consequences of his non-participation in sufficient time and in such a way as to enable him to arrange for his defence.

(13) Due to differences between the Member States as regards the rules of civil procedure and especially those governing the service of documents, it is necessary to lay down a specific and detailed definition of those minimum standards. In particular, any method of service that is based on a legal fiction as regards the fulfilment of those minimum standards cannot be considered sufficient for the certification of a judgment as a European Enforcement Order.

(14) All the methods of service listed in Articles 13 and 14 are characterized by either full certainty (Article 13) or a very high degree of likelihood (Article 14) that the document served has reached its addressee. In the second category, a judgment should only be certified as a European Enforcement Order if the Member State of origin has an appropriate mechanism in place enabling the debtor to apply for a full review of the judgment under the conditions set out in Article 19 in those exceptional cases where, in spite of compliance with Article 14, the document has not reached the addressee.

(15) Personal service on certain persons other than the debtor himself pursuant to Article 14(1)(a) and (b) should be understood to meet the requirements of those provisions only if those persons actually accepted/received the document in question.

(16) Article 15 should apply to situations where the debtor cannot represent himself in court, as in the case of a legal person, and where a person to represent him is determined by law as well as situations where the debtor has authorised another person, in particular a lawyer, to represent him in the specific court proceedings at issue.

(17) The courts competent for scrutinizing full compliance with the minimum procedural standards should, if satisfied, issue a standardized European Enforcement Order certificate that makes that scrutiny and its result transparent.

(18) Mutual trust in the administration of justice in the Member States justifies the assessment by the court of one Member State that all conditions for certification as a European Enforcement Order are fulfilled to enable a judgment to be enforced in all other Member States without judicial review of the proper application of the minimum procedural standards in the Member State where the judgment is to be enforced.

(19) This Regulation does not imply an obligation for the Member States to adapt their national legislation to the minimum procedural standards set out herein. It provides an incentive to that end by making available a more efficient and rapid enforceability of judgments in other Member States only if those minimum standards are met.

(20) Application for certification as a European Enforcement Order for uncontested claims should be optional for the creditor, who may instead choose the system of recognition and enforcement under Regulation (EC) No 44/2001 or other Community instruments.

(21) When a document has to be sent from one Member State to another for service there, this Regulation and in particular the rules on service set out herein should apply together with Council Regulation (EC) No 1348/2000 of 29 May 2000 on the service in the Member States of judicial and extrajudicial documents in civil or commercial

matters,[7] and in particular Article 14 thereof in conjunction with Member States declarations made under Article 23 thereof.

(22) Since the objectives of the proposed action cannot be sufficiently achieved by the Member States and can therefore, by reason of the scale or effects of the action, be better achieved at Community level, the Community may adopt measures, in accordance with the principle of subsidiarity as set out in Article 5 of the Treaty. In accordance with the principle of proportionality, as set out in that Article, this Regulation does not go beyond what is necessary in order to achieve those objectives.

(23) The measures necessary for the implementation of this Regulation should be adopted in accordance with Council Decision 1999/468/EC of 28 June 1999 laying down the procedures for the exercise of implementing powers conferred on the Commission.[8]

(24) In accordance with Article 3 of the Protocol on the position of the United Kingdom and Ireland annexed to the Treaty on European Union and the Treaty establishing the European Community, the United Kingdom and Ireland have notified their wish to take part in the adoption and application of this Regulation.

(25) In accordance with Articles 1 and 2 of the Protocol on the position of Denmark annexed to the Treaty on European Union and the Treaty establishing the European Community, Denmark does not take part in the adoption of this Regulation, and is therefore not bound by it or subject to its application.

(26) Pursuant to the second indent of Article 67(5) of the Treaty, the codecision procedure is applicable from 1 February 2003 for the measures laid down in this Regulation,

HAVE ADOPTED THIS REGULATION:

## CHAPTER I
## SUBJECT MATTER, SCOPE AND DEFINITIONS

### *Article 1*
### Subject matter

The purpose of this Regulation is to create a European Enforcement Order for uncontested claims to permit, by laying down minimum standards, the free circulation of judgments, court settlements and authentic instruments throughout all Member States without any intermediate proceedings needing to be brought in the Member State of enforcement prior to recognition and enforcement.

### *Article 2*
### Scope

1. This Regulation shall apply in civil and commercial matters, whatever the nature of the court or tribunal. It shall not extend, in particular, to revenue, customs or administrative matters or the liability of the State for acts and omissions in the exercise of State authority ('acta iure imperii').
2. This Regulation shall not apply to:
   (a) the status or legal capacity of natural persons, rights in property arising out of a matrimonial relationship, wills and succession;
   (b) bankruptcy, proceedings relating to the winding-up of insolvent companies or other legal persons, judicial arrangements, compositions and analogous proceedings;
   (c) social security;
   (d) arbitration.

[7] OJ L 160, 30.6.2000, p 37.
[8] OJ L 184, 17.7.1999, p 23.

3. In this Regulation, the term 'Member State' shall mean Member States with the exception of Denmark.

*Article 3*

**Enforcement titles to be certified as a European Enforcement Order**

1. This Regulation shall apply to judgments, court settlements and authentic instruments on uncontested claims. A claim shall be regarded as uncontested if:
   (a) the debtor has expressly agreed to it by admission or by means of a settlement which has been approved by a court or concluded before a court in the course of proceedings; or
   (b) the debtor has never objected to it, in compliance with the relevant procedural requirements under the law of the Member State of origin, in the course of the court proceedings; or
   (c) the debtor has not appeared or been represented at a court hearing regarding that claim after having initially objected to the claim in the course of the court proceedings, provided that such conduct amounts to a tacit admission of the claim or of the facts alleged by the creditor under the law of the Member State of origin; or
   (d) the debtor has expressly agreed to it in an authentic instrument.
2. This Regulation shall also apply to decisions delivered following challenges to judgments, court settlements or authentic instruments certified as European Enforcement Orders.

*Article 4*

**Definitions**

For the purposes of this Regulation, the following definitions shall apply:

1. 'judgment': any judgment given by a court or tribunal of a Member State, whatever the judgment may be called, including a decree, order, decision or writ of execution, as well as the determination of costs or expenses by an officer of the court;
2. 'claim': a claim for payment of a specific sum of money that has fallen due or for which the due date is indicated in the judgment, court settlement or authentic instrument;
3. 'authentic instrument':
   (a) a document which has been formally drawn up or registered as an authentic instrument, and the authenticity of which:
      (i) relates to the signature and the content of the instrument; and
      (ii) has been established by a public authority or other authority empowered for that purpose by the Member State in which it originates; or
   (b) an arrangement relating to maintenance obligations concluded with administrative authorities or authenticated by them;
4. 'Member State of origin': the Member State in which the judgment has been given, the court settlement has been approved or concluded or the authentic instrument has been drawn up or registered, and is to be certified as a European Enforcement Order;
5. 'Member State of enforcement': the Member State in which enforcement of the judgment, court settlement or authentic instrument certified as a European Enforcement Order is sought;
6. 'court of origin': the court or tribunal seised of the proceedings at the time of fulfilment of the conditions set out in Article 3(1)(a), (b) or (c);
7. in Sweden, in summary proceedings concerning orders to pay (betalningsföreläggande), the expression 'court' includes the Swedishen forcement service (kronofogdemyndighet).

## CHAPTER II
## EUROPEAN ENFORCEMENT ORDER

*Article 5*

**Abolition of exequatur**

A judgment which has been certified as a European Enforcement Order in the Member State of origin shall be recognised and enforced in the other Member States without the need for a declaration of enforceability and without any possibility of opposing its recognition.

*Article 6*

**Requirements for certification as a European Enforcement Order**

1. A judgment on an uncontested claim delivered in a Member State shall, upon application at any time to the court of origin, be certified as a European Enforcement Order if:
   (a) the judgment is enforceable in the Member State of origin; and
   (b) the judgment does not conflict with the rules on jurisdiction as laid down in sections 3 and 6 of Chapter II of Regulation (EC) No 44/2001; and
   (c) the court proceedings in the Member State of origin met the requirements as set out in Chapter III where a claim is uncontested within the meaning of Article 3(1)(b) or (c); and
   (d) the judgment was given in the Member State of the debtor's domicile within the meaning of Article 59 of Regulation (EC) No 44/2001, in cases where
      — a claim is uncontested within the meaning of Article 3(1)(b) or (c); and
      — it relates to a contract concluded by a person, the consumer, for a purpose which can be regarded as being outside his trade or profession; and
      — the debtor is the consumer.
2. Where a judgment certified as a European Enforcement Order has ceased to be enforceable or its enforceability has been suspended or limited, a certificate indicating the lack or limitation of enforceability shall, upon application at any time to the court of origin, be issued, using the standard form in Annex IV.
3. Without prejudice to Article 12(2), where a decision has been delivered following a challenge to a judgment certified as a European Enforcement Order in accordance with paragraph 1 of this Article, a replacement certificate shall, upon application at any time, be issued, using the standard form in Annex V, if that decision on the challenge is enforceable in the Member State of origin.

*Article 7*

**Costs related to court proceedings**

Where a judgment includes an enforceable decision on the amount of costs related to the court proceedings, including the interest rates, it shall be certified as a European Enforcement Order also with regard to the costs unless the debtor has specifically objected to his obligation to bear such costs in the course of the court proceedings, in accordance with the law of the Member State of origin.

*Article 8*

**Partial European Enforcement Order certificate**

If only parts of the judgment meet the requirements of this Regulation, a partial European Enforcement Order certificate shall be issued for those parts.

*Article 9*

**Issue of the European Enforcement Order certificate**

1. The European Enforcement Order certificate shall be issued using the standard form in Annex I.
2. The European Enforcement Order certificate shall be issued in the language of the judgment.

*Article 10*

**Rectification or withdrawal of the European Enforcement Order certificate**

1. The European Enforcement Order certificate shall, upon application to the court of origin, be
   (a) rectified where, due to a material error, there is a discrepancy between the judgment and the certificate;
   (b) withdrawn where it was clearly wrongly granted, having regard to the requirements laid down in this Regulation.
2. The law of the Member State of origin shall apply to the rectification or withdrawal of the European Enforcement Order certificate.
3. An application for the rectification or withdrawal of a European Enforcement Order certificate may be made using the standard form in Annex VI.
4. No appeal shall lie against the issuing of a European Enforcement Order certificate.

*Article 11*

**Effect of the European Enforcement Order certificate**

The European Enforcement Order certificate shall take effect only within the limits of the enforceability of the judgment.

## CHAPTER III
## MINIMUM STANDARDS FOR UNCONTESTED CLAIMS PROCEDURES

*Article 12*

**Scope of application of minimum standards**

1. A judgment on a claim that is uncontested within the meaning of Article 3(1)(b) or (c) can be certified as a European Enforcement Order only if the court proceedings in the Member State of origin met the procedural requirements as set out in this Chapter.
2. The same requirements shall apply to the issuing of a European Enforcement Order certificate or a replacement certificate within the meaning of Article 6(3) for a decision following a challenge to a judgment where, at the time of that decision, the conditions of Article 3(1)(b) or (c) are fulfilled.

*Article 13*

**Service with proof of receipt by the debtor**

1. The document instituting the proceedings or an equivalent document may have been served on the debtor by one of the following methods:
   (a) personal service attested by an acknowledgement of receipt, including the date of receipt, which is signed by the debtor;
   (b) personal service attested by a document signed by the competent person who effected the service stating that the debtor has received the document or refused to receive it without any legal justification, and the date of the service;
   (c) postal service attested by an acknowledgement of receipt including the date of receipt, which is signed and returned by the debtor;
   (d) service by electronic means such as fax or e-mail, attested by an acknowledgement of receipt including the date of receipt, which is signed and returned by the debtor.
2. Any summons to a court hearing may have been served on the debtor in compliance with paragraph 1 or orally in a previous court hearing on the same claim and stated in the minutes of that previous court hearing.

*Article 14*

**Service without proof of receipt by the debtor**

1. Service of the document instituting the proceedings or an equivalent document and any summons to a court hearing on the debtor may also have been effected by one of the following methods:

(a) personal service at the debtor's personal address on persons who are living in the same household as the debtor or are employed there;
(b) in the case of a self-employed debtor or a legal person, personal service at the debtor's business premises on persons who are employed by the debtor;
(c) deposit of the document in the debtor's mailbox;
(d) deposit of the document at a post office or with competent public authorities and the placing in the debtor's mailbox of written notification of that deposit, provided that the written notification clearly states the character of the document as a court document or the legal effect of the notification as effecting service and setting in motion the running of time for the purposes of time limits;
(e) postal service without proof pursuant to paragraph 3 where the debtor has his address in the Member State of origin;
(f) electronic means attested by an automatic confirmation of delivery, provided that the debtor has expressly accepted this method of service in advance.

2. For the purposes of this Regulation, service under paragraph 1 is not admissible if the debtor's address is not known with certainty.
3. Service pursuant to paragraph 1, (a) to (d), shall be attested by:
   (a) a document signed by the competent person who effected the service, indicating:
      (i) the method of service used; and
      (ii) the date of service; and
      (iii) where the document has been served on a person other than the debtor, the name of that person and his relation to the debtor, or
   (b) an acknowledgement of receipt by the person served, for the purposes of paragraphs 1(a) and (b).

*Article 15*
**Service on the debtor's representatives**

Service pursuant to Articles 13 or 14 may also have been effected on a debtor's representative.

*Article 16*
**Provision to the debtor of due information about the claim**

In order to ensure that the debtor was provided with due information about the claim, the document instituting the proceedings or the equivalent document must have contained the following:
(a) the names and the addresses of the parties;
(b) the amount of the claim;
(c) if interest on the claim is sought, the interest rate and the period for which interest is sought unless statutory interest is automatically added to the principal under the law of the Member State of origin;
(d) a statement of the reason for the claim.

*Article 17*
**Provision to the debtor of due information about the procedural steps necessary to contest the claim**

The following must have been clearly stated in or together with the document instituting the proceedings, the equivalent document or any summons to a court hearing:
(a) the procedural requirements for contesting the claim, including the time limit for contesting the claim in writing or the time for the court hearing, as applicable, the name and the address of the institution to which to respond or before which to appear, as applicable, and whether it is mandatory to be represented by a lawyer;
(b) the consequences of an absence of objection or default of appearance, in particular, where applicable, the possibility that a judgment may be given or enforced against the debtor and the liability for costs related to the court proceedings.

*Article 18*

**Cure of non-compliance with minimum standards**

1. If the proceedings in the Member State of origin did not meet the procedural requirements as set out in Articles 13 to 17, such non-compliance shall be cured and a judgment may be certified as a European Enforcement Order if:
   (a) the judgment has been served on the debtor in compliance with the requirements pursuant to Article 13 or Article 14; and
   (b) it was possible for the debtor to challenge the judgment by means of a full review and the debtor has been duly informed in or together with the judgment about the procedural requirements for such a challenge, including the name and address of the institution with which it must be lodged and, where applicable, the time limit for so doing; and
   (c) the debtor has failed to challenge the judgment in compliance with the relevant procedural requirements.
2. If the proceedings in the Member State of origin did not comply with the procedural requirements as set out in Article 13 or Article 14, such non-compliance shall be cured if it is proved by the conduct of the debtor in the court proceedings that he has personally received the document to be served in sufficient time to arrange for his defence.

*Article 19*

**Minimum standards for review in exceptional cases**

1. Further to Articles 13 to 18, a judgment can only be certified as a European Enforcement Order if the debtor is entitled, under the law of the Member State of origin, to apply for a review of the judgment where:
   (a) (i) the document instituting the proceedings or an equivalent document or, where applicable, the summons to a court hearing, was served by one of the methods provided for in Article 14; and
   (ii) service was not effected in sufficient time to enable him to arrange for his defence, without any fault on his part; or
   (b) the debtor was prevented from objecting to the claim by reason of force majeure, or due to extraordinary circumstances without any fault on his part,

   provided in either case that he acts promptly.
2. This Article is without prejudice to the possibility for Member States to grant access to a review of the judgment under more generous conditions than those mentioned in paragraph 1.

## CHAPTER IV
## ENFORCEMENT

*Article 20*

**Enforcement procedure**

1. Without prejudice to the provisions of this Chapter, the enforcement procedures shall be governed by the law of the Member State of enforcement.

   A judgment certified as a European Enforcement Order shall be enforced under the same conditions as a judgment handed down in the Member State of enforcement.
2. The creditor shall be required to provide the competent enforcement authorities of the Member State of enforcement with:
   (a) a copy of the judgment which satisfies the conditions necessary to establish its authenticity; and
   (b) a copy of the European Enforcement Order certificate which satisfies the conditions necessary to establish its authenticity; and
   (c) where necessary, a transcription of the European Enforcement Order certificate or a translation thereof into the official language of the Member State of enforcement or,

if there are several official languages in that Member State, the official language or one of the official languages of court proceedings of the place where enforcement is sought, in conformity with the law of that Member State, or into another language that the Member State of enforcement has indicated it can accept. Each Member State may indicate the official language or languages of the institutions of the European Community other than its own which it can accept for the completion of the certificate. The translation shall be certified by a person qualified to do so in one of the Member States.

3. No security, bond or deposit, however described, shall be required of a party who in one Member State applies for enforcement of a judgment certified as a European Enforcement Order in another Member State on the ground that he is a foreign national or that he is not domiciled or resident in the Member State of enforcement.

*Article 21*

**Refusal of enforcement**

1. Enforcement shall, upon application by the debtor, be refused by the competent court in the Member State of enforcement if the judgment certified as a European Enforcement Order is irreconcilable with an earlier judgment given in any Member State or in a third country, provided that:
   (a) the earlier judgment involved the same cause of action and was between the same parties; and
   (b) the earlier judgment was given in the Member State of enforcement or fulfils the conditions necessary for its recognition in the Member State of enforcement; and
   (c) the irreconcilability was not and could not have been raised as an objection in the court proceedings in the Member State of origin.
2. Under no circumstances may the judgment or its certification as a European Enforcement Order be reviewed as to their substance in the Member State of enforcement.

*Article 22*

**Agreements with third countries**

This Regulation shall not affect agreements by which Member States undertook, prior to the entry into force of Regulation (EC) No 44/2001, pursuant to Article 59 of the Brussels Convention on jurisdiction and the enforcement of judgments in civil and commercial matters, not to recognise judgments given, in particular in other Contracting States to that Convention, against defendants domiciled or habitually resident in a third country where, in cases provided for in Article 4 of that Convention, the judgment could only be founded on a ground of jurisdiction specified in the second paragraph of Article 3 of that Convention.

*Article 23*

**Stay or limitation of enforcement**

Where the debtor has

— challenged a judgment certified as a European Enforcement Order, including an application for review within the meaning of Article 19, or

— applied for the rectification or withdrawal of a European Enforcement Order certificate in accordance with Article 10,

the competent court or authority in the Member State of enforcement may, upon application by the debtor:

(a) limit the enforcement proceedings to protective measures; or

(b) make enforcement conditional on the provision of such security as it shall determine; or

(c) under exceptional circumstances, stay the enforcement proceedings.

## CHAPTER V
## COURT SETTLEMENTS AND AUTHENTIC INSTRUMENTS

*Article 24*

**Court settlements**

1. A settlement concerning a claim within the meaning of Article 4(2) which has been approved by a court or concluded before a court in the course of proceedings and is enforceable in the Member State in which it was approved or concluded shall, upon application to the court that approved it or before which it was concluded, be certified as a European Enforcement Order using the standard form in Annex II.
2. A settlement which has been certified as a European Enforcement Order in the Member State of origin shall be enforced in the other Member States without the need for a declaration of enforceability and without any possibility of opposing its enforceability.
3. The provisions of Chapter II, with the exception of Articles 5, 6(1) and 9(1), and of Chapter IV, with the exception of Articles 21(1) and 22, shall apply as appropriate.

*Article 25*

**Authentic instruments**

1. An authentic instrument concerning a claim within the meaning of Article 4(2) which is enforceable in one Member State shall, upon application to the authority designated by the Member State of origin, be certified as a European Enforcement Order, using the standard form in Annex III.
2. An authentic instrument which has been certified as a European Enforcement Order in the Member State of origin shall be enforced in the other Member States without the need for a declaration of enforceability and without any possibility of opposing its enforceability.
3. The provisions of Chapter II, with the exception of Articles 5, 6(1) and 9(1), and of Chapter IV, with the exception of Articles 21(1) and 22, shall apply as appropriate.

## CHAPTER VI
## TRANSITIONAL PROVISION

*Article 26*

**Transitional provision**

This Regulation shall apply only to judgments given, to court settlements approved or concluded and to documents formally drawn up or registered as authentic instruments after the entry into force of this Regulation.

## CHAPTER VII
## RELATIONSHIP WITH OTHER COMMUNITY INSTRUMENTS

*Article 27*

**Relationship with Regulation (EC) No 44/2001**

This Regulation shall not affect the possibility of seeking recognition and enforcement, in accordance with Regulation (EC) No 44/2001, of a judgment, a court settlement or an authentic instrument on an uncontested claim.

*Article 28*

**Relationship with Regulation (EC) No 1348/2000**

This Regulation shall not affect the application of Regulation (EC) No 1348/2000.

## CHAPTER VIII
## GENERAL AND FINAL PROVISIONS

*Article 29*

**Information on enforcement procedures and authorities**

The Member States shall cooperate to provide the general public and professional circles with information on:

(a) the methods and procedures of enforcement in the Member States; and

(b) the competent authorities for enforcement in the Member States,

in particular via the European Judicial Network in civil and commercial matters established in accordance with Decision 2001/470/EC.[9]

*Article 30*

**Information relating to redress procedures, languages and authorities**

1. The Member States shall notify the Commission of:
   (a) the procedures for rectification and withdrawal referred to in Article 10(2) and for review referred to in Article 19(1);
   (b) the languages accepted pursuant to Article 20(2)(c);
   (c) the lists of the authorities referred to in Article 25; and any subsequent changes thereof.
2. The Commission shall make the information notified in accordance with paragraph 1 publicly available through publication in the *Official Journal of the European Union* and through any other appropriate means.

*Article 31*

**Amendments to the Annexes**

Any amendment to the standard forms in the Annexes shall be adopted in accordance with the advisory procedure referred to in Article 32(2).

*Article 32*

**Committee**

1. The Commission shall be assisted by the committee provided for by Article 75 of Regulation (EC) No 44/2001.
2. Where reference is made to this paragraph, Articles 3 and 7 of Decision 1999/468/EC shall apply, having regard to the provisions of Article 8 thereof.
3. The Committee shall adopt its Rules of Procedure.

*Article 33*

**Entry into force**

This Regulation shall enter into force on 21 January 2004.

It shall apply from 21 October 2005, with the exception of Articles 30, 31 and 32, which shall apply from 21 January 2005.

This Regulation shall be binding in its entirety and directly applicable in the Member States in accordance with the Treaty establishing the European Community.

Done at Strasbourg, 21 April 2004.

| *For the European Parliament* | *For the Council* |
| --- | --- |
| *The President* | *The President* |
| P. COX | D. ROCHE |

[9] OJ L 174, 27.6.2001, p 25.

## ANNEX I
## EUROPEAN ENFORCEMENT ORDER CERTIFICATE — JUDGMENT

1. Member State of origin:
AT☐ BE☐ DE☐ EL☐ ES☐ FI☐ FR☐
IE☐ IT☐ LU☐ NL☐ PT☐ SE☐ UK☐

2. Court/Tribunal issuing the certificate
2.1. Name:
2.2. Address:
2.3. Tel./fax/e-mail:

3. If different, Court/Tribunal giving the judgment
3.1. Name:
3.2. Address:
3.3. Tel./fax/e-mail:

4. Judgment
4.1. Date:
4.2. Reference number:
4.3. The parties
4.3.1. Name and address of creditor(s):
4.3.2. Name and address of debtor(s):

5. Monetary claim as certified
5.1. Principal Amount:
5.1.1. Currency Euro ☐
Swedish Kronor ☐
Pounds Sterling ☐
Other (explain) ☐
5.1.2. If the claim is for periodical payments
5.1.2.1. Amount of each instalment:
5.1.2.2. Due date of first instalment:
5.1.2.3. Due dates of following instalments
weekly ☐ monthly ☐ other (explain) ☐
5.1.2.4. Period of the claim
5.1.2.4.1. Currently indefinite ☐ or
5.1.2.4.2. Due date of last instalment:
5.2. Interest
5.2.1. Interest rate
5.2.1.1. . . . % or
5.2.1.2. . . . % above the base rate of the ECB[10]
5.2.1.3. Other (explain)
5.2.2. Interest to be collected as from:
5.3. Amount of reimbursable costs if specified in the judgment:

[10] Interest rate applied by the European Central Bank to its main refinancing operations.

6. Judgment is enforceable in the Member State of origin ☐

7. Judgment is still subject to the possibility of a challenge
Yes ☐ No ☐

8. Judgment is on an uncontested claim under Article 3(1) ☐

9. Judgment is in compliance with Article 6(1) (b) ☐

10. The judgment concerns matters relating to consumer contracts
Yes ☐ No ☐

10.1. If yes:
The debtor is the consumer
Yes ☐ No ☐

10.2. If yes:
The debtor is domiciled in the Member State of origin (within the meaning of Article 59 of Regulation (EC) 44/2001) ☐

11. Service of the document instituting the proceedings under Chapter III, where applicable

Yes ☐ No ☐

11.1. Service was effected in compliance with Article 13 ☐
or service was effected in compliance with Article 14 ☐
or it is proved in accordance with Article 18(2) that the debtor has received the document ☐

11.2. Due information
The debtor was informed in compliance with Articles 16 and 17 ☐

12. Service of summons, where applicable
Yes ☐ No ☐

12.1. Service was effected in compliance with Article 13 ☐
or service was effected in compliance with Article 14 ☐
or it is proved in accordance with Article 18(2) that the debtor has received the summons ☐

12.2. Due information
The debtor was informed in compliance with Article 17 ☐

13. Cure of non-compliance with procedural minimum standards pursuant to Article 18(1)

13.1. Service of the judgment was effected in compliance with Article 13 ☐
or service of the judgment was effected in compliance with Article 14 ☐
or it is proved in accordance with Article 18(2) that the debtor has received the judgment ☐

13.2. Due information
The debtor was informed in compliance with Article 18(1)(b) ☐

13.3. It was possible for the debtor to challenge the judgment
Yes ☐ No ☐

13.4. The debtor failed to challenge the judgment in compliance with the relevant procedural requirements
Yes ☐ No ☐

Done at . . . . . . . . . . . . date . . . . . . . . . . . . .

. . . . . . . . . . . . . . . . . . . . . . . . . . . . . . . . . . . . . . . .
Signature and/or stamp

## ANNEX II
## EUROPEAN ENFORCEMENT ORDER CERTIFICATE —COURT SETTLEMENT

1. Member State of origin:
AT☐ BE☐ DE☐ EL☐ ES☐ FI☐ FR☐
IE☐ IT☐ LU☐ NL☐ PT☐ SE☐ UK☐
2. Court issuing the certificate
2.1. Name:
2.2. Address:
2.3. Tel./fax/e-mail:
3. If different, Court approving the settlement or before which it was concluded
3.1. Name:
3.2. Address:
3.3. Tel./fax/e-mail:
4. Court settlement
4.1. Date:
4.2. Reference number:
4.3. The parties
4.3.1. Name and address of creditor(s):
4.3.2. Name and address of debtor(s):
5. Monetary claim as certified
5.1. Principal Amount:
5.1.1. Currency Euro ☐
Swedish Kronor ☐
Pounds Sterling ☐
Other (explain) ☐
5.1.2. If the claim is for periodical payments
5.1.2.1. Amount of each instalment:
5.1.2.2. Due date of first instalment:
5.1.2.3. Due dates of following instalments
weekly ☐ monthly ☐ other (explain) ☐
5.1.2.4. Period of the claim
5.1.2.4.1. Currently indefinite ☐ or
5.1.2.4.2. Due date of last instalment:
5.2. Interest
5.2.1. Interest rate
5.2.1.1. . . . % or
5.2.1.2. . . . % above the base rate of the ECB[11]
5.2.1.3. Other (explain)
5.2.2. Interest to be collected as from:

[11] Interest rate applied by the European Central Bank to its main refinancing operations.

5.3. Amount of reimbursable costs if specified in the court settlement:

6. The court settlement is enforceable in the Member State of origin ☐

Done at ............. date .............

.......................................

Signature and/or stamp

## ANNEX III
## EUROPEAN ENFORCEMENT ORDER CERTIFICATE —AUTHENTIC INSTRUMENT

1. Member State of origin:
   AT☐ BE☐ DE☐ EL☐ ES☐ FI☐ FR☐
   IE☐ IT☐ LU☐ NL☐ PT☐ SE☐ UK☐

2. Court/Authority issuing the certificate

2.1. Name:

2.2. Address:

2.3. Tel./fax/e-mail:

3. If different, Court/Authority drawing up or registering the authentic instrument

3.1. Name:

3.2. Address:

3.3. Tel./fax/e-mail:

4. Authentic instrument

4.1. Date:

4.2. Reference number:

4.3. The parties

4.3.1. Name and address of creditor(s):

4.3.2. Name and address of debtor(s):

5. Monetary claim as certified

5.1. Principal Amount:

5.1.1. Currency Euro ☐
Swedish Kronor ☐
Pounds Sterling ☐
Other (explain) ☐

5.1.2. If the claim is for periodical payments

5.1.2.1. Amount of each instalment:

5.1.2.2. Due date of first instalment:

5.1.2.3. Due dates of following instalments
weekly ☐ monthly ☐ other (explain) ☐

5.1.2.4. Period of the claim

5.1.2.4.1. Currently indefinite ☐ or

5.1.2.4.2. Due date of last instalment

5.2. Interest

5.2.1. Interest rate

5.2.1.1. . . . % or

5.2.1.2. . . . % above the base rate of the ECB[12]

5.2.1.3. Other (explain)

5.2.2. Interest to be collected as from:

5.3. Amount of reimbursable costs if specified in the authentic instrument:

6. The authentic instrument is enforceable in the Member State of origin ☐

Done at . . . . . . . . . . . . date . . . . . . . . . . . . .

. . . . . . . . . . . . . . . . . . . . . . . . . . . . . . . . . . . . . . .
Signature and/or stamp

## ANNEX IV
## CERTIFICATE OF LACK OR LIMITATION OF ENFORCEABILITY
(Article 6(2))

1. Member State of origin:
AT☐ BE☐ DE☐ EL☐ ES☐ FI☐ FR☐
IE☐ IT☐ LU☐ NL☐ PT☐ SE☐ UK☐

2. Court/Authority issuing the certificate

2.1. Name:

2.2. Address:

2.3. Tel./fax/e-mail:

3. If different, Court/Authority issuing the judgment/court settlement/authentic instrument (*)

3.1. Name:

3.2. Address:

3.3. Tel./fax/e-mail:

4. Judgment/court settlement/authentic instrument *

4.1. Date:

4.2. Reference number:

4.3. The parties

4.3.1. Name and address of creditor(s):

4.3.2. Name and address of debtor(s):

5. This judgment/court settlement/authentic instrument * was certified as a European Enforcement Order but

5.1. the judgment/court settlement/authentic instrument * is no longer enforceable ☐

5.2. Enforcement is temporarily

5.2.1. stayed ☐

5.2.2 limited to protective measures ☐

5.2.3. conditional upon the provision of a security which is still outstanding ☐

[12] Interest rate applied by the European Central Bank to its main refinancing operations.

* Delete as appropriate.

5.2.3.1. Amount of the security:

5.2.3.2. Currency Euro ☐
Swedish Kronor ☐
Pounds Sterling ☐
Other (explain) ☐

5.2.4. Other (explain) ☐

Done at ............ date ............

.....................................
Signature and/or stamp

## ANNEX V
## EUROPEAN ENFORCEMENT ORDER REPLACEMENT CERTIFICATE FOLLOWING A CHALLENGE
(Article 6(3))

A. The following judgment/court settlement/authentic instrument* certified as a European Enforcement Order was challenged

1. Member State of origin:

AT☐ BE☐ DE☐ EL☐ ES☐ FI☐ FR☐
IE☐ IT☐ LU☐ NL☐ PT☐ SE☐ UK☐

2. Court/Authority issuing the certificate

2.1. Name:

2.2. Address:

2.3. Tel./fax/e-mail:

3. If different, Court/Authority issuing the judgment/court settlement/authentic instrument *

3.1. Name:

3.2. Address:

3.3. Tel./fax/e-mail:

4. Judgment/court settlement/authentic instrument *

4.1. Date:

4.2. Reference number:

4.3. The parties

4.3.1. Name and address of creditor(s):

4.3.2. Name and address of debtor(s):

B. Upon that challenge the following decision has been handed down and is hereby certified as a European Enforcement Order replacing the original European Enforcement Order.

1. Court

1.1. Name:

1.2. Address:

1.3. Tel./fax/e-mail:

* Delete as appropriate.

2. Decision

2.1. Date:

2.2. Reference number:

3. Monetary claim as certified

3.1. Principal Amount

3.1.1. Currency Euro ☐
Swedish Kronor ☐
Pounds Sterling ☐
Other (explain) ☐

3.1.2. If the claim is for periodic payments

3.1.2.1. Amount of each instalment:

3.1.2.2. Due date of first instalment:

3.1.2.3. Due dates of following instalments
weekly ☐ monthly ☐ other (explain) ☐

3.1.2.4. Period of the claim

3.1.2.4.1. Currently indefinite ☐ or

3.1.2.4.2. Due date of last instalment:

3.2. Interest

3.2.1. Interest rate

3.2.1.1. . . . % or

3.2.1.2. . . . % above the base rate of the ECB[13]

3.2.1.3. Other (explain)

3.2.2. Interest to be collected as from:

3.3. Amount of reimbursable costs if specified in the decision:

4. Decision is enforceable in the Member State of origin ☐

5. Decision is still subject to the possibility of a further appeal
Yes ☐ No ☐

6. Decision is in compliance with Article 6(1)(b) ☐

7. The decision concerns matters relating to consumer contracts
Yes ☐ No ☐

7.1. If yes:
The debtor is the consumer
Yes ☐ No ☐

7.2. If yes:
The debtor is domiciled in the Member State of origin in the meaning of Article 59 of Regulation (EC) No 44/2001 ☐

8. At the time of the decision following the challenge, the claim is uncontested within the meaning of Article 3(1)(b) or (c)
Yes ☐ No ☐
If yes:

8.1. Service of the document instituting the challenge.

[13] Interest rate applied by the European Central Bank to its main refinancing operations.

Did the creditor lodge the challenge?
Yes ☐No ☐
If yes:

8.1.1. Service was effected incompliance with Article 13 ☐
or service was effected in compliance with Article 14 ☐
or it is proved in accordance with Article 18(2) that the debtor has received the document ☐

8.1.2. Due information

The debtor was informed incompliance with Articles 16 and 17 ☐

8.2. Service of summons, where applicable

Yes ☐ No ☐

If yes:

8.2.1. Service was effected in compliance with Article 13 ☐

or service was effected in compliance with Article ☐

or it is proved in accordance with Article 18(2) that the debtor has received the summons ☐

8.2.2. Due information

The debtor was informed in compliance with Article 17 ☐

8.3. Cure of non-compliance with procedural minimum standards pursuant to Article 18(1)

8.3.1. Service of the decision was effected in compliance with Article 13 ☐
or Service of the decision was effected in compliance with Article 14 ☐
or it is proved in accordance with Article 18(2) that the debtor has received the decision ☐

8.3.2. Due information

The debtor was informed in compliance with Article 18(1)(b) ☐

Done at ............. date .............

.......................................
Signature and/or stamp

## ANNEX VI
## APPLICATION FOR RECTIFICATION OR WITHDRAWAL OF THE EUROPEAN ENFORCEMENT ORDER CERTIFICATE (Article 10(3))

THE FOLLOWING EUROPEAN ENFORCEMENT ORDER CERTIFICATE

1. Member State of origin:

AT☐ BE☐ DE☐ EL☐ ES☐ FI☐ FR☐
IE☐ IT☐ LU☐ NL☐ PT☐ SE☐ UK☐

2. Court/Authority issuing the certificate

2.1. Name:

2.2. Address:

2.3. Tel./fax/e-mail:

3. If different, Court/Authority issuing the judgment/court settlement/authentic instrument *

* Delete as appropriate.

3.1. Name:

3.2. Address:

3.3. Tel./fax/e-mail:

4. Judgment/court settlement/authentic instrument (*)

4.1. Date:

4.2. Reference number:

4.3. The parties

4.3.1. Name and address of creditor(s):

4.3.2. Name and address of debtor(s):

HAS TO BE

5. RECTIFIED as due to a material error there is the following discrepancy between the European Enforcement Order certificate and the underlying judgment/court settlement/authentic instrument (explain) ☐

6. WITHDRAWN because:

6.1. the certified judgment was related to a consumer contract but was given in a Member State where the consumer is not domiciled within the meaning of Article 59 of Regulation (EC) No 44/2001 ☐

6.2. the European Enforcement Order certificate was clearly wrongly granted for another reason (explain) ☐

Done at . . . . . . . . . . . . date . . . . . . . . . . . .

. . . . . . . . . . . . . . . . . . . . . . . . . . . . . . . . . . . . . .

Signature and/or stamp

## COMMISSION REGULATION (EC) No 1869/2005*

### of 16 November 2005

### replacing the Annexes to Regulation (EC) No 805/2004 of the European Parliament and of the Council creating a European Enforcement Order for uncontested claims

THE COMMISSION OF THE EUROPEAN COMMUNITIES,

Having regard to the Treaty establishing the European Community,

Having regard to Regulation (EC) No 805/2004 of the European Parliament and of the Council of 21 April 2004 creating a European Enforcement Order for uncontested claims,[1] and in particular Article 31 thereof,

After consulting the Committee established by Article 32 of Regulation (EC) No 805/2004,

Whereas:

(1) Annexes I to VI to Regulation (EC) No 805/2004 contain a series of standard forms to be used in the context of the European Enforcement Order procedure for uncontested claims.

(2) Following the accession of new Member States on 1 May 2004, Annexes I to VI to Regulation (EC) No 805/2004 should be replaced so as to adapt the standard forms for use in the new Member States.

(3) Regulation (EC) No 805/2004 should therefore be amended accordingly,

* This Regulation is reproduced with the kind permission of Europa and the European Communities from their website. Disclaimer: Only European Community Legislation printed in the paper edition of the Official Journal of the European Union is deemed authentic.

[1] OJ L 143, 30.4.23004, p.15.

HAS ADOPTED THIS REGULATION:

*Article 1*

Annexes I to VI to Regulation (EC) No 805/2004 are replaced by the corresponding Annexes to this Regulation.

*Article 2*

This Regulation shall enter into force on the seventh day following its publication in the *Official Journal of the European Union.*

This Regulation shall be binding in its entirety and directly applicable in all Member States.

Done at Brussels, 16 November 2005.

*For the Commission*
*Franco FRATTINI*
*Vice-President*

ANNEX I

EUROPEAN ENFORCEMENT ORDER CERTIFICATE—JUDGMENT

1. Member State of origin:

| | | | | |
|---|---|---|---|---|
| Belgium ☐ | Czech Republic ☐ | Germany ☐ | Estonia ☐ | Greece ☐ |
| Spain ☐ | France ☐ | Ireland ☐ | Italy ☐ | Cyprus ☐ |
| Latvia ☐ | Lithuania ☐ | Luxembourg ☐ | Hungary ☐ | Malta ☐ |
| Netherland ☐ | Austria ☐ | Poland ☐ | Portugal ☐ | Slovakia ☐ |
| Slovenia ☐ | Finland ☐ | Sweden ☐ | United Kingdom ☐ | |

2. Court/Tribunal issuing the certificate:

2.1. Name:

2.2. Address:

2.3. Tel./fax/e-mail:

3. If different, Court/Tribunal giving the judgment:

3.1. Name:

3.2. Address:

3.3. Tel./fax/e-mail:

4. Judgment:

4.1. Date:

4.2. Reference number:

4.3. The parties:

4.3.1. Name and address of creditor(s):

4.3.2. Name and address of debtor(s):

5. Monetary claim as certified:

5.1. Principal amount:

5.1.1. Currency:

| | | | |
|---|---|---|---|
| Euro ☐ | Cyprus pound ☐ | Czech koruna ☐ | Estonian kroon ☐ |
| Pound sterling ☐ | Hungarian forint ☐ | Lithuanian litas ☐ | Latvian lats ☐ |
| Maltese lira ☐ | Polish zloty ☐ | Swedish kronor ☐ | Slovak koruna ☐ |
| Slovenian tolar ☐ | | | |
| other (explain) ☐ | | | |

5.1.2. If the claim is for periodical payments

5.1.2.1. Amount of each instalment:

5.1.2.2. Due date of first instalment:

5.1.2.3. Due dates of following instalments

weekly ☐ monthly ☐ other (explain) ☐

5.1.2.4. Period of the claim

5.1.2.4.1. Currently indefinite ☐ or

5.1.2.4.2. Due date of last instalment:

5.2. Interest

5.2.1. Interest rate

5.2.1.1. . . . % or

5.2.1.2. . . . % above the base rate of the ECB[1]

5.2.1.3. Other (explain)

5.2.2. Interest to be collected as from:

5.3. Amount of reimbursable costs if specified in the judgment:

6. Judgment is enforceable in the Member State of origin ☐

7. Judgment is still subject to the possibility of a challenge

Yes ☐ No ☐

8. Judgment is on an uncontested claim under Article 3(1) ☐

9. Judgment is in compliance with Article 6(1)(b) ☐

10. The judgment concerns matters relating to consumer contracts

Yes ☐ No ☐

10.1. If yes:

The debtor is the consumer

Yes ☐ No ☐

10.2. If yes:

The debtor is domiciled in the Member State of origin (within the meaning of Article 59 of Regulation (EC) No 44/2001) ☐

11. Service of the document instituting the proceedings under Chapter III, where applicable

Yes ☐ No ☐

11.1. Service was effected in compliance with Article 13 ☐

or service was effected in compliance with Article 14 ☐

or it is proved in accordance with Article 18(2) that the debtor has received the document ☐

11.2. Due information

The debtor was informed in compliance with Articles 16 and 17 ☐

12. Service of summons, where applicable

Yes ☐ No ☐

[1] Interest rate applied by the European Central Bank to its main refinancing operations.

12.1. Service was effected in compliance with Article 13 ☐

or service was effected in compliance with Article 14 ☐

or it is proved in accordance with Article 18(2) that the debtor has received the summons ☐

12.2. Due information

The debtor was informed in compliance with Article 17 ☐

13. Cure of non-compliance with procedural minimum standards pursuant to Article 18(1)

13.1. Service of the judgment was effected in compliance with Article 13 ☐

or service of the judgment was effected in compliance with Article 14 ☐

or it is proved in accordance with Article 18(2) that the debtor has received the judgment ☐

13.2. Due information

The debtor was informed in compliance with Article 18(1)(b) ☐

13.3. It was possible for the debtor to challenge the judgment

Yes ☐ No ☐

13.4. The debtor failed to challenge the judgment in compliance with the relevant procedural requirements

Yes ☐ No ☐

Done at ............ date ............

......................................
Signature and/or stamp

## ANNEX II
## EUROPEAN ENFORCEMENT ORDER CERTIFICATE—COURT SETTLEMENT

1. Member State of origin:

| | | | | | | | | | |
|---|---|---|---|---|---|---|---|---|---|
| Belgium | ☐ | Czech Republic | ☐ | Germany | ☐ | Estonia | ☐ | Greece | ☐ |
| Spain | ☐ | France | ☐ | Ireland | ☐ | Italy | ☐ | Cyprus | ☐ |
| Latvia | ☐ | Lithuania | ☐ | Luxembourg | ☐ | Hungary | ☐ | Malta | ☐ |
| Netherland | ☐ | Austria | ☐ | Poland | ☐ | Portugal | ☐ | Slovakia | ☐ |
| Slovenia | ☐ | Finland | ☐ | Sweden | ☐ | United Kingdom | ☐ | | |

2. Court issuing the certificate

2.1. Name:

2.2. Address:

2.3. Tel./fax//e-mail:

3. If different, Court approving the settlement or before which it was concluded

3.1. Name:

3.2. Address:

3.3. Tel./fax/e-mail:

4. Court settlement

4.1. Date:

4.2. Reference number:

4.3. The parties

4.3.1. Name and address of creditor(s):

4.3.2. Name and address of debtor(s):

5. Monetary claim as certified

5.1. Principal Amount:

5.1.1. Currency:

| | | | |
|---|---|---|---|
| Euro ☐ | Cyprus pound ☐ | Czech koruna ☐ | Estonian kroon ☐ |
| Pound sterling ☐ | Hungarian forint ☐ | Lithuanian litas ☐ | Latvian lats ☐ |
| Maltese lira ☐ | Polish zloty ☐ | Swedish kronor ☐ | Slovak koruna ☐ |
| Slovenian tolar ☐ | | | |
| other (explain) ☐ | | | |

5.1.2. If the claim is for periodical payments

5.1.2.1. Amount of each instalment:

5.1.2.2. Due date of first instalment:

5.1.2.3. Due dates of following instalments
weekly ☐ monthly ☐ other (explain) ☐

5.1.2.4. Period of the claim

5.1.2.4.1. Currently indefinite ☐ or

5.1.2.4.2. Due date of last instalment:

5.2. Interest

5.2.1. Interest rate

5.2.1.1. . . . % or

5.2.1.2. . . . % above the base rate of the ECB[1]

5.2.1.3. Other (explain)

5.2.2. Interest to be collected as from:

5.3. Amount of reimbursable costs if specified in the court settlement:

6. The court settlement is enforceable in the Member State of origin ☐

Done at . . . . . . . . . . . . date . . . . . . . . . . . . .

. . . . . . . . . . . . . . . . . . . . . . . . . . . . . . . . . . . . . . .
Signature and/or stamp

## ANNEX III
## EUROPEAN ENFORCEMENT ORDER CERTIFICATE— AUTHENTIC INSTRUMENT

1. Member State of origin:

| | | | | |
|---|---|---|---|---|
| Belgium ☐ | Czech Republic ☐ | Germany ☐ | Estonia ☐ | Greece ☐ |
| Spain ☐ | France ☐ | Ireland ☐ | Italy ☐ | Cyprus ☐ |
| Latvia ☐ | Lithuania ☐ | Luxembourg ☐ | Hungary ☐ | Malta ☐ |
| Netherland ☐ | Austria ☐ | Poland ☐ | Portugal ☐ | Slovakia ☐ |
| Slovenia ☐ | Finland ☐ | Sweden ☐ | United Kingdom ☐ | |

[1] Interest rate applied by the European Central Bank to its main refinancing operations.

2. Court/Authority issuing the certificate
2.1. Name:
2.2. Address:
2.3. Tel./fax/e-mail:

3. If different, Court/Authority drawing up or registering the authentic instrument
3.1. Name:
3.2. Address:
3.3. Tel./fax/e-mail:

4. Authentic instrument
4.1. Date:
4.2. Reference number:
4.3. The parties
4.3.1. Name and address of creditor(s):
4.3.2. Name and address of debtor(s):

5. Monetary claim as certified
5.1. Principal Amount:

| | | | |
|---|---|---|---|
| Euro ☐ | Cyprus pound ☐ | Czech koruna ☐ | Estonian kroon ☐ |
| Pound sterling ☐ | Hungarian forint ☐ | Lithuanian litas ☐ | Latvian lats ☐ |
| Maltese lira ☐ | Polish zloty ☐ | Swedish kronor ☐ | Slovak koruna ☐ |
| Slovenian tolar ☐ | | | |
| other (explain) ☐ | | | |

5.1.2. If the claim is for periodical payments
5.1.2.1. Amount of each instalment:
5.1.2.2. Due date of first instalment:
5.1.2.3. Due dates of following instalments
weekly ☐ monthly ☐ other (explain) ☐
5.1.2.4. Period of the claim
5.1.2.4.1. Currently indefinite ☐ or
5.1.2.4.2. Due date of last-instalment:
5.2. Interest
5.2.1. Interest rate
5.2.1.1. . . . % or
5.2.1.2. . . . % above the base rate of the ECB[1]
5.2.1.3. Other (explain)
5.2.2. Interest to be collected as from:
5.3. Amount of reimbursable costs if specified in the authentic instrument:

6. The authentic instrument is enforceable in the Member State of origin ☐

Done at . . . . . . . . . . . . date . . . . . . . . . . . . .

. . . . . . . . . . . . . . . . . . . . . . . . . . . . . . . . . . . . . . .
Signature and/or stamp

[1] Interest rate applied by the European Central Bank to its main refinancing operations.

## ANNEX IV
## CERTIFICATE OF LACK OR LIMITATION OF ENFORCEABILITY
(Article 6(2))

1. Member State of origin:

| | | | | | | | | | |
|---|---|---|---|---|---|---|---|---|---|
| Belgium | ☐ | Czech Republic | ☐ | Germany | ☐ | Estonia | ☐ | Greece | ☐ |
| Spain | ☐ | France | ☐ | Ireland | ☐ | Italy | ☐ | Cyprus | ☐ |
| Latvia | ☐ | Lithuania | ☐ | Luxembourg | ☐ | Hungary | ☐ | Malta | ☐ |
| Netherland | ☐ | Austria | ☐ | Poland | ☐ | Portugal | ☐ | Slovakia | ☐ |
| Slovenia | ☐ | Finland | ☐ | Sweden | ☐ | United Kingdom | ☐ | | |

2. Court/Authority issuing the certificate

2.1. Name:

2.2. Address

2.3. Tel./fax/e-mail:

3. If different, Court/Authority issuing the judgment/Court settlement/Authentic instrument*

3.1. Name:

3.2. Address:

3.3. Tel./fax/e-mail:

4. Judgment/Court settlement/ Authentic instrument*

4.1. Date:

4.2. Reference number:

4.3. The parties

4.3.1. Name and address of creditor(s):

4.3.2. Name and address of debtor(s):

5. This judgment/Court settlement/Authentic instrument* was certified as a European Enforcement Order but

5.1. the judgment/Court settlement/Authentic instrument* is no longer enforceable ☐

5.2. Enforcement is temporarily

5.2.1. stayed ☐

5.2.2. limited to protective measures ☐

5.2.3. conditional upon the provision of a security which is still outstanding ☐

5.2.3.1. Amount of the security:

| | | | | | | | |
|---|---|---|---|---|---|---|---|
| Euro | ☐ | Cyprus pound | ☐ | Czech koruna | ☐ | Estonian kroon | ☐ |
| Pound sterling | ☐ | Hungarian forint | ☐ | Lithuanian litas | ☐ | Latvian lats | ☐ |
| Maltese lira | ☐ | Polish zloty | ☐ | Swedish kronor | ☐ | Slovak koruna | ☐ |
| Slovenian tolar | ☐ | | | | | | |
| other (explain) | ☐ | | | | | | |

5.2.4. Other (explain) ☐

Done at ............ date .............

........................................
Signature and/or stamp

* Delete as appropriate.

ANNEX V
EUROPEAN ENFORCEMENT ORDER REPLACEMENT CERTIFICATE FOLLOWING A CHALLENGE
(Article 6(3))

A. The following judgment/court settlement/authentic instrument * certified as a European Enforcement Order was challenged

1. Member State of origin:

| | | | | | | | | | |
|---|---|---|---|---|---|---|---|---|---|
| Belgium | ☐ | Czech Republic | ☐ | Germany | ☐ | Estonia | ☐ | Greece | ☐ |
| Spain | ☐ | France | ☐ | Ireland | ☐ | Italy | ☐ | Cyprus | ☐ |
| Latvia | ☐ | Lithuania | ☐ | Luxembourg | ☐ | Hungary | ☐ | Malta | ☐ |
| Netherland | ☐ | Austria | ☐ | Poland | ☐ | Portugal | ☐ | Slovakia | ☐ |
| Slovenia | ☐ | Finland | ☐ | Sweden | ☐ | United Kingdom | ☐ | | |

2. Court/Authority issuing the certificate

2.1. Name:

2.2. Address:

2.3. Tel./fax/e-mail:

3. If different, Court/Authority issuing the judgment/Court settlement/Authentic Instrument*

3.1. Name:

3.2. Address:

3.3. Tel./fax/e-mail:

4. Judgment/Court settlement/Authentic Instrument*

4.1. Date:

4.2. Reference number:

4.3. The parties

4.3.1. Name and address of creditor(s):

4.3.2. Name and address of debtor(s):

B. Upon that challenge the following decision has been handed down and is hereby certified as a European Enforcement Order replacing the original European Enforcement Order.

1. Court

1.1. Name:

1.2. Address:

1.3. Tel./fax/e-mail:

2. Decision

2.1. Date:

2.2. Reference number:

3. Monetary claim as certified

3.1. Principal amount

* Delete as appropriate.

3.1.1. Currency:
Euro ☐ Cyprus pound ☐ Czech koruna ☐ Estonian kroon ☐
Pound sterling ☐ Hungarian forint ☐ Lithuanian litas ☐ Latvian lats ☐
Maltese lira ☐ Polish zloty ☐ Swedish kronor ☐ Slovak koruna ☐
Slovenian tolar ☐
other (explain) ☐

3.1.2.4. Period of the claim

3.1.2.4.1. Currently indefinite ☐ or

3.1.2.4.2. Due date of last instalment:

3.2. Interest

3.2.1. Interest rate

3.2.1.1. . . . % or

3.2.1.2. . . . % above the base rate of the ECB

3.2.1.3. Other (explain)

3.2.2. Interest to be collected as from:

3.3. Amount of reimbursable costs if specified in the decision:

4. Decision is enforceable in the Member State of origin ☐

5. Decision is still subject to the possibility of a further appeal
Yes ☐ No ☐

6. Decision is in compliance with Article 6(1)(b) ☐

7. The decision concerns matters relating to consumer contracts
Yes ☐ No ☐

7.1. If yes:
The debtor is the consumer
Yes ☐ No ☐

7.2. If yes:
The debtor is domiciled in the Member State of origin in the meaning of Article 59 of Regulation (EC) No 44/2001 ☐

8. At the time of the decision following the challenge, the claim is uncontested within the meaning of Article 3(1)(b) or (c)
Yes ☐ No ☐
If yes:

8.1. Service of the document instituting the challenge.
Did the creditor lodge the challenge?
Yes ☐ No ☐
If yes:

8.1.1. Service was effected in compliance with Article 13 ☐
or service was effected in compliance with Article 14 ☐
or it is proved in accordance with Article 18(2) that the debtor has received the document ☐

8.1.2. Due information
The debtor was informed in compliance with Articles 16 and 17 ☐

8.2. Service of summons, where applicable
Yes ☐ No ☐
If yes:

8.2.1. Service was effected in compliance with Article 13 ☐
or service was effected in compliance with Article 14 ☐
or it is proved in accordance with Article 18(2) that the debtor has received the summons ☐

8.2.2. Due information
The debtor was informed in compliance with Article 17 ☐

8.3. Cure of non-compliance with procedural minimum standards pursuant to Article 18(1)

8.3.1. Service of the decision was effected in compliance with Article 13 ☐
or Service of the decision was effected in compliance with Article 14 ☐
or it is proved in accordance with Article 18(2) that the debtor has received the decision ☐

8.3.2. Due information
The debtor was informed in compliance with Article 18(1)(b) ☐

Done at ............. date .............

......................................
Signature and/or stamp

## ANNEX VI
## APPLICATION FOR RECTIFICATION OR WITHDRAWAL OF THE EUROPEAN ENFORCEMENT ORDER CERTIFICATE
(Article 10(3))

THE FOLLOWING EUROPEAN ENFORCEMENT ORDER CERTIFICATE

1. Member State of origin:

| | | | | |
|---|---|---|---|---|
| Belgium ☐ | Czech Republic ☐ | Germany ☐ | Estonia ☐ | Greece ☐ |
| Spain ☐ | France ☐ | Ireland ☐ | Italy ☐ | Cyprus ☐ |
| Latvia ☐ | Lithuania ☐ | Luxembourg ☐ | Hungary ☐ | Malta ☐ |
| Netherland ☐ | Austria ☐ | Poland ☐ | Portugal ☐ | Slovakia ☐ |
| Slovenia ☐ | Finland ☐ | Sweden ☐ | United Kingdom ☐ | |

2. Court/Authority issuing the certificate

2.1. Name:

2.2. Address:

2.3. Tel./fax/e-mail:

3. If different, Court/Authority issuing the judgment/Court settlement/Authentic Instrument*

3.1. Name:

3.2. Address:

3.3. Tel./fax/e-mail:

4. Judgment/Court settlement/Authentic Instrument

4.1. Date:

4.2. Reference number:

4.3. The parties

4.3.1. Name and address of creditor(s):

* Delete as appropriate.

4.3.2. Name and address of debtor(s):

HAS TO BE

5. RECTIFIED as due to a material error there is the following discrepancy between the European Enforcement Order certificate and the underlying judgment/court settlement/authentic instrument (explain) ☐

6. WITHDRAWN because:

6.1. the certified judgment was related to a consumer contract but was given in a Member State where the consumer is not domiciled within the meaning of Article 59 of Regulation (EC) No 44/2001 ☐

6.2. the European Enforcement Order certificate was clearly wrongly granted for another reason (explain) ☐

Done at ............. date .............

.........................................

Signature and/or stamp

# CPR Part 75 Traffic Enforcement



## 75.1 Scope and Interpretation

(1) The practice direction—
  (a) sets out the proceedings to which this Part applies; and
  (b) may apply this Part with modifications in relation to any particular category of those proceedings.
(2) In this Part—
  (a) 'the Centre' means the Traffic Enforcement Centre established under the direction of the Lord Chancellor;
  (b) 'no relevant return to the warrant' means that—
    (i) the bailiff has been unable to seize goods because he has been denied access to premises occupied by the defendant or because the goods have been removed from those premises;
    (ii) any goods seized under a warrant of execution are insufficient to satisfy the debt and the cost of execution; or
    (iii) the goods are insufficient to cover the cost of their removal and sale;
  (c) 'the 1993 Order' means the Enforcement of Road Traffic Debts Order 1993;
  (d) 'relevant period', in relation to any particular case, means—
    (i) the period allowed for serving a statutory declaration under any enactment which applies to that case; or
    (ii) where an enactment permits the court to extend that period, the period as extended;
  (e) 'specified debts' means the debts specified in article 2 of the 1993 Order or treated as so specified by any other enactment; and
  (f) 'the authority', 'notice of the amount due', 'order' and 'the respondent' have the meaning given by the practice direction.

## 75.2 The Centre

(1) Proceedings to which this Part applies must be started in the Centre.
(2) For any purpose connected with the exercise of the Centre's functions—
  (a) the Centre shall be deemed to be part of the office of the court whose name appears on the documents to which the functions relates or in whose name the documents are issued; and
  (b) any officer of the Centre, in exercising its functions, is deemed to act as an officer of that court.

## 75.3 Request

(1) The authority must file a request in the appropriate form scheduling the amount claimed to be due.

(2) The authority must, in that request or in another manner approved by the court officer—
 (a) certify—
  (i) that 14 days have elapsed since service of the notice of the amount due;
  (ii) the date of such service;
  (iii) the number of the notice of the amount due; and
  (iv) that the amount due remains unpaid;
 (b) specify the grounds (whether by reference to the appropriate code or otherwise), as stated in the notice, on which the authority claims to be entitled to claim that amount; and
 (c) state—
  (i) the name, title and address of the respondent;
  (ii) the registration number of the vehicle concerned;
  (iii) the authority's address for service;
  (iv) the court fee; and
  (v) such other matters as required by the practice direction.

(3) On receipt of a request that meets the requirements of paragraphs (1) and (2), the court officer will order that the amount due may be recovered as if it were payable under a county court order by sealing the request and returning it to the authority.

(4) On receipt of a sealed request the authority may draw up an order and must attach to it a form of statutory declaration for the respondent's use.

(5) Within 14 days of receipt of the sealed request, the authority must serve the order (and the form of statutory declaration) on the respondent in accordance with Part 6.

(6) Where an order is served by first class post (or an alternative service which provides for delivery on the next working day) rule 6.7 is modified so that the date of service will be deemed to be the seventh day after the date on which the order was sent to the respondent.

## 75.4 Electronic Delivery of Documents

(1) Where the authority is required to file any document other than the request, that requirement is satisfied if the information which would be contained in the document is delivered in computer-readable form.

(2) For the purposes of paragraph (1), information which would be contained in a document relating to one case may be combined with information of the same nature relating to another case.

(3) Where a document is required to be produced, that requirement will be satisfied if a copy of the document is produced from computer records.

## 75.5 Functions of Court Officer

(1) The practice direction sets out circumstances in which a court officer may exercise the functions of the court or a district judge.

(2) Any party may request any decision of a court officer to be reviewed by a district judge.

(3) Such a request must be made within 14 days of service of the decision.

## 75.6 Enforcement of Orders

Subject to the 1993 Order and this rule the following rules apply to the enforcement of specified debts—
(a) Parts 70 to 73;
(b) CCR Order 25, rules 1 and 9;
(c) CCR Order 26, rule 5; and
(d) CCR Order 27, rules 1 to 7, 7A, 7B, 9 to 16 and 18 to 22.

(Rule 30.2 provides for the transfer between courts in order to enforce a judgment.)

### 75.7 Warrant of Execution

(1) An authority seeking the issue of a warrant of execution must file a request—
  (a) certifying the amount remaining due under the order;
  (b) specifying the date of service of the order on the respondent; and
  (c) certifying that the relevant period has elapsed.
(2) The court will seal the request and return it to the authority.
(3) Within 7 days of the sealing of the request the authority must prepare the warrant in the appropriate form.
(4) No payment under a warrant will be made to the court.
(5) For the purposes of execution a warrant will be valid for 12 months beginning with the date of its issue.
(6) An authority may not renew a warrant issued in accordance with this Part.

### 75.8 Revocation of Order

Where, in accordance with any enactment, an order is deemed to have been revoked following the filing of a statutory declaration—
(a) the court will serve a copy of the statutory declaration on the authority;
(b) any execution issued on the order will cease to have effect; and
(c) if appropriate, the authority must inform any bailiff instructed to levy execution of the withdrawal of the warrant as soon as possible.

### 75.9 Transfer For Enforcement

If an authority requests the transfer of proceedings to another county court for enforcement, the request must—
(a) where the authority has not attempted to enforce by execution, give the reason why no such attempt was made;
(b) certify that there has been no relevant return to the warrant of execution;
(c) specify the date of service of the order on the respondent; and
(d) certify that the relevant period has elapsed.

### 75.10 Further Information Required

An application for—
(a) an attachment of earnings order;
(b) an order to obtain information from a debtor;
(c) a third party debt order; or
(d) a charging order,
must, in addition to the requirements of Parts 71, 72 or 73 or CCR Order 27—
  (i) where the authority has not attempted to enforce by execution, give the reasons no such attempt was made;
  (ii) certify that there has been no relevant return to the warrant of execution;
  (iii) specify the date of service of the order on the respondent; and
  (iv) certify that the relevant period has elapsed.

### 75.11 Combining Requests

If the court officer allows, an authority may combine information relating to different orders against the same defendant in any request or application made under rules 75.9 or 75.10.

# PD 75 Practice Direction — Traffic Enforcement

This practice direction supplements CPR Part 75.

## Interpretation and Scope

1.1 In this Practice Direction:

(1) 'the 1991 Act' means the Road Traffic Act 1991;

(2) 'the 1996 Act' means the London Local Authorities Act 1996;

(3) 'the Road User Charging Regulations' means the Road User Charging (Enforcement and Adjudication) (London) Regulations 2001 (SI 2001/2313);

(4) 'the Vehicle Emissions (England) Regulations' means the Road Traffic (Vehicle Emissions) (Fixed Penalty) (England) Regulations 2002 (SI 2002/1808);

(5) 'the Vehicle Emissions (Wales) Regulations' means the Road Traffic (Vehicle Emissions) (Fixed Penalty) (Wales) Regulations 2003 (SI 2003/300);

(6) 'the 2003 Act' means the London Local Authorities and Transport for London Act 2003.

1.2 Part 75 applies to proceedings for the recovery of:

(1) increased penalty charges provided for in parking charge certificates issued under para. 6 of Schedule 6 to the 1991 Act;

(2) amounts payable by a person other than an authority under an adjudication of a parking adjudicator pursuant to s. 73 of the 1991 Act;

(3) increased penalty charges provided for in a charge certificate issued under para. 8 of sch. 1 to the 1996 Act (relating to a contravention or failure to comply with an order made under a provision referred to in s. 4(2) of that Act reserving all or part of a carriageway of a road as a bus lane);

(4) increased fixed penalties to which reg. 17(6) of the Vehicle Emissions (England) Regulations refers;

(5) amounts payable by a person other than an authority under an adjudication of an adjudicator pursuant to the schedule to the Road User Charging Regulations;

(6) increased penalty charges provided for in charge certificates issued under reg. 17 of the Road User Charging Regulations; and

(7) increased fixed penalties to which reg. 17(6) of the Vehicle Emissions (Wales) Regulations refers.

1.3 In Part 75 and this practice direction:

(1) 'authority' means the authority entitled to recover amounts due under the enactments referred to in para. 1.2;

(2) 'notice of the amount due' means, as the case may be:

(a) a parking charge certificate issued under para. 6 of sch. 6 to the 1991 Act;

(b) a charge certificate issued under para. 8 of sch. 1 to the 1996 Act;

(c) a fixed penalty notice issued under reg. 10 or reg. 13 of the Vehicle Emissions (England) Regulations;

(d) a charge certificate issued under reg. 17 of the Road User Charging Regulations; or

(e) a fixed penalty notice issued under reg. 10 or reg. 13 of the Vehicle Emissions (Wales) Regulations.

(3) 'order' means an order made under:

(a) para. 7 of sch. 6 to the 1991 Act;

(b) para. 9 of sch. 1 to the 1996 Act;

(c) s. 73(15) of the 1991 Act;

(d) reg. 21 of the Vehicle Emissions (England) Regulations;

(e) reg. 7 of the Road User Charging Regulations;

(f) reg. 18 of the Road User Charging Regulations; or
(g) reg. 21 of the Vehicle Emissions (Wales) Regulations;
(4) 'respondent' means:
(a) the person on whom the notice of the amount due was served; or
(b) the person (other than an authority) by whom the amount due under an adjudication is payable.

## Traffic Enforcement Centre

2.1 All claims to which Part 75 applies must be started in the Traffic Enforcement Centre ('the Centre') at Northampton County Court.

## Request

3.1 Where an order in respect of amounts payable by a person other than an authority under an adjudication pursuant to s. 73 of the 1991 Act or the schedule to the Road User Charging Regulations is sought, r. 75.3 applies with the necessary modifications and, in addition, the request must:
(1) state the date on which the adjudication was made;
(2) provide details of the order made on the adjudication; and
(3) certify the amount awarded by way of costs and that the amount remains unpaid.

## Functions of Court Officer

4.1 A court officer may exercise the functions of:
(1) the district judge under:
(a) para. 8(4) and (5)(d) of sch. 6 to the 1991 Act;
(b) para. 10(4) and (5)(d) of sch. 1 to the 1996 Act; and
(c) reg. 19(4) and (5)(d) of the Road User Charging Regulations; and
(2) the court under:
(a) reg. 23(3) of the Vehicle Emissions (England) Regulations; and
(b) reg. 23(3) of the Vehicle Emissions (Wales) Regulations.

## Application for Longer Period for Filing of Statutory Declaration

5.1 Paragraphs 5.2 to 5.5 apply where the respondent applies under:
(1) para. 8(3) of sch. 6 to the Road Traffic Act 1991;
(2) para. 10(3) of sch. 1 to the London Local Authorities Act 1996;
(3) reg. 23(3) of the Vehicle Emissions (England) Regulations;
(4) reg. 19(3) of the Road User Charging Regulations; or
(5) reg. 23(3) of the Vehicle Emissions (Wales) Regulations,
for an order allowing a longer period than 21 days for service of the statutory declaration.

5.2 The respondent must send to the Centre:
(1) a completed application notice (form PE 2 may be used); and
(2) a completed statutory declaration in form PE 3.
(Forms PE 2 and PE 3 can be obtained from the Centre at Northampton County Court, Bulk Centre, 21/27 St Katharine's Street, Northampton NN1 2LH. Telephone number: 08457 045007.)

5.3 The court will serve a copy of the application notice and a copy of the statutory declaration on the authority that obtained the court order seeking representations on the application.

5.4 A court officer will deal with the application without a hearing. The matter will not be dealt with until at least 14 days after the date on which the application notice and statutory declaration were served on the authority.

5.5 If the proceedings have been transferred to another court the Centre will transfer the application to that court.

5.6 Paragraphs 5.3 to 5.5 shall not apply where the court receives an application notice that is accompanied by a statutory declaration that is invalid by virtue of para. 8(2A) of sch. 6 to the 1991 Act as inserted by s. 15 of the 2003 Act.

## Application to Review Order Made by Court Officer

6.1 Where any order is made by a court officer it will contain a statement of the right of either party to request a review of the decision by a district judge at a hearing.

6.2 Attention is drawn to r. 75.5(2) and (3).

## Hearing

7.1 When a hearing is to be held, the proceedings will be transferred to the county court for the district in which the respondent's address for service is situated. This transfer is only for the purposes of holding the hearing and serving any orders made as a result of the hearing.

7.2 The respondent's address for service is his address for service shown on the last of the following documents filed at court by the respondent:

(1) the application notice or, if more than one, the latest application notice; and

(2) the appellant's notice.

7.3 The court where the hearing is held will serve any orders made as a result of the hearing before returning the papers to the Centre, or, if the proceedings have been transferred, to the court where the proceedings have been transferred.

7.4 Evidence at any hearing may be given orally or by witness statement.

## Applications to Suspend a Warrant of Execution

8.1 Where:

(1) the respondent makes an application under para. 5; and

(2) before that application is determined, a warrant of execution is issued,

the local authority must suspend enforcement of the warrant of execution until the application for an extension order is determined.

(Rule 75.7(b) provides that, where a court order is revoked because a statutory declaration has been served, any execution issued on the order will cease to have effect.)

# CPR Part 76 Proceedings Under the Prevention of Terrorism Act 2005



## SECTION 1 APPLICATIONS OF THIS PART

### 76.1 Scope and Interpretation

(1) This Part contains rules about—
  (a) control order proceedings in the High Court; and
  (b) appeals to the Court of Appeal against an order of the High Court in such proceedings.

(2) In the case of proceedings brought by virtue of section 11(2) of the Act, the rules in this Part shall apply with any modification which the court considers necessary.

(3) In this Part—
  (a) 'the Act' means the Prevention of Terrorism Act 2005;
  (b) 'closed material' means any relevant material that the Secretary of State objects to disclosing to a relevant party;
  (c) 'control order proceedings' has the same meaning as in section 11(6) of the Act;
  (d) 'controlled person' has the same meaning as in section 15(1) of the Act;
  (e) 'legal representative' is to be construed in accordance with paragraph 11 of the Schedule to the Act;
  (f) 'open material' means any relevant material that the Secretary of State does not object to disclosing to a relevant party;

(g) 'relevant law officer' has the same meaning as in paragraph 7(6) of the Schedule to the Act;
(h) 'relevant material' has the same meaning as in paragraph 4(5) of the Schedule to the Act;
(i) 'relevant party' has the same meaning as in paragraph 11 of the Schedule to the Act;
(j) 'special advocate' means a person appointed under paragraph 7 of the Schedule to the Act.

(4) For the purposes of this Part, disclosure is contrary to the public interest if it is made contrary to the interests of national security, the international relations of the United Kingdom, the detection and prevention of crime, or in any other circumstances where disclosure is likely to harm the public interest.

### 76.2 Modification to the Overriding Objective

(1) Where this Part applies, the overriding objective in Part 1, and so far as relevant any other rule, must be read and given effect in a way which is compatible with the duty set out in paragraph (2).
(2) The court must ensure that information is not disclosed contrary to the public interest.
(3) Subject to paragraph (2), the court must satisfy itself that the material available to it enables it properly to determine proceedings.

## SECTION 2 APPLICATIONS TO THE HIGH COURT RELATING TO DEROGATING CONTROL ORDERS

### 76.3 Scope of this Section

(1) This section of this Part contains rules about applications relating to derogating control orders.
(2) Part 23 does not apply to an application made under this section of this Part.

### 76.4 Applications for the Making of a Derogating Control Order

An application for the making of a derogating control order under section 4(1) of the Act must be made by the Secretary of State by filing with the court—

(a) a statement of reasons to support the application for—
    (i) making such an order, and
    (ii) imposing each of the obligations to be imposed by that order;
(b) all relevant material;
(c) any written submissions; and
(d) a draft of the order sought.

### 76.5 Directions for a Full Hearing on Notice

(1) When the court makes a derogating control order under section 4(3) of the Act it must—
    (a) immediately fix a date, time and place for a further hearing at which the controlled person, his legal representative and a special advocate (if one has been appointed) can be present; and
    (b) unless the court otherwise directs, that date must be no later than 7 days from the date that the order is made.
(2) At the hearing referred to in paragraph (1)(a) the court must give directions—
    (a) for the holding of a full hearing under section 4(1)(b) of the Act to determine whether to confirm the control order (with or without modifications) or to revoke it; and
    (b) specifying the date and time by which the parties and special advocate must file and serve any written evidence or written submissions in accordance with rule 76.30.

(3) When giving directions under paragraph (2), the court must have regard to the need to expedite the full hearing.

### 76.6 Applications on Notice

(1) An application under section 4(9) for the renewal, or under section 7(4) of the Act, for the revocation of a control order or for the modification of obligations imposed by such an order, must be made in accordance with this rule.
(2) An application by the Secretary of State must be made by—
 (a) filing with the court—
  (i) a statement of reasons to support the application,
  (ii) all relevant material,
  (iii) any written submissions, and
  (iv) a draft of the order sought; and
 (b) serving on the controlled person or his legal representative any open material.
(3) An application by the controlled person must be made by filing with the court and serving on the Secretary of State—
 (a) a statement of reasons to support the application;
 (b) any written evidence upon which he relies;
 (c) any written submissions; and
 (d) where appropriate, a draft of the order sought.
(4) If the controlled person wishes to oppose an application made under this rule, he must as soon as practicable file with the court, and serve on the Secretary of State, any written evidence and any written submissions upon which he relies.
(5) If the Secretary of State wishes to oppose an application made under this rule, he must as soon as practicable—
 (a) file with the court—
  (i) all relevant material, and
  (ii) any written submissions; and
 (b) serve on the controlled person any open material.

(Attention is drawn to rule 76.18 relating to the address for issuing proceedings in the High Court. Rules 76.28 and 76.29 will apply where any closed material is filed by the Secretary of State.)

## SECTION 3 PERMISSION APPLICATIONS, REFERENCES AND APPEALS TO THE HIGH COURT RELATING TO NON-DEROGATING CONTROL ORDERS

### 76.7 Scope of this Section

This section of this Part contains rules about—
(a) applications under section 3(1)(a) of the Act (application for permission to make a non-derogating control order);
(b) references under section 3(3) of the Act (reference of a non-derogating control order made without permission); and
(c) appeals to the High Court under section 10 of the Act (appeals relating to non-derogating control orders).

### 76.8 Application for Permission to Make Non-derogating Control Order

An application under section 3(1)(a) for permission to make a non-derogating control order must be made by the Secretary of State by filing with the court—
(a) a statement of reasons to support the application;
(b) all relevant material;
(c) any written submissions; and
(d) the proposed control order.

### 76.9 References under Section 3(3) of the Act

(1) This rule applies where the Secretary of State makes a reference under section 3(3) of the Act (reference of a non-derogating control order).
(2) The Secretary of State must promptly file with the court—
  (a) a statement of the reasons for—
    (i) making the control order,
    (ii) imposing the obligations imposed by that order;
  (b) all relevant material; and
  (c) any written submissions.

### 76.10 Directions for Hearing on Application for Permission or on a Reference

(1) This rule applies where the court gives directions under section 3(2)(c) or (6)(b) or (c) of the Act.
(2) The court must immediately—
  (a) fix a date, time and place for a further hearing at which the controlled person, his legal representative and a special advocate (if one has been appointed) can be present; and
  (b) unless the court otherwise directs, that date must be no later than 7 days from the date that the order is made.
(3) At the hearing referred to in paragraph (2), the court must give directions—
  (a) for a hearing under section 3(10); and
  (b) specifying the date and time by which the parties and special advocate must file and serve any written evidence or written submissions in accordance with rule 76.30.
(4) When giving directions under paragraph (3), the court must have regard to the need to expedite that hearing.

(Rules 76.28 and 76.29 will apply where any closed material is filed by the Secretary of State.)

### 76.11 Appeals under Section 10 of the Act

This rule and rules 76.12 to 76.15 apply to an appeal under section 10 of the Act (appeals relating to a non-derogating control order).

### 76.12 Modification of Part 52 (Appeals)

(1) Part 52 (appeals) applies to an appeal under section 10 of the Act, subject to—
  (a) rule 76.2;
  (b) the rules in section 5 of this Part; and
  (c) the modifications set out in paragraphs (2) and (3) of this rule.
(2) The following rules do not apply to appeals under section 10 of the Act—
  (a) rule 52.3 (permission);
  (b) rule 52.4 (appellant's notice);
  (c) rule 52.5 (respondent's notice); and
  (d) rule 52.11 (hearing of appeals).
(3) Rule 52.2 (all parties to comply with the practice direction) applies, but the parties shall not be required to comply with paragraphs 5.6, 5.6A, 5.7, 5.9 and 5.10 of that practice direction.

### 76.13 Notice of Appeal

(1) The controlled person must give notice of appeal by—
  (a) filing it with the court; and
  (b) serving a copy of the notice and any accompanying documents on the Secretary of State.

(2) The notice of appeal must—
  (a) set out the grounds of the appeal; and
  (b) state the name and address of—
    (i) the controlled person, and
    (ii) any legal representative of that person.
(3) A notice of appeal may include an application for an order under rule 76.19 requiring anonymity.
(4) The notice of appeal must be filed with—
  (a) a copy of the order that is the subject of the appeal;
  (b) a copy of the Secretary of State's decision on an application for the revocation of the control order, or for the modification of an obligation imposed by such an order.

(Attention is drawn to rule 76.18 relating to the address for issuing proceedings in the High Court.)

### 76.14 Time Limit for Appealing

(1) Subject to paragraph (2), the controlled person must give notice of appeal no later than 28 days after receiving notice of—
  (a) the order that is the subject of the appeal; or
  (b) the decision by the Secretary of State on an application for the revocation of the control order, or for the modification of an obligation imposed by such an order.
(2) In a case where the Secretary of State has failed to determine an application for the revocation of the control order, or for the modification of an obligation imposed by such an order, the controlled person must file the notice of appeal—
  (a) no earlier than 28 days; and
  (b) no later than 42 days;
  after the date the application was made.

### 76.15 Secretary of State's Reply

If the Secretary of State wishes to oppose an appeal made under section 10 of the Act, he must no later than 14 days after he is served with the notice of appeal—
(a) file with the court—
  (i) all relevant material, and
  (ii) any written submissions; and
(b) serve on the controlled person any open material.

## SECTION 4 APPEALS TO THE COURT OF APPEAL

### 76.16 Modification of Part 52 (Appeals)

(1) Part 52 (appeals) applies to an appeal to the Court of Appeal against an order of the High Court in control order proceedings, subject to—
  (a) rule 76.2;
  (b) the rules in section 5 of this Part; and
  (c) paragraphs (2) and (3) of this rule.
(2) The following rules do not apply to appeals to the Court of Appeal—
  (a) rule 52.4(1) (appellant's notice); and
  (b) rule 52.5 (respondent's notice); but
  the provisions of rules 76.13 and 76.15 shall apply with appropriate modifications.
(3) Rule 52.2 (all parties to comply with the practice direction) applies, but the parties shall not be required to comply with paragraphs 5.6, 5.6A, 5.7, 6.3A, 15.2, 15.3, 15.4 and 15.6 of that practice direction.

## SECTION 5 GENERAL PROVISIONS

### .17 Scope of this Section

his section of this Part applies to—
(a) control order proceedings in the High Court; and
(b) appeals to the Court of Appeal against an order of the High Court in such proceedings.

### 76.18 Address for Issuing Proceedings in the High Court

Any control order proceedings must be issued at the Administrative Court Office, Room C315, Royal Courts of Justice, Strand, London, WC2A 2LL.

### 76.19 Applications for Anonymity

(1) The controlled person or the Secretary of State may apply for an order requiring the anonymity of the controlled person.
(2) An application under paragraph (1) may be made at any time, irrespective of whether any control order proceedings have been commenced.
(3) An application may be made without notice to the other party.
(4) References in this rule to an order requiring anonymity for the controlled person are to be construed in accordance with paragraph 5(3) of the Schedule to the Act.

### 76.20 Notification of Hearing

Unless the court orders otherwise, it must serve notice of the date, time and place fixed for any hearing on—
(a) every party, whether or not entitled to attend that hearing; and
(b) if one has been appointed for the purposes of the hearing, the special advocate or those instructing him.

### 76.21 Hearings

(1) The following proceedings must be determined at a hearing—
  (a) a hearing pursuant to directions given under section 4(1)(b) of the Act (derogating control orders);
  (b) a hearing pursuant to directions given under sections 3(2)(c) or (6)(b) or (c) of the Act (non-derogating control orders);
  (c) an appeal under section 10 of the Act (appeal relating to a non-derogating control order);
  (d) an appeal to the Court of Appeal from an order of the High Court made in any of the above proceedings; and
  (e) a hearing under rule 76.29(2) (consideration of Secretary of State's objection).
(2) Paragraph (1)(c) and (d) do not apply where—
  (a) the appeal is withdrawn by the controlled person;
  (b) the Secretary of State consents to the appeal being allowed; or
  (c) the controlled person is outside the United Kingdom or it is impracticable to give him notice of a hearing and, in either case, he is unrepresented.

### 76.22 Hearings in Private

(1) If the court considers it necessary for any relevant party and his legal representative to be excluded from a hearing or part of a hearing in order to secure that information is not disclosed contrary to the public interest, it must—
  (a) direct accordingly; and
  (b) conduct the hearing, or that part of it from which the relevant party and his legal representative are excluded, in private.
(2) The court may conduct a hearing or part of a hearing in private for any other good reason.

### 76.23 Appointment of a Special Advocate

(1) Subject to paragraph (2), the Secretary of State must immediately give notice of the proceedings to the relevant law officer upon—
  (a) making an application under section 4(1) of the Act (relating to a derogating control order);
  (b) making an application under section 3(1)(a) of the Act (application for permission to make a non-derogating control order);
  (c) making a reference under section 3(3) of the Act (reference of a non-derogating control order made without permission); or
  (d) being served with a copy of any application, claim, or notice of appeal in proceedings to which this Part applies.

(2) Paragraph (1) applies unless—
  (a) the Secretary of State does not intend to—
    (i) oppose the appeal or application; or
    (ii) withhold closed material from a relevant party; or
  (b) a special advocate has already been appointed to represent the interests of the relevant party in the proceedings and that special advocate is not prevented from communicating with that party by virtue of rule 76.25.

(3) Where notice is given to the relevant law officer under paragraph (1), the relevant law officer may appoint a special advocate to represent the interests of the relevant party in the proceedings.

(4) Where any proceedings to which this Part apply are pending but no special advocate has been appointed, a relevant party or the Secretary of State may request the relevant law officer to appoint a special advocate.

### 76.24 Functions of Special Advocate

The functions of a special advocate are to represent the interests of a relevant party by—
(a) making submissions to the court at any hearings from which the relevant party and his legal representatives are excluded;
(b) cross-examining witnesses at any such hearings; and
(c) making written submissions to the court.

### 76.25 Special Advocate: Communicating about Proceedings

(1) The special advocate may communicate with the relevant party or his legal representative at any time before the Secretary of State serves closed material on him.

(2) After the Secretary of State serves closed material on the special advocate, the special advocate must not communicate with any person about any matter connected with the proceedings, except in accordance with paragraph (3) or a direction of the court pursuant to a request under paragraph (4).

(3) The special advocate may, without directions from the court, communicate about the proceedings with—
  (a) the court;
  (b) the Secretary of State, or any person acting for him;
  (c) the relevant law officer, or any person acting for him; or
  (d) any other person, except for the relevant party or his legal representative, with whom it is necessary for administrative purposes for him to communicate about matters not connected with the substance of the proceedings.

(4) The special advocate may request directions from the court authorising him to communicate with the relevant party or his legal representative or with any other person.

(5) Where the special advocate makes a request for directions under paragraph (4)—
  (a) the court must notify the Secretary of State of the request; and

CPF

b) the Secretary of State must, within a period specified by the court, file with the court and serve on the special advocate notice of any objection which he has to the proposed communication, or to the form in which it is proposed to be made.

Paragraph (2) does not prohibit the relevant party from communicating with the special advocate after the Secretary of State has served material on him as mentioned in paragraph (1), but—

(a) the relevant party may only communicate with the special advocate through a legal representative in writing; and
(b) the special advocate must not reply to the communication other than in accordance with directions of the court, except that he may without such directions send a written acknowledgment of receipt to the legal representative of the relevant party.

## 76.26 Modification of the General Rules of Evidence and Disclosure

(1) Part 31 (disclosure and inspection of documents), Part 32 (evidence) and Part 33 (miscellaneous rules about evidence) do not apply to any proceedings to which this Part applies.
(2) Subject to the other rules in this Part, the evidence of a witness may be given either—
  (a) orally, before the court; or
  (b) in writing, in which case it shall be given in such manner and at such time as the court directs.
(3) The court may also receive evidence in documentary or any other form.
(4) The court may receive evidence that would not, but for this rule, be admissible in a court of law.
(5) Every party shall be entitled to adduce evidence and to cross-examine witnesses during any part of a hearing from which he and his legal representative are not excluded.
(6) The court may require a witness to give evidence on oath.

## 76.27 Filing and Service of Relevant Material

The Secretary of State is required to make a reasonable search for relevant material and to file and serve that material in accordance with the rules in this Part.

## 76.28 Closed Material

(1) The Secretary of State—
  (a) must apply to the court for permission to withhold closed material from a relevant party or his legal representative in accordance with this rule; and
  (b) may not rely on closed material at a hearing on notice unless a special advocate has been appointed to represent the interests of the relevant party.
(2) The Secretary of State must file with the court and serve, at such time as the court directs, on the special advocate—
  (a) the closed material;
  (b) a statement of his reasons for withholding that material from the relevant party; and
  (c) if he considers it possible to summarise that material without disclosing information contrary to the public interest, a summary of that material in a form which can be served on the relevant party.
(3) The Secretary of State may at any time amend or supplement material filed under this rule, but only with—
  (a) the agreement of the special advocate; or
  (b) the permission of the court.

## 76.29 Consideration of Secretary of State's Objection

(1) This rule applies where the Secretary of State has—
  (a) objected under rule 76.25(5)(b) to a proposed communication by the special advocate; or

(b) applied under rule 76.28 for permission to withhold closed material.

(2) The court must fix a hearing for the Secretary of State and the special advocate to make oral representations, unless—
  (a) the special advocate gives notice to the court that he does not challenge the objection or application;
  (b) the court has previously considered—
    (i) an objection under rule 76.25(5)(b), or
    (ii) an application under rule 76.28(1) for permission to withhold the same or substantially the same material, and

  is satisfied that it would be just to uphold that objection or to give permission without a hearing; or
  (c) the Secretary of State and the special advocate consent to the court deciding the issue without a hearing.

(3) If the special advocate does not challenge the objection or the application, he must give notice of that fact to the court and the Secretary of State within 14 days, or such other period as the court may direct, after the Secretary of State serves on him a notice under rule 76.25(5)(b) or material under rule 76.28(2).

(4) Where the court fixes a hearing under this rule, the Secretary of State and the special advocate must before the hearing file with the court a schedule identifying the issues which cannot be agreed between them, which must—
  (a) list the items or issues in dispute;
  (b) give brief reasons for their contentions on each; and
  (c) set out any proposals for the court to resolve the issues in contention.

(5) A hearing under this rule shall take place in the absence of the relevant party and his legal representative.

(6) Where the court gives permission to the Secretary of State to withhold closed material, the court must—
  (a) consider whether to direct the Secretary of State to serve a summary of that material on the relevant party or his legal representative; but
  (b) ensure that no such summary contains information or other material the disclosure of which would be contrary to the public interest.

(7) Where the court has not given permission to the Secretary of State to withhold closed material from, or has directed the Secretary of State to serve a summary of that material on, a relevant party or his legal representative—
  (a) the Secretary of State shall not be required to serve that material or summary; but
  (b) if he does not do so, at a hearing on notice the court may—
    (i) if it considers that the material or anything that is required to be summarised might be of assistance to the relevant party in relation to a matter under consideration by the court, direct that the matter be withdrawn from its consideration, and
    (ii) in any other case, direct that the Secretary of State shall not rely in the proceedings on that material or (as the case may be) on what is required to be summarised.

(8) The court must give permission to the Secretary of State to withhold closed material where it considers that the disclosure of that material would be contrary to the public interest.

## 76.30 Order of Filing and Serving Material and Written Submissions

Subject to any directions given by the court, the parties must file and serve any material and written submissions, and the special advocate must file and serve any written submissions, in the following order—

(a) the Secretary of State must file with the court all relevant material;

(b) the Secretary of State must serve on—

(i) the relevant party or his legal representative; and
(ii) the special advocate (as soon as one is appointed) or those instructing him,
any open material;
(c) the relevant party must file with the court and serve on the Secretary of State and special advocate (if one is appointed) or those instructing him any written evidence which he wishes the court to take into account at the hearing;
(d) the Secretary of State must file with the court any further relevant material;
(e) the Secretary of State must serve on—
(i) the relevant party or his legal representative, and
(ii) the special advocate (as soon as one is appointed) or those instructing him,
any open material filed with the court under paragraph (d);
(f) the Secretary of State must serve on the special advocate (if one has been appointed) any closed material;
(g) the parties and the special advocate (if one has been appointed) must file and serve any written submissions as directed by the court.

(Rules 76.28 and 76.29 will apply where any closed material is filed by the Secretary of State.)

## 76.31 Failure to Comply with Directions

(1) Where a party or the special advocate fails to comply with a direction of the court, the court may serve on him a notice which states—
(a) the respect in which he has failed to comply with the direction;
(b) a time limit for complying with the direction; and
(c) that the court may proceed to determine the proceedings before it, on the material available to it, if the party or the special advocate fails to comply with the relevant direction within the time specified.
(2) Where a party or special advocate fails to comply with such a notice, the court may proceed in accordance with paragraph (1)(c).

## 76.32 Judgments

(1) When the court gives judgment in any proceedings to which this Part applies, it may withhold any or part of its reasons if and to the extent that it is not possible to give reasons without disclosing information contrary to the public interest.
(2) Where the judgment of the court does not include the full reasons for its decision, the court must serve on the Secretary of State and the special advocate a separate written judgment including those reasons.

## 76.33 Application by Secretary of State for Reconsideration of Decision

(1) This rule applies where the court proposes, in any proceedings to which this Part applies, to serve notice on a relevant party of any—
(a) order or direction made or given in the absence of the Secretary of State; or
(b) any judgment.
(2) Before the court serves any such notice on the relevant party, it must first serve notice on the Secretary of State of its intention to do so.
(3) The Secretary of State may, within 5 days of being served with notice under paragraph (2), apply to the court to reconsider the terms of the order or direction or to review the terms of the proposed judgment if he considers that—
(a) his compliance with the order or direction; or
(b) the notification to the relevant party of any matter contained in the judgment, order or direction;
would cause information to be disclosed contrary to the public interest.
(4) Where the Secretary of State makes an application under paragraph (3), he must at the same time serve a copy of it on the special advocate, if one has been appointed.
(5) Rule 76.29 (except for paragraphs (6) and (7)) shall, if a special advocate has been

appointed, apply with any necessary modifications to the consideration of an application under paragraph (3) of this rule.

(6) The court must not serve notice on the relevant party as mentioned in paragraph (1) before the time for the Secretary of State to make an application under paragraph (3) has expired.

### 76.34 Supply of Court Documents

Unless the court otherwise directs, rule 5.4 (Register of Claims), rule 5.4B (Supply of documents from court records—a party) and rule 5.4C (Supply of documents from court record—a non-party) do not apply to any proceedings to which this Part applies.

# Glossary

## Scope

This glossary is a guide to the meaning of certain legal expressions as used in these Rules, but it does not give the expressions any meaning in the Rules which they do not otherwise have in the law.

| Expression | Meaning |
|---|---|
| Affidavit | A written, sworn statement of evidence. |
| Alternative dispute resolution | Collective description of methods of resolving disputes otherwise than through the normal trial process. |
| Base rate | The interest rate set by the Bank of England which is used as the basis for other banks' rates. |
| Contribution | A right of someone to recover from a third person all or part of the amount which he himself is liable to pay. |
| Counterclaim | A claim brought by a defendant in response to the claimant's claim, which is included in the same proceedings as the claimant's claim. |
| Cross-examination (and see 'evidence in chief') | Questioning of a witness by a party other than the party who called the witness. |
| Damages | A sum of money awarded by the court as compensation to the claimant. |
| • aggravated damages | Additional damages which the court may award as compensation for the defendant's objectionable behaviour. |
| • exemplary damages | Damages which go beyond compensating for actual loss and are awarded to show the court's disapproval of the defendant's behaviour. |
| Defence of tender before claim | A defence that, before the claimant started proceedings, the defendant unconditionally offered to the claimant the amount due or, if no specified amount is claimed, an amount sufficient to satisfy the claim. |
| Evidence in chief (and see 'cross-examination') | The evidence given by a witness for the party who called him. |
| Indemnity | A right of someone to recover from a third party the whole amount which he himself is liable to pay. |
| Injunction | A court order prohibiting a person from doing something or requiring a person to do something. |
| Joint liability (and see 'several liability') | Parties who are jointly liable share a single liability and each party can be held liable for the whole of it. |
| Limitation period | The period within which a person who has a right to claim against another person must start court proceedings to establish that right. The expiry of the period may be a defence to the claim. |
| List | Cases are allocated to different lists depending on the subject matter of the case. The lists are used for administrative purposes and may also have their own procedures and judges. |
| Official copy | A copy of an official document, supplied and marked as such by the office which issued the original. |

| Expression | Meaning |
|---|---|
| Practice form | Form to be used for a particular purpose in proceedings, the form and purpose being specified by a practice direction. |
| Pre-action protocol | Statements of understanding between legal practitioners and others about pre-action practice and which are approved by a relevant practice direction. |
| Privilege | The right of a party to refuse to disclose a document or produce a document or to refuse to answer questions on the ground of some special interest recognised by law. |
| Seal | A seal is a mark which the court puts on a document to indicate that the document has been issued by the court. |
| Service | Steps required by rules of court to bring documents used in court proceedings to a person's attention. |
| Set aside | Cancelling a judgment or order or a step taken by a party in the proceedings. |
| Several liability (and see 'joint liability') | A person who is severally liable with others may remain liable for the whole claim even where judgment has been obtained against the others. |
| Stay | A stay imposes a halt on proceedings, apart from taking any steps allowed by the Rules or the terms of the stay. Proceedings can be continued if a stay is lifted. |
| Strike out | Striking out means the court ordering written material to be deleted so that it may no longer be relied upon. |
| Without prejudice | Negotiations with a view to a settlement are usually conducted 'without prejudice', which means that the circumstances in which the content of those negotiations may be revealed to the court are very restricted. |

# Section 2

## CPR SCHEDULES AND SPECIALIST PRACTICE DIRECTIONS*

[* This section sets out the various Specialist Practice Directions (those not related to specific CPR parts) following the text of Schedule 2.]

# CPR Schedule 1

## RSC ORDER 17
## INTERPLEADER

### Rule 1 Entitlement to Relief by Way of Interpleader

(1) Where—

(a) a person is under a liability in respect of a debt or in respect of any money, goods or chattels and he is, or expects to be, sued for or in respect of that debt or money or those goods or chattels by two or more persons making adverse claims thereto; or

(b) claim is made to any money, goods or chattels taken or intended to be taken by a sheriff in execution under any process, or to the proceeds or value of any such goods or chattels, by a person other than the person against whom the process is issued,

the person under liability as mentioned in sub-paragraph (a) or (subject to rule 2) the sheriff, may apply to the court for relief by way of interpleader.

(2) References in this Order to a sheriff shall be construed as including references to—

(a) an individual authorised to act as an enforcement officer under the Courts Act 2003; and

(b) any other officer charged with the execution of process by or under the authority of the High Court.

### Rule 2 Claim to Goods, etc., Taken in Execution

(1) Any person making a claim to or in respect of any money, goods or chattels taken or intended to be taken in execution under process of the court, or to the proceeds or value of any such goods or chattels, must give notice of his claim to the sheriff charged with the execution of the process and must include in his notice a statement of his address, and that address shall be his address for service.

(2) On receipt of a claim made under this rule the sheriff must forthwith give notice thereof to the execution creditor and the execution creditor must, within seven days after receiving the notice, give notice to the sheriff informing him whether he admits or disputes the claim. An execution creditor who gives notice in accordance with this paragraph admitting a claim shall only be liable to the sheriff for any fees and expenses incurred by the sheriff before receipt of that notice.

(3) Where—

(a) the sheriff receives a notice from an execution creditor under paragraph (2) disputing a claim, or the execution creditor fails, within the period mentioned in that paragraph, to give the required notice; and

(b) the claim made under this rule is not withdrawn,

the sheriff may apply to the court for relief under this order.

(4) A sheriff who receives a notice from an execution creditor under paragraph (2) admitting a claim made under this rule shall withdraw from possession of the money, goods or chattels claimed and may apply to the court for relief under this order of the following kind, that is to say, an order restraining the bringing of a claim against him for or in respect of his having taken possession of that money or those goods or chattels.

### Rule 2A Claim in Respect of Goods Protected from Seizure

(1) Where a judgment debtor whose goods have been seized, or are intended to be seized, by a sheriff under a writ of execution claims that such goods are not liable to execution by virtue of section 138(3A) of the Act, he must within 5 days of the seizure give notice in writing to the sheriff identifying all those goods in respect of which he makes such a claim and the grounds of such claim in respect of each item.

(2) Upon receipt of a notice of claim under paragraph (1), the sheriff must forthwith give notice thereof to the execution creditor and to any person who has made a claim to, or

in respect of, the goods under rule 2(1) and the execution creditor and any person who has made claim must, within 7 days of receipt of such notice, inform the sheriff in writing whether he admits or disputes the judgment debtor's claim in respect of each item.

(3) The sheriff shall withdraw from possession of any goods in respect of which the judgment debtor's claim is admitted or if the execution creditor or any person claiming under rule 2(1) fails to notify him in accordance with paragraph (2) and the sheriff shall so inform the parties in writing.

(4) Where the sheriff receives notice from—
   (a) the execution creditor; or
   (b) any such person to whom notice was given under paragraph (2),

   that the claim or any part thereof is disputed, he must forthwith seek the directions of the court and may include therein an application for an order restraining the bringing of any claim against him for, or in respect of, his having seized any of those goods or his having failed so to do.

(5) The sheriff's application for directions under paragraph (4) shall be made by an application in accordance with CPR Part 23 and, on the hearing of the application, the court may—
   (a) determine the judgment debtor's claim summarily; or
   (b) give such directions for the determination of any issue raised by such claim as may be just.

(6) A Master and a district judge of a district registry shall have power to make an order of the kind referred to in paragraph (4) and the reference to Master shall be construed in accordance with rule 4.

## Rule 3 Mode of Application

(1) An application for relief under this order must be made by claim form unless made in an existing claim, in which case it must be made by accordance with CPR Part 23.

(2) Where the applicant is a sheriff who has withdrawn from possession of money, goods or chattels taken in execution and who is applying for relief under rule 2(4) the claim form must be served on any person who made a claim under that rule to or in respect of that money or those goods or chattels, and that person may attend the hearing of the application.

(4) Subject to paragraph (5) a claim form or application notice under this rule must be supported by evidence that the applicant—
   (a) claims no interest in the subject-matter in dispute other than for charges or costs;
   (b) does not collude with any of the claimants to that subject-matter; and
   (c) is willing to pay or transfer that subject-matter into court or to dispose of it as the court may direct.

(5) Where the applicant is a sheriff, he shall not provide such evidence as is referred to in paragraph (4) unless directed by the court to do so.

(6) Any person who makes a claim under rule 2 and who is served with a claim form under this rule shall within 14 days serve on the execution creditor and the sheriff a witness statement or affidavit specifying any money and describing any goods and chattels claimed and setting out the grounds upon which such claim is based.

(7) Where the applicant is a sheriff a claim form under this rule must give notice of the requirement in paragraph (6).

## Rule 4 To Whom Sheriff May Apply for Relief

An application to the court for relief under this order may, if the applicant is a sheriff, be made—

(a) where the claim in question is proceeding in the Royal Courts of Justice, to a Master or, if the execution to which the application relates has been or is to be levied in the district of a District Registry, either to a Master or to the district judge of that Registry;

(b) where the claim in question is proceeding in a District Registry, to the district judge of that Registry or, if such execution has been or is to be levied in the district of some other District Registry or outside the district of any District Registry, either to the said district judge or to the district judge of that other registry or to a Master as the case may be.

Where the claim in question is proceeding in the Admiralty Court or the Family Division, references in this rule to a Master shall be construed as references to the Admiralty Registrar or to a Registrar of that Division.

## Rule 5 Powers of Court Hearing Claim

(1) Where on the hearing of a claim under this order all the persons by whom adverse claims to the subject-matter in dispute (hereafter in this Order referred to as 'the interpleader claimants') appear, the court may order—
   (a) that any interpleader claimant be made a defendant in any claim pending with respect to the subject-matter in dispute in substitution for or in addition to the applicant for relief under this order; or
   (b) that an issue between the interpleader claimants be stated and tried and may direct which of the interpleader claimants is to be claimant and which defendant.

(2) Where—
   (a) the applicant under this order is a sheriff; or
   (b) all the interpleader claimants consent or any of them so requests; or
   (c) the question at issue between the interpleader claimants is a question of law and the facts are not in dispute,

   the court may summarily determine the question at issue between the interpleader claimants and make an order accordingly on such terms as may be just.

(3) Where an interpleader claimant, having been duly served with a claim form under this order, does not appear at the hearing or, having appeared, fails or refuses to comply with an order made in the proceedings, the court may make an order declaring the interpleader claimant, and all persons claiming under him, for ever barred from prosecuting his claim against the applicant for such relief and all persons claiming under him, but such an order shall not affect the rights of the interpleader claimants as between themselves.

## Rule 6 Power to Order Sale of Goods Taken in Execution

Where an application for relief under this order is made by a sheriff who has taken possession of any goods or chattels in execution under any process, and an interpleader claimant alleges that he is entitled, under a bill of sale or otherwise. to the goods or chattels by way of security for debt, the court may order those goods or chattels or any part thereof to be sold and may direct that the proceeds of sale be applied in such manner and on such terms as may be just and as may be specified in the order.

## Rule 7 Power to Stay Proceedings

Where a defendant to a claim applies for relief under this Order in the claim, the court may by order stay all further proceedings in the claim.

## Rule 8 Other Powers

(1) Subject to the foregoing rules of this Order, the court may in or for the purposes of any interpleader proceedings make such order as to costs or any other matter as it thinks just.

(2) Where the interpleader claimant fails to appear at the hearing, the Court may direct that the sheriff's and execution creditor's costs shall be assessed by a master or, where the hearing was heard in a district registry, by a district judge of that registry and the following CPR rules shall apply—
   (a) 44.4 (basis of assessment);
   (b) 44.5 (factors to be taken into account in deciding the amount of costs);

(c) 48.4 (limitations on court's power to award costs in favour of trustee or personal representative); and
(d) 48.6 (litigants in person).

(3) Where the claim in question is proceeding in the Admiralty Court or the Family Division, references in this rule to a Master shall be construed as references to the Admiralty Registrar or to a Registrar of that Division.

### Rule 9 One Order in Several Proceedings

Where the Court considers it necessary or expedient to make an order in any interpleader proceedings in several proceedings pending in several Divisions, or before different judges of the same Division, the court may make such an order; and the order shall be entitled in all those causes or matters and shall be binding on all the parties to them.

### Rule 10 Disclosure

CPR Parts 31 and 18 shall, with the necessary modifications, apply in relation to an interpleader issue as they apply in relation to any other proceedings.

### Rule 11 Trial of Interpleader Issue

(1) CPR Part 39 shall, with the necessary modifications, apply to the trial of an interpleader issue as it applies to the trial of a claim.

(2) The court by whom an interpleader issue is tried may give such judgment or make such order as finally to dispose of all questions arising in the interpleader proceedings.

## RSC ORDER 45
## ENFORCEMENT OF JUDGMENTS AND ORDERS: GENERAL

### Rule 1 Enforcement of Judgment, etc., For Payment of Money

(4) In this Order references to any writ shall be construed as including references to any further writ in aid of the first mentioned writ.

### Rule 1A Interpretation

In this Order, and in RSC Orders 46 and 47—

(a) 'enforcement officer' means an individual who is authorised to act as an enforcement officer under the Courts Act 2003; and
(b) 'relevant enforcement officer' means—
  (i) in relation to a writ of execution which is directed to a single enforcement officer, that officer;
  (ii) in relation to a writ of execution which is directed to two or more enforcement officers, the officer to whom the writ is allocated.

### Rule 2 Notice of Seizure

When first executing a writ of fieri facias, the Sheriff or his officer or the relevant enforcement officer shall deliver to the debtor or leave at each place where execution is levied a notice in Form No. 55 in the relevant Practice Direction informing the debtor of the execution.

### Rule 3 Enforcement of Judgment for Possession of Land

(1) Subject to the provisions of these rules, a judgment or order for the giving of possession of land may be enforced by one or more of the following means, that is to say—
  (a) writ of possession;
  (b) in a case in which rule 5 applies, an order of committal;
  (c) in such a case, writ of sequestration.

(2) A writ of possession to enforce a judgment or order for the giving of possession of any

land shall not be issued without the permission of the court except where the judgment or order was given or made in proceedings by a mortgagee or mortgagor or by any person having the right to foreclose or redeem any mortgage, being proceedings in which there is a claim for—

(a) payment of moneys secured by the mortgage;
(b) sale of the mortgaged property;
(c) foreclosure;
(d) delivery of possession (whether before or after foreclosure or without foreclosure) to the mortgagee by the mortgagor or by any other person who is alleged to be in possession of the property;
(e) redemption;
(f) reconveyance of the land or its release from the security; or
(g) delivery of possession by the mortgagee.

(2A) In paragraph (2) 'mortgage' includes a legal or equitable mortgage and a legal or equitable charge, and reference to a mortgagor, a mortgagee and mortgaged land is to be interpreted accordingly.

(3) Such permission as is referred to in paragraph (2) shall not be granted unless it is shown—

(a) that every person in actual possession of the whole or any part of the land has received such notice of the proceedings as appears to the court sufficient to enable him to apply to the court for any relief to which he may be entitled; and
(b) if the operation of the judgment or order is suspended by subsection (2) of section 16 of the Landlord and Tenant Act, 1954, that the applicant has not received notice in writing from the tenant that he desires that the provisions of paragraphs (a) and (b) of that subsection shall have effect.

(4) A writ of possession may include provision for enforcing the payment of any money adjudged or ordered to be paid by the judgment or order which is to be enforced by the writ.

## Rule 4 Enforcement of Judgment for Delivery of Goods

(1) Subject to the provisions of these rules, a judgment or order for the delivery of any goods which does not give a person against whom the judgment is given or order made the alternative of paying the assessed value of the goods may be enforced by one or more of the following means, that is to say—

(a) writ of delivery to recover the goods without alternative provision for recovery of the assessed value thereof (hereafter in this rule referred to as a 'writ of specific delivery');
(b) in a case in which rule 5 applies, an order of committal;
(c) in such a case, writ of sequestration.

(2) Subject to the provisions of these rules, a judgment or order for the delivery of any goods or payment of their assessed value may be enforced by one or more of the following means, that is to say—

(a) writ of delivery to recover the goods or their assessed value;
(b) by order of the court, writ of specific delivery;
(c) in a case in which rule 5 applies, writ of sequestration.

An application for an order under sub-paragraph (b) shall be made in accordance with CPR Part 23, which must be served on the defendant against whom the judgment or order sought to be enforced was given or made.

(3) A writ of specific delivery, and a writ of delivery to recover any goods or their assessed value, may include provision for enforcing the payment of any money adjudged or ordered to be paid by the judgment or order which is to be enforced by the writ.

(4) A judgment or order for the payment of the assessed value of any goods may be enforced by the same means as any other judgment or order for the payment of money.

## Rule 5 Enforcement of Judgment to Do or Abstain from Doing Any Act

(1) Where—
  (a) a person required by a judgment or order to do an act within a time specified in the judgment or order refuses or neglects to do it within that time or, as the case may be, within that time as extended or abridged under a court order or CPR rule 2.11; or
  (b) a person disobeys a judgment or order requiring him to abstain from doing an act, then, subject to the provisions of these rules, the judgment or order may be enforced by one or more of the following means, that is to say—
    (i) with the permission of the court, a writ of sequestration against the property of that person;
    (ii) where that person is a body corporate, with the permission of the court, a writ of sequestration against the property of any director or other officer of the body;
    (iii) subject to the provisions of the Debtors Act 1869 and 1878, an order of committal against that person or, where that person is a body corporate, against any such officer.

(2) Where a judgment or order requires a person to do an act within a time therein specified and an order is subsequently made under rule 6 requiring the act to be done within some other time, references in paragraph (1) of this rule to a judgment or order shall be construed as references to the order made under rule 6.

(3) Where under any judgment or order requiring the delivery of any goods the person liable to execution has the alternative of paying the assessed value of the goods, the judgment or order shall not be enforceable by order of committal under paragraph (1), but the court may, on the application of the person entitled to enforce the judgment or order, make an order requiring the first mentioned person to deliver the goods to the applicant within a time specified in the order, and that order may be so enforced.

## Rule 6 Judgment, etc. Requiring Act to be Done: Order Fixing Time for Doing It

(1) Notwithstanding that a judgment or order requiring a person to do an act specifies a time within which the act is to be done, the court shall have power to make an order requiring the act to be done within another time, being such time after service of that order, or such other time, as may be specified therein.

(2) Where a judgment or order requiring a person to do an act does not specify a time within which the act is to be done, the court shall have power subsequently to make an order requiring the act to be done within such time after service of that order, or such other time, as may be specified therein.

(3) An application for an order under this rule must be made in accordance with CPR Part 23 and the application notice must, be served on the person required to do the act in question.

## Rule 7 Service of Copy of Judgment, etc., Prerequisite to Enforcement Under Rule 5

(1) In this rule references to an order shall be construed as including references to a judgment.

(2) Subject to paragraphs (6) and (7) of this rule, an order shall not be enforced under rule 5 unless—
  (a) a copy of the order has been served personally on the person required to do or abstain from doing the act in question; and
  (b) in the case of an order requiring a person to do an act, the copy has been so served before the expiration of the time within which he was required to do the act.

(3) Subject as aforesaid, an order requiring a body corporate to do or abstain from doing an act shall not be enforced as mentioned in rule 5(1)(b)(ii) or (iii) unless—
  (a) a copy of the order has also been served personally on the officer against whose

property permission is sought to issue a writ of sequestration or against whom an order of committal is sought; and

(b) in the case of an order requiring the body corporate to do an act, the copy has been so served before the expiration of the time within which the body was required to do the act.

(4) There must be prominently displayed on the front of the copy of an order served under this rule a warning to the person on whom the copy is served that disobedience to the order would be a contempt of court punishable by imprisonment, or (in the case of an order requiring a body corporate to do or abstain from doing an act) punishable by sequestration of the assets of the body corporate and by imprisonment of any individual responsible.

(5) With the copy of an order required to be served under this rule, being an order requiring a person to do an act, there must also be served a copy of any order or agreement under CPR rule 2.11 extending or abridging the time for doing the act and, where the first-mentioned order was made under rule 5(3) or 6 of this Order, a copy of the previous Order requiring the act to be done.

(6) An order requiring a person to abstain from doing an act may be enforced under rule 5 notwithstanding that service of a copy of the order has not been effected in accordance with this rule if the court is satisfied that pending such service, the person against whom or against whose property is sought to enforce the order has had notice thereof either—

(a) by being present when the order was made; or

(b) by being notified of the terms of the order, whether by telephone, telegram or otherwise.

(7) The court may dispense with service of a copy of an order under this rule if it thinks it just to do so.

## Rule 8 Court May Order Act to be Done at Expense of Disobedient Party

If a mandatory order, an injunction or a judgment or order for the specific performance of a contract is not complied with, then, without prejudice to its powers under section 39 of the Act and its powers to punish the disobedient party for contempt, the court may direct that the act required to be done may, so far as practicable, be done by the party by whom the order or judgment was obtained or some other person appointed by the court, at the cost of the disobedient party, and upon the act being done the expenses incurred may be ascertained in such manner as the court may direct and execution may issue against the disobedient party for the amount so ascertained and for costs.

## Rule 11 Matters Occurring After Judgment: Stay of Execution, etc.

Without prejudice to Order 47, rule 1, a party against whom a judgment has been given or an order made may apply to the court for a stay of execution of the judgment or order or other relief on the ground of matters which have occurred since the date of the judgment or order, and the court may by order grant such relief, and on such terms, as it thinks just.

## Rule 12 Forms of Writs

(1) A writ of fieri facias must be in such of the Forms Nos. 53 to 63 in the relevant practice direction as is appropriate in the particular case.

(2) A writ of delivery must be in Form No. 64 or 65 in the relevant practice direction, whichever is appropriate.

(3) A writ of possession must be in Form No. 66 or 66A in the relevant practice direction, whichever is appropriate.

(4) A writ of sequestration must be in Form No. 67 in the relevant practice direction.

# RSC ORDER 46
# WRITS OF EXECUTION: GENERAL

## Rule 1 Definition

In this Order, unless the context otherwise requires, 'writ of execution' includes a writ of fieri facias, a writ of possession, a writ of delivery, a writ of sequestration and any further writ in aid of any of the aforementioned writs.

## Rule 2 When Permission to Issue Any Writ of Execution is Necessary

(1) A writ of execution to enforce a judgment or order may not issue without the permission of the court in the following cases, that is to say—
   (a) where 6 years or more have elapsed since the date of the judgment or order;
   (b) where any change has taken place, whether by death or otherwise, in the parties entitled or liable to execution under the judgment or order;
   (c) where the judgment or order is against the assets of a deceased person coming to the hands of his executors or administrators after the date of the judgment or order, and it is sought to issue execution against such assets;
   (d) where under the judgment or order any person is entitled to a remedy subject to the fulfilment of any condition which it is alleged has been fulfilled;
   (e) where any goods sought to be seized under a writ of execution are in the hands of a receiver appointed by the court or a sequestrator.

(2) Paragraph (1) is without prejudice to section 2 of the Reserve and Auxiliary Forces (Protection of Civil Interests) Act 1951, or any other enactment or rule by virtue of which a person is required to obtain the permission of the court for the issue of a writ of execution or to proceed to execution on or otherwise to the enforcement of a judgment or order.

(3) Where the court grants permission, whether under this rule or otherwise, for the issue of a writ of execution and the writ is not issued within one year after the date of the order granting such permission, the order shall cease to have effect, without prejudice, however, to the making of a fresh order.

## Rule 3 Permission Required for Issue of Writ in Aid of Other Writ

A writ of execution in aid of any other writ of execution shall not issue without the permission of the court.

## Rule 4 Application for Permission to Issue Writ

(1) An application for permission to issue a writ of execution may be made in accordance with CPR Part 23 but the application notice need not be served on the respondent unless the court directs.

(2) Such an application must be supported by a witness statement or affidavit—
   (a) identifying the judgment or order to which the application relates and, if the judgment or order is for the payment of money, stating the amount originally due thereunder and the amount due thereunder at the date the application notice is filed;
   (b) stating, where the case falls within rule 2(1)(a), the reasons for the delay in enforcing the judgment or order;
   (c) stating, where the case falls within rule 2(1)(b), the change which has taken place in the parties entitled or liable to execution since the date of the judgment or order;
   (d) stating, where the case falls within rule 2(1)(c) or (d), that a demand to satisfy the judgment or order was made on the person liable to satisfy it and that he has refused or failed to do so;
   (e) giving such other information as is necessary to satisfy the court that the applicant is entitled to proceed to execution on the judgment or order in question and that the person against whom it is sought to issue execution is liable to execution on it.

(3) The court hearing such application may grant permission in accordance with the application or may order that any issue or question, a decision on which is necessary to determine the rights of the parties, be tried in any manner in which any question of fact or law arising in proceedings may be tried and, in either case, may impose such terms as to costs or otherwise as it thinks just.

## Rule 5 Application for Permission to Issue Writ of Sequestration

(1) Notwithstanding anything in rules 2 and 4, an application for permission to issue a writ of sequestration must be made in accordance with CPR Part 23 and be heard by a judge.
(2) Subject to paragraph (3), the application notice, stating the grounds of the application and accompanied by a copy of the witness statement or affidavit in support of the application, must be served personally on the person against whose property it is sought to issue the writ.
(3) The court may dispense with service of the application notice under this rule if it thinks it just to do so.
(4) The judge hearing an application for permission to issue a writ of sequestration may sit in private in any case in which, if the application were for an order of committal, he would be entitled to do so by virtue of Order 52, rule 6 but, except in such a case, the application shall be heard in public.

## Rule 6 Issue of Writ of Execution

(1) Issue of a writ of execution takes place on its being sealed by a court officer of the appropriate office.
(2) Before such a writ is issued, a praecipe for its issue must be filed.
(3) The praecipe must be signed by or on behalf of the solicitor of the person entitled to execution or, if that person is acting in person, by him.
(4) No such writ shall be sealed unless at the time of the tender thereof for sealing—
  (a) the person tendering it produces—
    (i) the judgment or order on which the writ is to issue, or an office copy thereof;
    (ii) where the writ may not issue without the permission of the court, the order granting such permission or evidence of the granting of it;
    (iii) where judgment on failure to acknowledge service has been entered against a State, as defined in section 14 of the State Immunity Act 1978, evidence that the State has been served in accordance with CPR rule 40.10 and that the judgment has taken effect; and
  (b) the court officer authorised to seal it is satisfied that the period, if any, specified in the judgment or order for the payment of any money or the doing of any other act thereunder has expired.
(5) Every writ of execution shall bear the date of the day on which it is issued.
(6) In this rule 'the appropriate office' means—
  (a) where the proceedings in which execution is to issue are in a District Registry, that Registry;
  (b) where the proceedings are in the Principal Registry of the Family Division, that Registry;
  (c) where the proceedings are Admiralty proceedings or commercial proceedings which are not in a District Registry, the Admiralty and Commercial Registry;
  (ca) where the proceedings are in the Chancery Division, Chancery Chambers;
  (d) in any other case, the Central Office of the Supreme Court.

## Rule 8 Duration and Renewal of Writ of Execution

(1) For the purpose of execution, a writ of execution is valid in the first instance for 12 months beginning with the date of its issue.
(2) Where a writ has not been wholly executed the court may by order extend the validity of the writ from time to time for a period of 12 months at any one time beginning with the

day on which the order is made, if an application for extension is made to the court before the day next following that on which the writ would otherwise expire or such later day, if any, as the court may allow.

(3) Before a writ the validity of which had been extended under paragraph (2) is executed either the writ must be sealed with the seal of the office out of which it was issued showing the date on which the order extending its validity was made or the applicant for the order must serve a notice (in Form No. 71 in the relevant practice direction) sealed as aforesaid, on the sheriff to whom the writ is directed or the relevant enforcement officer informing him of the making of the order and the date thereof.

(4) The priority of a writ, the validity of which has been extended under this rule, shall be determined by reference to the date on which it was originally delivered to the sheriff or the relevant enforcement officer.

(5) The production of a writ of execution, or of such a notice as is mentioned in paragraph (3) purporting in either case to be sealed as mentioned in that paragraph, shall be evidence that the validity of that writ, or, as the case may be, of the writ referred to in that notice, has been extended under paragraph (2).

(6) If, during the validity of a writ of execution, an interpleader summons is issued in relation to an execution under that writ, the validity of the writ shall be extended until the expiry of 12 months from the conclusion of the interpleader proceedings.

### Rule 9 Return to Writ of Execution

(1) Any party at whose instance or against whom a writ of execution was issued may serve a notice on the sheriff to whom the writ was directed or the relevant enforcement officer requiring him, within such time as may be specified in the notice, to indorse on the writ a statement of the manner in which he has executed it and to send to that party a copy of the statement.

(2) If a sheriff or enforcement officer on whom such a notice is served fails to comply with it the party by whom it was served may apply to the court for an order directing the sheriff or enforcement officer to comply with the notice.

## RSC ORDER 47
## WRITS OF FIERI FACIAS

### Rule 1 Power to Stay Execution by Writ of Fieri Facias

(1) Where a judgment is given or an order made for the payment by any person of money, and the court is satisfied, on an application made at the time of the judgment or order, or at any time thereafter, by the judgment debtor or other party liable to execution—

(a) that there are special circumstances which render it inexpedient to enforce the judgment or order; or

(b) that the applicant is unable from any cause to pay the money,

then, notwithstanding anything in rule 2 or 3, the court may by order stay the execution of the judgment or order by writ of fieri facias either absolutely or for such period and subject to such conditions as the court thinks fit.

(2) An application under this rule, if not made at the time the judgment is given or order made, must be made in accordance with CPR Part 23 and may be so made notwithstanding that the party liable to execution did not acknowledge service of the claim form or serve a defence or take any previous part in the proceedings.

(3) The grounds on which an application under this rule is made must be set out in the application notice and be supported by a witness statement or affidavit made by or on behalf of the applicant substantiating the said grounds and, in particular, where such application is made on the grounds of the applicant's inability to pay, disclosing his income, the nature and value of any property of his and the amount of any other liabilities of his.

(4) The application notice and a copy of the supporting witness statement or affidavit must,

not less than 4 clear days before the hearing, be served on the party entitled to enforce the judgment or order.

(5) An order staying execution under this rule may be varied or revoked by a subsequent order.

### Rule 2 [*Revoked*]

### Rule 3 Separate Writs to Enforce Payment of Costs, etc.

(1) Where only the payment of money, together with costs to be assessed in accordance with CPR Part 47 (detailed costs assessment), is adjudged or ordered, then, if when the money becomes payable under the judgment or order the costs have not been assessed, the party entitled to enforce that judgment or order may issue a writ of fieri facias to enforce payment of the sum (other than for costs) adjudged or ordered and, not less than 8 days after the issue of that writ, he may issue a second writ to enforce payment of the assessed costs.

(2) A party entitled to enforce a judgment or order for the delivery of possession of any property (other than money) may, if he so elects, issue a separate writ of fieri facias to enforce payment of any damages or costs awarded to him by that judgment or order.

### Rule 4 No Expenses of Execution in Certain Cases

Where a judgment or order is for less than £600 and does not entitle the claimant to costs against the person against whom the writ of fieri facias to enforce the judgment or order is issued, the writ may not authorise the sheriff or enforcement officer to whom it is directed to levy any fees, poundage or other costs of execution.

### Rule 5 Writ of Fieri Facias De Bonis Ecclesiasticis, etc.

(1) Where it appears upon the return of any writ of fieri facias that the person against whom the writ was issued has no goods or chattels in the county of the sheriffs to whom the writ was directed or the district of the relevant enforcement officer but that he is the incumbent of a benefice named in the return, then, after the writ and return have been filed, the party by whom the writ of fieri facias was issued may issue a writ of fieri facias de bonis ecclesiasticis or a writ of sequestrari de bonis ecclesiasticis directed to the bishop of the diocese within which that benefice is.

(2) Any such writ must be delivered to the bishop to be executed by him.

(3) Only such fees for the execution of any such writ shall be taken by or allowed to the bishop or any diocesan officer as are for the time being authorised by or under any enactment, including any measure of the General Synod.

### Rule 6 Order For Sale Otherwise Than by Auction

(1) An order of the court under paragraph 10 of Schedule 7 to the Courts Act 2003 that a sale of goods seized under an execution may be made otherwise than by public auction may be made on the application of—
   (a) the person at whose instance the writ of execution under which the sale is to be made was issued;
   (b) the person against whom that writ was issued (in this rule referred to as 'the judgment debtor');
   (c) if the writ was directed to a sheriff, that sheriff; and
   (d) if the writ was directed to one or more enforcement officers, the relevant enforcement officer.

(2) Such an application must be made in accordance with CPR Part 23 and the application notice must contain a short statement of the grounds of the application.

(3) Where the applicant for an order under this rule is not the sheriff or enforcement officer, the sheriff or enforcement officer must, on the demand of the applicant, send to the applicant a list stating—

(a) whether he has notice of the issue of another writ or writs of execution against the goods of the judgment debtor; and
(b) so far as is known to him, the name and address of every creditor who has obtained the issue of another such writ of execution,

and where the sheriff or enforcement officer is the applicant, he must prepare such a list.

(4) Not less than 4 clear days before the hearing the applicant must serve the application notice on each of the other persons by whom the application might have been made and on every person named in the list under paragraph (3).

(5) Service of the application notice on a person named in the list under paragraph (3) is notice to him for the purpose of paragraph 10(3) of Schedule 7 to the Courts Act 2003.

(Paragraph 10(3) provides that if the person who seized the goods has notice of another execution or other executions, the court must not consider an application for leave to sell privately until the notice prescribed by Civil Procedure Rules has been given to the other execution creditor or creditors.)

(6) The applicant must produce the list under paragraph (3) to the court on the hearing of the application.

(7) Every person on whom the application notice was served may attend and be heard on the hearing of the application.

## RSC ORDER 52
## COMMITTAL

### Rule 1 Committal for Contempt of Court

(1) The power of the High Court or Court of Appeal to punish for contempt of court may be exercised by an order of committal.

(2) Where contempt of court—
(a) is committed in connection with—
(i) any proceedings before a Divisional Court of the Queen's Bench Division; or
(ii) criminal proceedings, except where the contempt is committed in the face of the court or consists of disobedience to an order of the court or a breach of an undertaking to the court; or
(iii) proceedings in an inferior court; or
(b) is committed otherwise than in connection with any proceedings, then, subject to paragraph (4), an order of committal may be made only by a Divisional Court of the Queen's Bench Division.

This paragraph shall not apply in relation to contempt of the Court of Appeal.

(3) Where contempt of court is committed in connection with any proceedings in the High Court, then, subject to paragraph (2), an order of committal may be made by a single judge of the Queen's Bench Division except where the proceedings were assigned or subsequently transferred to some other Division, in which case the order may be made only by a single judge of that other Division.

The reference in this paragraph to a single judge of the Queen's Bench Division shall, in relation to proceedings in any court the judge or judges of which are, when exercising the jurisdiction of that court, deemed by virtue of any enactment to constitute a court of the High Court, be construed as a reference to a judge of that court.

(4) Where by virtue of any enactment the High Court has power to punish or take steps for the punishment of any person charged with having done anything in relation to a court, tribunal or person which would, if it had been done in relation to the High Court, have been a contempt of that court, an order of committal may be made—
(a) on an application under section 88 of the Charities Act 1993, by a single judge of the Chancery Division; and
(b) in any other case, by a single judge of the Queen's Bench Division.

## Rule 2 Application to Divisional Court

(1) No application to a Divisional Court for an order of committal against any person may be made unless permission to make such an application has been granted in accordance with this rule.

(2) An application for such permission must be made without notice to a Divisional Court, except in vacation when it may be made to a judge in chambers and must be supported by a statement setting out the name and description of the applicant, the name, description and address of the person sought to be committed and the grounds on which his committal is sought, and by an affidavit, to be filed before the application is made, verifying the facts relied on.

(3) The applicant must give notice of the application for permission not later than the preceding day to the Crown Office and must at the same time lodge in that office copies of the statement and affidavit.

(4) Where an application for permission under this rule is refused by a judge in chambers, the applicant may make a fresh application for such permission to a Divisional Court.

(5) An application made to a Divisional Court by virtue of paragraph (4) must be made within 8 days after the judge's refusal to give permission or, if a Divisional Court does not sit within that period, on the first day on which it sits thereafter.

## Rule 3 Application for Order After Leave to Apply Granted

(1) When permission has been granted under rule 2 to apply for an order of committal, the application for the order must be made to a Divisional Court and, unless the court or judge granting permission has otherwise directed, there must be at least 14 clear days between the service of the claim form and the day named therein for the hearing.

(2) Unless within 14 days after such permission was granted, the claim form is issued the permission shall lapse.

(3) Subject to paragraph 4, the claim form, accompanied by a copy of the statement and affidavit in support of the application for permission, must be served personally on the person sought to be committed.

(4) Without prejudice to the powers of the court or judge under Part 6 of the CPR, the court or judge may dispense with service under this rule if it or he thinks it just to do so.

## Rule 4 Application to Court Other Than Divisional Court

(1) Where an application for an order of committal may be made to a court other than a Divisional Court, the application must be made by claim form or application notice and be supported by an affidavit.

(2) Subject to paragraph (3) the claim form or application notice, stating the grounds of the application and accompanied by a copy of the affidavit in support of the application, must be served personally on the person sought to be committed.

(3) Without prejudice to its powers under Part 6 of the CPR, the court may dispense with service under this rule if it thinks it just to do so.

(4) This rule does not apply to committal applications which under rules 1(2) and 3(1) should be made to a Divisional Court but which, in vacation, have been properly made to a single judge in accordance with RSC Order 64, rule 4.

## Rule 5 Saving for Power to Commit Without Application For Purpose

Nothing in the foregoing provisions of this Order shall be taken as affecting the power of the High Court or Court of Appeal to make an order of committal of its own initiative against a person guilty of contempt of court.

## Rule 6 Provisions as to Hearing

(1) Subject to paragraph (2), the court hearing an application for an order of committal may sit in private in the following cases, that is to say—

(a) where the application arises out of proceedings relating to the wardship or adoption of an infant or wholly or mainly to the guardianship, custody, maintenance or upbringing of an infant, or rights of access to an infant;
(b) where the application arises out of proceedings relating to a person suffering or appearing to be suffering from mental disorder within the meaning of the Mental Health Act 1983;
(c) where the application arises out of proceedings in which a secret process, discovery or invention was in issue;
(d) where it appears to the court that in the interests of the administration of justice or for reasons of national security the application should be heard in private;

but, except as aforesaid, the application shall be heard in public.

(2) If the court hearing an application in private by virtue of paragraph (1) decides to make an order of committal against the person sought to be committed, it shall in public state—
(a) the name of that person;
(b) in general terms the nature of the contempt of court in respect of which the order of committal is being made; and
(c) the length of the period for which he is being committed.

(3) Except with the permission of the court hearing an application for an order of committal, no grounds shall be relied upon at the hearing except the grounds set out in the statement under rule 2 or, as the case may be, in the claim form or application notice under rule 4.

(4) If on the hearing of the application the person sought to be committed expresses a wish to give oral evidence on his own behalf, he shall be entitled to do so.

## Rule 7 Power to Suspend Execution of Committal Order

(1) The court by whom an order of committal is made may by order direct that the execution of the order of committal shall be suspended for such period or on such terms or conditions as it may specify.

(2) Where execution of an order of committal is suspended by an order under paragraph (1), the applicant for the order of committal must, unless the court otherwise directs, serve on the person against whom it was made a notice informing him of the making and terms of the order under that paragraph.

## Rule 7A Warrant for arrest

A warrant for the arrest of a person against whom an order of committal has been made shall not, without further order of the court, be enforced more than 2 years after the date on which the warrant is issued.

## Rule 8 Discharge of Person Committed

(1) The court may, on the application of any person committed to prison for any contempt of court, discharge him.

(2) Where a person has been committed for failing to comply with a judgment or order requiring him to deliver any thing to some other person or to deposit it in court or elsewhere, and a writ of sequestration has also been issued to enforce that judgment or order, then, if the thing is in the custody or power of the person committed, the commissioners appointed by the writ of sequestration may take possession of it as if it were the property of that person and, without prejudice to the generality of paragraph (1), the court may discharge the person committed and may give such directions for dealing with the thing taken by the commissioners as it thinks fit.

(RSC Order 46, rule 5 contains rules relating to writs of sequestration.)

## Rule 9 Saving For Other Powers

Nothing in the foregoing provisions of this Order shall be taken as affecting the power of the court to make an order requiring a person guilty of contempt of court, or a person punishable by virtue of any enactment in like manner as if he had been guilty of contempt of the High Court, to pay a fine or to give security for his good behaviour, and those provisions, so far as applicable, and with the necessary modifications, shall apply in relation to an application for such an order as they apply in relation to an application for an order of committal.

## RSC ORDER 54
## APPLICATIONS FOR WRIT OF HABEAS CORPUS

### Rule 1 Application for Writ of Habeas Corpus Ad Subjiciendum

(1) Subject to rule 11, an application for a writ of habeas corpus ad subjiciendum shall be made to a judge in court, except that—
   (a) it shall be made to a Divisional Court of the Queen's Bench Division if the court so directs;
   (b) it may be made to a judge otherwise than in court at any time when no judge is sitting in court; and
   (c) any application on behalf of a child must be made in the first instance to a judge otherwise than in court.

(2) An application for such writ may be made without notice being served on any other party and, subject to paragraph (3) must be supported by a witness statement or affidavit by the person restrained showing that it is made at his instance and setting out the nature of the restraint.

(3) Where the person restrained is unable for any reason to make the witness statement or affidavit required by paragraph (2) the witness statement or affidavit may be made by some other person on his behalf and that witness statement or affidavit must state that the person restrained is unable to make the witness statement or affidavit himself and for what reason.

### Rule 2 Power of Court to Whom Application Made Without Notice Being Served on Any Other Party

(1) The court or judge to whom an application under rule 1 is made without notice being served on any other party may make an order forthwith for the writ to issue, or may—
   (a) where the application is made to a judge otherwise than in court, direct the issue of a claim form seeking the writ, or that an application therefor be made by claim form to a Divisional Court or to a judge in court;
   (b) where the application is made to a judge in court, adjourn the application so that notice thereof may be given, or direct that an application be made by claim form to a Divisional Court;
   (c) where the application is made to a Divisional Court, adjourn the application so that notice thereof may be given.

(2) The claim form must be served on the person against whom the issue of the writ is sought and on such other persons as the court or judge may direct, and, unless the court or judge otherwise directs, there must be at least 8 clear days between the service of the claim form and the date named therein for the hearing of the application.

### Rule 3 Copies of Witness Statements or Affidavits to be Supplied

Every party to an application under rule 1 must supply to every other party on demand and on payment of the proper charges copies of the witness statements or affidavits which he proposes to use at the hearing of the application.

### Rule 4 Power to Order Release of Person Restrained

(1) Without prejudice to rule 2(1), the court or judge hearing an application for a writ of habeas corpus ad subjiciendum may in its or his discretion order that the person

restrained be released, and such order shall be a sufficient warrant to any governor of a prison, constable or other person for the release of the person under restraint.

(2) Where such an application in criminal proceedings is heard by a judge and the judge does not order the release of the person restrained, he shall direct that the application be made by claim form to a Divisional Court of the Queen's Bench Division.

### Rule 5 Directions as to Return to Writ

Where a writ of habeas corpus ad subjiciendum is ordered to issue, the court or judge by whom the order is made shall give directions as to the court or judge before whom, and the date on which, the writ is returnable.

### Rule 6 Service of Writ and Notice

(1) Subject to paragraphs (2) and (3), a writ of habeas corpus ad subjiciendum must be served personally on the person to whom it is directed.

(2) If it is not possible to serve such writ personally, or if it is directed to a governor of a prison or other public official, it must be served by leaving it with a servant or agent of the person to whom the writ is directed at the place where the person restrained is confined or restrained.

(3) If the writ is directed to more than one person, the writ must be served in manner provided by this rule on the person first named in the writ, and copies must be served on each of the other persons in the same manner as the writ.

(4) There must be served with the writ a notice (in Form No. 90 in the relevant practice direction) stating the court or judge before whom and the date on which the person restrained is to be brought and that in default of obedience proceedings for committal of the party disobeying will be taken.

### Rule 7 Return to the Writ

(1) The return to a writ of habeas corpus ad subjiciendum must be indorsed on or annexed to the writ and must state all the causes of the detainer of the person restrained.

(2) The return may be amended, or another return substituted therefor, by permission of the court or judge before whom the writ is returnable.

### Rule 8 Procedure at Hearing of Writ

When a return to a writ of habeas corpus ad subjiciendum is made, the return shall first be read, and motion then made for discharging or remanding the person restrained or amending or quashing the return, and where that person is brought up in accordance with the writ, his counsel shall be heard first, then the counsel for the Crown, and then one counsel for the person restrained in reply.

### Rule 9 Bringing Up Prisoner to Give Evidence, etc.

(1) An application for a writ of habeas corpus ad testificandum or of habeas corpus ad respondendum must be made on witness statement or affidavit to a judge.

(2) An application for an order to bring up a prisoner, otherwise than by writ of habeas corpus, to give evidence in any proceedings, civil or criminal, before any court, tribunal or justice, must be made on witness statement or affidavit to a judge.

### Rule 10 Form of Writ

A writ of habeas corpus must be in Form No. 89, 91 or 92 in the relevant practice direction, whichever is appropriate.

### Rule 11 Applications Relative to the Custody, etc., of Child

An application by a parent or guardian of a child for a writ of habeas corpus ad subjiciendum relative to the custody, care or control of the child must be made in the Family Division, and this Order shall accordingly apply to such applications with the appropriate modifications.

# RSC ORDER 64
# SITTINGS, VACATIONS AND OFFICE HOURS

## Rule 4 Divisional Court Business During Vacation

Proceedings which require to be immediately or promptly heard and which by virtue of the following provisions must be brought in a Divisional Court may, in vacation, be brought before a single judge:

(a) Order 52, rules 1(2) and 3(1).

# RSC ORDER 79
# CRIMINAL PROCEEDINGS

## Rule 8 Estreat of Recognisances

(1) No recognisance acknowledged in or removed into the Queen's Bench Division shall be estreated without the order of a judge.

(2) Every application to estreat a recognisance in the Queen's Bench Division must be made by claim form and will be heard by a judge and must be supported by a witness statement or affidavit showing in what manner the breach has been committed and proving that the claim form was duly served.

(2A) When it issues the claim form the court will fix a date for the hearing of the application.

(3) A claim form under this rule must be served at least 2 clear days before the day named therein for the hearing.

(4) On the hearing of the application the judge may, and if requested by any party shall, direct any issue of fact in dispute to be tried by a jury.

(5) If it appears to the judge that a default has been made in performing the conditions of the recognisance, the judge may order the recognisance to be estreated.

## Rule 9 Bail

(1) Subject to the provisions of this rule, every application to the High Court in respect of bail in any criminal proceeding—
   (a) where the defendant is in custody, must be made by claim form to a judge to show cause why the defendant should not be granted bail;
   (b) where the defendant has been admitted to bail, must be made by claim form to a judge to show cause why the variation in the arrangements for bail proposed by the applicant should not be made.

(2) Subject to paragraph (5), the claim form (in Form No. 97 or 97A in the relevant practice direction) must, at least 24 hours before the day named therein for the hearing, be served—
   (a) where the application was made by the defendant, on the prosecutor and on the Director of Public Prosecutions, if the prosecution is being carried on by him;
   (b) where the application was made by the prosecutor or a constable under section 3(8) of the Bail Act 1976, on the defendant.

(3) Subject to paragraph (5), every application must be supported by witness statement or affidavit.

(4) Where a defendant in custody who desires to apply for bail is unable through lack of means to instruct a solicitor, he may give notice in writing to the court stating his desire to apply for bail and requesting that the Official Solicitor shall act for him in the application, and the court may assign the Official Solicitor to act for the applicant accordingly.

(5) Where the Official Solicitor has been so assigned the court may dispense with the requirements of paragraphs (1) to (3) and deal with the application in a summary manner.

(6) Where the court grants the defendant bail, the order must be in Form No. 98 in the relevant practice direction and a copy of the order shall be transmitted forthwith—
- (a) where the proceedings in respect of the defendant have been transferred to the Crown Court for trial or where the defendant has been committed to the Crown Court to be sentenced or otherwise dealt with, to the appropriate officer of the Crown Court;
- (b) in any other case, to the justices' chief executive for the court which committed the defendant.

(6A) The recognisance of any surety required as a condition of bail granted as aforesaid may, where the defendant is in a prison or other place of detention, be entered into before the governor or keeper of the prison or place as well as before the persons specified in section 8(4) of the Bail Act 1976.

(6B) Where under section 3(5) or (6) of the Bail Act 1976 the court imposes a requirement to be complied with before a person's release on bail, it may give directions as to the manner in which and the person or persons before whom the requirement may be complied with.

(7) A person who in pursuance of an order for the grant of bail made by the court under this rule proposes to enter into a recognisance or give security must, unless the court otherwise directs, give notice (in Form No. 100 in the relevant practice direction) to the prosecutor at least 24 hours before he enters into the recognisance or complies with the requirements as aforesaid.

(8) Where in pursuance of such an order as aforesaid a recognisance is entered into or requirement complied with before any person, it shall be the duty of that person to cause the recognisance or, as the case may be, a statement of the requirement complied with to be transmitted forthwith—
- (a) where the proceedings in respect of the defendant have been transferred to the Crown Court for trial or where the defendant has been committed to the Crown Court to be sentenced or otherwise dealt with, to the appropriate officer of the Crown Court;
- (b) in any other case, to the justices' chief executive for the court which committed the defendant,

and a copy of such recognisance or statement shall at the same time be sent to the governor or keeper of the prison or other place of detention in which the defendant is detained, unless the recognisance was entered into or the requirement complied with before such governor or keeper.

(10) An order varying the arrangements under which the defendant has been granted bail shall be in Form 98A in the relevant practice direction and a copy of the order shall be transmitted forthwith—
- (a) where the proceedings in respect of the defendant have been transferred to the Crown Court for trial or where the defendant has been committed to the Crown Court to be sentenced or otherwise dealt with, to the appropriate officer of the Crown Court;
- (b) in any other case, to the justices' chief executive for the court which committed the defendant.

(11) Where in pursuance of an order of the High Court or the Crown Court a person is released on bail in any criminal proceeding pending the determination of an appeal to the High Court or House of Lords or an application for a quashing order, then, upon the abandonment of the appeal or application, or upon the decision of the High Court or House of Lords being given, any justice (being a justice acting for the same petty sessions area as the magistrates' court by which that person was convicted or sentenced) may issue process for enforcing the decision in respect of which such appeal or application was brought or, as the case may be, the decision of the High Court or House of Lords.

(12) If an applicant to the High Court in any criminal proceedings is refused bail, the

applicant shall not be entitled to make a fresh application for bail to any other judge or to a Divisional Court.

(13) The record required by section 5 of the Bail Act 1976 to be made by the High Court shall be made by including in the file relating to the case in question a copy of the relevant order of the Court and shall contain the particulars set out in Form No. 98 or 98A in the relevant practice direction, whichever is appropriate, except that in the case of a decision to withhold bail the record shall be made by inserting a statement of the decision on the court's copy of the relevant claim form and including it in the file relating to the case in question.

(14) In the case of a person whose return or surrender is sought under the Extradition Act 1989, this rule shall apply as if references to the defendant were references to that person and references to the prosecutor were references to the state seeking the return or surrender of that person.

## RSC ORDER 93
## APPLICATIONS AND APPEALS TO HIGH COURT UNDER VARIOUS ACTS: CHANCERY DIVISION

### Rule 4 Proceedings Under the Trustee Act 1925

All proceedings brought in the High Court under the Trustee Act 1925, shall be assigned to the Chancery Division.

### Rule 5 Application Under Section 2(3) of the Public Order Act 1936

(1) Proceedings by which an application is made to the High Court under section 2(3) of the Public Order Act 1936, shall be assigned to the Chancery Division.

### Rule 9 Right of Appeal Under the Law of Property Act

An appeal shall lie to the High Court against a decision of the Minister of Agriculture, Fisheries and Food under paragraph 16 of Schedule 15 to the Law of Property Act 1922.

### Rule 10 Determination of Appeal or Case Stated Under Various Acts

(1) An appeal to the High Court against an order of a county court made under the Land Registration Act 1925 shall be heard and determined by a Divisional Court of the Chancery Division.

### Rule 16 Proceedings Under the Commons Registration Act 1965

(1) Proceedings in the High Court under section 14 or 18 of the Commons Registration Act 1965 shall be assigned to the Chancery Division.

### Rule 17 Proceedings Under Section 21 or 25 of the Law of Property Act 1969

Proceedings in the High Court under section 21 or 25 of the Law of Property Act 1969 shall be assigned to the Chancery Division.

### Rule 18 Proceedings Under Section 86 of the Civil Aviation Act 1982

(1) Proceedings in the High Court for the amendment of any register of aircraft mortgages kept pursuant to an Order in Council made under section 86 of the Civil Aviation Act 1982 shall be assigned to the Chancery Division.

(2) Such proceedings shall be brought by claim form and every person, other than the claimant, appearing in the register as mortgagee or mortgagor of the aircraft in question shall be made a defendant to the claim.

(3) A copy of the claim form shall also be sent to the Civil Aviation Authority and the Authority shall be entitled to be heard in the proceedings.

### Rule 19 Proceedings Under Section 85(7) of the Fair Trading Act 1973 and the Control of Misleading Advertisements Regulations 1988

(1) Proceedings to which this rule applies shall be assigned to the Chancery Division and may be begun by claim form.
(2) This rule applies to any application to the High Court for an order under section 85(7) of the Fair Trading Act 1973, or under any provision to which that section applies or under the Control of Misleading Advertisements Regulations 1988.

## RSC ORDER 94
## APPLICATIONS AND APPEALS TO HIGH COURT UNDER VARIOUS ACTS: QUEEN'S BENCH DIVISION

### Rule 4 Rectification of Register of Deeds of Arrangement

(1) Every application to the Court under section 7 of the Deeds of Arrangement Act 1914, for an order—
 (a) that any omission to register a deed of arrangement within the time prescribed by that Act be rectified by extending the time for such registration; or
 (b) that any omission or misstatement of the name, residence or description of any person be rectified by the insertion in the register of his true name, residence or description,

 must be made by witness statement or affidavit without notice being served on any other party to a master of the Queen's Bench Division.
(2) The witness statement or affidavit must set out particulars of the deed of arrangement and of the omission or misstatement in question and must state the grounds on which the application is made.

### Rule 5 Exercise of Jurisdiction Under Representation of the People Acts

(1) Proceedings in the High Court under the Representation of the People Acts shall be assigned to the Queen's Bench Division.
(2) Subject to paragraphs (3) and (4) the jurisdiction of the High Court under the said Acts in matters relating to parliamentary and local government elections shall be exercised by a Divisional Court.
(3) Paragraph (2) shall not be construed as taking away from a single judge or a Master any jurisdiction under the said Acts which, but for that paragraph, would be exercisable by a single judge or, as the case may be, by a Master.
(4) Where the jurisdiction of the High Court under the said Acts is by a provision of any of those Acts made exercisable in matters relating to parliamentary elections by a single judge, that jurisdiction in matters relating to local government elections shall also be exercisable by a single judge.

### Rule 8 Tribunals and Inquiries Act 1992: Appeal From Tribunal

(1) A person who was a party to proceedings before any such tribunal as is mentioned in section 11(1) of the Tribunals and Inquiries Act 1992 and is dissatisfied in point of law with the decision of the tribunal may appeal to the High Court.
(2) The appellant's notice must be served—
 (a) on the chairman of the tribunal;
 (b) in the case of a tribunal which has no chairman or member who acts as a chairman, on the member or members of that tribunal; or
 (c) in the case of any such tribunal as is specified in paragraph 16 of Schedule 1 to the said Act of 1992, on the secretary of the tribunal.
(3) Where an appeal is against the decision of the tribunal constituted under section 46 of the National Health Service Act 1977 the appellant's notice must be filed at the High Court within 14 days after the date of that decision.

(4) Where an appeal is against the decision of a tribunal established under section 1 of the Employment Tribunals Act 1996 the appellant's notice must be filed at the High Court within 42 days after the date of that decision.

## Rule 9 Tribunals and Inquiries Act 1992: Case Stated by Tribunal

(1) Any such tribunal as is mentioned in section 11(1) of the Tribunals and Inquiries Act 1992 may, of its own initiative or at the request of any party to proceedings before it, state in the course of proceedings before it in the form of a special case for the decision of the High Court any question of law arising in the proceedings.
(2) Any party to proceedings before any such tribunal who is aggrieved by the tribunal's refusal to state such a case may apply to the High Court for an order directing the tribunal to do so.
(3) A case stated by any such tribunal which has no chairman or member who acts as a chairman must be signed by the member or members of the tribunal.

## Rule 12 Applications for Permission Under Section 289(6) of the Town and Country Planning Act 1990 and Section 65(5) of the Planning (Listed Buildings and Conservation Areas) Act 1990

(1) An application for permission to appeal to the High Court under section 289 of the Town and Country Planning Act 1990 or section 65 of the Planning (Listed Buildings and Conservation Areas) Act 1990 shall be made within 28 days after the date on which notice of the decision was given to the applicant.
(2) An application shall—
  (a) include, where necessary, any application to extend the time for applying;
  (b) be in writing setting out the reasons why permission should be granted, and if the time for applying has expired, the reasons why the application was not made within that time;
  (c) be made by filing it in the Crown Office together with the decision, a draft claim form, and a witness statement or affidavit verifying any facts relied on;
  (d) before being filed under sub-paragraph (c), be served together with the draft appellant's notice and a copy of the witness statement or affidavit to be filed with the application, upon the persons who are referred to in rule 13(5); and
  (e) be accompanied by a witness statement or affidavit giving the names and addresses of, and the places and dates of service on, all persons who have been served with the application and, if any person who ought to be served has not been served, the witness statement or affidavit must state that fact and the reason for it.
(3) An application shall be heard—
  (a) by a single judge;
  (b) unless the court otherwise orders, not less than 21 days after it was filed at the Crown Office.

  Any person served with the application shall be entitled to appear and be heard.
(4) If on the hearing of an application the court is of opinion that any person who ought to have been served has not been served, the court may adjourn the hearing on such terms (if any) as it may direct in order that the application may be served on that person.
(5) If the court grants permission—
  (a) it may impose such terms as to costs and as to giving security as it thinks fit;
  (b) it may give directions; and
  (c) the appellant's notice by which the appeal is to be brought shall be served and filed within 7 days of the grant.
(6) Any respondent who intends to use a witness statement or affidavit at the hearing shall file it in the Crown Office and serve a copy thereof on the applicant as soon as is

practicable and in any event, unless the court otherwise allows, at least 2 days before the hearing.

The court may allow the applicant to use a further witness statement or affidavit.

### Rule 13 Proceedings Under Sections 289 And 290 of the Town and Country Planning Act 1990 and Under Section 65 of the Planning (Listed Buildings and Conservation Areas) Act 1990

(1) In this rule a reference to 'section 65' is a reference to section 65 of the Planning (Listed Buildings and Conservation Areas) Act 1990, but, save as aforesaid, a reference to a section by number is a reference to the section so numbered in the Town and Country Planning Act 1990.

(2) An appeal shall lie to the High Court on a point of law against a decision of the Secretary of State under subsection (1) or (2) of section 289 or under subsection (1) of section 65 at the instance of any person or authority entitled to appeal under any of those subsections respectively.

(3) In the case of a decision to which section 290 applies, the person who made the application to which the decision relates, or the local planning authority, if dissatisfied with the decision in point of law, may appeal against the decision to the High Court.

(4) Any appeal under section 289(1) or (2), section 65(1) or section 290, and any case stated under section 289(3) or section 65(2), shall be heard and determined by a single judge unless the court directs that the matter shall be heard and determined by a Divisional Court.

(5) The persons to be served with the appellant's notice by which an appeal to the High Court is brought by virtue of section 289(1) or (2), section 65(1) or section 290 are—

(a) the Secretary of State;

(b) the local planning authority who served the notice or gave the decision, as the case may be, or, where the appeal is brought by that authority, the appellant or applicant in the proceedings in which the decision appealed against was given;

(c) in the case of an appeal brought by virtue of section 289(1) or section 65(1), any other person having an interest in the land to which the notice relates, and;

(d) in the case of an appeal brought by virtue of section 289(2), any other person on whom the notice to which those proceedings related was served.

(6) The court hearing any such appeal may remit the matter to the Secretary of State to the extent necessary to enable him to provide the court with such further information in connection with the matter as the court may direct.

(7) Where the court is of opinion that the decision appealed against was erroneous in point of law, it shall not set aside or vary that decision but shall remit the matter to the Secretary of State with the opinion of the court for re-hearing and determination by him.

(9) The court may give directions as to the exercise, until an appeal brought by virtue of section 289(1) is finally concluded and any rehearing and determination by the Secretary of State has taken place, of the power to serve, and institute proceedings (including criminal proceedings) concerning—

(a) a stop notice under section 183; and

(b) a breach of condition notice under section 187A.

## RSC ORDER 95
## BILLS OF SALE ACTS 1878 AND 1882 AND THE INDUSTRIAL AND PROVIDENT SOCIETIES ACT 1967

### Rule 1 Rectification of Register

(1) Every application to the court under section 14 of the Bills of Sale Act 1878, for an order—

(a) that any omission to register a bill of sale or a witness statement or affidavit of renewal thereof within the time prescribed by that Act be rectified by extending the time for such registration; or

(b) that any omission or misstatement of the name, residence or occupation of any person be rectified by the insertion in the register of his true name, residence or occupation,

must be made by witness statement or affidavit to a Master of the Queen's Bench Division, and a copy of the witness statement or affidavit need not be served on any other person.

(2) Every application for such an order as is described in paragraph (1) shall be supported by a witness statement or affidavit setting out particulars of the bill of sale and of the omission or misstatement in question and stating the grounds on which the application is made.

### Rule 4 Search of Register

Any Master of the Queen's Bench Division shall, on a request in writing giving sufficient particulars, and on payment of the prescribed fee, cause a search to be made in the register of bills of sale and issue a certificate of the result of the search.

### Rule 5 Application Under Section 1(5) of the Industrial and Provident Societies Act 1967

Every application to the court under section 1(5) of the Industrial and Provident Societies Act 1967 for an order—

(a) that the period for making an application for recording a charge be extended; or

(b) that any omission from or misstatement in such an application be rectified,

must be made to a Master of the Queen's Bench Division by witness statement or affidavit setting out particulars of the charge and of the omission or misstatement in question and stating the grounds of the application, and need not be served on any other person.

### Rule 6 Assignment of Book Debts

(1) There shall continue to be kept in the Central Office, under the supervision of the registrar, a register of assignments of book debts.

(2) Every application for registration of an assignment of a book debt under section 344 of the Insolvency Act 1986 shall be made by producing at the Filing and Record Department of the Central Office—

(a) a true copy of the assignment, and of every schedule thereto; and

(b) a witness statement or affidavit verifying the date and the time, and the due execution of the assignment in the presence of the witness, and setting out the particulars of the assignment and the parties thereto.

(3) On an application being made in accordance with the preceding paragraph, the documents there referred to shall be filed, and the particulars of the assignment, and of the parties to it, shall be entered in the register.

(4) In this rule, 'the registrar' has the meaning given in section 13 of the Bills of Sale Act 1878.

## RSC ORDER 96
## THE MINES (WORKING FACILITIES AND SUPPORT) ACT 1966 ETC.

### Rule 1 Assignment to Chancery Division

Any proceedings in which the jurisdiction conferred on the High Court by section 1 of the Railway and Canal Commission (Abolition) Act 1949 is invoked shall be assigned to the Chancery Division and be begun by claim form which need not be served on any other party.

# RSC ORDER 109
# THE ADMINISTRATION OF JUSTICE ACT 1960

## Rule 1 Applications Under Act

(1) Any of the following applications, that is to say—
  (a) an application under section 2 of the Administration of Justice Act 1960, or under that section as applied by section 13 of that Act, to extend the time within which an application may be made to a Divisional Court for permission to appeal to the House of Lords under section 1 of that Act, or section 13 thereof, from an order or decision of that court, and
  (b) an application by a defendant under section 9(3) of that Act to a Divisional Court for permission to be present on the hearing of any proceedings preliminary or incidental to an appeal to the House of Lords under section 1 of that Act from a decision of that court

must be made to a Divisional Court except in vacation when it may be made to a judge.

(2) Any such application to a Divisional Court, if not made in the proceedings before the Divisional Court from whose order or decision the appeal in question is brought, must be made by the issue of a claim form.

(3) Any such application to a judge must, in the case of such an application as is referred to in paragraph (1)(a) be made by the issue of a claim form and, in the case of such an application as is referred to in paragraph (1)(b) need not be served on any other person unless, in the latter case, the judge otherwise directs.

(4) No application notice or copy of the claim form (as the case may be) by which such an application as is referred to in paragraph (1)(b) is made, need be given to any party affected thereby unless the Divisional Court otherwise directs.

(5) Where any application to which this rule applies is made in vacation to a single judge and the judge refuses the application, the applicant shall be entitled to have the application determined by a Divisional Court.

## Rule 2 Appeals Under Section 13 of Act

(1) An appeal to a Divisional Court of the High Court under section 13 of the Administration of Justice Act 1960, shall be heard and determined by a Divisional Court of the Queen's Bench Division.

(4) Unless the court gives permission, there shall be not more than 4 clear days between the date on which the order or decision appealed against was made and the day named in the notice of appeal for the hearing of the appeal.

(5) The notice must be served, and the appeal entered, not less than one clear day before the day named in the notice for the hearing of the appeal.

## Rule 3 Release of Appellant on Bail

(1) Where, in the case of an appeal under section 13 of the Administration of Justice Act 1960, to a Divisional Court or to the House of Lords from a Divisional Court, the appellant is in custody, the High Court may order his release on his giving security (whether by recognisance, with or without sureties, or otherwise and for such reasonable sum as the court may fix) for his appearance, within 10 days after the judgment of the Divisional Court or, as the case may be, of the House of Lords, on the appeal before the court from whose order or decision the appeal is brought unless the order or decision is reversed by that judgment.

(2) Order 79, rule 9(1) to (6) and (8) shall apply in relation to an application to the High Court for bail pending an appeal under the said section 13 to which this rule applies, and to the admission of a person to bail in pursuance of an order made on the application, as they apply in relation to an application to that court for bail in criminal proceedings, and to the admission of a person to bail in pursuance of an order made on

the application, but with the substitution, for references to the defendant, of references to the appellant, and, for references to the prosecutor, of references to the court officer of the court from whose order or decision the appeal is brought and to the parties to the proceedings in that court who are directly affected by the appeal.

### Rule 4 Release of Appellant on Bail by the Court of Appeal

(1) Where, in the case of an appeal under section 13 of the Administration of Justice Act 1960 to the Court of Appeal or to the House of Lords from the Court of Appeal, the appellant is in custody, the Court of Appeal may order his release on his giving security (whether by recognisance, with or without sureties, or otherwise and for such reasonable sum as that court may fix) for his appearance within 10 days after the judgment of the Court of Appeal or, as the case may be, of the House of Lords on the appeal shall have been given, before the court from whose order or decision the appeal is brought unless the order or decision is reversed by that judgment.

(2) An application for the release of a person under paragraph (1) pending an appeal to the Court of Appeal or House of Lords under the said section 13 must be made in accordance with CPR Part 23, and the application notice must, at least 24 hours before the day named therein for the hearing, be served on the court from whose order or decision the appeal is brought and on all parties to the proceedings in that court who are directly affected by the appeal.

(3) Order 79, rules 9(6), (6A), (6B) and (8) shall apply in relation to the grant of bail under this rule by the Court of Appeal in a case of criminal contempt of court as they apply in relation to the grant of bail in criminal proceedings by the High Court, but with the substitution for references to a judge of references to the Court of Appeal and for references to the defendant of references to the appellant.

(4) When granting bail under this rule in a case of civil contempt of court, the Court of Appeal may order that the recognisance or other security to be given by the appellant or the recognisance of any surety shall be given before any person authorised by virtue of section 119(1) of the Magistrates' Courts Act 1980 to take a recognisance where a magistrates' court having power to take it has, instead of taking it, fixed the amount in which the principal and his sureties, if any, are to be bound. An order by the Court of Appeal granting bail as aforesaid must be in Form 98 in the relevant Practice Direction with the necessary adaptations.

(5) Where in pursuance of an order of the Court of Appeal under paragraph (4) of this rule a recognisance is entered into or other security given before any person, it shall be the duty of that person to cause the recognisance of the appellant or any surety or, as the case may be, a statement of the other security given, to be transmitted forthwith to the justices' chief executive for the court which committed the appellant; and a copy of such recognisance or statement shall at the same time be sent to the governor or keeper of the prison or other place of detention in which the appellant is detained, unless the recognisance or security was given before such governor or keeper.

(6) The powers conferred on the Court of Appeal by paragraphs (1), (3) and (4) of this rule may be exercised by a single judge.

## RSC ORDER 113
## SUMMARY PROCEEDINGS FOR POSSESSION OF LAND

### Rule 7 Writ of Possession

(1) Order 45, rule 3(2) shall not apply in relation to an order for possession in a possession claim against trespassers under Part 55 but no writ of possession to enforce such an order shall be issued after the expiry of three months from the date of the order without the permission of the court.

An application for permission may be made without notice being served on any other party unless the court otherwise directs.

(2) The writ of possession shall be in Form No. 66A.

# RSC ORDER 115
# CONFISCATION AND FORFEITURE IN CONNECTION WITH CRIMINAL PROCEEDINGS

## I Drug Trafficking Act 1994 and Criminal Justice (International Co-operation) Act 1990

### Rule 1 Interpretation

(1) In this Part of this Order, 'The Act' means the Drug Trafficking Act 1994 and a section referred to by number means the section so numbered in the Act.

(2) Expressions used in this Part of this Order which are used in the Act have the same meanings in this Part of this Order as in the Act and include any extended meaning given by the Criminal Justice (Confiscation) (Northern Ireland) Order 1990.

### Rule 2 Assignment of Proceedings

Subject to rule 12, the jurisdiction of the High Court under the Act shall be exercised by a judge of the Chancery Division or of the Queen's Bench Division.

### Rule 2A Title of Proceedings

An application made in accordance with CPR Part 23, or a claim form issued in relation to proceedings under this Part of this Order shall be entitled in the matter of the defendant, naming him, and in the matter of the Act, and all subsequent documents in the matter shall be so entitled.

### Rule 2B Application for Confiscation Order

(1) An application by the prosecutor for a confiscation order under section 19 shall be made in accordance with CPR Part 23 where there have been proceedings against the defendant in the High Court, and shall otherwise be made by the issue of a claim form.

(2) The application shall be supported by a witness statement or affidavit giving full particulars of the following matters—
   (a) the grounds for believing that the defendant has died or absconded;
   (b) the date or approximate date on which the defendant died or absconded;
   (c) where the application is made under section 19(2), the offence or offences of which the defendant was convicted, and the date and place of conviction;
   (d) where the application is made under section 19(4), the proceedings which have been initiated against the defendant (including particulars of the offence and the date and place of institution of those proceedings); and
   (e) where the defendant is alleged to have absconded, the steps taken to contact him.

(3) The prosecutor's statement under section 11 shall be exhibited to the witness statement or affidavit and shall include the following particulars—
   (a) the name of the defendant;
   (b) the name of the person by whom the statement is given;
   (c) such information known to the prosecutor as is relevant to the determination whether the defendant has benefited from drug trafficking and to the assessment of the value of his proceeds of drug trafficking.

(4) Unless the court otherwise orders, a witness statement or affidavit under paragraph (2) may contain statements of information and belief, with their sources and grounds.

(5) The application and the witness statement or affidavit in support shall be served not less than 7 days before the date fixed for the hearing of the application on—
(a) the defendant (or on the personal representatives of a deceased defendant);
(b) any person who the prosecutor reasonably believes is likely to be affected by the making of a confiscation order; and
(c) the receiver, where one has been appointed in the matter.

## Rule 3 Application for Restraint Order or Charging Order

(1) An application for a restraint order under section 26 or for a charging order under section 27 (to either of which may be joined an application for the appointment of a receiver) may be made by the prosecutor by the issue of a claim form notice of which need not be served on any other party.
(2) An application under paragraph (1) shall be supported by a witness statement or affidavit, which shall—
(a) give the grounds for the application; and
(b) to the best of the witness's ability, give full particulars of the realisable property in respect of which the order is sought and specify the person or persons holding such property.
(3) Unless the court otherwise directs, a witness statement or affidavit under paragraph (2) may contain statements of information or belief with the sources and grounds thereof.

## Rule 4 Restraint Order and Charging Order

(1) A restraint order may be made subject to conditions and exceptions, including but not limited to conditions relating to the indemnifying of third parties against expenses incurred in complying with the order, and exceptions relating to living expenses and legal expenses of the defendant, but the prosecutor shall not be required to give an undertaking to abide by any order as to damages sustained by the defendant as a result of the restraint order.
(2) Unless the court otherwise directs, a restraint order made where notice of it has not been served on any person shall have effect until a day which shall be fixed for the hearing where all parties may attend on the application and a charging order shall be an order to show cause, imposing the charge until such day.
(3) Where a restraint order is made the prosecutor shall serve copies of the order and of the witness statement or affidavit in support on the defendant and on all other named persons restrained by the order and shall notify all other persons or bodies affected by the order of its terms.
(4) Where a charging order is made the prosecutor shall serve copies of the order and of the witness statement or affidavit in support on the defendant and, where the property to which the order relates is held by another person, on that person and shall serve a copy of the order on such of the persons or bodies specified in CPR rule 73.5(1)(c) to (e) as shall be appropriate.

## Rule 5 Discharge or Variation of Order

(1) Any person or body on whom a restraint order or a charging order is served or who is notified of such an order may make an application in accordance with CPR Part 23 to discharge or vary the order.
(2) The application notice and any witness statement or affidavit in support shall be lodged with the court and served on the prosecutor and, where he is not the applicant, on the defendant, not less than two clear days before the date fixed for the hearing of the application.
(3) Upon the court being notified that proceedings for the offences have been concluded or that the amount, payment of which is secured by a charging order has been paid into court, any restraint order or charging order, as the case may be, shall be discharged.
(4) The court may also discharge a restraint order or a charging order upon receiving notice

from the prosecutor that it is no longer appropriate for the restraint order or the charging order to remain in place.

### Rule 6 Further Application by Prosecutor

(1) Where a restraint order or a charging order has been made the prosecutor may apply by an application in accordance with CPR Part 23 with notice or, where the case is one of urgency or the giving of notice would cause a reasonable apprehension of dissipation of assets, without notice—
  (a) to vary such order; or
  (b) for a restraint order or a charging order in respect of other realisable property; or
  (c) for the appointment of a receiver.
(2) An application under paragraph (1) shall be supported by a witness statement or affidavit which, where the application is for a restraint order or a charging order, shall to the best of the witness's ability give full particulars of the realisable property in respect of which the order is sought and specify the person or persons holding such property.
(3) The application and witness statement or affidavit in support shall be lodged with the court and served on the defendant and, where one has been appointed in the matter, on the receiver, not less than two clear days before the date fixed for the hearing of the application.
(4) Rule 4(3) and (4) shall apply to the service of restraint orders and charging orders respectively made under this rule on persons other than the defendant.

### Rule 7 Realisation of Property

(1) An application by the prosecutor under section 29 shall, where there have been proceedings against the defendant in the High Court, be made by an application in accordance with CPR Part 23 and shall otherwise be made by the issue of a claim form
(2) The application notice or claim form, as the case may be, shall be served with the evidence in support not less than 7 days before the date fixed for the hearing of the application or claim on—
  (a) the defendant;
  (b) any person holding any interest in the realisable property to which the application relates; and
  (c) the receiver, where one has been appointed in the matter.
(3) The application shall be supported by a witness statement or affidavit, which shall, to the best of the witness's ability, give full particulars of the realisable property to which it relates and specify the person or persons holding such property, and a copy of the confiscation order, of any certificate issued by the Crown Court under section 5(2) and of any charging order made in the matter shall be exhibited to such witness statement or affidavit.
(4) The Court may, on an application under section 29—
  (a) exercise the power conferred by section 30(2) to direct the making of payments by a receiver;
  (b) give directions in respect of the property interests to which the application relates; and
  (c) make declarations in respect of those interests.

### Rule 8 Receivers

(1) Subject to the provisions of this rule, the provisions of CPR Part 69 shall apply where a receiver is appointed in pursuance of a charging order or under sections 26 or 29.
(2) Where the receiver proposed to be appointed has been appointed receiver in other proceedings under the Act, it shall not be necessary for a witness statement or affidavit of fitness to be sworn or for the receiver to give security, unless the court otherwise orders.
(3) Where a receiver has fully paid the amount payable under the confiscation order and any

sums remain in his hands, he shall make an application to the court for directions in accordance with CPR Part 23, as to the distribution of such sums.

(4) An application under paragraph (3) shall be served with any evidence in support not less than 7 days before the date fixed for the hearing of the application on—
  (a) the defendant; and
  (b) any other person who held property realised by the receiver.

(5) A receiver may apply for an order to discharge him from his office by making an application in accordance with CPR Part 23, which shall be served, together with any evidence in support, on all persons affected by his appointment not less than 7 days before the day fixed for the hearing of the application.

## Rule 9 Certificate of Inadequacy

(1) The defendant or a receiver appointed under section 26 or 29 or in pursuance of a charging order may apply in accordance with CPR Part 23 for a certificate under section 17(1).

(2) An application under paragraph (1) shall be served with any supporting evidence not less than 7 days before the date fixed for the hearing of the application on the prosecutor and, as the case may be, on either the defendant or the receiver (where one has been appointed).

## Rule 9A Certificate Under Section 16

An application under section 16(2) (increase in realisable property) shall be served with any supporting evidence not less than 7 days before the date fixed for the hearing of the application on the defendant and, as the case may be, on either the prosecutor or (where one has been appointed in the matter) on the receiver.

## Rule 10 Compensation

An application for an order under section 18 shall be made in accordance with CPR Part 23, which shall be served, with any supporting evidence, on the person alleged to be in default and on the relevant authority under section 18(5) not less than 7 days before the date fixed for the hearing of the application.

## Rule 11 Disclosure of Information

(1) An application by the prosecutor under section 59 shall be made in accordance with CPR Part 23 and the application notice shall state the nature of the order sought and whether material sought to be disclosed is to be disclosed to a receiver appointed under section 26 or 29 or in pursuance of a charging order or to a person mentioned in section 59(8).

(2) The application notice and witness statement or affidavit in support shall be served on the authorised Government Department in accordance with Order 77, rule 4 not less than 7 days before the date fixed for the hearing of the application.

(3) The witness statement or affidavit in support of an application under paragraph (1) shall state the grounds for believing that the conditions in section 59(4) and, if appropriate, section 59(7) are fulfilled.

## Rule 11A Compensation for, Discharge and Variation of Confiscation Order

(1) An application under section 21, 22 or 23 shall be made in accordance with CPR Part 23 which, together with any evidence in support, shall be lodged with the court and served on the prosecutor not less than 7 days before the day fixed for the hearing of the application.

(2) Notice shall also be served on any receiver appointed in pursuance of a charging order or under section 26 or 29.

(3) An application for an order under section 22 shall be supported by a witness statement or affidavit giving details of—
  (a) the confiscation order made under section 19(4);
  (b) the acquittal of the defendant;

(c) the realisable property held by the defendant; and
(d) the loss suffered by the applicant as a result of the confiscation order.

(4) An application for an order under section 23 shall be supported by a witness statement or affidavit giving details of—
(a) the confiscation order made under section 19(4);
(b) the date on which the defendant ceased to be an absconder;
(c) the date on which proceedings against the defendant were instituted and a summary of the steps taken in the proceedings since then; and
(d) any indication given by the prosecutor that he does not intend to proceed against the defendant.

(5) An application made under section 21 shall be supported by a witness statement or affidavit giving details of—
(a) the confiscation order made under section 19(4);
(b) the circumstances in which the defendant ceased to be an absconder; and
(c) the amounts referred to in section 21(2).

(6) Where an application is made for an order under section 23(3) or 24(2)(b), the witness statement or affidavit shall also include—
(a) details of the realisable property to which the application relates; and
(b) details of the loss suffered by the applicant as a result of the confiscation order.

(7) Unless the court otherwise orders, a witness statement or affidavit under paragraphs (3) to (6) may contain statements of information and belief, with the sources and grounds thereof.

## Rule 12 Exercise of Powers Under Sections 37 and 40

The powers conferred on the High Court by sections 37 and 40 may be exercised by a judge or a Master of the Queen's Bench Division.

## Rule 13 Application for Registration

An application for registration of an order specified in an Order in Council made under section 37 or of an external confiscation order under section 40(1) must be made in accordance with CPR Part 23, and may be made without notice.

## Rule 14 Evidence in Support of Application Under Section 37

An application for registration of an order specified in an Order in Council made under section 37 must be made in accordance with CPR Part 23, and be supported by a witness statement or affidavit—

(i) exhibiting the order or a certified copy thereof; and
(ii) stating, to the best of the witness's knowledge, particulars of what property the person against whom the order was made holds in England and Wales, giving the source of the witness's knowledge.

## Rule 15 Evidence in Support of Application Under Section 40(1)

(1) An application for registration of an external confiscation order must be made in accordance with CPR Part 23, and be supported by a witness statement or affidavit—
(a) exhibiting the order or a verified or certified or otherwise duly authenticated copy thereof and, where the order is not in the English language, a translation thereof into English certified by a notary public or authenticated by witness statement or affidavit; and
(b) stating—
(i) that the order is in force and is not subject to appeal;
(ii) where the person against whom the order was made did not appear in the proceedings, that he received notice thereof in sufficient time to enable him to defend them;
(iii) in the case of money, either that at the date of the application the sum payable

under the order has not been paid or the amount which remains unpaid, as may be appropriate, or, in the case of other property, the property which has not been recovered; and

(iv) to the best of the witness's knowledge, particulars of what property the person against whom the order was made holds in England and Wales, giving the source of the witness's knowledge.

(2) Unless the court otherwise directs, a witness statement or affidavit for the purposes of this rule may contain statements of information or belief with the sources and grounds thereof.

### Rule 16 Register of Orders

(1) There shall be kept in the Central Office under the direction of the Master of the Crown Office a register of the orders registered under the Act.

(2) There shall be included in such register particulars of any variation or setting aside of a registration and of any execution issued on a registered order.

### Rule 17 Notice of Registration

(1) Notice of the registration of an order must be served on the person against whom it was obtained by delivering it to him personally or by sending it to him at his usual or last known address or place of business or in such other manner as the court may direct.

(2) Permission is not required to serve such a notice out of the jurisdiction and CPR rules 6.24, 6.25 and 6.29 shall apply in relation to such notice as they apply in relation to a claim form.

### Rule 18 Application to Vary or Set Aside Registration

An application made in accordance with CPR Part 23 by the person against whom an order was made to vary or set aside the registration of an order must be made to a judge and be supported by witness statement or affidavit.

### Rule 19 Enforcement of Order

(2) If an application is made under rule 18, an order shall not be enforced until after such application is determined.

### Rule 20 Variation, Satisfaction and Discharge of Registered Order

Upon the court being notified by the applicant for registration that an order which has been registered has been varied, satisfied or discharged, particulars of the variation, satisfaction or discharge, as the case may be, shall be entered in the register.

### Rule 21 Rules to Have Effect Subject to Orders in Council

Rules 12 to 20 shall have effect subject to the provisions of the Order in Council made under section 37 or, as the case may be, of the Order in Council made under section 39.

### Rule 21A Criminal Justice (International Co-operation) Act 1990: External Forfeiture Orders

The provisions of this Part of this Order shall, with such modifications as are necessary and subject to the provisions of any Order in Council made under section 9 of the Criminal Justice (International Co-operation) Act 1990, apply to proceedings for the registration and enforcement of external forfeiture orders as they apply to such proceedings in relation to external confiscation orders.

For the purposes of this rule, an external forfeiture order is an order made by a court in a country or territory outside the United Kingdom which is enforceable in the United Kingdom by virtue of any such Order in Council.

## II Part VI of the Criminal Justice Act 1988

### Rule 22 Interpretation

(1) In this Part of this Order, 'the 1988 Act' means the Criminal Justice Act 1988 and a section referred to by number means the section so numbered in that Act.
(2) Expressions which are used in this Part of this Order which are used in the 1988 Act have the same meanings in this Part of this Order as in the 1988 Act and include any extended meaning given by the Criminal Justice (Confiscation) (Northern Ireland) Order 1990.

### Rule 23 Application of Part I of Order 115

Part I of Order 115 (except rule 11) shall apply for the purposes of proceedings under Part VI of the 1988 Act with the necessary modifications and, in particular—

(a) references to drug trafficking offences and to drug trafficking shall be construed as references to offences to which Part VI of the 1988 Act applies and to committing such an offence;
(b) references to the Drug Trafficking Act 1994 shall be construed as references to the 1988 Act and references to sections 5(2), 26, 27, 29, 30(2), 17(1), 18, 18(5), 39 and 40 of the 1994 Act shall be construed as references to sections 73(6), 77, 78, 80, 81, 81(1), 83(1), 89, 89(5), 96 and 97 of the 1988 Act respectively;
(c) rule 3(2) shall have effect as if the following sub-paragraphs were substituted for sub-paragraphs (a) and (b)—
  '(a) state, as the case may be, either that proceedings have been instituted against the defendant for an offence to which Part VI of the 1988 Act applies (giving particulars of the offence) and that they have not been concluded or that, whether by the laying of an information or otherwise, a person is to be charged with such an offence;
  (b) state, as the case may be, either that a confiscation order has been made or the grounds for believing that such an order may be made;'
(d) rule 7(3) shall have effect as if the words 'certificate issued by a magistrates' court or the Crown Court' were substituted for the words 'certificate issued by the Crown Court';
(e) rule 8 shall have effect as if the following paragraph were added at the end—
  '(6) Where a receiver applies in accordance with CPR Part 23 for the variation of a confiscation order, the application notice shall be served, with any supporting evidence, on the defendant and any other person who may be affected by the making of an order under section 83 of the 1988 Act, not less than 7 days before the date fixed for the hearing of the application.';
(f) rule 11 shall apply with the necessary modifications where an application is made under section 93J of the 1988 Act for disclosure of information held by government departments.

## III Terrorism Act 2000

### Rule 24 Interpretation

In this Part of this Order—

(a) 'the Act' means the Terrorism Act 2000;
(b) 'Schedule 4' means Schedule 4 to the Act;
(ba) 'the prosecutor' means the person with conduct of proceedings which have been instituted in England and Wales for an offence under any of sections 15 to 18 of the Act, or the person who the High Court is satisfied will have the conduct of any proceedings for such an offence; and
(c) other expressions used have the same meanings as they have in Schedule 4 to the Act.

## Rule 25 Assignment of Proceedings

(1) Subject to paragraph (2), the jurisdiction of the High Court under the Act shall be exercised by a judge of the Queen's Bench Division or of the Chancery Division sitting in private.

(2) The jurisdiction conferred on the High Court by paragraph 9 of Schedule 4 may also be exercised by a Master of the Queen's Bench Division.

## Rule 26 Application for Restraint Order

(1) An application for a restraint order under paragraph 5 of Schedule 4 may be made by the prosecutor by a claim form, which need not be served on any person.

(2) An application under paragraph (1) shall be supported by a witness statement or affidavit, which shall—

(a) state, as the case may be, either—

(i) that proceedings have been instituted against a person for an offence under any of sections 15 to 18 of the Act and that they have not been concluded; or

(ii) that a criminal investigation has been started in England and Wales with regard to such an offence,

and in either case give details of the alleged or suspected offence and of the defendant's involvement;

(b) where proceedings have been instituted, state, as the case may be, that a forfeiture order has been made in the proceedings or the grounds for believing that such an order may be made;

(ba) where proceedings have not been instituted—

(i) indicate the state of progress of the investigation and when it is anticipated that a decision will be taken on whether to institute proceedings against the defendant;

(ii) state the grounds for believing that a forfeiture order may be made in any proceedings against the defendant; and

(iii) verify that the prosecutor is to have the conduct of any such proceedings;

(c) to the best of the witness's ability, give full particulars of the property in respect of which the order is sought and specify the person or persons holding such property and any other persons having an interest in it.

(3) A claim form under paragraph (1) shall be entitled in the matter of the defendant, naming him, and in the matter of the Act, and all subsequent documents in the matter shall be so entitled.

(4) Unless the court otherwise directs, a witness statement or affidavit under paragraph (2) may contain statements of information or belief with the sources and grounds thereof.

## Rule 27 Restraint Order

(1) A restraint order may be made subject to conditions and exceptions, including but not limited to conditions relating to the indemnifying of third parties against expenses incurred in complying with the order, and exceptions relating to living expenses and legal expenses of the defendant; but the prosecutor shall not be required to give an undertaking to abide by any order as to damages sustained by the defendant as a result of the restraint order.

(2) Unless the court otherwise directs, the application for it being served on any person shall have effect until a day which shall be fixed for the hearing where all parties may attend on the application.

(3) Where a restraint order is made the prosecutor shall serve copies of the order and, unless the court otherwise orders, of the witness statement or affidavit in support on the defendant and on all other persons affected by the order.

## Rule 28 Discharge or Variation of Order

(1) Subject to paragraph (2), an application to discharge or vary a restraint order shall be made in accordance with CPR Part 23.
(2) Where the case is one of urgency, an application under this rule by the prosecutor may be made without notice.
(3) The application and any witness statement or affidavit in support shall be lodged with the court and, where the application is made in accordance with CPR Part 23 the application notice shall be served on the following persons (other than the applicant)—
  (a) the prosecutor;
  (b) the defendant; and
  (c) all other persons restrained or otherwise affected by the order;
  not less than two clear days before the date fixed for the hearing of the application.
(4) Where a restraint order has been made and has not been discharged, the prosecutor shall notify the court when proceedings for the offence have been concluded, and the court shall thereupon discharge the restraint order.
(5) Where an order is made discharging or varying a restraint order, the applicant shall serve copies of the order of discharge or variation on all persons restrained by the earlier order and shall notify all other persons affected of the terms of the order of discharge or variation.

## Rule 29 Compensation

An application for an order under paragraph 9 or 10 of Schedule 4 shall be made in accordance with CPR Part 23, and the application notice, shall be served, with any supporting evidence, on the person alleged to be in default and on the person or body by whom compensation, if ordered, will be payable under paragraph 9(6) or 10(4) not less than 7 days before the date fixed for the hearing of the application.

## Rule 30 Application for Registration

An application for registration of a Scottish order, a Northern Ireland order or an Islands order must be made in accordance with CPR Part 23 and may be made without notice.

## Rule 31 Evidence in Support of Application

(1) An application for registration of any such order as is mentioned in rule 30 must be supported by a witness statement or affidavit—
  (a) exhibiting the order or a certified copy thereof; and
  (b) which shall, to the best of the witness's ability, give particulars of such property in respect of which the order was made as is in England and Wales, and specify the person or persons holding such property.
(2) Unless the court otherwise directs, a witness statement or affidavit for the purposes of this rule may contain statements of information or belief with the sources and grounds thereof.

## Rule 32 Register of Orders

(1) There shall be kept in the Central Office under the direction of the Master of the Administrative Court a register of the orders registered under the Act.
(2) There shall be included in such register particulars of any variation or setting aside of a registration, and of any execution issued on a registered order.

## Rule 33 Notice of Registration

(1) Notice of the registration of an order must be served on the person or persons holding the property referred to in rule 3 1 (1)(b) and any other persons appearing to have an interest in that property.
(2) Permission is not required to serve such a notice out of the jurisdiction and CPR rules

6.24, 6.25 and 6.29 shall apply in relation to such notice as they apply in relation to a claim form.

### Rule 34 Application to Vary or Set Aside Registration

An application to vary or set aside the registration of an order must be made to a judge in accordance with CPR Part 23 and be supported by a witness statement or affidavit.

This rule does not apply to a variation or cancellation under rule 36.

### Rule 35 Enforcement of Order

(2) If an application is made under rule 34, an order shall not be enforced until after such application is determined.
(3) This rule does not apply to the taking of steps under paragraph 7 or 8 of Schedule 4, as applied by paragraph 13(6) of that Schedule.

### Rule 36 Variation and Cancellation of Registration

If effect has been given (whether in England or Wales or elsewhere) to a Scottish, Northern Ireland or Islands order, or if the order has been varied or discharged by the court by which it was made, the applicant for registration shall inform the court and—
(a) if such effect has been given in respect of all the money or other property to which the order applies, or if the order has been discharged by the court by which it was made, registration of the order shall be cancelled;
(b) if such effect has been given in respect of only part of the money or other property, or if the order has been varied by the court by which it was made, registration of the order shall be varied accordingly.

## IV International Criminal Court Act 2001: Fines, Forfeitures and Reparation Orders

### Rule 37 Interpretation

In this Part of this Order—
(a) 'the Act' means the International Criminal Court Act 2001;
(b) 'the ICC' means the International Criminal Court;
(c) 'an order of the ICC' means—
  (i) a fine or forfeiture ordered by the ICC; or
  (ii) an order by the ICC against a person convicted by the ICC specifying a reparation to, or in respect of, a victim.

### Rule 38 Registration of ICC Orders for Enforcement

(1) An application to the High Court to register an order of the ICC for enforcement, or to vary or set aside the registration of an order, may be made to a judge or a Master of the Queen's Bench Division.
(2) Rule 13 and rules 15 to 20 in Part I of this Order shall, with such modifications as are necessary and subject to the provisions of any regulations made under section 49 of the Act, apply to the registration for enforcement of an order of the ICC as they apply to the registration of an external confiscation order.

# RSC ORDER 116
# THE CRIMINAL PROCEDURE AND INVESTIGATIONS ACT 1996

### Rule 1 Application

This Order shall apply in relation to acquittals in respect of offences alleged to be committed on or after 15th April 1997.

## Rule 2 Interpretation

In this Order, unless the context otherwise requires—

'the Act' means the Criminal Procedure and Investigations Act 1996;

'acquitted person' means a person whose acquittal of an offence is the subject of a certification under section 54(2) of the Act, and 'acquittal' means the acquittal of that person of that offence;

'magistrates' court' has the same meaning as in section 148 of the Magistrates' Courts Act 1980;

'prosecutor' means the individual or body which acted as prosecutor in the proceedings which led to the acquittal;

'record of court proceedings' means—

(a) (where the proceedings took place in the Crown Court) a transcript of the evidence, or
(b) a note of the evidence made by the justices' clerk,

in the proceedings which led to the conviction for the administration of justice offence referred to in section 54(1)(b) of the Act or, as the case may be, the proceedings which led to the acquittal;

'single judge' means a judge of the Queen's Bench Division;

'witness' means a witness whose evidence is contained in a witness statement or affidavit filed under rule 5, 7, 8 or 9.

## Rule 3 Assignment of Proceedings

The jurisdiction of the High Court under section 54(3) of the Act shall be exercised by a single judge.

## Rule 4 Time Limit For Making Application

An application under section 54(3) of the Act shall be made not later than 28 days after—

(a) the expiry of the period allowed for appealing (whether by case stated or otherwise), or making an application for leave to appeal, against the conviction referred to in section 54(1)(b) of the Act; or
(b) where notice of appeal or application for leave to appeal against the conviction is given, the determination of the appeal or application for leave to appeal and, for this purpose, 'determination' includes abandonment (within the meaning of rule 10 of the Criminal Appeal Rules 1968 or, as the case may be, rule 11 of the Crown Court Rules 1982).

## Rule 5 Application

(1) An application under section 54(3) of the Act shall be made by claim form which shall be issued out of the Crown Office by the prosecutor.
(2) The application shall be accompanied by—
  (a) a witness statement or affidavit which deals with the conditions in section 55(1), (2) and (4) of the Act and which exhibits any relevant documents (which may include a copy of any record of court proceedings);
  (b) a copy of the certification under section 54(2) of the Act.

## Rule 6 Notice to the Acquitted Person

(1) The prosecutor shall, within 4 days of the issue of the application, serve written notice on the acquitted person that the application has been issued.
(2) The notice given under paragraph (1) shall—
  (a) specify the date on which the application was issued;
  (b) be accompanied by a copy of the application and of the documents which accompanied it;
  (c) inform the acquitted person that—
    (i) the result of the application may be the making of an order by the High Court quashing the acquittal, and

(ii) if he wishes to respond to the application, he must, within 28 days of the date of service on him of the notice, file in the Crown Office any witness statement or affidavit on which he intends to rely.

### Rule 7 Witness Statement or Affidavit of Service on an Acquitted Person

The prosecutor shall, as soon as practicable after service of the notice under rule 6, file at the Crown Office a witness statement or affidavit of service which exhibits a copy of the notice.

### Rule 8 Response of Acquitted Person

(1) If the acquitted person wishes to respond to the application, he shall, within 28 days of service on him of notice under rule 6, file in the Crown Office a witness statement or affidavit which—
(a) deals with the conditions in section 55(1), (2) and (4) of the Act; and
(b) exhibits any relevant documents (which may include a copy of any record of court proceedings).

(2) The acquitted person shall, within 4 days of the filing of the documents mentioned in paragraph (1), serve copies of them on the prosecutor.

### Rule 9 Evidence

(1) A witness statement or affidavit filed under rule 5, 7, 8 or this rule may contain statements of information or belief with the sources and grounds thereof.

(2) The prosecutor may, not later than 10 days after expiry of the period allowed under rule 8(1), apply for an order granting permission to file further evidence without notice being served on any other party.

(3) If the single judge grants permission, the order shall specify a period within which further evidence or records are to be filed, and the Crown Office shall serve a copy of the order on the prosecutor and on the acquitted person.

(4) The prosecutor shall, within 4 days of filing further evidence in the Crown Office, serve a copy of that evidence on the acquitted person.

### Rule 10 Determination of the Application

(1) Subject to paragraph (3), the single judge shall determine whether or not to make an order under section 54(3) of the Act on the basis of the written material provided under rules 5, 7, 8 and 9 in the absence of the prosecutor, the acquitted person, or of any witness.

(2) The determination shall not be made, and any hearing under paragraph (3) shall not take place, before the expiry of—
(a) 10 days after the expiry of the period allowed under rule 8(1), or
(b) 10 days after the expiry of the period allowed by any order made under rule 9(3).

(3) The single judge may, of his own initiative or on the application of the prosecutor or acquitted person, order a hearing of the application if he thinks fit.

(4) An application under paragraph (3) shall state whether a hearing is desired in order for a deponent for the other party to attend and be cross-examined, and, if so, the reasons for wishing the witness to attend.

(5) An application under paragraph (3) shall be made no later than 7 days after the expiry of the period allowed—
(a) under rule 8(1), or
(b) by any order made under rule 9(3).

(6) Where a hearing is ordered, the single judge may, of his own initiative or on the application of the prosecutor or acquitted person, order a witness to attend in order to be cross-examined.

(7) The prosecutor or the acquitted person, as the case may be, shall within 4 days after filing the application under paragraph (3), serve a copy of it on the other party, and file in the Crown Office a witness statement or affidavit of service.

(8) A party served under paragraph (7) shall, within 5 days of service, file any representations he wishes to make as to whether or not a hearing should be ordered.

(9) Subject to paragraph (10) below—
  (a) the single judge shall not determine an application for a hearing under paragraph (3) unless—
    (i) a witness statement or affidavit of service has been filed as required by paragraph (7), and
    (ii) the period for filing representations allowed under paragraph (8) has elapsed, or
    (iii) representations have been filed under paragraph (8).
  (b) The requirements imposed by sub-paragraph (a)(i) and (iii) are satisfied even though the witness statement or affidavit of service or, as the case may be, the representations are filed outside the time limits allowed.

(10) Where after an application for a hearing has been made—
  (a) no witness statement or affidavit or service has been filed, and
  (b) no representations under paragraph (8) have been received after the expiry of 7 days from the filing of the application,

  the single judge may reject the application.

(11) Where after a hearing is ordered, either the prosecutor or the acquitted person desires a witness for the other party to attend the hearing in order to be cross-examined, he must apply for an order under paragraph (5) giving his reasons without notice being served on any other party.

(12) The Crown Office shall serve notice on the prosecutor and the acquitted person of any order made under the foregoing paragraphs of this rule and, where a hearing is ordered, the notice shall—
  (a) set out the date, time and place of the hearing, and
  (b) give details of any witness ordered to attend for cross-examination.

(13) A hearing ordered under paragraph (3) above shall be in public unless the single judge otherwise directs.

(14) The Crown Office shall serve notice of any order made under section 54(3) of the Act quashing the acquittal or of a decision not to make such an order on the prosecutor, the acquitted person and—
  (a) where the court before which the acquittal or conviction occurred was a magistrates' court, on the justices' chief executive;
  (b) where the court before which the acquittal or conviction occurred was the Crown Court, on the appropriate officer of the Crown Court sitting at the place where the acquittal or conviction occurred.

# PD RSC Ord. 46 & CCR Ord. 26 Practice Direction — Execution

This practice direction supplements RSC Order 46 (Schedule 1 to the CPR) and CCR Order 26 (Schedule 2 to the CPR).

## Levying Execution on Certain Days

1.1 Unless the court orders otherwise, a writ of execution or a warrant of execution to enforce a judgment or order must not be executed on a Sunday, Good Friday or Christmas Day.

1.2 Paragraph 1.1 does not apply to an Admiralty claim in rem.

# PD RSC Ord. 52 & CCR Ord. 29 Practice Direction — Committal

This practice direction is supplemental to RSC Order 52 (Schedule 1 to the CPR) and CCR Order 29 (Schedule 2 to the CPR).

## General

1.1 Part I of this practice direction applies to any application for an order for committal of a person to prison for contempt of court (a 'committal application'). Part II makes additional provision where the committal application relates to a contempt in the face of the court.

1.2 Where the alleged contempt of court consists of or is based upon disobedience to an order made in a county court or breach of an undertaking given to a county court or consists of an act done in the course of proceedings in a county court, or where in any other way the alleged contempt is a contempt which the county court has power to punish, the committal application may be made in the county court in question.

1.3 In every other case (other than one within Part II of this practice direction), a committal application must be made in the High Court.

1.4 In all cases the Convention rights of those involved should particularly be borne in mind. It should be noted that the burden of proof, having regard to the possibility that a person may be sent to prison, is that the allegation be proved beyond reasonable doubt. (Section 1 of the Human Rights Act 1998 defines 'the Convention rights'.)

## PART I

## Commencement of Committal Proceedings

2.1 A committal application must, subject to para. 2.2, be commenced by the issue of a Part 8 claim form (see para. 2.5).

2.2 (1) If the committal application is made in existing proceedings it must be commenced by the filing of an application notice in those proceedings.
(2) An application to commit for breach of an undertaking or order must be commenced by the filing of an application notice in the proceedings in which the undertaking was given or the order was made.
(3) The application notice must state that the application is made in the proceedings in question and its title and reference number must correspond with the title and reference number of those proceedings.

2.3 If the committal application is one which cannot be made without permission, the claim form or application notice, as the case may be, may not be issued or filed until the requisite permission has been granted.

2.4 If the permission of the court is needed in order to make a committal application:
(1) the permission must be applied for by filing an application notice (see r. 23.2(4));
(2) the application notice need not be served on the respondent;
(3) the date on which and the name of the judge by whom the requisite permission was granted must be stated on the claim form or application notice by which the committal application is commenced;
(4) the permission may only be granted by a judge who, under para. 11, would have power to hear the committal application if permission were granted; and
(5) r. 23.9 and 23.10 do not apply.

2.5 If the committal application is commenced by the issue of a claim form, Part 8 shall, subject to the provisions of this practice direction, apply as though references to 'claimant' were references to the person making the committal application and references to 'defendant' were references to the person against whom the committal application is made (in this practice direction referred to as 'the respondent') but:

(1) the claim form together with copies of all written evidence in support must, unless the court otherwise directs, be served personally on the respondent,
(2) the claim form must set out in full the grounds on which the committal application is made and must identify, separately and numerically, each alleged act of contempt including, if known, the date of each alleged act,
(3) an amendment to the claim form can be made with the permission of the court but not otherwise,
(4) r. 8.4 does not apply, and
(5) the claim form must contain a prominent notice stating the possible consequences of the court making a committal order and of the respondent not attending the hearing. A form of notice, which may be used, is annexed to this practice direction.

2.6 If a committal application is commenced by the filing of an application notice, Part 23 shall, subject to the provisions of this practice direction, apply, but:

(1) the application notice together with copies of all written evidence in support must, unless the court otherwise directs, be served personally on the respondent,
(2) the application notice must set out in full the grounds on which the committal application is made and must identify, separately and numerically, each alleged act of contempt including, if known, the date of each of the alleged acts,
(3) an amendment to the application notice can be made with the permission of the court but not otherwise,
(4) the court may not dispose of the committal application without a hearing, and
(5) the application notice must contain a prominent notice stating the possible consequences of the court making a committal order and of the respondent not attending the hearing. A form of notice, which may be used, is annexed to this practice direction.

## Written Evidence

3.1 Written evidence in support of or in opposition to a committal application must be given by affidavit.

3.2 Written evidence served in support of or in opposition to a committal application must, unless the court otherwise directs, be filed.

3.3 A respondent may give oral evidence at the hearing, whether or not he has filed or served any written evidence. If he does so, he may be cross-examined.

3.4 A respondent may, with the permission of the court, call a witness to give oral evidence at the hearing whether or not the witness has sworn an affidavit.

## Case Management and Date of Hearing

4.1 The applicant for the committal order must, when lodging the claim form or application notice with the court for issuing or filing, as the case may be, obtain from the court a date for the hearing of the committal application.

4.2 Unless the court otherwise directs, the hearing date of a committal application shall be not less than 14 days after service of the claim form or of the application notice, as the case may be, on the respondent. The hearing date must be specified in the claim form or application notice or in a notice of hearing or application attached to and served with the claim form or application notice.

4.3 The court may, however, at any time give case management directions, including directions for the service of written evidence by the respondent and written evidence in reply by the applicant, or may hold a directions hearing.

4.4 The court may on the hearing date:

(1) give case management directions with a view to a hearing of the committal application on a future date, or
(2) if the committal application is ready to be heard, proceed forthwith to hear it.

4.5 In dealing with any committal application, the court will have regard to the need for the respondent to have details of the alleged acts of contempt and the opportunity to respond to the committal application.

4.6 The court should also have regard to the need for the respondent to be:
(1) allowed a reasonable time for responding to the committal application including, if necessary, preparing a defence;
(2) made aware of the availability of assistance from the Community Legal Service and how to contact the Service;
(3) given the opportunity, if unrepresented, to obtain legal advice; and
(4) if unable to understand English, allowed to make arrangements, seeking the assistance of the court if necessary, for an interpreter to attend the hearing.

## Striking Out

5 The court may, on application by the respondent or on its own initiative, strike out a committal application if it appears to the court:
(1) that the committal application and the evidence served in support of it disclose no reasonable ground for alleging that the respondent is guilty of a contempt of court,
(2) that the committal application is an abuse of the court's process or, if made in existing proceedings, is otherwise likely to obstruct the just disposal of those proceedings, or
(3) that there has been a failure to comply with a rule, practice direction or court order.
(Part 3 contains general powers for the management by the court.)

## Miscellaneous

6 Rules 35.7 (court's power to direct that evidence is to be given by a single joint expert), 35.8 (instructions to single joint expert) and 35.9 (power of court to direct a party to provide information) do not apply to committal applications.

7 An order under r. 18.1 (order for a party to give additional information) may not be made against a respondent to a committal application.

8 A committal application may not be discontinued without the permission of the court.

9 A committal application should normally be heard in public (see r. 39.2), but if it is heard in private and the court finds the respondent guilty of contempt of court, the judge shall, when next sitting in public, state:
(1) the name of the respondent,
(2) in general terms the nature of the contempt or contempts found proved, and
(3) the penalty (if any) imposed.

10 The court may waive any procedural defect in the commencement or conduct of a committal application if satisfied that no injustice has been caused to the respondent by the defect.

11 Except where under an enactment a master or district judge has power to make a committal order,[1] a committal order can only be made:
(1) in High Court proceedings, by a High Court judge or a person authorised to act as such,[2]
(2) in county court proceedings by a circuit judge or a person authorised to act or capable by virtue of his office of acting as such.[3]

## PART II

12 Where the committal application relates to a contempt in the face of the court the following matters should be given particular attention. Normally, it will be appropriate

[1] E.g. County Courts Act 1984, sections 14 and 118.
[2] See Supreme Court Act 1981, section 9(1).
[3] See County Courts Act 1984, section 5(3).

to defer consideration of the behaviour to allow the respondent time to reflect on what has occurred. The time needed for the following procedures should allow such a period of reflection.

13 A Part 8 claim form and an application notice are not required for Part II, but other provisions of this practice direction should be applied, as necessary, or adapted to the circumstances. In addition the judge should:

(1) tell the respondent of the possible penalty he faces;
(2) inform the respondent in detail, and preferably in writing, of the actions and behaviour of the respondent which have given rise to the committal application;
(3) if he considers that an apology would remove the need for the committal application, tell the respondent;
(4) have regard to the need for the respondent to be:
  (a) allowed a reasonable time for responding to the committal application, including, if necessary, preparing a defence;
  (b) made aware of the availability of assistance from the Community Legal Service and how to contact the Service;
  (c) given the opportunity, if unrepresented, to obtain legal advice;
  (d) if unable to understand English, allowed to make arrangements, seeking the court's assistance if necessary, for an interpreter to attend the hearing; and
  (e) brought back before the court for the committal application to be heard within a reasonable time;
(5) allow the respondent an opportunity to:
  (a) apologise to the court;
  (b) explain his actions and behaviour; and,
  (c) if the contempt is proved, to address the court on the penalty to be imposed on him;
(6) if there is a risk of the appearance of bias, ask another judge to hear the committal application;
(7) where appropriate, nominate a suitable person to give the respondent the information.

(It is likely to be appropriate to nominate a person where the effective communication of information by the judge to the respondent was not possible when the incident occurred.)

14 Where the committal application is to be heard by another judge, a written statement by the judge before whom the actions and behaviour of the respondent which have given rise to the committal application took place may be submitted as evidence of those actions and behaviour.

## ANNEX

### Important Notice

The court has power to send you to prison and to fine you if it finds that any of the allegations made against you are true and amount to a contempt of court.

**You must attend court** on the date shown on the front of this form. It is in your own interest to do so. You should bring with you any witnesses and documents which you think will help you put your side of the case.

If you consider the allegations are not true you must tell the court why. If it is established that they are true, you must tell the court of any good reason why they do not amount to a contempt of court, or, if they do, why you should not be punished.

If you need advice you should show this document at once to your solicitor or go to a Citizens' Advice Bureau.

# PD RSC Ord. 54 Practice Direction — Application for Writ of Habeas Corpus

This practice direction supplements CPR Part 50, and Schedule 1 to the CPR.

## Terminology

1.1 In this practice direction:

(1) 'Order 54' means those provisions contained in Schedule 1, RSC Order 54 which were previously contained in the Rules of the Supreme Court (1965);

(2) a reference to a rule or Part prefixed with CPR is a reference to a rule or Part contained in the CPR rules; and

(3) a reference to a rule number alone is a reference to the rule so numbered in Order 54.

## Scope

2.1 This practice direction supplements Order 54 (which sets out how to apply for a writ of habeas corpus) by providing further detail about the application.

2.2 This practice direction must be read together with Order 54.

2.3 It also lists at paragraph 7 other practice directions which governed procedure relating to Order 54 before 26 April 1999 and which will continue to do so.

## Form to be Used Where Court Directs Claim Form to be Used

3.1 Where the court directs that an application be made by claim form, under:

(1) rule 2, (on hearing application under rule 1); or

(2) rule 4(2) (application in criminal proceedings ordered to be made to Divisional Court of the Queen's Bench Division),

the claimant must use Form 87 modified in accordance with the guidance set out in the Forms practice direction.

## Form to be Used for Notice of Adjourned Application Directed by Court

4.1 Where the court directs under rule 2(1)(c) that an application made under rule 1 is adjourned to allow for service of notice of the application, such notice must be given in modified Form 88.

## Service

5.1 The party seeking the writ must serve:

(1) the claim form in accordance with rule 2(2); and

(2) the writ of habeas corpus ad subjiciendum and notice in Form 90, as modified, in accordance with rule 6.

(CPR rule 6.3 provides that the court will normally serve a document which it has issued or prepared.)

## The Administrative Court

6.1 When the court directs that an application is to be made by claim form under:

(1) rule 2(1) (powers of court to whom application made under rule 1); or

(2) rule 4(2) (power of court where application made in criminal proceedings)

the application must be entered in the Administrative Court List in accordance with Practice Direction (Crown Office List) [1987] 1 WLR 232, [1987] 1 All ER 368.

## Practice Directions etc., Which Apply to Order 54

7.1 On and after 26 April 1999, the practice directions, statements and practice notes set out in Table 1 continue to apply to proceedings under Order 54.

**Table 1**

| Practice Direction etc. | Content |
|---|---|
| Practice Direction (Crown Office List: Criminal Proceedings) [1983] 1 WLR 925, [1983] 2 All ER 1020. | Urgent matters outside London—consultation of Crown Office and continuation in London |
| Practice Note (Crown Office List: Estimated Length of Hearing) [1987] 1 All ER 1184. | Need for accuracy in time estimates |
| Practice Direction (Crown Office List) [1987] 1 WLR 232, [1987] 1 All ER 368. | Parts of the List |
| Practice Direction (Crown Office List: Preparation for Hearings) [1994] 1 WLR 1551, [1994] 4 All ER 671. | Preparation for hearings; documentation; time limits; skeleton arguments; amendment of grounds |
| Practice Direction (Crown Office List: Consent Orders) [1997] 1 WLR 825, [1997] 2 All ER 799. | Consent orders |
| Practice Statement (Supreme Court: Judgments) [1998] 1 WLR 825, [1998] 2 All ER 667. | Judgments |

# PD RSC Ord. 95 Practice Direction — Bills of Sale

This practice direction supplements RSC Order 95 (Schedule 1 to the CPR).

## Entry of Satisfaction

1. Notwithstanding the provisions of RSC Order 95, rule 2(1), (1A) and (2), if a consent to the satisfaction signed by the person entitled to the benefit of the bill of sale can be obtained, the application under RSC Order 95, rule 2(1) can be made by affidavit or witness statement instead of by claim form.
2. If paragraph 1 applies and the application is made by affidavit or witness statement:
   (1) CPR Part 23 will apply to the application;
   (2) the affidavit or witness statement will constitute the application notice;
   (3) the affidavit or witness statement need not be served on any other person; and
   (4) the application will normally be dealt with without a hearing.
3. Where the consent of the person entitled to the benefit of the bill of sale cannot be obtained, the application under RSC Order 95, rule 2(1) must be made by claim form in accordance with CPR Part 8 and RSC Order 95, rule 2(3) will apply.

# PD RSC Ord. 115 Practice Direction — Restraint Orders and Appointment of Receivers in Connection with Criminal Proceedings and Investigations

This practice direction supplements RSC Order 115 (Schedule 1 to the CPR).

## Scope and Interpretation

1.1 This practice direction applies to applications to the High Court for a restraint order or the appointment of a receiver under:

(1) part VI of the Criminal Justice Act 1988 ('the 1988 Act');

(2) part I of the Drug Trafficking Act 1994 ('the 1994 Act'); or

(3) sch. 4 to the Terrorism Act 2000 ('the 2000 Act').

(Part VI of the 1988 Act and Part I of the 1994 Act are repealed by the Proceeds of Crime Act 2002 from a day to be appointed, but will continue to apply to pending and transitional cases. Following their repeal, applications for a restraint order or the appointment of a receiver which would previously have been made under those Acts will instead be made to the Crown Court under part 2 of the 2002 Act.)

1.2 In this practice direction:

(1) 'the prosecutor' means the person applying for a restraint order or the appointment of a receiver; and

(2) 'the defendant' means the person against whom criminal proceedings have been brought or a criminal investigation is taking place, and against whom a confiscation order or forfeiture order has been or might be made.

## I RESTRAINT ORDERS

### Form of Restraint Order

2 An example of a restraint order is annexed to this practice direction. This example may be modified as appropriate in any particular case.

### Amount Under Restraint

3.1 A restraint order may, where appropriate, apply to:

(1) all of the defendant's realisable property;

(2) the defendant's realisable property up to a specified value; or

(3) one or more particular specified assets.

3.2 Where:

(1) a confiscation order or forfeiture order has already been made against the defendant in a particular amount; or

(2) the prosecutor is able to make a reasonably accurate estimate of the amount of any confiscation order or forfeiture order that might be made against him,

and, in either case, it is clear that the defendant's realisable property is greater in value than the amount or estimated amount of that order, the court will normally limit the application of the restraint order in accordance with para. 3.1(2) or (3).

3.3 In such cases the prosecutor's draft order should normally either include an appropriate financial limit or specify the particular assets to which the order should apply.

### Living Expenses and Legal Fees

4 A restraint order will normally, unless it is clear that a person restrained has sufficient assets which are not subject to the order, include an exception to the order permitting that person to spend assets:

(1) in the case of an individual, for reasonable living expenses; and
(2) in the case of either an individual or a company, to pay reasonable legal fees so that they may take advice in relation to the order and if so advised apply for its variation or discharge.

### Restraint Orders Against Third Parties

5.1 Where a restraint order applies to property held in the name of a person other than the defendant:
(1) the order must be addressed to that person in addition to the defendant; and
(2) in applying for the order, the prosecutor must consider the guidance given in *Re G (Restraint Order)* [2001] EWHC Admin 606.

5.2 Examples of additional persons to whom an order must, where appropriate, be addressed include:
(1) a person who has a joint bank account with the defendant;
(2) in proceedings under the 1988 Act or the 1994 Act, a person to whom the defendant is alleged to have made a gift which may be treated as realisable property of the defendant under the provisions of the relevant Act; or
(3) a company, where the prosecutor alleges that assets apparently belonging to the company are in reality those of the defendant.

5.3 However, an order should not normally be addressed:
(1) to a bank with whom a defendant has an account; or
(2) to the business name of a defendant who carries on an unincorporated business (such business not being a separate legal entity from the defendant).

### Restraint Orders Against Businesses

6 If an application for a restraint order is made against a company, partnership or individual apparently carrying on a legitimate business:
(1) the court will take into account the interests of the employees, creditors and customers of the business and, in the case of a company, any shareholders other than the defendant, before making an order which would or might prevent the business from being continued; and
(2) any restraint order made against that person will normally contain an exception enabling it to deal with its assets in the ordinary course of business.

### Duration of Order Made on Application Without Notice (Rules 4(2) and 27(2))

7.1 Rules 4(2) and 27(2) of RSC, ord. 115 in CPR, sch. 1, provide that, unless the court otherwise directs, a restraint order made without notice shall have effect until a day which shall be fixed for a further hearing where all parties may attend ('the return date').

7.2 Where a return date is fixed, it will normally be no more than 14 days after the date of the order.

7.3 Where no return date is fixed, the court will always include in the order a provision giving the defendant or anyone affected by the order permission to apply to vary or discharge the order (see para. 14 of the sample form of order).

## II APPOINTMENT OF RECEIVER

8.1 Part 69 and PD 69 apply to the appointment of a receiver under the 1988, 1994 or 2000 Act, subject to the provisions of RSC, ord. 115, rr. 8 and 23(e) in CPR, sch. 1, where applicable.

8.2 In particular, r. 69.7, and PD 69, para. 9, apply in relation to the remuneration of the receiver.

8.3 Where no confiscation or forfeiture order has been made:

(1) an application for the appointment of a receiver should not be made without notice, unless the application is urgent or there is some other good reason for not giving notice to the defendant; and
(2) if the application is made without notice, the prosecutor's written evidence should explain the reasons for doing so.

8.4 Where the court appoints a receiver on an application without notice in the circumstances set out in para. 8.3, the order will normally limit the receiver's powers to manage, deal with or sell property (other than with the defendant's consent) to the extent that is shown to be urgently necessary. If the receiver seeks further powers, he should apply on notice for further directions.

## [APPENDIX

The appendix, which consists of an example of a restraint order prohibiting disposal of assets, is not reproduced in this work but may be accessed via the DCA website at <http://www.dca.gov.uk>.]

# CPR Schedule 2

## CCR ORDER 1
## CITATION, APPLICATION AND INTERPRETATION

Where by virtue of these rules or section 76 of the Act or otherwise any provision of the RSC is applied in relation to proceedings in a county court, that provision shall have effect with the necessary modifications and in particular—

(b) any reference in that provision to a master, district judge of the Principal Registry of the Family Division, the Admiralty registrar, or a district judge or taxing officer shall be construed as a reference to the district judge of the county court; and

(d) any reference in that provision to an office of the Supreme Court having the conduct of the business of a division or court or a district registry shall be construed as a reference to the county court office.

## CCR ORDER 16
## TRANSFER OF PROCEEDINGS

### Rule 7 Interpleader Proceedings Under Execution

(1) This rule applies to interpleader proceedings under an execution which are ordered to be transferred from the High Court.

(1A) In this rule references to the sheriff shall be interpreted as including references to an individual authorised to act as an enforcement officer under the Courts Act 2003.

(2) Notice of the hearings or pre-trial review of the proceedings shall be given by the court officer to the sheriff as well as to every other party to the proceedings.

(3) The interpleader claimant shall, within 8 days of the receipt by him of the notice referred to in paragraph (2), file in triplicate particulars of any goods alleged to be his property and the grounds of his interpleader claim and the court officer shall send a copy to the execution creditor and to the sheriff, but the judge may hear the proceedings or, as the case may be, the district judge may proceed with the pre-trial review, if he thinks fit, notwithstanding that the particulars have not been filed.

(4) Subject to any directions in the order of the High Court, damages may be claimed against the execution creditor in the same manner as in interpleader proceedings commenced in a county court.

(5) On any day fixed for the pre-trial review of the proceedings or for the hearing of any application by the sheriff or other party for directions the court may order the sheriff—

   (a) to postpone the sale of the goods seized;

   (b) to remain in possession of such goods until the hearing of the proceedings; or

   (c) to hand over possession of such goods to the district judge,

   and, where a direction is given under sub-paragraph (c), the district judge shall be allowed reasonable charges for keeping possession of the goods, not exceeding those which might be allowed to the sheriff, and, if the district judge is directed to sell the goods, such charges for the sale as would be allowed under an execution issued by the county court.

(6) No order made in the proceedings shall prejudice or affect the rights of the sheriff to any proper charges and the judge may make such order with respect to them as may be just.

(7) The charges referred to in paragraphs (5) and (6) shall ultimately be borne in such manner as the judge shall direct.

(8) The order made at the hearing of the proceedings shall direct how any money in the hands of the sheriff is to be disposed of.

# CCR ORDER 22
# JUDGMENTS AND ORDERS

## Rule 8 Certificate of Judgment

(1) Any person who wishes to have a certificate of any judgment or order given or made in a claim shall make a request in writing to the court stating—
   (a) if he is a party to the claim whether the certificate—
      (i) is required for the purpose of taking proceedings on the judgment or order in another court;
      (ii) is required for the purpose of enforcing the judgment or order in the High Court; or
      (iii) is for the purpose of evidence only;
   (b) if he is not a party to the claim, the purpose for which the certificate is required, the capacity in which he asks for it and any other facts showing that the certificate may properly be granted.

(1A) Where the certificate is required for the purpose of enforcing the judgment or order in the High Court, the applicant shall also either—
   (a) state that—
      (i) it is intended to enforce the judgment or order by execution against goods; or
      (ii) the judgment or order to be enforced is an order for possession of land made in a possession claim against trespassers; or
   (b) confirm that an application has been made for an order under section 42 of the Act (transfer to High Court by order of a county court) and attach a copy of the application to the request for a certificate.

(2) Where the request is made by a person who is not a party to the claim, the request shall be referred to the district judge, who may, if he thinks fit, refer it to the judge.

(3) Without prejudice to paragraph (2), for the purposes of section 12(2) of the Act a certificate under this rule may be signed by the court manager or any other officer of the court acting on his behalf.

## Rule 10 Variation of Payment

(1) Where a judgment or order has been given or made for the payment of money, the person entitled to the benefit of the judgment or order or, as the case may be, the person liable to make the payment (in this rule referred to as 'the judgment creditor' and 'the debtor' respectively) may apply in accordance with the provisions of this rule for a variation in the date or rate of payment.

(2) The judgment creditor may apply in writing, without notice being served on any other party, for an order that the money, if payable in one sum, be paid at a later date than that by which it is due or by instalments or, if the money is already payable by instalments, that it be paid by the same or smaller instalments, and the court officer may make an order accordingly unless no payment has been made under the judgment or order for 6 years before the date of the application in which case he shall refer the application to the district judge.

(3) The judgment creditor may apply to the district judge on notice for an order that the money, if payable in one sum, be paid at an earlier date than that by which it is due or, if the money is payable by instalments, that it be paid in one sum or by larger instalments, and any such application shall be made in writing stating the proposed terms and the grounds on which it is made.

(4) Where an application is made under paragraph (3)—
   (a) the proceedings shall be automatically transferred to the debtor's home court if the judgment or order was not given or made in that court; and
   (b) the court officer shall fix a day for the hearing of the application before the district

judge and give to the judgment creditor and the debtor not less than 8 days' notice of the day so fixed,

and at the hearing the district judge may make such order as seems just.

(5) The debtor may apply for an order that the money, if payable in one sum, be paid at a later date than that by which it is due or by instalments or, if the money is already payable by instalments, that it be paid by smaller instalments, and any such application shall be in the appropriate form stating the proposed terms, the grounds on which it is made and including a signed statement of the debtor's means.

(6) Where an application is made under paragraph (5), the court officer shall—
   (a) send the judgment creditor a copy of the debtor's application (and statement of means); and
   (b) require the judgment creditor to notify the court in writing, within 14 days of service of notification upon him, giving his reasons for any objection he may have to the granting of the application.

(7) If the judgment creditor does not notify the court of any objection within the time stated, the court officer shall make an order in the terms applied for.

(8) Upon receipt of a notice from the judgment creditor under paragraph (6), the court officer may determine the date and rate of payment and make an order accordingly.

(9) Any party affected by an order made under paragraph (8) may, within 14 days of service of the order on him and giving his reasons, apply on notice for the order to be reconsidered and, where such an application is made—
   (a) the proceedings shall be automatically transferred to the debtor's home court if the judgment or order was not given or made in that court; and
   (b) the court officer shall fix a day for the hearing of the application before the district judge and give to the judgment creditor and the debtor not less than 8 days' notice of the day so fixed.

(10) On hearing an application under paragraph (9), the district judge may confirm the order or set it aside and make such new order as he thinks fit and the order so made shall be entered in the records of the court.

(11) Any order made under any of the foregoing paragraphs may be varied from time to time by a subsequent order made under any of those paragraphs.

## Rule 11 Set-off of Cross-judgments

(1) An application under section 72 of the Act for permission to set off any sums, including costs, payable under several judgments or orders each of which was obtained in a county court shall be made in accordance with this rule.

(2) Where the judgments or orders have been obtained in the same county court, the application may be made to that court on the day when the last judgment or order is obtained, if both parties are present, and in any other case shall be made on notice.

(3) Where the judgments or orders have been obtained in different county courts, the application may be made to either of them on notice, and notice shall be given to the other court.

(4) The district judge of the court to which the application is made and the district judge of any other court to which notice is given under paragraph (3) shall forthwith stay execution on any judgment or order in his court to which the application relates and any money paid into court under the judgment or order shall be retained until the application has been disposed of.

(5) The application may be heard and determined by the court and any order giving permission shall direct how any money paid into court is to be dealt with.

(6) Where the judgments or orders have been obtained in different courts, the court in which an order giving permission is made shall send a copy of the order to the other court, which shall deal with any money paid into that court in accordance with the order.

(7) The court officer or, as the case may be, each of the court officers affected shall enter

satisfaction in the records of his court for any sums ordered to be set off, and execution or other process for the enforcement of any judgment or order not wholly satisfied shall issue only for the balance remaining payable.

(8) Where an order is made by the High Court giving permission to set off sums payable under several judgments and orders obtained respectively in the High Court and a county court, the court officer of the county court shall, on receipt of a copy of the order, proceed in accordance with paragraph (7).

### Rule 13 Order of Appellate Court

Where the Court of Appeal or High Court has heard and determined an appeal from a county court, the party entitled to the benefit of the order of the Court of Appeal or High Court shall deposit the order or an office copy thereof in the office of the county court.

## CCR ORDER 24
## SUMMARY PROCEEDINGS FOR THE RECOVERY OF LAND

### Part I Land

### Rule 6 Warrant of Possession

(1) Subject to paragraphs (2) and (3), a warrant of possession to enforce an order for possession in a possession claim against trespassers under Part 55 may be issued at any time after the making of the order and subject to the provisions of Order 26, rule 17, a warrant of restitution may be issued in aid of the warrant of possession.

(2) No warrant of possession shall be issued after the expiry of 3 months from the date of the Order without the permission of the court, and an application for such permission may be made without notice being served on any other party unless the court otherwise directs.

(3) Nothing in this rule shall authorise the issue of a warrant of possession before the date on which possession is ordered to be given.

## CCR ORDER 25
## ENFORCEMENT OF JUDGMENTS AND ORDERS: GENERAL

### Rule 1 Judgment Creditor and Debtor

In this Order and Orders 26 to 29 judgment creditor' means the person who has obtained or is entitled to enforce a judgment or order and 'debtor' means the person against whom it was given or made.

### Rule 6 Description of Parties

Where the name or address of the judgment creditor or the debtor as given in the request for the issue of a warrant of execution or delivery, judgment summons or warrant of committal differs from his name or address in the judgment or order sought to be enforced and the judgment creditor satisfies the court officer that the name or address as given in the request is applicable to the person concerned, the judgment creditor or the debtor, as the case may be, shall be described in the warrant or judgment summons as 'C.D. of [name and address as given in the request] suing [or sued] as A.D. of [name and address in the judgment or order]'.

### Rule 7 Recording and Giving Information as to Warrants and Orders

(1) Subject to paragraph (1A), every district judge by whom a warrant or order is issued or received for execution shall from time to time state in the records of his court what has been done in the execution of the warrant or order.

(1A) Where a warrant of execution issued by a court ('the home court') is sent to another court for execution ('the foreign court'), paragraph (1) shall not apply to the district judge of the home court, but when such a warrant is returned to the home court under paragraph (7), the court officer of the home court shall state in the records of his court what has been done in the execution of the warrant or order.

(2) If the warrant or order has not been executed within one month from the date of its issue or receipt by him, the court officer of the court responsible for its execution shall, at the end of that month and every subsequent month during which the warrant remains outstanding, send notice of the reason for non-execution to the judgment creditor and, if the warrant or order was received from another court, to that court.

(3) The district judge responsible for executing a warrant or order shall give such information respecting it as may reasonably be required by the judgment creditor and, if the warrant or order was received by him from another court, by the district judge of that court.

(4) Where money is received in pursuance of a warrant of execution or committal sent by one court to another court, the foreign court shall, subject to paragraph (5) and to section 346 of Insolvency Act 1986 and section 326 of the Companies Act 1948 send the money to the judgment creditor in the manner prescribed by the Court Funds Rules 1987 and, where the money is received in pursuance of a warrant of committal, make a return to the home court.

(5) Where interpleader proceedings are pending, the court shall not proceed in accordance with paragraph (4) until the interpleader proceedings are determined and the district judge shall then make a return showing how the money is to be disposed of and, if any money is payable to the judgment creditor, the court shall proceed in accordance with paragraph (4).

(6) Where a warrant of committal has been received from another court, the foreign court shall, on the execution of the warrant, send notice thereof to the home court.

(7) Where a warrant of execution has been received from another court, either—
- (a) on the execution of the warrant; or
- (b) if the warrant is not executed—
  - (i) on the making of a final return to the warrant; or
  - (ii) on suspension of the warrant under rule 8 (suspension of judgment or execution) or Order 26, rule 10 (withdrawal and suspension of warrant at creditor's request),

the foreign court shall return the warrant to the home court.

## Rule 8 Suspension of Judgment or Execution

(1) The power of the court to suspend or stay a judgment or order or to stay execution of any warrant may be exercised by the district judge or, in the case of the power to stay execution of a warrant of execution and in accordance with the provisions of this rule, by the court officer.

(2) An application by the debtor to stay execution of a warrant of execution shall be in the appropriate form stating the proposed terms, the grounds on which it is made and including a signed statement of the debtor's means.

(3) Where the debtor makes an application under paragraph (2), the court shall—
- (a) send the judgment creditor a copy of the debtor's application (and statement of means); and
- (b) require the creditor to notify the court in writing, within 14 days of service of notification upon him, giving his reasons for any objection he may have to the granting of the application.

(4) If the judgment creditor does not notify the court of any objection within the time stated, the court officer may make an order suspending the warrant on terms of payment.

(5) Upon receipt of a notice by the judgment creditor under paragraph (3)(b), the court officer may, if the judgment creditor objects only to the terms offered, determine the date and rate of payment and make an order suspending the warrant on terms of payment.

(6) Any party affected by an order made under paragraph (5) may, within 14 days of service of the order on him and giving his reasons, apply on notice for the order to be reconsidered and the court shall fix a day for the hearing of the application before the district judge and give to the judgment creditor and the debtor not less than 8 days' notice of the day so fixed.
(7) On hearing an application under paragraph (6), the district judge may confirm the order or set it aside and make such new order as he thinks fit and the order so made shall be entered in the records of the court.
(8) Where the judgment creditor states in his notice under paragraph (3)(b) that he wishes the bailiff to proceed to execute the warrant, the court shall fix a day for a hearing before the district judge of the debtor's application and give to the judgment creditor and to the debtor not less than 2 days' notice of the day so fixed.
(9) Subject to any directions given by the district judge, where a warrant of execution has been suspended, it may be re-issued on the judgment creditor's filing a request showing that any condition subject to which the warrant was suspended has not been complied with.
(10) Where an order is made by the district judge suspending a warrant of execution, the debtor may be ordered to pay the costs of the warrant and any fees or expenses incurred before its suspension and the order may authorise the sale of a sufficient portion of any goods seized to cover such costs, fees and expenses and the expenses of sale.

### Rule 13 Transfer to High Court for Enforcement

(1) Where the judgment creditor makes a request for a certificate of judgment under Order 22, rule 8(1) for the purpose of enforcing the judgment or order in the High Court—
  (a) by execution against goods; or
  (b) where the judgment or order to be enforced is an order for possession of land made in a possession claim against trespassers,

the grant of a certificate by the court shall take effect as an order to transfer the proceedings to the High Court and the transfer shall have effect on the grant of that certificate.
(2) On the transfer of proceedings in accordance with paragraph (1), the court shall give notice to the debtor or the person against whom the possession order was made that the proceedings have been transferred and shall make an entry of that fact in the records of his court.
(3) In a case where a request for a certificate of judgment is made under Order 22, rule 8(1) for the purpose of enforcing a judgment or order in the High Court and—
  (a) an application for a variation in the date or rate of payment of money due under a judgment or order;
  (b) an application under either CPR rule 39.3(3) or CPR rule 13.4;
  (c) a request for an administration order; or
  (d) an application for a stay of execution under section 88 of the Act,

is pending, the request for the certificate shall not be dealt with until those proceedings are determined.

## CCR ORDER 26
## WARRANTS OF EXECUTION, DELIVERY AND POSSESSION

### Rule 1 Application for Warrant of Execution

(1) A judgment creditor desiring a warrant of execution to be issued shall file a request in that behalf certifying—
  (a) the amount remaining due under the judgment or order; and
  (b) where the order made is for payment of a sum of money by instalments—
    (i) that the whole or part of any instalment due remains unpaid; and
    (ii) the amount for which the warrant is to be issued.

(1A) The court officer shall discharge the functions—
  (a) under section 85(2) of the Act of issuing a warrant of execution;
  (b) under section 85(3) of the Act of entering in the record mentioned in that subsection and on the warrant the precise time of the making of the application to issue the warrant, and
  (c) under section 103(1) of the Act of sending the warrant of execution to another county court.

(2) Where the court has made an order for payment of a sum of money by instalments and default has been made in payment of such an instalment, a warrant of execution may be issued for the whole of the said sum of money and costs then remaining unpaid or, subject to paragraph (3), for such part as the judgment creditor may request, not being in the latter case less than £50 or the amount of one monthly instalment or, as the case may be, 4 weekly instalments, whichever is the greater.

(3) In any case to which paragraph (2) applies no warrant shall be issued unless at the time when it is issued—
  (a) the whole or part of an instalment which has already become due remains unpaid; and
  (b) any warrant previously issued for part of the said sum of money and costs has expired or has been satisfied or abandoned.

(4) Where a warrant is issued for the whole or part of the said sum of money and costs, the court officer shall, unless the district judge responsible for execution of the warrant directs otherwise, send a warning notice to the person against whom the warrant is issued and, where such a notice is sent, the warrant shall not be levied until 7 days thereafter.

(5) Where judgment is given or an order made for payment otherwise than by instalments of a sum of money and costs to be assessed in accordance with CPR Part 47 (detailed assessment procedure) and default is made in payment of the sum of money before the costs have been assessed, a warrant of execution may issue for recovery of the sum of money and a separate warrant may issue subsequently for the recovery of the costs if default is made in payment of them.

## Rule 2 Execution of High Court Judgment

(1) Where it is desired to enforce by warrant of execution a judgment or order of the High Court, or a judgment, order, decree or award which is or has become enforceable as if it were a judgment of the High Court, the request referred to in rule 1(1) may be filed in any court in the district of which execution is to be levied.

(2) Subject to Order 25, rule 9(5), any restriction imposed by these rules on the issue of execution shall apply as if the judgment, order, decree or award were a judgment or order of the county court, but permission to issue execution shall not be required if permission has already been given by the High Court.

(3) Notice of the issue of the warrant shall be sent by the county court to the High Court.

## Rule 3 Execution Against Farmer

If after the issue of a warrant of execution the district judge for the district in which the warrant is to be executed has reason to believe that the debtor is a farmer, the execution creditor shall, if so required by the district judge, furnish him with an official certificate, dated not more than three days beforehand, of the result of a search at the Land Registry as to the existence of any charge registered against the debtor under the Agricultural Credits Act 1928.

## Rule 4 Concurrent Warrants

Two or more warrants of execution may be issued concurrently for execution in different districts, but—

(a) no more shall be levied under all the warrants together than is authorised to be levied under one of them; and

(b) the costs of more than one such warrant shall not be allowed against the debtor except by order of the court.

## Rule 5 Permission to Issue Certain Warrants

(1) A warrant of execution shall not issue without the permission of the court where—
  (a) six years or more have elapsed since the date of the judgment or order;
  (b) any change has taken place, whether by death or otherwise in the parties entitled to enforce the judgment or order or liable to have it enforced against them;
  (c) the judgment or order is against the assets of a deceased person coming into the hands of his executors or administrators after the date of the judgment or order and it is sought to issue execution against such assets; or
  (d) any goods to be seized under a warrant of execution are in the hands of a receiver appointed by a court.

(2) An application for permission shall be supported by a witness statement or affidavit establishing the applicant's right to relief and may be made without notice being served on any other party in the first instance but the court may direct the application notice to be served on such persons as it thinks fit.

(3) Where, by reason of one and the same event, a person seeks permission under paragraph (1)(b) to enforce more judgments or orders than one, he may make one application only, specifying in a schedule all the judgments or orders in respect of which it is made, and if the application notice is directed to be served on any person, it need set out only such part of the application as affects him.

(4) Paragraph (1) is without prejudice to any enactment, rule or direction by virtue of which a person is required to obtain the permission of the court for the issue of a warrant or to proceed to execution or otherwise to the enforcement of a judgment or order.

## Rule 6 Duration and Renewal of Warrant

(1) A warrant of execution shall, for the purpose of execution, be valid in the first instance for 12 months beginning with the date of its issue, but if not wholly executed, it may be renewed from time to time, by order of the court, for a period of 12 months at any one time, beginning with the day next following that on which it would otherwise expire, if an application for renewal is made before that day or such later day (if any) as the court may allow.

(2) A note of any such renewal shall be indorsed on the warrant and it shall be entitled to priority according to the time of its original issue or, where appropriate, its receipt by the district judge responsible for its execution.

## Rule 7 Notice on Levy

Any bailiff upon levying execution shall deliver to the debtor or leave at the place where execution is levied a notice of the warrant.

## Rule 8 Bankruptcy or Winding Up of Debtor

(1) Where the district judge responsible for the execution of a warrant is required by any provision of the Insolvency Act 1986 or any other enactment relating to insolvency to retain the proceeds of sale of goods sold under the warrant or money paid in order to avoid a sale, the court shall, as soon as practicable after the sale or the receipt of the money, send notice to the execution creditor and, if the warrant issued out of another court, to that court.

(2) Where the district judge responsible for the execution of a warrant—
  (a) receives notice that a bankruptcy order has been made against the debtor or, if the debtor is a company, that a provisional liquidator has been appointed or that an order has been made or a resolution passed for the winding up of the company; and
  (b) withdraws from possession of goods seized or pays over to the official receiver or trustee in bankruptcy or, if the debtor is a company, to the liquidator the proceeds

of sale of goods sold under the warrant or money paid in order to avoid a sale or seized or received in part satisfaction of the warrant,

the court shall send notice to the execution creditor and, if the warrant issued out of another court, to that court.

(3) Where the court officer of a court to which a warrant issued out of another court has been sent for execution receives any such notice as is referred to in paragraph (2)(a) after he has sent to the home court any money seized or received in part satisfaction of the warrant, he shall forward the notice to that court.

## Rule 10 Withdrawal and Suspension of Warrant at Creditor's Request

(1) Where an execution creditor requests the district judge responsible for executing a warrant to withdraw from possession, he shall, subject to the following paragraphs of this rule, be treated as having abandoned the execution, and the court shall mark the warrant as withdrawn by request of the execution creditor.

(2) Where the request is made in consequence of a claim having been made under Order 33, rule 1, to goods seized under the warrant, the execution shall be treated as being abandoned in respect only of the goods claimed.

(3) If the district judge responsible for executing a warrant is requested by the execution creditor to suspend it in pursuance of an arrangement between him and the debtor, the court shall mark the warrant as suspended by request of the execution creditor and the execution creditor may subsequently apply to the district judge holding the warrant for it to be re-issued and, if he does so, the application shall be deemed for the purpose of section 85(3) of the Act to be an application to issue the warrant.

(4) Nothing in this rule shall prejudice any right of the execution creditor to apply for the issue of a fresh warrant or shall authorise the re-issue of a warrant which has been withdrawn or has expired or has been superseded by the issue of a fresh warrant.

## Rule 11 Suspension of Part Warrant

Where a warrant issued for part of a sum of money and costs payable under a judgment or order is suspended on payment of instalments, the judgment or order shall, unless the court otherwise directs, be treated as suspended on those terms as respects the whole of the sum of money and costs then remaining unpaid.

## Rule 12 Inventory and Notice Where Goods Removed

(1) Where goods seized in execution are removed, the court shall forthwith deliver or send to the debtor a sufficient inventory of the goods removed and shall, not less than 4 days before the time fixed for the sale, give him notice of the time and place at which the goods will be sold.

(2) The inventory and notice shall be given to the debtor by delivering them to him personally or by sending them to him by post at his place of residence or, if his place of residence is not known, by leaving them for him, or sending them to him by post, at the place from which the goods were removed.

## Rule 13 Account of Sale

Where goods are sold under an execution, the court shall furnish the debtor with a detailed account in writing of the sale and of the application of the proceeds.

## Rule 14 Notification to Foreign Court of Payment Made

Where, after a warrant has been sent to a foreign court for execution but before a final return has been made to the warrant, the home court is notified of a payment made in respect of the sum for which the warrant is issued, the home court shall send notice of the payment to the foreign court.

### Rule 15 Order for Private Sale

(1) Subject to paragraph (6), an order of the court under section 97 of the Act that a sale under an execution may be made otherwise than by public auction may be made on the application of the execution creditor or the debtor or the district judge responsible for the execution of the warrant.
(2) Where he is not the applicant for an order under this rule, the district judge responsible for the execution of the warrant shall, on the demand of the applicant, furnish him with a list containing the name and address of every execution creditor under any other warrant or writ of execution against the goods of the debtor of which the district judge has notice, and where the district judge is the applicant, he shall prepare such a list.
(3) Not less than 4 days before the day fixed for the hearing of the application, the applicant shall give notice of the application to each of the other persons by whom the application might have been made and to every person named in the list referred to in paragraph (2).
(4) The applicant shall produce the list to the court on the hearing of the application.
(5) Every person to whom notice of the application was given may attend and be heard on the hearing of the application.
(6) Where the district judge responsible for the execution of the warrant is the district judge by whom it was issued and he has no notice of any other warrant or writ of execution against the goods of the debtor, an order under this rule may be made by the court of its own motion with the consent of the execution creditor and the debtor or after giving them an opportunity of being heard.

### Rule 16 Warrant of Delivery

(1) Except where an Act or rule provides otherwise, a judgment or order for the delivery of any goods shall be enforceable by warrant of delivery in accordance with this rule.
(2) If the judgment or order does not give the person against whom it was given or made the alternative of paying the value of the goods, it may be enforced by a warrant of specific delivery, that is to say, a warrant to recover the goods without alternative provision for recovery of their value.
(3) If the judgment or order is for the delivery of the goods or payment of their value, it may be enforced by a warrant of delivery to recover the goods or their value.
(4) Where a warrant of delivery is issued, the judgment creditor shall be entitled, by the same or a separate warrant, to execution against the debtor's goods for any money payable under the judgment or order which is to be enforced by the warrant of delivery.
(4A) Where a judgment or order is given or made for the delivery of goods or payment of their value and a warrant is issued to recover the goods or their value, money paid into court under the warrant shall be appropriated first to any sum of money and costs awarded.
(5) The foregoing provisions of this Order, so far as applicable, shall have effect, with the necessary modifications, in relation to warrants of delivery as they have effect in relation to warrants of execution.

### Rule 17 Warrant of Possession

(1) A judgment or order for the recovery of land shall be enforceable by warrant of possession.
(2) Without prejudice to paragraph (3A), the person desiring a warrant of possession to be issued shall file a request in that behalf certifying that the land has not been vacated in accordance with the judgment or order for the recovery of the said land.
(3) Where a warrant of possession is issued, the judgment creditor shall be entitled, by the same or a separate warrant, to execution against the debtor's goods for any money payable under the judgment or order which is to be enforced by the warrant of possession.

(3A) In a case to which paragraph (3) applies or where an order for possession has been suspended on terms as to payment of a sum of money by instalments, the judgment creditor shall in his request certify—
(a) the amount of money remaining due under the judgment or order; and
(b) that the whole or part of any instalment due remains unpaid.
(4) A warrant of restitution may be issued, with the permission of the court, in aid of any warrant of possession.
(5) An application for permission under paragraph (4) may be made without notice being served on any other party and shall be, supported by evidence of wrongful re-entry into possession following the execution of the warrant of possession and of such further facts as would, in the High Court, enable the judgment creditor to have a writ of restitution issued.
(6) Rules 5 and 6 shall apply, with the necessary modifications, in relation to a warrant of possession and any further warrant in aid of such a warrant as they apply in relation to a warrant of execution.

### Rule 18 Saving for Enforcement by Committal

Nothing in rule 16 or 17 shall prejudice any power to enforce a judgment or order for the delivery of goods or the recovery of land by an order of committal.

## CCR ORDER 27
## ATTACHMENT OF EARNINGS

### Part I General

### Rule 1 Interpretation

(1) In this Order—
'the Act of 1971' means the Attachment of Earnings Act 1971 and, unless the context otherwise requires, expressions used in that Act have the same meanings as in that Act.

### Rule 2 Index of Orders

(1) The court officer of every court shall keep a nominal index of the debtors residing within the district of his court in respect of whom there are in force attachment of earnings orders which have been made by that court or of which the court officer has received notice from another court.
(2) Where a debtor in respect of whom a court has made an attachment of earnings order resides within the district of another court, the court officer of the first-mentioned court shall send a copy of the order to the court officer of the other court for entry in his index.
(3) The court officer shall, on the request of any person having a judgment or order against a person believed to be residing within the district of the court, cause a search to be made in the index of the court and issue a certificate of the result of the search.

### Rule 3 Appropriate Court

(1) Subject to paragraphs (2) and (3), an application for an attachment of earnings order may be made to the court for the district in which the debtor resides.
(2) If the debtor does not reside within England or Wales, or the creditor does not know where he resides, the application may be made to the court in which, or for the district in which, the judgment or order sought to be enforced was obtained.
(3) Where the creditor applies for attachment of earnings orders in respect of two or more debtors jointly liable under a judgment or order, the application may be made to the court for the district in which any of the debtors resides, so however that if the judgment or order was given or made by any such court, the application shall be made to that court.

### Rule 4 Mode of Applying

(1) A judgment creditor who desires to apply for an attachment of earnings order shall file his application certifying the amount of money remaining due under the judgment or order and that the whole or part of any instalment due remains unpaid and, where it is sought to enforce an order of a magistrates' court—
(a) a certified copy of the order; and
(b) a witness statement or affidavit verifying the amount due under the order or, if payments under the order are required to be made to the justices' chief executive for the magistrates' court, a certificate by that chief executive to the same effect.

(2) On the filing of the documents mentioned in paragraph (1) the court officer shall, where the order to be enforced is a maintenance order, fix a day for the hearing of the application.

### Rule 5 Service and Reply

(1) Notice of the application together with a form of reply in the appropriate form, shall be served on the debtor in the manner set out in CPR rule 6.2.

(2) The debtor shall, within 8 days after service on him of the documents mentioned in paragraph (1), file a reply in the form provided, and the instruction to that effect in the notice to the debtor shall constitute a requirement imposed by virtue of section 14(4) of the Act of 1971:
Provided that no proceedings shall be taken for an offence alleged to have been committed under section 23(2)(c) or (f) of the Act of 1971 in relation to the requirement unless the said documents have been served on the debtor personally or the court is satisfied that they came to his knowledge in sufficient time for him to comply with the requirement.

(2A) Nothing in paragraph (2) shall require a defendant to file a reply if, within the period of time mentioned in that paragraph, he pays to the judgment creditor the money remaining due under the judgment or order and, where such payment is made, the judgment creditor shall so inform the court officer.

(3) On receipt of a reply the court officer shall send a copy to the applicant.

### Rule 6 Notice to Employer

Without prejudice to the powers conferred by section 14(1) of the Act of 1971, the court officer may, at any stage of the proceedings, send to any person appearing to have the debtor in his employment a notice requesting him to give to the court, within such period as may be specified in the notice, a statement of the debtor's earnings and anticipated earnings with such particulars as may be so specified.

### Rule 7 Attachment of Earnings Order

(1) On receipt of the debtor's reply, the court officer may, if he has sufficient information to do so, make an attachment of earnings order and a copy of the order shall be sent to the parties and to the debtor's employer.

(2) Where an order is made under paragraph (1), the judgment creditor or the debtor may, within 14 days of service of the order on him and giving his reasons, apply on notice for the order to be re-considered and the court officer shall fix a day for the hearing of the application and give to the judgment creditor and the debtor not less than 2 days' notice of the day so fixed.

(3) On hearing an application under paragraph (2), the district judge may confirm the order or set it aside and make such new order as he thinks fit and the order so made shall be entered in the records of the court.

(4) Where an order is not made under paragraph (1), the court officer shall refer the application to the district judge who shall, if he considers that he has sufficient information to do so without the attendance of the parties, determine the application.

(5) Where the district judge does not determine the application under paragraph (4), he shall direct that a day be fixed for the hearing of the application whereupon the court officer shall fix such a day and give to the judgment creditor and the debtor not less than 8 days' notice of the day so fixed.
(6) Where an order is made under paragraph (4), the judgment creditor or the debtor may, within 14 days of service of the order on him and giving his reasons, apply on notice for the order to be re-considered; and the court officer shall fix a day for the hearing of the application and give to the judgment creditor and the debtor not less than 2 days' notice of the day so fixed.
(7) On hearing an application under paragraph (6), the district judge may confirm the order or set it aside and make such new order as he thinks fit and the order so made shall be entered in the records of the court.
(8) If the creditor does not appear at the hearing of the application under paragraph (5) but—
 (a) the court has received a witness statement or affidavit of evidence from him; or
 (b) the creditor requests the court in writing to proceed in his absence,
 the court may proceed to hear the application and to make an order thereon.
(9) An attachment of earnings order may be made to secure the payment of a judgment debt if the debt is—
 (a) of not less than £50; or
 (b) for the amount remaining payable under a judgment for a sum of not less than £50.

## Rule 7A Failure by Debtor

(1) If the debtor has failed to comply with rule 5(2) or to make payment to the judgment creditor, the court officer may issue an order under section 14(1) of the Act of 1971 which shall—
 (a) be indorsed with or incorporate a notice warning the debtor of the consequences of disobedience to the order;
 (b) be served on the debtor personally; and
 (c) direct that any payments made thereafter shall be paid into the court and not direct to the judgment creditor.
(2) Without prejudice to rule 16, if the person served with an order made pursuant to paragraph (1) fails to obey it or to file a statement of his means or to make payment, the court officer shall issue a notice calling on that person to show good reason why he should not be imprisoned and any such notice shall be served on the debtor personally not less than 5 days before the hearing.
(3) Order 29, rule 1 shall apply, with the necessary modifications and with the substitution of references to the district judge for references to the judge, where a notice is issued under paragraph (2) or (4) of that rule.
(4) In this rule 'statement of means' means a statement given under section 14(1) of the Act of 1971.

## Rule 7B Suspended Committal Order

(1) If the debtor fails to attend at an adjourned hearing of an application for an attachment of earnings order and a committal order is made, the judge or district judge may direct that the committal order shall be suspended so long as the debtor attends at the time and place specified in the committal order and paragraphs (2), (4) and (5) of Order 28, rule 7 shall apply, with the necessary modifications, where such a direction is given as they apply where a direction is given under paragraph (1) of that rule.
(2) Where a committal order is suspended under paragraph (1) and the debtor fails to attend at the time and place specified under paragraph (1), a certificate to that effect given by the court officer shall be sufficient authority for the issue of a warrant of committal.

## Rule 8 Failure by Debtor—Maintenance Orders

(1) An order made under section 23(1) of the Act of 1971 for the attendance of the debtor at an adjourned hearing of an application for an attachment of earnings order to secure payments under a maintenance order shall—
  (a) be served on the debtor personally not less than 5 days before the day fixed for the adjourned hearing; and
  (b) direct that any payments made thereafter shall be paid into the court and not direct to the judgment creditor.

(2) An application by a debtor for the revocation of an order committing him to prison and, if he is already in custody, for his discharge under subsection (7) of the said section 23 shall be made to the judge or district judge in writing without notice to any other party showing the reasons for the debtor's failure to attend the court or his refusal to be sworn or to give evidence, as the case may be, and containing an undertaking by the debtor to attend the court or to be sworn or to give evidence when next ordered or required to do so.

(3) The application shall, if the debtor has already been lodged in prison, be attested by the governor of the prison (or any other officer of the prison not below the rank of principal officer) and in any other case be made on witness statement or affidavit.

(4) Before dealing with the application the judge or district judge may, if he thinks fit, cause notice to be given to the judgment creditor that the application has been made and of a day and hour when he may attend and be heard.

## Rule 9 Costs

(1) Where costs are allowed to the judgment creditor on an application for an attachment of earnings order, there may be allowed—
  (a) a charge of a solicitor for attending the hearing and, if the court so directs, for serving the application;
  (b) if the court certifies that the case is fit for counsel, a fee to counsel; and
  (c) the court fee on the issue of the application.

(2) For the purpose of paragraph (1)(a) a solicitor who has prepared on behalf of the judgment creditor a witness statement or affidavit or request under rule 7(8) shall be treated as having attended the hearing.

(3) The costs may be fixed and allowed without detailed assessment under CPR Part 47.

## Rule 10 Contents and Service of Order

(1) An attachment of earnings order shall contain such of the following particulars relating to the debtor as are known to the court, namely—
  (a) his full name and address;
  (b) his place of work; and
  (c) the nature of his work and his works number, if any, and those particulars shall be the prescribed particulars for the purposes of section 6(3) of the Act of 1971.

(2) An attachment of earnings order and any order varying or discharging such an order shall be served on the debtor and on the person to whom the order is directed, and CPR Part 6 and CPR rules 40.4 and 40.5 shall apply with the further modification that where the order is directed to a corporation which has requested the court that any communication relating to the debtor or to the class of persons to whom he belongs shall be directed to the corporation at a particular address, service may, if the district judge thinks fit, be effected on the corporation at that address.

(3) Where an attachment of earnings order is made to enforce a judgment or order of the High Court or a magistrates' court, a copy of the attachment of earnings order and of any order discharging it shall be sent by the court officer of the county court to the court officer of the High Court, or, as the case may be, the justices' chief executive for the magistrates' court.

### Rule 11 Application to Determine Whether Particular Payments Are Earnings

An application to the court under section 16 of the Act of 1971 to determine whether payments to the debtor of a particular class or description are earnings for the purpose of an attachment of earnings order may be made to the district judge in writing and the court officer shall thereupon fix a date and time for the hearing of the application by the court and give notice thereof to the persons mentioned in the said section 16(2)(a), (b) and (c).

### Rule 12 Notice of Cesser

Where an attachment of earnings order ceases to have effect under section 8(4) of the Act of 1971, the court officer of the court in which the matter is proceeding shall give notice of the cesser to the person to whom the order was directed.

### Rule 13 Variation and Discharge by Court of Own Motion

(1) Subject to paragraph (9), the powers conferred by section 9(1) of the Act of 1971 may be exercised by the court of its own motion in the circumstances mentioned in the following paragraphs.
(2) Where it appears to the court that a person served with an attachment of earnings order directed to him has not the debtor in his employment, the court may discharge the order.
(3) Where an attachment of earnings order which has lapsed under section 9(4) of the Act of 1971 is again directed to a person who appears to the court to have the debtor in his employment, the court may make such consequential variations in the order as it thinks fit.
(4) Where, after making an attachment of earnings order, the court makes or is notified of the making of another such order in respect of the same debtor which is not to secure the payment of a judgment debt or payments under an administration order, the court may discharge or vary the first-mentioned order having regard to the priority accorded to the other order by paragraph 8 of Schedule 3 to the Act of 1971.
(5) Where, after making an attachment of earnings order, the court makes an order under section 4(1)(b) of the Act of 1971 or makes an administration order, the court may discharge the attachment of earnings order or, if it exercises the power conferred by section 5(3) of the said Act, may vary the order in such manner as it thinks fit.
(6) On making a consolidated attachment of earnings order the court may discharge any earlier attachment of earnings order made to secure the payment of a judgment debt by the same debtor.
(7) Where it appears to the court that a bankruptcy order has been made against a person in respect of whom an attachment of earnings order is in force to secure the payment of a judgment debt, the court may discharge the attachment of earnings order.
(8) Where an attachment of earnings order has been made to secure the payment of a judgment debt and the court grants permission to issue execution for the recovery of the debt, the court may discharge the order.
(9) Before varying or discharging an attachment of earnings order of its own motion under any of the foregoing paragraphs of this rule, the court shall, unless it thinks it unnecessary in the circumstances to do so, give the debtor and the person on whose application the order was made an opportunity of being heard on the question whether the order should be varied or discharged, and for that purpose the court officer may give them notice of a date, time and place at which the question will be considered.

### Rule 14 Transfer of Attachment Order

(1) Where the court by which the question of making a consolidated attachment order falls to be considered is not the court by which any attachment of earnings order has been made to secure the payment of a judgment debt by the debtor, the district judge of the

last-mentioned court shall, at the request of the district judge of the first-mentioned court, transfer to that court the matter in which the attachment of earnings order was made.

(2) Without prejudice to paragraph (1), if in the opinion of the judge or district judge of any court by which an attachment of earnings order has been made, the matter could more conveniently proceed in some other court, whether by reason of the debtor having become resident in the district of that court or otherwise, he may order the matter to be transferred to that court.

(3) The court to which proceedings arising out of an attachment of earnings are transferred under this rule shall have the same jurisdiction in relation to the order as if it has been made by that court.

### Rule 15 Exercise of Power to Obtain Statement of Earnings etc.

(1) An order under section 14(1) of the Act of 1971 shall be indorsed with or incorporate a notice warning the person to whom it is directed of the consequences of disobedience to the order and shall be served on him personally.

(2) Order 34, rule 2, shall apply, with the necessary modifications, in relation to any penalty for failure to comply with an order under the said section 14(1) or, subject to the proviso to rule 5(2), any penalty for failure to comply with a requirement mentioned in that rule, as it applies in relation to a fine under section 55 of the County Courts Act 1984.

### Rule 16 Offences

(1) Where it is alleged that a person has committed any offence mentioned in section 23(2)(a), (b), (d), (e) or (f) of the Act of 1971 in relation to proceedings in, or to an attachment of earnings order made by, a county court, the district judge shall, unless it is decided to proceed against the alleged offender summarily, issue a summons calling upon him to show cause why he should not be punished for the alleged offence.
The summons shall be served on the alleged offender personally not less than 14 days before the return day.

(2) Order 34, rules 3 and 4, shall apply, with the necessary modifications, to proceedings for an offence under section 23(2) of the Act of 1971 as they apply to proceedings for offences under the County Courts Act 1984.

### Rule 17 Maintenance Orders

(1) The foregoing rules of this Order shall apply in relation to maintenance payments as they apply in relation to a judgment debt, subject to the following paragraphs.

(2) An application for an attachment of earnings order to secure payments under a maintenance order made by a county court shall be made to that county court.

(3) Any application under section 32 of the Matrimonial Causes Act 1973 for permission to enforce the payment of arrears which became due more than 12 months before the application for an attachment of earnings order shall be made in that application.

(3A) Notice of the application together with a form of reply in the appropriate form, shall be served on the debtor in the manner set out in CPR rule 6.2.

(3B) Service of the notice shall be effected not less than 21 days before the hearing, but service may be effected at any time before the hearing on the applicant satisfying the court by witness statement or affidavit that the respondent is about to remove from his address for service.

(3C) Rule 5(2A) shall not apply.

(4) An application by the debtor for an attachment of earnings order to secure payments under a maintenance order may be made on the making of the maintenance order or an order varying the maintenance order, and rules 4 and 5 shall not apply.

(5) Rule 7 shall have effect as if for paragraphs (1) to (8) there were substituted the following paragraph—

'(1) An application for an attachment of earnings order may be heard and determined by the district judge, who shall hear the application in private.'

(6) Rule 9 shall apply as if for the reference to the amount payable under the relevant adjudication there were substituted a reference to the arrears due under the related maintenance order.

(7) Where an attachment of earnings order made by the High Court designates the court officer of a county court as the collecting officer, that officer shall, on receipt of a certified copy of the order from the court officer of the High Court, send to the person to whom the order is directed a notice as to the mode of payment.

(8) Where an attachment of earnings order made by a county court to secure payments under a maintenance order ceases to have effect and—
  (a) the related maintenance order was made by that court; or
  (b) the related maintenance order was an order of the High Court and—
    (i) the court officer of the county court has received notice of the cessation from the court officer of the High Court; or
    (ii) a committal order has been made in the county court for the enforcement of the related maintenance order,

the court officer of the county court shall give notice of the cessation to the person to whom the attachment of earnings order was directed.

(9) Where an attachment of earnings order has been made by a county court to secure payments under a maintenance order, notice under section 10(2) of the Act of 1971 to the debtor and to the person to whom the district judge is required to pay sums received under the order shall be in the form provided for that purpose, and if the debtor wishes to request the court to discharge the attachment of earnings order or to vary it otherwise than by making the appropriate variation, he shall apply to the court, within 14 days after the date of the notice, for the remedy desired.

(10) Rule 13 shall have effect as if for paragraphs (4) to (7) there were substituted the following paragraph—

'(4) Where it appears to the court by which an attachment of earnings order has been made that the related maintenance order has ceased to have effect, whether by virtue of the terms of the maintenance order or under section 28 of the Matrimonial Causes Act 1973 or otherwise, the court may discharge or vary the attachment of earnings order.'

## Part II Consolidated Attachment of Earnings Orders

### Rule 18 Cases in Which Consolidated Order May be Made

Subject to the provisions of rules 19 to 21, the court may make a consolidated attachment order where—

(a) two or more attachment of earnings orders are in force to secure the payment of judgment debts by the same debtor; or

(b) on an application for an attachment of earnings order to secure the payment of a judgment debt, or for a consolidated attachment order to secure the payment of two or more judgment debts, it appears to the court that an attachment of earnings order is already in force to secure the payment of a judgment debt by the same debtor.

### Rule 19 Application for Consolidated Order

(1) An application for a consolidated attachment order may be made—
  (a) by the debtor in respect of whom the order is sought; or
  (b) by any person who has obtained or is entitled to apply for an attachment of earnings order to secure the payment of a judgment debt by that debtor.

(2) An application under paragraph (1) may be made in the proceedings in which any attachment of earnings order (other than a priority order) is in force and rules 3, 4 and 5 of this Order shall not apply.

(3) Where the judgment which it is sought to enforce was not given by the court which made the attachment of earnings order, the judgment shall be automatically transferred to the court which made the attachment of earnings order.

(3A) An application under paragraph (1)(b) shall certify the amount of money remaining due under the judgment or order and that the whole or part of any instalment due remains unpaid.

(3B) Where an application for a consolidated attachment of earnings order is made, the court officer shall—

(a) notify any party who may be affected by the application of its terms; and

(b) require him to notify the court in writing, within 14 days of service of notification upon him, giving his reasons for any objection he may have to the granting of the application.

(3C) If notice of any objection is not given within the time stated, the court officer shall make a consolidated attachment of earnings order.

(3D) If any party objects to the making of a consolidated attachment of earnings order, the court officer shall refer the application to the district judge who may grant the application after considering the objection made and the reasons given.

(3E) In the foregoing paragraphs of this rule, a party affected by the application means—

(a) where the application is made by the debtor, the creditor in the proceedings in which the application is made and any other creditor who has obtained an attachment of earnings order which is in force to secure the payment of a judgment debt by the debtor;

(b) where the application is made by the judgment creditor, the debtor and every person who, to the knowledge of the applicant, has obtained an attachment of earnings order which is in force to secure the payment of a judgment debt by the debtor.

(4) A person to whom two or more attachment of earnings orders are directed to secure the payment of judgment debts by the same debtor may request the court in writing to make a consolidated attachment order to secure the payment of those debts, and on receipt of such a request paragraphs (3B) to (3E) shall apply, with the necessary modifications, as if the request were an application by the judgment creditor.

## Rule 20 Making of Consolidated Order by Court of its Own Motion

Where an application is made for an attachment of earnings order to secure the payment of a judgment debt by a debtor in respect of whom an attachment of earnings order is already in force to secure the payment of another judgment debt and no application is made for a consolidated attachment order, the court officer may make such an order of his own motion after giving all persons concerned an opportunity of submitting written objections.

## Rule 21 Extension of Consolidated Order

(1) Where a consolidated attachment order is in force to secure the payment of two or more judgment debts, any creditor to whom another judgment debt is owed by the same judgment debtor may apply to the court by which the order was made for it to be extended so as to secure the payment of that debt as well as the first-mentioned debts and, if the application is granted, the court may either vary the order accordingly or may discharge it and make a new consolidated attachment order to secure payment of all the aforesaid judgment debts.

(2) An application under this rule shall be treated for the purposes of rules 19 and 20 as an application for a consolidated attachment order.

## Rule 22 Payments Under Consolidated Order

Instead of complying with section 13 of the Act of 1971, a court officer who receives payments made to him in compliance with a consolidated attachment order shall, after deducting such court fees, if any, in respect of proceedings for or arising out of the order as are deductible from those payments, deal with the sums paid as he would if they had been paid by the debtor to satisfy the relevant adjudications in proportion to the amounts payable thereunder, and for that purpose dividends may from time to time be declared and distributed among the creditors entitled thereto.

# CCR ORDER 28
# JUDGMENT SUMMONSES

## Rule 1 Application for Judgment Summons

(1) An application for the issue of a judgment summons may be made to the court for the district in which the debtor resides or carries on business or, if the summons is to issue against two or more persons jointly liable under the judgment or order sought to be enforced, in the court for the district in which any of the debtors resides or carries on business.

(2) The judgment creditor shall make his application by filing a request in that behalf certifying the amount of money remaining due under the judgment or order, the amount in respect of which the judgment summons is to issue and that the whole or part of any instalment due remains unpaid.

(3) The judgment creditor must file with the request all written evidence on which he intends to rely.

## Rule 2 Mode of Service

(1) Subject to paragraph (2), a judgment summons shall be served personally on every debtor against whom it is issued.

(2) Where the judgment creditor or his solicitor gives a certificate for postal service in respect of a debtor residing or carrying on business within the district of the court, the judgment summons shall, unless the district judge otherwise directs, be served on that debtor by an officer of the court sending it to him by first-class post at the address stated in the request for the judgment summons and, unless the contrary is shown, the date of service shall be deemed to be the seventh day after the date on which the judgment summons was sent to the debtor.

(3) Where a judgment summons has been served on a debtor in accordance with paragraph (2), no order of commitment shall be made against him unless—
(a) he appears at the hearing; or
(b) it is made under section 110(2) of the Act.

(4) The written evidence on which the judgment creditor intends to rely must be served with the judgment summons.

## Rule 3 Time for Service

(1) The judgment summons and written evidence must be served not less than 14 days before the day fixed for the hearing.

(2) A notice of non-service shall be sent pursuant to CPR rule 6.11 in respect of a judgment summons which has been sent by post under rule 2(2) and has been returned to the court office undelivered.

(3) CPR rules 7.5 and 7.6 shall apply, with the necessary modifications, to a judgment summons as they apply to a claim form.

## Rule 4 Enforcement of Debtor's Attendance

(1) Order 27, rules 711 and 8, shall apply, with the necessary modifications, to an order made under section 110(1) of the Act for the attendance of the debtor at an adjourned hearing of a judgment summons as they apply to an order made under section 23(1) of the Attachment of Earnings Act 1971 for the attendance of the debtor at an adjourned hearing of an application for an attachment of earnings order.

(1A) An order made under section 110(1) of the Act must be served personally on the judgment debtor.

(1B) Copies of—

(a) the judgment summons; and

(b) the written evidence,

must be served with the order.

(2) At the time of service of the order there shall be paid or tendered to the debtor a sum reasonably sufficient to cover his expenses in travelling to and from the court, unless such a sum was paid to him at the time of service of the judgment summons.

## Rule 5 Evidence

(1) No person may be committed on an application for a judgment summons unless—

(a) the order is made under section 110(2) of the Act; or

(b) the judgment creditor proves that the debtor—

(i) has or has had since the date of the judgment or order the means to pay the sum in respect of which he has made default; and

(ii) has refused or neglected or refuses or neglects to pay that sum.

(2) The debtor may not be compelled to give evidence.

## Rule 7 Suspension of Committal Order

(1) If on the hearing of a judgment summons a committal order is made, the judge may direct execution of the order to be suspended to enable the debtor to pay the amount due.

(2) A note of any direction given under paragraph (1) shall be entered in the records of the court and notice of the suspended committal order shall be sent to the debtor.

(3) Where a judgment summons is issued in respect of one or more but not all of the instalments payable under a judgment or order for payment by instalments and a committal order is made and suspended under paragraph (1), the judgment or order shall, unless the judge otherwise orders, be suspended for so long as the, execution of the committal order is suspended.

(4) Where execution of a committal order is suspended under paragraph (1) and the debtor subsequently desires to apply for a further suspension, the debtor shall attend at or write to the court office and apply for the suspension he desires, stating the reasons for his inability to comply with the terms of the original suspension, and the court shall fix a day for the hearing of the application by the judge and give at least 3 days' notice thereof to the judgment creditor and the debtor.

(5) The district judge may suspend execution of the committal order pending the hearing of an application under paragraph (4).

## Rule 8 New Order on Judgment Summons

(1) Where on the hearing of a judgment summons, the judge makes a new order for payment of the amount of the judgment debt remaining unpaid, there shall be included in the amount payable under the order for the purpose of any enforcement proceedings, otherwise than by judgment summons, any amount in respect of which a committal order has already been made and the debtor imprisoned.

(2) No judgment summons under the new order shall include any amount in respect of which the debtor was imprisoned before the new order was made, and any amount subsequently paid shall be appropriated in the first instance to the amount due under the new order.

## Rule 9 Notification of Order on Judgment of High Court

(1) Notice of the result of the hearing of a judgment summons on a judgment or order of the High Court shall be sent by the county court to the High Court.

(2) If a committal order or a new order for payment is made on the hearing, the office copy

of the judgment or order filed in the county court shall be deemed to be a judgment or order of the court in which the judgment summons is heard.

### Rule 10 Costs on Judgment Summons

(1) No costs shall be allowed to the judgment creditor on the hearing of a judgment summons unless—
  (a) a committal order is made; or
  (b) the sum in respect of which the judgment summons was issued is paid before the hearing.
(2) Where costs are allowed to the judgment creditor,
  (a) there may be allowed—
    (i) a charge of the judgment creditor's solicitor for attending the hearing and, if the judge so directs, for serving the judgment summons;
    (ii) a fee to counsel if the court certifies that the case is fit for counsel;
    (iii) any travelling expenses paid to the debtor, and
    (iv) the court fee on the issue of the judgment summons.,
  (b) the costs may be fixed and allowed without detailed assessment under CPR Part 47.

### Rule 11 Issue of Warrant of Committal

(1) A judgment creditor desiring a warrant to be issued pursuant to a committal order shall file a request in that behalf.
(2) Where two or more debtors are to be committed in respect of the same judgment or order, a separate warrant of committal shall be issued for each of them.
(3) Where a warrant of committal is sent to a foreign court for execution, that court shall indorse on it a notice as to the effect of section 122(3) of the Act addressed to the governor of the prison of that court.

### Rule 12 Notification to Foreign Court of Part Payment Before Debtor Lodged in Prison

Where, after a warrant of committal has been sent to a foreign court for execution but before the debtor is lodged in prison, the home court is notified that an amount which is less than the sum on payment of which the debtor is to be discharged has been paid, the home court shall send notice of the payment to the foreign court.

### Rule 13 Payment After Debtor Lodged in Prison

(1) Where, after the debtor has been lodged in prison under a warrant of committal, payment is made of the sum on payment of which the debtor is to be discharged, then—
  (a) if the payment is made to the court responsible for the execution of the warrant, the court officer shall make and sign a certificate of payment and send it by post or otherwise to the gaoler;
  (b) if the payment is made to the court which issued the warrant of committal after the warrant has been sent to a foreign court for execution, the home court shall send notice of the payment to the foreign court, and the court officer at the foreign court shall make and sign a certificate of payment and send it by post or otherwise to the gaoler;
  (c) if the payment is made to the gaoler, he shall sign a certificate of payment and send the amount to the court which made the committal order.
(2) Where, after the debtor has been lodged in prison under a warrant of committal, payment is made of an amount less than the sum on payment of which the debtor is to be discharged, then subject to paragraph (3), paragraph (1)(a) and (b) shall apply with the substitution of references to a notice of payment for the references to a certificate of payment and paragraph (1)(c) shall apply with the omission of the requirement to make and sign a certificate of payment.

(3) Where, after the making of a payment to which paragraph (2) relates, the balance of the sum on payment of which the debtor is to be discharged is paid, paragraph (1) shall apply without the modifications mentioned in paragraph (2).

### Rule 14 Discharge of Debtor Otherwise than on Payment

(1) Where the judgment creditor lodges with the district judge a request that a debtor lodged in prison under a warrant of committal may be discharged from custody, the district judge shall make an order for the discharge of the debtor in respect of the warrant of committal and the court shall send the gaoler a certificate of discharge.
(2) Where a debtor who has been lodged in prison under a warrant of committal desires to apply for his discharge under section 121 of the Act, the application shall be made to the judge in writing and without notice showing the reasons why the debtor alleges that he is unable to pay the sum in respect of which he has been committed and ought to be discharged and stating any offer which he desires to make as to the terms on which his discharge is to be ordered, and Order 27, rule 8(3) and (4), shall apply, with the necessary modifications, as it applies to an application by a debtor for his discharge from custody under section 23(7) of the Attachment of Earnings Act 1971.
(3) If in a case to which paragraph (2) relates the debtor is ordered to be discharged from custody on terms which include liability to re-arrest if the terms are not complied with, the judge may, on the application of the judgment creditor if the terms are not complied with, order the debtor to be re-arrested and imprisoned for such part of the term of imprisonment as remained unserved at the time of discharge.
(4) Where an order is made under paragraph (3), a duplicate warrant of committal shall be issued, indorsed with a certificate signed by the court officer as to the order of the judge.

## CCR ORDER 29
## COMMITTAL FOR BREACH OF ORDER OR UNDERTAKING

### Rule 1 Enforcement of Judgment to Do or Abstain From Doing Any Act

(1) Where a person required by a judgment or order to do an act refuses or neglects to do it within the time fixed by the judgment or order or any subsequent order, or where a person disobeys a judgment or order requiring him to abstain from doing an act, then, subject to the Debtors Acts 1869 and 1878 and to the provisions of these rules, the judgment or order may be enforced, by order of the judge, by a committal order against that person or, if that person is a body corporate, against any director or other officer of the body.
(2) Subject to paragraphs (6) and (7), a judgment or order shall not be enforced under paragraph (1) unless—
 (a) a copy of the judgment or order has been served personally on the person required to do or abstain from doing the act in question and also, where that person is a body corporate, on the director or other officer of the body against whom a committal order is sought; and
 (b) in the case of a judgment or order requiring a person to do an act, the copy has been so served before the expiration of the time within which he was required to do the act and was accompanied by a copy of any order, made between the date of the judgment or order and the date of service, fixing that time.
(3) Where a judgment or order enforceable by committal order under paragraph (1) has been given or made, the court officer shall, if the judgment or order is in the nature of an injunction, at the time when the judgment or order is drawn up, and in any other case on the request of the judgment creditor, issue a copy of the judgment or order, indorsed with or incorporating a notice as to the consequences of disobedience, for service in accordance with paragraph (2).
(4) If the person served with the judgment or order fails to obey it, the judgment creditor

may issue a claim form or, as the case may be, an application notice seeking the committal for contempt of court of that person and subject to paragraph (7), the claim form or application notice shall be served on him personally.

(4A) The claim form or application notice (as the case may be) shall—
- (a) identify the provisions of the injunction or undertaking which it is alleged have been disobeyed or broken;
- (b) list the ways in which it is alleged that the injunction has been disobeyed or the undertaking has been broken;
- (c) be supported by an affidavit stating the grounds on which the application is made, and unless service is dispensed with under paragraph (7), a copy of the affidavit shall be served with the claim form or application notice.

(5) If a committal order is made, the order shall be for the issue of a warrant of committal and, unless the judge otherwise orders—
- (a) a copy of the order shall be served on the person to be committed either before or at the time of the execution of the warrant; or
- (b) where the warrant has been signed by the judge, the order for issue of the warrant may be served on the person to be committed at any time within 36 hours after the execution of the warrant.

(5A) A warrant of committal shall not, without further order of the court, be enforced more than 2 years after the date on which the warrant is issued.

(6) A judgment or order requiring a person to abstain from doing an act may be enforced under paragraph (1) notwithstanding that service of a copy of the judgment or order has not been effected in accordance with paragraph (2) if the judge is satisfied that, pending such service, the person against whom it is sought to enforce the judgment or order has had notice thereof either—
- (a) by being present when the judgment or order was given or made; or
- (b) by being notified of the terms of the judgment or order whether by telephone, telegram or otherwise.

(7) Without prejudice to its powers under Part 6 of the CPR, the court may dispense with service of a copy of a judgment or order under paragraph (2) or a claim form or application notice under paragraph (4) if the court thinks it just to do so.

(8) Where service of the claim form or application notice has been dispensed with under paragraph (7) and a committal order is made in the absence of the respondent, the judge may on his own initiative fix a date and time when the person to be committed is to be brought before him or before the court.

## Rule 1A Undertaking Given by Party

Rule 1 (except paragraph (6)) shall apply to undertakings as it applies to orders with the necessary modifications and as if—

(a) for paragraph (2) of that rule there were substituted the following—

'(2) A copy of the document recording the undertaking shall be delivered by the court officer to the party giving the undertaking—
- (a) by handing a copy of the document to him before he leaves the court building; or
- (b) where his place of residence is known, by posting a copy to him at his place of residence; or
- (c) through his solicitor,

and, where delivery cannot be effected in this way, the court officer shall deliver a copy of the document to the party for whose benefit the undertaking is given and that party shall cause it to be served personally as soon as is practicable'.

(b) in paragraph (7), the words from 'a copy of' to 'paragraph (2) or' were omitted.

## Rule 2 Solicitor's Undertaking

(1) An undertaking given by a solicitor in relation to any proceeding in a county court may be enforced, by order of the judge of that court, by committal order against the solicitor.

(2) Where it appears to the judge that a solicitor has failed to carry out any such undertaking, he may of his own initiative direct the court officer to issue a notice calling on the solicitor to show cause why he should not be committed to prison.

(3) Where any party to the proceedings desires to have the undertaking enforced by committal order, the court officer shall, on the application of the party supported by an affidavit setting out the facts on which the application is based, issue such a notice as is referred to in paragraph (2).

### Rule 3 Discharge of Person in Custody

(1) Where a person in custody under a warrant or order, other than a warrant of committal to which Order 27, rule 8, or Order 28, rule 4 or 14, relates, desires to apply to the court for his discharge, he shall make his application in writing attested by the governor of the prison (or any other officer of the prison not below the rank of principal officer) showing that he has purged or is desirous of purging his contempt and shall, not less than one day before the application is made, serve notice of it on the party, if any, at whose instance the warrant or order was issued.

(2) If the committal order—

(a) does not direct that any application for discharge shall be made to a judge; or

(b) was made by the district judge under section 118 of the Act,

any application for discharge may be made to the district judge.

(3) Nothing in paragraph (1) shall apply to an application made by the Official Solicitor in his official capacity for the discharge of a person in custody.

## CCR ORDER 33
## INTERPLEADER PROCEEDINGS

### Part I Under Execution

### Rule 1 Notice of Claim

(A1) In this Part of this Order 'the interpleader claimant' means any person making a claim to or in respect of goods seized in execution or the proceeds or value thereof and 'the interpleader claim' means that claim.

(1) The interpleader claimant shall deliver to the bailiff holding the warrant of execution, or file in the office of the court for the district in which the goods were seized, notice of his claim stating—

(a) the grounds of the interpleader claim or, in the case of a claim for rent, the particulars required by section 102(2) of the Act; and

(b) the interpleader claimant's full name and address.

(2) On receipt of an interpleader claim made under this rule, the court shall—

(a) send notice thereof to the execution creditor; and

(b) except where the interpleader claim is to the proceeds or value of the goods, send to the interpleader claimant a notice requiring him to make a deposit or give security in accordance with section 100 of the Act.

### Rule 2 Reply to Interpleader Claim

(1) Within 4 days after receiving notice of an interpleader claim under rule 1(2) the execution creditor shall give notice to the court informing him whether he admits or disputes the interpleader claim or requests the district judge to withdraw from possession of the goods or money claimed.

(2) If, within the period aforesaid, the execution creditor gives notice to the court admitting the interpleader claim or requesting the district judge to withdraw from possession of the goods or money claimed, the execution creditor shall not be liable to the district judge for any fees or expenses incurred after receipt of the notice.

### Rule 3 Order Protecting District Judge

Where the execution creditor gives the court such a notice as is mentioned in rule 2(2), the district judge shall withdraw from possession of the goods or money claimed and may apply to the judge, on notice to the interpleader claimant, for an order restraining the bringing of a claim against the district judge for or in respect of his having taken possession of the goods or money and on the hearing of the application the judge may make such order as may be just.

### Rule 4 Issue of Interpleader Proceedings

(1) Where the execution creditor gives notice under rule 2(1) disputing an interpleader claim made under rule 1 or fails, within the period mentioned in rule 2(1), to give the notice required by that rule, the district judge shall, unless the interpleader claim is withdrawn, issue an interpleader notice to the execution creditor and the interpleader claimant.

(2) On the issue of an interpleader notice under paragraph (1) the court officer shall enter the proceedings in the records of the court, fix a day for the hearing by the judge and prepare sufficient copies of the notice for service under this rule.

(3) Subject to paragraph (4) the notice shall be served on the execution creditor and the interpleader claimant in the manner set out in CPR rule 6.2.

(4) Service shall be effected not less than 14 days before the return day.

### Rule 5 Claim for Damages

Where in interpleader proceedings under an execution the interpleader claimant claims from the execution creditor or the district judge, or the execution creditor claims from the district judge, damages arising or capable of arising out of the execution—

(a) the party claiming damages shall, within 8 days after service of the notice on him under rule 4(3), give notice of this claim to the court and to any other party against whom the claim is made, stating the amount and the grounds of the claim; and

(b) the party from whom damages are claimed may pay money into court in satisfaction of the claim as if the interpleader proceedings were a claim brought in accordance with CPR Part 7 by the person making the claim.

## Part II Otherwise Than Under Execution

### Rule 6 Application for Relief

(1) Where a person (in this Part of this Order called 'the applicant') is under a liability in respect of a debt or any money or goods and he is, or expects to be, sued for or in respect of the debt, money or goods by two or more persons making adverse claims thereto ('the interpleader claimants'), he may apply to the court, in accordance with these rules, for relief by way of interpleader.

(2) The application shall be made to the court in which the claim is pending against the applicant or, if no claim is pending against him, to the court in which he might be sued.

(3) The application shall be made by filing a witness statement or affidavit showing that—

  (a) the applicant claims no interest in the subject-matter in dispute other than for charges or costs;

  (b) the applicant does not collude with any of the interpleader claimants; and

  (c) the applicant is willing to pay or transfer the subject-matter into court or to dispose of it as the court may direct,

together with as many copies of the witness statement or affidavit as there are interpleader claimants.

### Rule 7 Relief in Pending Claim

Where the applicant is a defendant in a pending claim—

(a) the witness statement or affidavit and copies required by rule 6(3) shall be filed within 14 days after service on him of the claim form;
(b) the return day of the application shall be a day fixed for the pre-trial review of the claim including the interpleader proceedings and, if a day has already been fixed for the pre-trial review or hearing of the claim, the court shall, if necessary, postpone it;
(c) the interpleader claimant, the applicant and the claimant in the claim shall be given notice of the application, which shall be prepared by the court together with sufficient copies for service;
(d) the notice to the interpleader claimant shall be served on him, together with a copy of the witness statement or affidavit filed under rule 6(3) and of the claim form and particulars of claim in the claim, not less than 21 days before the return day in the same manner as an interpleader notice in accordance with rule 4(3);
(e) the notices to the applicant and the claimant shall be sent to them by the court and the notice to the claimant shall be accompanied by a copy of the said witness statement or affidavit.

### Rule 8 Relief Otherwise Than in Pending Claim

Where the applicant is not a defendant in a pending claim—
(a) the court shall enter the proceedings in the records of the court;
(b) the court shall fix a day for the pre-trial review or, if the court so directs, a day for the hearing of the proceedings and shall prepare and issue an interpleader notice, together with sufficient copies for service;
(c) the notice together with a copy of the witness statement or affidavit filed under rule 6(3), shall be served on each of the claimants not less than 21 days before the return day in the same manner as an interpleader notice to be served under rule 4(3); and
(d) the court shall deliver or send a notice of issue to the applicant.

### Rule 9 Payment into Court etc.

Before or after the court officer proceeds under rule 7 or 8 the district judge may direct the applicant to bring the subject-matter of the proceedings into court, or to dispose of it in such manner as the district judge thinks fit, to abide the order of the court.

### Rule 10 Reply by Interpleader Claimant

(1) An interpleader claimant shall, within 14 days after service on him of the notice under rule 7(c) or the interpleader notice under rule 8(c), file—
  (a) a notice that he makes no interpleader claim; or
  (b) particulars stating the grounds of his interpleader claim to the subject matter,
  together in either case with sufficient copies for service under paragraph (2).
(2) The court shall send to each of the other parties a copy of any notice or particulars filed under paragraph (1).
(3) The court may, if it thinks fit, hear the proceedings although no notice or particulars have been filed.

### Rule 11 Order Barring Interpleader Claim etc.

(1) Where an interpleader claimant does not appear on any day fixed for a pre-trial review or the hearing of interpleader proceedings, or fails or refuses to comply with an order made in the proceedings, the court may make an order barring his interpleader claim.
(2) If, where the applicant is a defendant in a pending claim, the claimant does not appear on any day fixed for a pre-trial review or the hearing of the interpleader proceedings, the claim including the interpleader proceedings may be struck out.
(3) In any other case where a day is fixed for the hearing of interpleader proceedings, the court shall hear and determine the proceedings and give judgment finally determining the rights and claims of the parties.

(4) Where the court makes an order barring the interpleader claim of an interpleader claimant, the order shall declare the interpleader claimant, and all persons claiming under him, forever barred from prosecuting his interpleader claim against the applicant and all persons claiming under him, but unless the interpleader claimant has filed a notice under rule 10 that he makes no interpleader claim, such an order shall not affect the rights of the interpleader claimants as between themselves.

## CCR ORDER 34
## PENAL AND DISCIPLINARY PROVISIONS

### Rule 1 Issue and Service of Summons for Offence Under Section 14, 92 or 124 of the Act

Where—

(a) it is alleged that any person has committed an offence under section 14, 92 or 118 of the Act by assaulting an officer of the court while in the execution of his duty, or by rescuing or attempting to rescue any goods seized in execution, or by wilfully insulting a judge, juror, witness or any officer of the court, and the alleged offender has not been taken into custody and brought before the judge; or

(b) a complaint is made against an officer of the court under section 124 of the Act for having lost the opportunity of levying execution,

the court officer shall issue a summons, which shall be served on the alleged offender personally not less than 8 days before the return day appointed in the summons.

### Rule 1A Committal Under Section 14, 92 or 118 of the Act

Rule 1(5) of Order 29 shall apply, with the necessary modifications, where an order is made under section 14, 92 or 118 of the Act committing a person to prison.

### Rule 2 Notice to Show Cause Before or After Fine Under Section 55 of the Act

Before or after imposing a fine on any person under section 55 of the Act for disobeying a witness summons or refusing to be sworn or give evidence, the judge may direct the court officer to give to that person notice that if he has any cause to show why a fine should not be or should not have been imposed on him, he may show cause in person or by witness statement or affidavit or otherwise on a day named in the notice, and the judge after considering the cause shown may make such order as he thinks fit.

### Rule 3 Non-payment of Fine

(1) If a fine is not paid in accordance with the order imposing it, the court officer shall forthwith report the matter to the judge.

(2) Where by an order imposing a fine, the amount of the fine is directed to be paid by instalments and default is made in the payment of any instalment, the same proceedings may be taken as if default had been made in payment of the whole of the fine.

(3) If the judge makes an order for payment of a fine to be enforced by warrant of execution, the order shall be treated as an application made to the district judge for the issue of the warrant at the time when the order was received by him.

### Rule 4 Repayment of Fine

If, after a fine has been paid, the person on whom it was imposed shows cause sufficient to satisfy the judge that, if it had been shown at an earlier date, he would not have imposed a fine or would have imposed a smaller fine or would not have ordered payment to be enforced, the judge may order the fine or any part thereof to be repaid.

# CCR ORDER 39
# ADMINISTRATION ORDERS

## Rule 1 Exercise of Powers by District Judge

Any powers conferred on the court by Part VI of the Act, section 4 of the Attachment of Earnings Act 1971 or this Order may be exercised by the district judge or, in the circumstances mentioned in this Order, by the court officer.

## Rule 2 Request and List of Creditors

(1) A debtor who desires to obtain an administration order under Part VI of the Act shall file a request in that behalf in the court for the district in which he resides or carries on business.

(2) Where on his examination under CPR Part 71, or otherwise, a debtor furnishes to the court on oath a list of his creditors and the amounts which he owes to them respectively and sufficient particulars of his resources and needs, the court may proceed as if the debtor had filed a request under paragraph (1).

(3) Where a debtor is ordered to furnish a list under section 4(1)(b) of the said Act of 1971, then, unless otherwise directed, the list shall be filed within 14 days after the making of the order.

## Rule 3 Verification on Oath

The statements in the request mentioned in rule 2(1) and the list mentioned in rule 2(3) shall be verified by the debtor on oath.

## Rule 5 Orders Made by the Court Officer

(1) The question whether an administration order should be made, and the terms of such an order, may be decided by the court officer in accordance with the provisions of this rule.

(2) On the filing of a request or list under rule 2, the court officer may, if he considers that the debtor's means are sufficient to discharge in full and within a reasonable period the total amount of the debts included in the list, determine the amount and frequency of the payments to be made under such an order ('the proposed rate') and—

(a) notify the debtor of the proposed rate requiring him to give written reasons for any objection he may have to the proposed rate within 14 days of service of notification upon him;

(b) send to each creditor mentioned in the list provided by the debtor a copy of the debtor's request or of the list together with the proposed rate;

(c) require any such creditor to give written reasons for any objection he may have to the making of an administration order within 14 days of service of the documents mentioned in sub-paragraph (b) upon him.

Objections under sub-paragraph (c) may be to the making of an order, to the proposed rate or to the inclusion of a particular debt in the order.

(3) Where no objection under paragraph (2)(a) or (c) is received within the time stated, the court officer may make an administration order providing for payment in full of the total amount of the debts included in the list.

(4) Where the debtor or a creditor notifies the court of any objection within the time stated, the court officer shall fix a day for a hearing at which the district judge will decide whether an administration order should be made and the court officer shall give not less than 14 days' notice of the day so fixed to the debtor and to each creditor mentioned in the list provided by the debtor.

(5) Where the court officer is unable to fix a rate under paragraph (2) (whether because he considers that the debtor's means are insufficient or otherwise), he shall refer the request to the district judge.

(6) Where the district judge considers that he is able to do so without the attendance of the parties, he may fix the proposed rate providing for payment of the debts included in the list in full or to such extent and within such a period as appears practicable in the circumstances of the case.

(7) Where the proposed rate is fixed under paragraph (6), paragraphs (2) to (4) shall apply with the necessary modifications as if the rate had been fixed by the court officer.

(8) Where the district judge does not fix the proposed rate under paragraph (6), he shall direct the court officer to fix a day for a hearing at which the district judge will decide whether an administration order should be made and the court officer shall give not less than 14 days' notice of the day so fixed to the debtor and to each creditor mentioned in the list provided by the debtor.

(9) Where an administration order is made under paragraph (3), the court officer may exercise the power of the court under section 5 of the Attachment of Earnings Act 1971 to make an attachment of earnings order to secure the payments required by the administration order.

## Rule 6 Notice of Objection by Creditor

(1) Any creditor to whom notice has been given under rule 5(8) and who objects to any debt included in the list furnished by the debtor shall, not less than 7 days before the day of hearing, give notice of his objection, stating the grounds thereof, to the court officer, to the debtor and to the creditor to whose debt he objects.

(2) Except with the permission of the court, no creditor may object to a debt unless he has given notice of his objection under paragraph (1).

## Rule 7 Procedure on Day of Hearing

On the day of the hearing—

(a) any creditor, whether or not he is mentioned in the list furnished by the debtor, may attend and prove his debt or, subject to rule 6, object to any debt included in that list;

(b) every debt included in that list shall be taken to be proved unless it is objected to by a creditor or disallowed by the court or required by the court to be supported by evidence;

(c) any creditor whose debt is required by the court to be supported by evidence shall prove his debt;

(d) the court may adjourn proof of any debt and, if it does so, may either adjourn consideration of the question whether an administration order should be made or proceed to determine the question, in which case, if an administration order is made, the debt, when proved, shall be added to the debts scheduled to the order;

(e) any creditor whose debt is admitted or proved, and, with the permission of the court, any creditor the proof of whose debt has been adjourned, shall be entitled to be heard and to adduce evidence on the question whether an administration order should be made and, if so, in what terms.

## Rule 8 Direction for Order to be Subject to Review

(1) The court may, on making an administration order or at any subsequent time, direct that the order shall be subject to review at such time or at such intervals as the court may specify.

(2) Where the court has directed that an administration order shall be subject to review, the court officer shall give to the debtor and to every creditor who appeared when the order was made not less than 7 days' notice of any day appointed for such a review.

(3) Nothing in this rule shall require the court officer to fix a day for a review under rule 13A.

## Rule 9 Service of Order

Where an administration order is made, the court officer shall send a copy to—

(a) the debtor;

(b) every creditor whose name was included in the list furnished by the debtor;
(c) any other creditor who has proved his debt; and
(d) every other court in which, to the knowledge of the district judge, judgment has been obtained against the debtor or proceedings are pending in respect of any debt scheduled to the order.

### Rule 10 Subsequent Objection by Creditor

(1) After an administration order has been made, a creditor who has not received notice under rule 5 and who wishes to object to a debt scheduled to the order, or to the manner in which payment is directed to be made by instalments, shall give notice to the court officer of his objection and of the grounds thereof.
(2) On receipt of such notice the court shall consider the objection and may—
   (a) allow it;
   (b) dismiss it; or
   (c) adjourn it for hearing on notice being given to such persons and on such terms as to security for costs or otherwise as the court thinks fit.
(3) Without prejudice to the generality of paragraph (2), the court may dismiss an objection if it is not satisfied that the creditor gave notice of it within a reasonable time of his becoming aware of the administration order.

### Rule 11 Subsequent Proof by Creditor

(1) Any creditor whose debt is not scheduled to an administration order, and any person who after the date of the order became a creditor of the debtor, shall, if he wishes to prove his debt, send particulars of his claim to the court officer, who shall give notice of it to the debtor and to every creditor whose debt is so scheduled.
(2) If neither the debtor nor any creditor gives notice to the court officer, within 7 days after receipt of notice under paragraph (1), that he objects to the claim, then, unless it is required by the court to be supported by evidence, the claim shall be taken to be proved.
(3) If the debtor or a creditor gives notice of objection within the said period of 7 days or the court requires the claim to be supported by evidence, the court officer shall fix a day for consideration of the claim and give notice of it to the debtor, the creditor by whom the claim was made and the creditor, if any, making the objection, and on the hearing the court may either disallow the claim or allow it in whole or in part.
(4) If a claim is taken to be proved under paragraph (2) or allowed under paragraph (3), the debt shall be added to the schedule to the order and a copy of the order shall then be sent to the creditor by whom the claim was made.

### Rule 12 Permission to Present Bankruptcy Petition

An application by a creditor under section 112(4) of the Act for permission to present or join in a bankruptcy petition shall be made on notice to the debtor in accordance with CPR Part 23, but the court may, if it thinks fit, order that notice be given to any other creditor whose debt is scheduled to the administration order.

### Rule 13 Conduct of Order

(1) The court manager or such other officer of the court as the court making an administration order shall from time to time appoint shall have the conduct of the order and shall take all proper steps to enforce the order (including exercising the power of the court under section 5 of the Attachment of Earnings Act 1971 to make an attachment of earnings order to secure payments required by the administration order) or to bring to the attention of the court any matter which may make it desirable to review the order.
(2) Without prejudice to section 115 of the Act, any creditor whose debt is scheduled to the order may, with the permission of the court, take proceedings to enforce the order.
(3) The debtor or, with the permission of the court, any such creditor may apply to the court to review the order.

(4) When on a matter being brought to its attention under paragraph (1) the court so directs or the debtor or a creditor applies for the review of an administration order, rule 8(2) shall apply as if the order were subject to review under that rule.
(5) Nothing in this rule shall require the court officer to fix a day for a review under rule 13A.

## Rule 13A Review by Court Officer in Default of Payment

(1) Where it appears that the debtor is failing to make payments in accordance with the order, the court officer shall (either of his own initiative or on the application of a creditor whose debt is scheduled to the administration order) send a notice to the debtor—
  (a) informing him of the amounts which are outstanding; and
  (b) requiring him (within 14 days of service of the notice upon him) to—
    (i) make the payments as required by the order; or
    (ii) explain his reasons for failing to make the payments; and
    (iii) make a proposal for payment of the amounts outstanding; or
    (iv) make a request to vary the order.
(2) If the debtor does not comply with paragraph (1)(b) within the time stated, the court officer shall revoke the administration order.
(3) The court officer shall refer a notice given by a debtor under paragraph (1)(b)(ii), (iii) or (iv) to the district judge who may—
  (a) without requiring the attendance of the parties—
    (i) revoke the administration order or vary it so as to provide for payment of the debts included in the order in full or to such extent and within such a period as appears practicable in the circumstances of the case; or
    (ii) suspend the operation of the administration order for such time and on such terms as he thinks fit; or
  (b) require the court officer to fix a day for the review of the administration order and to give to the debtor and to every creditor whose debt is scheduled to the administration order not less than 8 days' notice of the day so fixed.
(4) Any party affected by an order made under paragraph (2) or (3)(a) may, within 14 days of service of the order on him and giving his reasons, apply on notice for the district judge to consider the matter afresh and the court officer shall fix a day for the hearing of the application before the district judge and give to the debtor and to every creditor whose debt is scheduled to the administration order not less than 8 days' notice of the day so fixed.
(5) On hearing an application under paragraph (4), the district judge may confirm the order or set it aside and make such new order as he thinks fit and the order so made shall be entered in the records of the court.

## Rule 14 Review of Order

(1) On the review of an administration order the court may—
  (a) if satisfied that the debtor is unable from any cause to pay any instalment due under the order, suspend the operation of the order for such time and on such terms as it thinks fit;
  (b) if satisfied that there has been a material change in any relevant circumstances since the order was made, vary any provision of the order made by virtue of section 112(6) of the Act;
  (c) if satisfied that the debtor has failed without reasonable cause to comply with any provision of the order or that it is otherwise just and expedient to do so, revoke the order, either forthwith or on failure to comply with any condition specified by the court; or
  (d) make an attachment of earnings order to secure the payments required by the administration order or vary or discharge any such attachment of earnings order already made.

(2) The court officer shall send a copy of any order varying or revoking an administration order to the debtor, to every creditor whose debt is scheduled to the administration order and, if the administration order is revoked, to any other court to which a copy of the administration order was sent pursuant to rule 9.

### Rule 16 Discharge of Attachment of Earnings Order

On the revocation of an administration order any attachment of earnings order made to secure the payments required by the administration order shall be discharged.

### Rule 17 Declaration of Dividends

(1) The officer having the conduct of an administration order shall from time to time declare dividends and distribute them among the creditors entitled to them.
(2) When a dividend is declared, notice shall be sent by the officer to each of the creditors.

### Rule 18 Creditors to Rank Equally

All creditors scheduled under section 113(d) of the Act before an administration order is superseded under section 117(2) of the Act shall rank equally in proportion to the amount of their debts subject to the priority given by the said paragraph (d) to those scheduled as having been creditors before the date of the order, but no payment made to any creditor by way of dividend or otherwise shall be disturbed by reason of any subsequent proof by any creditor under the said paragraph (d).

### Rule 19 Change of Debtor's Address

(1) A debtor who changes his residence shall forthwith inform the court of his new address.
(2) Where the debtor becomes resident in the district of another court, the court in which the administration order is being conducted may transfer the proceedings to that other court.

## CCR ORDER 44
## THE AGRICULTURAL HOLDINGS ACT 1986

### Rule 4 Enforcement of Order Imposing Penalty

(1) When taking any proceedings for the enforcement in a county court of an order under section 27 of the Agricultural Holdings Act 1986, the party in whose favour the order was made shall file—
   (a) a certified copy of the order; and
   (b) a certificate specifying the amount due under the order and stating whether any previous proceedings have been taken for its enforcement and, if so, the nature of the proceedings and their result.
(2) Where it is desired to enforce the order by warrant of execution, the proceedings may be taken in any court in the district of which execution is to be levied.

## CCR ORDER 45
## THE REPRESENTATION OF THE PEOPLE ACT 1983

### Rule 2 Appeal from Decision of Registration Officer

(1) Where notice of appeal from a decision of a registration officer is given pursuant to regulations made under section 53 of the said Act of 1983 the registration officer shall, within 7 days after receipt of the notice by him, forward the notice by post to the court in which the appeal is required to be brought, together with the statement mentioned in those regulations.
(2) The appeal shall be brought in the court for the district in which the qualifying premises are situated.

In this paragraph 'qualifying premises' means the premises in respect of which—
(a) the person whose right to be registered in the register of electors is in question on the appeal is entered on the electors' list or is registered or claims to be entitled to be registered; or
(b) the person whose right to vote by proxy or by post is in question on the appeal is or will be registered in the register of electors; or
(c) the elector whose proxy's right to vote by post is in question on the appeal is or will be registered in the register of electors, as the case may be.

(3) The respondents to the appeal shall be the registration officer and the party (if any) in whose favour the decision of the registration officer was given.

(4) On the hearing of the appeal—
(a) the statement forwarded to the court by the registration officer and any document containing information furnished to the court by the registration officer pursuant to the regulations mentioned in paragraph (1) shall be admissible as evidence of the facts stated therein; and
(b) the judge shall have power to draw all inferences of fact which might have been drawn by the registration officer and to give any decision and make any order which ought to have been given or made by the registration officer.

(5) A respondent to an appeal other than the registration officer shall not be liable for or entitled to costs, unless he appears before the court in support of the decision of the registration officer.

### Rule 3 Selected Appeals

(1) Where two or more appeals to which rule 2 relates involve the same point of law, the judge may direct that one appeal shall be heard in the first instance as a test case and thereupon the court shall send a notice of the direction to the parties to the selected appeal and the parties to the other appeals.

(2) If within 7 days after service of such notice on him any party to an appeal other than the selected appeal gives notice to the court that he desires the appeal to which he is a party to be heard—
(a) the appeal shall be heard after the selected appeal is disposed of;
(b) the court shall give the parties to the appeal notice of the day on which it will be heard;
(c) the party giving notice under this paragraph shall not be entitled to receive any costs occasioned by the separate hearing of the appeal to which he is a party, unless the judge otherwise orders.

(3) If no notice is given under paragraph (2) within the time limited—
(a) the decision on the selected appeal shall bind the parties to each other appeal without prejudice to their right to appeal to the Court of Appeal;
(b) an order similar to the order in the selected appeal shall be made in each other appeal without further hearing;
(c) the party to each other appeal who is in the same interest as the unsuccessful party to the selected appeal shall be liable for the costs of the selected appeal in the same manner and to the same extent as the unsuccessful party to that appeal and an order directing him to pay such costs may be made and enforced accordingly.

## CCR ORDER 49
## MISCELLANEOUS STATUTES

### Rule 18A Telecommunications Act 1984

CPR Rule 35.15 applies to proceedings under paragraph 5 of Schedule 2 to the Telecommunications Act 1984.

## Rule 19 Trade Union and Labour Relations Consolidation Act 1992

(1) Where a complainant desires to have an order of the Certification Officer under section 82 of the Trade Union and Labour Relations Consolidation Act 1992 recorded in the county court, he shall produce the order and a copy thereof to the court for the district in which he resides or the head or main office of the trade union is situate.
(2) The order shall be recorded by filing it, and the copy shall be sealed and dated and returned to the complainant.
(3) The sealed copy shall be treated as if it were the notice of issue in a claim begun by the complainant.
(4) The costs, if any, allowed for recording the order shall be recoverable as if they were payable under the order.
(5) The order shall not be enforced until proof is given to the satisfaction of the court that the order has not been obeyed and, if the order is for payment of money, of the amount remaining unpaid.

# Practice Direction — Competition Law — Claims Relating to the Application of Articles 81 and 82 of the EC Treaty and Chapters I and II of Part I of the Competition Act 1998

## Scope and Interpretation

1.1 This practice direction applies to any claim relating to the application of—
   (a) Article 81 or Article 82 of the Treaty establishing the European Community; or
   (b) Chapter I or Chapter II of Part I of the Competition Act 1998.

1.2 In this practice direction—
   (a) 'the Act' means the Competition Act 1998;
   (b) 'the Commission' means the European Commission;
   (c) 'the Competition Regulation' means Council Regulation (EC) No. 1/2003 of 16 December 2002 on the implementation of the rules on competition laid down in Articles 81 and 82 of the Treaty;
   (d) 'national competition authority' means—
      (i) the Office of Fair Trading; and
      (ii) any other person or body designated pursuant to Article 35 of the Competition Regulation as a national competition authority of the United Kingdom;
   (e) 'the Treaty' means the Treaty establishing the European Community.

## Venue

2.1 A claim to which this Practice Direction applies—
   (a) must be commenced in the High Court at the Royal Courts of Justice; and
   (b) will be assigned to the Chancery Division, unless it comes within the scope of rule 58.1(2), in which case it will be assigned to the Commercial Court of the Queen's Bench Division.

2.2 Any party whose statement of case raises an issue relating to the application of Article 81 or 82 of the Treaty, or Chapter I or II of Part I of the Act, must—
   (a) state that fact in his statement of case; and
   (b) apply for the proceedings to be transferred to the Chancery Division at the Royal Courts of Justice, if they have not been commenced there, or in the Commercial or Admiralty Courts; or
   (c) apply for the transfer of the proceedings to the Commercial Court, in accordance with rules 58.4(2) and 30.5(3). If such application is refused, the proceedings must be transferred to the Chancery Division of the High Court at the Royal Courts of Justice.

2.3 Rule 30.8 provides that where proceedings are taking place in the Queen's Bench Division (other than proceedings in the Commercial or Admiralty Courts), a district registry of the High Court or a county court, the court must transfer the proceedings to the Chancery Division at the Royal Courts of Justice if the statement of case raises an issue relating to the application of Article 81 or 82, or Chapter I or II.
However, if any such proceedings which have been commenced in the Queen's Bench Division or a mercantile court fall within the scope of rule 58.1(2), any party to those proceedings may apply for the transfer of the proceedings to the Commercial Court, in accordance with rules 58.4(2) and 30.5(3). If the application is refused, the proceedings must be transferred to the Chancery Division of the High Court at the Royal Courts of Justice.

2.4 Where proceedings are commenced in or transferred to the Chancery Division at the Royal Courts of Justice in accordance with this paragraph, that court may transfer the proceedings or any part of the proceedings to another court if—
(a) the issue relating to the application of Article 81 or 82, or Chapter I or II, has been resolved; or
(b) the judge considers that the proceedings or part of the proceedings to be transferred does not involve any issue relating to the application of Article 81 or 82, or Chapter I or II.
(Rule 30.3 sets out the matters to which the court must have regard when considering whether to make a transfer order.)

## Notice of Proceedings

3 Any party whose statement of case raises or deals with an issue relating to the application of Article 81 or 82, or Chapter I or II, must serve a copy of the statement of case on the Office of Fair Trading at the same time as it is served on the other parties to the claim (addressed to the Director of Competition Policy Co-ordination, Office of Fair Trading, Fleetbank House, 2–6 Salisbury Square, London EC4Y 8JX).

## Case Management

4.1 Attention is drawn to the provisions of article 15.3 of the Competition Regulation (co-operation with national courts), which entitles competition authorities and the Commission to submit written observations to national courts on issues relating to the application of Article 81 or 82 and, with the permission of the court in question, to submit oral observations to the court.

4.1A A national competition authority may also make written observations to the court, or apply for permission to make oral observations, on issues relating to the application of Chapter I or II.

4.2 If a national competition authority or the Commission intends to make written observations to the court, it must give notice of its intention to do so by letter to Chancery Chambers at the Royal Courts of Justice (including the claim number and addressed to the Court Manager, Room TM 6.06, Royal Courts of Justice, Strand, London WC2A 2LL) at the earliest reasonable opportunity.

4.3 An application by a national competition authority or the Commission for permission to make oral representations at the hearing of a claim must be made by letter to Chancery Chambers (including the claim number and addressed to the Court Manager, Room TM 6.06, Royal Courts of Justice, Strand, London WC2A 2LL) at the earliest reasonable opportunity, identifying the claim and indicating why the applicant wishes to make oral representations.

4.4 If a national competition authority or the Commission files a notice under paragraph 4.2 or an application under paragraph 4.3, it must at the same time serve a copy of the notice or application on every party to the claim.

4.5 Any request by a national competition authority or the Commission for the court to send it any documents relating to a claim should be made at the same time as filing a notice under paragraph 4.2 or an application under paragraph 4.3.

4.6 Where the court receives a notice under paragraph 4.2 it may give case management directions to the national competition authority or the Commission, including directions about the date by which any written observations are to be filed.

4.7 The court will serve on every party to the claim a copy of any directions given or order made—
(a) on an application under paragraph 4.3; or
(b) under paragraph 4.6.

4.8 In any claim to which this practice direction applies, the court shall direct a pre-trial review to take place shortly before the trial, if possible before the judge who will be conducting the trial.

## Avoidance of Conflict with Commission Decisions

5.1 In relation to claims which raise an issue relating to the application of Article 81 or 82 of the Treaty, attention is drawn to the provisions of article 16 of the Competition Regulation (uniform application of Community competition law).

5.2 Every party to such a claim, and any national competition authority which has been served with a copy of a party's statement of case, is under a duty to notify the court at any stage of the proceedings if they are aware that—

(a) the Commission has adopted, or is contemplating adopting, a decision in relation to proceedings which it has initiated; and

(b) the decision referred to in (a) above has or would have legal effects in relation to the particular agreement, decision or practice in issue before the court.

5.3 Where the court is aware that the Commission is contemplating adopting a decision as mentioned in paragraph 5.2(a), it shall consider whether to stay the claim pending the Commission's decision.

## Judgments

6 Where any judgment is given which decides on the application of Article 81 or Article 82 of the Treaty, the judge shall direct that a copy of the transcript of the judgment shall be sent to the Commission.

Judgments may be sent to the Commission electronically to comp-amicus@cec.eu.int or by post to the European Commission—DG Competition, B-1049, Brussels.

# CPR Specialist Practice Direction

# Practice Direction — Insolvency Proceedings

## PART ONE

### 1. General

1.1 In this practice direction:

(1) 'the Act' means the Insolvency Act 1986 and includes the Act as applied to limited liability partnerships by the Limited Liability Partnerships Regulations 2001 (SI 2001/1090);

(2) 'the Insolvency Rules' means the rules for the time being in force and made under s. 411 and s. 412 of the Act in relation to insolvency proceedings;*

(3) 'CPR' means the Civil Procedure Rules and 'CPR' followed by a Part or rule by number means the Part or rule with that number in those Rules;

(4) 'RSC' followed by an Order by number means the Order with that number set out in sch. 1 to the CPR;

(5) 'insolvency proceedings' means any proceedings under the Act, the Insolvency Rules, the Administration of Insolvent Estates of Deceased Persons Order 1986 (SI 1986/1999), the Insolvent Partnerships Order 1986 (SI 1986/2124), the Insolvent Partnerships Order 1994 (SI 1994/2421) or the Limited Liability Partnerships Regulations 2001.

(6) references to a 'company' shall include a limited liability partnership and references to a 'contributory' shall include a member of a limited liability partnership.

1.2 This practice direction shall come into effect on 26 April 1999 and shall replace all previous practice notes and practice directions relating to insolvency proceedings.

1.3 Except where the Insolvency Rules otherwise provide, service of documents in insolvency proceedings in the High Court will be the responsibility of the parties and will not be undertaken by the court.

1.4 Where r. 2.4 of the CPR provides for the court to perform any act, that act may be performed by a registrar in bankruptcy for the purpose of insolvency proceedings in the High Court.

1.5 A writ of execution to enforce any order made in insolvency proceedings in the High Court may be issued on the authority of a registrar.

1.6 (1) This paragraph applies where an insolvency practitioner ('the outgoing office holder') holds office as a liquidator, administrator, trustee or supervisor in more than one case and dies, retires from practice as an insolvency practitioner or is otherwise unable or unwilling to continue in office.

(2) A single application may be made to a judge of the Chancery Division of the High Court by way of ordinary application in form 7.2 for the appointment of a substitute office holder or office holders in all cases in which the outgoing office holder holds office, and for the transfer of each such case to the High Court for the purpose only of making such an order.

(3) The application may be made by any of the following:

(i) the outgoing office holder (if he is able and willing to do so);

(ii) any person who holds office jointly with the outgoing office holder;

(iii) any person who is proposed to be appointed as a substitute for the outgoing office holder; or

(iv) any creditor in the cases where the substitution is proposed to be made.

[* The text issued by the Department for Constitutional Affairs refers to an earlier version of the practice direction.]

(4) The outgoing office holder (if he is not the applicant) and every person who holds office jointly with the office holder must be made a respondent to the application, but it is not necessary to join any other person as a respondent or to serve the application upon any other person unless the judge or registrar in the High Court so directs.

(5) The application should contain schedules setting out the nature of the office held, the identity of the court currently having jurisdiction over each case and its name and number.

(6) The application must be supported by evidence setting out the circumstances which have given rise to the need to make a substitution and exhibiting the written consent to act of each person who is proposed to be appointed in place of the outgoing office holder.

(7) The judge will in the first instance consider the application on paper and make such order as he thinks fit. In particular he may do any of the following:

(i) make an order directing the transfer to the High Court of those cases not already within its jurisdiction for the purpose only of the substantive application;

(ii) if he considers that the papers are in order and that the matter is straightforward, make an order on the substantive application;

(iii) give any directions which he considers to be necessary including (if appropriate) directions for the joinder of any additional respondents or requiring the service of the application on any person or requiring additional evidence to be provided;

(iv) if he does not himself make an order on the substantive application when the matter is first before him, give directions for the further consideration of the substantive application by himself or another judge of the Chancery Division or adjourn the substantive application to the registrar for him to make such order upon it as is appropriate.

(8) An order of the kind referred to in [sub-paragraph (7)(i)*] shall follow the draft order in form PDIP 3 set out in the schedule hereto and an order granting the substantive application shall follow the draft order in form PDIP 4 set out in the schedule hereto (subject in each case to such modifications as may be necessary or appropriate).

(9) It is the duty of the applicant to ensure that a sealed copy of every order transferring any case to the High Court and of every order which is made on a substantive application is lodged with the court having jurisdiction over each case affected by such order for filing on the court file relating to that case.

(10) It will not be necessary for the file relating to any case which is transferred to the High Court in accordance with this paragraph to be sent to the High Court unless a judge or registrar so directs.

## PART TWO COMPANIES

### 2. Advertisement of Winding-up Petition

2.1 Rule 4.11(2)(b) of IR 1986 is mandatory, and designed to ensure that the class remedy of winding up by the court is made available to all creditors, and is not used as a means of putting pressure on the company to pay the petitioner's debt. Failure to comply with the rule, without good reason accepted by the court, may lead to the summary dismissal of the petition on the return date (IR 1986, r. 4.11(5)). If the court, in its discretion, grants an adjournment, this will be on condition that the petition is advertised in due

[* These are the Insolvency Rules 1986 (SI 1986/1925), abbreviated as IR 1986.]

time for the adjourned hearing. No further adjournment for the purpose of advertisement will normally be granted.

2.2 Copies of every advertisement published in connection with a winding-up petition must be lodged with the court as soon as possible after publication and in any event not later than the day specified in IR 1986, r. 4.14. This direction applies even if the advertisement is defective in any way (eg is published at a date not in accordance with the Insolvency Rules, or omits or misprints some important words) or if the petitioner decides not to pursue the petition (eg on receiving payment).

## 3. Certificate of Compliance—Time For Filing

3.1 In the High Court in order to assist practitioners and the court the time laid down by IR 1986, r. 4.14, for filing a certificate of compliance and a copy of the advertisement, is hereby extended to not later than 4.30 p.m. on the Friday preceding the day on which the petition is to be heard. Applications to file the certificate and the copy advertisement after 4.30 p.m. on the Friday will only be allowed if some good reason is shown for the delay.

## 4. Errors in Petitions

4.1 Applications for leave to amend errors in petitions which are discovered subsequent to a winding-up order being made should be made to the court manager in the High Court and to the district judge in the county court.

4.2 Where the error is an error in the name of the company, the court manager in the High Court and the district judge in the county court may make any necessary amendments to ensure that the winding-up order is drawn with the correct name of the company inserted. If there is any doubt, e.g. where there might be another company in existence which could be confused with the company to be wound up, the court manager will refer the application to the registrar and the district judge may refer it to the judge.

4.3 Where an error is an error in the registered office of the company and any director or member of the company claims that the company was unaware of the petition by reason of it having been served at the wrong registered office, it will be open to them to apply to rescind the winding-up order in the usual way.

4.4 Where it is discovered that the company had been struck off the register of companies prior to the winding-up order being made, the matter must be restored to the list before the order is entered to enable an order for the restoration of the name to be made as well as the order to wind up.

## 5. Distribution of Business

5.1 The following applications shall be made direct to the judge and, unless otherwise ordered, shall be heard in public:

(1) applications to commit any person to prison for contempt;
(2) applications for urgent interim relief (e.g. applications pursuant to s. 127 of the Act prior to any winding-up order being made);
(3) applications to restrain the presentation or advertisement of a petition to wind up; or
(4) applications for the appointment of a provisional liquidator;
(5) petitions for administration orders or an interim order upon such a petition;
(6) applications after an administration order has been made pursuant to s. 14(3) of the Act (for directions) or s. 18(3) of the Act (to vary or discharge the order);
(7) petitions to discharge administration orders and to wind up;
(8) applications pursuant to s. 5(3) of the Act (to stay a winding up or discharge an administration order or for directions) where a voluntary arrangement has been approved;
(9) appeals from a decision made by a county court or by a registrar of the High Court.

5.2 Subject to para. 5.4 below all other applications shall be made to the registrar or the district judge in the first instance who may give any necessary directions and may, in the exercise of his discretion, either hear and determine it himself or refer it to the judge.

5.3 The following matters will also be heard in public:
(1) petitions to wind up;
(2) public examinations;
(3) all matters and applications heard by the judge, except those referred by the registrar or the district judge to be heard in private or so directed by the judge to be heard.

5.4 In accordance with directions given by the Lord Chancellor the registrar has authorised certain applications in the High Court to be dealt with by the court manager of the Companies Court, pursuant to IR 1986, r. 13.2(2). The applications are:
(1) to extend or abridge time prescribed by the Insolvency Rules in connection with winding up (IR 1986, rr. 4.3 and 12.9);
(2) for substituted service of winding-up petitions (IR 1986, r. 4.8(6));
(3) to withdraw petitions (IR 1986, r. 4.15);
(4) for the substitution of a petitioner (IR 1986, r. 4.19);
(5) by the official receiver for limited disclosure of a statement of affairs (IR 1986, r. 4.35);
(6) by the official receiver for relief from duties imposed upon him by the rules (IR 1986, r. 4.47);
(7) by the official receiver for permission to give notice of a meeting by advertisement only (IR 1986, r. 4.59);
(8) to transfer proceedings from the High Court to a county court (IR 1986, r. 7.11);
(9) for permission to amend any originating application.

(NB In district registries all such applications must be made to the district judge.)

## 6. Drawing Up of Orders

6.1 The court will draw up all orders except orders on the application of the official receiver or for which the Treasury Solicitor is responsible under the existing practice.

## 7. Rescission of a Winding-up Order

7.1 Any application for the rescission of a winding-up order shall be made within 7 days after the date on which the order was made (IR 1986, r. 7.47(4)). Notice of any such application must be given to the official receiver.

7.2 Applications will only be entertained if made (a) by a creditor, or (b) by a contributory, or (c) by the company jointly with a creditor or with a contributory. The application must be supported by written evidence of assets and liabilities.

7.3 In the case of an unsuccessful application the costs of the petitioning creditor, the supporting creditors and of the official receiver will normally be ordered to be paid by the creditor or the contributory making or joining in the application. The reason for this is that if the costs of an unsuccessful application are made payable by the company, they fall unfairly on the general body of creditors.

7.4 Cases in which the making of the winding-up order has not been opposed may, if the application is made promptly, be dealt with on a statement by the applicant's legal representative of the circumstances; but apart from such cases, the court will normally require any application to be supported by written evidence.

7.5 There is no need to issue a form of application (form 7.2) as the petition is restored before the court.

## 8. Restraint of Presentation of a Winding-up Petition

8.1 An application to restrain presentation of a winding-up petition must be made to the judge by the issue of an originating application (form 7.1).

## PART THREE PERSONAL INSOLVENCY — BANKRUPTCY

### 9. Distribution of Business

9.1 The following applications shall be made direct to the judge and unless otherwise ordered shall be heard in public:
(1) applications for the committal of any person to prison for contempt;
(2) application for injunctions or for the modification or discharge of injunctions;
(3) applications for interlocutory relief or directions after the matter has been referred to the judge.

9.2 All other applications shall be made to the registrar or the district judge in the first instance. He shall give any necessary directions and may, if the application is within his jurisdiction to determine, in his discretion either hear and determine it himself or refer it to the judge.

9.3 The following matters shall be heard in public:
(1) the public examination of debtors;
(2) opposed applications for discharge or for the suspension or lifting of the suspension of discharge;
(3) opposed applications for permission to be a director;
(4) in any case where the petition was presented or the receiving order or order for adjudication was made before the appointed day, those matters and applications specified in r. 8 of the Bankruptcy Rules 1952;
(5) all matters and applications heard by the judge, except matters and applications referred by the registrar or the district judge to be heard by the judge in private or directed by the judge to be so heard.

9.4 All petitions presented will be listed under the name of the debtor.

9.5 In accordance with directions given by the Lord Chancellor the registrar has authorised certain applications in the High Court to be dealt with by the court manager of the Bankruptcy Court pursuant to IR 1986, r. 13.2(2). The applications are:
(1) by petitioning creditors: to extend time for hearing petitions (s. 376 of the Act);
(2) by the official receiver:
(a) to transfer proceedings from the High Court to a county court (IR 1986, r. 7.13);
(b) to amend the full title of the proceedings (IR 1986, rr. 6.35 and 6.47).

(NB In district registries all such applications must be made to the district judge.)

### 10. Service Abroad of Statutory Demand

10.1 A statutory demand is not a document issued by the court. Leave to serve out of the jurisdiction is not, therefore, required.

10.2 Rule 6.3(2) of IR 1986 (requirements as to service) applies to service of the statutory demand whether outside or within the jurisdiction.

10.3 A creditor wishing to serve a statutory demand outside the jurisdiction in a foreign country with which a civil procedure convention has been made (including the Hague Convention) may and, if the assistance of a British consul is desired, must adopt the procedure prescribed by CPR, r. 6.25. In the case of any doubt whether the country is a 'convention country', enquiries should be made of the Queen's Bench Masters' Secretary Department, Room E216, Royal Courts of Justice.

10.4 In all other cases, service of the demand must be effected by private arrangement in accordance with IR 1986, r. 6.3(2), and local foreign law.

10.5 When a statutory demand is to be served out of the jurisdiction, the time limits of 21 days and 18 days respectively referred to in the demand must be amended. For this purpose reference should be made to the table set out in PD 6B.

10.6 A creditor should amend the statutory demand as follows:

(1) for any reference to 18 days there must be substituted the appropriate number of days set out in the table plus 4 days, and
(2) for any reference to 21 days must be substituted the appropriate number of days in the table plus 7 days.

Attention is drawn to the fact that in all forms of the statutory demand the figure 18 and the figure 21 occur in more than one place.

## 11. Substituted Service

*Statutory Demands*

11.1 The creditor is under an obligation to do all that is reasonable to bring the statutory demand to the debtor's attention and, if practicable, to cause personal service to be effected. Where it is not possible to effect prompt personal service, service may be effected by other means such as first class post or by insertion through a letter box.

11.2 Advertisement can only be used as a means of substituted service where:
(1) the demand is based on a judgment or order of any court;
(2) the debtor has absconded or is keeping out of the way with a view to avoiding service; and
(3) there is no real prospect of the sum due being recovered by execution or other process.

As there is no statutory form of advertisement, the court will accept an advertisement in the following form:

STATUTORY DEMAND

(Debt for liquidated sum payable immediately following a judgment or order of the court)

---

To (Block letters)

of

TAKE NOTICE that a statutory demand has been issued by:

Name of Creditor:

Address:

The creditor demands payment of £ the amount now due on a judgment or order of the (High Court of Justice Division) (........... County Court) dated the day of 200 .

The statutory demand is an important document and it is deemed to have been served on you on the date of the first appearance of this advertisement. You must deal with this demand within 21 days of the service upon you or you could be made bankrupt and your property and goods taken away from you. If you are in any doubt as to your position, you should seek advice immediately from a solicitor or your nearest Citizens' Advice Bureau. The statutory demand can be obtained or is available for inspection and collection from:

Name:

Address:

(Solicitor for) the Creditor

Tel. No. Reference:

You have only 21 days from the date of the first appearance of this advertisement before the creditor may present a bankruptcy petition. You have only 18 days from that date within which to apply to the court to set aside the demand.

11.3 In all cases where substituted service is effected, the creditor must have taken all those steps which would justify the court making an order for substituted service of a petition. The steps to be taken to obtain an order for substituted service of a petition are set out below. Failure to comply with these requirements may result in the court declining to file the petition (IR 1986, r. 6.11(9)).

*Petitions*

11.4 In most cases, evidence of the following steps will suffice to justify an order for substituted service:

(1) One personal call at the residence and place of business of the debtor where both are known or at either of such places as is known. Where it is known that the debtor has more than one residential or business address, personal calls should be made at all the addresses.

(2) Should the creditor fail to effect service, a first class prepaid letter should be written to the debtor referring to the call(s), the purpose of the same and the failure to meet with the debtor, adding that a further call will be made for the same purpose on the day of 20 at hours at (place). At least two business days' notice should be given of the appointment and copies of the letter sent to all known addresses of the debtor. The appointment letter should also state that:

(a) in the event of the time and place not being convenient, the debtor is to name some other time and place reasonably convenient for the purpose;

(b) (Statutory Demands) if the debtor fails to keep the appointment the creditor proposes to serve the debtor by [advertisement] [post] [insertion through a letter box] or as the case may be, and that, in the event of a bankruptcy petition being presented, the court will be asked to treat such service as service of the demand on the debtor;

(c) (Petitions) if the debtor fails to keep the appointment, application will be made to the court for an order for substituted service either by advertisement, or in such other manner as the court may think fit.

(3) In attending any appointment made by letter, inquiry should be made as to whether the debtor has received all letters left for him. If the debtor is away, inquiry should also be made as to whether or not letters are being forwarded to an address within the jurisdiction (England and Wales) or elsewhere.

(4) If the debtor is represented by a solicitor, an attempt should be made to arrange an appointment for personal service through such solicitor. The Insolvency Rules enable a Solicitor to accept service of a statutory demand on behalf of his client but there is no similar provision in respect of service of a bankruptcy petition.

(5) The written evidence filed pursuant to IR 1986, r. 6.11, should deal with all the above matters including all relevant facts as to the debtor's whereabouts and whether the appointment letter(s) have been returned.

11.5 Where the court makes an order for service by first class ordinary post, the order will normally provide that service be deemed to be effected on the seventh day after posting. The same method of calculating service may be applied to calculating the date of service of a statutory demand.

## 12. Setting Aside a Statutory Demand

12.1 The application (form 6.4) and written evidence in support (form 6.5) exhibiting a copy of the statutory demand must be filed in court within 18 days of service of the statutory demand on the debtor. Where service is effected by advertisement in a newspaper the period of 18 days is calculated from the date of the first appearance of the advertisement. Three copies of each document must be lodged with the application to enable the court to serve notice of the hearing date on the applicant, the creditor and the person named in part B of the statutory demand.

12.2 Where, to avoid expense, copies of the documents are not lodged with the application in the High Court, any order of the registrar fixing a venue is conditional upon copies of the documents being lodged on the next business day after the registrar's order otherwise the application will be deemed to have been dismissed.

12.3 Where the statutory demand is based on a judgment or order, the court will not at this stage go behind the judgment or order and inquire into the validity of the debt nor, as a general rule, will it adjourn the application to await the result of an application to set aside the judgment or order.

12.4 Where the debtor (a) claims to have a counterclaim, set-off or cross-demand (whether or not he could have raised it in the action in which the judgment or order was obtained) which equals or exceeds the amount of the debt or debts specified in the statutory demand or (b) disputes the debt (not being a debt subject to a judgment or order) the court will normally set aside the statutory demand if, in its opinion, on the evidence there is a genuine triable issue.

12.5 A debtor who wishes to apply to set aside a statutory demand after the expiration of 18 days from the date of service of the statutory demand must apply for an extension of time within which to apply. If the applicant wishes to apply for an injunction to restrain presentation of a petition the application must be made to the judge. Paragraphs 1 and 2 of form 6.5 (affidavit in support of application to set aside statutory demand) should be used in support of the application for an extension of time with the following additional paragraphs:

'3. That to the best of my knowledge and belief the creditor(s) named in the demand has/have not presented a petition against me.

4. That the reasons for my failure to apply to set aside the demand within 18 days after service are as follows: . . .'

If application is made to restrain presentation of a bankruptcy petition the following additional paragraph should be added:

'5. Unless restrained by injunction the creditor(s) may present a bankruptcy petition against me.'

## 13. Proof of Service of a Statutory Demand

13.1 Rule 6.11(3) of IR 1986 provides that, if the statutory demand has been served personally, the written evidence must be provided by the person who effected that service. Rule 6.11(4) of IR 1986 provides that, if service of the demand (however effected) has been acknowledged in writing, the evidence of service must be provided by the creditor or by a person acting on his behalf. Rule 6.11(5) of IR 1986 provides that, if neither paras (3) or (4) apply, the written evidence must be provided by a person having direct knowledge of the means adopted for serving the demand.

13.2 Form 6.11 (evidence of personal service of the statutory demand): this form should only be used where the demand has been served personally and acknowledged in writing (see IR 1986, r. 6.11(4)). If the demand has not been acknowledged in writing, the written evidence should be provided by the process server and paras 2 and 3 (part of form 6.11) should be omitted (see IR 1986, r. 6.11(3)).

13.3 Form 6.12 (evidence of substituted service of the statutory demand): this form can be used whether or not service of the demand has been acknowledged in writing. Paragraphs 4 and 5 (part) provide for the alternatives. Practitioners are reminded, however, that the appropriate person to provide the written evidence may not be the same in both cases. If the demand has been acknowledged in writing, the appropriate person is the creditor or a person acting on his behalf. If the demand has not been acknowledged, that person must be someone having direct knowledge of the means adopted for serving the demand.

Practitioners may find it more convenient to allow process servers to carry out the necessary investigation whilst reserving to themselves the service of the demand. In these circumstances para. 1 should be deleted and the following paragraph substituted:

'1. Attempts have been made to serve the demand, full details of which are set out in the accompanying affidavit of . . .'.

13.4 'Written evidence' means an affidavit or a witness statement.

## 14. Extension of Hearing Date of Petition

14.1 Late applications for extension of hearing dates under IR 1986, r. 6.28, and failure to attend on the listed hearing of a petition, will be dealt with as follows:

(1) If an application is submitted less than two clear working days before the hearing date (for example, later than Monday for Thursday, or Wednesday for Monday) the costs of the application will not be allowed under IR 1986, r. 6.28(3).

(2) If the petition has not been served and no extension has been granted by the time fixed for the hearing of the petition, and if no one attends for the hearing, the petition will be re-listed for hearing about 21 days later. The court will notify the petitioning creditor's solicitors (or the petitioning creditor in person), and any known supporting or opposing creditors or their solicitors, of the new date and times. Written evidence should then be filed on behalf of the petitioning creditor explaining fully the reasons for the failure to apply for an extension or to appear at the hearing, and (if appropriate) giving reasons why the petition should not be dismissed.

(3) On the re-listed hearing the court may dismiss the petition if not satisfied it should be adjourned or a further extension granted.

14.2 All applications for extension should include a statement of the date fixed for the hearing of the petition.

14.3 The petitioning creditor should attend (by solicitors or in person) on or before the hearing date to ascertain whether the application has reached the file and been dealt with. It should not be assumed that an extension will be granted.

## 15. Bankruptcy Petition

To help in the completion of the form of a creditor's bankruptcy petition, attention is drawn to the following points:

15.1 The petition does not require dating, signing or witnessing.

15.2 In the title it is only necessary to recite the debtor's name e.g. Re John William Smith or Re J W Smith (Male). Any alias or trading name will appear in the body of the petition. This also applies to all other statutory forms other than those which require the 'full title'.

15.3 Where the petition is based on a statutory demand, only the debt claimed in the demand may be included in the petition.

15.4 In completing para. 2 of the petition, attention is drawn to IR 1986, r. 6.8(1)(a) to (c), particularly where the 'aggregate sum' is made up of a number of debts.

15.5 Date of service of the statutory demand (para. 4 of the petition):

(1) In the case of personal service, the date of service as set out in the affidavit of service should be recited and whether service is effected *before/after* 1700 hours on Monday to Friday or at any time on a Saturday or a Sunday: see CPR, r. 6.7(2) and (3).

(2) In the case of substituted service (otherwise than by advertisement), the date alleged in the affidavit of service should be recited: see para. 11 above.

(3) In the strictly limited case of service by advertisement under IR 1986, r. 6.3, the date to be alleged is the date of the advertisement's appearance or, as the case may be, its first appearance: see IR 1986, rr. 6.3(3) and 6.11(8).

15.6 There is no need to include in the petition details of the person authorised to present it.

15.7 Certificates at the end of the petition:

(1) The period of search for prior petitions has been reduced to 18 months.

(2) Where a statutory demand is based wholly or in part on a county court judgment, the following certificate is to be added:
'I/We certify that on the day of 20 I/We attended on the County Court and was/were informed by an officer of the Court that no money

had been paid into Court in the action or matter v Claim No. pursuant to the statutory demand.'

This certificate will not be required when the demand also requires payment of a separate debt, not based on a county court judgment, the amount of which exceeds the bankruptcy level (at present £750).

15.8 Deposit on petition: the deposit will be taken by the court and forwarded to the official receiver. In the High Court, the petition fee and deposit should be handed to the Supreme Court Accounts Office, Fee Stamping Room, who will record the receipt and will impress two entries on the original petition, one in respect of the court fee and the other in respect of the deposit. In the county court, the petition fee and deposit should be handed to the duly authorised officer of the court's staff who will record its receipt.

In all cases cheque(s) for the whole amount should be made payable to 'HM Pay-master General'.

15.9 On the hearing of a petition for a bankruptcy order, in order to satisfy the court that the debt on which the petition is founded has not been paid or secured or compounded the court will normally accept as sufficient a certificate signed by the person representing the petitioning creditor in the following form:

'I certify that I have/my firm has made enquiries of the petitioning creditor(s) within the last business day prior to the hearing/adjourned hearing and to the best of my knowledge and belief the debt on which the petition is founded is still due and owing and has not been paid or secured or compounded save as to ................

Signed .............. Dated ................'

For convenience in the High Court this certificate will be incorporated in the attendance slip, which will be filed after the hearing. A fresh certificate will be required on each adjourned hearing.

15.10 On the occasion of the adjourned hearing of a petition for a bankruptcy order, in order to satisfy the court that the petitioner has complied with IR 1986, r. 6.29, the petitioner will be required to file written evidence of the manner in which notice of the making of the order of adjournment and of the venue for the adjourned hearing has been sent to:

(i) the debtor, and
(ii) any creditor who has given notice under IR 1986, r. 6.23, but was not present at the hearing when the order for adjournment was made.

## 16. Orders Without Attendance

16.1 In suitable cases the court will normally be prepared to make orders under Part VIII of the Act (individual voluntary arrangements), without the attendance of either party, provided there is no bankruptcy order in existence and (so far as is known) no pending petition. The orders are:

(1) A 14-day interim order with the application adjourned 14 days for consideration of the nominee's report, where the papers are in order, and the nominee's signed consent to act includes a waiver of notice of the application or a consent by the nominee to the making of an interim order without attendance.
(2) A standard order on consideration of the nominee's report, extending the interim order to a date seven weeks after the date of the proposed meeting, directing the meeting to be summoned and adjourning to a date about three weeks after the meeting. Such an order may be made without attendance if the nominee's report has been delivered to the court and complies with s. 256(1) of the Act and IR 1986, r. 5.10(2) and (3), and proposes a date for the meeting not less than 14 days from that on which the nominee's report is filed in court under IR 1986, r. 5.10, nor more than 28 days from that on which that report is considered by the court under IR 1986, r. 5.12.

(3) A 'concertina' order, combining orders as under (1) and (2) above. Such an order may be made without attendance if the initial application for an interim order is accompanied by a report of the nominee and the conditions set out in (1) and (2) above are satisfied.
(4) A final order on consideration of the chairman's report. Such an order may be made without attendance if the chairman's report has been filed and complies with IR 1986, r. 5.22(1). The order will record the effect of the chairman's report and may discharge the interim order.

16.2 Provided that the conditions as under para. 16.1(2) and (4) above are satisfied and that the appropriate report has been lodged with the court in due time the parties need not attend or be represented on the adjourned hearing for consideration of the nominee's report or of the chairman's report (as the case may be) unless they are notified by the court that attendance is required. Sealed copies of the order made (in all four cases as above) will be posted by the court to the applicant or his solicitor and to the nominee.

16.3 In suitable cases the court may also make consent orders without attendance by the parties. The written consent of the parties will be required. Examples of such orders are as follows:

(1) On applications to set aside a statutory demand, orders:
  (a) dismissing the application, with or without an order for costs as may be agreed (permission will be given to present a petition on or after the seventh day after the date of the order, unless a different date is agreed);
  (b) setting aside the demand, with or without an order for costs as may be agreed; or
  (c) giving permission to withdraw the application with or without an order for costs as may be agreed.
(2) On petitions: where there is a list of supporting or opposing creditors in form 6.21, or a statement signed by or on behalf of the petitioning creditor that no notices have been received from supporting or opposing creditors, orders:
  (a) dismissing the petition, with or without an order for costs as may be agreed; or
  (b) if the petition has not been served, giving permission to withdraw the petition (with no order for costs).
(3) On other applications, orders:
  (a) for sale of property, possession of property, disposal of proceeds of sale;
  (b) giving interim directions;
  (c) dismissing the application, with or without an order for costs as may be agreed;
  (d) giving permission to withdraw the application, with or without an order for costs as may be agreed.

If (as may often be the case with orders under sub-paras (3)(a) or (b) above) an adjournment is required, whether generally with liberty to restore or to a fixed date, the order by consent may include an order for the adjournment. If adjournment to a date is requested, a time estimate should be given and the court will fix the first available date and time on or after the date requested.

16.4 The above lists should not be regarded as exhaustive, nor should it be assumed that an order will be made without attendance as requested.

16.5 The procedure outlined above is designed to save time and costs but is not intended to discourage attendance.

16.6 Applications for consent orders without attendance should be lodged at least two clear working days (and preferably longer) before any fixed hearing date.

16.7 Whenever a document is lodged or a letter sent, the correct case number, code (if any) and year (for example 123/SD/99 or 234/99) should be quoted. A note should also be given of the date and time of the next hearing (if any).

16.8 Attention is drawn to [PD 43–48, para. 13.4*].

## 16A. Bankruptcy Restrictions Orders

*Making the application*

16A.1 An application for a bankruptcy restrictions order is made as an ordinary application in the bankruptcy.

16A.2 The application must be made within one year beginning with the date of the bankruptcy order unless the court gives permission for the application to be made after that period. The one year period does not run while the bankrupt's discharge has been suspended under section 279(3) of the Insolvency Act 1986.

16A.3 An application for a bankruptcy restrictions order may be made by the Secretary of State or the Official Receiver ('the Applicant'). The application must be supported by a report which must include:

(a) a statement of the conduct by reference to which it is alleged that it is appropriate for a bankruptcy restrictions order to be made; and

(b) the evidence relied on in support of the application (r. 6.241 of the Insolvency Rules 1986).

16A.4 The report is treated as if it were an affidavit (r. 7.9(2) of the Insolvency Rules 1986) and is prima facie evidence of any matter contained in it (r. 7.9(3)).

16A.5 The application may be supported by evidence from other witnesses which may be given by affidavit or (by reason of r. 7.57(5) of the Insolvency Rules 1986) by witness statement verified by a statement of truth.

16A.6 The court will fix a first hearing which must be not less than 8 weeks from the date when the hearing is fixed (r. 6.241(4) of the Insolvency Rules 1986).

16A.7 Notice of the application and the venue fixed by the court must be served by the Applicant on the bankrupt not more than 14 days after the application is made. Service of notice must be accompanied by a copy of the application together with the evidence in support and a form of acknowledgment of service.

16A.8 The bankrupt must file in court an acknowledgment of service not more than 14 days after service of the application on him, indicating whether or not he contests the application. If he fails to do so he may attend the hearing of the application but may not take part in the hearing unless the court gives permission.

*Opposing the application*

16A.9 If the bankrupt wishes to oppose the application, he must within 28 days of service on him of the application and the evidence in support (or such longer period as the court may allow) file in court and (within three days thereof) serve on the Applicant any evidence which he wishes the court to take into consideration. Such evidence should normally be in the form of an affidavit or a witness statement verified by a statement of truth.

16A.10 The Applicant must file any evidence in reply within 14 days of receiving the evidence of the bankrupt (or such longer period as the court may allow) and must serve it on the bankrupt as soon as reasonably practicable.

*Hearings*

16A.11 Any hearing of an application for a bankruptcy restrictions order must be in public (r. 6.241(5) Insolvency Rules 1986). The hearing will generally be before the registrar or district judge in the first instance who may:

(1) adjourn the application and give directions;

(2) make a bankruptcy restrictions order; or

(3) adjourn the application to the judge.

[* The text issued by the Department for Constitutional Affairs mistakenly refers to sub-paragraph (6)(i).]

*Making a bankruptcy restrictions order*

16A.12 When the court is considering whether to make a bankruptcy restrictions order, it must not take into account any conduct of the bankrupt prior to 1 April 2004 (art. 7 of the Enterprise Act (Commencement No 4 and Transitional Provisions and Savings) Order 2003).

16A.13 The court may make a bankruptcy restrictions order in the absence of the bankrupt and whether or not he has filed evidence (r. 6.244 of the Insolvency Rules 1986).

16A.14 When a bankruptcy restrictions order is made the court must send two sealed copies of the order to the Applicant (r. 6.244(2) of the Insolvency Rules 1986), and as soon as reasonably practicable after receipt, the Applicant must send one sealed copy to the bankrupt (r. 6.244(3)).

16A.15 A bankruptcy restrictions order comes into force when it is made and must specify the date on which it will cease to have effect, which must be between two and 15 years from the date on which it is made.

*Interim bankruptcy restrictions orders*

16A.16 An application for an interim bankruptcy restrictions order may be made any time between the institution of an application for a bankruptcy restrictions order and the determination of that application (Sch 4A, para. 5 of the Insolvency Act 1986). The application is made as an ordinary application in the bankruptcy.

16A.17 The application must be supported by a report as evidence in support of the application (rule 6.246(1) of the Insolvency Rules 1986) which must include evidence of the bankrupt's conduct which is alleged to constitute the grounds for making an interim bankruptcy restrictions order and evidence of matters relating to the public interest in making the order.

16A.18 Notice of the application must be given to the bankrupt at least two business days before the date fixed for the hearing unless the court directs otherwise (r. 6.245).

16A.19 Any hearing of the application must be in public (r. 6.245).

16A.20 The court may make an interim bankruptcy restrictions order in the absence of the bankrupt and whether or not he has filed evidence (r. 6.247).

16A.21 The bankrupt may apply to the court to set aside an interim bankruptcy restrictions order. The application is made by ordinary application in the bankruptcy and must be supported by an affidavit or witness statement verified by a statement of truth stating the grounds on which the application is made (r. 6.248(2)).

16A.22 The bankrupt must send the Secretary of State, not less than 7 days before the hearing, notice of his application, notice of the venue, a copy of his application and a copy of the supporting affidavit. The Secretary of State may attend the hearing and call the attention of the court to any matters which seem to him to be relevant, and may himself give evidence or call witnesses.

16A.23 Where the court sets aside an interim bankruptcy restrictions order, two sealed copies of the order must be sent by the court, as soon as reasonably practicable, to the Secretary of State.

16A.24 As soon as reasonably practicable after receipt of sealed copies of the order, the Secretary of State must send a sealed copy to the bankrupt.

*Bankruptcy restrictions undertakings*

16A.25 Where a bankrupt has given a bankruptcy restrictions undertaking, the Secretary of State must file a copy in court and send a copy to the bankrupt as soon as reasonably practicable (r. 6.250).

16A.26 The bankrupt may apply to annul a bankruptcy restrictions undertaking. The application is made as an ordinary application in the bankruptcy and must be supported by an affidavit or witness statement verified by a statement of truth stating the grounds on which it is made.

16A.27 The bankrupt must give notice of his application and the venue together with a copy of his affidavit in support to the Secretary of State at least 28 days before the date fixed for the hearing.

16A.28 The Secretary of State may attend the hearing and call the attention of the court to any matters which seem to him to be relevant and may himself give evidence or call witnesses.

16A.29 The court must send a sealed copy of any order annulling or varying the bankruptcy restrictions undertaking to the Secretary of State and the bankrupt.

## PART 4

### 17. Appeals in Insolvency Proceedings

17.1 This Part shall come into effect on 2 May 2000 and shall replace and revoke para. 17 of, and be read in conjunction with PD Insolvency Proceedings which came into effect on 26 April 1999 as amended.

17.2 (1) An appeal from a decision of a county court (whether made by a district judge or a circuit judge) or of a registrar of the High Court in insolvency proceedings ('a first appeal') lies to a judge of the High Court pursuant to s. 375(2) of the Act and IR 1986, rr. 7.47(2) and 7.48(2) (as amended by s. 55 of the Access to Justice Act 1999).

(2) The procedure and practice for a first appeal are governed by IR 1986, r. 7.49, which imports the procedure and practice of the Court of Appeal. The procedure and practice of the Court of Appeal are governed by CPR, Part 52, and PD 52, which are subject to the provisions of the Act, the Insolvency Rules and this practice direction: see CPR, r. 52.1(4).

(3) A first appeal (as defined above) does not include an appeal from a decision of a judge of the High Court.

17.3 (1) Section 55 of the Access to Justice Act 1999 has amended s. 375(2) of the Act and IR 1986, rr. 7.47(2) and 7.48(2), so that an appeal from a decision of a judge of the High Court made on a first appeal lies, with the permission of the Court of Appeal, to the Court of Appeal.

(2) An appeal from a judge of the High Court in insolvency proceedings which is not a decision on a first appeal lies, with the permission of the judge or of the Court of Appeal, to the Court of Appeal (see CPR, r. 52.3).

(3) The procedure and practice for appeals from a decision of a judge of the High Court in insolvency proceedings (whether made on a first appeal or not) are also governed by IR 1986, r. 7.49, which imports the procedure and practice of the Court of Appeal as stated at para. 17.2(2) above.

17.4 Part 52 of the CPR and its practice direction [PD 52] and forms apply to appeals from a decision of a judge of the High Court in insolvency proceedings.

17.5 An appeal from a decision of a judge of the High Court in insolvency proceedings requires permission as set out in para. 17.3(1) and (2) above.

17.6 A first appeal is subject to the permission requirement in CPR Part 52, rule 3.

17.7 Except as provided in this Part, CPR, Part 52, and its practice direction [PD 52] and forms do not apply to first appeals, but paras 17.8 to 17.23 inclusive of this Part apply only to first appeals.

17.8 Interpretation:

(a) the expressions 'appeal court', 'lower court', 'appellant', 'respondent' and 'appeal notice' have the meanings given in CPR, r. 52.1(3);

(b) 'registrar of appeals' means in relation to an appeal filed at the Royal Courts of Justice in London a bankruptcy registrar, and in relation to an appeal filed in a district registry in accordance with para. 17.10(2) and (3) below a district judge of the relevant district registry.

(c) 'appeal date' means the date fixed by the appeal court for the hearing of the appeal or the date fixed by the appeal court upon which the period within which the appeal will be heard commences.

17.9 An appellant's notice and a respondent's notice shall be in form PDIP 1 and PDIP 2 set out in the schedule hereto.

17.10 (1) An appeal from a decision of a Registrar in Bankruptcy shall, or from any decision made in any county court may, be filed at the Royal Courts of Justice in London.

(2) An appeal from a decision made in the county court exercising jurisdiction over an area within the Birmingham, Bristol, Cardiff, Leeds, Liverpool, Manchester, Newcastle upon Tyne or Preston Chancery district registries may be filed in the Chancery district registry of the High Court appropriate to the area in which the decision was made.

17.11 (1) Where a party seeks an extension of time in which to file an appeal notice it must be requested in the appeal notice and the appeal notice should state the reason for the delay and the steps taken prior to the application being made; the court will fix a date for the hearing of the application and notify the parties of the date and place of hearing;

(2) The appellant must file the appellant's notice at the appeal court within:
   (a) such period as may be directed by the lower court; or
   (b) where the court makes no such direction, 14 days after the date of the decision of the lower court which the appellant wishes to appeal.

(3) Unless the appeal court orders otherwise, an appeal notice must be served by the appellant on each respondent:
   (a) as soon as practicable; and
   (b) in any event not later than seven days, after it is filed.

17.12 (1) A respondent may file and serve a respondent's notice.

(2) A respondent who wishes to ask the appeal court to uphold the order of the lower court for reasons different from or additional to those given by the lower court must file a respondent's notice.

(3) A respondents notice must be filed within:
   (a) such period as may be directed by the lower court; or
   (b) where the court makes no such direction, 14 days after the date on which the respondent is served with the appellant's notice.

(4) Unless the appeal court orders otherwise a respondent's notice must be served by the respondent on the appellant and any other respondent:
   (a) as soon as practicable; and
   (b) in any event not later than seven days, after it is filed.

17.13 (1) An application to vary the time limit for filing an appeal notice must be made to the appeal court.

(2) The parties may not agree to extend any date or time limit set by:
   (a) this practice direction; or
   (b) an order of the appeal court or the lower court.

17.14 Unless the appeal court or the lower court orders otherwise an appeal shall not operate as a stay of any order or decision of the lower court.

17.15 An appeal notice may not be amended without the permission of the appeal court.

17.16 A judge of the appeal court may strike out the whole or part of an appeal notice where there is compelling reason for doing so.

17.17 (1) In relation to an appeal the appeal court has all the powers of the lower court.

(2) The appeal court has power to:
   (a) affirm, set aside or vary any order or judgment made or given by the lower court;
   (b) refer any claim or issue for determination by the lower court;
   (c) order a new trial or hearing;
   (d) make a costs order.

(3) The appeal court may exercise its powers in relation to the whole or part of an order of the lower court.

17.18 (1) Every appeal shall be limited to a review of the decision of the lower court.
(2) Unless it orders otherwise, the appeal court will not receive:
(a) oral evidence; or
(b) evidence which was not before the lower court.
(3) The appeal court will allow an appeal where the decision of the lower court was:
(a) wrong; or
(b) unjust because of a serious procedural or other irregularity in the proceedings in the lower court.
(4) The appeal court may draw any inference of fact which it considers justified on the evidence.
(5) At the hearing of the appeal a party may not rely on a matter not contained in his appeal notice unless the appeal court gives permission.

17.19 The following applications shall be made to a judge of the appeal court:
(1) for injunctions pending a substantive hearing of the appeal;
(2) for expedition or vacation of the hearing date of an appeal;
(3) for an order striking out the whole or part of an appeal notice pursuant to para.17.16 above;
(4) for a final order on paper pursuant to para. 17.22(8) below.

17.20 (1) All other interim applications shall be made to the registrar of appeals in the first instance who may in his discretion either hear and determine it himself or refer it to the judge.
(2) An appeal from a decision of a registrar of appeals lies to a judge of the appeal court and does not require the permission of either the registrar of appeals or the judge.

17.21 The procedure for interim applications is by way of ordinary application (see IR 1986, r. 12.7 and sch. 4, form 7.2).

17.22 The following practice applies to all first appeals to a judge of the High Court whether filed at the Royal Courts of Justice in London, or filed at one of the other venues referred to in para. 17.10 above:
(1) on filing an appellant's notice in accordance with para. 17.11(2) above, the appellant must file:
(a) two copies of the appeal notice for the use of the court, one of which must be stamped with the appropriate fee, and a number of additional copies equal to the number of persons who are to be served with it pursuant to para. 17.22(4) below;
(b) a copy of the order under appeal; and
(c) an estimate of time for the hearing.
(2) The above documents may be lodged personally or by post and shall be lodged at the address of the appropriate venue listed below:
(a) if the appeal is to be heard at the Royal Courts of Justice in London the documents must be lodged at Room 110, Thomas More Building, The Royal Courts of Justice, Strand, London WC2A 2LL;
(b) if the appeal is to be heard in Birmingham, the documents must be lodged at the District Registry of the Chancery Division of the High Court, 33 Bull Street, Birmingham B4 6DS;
(c) if the appeal is to be heard in Bristol the documents must be lodged at the District Registry of the Chancery Division of the High Court, Third Floor, Greyfriars, Lewins Mead, Bristol BS1 2NR;
(d) if the appeal is to be heard in Cardiff the documents must be lodged at the District Registry of the Chancery Division of the High Court, First Floor, 2 Park Street, Cardiff CF10 1ET;
(e) if the appeal is to be heard in Leeds the documents must be lodged at the

District Registry of the Chancery Division of the High Court, The Court House, 1 Oxford Row, Leeds LS1 3BG;

(f) if the appeal is to be heard in Liverpool the documents must be lodged at the District Registry of the Chancery Division of the High Court, Liverpool Combined Court Centre, Derby Square, Liverpool L2 1XA;

(g) if the appeal is to be heard in Manchester the documents must be lodged at the District Registry of the Chancery Division of the High Court, Courts of Justice, Crown Square, Manchester M60 9DJ;

(h) if the appeal is to be heard at Newcastle upon Tyne the documents must be lodged at the District Registry of the Chancery Division of the High Court, The Law Courts, Quayside, Newcastle upon Tyne NE1 3LA;

(i) if the appeal is to be heard in Preston the documents must be lodged at the District Registry of the Chancery Division of the High Court, The Combined Court Centre, Ringway, Preston PR1 2LL.

(3) If the documents are correct and in order the court at which the documents are filed will fix the appeal date and will also fix the place of hearing. That court will send letters to all the parties to the appeal informing them of the appeal date and of the place of hearing and indicating the time estimate given by the appellant. The parties will be invited to notify the court of any alternative or revised time estimates. In the absence of any such notification the estimate of the appellant will be taken as agreed. The court will also send to the appellant a document setting out the courts requirement concerning the form and content of the bundle of documents for the use of the judge. Not later than seven days before the appeal date the bundle of documents must be filed by the appellant at the address of the relevant venue as set out in sub-para. 17.22(2) above and a copy of it must be served by the appellant on each respondent. The bundle should include an approved transcript of the judgment of the lower court or, where there is no officially recorded judgment, the document(s) referred to in PD 52, para. 5.12.

(4) The appeal notice must be served on all parties to the proceedings in the lower court who are directly affected by the appeal. This may include the official receiver, liquidator or trustee in bankruptcy.

(5) The appeal notice must be served by the appellant or by the legal representative of the appellant and may be effected by:

(a) any of the methods referred to in CPR, r. 6.2; or

(b) with permission of the court, an alternative method pursuant to CPR, r. 6.8.

(6) Service of an appeal notice shall be proved by a certificate of service in accordance with CPR, r. 6.10 (CPR form N215) which must be filed at the relevant venue referred to at para. 17.22(2) above immediately after service.

(7) Skeleton arguments, accompanied by a written chronology of events relevant to the appeal, should be filed at the address of the appropriate venue as set out in para. 17.22(2) above, at least two clear days before the date fixed for the hearing. Failure to lodge may result in an adverse costs order being made by the judge on the hearing of the appeal.

(8) Where an appeal has been settled or where an appellant does not wish to continue with the appeal, the appeal may be disposed of on paper without a hearing. It may be dismissed by consent but the appeal court will not make an order allowing an appeal unless it is satisfied that the decision of the lower court was wrong. Any consent order signed by each party or letters of consent from each party must be lodged not later than 24 hours before the date fixed for the hearing of the appeal at the address of the appropriate venue as set out in para. 17.22(2) above and will be dealt with by the judge of the appeal court. Attention is drawn

to [PD 43–48, para. 13.4*] regarding costs where an order is made by consent without attendance.

17.23 Only the following paragraphs of PD 52, with any necessary modifications, shall apply to first appeals: 5.12 and 5.14 to 5.20 inclusive.

17.24 (1) Where, under the procedure relating to appeals in, insolvency proceedings prior to the coming into effect of this part of this practice direction, an appeal has been set down in the High Court or permission to appeal to the Court of Appeal has been granted before 2 May 2000, the procedure and practice set out in this part of this practice direction shall apply to such an appeal after that date.

(2) Where, under the procedure relating to appeals in insolvency proceedings prior to the coming into effect of this part of this practice direction, any person has failed before 2 May 2000 either:

(a) in the case of a first appeal, to set down in the High Court an appeal which relates to an order made (county court) or sealed (High Court) after 27 March 2000 and before 2 May 2000, or

(b) in the case of an appeal from a decision of a judge of the High Court, to obtain any requisite permission to appeal to the Court of Appeal which relates to an order sealed in the same period,

the time for filing an appeal notice is extended to 16 May 2000 and application for any such permission should be made in the appeal notice.

17.25 This paragraph applies where a judge of the High Court has made a bankruptcy order or a winding-up order or dismissed an appeal against such an order and an application is made for a stay of proceedings pending appeal.

(1) The judge will not normally grant a stay of all proceedings but will confine himself to a stay of advertisement of the proceedings.

(2) Where the judge has granted permission to appeal any stay of advertisement will normally be until the hearing of the appeal but on terms that the stay will determine without further order if an appellant's notice is not filed within the period prescribed by the rules.

(3) Where the judge has refused permission to appeal any stay of advertisement will normally be for a period not exceeding 28 days. Application for any further stay of advertisement should be made to the Court of Appeal.

## The Schedule

[The schedule consists of forms which are not reproduced in this work but may be accessed via the DCA website at <http://www.dca.gov.uk>.

PDIP1 Appellant's Notice—Insolvency Proceedings
PDIP2 Respondent's Notice—Insolvency Proceedings
PDIP3 Draft Order—Multiple Transfer of Proceedings
PDIP4 Draft Order—Multiple Appointments of Office Holder]

[* The text issued by the Department for Constitutional Affairs refers to an earlier version of the practice direction.]

# Practice Direction — Directors Disqualification Proceedings

## PART ONE

### 1. Application and Interpretation

1.1 In this practice direction:

(1) 'the Act' means the Company Directors Disqualification Act 1986;

(2) 'the Disqualification Rules' means the rules for the time being in force made under s. 411 of the Insolvency Act 1986 in relation to disqualification proceedings;[1]

(3) 'the Insolvency Rules' means the rules for the time being in force made under ss. 411 and 412 of the Insolvency Act 1986 in relation to insolvency proceedings;

(4) 'CPR' means the Civil Procedure Rules 1998 and 'CPR' followed by 'Part' or 'rule' and a number means the Part or rule with that number in those Rules;

(5) 'disqualification proceedings' has the meaning set out in para. 1.3 below;

(6) 'a disqualification application' is an application under the Act for the making of a disqualification order;

(7) 'registrar' means any judge of the High Court or the county court who is a registrar within the meaning of the Insolvency Rules;

(8) 'Companies Court registrar' means any judge of the High Court sitting in the Royal Courts of Justice in London who is a registrar within the meaning of the Insolvency Rules;

(9) except where the context otherwise requires references to:

(a) 'company' or 'companies' shall include references to 'partnership' or 'partnerships' and to 'limited liability partnership' and 'limited liability partnerships';

(b) 'director' shall include references to an 'officer' of a partnership and to a 'member' of a limited liability partnership;

(c) 'shadow director' shall include references to a 'shadow member' of a limited liability partnership

and, in appropriate cases, the forms annexed to this practice direction shall be varied accordingly;

(10) 'disqualification order' has the meaning set out in section 1 of the Act and 'disqualification undertaking' has the meaning set out in section 1A or section 9B of the Act (as the context requires);

(11) a 'section 8A application' is an application under s. 8A of the Act to reduce the period for which a disqualification undertaking is in force or to provide for it to cease to be in force;

(12) 'specified regulator' has the meaning set out in section 9E(2) of the Act.

1.2 This practice direction shall come into effect on 26 April 1999 and shall replace all previous practice directions relating to disqualification proceedings.

1.3 This practice direction applies to the following proceedings ('disqualification proceedings'):

---

[1] The current rules are the Insolvent Companies (Disqualification of Unfit Directors) Proceedings Rules 1987 (SI 1987/2023). For convenience relevant references to the Insolvent Companies (Disqualification of Unfit Directors) Proceedings Rules 1987, which apply to disqualification applications under sections 7, 8 and 9A of the Act (see rule 1(3)) are set out in footnotes to this practice direction. This practice direction applies certain provisions contained in the Insolvent Companies (Disqualification of Unfit Directors) Proceedings Rules 1987 to disqualification proceedings other than applications under sections 7, 8 and 9A of the Act.

(1) disqualification applications made:
   (a) under s. 2(2)(a) of the Act (after the person's conviction of an indictable offence in connection with the affairs of a company);
   (b) under s. 3 of the Act (on the ground of persistent breaches of provisions of companies legislation);
   (c) under s. 4 of the Act (on the ground of fraud etc.);
   (d) by the Secretary of State or the official receiver under section 7(1) of the Act (on the ground that the person is or has been a director of a company which has at any time become insolvent and his conduct makes him unfit to be concerned in the management of a company);
   (e) by the Secretary of State under section 8 of the Act (on it appearing to the Secretary of State from investigative material that it is expedient in the public interest that a disqualification order should be made); or
   (f) by the Office of Fair Trading or a specified regulator under section 9A of the Act (on the ground of breach of competition law by an undertaking and unfitness to be concerned in the management of a company);

(2) any application made under s. 7(2) or 7(4) of the Act;

(3) any application for permission to act made under section 17 of the Act for the purposes of any of sections 1(1)(a), 1A(1)(a) or 9B(4), or made under section 12(2) of the Act;

(4) any application for a court order made under CPR Part 23 in the course of any of the proceedings set out in sub-paras (1) to (3) above;

(5) any application under the Act to the extent provided for by subordinate legislation;[2]

(6) any section 8A application.

## 2. Multi-track

2.1 All disqualification proceedings are allocated to the multi-track. The CPR relating to allocation questionnaires and track allocation shall not apply.

## 3. Rights of Audience

3.1 Official receivers and deputy official receivers have right of audience in any proceedings to which this practice direction applies, including cases where a disqualification application is made by the Secretary of State or by the official receiver at his direction, and whether made in the High Court or a county court.[3]

# PART TWO DISQUALIFICATION APPLICATIONS

## 4. Commencement

4.1 Sections 2(2)(a), 3(4), 4(2), 6(3), 8(3) and 9E(3) of the Act identify the civil courts which have jurisdiction to deal with disqualification applications.

4.1A A disqualification application must be commenced by a claim form issued:

(1) in the case of a disqualification application under section 9A of the Act, in the High Court out of the office of the companies court registrar at the Royal Courts of Justice;

(2) in any other case,
   (a) in the High Court out of the office of the companies court registrar or a chancery district registry; and
   (b) in the county court, out of a county court office.

---

[2] Current subordinate legislation includes the Insolvent Partnerships Order 1994 (SI 1994/2421) and the Limited Liability Partnerships Regulations 2001 (SI 2001/1090).

[3] Rule 10 of the Insolvent Companies (Disqualification of Unfit Directors) Proceedings Rules 1987.

4.2 Disqualification applications shall be made by the issue of a claim form in the form annexed hereto and the use of the procedure set out in CPR, Part 8,[4] subject to any modification of that procedure under this practice direction and (where the application is made under sections 7, 8 or 9A of the Act) the Disqualification Rules. CPR rule 8.1(3) (power of the court to order the application to continue as if the claimant had not used the Part 8 procedure) shall not apply.

4.3 When the claim form is issued, the claimant will be given a date for the first hearing of the disqualification application. This date is to be not less than eight weeks from the date of issue of the claim form.[5] The first hearing will be before a registrar.

## 5. Headings

5.1 Every claim form by which an application under the Act is begun and all affidavits, notices and other documents in the proceedings must be entitled in the matter of the company or companies in question and in the matter of the Act. In the case of any disqualification application under section 7 or 9A of the Act it is not necessary to mention in the heading any company other than that referred to in section 6(1)(a) or 9A(2) of the Act (as the case may be).

## 6. The Claim Form

6.1 CPR rule 8.2 does not apply. The claim form must state:

(1) that CPR, Part 8 (as modified by this practice direction), applies, and (if the application is made under sections 7, 8 or 9A of the Act) that the application is made in accordance with the Disqualification Rules;[6]

(2) that the claimant seeks a disqualification order, and the section of the Act pursuant to which the disqualification application is made;

(3) the period for which, in accordance with the Act, the court has power to impose a disqualification period.

The periods are as follows:

(a) where the application is under s. 2 of the Act, for a period of up to 15 years;

(b) where the application is under s. 3 of the Act, for a period of up to 5 years;

(c) where the application is under s. 4 of the Act, for a period of up to 15 years;

(d) where the application is under section 7 of the Act, for a period of not less than 2, and up to 15, years;[7]

(e) where the application is under section 8 or 9A of the Act, for a period of up to 15 years,[8]

(4) in cases where the application is made under sections 7, 8 or 9A of the Act, that on the first hearing of the application, the court may hear and determine it summarily, without further or other notice to the defendant, and that, if the application is so determined, the court may impose a period of disqualification of up to 5 years but that if at the hearing of the application the court, on the evidence then before it, is minded to impose, in the case of any defendant, disqualification for any period longer than 5 years, it will not make a disqualification order on that occasion but will adjourn the application to be heard (with further evidence, if any) at a later date that will be notified to the defendant;[9]

[4] Rule (2) of the Insolvent Companies (Disqualification of Unfit Directors) Proceedings Rules 1987 as amended.

[5] Rule 7(1) of the Insolvent Companies (Disqualification of Unfit Directors) Proceedings Rules 1987.

[6] Rule 4(a) of the Insolvent Companies (Disqualification of Unfit Directors) Proceedings Rules 1987.

[7] Rule 4(b)(i) of the Insolvent Companies (Disqualification of Unfit Directors) Proceedings Rules 1987.

[8] Rule 4(b)(ii) of the Insolvent Companies (Disqualification of Unfit Directors) Proceedings Rules 1987.

[9] Rule 4(c) and (d) of the Insolvent Companies (Disqualification of Unfit Directors) Proceedings Rules 1987.

(5) that any evidence which the defendant wishes the court to take into consideration must be filed in court in accordance with the time limits set out in para. 9 below (which time limits shall be set out in the notes to the claim form).[10]

## 7. Service of the Claim Form

7.1 Service of claim forms in disqualification proceedings will be the responsibility of the parties and will not be undertaken by the court.

7.2 The claim form shall be served by the claimant on the defendant. It may be served by sending it by first class post to his last known address; and the date of service shall, unless the contrary is shown, be deemed to be the seventh day following that on which the claim form was posted.[11] Rule 6.7(1) of the CPR shall be modified accordingly. Otherwise Sections I and II of CPR Part 6 apply.[12]

7.3 Where any claim form or order of the court or other document is required under any disqualification proceedings to be served on any person who is not in England and Wales, the court may order service on him to be effected within such time and in such manner as it thinks fit, may require such proof of service as it thinks fit,[13] and may give such directions as to acknowledgment of service as it thinks fit. Section III of CPR Part 6 shall not apply.

7.4 The claim form served on the defendant shall be accompanied by an acknowledgment of service.

## 8. Acknowledgment of Service

8.1 The form of acknowledgment of service is annexed to this practice direction. CPR rules 8.3(2) and 8.3(3)(a) do not apply to disqualification applications.

8.2 In cases brought under sections 7, 8 or 9A of the Act, the form of acknowledgment of service shall state that the defendant should indicate:[14]

(1) whether he contests the application on the grounds that, in the case of any particular company:

(a) he was not a director or shadow director of that company at a time when conduct of his, or of other persons, in relation to that company is in question; or

(b) his conduct as director or shadow director of that company was not as alleged in support of the application for a disqualification order;

(c) in the case of an application made under section 7 of the Act, the company has at no time become insolvent within the meaning of section 6; or

(d) in the case of an application under section 9A of the Act, the undertaking which is a company did not commit a breach of competition law within the meaning of that section.

(2) whether, in the case of any conduct of his, he disputes the allegation that such conduct makes him unfit to be concerned in the management of a company; and

(3) whether he, while not resisting the application for a disqualification order, intends to adduce mitigating factors with a view to reducing the period of disqualification.

8.3 The defendant shall:

(1) (subject to any directions to the contrary given under para. 7.3 above) file an acknowledgment of service in the prescribed form not more than 14 days after service of the claim form; and

(2) serve the acknowledgment of service on the claimant and any other party.

---

[10] Rule 4(e) of the Insolvent Companies (Disqualification of Unfit Directors) Proceedings Rules 1987.

[11] Rule 5(1) of the Insolvent Companies (Disqualification of Unfit Directors) Proceedings Rules 1987.

[12] Attention is drawn to CPR, r. 6.14(2), regarding a certificate of service of the claim form.

[13] Rule 5(2) of the Insolvent Companies (Disqualification of Unfit Directors) Proceedings Rules 1987.

[14] Rule 5(4) of the Insolvent Companies (Disqualification of Unfit Directors) Proceedings Rules 1987.

8.4 Where the defendant has failed to file an acknowledgment of service and the time period for doing so has expired, the defendant may attend the hearing of the application but may not take part in the hearing unless the court gives permission.

## 9. Evidence

9.1 Evidence in disqualification applications shall be by affidavit, except where the official receiver is a party, in which case his evidence may be in the form of a written report (with or without affidavits by other persons) which shall be treated as if it had been verified by affidavit by him and shall be prima facie evidence of any matter contained in it.[15]

9.2 In the affidavits or (as the case may be) the official receiver's report in support of the application, there shall be included:

(1) a statement of the matters by reference to which it is alleged that a disqualification order should be made against the defendant;[16] and

(2) a statement of the steps taken to comply with any requirements imposed by sections 16(1) and 9C(4) of the Act.

9.3 When the claim form is issued:

(1) the affidavit or report in support of the disqualification application must be filed in court;

(2) exhibits must be lodged with the court where they shall be retained until the conclusion of the proceedings; and

(3) copies of the affidavit/report and exhibits shall be served with the claim form on the defendant.[17]

9.4 The defendant shall, within 28 days from the date of service of the claim form:[18]

(1) file in court any affidavit evidence in opposition to the disqualification application that he or she wishes the court to take into consideration; and

(2) lodge the exhibits with the court where they shall be retained until the conclusion of the proceedings; and

(3) at the same time, serve upon the claimant a copy of the affidavits and exhibits.

9.5 In cases where there is more than one defendant, each defendant is required to serve his evidence on the other defendants unless the court otherwise orders.

9.6 The claimant shall, within 14 days from receiving the copy of the defendant's evidence:[19]

(1) file in court any further affidavit or report in reply he wishes the court to take into consideration; and

(2) lodge the exhibits with the court where they shall be retained until the conclusion of the proceedings; and

(3) at the same time serve a copy of the affidavits/reports and exhibits upon the defendant.

9.7 Prior to the first hearing of the disqualification application, the time for serving evidence may be extended by written agreement between the parties. After the first hearing, the extension of time for serving evidence is governed by CPR rules 2.11 and 29.5.

9.8 So far as is possible all evidence should be filed before the first hearing of the disqualification application.

---

[15] Rule 3(2) of the Insolvent Companies (Disqualification of Unfit Directors) Proceedings Rules 1987. Section 441 of the Companies Act 1985 makes provision for the admissibility in legal proceedings of a certified copy of a report of inspectors appointed under part XIV of the Companies Act 1985. Note that the requirements of para. 8.1(2)(c) and (d) of this practice direction are additional to the provisions in the said r. 5(4).

[16] Rule 3(3) of the Insolvent Companies (Disqualification of Unfit Directors) Proceedings Rules 1987.

[17] Ibid, rule 3(1).

[18] Ibid, rule 6(1).

[19] Ibid, rule 6(2).

## 10. The First Hearing of the Disqualification Application

10.1 The date fixed for the hearing of the disqualification application shall be not less than eight weeks from the date of issue of the claim form.[20]

10.2 The hearing shall in the first instance be before the registrar.[21]

10.3 The registrar shall either determine the case on the date fixed or give directions and adjourn it.[22]

10.4 All interim directions should in so far as possible be sought at the first hearing of the disqualification application so that the disqualification application can be determined at the earliest possible date. The parties should take all such steps as they respectively can to avoid successive directions hearings.

10.5 In the case of a disqualification application, applications made under sections 7, 8 or 9A of the Act, the registrar shall adjourn the case for further consideration if:

(1) he forms the provisional opinion that a disqualification order ought to be made, and that a period of disqualification longer than 5 years is appropriate,[23]

or

(2) he is of opinion that questions of law or fact arise which are not suitable for summary determination.[24]

10.6 If the registrar adjourns the application for further consideration he shall:

(1) direct whether the application is to be heard by a registrar or by a judge.[25] This direction may at any time be varied by the court either on application or of its own initiative. If the court varies the direction in the absence of any of the parties, notice will be given to the parties;

(2) consider whether or not to adjourn the application to a judge so that the judge can give further directions;

(3) consider whether or not to make any direction with regard to fixing the trial date or a trial window;

(4) state the reasons for the adjournment.[26]

## 11. Case Management

11.1 On the first or any subsequent hearing of the disqualification application, the registrar may also give directions as to the following matters:

(1) the filing in court and the service of further evidence (if any) by the parties;[27]

(2) the timetable for the steps to be taken between the giving of directions and the hearing of the application;

(3) such other matters as the registrar thinks necessary or expedient with a view to an expeditious disposal of the application or the management of it generally;[28]

(4) the time and place of the adjourned hearing;[29] and

(5) the manner in which and the time within which notice of the adjournment and the reasons for it are to be given to the parties.[30]

11.2 Where a case is adjourned other than to a judge, it may be heard by the registrar who originally dealt with the case or by another registrar.[31]

---

[20] Ibid, rule 7(1).
[21] Ibid, rule 7(2).
[22] Ibid, rule 7(3).
[23] Ibid, rule 7(4)(a).
[24] Ibid, rule 7(4)(b).
[25] Ibid, rule 7(5)(a).
[26] Ibid, rule 7(5)(b).
[27] Ibid, rule 7(5)(c)(ii).
[28] Ibid, rule 7(5)(c)(iii).
[29] Ibid, rule 7(5)(c)(iv).
[30] Ibid, rule 7(5)(c)(i).
[31] Ibid, rule 7(6).

11.3 If the Companies Court registrar adjourns the application to a judge, all directions having been complied with and the evidence being complete, the application will be referred to the Listing Office and any practice direction relating to listing shall apply accordingly.

11.4 In all disqualification applications, the court may direct a pre-trial review ('PTR'), a case management conference or pre-trial checklists (listing questionnaires) (in the form annexed to this practice direction) and will fix a trial date or trial period in accordance with the provisions of CPR, Part 29 (the multi-track), as modified by any relevant practice direction made thereunder.

11.5 At the hearing of the PTR, the registrar may give any further directions as appropriate and, where the application is to be heard in the Royal Courts of Justice in London, unless the trial date has already been fixed, may direct the parties (by counsel's clerks if applicable) to attend the registrar at a specified time and place in order solely to fix a trial date. The court will give notice of the date fixed for the trial to the parties.

11.6 In all cases, the parties must inform the court immediately of any material change to the information provided in a pre-trial checklist.

## 12. The Trial

12.1 Trial bundles containing copies of:
(1) the claim form;
(2) the acknowledgment of service;
(3) all evidence filed by or on behalf of each of the parties to the proceedings, together with the exhibits thereto;
(4) all relevant correspondence; and
(5) such other documents as the parties consider necessary; shall be lodged with the court.

12.2 Skeleton arguments should be prepared by all the parties in all but the simplest cases whether the case is to be heard by a registrar or a judge. They should comply with all relevant guidelines.

12.3 The advocate for the claimant should also in all but the simplest cases provide: (a) a chronology; (b) a dramatis personae; (c) in respect of each defendant, a list of references to the relevant evidence.

12.4 The documents mentioned in paras 12.1–12.3 above must be delivered to the court in accordance with any order of the court and/or any relevant practice direction.[32]
(1) If the case is to be heard by a judge sitting in the Royal Courts of Justice, London, but the name of the judge is not known, or the judge is a deputy judge, these documents must be delivered to the Clerk of the Lists. If the name of the judge (other than a deputy judge) is known, these documents must be delivered to the judge's clerk.
(2) If the case is to be heard by a Companies Court registrar, these documents must be delivered to Room 409, Thomas More Building, Royal Courts of Justice. Copies must be provided to the other party so far as possible when they are delivered to the court.
(3) If the case is to be heard in the Chancery district registries in Birmingham, Bristol, Cardiff, Leeds, Liverpool, Manchester or Newcastle, the addresses for delivery are set out in annex 1.
(4) If the case is to be heard in a county court, the documents should be delivered to the relevant county court office.

[32] Attention is drawn to the provisions of the Chancery Guide. Chapter 7 of that Guide dated September 2000 provides guidance on the preparation of trial bundles and skeleton arguments. Unless the court otherwise orders, para. 7.16 of the Chancery Guide requires that trial bundles be delivered to the court 7 days before trial and para. 7.21 requires that skeleton arguments be delivered to the court not less than 2 clear days before trial.

12.5 Copies of documents delivered to the court must, so far as possible, be provided to each of the other parties to the claim.

12.6 The provisions in paras 12.1 to 12.5 above are subject to any order of the court making different provision.

## 13. Summary Procedure

13.1 If the parties decide to invite the court to deal with the application under the procedure adopted in *Re Carecraft Construction Co. Ltd* [1994] 1 WLR 172, they should inform the court immediately and obtain a date for the hearing of the application.

13.2 Whenever the *Carecraft* procedure is adopted, the claimant must:

(1) except where the court otherwise directs, submit a written statement containing in respect of each defendant any material facts which (for the purposes of the application) are either agreed or not opposed (by either party); and

(2) specify in writing the period of disqualification which the parties accept that the agreed or unopposed facts justify or the band of years (e.g. 4 to 6 years) or bracket (i.e. 2 to 5 years; 6 to 10 years; 11 to 15 years) into which they will submit the case falls.

13.3 Paragraph 12.4 above applies to the documents mentioned in para. 13.2 above unless the court otherwise directs.

13.4 Unless the court otherwise orders, a hearing under the *Carecraft* procedure will be held in private.

13.5 If the court is minded to make a disqualification order having heard the parties' representations, it will usually give judgment and make the disqualification order in public. Unless the court otherwise orders, the written statement referred to in para. 13.2 shall be annexed to the disqualification order.

13.6 If the court refuses to make the disqualification order under the *Carecraft* procedure, the court shall give further directions for the hearing of the application.

## 14. Making and Setting Aside of Disqualification Order

14.1 The court may make a disqualification order against the defendant, whether or not the latter appears, and whether or not he has completed and returned the acknowledgment of service of the claim form, or filed evidence.[33]

14.2 Any disqualification order made in the absence of the defendant may be set aside or varied by the court on such terms as it thinks just.[34]

## 15. Service of Disqualification Orders

15.1 Service of disqualification orders will be the responsibility of the claimant.

## 16. Commencement of Disqualification Order

16.1 Unless the court otherwise orders, the period of disqualification imposed by a disqualification order shall begin at the end of the period of 21 days beginning with the date of the order.[35]

# PART THREE APPLICATIONS UNDER SECTIONS 7(2) AND 7(4) OF THE ACT

## 17. Applications for Permission to Make a Disqualification Application After the End of the Period of 2 Years Specified in Section 7(2) of the Act

17.1 Such applications shall be made by Practice Form N208 under CPR Part 8 save where it is sought to join a director or former director to existing proceedings, in which case

[33] Rule 8(1) of the Insolvent Companies (Disqualification of Unfit Directors) Proceedings Rules 1987.

[34] Ibid, rule 8(2).

[35] Section 1(2) of the Act (as amended).

such application shall be made by Application Notice under CPR Part 23, and the Part 23 Practice Direction shall apply save as modified below.

## 18. Applications for Extra Information Made Under Section 7(4) of the Act

18.1 Such applications may be made:
(1) by form N208 under CPR, Part 8;
(2) by application notice in existing disqualification proceedings; or
(3) by application under the Insolvency Rules in the relevant insolvency, if the insolvency practitioner against whom the application is made remains the officeholder.

## 19. Provisions Applicable to Applications Under Sections 7(2) and 7(4) of the Act

19.1 *Headings:*
Every claim form and notice by which such an application is begun and all affidavits, notices and other documents in relation thereto must be entitled in the matter of the company or companies in question and in the matter of the Act.
19.2 *Service:*
(1) Service of claim forms and application notices seeking orders under s. 7(2) or 7(4) of the Act will be the responsibility of the applicant and will not be undertaken by the court.
(2) Where any claim form, application notice or order of the court or other document is required in any application under s. 7(2) or s. 7(4) of the Act to be served on any person who is not in England and Wales, the court may order service on him to be effected within such time and in such manner as it thinks fit, may require such proof of service as it thinks fit, and may make such directions as to acknowledgment of service as it thinks fit. Section III of CPR Part 6 does not apply.

# PART FOUR APPLICATIONS FOR PERMISSION TO ACT

## 20. Commencing an Application for Permission to Act

20.1 This practice direction governs applications for permission to act made under:
(1) section 17 of the Act for the purposes of any of sections 1(1)(a), 1A(1)(a) or 9B(4); and
(2) section 12(2) of the Act.
20.2 Sections 12 and 17 of the Act identify the courts which have jurisdiction to deal with applications for permission to act. Subject to these sections, such applications may be made:
(1) by form N208 under CPR, Part 8; or
(2) by application notice in an existing disqualification application.
20.3 In the case of a person subject to disqualification under section 12A or 12B of the Act (by reason of being disqualified in Northern Ireland), permission to act notwithstanding disqualification can only be granted by the High Court of Northern Ireland.

## 21. Headings

21.1 Every claim form or application notice by which an application for permission to act is begun, and all affidavits, notices and other documents in the application must be entitled in the matter of the company or companies in question and in the matter of the Act.
21.2 Every application notice by which an application for permission to act is made and all affidavits, notices and other documents in the application shall be entitled in the same manner as the heading of the claim form in the existing disqualification application.

## 22. Evidence

22.1 Evidence in support of an application for permission to act shall be by affidavit.

## 23. Service[36]

23.1 Where a disqualification application has been made under section 9A of the Act or a disqualification undertaking has been accepted under section 9B of the Act, the claim form or application notice (as appropriate), together with the evidence in support thereof, must be served on the Office of Fair Trading or specified regulator which made the relevant disqualification application or accepted the disqualification undertaking (as the case may be).

23.2 In all other cases, the claim form or application notice (as appropriate), together with the evidence in support thereof, must be served on the Secretary of State.

# PART FIVE APPLICATIONS

## 24. Form of Application

24.1 CPR, Part 23, and PD 23 (general rules about applications for court orders) shall apply in relation to applications governed by this practice direction (see para. 1.3(4) above) save as modified below.

## 25. Headings

25.1 Every notice and all affidavits in relation thereto must be entitled in the same manner as the claim form in the proceedings in which the application is made.

## 26. Service

26.1 Service of application notices in disqualification proceedings will be the responsibility of the parties and will not be undertaken by the court.

26.2 Where any application notice or order of the court or other document is required in any application to be served on any person who is not in England and Wales, the court may order service on him to be effected within such time and in such manner as it thinks fit, and may also require such proof of service as it thinks fit. Section III of CPR Part 6 does not apply.

# PART SIX DISQUALIFICATION PROCEEDINGS OTHER THAN IN THE ROYAL COURTS OF JUSTICE

27.1 Where a disqualification application or a section 8A application is made by a claim form issued other than in the Royal Courts of Justice this practice direction shall apply with the following modifications:

(1) Upon the issue of the claim form the court shall endorse it with the date and time for the first hearing before a district judge. The powers exercisable by a registrar under this practice direction shall be exercised by a district judge.

(2) If the district judge (either at the first hearing or at any adjourned hearing before him) directs that the disqualification claim or section 8A application is to be heard by a High Court judge or by an authorised circuit judge he will direct that the case be entered forthwith in the list for hearing by that judge and the court will allocate (i) a date for the hearing of the trial by that judge and (ii) unless the district judge directs otherwise a date for the hearing of a PTR by the trial judge.

# PART SEVEN DISQUALIFICATION UNDERTAKINGS

## 28. Costs

28.1 The general rule is that the court will order the defendant to pay—

[36] Addresses for service on government departments are set out in the List of Authorised Government Departments issued by the Cabinet Office under section 17 of the Crown Proceedings Act 1947, which is annexed to the practice direction supplementing Part 66.

(1) the costs of the Secretary of State (and, in the case of a disqualification application made under section 7(1)(b) of the Act, the costs of the official receiver) if:
 (a) a disqualification application under section 7 or 8 of the Act has been commenced; and
 (b) that application is discontinued because the Secretary of State has accepted a disqualification undertaking under section 1A of the Act;

(2) the costs of the Office of Fair Trading or a specified regulator if:
 (a) a disqualification application under section 9A of the Act has been commenced; and
 (b) that application is discontinued because the Office of Fair Trading or specified regulator (as the case may be) has accepted a disqualification undertaking under section 9B of the Act.

28.2 The general rule will not apply where the court considers that the circumstances are such that it should make another order.

## APPLICATIONS UNDER SECTION 8A OF THE ACT TO REDUCE THE PERIOD FOR WHICH A DISQUALIFICATION UNDERTAKING IS IN FORCE OR TO PROVIDE FOR IT TO CEASE TO BE IN FORCE

### 29. Headings

29.1 Every claim form by which a section 8A application is begun and all affidavits, notices and other documents in the proceedings must be entitled in the matter of a disqualification undertaking and its date and in the matter of the Act.

### 30. Commencement: The Claim Form

30.1 Section 8A(3) of the Act identifies the courts which have jurisdiction to deal with section 8A applications.

30.1A A section 8A application must be commenced by a claim form issued:
 (1) in the case of a disqualification undertaking given under section 9B of the Act, in the High Court out of the office of the companies court registrar at the Royal Courts of Justice;
 (2) in any other case,
  (a) in the High Court out of the office of the companies court registrar or a chancery district registry; and
  (b) in the county court, out of a county court office.

30.2 A section 8A application shall be made by the issue of a Part 8 claim form in the form annexed hereto and the use of the procedure set out in CPR, Part 8, as modified by this practice direction. Rule 8.1(3) of the CPR (power of the court to order the application to continue as if the claimant had not used the Part 8 procedure) shall not apply.

30.3 When the claim form is issued, the claimant will be given a date for the first hearing of the section 8A application. This date is to be not less than eight weeks from the date of issue of the claim form. The first hearing will be before [a] registrar.

30.4 Rule 8.2 of the CPR does not apply. The claim form must state:
 (1) that CPR, Part 8 (as modified by this practice direction), applies;
 (2) the form of order the claimant seeks.

30.5 In the case of a disqualification undertaking given under section 9B of the Act, the defendant to the section 8A application shall be the Office of Fair Trading or specified regulator which accepted the undertaking. In all other cases, the Secretary of State shall be made the defendant to the section 8A application.

30.6 Service of claim forms in section 8A applications will be the responsibility of the claimant and will not be undertaken by the court. The claim form may be served by sending it by first-class post and the date of service shall, unless the contrary is shown, be deemed to be the seventh day following that on which the claim form was posted.

Rule 6.7(1) of the CPR shall be modified accordingly. Otherwise Part 6 of the CPR applies. Otherwise Sections I and II of CPR Part 6 apply.[37]

30.7 Where any order of the court or other document is required to be served on any person who is not in England and Wales, the court may order service on him to be effected within such time and in such manner as it thinks fit and may require such proof of service as it thinks fit. Section III of CPR Part 6 shall not apply.

30.8 The claim form served on the defendant shall be accompanied by an acknowledgment of service in the form annexed hereto.

## 31. Acknowledgment of Service

31.1 The defendant shall:

(1) file an acknowledgment of service in the relevant practice form not more than 14 days after service of the claim form; and

(2) serve a copy of the acknowledgment of service on the claimant and any other party.

31.2 Where the defendant has failed to file an acknowledgment of service and the time period for doing so has expired, the defendant may nevertheless attend the hearing of the application and take part in the hearing as provided for by s. 8A(2) or (2A) of the Act. However, this is without prejudice to the court's case management powers and its powers to make costs orders.

## 32. Evidence

32.1 Evidence in section 8A applications shall be by affidavit. The undertaking (or a copy) shall be exhibited to the affidavit.

32.2 When the claim form is issued:

(1) the affidavit in support of the section 8A application must be filed in court;

(2) exhibits must be lodged with the court where they shall be retained until the conclusion of the proceedings; and

(3) copies of the affidavit and exhibits shall be served with the claim form on the defendant.

32.3 The defendant shall, within 28 days from the date of service of the claim form:

(1) file in court any affidavit evidence that he wishes the court to take into consideration on the application; and

(2) lodge the exhibits with the court where they shall be retained until the conclusion of the proceedings; and

(3) at the same time, serve upon the claimant a copy of the affidavits and exhibits.

32.4 The claimant shall, within 14 days from receiving the copy of the defendant's evidence:

(1) file in court any further affidavit evidence in reply he wishes the court to take into consideration; and

(2) lodge the exhibits with the court where they shall be retained until the conclusion of the proceedings; and

(3) at the same time serve a copy of the affidavits and exhibits upon the defendant.

32.5 Prior to the first hearing of the section 8A application, the time for serving evidence may be extended by written agreement between the parties. After the first hearing, the extension of time for serving evidence is governed by CPR, rr. 2.11 and 29.5.

32.6 So far as is possible all evidence should be filed before the first hearing of the section 8A application.

## 33. Hearings and Case Management

33.1 The date fixed for the first hearing of the section 8A application shall be not less than eight weeks from the date of issue of the claim form.

[37] Attention is drawn to CPR, r. 6.14(2), regarding a certificate of service of the claim form.

33.2 The hearing shall in the first instance be before the registrar.

33.3 The registrar shall either determine the case on the date fixed or give directions and adjourn it.

33.4 All interim directions should in so far as possible be sought at the first hearing of the section 8A application so that the section 8A application can be determined at the earliest possible date. The parties should take all such steps as they respectively can to avoid successive directions hearings.

33.5 If the registrar adjourns the application for further consideration he shall:

(1) direct whether the application is to be heard by a registrar or by a judge. This direction may at any time be varied by the court either on application or of its own initiative. If the court varies the direction in the absence of any of the parties, notice will be given to the parties;

(2) consider whether or not to adjourn the application to a judge so that the judge can give further directions;

(3) consider whether or not to make any direction with regard to fixing the trial date or a trial window.

33.6 On the first or any subsequent hearing of the section 8A application, the registrar may also give directions as to the following matters:

(1) the filing in court and the service of further evidence (if any) by the parties;

(2) the timetable for the steps to be taken between the giving of directions and the hearing of the section 8A application;

(3) such other matters as the registrar thinks necessary or expedient with a view to an expeditious disposal of the section 8A application or the management of it generally;

(4) the time and place of the adjourned hearing.

33.7 Where a case is adjourned other than to a judge, it may be heard by the registrar who originally dealt with the case or by another registrar.

33.8 If the Companies Court registrar adjourns the application to a judge, all directions having been complied with and the evidence being complete, the application will be referred to the Listing Office and any practice direction relating to listing shall apply accordingly.

33.9 In all section 8A applications, the court may direct a pre-trial review ('PTR'), a case management conference or pre-trial checklists (listing questionnaires) (in the form annexed to this practice direction) and will fix a trial date or trial period in accordance with the provisions of CPR, Part 29, as modified by any relevant practice direction made thereunder.

33.10 At the hearing of the PTR, the registrar may give any further directions as appropriate and, where the application is to be heard in the Royal Courts of Justice in London, unless the trial date has already been fixed, may direct the parties (by counsel's clerks, if applicable) to attend the registrar at a specified time and place in order solely to fix a trial date. The court will give notice of the date fixed for the trial to the parties.

33.11 In all cases, the parties must inform the court immediately of any material change to the information provided in a pre-trial checklist.

## 34. The Trial

34.1 Trial bundles containing copies of:

(1) the claim form;

(2) the acknowledgment of service;

(3) all evidence filed by or on behalf of each of the parties to the proceedings, together with the exhibits thereto;

(4) all relevant correspondence; and

(5) such other documents as the parties consider necessary;

shall be lodged with the court.

34.2 Skeleton arguments should be prepared by all the parties in all but the simplest cases whether the case is to be heard by a registrar or a judge. They should comply with all relevant guidelines.

34.3 The advocate for the claimant should also in all but the simplest cases provide: (a) chronology; (b) a dramatis personae.

34.4 The documents mentioned in paras 34.1 to 34.3 above must be delivered to the court in accordance with any order of the court and/or [any] relevant practice direction.[38]

(1) If the case is to be heard by a judge sitting in the Royal Courts of Justice, London, but the name of the judge is not known, or the judge is a deputy judge, these documents must be delivered to the Clerk of the Lists. If the name of the judge (other than a deputy judge) is known, these documents must be delivered to the judge's clerk.

(2) If the case is to be heard by a Companies Court registrar, these documents must be delivered to Room 409, Thomas More Building, Royal Courts of Justice. Copies must be provided to the other party so far as possible when they are delivered to the court.

(3) If the case is to be heard in the Chancery district registries in Birmingham, Bristol, Cardiff, Leeds, Liverpool, Manchester, Newcastle, or Preston, the addresses for delivery are set out in Annex 1.

(4) If the case is to be heard in a county court, the documents should be delivered to the relevant county court office.

34.5 Copies of documents delivered to the court must, so far as possible, be provided to each of the other parties to the claim.

34.6 The provisions in paras 34.1 to 34.5 above are subject to any order of the court making different provision.

## 35. Appeals

35.1 Rules 7.47 and 7.49 of the Insolvency Rules, as supplemented by Part Four of the Insolvency Proceedings Practice Direction, apply to an appeal from, or review of, a decision made by the court in the course of:

(1) disqualification proceedings under any of sections 6 to 8A or 9A of the Act;

(2) an application made under section 17 of the Act for the purposes of any of sections 1(1)(a), 1A(1)(a) or 9B(4), for permission to act notwithstanding a disqualification order made, or a disqualification undertaking accepted, under any of sections 6 to 10.

Any such decision, and any appeal from it, constitutes 'insolvency proceedings' for the purposes of the Insolvency Proceedings Practice Direction.[39]

35.2 An appeal from a decision made by the court in the course of disqualification proceedings under any of sections 2(2)(a), 3 or 4 of the Act or on an application for permission to act notwithstanding a disqualification order made under any of those sections is governed by CPR Part 52 and the practice direction supplementing that Part.

---

[38] Attention is drawn to the provisions of the Chancery Guide. Chapter 7 of that Guide dated September 2000 provides guidance on the preparation of trial bundles and skeleton arguments. Unless the court otherwise orders, para. 7.16 of the Chancery Guide requires that trial bundles be delivered to the court 7 days before trial and para. 7.21 requires that skeleton arguments be delivered to the court not less than 2 clear days before trial. Addresses for service on government departments are set out in the List of Authorised Government Departments issued by the Cabinet Office under section 17 of the Crown Proceedings Act 1947, which is annexed to the practice direction supplementing Part 66.

[39] CPR rule 2.1(2) and section 21(2) of the Act. See also r. 2(4) of the Insolvent Companies (Disqualification of Unfit Directors) Proceedings Rules 1987 and *Re Tasbian Limited, Official Receiver* v *Nixon* [1991] BCLC 59; [1990] BCC 322; *Re Probe Data Systems Limited (No 3), Secretary of State for Trade and Industry* v *Desai* [1992] BCLC 405; [1992] BCC 110 and *Re The Premier Screw & Repetition Company Ltd, Secretary of State for Trade and Industry* v *Paulin* [2005] EWCH 888 (Ch).

## ANNEX 1

*Birmingham:* The Chancery Listing Officer, The District Registry of the Chancery Division of the High Court, 33 Bull Street, Birmingham B4 6DS.

*Bristol:* The Chancery Listing Officer, The District Registry of the Chancery Division of the High Court, 3rd Floor, Greyfriars, Lewins Mead, Bristol BS1 2NR.

*Cardiff:* The Chancery Listing Officer, The District Registry of the Chancery Division of the High Court, 1st Floor, 2 Park Street, Cardiff CF10 1EE.

*Leeds:* The Chancery Listing Officer, The District Registry of the Chancery Division of the High Court, Leeds Combined Court Centre, The Court House, 1 Oxford Row, Leeds LS1 3BG.

*Liverpool and Manchester:* The Chancery Listing Officer, The District Registry of the Chancery Division of the High Court, Manchester Courts of Justice, Crown Square, Manchester M60 9DJ.

*Newcastle:* The Chancery Listing Officer, The District Registry of the Chancery Division of the High Court, The Law Courts, Quayside, Newcastle upon Tyne NE1 3LA.

*Preston:* The Chancery Listing Officer, The District Registry of the Chancery Division of the High Court, The Combined Court Centre, Ringway, Preston PR1 2LL.

## [FORMS

**Claim Form (Part 8)**
Claim Form N500
Notes for claimant N500a
Notes for defendant N500b
Claim Form section 8a application N501
Notes for claimant section 8a application N501a
Notes for defendant section 8a application N501b
Acknowledgment of service N502
Acknowledgment of service section 8a application N503
Pre-trial check list N504

The forms are not reproduced in this work but may be accessed via the DCA website at <http://www.dca.gov.uk>.]

# Practice Direction Relating to the Use of the Welsh Language in Cases in the Civil Courts in Wales*

The purpose of this practice direction is to reflect the principle of the Welsh Language Act 1993 that in the administration of justice in Wales, the English and Welsh languages should be treated on the basis of equality.

## 1. General

1.1 This practice direction applies to civil proceedings in courts in Wales.

1.2 The existing practice of conducting a hearing entirely in the Welsh language on an ad hoc basis and without notice will continue to apply when all parties and witnesses directly involved at the time consent to the proceedings being so conducted.

1.3 In every case in which it is possible that the Welsh language may be used by any party or witness (or in any document which may be placed before the court), the parties or their legal representatives must inform the court of that fact so that appropriate arrangements can be made for the management and listing of the case.

1.4 If costs are incurred as a result of a party failing to comply with this direction, a costs order may be made against him or his legal representative.

1.5 Where a case is tried with a jury, the law does not permit the selection of jurors in a manner which enables the court to discover whether a juror does or does not speak Welsh or to secure a jury whose members are bilingual to try a case in which the Welsh language may be used.

## 2. The Allocation Questionnaire

2.1 In any proceedings in which a party is required to complete an allocation questionnaire, he must include details relating to the possible use of Welsh i.e. details of any person wishing to give oral evidence in Welsh and of any documents in Welsh (e.g. documents to be disclosed under Part 31 or witness statements) which that party expects to use.

2.2 A party must include the details mentioned in para. 2.1 in the allocation questionnaire even if he has already informed the court of the possible use of Welsh in accordance with the provisions of section 1 above.

## 3. Case Management

3.1 At any interlocutory hearing, the court will take the opportunity to consider whether it should give case management directions. To assist the court, a party or his legal representative should draw the court's attention to the possibility of Welsh being used in the proceedings, even where he has already done so in compliance with other provisions of this direction.

3.2 In any case where a party is required to complete a pre-trial checklist (listing questionnaire) and has already intimated the intention to use Welsh, he should confirm the intended use of Welsh in the pre-trial checklist and provide any details which have not been set out in the allocation questionnaire.

## 4. Listing by the Court

4.1 The diary manager, in consultation with the designated civil judge, will ensure that a case in which the Welsh language is to be used is listed:

(a) wherever practicable before a Welsh speaking judge; and

---

* A Welsh language version of this Practice Direction is available via <http://www.dca.gov.uk> entitled Cyfarwyddiadau Ymarfer Ar Ddefnyddio'r laith Gymraeg Mewn Achosion yn y Llysoedd Sifil Yng Nghymru.

(b) where translation facilities are needed, at a court with simultaneous translation facilities.

## 5. Interpreters

5.1 Whenever an interpreter is needed to translate evidence from English to Welsh or from Welsh to English, the court manager in whose court the case is to be heard will take steps to secure the attendance of an interpreter whose name is included in the list of approved court interpreters.

## 6. Witnesses and Jurors

6.1 When each witness is called, the court officer administering the oath or affirmation will inform the witness that he or she may be sworn or may affirm in Welsh or English as he or she wishes.

6.2 Where a case is tried with a jury, the court officer swearing in the jury will inform the jurors in open court that each juror may take the oath or may affirm in Welsh or English as he or she wishes.

## 7. Role of the Liaison Judge

7.1 If any question or difficulty arises concerning the implementation of this practice direction, contact should in the first place be made with the Liaison Judge for the Welsh language.

# Practice Direction — Devolution Issues*

This Practice Direction is divided into 4 parts:

Part I Introduction
Part II Directions applicable to all proceedings
Part III Directions applicable to specific proceedings
Part IV Appeals

## PART I INTRODUCTION

### Definitions

1. In this Practice Direction:

   'the Assembly' means the National Assembly for Wales or Cynulliad Cenedlaethol Cymru
   'the GWA' means the Government of Wales Act 1998
   'the NIA' means the Northern Ireland Act 1998
   'the SA' means the Scotland Act 1998
   'the Acts' mean the GWA, the NIA and the SA
   'the Judicial Committee' means the Judicial Committee of the Privy Council
   'the CPR' means the Civil Procedure Rules 1998
   'the FPR' means the Family Proceedings Rules 1991
   'the FPC' means the Family Proceedings Courts (Children Act 1989) Rules 1991
   'devolution issue' has the same meaning as in paragraph 1, schedule 8 to the GWA; paragraph 1, schedule 10 to the NIA; and paragraph 1, schedule 6 of the SA
   'devolution issue notice' means a notice that a devolution issue has arisen in proceedings.

### Scope

2.1 This Practice Direction supplements the provisions dealing with devolution issues in the Acts. It deals specifically with the position if a devolution issue arises under the GWA. If a devolution issue arises under the NIA or the SA the procedure laid down in this Practice Direction should be adapted as required.

### The Devolution Legislation

3.1 Schedule 8 to the GWA contains provisions dealing with devolution issues arising out of the GWA; schedule 10 to the NIA contains provisions dealing with devolution issues arising out of the NIA; and schedule 6 to the SA contains provisions dealing with devolution issues arising out of the SA.

3.2 Broadly a devolution issue will involve a question whether a devolved body has acted or proposes to act within its powers (which includes not acting incompatibly with Convention rights[1] and Community law[2]) or has failed to comply with a duty imposed on it. Reference should be made to the Acts where 'devolution issue' is defined.

---

* Editorial note: the Welsh language version of this practice direction (Cyfarwyddyd Ymarfer–Materion yn Ymwneud â Datganoli) can be found at the DCA website.

[1] The rights and fundamental freedoms set out in: (a) Articles 2 to 12 and 14 of the European Convention on Human Rights ('ECHR'), (b) Articles 1 to 3 of the First Protocol (agreed at Paris on 20th March 1952), and (c) Articles 1 and 2 of the Sixth Protocol (agreed at Strasbourg on 11th May 1994), as read with Articles 16 and 18 of the ECHR (Section 1 Human Rights Act 1998; s. 107(1) and (5) GWA; sections 6(2); 24(1) and 98(1) NIA; sections 29(2); 57(2) and 126(1) SA).

[2] All the rights, powers, liabilities, obligations and restrictions from time to time created or arising by or under the Community Treaties; and all the remedies and procedures from time to time provided for by or under the Community Treaties (sections 106(7) and 155(1), GWA; sections 6(2); 24(1) and 98(1), NIA; sections 29(2); 57(2) and 126(9) SA).

3.3 (1) If a devolution issue under the GWA arises in proceedings, the court must order notice of it to be given to the Attorney General and the Assembly if they are not already a party. They have a right to take part as a party in the proceedings so far as they relate to a devolution issue, if they are not already a party (paragraph 5, schedule 8 to the GWA.) If they do take part, they may require the court to refer the devolution issue to the Judicial Committee (paragraph 30, schedule 8 to the GWA).[3]

(2) There are similar provisions in the NIA and the SA although the persons to be notified are different (paragraphs 13, 14, and 33, schedule 10 to the NIA; paragraphs 16, 17 and 33, schedule 6 to the SA).

3.4 Under all the Acts the court may refer a devolution issue to another court as follows:

(1) A magistrates' court may refer a devolution issue arising in civil or summary proceedings to the High Court (paragraphs 6 and 9, schedule 8 to the GWA; paragraphs 15 and 18, schedule 10 to the NIA; and paragraphs 18 and 21, schedule 6 to the SA).

(2) The Crown Court may refer a devolution issue arising in summary proceedings to the High Court and a devolution issue arising in proceedings on indictment to the Court of Appeal (paragraph 9, schedule 8 to the GWA; paragraph 18, schedule 10 to the NIA; paragraph 21, schedule 6 to the SA).

(3) A county court, the High Court (unless the devolution issue has been referred to the High Court),[4] and the Crown Court[5] may refer a devolution issue arising in civil proceedings to the Court of Appeal (paragraph 7, schedule 8 to the GWA; paragraph 16, schedule 10 to the NIA; paragraph 19, schedule 6 to the SA).

(4) A tribunal from which there is no appeal must, and any other tribunal may, refer a devolution issue to the Court of Appeal (paragraph 8, schedule 8 to the GWA; paragraph 17, schedule 10 to the NIA; paragraph 20, schedule 6 to the SA).

(5) The Court of Appeal may refer a devolution issue to the Judicial Committee, unless the devolution issue was referred to it by another court (paragraph 10, schedule 8 to the GWA; paragraph 19, schedule 10 to the NIA; paragraph 22, schedule 6 to the SA).

(6) An appeal against the determination of a devolution issue by the High Court or the Court of Appeal on a reference lies to the Judicial Committee with the leave of the court concerned, or, failing such leave, with special leave of the Judicial Committee (paragraph 11, schedule 8 to the GWA; paragraph 20, schedule 10 to the NIA; paragraph 23, schedule 6 to the SA).

3.5 A court may take into account additional expense which the court considers that a party has incurred as a result of the participation of the Attorney General or the Assembly in deciding any question as to costs (paragraph 35, schedule 8 to the GWA).

---

[3] If the Attorney General or the Assembly had become a party to the original proceedings but did not exercise their right to require the devolution issue to be referred to the Judicial Committee and the court decided the case, they would have the same rights of appeal as parties. These would not allow them to appeal a decision made in proceedings on indictment, although the Attorney General has a power under section 36 of the Criminal Justice Act 1972 to refer a point of law to the Court of Appeal where the defendant has been acquitted in a trial on indictment.

Paragraph 31, schedule 8 to the GWA, allows the Attorney General and Assembly to refer to the Judicial Committee any devolution issue which is not the subject of proceedings. This power could possibly be used if a court reached a decision where they had not been parties and so had no rights of appeal but such a reference could not affect the decision of the court.

[4] If an appeal by way of case stated in criminal proceedings goes to the Divisional Court there appears to be no power for the Divisional Court to refer a devolution issue to the Court of Appeal.

[5] E.g. in appeals from a magistrates' court in a licensing matter.

## PART II DIRECTIONS APPLICABLE TO ALL PROCEEDINGS

### Scope

4 Paragraphs 5 to 13 apply to proceedings in England and Wales in the magistrates' courts, the county courts, the Crown Court, the High Court and the Court of Appeal (Civil and Criminal Division). Paragraph 10 also applies to the form and procedure for a reference to the Court of Appeal by a tribunal.

### Raising the Question as to Whether a Devolution Issue Arises

5.1 Where a party to any form of proceedings wishes to raise an issue which may be a devolution issue whether as a claim (or part of a claim) to enforce or establish a legal right or to seek a remedy or as a defence (or part of a defence), the provisions of this Practice Direction apply in addition to the rules of procedure applicable to the proceedings in which the issue arises.

5.2 A court may, of its own volition, require the question of whether a devolution issue arises to be considered, if the materials put before the court indicate such an issue may arise, even if the parties have not used the term 'devolution issue'.

### Determination by a Court of Whether a Devolution Issue Arises

6.1 The court may give such directions as it considers appropriate to obtain clarification or additional information to establish whether a devolution issue arises.

6.2 In determining whether a devolution issue arises the court, notwithstanding the contention of a party to the proceedings, may decide that a devolution issue shall *not* be taken to arise if the contention appears to the court to be frivolous or vexatious (paragraph 2 of schedule 8 to the GWA).

6.3 If the court determines that a devolution issue arises it must state what that devolution issue is clearly and concisely.

### Notice of Devolution Issue to the Attorney General and the Assembly

7.1 If a court determines that a devolution issue arises in the proceedings, it must order a devolution issue notice substantially in the form numbered 'DI 1' in Annex 1 to be given to the Attorney General and the Assembly unless they are already a party to the proceedings (paragraph 5(1), schedule 8 to the GWA).

7.2 A court receiving a reference does not have to serve a devolution issue notice unless it determines that a devolution issue that was not identified by the court making the reference has arisen. In that case the court receiving the reference must serve a devolution issue notice which must:

(1) state what devolution issue has been referred to it;
(2) state what further devolution issue has arisen; and
(3) identify the referring court.

7.3 If the devolution issue has arisen in criminal proceedings, the devolution issue notice must state:

(1) whether the proceedings have been adjourned;
(2) whether the defendant is remanded in custody; and
(3) if the defendant has been remanded in custody and his trial has not commenced, when the custody time limit expires.[6]

7.4 If the devolution issue arises in an appeal, the devolution issue notice must:

(1) state that the devolution issue arises in an appeal;
(2) identify the court whose decision is being appealed; and
(3) state whether the devolution issue is raised for the first time on appeal; or, if

---

[6] Custody time limits are imposed by the Prosecution of Offences (Custody Time Limits) Regulations 1987 as amended.

it is not, state that the devolution issue was raised in the court whose decision is being appealed, what decision was reached by that court, and the date of the previous notice to the Attorney General and the Assembly.

7.5 The devolution issue notice will specify a date which will be 14 days, or such longer period as the court may direct (see below), after the date of the devolution issue notice as the date by which the Attorney General or the Assembly must notify the court that he or it wishes to take part as a party to the proceedings, so far as they relate to a devolution issue.

7.6 The court may, in exceptional circumstances, specify a date longer than 14 days after the date of the devolution issue notice as the date by which the Attorney General and the Assembly must notify the court that he or it wishes to take part as a party to the proceedings. The court may do this before the notice is given, or before or after the expiry of the period given in the notice.

7.7 (1) On the date of the devolution issue notice,
  (a) the devolution issue notice for the Attorney General must be faxed to him by the court;[7] and
  (b) the devolution issue notice for the Assembly must be faxed by the court to the Counsel General for the Assembly.
(2) On the same day as a fax is sent a copy of the devolution issue notice must be sent by the court by first class post to the Attorney General and the Counsel General for the Assembly.

7.8 The court may, on such terms as it considers appropriate, order such additional documents to be served (in civil proceedings, the claim form) or additional information to be supplied with the devolution issue notice.

7.9 (1) When a court orders a devolution issue notice to be given the court may make such further orders as it thinks fit in relation to any adjournment, stay, continuance of the proceedings, or interim measures, during the period within which the Attorney General and the Assembly have to notify the court if they intend to take part as a party to the proceedings.
(2) Before ordering an adjournment in criminal proceedings, the court will consider all material circumstances, including whether it would involve delay that might extend beyond the custody time limits if the defendant is remanded in custody and his trial has not commenced.

7.10 If neither the Attorney General nor the Assembly notify the court within the specified time that he or it wishes to take part as a party to the proceedings:
(1) the proceedings should immediately continue on expiry of the period within which they had to notify the court; and
(2) the court has no duty to inform them of the outcome of the proceedings apart from the duty to notify them if the court decides to refer the devolution issue to another court (see paragraph 10.3(5)).[8]

## Adding the Attorney General or the Assembly to the Proceedings and Their Right to Require Referral of a Devolution Issue to the Judicial Committee

8.1 If the Attorney General or the Assembly wishes to take part as a party to the proceedings so far as they relate to a devolution issue, he or it must send to the court and the other parties (and to each other if only one of them has become a party) a notice substantially in the form numbered 'DI 2' shown in Annex 1 within the time specified in the devolution issue notice.

8.2 On receipt of this form the court may give such consequential directions as it considers necessary.

[7] See Annex 2 for information about fax numbers and addresses.

[8] If there is an appeal, the appeal court will serve a devolution issue notice on the Attorney General and the Assembly (see paragraph 7.4).

8.3 If the Attorney General or the Assembly is a party to the proceedings, and either of them wishes to require the court to refer the devolution issue to the Judicial Committee, he or it must as soon as practicable send to the court and the other parties (and to each other if only one of them has become a party) a notice substantially in the form numbered 'DI 3' shown in Annex 1.

## Determination by the Court of Whether or Not to Make a Reference of a Devolution Issue if the Attorney General or the Assembly Do Not Require a Reference

9.1 If the court is not required to refer the devolution issue to the Judicial Committee, the court will decide whether it should refer the devolution issue to the relevant court as specified in paragraph 3.4.

9.2 Before deciding whether to make a reference the court may hold a directions hearing or give written directions as to the making of submissions on the question of whether to make a reference.

9.3 The court may make a decision on the basis of written submissions if its procedures permit this and it wishes to do so, or the court may have a hearing before making a decision.

9.4 In exercising its discretion as to whether to make a reference, the court will have regard to all relevant circumstances and in particular to:

(1) the importance of the devolution issue to the public in general;
(2) the importance of the devolution issue to the original parties to the proceedings;
(3) whether a decision on the reference of the devolution issue will be decisive of the matters in dispute between the parties;
(4) whether all the relevant findings of fact have been made (a devolution issue will not, unless there are exceptional circumstances, be suitable for a reference if it has to be referred on the basis of assumed facts);
(5) the delay that a reference would entail particularly in cases involving children and criminal cases (including whether the reference is likely to involve delay that would extend beyond the expiry of the custody time limits if the defendant is remanded in custody and his trial has not commenced); and
(6) additional costs that a reference might involve.[9]

9.5 The court should state its reasons for making or declining to make a reference.

9.6 If the court decides not to refer the case, it will give directions for the future conduct of the action, which will include directions as to the participation of the Attorney General and the Assembly if they are parties.

## Form and Procedure for References

10.1 If the court or tribunal is required by the Attorney General or the Assembly (in relation to any proceedings before the court to which he or it is a party) to refer the devolution issue to the Judicial Committee:

(1) the court or tribunal will make the reference as soon as practicable after receiving the notice from the Attorney General or the Assembly substantially in the form numbered 'DI 3' shown in Annex 1, and follow the procedure for references in the Judicial Committee (Devolution Issues) Rules Order 1999; and
(2) the court or tribunal may order the parties, or any of them, to draft the reference.

10.2 If the Court of Appeal decides to refer the devolution issue to the Judicial Committee:

(1) It will follow the procedure in the Judicial Committee (Devolution Issues) Rules Order 1999; and

[9] In criminal cases section 16 of the Prosecution of Offences Act 1985 does not enable a court receiving a reference to make a defendant's costs order. If the defendant is subsequently acquitted by the court who made the reference that court can make a defendant's costs order. However it would not cover the costs of the reference as 'proceedings' is defined in section 21 as including proceedings in any court below but makes no mention of proceedings on a reference.

(2) the court may order the parties, or any of them, to draft the reference.

10.3 If any other court or tribunal decides, or if a tribunal is required, to refer the devolution issue to another court:

(1) the reference must be substantially in the form numbered 'DI 4' shown in Annex 1 and must set out the following:
   (a) the question referred;
   (b) the addresses of the parties, except in the case of family proceedings, for which see paragraphs 15.2–4;
   (c) a concise statement of the background of the matter including:
      (i) the facts of the case, including any relevant findings of fact by the referring court or lower courts; and
      (ii) the main issues in the case and the contentions of the parties with regard to them;
   (d) the relevant law, including the relevant provisions of the GWA;
   (e) the reasons why an answer to the question is considered necessary for the purpose of disposing of the proceedings;

(2) all judgments already given in the proceedings will be annexed to the reference;

(3) the court may order the parties, or any of them, to draft the reference;

(4) the court or tribunal will transmit the reference to:
   (a) the Civil Appeals Office Registry if the reference is to the Court of Appeal from a county court, the High Court or the Crown Court in civil proceedings, or from a tribunal;
   (b) the Registrar of Criminal Appeals if the reference is to the Court of Appeal from the Crown Court in proceedings on indictment; and
   (c) the Administrative Court Office if the reference is to the High Court from a magistrates' court in civil or summary proceedings or from the Crown Court in summary proceedings.[10]

   If the reference is transmitted to Cardiff an additional copy of the reference must be filed so that it can be retained by the Cardiff Office. The original reference will be forwarded to the Administrative Court Office in London.

(5) at the same time as the reference is transmitted to the court receiving the reference a copy of the reference will be sent by first class post to:
   (a) the parties;
   (b) the Attorney General if he is not already a party; and
   (c) the Assembly if it is not already a party;

(6) each person on whom a copy of the reference is served must within 21 days notify the court to which the reference is transmitted and the other persons on whom the reference is served whether they wish to be heard on the reference;

(7) the court receiving the reference (either the Court of Appeal or the High Court) will give directions for the conduct of the reference, including the lodging of cases or skeleton arguments; and transmit a copy of the determination on the reference to the referring court; and

(8) if there has been an appeal to the Judicial Committee against a decision of the High Court or the Court of Appeal on a reference, and a copy of the Judicial Committee's decision on that appeal has been sent to the High Court or Court of Appeal (as the case may be), that court will send a copy to the court which referred the devolution issue to it.

10.4 When a court receives notification of the decision on a reference, it will determine how to proceed with the remainder of the case.

---

[10] See Annex 2 for the relevant addresses. It shows The Law Courts, Cathays Park, Cardiff CF10 3PG and the Royal Courts of Justice, Strand, London WC2A 2LL as alternative addresses for transmitting documents to the Administrative Court Office. If the order is transmitted to Cardiff, the additional copy will be forwarded by the Cardiff Office to the Administrative Court Office in London.

### Power of the Court to Deal With Pending Proceedings if a Reference is Made (Whether by the Attorney General, the Assembly or the Court)

11 If a reference is made the court will adjourn or stay the proceedings in which the devolution issue arose, unless it otherwise orders; and will make such further orders as it thinks fit in relation to any adjournment or stay.

### The Welsh Language

12.1 If any party wishes to put forward a contention in relation to a devolution issue that involves comparison of the Welsh and English texts of any Assembly subordinate legislation, that party must give notice to the court as soon as possible.

12.2 Upon receipt of the notification, the court will consider the appropriate means of determining the issue, including, if necessary, the appointment of a Welsh speaking judicial assessor to assist the court.

12.3 Parties to any proceedings in which the Welsh language may be used must also comply with the Practice Direction of 16th October 1998 (relating to proceedings in the Crown Court) and the Practice Direction of 26th April 1999 (relating to civil proceedings). These Practice Directions apply, as appropriate, to proceedings involving a devolution issue in which the Welsh language may be used.

### Crown Proceedings Act 1947 (Section 19)

13 Where the court has determined that a devolution issue arises, the Attorney General will give any necessary consent to:

(1) the proceedings being transferred to The Law Courts, Cathays Park, Cardiff CF10 3PG, or to such other district registry as shall (exceptionally) be directed by the court; and

(2) to the trial taking place at Cardiff or at such other trial location as shall (exceptionally) be directed by the court.

## PART III DIRECTIONS APPLICABLE TO SPECIFIC PROCEEDINGS

### Judicial Review Proceedings in Wales

14.1 PD 54 (judicial review) contains provisions about when judicial review proceedings may be brought in the Administrative Court in Wales.

### Family Proceedings in the Magistrates' Courts, the County Courts and the High Court

15.1 In any proceedings in which any question with respect to the upbringing of a child arises, the court shall have regard to the general principle that any delay in determining the question is likely to prejudice the welfare of the child.[11]

15.2 If the FPR apply, the court will comply with rule 10.21.[12]

15.3 If Part IV of the FPR applies, the court will comply with rule 4.23.[13]

---

[11] Section 1(2), Children Act 1989.

[12] Rule 10.21 states: (1) Subject to rule 2.3 [of the FPR] nothing in these rules shall be construed as requiring any party to reveal the address of their private residence (or that of any child) save by order of the court. (2) Where a party declines to reveal an address in reliance upon paragraph (1) above, he shall give notice of that address to the court in Form C8 and that address shall not be revealed to any person save by order of the court.

[13] Rule 4.23 states: (1) Notwithstanding any rule of court to the contrary, no document, other than a record of an order, held by the court and relating to proceedings to which [Part IV] applies shall be disclosed, other than to—(a) a party, (b) the legal representative of a party, (c) the guardian ad litem, (d) the Legal Aid Board, or (e) a welfare officer, without the leave of the judge or the district judge. (2) Nothing in this rule shall prevent the notification by the court or the proper officer of a direction under section 37(1) to the authority concerned. (3) Nothing in this rule shall prevent the disclosure of a document prepared by a guardian ad litem for the purpose of—(a) enabling a person to perform functions required by regulations made under section 41(7); (b) assisting a guardian ad litem or a reporting

15.4 If the FPC apply, the court will comply with Rules 23 and 33A.[14]

15.5 If the proceedings are listed in column (1) of Appendix 3 to the FPR or Schedule 2 to the FPC, a copy of any notice to be given to the parties must also be given to the persons set out in column (iv) of Appendix 3 or Schedule 2 as the case may be.

15.6 A party wishing to raise a devolution issue must, wherever possible, raise it (giving full particulars of the provisions relied on) in the application or answer or at the first directions hearing where appropriate.

15.7 If a party has not raised a devolution issue as above, the party must seek the permission of the court to raise it at a later stage.

15.8 Where a court has referred the devolution issue to another court and has received notification of the decision on the reference, the matter should so far as is practicable be placed before the same judge or magistrates who dealt with the case before the reference.

## Civil Proceedings in the County Courts and the High Court

16.1 A party wishing to raise a devolution issue must specify in the claim form, or if he is a defendant, in the defence (or written evidence filed with the acknowledgement of service in a Part 8 claim) that the claim raises a devolution issue and the relevant provisions of the GWA.

16.2 The particulars of claim or defence if the devolution issue is raised by the defendant (or written evidence filed with the acknowledgement of service in a Part 8 claim) must contain the facts and circumstances and points of law on the basis of which it is alleged that a devolution issue arises in sufficient detail to enable the court to determine whether a devolution issue arises in the proceedings.

16.3 Whether or not the allocation rules apply, if a question is raised during the proceedings that might be a devolution issue, then a directions hearing must take place and the matter must be referred to a circuit judge (in county court actions) or a High Court judge (in High Court actions) for determination as to whether a devolution issue arises and for further directions.

16.4 If a party fails to specify in the appropriate document that a devolution issue arises but that party subsequently wishes to raise a devolution issue, that party must seek the permission of the court.

16.5 Where any party has specified that a devolution issue arises, no default judgment can be obtained.

## Criminal Proceedings in the Crown Court

17 If the defendant wishes to raise a devolution issue he should do so at the Plea and Directions Hearing.

---

officer (within the meaning of section 65(1)(b) of the Adoption Act 1976) who is appointed under any enactment to perform his functions.

[14] Rule 23 states: (1) No document, other than a record of an order, held by the court and relating to relevant proceedings shall be disclosed, other than to—(a) a party, (b) the legal representative of a party, (c) the guardian ad litem, (d) the Legal Aid Board, or (e) a welfare officer, without leave of the justices' clerk or the court. (2) Nothing in this rule shall prevent the notification by the court or the justices' clerk of a direction under section 37(1) to the authority concerned. (3) Nothing in this rule shall prevent the disclosure of a document prepared by a guardian ad litem for the purpose of—(a) enabling a person to perform functions required by regulations made under section 41(7); (b) assisting a guardian ad litem or a reporting officer (within the meaning of section 65(1)(b) of the Adoption Act 1976) who is appointed under any enactment to perform his functions.

Rule 33A states: (1) Nothing in these Rules shall be construed as requiring any party to reveal the address of their private residence (or that of any child) except by order of the court. (2) Where a party declines to reveal an address in reliance upon paragraph (1) he shall give notice of that address to the court in Form C8 and that address shall not be revealed to any person except by order of the court.

## Criminal and Civil Proceedings in the Magistrates' Courts

18.1 (1) Where a defendant, who has been charged or has had an information laid against him in respect of a criminal offence and has entered a plea of 'Not Guilty', wishes to raise a devolution issue he should, wherever possible, give full particulars of the provisions relied on by notice in writing.

(2) Where a party to a complaint, or applicant for a licence wishes to raise a devolution issue he should, wherever possible, give full particulars of the provisions relied on by notice in writing.

(3) Such notice should be given to the prosecution (and other party if any) and the court as soon as practicable after the 'Not Guilty' plea is entered or the complaint or application is made as the case may be.

18.2 Where proceedings are to be committed or transferred to the Crown Court by the magistrates, the question as to whether a devolution issue arises shall be a matter for the Crown Court.

# PART IV APPEALS

## Appeals to the Court of Appeal (Civil and Criminal Division)

19.1 This paragraph applies if a devolution issue is raised in any appeal to either the Civil or the Criminal Division of the Court of Appeal.

19.2 The devolution issue may already have been raised in the court whose decision is being appealed. The devolution issue may, however, be raised for the first time on appeal.

19.3 Where an application for permission to appeal is made, or an appeal is brought where permission is not needed, the appellant must specify in the application notice (or the notice of appeal or notice of motion as the case may be):

(1) that the appeal raises a devolution issue and the relevant provisions of the GWA;

(2) the facts and circumstances and points of law on the basis of which it is alleged that a devolution issue arises in sufficient detail to enable the court to determine whether a devolution issue arises; and

(3) whether the devolution issue was considered in the court below, and, if so, provide details of the decision.

19.4 An appellant may not seek to raise a devolution issue without the permission of the court after he has filed an application notice; or a notice of appeal or notice of motion (if no application notice).

19.5 Where permission to appeal is sought and a party to the appeal wishes to raise a devolution issue which was not raised in the lower court, the court will determine if a devolution issue arises before deciding whether to grant leave to appeal.

## Appeals to the Crown Court

20 A notice of appeal from a decision of the magistrates' courts to the Crown Court must specify whether the devolution issue was considered in the court below and if so, provide details of the decision. If it was not so considered, the notice should specify:

(1) that the appeal raises a devolution issue and the relevant provisions of the GWA; and

(2) the facts and circumstances and points of law on the basis of which it is alleged that a devolution issue arises in sufficient detail to enable the court to determine whether a devolution issue arises.

# ANNEX 1

## DI 1 Devolution Issues

*Notice of Devolution Issue to Attorney General and The National Assembly For Wales*

[NAME OF CASE]

Take notice that the above mentioned case has raised a devolution issue as defined by

Schedule 8 to the Government of Wales Act 1998. Details of the devolution issue are given in the attached schedule.

This notice meets the notification requirements under paragraph 5(1) of Schedule 8 to the Government of Wales Act 1998. You may take part as a party to these proceedings, so far as they relate to a devolution issue (paragraph 5(2) of Schedule 8). If you want to do this you must notify the court by completing the attached form, and returning it to the court at [address] by [date].

DATED

To: The Attorney General
The National Assembly for Wales
Other parties (where appropriate)

## DI 2 Devolution Issues

*Notice of Intention of Attorney General or The National Assembly For Wales to Become Party to Proceedings, So Far As They Relate To a Devolution Issue, Under Paragraph 5(2) Schedule 8 to The Government of Wales Act 1998*

In the [name of court]

[case name]

Take notice that the [Attorney General] [the National Assembly for Wales] intends to take part as a party to proceedings so far as they relate to a devolution issue as permitted by paragraph 5(2) of Schedule 8 to the Government of Wales Act 1998 in relation to the devolution issue raised by [ ], of which notice was received by the [Attorney General] [Assembly] on [ ].

[The [ ] also gives notice that it [requires the matter to be referred to] [is still considering whether to require the matter to be referred to] the Judicial Committee of the Privy Council under paragraph 30 of Schedule 8 to the Government of Wales Act 1998.]

[DATE]

On behalf of the [Attorney General]
[National Assembly for Wales]

To: The clerk of the court at [ ]
The parties to the case
[Attorney General] [National Assembly for Wales]

## DI 3 Devolution Issues

*Notice by Attorney General or National Assembly For Wales That They Require Devolution Issue to be Referred to The Judicial Committee of the Privy Council*

In the [court]

[case name]

The [Attorney General] [National Assembly for Wales] gives notice that the devolution issue, which has been raised in the above case and to which [he] [it] is a party, must be referred to the Judicial Committee of the Privy Council under paragraph 30 of Schedule 8 to the Government of Wales Act 1998.

[Date]

On behalf of the [Attorney General]
[National] Assembly for Wales]

To: The clerk of the court at [ ]
The parties to the case
[Attorney General] [National Assembly for Wales]

## DI 4 Devolution Issues

*Reference by The Court or Tribunal of Devolution Issue to [High Court] [Court of Appeal] [Judicial Committee of The Privy Council]*

In the [court]

[case name]

It is ordered that the devolution issue(s) set out in the schedule be referred to the [High Court] [Court of Appeal] [Judicial Committee of the Privy Council] for determination in accordance with paragraph [ ] of Schedule 8 to the Government of Wales Act 1998.

It is further ordered that the proceedings be stayed until the [High Court] [Court of Appeal] [Judicial Committee of the Privy Council] determine the devolution issue[s] or until further order.

DATED

Judge/clerk to the magistrates' court
Chairman of the Tribunal
[Address]

## Skeleton Reference to be Attached to Form DI 4

In the [court]

[case name]

(a) [The question referred.]
(b) [The addresses of the parties]
(c) [A concise statement of the background to the matters including—
    (i) The facts of the case including any relevant findings of fact by the referring court or lower courts; and
    (ii) The main issues in the case and the contentions of the parties with regard to them;]
(d) [the relevant law including the relevant provisions of the Government of Wales Act 1998]
(e) [the reasons why an answer to the question is considered necessary for the purpose of disposing of the proceedings.]

[All judgments already given in the proceedings are annexed to this reference.]

# ANNEX 2
# ADDRESSES

1. Notices to the National Assembly for Wales (Cynulliad Cenedlaethol Cymru) must be sent to the Counsel General to the National Assembly for Wales, Crown Buildings, Cathays Park, Cardiff CF99 1NA. Fax number: (01222) 826798.
2. Notices to the Attorney General must be sent to the Attorney General's Chambers, 9 Buckingham Gate, London SW1E 6JP. Fax number (0207) 271 2433.
3. References to the Crown Office under paragraph 9.3(1)c of the Practice Direction may be sent to the Crown Office, Royal Courts of Justice, Strand, London WC2A 2LL; or the Law Courts, Cathays Park, Cardiff CF10 3PG (2 copies).

## Explanatory Note

4. The addresses and fax numbers above are the best information available. However it is possible that these (particularly the fax numbers and address for Notices to the Assembly) may change. It would therefore be advisable to confirm the numbers before sending information.

# Practice Direction — Application for a Warrant under the Competition Act 1998

## Interpretation

1.1 In this practice direction—
 (1) 'the Act' means the Competition Act 1998;
 (2) 'the Commission' means the European Commission;
 (3) 'Commission official' means a person authorised by the Commission for any of the purposes set out in section 62(10), 62A(12) or 63(10) of the Act;
 (4) 'the OFT' means the Office of Fair Trading;
 (5) 'officer' means an officer of the OFT;
 (6) 'named officer' means the person identified in a warrant as the principal officer in charge of executing that warrant, and includes a named authorised officer under section 63 of the Act; and
 (7) 'warrant' means a warrant under section 28, 28A, 62, 62A, 63, 65G or 65H of the Act.

1.2 In relation to an application for a warrant by a regulator entitled pursuant to section 54 and Schedule 10 of the Act to exercise the functions of the OFT, references to the OFT shall be interpreted as referring to that regulator.

## Application for a Warrant

2.1 An application by the OFT for a warrant must be made to a High Court judge using the Part 8 procedure as modified by this practice direction.

2.2 The application should be made to a judge of the Chancery Division at the Royal Courts of Justice (if available).

2.3 The application is made without notice and the claim form may be issued without naming a defendant. Rules 8.1(3), 8.3, 8.4, 8.5(2)–(6), 8.6(1), 8.7 and 8.8 do not apply.

## Confidentiality of Court Documents

3.1 The court will not effect service of any claim form, warrant, or other document filed or issued in an application to which this practice direction applies, except in accordance with an order of the judge hearing the application.

3.2 CPR rules 5.4, 5.4B and 5.4C do not apply, and paragraphs 3.3 and 3.4 have effect in [their*] place.

3.3 When a claim form is issued the court file will be marked 'Not for disclosure' and, unless a High Court judge grants permission, the court records relating to the application (including the claim form and documents filed in support and any warrant or order that is issued) will not be made available by the court for any person to inspect or copy, either before or after the hearing of the application.

3.4 An application for permission under paragraph 3.3 must be made on notice to the OFT in accordance with Part 23.

(Rule 23.7(1) requires a copy of the application notice to be served as soon as practicable after it is filed, and in any event at least 3 days before the court is to deal with the application.)

## Contents of Claim Form, Affidavit and Documents in Support

4.1 The claim form must state—
 (1) the section of the Act under which the OFT is applying for a warrant;
 (2) the address or other identification of the premises to be subject to the warrant; and
 (3) the anticipated date or dates for the execution of the warrant.

* Editorial note: the official text states 'its', but it is presumed that such is an error and should state 'their'.

4.2 The application must be supported by affidavit evidence, which must be filed with the claim form.

4.3 The evidence must set out all the matters on which the OFT relies in support of the application, including all material facts of which the court should be made aware. In particular it must state—

(1) the subject matter (i.e. the nature of the suspected infringement of the Chapter I or II prohibitions in the Act, or of Articles 81 or 82 of the Treaty establishing the European Community) and purpose of the investigation to which the application relates;

(2) the identity of the undertaking or undertakings suspected to have committed the infringement;

(3) the grounds for applying for the issue of the warrant and the facts relied upon in support;

(4) details of the premises to be subject to the warrant and of the possible occupier or occupiers of those premises;

(5) the connection between the premises and the undertaking or undertakings suspected to have committed the infringement;

(6) the name and position of the officer who it is intended will be the named officer;

(7) if it is intended that the warrant may pursuant to a relevant provision of the Act authorise any person (other than an officer or a Commission official) to accompany the named officer in executing the warrant, the name and job title of each such person and the reason why it is intended that he may accompany the named officer.

4.4 There must be exhibited to an affidavit in support of the application—

(1) the written authorisation of the OFT containing the names of—

(a) the officer who it is intended will be the named officer;

(b) the other persons who it is intended may accompany him in executing the warrant; and

(2) in the case of an application under section 62, 62A or 63 of the Act, if it is intended that Commission officials will accompany the named officer in executing the warrant, the written authorisations of the Commission containing the names of the Commission officials.

4.5 There must also be filed with the claim form—

(1) drafts of—

(a) the warrant; and

(b) an explanatory note to be produced and served with it; and

(2) the written undertaking by the named officer required by paragraph 6.2 of this practice direction.

(Examples of forms of warrant under sections 28 and 62 of the Act, and explanatory notes to be produced and served with them, are annexed to this practice direction. These forms and notes should be used with appropriate modifications in applications for warrants under other sections of the Act.)

4.6 If possible the draft warrant and explanatory note should also be supplied to the court on disk in a form compatible with the word processing software used by the court.

## Listing

5 The application will be listed by the court on any published list of cases as 'An application by D'.

## Hearing of the Application

6.1 An application for a warrant will be heard and determined in private, unless the judge hearing it directs otherwise.

6.2 The court will not issue a warrant unless there has been filed a written undertaking, signed by the named officer, to comply with paragraph 8.1 of this practice direction.

## The Warrant

7.1 The warrant must—
- (1) contain the information required by section 29(1), 64(1) or 65I(1) of the Act;
- (2) state the address or other identification of the premises to be subject to the warrant;
- (3) state the names of—
  - (a) the named officer; and
  - (b) any other officers, Commission officials or other persons who may accompany him in executing the warrant;
- (4) set out the action which the warrant authorises the persons executing it to take under the relevant section of the Act;
- (5) give the date on which the warrant is issued;
- (6) include a statement that the warrant continues in force until the end of the period of one month beginning with the day on which it is issued; and
- (7) state that the named officer has given the undertaking required by paragraph 6.2.

7.2 Rule 40.2 applies to a warrant.

(Rule 40.2 requires every judgment or order to state the name and judicial title of the person making it, to bear the date on which it is given or made, and to be sealed by the court.)

7.3 Upon the issue of a warrant the court will provide to the OFT—
- (1) the sealed warrant and sealed explanatory note; and
- (2) a copy of the sealed warrant and sealed explanatory note for service on the occupier or person in charge of the premises subject to the warrant.

## Execution of Warrant

8.1 A named officer attending premises to execute a warrant must, if the premises are occupied—
- (1) produce the warrant and an explanatory note on arrival at the premises; and
- (2) as soon as possible thereafter personally serve a copy of the warrant and the explanatory note on the occupier or person appearing to him to be in charge of the premises.

8.2 The named officer must also comply with any order which the court may make for service of any other documents relating to the application.

8.3 Unless the court otherwise orders—
- (1) the initial production of a warrant and entry to premises under the authority of the warrant must take place between 9.30 a.m. and 5.30 p.m. Monday to Friday; but
- (2) once persons named in the warrant have entered premises under the authority of a warrant, they may, whilst the warrant remains in force—
  - (a) remain on the premises; or
  - (b) re-enter the premises to continue executing the warrant, outside those times.

8.4 If the persons executing a warrant propose to remove any items from the premises pursuant to the warrant they must, unless it is impracticable—
- (1) make a list of all the items to be removed;
- (2) supply a copy of the list to the occupier or person appearing to be in charge of the premises; and
- (3) give that person a reasonable opportunity to check the list before removing any of the items.

## Application to Vary or Discharge Warrant

9.1 The occupier or person in charge of premises in relation to which a warrant has been issued may apply to vary or discharge the warrant.

9.2 An application under paragraph 9.1 to stop a warrant from being executed must be made immediately upon the warrant being served.

9.3 A person applying to vary or discharge a warrant must first inform the named officer that he is making the application.

9.4 The application should be made to the judge who issued the warrant, or, if he is not available, to another High Court judge.

### Application under s. 59 Criminal Justice and Police Act 2001

10.1 Attention is drawn to section 59 of the Criminal Justice and Police Act 2001, which makes provision about applications relating to property seized in the exercise of the powers conferred by (among other provisions) section 28(2) of the Act.

10.2 An application under section 59—

(1) must be made by application notice in accordance with CPR Part 23; and

(2) should be made to a judge of the Chancery Division at the Royal Courts of Justice (if available).

### Warrant

*[The form of the warrant is not reproduced here but may be accessed via the DCA website, <http://www.dca.gov.uk>.]*

## EXPLANATORY NOTE TO WARRANT UNDER SECTIONS 28 AND 29 OF THE COMPETITION ACT 1998 ('THE ACT')

This Explanatory Note is provided for information only. It is not a detailed note of the powers under the Act which are subject to interpretation by the courts.

### Subject Matter and Powers

Officers of the Office of Fair Trading ('the OFT') [[*if the Judge so orders pursuant to section 28(3A), insert the following here and elsewhere as indicated*] and other persons] have been authorised under Warrant to enter and search the premises identified in the Warrant in connection with an investigation under the Act. The subject matter of this investigation is set out in paragraph 2 of the Warrant. The officers [and other persons] will not elaborate on this.

Paragraph 4 of the Warrant sets out the powers of the named officer[1] and other officers [and other persons] under section 28 of the Act for the purposes of the present investigation. On entering the premises, the named officer will, as a matter of practice, produce evidence of the identity of the other officers in addition to his identity when producing the Warrant.

Unless the Court has ordered otherwise, the initial production of the Warrant and entry to premises must take place between 9.30 a.m. and 5.30 p.m. Monday to Friday and, once officers [and other persons] have entered premises under the authority of the Warrant, they may outside those times and whilst the Warrant remains in force, remain on the premises or re-enter the premises to continue executing the Warrant.

### Access to Legal Advice

You are advised to seek legal advice. If the named officer and other officers consider it reasonable in the circumstances to do so and if they are satisfied that you are complying with, or will comply with, such conditions as they consider it appropriate to impose, the named officer and other officers will grant a request to allow a reasonable time for your legal adviser to arrive at the premises before the inspection continues.

If you decide to seek legal advice you should do so promptly and this must not unduly delay or impede the inspection. Any delay must be kept to a strict minimum.

If you have an in-house legal adviser on the premises, or if you have received prior notice of the inspection, the named officer and other officers [and other persons] will not wait for your external legal adviser to arrive.

[1] The named officer is the principal officer of the OFT who, together with the other officers [and other persons], is authorised by the Warrant to exercise the powers under section 28 of the Act. His name and the names of the other officers [and other persons] are set out in Schedule B to the Warrant.

## Self-incrimination

The named officer and other officers [and other persons] have powers, among other matters, to search and take copies of, or extracts from, documents covered by the Warrant, to require you to produce relevant information which is stored in any electronic form and to require you to provide an explanation of any such documents (which the Act defines as including information recorded in any form). However, if your undertaking is suspected of having committed an infringement of the Act, they cannot require you to provide answers or statements that might involve an admission on your part of the existence of that infringement.

You should note also that, any statement made by a person in response to a requirement imposed by the named officer or other officers [or other persons] in exercise of their powers under paragraph 4 of the Warrant, may not be used in evidence against him on a prosecution for an offence under section 188 of the Enterprise Act 2002 (the cartel offence) unless, in the proceedings—

(a) in giving evidence, he makes a statement inconsistent with it, and
(b) evidence relating to it is adduced, or a question relating to it is asked, by him or on his behalf.

## Legally Privileged Communications

The powers under section 28 of the Act to search, take copies etc. (set out in paragraph 4(b) onwards in the Warrant) do not apply in respect of any 'privileged communication'. This is defined in section 30 of the Act to mean a communication

(a) between a professional legal adviser and his client, or
(b) made in connection with, or in contemplation of, legal proceedings and for the purposes of those proceedings,

which would be protected from disclosure in proceedings in the High Court on grounds of legal professional privilege.

For the purposes of section 30, a 'professional legal adviser' includes both an external and an in-house qualified legal adviser.

If you consider that a document or information is privileged, you should provide the named officer or other officer [or other person] with material of such a nature as to demonstrate to his satisfaction that the document or information, or parts of it, for which privilege is claimed, fulfil the conditions for it being privileged.

If you fail to do so, you should gather together the items for which privilege is claimed. These items will not be examined or copied unless you reach an agreement with the named officer that they may be examined or copied. If no agreement is reached on the day of the inspection, the named officer will request that you make a copy of the items and place this in a sealed envelope or package in his presence. The named officer will then discuss with you appropriate arrangements for the safe-keeping of these items pending resolution of the issue of privilege. For example, such arrangements may include a request that your legal adviser should give (or if no legal adviser is present, that you give), a written undertaking that the envelope or package will be retained safely and that its contents will not be concealed, removed, tampered with or destroyed until the issue of privilege is resolved.

## Listing of Items

Unless it is impracticable in all the circumstances, no item may be removed from the premises by the named officer or other officers [or other persons] until they have prepared a list of all the items to be removed, a copy of the list has been supplied to you, and you have been given a reasonable opportunity to check that the list relates to all the items concerned, and only to those items. This does not entitle you or your legal adviser to insist that the list or its contents should take any particular form.

## Confidentiality

You should note that, subject to the safeguards in relation to self-incrimination and legal privilege, you are **not** entitled to withhold a document or information by claiming that it is confidential.

Where it is possible to do so, it is suggested that after the inspection on the premises you should identify any part or parts of any information or document copied or taken that you consider to be confidential and provide a written explanation as to why it should be treated as such. For these purposes information is confidential if it is:

(i) commercial information the disclosure of which would, or might, significantly harm the legitimate business interests of the undertaking to which it relates; or

(ii) information relating to the private affairs of an individual the disclosure of which would, or might, significantly harm his interests.[2]

A document will be treated as confidential to the extent that it contains confidential information.

It is for the OFT to determine whether or not the information is to be disclosed in accordance with Part 9 of the Enterprise Act 2002 and any applicable obligation or power to disclose information pursuant to Council Regulation (EC) No. 1/2003.[3]

## Application to Vary or Discharge the Warrant

You are entitled to apply to the Court to vary or discharge the Warrant. If you intend to make such an application, you must first inform the named officer. An application to stop the Warrant from being executed must be made immediately upon it being served.

The application must be made to the judge who issued the Warrant, or if he is not available, to another High Court judge.

If you are making an immediate application to stop the Warrant from being executed, the named officer will delay starting or continuing a search of the premises for a reasonable period (not exceeding two hours) while you make your application, provided that you

(1) permit the named officer and other officers [and other persons] to enter and remain on the premises;

(2) keep the named officer informed of the steps you are taking in relation to the application; and

(3) comply with any other conditions that the named officer imposes.

Examples of conditions that the named officer may impose pursuant to (3) above include: that you do not disturb or move any document or information that is the subject of the Warrant; and/or you do not tell anyone other than your legal adviser about the Warrant or the investigation.

## Application under Section 59 Criminal Justice and Police Act 2001

Your attention is drawn to section 59 of the Criminal Justice and Police Act 2001, which makes provision about applications relating to property seized in the exercise of the powers conferred by (among other provisions) section 28(2) of the Act.

An application under section 59—

(1) must be made by application notice in accordance with Part 23 of the Civil Procedure Rules; and

(2) should be made to a judge of the Chancery Division at the Royal Courts of Justice (if available).

---

[2] The relevant terms of this offence are set out in Schedule C to the Warrant.

[3] Council Regulation (EC) No. 1/2003 of 16 December 2002 on the implementation of the rules on competition laid down in Articles 81 and 82 of the Treaty, OJ L 1, 4.1.2003, p.1.

## Warrant

*[The form of the warrant is not reproduced here but may be accessed via the DCA website, <http://www.dca.gov.uk>.]*

# EXPLANATORY NOTE TO WARRANT UNDER SECTIONS 62 AND 64 OF THE COMPETITION ACT 1998 ('THE ACT')

This Explanatory Note is provided for information only. It is not a detailed note of the powers under the Act or of the European Commission's powers of enquiry and investigation which are subject to interpretation respectively by the courts and the Court of Justice of the European Communities.

## Subject Matter and Powers

Officers of the Office of Fair Trading (the 'OFT') [*[if the Judge so orders pursuant to section 62(5A), insert the following here and elsewhere as indicated]*, other persons] and European Commission officials ('Commission officials') have been authorised under Warrant to enter and search the premises identified in the Warrant in connection with an investigation under the EC competition rules. The inspection of the premises has been ordered by a decision of the European Commission. The subject matter of this inspection is set out in paragraph 1 of the Warrant and in the European Commission's decision. The officers [, other persons] and Commission officials will not elaborate on this.

Paragraph 3 of the Warrant sets out the powers of the named officer,[4] the other officers [, other persons] and the Commission officials under section 62 of the Act for the purposes of the present inspection. On entering the premises, the named officer and the Commission officials will, as a matter of practice, produce evidence of the identity of the other officers in addition to their identity when producing the Warrant.

Unless the Court has ordered otherwise, the initial production of the Warrant and entry to premises must take place between 9.30 a.m. and 5.30 p.m. Monday to Friday and, once the officers [, the other persons] and Commission officials have entered premises under the authority of the Warrant, they may outside those times and whilst the Warrant remains in force, remain on the premises or re-enter the premises to continue executing the Warrant.

## Access to Legal Advice

You are advised to seek legal advice as explained in the European Commission's explanatory note to their Authorisation to Investigate, a copy of which will be produced to you by the Commission officials.

## Self-incrimination

You may be requested to provide explanations on facts or documents relating to the subject matter and purpose of the inspection. However, if your undertaking is suspected of having committed an infringement of EC competition laws, or you have committed the offence of intentional obstruction under section 65 of the Act,[5] you cannot be compelled to provide answers or statements that might involve an admission on your part of the existence of that infringement or offence.

## Legally Privileged Communications

The powers under section 62 of the Act (set out in paragraph 3(b) onwards in the Warrant) do not apply in respect of documents or information that are legally privileged. The Court of

[4] The named officer is the principal officer of the OFT who, together with the other officers [, other persons] and Commission officials, is authorised by the Warrant to exercise the powers under section 62 of the Act. His name and the names of the other officers [, other persons] and Commission officials are set out in Schedule B to the Warrant.

[5] The relevant terms of this offence are set out in Schedule C to the Warrant.

Justice of the European Communities has recognised that correspondence between a client and an external legal adviser, entitled to practise in one of the Member States, is privileged where

(a) the correspondence follows the initiation of proceedings by the European Commission and concerns the defence of the client; or
(b) the correspondence existed before the initiation of proceedings but is closely linked with the subject matter of the proceedings.

Correspondence between a client and an external legal adviser who is not entitled to practise in one of the Member States or between a client and an in-house legal adviser is not recognised by the Court of Justice as being protected by legal privilege. However, where the in-house legal adviser is simply reporting the statement of an external legal adviser who is entitled to practise in one of the Member States, privilege will apply.

If you consider that a document or information is privileged, you should provide the Commission officials with material of such a nature as to demonstrate to their satisfaction that the document or information, or parts of it, for which privilege is claimed, fulfil the conditions for it being privileged.

If you fail to do so, you should gather together the items for which privilege is claimed. These items will not be examined or copied unless you reach an agreement with the named officer or the Commission officials that they may be examined or copied. If no agreement is reached on the day of the inspection, the named officer or the Commission officials will request that you make a copy of the items and place this in a sealed envelope or package in his or their presence. They will then discuss with you appropriate arrangements for the safe-keeping of these items pending resolution of the issue of privilege. For example, such arrangements may include a request that your legal adviser should give (or if no legal adviser is present, that you give), a written undertaking that the envelope or package will be retained safely and that its contents will not be concealed, removed, tampered with or destroyed until the issue of privilege is resolved. The European Commission may adopt a decision requiring the documents to be handed over. You can challenge this by bringing proceedings for review of that decision before the Court of First Instance of the European Communities.

## Listing of Items

Unless it is impracticable in all the circumstances, no item may be removed from the premises by the named officer or the Commission officials until they have prepared a list of all the items to be removed, a copy of the list has been supplied to you, and you have been given a reasonable opportunity to check that the list relates to all the items concerned, and only to those items. This does not entitle you or your legal adviser to insist that the list or its contents should take any particular form.

## Confidentiality

You should note that, subject to the safeguards in relation to self-incrimination and legal privilege, you are **not** entitled to withhold a document or information by claiming that it is confidential.

Where it is possible to do so, it is suggested that after the inspection on the premises you should identify any information or document copied that you consider to be confidential and provide a written explanation to the European Commission as to why it should be treated as such.

A document will be treated as confidential to the extent that it contains confidential information.

It is for the European Commission to determine, subject to review by the Court of Justice, whether or not the information is to be disclosed, subject to the duty not to disclose information of the kind covered by the obligation of professional secrecy (Article 287 (ex

214) of the Treaty establishing the European Community and Article 28 of Council Regulation (EC) No. 1/2003[6]).

## Application to Vary or Discharge the Warrant

You are entitled to apply to the Court to vary or discharge the Warrant. If you intend to make such an application, you must first inform the named officer. An application to stop the Warrant from being executed must be made immediately upon it being served.

The application must be made to the judge who issued the Warrant, or if he is not available, to another High Court judge.

If you are making an immediate application to stop the Warrant from being executed, the named officer will delay starting or continuing a search of the premises for a reasonable period (not exceeding two hours) while you make your application, provided that you

(1) permit the named officer, the other officers [, other persons] and the Commission officials to enter and remain on the premises;
(2) keep the named officer informed of the steps you are taking in relation to the application; and
(3) comply with any other conditions that the named officer imposes.

Examples of conditions that the named officer may impose pursuant to (3) above include: that you do not disturb or move any document or information that is the subject of the Warrant; and/or you do not tell anyone other than your legal adviser about the Warrant, the inspection or the investigation.

In issuing the Warrant the judge was satisfied that the applicable statutory grounds were met, in particular that the measures authorised by the Warrant are neither arbitrary nor excessive having regard to the subject matter of the inspection ordered by the European Commission's decision specified in paragraph 1 of the Warrant. The Court cannot question the need for the inspection or the investigation, nor the lawfulness of the assessments of fact and law made by the European Commission in adopting the decision to order the inspection. Such issues may be raised only in proceedings for review of that decision brought before the Court of First Instance of the European Communities.

[6] Council Regulation (EC) No. 1/2003 of 16 December 2002 on the implementation of the rules on competition laid down in Articles 81 and 82 of the Treaty, OJ L 1, 4.1.2003, p.1.

# Practice Direction — Civil Recovery Proceedings

## Scope and Interpretation

1.1 Section I of this practice direction contains general provisions about proceedings in the High Court under parts 5 and 8 of the Proceeds of Crime Act 2002 and Part 5 of the Proceeds of Crime Act 2002 (External Requests and Orders) Order 2005.

1.2 Section II contains provisions about—
- (1) applications to the High Court under Part 5 of the Act and Part 5 of the Order in Council for—
  - (a) a recovery order;
  - (b) a property freezing order; and
  - (c) an interim receiving order; and
- (2) the register of external orders.

1.3 Section III contains provisions about applications to the High Court under part 8 of the Act for any of the following types of order or warrant in connection with a civil recovery investigation:
- (a) a production order;
- (b) a search and seizure warrant;
- (c) a disclosure order;
- (d) a customer information order; and
- (e) an account monitoring order.

1.4 Section IV of this practice direction contains further provisions about applications for each of the specific types of order and warrant listed in para. 1.3 above.

1.5 In this practice direction:
- (1) 'the Act' means the Proceeds of Crime Act 2002;
- (2) 'the Director' means the Director of the Assets Recovery Agency, or any person authorised by him to act on his behalf in accordance with s. 1(6) of the Act;
- (3) 'the Order in Council' means the Proceeds of Crime Act 2002 (External Requests and Orders) Order 2005;
- (4) 'civil recovery proceedings' means proceedings under Part 5 of the Act or Part 5 of the Order in Council (as appropriate);
- (5) 'the Regulations' means the Proceeds of Crime Act 2002 (Legal Expenses in Civil Recovery Proceedings) Regulations 2005; and
- (6) other expressions used have the same meaning as in the Act or the Order in Council (as appropriate).

## I GENERAL PROVISIONS

### Venue

2.1 A claim or application to the High Court under part 5 or part 8 of the 2002 Act or Part 5 of the Order in Council must be issued in the Administrative Court.

2.2 The Administrative Court will thereupon consider whether to transfer the claim or application to another Division or Court of the High Court.

### Use of Pseudonyms by Agency Staff

3.1 If a member of staff of the Assets Recovery Agency gives written or oral evidence in any proceedings using a pseudonym in accordance with s. 449 of the Act:
- (1) the court must be informed that the witness is using a pseudonym; and
- (2) a certificate under s. 449(3) of the Act must be filed or produced.

## II CIVIL RECOVERY PROCEEDINGS UNDER PART 5 OF THE ACT OR PART 5 OF THE ORDER IN COUNCIL

### Claim for a recovery order

4.1 A claim by the Director for a recovery order must be made using the CPR Part 8 procedure.

4.2 In a claim for a recovery order based on an external order, the claim must include an application to register the external order.

4.3 The claim form must—

(1) identify the property in relation to which a recovery order is sought;

(2) state, in relation to each item or description of property—

(a) whether the property is alleged to be recoverable property or associated property; and

(b) either—

(i) who is alleged to hold the property; or

(ii) where the Director is unable to identify who holds the property, the steps that have been taken to try to establish their identity;

(3) set out the matters relied upon in support of the claim;

(4) give details of the person nominated by the Director to act as trustee for civil recovery in accordance with section 267 of the Act or article 178 of the Order in Council; and

(5) in a claim which includes an application to register an external order, be accompanied by a copy of the external order.

4.4 The evidence in support of the claim must include the signed, written consent of the person nominated by the Director to act as trustee for civil recovery if appointed by the court.

4.5 In a claim which includes an application to register an external order, where—

(1) the sum specified in the external order is expressed in a currency other than sterling; and

(2) there are not funds held in the United Kingdom in the currency in which the sum specified is expressed sufficient to satisfy the external order,

the claim form, or particulars of claim if served subsequently, must state the sterling equivalent of the sum specified.

(Article 145(2) of the Order in Council provides that the sterling equivalent is to be calculated in accordance with the exchange rate prevailing at end of the day on which the external order is made.)

### Application for property freezing order or interim receiving order

5.1 An application for a property freezing order or an interim receiving order must be made—

(1) to a High Court judge; and

(2) in accordance with Part 23.

5.2 Rule 23.10(2) and Section I of Part 25 do not apply to applications for property freezing orders and interim receiving orders.

5.3 The application may be made without notice in the circumstances set out in—

(1) section 245A(3) of the Act and Article 147(3) of the Order in Council (in the case of an application for a property freezing order); and

(2) section 246(3) of the Act and Article 151(3) of the Order in Council (in the case of an application for an interim receiving order).

5.4 An application for a property freezing order must be supported by written evidence which must—

(1) set out the grounds on which the order is sought; and

(2) give details of each item or description of property in respect of which the order is sought, including—

(a) an estimate of the value of the property; and
(b) the additional information referred to in paragraph 5.5(2).

5.5 Part 69 (court's power to appoint a receiver) and its practice direction apply to an application for an interim receiving order with the following modifications—
(1) paragraph 2.1 of the practice direction supplementing Part 69 does not apply;
(2) the Director's written evidence must, in addition to the matters required by paragraph 4.1 of that practice direction, also state in relation to each item or description of property in respect of which the order is sought—
(a) whether the property is alleged to be—
(i) recoverable property; or
(ii) associated property,
and the facts relied upon in support of that allegation; and
(b) in the case of any associated property—
(i) who is believed to hold the property; or
(ii) if the Director is unable to establish who holds the property, the steps that have been taken to establish their identity; and
(3) the Director's written evidence must always identify a nominee and include the information in paragraph 4.2 of that practice direction.

5.6 A draft of the order which is sought must be filed with the application notice. This should if possible also be supplied to the court in an electronic form compatible with the word processing software used by the court.

## Property freezing order or interim receiving order made before commencement of claim for recovery order

5A A property freezing order or interim receiving order which is made before a claim for a recovery order has been commenced shall—
(1) specify a period within which the Director must either start the claim or apply for the continuation of the order while he carries out his investigation; and
(2) provide that the order shall be set aside if the Director does not start the claim or apply for its continuation before the end of that period.

## Exclusions when making property freezing order or interim receiving order

5B.1 When the court makes a property freezing order or interim receiving order on an application without notice, it will normally make an initial exclusion from the order for the purpose of enabling the respondent to meet his reasonable legal costs so that he may—
(1) take advice in relation to the order;
(2) prepare a statement of assets in accordance with paragraph 7A.3; and
(3) if so advised, apply for the order to be varied or set aside.
The total amount specified in the initial exclusion will not normally exceed £3,000.

5B.2 When it makes a property freezing order or interim receiving order before a claim for a recovery order has been commenced, the court may also make an exclusion to enable the respondent to meet his reasonable legal costs so that (for example) when the claim is commenced—
(1) he may file an acknowledgment of service and any written evidence on which he intends to rely; or
(2) he may apply for a further exclusion for the purpose of enabling him to meet his reasonable costs of the proceedings.

5B.3 Paragraph 7A contains general provisions about exclusions made for the purpose of enabling a person to meet his reasonable legal costs.

## Interim receiving order: application for directions

6.1 An application for directions as to the exercise of the interim receiver's functions may, under section 251 of the Act or article 156 of the Order in Council, be made at any time by—

(1) the interim receiver;
(2) any party to the proceedings; and
(3) any person affected by any action taken by the interim receiver, or who may be affected by any action proposed to be taken by him.

6.2 The application must always be made by application notice, which must be served on—
(1) the interim receiver (unless he is the applicant);
(2) every party to the proceedings; and
(3) any other person who may be interested in the application.

## Application to vary or set aside property freezing order or interim receiving order

7.1 An application to vary or set aside a property freezing order or an interim receiving order (including an application for, or relating to, an exclusion from the order) may be made at any time by—
(1) the Director; or
(2) any person affected by the order.

7.2 Unless the court otherwise directs or exceptional circumstances apply, a copy of the application notice must be served on—
(1) every party to the proceedings;
(2) in the case of an application to vary or set aside an interim receiving order, the interim receiver; and
(3) any other person who may be affected by the court's decision.

7.3 The evidence in support of an application for an exclusion from a property freezing order or interim receiving order for the purpose of enabling a person to meet his reasonable legal costs must—
(1) contain full details of the stage or stages in civil recovery proceedings in respect of which the costs in question have been or will be incurred;
(2) include an estimate of the costs which the person has incurred and will incur in relation to each stage to which the application relates, substantially in the form illustrated in Precedent H in the Schedule of Costs Precedents annexed to the Practice Direction about Costs;
(3) include a statement of assets containing the information set out in paragraph 7A.3 (unless the person has previously filed such a statement in the same civil recovery proceedings and there has been no material change in the facts set out in that statement);
(4) where the court has previously made an exclusion in respect of any stage to which the application relates, explain why the person's costs will exceed the amount specified in the exclusion for that stage; and
(5) state whether the terms of the exclusion have been agreed with the Director.

## Exclusions for the purpose of meeting legal costs: general provisions

7A.1 Subject to paragraph 7A.2, when the court makes an order or gives directions in civil recovery proceedings it will at the same time consider whether it is appropriate to make or vary an exclusion for the purpose of enabling any person affected by the order or directions to meet his reasonable legal costs.

7A.2 The court will not make an exclusion for the purpose of enabling a person to meet his reasonable legal costs, other than an exclusion to meet the costs of taking any of the steps referred to in paragraph 5B.1, unless that person has made and filed a statement of assets.

7A.3 A statement of assets is a witness statement which sets out all the property which the maker of the statement owns, holds or controls, or in which he has an interest, giving the value, location and details of all such property. Information given in a statement of assets under this practice direction will be used only for the purpose of the civil recovery proceedings.

7A.4 The court—

(1) will not make an exclusion for the purpose of enabling a person to meet his reasonable legal costs (including an initial exclusion under paragraph 5B.1); and
(2) may set aside any exclusion which it has made for that purpose or reduce any amount specified in such an exclusion,

if it is satisfied that the person has property to which the property freezing order or interim receiving order does not apply from which he may meet those costs.

7A.5 The court will normally refer to a costs judge any question relating to the amount which an exclusion should allow for reasonable legal costs in respect of proceedings or a stage in proceedings.

7A.6 Attention is drawn to section 245C of the Act and article 149 of the Order in Council (in relation to exclusions from property freezing orders) and to section 252 of the Act and article 157 of the Order in Council (in relation to exclusions from interim receiving orders). An exclusion for the purpose of enabling a person to meet his reasonable legal costs must be made subject to the 'required conditions' specified in Part 2 of the Regulations.

7A.7 An exclusion made for the purpose of enabling a person to meet his reasonable legal costs will specify—

(1) the stage or stages in civil recovery proceedings to which it relates;
(2) the maximum amount which may be released in respect of legal costs for each specified stage; and
(3) the total amount which may be released in respect of legal costs pursuant to the exclusion.

7A.8 A person who becomes aware that his legal costs—

(1) in relation to any stage in civil recovery proceedings have exceeded or will exceed the maximum amount specified in the exclusion for that stage; or
(2) in relation to all the stages to which the exclusion relates have exceeded or will exceed the total amount that may be released pursuant to the exclusion,

should apply for a further exclusion or a variation of the existing exclusion as soon as reasonably practicable.

### Assessment of costs where recovery order is made

7B.1 Where the court—

(1) makes a recovery order in respect of property which was the subject of a property freezing order or interim receiving order; and
(2) had made an exclusion from the property freezing order or interim receiving order for the purpose of enabling a person to meet his reasonable legal costs,

the recovery order will make provision under section 266(8A) of the Act or article 177(10) of the Order in Council (as appropriate) for the payment of those costs.

7B.2 Where the court makes a recovery order which provides for the payment of a person's reasonable legal costs in respect of civil recovery proceedings, it will at the same time order the detailed assessment of those costs. Parts 4 and 5 of the Regulations, Part 47 of the Civil Procedure Rules and Section 49A of the Practice Direction about Costs apply to a detailed assessment pursuant to such an order.

### Registers

7C. There will be kept in the Central Office of the Supreme Court at the Royal Courts of Justice, under the direction of the Senior Master, a register of external orders which the High Court has ordered to be registered.

## III APPLICATIONS UNDER PART 8 OF THE ACT

### How to Apply for an Order or Warrant

8.1 An application by the Director for an order or warrant under part 8 of the Act in connection with a civil recovery investigation must be made:

(1) to a High Court judge;
(2) by filing an application notice.

8.2 The application may be made without notice.

## Confidentiality of Court Documents

9.1 CPR rules 5.4, 5.4B and 5.4C do not apply to an application under part 8 of the Act, and paras 9.2 and 9.3 below have effect in [their*] place.

9.2 When an application is issued, the court file will be marked 'Not for disclosure' and, unless a High Court judge grants permission, the court records relating to the application (including the application notice, documents filed in support, and any order or warrant that is made) will not be made available by the court for any person to inspect or copy, either before or after the hearing of the application.

9.3 An application for permission under para. 9.2 must be made on notice to the Director in accordance with Part 23.
(Rule 23.7(1) requires a copy of the application notice to be served as soon as practicable after it is filed, and in any event at least three days before the court is to deal with the application.)

## Application Notice and Evidence

10.1 The application must be supported by written evidence, which must be filed with the application notice.

10.2 The evidence must set out all the matters on which the Director relies in support of the application, including any matters required to be stated by the relevant sections of the Act, and all material facts of which the court should be made aware.

10.3 There must also be filed with the application notice a draft of the order sought. This should if possible also be supplied to the court on disk in a form compatible with the word processing software used by the court.

## Hearing of the Application

11.1 The application will be heard and determined in private, unless the judge hearing it directs otherwise.

## Variation or Discharge of Order or Warrant

12.1 An application to vary or discharge an order or warrant may be made by:
(1) the Director; or
(2) any person affected by the order or warrant.

12.2 An application under para. 12.1 to stop an order or warrant from being executed must be made immediately upon it being served.

12.3 A person applying to vary or discharge a warrant must first inform the Director that he is making the application.

12.4 The application should be made to the judge who made the order or issued the warrant or, if he is not available, to another High Court judge.

# IV FURTHER PROVISIONS ABOUT SPECIFIC APPLICATIONS UNDER PART 8 OF THE ACT

## Production Order

13.1 The application notice must name as a respondent the person believed to be in possession or control of the material in relation to which a production order is sought.

13.2 The application notice must specify:

* Editorial note: the official text states 'its', but it is presumed that such is an error and should state 'their'.

(1) whether the application is for an order under para. (a) or (b) of s. 345(4) of the Act;
(2) the material, or description of material, in relation to which the order is sought; and
(3) the person who is believed to be in possession or control of the material.

13.3 An application under s. 347 of the Act for an order to grant entry may be made either:
(1) together with an application for a production order; or
(2) by separate application, after a production order has been made.

13.4 An application notice for an order to grant entry must:
(1) specify the premises in relation to which the order is sought; and
(2) be supported by written evidence explaining why the order is needed.

13.5 A production order, or an order to grant entry, must contain a statement of the right of any person affected by the order to apply to vary or discharge the order.

## Search and Seizure Warrant

14.1 The application notice should name as respondent the occupier of the premises to be subject to the warrant, if known.

14.2 The evidence in support of the application must state:
(1) the matters relied on by the Director to show that one of the requirements in s. 352(6) of the Act for the issue of a warrant is satisfied;
(2) details of the premises to be subject to the warrant, and of the possible occupier or occupiers of those premises;
(3) the name and position of the member of the staff of the Agency who it is intended will execute the warrant.

14.3 There must be filed with the application notice drafts of:
(1) the warrant; and
(2) a written undertaking by the person who is to execute the warrant to comply with para. 13.8 of this practice direction.

14.4 A search and seizure warrant must:
(1) specify the statutory power under which it is issued and, unless the court orders otherwise, give an indication of the nature of the investigation in respect of which it is issued;
(2) state the address or other identification of the premises to be subject to the warrant;
(3) state the name of the member of staff of the Agency who is authorised to execute the warrant;
(4) set out the action which the warrant authorises the person executing it to take under the relevant sections of the Act;
(5) give the date on which the warrant is issued;
(6) include a statement that the warrant continues in force until the end of the period of one month beginning with the day on which it is issued;
(7) contain a statement of the right of any person affected by the order to apply to discharge or vary the order.

14.5 An example of a search and seizure warrant is annexed to this practice direction. This example may be modified as appropriate in any particular case.

14.6 CPR, r. 40.2, applies to a search and seizure warrant.

(Rule 40.2 requires every judgment or order to state the name and judicial title of the person making it, to bear the date on which it is given or made, and to be sealed by the court.)

14.7 Upon the issue of a warrant the court will provide to the Director:
(1) the sealed warrant; and
(2) a copy of it for service on the occupier or person in charge of the premises subject to the warrant.

14.8 A person attending premises to execute a warrant must, if the premises are occupied produce the warrant on arrival at the premises, and as soon as possible thereafter personally serve a copy of the warrant and an explanatory notice on the occupier or the person appearing to him to be in charge of the premises.

14.9 The person executing the warrant must also comply with any order which the court may make for service of any other documents relating to the application.

## Disclosure Order

15.1 The application notice should normally name as respondents the persons on whom the Director intends to serve notices under the disclosure order sought.

15.2 A disclosure order must:
(1) give an indication of the nature of the investigation for the purposes of which the order is made;
(2) set out the action which the order authorises the Director to take in accordance with s. 357(4) of the Act;
(3) contain a statement of:
(a) the offences relating to disclosure orders under s. 359 of the Act; and
(b) the right of any person affected by the order to apply to discharge or vary the order.

15.3 Where, pursuant to a disclosure order, the Director gives to any person a notice under s. 357(4) of the Act, he must also at the same time serve on that person a copy of the disclosure order.

## Customer Information Order

16.1 The application notice should normally (unless it is impracticable to do so because they are too numerous) name as respondents the financial institution or institutions to which it is proposed that an order should apply.

16.2 A customer information order must:
(1) specify the financial institution, or description of financial institutions, to which it applies;
(2) state the name of the person in relation to whom customer information is to be given, and any other details to identify that person;
(3) contain a statement of:
(a) the offences relating to disclosure orders under s. 366 of the Act; and
(b) the right of any person affected by the order to apply to discharge or vary the order.

16.3 Where, pursuant to a customer information order, the Director gives to a financial institution a notice to provide customer information, he must also at the same time serve a copy of the order on that institution.

## Account Monitoring Order

17.1 The application notice must name as a respondent the financial institution against which an account monitoring order is sought.

17.2 The application notice must:
(1) state the matters required by s. 370(2) and (3) of the Act; and
(2) give details of:
(a) the person whose account or accounts the application relates to;
(b) each account or description of accounts in relation to which the order is sought, including if known the number of each account and the branch at which it is held;
(c) the information sought about the account or accounts;
(d) the period for which the order is sought;
(e) the manner in which, and the frequency with which, it is proposed that the financial institution should provide account information during that period.

17.3 An account monitoring order must contain a statement of the right of any person affected by the order to apply to vary or discharge the order.

## [ANNEX

The annex, which contains an example of a search and seizure warrant, is not reproduced in this work but may be accessed via the DCA website at <http://www.dca.gov.uk>]

# Practice Direction—Proceedings under Enactments Relating to Discrimination

## Scope and Interpretation

1.1 This Practice Direction applies to certain county court proceedings under the enactments defined in paragraph 1.2.

1.2 In this Practice Direction—

(1) 'the 1975 Act' means the Sex Discrimination Act 1975;
(2) 'the 1976 Act' means the Race Relations Act 1976;
(3) 'the 1995 Act' means the Disability Discrimination Act 1995;
(4) 'the 1999 Act' means the Disability Rights Commission Act 1999;
(5) 'the 2006 Act' means the Equality Act 2006;
(6) 'the Age Regulations' means the Employment Equality (Age) Regulations 2006;
(7) 'the Religion or Belief Regulations' means the Employment Equality (Religion or Belief) Regulations 2003;
(8) 'the Sexual Orientation Regulations' means the Employment Equality (Sexual Orientation) Regulations 2003.

1.3 In this Practice Direction—

(1) a reference to 'the Commission', in relation to proceedings under a particular Act is a reference to the Commission as defined in that Act;
(2) where it applies to proceedings under the 1976 Act, 'court' means a designated county court under section 67(1) of that Act.

## Commission to be given notice of claims

2.1 This paragraph applies to claims under—

(a) section 66 of the 1975 Act;
(b) section 57 of the 1976 Act; or
(c) section 25 of the 1995 Act.

2.2 When a claim to which this paragraph applies is commenced, the claimant must—

(a) give notice of the commencement of the proceedings to the Commission;
(b) file a copy of that notice.

## Assessors

3. Rule 35.15 shall have effect in relation to an assessor who is to be appointed in proceedings under section 66 (1) of the Act of 1975.

## Admissibility of Evidence

4.1 This paragraph applies where a claimant in a claim alleging discrimination has questioned the defendant under—

(a) section 74 of the 1975 Act;
(b) section 65 of the 1976 Act;
(c) section 56 of the 1995 Act;
(d) regulation 41 of the Age Regulations;
(e) regulation 33 of the Religion or Belief Regulations; or
(f) regulation 33 of the Sexual Orientation Regulations.

4.2 Either party may apply to the court to determine whether the question or any reply is admissible under that section.

(Part 23 contains general rules about making applications.)

4.3 Rule 3.4 (power to strike out a statement of case) applies to the question and any answer as it applies to a statement of case.

## Exclusion of persons from certain proceedings

5.1 In a claim—
  (1) brought under section 66(1) of the 1975 Act;
  (2) brought under section 57(1) of the 1976 Act;
  (3) alleging discrimination under the 1995 Act; or
  (4) brought under section 66 of the 2006 Act, the court may, where it considers it expedient in the interests of national security—
    (a) exclude from all or part of the proceedings—
      (i) the claimant;
      (ii) the claimant's representatives; or
      (iii) any assessors
    (Section 67(4) of the Race Relations Act 1975 allows an assessor to be appointed in proceedings under that Act);
    (b) permit a claimant or representative to make a statement to the court before the start of the proceedings (or the part of the proceedings) from which he is excluded; or
    (c) take steps to keep secret all or part of the reasons for its decision in the claim.

5.2 In this paragraph, a 'special advocate' means a person appointed under—
  (1) section 66B(2) of the 1975 Act;
  (2) section 67A(2) of the 1976 Act;
  (3) section 59A(2) of the 1995 Act; or
  (4) section 71(2) of the 2006 Act to represent the claimant.

5.3 In proceedings to which this paragraph refers, where the claimant or his representatives have been excluded from all or part of the proceedings—
  (a) the court will inform the Attorney-General of the proceedings; and
  (b) the Attorney-General may appoint a special advocate to represent the claimant in respect of those parts of the proceedings from which he or his representative have been excluded.

5.4 In exercise of its powers under paragraph 5.1(c), the court may order the special advocate not to communicate (directly or indirectly) with any persons (including the excluded claimant)—
  (a) on any matter discussed or referred to; or
  (b) with regard to any material disclosed,
  during or with reference to any part of the proceedings from which the claimant or his representative are excluded.

5.5 Where the court makes an order referred to in paragraph 5.4 (or any similar order), the special advocate may apply to the court for directions enabling him to seek instructions from, or otherwise to communicate with an excluded person.

## Expenses of Commission

6.1 This paragraph applies where the Commission have, in respect of a claim, provided a claimant with assistance under—
  (a) section 75 of the 1975 Act;
  (b) section 66 of the 1976 Act; or
  (c) section 7 of the 1999 Act.

6.2 If the Commission claims a charge for expenses incurred by it in providing such assistance, it shall give notice of the claim to—
  (a) the court; and
  (b) the claimant,
within 14 days of determination of the proceedings.

6.3 If notice is given to the court under paragraph 6.2—
  (a) money paid into court for the benefit of the claimant that relates to costs and expenses shall not be paid out unless this is permitted by an order of the court; and

(b) the court may order the expenses incurred by the Commission to be assessed as if they were costs payable by the claimant to his own solicitor for work done in connection with the proceedings.

6.4 The court may either—

(a) make a summary assessment of the expenses; or

(b) order detailed assessment of the expenses by a costs officer.

## Applications to vary terms of certain agreements

7.1 This paragraph applies to an application to remove or modify a term of a contract to which any of the following apply—

(a) section 77(2) of the 1975 Act;

(b) section 72(2) of the 1976 Act;

(c) section 26 of or Schedule 3A to the 1995 Act;

(d) section 72(5) of the 2006 Act;

(e) paragraph 1(1) or (2) of Schedule 5 to the Age Regulations;

(f) paragraph 1(1) or (2) of Schedule 4 to the Religion or Belief Regulations;

(g) paragraph 1(1) or (2) of Schedule 4 to the Sexual Orientation Regulations.

7.2 A person affected by the proposed variation must be made a respondent to the application unless the court orders otherwise.

# Practice Direction—Application for a Warrant under the Enterprise Act 2002

## Interpretation

1.1 In this practice direction—
   (1) 'the Act' means the Enterprise Act 2002;
   (2) 'the OFT' means the Office of Fair Trading;
   (3) 'officer' means an officer of the OFT;
   (4) 'named officer' means the person identified in a warrant as the principal officer or person in charge of executing that warrant;
   (5) 'Notice' means the Notice of the powers to search premises and the rights of occupiers; and
   (6) 'warrant' means a warrant under section 194 of the Act.

## Application for a Warrant

2.1 An application by the OFT for a warrant must be made to a High Court judge using the Part 8 procedure as modified by this practice direction.

2.2 The application must be made to a judge of the Chancery Division at the Royal Courts of Justice.

2.3 The application is made without notice and the claim form may be issued without naming a defendant. Rules 8.1(3), 8.3, 8.4, 8.5(2)–(6), 8.6(1), 8.7 and 8.8 do not apply.

## Confidentiality of Court Documents

3.1 The court will not serve any claim form, warrant, or other document filed or issued in an application to which this practice direction applies, except in accordance with an order of the judge hearing the application.

3.2 CPR rules 5.4(2), 5.4B and 5.4C do not apply, and paragraphs 3.3 and 3.4 have effect in their place.

3.3 When a claim form is issued the court file will be marked 'Not for disclosure' and, unless a High Court judge grants permission, the court records relating to the application (including the claim form and documents filed in support and any warrant or order that is issued) will not be made available by the court for any person to inspect or copy, either before or after the hearing of the application.

3.4 An application for permission under paragraph 3.3 must be made on notice to the OFT in accordance with Part 23.

(Rule 23.7(1) requires a copy of the application notice to be served as soon as practicable after it is filed, and in any event at least 3 days before the court is to deal with the application.)

## Contents of Claim Form, Affidavit and Documents in Support

4.1 The claim form must state—
   (1) that the OFT is applying for a warrant under section 194 of the Act;
   (2) the address or other identification of the premises to be subject to the warrant; and
   (3) the anticipated date or dates for the execution of the warrant.

4.2 The application must be supported by affidavit evidence, which must be filed with the claim form.

4.3 The evidence must set out all the matters on which the OFT relies in support of the application, including all material facts of which the court should be made aware. In particular it must state—
   (1) the subject matter (i.e. the nature of the suspected offence under section 188 of the Act) and purpose of the investigation to which the application relates;

(2) the identity of the person or persons suspected to have committed the offence;
(3) the grounds for applying for the issue of the warrant and the facts relied upon in support;
(4) details of the premises to be subject to the warrant and of the possible occupier or occupiers of those premises;
(5) the connection between the premises and the person or persons suspected to have committed the offence;
(6) the name and position of the officer who it is intended will be the named officer;
(7) the name and position of the officer or officers who it is intended will accompany the named officer;
(8) if it is intended that the named officer is to be a person who is not an officer and who has been authorised by the OFT pursuant to section 195(1) of the Act to exercise on its behalf all or any of the powers conferred by section 194 of the Act and to act as the named officer, the name and job title of such person and the reason why it is intended that he may act as the named officer and exercise the relevant powers conferred by section 194 of the Act;
(9) if it is intended that the warrant may pursuant to section 194(4) of the Act authorise any person (other than an officer) to accompany the named officer in executing the warrant, the name and job title of each such person and the reason why it is intended that he may accompany the named officer; and
(10) if it is intended that any competent person who is not an officer will be authorised by the OFT pursuant to section 195(1) to exercise on its behalf all or any of the powers conferred by section 194, the name and job title of each such person and the reason why it is intended that he may exercise such powers.

4.4 There must be exhibited to an affidavit in support of the application the written authorisation of the OFT containing the names of all persons falling within the categories described at subparagraphs (6) to (10) of paragraph 4.3 above.

4.5 There must also be filed with the claim form—
(1) a draft of the warrant;
(2) the Notice to be produced and served with it; and
(3) the written undertaking by the named officer required by paragraph 6.2 of this practice direction.

(An example of the form of a warrant under section 194 of the Act, and the Notice to be produced and served with it, are annexed to this practice direction).

4.6 If possible the draft warrant and the Notice should also be supplied to the court on disk or electronically in a form compatible with the word processing software used by the court.

## Listing

5. The application will be listed by the court on any published list of cases as 'An application by [D]'.

## Hearing of the Application

6.1 An application for a warrant will be heard and determined in private, unless the judge hearing it directs otherwise.

6.2 The court will not issue a warrant unless there has been filed a written undertaking, signed by the named officer, to comply with paragraph 8.1 of this practice direction.

## The Warrant

7.1 The warrant must—
(1) state the address or other identification of the premises to be subject to the warrant;
(2) state the names of—
(a) the named officer; and
(b) any other officers or other persons who may accompany him in executing the warrant;

(3) set out the action which the warrant authorises the persons executing it to take under section 194 of the Act;
(4) give the date on which the warrant is issued; and
(5) state that the named officer has given the undertaking required by paragraph 6.2.

7.2 Rule 40.2 applies to a warrant.

(Rule 40.2 requires every judgment or order to state the name and judicial title of the person making it, to bear the date on which it is given or made, and to be sealed by the court.)

7.3 Upon the issue of a warrant the court will provide to the OFT—
(1) the sealed warrant and the Notice; and
(2) a copy of the sealed warrant and the Notice for service on the occupier or person in charge of the premises subject to the warrant.

## Execution of Warrant

8.1 A named officer attending premises to execute a warrant must, if the premises are occupied—
(1) produce the warrant and Notice immediately upon arrival at the premises to the occupier or any other person entitled to grant access to the premises, explaining the authority under which entry is sought; and
(2) as soon as possible after his arrival at the premises, personally serve a copy of the warrant and Notice on the occupier or person appearing to him to be in charge of the premises.

The named officer is not required to serve the warrant and Notice personally if he reasonably believes this would frustrate the object of the search or endanger officers or other people.

8.2 If the occupier is not present, the named officer shall leave copies of the warrant and Notice of the powers to search premises and of the rights of occupiers in a prominent place on the premises or appropriate part of the premises, recording the name of the named officer in charge of the search and the date and time of the search, unless the named officer reasonably believes recording or disclosing his name might put him in danger.

8.3 The named officer must also comply with any order which the court may make for service of any other documents relating to the application.

8.4 Unless the court otherwise orders—
(1) the initial production of a warrant and entry to premises under the authority of the warrant must take place at a reasonable hour, unless this might frustrate the purpose of the search; but
(2) once persons named in the warrant have entered premises under the authority of a warrant, they may, whilst the warrant remains in force—
(a) remain on the premises; or
(b) re-enter the premises to continue executing the warrant.

8.5 If the persons executing a warrant propose to remove any items from the premises pursuant to the warrant they must, unless it is impracticable—
(1) make a list of all the items to be removed;
(2) supply a copy of the list to the occupier or person appearing to be in charge of the premises; and
(3) give that person a reasonable opportunity to check the list before removing any of the items.

## Application to Vary or Discharge Warrant

9.1 The occupier or person in charge of premises in relation to which a warrant has been issued may apply to vary or discharge the warrant.

9.2 An application under paragraph 9.1 to stop a warrant from being executed must be made immediately upon the warrant being served.

9.3 A person applying to vary or discharge a warrant must first inform the named officer that he is making the application.

9.4 The application should be made to the judge who issued the warrant, or, if he is not available, to another judge of the Chancery Division.

## Expiry of the Warrant

10. The warrant will expire one month after the date on which it is issued.

## Application under Section 59 Criminal Justice and Police Act 2001

11. Attention is drawn to section 59 of the Criminal Justice and Police Act 2001, which makes provision about applications relating to property seized in the exercise of the powers conferred by (among other provisions) section 194(2) of the Act.

## WARRANT

**IN THE HIGH COURT OF JUSTICE** **CLAIM No. of 20**
**CHANCERY DIVISION**

**CLAIMANT:**

**OFFICE OF FAIR TRADING**

[insert address]

**PREMISES TO WHICH THIS WARRANT RELATES:**

[insert address]

**WARRANT TO ENTER PREMISES AND EXERCISE POWERS UNDER SECTION 194 ENTERPRISE ACT 2002**

To the occupier of the premises described above ("the premises") and to any person in charge of, or operating at or from, the premises:

You should read the terms of this Warrant and the accompanying Notice of the powers to search premises and of the rights of occupiers ("the Notice") very carefully. If you intentionally obstruct an officer or fail to comply with any requirement of the officers or other persons exercising their powers under the Warrant, you may be committing a criminal offence under section 201 of the Enterprise Act 2002, the relevant terms of which are set out in Schedule C to this Warrant.

An application was made on [insert date] by Counsel for the Office of Fair Trading ("the OFT") to The Honourable Mr Justice [insert name] ("the Judge"), for a warrant under section 194(1)(a) and (b)[insert the relevant sub-paragraph (i), (ii) or (iii)] of the Enterprise Act 2002 ("the Act") on the basis that there are reasonable grounds for believing:

(a) that there are on the premises documents which the OFT has power under section 193 of the Act to require to be produced for the purposes of an investigation under section 192(1) of the Act; and

(b) that [insert the text of the relevant sub-paragraph (i), (ii) or (iii)].

[In the remainder of this Warrant, references to an officer or officers of the OFT shall be taken to include any competent persons authorised by the OFT under section 195(1 )of the Act to exercise on its behalf all or any of the powers conferred by section 194.] The Judge read the evidence in support of the application and was satisfied that the grounds in section

194(1)(a) and (b)[insert the relevant subparagraph (i), (ii) or (iii)] of the Act have been met and accepted the undertakings by [insert name], an officer of the OFT authorised to act as the "named officer", set out in Schedule A to this Warrant. The named officer is the principal officer of the OFT in charge of executing this Warrant.

As a result of the application, this Warrant in relation to the premises was issued by the Judge on [insert date].

1. This Warrant is issued in respect of an investigation under section 192(1) of the Act by the OFT on the basis that there are reasonable grounds for suspecting that an offence under section 188 (cartel offence) of the Act has been committed and, under section 192(2) of the Act, it appears to the OFT that there is good reason to exercise the powers under section 194 of the Act for the purpose of investigating the affairs, or any aspect of the affairs, of any person ("the person under investigation").
2. [Set out the subject matter and purpose of the investigation].
3. By this Warrant the named officer and the other officers [and person(s)] [The words in brackets shall be included if the Judge so orders pursuant to section 194(4).] named in Schedule B and authorised in writing by the OFT to accompany the named officer, are authorised to produce the Warrant at any reasonable time [unless the Judge has ordered otherwise] and on producing the Warrant:
   (a) to enter the premises, using such force as is reasonably necessary for the purpose;
   (b) to search the premises and—
      (i) take possession of any documents appearing to be of a kind in respect of which the application referred to in this Warrant was granted ("the relevant kind"), or
      (ii) take, in relation to any documents appearing to be of the relevant kind, any other steps which may appear to be necessary for preserving them or preventing interference with them;
   (c) to require any person to provide an explanation of any document appearing to be of the relevant kind or to state, to the best of his knowledge and belief, where it may be found;
   (d) to require any information which is stored in any electronic form and is accessible from the premises and which the named officer considers relates to any matter relevant to the investigation, to be produced in a form—
      (i) in which it can be taken away, and
      (ii) in which it is visible and legible or from which it can readily be produced in a visible and legible form.
4. The Warrant will expire one month after the date on which it is issued.
5. Pursuant to section 50 of the Criminal Justice and Police Act 2001, the powers set out in paragraph 3(b)(i) of this Warrant include the powers—
   (a) to take possession of any document in order to determine later and elsewhere whether (or the extent to which) the document is of the relevant kind, where in all the circumstances it is not reasonably practicable to determine this on the premises; and
   (b) to take possession of any document comprised in something else where in all the circumstances it is not reasonably practicable to separate, on the premises, the document which is of the relevant kind from a document which is not but in which it is comprised.
6. Terms used in this Warrant have the following meanings in accordance with the Act: "documents" include information recorded in any form and, in relation to information recorded otherwise than in a form in which it is visible and legible, references to its production include references to producing it in a form in which it is visible and legible or from which it can readily be produced in a visible and legible form.

## SCHEDULE A

## UNDERTAKINGS GIVEN TO THE COURT BY THE NAMED OFFICER

If the premises are occupied when the Warrant is to be executed—

1. To produce the Warrant and the Notice on arrival at the premises; and
2. As soon as possible thereafter to serve personally a copy of the Warrant and the Notice on the occupier or person appearing to him to be in charge of the premises.

The Notice was produced to the Court with the application for the Warrant.

## SCHEDULE B

## NAMES OF PERSONS AUTHORISED TO EXECUTE THE WARRANT

[insert name of the named officer] who is the OFT's officer authorised in writing by the OFT to be the named officer.

[insert name of each of the other officers] who are the OFT's other officers authorised in writing by the OFT to accompany the named officer.

[insert name of each of the other person(s)] who is [insert job title of each person] and who [is/are] authorised in writing by the OFT to accompany the named officer. [This paragraph shall be included if the Judge so orders pursuant to section 194(4).]

[insert name of each of the other person(s)] who is [insert job title of each person] and who [is/are] authorised in writing by the OFT pursuant to section 195 to exercise on its behalf all or any of the powers conferred by section 194. [This paragraph shall be included if the Judge so orders pursuant to section 194(4).]

## SCHEDULE C

## OFFENCES CREATED BY SECTION 201 OF THE ACT

The offences created by section 201 of the Act in connection with the execution of a warrant under section 194 are set out below. Text marked as [. . .] denotes the omission of provisions that are not relevant for section 194 purposes.

201 (1) Any person who without reasonable excuse fails to comply with a requirement imposed on him under section [. . .] 194 is guilty of an offence and liable on summary conviction to imprisonment for a term not exceeding six months or to a fine not exceeding level 5 on the standard scale or to both.

(2) A person who, in purported compliance with a requirement under section [. . .] 194—

(a) makes a statement which he knows to be false or misleading in a material particular; or

(b) recklessly makes a statement which is false or misleading in a material particular, is guilty of an offence.

(3) A person guilty of an offence under subsection (2) is liable—

(a) on conviction on indictment, to imprisonment for a term not exceeding two years or to a fine or to both; and

(b) on summary conviction, to imprisonment

for a term not exceeding six months or to a fine not exceeding the statutory maximum, or to both.

(4) Where any person—

(a) knows or suspects that an investigation by the Serious Fraud Office or the OFT into an offence under section 188 is being or is likely to be carried out; and

(b) falsifies, conceals, destroys or otherwise disposes of, or causes or permits the falsification, concealment, destruction or disposal of documents which he knows or suspects or would be relevant to such an investigation, he is guilty of an offence unless he proves that he had no intention of concealing the facts disclosed by the documents from the persons carrying out such an investigation.

(5) A person guilty of an offence under subsection (4) is liable—
   (a) on conviction on indictment, to imprisonment for a term not exceeding 5 years or to a fine or to both; and
   (b) on summary conviction, to imprisonment for a term not exceeding six months or to a fine not exceeding the statutory maximum, or to both.

(6) A person who intentionally obstructs a person in the exercise of his powers under a warrant issued under section 194 is guilty of an offence and liable—
   (a) on conviction on indictment, to imprisonment for a term not exceeding 2 years or to a fine or to both; and
   (b) on summary conviction, to a fine not exceeding the statutory maximum.
   The statutory maximum fine on summary conviction is currently £5,000 and the fine at level 5 is currently also £5,000. The fine on conviction on indictment is unlimited.

DATED this [ ] day of [ ] 20

THE HONOURABLE MR JUSTICE [ ]

## Notice of the Powers to search premises and of the rights of occupiers under section 194 of the Enterprise Act 2002 ('the Act')

### Subject matter and powers

[In this notice, references to 'an officer or officers of the OFT' shall be taken to include any competent person authorised by the OFT under section 195(1) of the Act to exercise on its behalf all or any of the powers conferred by section 194 of the Act.] Officers of the Office of Fair Trading ('the OFT') have been authorised under Warrant to enter and search the premises identified in the Warrant in connection with an investigation under the Act. OFT officers can be accompanied by one or more named individuals authorised to assist them to execute the warrant under section 194(4) of the Act. The subject matter of this investigation is set out in paragraph 2 of the Warrant. The officers and any accompanying persons will not elaborate on this.

Paragraph 3 of the Warrant sets out the powers of the named officer[1] and other officers and any accompanying persons under section 194 of the Act for the purposes of the present investigation. On entering the premises, the named officer will, as a matter of practice, produce evidence of his identity when producing the Warrant, and identify and introduce all other officers and any accompanying persons, unless he has reasonable grounds for believing that alerting the occupier or any other person entitled to grant access would frustrate the object of the search or endanger any officers or accompanying persons.

Officers of the OFT and any accompanying persons shall have regard to the provisions of Code B of the Code of Practice under the Police and Criminal Evidence Act 1984, including in Scotland. A copy of Code B of the Codes of Practice will be made available on request. Reasonable and proportionate force may be used to enter premises if the named officer in charge of the search is satisfied that premises are those specified in the warrant and the occupier or any other person entitled to grant access has refused entry or it is impossible to communicate with the occupier or any other person entitled to grant access. If the occupier is not present, a copy of the warrant and of the notice of the powers to search premises and

---

[1] The named officer is the principal officer of the OFT who, together with other officers and accompanying persons, is authorised by the Warrant to exercise the powers under section 194 of the Act. His name and the names of the other officers and accompanying persons are set out in Schedule B to the Warrant.

the rights of occupiers shall be left in a prominent place on the premises, recording the date and time of the search and the name of the named officer.
If premises have been entered by force, before leaving the named officer must make sure that they are secure either by arranging for the occupier or the occupier's representative to be present or by any other appropriate means.

Unless the Court has ordered otherwise, the initial production of the Warrant and entry to premises must take place at a reasonable hour unless this might frustrate the purpose of the search; and, once officers and any accompanying persons have entered premises under the authority of the Warrant, they may remain on the premises or re-enter the premises to continue executing the Warrant.

The named officer shall also provide the occupier with this Notice of the powers to search premises and the rights of occupiers.

OFT officers also have the power in accordance with section 50 of the Criminal Justice and Police Act 2001 to seize material where it is not reasonably practicable, while on the premises, to determine the extent to which it may be seized, if at all, or for the seizable material to be separated from the non-seizable material in which it is comprised. Where this power is to be exercised, the occupier will be given a Notice which sets out the grounds for the exercise of the power and the rights of persons who have an interest in the property to be seized pursuant to the power.

## Access to legal advice

When executing a warrant OFT officers are not required to wait for an occupier or other person's legal adviser to be present before commencing the search.
However, generally the OFT officers will wait for a legal adviser before commencing a search provided the search is not unreasonably delayed. Where the OFT officers do wait for the legal adviser's arrival, they will wait on the premises and all persons on the premises will be required to adhere to appropriate instructions to ensure that material on the premises, or on other premises, which may be relevant to the investigation, is not interfered or tampered with. Furthermore, in cases where the OFT has commenced the search without waiting for a legal adviser to arrive, the OFT would avoid removing any material from the premises until the person's legal adviser has arrived and had the opportunity to make representations. This is provided that the conclusion of the search is not unreasonably delayed.

## Witness to the search

A friend, neighbour or other person will be allowed to witness the search if the occupier wishes unless the named officer in charge of the search has reasonable grounds for believing that the presence of such person would unreasonably delay the investigation or endanger officers or other people.
A record of the action taken, including the grounds for refusing a request from the occupier to have a witness to the search, will be made on the premises search record.

## Protection against self-incrimination

The OFT has the power to require any person at the premises to provide an explanation of any document appearing to be of the relevant kind or to state, to the best of his or her knowledge and belief, where it may be found. This power is used to enable the OFT to direct its search efficiently and effectively.
It should be noted that, any statement made by a person in response to any such requirement imposed by the named officer or other officers or accompanying persons in exercise of their powers under paragraph 3(c) of the Warrant (the 'earlier statement'), may only be used in evidence against that person in the following circumstances.

## On a prosecution for an offence under section 201(2) of the Act

Where that person has knowingly or recklessly made a statement that is false or misleading in a material particular in response to that requirement.

## On a prosecution for some other offence

Where he makes a statement inconsistent with the earlier statement provided evidence relating to the earlier statement is adduced or a question relating to it is asked by him or on his behalf in that prosecution.[2]

## Privileged communications

The powers under section 194 of the Act in relation to documents and information (set out in paragraph 3(b) onwards in the Warrant) do not apply to communications benefiting from legal professional privilege ('privilege'). A person may not be required to disclose any information or produce any document which he would be entitled to refuse to disclose or produce on grounds of privilege in proceedings in the High Court. However, a lawyer may be required to provide the name and address of his client as part of an investigation being conducted under the powers in the Act. Privilege does not apply to communications made with the intention of furthering a criminal purpose (whether the lawyer is acting unwittingly or culpably).

The Act also provides a safeguard in respect of confidential banking information. A person may not be required to disclose any information or produce any document in respect of which he owes an obligation of confidence by virtue of carrying on any banking business, unless the person to whom the obligation of confidence is owed consents to the disclosure or production or the OFT has authorised the making of the requirement.

If you consider that a document or information is subject to privilege, you should provide the named officer or other officer or accompanying person with a sufficient explanation such as to demonstrate to his satisfaction that the document or information, or parts of it, for which privilege is claimed, fulfil the conditions for it being privileged.

If no agreement is reached during the search as to whether the conditions for privilege have been made out in relation to particular documents or information, the named officer will request that the documents or information are placed in a sealed opaque bag in his presence. The named officer will then discuss with you appropriate arrangements for the safe-keeping of the documents or information by the OFT pending resolution of the issue of privilege.

## Listing of items

Unless it is impracticable in all the circumstances, items will not be removed from the premises by the named officer or other officers or accompanying persons until a list has been prepared by the named officer (or other officers or accompanying persons) of all the items to be removed, a copy of the list has been supplied to you, and you have been given a reasonable opportunity to check that the list relates to all the items concerned, and only to those items.

## Retention and copying of items

Items seized during the search will be retained by the OFT only for as long as is necessary in all the circumstances. For example, material seized may be retained if it will be needed—

(1) for use in evidence in a criminal trial;
(2) to satisfy the OFT's criminal disclosure obligations; or
(3) so that it may be subjected to forensic examination.

Material may also be retained under the provisions of the Criminal Justice and Police Act 2001.

On request, the OFT will, where practicable, provide a copy of such material to the person from whom the material was seized as soon as reasonably practicable.

[2] See section 197 of the Enterprise Act 2002.

### Confidentiality

You should note that, subject to the safeguards in relation to self-incrimination and communications subject to privilege, you are not entitled to withhold a document or information by claiming that it is confidential.

However, section 237 of the Act imposes limits on the disclosure of information that relates to the affairs of any individual or any business which has been obtained by the OFT as a result of using its powers of investigation under the Act, subject to certain exceptions. Those exceptions include the right of the OFT to disclose information for the purpose of facilitating the exercise by the OFT of its statutory function and the investigation of any criminal offence in any part of the UK. The relevant provisions are in Part 9 of the Act.

### Application to vary or discharge the Warrant

You are entitled to apply to the Court to vary or discharge the Warrant. If you intend to make such an application, you must first inform the named officer. An application to stop the Warrant from being executed must be made immediately upon it being served.

The application must be made to the judge who issued the Warrant, or if he is not available, to another judge of the Chancery Division.

If you are making an immediate application to stop the Warrant from being executed, the named officer will delay starting or continuing a search of the premises for a reasonable period (not exceeding two hours) while you make your application, provided that you—

(1) permit the named officer and other officers [and other accompanying persons] to enter and remain on the premises;

(2) keep the named officer informed of the steps you are taking in relation to the application;

(3) provide the named officer with contact details of the solicitor, if any, who is in receipt of your formal instructions in relation to an application to stop the Warrant being executed; and

(4) comply with any other conditions that the named officer imposes.

Examples of conditions that the named officer may impose pursuant to (4) above include—

(1) that you do not disturb or move any document or information that is the subject of the Warrant; and/or

(2) you do not tell anyone other than your legal adviser about the Warrant or the investigation.

### Application under Section 59 Criminal Justice and Police Act 2001

Your attention is drawn to section 59 of the Criminal Justice and Police Act 2001, which makes provision about applications relating to property seized in the exercise of the powers conferred by (among other provisions) section 194(2) of the Act. An application under section 59 should be made to a judge of the Crown Court.

## House of Lords Practice Direction and Standing Orders Applicable to Civil Appeals [*not reproduced*]

(available at <http://www.parliament.uk/judicial_work/judicial_work2.cfm>)



# Section 3

## PRE-ACTION PROTOCOLS

At the beginning of each protocol there is a contents list for that protocol.



# Practice Direction — Protocols

## GENERAL

1.1 This practice direction applies to the pre-action protocols which have been approved by the Head of Civil Justice.

1.2 The pre-action protocols which have been approved are set out in para. 5.1. Other pre- action protocols may subsequently be added.

1.3 Pre-action protocols outline the steps parties should take to seek information from and to provide information to each other about a prospective legal claim.

1.4 The objectives of pre-action protocols are:

(1) to encourage the exchange of early and full information about the prospective legal claim,

(2) to enable parties to avoid litigation by agreeing a settlement of the claim before the commencement of proceedings,

(3) to support the efficient management of proceedings where litigation cannot be avoided.

## COMPLIANCE WITH PROTOCOLS

2.1 The Civil Procedure Rules enable the court to take into account compliance or non-compliance with an applicable protocol when giving directions for the management of proceedings (see rr. 3.1(4) and (5) and 3.9(e)) and when making orders for costs (see r. 44.3(5)(a)).

2.2 The court will expect all parties to have complied in substance with the terms of an approved protocol.

2.3 If, in the opinion of the court, non-compliance has led to the commencement of proceedings which might otherwise not have needed to be commenced, or has led to costs being incurred in the proceedings that might otherwise not have been incurred, the orders the court may make include:

(1) an order that the party at fault pay the costs of the proceedings, or part of those costs, of the other party or parties;

(2) an order that the party at fault pay those costs on an indemnity basis;

(3) if the party at fault is a claimant in whose favour an order for the payment of damages or some specified sum is subsequently made, an order depriving that party of interest on such sum and in respect of such period as may be specified, and/or awarding interest at a lower rate than that at which interest would otherwise have been awarded;

(4) if the party at fault is a defendant and an order for the payment of damages or some specified sum is subsequently made in favour of the claimant, an order awarding interest on such sum and in respect of such period as may be specified at a higher rate, not exceeding 10 per cent above base rate (cf r. 36.21(2)), than the rate at which interest would otherwise have been awarded.

2.4 The court will exercise its powers under paras 2.1 and 2.3 with the object of placing the innocent party in no worse a position than he would have been in if the protocol had been complied with.

3.1 A claimant may be found to have failed to comply with a protocol by, for example:

(a) not having provided sufficient information to the defendant, or

(b) not having followed the procedure required by the protocol to be followed (e.g. not having followed the medical expert instruction procedure set out in the Personal Injury Protocol).

3.2 A defendant may be found to have failed to comply with a protocol by, for example:

(a) not making a preliminary response to the letter of claim within the time fixed for that purpose by the relevant protocol (21 days under the Personal Injury Protocol, 14 days under the Clinical Negligence Protocol),

(b) not making a full response within the time fixed for that purpose by the relevant protocol (three months of the letter of claim under the Clinical Negligence Protocol, three months from the date of acknowledgment of the letter of claim under the Personal Injury Protocol),

(c) not disclosing documents required to be disclosed by the relevant protocol.

3.3 The court is likely to treat this practice direction as indicating the normal, reasonable way of dealing with disputes. If proceedings are issued and parties have not complied with this practice direction or a specific protocol, it will be for the court to decide whether sanctions should be applied.

3.4 The court is not likely to be concerned with minor infringements of the practice direction or protocols. The court is likely to look at the effect of non-compliance on the other party when deciding whether to impose sanctions.

3.5 This practice direction does not alter the statutory time limits for starting court proceedings. A claimant is required to start proceedings within those time limits and to adhere to subsequent time limits required by the rules or ordered by the court. If proceedings are for any reason started before the parties have followed the procedures in this practice direction, the parties are encouraged to agree to apply to the court for a stay of the proceedings while they follow the practice direction.

## PRE-ACTION BEHAVIOUR IN OTHER CASES

4.1 In cases not covered by any approved protocol, the court will expect the parties, in accordance with the overriding objective and the matters referred to in r. 1.1(2)(a), (b) and (c), to act reasonably in exchanging information and documents relevant to the claim and generally in trying to avoid the necessity for the start of proceedings.

4.2 Parties to a potential dispute should follow a reasonable procedure, suitable to their particular circumstances, which is intended to avoid litigation. The procedure should not be regarded as a prelude to inevitable litigation. It should normally include:

(a) the claimant writing to give details of the claim;

(b) the defendant acknowledging the claim letter promptly;

(c) the defendant giving within a reasonable time a detailed written response; and

(d) the parties conducting genuine and reasonable negotiations with a view to settling the claim economically and without court proceedings.

4.3 The claimant's letter should:

(a) give sufficient concise details to enable the recipient to understand and investigate the claim without extensive further information;

(b) enclose copies of the essential documents which the claimant relies on;

(c) ask for a prompt acknowledgment of the letter, followed by a full written response within a reasonable stated period;
(For many claims, a normal reasonable period for a full response may be one month.)

(d) state whether court proceedings will be issued if the full response is not received within the stated period;

(e) identify and ask for copies of any essential documents, not in his possession, which the claimant wishes to see;

(f) state (if this is so) that the claimant wishes to enter into mediation or another alternative method of dispute resolution; and

(g) draw attention to the court's powers to impose sanctions for failure to comply with this practice direction and, if the recipient is likely to be unrepresented, enclose a copy of this practice direction.

4.4 The defendant should acknowledge the claimant's letter in writing within 21 days of receiving it. The acknowledgment should state when the defendant will give a full written response. If the time for this is longer than the period stated by the claimant, the defendant should give reasons why a longer period is needed.

4.5 The defendant's full written response should as appropriate:

(a) accept the claim in whole or in part and make proposals for settlement; or

(b) state that the claim is not accepted.

If the claim is accepted in part only, the response should make clear which part is accepted and which part is not accepted.

4.6 If the defendant does not accept the claim or part of it, the response should:

(a) give detailed reasons why the claim is not accepted, identifying which of the claimant's contentions are accepted and which are in dispute;

(b) enclose copies of the essential documents which the defendant relies on;

(c) enclose copies of documents asked for by the claimant, or explain why they are not enclosed;

(d) identify and ask for copies of any further essential documents, not in his possession, which the defendant wishes to see; and

(The claimant should provide these within a reasonably short time or explain in writing why he is not doing so.)

(e) state whether the defendant is prepared to enter into mediation or another alternative method of dispute resolution.

4.7 The parties should consider whether some form of alternative dispute resolution procedure would be more suitable than litigation, and if so, endeavour to agree which form to adopt. Both the claimant and defendant may be required by the court to provide evidence that alternative means of resolving their dispute were considered. The courts take the view that litigation should be a last resort, and that claims should not be issued prematurely when a settlement is still actively being explored. Parties are warned that if this paragraph is not followed then the court must have regard to such conduct when determining costs.

It is not practicable in this Practice Direction to address in detail how the parties might decide which method to adopt to resolve their particular dispute. However, summarized below are some of the options for resolving disputes without litigation:

- discussion and negotiation;
- early neutral evaluation by an independent third party (for example, a lawyer experienced in that field or an individual experienced in the subject matter of the claim);
- mediation—a form of facilitated negotiation assisted by an independent neutral party.

The Legal Services Commission has published a booklet on 'Alternatives to Court', CLS Direct Information Leaflet 23 (<http://www.clsdirect.org.uk/legalhelp/leaflet23.jsp>), which lists a number of organisations that provide alternative dispute resolution services.

It is expressly recognised that no party can or should be forced to mediate or enter into any form of ADR.

4.8 Documents disclosed by either party in accordance with this practice direction may not be used for any purpose other than resolving the dispute, unless the other party agrees.

4.9 The resolution of some claims, but by no means all, may need help from an expert. If an expert is needed, the parties should wherever possible and to save expense engage an agreed expert.

4.10 Parties should be aware that, if the matter proceeds to litigation, the court may not allow the use of an expert's report, and that the cost of it is not always recoverable.

## INFORMATION ABOUT FUNDING ARRANGEMENTS

4A.1 Where a person enters into a funding arrangement within the meaning of r. 43.2(1)(k) he should inform other potential parties to the claim that he has done so.

4A.2 Paragraph 4A.1 applies to all proceedings whether proceedings to which a pre-action protocol applies or otherwise.

(Rule 44.3B(1)(c) provides that a party may not recover any additional liability for any period in the proceedings during which he failed to provide information about a funding arrangement in accordance with a rule, practice direction or court order.)

## COMMENCEMENT

5.1 The following table sets out the protocols currently in force, the date they came into force and their date of publication:

| Protocol | Coming into force | Publication |
|---|---|---|
| Personal Injury | 26 April 1999 | January 1999 |
| Clinical Negligence | 26 April 1999 | January 1999 |
| Construction and Engineering Disputes | 2 October 2000 | September 2000 |
| Defamation | 2 October 2000 | September 2000 |
| Professional Negligence | 16 July 2001 | May 2001 |
| Judicial Review | 4 March 2002 | 3 December 2001 |
| Disease and Illness | 8 December 2003 | September 2003 |
| Possession Claims based on rent arrears | 2 October 2006 | September 2006 |

5.2 The court will take compliance or non-compliance with a relevant protocol into account where the claim was started after the coming into force of that protocol but will not do so where the claim was started before that date.

5.3 Parties in a claim started after a relevant protocol came into force, who have, by work done before that date, achieved the objectives sought to be achieved by certain requirements of that protocol, need not take any further steps to comply with those requirements. They will not be considered to have not complied with the protocol for the purposes of paras 2 and 3.

5.4 Parties in a claim started after a relevant protocol came into force, who have not been able to comply with any particular requirements of that protocol because the period of time between the publication date and the date of coming into force was too short, will not be considered to have not complied with the protocol for the purposes of paras 2 and 3.

# Pre-action Protocol for Construction and Engineering Disputes

## 1 Introduction

1.1 This Pre-Action Protocol applies to all construction and engineering disputes (including professional negligence claims against architects, engineers and quantity surveyors).

*Exceptions*

1.2 A claimant shall not be required to comply with this Protocol before commencing proceedings to the extent that the proposed proceedings (i) are for the enforcement of the decision of an adjudicator to whom a dispute has been referred pursuant to section 108 of the Housing Grants, Construction and Regeneration Act 1996 ("the 1996 Act"), (ii) include a claim for interim injunctive relief, (iii) will be the subject of a claim for summary judgment pursuant to Part 24 of the Civil Procedure Rules, or (iv) relate to the same or substantially the same issues as have been the subject of recent adjudication under the 1996 Act, or some other formal alternative dispute resolution procedure.

*Objectives*

1.3 The objectives of this Protocol are as set out in the Practice Direction relating to Civil Procedure Pre-Action Protocols, namely:

- (i) to encourage the exchange of early and full information about the prospective legal claim;
- (ii) to enable parties to avoid litigation by agreeing a settlement of the claim before commencement of proceedings; and
- (iii) to support the efficient management of proceedings where litigation cannot be avoided.

*Compliance*

1.4 If proceedings are commenced, the court will be able to treat the standards set in this Protocol as the normal reasonable approach to pre-action conduct. If the court has to consider the question of compliance after proceedings have begun, it will be concerned with substantial compliance and not minor departures, e.g. failure by a short period to provide relevant information. Minor departures will not exempt the "innocent" party from following the Protocol. The court will look at the effect of non-compliance on the other party when deciding whether to impose sanctions. For sanctions generally, see paragraph 2 of the Practice Direction-Protocols "Compliance with Protocols".

*Proportionality*

1.5 The overriding objective (CPR rule 1.1) applies to the pre-action period. The Protocol must not be used as a tactical device to secure advantage for one party or to generate unnecessary costs. In lower value claims (such as those likely to proceed in the county court), the letter of claim and the response should be simple and the costs of both sides should be kept to a modest level. In all cases the costs incurred at the Protocol stage should be proportionate to the complexity of the case and the amount of money which is at stake. The Protocol does not impose a requirement on the parties to marshal and disclose all the supporting details and evidence that may ultimately be required if the case proceeds to litigation.

## 2 Overview of the Protocol

*General Aim*

2 The general aim of this Protocol is to ensure that before court proceedings commence:

- (i) the claimant and the defendant have provided sufficient information for each party to know the nature of the other's case;

(ii) each party has had an opportunity to consider the other's case, and to accept or reject all or any part of the case made against him at the earliest possible stage;
(iii) there is more pre-action contact between the parties;
(iv) better and earlier exchange of information occurs;
(v) there is better pre-action investigation by the parties;
(vi) the parties have met formally on at least one occasion with a view to
- defining and agreeing the issues between them; and
- exploring possible ways by which the claim may be resolved;

(vii) the parties are in a position where they may be able to settle cases early and fairly without recourse to litigation; and
(vii) proceedings will be conducted efficiently if litigation does become necessary.

## 3 The Letter of Claim

3 Prior to commencing proceedings, the claimant or his solicitor shall send to each proposed defendant (if appropriate to his registered address) a copy of a letter of claim which shall contain the following information:
(i) the claimant's full name and address;
(ii) the full name and address of each proposed defendant;
(iii) a clear summary of the facts on which each claim is based;
(iv) the basis on which each claim is made, identifying the principal contractual terms and statutory provisions relied on;
(v) the nature of the relief claimed: if damages are claimed, a breakdown showing how the damages have been quantified; if a sum is claimed pursuant to a contract, how it has been calculated; if an extension of time is claimed, the period claimed;
(vi) where a claim has been made previously and rejected by a defendant, and the claimant is able to identify the reason(s) for such rejection, the claimant's grounds of belief as to why the claim was wrongly rejected;
(vii) the names of any experts already instructed by the claimant on whose evidence he intends to rely, identifying the issues to which that evidence will be directed.

## 4 The Defendant's Response

*The defendant's acknowledgment*

4.1 Within 14 calendar days of receipt of the letter of claim, the defendant should acknowledge its receipt in writing and may give the name and address of his insurer (if any). If there has been no acknowledgment by or on behalf of the defendant within 14 days, the claimant will be entitled to commence proceedings without further compliance with this Protocol.

4.2 Objections to the court's jurisdiction or the named defendant

4.2.1 If the defendant intends to take any objection to all or any part of the claimant's claim on the grounds that (i) the court lacks jurisdiction, (ii) the matter should be referred to arbitration, or (iii) the defendant named in the letter of claim is the wrong defendant, that objection should be raised by the defendant within 28 days after receipt of the letter of claim. The letter of objection shall specify the parts of the claim to which the objection relates, setting out the grounds relied on, and, where appropriate, shall identify the correct defendant (if known). Any failure to take such objection shall not prejudice the defendant's rights to do so in any subsequent proceedings, but the court may take such failure into account when considering the question of costs.

4.2.2 Where such notice of objection is given, the defendant is not required to send a letter of response in accordance with paragraph 4.3.1 in relation to the claim or those parts of it to which the objection relates (as the case may be).

4.2.3 If at any stage before the claimant commences proceedings, the defendant withdraws his objection, then paragraph 4.3 and the remaining part of this Protocol will apply to the claim or those parts of it to which the objection related as if the letter of claim had been received on the date on which notice of withdrawal of the objection had been given.

4.3 The defendant's response

4.3.1 Within 28 days from the date of receipt of the letter of claim, or such other period as the parties may reasonably agree (up to a maximum of 3 months), the defendant shall send a letter of response to the claimant which shall contain the following information:

(i) the facts set out in the letter of claim which are agreed or not agreed, and if not agreed, the basis of the disagreement;

(ii) which claims are accepted and which are rejected, and if rejected, the basis of the rejection;

(iii) if a claim is accepted in whole or in part, whether the damages, sums or extensions of time claimed are accepted or rejected, and if rejected, the basis of the rejection;

(iv) if contributory negligence is alleged against the claimant, a summary of the facts relied on;

(v) whether the defendant intends to make a counterclaim, and if so, giving the information which is required to be given in a letter of claim by paragraph 3(iii) to (vi) above;

(vi) the names of any experts already instructed on whose evidence it is intended to rely, identifying the issues to which that evidence will be directed;

4.3.2 If no response is received by the claimant within the period of 28 days (or such other period as has been agreed between the parties), the claimant shall be entitled to commence proceedings without further compliance with this Protocol.

*Claimant's response to counter claim*

4.4 The claimant shall provide a response to any counterclaim within the equivalent period allowed to the defendant to respond to the letter of claim under paragraph 4.3.1 above.

## 5 Pre-Action Meeting

5.1 Within 28 days after receipt by the claimant of the defendant's letter of response, or (if the claimant intends to respond to the counterclaim) after receipt by the defendant of the claimant's letter of response to the counterclaim, the parties should normally meet.

5.2 The aim of the meeting is for the parties to agree what are the main issues in the case, to identify the root cause of disagreement in respect of each issue, and to consider (i) whether, and if so how, the issues might be resolved without recourse to litigation, and (ii) if litigation is unavoidable, what steps should be taken to ensure that it is conducted in accordance with the overriding objective as defined in rule 1.1 of the Civil Procedure Rules.

5.3 In some circumstances, it may be necessary to convene more than one meeting. It is not intended by this Protocol to prescribe in detail the manner in which the meetings should be conducted. But the court will normally expect that those attending will include:

(i) where the party is an individual, that individual, and where the party is a corporate body, a representative of that body who has authority to settle or recommend settlement of the dispute;

(ii) a legal representative of each party (if one has been instructed);

(iii) where the involvement of insurers has been disclosed, a representative of the insurer (who may be its legal representative); and

(iv) where a claim is made or defended on behalf of some other party (such as, for example, a claim made by a main contractor pursuant to a contractual obligation to pass on subcontractor claims), the party on whose behalf the claim is made or defended and/or his legal representatives.

5.4 In respect of each agreed issue or the dispute as a whole, the parties should consider whether some form of alternative dispute resolution procedure would be more suitable than litigation, and if so, endeavour to agree which form to adopt. It is expressly recognised that no party can or should be forced to mediate or enter into any form of alternative dispute resolution.

5.5 If the parties are unable to agree on a means of resolving the dispute other than by litigation they should use their best endeavours to agree:

(i) if there is any area where expert evidence is likely to be required, how the relevant issues are to be defined and how expert evidence is to be dealt with including whether a joint expert might be appointed, and if so, who that should be; and (so far as is practicable)

(ii) the extent of disclosure of documents with a view to saving costs; and

(iii) the conduct of the litigation with the aim of minimising cost and delay.

5.6 Any party who attended any pre-action meeting shall be at liberty and may be required to disclose to the court:

(i) that the meeting took place, when and who attended;

(ii) the identity of any party who refused to attend, and the grounds for such refusal;

(iii) if the meeting did not take place, why not; and

(iv) any agreements concluded between the parties.

(v) the fact of whether alternative means of resolving the dispute were considered or agreed.

5.7 Except as provided in paragraph 5.6, everything said at a pre-action meeting shall be treated as "without prejudice".

## 6 Limitation of Action

6 If by reason of complying with any part of this protocol a claimant's claim may be time-barred under any provision of the Limitation Act 1980, or any other legislation which imposes a time limit for bringing an action, the claimant may commence proceedings without complying with this Protocol. In such circumstances, a claimant who commences proceedings without complying with all, or any part, of this Protocol must apply to the court on notice for directions as to the timetable and form of procedure to be adopted, at the same time as he requests the court to issue proceedings. The court will consider whether to order a stay of the whole or part of the proceedings pending compliance with this Protocol.

# Pre-action Protocol for Defamation



## 1 INTRODUCTION

1.1 Lord Irvine of Lairg, in his foreword to the Pre-Action Protocol for Personal Injury Claims identified the value of creating pre-action protocols as a key part of the civil justice reforms. He hoped that pre-action protocols would set effective and enforceable standards for the efficient conduct of pre-action litigation.

1.2 Lord Irvine went on to state that:

> The protocol aims to improve pre-action communication between the parties by establishing a timetable for the exchange of information relevant to the dispute and by setting standards for the content of correspondence. Compliance with the protocol will enable parties to make an informed judgement on the merits of their cases earlier than tends to happen today, because they will have earlier access to the information they need. This will provide every opportunity for improved communications between the parties designed to lead to an increase in the number of pre-action settlements.

1.3 It is against this background that a Pre-Action Protocol for Claims in Defamation is submitted. This protocol is intended to encourage exchange of information between parties at an early, stage and to provide a clear framework within which parties to a claim in defamation, acting in good faith, can explore the early and appropriate resolution of that claim.

1.4 There are important features which distinguish defamation claims from other areas of civil litigation, and these must be borne in mind when both applying, and reviewing the application of, the pre-action protocol. In particular, time is always 'of the essence' in defamation claims; the limitation period is (uniquely) only one year, and almost invariably, a claimant will be seeking an immediate correction and/or apology as part of the process of restoring his/her reputation.

1.5 This pre-action protocol embraces the spirit of the reforms to the civil justice system envisaged by Lord Woolf, and now enacted in the Civil Procedure Rules. It aims to incorporate the concept of the overriding objective, as provided by the Rules at Part 1, before the commencement of any court proceedings, namely:

dealing with a case justly includes, so far as is practicable:

- ensuring that the parties are on an equal footing;
- saving expense;

dealing with the case in ways which are proportionate:

- to the amount of money involved;
- to the importance of the case;
- to the complexity of the issues; and
- to the financial position of each party;
- ensuring that it is dealt with expeditiously and fairly; and
- allotting to it an appropriate share of the court's resources, while taking into account the need to allot resources to other cases.

## 2 AIMS OF THE PROTOCOL

- This protocol aims to set out a code of good practice which parties should follow when litigation is being considered.

- It encourages early communication of a claim.
- It aims to encourage both parties to disclose sufficient information to enable each to understand the other's case and to promote the prospect of early resolution.
- It sets a timetable for the exchange of information relevant to the dispute.
- It sets standards for the content of correspondence.
- It identifies options which either party might adopt to encourage settlement of the claim.
- Should a claim proceed to litigation, the extent to which the protocol has been followed both in practice and in spirit by the parties will assist the court in dealing with liability for costs and making other orders.
- Letters of claim and responses sent pursuant to this protocol are not intended to have the same status as a statement of case in proceedings.
- It aims to keep the costs of resolving disputes subject to this protocol proportionate.

## 3 PRE-ACTION PROTOCOL

### Letter of Claim

3.1 The claimant should notify the defendant of his/her claim in writing at the earliest reasonable opportunity.

3.2 The letter of claim should include the following information:

- name of claimant;
- sufficient details to identify the publication or broadcast which contained the words complained of;
- the words complained of and, if known, the date of publication; where possible, a copy or transcript of the words complained of should be enclosed;
- factual inaccuracies or unsupportable comment within the words complained of; the claimant should give a sufficient explanation to enable the defendant to appreciate why the words are inaccurate or unsupportable;
- the nature of the remedies sought by the claimant.

Where relevant, the letter of claim should also include:

- any facts or matters which make the claimant identifiable from the words complained of;
- details of any special facts relevant to the interpretation of the words complained of and/or any particular damage caused by the words complained of.

3.3 It is desirable for the claimant to identify in the letter of claim the meaning(s) he/she attributes to the words complained of.

### Defendant's Response to Letter of Claim

3.4 The defendant should provide a full response to the letter of claim as soon as reasonably possible. If the defendant believes that he/she will be unable to respond within 14 days (or such shorter time limit as specified in the letter of claim), then he/she should specify the date by which he/she intends to respond.

3.5 The response should include the following:

- whether or to what extent the claimant's claim is accepted, whether more information is required or whether it is rejected;
- if the claim is accepted in whole or in part, the defendant should indicate which remedies it is willing to offer;
- if more information is required, then the defendant should specify precisely what information is needed to enable the claim to be dealt with and why;
- if the claim is rejected, then the defendant should explain the reasons why it is rejected, including a sufficient indication of any facts on which the defendant is likely to rely in support of any substantive defence.

It is desirable for the defendant to include in the response to the letter of claim the meaning(s) he/she attributes to the words complained of.

## Proportionality of Costs

3.6 In formulating both the letter of claim and response and in taking any subsequent steps, the parties should act reasonably to keep costs proportionate to the nature and gravity of the case and the stage the complaint has reached.

## Alternative Dispute Resolution

3.7 The parties should consider whether some form of alternative dispute resolution procedure would be more suitable than litigation, and if so, endeavour to agree which form to adopt. Both the claimant and defendant may be required by the court to provide evidence that alternative means of resolving their dispute were considered. The courts take the view that litigation should be a last resort, and that claims should not be issued prematurely when a settlement is still actively being explored. Parties are warned that if the protocol is not followed (including this paragraph) then the court must have regard to such conduct when determining costs.

3.8 It is not practicable in this protocol to address in detail how the parties might decide which method to adopt to resolve their particular dispute. However, summarised below are some of the options for resolving disputes without litigation:

- discussion and negotiation;
- early neutral evaluation by an independent third party (for example, a lawyer experienced in the field of defamation or an individual experienced in the subject matter of the claim);
- mediation—a form of facilitated negotiation assisted by an independent neutral party;
- reference to the Press Complaints Commission (an independent body which deals with complaints from members of the public about the editorial content of newspapers and magazines).

The Legal Services Commission has published a booklet on 'Alternatives to Court', CLS Direct Information Leaflet 23 (<http://www.clsdirect.org.uk/legalhelp/leaflet23.jsp>), which lists a number of organisations that provide alternative dispute resolution services.

3.9 It is expressly recognised that no party can or should be forced to mediate or enter into any form of ADR.

# Pre-action Protocol for Personal Injury Claims



## 1 INTRODUCTION

1.1 Lord Woolf in his final Access to Justice Report of July 1996 recommended the development of pre-action protocols:
'To build on and increase the benefits of early but well informed settlement which genuinely satisfy both parties to dispute.'

1.2 The aims of pre-action protocols are:
- more pre-action contact between the parties
- better and earlier exchange of information
- better pre-action investigation by both sides
- to put the parties in a position where they may be able to settle cases fairly and early without litigation
- to enable proceedings to run to the court's timetable and efficiently, if litigation does become necessary
- to promote the provision of medical or rehabilitation treatment (not just in high value cases) to address the needs of the claimant.

1.3 The concept of protocols is relevant to a range of initiatives for good litigation and pre-litigation practice, especially:
- predictability in the time needed for steps pre-proceedings
- standardisation of relevant information, including documents to be disclosed.

1.4 The courts will be able to treat the standards set in protocols as the normal reasonable approach to pre-action conduct. If proceedings are issued, it will be for the court to decide whether non-compliance with a protocol should merit adverse consequences. Guidance on the court's likely approach will be given from time to time in practice directions.

1.5 If the court has to consider the question of compliance after proceedings have begun, it will not be concerned with minor infringements, e.g. failure by a short period to provide relevant information. One minor breach will not exempt the 'innocent' party from following the protocol. The court will look at the effect of non-compliance on the other party when deciding whether to impose sanctions.

## 2 NOTES OF GUIDANCE

2.1 The protocol has been kept deliberately simple to promote ease of use and general acceptability. The notes of guidance which follows relate particularly to issues which arose during the piloting of the protocol.

### Scope of the Protocol

2.2 This protocol is intended to apply to all claims which include a claim for personal injury (except those claims covered by the Clinical Disputes and Disease and Illness Protocols) and to the entirety of those claims: not only to the personal injury element of a claim which also includes, for instance, property damage.

2.3 This protocol is primarily designed for those road traffic, tripping and slipping and accident at work cases which include an element of personal injury with a value of less than £15,000 which are likely to be allocated to the fast track. This is because time will be of the essence, after proceedings are issued, especially for the defendant, if a case is to be ready for trial within 30 weeks of allocation. Also, proportionality of work and costs to the value of what is in dispute is particularly important in lower value claims. For some claims within the value 'scope' of the fast track some flexibility in the timescale of the protocol may be necessary, see also paragraph 3.8.

2.4 However, the 'cards on the table' approach advocated by the protocol is equally appropriate to higher value claims. The spirit, if not the letter of the protocol, should still be followed for multi-track type claims. In accordance with the sense of the civil justice reforms, the court will expect to see the spirit of reasonable pre-action behaviour applied in all cases, regardless of the existence of a specific protocol. In particular with regard to personal injury cases worth more than £15,000, with a view to avoiding the necessity of proceedings parties are expected to comply with the protocol as far as possible e.g. in respect of letters before action, exchanging information and documents and agreeing experts.

2.5 The timetable and the arrangements for disclosing documents and obtaining expert evidence may need to be varied to suit the circumstances of the case. Where one or both parties consider the detail of the protocol is not appropriate to the case, and proceedings are subsequently issued, the court will expect an explanation as to why the protocol has not been followed, or has been varied.

## Early Notification

2.6 The claimant's legal representative may wish to notify the defendant and/or his insurer as soon as they know a claim is likely to be made, but before they are able to send a detailed letter of claim, particularly for instance, when the defendant has no or limited knowledge of the incident giving rise to the claim or where the claimant is incurring significant expenditure as a result of the accident which he hopes the defendant might pay for, in whole or in part. If the claimant's representative chooses to do this, it will not start the timetable for responding.

## The Letter of Claim

2.7 The specimen letter of claim at Annex A will usually be sent to the individual defendant. In practice, he/she may have no personal financial interest in the financial outcome of the claim/dispute because he/she is insured. Court imposed sanctions for non-compliance with the protocol may be ineffective against an insured. This is why the protocol emphasises the importance of passing the letter of claim to the insurer and the possibility that the insurance cover might be affected. If an insurer receives the letter of claim only after some delay by the insured, it would not be unreasonable for the insurer to ask the claimant for additional time to respond.

2.8 In road traffic cases, the letter of claim should always contain the name and address of the hospital where the claimant was treated and, where available, the claimant's hospital reference number.

2.9 The priority at letter of claim stage is for the claimant to provide sufficient information for the defendant to assess liability. Sufficient information should also be provided to enable the defendant to estimate the likely size of the claim.

2.10 Once the claimant has sent the letter of claim no further investigation on liability should normally be carried out until a response is received from the defendant indicating whether liability is disputed.

## Reasons for Early Issue

2.11 The protocol recommends that a defendant be given three months to investigate and respond to a claim before proceedings are issued. This may not always be possible, particularly where a claimant only consults a solicitor close to the end of any relevant limitation period. In these circumstances, the claimant's solicitor should give as much notice of the intention to issue proceedings as is practicable and the parties should consider whether the court might be invited to extend time for service of the claimant's supporting documents and for service of any defence, or alternatively, to stay the proceedings while the recommended steps in the protocol are followed.

## Status of Letters of Claim and Response

2.12 Letters of claim and response are not intended to have the same status as a statement of case in proceedings. Matters may come to light as a result of investigation after the letter of claim has been sent, or after the defendant has responded, particularly if disclosure of documents takes place outside the recommended three-month period. These circumstances could mean that the 'pleaded' case of one or both parties is presented slightly differently than in the letter of claim and response. It would not be consistent with the spirit of the protocol for a party to 'take a point' on this in the proceedings, provided that there was no obvious intention by the party who changed their position to mislead the other party.

## Disclosure of Documents

2.13 The aim of the early disclosure of documents by the defendant is not to encourage 'fishing expeditions' by the claimant, but to promote an early exchange of relevant information to help in clarifying or resolving issues in dispute. The claimant's solicitor can assist by identifying in the letter of claim or in a subsequent letter the particular categories of documents which they consider are relevant.

## Experts

2.14 The protocol encourages joint selection of, and access to, experts. The report produced is not a joint report for the purposes of CPR Part 35. Most frequently this will apply to the medical expert, but on occasions also to liability experts, e.g. engineers. The protocol promotes the practice of the claimant obtaining a medical report, disclosing it to the defendant who then asks questions and/or agrees it and does not obtain his own report. The protocol provides for nomination of the expert by the claimant in personal injury claims because of the early stage of the proceedings and the particular nature of such claims. If proceedings have to be issued, a medical report must be attached to these proceedings. However, if necessary after proceedings have commenced and with the permission of the court, the parties may obtain further expert reports. It would be for the court to decide whether the costs of more than one expert's report should be recoverable.

2.15 Some solicitors choose to obtain medical reports through medical agencies, rather than directly from a specific doctor or hospital. The defendant's prior consent to the action should be sought and, if the defendant so requests, the agency should be asked to provide in advance the names of the doctor(s) whom they are considering instructing.

## Alternative Dispute Resolution

2.16 The parties should consider whether some form of alternative dispute resolution procedure would be more suitable than litigation, and if so, endeavour to agree which form to adopt. Both the claimant and defendant may be required by the court to provide evidence that alternative means of resolving their dispute were considered. The courts take the view that litigation should be a last resort, and that claims should not be issued prematurely when a settlement is still actively being explored. Parties are warned that if the protocol is not followed (including this paragraph) then the court must have regard to such conduct when determining costs.

2.17 It is not practicable in this protocol to address in detail how the parties might decide which method to adopt to resolve their particular dispute. However, summarised below are some of the options for resolving disputes without litigation:

- discussion and negotiation;
- early neutral evaluation by an independent third party (for example, a lawyer experienced in the field of personal injury or an individual experienced in the subject matter of the claim);
- mediation—a form of facilitated negotiation assisted by an independent neutral party.

2.18 The Legal Services Commission has published a booklet on 'Alternatives to Court', CLS Direct Information Leaflet 23 (<http://www.clsdirect.org.uk/legalhelp/leaflet 23.jsp>),which lists a number of organisations that provide alternative dispute resolution services.

2.19 It is expressly recognised that no party can or should be forced to mediate or enter into any form of ADR.

### Stocktake

2.20 Where a claim is not resolved when the protocol has been followed, the parties might wish to carry out a 'stocktake' of the issues in dispute, and the evidence that the court is likely to need to decide those issues, before proceedings are started. Where the defendant is insured and the pre-action steps have been conducted by the insurer, the insurer would normally be expected to nominate solicitors to act in the proceedings and the claimant's solicitor is recommended to invite the insurer to nominate solicitors to act in the proceedings and do so 7–14 days before the intended issue date.

## 3 THE PROTOCOL

### Letter of Claim

3.1 The claimant shall send to the proposed defendant two copies of a letter of claim, immediately sufficient information is available to substantiate a realistic claim and before issues of quantum are addressed in detail. One copy of the letter is for the defendant, the second for passing on to his insurers.

3.2 The letter shall contain **a clear summary of the facts** on which the claim is based together with an indication of the **nature of any injuries** suffered and of **any financial loss incurred**. In cases of road traffic accidents, the letter should provide the name and address of the hospital where treatment has been obtained and the claimant's hospital reference number. Where the case is funded by a conditional fee agreement (or collective conditional fee agreement), notification should be given of the existence of the agreement and where appropriate, that there is a success fee and/or insurance premium, although not the level of the success fee or premium.

3.3 Solicitors are recommended to use a **standard format** for such a letter—an example is at Annex A: this can be amended to suit the particular case.

3.4 The letter should ask for **details of the insurer** and that a copy should be sent by the proposed defendant to the insurer where appropriate. If the insurer is known, a copy shall be sent directly to the insurer. Details of the claimant's National Insurance number and date of birth should be supplied to the defendant's insurer once the defendant has responded to the letter of claim and confirmed the identity of the insurer. This information should not be supplied in the letter of claim.

3.5 **Sufficient information** should be given in order to enable the defendant's insurer/solicitor to commence investigations and at least put a broad valuation on the 'risk'.

3.6 The **defendant should reply within 21 calendar days** of the date of posting of the letter identifying the insurer (if any) and, if necessary, identifying specifically any significant omissions from the letter of claim. If there has been no reply by the defendant or insurer within 21 days, the claimant will be entitled to issue proceedings.

3.7 The **defendant**('s insurers) will have a **maximum of three months** from the date of acknowledgment of the claim **to investigate**. No later than the end of that period the defendant (insurer) shall reply, stating whether liability is denied and, if so, giving reasons for their denial of liability including any alternative version of events relied upon.

3.8 Where the accident occurred outside England and Wales and/or where the defendant is outside the jurisdiction, the time periods of 21 days and three months should normally be extended up to 42 days and six months.

3.9 Where the claimant's investigation indicates that the value of the claim has increased to more than £15,000 since the letter of claim, the claimant should notify the defendant as soon as possible.

## Documents

3.10 If the **defendant denies liability**, he should enclose with the letter of reply, **documents** in his possession which are **material to the issues** between the parties, and which would be likely to be ordered to be disclosed by the court, either on an application for pre-action disclosure, or on disclosure during proceedings.

3.11 Attached at Annex B are **specimen**, but non-exhaustive, **lists** of documents likely to be material in different types of claim. Where the claimant's investigation of the case is well advanced, the letter of claim could indicate which classes of documents are considered relevant for early disclosure. Alternatively these could be identified at a later stage.

3.12 Where the defendant admits primary liability, but alleges contributory negligence by the claimant, the defendant should give reasons supporting those allegations and disclose those documents from Annex B which are relevant to the issues in dispute. The claimant should respond to the allegations of contributory negligence before proceedings are issued.

3.13 No charge will be made for providing copy documents under the Protocol.

## Special Damages

3.14 The claimant will send to the defendant as soon as practicable a Schedule of Special Damages with supporting documents, particularly where the defendant has admitted liability.

## Experts

3.15 Before any party instructs an expert he should give the other party a list of the **name**(s) of **one or more experts** in the relevant speciality whom he considers are suitable to instruct.

3.16 Where a medical expert is to be instructed the claimant's solicitor will organise access to relevant medical records—see specimen letter of instruction at Annex C.

3.17 **Within 14 days** the other party may indicate **an objection** to one or more of the named experts. The first party should then instruct a mutually acceptable expert (which is not the same as a joint expert). It must be emphasised that if the Claimant nominates an expert in the original letter of claim, the defendant has 14 days to object to one or more of the named experts after expiration of the period of 21 days within which he has to reply to the letter of claim, as set out in paragraph 3.6.

3.18 If the second party objects to all the listed experts, the parties may then instruct **experts of their own choice**. It would be for the court to decide subsequently, if proceedings are issued, whether either party had acted unreasonably.

3.19 If the **second party does not object to an expert nominated**, he shall not be entitled to rely on his own expert evidence within that particular speciality unless:
(a) the first party agrees,
(b) the court so directs, or
(c) the first party's expert report has been amended and the first party is not prepared to disclose the original report.

3.20 **Either party may send to an agreed expert written questions** on the report, relevant to the issues, via the first party's solicitors. The expert should send answers to the questions separately and directly to each party.

3.21 The cost of a report from an agreed expert will usually be paid by the instructing first party: the costs of the expert replying to questions will usually be borne by the party which asks the questions.

## 4 REHABILITATION

4.1 The claimant or the defendant or both shall consider as early as possible whether the claimant has reasonable needs that could be met by rehabilitation treatment or other measures.

4.2 The parties shall consider, in such cases, how those needs might be addressed. The Rehabilitation Code (which is attached at Annex D) may be helpful in considering how to identify the claimant's needs and how to address the cost of providing for those needs.

4.3 The time limit set out in paragraph 3.7 of this Protocol shall not be shortened, except by consent to allow these issues to be addressed.

4.4 The provision of any report obtained for the purposes of assessment of provision of a party's rehabilitation needs shall not be used in any litigation arising out of the accident, the subject of the claim, save by consent and shall in any event be exempt from the provisions of paragraphs 3.15 to 3.21 inclusive of this protocol.

## 5 RESOLUTION OF ISSUES

5.1 Where the defendant admits liability in whole or in part, before proceedings are issued, any medical reports obtained under this protocol on which a party relies should be disclosed to the other party. The claimant should delay issuing proceedings for 21 days from disclosure of the report (unless such delay would cause his claim to become time-barred), to enable the parties to consider whether the claim is capable of settlement.

5.2 The Civil Procedure Rules Part 36 permit claimants and defendants to make offers to settle pre-proceedings. Parties should always consider before issuing if it is appropriate to make Part 36 Offer. If such an offer is made, the party making the offer must always supply sufficient evidence and/or information to enable the offer to be properly considered.

5.3 Where the defendant has admitted liability, the claimant should send to the defendant schedules of special damages and loss at least 21 days before proceedings are issued (unless that would cause the claimant's claim to become time-barred).

## ANNEX A
## LETTER OF CLAIM

To
Defendant

Dear Sirs

**Re: Claimant's full name**
**Claimant's full address**
**Claimant's Clock or Works Number**
**Claimant's Employer (name and address)**

We are instructed by the above named to claim damages in connection with an *accident at work/road traffic accident/tripping accident* on
day of *(year)* at *(place of accident which must be sufficiently detailed to establish location)*

Please confirm the identity of your insurers. Please note that the insurers will need to see this letter as soon as possible and it may affect your insurance cover and/or the conduct of any subsequent legal proceedings if you do not send this letter to them.

The circumstances of the accident are:—
*(brief outline)*

The reason why we are alleging fault is:
*(simple explanation e.g. defective machine, broken ground)*

A description of our client's injuries is as follows:—
***(brief outline)***

*(In cases of road traffic accidents)*
Our client (state hospital reference number) received treatment for the injuries at name and address of hospital).

*Our client is still suffering from the effects of his/her injury. We invite you to participate with us in addressing his/her immediate needs by use of rehabilitation.*

He is employed as *(occupation)* and has had the following time off work *(dates of absence)*. His approximate weekly income is (insert if known).

*If you are our client's employers, please provide us with the usual earnings details which will enable us to calculate his financial loss.*

*We are obtaining a police report and will let you have a copy of the same upon your undertaking to meet half the fee.*

We have also sent a letter of claim to *(name and address)* and a copy of that letter is attached. We understand their insurers are *(name, address and claims number if known)*.

At this stage of our enquiries we would expect the documents contained in parts *(insert appropriate parts of standard disclosure list)* to be relevant to this action.

*Please note that we have entered into a conditional fee agreement with our client dated in relation to this claim which provides for a success fee within the meaning of section 58(2) of the Courts and Legal Services Act 1990. Our client has taken out an insurance policy with [name of insurance company] of [address of insurance company] to which section 29 of the Access to Justice Act 1999 applies. The policy number is and the policy is dated . Where the funding arrangement is an insurance policy, the party must state the name and address of the insurer, the policy number and the date of the policy, and must identify the claim or claims to which it relates (including Part 20 claims if any).*

A copy of this letter is attached for you to send to your insurers. Finally we expect an acknowledgment of this letter within 21 days by yourselves or your insurers.

Yours faithfully

## ANNEX B
## PRE-ACTION PERSONAL INJURY PROTOCOL
## STANDARD DISCLOSURE LISTS

## FAST TRACK DISCLOSURE

### RTA Cases

### Section A

In all cases where liability is at issue—

(i) Documents identifying nature, extent and location of damage to defendant's vehicle where there is any dispute about point of impact.
(ii) MOT certificate where relevant.
(iii) Maintenance records where vehicle defect is alleged or it is alleged by defendant that there was an unforeseen defect which caused or contributed to the accident.

### Section B

Accident involving commercial vehicle as defendant—

(i) Tachograph charts or entry from individual control book.
(ii) Maintenance and repair records required for operators' licence where vehicle defect is alleged or it is alleged by defendant that there was an unforeseen defect which caused or contributed to the accident.

## Section C

Cases against local authorities where highway design defect is alleged.
(i) Documents produced to comply with section 39 of the Road Traffic Act 1988 in respect of the duty designed to promote road safety to include studies into road accidents in the relevant area and documents relating to measures recommended to prevent accidents in the relevant area.

*Highway tripping claims*
Documents from Highway Authority for a period of 12 months prior to the accident—
(i) Records of inspection for the relevant stretch of highway.
(ii) Maintenance records including records of independent contractors working in relevant area.
(iii) Records of the minutes of Highway Authority meetings where maintenance or repair policy has been discussed or decided.
(iv) Records of complaints about the state of highways.
(v) Records of other accidents which have occurred on the relevant stretch of highway.

*Workplace claims*
(i) Accident book entry.
(ii) First aider report.
(iii) Surgery record.
(iv) Foreman/supervisor accident report.
(v) Safety representatives accident report.
(vi) RIDDOR (Reporting of Injuries, Diseases and Dangerous Occurrences Regulations) report to HSE.
(vii) Other communications between defendants and HSE.
(viii) Minutes of Health and Safety Committee meeting(s) where accident/matter considered.
(ix) Report to DSS.
(x) Documents listed above relative to any previous accident/matter identified by the claimant and relied upon as proof of negligence.
(xi) Earnings information where defendant is employer.
Documents produced to comply with requirements of the Management of Health and Safety at Work Regulations 1992—
(i) Pre-accident Risk Assessment required by regulation 3.
(ii) Post-accident Re-Assessment required by regulation 3.
(iii) Accident Investigation Report prepared in implementing the requirements of regulations 4, 6 and 9.
(iv) Health Surveillance Records in appropriate cases required by regulation 5.
(v) Information provided to employees under regulation 8.
(vi) Documents relating to the employees health and safety training required by regulation 11.

# WORKPLACE CLAIMS—DISCLOSURE WHERE SPECIFIC REGULATIONS APPLY

## Section A—Workplace (Health Safety and Welfare) Regulations 1992

(i) Repair and maintenance records required by regulation 5.
(ii) Housekeeping records to comply with the requirements of regulation 9.
(iii) Hazard warning signs or notices to comply with regulation 17 (Traffic Routes).

### Section B—Provision and Use of Work Equipment Regulations 1998

(i) Manufacturers' specifications and instructions in respect of relevant work equipment establishing its suitability to comply with regulation 5.
(ii) Maintenance log/maintenance records required to comply with regulation 6.
(iii) Documents providing information and instructions to employees to comply with regulation 8.
(iv) Documents provided to the employee in respect of training for use to comply with regulation 9.
(v) Any notice, sign or document relied upon as a defence to alleged breaches of regulations 14 to 18 dealing with controls and control systems.
(vi) Instruction/training documents issued to comply with the requirements of regulation 22 insofar as it deals with maintenance operations where the machinery is not shut down.
(vii) Copies of markings required to comply with regulation 23.
(viii) Copies of warnings required to comply with regulation 24.

### Section C—Personal Protective Equipment at Work Regulations 1992

(i) Documents relating to the assessment of the Personal Protective Equipment to comply with regulation 6.
(ii) Documents relating to the maintenance and replacement of Personal Protective Equipment to comply with regulation 7.
(iii) Record of maintenance procedures for Personal Protective Equipment to comply with regulation 7.
(iv) Records of tests and examinations of Personal Protective Equipment to comply with regulation 7.
(v) Documents providing information, instruction and training in relation to the Personal Protective Equipment to comply with regulation 9.
(vi) Instructions for use of Personal Protective Equipment to include the manufacturers' instructions to comply with regulation 10.

### Section D—Manual Handling Operations Regulations 1992

(i) Manual Handling Risk Assessment carried out to comply with the requirements of regulation 4(1)(b)(i).
(ii) Re-assessment carried out post-accident to comply with requirements of regulation 4(1)(b)(i).
(iii) Documents showing the information provided to the employee to give general indications related to the load and precise indications on the weight of the load and the heaviest side of the load if the centre of gravity was not positioned centrally to comply with regulation 4(1)(b)(iii).
(iv) Documents relating to training in respect of manual handling operations and training records.

### Section E—Health and Safety (Display Screen Equipment) Regulations 1992

(i) Analysis of work stations to assess and reduce risks carried out to comply with the requirements of regulation 2.
(ii) Re-assessment of analysis of work stations to assess and reduce risks following development of symptoms by the claimant.
(iii) Documents detailing the provision of training including training records to comply with the requirements of regulation 6.
(iv) Documents providing information to employees to comply with the requirements of regulation 7.

## Section F—Control of Substances Hazardous to Health Regulations 1999

(i) Risk assessment carried out to comply with the requirements of regulation 6.
(ii) Reviewed risk assessment carried out to comply with the requirements of regulation 6.
(iii) Copy labels from containers used for storage handling and disposal of carcinogenics to comply with the requirements of regulation 7(2A)(h).
(iv) Warning signs identifying designation of areas and installations which may be contaminated by carcinogenics to comply with the requirements of regulation 7(2A)(h).
(v) Documents relating to the assessment of the Personal Protective Equipment to comply with regulation 7(3A).
(vi) Documents relating to the maintenance and replacement of Personal Protective Equipment to comply with regulation 7(3A).
(vii) Record of maintenance procedures for Personal Protective Equipment to comply with regulation 7(3A).
(viii) Records of tests and examinations of Personal Protective Equipment to comply with regulation 7(3A).
(ix) Documents providing information, instruction and training in relation to the Personal Protective Equipment to comply with regulation 7(3A).
(x) Instructions for use of Personal Protective Equipment to include the manufacturers' instructions to comply with regulation 7(3A).
(xi) Air monitoring records for substances assigned a maximum exposure limit or occupational exposure standard to comply with the requirements of regulation 7.
(xii) Maintenance examination and test of control measures records to comply with regulation 9.
(xiii) Monitoring records to comply with the requirements of regulation 10.
(xiv) Health surveillance records to comply with the requirements of regulation 11.
(xv) Documents detailing information, instruction and training including training records for employees to comply with the requirements of regulation 12.
(xvi) Labels and Health and Safety data sheets supplied to the employers to comply with the CHIP Regulations.

## Section G—Construction (Design and Management) (Amendment) Regulations 2000

(i) Notification of a project form (HSE F10) to comply with the requirements of regulation 7.
(ii) Health and Safety Plan to comply with requirements of regulation 15.
(iii) Health and Safety file to comply with the requirements of regulations 12 and 14.
(iv) Information and training records provided to comply with the requirements of regulation 17.
(v) Records of advice from and views of persons at work to comply with the requirements of regulation 18.

## Section H—Pressure Systems and Transportable Gas Containers Regulations 1989

(i) Information and specimen markings provided to comply with the requirements of regulation 5.
(ii) Written statements specifying the safe operating limits of a system to comply with the requirements of regulation 7.
(iii) Copy of the written scheme of examination required to comply with the requirements of regulation 8.
(iv) Examination records required to comply with the requirements of regulation 9.
(v) Instructions provided for the use of operator to comply with regulation 11.
(vi) Records kept to comply with the requirements of regulation 13.
(vii) Records kept to comply with the requirements of regulation 22.

### Section I—Lifting Operations and Lifting Equipment Regulations 1998

(i) Record kept to comply with the requirements of regulation 6.

### Section J—The Noise at Work Regulations 1989

(i) Any risk assessment records required to comply with the requirements of regulations 4 and 5.
(ii) Manufacturers' literature in respect of all ear protection made available to claimant to comply with the requirements of regulation 8.
(iii) All documents provided to the employee for the provision of information to comply with regulation 11.

### Section K—Construction (Head Protection) Regulations 1989

(i) Pre-accident assessment of head protection required to comply with regulation 3(4).
(ii) Post-accident re-assessment required to comply with regulation 3(5).

### Section L—The Construction (General Provisions) Regulations 1961

(i) Report prepared following inspections and examinations of excavations etc. to comply with the requirements of regulation 9.

### Section M—Gas Containers Regulations 1989

(i) Information and specimen markings provided to comply with the requirements of regulation 5.
(ii) Written statements specifying the safe operating limits of a system to comply with the requirements of regulation 7.
(iii) Copy of the written scheme of examination required to comply with the requirements of regulation 8.
(iv) Examination records required to comply with the requirements of regulation 9.
(v) Instructions provided for the use of operator to comply with regulation 11.

## ANNEX C
## LETTER OF INSTRUCTION TO MEDICAL EXPERT

Dear Sir,
Re: *(Name and Address)*
D.O.B.—
Telephone No.—
Date of Accident—

We are acting for the above named in connection with injuries received in an accident which occurred on the above date. The main injuries appear to have been **(main injuries)**.

We should be obliged if you would examine our Client and let us have a full and detailed report dealing with any relevant pre-accident medical history, the injuries sustained, treatment received and present condition, dealing in particular with the capacity for work and giving a prognosis.

It is central to our assessment of the extent of our Client's injuries to establish the extent and duration of any continuing disability. Accordingly, in the prognosis section we would ask you to specifically comment on any areas of continuing complaint or disability or impact on daily living. If there is such continuing disability you should comment upon the level of suffering or inconvenience caused and, if you are able, give your view as to when or if the complaint or disability is likely to resolve.

Please send our Client an appointment direct for this purpose. Should you be able to offer a cancellation appointment please contact our Client direct. We confirm we will be responsible for your reasonable fees.

*We are obtaining the notes and records from our Client's GP and Hospitals attended and will forward them to you when they are to hand/or please request the GP and Hospital records direct and advise that any invoice for the provision of these records should be forwarded to us.*

In order to comply with Court Rules we would be grateful if you would insert above your signature a statement that the contents are true to the best of your knowledge and belief.

In order to avoid further correspondence we can confirm that on the evidence we have there is no reason to suspect we may be pursuing a claim against the hospital or its staff.

We look forward to receiving your report within ________ weeks. If you will not be able to prepare your report within this period please telephone us upon receipt of these instructions.

When acknowledging these instructions it would assist if you could give an estimate as to the likely time scale for the provision of your report and also an indication as to your fee.

Yours faithfully

## ANNEX D
## THE REHABILITATION CODE[1]

### 4.11 The revised Rehabilitation Code

THE REHABILITATION CODE

**(Code of Best Practice on Rehabilitation, Early Intervention and Medical Treatment in Personal Injury Claims)**

The main aim of this Code, first introduced in 1999, is to promote the use of rehabilitation and early intervention in the claims process so that the injured person makes the best and quickest possible medical, social and psychological recovery. This objective applies whatever the severity of the injury sustained by the claimant. The Code provides a framework supported by all the main associations for insurers and personal injury lawyers in the UK, but is neither compulsory nor the only way to approach rehabilitation. The objectives of the Rehabilitation Code will be met whenever the parties co-operate to assess and then provide for the claimant's rehabilitation needs.

## 1 INTRODUCTION

1.1 It is recognised that, in many claims for damages for personal injuries, the claimant's current medical situation, and/or the long-term prognosis, may be improved by appropriate medical treatment, including surgery, being given at the earliest practicable opportunity, rather than waiting until the claim has been settled. Similarly, claims may involve a need for non-medical treatment, such as physiotherapy, counselling, occupational therapy, speech therapy and so forth ('rehabilitation'): again, there is a benefit in these services being provided as early as practicable.

1.2 It is also recognised that (predominantly in cases of serious injury) the claimant's quality of life can be immediately improved by undertaking some basic home adaptations and/or by the provision of aids and equipment and/or appropriate medical treatment as soon as these are needed ('early intervention'), rather than when the claim is finally settled.

1.3 It is further recognised that, where these medical or other issues have been dealt with, there may be employment issues that can be addressed for the benefit of the claimant, to enable the claimant to keep his/her existing job, to obtain alternative suitable employment with the same employer or to retrain for new employment. Again, if these needs are addressed at the proper time, the claimant's quality of life and long-term prospects may be greatly improved.

[1] The wording of the Code reproduced here is the version promulgated by the DCA.

1.4 Solicitors acting for claimants understand that, taking all these matters into account, they can achieve more for the claimant—by making rehabilitation available—than just the payment of compensation. The insurance industry realises that great benefit may be had in considering making funds available for these purposes.

1.5 The aim of this Rehabilitation Code is therefore to ensure that the claimant's solicitor and the insurer (and the insurer's solicitor or handling agent) both actively consider the use of rehabilitation services and the benefits of an early assessment of the claimant's needs. The further aim is that both should treat the possibility of improving the claimant's quality of life and their present and long-term physical and mental well-being as issues equally as important as the payment of just, full and proper compensation.

1.6 The report mentioned in section 6 of the Code focuses on the early assessment of the claimant's needs in terms of treatment and/or rehabilitation. The assessment report is not intended to determine the claimant's long-term needs for care or medical treatment, other than by way of general indication and comment.

## 2 THE CLAIMANT'S SOLICITOR'S DUTY

2.1 It shall be the duty of every claimant's solicitor to consider, from the earliest practicable stage, and in consultation with the claimant and/or the claimant's family, whether it is likely or possible that early intervention, rehabilitation or medical treatment would improve their present and/or long-term physical or mental well-being. This duty is ongoing throughout the life of the case but is of most importance in the early stages.

2.2 It shall be the duty of a claimant's solicitor to consider, with the claimant and/or the claimant's family, whether there is an immediate need for aids, adaptations or other matters that would seek to alleviate problems caused by disability, and then to communicate with the insurer as soon as practicable about any rehabilitation needs, with a view to putting this Code into effect.

2.3 It shall not be the responsibility of the solicitor to decide on the need for treatment or rehabilitation or to arrange such matters without appropriate medical consultation. Such medical consultation should involve the claimant and/or the claimant's family, the claimant's primary care physician and, where appropriate, any other medical practitioner currently treating the claimant.

2.4 Nothing in this Code shall in any way affect the obligations placed on a claimant's solicitor by the Pre-Action Protocol for Personal Injury Claims ('the Protocol'). However, it must be appreciated that very early communication with the insurer will enable the matters dealt with here to be addressed more effectively.

2.5 It must be recognised that the insurer will need to receive from the claimant's solicitor sufficient information for the insurer to make a proper decision about the need for intervention, rehabilitation or treatment. To this extent, the claimant's solicitor must comply with the requirements of the Protocol to provide the insurer with full and adequate details of the injuries sustained by the claimant, the nature and extent of any, or any likely, continuing disability and any suggestions that may already have been made concerning rehabilitation and/or early intervention. There is no requirement under the Protocol, or this Code, for the claimant's solicitor to have obtained a full medical report. It is recognised that many cases will be identified for consideration under this Code before medical evidence has actually been commissioned.

## 3 THE INSURER

3.1 It shall be the duty of the insurer to consider, from the earliest practicable stage in any appropriate case, whether it is likely that the claimant will benefit in the immediate, medium or longer term from further medical treatment, rehabilitation or early intervention. This duty is ongoing throughout the life of the case but is of most importance in the early stages.

3.2 If the insurer considers that a particular claim might be suitable for intervention, rehabilitation or treatment, the insurer will communicate this to the claimant's solicitor as soon as practicable.

3.3 On receipt of such communication, the claimant's solicitor will immediately discuss these issues with the claimant and/or the claimant's family pursuant to his duty as set out above and, where appropriate, will seek advice from the claimant's treating physicians/surgeons.

3.4 Nothing in this or any other Code of Practice shall in any way modify the obligations of the insurer under the protocol to investigate claims rapidly and in any event within 3 months (except where time is extended by the claimant's solicitor) from the date of the formal claim letter. It is recognised that, although the rehabilitation assessment can be done even where liability investigations are outstanding, it is essential that such investigations proceed with the appropriate speed.

## 4 ASSESSMENT

4.1 Unless the need for intervention, rehabilitation or treatment has already been identified by medical reports obtained and disclosed by either side, the need for and extent of such intervention, rehabilitation or treatment will be considered by means of an independent assessment.

4.2 'Independent assessment' in this context means that the assessment will be carried out by either:

a. One or more of the treating physicians/surgeons, or

b. By an agency suitably qualified and/or experienced in such matters, which is financially and managerially independent of the claimant's solicitor's firm and the insurers dealing with the claim.

4.3 It is essential that the process of assessment and recommendation be carried out by those who have an appropriate qualification (to include physiotherapists, occupational therapists, psychologists, psychotherapists and so forth). It would be inappropriate for assessments to be done by someone who does not have a medical or other appropriate qualification. Those doing the assessments should not only have an appropriate qualification but should have experience in treating the type of disability from which the individual claimant suffers.

## 5 THE ASSESSMENT PROCESS

5.1 Where possible, the agency to be instructed to provide the assessment should be agreed between the claimant's solicitor and the insurer. The instruction letter will be sent by the claimant's solicitor to the medical agency and a copy of the instruction letter will be sent to the insurer.

5.2 The medical agency will be asked to interview the claimant at home (or in hospital, if the claimant is still in hospital, with a subsequent visit to the claimant's home) and will be asked to produce a report, which covers the following headings:

1. The injuries sustained by the claimant
2. The claimant's present medical condition (medical conditions that do not arise from the accident should also be noted where relevant to the overall picture of the claimant's needs)
3. The claimant's domestic circumstances (including mobility, accommodation and employment), where relevant
4. The injuries/disability in respect of which early intervention or early rehabilitation is suggested
5. The type of intervention or treatment envisaged
6. The likely cost
7. The likely short/medium-term benefit to the claimant

5.3 The report will not deal with diagnostic criteria, causation issues or long-term care requirements.

## 6 THE ASSESSMENT REPORT

6.1 The reporting agency will, on completion of the report, send copies to both the instructing solicitor and the insurer simultaneously. Both parties will have the right to raise queries on the report, disclosing such correspondence to the other party.

6.2 It is recognised that for this independent assessment report to be of benefit to the parties, it should be prepared and used wholly outside the litigation process. Neither side can therefore rely on its contents in any subsequent litigation. With that strict proviso, to be confirmed in writing by the individual solicitor and insurer if required, the report shall be disclosed to both parties.

6.3 The report, any correspondence relating to it and any notes created by the assessing agency will be covered by legal privilege and will not under any circumstances be disclosed in any legal proceedings. Any notes or documents created in connection with the assessment process will not be disclosed in any litigation, and any person involved in the preparation of the report or involved in the assessment process shall not be a compellable witness at court.

6.4 The provision in paragraph 6.3 above as to treating the report, etc. as outside the litigation process is limited to the assessment report and any notes relating to it. Once the parties have agreed, following an assessment report, that a particular regime of rehabilitation or treatment should be put in place, the case management of that regime falls outside this Code and paragraph 6.3 does not therefore apply. Any notes and reports created during the subsequent case management will be governed by the usual principles relating to disclosure of documents and medical records relating to the claimant.

6.5 The insurer will pay for the report within 28 days of receipt.

6.6 The need for any further or subsequent assessment shall be agreed between the claimant's solicitor and the insurer. The provisions of this Code shall apply to such assessments.

## 7 RECOMMENDATIONS

7.1 When the assessment report is disclosed to the insurer, the insurer will be under a duty to consider the recommendations made and the extent to which funds will be made available to implement all or some of the recommendations. The insurer will not be required to pay for intervention or treatment that is unreasonable in nature, content or cost. The claimant will be under no obligation to undergo intervention, medical investigation or treatment that is unreasonable in all the circumstances of the case.

7.2 Any funds made available shall be treated as an interim payment on account of damages. However, if the funds are provided to enable specific intervention, rehabilitation or treatment to occur, the insurers warrant that they will not, in any legal proceedings connected with the claim, dispute the reasonableness of that treatment nor the agreed cost, provided of course that the claimant has had the recommended treatment.

# Pre-action Protocol for the Resolution of Clinical Disputes

## Clinical Disputes Forum



## EXECUTIVE SUMMARY

1 The Clinical Disputes Forum is a multi-disciplinary body which was formed in 1997, as a result of Lord Woolf's 'Access to Justice' inquiry. One of the aims of the Forum is to find less adversarial and more cost-effective ways of resolving disputes about healthcare and medical treatment. The names and addresses of the Chairman and Secretary of the Forum can be found at Annex E.

2 This protocol is the Forum's first major initiative. It has been drawn up carefully, including extensive consultations with most of the key stakeholders in the medico-legal system.

3 The protocol—

- encourages a climate of openness when something has 'gone wrong' with a patient's treatment or the patient is dissatisfied with that treatment and/or the outcome. This reflects the new and developing requirements for clinical governance within healthcare;
- provides **general guidance** on how this more open culture might be achieved when disputes arise;
- recommends a **timed sequence** of steps for patients and healthcare providers, and their advisers, to follow when a dispute arises. This should facilitate and speed up exchanging relevant information and increase the prospects that disputes can be resolved without resort to legal action.

4 This protocol has been prepared by a working party of the Clinical Disputes Forum. It has support of the Lord Chancellor's Department, the Department of Health and NHS Executive, the Law Society, the Legal Aid Board and many other key organisations.

## 1 WHY THIS PROTOCOL?

### Mistrust in Healthcare Disputes

1.1 The number of complaints and claims against hospitals, GPs, dentists and private healthcare providers is growing as patients become more prepared to question the treatment they are given, to seek explanations of what happened, and to seek appropriate redress. Patients may require further treatment, an apology, assurances about future action, or compensation. These trends are unlikely to change. The Patients' Charter encourages patients to have high expectations, and a revised NHS Complaints Procedure was implemented in 1996. The civil justice reforms and new Rules of Court should make litigation quicker, more user friendly and less expensive.

1.2 It is clearly in the interests of patients, healthcare professionals and providers that patients' concerns, complaints and claims arising from their treatment are resolved as quickly, efficiently and professionally as possible. A climate of mistrust and lack of openness can seriously damage the patient/clinician relationship, unnecessarily prolong disputes (especially litigation), and reduce the resources available for treating patients. It may also cause additional work for, and lower the morale of, healthcare professionals.

1.3 At present there is often mistrust by both sides. This can mean that patients fail to raise their concerns with the healthcare provider as early as possible. Sometimes patients may pursue a complaint or claim which has little merit, due to a lack of sufficient information and understanding. It can also mean that patients become reluctant, once advice has been taken on a potential claim, to disclose sufficient information to enable the provider to investigate that claim efficiently and, where appropriate, resolve it.

1.4 On the side of the healthcare provider this mistrust can be shown in a reluctance to be honest with patients, a failure to provide prompt clear explanations, especially of adverse outcomes (whether or not there may have been negligence) and a tendency to 'close ranks' once a claim is made.

## What Needs to Change

1.5 If that mistrust is to be removed, and a more cooperative culture is to develop—
- healthcare professionals and providers need to adopt a constructive approach to complaints and claims. They should accept that concerned patients are entitled to an explanation and an apology, if warranted, and to appropriate redress in the event of negligence. An overly defensive approach is not in the long-term interest of their main goal: patient care;
- patients should recognise that unintended and/or unfortunate consequences of medical treatment can only be rectified if they are brought to the attention of the healthcare provider as soon as possible.

1.6 A protocol which sets out 'ground rules' for the handling of disputes at their early stages should, if it is to be subscribed to, and followed—
- encourage greater openness between the parties;
- encourage parties to find the most appropriate way of resolving the particular dispute;
- reduce delay and costs;
- reduce the need for litigation.

## Why This Protocol Now?

1.7 Lord Woolf in his Access to Justice Report in July 1996, concluded that major causes of costs and delay in medical negligence litigation occur at the pre-action stage. He recommended that patients and their advisers, and healthcare providers, should work more closely together to try to resolve disputes cooperatively, rather than proceed to litigation. He specifically recommended a pre-action protocol for medical negligence cases.

1.8 A fuller summary of Lord Woolf's recommendations is at Annex D.

## Where the Protocol Fits In

1.9 Protocols serve the needs of litigation and pre-litigation practice, especially—
- predictability in the time needed for steps pre-proceedings;
- standardisation of relevant information, including records and documents to be disclosed.

1.10 Building upon Lord Woolf's recommendations, the Lord Chancellor's Department is promoting the adoption of protocols in specific areas, including medical negligence.

1.11 It is recognised that contexts differ significantly. For example: patients tend to have an ongoing relationship with a GP, more so than with a hospital; clinical staff in the National Health Service are often employees, while those in the private sector may be contractors; providing records quickly may be relatively easy for GPs and dentists, but can be a complicated procedure in a large multi-department hospital. The protocol which follows is intended to be sufficiently broadly based, and flexible, to apply to all aspects of the health service: primary and secondary; public and private sectors.

### Enforcement of the Protocol and Sanctions

1.12 The civil justice reforms will be implemented in April 1999. One new set of Court Rules and procedures is replacing the existing rules for both the High Court and county courts. This and the personal injury protocol are being published with the Rules, practice directions and key court forms. The courts will be able to treat the standards set in protocols as the normal reasonable approach to pre-action conduct.

1.13 If proceedings are issued it will be for the court to decide whether non-compliance with a protocol should merit sanctions. Guidance on the court's likely approach will be given from time to time in practice directions.

1.14 If the court has to consider the question of compliance after proceedings have begun it will not be concerned with minor infringements, e.g. failure by a short period to provide relevant information. One minor breach will not entitle the 'innocent' party to abandon following the protocol. The court will look at the effect of non-compliance on the other party when deciding whether to impose sanctions.

## 2 THE AIMS OF THE PROTOCOL

2.1 The *general* aims of the protocol are—
- to maintain/restore the patient/healthcare provider relationship;
- to resolve as many disputes as possible without litigation.

2.2 The *specific* objectives are—

### Openness

- to encourage early communication of the perceived problem between patients and healthcare providers;
- to encourage patients to voice any concerns or dissatisfaction with their treatment as soon as practicable;
- to encourage healthcare providers to develop systems of early reporting and investigation for serious adverse treatment outcomes and to provide full and prompt explanations to dissatisfied patients;
- to ensure that sufficient information is disclosed by both parties to enable each to understand the other's perspective and case, and to encourage early resolution.

### Timeliness

- to provide an early opportunity for healthcare providers to identify cases where an investigation is required and to carry out that investigation promptly;
- to encourage primary and private healthcare providers to involve their defence organisations or insurers at an early stage;
- to ensure that all relevant medical records are provided to patients or their appointed representatives on request, to a realistic timetable by any healthcare provider;
- to ensure that relevant records which are not in healthcare providers' possession are made available to them by patients and their advisers at an appropriate stage;
- where a resolution is not achievable to lay the ground to enable litigation to proceed on a reasonable timetable, at a reasonable and proportionate cost and to limit the matters in contention;
- to discourage the prolonged pursuit of unmeritorious claims and the prolonged defence of meritorious claims.

### Awareness of Options

- to ensure that patients and healthcare providers are made aware of the available options to pursue and resolve disputes and what each might involve.

2.3 This protocol does not attempt to be prescriptive about a number of related clinical governance issues which have a bearing on healthcare providers' ability to meet the standards within the protocol. Good clinical governance requires the following to be considered—

(a) **Clinical risk management:** the protocol does not provide any detailed guidance to healthcare providers on clinical risk management or the adoption of risk management systems and procedures. This must be a matter for the NHS Executive, the National Health Service Litigation Authority, individual trusts and providers, including GPs, dentists and the private sector. However, effective co-ordinated, focused clinical risk management strategies and procedures can help in managing risk and in the early identification and investigation of adverse outcomes.

(b) **Adverse outcome reporting:** the protocol does not provide any detailed guidance on which adverse outcomes should trigger an investigation. However, healthcare providers should have in place procedures for such investigations, including recording of statements of key witnesses. These procedures should also cover when and how to inform patients that an adverse outcome has occurred.

(c) **The professional's duty to report:** the protocol does not recommend changes to the codes of conduct of professionals in healthcare, or attempt to impose a specific duty on those professionals to report known adverse outcomes or untoward incidents. Lord Woolf in his final report suggested that the professional bodies might consider this. The General Medical Council is preparing guidance to doctors about their duty to report adverse incidents and to cooperate with inquiries.

## 3 THE PROTOCOL

3.1 This protocol is not a comprehensive code governing all the steps in clinical disputes. Rather it attempts to set out **a code of good practice** which parties should follow when litigation might be a possibility.

3.2 The **commitments** section of the protocol summarises the guiding principles which healthcare providers and patients and their advisers are invited to endorse when dealing with patient dissatisfaction with treatment and its outcome, and with potential complaints and claims.

3.3 The **steps** section sets out in a more prescriptive form, a recommended sequence of actions to be followed if litigation is a prospect.

### Good Practice Commitments

3.4 Healthcare providers should—

(i) ensure that **key staff**, including claims and litigation managers, are appropriately trained and have some knowledge of healthcare law, and of complaints procedures and civil litigation practice and procedure;

(ii) develop an approach to **clinical governance** that ensures that clinical practice is delivered to commonly accepted standards and that this is routinely monitored through a system of clinical audit and clinical risk management (particularly adverse outcome investigation);

(iii) set up **adverse outcome reporting systems** in all specialties to record and investigate unexpected serious adverse outcomes as soon as possible. Such systems can enable evidence to be gathered quickly, which makes it easier to provide an accurate explanation of what happened and to defend or settle any subsequent claims;

(iv) use the results of **adverse incidents and complaints positively** as a guide to how to improve services to patients in the future;

(v) ensure **that patients receive clear and comprehensible information** in an accessible form about how to raise their concerns or complaints;

(vi) establish **efficient and effective systems of recording and storing patient records**, notes, diagnostic reports and X-rays, and to retain these in accordance with Department of Health guidance (currently for a minimum of eight years for adults, and all obstetric and paediatric notes for children until they reach the age of 25);

(vii) **advise patients** of a serious adverse outcome and provide on request to the patient or the patient's representative an oral or written explanation of what happened, information on further steps open to the patient, including where appropriate an offer of future treatment to rectify the problem, an apology, changes in procedure which will benefit patients and/or compensation.

3.5 Patients and their advisers should—

(i) **report any concerns and dissatisfaction** to the healthcare provider as soon as is reasonable to enable that provider to offer clinical advice where possible, to advise the patient if anything has gone wrong and take appropriate action;

(ii) consider the **full range of options** available following an adverse outcome with which a patient is dissatisfied, including a request for an explanation, a meeting, a complaint, and other appropriate dispute resolution methods (including mediation) and negotiation, not only litigation;

(iii) **inform the healthcare provider when the patient is satisfied** that the matter has been concluded: legal advisers should notify the provider when they are no longer acting for the patient, particularly if proceedings have not started.

## Protocol Steps

3.6 The steps of this protocol which follow have been kept deliberately simple. An illustration of the likely sequence of events in a number of healthcare situations is at Annex A.

## Obtaining the Health Records

3.7 Any request for records by the **patient** or their adviser should—

- **provide sufficient information** to alert the healthcare provider where an adverse outcome has been serious or had serious consequences;
- be as specific **as possible** about the records which are required.

3.8 Requests for copies of the patient's clinical records should be made using the Law Society and Department of Health approved **standard forms** (enclosed at Annex B), adapted as necessary.

3.9 The copy records should be provided **within 40 days** of the request and for a cost not exceeding the charges permissible under the Access to Health Records Act 1990 (currently a maximum of £10 plus photocopying and postage).

3.10 In the rare circumstances that the healthcare provider is in difficulty in complying with the request within 40 days, the **problem should be explained** quickly and details given of what is being done to resolve it.

3.11 It will not be practicable for healthcare providers to investigate in detail each case when records are requested. But healthcare providers should **adopt a policy on which cases will be investigated** (see paragraph 3.5 on clinical governance and adverse outcome reporting).

3.12 If the healthcare provider fails to provide the health records within 40 days, the patient or their adviser can then apply to the court for an **order for pre-action disclosure**. The new Civil Procedure Rules should make pre-action applications to the court easier. The court will also have the power to impose costs sanctions for unreasonable delay in providing records.

3.13 If either the patient or the healthcare provider considers **additional health records are required from a third party**, in the first instance these should be requested by or through the patient. Third party healthcare providers are expected to co-operate. The Civil Procedure Rules will enable patients and healthcare providers to apply to the court for pre-action disclosure by third parties.

## Letter of Claim

3.14 Annex C1 to this protocol provides **a template for the recommended contents of a letter of claim:** the level of detail will need to be varied to suit the particular circumstances.

3.15 If, following the receipt and analysis of the records, and the receipt of any further advice (including from experts if necessary—see Section 4), the patient/adviser decides that there are grounds for a claim, they should then send, as soon as practicable, to the healthcare provider/potential defendant, a **letter of claim**.

3.16 This letter should contain a **clear summary of the facts** on which the claim is based, including the alleged adverse outcome, and the **main allegations of negligence**. It should also describe the **patient's injuries**, and present condition and prognosis. The **financial loss** incurred by the plaintiff should be outlined with an indication of the heads of damage to be claimed and the scale of the loss, unless this is impracticable.

3.17 In more complex cases a **chronology** of the relevant events should be provided, particularly if the patient has been treated by a number of different healthcare providers.

3.18 The letter of claim **should refer to any relevant documents**, including health records, and if possible enclose copies of any of those which will not already be in the potential defendant's possession, e.g. any relevant general practitioner records if the plaintiff's claim is against a hospital.

3.19 **Sufficient information** must be given to enable the healthcare provider defendant to **commence investigations** and to put an initial valuation on the claim.

3.20 Letters of claim are **not** intended to have the same formal status as a **pleading**, nor should any sanctions necessarily apply if the letter of claim and any subsequent statement of claim in the proceedings differ.

3.21 **Proceedings should not be issued until after three months from the letter of claim**, unless there is a limitation problem and/or the patient's position needs to be protected by early issue.

3.22 The patient or their adviser may want to make an **offer to settle** the claim at this early stage by putting forward an amount of compensation which would be satisfactory (possibly including any costs incurred to date). If an offer to settle is made, generally this should be supported by a medical report which deals with the injuries, condition and prognosis, and by a schedule of loss and supporting documentation. The level of detail necessary will depend on the value of the claim. Medical reports may not be necessary where there is no significant continuing injury, and a detailed schedule may not be necessary in a low value case. The Civil Procedure Rules are expected to set out the legal and procedural requirements for making offers to settle.

## The Response

3.23 Attached at Annex C2 is a template for the suggested contents of the **letter of response**.

3.24 The healthcare provider should **acknowledge** the letter of claim **within 14 days of receipt** and should identify who will be dealing with the matter.

3.25 The healthcare provider should, **within three months** of the letter of claim, provide a **reasoned answer**—

- if the **claim is admitted** the healthcare provider should say so in clear terms;
- if only **part of** the **claim is admitted** the provider should make clear which issues of breach of duty and/or causation are admitted and which are denied and why;
- if it is intended that any admissions **will be binding**;
- if the claim is denied, this should include specific comments on the allegations of negligence, and if a synopsis or chronology of relevant events has been provided and is disputed, the healthcare provider's version of those events;
- where additional documents are relied upon, e.g. an internal protocol, copies should be provided.

3.26 If the patient has made an offer to settle, the healthcare provider should **respond to that offer** in the response letter, preferably with reasons. The provider may make its own offer to settle at this stage, either as a counter-offer to the patient's, or of its own accord, but should accompany any offer by any supporting medical evidence, and/or by any other evidence in relation to the value of the claim which is in the healthcare provider's possession.

3.27 If the parties reach agreement on liability, but time is needed to resolve the value of the claim, they should aim to agree a reasonable period.

## 4 EXPERTS

4.1 In clinical negligence disputes **expert opinions** may be needed—
- on breach of duty and causation;
- on the patient's condition and prognosis;
- to assist in valuing aspects of the claim.

4.2 The civil justice reforms and the new **Civil Procedure Rules** will encourage economy in the use of experts and a **less adversarial expert culture**. It is recognised that in clinical negligence disputes, the parties and their advisers will require flexibility in their approach to expert evidence. Decisions on whether experts might be instructed jointly, and on whether reports might be disclosed sequentially or by exchange, should rest with the parties and their advisers. Sharing expert evidence may be appropriate on issues relating to the value of the claim. However, this protocol does not attempt to be prescriptive on issues in relation to expert evidence.

4.3 Obtaining expert evidence will often be an expensive step and may take time, especially in specialised areas of medicine where there are limited numbers of suitable experts. Patients and healthcare providers, and their advisers, will therefore need to consider carefully how best to obtain any necessary expert help quickly and cost-effectively. Assistance with locating a suitable expert is available from a number of sources.

## 5 ALTERNATIVE DISPUTE RESOLUTION

5.1 The parties should consider whether some form of alternative dispute resolution procedure would be more suitable than litigation, and if so, endeavour to agree which form to adopt. Both the claimant and defendant may be required by the court to provide evidence that alternative means of resolving their dispute were considered. The courts take the view that litigation should be a last resort, and that claims should not be issued prematurely when a settlement is still actively being explored. Parties are warned that if the protocol is not followed (including this paragraph) then the court must have regard to such conduct when determining costs.

5.2 It is not practicable in this protocol to address in detail how the parties might decide which method to adopt to resolve their particular dispute. However, summarised below are some of the options for resolving disputes without litigation:
- Discussion and negotiation. Parties should bear in mind that carefully planned face-to-face meetings may be particularly helpful in exploring further treatment for the patient, in reaching understandings about what happened, and on both parties' positions, in narrowing the issues in dispute and, if the timing is right, in helping to settle the whole matter especially if the patient wants an apology, explanation, or assurances about how other patients will be affected.
- Early neutral evaluation by an independent third party (for example, a lawyer experienced in the field of clinical negligence or an individual experienced in the subject matter of the claim).
- Mediation—a form of facilitated negotiation assisted by an independent neutral party. The Clinical Disputes Forum has published a Guide to Mediation which will assist—available on the Clinical Disputes Forum website at http://www.clinicaldisputesforum.org.uk.
- The **NHS Complaints Procedure** is designed to provide patients with an explanation of what happened and an apology if appropriate. It is not designed to provide compensation for cases of negligence. However, patients might choose to use the procedure if their only, or main, goal is to obtain an explanation, or to obtain more information to help them decide what other action might be appropriate.

5.3 The Legal Services Commission has published a booklet on 'Alternatives to Court', CLS Direct Information Leaflet 23 (http://www.clsdirect.org.uk/legalhelp/leaflet23.jsp), which lists a number of organisations that provide alternative dispute resolution services.

5.4 It is expressly recognised that no party can or should be forced to mediate or enter into any form of ADR.

## ANNEX A
## ILLUSTRATIVE FLOWCHART

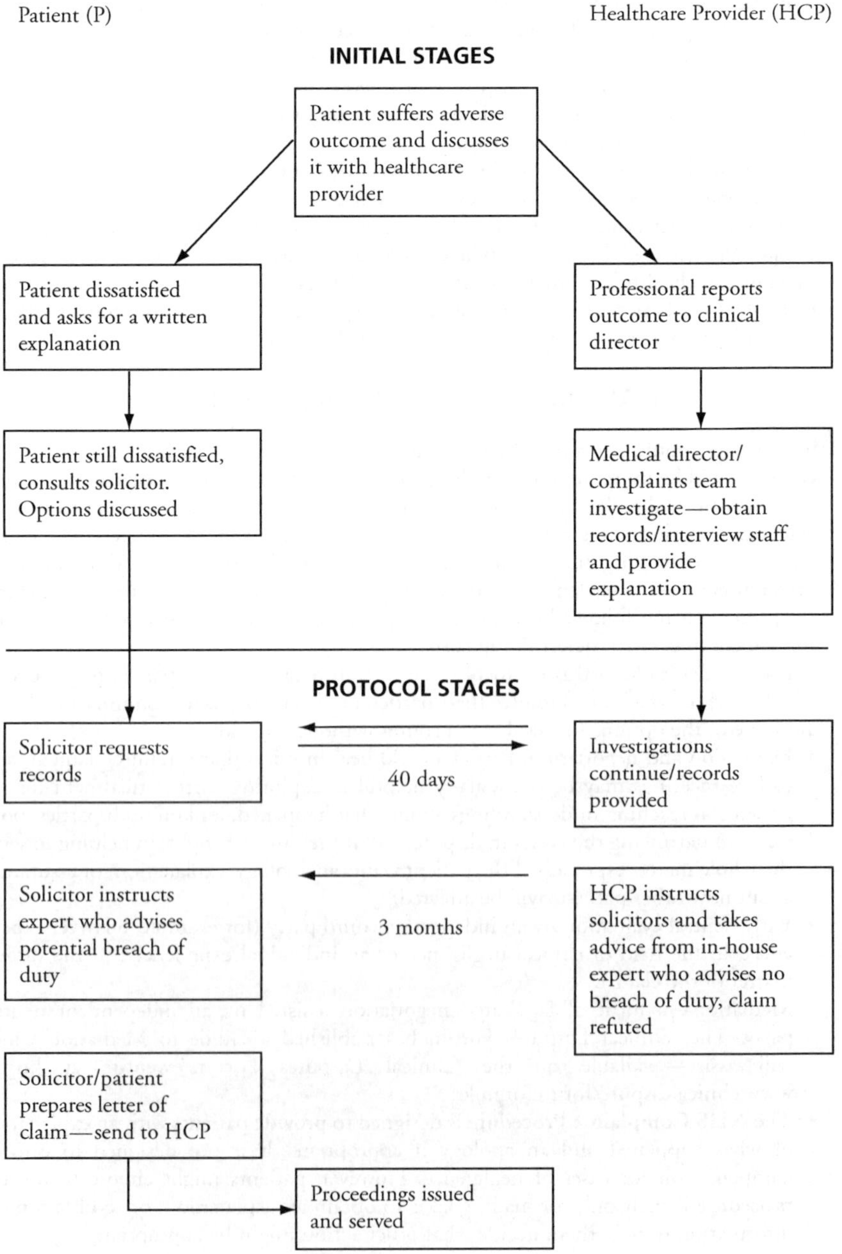

# ANNEX B
# MEDICAL NEGLIGENCE AND PERSONAL INJURY CLAIMS

## A PROTOCOL FOR OBTAINING HOSPITAL MEDICAL RECORDS

### Application on Behalf of a Patient for Hospital Medical Records for Use When Court Proceedings are Contemplated

### Purpose of the Forms

This application form and response forms have been prepared by a working party of the Law Society's Civil Litigation Committee and approved by the Department of Health for use in NHS and Trust hospitals.

The purpose of the forms is to standardise and streamline the disclosure of medical records to a patient's solicitors, who are investigating pursuing a personal injury claim against a third party, or a medical negligence claim against the hospital to which the application is addressed and/or other hospitals or general practitioners.

### Use of the Forms

Use of the forms is entirely voluntary and does not prejudice any party's right under the Access to Health Records Act 1990, the Data Protection Act 1984, or ss. 33 and 34 of the Supreme Court Act 1981. However, it is Department of Health policy that patients be permitted to see what has been written about them, and that healthcare providers should make arrangements to allow patients to see all their records, not only those covered by the Access to Health Records Act 1990. The aim of the forms is to save time and costs for all concerned for the benefit of the patient and the hospital and in the interests of justice. Use of the forms should make it unnecessary in most cases for there to be exchanges of letters or other enquiries. If there is any unusual matter not covered by the form, the patient's solicitor may write a separate letter at the outset.

### Charges for Records

The Access to Health Records Act 1990 prescribes a maximum fee of £10. Photocopying and postage costs can be charged in addition. No other charges may be made.

The NHS Executive guidance makes it clear to healthcare providers that 'it is a perfectly proper use' of the 1990 Act to request records in that framework for the purpose of potential or actual litigation, whether against a third party or against the hospital or trust.

The 1990 Act does not permit differential rates of charges to be levied if the application is made by the patient, or by a solicitor on his or her behalf, or whether the response to the application is made by the healthcare provider directly (the medical records manager or a claims manager) or by a solicitor.

The NHS Executive guidance recommends that the same practice should be followed with regard to charges when the records are provided under a voluntary agreement as under the 1990 Act, except that in those circumstances the £10 access fee will not be appropriate.

The NHS Executive also advises—

- that the cost of photocopying may include 'the cost of staff time in making copies' and the costs of running the copier (but not costs of locating and sifting records);
- that the common practice of setting a standard rate for an application or charging an administration fee is not acceptable because there will be cases when this fails to comply with the 1990 Act.

### Records: What Might be Included

X-rays and test results form part of the patient's records. Additional charges for copying X-rays are permissible. If there are large numbers of X-rays, the records officer should check with the patient/solicitor before arranging copying.

Reports on an 'adverse incident' and reports on the patient made for risk management and audit purposes may form part of the records and be disclosable: the exception will be any specific record or report made solely or mainly in connection with an actual or potential claim.

## Records: Quality Standards

When copying records healthcare providers should ensure—

1. All documents are legible, and complete, if necessary by photocopying at less than 100% size.
2. Documents larger than A4 in the original, e.g. ITU charts, should be reproduced in A3, or reduced to A4 where this retains readability.
3. Documents are only copied on one side of paper, unless the original is two sided.
4. Documents should not be unnecessarily shuffled or bound and holes should not be made in the copied papers.

## Enquiries/Further Information

Any enquiries about the forms should be made initially to the solicitors making the request. Comments on the use and content of the forms should be made to the Secretary, Civil Litigation Committee, The Law Society, 113 Chancery Lane, London WC2A 1PL, telephone (020) 7320 5739, or to the NHS Management Executive, Quarry House, Quarry Hill, Leeds LS2 7UE.

The Law Society

May 1998

## Application on Behalf of a Patient for Hospital Medical Records for Use When Court Proceedings are Contemplated

This should be completed as fully as possible

Insert Hospital Name and Address

| |
|---|
| **TO: Medical Records Officer** |
| **Hospital** |

| | | |
|---|---|---|
| 1 | (a) Full name of patient (including previous surnames) | |
| | (b) Address now | |
| | (c) Address at start of treatment | |
| | (d) Date of birth (and death, if applicable) | |
| | (e) Hospital ref. no if available | |
| | (f) N.I. number, if available | |
| 2 | This application is made because the patient is considering | |
| | (a) a claim against your hospital as detailed in para. 7 overleaf | YES/NO |
| | (b) pursuing an action against someone else | YES/NO |
| 3 | Department(s) where treatment was received | |
| 4 | Name(s) of consultant(s) at your hospital in charge of the treatment | |
| 5 | Whether treatment at your hospital was private or NHS, wholly or in part | |
| 6 | A description of the treatment received, with approximate dates | |
| 7 | If the answer to Q2(a) is 'Yes' details of | |
| | (a) the likely nature of the claim | |
| | (b) grounds for the claim | |
| | (c) approximate dates of the events involved | |
| 8 | If the answer to Q2(b) is 'Yes' insert | |
| | (a) the names of the proposed defendants | |
| | (b) whether legal proceedings yet begun | YES/NO |
| | (c) if appropriate, details of the claim and action number | |
| 9 | We confirm we will pay reasonable copying charges | |
| 10 | We request prior details of<br>(a) photocopying and administration charges for medical records | YES/NO |
| | (b) number of and cost of copying X-ray and scan films | YES/NO |

| | | |
|---|---|---|
| 11 | Any other relevant information, particular requirements, or any particular documents *not* required (e.g. copies of computerised records) | |
| | Signature of solicitor | |
| | Name | |
| | Address | |
| | Ref. | |
| | Telephone number | |
| | Fax number | |

*Please print name beneath each signature. Signature by child over 12 but under 18 years also requires signature by parent*

Signature of patient

---

Signature of parent or
next friend if appropriate

---

Signature of personal representative
where patient has died

---

## First Response to Application for Hospital Records

| | | |
|---|---|---|
| NAME OF PATIENT<br>Our ref<br>Your ref | | |
| 1 | Date of receipt of patient's application | |
| 2 | We intend that copy medical records will be dispatched within 6 weeks of that date | YES/NO |
| 3 | We require pre-payment of photocopying charges | YES/NO |
| 4 | If estimate of photocopying charges requested or pre-payment required the amount will be | £ /notified to you |
| 5 | The cost of X-ray and scan films will be | £ /notified to you |
| 6 | If there is any problem, we shall write to you within those 6 weeks | YES/NO |
| 7 | Any other information | |
| | Please address further correspondence to | |
| | Signed | |
| | Direct telephone number | |
| | Direct fax number | |
| | Dated | |

### Second Response Enclosing Patient's Hospital Medical Records

Address Our Ref.

Your Ref.

| | | |
|---|---|---|
| 1 | NAME OF PATIENT:<br>We confirm that the enclosed copy medical records are all those within the control of the hospital, relevant to the application which you have made to the best of our knowledge and belief, subject to paras 2–5 below | YES/NO |
| 2 | Details of any other documents which have not yet been located | |
| 3 | Date by when it is expected that these will be supplied | |
| 4 | Details of any records which we are not producing | |
| 5 | The reasons for not doing so | |
| 6 | An invoice for copying and administration charges is attached | YES/NO |
| | Signed | |
| | Date | |

## ANNEX C
## TEMPLATES FOR LETTERS OF CLAIM AND RESPONSE

### C1 Letter of Claim

*Essential contents*

1. **Client's name, address, date of birth, etc.**
2. **Dates of allegedly negligent treatment**
3. **Events giving rise to the claim:**
   - an outline of what happened, including details of other relevant treatments to the client by other healthcare providers.
4. **Allegation of negligence and causal link with injuries:**
   - an outline of the allegations or a more detailed list in a complex case;
   - an outline of the causal link between allegations and the injuries complained of.
5. **The Client's injuries, condition and future prognosis**
6. **Request for clinical records (if not previously provided)**
   - use the Law Society form if appropriate or adapt;
   - specify the records required;
   - if other records are held by other providers, and may be relevant, say so;
   - state what investigations have been carried out to date, e.g. information from client and witnesses, any complaint and the outcome, if any clinical records have been seen or experts advice obtained.
7. **The likely value of the claim**
   - an outline of the main heads of damage, or, in straightforward cases, the details of loss.

*Optional information*

What investigations have been carried out

An offer to settle without supporting evidence

Suggestions for obtaining expert evidence

Suggestions for meetings, negotiations, discussion or mediation

Possible enclosures

Chronology
Clinical records request form and client's authorisation
Expert report(s)
Schedules of loss and supporting evidence

## C2 Letter of Response

*Essential contents*

1. Provide **requested records** and invoice for copying:
   - explain if records are incomplete or extensive records are held and ask for further instructions;
   - request additional records from third parties.
2. **Comments on events and/or chronology:**
   - if events are disputed or the healthcare provider has further information or documents on which they wish to rely, these should be provided, e.g. internal protocol;
   - details of any further information needed from the patient or a third party should be provided.
3. **If breach of duty and causation are accepted:**
   - suggestions might be made for resolving the claim and/or requests for further information;
   - a response should be made to any offer to settle.
4. **If breach of duty and/or causation are denied:**
   - a bare denial will not be sufficient. If the healthcare provider has other explanations for what happened, these should be given at least in outline;
   - suggestions might be made for the next steps, e.g. further investigations, obtaining expert evidence, meetings/ negotiations or mediation, or an invitation to issue proceedings.

*Optional matters*
An offer to settle if the patient has not made one, or a counter offer to the patient's with supporting evidence

*Possible enclosures:*
Clinical records
Annotated chronology
Expert reports

## ANNEX D
## LORD WOOLF'S RECOMMENDATIONS

1. Lord Woolf in his Access to Justice Report in July 1996, following a detailed review of the problems of medical negligence claims, identified that one of the major sources of **costs and delay is at the pre-litigation** stage because—
   (a) Inadequate incident reporting and record keeping in hospitals, and mobility of staff, make it difficult to establish facts, often several years after the event.
   (b) Claimants must incur the cost of an expert in order to establish whether they have a viable claim.
   (c) There is often a long delay before a claim is made.
   (d) Defendants do not have sufficient resources to carry out a full investigation of every incident, and do not consider it worthwhile to start an investigation as soon as they receive a request for records, because many cases do not proceed beyond that stage.
   (e) Patients often give the defendant little or no notice of a firm intention to pursue a claim. Consequently, many incidents are not investigated by the defendants until after proceedings have started.

(f) Doctors and other clinical staff are traditionally reluctant to admit negligence or apologise to, or negotiate with, claimants for fear of damage to their professional reputations or career prospects.

2. Lord Woolf acknowledged that under the present arrangements **healthcare providers**, faced with possible medical negligence claims, have a number of **practical problems** to contend with—
   (a) Difficulties of finding patients' records and tracing former staff, which can be exacerbated by late notification and by the health care provider's own failure to identify adverse incidents.
   (b) The healthcare provider may have only treated the patient for a limited time or for a specific complaint: the patient's previous history may be relevant but the records may be in the possession of one of several other healthcare providers.
   (c) The large number of potential claims which do not proceed beyond the stage of a request for medical records, or an explanation; and that it is difficult for healthcare providers to investigate fully every case whenever a patient asks to see the records.

## ANNEX E
## HOW TO CONTACT THE FORUM

### The Clinical Disputes Forum

**Chairman**
Dr Alastair Scotland
Medical Director and Chief Officer
National Clinical Assessment Authority
9th Floor, Market Towers
London
SW8 5NQ Telephone: (020) 7273 0850

**Secretary**
Sarah Leigh
c/o Margaret Dangoor
3 Clydesdale Gardens
Richmond
Surrey
TW10 5EG Telephone: (020) 8408 1012

# Professional Negligence Pre-action Protocol

This protocol merges the two protocols previously produced by the Solicitors Indemnity Fund (SIF) and Claims against Professionals (CAP).



## A INTRODUCTION

A1 This protocol is designed to apply when a claimant wishes to claim against a professional (other than construction professionals and healthcare providers) as a result of that professional's alleged negligence or equivalent breach of contract or breach of fiduciary duty. Although these claims will be the usual situation in which the protocol will be used, there may be other claims for which the protocol could be appropriate. For a more detailed explanation of the scope of the protocol see Guidance Note C2.

A2 The aim of this protocol is to establish a framework in which there is an early exchange of information so that the claim can be fully investigated and, if possible, resolved without the need for litigation. This includes:
- (a) ensuring that the parties are on an equal footing;
- (b) saving expense;
- (c) dealing with the dispute in ways which are proportionate:
  - (i) to the amount of money involved;
  - (ii) to the importance of the case;
  - (iii) to the complexity of the issues;
  - (iv) to the financial position of each party;
- (d) ensuring that it is dealt with expeditiously and fairly.

A3 This protocol is not intended to replace other forms of pre-action dispute resolution (such as internal complaints procedures, the Surveyors and Valuers Arbitration Scheme, etc.). Where such procedures are available, parties are encouraged to consider whether they should be used. If, however, these other procedures are used and fail to resolve the dispute, the protocol should be used before litigation is started, adapting it where appropriate. See also Guidance Note C3.

A4 The courts will be able to treat the standards set in this protocol as the normal reasonable approach. If litigation is started, it will be for the court to decide whether sanctions should be imposed as a result of substantial non-compliance with a protocol. Guidance on the courts' likely approach is given in PD Protocols. The court is likely to disregard minor departures from this protocol and so should the parties as between themselves.

A5 Both in operating the timetable and in requesting and providing information during the protocol period, the parties are expected to act reasonably, in line with the court's expectations of them. See also Guidance Note C1.2.

## B THE PROTOCOL

### B1 Preliminary Notice

(See also Guidance Note C3.1.)

B1.1 As soon as the claimant decides there is a reasonable chance that he will bring a claim against a professional, the claimant is encouraged to notify the professional in writing.

B1.2 This letter should contain the following information:
- (a) the identity of the claimant and any other parties;

(b) a brief outline of the claimant's grievance against the professional;
(c) if possible, a general indication of the financial value of the potential claim.

B1.3 This letter should be addressed to the professional and should ask the professional to inform his professional indemnity insurers, if any, immediately.

B1.4 The professional should acknowledge receipt of the claimant's letter within 21 days of receiving it. Other than this acknowledgment, the protocol places no obligation upon either party to take any further action.

## B2 Letter of Claim

B2.1 As soon as the claimant decides there are grounds for a claim against the professional, the claimant should write a detailed letter of claim to the professional.

B2.2 The letter of claim will normally be an open letter (as opposed to being 'without prejudice') and should include the following:

(a) The identity of any other parties involved in the dispute or a related dispute.
(b) A clear chronological summary (including key dates) of the facts on which the claim is based. Key documents should be identified, copied and enclosed.
(c) The allegations against the professional. What has he done wrong? What has he failed to do?
(d) An explanation of how the alleged error has caused the loss claimed.
(e) An estimate of the financial loss suffered by the claimant and how it is calculated. Supporting documents should be identified, copied and enclosed. If details of the financial loss cannot be supplied, the claimant should explain why and should state when he will be in a position to provide the details. This information should be sent to the professional as soon as reasonably possible. If the claimant is seeking some form of non-financial redress, this should be made clear.
(f) Confirmation whether or not an expert has been appointed. If so, providing the identity and discipline of the expert, together with the date upon which the expert was appointed.
(g) A request that a copy of the letter of claim be forwarded immediately to the professional's insurers, if any.

B2.3 The letter of claim is not intended to have the same formal status as a statement of case. If, however, the letter of claim differs materially from the statement of case in subsequent proceedings, the court may decide, in its discretion, to impose sanctions.

B2.4 If the claimant has sent other letters of claim (or equivalent) to any other party in relation to this dispute or related dispute, those letters should be copied to the professional. (If the claimant is claiming against someone else to whom this protocol does not apply, please see Guidance Note C4.)

## B3 The Letter of Acknowledgment

B3.1 The professional should acknowledge receipt of the letter of claim within 21 days of receiving it.

## B4 Investigations

B4.1 The professional will have three months from the date of the letter of acknowledgment to investigate.

B4.2 If the professional is in difficulty in complying with the three-month time period, the problem should be explained to the claimant as soon as possible. The professional should explain what is being done to resolve the problem and when the professional expects to complete the investigations. The claimant should agree to any reasonable request for an extension of the three-month period.

B4.3 The parties should supply promptly, at this stage and throughout, whatever relevant information or documentation is reasonably requested. (Please see Guidance Note C5). (If the professional intends to claim against someone who is not currently a party to the dispute, please see Guidance Note C4.)

## B5 Letter of Response and Letter of Settlement

B5.1 As soon as the professional has completed his investigations, the professional should send to the claimant:

(a) a letter of response; or

(b) a letter of settlement; or

(c) both.

The letters of response and settlement can be contained within a single letter.

*The letter of response*

B5.2 The letter of response will normally be an open letter (as opposed to being 'without prejudice') and should be a reasoned answer to the claimant's allegations:

(a) If the claim is admitted the professional should say so in clear terms.

(b) If only part of the claim is admitted the professional should make clear which parts of the claim are admitted and which are denied.

(c) If the claim is denied in whole or in part, the letter of response should include specific comments on the allegations against the professional and, if the claimant's version of events is disputed, the professional should provide his version of events.

(d) If the professional is unable to admit or deny the claim, the professional should identify any further information which is required.

(e) If the professional disputes the estimate of the claimant's financial loss, the letter of response should set out the professional's estimate. If an estimate cannot be provided, the professional should explain why and should state when he will be in a position to provide an estimate. This information should be sent to the claimant as soon as reasonably possible.

(f) Where additional documents are relied upon, copies should be provided.

B5.3 The letter of response is not intended to have the same formal status as a defence. If, however, the letter of response differs materially from the defence in subsequent proceedings, the court may decide, in its discretion, to impose sanctions.

*The letter of settlement*

B5.4 The letter of settlement will normally be a without prejudice letter and should be sent if the professional intends to make proposals for settlement. It should:

(a) Set out the professional's views to date on the claim identifying those issues which the professional believes are likely to remain in dispute and those which are not. (The letter of settlement does not need to include this information if the professional has sent a letter of response.)

(b) Make a settlement proposal or identify any further information which is required before the professional can formulate its proposals.

(c) Where additional documents are relied upon, copies should be provided.

*Effect of letter of response and/or letter of settlement*

B5.5 If the letter of response denies the claim in its entirety and there is no letter of settlement, it is open to the claimant to commence proceedings.

B5.6 In any other circumstance, the professional and the claimant should commence negotiations with the aim of concluding those negotiations within six months of the date of the letter of acknowledgment (*not* from the date of the letter of response).

B5.7 If the claim cannot be resolved within this period:

(a) The parties should agree within 14 days of the end of the period whether the period should be extended and, if so, by how long.

(b) The parties should seek to identify those issues which are still in dispute and those which can be agreed.

(c) If an extension of time is not agreed it will then be open to the claimant to commence proceedings.

## B6 Alternative Dispute Resolution

B6.1 The parties should consider whether some form of alternative dispute resolution procedure would be more suitable than litigation, and if so, endeavour to agree which form to adopt. Both the claimant and professional may be required by the court to provide evidence that alternative means of resolving their dispute were considered. The courts take the view that litigation should be a last resort, and that claims should not be issued prematurely when a settlement is still actively being explored. Parties are warned that if the protocol is not followed (including this paragraph) then the court must have regard to such conduct when determining costs.

B6.2 It is not practicable in this protocol to address in detail how the parties might decide which method to adopt to resolve their particular dispute. However, summarised below are some of the options for resolving disputes without litigation:

- discussion and negotiation;
- early neutral evaluation by an independent third party (for example, a lawyer experienced in the field of professional negligence or an individual experienced in the subject matter of the claim);
- mediation—a form of facilitated negotiation assisted by an independent neutral party.

B6.3 The Legal Services Commission has published a booklet on 'Alternatives to Court', CLS Direct Information Leaflet 23 (<http://www.clsdirect.org.uk/legalhelp/leaflet23.jsp>), which lists a number of organisations that provide alternative dispute resolution services.

B6.4 It is expressly recognised that no party can or should be forced to mediate or enter into any form of ADR.

## B7 Experts

(The following provisions apply where the claim raises an issue of professional expertise whose resolution requires expert evidence.)

B7.1 If the claimant has obtained expert evidence prior to sending the letter of claim, the professional will have equal right to obtain expert evidence prior to sending the letter of response/letter of settlement.

B7.2 If the claimant has not obtained expert evidence prior to sending the letter of claim, the parties are encouraged to appoint a joint expert. If they agree to do so, they should seek to agree the identity of the expert and the terms of the expert's appointment.

B7.3 If agreement about a joint expert cannot be reached, all parties are free to appoint their own experts.
(For further details on experts see Guidance Note C6.)

## B8 Proceedings

B8.1 Unless it is necessary (for example, to obtain protection against the expiry of a relevant limitation period) the claimant should not start court proceedings until:

(a) the letter of response denies the claim in its entirety and there is no letter of settlement (see para. B5.5 above); or

(b) the end of the negotiation period (see paras B5.6 and B5.7 above).
(For further discussion of statutory time limits for the commencement of litigation, please see Guidance Note C7.)

B8.2 Where possible 14 days' written notice should be given to the professional before proceedings are started, indicating the court within which the claimant is intending to commence litigation.

B8.3 Proceedings should be served on the professional, unless the professional's solicitor has notified the claimant in writing that he is authorised to accept service on behalf of the professional.

# C GUIDANCE NOTES

## C1 Introduction

C1.1 The protocol has been kept simple to promote ease of use and general acceptability. The guidance notes which follow relate particularly to issues on which further guidance may be required.

C2.2 The Woolf reforms envisages that parties will act reasonably in the pre-action period. Accordingly, in the event that the protocol and the guidelines do not specifically address a problem, the parties should comply with the spirit of the protocol by acting reasonably.

## C2 Scope of Protocol

C2.1 The protocol is specifically designated for claims of negligence against professionals. This will include claims in which the allegation against a professional is that they have breached a contractual term to take reasonable skill and care. The protocol is also appropriate for claims of breach of fiduciary duty against professionals.

C2.2 The protocol is not intended to apply to claims:

(a) against architects, engineers and quantity surveyors—parties should use the Construction and Engineering Disputes (CED) protocol;

(b) against healthcare providers—parties should use the Pre-action Protocol for the Resolution of Clinical Disputes;

(c) concerning defamation—parties should use the Pre-action Protocol for Defamation.

C2.3 'Professional' is deliberately left undefined in the protocol. If it becomes an issue as to whether a defendant is or is not a professional, parties are reminded of the overriding need to act reasonably (see paras A4 and C1.2 above). Rather than argue about the definition of 'professional', therefore, the parties are invited to use this protocol, adapting it where appropriate.

C2.4 The protocol may not be suitable for disputes with professionals concerning intellectual property claims, etc. Until specific protocols are created for those claims, however, parties are invited to use this protocol, adapting it where necessary.

C2.5 Allegations of professional negligence are sometimes made in response to an attempt by the professional to recover outstanding fees. Where possible these allegations should be raised before litigation has commenced, in which case the parties should comply with the protocol before either party commences litigation. If litigation has already commenced it will be a matter for the court whether sanctions should be imposed against either party. In any event, the parties are encouraged to consider applying to the court for a stay to allow the protocol to be followed.

## C3 Interaction With Other Pre-action Methods of Dispute Resolution

C3.1 There are a growing number of methods by which disputes can be resolved without the need for litigation, e.g., internal complaints procedures, the Surveyors and Valuers Arbitration Scheme, and so on. The preliminary notice procedure of the protocol (see para. B1) is designed to enable both parties to take stock at an early stage and to decide before work starts on preparing a letter of claim whether the grievance should be referred to one of these other dispute resolution procedures. (For the avoidance of doubt, however, there is no obligation on either party under the protocol to take any action at this stage other than giving the acknowledgment provided for in para. B1.4.)

C3.2 Accordingly, parties are free to use (and are encouraged to use) any of the available pre-action procedures in an attempt to resolve their dispute. If appropriate, the parties can agree to suspend the protocol timetable whilst the other method of dispute resolution is used.

C3.3 If these methods fail to resolve the dispute, however, the protocol should be used before litigation is commenced. Because there has already been an attempt to resolve the dispute, it may be appropriate to adjust the protocol's requirements. In particular, unless the parties agree otherwise, there is unlikely to be any benefit in duplicating a stage which has in effect already been undertaken. However, if the protocol adds anything to the earlier method of dispute resolution, it should be used, adapting it where appropriate. Once again, the parties are expected to act reasonably.

### C4 Multi-party Disputes

C4.1 Paragraph B2.2(a) of the protocol requires a claimant to identify any other parties involved in the dispute or a related dispute. This is intended to ensure that all relevant parties are identified as soon as possible.

C4.2 If the dispute involves more than two parties, there are a number of potential problems. It is possible that different protocols will apply to different defendants. It is possible that defendants will claim against each other. It is possible that other parties will be drawn into the dispute. It is possible that the protocol timetable against one party will not be synchronised with the protocol timetable against a different party. How will these problems be resolved?

C4.3 As stated in para. C1.2 above, the parties are expected to act reasonably. What is 'reasonable' will, of course, depend upon the specific facts of each case. Accordingly, it would be inappropriate for the protocol to set down generalised rules. Whenever a problem arises, the parties are encouraged to discuss how it can be overcome. In doing so, parties are reminded of the protocol's aims which include the aim to resolve the dispute without the need for litigation (para. A2 above).

### C5 Investigations

C5.1 Paragraph B4.3 is intended to encourage the early exchange of relevant information, so that issues in the dispute can be clarified or resolved. It should not be used as a 'fishing expedition' by either party. No party is obliged under para. B4.3 to disclose any document which a court could not order them to disclose in the pre-action period.

C5.2 This protocol does not alter the parties' duties to disclose documents under any professional regulation or under general law.

### C6 Experts

C6.1 Expert evidence is not always needed, although the use and role of experts in professional negligence claims is often crucial. However, the way in which expert evidence is used in, say, an insurance brokers' negligence case, is not necessarily the same as in, say, an accountants' case. Similarly, the approach to be adopted in a £10,000 case does not necessarily compare with the approach in a £10 million case. The protocol therefore is designed to be flexible and does not dictate a standard approach. On the contrary it envisages that the parties will bear the responsibility for agreeing how best to use experts.

C6.2 If a joint expert is used, therefore, the parties are left to decide issues such as: the payment of the expert, whether joint or separate instructions are used, how and to whom the expert is to report, how questions may be addressed to the expert and how the expert should respond, whether an agreed statement of facts is required, and so on.

C6.3 If separate experts are used, the parties are left to decide issues such as: whether the experts' reports should be exchanged, whether there should be an experts' meeting, and so on.

C6.4 Even if a joint expert is appointed, it is possible that parties will still want to instruct their own experts. The protocol does not prohibit this.

## C7 Proceedings

C7.1 This protocol does not alter the statutory time limits for starting court proceedings. A claimant is required to start proceedings within those time limits.

C7.2 If proceedings are for any reason started before the parties have followed the procedures in this protocol, the parties are encouraged to agree to apply to the court for a stay whilst the protocol is followed.

# Pre-action Protocol for Judicial Review



## INTRODUCTION

This protocol applies to proceedings within England and Wales only. It does not affect the time limit specified by CPR, r. 54.5(1), which requires that any claim form in an application for judicial review must be filed promptly and in any event not later than three months after the grounds to make the claim first arose.[1]

1. Judicial review allows people with a sufficient interest in a decision or action by a public body to ask a judge to review the lawfulness of:
   - an enactment; or
   - a decision, action or failure to act in relation to the exercise of a public function.[2]
2. Judicial review may be used where there is no right of appeal or where all avenues of appeal have been exhausted.

### Alternative Dispute Resolution

3.1 The parties should consider whether some form of alternative dispute resolution procedure would be more suitable than litigation, and if so, endeavour to agree which form to adopt. Both the claimant and defendant may be required by the court to provide evidence that alternative means of resolving their dispute were considered. The Courts take the view that litigation should be a last resort, and that claims should not be issued prematurely when a settlement is still actively being explored. Parties are warned that if the protocol is not followed (including this paragraph) then the court must have regard to such conduct when determining costs. However, parties should also note that a claim for judicial review 'must be filed promptly and in any event not later than 3 months after the grounds to make the claim first arose'.

3.2 It is not practicable in this protocol to address in detail how the parties might decide which method to adopt to resolve their particular dispute. However, summarised below are some of the options for resolving disputes without litigation:
- discussion and negotiation.
- Ombudsmen—the Parliamentary and Health Service and the Local Government Ombudsmen have discretion to deal with complaints relating to maladministration. The British and Irish Ombudsman Association provide information about Ombudsman schemes and other complaint handling bodies and this is available from their website at <http://www.bioa.org.uk>. Parties may wish to note that the Ombudsmen are not able to look into a complaint once court action has been commenced.
- Early neutral evaluation by an independent third party (for example, a lawyer experienced in the field of administrative law or an individual experienced in the subject matter of the claim).
- Mediation—a form of facilitated negotiation assisted by an independent neutral party.

[1] While the court does have the discretion under r. 3.1(2)(a) to allow a late claim, this is only used in exceptional circumstances. Compliance with the protocol alone is unlikely to be sufficient to persuade the court to allow a late claim.

[2] Rule 54.1(2).

3.3 The Legal Services Commission has published a booklet on 'Alternatives to Court', CLS Direct Information Leaflet 23 (<http://www.clsdirect.org.uk/legalhelp/leaflet23.jsp>), which lists a number of organisations that provide alternative dispute resolution services.

3.4 It is expressly recognised that no party can or should be forced to mediate or enter into any form of ADR.

4. **Judicial review may not be appropriate in every instance.**

**Claimants are strongly advised to seek appropriate legal advice when considering such proceedings and, in particular, before adopting this protocol or making a claim. Although the Legal Services Commission will not normally grant Full Representation before a letter before claim has been sent and the proposed defendant given a reasonable time to respond, initial funding may be available, for eligible claimants, to cover the work necessary to write this. (See Annex C for more information.)**

5. This protocol sets out a code of good practice and contains the steps which parties should generally follow before making a claim for judicial review.

6. This protocol does not impose a greater obligation on a public body to disclose documents or give reasons for its decision than that already provided for in statute or common law. However, where the court considers that a public body should have provided *relevant* documents and/or information, particularly where this failure is a breach of a statutory or common law requirement, it may impose sanctions.

**This protocol *will not be appropriate* where the defendant does not have the legal power to change the decision being challenged, for example decisions issued by tribunals such as the Asylum and Immigration Tribunal.**

**This protocol *will not be appropriate* in urgent cases, for example, when directions have been set, or are in force, for the claimant's removal from the UK, or where there is an urgent need for an interim order to compel a public body to act where it has unlawfully refused to do so (for example, the failure of a local housing authority to secure interim accommodation for a homeless claimant) a claim should be made immediately. A letter before claim will not stop the implementation of a disputed decision in all instances.**

7. All claimants will need to satisfy themselves whether they should follow the protocol, depending upon the circumstances of his or her case. Where the use of the protocol is appropriate, the court will normally expect all parties to have complied with it and will take into account compliance or non-compliance when giving directions for case management of proceedings or when making orders for costs.[3] However, even in emergency cases, it is good practice to fax to the defendant the draft claim form which the claimant intends to issue. A claimant is also normally required to notify a defendant when an interim mandatory order is being sought.

## THE LETTER BEFORE CLAIM

8. Before making a claim, the claimant should send a letter to the defendant. The purpose of this letter is to identify the issues in dispute and establish whether litigation can be avoided.

9. Claimants should normally use the suggested **standard format** for the letter outlined at Annex A.

10. The letter should contain **the date and details of the decision, act or omission being challenged and a clear summary of the facts** on which the claim is based. It should also contain the **details of any relevant information** that the claimant is seeking and an explanation of why this is considered relevant.

11. The letter should normally contain the **details of any interested parties**[4] known to the claimant. They should be sent a **copy** of the letter before claim for **information. Claim-**

[3] PD 43–48.

[4] See CPR, r. 54.1(2)(f).

**ants are strongly advised to seek appropriate legal advice when considering such proceedings and, in particular, before sending the letter before claim to other interested parties or making a claim.**

12. A claim should not normally be made until the proposed reply date given in the letter before claim has passed, unless the circumstances of the case require more immediate action to be taken.

## THE LETTER OF RESPONSE

13. Defendants should normally respond within 14 days using the **standard format** at Annex B. Failure to do so will be taken into account by the court and sanctions may be imposed unless there are good reasons.[5]
14. Where it is not possible to reply within the proposed time limit the defendant should send an interim reply and propose a reasonable extension. Where an extension is sought, reasons should be given and, where required, additional information requested. **This will not affect the time limit for making a claim for judicial review**[6] nor will it bind the claimant where he or she considers this to be unreasonable. However, where the court considers that a subsequent claim is made prematurely it may impose sanctions.
15. If the **claim is being conceded in full**, the reply should say so in clear and unambiguous terms.
16. If the **claim is being conceded in part or not being conceded at all**, the reply should say so in clear and unambiguous terms, and:
    (a) where appropriate, contain a new decision, clearly identifying what aspects of the claim are being conceded and what are not, or, give a clear timescale within which the new decision will be issued;
    (b) provide a fuller explanation for the decision, if considered appropriate to do so;
    (c) address any points of dispute, or explain why they cannot be addressed;
    (d) enclose any **relevant** documentation requested by the claimant, or explain why the documents are not being enclosed; and
    (e) where appropriate, confirm whether or not they will oppose any application for an interim remedy.
17. The response should be sent to **all interested parties**[7] identified by the claimant and contain details of any other parties who the defendant considers also have an interest.

## ANNEX A
## LETTER BEFORE CLAIM

### Section 1 Information Required in a Letter Before Claim

### Proposed Claim for Judicial Review

1. To (Insert the name and address of the proposed defendant—see details in section 2)
2. The claimant (Insert the title, first and last name and the address of the claimant)
3. Reference details (When dealing with large organisations it is important to understand that the information relating to any particular individual's previous dealings with it may not be immediately available, therefore it is important to set out the relevant reference numbers for the matter in dispute and/or the identity of those within the public body who have been handling the particular matter in dispute—see details in section 3)
4. The details of the matter being challenged (Set out clearly the matter being challenged, particularly if there has been more than one decision)

[5] See PD Protocols, paras 2 and 3.
[6] See CPR, r. 54.5(1).
[7] See CPR, r. 54.1(2)(f).

5. The issue (Set out the date and details of the decision, or act or omission being challenged, a brief summary of the facts and why it is contended to be wrong)
6. The details of the action that the defendant is expected to take (Set out the details of the remedy sought, including whether a review or any interim remedy is being requested)
7. The details of the legal advisers, if any, dealing with this claim (Set out the name, address and reference details of any legal advisers dealing with the claim)
8. The details of any interested parties (Set out the details of any interested parties and confirm that they have been sent a copy of this letter)
9. The details of any information sought (Set out the details of any information that is sought. This may include a request for a fuller explanation of the reasons for the decision that is being challenged)
10. The details of any documents that are considered relevant and necessary (Set out the details of any documentation or policy in respect of which the disclosure is sought and explain why these are relevant. If you rely on a statutory duty to disclose, this should be specified)
11. The address for reply and service of court documents (Insert the address for the reply)
12. Proposed reply date (The precise time will depend upon the circumstances of the individual case. However, although a shorter or longer time may be appropriate in a particular case, 14 days is a reasonable time to allow in most circumstances.)

## Section 2 Address for Sending the Letter Before Claim

Public bodies have requested that, for certain types of cases, in order to ensure a prompt response, letters before claim should be sent to specific addresses.

Where the claim concerns a decision in an immigration, asylum or nationality case:

The Judicial Review Management Unit
Immigration and Nationality Directorate
1st Floor
Green Park House
29 Wellesley Road
Croydon
CR0 2AJ

Where the claim concerns a decision by the Legal Services Commission:

The address on the decision letter/notification; and
Policy and Legal Department
Legal Services Commission
85 Gray's Inn Road
London WC1X 8TX

Where the claim concerns a decision by a local authority:

The address on the decision letter/notification; and
Their legal department[8]

Where the claim concerns a decision by a department or body for whom Treasury Solicitor acts *and the Treasury Solicitor has already been involved in the case* a copy should also be sent, quoting the Treasury Solicitor's reference, to:

The Treasury Solicitor
One Kemble Street
London WC2B 4TS

In all other circumstances, the letter should be sent to the address on the letter notifying the decision.

[8] The relevant address should be available from a range of sources such as the *Phone Book, Business and Services Directory, Thomson Local*, CAB, etc.

### Section 3 Specific Reference Details Required

Public bodies have requested that the following information should be provided in order to ensure prompt response.

Where the claim concerns an immigration, asylum or nationality case, dependent upon the nature of the case:

The Home Office reference number
The port reference number
The Immigration Appellate Authority reference number
The National Asylum Support Service reference number

Or, if these are unavailable:

The full name, nationality and date of birth of the claimant.

Where the claim concerns a decision by the Legal Services Commission:

The certificate reference number.

## ANNEX B
## RESPONSE TO A LETTER BEFORE CLAIM

### Information Required in a Response to a Letter Before Claim

### Proposed Claim for Judicial Review

1. The claimant (Insert the title, first and last names and the address to which any reply should be sent)
2. From (Insert the name and address of the defendant)
3. Reference details (Set out the relevant reference numbers for the matter in dispute and the identity of those within the public body who have been handling the issue)
4. The details of the matter being challenged (Set out details of the matter being challenged, providing a fuller explanation of the decision, where this is considered appropriate)
5. Response to the proposed claim (Set out whether the issue in question is conceded in part, or in full, or will be contested. Where it is not proposed to disclose any information that has been requested, explain the reason for this. Where an interim reply is being sent and there is a realistic prospect of settlement, details should be included)
6. Details of any other interested parties (Identify any other parties who you consider have an interest who have not already been sent a letter by the claimant)
7. Address for further correspondence and service of court documents (Set out the address for any future correspondence on this matter)

## ANNEX C
## NOTES ON PUBLIC FUNDING FOR LEGAL COSTS IN JUDICIAL REVIEW

Public funding for legal costs in judicial review is available from legal professionals and advice agencies which have contracts with the Legal Services Commission as part of the Community Legal Service. Funding may be provided for:

- Legal Help to provide initial advice and assistance with any legal problem; or
- Legal Representation to allow you to be represented in court if you are taking or defending court proceedings. This is available in two forms:
  - Investigative Help is limited to funding to investigate the strength of the proposed claim. It includes the issue and conduct of proceedings only so far as is necessary to obtain disclosure of relevant information or to protect the client's position in relation to any urgent hearing or time limit for the issue of proceedings. This includes the work necessary to write a letter before claim to the body potentially under challenge, setting out the grounds of challenge, and giving that body a reasonable opportunity, typically 14 days, in which to respond.

— Full Representation is provided to represent you in legal proceedings and includes litigation services, advocacy services, and all such help as is usually given by a person providing representation in proceedings, including steps preliminary or incidental to proceedings, and/or arriving at or giving affect to a compromise to avoid or bring to an end any proceedings. Except in emergency cases, a proper letter before claim must be sent and the other side must be given an opportunity to respond before Full Representation is granted.

Further information on the type(s) of help available and the criteria for receiving that help may be found in the *Legal Service Manual*, vol. 3, *The Funding Code*. This may be found on the Legal Services Commission website at:

<http://www.legalservices.co.uk/>

A list of contracted firms and advice agencies may be found on the Community Legal Service website at: <http://www.justask.org.uk/>

# Pre-action Protocol for Disease and Illness Claims



## 1 INTRODUCTION

1.1 Lord Woolf in his *Final Report* of July 1996 recommended the development of protocols: 'to build on and increase the benefits of early but well-informed settlements which genuinely satisfy both parties to a dispute'.

1.2 The aims of these protocols are:
- more contact between the parties;
- better and earlier exchange of information;
- better investigation by both sides;
- to put the parties in a position where they may be able to settle cases fairly and early without litigation;
- to enable proceedings to run to the court's timetable and efficiently, if litigation does become necessary.

1.3 The concept of protocols is relevant to a range of initiatives for good claims practice, especially:
- predictability in the time needed for steps to be taken;
- standardisation of relevant information, including documents to be disclosed.

1.4 The courts will be able to treat the standards set in protocols as the normal reasonable approach. If proceedings are issued, it will be for the court to decide whether non-compliance with a protocol should merit adverse consequences. Guidance on the court's likely approach will be given from time to time in practice directions.

1.5 If the court has to consider the question of compliance after proceedings have begun, it will not be concerned with minor infringements, e.g. failure by a short period to provide relevant information. One minor breach will not exempt the 'innocent' party from following the protocol. The court will look at the effect of non-compliance on the other party when deciding whether to impose sanctions.

## 2 NOTES OF GUIDANCE

### Scope of the Protocol

2.1 This protocol is intended to apply to all personal injury claims where the injury is not as the result of an accident but takes the form of an illness or disease.

2.2 This protocol covers disease claims which are likely to be complex and frequently not suitable for fast track procedures even though they may fall within fast track limits. Disease for the purpose of this protocol primarily covers any illness physical or psychological, any disorder, ailment, affliction, complaint, malady, or derangement other than a physical or psychological injury solely caused by an accident or other similar single event.

2.3 This protocol is not limited to diseases occurring in the workplace but will embrace diseases occurring in other situations for example through occupation of premises or the use of products. It is not intended to cover those cases, which are dealt with as a 'group' or 'class' action.

2.4 The 'cards on the table' approach advocated by the personal injury protocol is equally appropriate to disease claims. The spirit of that protocol, and of the clinical negligence protocol is followed here, in accordance with the sense of the civil justice reforms.

2.5 The timetable and the arrangements for disclosing documents and obtaining expert evidence may need to be varied to suit the circumstances of the case. If a party considers the detail of the protocol to be inappropriate they should communicate their reasons to all of the parties at that stage. If proceedings are subsequently issued, the court will expect an explanation as to why the protocol has not been followed, or has been varied. In a terminal disease claim with short life expectancy, for instance for a claimant who has a disease such as mesothelioma, the timescale of the protocol is likely to be too long. In such a claim, the claimant may not be able to follow the protocol and the defendant would be expected to treat the claim with urgency.

### Alternative Dispute Resolution

2A.1 The parties should consider whether some form of alternative dispute resolution procedure would be more suitable than litigation, and if so, endeavour to agree which form to adopt. Both the claimant and defendant may be required by the court to provide evidence that alternative means of resolving their dispute were considered. The courts take the view that litigation should be a last resort, and that claims should not be issued prematurely when a settlement is still actively being explored. Parties are warned that if the protocol is not followed (including this paragraph) then the court must have regard to such conduct when determining costs.

2A.2 It is not practicable in this protocol to address in detail how the parties might decide which method to adopt to resolve their particular dispute. However, summarised below are some of the options for resolving disputes without litigation:

- discussion and negotiation;
- early neutral evaluation by an independent third party (for example, a lawyer experienced in the field of disease or illness, or an individual experienced in the subject matter of the claim);
- mediation—a form of facilitated negotiation assisted by an independent neutral party.

2A.3 The Legal Services Commission has published a booklet on 'Alternatives to Court', CLS Direct Information Leaflet 23 (<http://www.clsdirect.org.uk/legalhelp/leaflet23.jsp>), which lists a number of organisations that provide alternative dispute resolution services.

2A.4 It is expressly recognised that no party can or should be forced to mediate or enter into any form of ADR.

## 3 THE AIMS OF THE PROTOCOL

3.1 The *general* aims of the protocol are:

- to resolve as many disputes as possible without litigation;
- where a claim cannot be resolved to identify the relevant issues which remain in dispute.

3.2 The *specific* objectives are:

*Openness*

- to encourage early communication of the perceived problem between the parties or their insurers;
- to encourage employees to voice any concerns or worries about possible work-related illness as soon as practicable;

- to encourage employers to develop systems of early reporting and investigation of suspected occupational health problems and to provide full and prompt explanations to concerned employees or former employees;
- to apply such principles to perceived problems outside the employer/employee relationship, for example occupiers of premises or land and producers of products;
- to ensure that sufficient information is disclosed by both parties to enable each to understand the other's perspective and case, and to encourage early resolution;

*Timeliness*

- to provide an early opportunity for employers (past or present) or their insurers to identify cases where an investigation is required and to carry out that investigation promptly;
- to encourage employers (past or present) or other defendants to involve and identify their insurers at an early stage;
- to ensure that all relevant records including health and personnel records are provided to employees (past or present) or their appointed representatives promptly on request, by any employer (past or present) or their insurers. This should be complied with to a realistic timetable;
- to ensure that relevant records which are in the claimant's possession are made available to the employers or their insurers by claimants or their advisers at an appropriate stage;
- to proceed on a reasonable timetable where a resolution is not achievable to lay the ground to enable litigation to proceed at a reasonable and proportionate cost, and to limit the matters in contention;
- to communicate promptly where any of the requested information is not available or does not exist;
- to discourage the prolonged pursuit of unmeritorious claims and the prolonged defence of meritorious claims;
- to encourage all parties, at the earliest possible stage, to disclose voluntarily any additional documents which will assist in resolving any issue.

## 4 THE PROTOCOL

This protocol is not a comprehensive code governing all the steps in disease claims. Rather it attempts to set out *a code of good practice* which parties should follow.

### Obtaining Occupational Records Including Health Records

4.1 In appropriate cases, a *potential claimant* may request occupational records including health records and personnel records before sending a letter of claim.

4.2 Any request for records by the *potential claimant* or his adviser should *provide sufficient information* to alert the *potential defendant* or his insurer where a possible disease claim is being investigated. Annex A1 provides a suggested form for this purpose for use in cases arising from employment. Similar forms can be prepared and used in other situations.

4.3 The copy records should be provided *within a maximum of 40 days* of the request at no cost. Although these will primarily be occupational records, it will be good practice for a *potential defendant* to disclose product data documents identified by a *potential claimant* at this stage which may resolve a causation issue.

4.4 In the rare circumstances that the *potential defendant* or his insurer is in difficulty in providing information quickly details should be given of what is being done to resolve it with a reasonable time estimate for doing so.

4.5 If the *potential defendant* or his insurer fails to provide the records including health records within 40 days and fails to comply with para. 4.4 above, the *potential claimant* or his adviser may then apply to the court for an *order for pre-action disclosure*. The CPR make pre-action applications to the court easier. The court also has the power to impose costs sanctions for unreasonable delay in providing records.

## 5 COMMUNICATION

5.1 If either the *potential claimant* or his adviser considers *additional records are required from a third party*, such as records from previous employers or general practitioner records, in the first instance these should be requested by the *potential claimant* or their advisers. Third party record holders would be expected to cooperate. The CPR enable parties to apply to the court for pre-action disclosure by third parties.

5.2 As soon as the records have been received and analysed, the *potential claimant* or his adviser should consider whether a claim should be made. General practitioner records will normally be obtained before a decision is reached.

5.3 If a decision is made not to proceed further at this stage against a party identified as a *potential defendant*, the *potential claimant* or his adviser should notify that *potential defendant* as soon as practicable.

## 6 LETTER OF CLAIM

6.1 Where a decision is made to make a claim, the claimant shall send to the proposed defendant two copies of a letter of claim, as soon as sufficient information is available to substantiate a realistic claim and before issues of quantum are addressed in detail. One copy is for the defendants, the second for passing on to his insurers.

6.2 This letter shall contain a *clear summary of the facts* on which the claim is based, including details of the illness alleged, and the *main allegations of fault*. It shall also give details of present condition and prognosis. The *financial loss* incurred by the claimant should be outlined. Where the case is funded by a conditional fee agreement, notification should be given of the existence of the agreement and where appropriate, that there is a success fee and insurance premium, although not the level of the success fee or premium.

6.3 Solicitors are recommended to use *a standard format* for such a letter—an example is at annex B: this can be amended to suit the particular case, for example, if the client has rehabilitation needs these can also be detailed in the letter.

6.4 A *chronology* of the relevant events (e.g. dates or periods of exposure) should be provided. In the case of alleged occupational disease an appropriate employment history should also be provided, particularly if the claimant has been employed by a number of different employers and the illness in question has a long latency period.

6.5 The letter of claim should identify any *relevant documents*, including health records not already in the defendant's possession e.g. any relevant general practitioner records. These will need to be disclosed in confidence to the nominated insurance manager or solicitor representing the defendant following receipt of their letter of acknowledgment. Where the action is brought under the Law Reform (Miscellaneous Provisions) Act 1934 or the Fatal Accidents Act 1976 then *relevant documents* will normally include copies of the death certificate, the post mortem report, the inquest depositions and if obtained by that date the grant of probate or letters of administration.

6.6 The letter of claim should indicate whether a claim is also being made against any *other potential defendant* and identify any known insurer involved.

6.7 Sufficient information should be given to enable the defendant's insurer/solicitor to commence *investigations* and at least to put a broad valuation on the 'risk'.

6.8 It is not a requirement for the claimant to provide *medical evidence* with the letter of claim, but the claimant may choose to do so in very many cases.

6.9 *Letters of claim and response* are not intended to have the same *status* as a statement of case in proceedings. Matters may come to light as a result of investigation after the letter of claim has been sent, or after the defendant has responded, particularly if disclosure of documents takes place outside the recommended three-month period. These circumstances could mean that the 'pleaded' case of one or both parties is presented slightly differently than in the letter of claim or response. It would not be consistent with the spirit of the protocol for a party to 'take a point' on this in the proceedings, provided that there was no obvious intention by the party who changed their position to mislead the other party.

6.10 *Proceedings should not be issued until after three months from the date of acknowledgment* (see para. 7), unless there is a limitation problem and/or the claimant's position needs to be protected by early issue (see para. 2.5).

## 7 THE RESPONSE

7.1 The defendant should *send an acknowledgment within 21 calendar days* of the date of posting of the letter of claim, identifying the liability insurer (if any) who will be dealing with the matter and, if necessary, identifying specifically any significant omissions from the letter of claim. If there has been no acknowledgment by the defendant or insurer within 21 days, the claimant will be entitled to issue proceedings.

7.2 The identity of all relevant insurers, if more than one, should be notified to the claimant by the insurer identified in the acknowledgment letter, within one calendar month of the date of that acknowledgment.

7.3 The defendant or his representative should, *within three months of the date of the acknowledgment letter*, provide a *reasoned answer*:

- if the *claim is admitted*, they should say so in clear terms;
- if only *part of the claim is admitted* they should make clear which issues of fault and/or causation and/or limitation are admitted and which remain in issue and why;
- if the *claim is not admitted in full*, they should explain why and should, for example, include comments on the employment status of the claimant (including job description(s) and details of the department(s) where the claimant worked), the allegations of fault, causation and of limitation, and if a synopsis or chronology of relevant events has been provided and is disputed, their version of those events;
- if the *claim is not admitted in full*, the defendant should enclose with his letter of reply *documents* in his possession which are *material to the issues* between the parties and which would be likely to be ordered to be disclosed by the court, either on an application for pre-action disclosure, or on disclosure during proceedings. Reference can be made to the documents annexed to the personal injury protocol.
- where more than one defendant receives a letter of claim, the timetable will be activated for each defendant by the date on the letter of claim addressed to them. If any defendant wishes to extend the timetable because the number of defendants will cause complications, they should seek agreement to a different timetable as soon as possible.

7.4 If the parties reach agreement on liability and/or causation, but time is needed to resolve other issues including the value of the claim, they should aim to agree a reasonable period.

7.5 Where it is not practicable for the defendant to complete his investigations within three months, the defendant should indicate the difficulties and outline the further time needed. Any request for an extension of time should be made, with reasons, as soon as the defendant becomes aware that an extension is needed and normally before the three-month period has expired. Such an extension of time should be agreed in circumstances where reasonable justification has been shown. Lapse of many years since the circumstances giving rise to the claim does not, by itself, constitute reasonable justification for further time.

7.6 Where the relevant negligence occurred outside England and Wales and/or where the defendant is outside the jurisdiction, the time periods of 21 days and three months should normally be extended up to 42 days and six months.

## 8 SPECIAL DAMAGES

8.1 The claimant will send to the defendant as soon as practicable a schedule of special damages with supporting documents, particularly where the defendant has admitted liability.

## 9 EXPERTS

9.1 In disease claims expert opinions will usually be needed:
- on knowledge, fault and causation;
- on condition and prognosis;
- to assist in valuing aspects of the claim.

9.2 The civil justice reforms and the CPR encourage economy in the use of experts and a less adversarial expert culture. It is recognised that in disease claims, the parties and their advisers will require flexibility in their approach to expert evidence. Decisions on whether experts might be instructed jointly, and on whether reports might be disclosed sequentially or by exchange, should rest with the parties and their advisers. Sharing expert evidence may be appropriate on various issues including those relating to the value of the claim. However, this protocol does not attempt to be prescriptive on issues in relation to expert evidence.

9.3 Obtaining expert evidence will often be an expensive step and may take time, especially in specialised areas where there are limited numbers of suitable experts. Claimants, defendants and their advisers, will therefore need to consider carefully how best to obtain any necessary expert help quickly and cost-effectively.

9.4 The protocol recognises that a flexible approach must be adopted in the obtaining of medical reports in claims of this type. There will be very many occasions where the claimant will need to obtain a medical report before writing the letter of claim. In such cases the defendant will be entitled to obtain their own medical report. In some other instances it may be more appropriate to send the letter of claim before the medical report is obtained. Defendants will usually need to see a medical report before they can reach a view on causation.

9.5 Where the parties agree the nomination of a single expert is appropriate, before any party instructs an expert he should give the other party a list of the *name(s) of one or more experts* in the relevant speciality whom he considers are suitable to instruct. The parties are encouraged to agree the instruction of a single expert to deal with discrete areas such as cost of care.

9.6 *Within 14 days* the other party may indicate an objection to one or more of the named experts. The first party should then instruct a mutually acceptable expert. If the Claimant nominates an expert in the original letter of claim, the 14 days is in addition to the 21 days in para. 7.1.

9.7 If the second party objects to all the listed experts, the parties may then instruct *experts of their own choice*. It would be for the court to decide subsequently, if proceedings are issued, whether either party had acted unreasonably.

9.8 If the *second party does not object to an expert nominated*, he shall not be entitled to rely on his own expert evidence within that particular speciality unless:
(a) the first party agrees,
(b) the court so directs, or
(c) the first party's expert report has been amended and the first party is not prepared to disclose the original report.

9.9 *Either party may send to an agreed expert written questions* on the report, relevant to the issues, via the first party's solicitors. The expert should send answers to the questions separately and directly to each party.

9.10 The cost of a report from an agreed expert will usually be paid by the instructing first party: the costs of the expert replying to questions will usually be borne by the party which asks the questions.

9.11 Where the defendant admits liability in whole or in part, before proceedings are issued, any medical report obtained under this protocol which *the claimant* relies upon, should be disclosed to the other party.

9.12 Where the defendant admits liability in whole or in part before proceedings are issued, any medical report obtained under this protocol which *the defendant* relies upon, should be disclosed to the claimant.

## 10 RESOLUTION OF ISSUES

10.1 Part 36 of the CPR enables claimants and defendants to make formal offers to settle before proceedings are started. Parties should consider making such an offer, since to do so often leads to settlement. If such an offer is made, the party making the offer must always supply sufficient evidence and/or information to enable the offer to be properly considered.

10.2 Where a claim is not resolved when the protocol has been followed, the parties might wish to carry out a 'stocktake' of the issues in dispute, and the evidence that the court is likely to need to decide those issues, before proceedings are started.

10.3 Prior to proceedings it will be usual for all parties to disclose those expert reports relating to liability and causation upon which they propose to rely.

10.4 The claimant should delay issuing proceedings for 21 days from disclosure of reports to enable the parties to consider whether the claim is capable of settlement.

10.5 Where the defendant is insured and the pre-action steps have been conducted by the insurer, the insurer would normally be expected to nominate solicitors to act in the proceedings and the claimant's solicitor is recommended to invite the insurer to nominate solicitors to act in the proceedings and to do so seven to 14 days before the intended issue date.

## 11 LIMITATION

11.1 If by reason of complying with any part of this protocol a claimant's claim may be time-barred under any provision of the Limitation Act 1980, or any other legislation which imposes a time limit for bringing an action, the claimant may commence proceedings without complying with this protocol. In such circumstances, a claimant who commences proceedings without complying with all, or any part, of this protocol may apply to the court on notice for directions as to the timetable and form of procedure to be adopted, at the same time as he requests the court to issue proceedings. The court will consider whether to order a stay of the whole or part of the proceedings pending compliance with this protocol.

## ANNEX A
## LETTER REQUESTING OCCUPATIONAL RECORDS INCLUDING HEALTH RECORDS

Dear Sirs,

We are acting on behalf of the above-named who has developed the following *(with name of disease)*. We are investigating whether this disease may have been caused:

- during the course of his employment with you (*name of employer if different*);
- whilst at your premises at *(address)*;
- as a result of your product *(name)*.

We are writing this in accordance with the Pre-action Protocol for Disease and Illness Claims.

We seek the following records:

(details, e.g., personnel, occupational health)

Please note your insurers may require you to advise them of this request.

We enclose a request form and expect to receive the records within 40 days.

If you are not able to comply with this request within this time, please advise us of the reason.

Yours faithfully

## ANNEX A1
## APPLICATION ON BEHALF OF A POTENTIAL CLAIMANT FOR USE WHERE A DISEASE CLAIM IS BEING INVESTIGATED

This should be completed as fully as possible.

Company

Name

Address

1 (a) Full name of claimant (including previous surnames)
   (b) Address now
   (c) Address at date of termination of employment, if different
   (d) Date of birth (and death, if applicable)
   (e) National Insurance number, if available

2 Department(s) where claimant worked

3 This application is made because the claimant is considering:
   (a) a claim against you as detailed in point 4 YES/NO
   (b) pursuing an action against someone else YES/NO

4 If the answer to point 3(a) is 'Yes' details of:
   (a) the likely nature of the claim, e.g., dermatitis
   (b) grounds for the claim, e.g., exposure to chemical
   (c) approximate dates of the events involved

5 If the answer to point 3(b) is 'Yes' insert:
   (a) the names of the proposed defendants
   (b) have legal proceedings been started? YES/NO
   (c) if appropriate, details of the claim and action number

6 Any other relevant information or documents requested

Signature of solicitor

Name

Address

Ref.

Telephone number

Fax number

I authorise you to disclose all of your records relating to me/the claimant to my solicitor and to your legal and insurance representatives.

Signature of claimant

Signature of personal representative where claimant has died

## ANNEX B
## TEMPLATE FOR LETTER OF CLAIM

To Defendant

Dear Sirs

Re: *(Claimant's full name)*

(Claimant's full address)

National Insurance number:

Date of birth:

Clock or works number:

Employer: *(name and address)*

We are instructed by the above named to claim damages in connection with a claim for:

(specify occupational disease.)

We are writing this letter in accordance with the Pre-action Protocol for Disease and Illness Claims.

Please confirm the identity of your insurers. Please note that your insurers will need to see this letter as soon as possible and it may affect your insurance cover if you do not send this to them.

The Claimant was employed by you *(if the claim arises out of public or occupiers' liability give appropriate details)* as *(job description)* from *(date)* to *(date)*. During the relevant period of his employment he worked:

(description of precisely where the claimant worked and what he did to include a description of any machines used and details of any exposure to noise or substances.)

The circumstances leading to the development of this condition are as follows:

(give chronology of events.)

The reason why we are alleging fault is:

(details should be given of contemporary and comparable employees who have suffered from similar problems if known; any protective equipment provided; complaints; the supervisors concerned, if known.)

Our client's employment history is attached.

[We have also made a claim against:

(insert details)

Their insurers' details are:

*(insert if known)*]

We have the following documents in support of our client's claim and will disclose these in confidence to your nominated insurance manager or solicitor when we receive their acknowledgment letter:

(e.g., occupational health notes; GP notes.)

[We have obtained a medical report from *(name)* and will disclose this when we receive your acknowledgment of this letter.

*(This is optional at this stage.)*]

From the information we presently have:

(i) the Claimant first became aware of symptoms on *(insert approximate date)*;

(ii) the Claimant first received medical advice about those symptoms on *(insert date) (give details of advice given if appropriate)*.

(iii) the Claimant first believed that those symptoms might be due to exposure leading to this claim on *(insert approximate date)*.

A description of our client's condition is as follows:

(this should be sufficiently detailed to allow the defendant to put a broad value on the claim.)

He has the following time off work:

(insert dates.)

He is presently employed as a *(job description)* and his average net weekly income is £___.

If you are our client's employers, please provide us with the usual earnings details, which will enable us to calculate his financial loss.

[Please note that we have entered into a conditional fee agreement with our client dated___ in relation to this claim which provides for a success fee within the meaning of section 58(2) of the Courts and Legal Services Act 1990. Our client has taken out an insurance policy dated with *(name of insurance company)* to which section 29 of the Access to Justice Act 1999 applies in respect of this claim.]

A copy of this letter is attached for you to send to your insurers. Finally we expect an acknowledgment of this letter within 21 days by yourselves or your insurers.

Yours faithfully

# Pre-action Protocol for Housing Disrepair Cases



## 1 INTRODUCTION

Following a review of the problems of civil housing disrepair claims, Lord Woolf recommended in his *Final Report* in July 1996 that there should be a pre-action protocol.

The protocol, which covers claims in England and Wales, is intended to encourage the exchange of information between parties at an early stage and to provide a clear framework within which parties in a housing disrepair claim can attempt to achieve an early and appropriate resolution of the issues. An attempt has been made to draft the protocol in plain English and to keep the contents straightforward in order to make the protocol accessible and easy to use by all, including those representing themselves.

The protocol embraces the spirit of the Woolf reforms to the civil justice system. As Lord Woolf noted, landlords and tenants have a common interest in maintaining housing stock in good condition. It is generally common ground that in principle court action should be treated as a last resort, and it is hoped that the protocol will lead to the avoidance of unnecessary litigation. Before using the protocol tenants should therefore ensure that the landlord is aware of the disrepair. Tenants should also consider whether other options for having repairs carried out and/or obtaining compensation are more appropriate. Examples of other options are set out in para. 4.1(a).

Should a claim proceed to litigation, the court will expect all parties to have complied with the protocol as far as possible. The court has the power to order parties who have unreasonably failed to comply with the protocol to pay costs or be subject to other sanctions.

## 2 AIMS OF THE PROTOCOL

PD Protocols provides that the objectives of pre-action protocols are:

(1) to encourage the exchange of early and full information about the prospective legal claim,

(2) to enable parties to avoid litigation by agreeing a settlement of the claim before the commencement of proceedings,

(3) to support the efficient management of proceedings where litigation cannot be avoided.

The specific aims of this protocol are:

- To avoid unnecessary litigation.
- To promote the speedy and appropriate carrying out of any repairs which are the landlord's responsibility.
- To ensure that tenants receive any compensation to which they are entitled as speedily as possible.
- To promote good pre-litigation practice, including the early exchange of information and to give guidance about the instruction of experts.
- To keep the costs of resolving disputes down.

## 3 PROTOCOL

When using this protocol, please refer to the guidance notes in para. 4.

### 3.1 Definitions

For the purposes of this protocol:

(a) A disrepair claim is a civil claim arising from the condition of residential premises and may include a related personal injury claim. (See para. 4.4 (c), (d) and (e) of the guidance notes.) It does not include disrepair claims which originate as counterclaims or set-offs in other proceedings.

(b) The types of claim which this protocol is intended to cover include those brought under the Landlord and Tenant Act 1985, s. 11, the Defective Premises Act 1972, s. 4, common law nuisance and negligence, and those brought under the express terms of a tenancy agreement or lease. It does not cover claims brought under the Environmental Protection Act 1990, s. 82 (which are heard in the magistrates' court).

(c) This protocol covers claims by any person with a disrepair claim as referred to in paragraphs (a) and (b) above, including tenants, lessees and members of the tenant's family. The use of the term 'tenant' in this protocol is intended to cover all such people. (See also paragraph 4.4(e).)

### 3.2 Early Notification Letter

(a) Notice of the claim should be given to the landlord as soon as possible. In order to avoid delay in notifying the landlord it may be appropriate to send a letter notifying the landlord of the claim (early notification letter) before sending a letter setting out the full details of the claim (letter of claim). An early notification letter is intended to be a helpful tool, but it will not be necessary in every case. It might be appropriate where, for example, a repair is urgent or there is likely to be some delay before enough details are available to make a claim. The early notification letter to the landlord should give the following information:
   (i) tenant's name, the address of the property, tenant's address if different, tenant's telephone number and when access is available;
   (ii) details of the defects, including any defects outstanding, in the form of a schedule, if appropriate. Attached at annex G is a specimen schedule which can be used to inform the landlord of the disrepair;
   (iii) details of any notification previously given to the landlord of the need for repair or information as to why the tenant believes that the landlord has knowledge of the need for repair;
   (iv) proposed expert (see para. 3.6);
   (v) proposed letter of instruction to expert (see annex C);
   (vi) tenant's disclosure of such relevant documents as are readily available.

(b) The early notification letter should also request the following disclosure from the landlord: All relevant records or documents including:
   (i) copy of tenancy agreement including tenancy conditions;
   (ii) documents or computerised records relating to notice given, disrepair reported, inspection reports or repair works to the property.

(c) The early notification letter should include the authorisation for release of the information (except in a case where the tenant is acting in person).

(d) Specimen early notification letters are attached at annex A. They may be suitably adapted as appropriate.

### 3.3 Letter of Claim

(a) The tenant should send to the landlord a letter of claim at the earliest reasonable opportunity. The letter of claim should contain the following details *(if they have not already been provided in an early notification letter)*:
   (i) tenant's name, the address of the property, tenant's address if different, the tenant's telephone number and when access is available;
   (ii) details of the defects, including any defects outstanding, in the form of a schedule,

if appropriate. Attached at annex G is a specimen schedule which can be used to inform the landlord of the disrepair;
(iii) history of the defects, including attempts to rectify them;
(iv) details of any notification previously given to the landlord of the need for repair or information as to why the tenant believes that the landlord has knowledge of the need for repair;
(v) the effect of the defects on the tenant (see para. 4.4(c), (d) and (e) regarding personal injury claims);
(vi) details of any special damages (see form attached at annex E and definition of 'special damages' at para. 4.10);
(vii) proposed expert (see para. 3.6);
(viii) proposed letter of instruction to the expert (see annex C);
(ix) tenant's disclosure of relevant documents.

(b) If not already requested in an early notification letter, the letter of claim should also request the following disclosure from the landlord:
All relevant records or documents including:
(i) copy of tenancy agreement including tenancy conditions;
(ii) tenancy file;
(iii) documents relating to notice given, disrepair reported, inspection reports or requirements to the property;
(iv) computerised records.

(c) If not requested in an early notification letter, the letter of claim should also include the authorisation for release of the information (except in a case where the tenant is acting in person).

(d) Specimen letters of claim are attached at annex B. It will be seen that there are different versions depending on whether or not an early notification letter has been sent. The letters may be suitably adapted as appropriate.

## 3.4 Limitation Period

The procedures in this protocol do not extend statutory limitation periods. If a limitation period is about to expire, the tenant may need to issue proceedings immediately unless the landlord confirms that they will not rely on limitation as a defence in subsequent proceedings. (See para. 4.8 for guidance about the limitation period, and para. 4.10 for a definition of 'limitation period'.) Alternatively the tenant can ask the landlord to agree to extend the limitation period.

## 3.5 Landlord's Response

*3.5.1 Response to first letter*
The landlord should normally reply within 20 working days of the date of receipt of the first letter from the tenant, i.e., the early notification letter or the letter of claim if no early notification letter is sent. (See para. 4.10 for a definition of 'working days'.) The landlord's response to the first letter, whether an early notification letter or a letter of claim, should include the following:

*Disclosure*

(a) All relevant records or documents including:
(i) copy of tenancy agreement including tenancy conditions;
(ii) documents or computerised records relating to notice given, disrepair reported, inspection reports or requirements to the property.

*Expert*

(b) A response to the tenant's proposals for instructing an expert including:
(i) whether or not the proposed single joint expert is agreed;
(ii) whether the letter of instruction is agreed;

(iii) if the single joint expert is agreed but with separate instructions, a copy of the letter of instruction;
(iv) if the appointment of a single joint expert is not agreed, whether the landlord agrees to a joint inspection.

*3.5.2 Response to letter of claim*

(a) The landlord's response to the tenant's letter of claim should include:
  (i) whether liability is admitted and if so, in respect of which defects. If liability is disputed in respect of some or all of the defects, the reasons for this;
  (ii) any point which the landlord wishes to make regarding lack of notice of the repair or regarding any difficulty in gaining access;
  (iii) a full schedule of intended works including anticipated start and completion dates and a timetable for the works;
  (iv) any offer of compensation;
  (v) any offer in respect of costs;
  (vi) the information set out at para. 3.5.1(a) and (b), if it has not already been provided.
(b) On receipt of the letter of claim (whether or not an early notification letter was sent), the landlord may provide a response to the issues set out at paragraph (a) above either:
  (i) within 20 working days of the date of receipt of the letter of claim (see para. 4.10 for a definition of 'working days'); or
  (ii) within 20 working days of the date of receipt of the report of the single joint expert (see para. 3.6(h)) or date of receipt of the experts' agreed schedule following a joint inspection (see para. 3.6(g)).

*3.5.3 If landlord does not respond*

(a) If no response is received from the landlord to the early notification letter within 20 working days, the tenant should send a letter of claim giving as many of the details outlined at para. 3.3 as possible, on the basis of the information the tenant has to hand.
(b) Failure to respond within the time limits set out in paras 3.5.1 and 3.5.2, or at all, to the early notification letter or the letter of claim will be a breach of the protocol. (See para. 4.7(a) and (b) regarding time limits and the power of the court if the protocol is breached.)

## 3.6 Experts

*General*

See para. 4.6 for guidance regarding the use of experts.

(a) Tenants should remember that in some cases it might not be necessary to instruct an expert to provide evidence of disrepair, for example, if the only issue relates to the level of any damages claimed. It may be advisable to take photographs of any defects before and after works, and consideration should be given to the use of video footage, particularly if an expert has not been instructed.
(b) The expert should be instructed to report on all items of disrepair which the landlord ought reasonably to know about, or which the expert ought reasonably to report on. The expert should be asked to provide a schedule of works, an estimate of the costs of repair, and to list any urgent works.
(c) Information is given at para. 4.6(a) about obtaining lists of independent experts who can be instructed in disrepair cases.

*Single joint expert*

(d) If the landlord does not raise an objection to the proposed expert or letter of instruction within 20 working days of the date of receipt of the early notification letter or letter of claim, the expert should be instructed as a single joint expert, using the tenant's proposed letter of instruction. Attached at annex C are specimen letters of instruction to an expert. Alternatively, if the parties cannot agree joint instructions, the landlord and tenant should send their own separate instructions to the single joint expert. If sending separate instructions, the landlord should send the tenant a copy of the landlord's letter of instruction with their response to the first letter. (The tenant has already forwarded the proposed letter of instruction to the landlord.)

*Joint inspection*

(e) If it is not possible to reach agreement to instruct a single joint expert, even with separate instructions, the parties should attempt to arrange a joint inspection, i.e., an inspection by different experts instructed by each party to take place at the same time. If the landlord wishes to send their own expert to a joint inspection, they should inform both the tenant's expert and the tenant's solicitor. If the landlord instructs their own expert to inspect then the tenant can also instruct their own expert. It will be for the court to decide subsequently, if proceedings are issued, whether or not either party has acted reasonably.

*Time limits*

(f) Whether a single joint expert or a joint inspection is used, the property should be inspected within 20 working days of the date that the landlord responds to the tenant's first letter.

(g) If there is a joint inspection, the experts should produce an agreed schedule of works detailing:
  (i) the defects and required works which are agreed and a timetable for the agreed works;
  (ii) the areas of disagreement and the reasons for disagreement.

  The agreed schedule should be sent to both the landlord and the tenant within 10 working days of the joint inspection.

(h) If there is a single joint expert, a copy of the report should be sent to both the landlord and the tenant within 10 working days of the inspection. Either party can ask relevant questions of the expert.

(i) At annex D are flowcharts showing the time limits in the protocol.

*Urgent cases*

(j) The protocol does not prevent a tenant from instructing an expert at an earlier stage if this is considered necessary for reasons of urgency, and the landlord should give access in such cases. Appropriate cases may include:
  (i) where the tenant reasonably considers that there is a significant risk to health and safety;
  (ii) where the tenant is seeking an interim injunction;
  (iii) where it is necessary to preserve evidence.

*Access*

(k) Tenants must give reasonable access to the landlord for inspection and repair in line with the tenancy agreement. The landlord should give reasonable notice of the need for access, except in the case of an emergency. The landlord must give access to common parts as appropriate, e.g., for the inspection of a shared heating system.

*Costs*

(l) Terms of appointment should be agreed at the outset and should include:
  (i) the basis of the expert's charges (either daily or hourly rates and an estimate of the time likely to be required, or a fee for the services);
  (ii) any travelling expenses and other relevant expenses;
  (iii) rates for attendance at court should this become necessary, and provisions for payment on late notice of cancellation of a court hearing;
  (iv) time for delivery of report;
  (v) time for making payment;
  (vi) whether fees are to be paid by a third party; and

(vii) arrangements for dealing with questions for experts and discussions between experts and for providing for the cost involved.

(m) If a single joint expert is instructed, each party will pay one half of the cost of the report. If a joint inspection is carried out, each party will pay the full cost of the report from their own expert. (See para. 3.7.)

(n) The expert should send separately and directly to both parties answers to any questions asked.

### 3.7 Costs

(a) If the tenant's claim is settled without litigation on terms which justify bringing it, the landlord will pay the tenant's reasonable costs or out-of-pocket expenses. (See para. 4.10 for a definition of 'costs' and 'out-of-pocket expenses'.)

(b) Attached at annex F is a statement of costs form which can be used to inform the landlord of the costs of the claim.

## 4 GUIDANCE NOTES

### 4.1 Alternative Dispute Resolution

(a) The parties should consider whether some form of alternative dispute resolution procedure (see paragraph 4.10 for a definition of alternative dispute resolution) would be more suitable than litigation, and if so, endeavour to agree which form to adopt. Both the claimant and defendant may be required by the court to provide evidence that alternative means of resolving their dispute were considered. The courts take the view that litigation should be a last resort, and that claims should not be issued prematurely when a settlement is still actively being explored. Parties are warned that if the protocol is not followed (including this paragraph) then the court must have regard to such conduct when determining costs.

(b) It is not practicable in this protocol to address in detail how the parties might decide which method to adopt to resolve their particular dispute. However, summarised below are some of the options for resolving disputes without litigation:

- discussion and negotiation;
- early neutral evaluation by an independent third party (for example, a lawyer experienced in the field of housing disrepair or an individual experienced in the subject matter of the claim);
- mediation—a form of facilitated negotiation assisted by an independent neutral party;
- other options in respect of the following specific categories:

  (i) For council tenants:

  - local authority repairs, complaints and/or arbitration procedures.
  - the Right to Repair Scheme. The scheme is only suitable for small, urgent repairs of less than £250 in value.

    Information and leaflets about the scheme in England can be obtained from the Office of the Deputy Prime Minister, Eland House, Bressenden Place, London SW1E 5DU. Tel. 020 7944 3672.

    Information about the scheme in Wales can be obtained from the National Assembly for Wales, Cathays Park, Cardiff, CF10 3NQ. Tel. 029 2082 5111.
  - Commission for Local Administration in England. Tel. 0845 602 1983.
  - the Local Government Ombudsman for Wales. Tel. 01656 661325.

  (ii) For tenants of social landlords who are not council tenants, and for tenants of qualifying private landlords

  - In England, the Independent Housing Ombudsman. 3rd Floor, Norman House, 105–109 Strand, London WC2R 0AA. Tel. 020 7836 3630.

In Wales, the National Assembly for Wales, Cathays Park, Cardiff CF10 3NQ. Tel. 029 2082 5111.

- Local authority environmental health officers.

(iii) For private tenants:

- Local authority environmental health officers.

(c) The Legal Services Commission has published a booklet on 'Alternatives to Court', CLS Direct Information Leaflet 23 (http://www.clsdirect.org.uk/legalhelp/leaflet23.jsp), which lists a number of organisations that provide alternative dispute resolution services.

(d) It is expressly recognised that no party can or should be forced to mediate or enter into any form of ADR.

(e) Information about repair rights generally is available free of charge from the following web pages: <http://www.shelter.org.uk/housingadvice/index.asp> and <http://www.legalservices.gov.uk/leaflets/cls/index.htm>.

(f) The former Department for Transport, Local Government and the Regions issued *Good Practice Guidance on Housing Disrepair Legal Obligations* in January 2002. Copies of the Guidance (ISBN 185112 523X) can be obtained from ODPM Publications Sales Centre, Cambertown House, Goldthorpe Industrial Estate, Rotherham, S63 9BL. A summary, Housing Research Summary No. 154, is available free from the Housing Support Unit, ODPM, Zone 2/C6, Eland House, Bressenden Place, London SW1E 5DU (Fax 020 7944 4527). The ODPM housing website <http://www.housing.odpm.gov.uk> is a general source of information for landlords and tenants.

## 4.2 Scope of the Protocol

(a) This protocol is intended to apply to all civil law claims which include a claim for disrepair, but not to counterclaims or set-offs in disrepair claims which originate as other proceedings. (See para. 4.10 for an explanation of 'counterclaim' and 'set-off'.) In cases which involve a counterclaim or set-off, the landlord and tenant will still be expected to act reasonably in exchanging information and trying to settle the case at an early stage.

(b) In practice, most disrepair cases will have a value of more than £1,000 but less than £15,000 and so are likely to be allocated to the fast track if they come to court. (See para. 4.10 for an explanation of 'the fast track'.) The protocol is aimed at this type of case. The need to keep costs down is especially important in claims of lower value. The approach of the protocol is however, equally appropriate to all claims and the protocol should also be followed in small claims track and multi-track claims. (See para. 4.10 for an explanation of 'small claims track' and 'multi-track'.) The court will expect to see reasonable pre-action behaviour applied in all cases.

## 4.3 Early Notification Letter

(a) The early notification letter is not intended to replace the direct reporting of defects to the landlord at an early stage, using any procedure the landlord may have established. The protocol is for use in those cases where, despite the landlord's knowledge of the disrepair, the matter remains unresolved.

(b) It is recognised that disrepair cases can range from straightforward to highly complex, and that it is not always possible to obtain detailed information at an early stage. In order to avoid unnecessary delay and to ensure that notice of the claim is given to the landlord at the earliest possible opportunity, the protocol suggests the use of two letters in some cases; an early notification letter and a later letter of claim. (See para. 3.2(a) and annexes A and B.)

(c) A copy of the protocol need only be sent to the landlord if the tenant has reason to believe that the landlord will not have access to the protocol, e.g. because the landlord is an individual or small organisation. If in doubt, a copy should be sent.

## 4.4 Letters of Claim and Landlord's Response

(a) Letters of claim and a landlord's response are not intended to have the same status as a statement of case in court proceedings. Matters may come to light after the letter of claim has been sent, or after the landlord has responded, which could mean that the case of one or both parties is presented slightly differently than in the letters of claim or in the landlord's response. It would be inconsistent with the spirit of the protocol to seek to capitalise on this in the proceedings, provided that there was no intention to mislead. In particular, advantage should not be taken regarding discrepancies relating to the general details of notice given in the early notification letter.

(b) See para. 4.3(c) regarding the sending of a copy of the protocol by the tenant to the landlord.

*Cases with a personal injury element*

(c) Housing disrepair claims may contain a personal injury element. This should be set out in the letter of claim, as should a clear indication of the identities of all persons who plan to make a personal injury claim.

(d) There is also a Pre-action Protocol for Personal Injury Claims. This protocol should be followed for that part of the disrepair claim which forms a personal injury claim, unless it is insufficient to warrant separate procedures and would therefore be dealt with only as part of the disrepair claim and evidenced by a general practitioner's letter. The Pre-action Protocol for Personal Injury Claims should be followed for any claim which requires expert evidence other than a general practitioner's letter. If the disrepair claim is urgent, it would be reasonable to pursue separate disrepair and personal injury claims, which could then be case-managed or consolidated at a later date.

(e) Paragraph 3.3(a)(v) refers to the effect of the defects on 'the tenant'. This should be taken to include all persons who have a personal injury claim. The details of any such claim and of all likely claimants should be set out in the letter of claim.

## 4.5 Disclosure of Documents

(a) When giving disclosure, the landlord should copy all relevant documents. In housing disrepair claims, this includes any and all documents relating in particular to the disrepair and to notice given by the tenant to the landlord of the disrepair. Notice is often given by personal attendance at the landlord's office, and copies of any notes of meetings and oral discussions should also be copied, along with other relevant documents. Documents regarding rent arrears or tenants' disputes will not normally be relevant.

(b) The aim of the early disclosure of documents by the landlord is not to encourage 'fishing expeditions' by the tenant, but to promote an early exchange of relevant information to help in clarifying or resolving issues in dispute. The tenant should assist by identifying the particular categories of documents which they consider relevant.

(c) The 20 working days time limit specified in para. 3.5 runs from the date of receipt of either letter. Receipt of the letter is deemed to have taken place two days after the date of the letter. If necessary, a written request for extra time should be made by the landlord to the tenant. Should a case come to court, the court will decide whether the parties have acted reasonably, and whether any sanctions, including costs orders, are appropriate. The principles regarding time limits are referred to again at para. 4.7.

(d) Nothing in the protocol restricts the right of the tenant to look personally at their file or to request a copy of the whole file. Neither is the landlord prevented from sending to the tenant a copy of the whole file, should the landlord wish.

## 4.6 Experts

(a) Information about independent experts can be obtained from:
   (i) The Chartered Institute of Environmental Health, Chadwick Court, 15 Hatfields, London SE1 8DJ Tel: (020) 7928 6006. Ask for a copy of the Consultants and Trainers Directory.

(ii) The Law Society, 113 Chancery Lane, London WC2A 1PL, Tel: (020) 7831 0344. Refer to the Society's Expert Witness Directory.
(iii) The Royal Institution of Chartered Surveyors, 12 Great George Street, Parliament Square, London SW1P 3AD, Tel: 0845 304 4111. Ask for a copy of the relevant regional directory.

(b) The protocol encourages the use of a single joint expert. In order to make it less likely that a second expert will be necessary, the protocol provides for the landlord to forward their own instructions directly to the single joint expert if they cannot agree joint instructions. Both parties can ask relevant questions of the expert. If the parties cannot agree on a single joint expert, either with joint or separate instructions, the protocol suggests a joint inspection by each party's expert.
(c) The specimen letters at annexes A and B ask for reasons to be given as to why the landlord objects to the expert proposed by the tenant. Should a case come to court, it will be for the court to decide whether the parties have acted reasonably and whether the costs of more than one expert should be recoverable.
(d) Parties should bear in mind that it may not always be necessary to obtain expert evidence of disrepair, and in view of this, the protocol encourages the use of photos before and after works, and if appropriate, video evidence.
(e) Parties are reminded that the CPR provide that expert evidence should be restricted to that which is necessary and that the court's permission is required to use an expert's report. The court may limit the amount of experts' fees and expenses recoverable from another party.
(f) When instructing an expert, regard should be had to any approved Code of Guidance for Experts and whether a copy of the protocol should be sent to the expert.

### 4.7 Time Limits

(a) The timescales given in the protocol are longstops and every attempt should be made to comply with the protocol as soon as possible. If parties are able to comply earlier than the timescales provided, they should do so.
(b) Time limits in the protocol may be changed by agreement. However, it should always be borne in mind that the court will expect an explanation as to why the protocol has not been followed or has been varied and breaches of the protocol may lead to costs or other orders being made by the court.

### 4.8 Limitation Period

(a) In cases where the limitation period will shortly expire, the tenant should ask in the first letter for an extension of the limitation period. The extension requested should be only so long as is necessary to avoid the cost of starting court proceedings.
(b) It will be for the court to decide whether refusal to grant the request is reasonable and whether any sanctions, including costs orders, are appropriate.

### 4.9 Contact Point

Where a landlord is not an individual, a person should be designated to act as a point of contact for the tenant as soon as possible after the landlord receives the first letter from the tenant and (if one is involved) their solicitor. The appointee's name and contact details should be sent to the tenant and their solicitor as soon as possible after the appointment is made.

### 4.10 Glossary

**alternative dispute resolution**. Mediation, or other dispute resolution method, which seeks to settle disputes without the need for court proceedings.
**counterclaim**. A claim that either party makes in response to an initial claim by the other.
**costs**. Legal fees or, in a small track claim, out-of-pocket expenses incurred as a result of a claim. (See **out-of-pocket expenses** below.)

**damages.** Money obtained as the result of a claim to compensate for inconvenience and/or distress suffered because of the condition of the property. (See also **special damages** below.)

**defect/disrepair.** A fault or problem with a property, for which the landlord is responsible.

**disclosure.** The making available by one party to the other of documentation relevant to the claim.

**fast track/multi-track/small claims track.** Cases which proceed to court will be allocated to separate tracks depending on their value. The separate tracks have different rules and procedures. Housing cases worth between £1,000 and £15,000 where there is a claim for works to be done will usually be allocated to the **fast track.** Housing cases where the costs of the repairs and/or the damages do not exceed £1,000 will usually be dealt with on the **small claims track.** Cases over £15,000 will usually be allocated to the **multi-track.**

**joint inspection.** An inspection of a property carried out at the same time by one expert instructed by the tenant and by one expert instructed by the landlord.

**limitation period.** The time limit after which a legal action cannot be started. In most housing cases it is six years. In personal injury cases it is three years.

**litigation.** A court case or court proceedings. The taking of legal action by someone.

**notice.** Notification of a disrepair, either directly by the tenant in writing or orally to the landlord or his employee, or indirectly, by inspection of the property by the landlord or his employee.

**out-of-pocket expenses.** Expenses incurred in a small track claim as a result of the claim, such as loss of earnings and experts' fees.

**protocol.** A code or procedure—in this case for dealing with housing disrepair.

**set-off.** Where one party agrees with the other's claim or part of it, but sets up one which counterbalances it.

**single joint expert.** An expert who is instructed by both the tenant and the landlord, either with joint or separate instructions.

**special damages.** Compensation for loss of or damage to specific items, e.g., clothes, carpets, curtains, wallpaper, bedding or extra electricity costs.

**tenant.** Someone who rents land (including property) owned by another. (See also the definition at para. 3.1(c).)

**third party.** Someone other than the landlord or tenant.

**working days.** All days other than Saturdays, Sundays and bank holidays.

## 5 ANNEXES

### Specimen Letters

It will be noted that the attached specimen letters are in pairs for use by solicitors and by tenants acting in person respectively.

It is emphasised that they may be suitably adapted as appropriate.

The letters, with the paragraph of the protocol to which each one relates, are as follows:

Annex A early notification letter (see para. 3.2.).
Annex B letter of claim (see para. 3.3.).
  Note: There are two versions of this:
    (a) for use where an early notification letter has been sent;
    (b) for other cases.
Annex C letter of instruction to expert (see para. 3.6).
Annex D early notification letter flowchart.
Annex E special damages form.
Annex F statement of costs.
Annex G schedule.

## ANNEX A
## EARLY NOTIFICATION LETTER

### (i) Letter from Solicitor

To Landlord

Dear Sirs,

Re: *(tenant's name and address of property)*

We are instructed by your above-named tenant. *(Include a sentence stating how the case is being funded.)* We are using the Housing Disrepair Protocol. [We enclose a copy of the protocol for your information.*]

REPAIRS

Your tenant complains of the following defects at the property *(set out nature of defects)*.

[We enclose a schedule, which sets out the disrepair in each room.*]

You received notice of the defects as follows: *(list details of notice relied on)*.

Please arrange to inspect the property as soon as possible. Access will be available on the following dates and times: *(list dates and times as appropriate)*

Please let us know what repairs you propose to carry out and the anticipated date for completion of the works.

DISCLOSURE

Please also provide within 20 working days of receipt of this letter, the following:

All relevant records or documents including:
(i) copy of tenancy agreement including tenancy conditions;
(ii) documents or computerised records relating to notice given, disrepair, reported, inspection reports or repair works to the property.

We enclose a signed authority from our clients for you to release this information to ourselves.

We also enclose copies of the following relevant documents from our client: *(list documents enclosed)*

EXPERT

If agreement is not reached about the carrying out of repairs within 20 working days of this letter, we propose to jointly instruct a single joint expert *(insert expert's name and address)* to carry out an inspection of the property and provide a report. We enclose a copy of their CV, plus a draft letter of instruction. Please let us know if you agree to his/her appointment. If you object, please let us know your reasons within 20 working days.

If you do not object to the expert being instructed as a single joint expert, but wish to provide your own instructions, you should send those directly to *(insert expert's name)* within 20 working days of this letter. Please send to ourselves a copy of your letter of instruction. If you do not agree to a single joint expert, we will instruct *(insert expert's name)* to inspect the property in any event. In those circumstances, if you wish to instruct your expert to attend at the same time, please let ourselves and *(insert expert's name)* know within 20 working days of this letter.

CLAIM

Our client's disrepair claim requires further investigation. We will write to you as soon as possible with further details of the history of the defects and of notice relied on, along with details of our client's claim for general and special damages.

Yours faithfully,

---

* Delete as appropriate.

### (ii) Letter from Tenant

To Landlord

Dear

Re: *(your name and address of property)*

I write regarding disrepair at the above address. I am using the Housing Disrepair Protocol. [I enclose a copy of the protocol for your information.*]

REPAIRS

The following defects exist at the property *(set out nature of defects).*

[I enclose a schedule which sets out the disrepair in each room.*]

Please arrange to inspect the property as soon as possible. Access will be available on the following dates and times: *(list dates and time as appropriate)*

You received notice of the defects as follows: *(list details of notice relied on).*

Please let me know what repairs you propose to carry out and the anticipated date for completion of the works.

DISCLOSURE

Please also provide within 20 working days of receipt of this letter, the following:

All relevant records or documents including:
(i) copy of tenancy agreement including tenancy conditions;
(ii) documents or computerised records relating to notice given, disrepair reported, inspection reports or repair works to the property.

I also enclose copies of the following relevant documents: *(list documents enclosed)*

EXPERT

If agreement is not reached about the carrying out of repairs within 20 working days, I propose that we jointly instruct a single joint expert *(insert expert's name and address)* to carry out an inspection of the property and provide a report. I enclose a copy of their CV, plus a draft letter of instruction. Please let me know if you agree to his/her appointment. If you object, please let me know your reasons within 20 working days.

If you do not object to the expert being appointed as a single joint expert but wish to provide your own instructions, you should send those directly to *(insert expert's name)* within 20 working days. Please send a copy of your letter of instruction to me. If you do not agree to a single joint expert I will instruct *(insert expert's name)* to inspect the property in any event. In those circumstances if you wish your expert to attend at the same time, please let me and *(insert expert's name)* know within 20 working days.

CLAIM

I will write to you as soon as possible with further details of the history of the defects and of notice relied on, along with details of my claim for general and special damages.

Yours sincerely

* Delete as appropriate.

# ANNEX B

# LETTER OF CLAIM

## (a) For Use Where an Early Notification Letter Has Been Sent (As Set Out In Annex A)

### (i) Letter from Solicitor

To Landlord

Dear Sirs,

Re: *(tenant's name and address of property)*

We write further to our letter of *(insert date)* regarding our client's housing disrepair claim. We have now taken full instructions from our client.

REPAIRS

The history of the disrepair is as follows: *(set out history of defects).*

[I enclose a schedule which sets out the disrepair in each room.*]

You received notice of the defects as follows: *(list details of notice relied on).*

The defects at the property are causing *(set out the effects of the disrepair on the client and their family, including any personal injury element; specify if there will be any additional claimant).*

Please forward to us within 20 working days of receipt of this letter a full schedule of works together with the anticipated date for completion of the works proposed.

CLAIM

We take the view that you are in breach of your repairing obligations. Please provide us with your proposals for compensation. *(Alternatively, set out suggestions for general damages, e.g., £x for x years).* [Our client also requires compensation for special damages, and we attach a schedule of the special damages claimed.*]

Yours faithfully,

### (ii) Letter from Tenant

To Landlord

Dear

Re: *(your name and address of property)*

I write further to my letter of *(insert date)* regarding my housing disrepair claim. I am now able to provide you with further details.

REPAIRS

The history of the disrepair is as follows: *(set out history of defects).*

You received notice of the defects as follows: *(list details of notice relied on).*

The defects at the property are causing *(set out the effects of the disrepair on you and your family, including any personal injury element; specify if there will be any additional claimant).*

Please forward to me within 20 working days of receipt of this letter a full schedule of works together with the anticipated date for completion of the works proposed.

CLAIM

I take the view that you are in breach of your repairing obligations. Please provide me with

* Delete as appropriate.

your proposals for compensation. *(Alternatively, set out suggestions for general damages, e.g., £x for x years).* [I also require compensation for special damages, and I attach a schedule of the special damages claimed.*]

Yours sincerely,

### (b) For Use Where an Early Notification Letter Has Not Been Sent

#### (i) Letter from Solicitor

To Landlord

Dear Sirs,

Re: *(tenant's name and address of property)*

We are instructed by your above-named tenant. *(Insert a sentence stating how the case is being funded.)* We are using the Housing Disrepair Protocol. [We enclose a copy of the protocol for your information.*]

REPAIRS

Your tenant complains of the following defects at the property: *(set out nature and history of defects).*

[We enclose a schedule which sets out the disrepair in each room.*]

You received notice of the defects as follows: *(list details of notice relied on).*

The defects at the property are causing *(set out the effects of the disrepair on the client and their family, including any personal injury element, specifying if there are any additional claimants).*

Please provide within 20 working days of receipt of this letter a full schedule of the works you propose to carry out to remedy the above defects and the anticipated date for completion of the works.

DISCLOSURE

Please also provide within 20 working days of this letter the following:

All relevant records or documents including:

(i) copy of tenancy agreement including tenancy conditions;
(ii) tenancy file;
(iii) documents relating to notice given, disrepair reported, inspection reports or repair works to the property;
(iv) computerised records.

We enclose a signed authority from our clients for you to release this information to ourselves.

We also enclose copies of the following relevant documents: *(list documents enclosed)*

EXPERT

If agreement is not reached about the carrying out of repairs within 20 working days of receipt of this letter, we propose to jointly instruct a single joint expert *(insert expert's name and address)* to carry out an inspection of the property and provide a report. We enclose a copy of their CV, plus a draft letter of instruction. Please let me know if you agree to his/her appointment. If you object, please let me know your reasons within 20 working days.

If you do not object to the expert being instructed a single joint expert, but wish to provide your own instructions, you should send those directly to *(insert expert's name)* within 20 working days. Please send a copy of your letter of instruction to ourselves. If you do not agree to a single joint expert, we will instruct *(insert expert's name)* to inspect the property in any event. In those circumstances, if you wish to instruct your expert to attend at the same time please let ourselves and *(insert expert's name)* know within 20 working days.

* Delete as appropriate.

CLAIM

We take the view that you are in breach of your repairing obligations. Please provide us with your proposals for compensation. *(Alternatively, set out suggestions for general damages, e.g., £x for x years.)* [Our client also requires compensation for the special damages, and we attach a schedule of the special damages claimed.*]

Yours faithfully,

### (ii) Letter from Tenant

To Landlord

Dear

Re: *(your name and address of property)*

I write regarding the disrepair at the above address. I am using the Housing Disrepair Protocol. [I enclose a copy of the protocol for your information.*]

REPAIRS

The property has the following defects: *(set out nature and history of defects).*

[I enclose a schedule which sets out the disrepair in each room.*]

You received notice of the defects as follows: *(list details of notice relied on).*

The defects at the property are causing *(set out the effects of the disrepair on you and your family, including any personal injury element, specifying if there are any additional claimants).*

Please provide within 20 working days of receipt of this letter a full schedule of the works you propose to carry out to remedy the above defects and the anticipated date for completion of the works.

DISCLOSURE

Please also provide within 20 working days of receipt of this letter the following:

All relevant records or documents including:
(i) copy of tenancy agreement including tenancy conditions;
(ii) tenancy file;
(iii) documents relating to notice given, disrepair reported, inspection reports or repair works to the property;
(iv) computerised records.

I also enclose copies of the following relevant documents: *(list documents enclosed).*

EXPERT

If agreement is not reached about the carrying out of repairs within 20 working days of receipt of this letter, I propose that we jointly instruct a single joint expert *(insert expert's name and address)* to carry out an inspection of the property and provide a report. I enclose a copy of their CV, plus a draft letter of instruction. Please let me know if you agree to his/her appointment. If you object, please let me know your reasons within 20 working days.

If you do not object to the expert being instructed as a single joint expert, but wish to provide your own instructions, you should send those directly to *(insert expert's name)* within 20 working days. Please also send a copy of the letter of instruction to me. If you do not agree to a single joint expert, I will instruct *(insert expert's name)* to inspect the property in any event. In those circumstances, if you wish to instruct your expert to attend at the same time please let me and *(insert expert's name)* know within 20 working days.

* Delete as appropriate.

CLAIM

I take the view that you are in breach of your repairing obligations. Please provide me with your proposals for compensation. *(Alternatively, set out suggestions for general damages, e.g. £x for x years.)* [I also require compensation for special damages, and I attach a schedule of the special damages claimed.*]

Yours sincerely

## ANNEX C
## LETTER OF INSTRUCTION TO EXPERT

### (i) Letter from Solicitor

Dear

Re: *(tenant's name and address of property)*

We act for the above-named in connection with a housing disrepair claim at the above property. We are using the Housing Disrepair Protocol. [We enclose a copy of the Protocol for your information.*]

Please carry out an inspection of the above property by (*date*†) and provide a report covering the following points:

(a) whether you agree that the defects are as claimed;
(b) whether any of the defects is structural;
(c) the cause of the defect(s);
(d) the age, character and prospective life of the property.

Access will be available on the following dates and times: *(list dates and times as appropriate)*

[You are instructed as a single joint expert.] [The landlord is *(landlord's name and details)*.] [The landlord will be providing you with their own instructions direct.] [The landlord will contact you to confirm that their expert will attend at the same time as you to carry out a joint inspection.]*

Please provide the report within 10 working days of the inspection. Please contact us immediately if there are any works which require an interim injunction.

If the case proceeds to court, the report may be used in evidence. In order to comply with court rules we would be grateful if you would insert above your signature a statement that the contents are true to the best of your knowledge and belief. We refer you to Part 35 of the Civil Procedure Rules which specifies experts' responsibilities, the contents of any report, and the statements experts must sign.

*(Insert details as to cost and payment.)*

Yours sincerely

### (ii) Letter from Tenant

Dear

Re: *(your name and address of property)*

I am currently in dispute with my landlord about disrepair at the above property. I am using the Housing Disrepair Protocol. [I enclose a copy of the protocol for your information.*]

Please carry out an inspection of the above property by (*date*†) and provide a report covering the following points:

(a) whether you agree that the defects are as claimed;

* Delete as appropriate.

† The date to be inserted should be 20 working days from the date of the letter, in accordance with para. 3.6(f) of the protocol.

(b) whether any of the defects is structural;
(c) the cause of the defect(s);
(d) the age, character and prospective life of the property.

Access will be available on the following dates and times: *(list dates and times as appropriate).* [You are instructed as a single joint expert.] [The landlord is *(landlord's name and details).*] [The landlord will be providing you with their own instructions direct.] [The landlord will contact you to confirm that their expert will attend at the same time as you to carry out a joint inspection.]*

Please provide the report within 10 working days of the inspection. Please contact me immediately if there are any works which require an interim injunction.

If the case proceeds to court, the report may be used in evidence. In order to comply with court rules I would be grateful if you would insert above your signature a statement that the contents are true to the best of your knowledge and belief. I refer you to Part 35 of the Civil Procedure Rules which specifies experts' responsibilities, the contents of any report, and the statements experts must sign.

*(Insert details as to cost and payment.)*

Yours sincerely

* Delete as appropriate.

## ANNEX D
## EARLY NOTIFICATION LETTER FLOWCHART

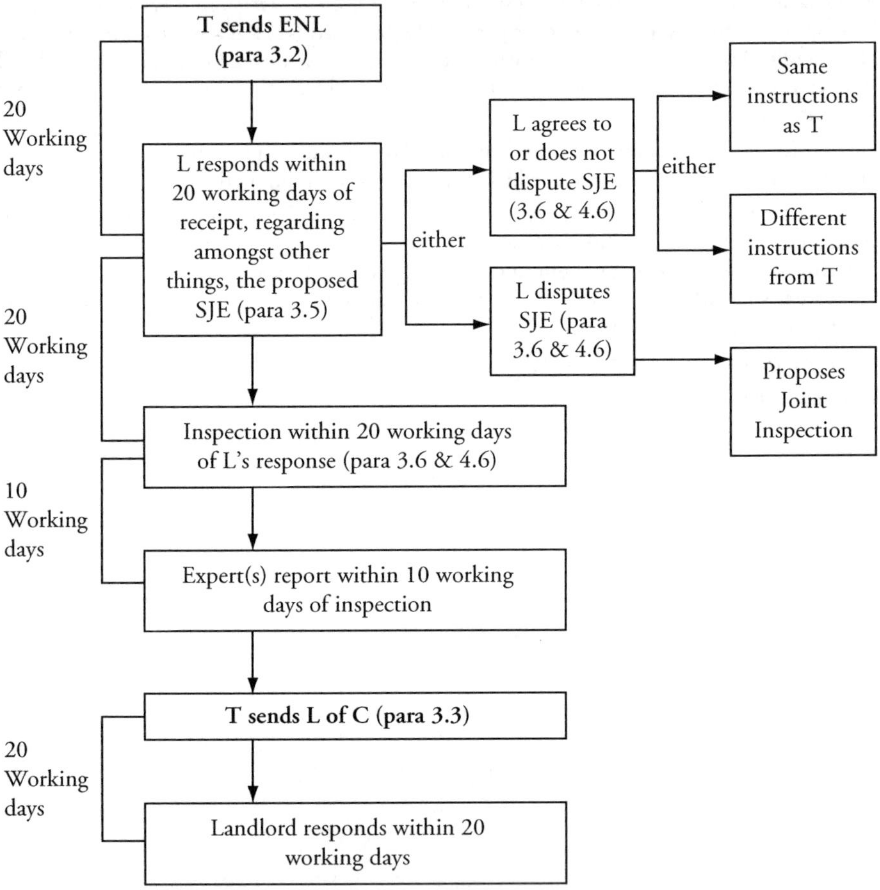


## ANNEX E
## SPECIAL DAMAGES FORM

| | ITEM | DATE PURCHASED | WHERE PURCHASED | PRICE | RECEIPTS—YES/NO | HOW DAMAGED |
|---|---|---|---|---|---|---|
| 1 | | | | | | |
| 2 | | | | | | |
| 3 | | | | | | |
| 4 | | | | | | |
| 5 | | | | | | |
| 6 | | | | | | |
| 7 | | | | | | |
| 8 | | | | | | |
| 9 | | | | | | |
| 10 | | | | | | |

## ANNEX F
## STATEMENT OF COSTS

Annex F is not reproduced here, because it is form N260, which may be accessed via the DCA website at <http://www.dca.gov.uk>.

## ANNEX G
## SCHEDULE

**Schedule**
**Disrepair Protocol**

**TENANT**

| | Item Number | Room (tick where appropriate) | Disrepair (Identify briefly) | Notice given (How was the landlord made aware of the problem) | Inconvenience suffered (How has the disrepair affected you) |
|---|---|---|---|---|---|
| Exterior of premises, roof and access<br>Comment: | | | | | |
| Entrance, hall and storage<br>Comment: | | | | | |
| Living room (s)<br>Comment: | | | | | |
| Kitchen<br>Comment: | | | | | |
| Bathroom<br>Comment: | | | | | |
| Bedroom 1<br>Comment: | | | | | |
| Bedroom 2<br>Comment: | | | | | |
| Bedroom 3<br>Comment: | | | | | |
| Other<br>Comment | | | | | |

# Pre-action Protocol for Possession Claims Based on Rent Arrears

## Aims and Scope of the Protocol

This protocol applies to residential possession claims by social landlords (such as local authorities, Registered Social Landlords and Housing Action Trusts) which are based solely on claims for rent arrears. The protocol does not apply to claims in respect of long leases or to claims for possession where there is no security of tenure.

The protocol reflects the guidance on good practice given to social landlords in the collection of rent arrears. It recognises that it is in the interests of both landlords and tenants to ensure that rent is paid promptly and to ensure that difficulties are resolved wherever possible without court proceedings.

Its aim is to encourage more pre-action contact between landlords and tenants and to enable court time to be used more effectively.

Courts should take into account whether this protocol has been followed when considering what orders to make. Registered Social Landlords and local authorities should also comply with guidance issued from time to time by the Housing Corporation and the Department for Communities and Local Government.

## Initial Contact

1. The landlord should contact the tenant as soon as reasonably possible if the tenant falls into arrears to discuss the cause of the arrears, the tenant's financial circumstances, the tenant's entitlement to benefits and repayment of the arrears. Where contact is by letter, the landlord should write separately to each named tenant.
2. The landlord and tenant should try to agree affordable sums for the tenant to pay towards arrears, based upon the tenant's income and expenditure (where such information has been supplied in response to the landlord's enquiries). The landlord should clearly set out in pre-action correspondence any time limits with which the tenant should comply.
3. The landlord should provide, on a quarterly basis, rent statements in a comprehensible format showing rent due and sums received for the past 13 weeks. The landlord should, upon request, provide the tenant with copies of rent statements in a comprehensible format from the date when arrears first arose showing all amounts of rent due, the dates and amounts of all payments made, whether through housing benefit or by the tenant, and a running total of the arrears.
4. (a) If the landlord is aware that the tenant has difficulty in reading or understanding information given, the landlord should take reasonable steps to ensure that the tenant understands any information given. The landlord should be able to demonstrate that reasonable steps have been taken to ensure that the information has been appropriately communicated in ways that the tenant can understand.
   (b) If the landlord is aware that the tenant is under 18 or is particularly vulnerable, the landlord should consider at an early stage—
      (i) whether or not the tenant has the mental capacity to defend possession proceedings and, if not, make an application for the appointment of a litigation friend in accordance with CPR 21;
      (ii) whether or not any issues arise under Disability Discrimination Act 1995; and
      (iii) in the case of a local authority landlord, whether or not there is a need for a community care assessment in accordance with National Health Service and Community Care Act 1990.
5. If the tenant meets the appropriate criteria, the landlord should arrange for arrears to be paid by the Department for Work and Pensions from the tenant's benefit.

6. The landlord should offer to assist the tenant in any claim the tenant may have for housing benefit.
7. Possession proceedings for rent arrears should not be started against a tenant who can demonstrate that he has—
   (a) provided the local authority with all the evidence required to process a housing benefit claim;
   (b) a reasonable expectation of eligibility for housing benefit; and
   (c) paid other sums due not covered by housing benefit.

The landlord should make every effort to establish effective ongoing liaison with housing benefit departments and, with the tenant's consent, make direct contact with the relevant housing benefit department before taking enforcement action.

The landlord and tenant should work together to resolve any housing benefit problems.

8. Bearing in mind that rent arrears may be part of a general debt problem, the landlord should advise the tenant to seek assistance from CAB, debt advice agencies or other appropriate agencies as soon as possible.

## After Service of Statutory Notices

9. After service of a statutory notice but before the issue of proceedings, the landlord should make reasonable attempts to contact the tenant, to discuss the amount of the arrears, the cause of the arrears, repayment of the arrears and the housing benefit position.
10. If the tenant complies with an agreement to pay the current rent and a reasonable amount towards arrears, the landlord should agree to postpone court proceedings so long as the tenant keeps to such agreement. If the tenant ceases to comply with such agreement, the landlord should warn the tenant of the intention to bring proceedings and give the tenant clear time limits within which to comply.

## Alternative Dispute Resolution

11. The parties should consider whether it is possible to resolve the issues between them by discussion and negotiation without recourse to litigation. The parties may be required by the court to provide evidence that alternative means of resolving the dispute were considered. Courts take the view that litigation should be a last resort, and that claims should not be issued prematurely when a settlement is still actively being explored.

The Legal Services Commission has published a booklet on 'Alternatives to Court', CLS Direct Information Leaflet 23 (<http://www.clsdirect.org.uk/legalhelp/leaflet23.jsp>), which lists a number of organisations that provide alternative dispute resolution services.

## Court Proceedings

12. Not later than ten days before the date set for the hearing, the landlord should—
    (a) provide the tenant with up to date rent statements;
    (b) disclose what knowledge he possesses of the tenant's housing benefit position to the tenant.
13. (a) The landlord should inform the tenant of the date and time of any court hearing and the order applied for. The landlord should advise the tenant to attend the hearing as the tenant's home is at risk. Records of such advice should be kept.
    (b) If the tenant complies with an agreement made after the issue of proceedings to pay the current rent and a reasonable amount towards arrears, the landlord should agree to postpone court proceedings so long as the tenant keeps to such agreement.
    (c) If the tenant ceases to comply with such agreement, the landlord should warn the tenant of the intention to restore the proceedings and give the tenant clear time limits within which to comply.
14. If the landlord unreasonably fails to comply with the terms of the protocol, the court may impose one or more of the following sanctions—
    (a) an order for costs;

(b) in cases other than those brought solely on mandatory grounds, adjourn, strike out or dismiss claims.

15. If the tenant unreasonably fails to comply with the terms of the protocol, the court may take such failure into account when considering whether it is reasonable to make possession orders.

# Appendix

# FORMS

# Claim Form

| In the |
|---|
| |

| | for court use only |
|---|---|
| Claim No. | |
| Issue date | |

Claimant

SEAL

Defendant(s)

Brief details of claim

Value

Defendant's name and address

| | £ |
|---|---|
| Amount claimed | |
| Court fee | |
| Solicitor's costs | |
| Total amount | |

The court office at

is open between 10 am and 4 pm Monday to Friday. When corresponding with the court, please address forms or letters to the Court Manager and quote the claim number.

**N1** Claim form (CPR Part 7) (01.02) *Printed on behalf of The Court Service*

| Claim No. | |
|---|---|

Does, or will, your claim include any issues under the Human Rights Act 1998? ☐ Yes ☐ No

Particulars of Claim (attached)(to follow)

Statement of Truth
*(I believe)(The Claimant believes) that the facts stated in these particulars of claim are true.
* I am duly authorised by the claimant to sign this statement

Full name ______________________________

Name of claimant's solicitor's firm ______________________________

signed ______________________ position or office held ______________________
*(Claimant)(Litigation friend)(Claimant's solicitor) (if signing on behalf of firm or company)

*delete as appropriate*

Claimant's or claimant's solicitor's address to which documents or payments should be sent if different from overleaf including (if appropriate) details of DX, fax or e-mail.

# Part 23 Application Notice (N244)

## Application Notice

**You should provide this information for listing the application**

1. How do you wish to have your application dealt with
   - a) at a hearing? ☐ } *complete all questions below*
   - b) at a telephone conference? ☐ }
   - c) without a hearing? ☐ *complete Qs 5 and 6 below*
2. Give a time estimate for the hearing/conference
   _________(hours)_____(mins)
3. Is this agreed by all parties? ☐ Yes ☐ No
4. Give dates of any trial period or fixed trial date ______________
5. Level of judge ______________
6. Parties to be served ______________

| In the | |
|---|---|
| **Claim no.** | |
| **Warrant no.** (If applicable) | |
| **Claimant** (including ref.) | |
| **Defendant(s)** (including ref.) | |
| **Date** | |

**Note** You must complete Parts A **and** B, **and** Part C if applicable. Send any relevant fee and the completed application to the court with any draft order, witness statement or other evidence; and sufficient copies for service on each respondent.

**Part A**

1. Enter your full name, or name of solicitor

I (We)(1) (on behalf of)(the claimant)(the defendant)

2. State clearly what order you are seeking and if possible attach a draft

intend to apply for an order ( a draft of which is attached) that(2)

because(3)

3. Briefly set out why you are seeking the order. Include the material facts on which you rely, identifying any rule or statutory provision

**Part B**

I (We) wish to rely on: *tick one box*

the attached (witness statement)(affidavit) ☐ my statement of case ☐

evidence in Part C in support of my application ☐

4. If you are not already a party to the proceedings, you must provide an address for service of documents

**Signed** ______________ **Position or office held** ______________

(Applicant)('s Solicitor)('s litigation friend) (if signing on behalf of firm or company)

Address to which documents about this claim should be sent (including reference if appropriate)(4)

| | if applicable |
|---|---|
| | fax no. |
| | DX no. |
| Tel. no. Postcode | e-mail |

The court office at

is open from 10am to 4pm Monday to Friday. When corresponding with the court please address forms or letters to the Court Manager and quote the claim number.

**N244** Application Notice (4.00) *Printed on behalf of The Court Service*

**Part C**

Claim No.

I (We) wish to rely on the following evidence in support of this application:

**Statement of Truth**

*(I believe) *(The applicant believes) that the facts stated in Part C are true

**delete as appropriate*

**Signed**

(Applicant)('s Solicitor)('s litigation friend)

**Position or office held**

(if signing on behalf of firm or company)

**Date**

# SD Pro-forma Order (PF52)

**PF 52**
**Order for case management directions in the multi-track (Part 29)**

**IN THE HIGH COURT OF JUSTICE**
**QUEEN'S BENCH DIVISION**

**Claim No.**

**Before** [sitting in Private]

**Claimant**

**Defendant**

**An Application** was made by application letter dated *or* by Solicitor for and was attended by

**The Master** [**District Judge**] read the written evidence filed

**[The parties** having agreed the directions set out in paragraph(s) below which are made by consent],

**IT IS ORDERED** that:

1. ALLOCATION
the case be allocated to the multi-track.

2. TRANSFER
(1) the claim be transferred to;
(a) the Division of the High Court,
(b) the District Registry [Mercantile List], or
(c) the County Court [Chancery List][Business List],
(2) the issue(s) be transferred to the County Court [Chancery List][Business List] for determination.
(3) the apply by to a Judge of the Technology and Construction Court [or other Specialist List] for an order to transfer the claim to that court.

(4) the claim commenced in the County Court be transferred from that court to the Queen's Bench Division of the High Court.

3. ALTERNATIVE DISPUTE RESOLUTION
the claim be stayed until while the parties try to settle it by mediation or other means. [The parties shall notify the Court in writing at the end of that period whether settlement has or has not been reached, and shall submit a draft consent order of any settlement]. The claim will be listed on for the court to make further directions unless;

(a) the claim has been settled and the claimant advises the court of the settlement in writing and files a draft consent order, or
(b) the parties apply not later than 3 days before the hearing for further directions without a hearing, or
(c) the parties apply for an extension of the stay and the extension is granted, upon which the hearing will be relisted on the date to which the extension is granted.

4. PROBATE CASES ONLY
the Defendant file his witness statement or affidavit of testamentary scripts and lodge any testamentary script at Room TM7.09 Thomas More Building, Royal Courts of Justice, Strand WC2A 2LL [ District Registry/ County Court, at ] by

5. CASE SUMMARY
the by prepare and serve a Case Summary [not exceeding words] on all other parties, to be agreed by and filed by and if it is not agreed the parties by that date file their own Case Summaries.

6. CASE MANAGEMENT CONFERENCE etc.

[*(a)* there be a [further] Case Management Conference/Listing Hearing before the Master/District Judge in [Court/Room No ] [[Thomas More Building] Royal Courts of Justice][ Court (trial centre)] on at of hours/minutes duration.] *or*

[*(b)* there be a Case Management Conference/Listing Hearing of hours/minutes duration. In order for the Court to fix a date the parties are to complete the accompanying questionnaire and file it by .] *or*

[*(c)* the apply for an appointment for a [further] Case Management Conference/Listing Hearing by .]

At the Case Management Conference, except for urgent matters in the meantime, the Court will hear any further applications for Directions or Orders and any party must file an Application Notice for any such Directions or Orders and serve it and supporting evidence (if any) by .

7. AMENDMENTS TO STATEMENTS OF CASE
(1) the has permission to amend his statement of case in accordance with the attached draft initialled by the District Judge
(2) the amended statement of case be verified by a statement of truth.
(3) the amended statement of case be filed by
(4) the amended statement of case be served by *or* service of the amended statement of case be dispensed with.
(5) any consequential amendments to other statements of case be filed and served by
(6) the costs of and caused by the amendment to the statement of case be in any event *or* are assessed in the sum of £ and are to be paid by

8. ADDITION OF PARTIES
(1) the has permission;
(a) to substitute as a ,and
(b) to amend his statement of case in accordance with the attached draft initialled by the District Judge
(2) the amended statement of case be verified by a statement of truth.
(3) the amended statement of case be;
(a) filed by and
(b) served on by
(4) a copy of this order be served on by
(5) any consequential amendments to other statements of case be filed and served by
(6) the costs of and caused by the amendment to the statement of case be in any event *or* are assessed in the sum of £ and are to be paid by

9. CONSOLIDATION
this claim be consolidated with claim number ,the lead claim to be claim number . [The title to the consolidated case shall be as set out in the Schedule to this order.]

10. TRIAL OF ISSUE
the issue of be tried as follows;
(1) with the consent of the parties, before a Master
(a) on in Room at the Royal Courts of Justice,
(b) with an estimated length of hearing hours,
(c) with the filing of listing questionnaires dispensed with,

*or*

(2) before a Judge

(a) with the trial of the issue to take place within after ("the trial window")

(b) with the to apply to the Clerk of the Lists at Room W15 by for a trial date within the trial window

(c) with the issue

(i) to be entered in the General List category "A" "B" or "C", with a time estimate of ,and

(ii) to take place in London

[(d) the filing of listing questionnaires be dispensed with [unless directed by the Clerk of the Lists] *or* each party file his completed listing questionnaire by ], *or*

(3) before a [District Judge, with the consent of the parties] [Circuit Judge] [High Court Judge] [listing category [A][B][C]], at a hearing details of which [accompany this order][will be sent shortly] with an estimated length of hearing hours.

11. FURTHER INFORMATION

(1) the provide by the clarification sought in the Request dated attached and initialled by the District Judge

(2) any request for clarification ɔe served by

12. DISCLOSURE OF DOCUMENTS

(1) no disclosure is required.

(2) each party give by standard disclosure to every other party by list [by categories].

(3) the give specific disclosure of documents [limited to the issues of ] described in the Schedule to this order [initialled by the Master/District Judge] by list [by categories] by

(4) the give by standard disclosure by list [by categories] to of documents limited to the issue(s) of by list.

13. INSPECTION OF DOCUMENTS

Any requests for inspection or copies of disclosed documents shall be made within days after service of the list.

14. PRESERVATION OF PROPERTY

the preserve until trial of the claim or further order *or other remedy under rule 25.1(1).*

15. WITNESS STATEMENTS

(1) each party serve on every other party the witness statement of the oral evidence which the party serving the statement intends to rely on in relation to [any issues of fact][the following issues of fact ] to be decided at the trial, those statements and any Notices of intention to rely on hearsay evidence to be

(a) exchanged by *or*

(b) served by by and by by

(2) the has permission to serve a witness summary relating to the evidence of of on every other party by

16. NO EXPERT EVIDENCE

(1) no expert evidence being necessary, [no party has permission to call or rely on expert evidence][permission to call or rely on expert evidence is refused].

17. SINGLE EXPERT

(1) evidence be given by the report of a single expert in the field of ,instructed jointly by the parties, on the issue of [and his fees shall be limited to £ ].

(2) the claimant advise the court in writing by whether or not the single expert has been instructed.

(3) if the parties are unable to agree [by that date] who that expert is to be and about the payment of his fees any party may apply for further directions.

(4) unless the parties agree in writing or the court orders otherwise, the fees and expenses of the single expert shall be paid to him [by the parties equally](*or as ordered*).

(5) each party give his instructions to the single expert by

(6) the report of the single expert be filed by

(7) the evidence of the expert be given at the trial by written report/oral evidence of the expert.

18. SEPARATE EXPERTS

[(1) each party has permission to adduce [oral] expert evidence in the field of [limited to expert(s) [per party] [on each side]].

(2) the experts reports shall be exchanged by

(3) the experts shall hold a discussion for the purpose of:

(a) identifying the issues, if any, between them; and

(b) where possible, reaching agreement on those issues.

(4) the experts shall by prepare and file a statement for the Court showing:

(a) those issues on which they did agree; and

(b) those issues on which they disagree and a summary of their reasons for disagreeing.

(5) no party shall be entitled to recover by way of costs from any other party more than £ for the fees or expenses of an expert.]

*or*

[(1) the parties have permission to rely on expert evidence as follows:

| Party | Identity of Expert | Field of Expertise | Issue to be addressed |
| --- | --- | --- | --- |
| Claimant | | | |
| Defendant | | | |
| (*other parties*) | | | |
| | | | |
| | | | |
| | | | |
| | | | |

(2) the number of expert witnesses in each field be limited to for the and to for the .

[(3) the amount of the fees and expenses of the experts in the field[s] of that the may recover from the be limited to £ .

(4) the experts in the field(s) of prepare reports which are to be served as follows:

(a) by simultaneous exchange by

(b) by by and by by

(5) the reports be agreed if possible by .

(6) (a) if the reports are not agreed by that date, then the experts in the same field(s) shall, by seek to identify, by "without prejudice" discussion, the issues between them and, where possible, to reach agreement on all/any issue(s),

(b) the experts shall by prepare and file a statement showing those issues on which they are agreed, those issues on which they disagree and a summary of their reasons for disagreeing.

(7) the expert evidence relied on by the in the field of be given at the trial by written report(s)/written summary of agreement/oral evidence of the expert(s).

(8) no party shall be entitled to recover by way of costs from any other party more than £ for the fees or expenses of an expert.]

19. TRIAL AND LISTING QUESTIONNAIRES

(1) (a) the trial of the claim/issue(s) take place [within after ][between and ("the trial window").

(b) the make an appointment to attend on the Clerk of the Lists/Listing Officer at Room [W14][W15] in order to fix a trial date within the trial window, such appointment to be [within 14 days after][on] [not later than] and give notice of the appointment to all other parties.

(c) the claim
(i) be entered in the General List category "A" "B" or "C", with a time estimate of ,and
(ii) take place in London , *or*

(2) (a) Trial Date - the trial take place on a date to be fixed , a Notice of Hearing will be sent shortly at a venue to be notified *or*
(b) Trial Window - the trial take place during the period beginning on and ending on at a venue to be notified,
(c) the present estimate of the time to be allowed for the trial is

(3) Listing Questionnaires -
[(a) the filing of listing questionnaires be dispensed with [unless directed by the Clerk of the Lists/Listing Officer]], *or*
[(b) each party file his completed listing questionnaire by 4.00pm on ],

(4) the parties inform the Court forthwith of any change in the trial time estimate.

20. PRE TRIAL REVIEW
[[The trial being estimated to last more than 10 days], There be a Pre Trial Review on a date to be arranged by the Clerk of the Lists/Listing Officer in Room [W14][W15]] [there be a Pre-Trial Review on at ] before the Judge at the Court at which, except for urgent matters in the meantime, the Court will hear any further applications for Directions or Orders.

21. DEFINITION AND REDUCTION OF ISSUES
by the parties list and discuss the issues in the claim [including the experts' reports and statements] and attempt to define and narrow the issues [including those issues the subject of discussion by the experts].

22. TRIAL BUNDLE
The parties agree and file a trial bundle and exchange and file skeleton arguments and chronologies not more than 7 and not less than 3 days before the start of the trial.

23. TRIAL TIMETABLE (*only for use at final CMC or PTR*)
(1) the parties agree a timetable for the trial, subject to the approval of the trial Judge, and file it with the trial bundle.
(2) subject to the approval of the trial Judge, the timetable for the trial will be:
(a) opening speeches to last no more than minutes,
(b) the statements served stand as the evidence in chief of the Claimants' witnesses of fact who are to give evidence on the [first] morning/afternoon/day of the trial,

(c) the statements served stand as the evidence in chief of the Defendants' witnesses of fact who are to give evidence on the morning/afternoon/day of the trial,
(d) the reports of the experts served stand as their evidence in chief and the experts in the field(s) of give oral evidence on the morning /afternoon/day of the trial,
(e) closing submissions be made on the morning /afternoon/day of the trial.

24. SETTLEMENT
If the claim or part of the claim is settled the parties must immediately inform the Court, whether or not it is then possible to file a draft Consent Order to give effect to the settlement.

25. OTHER DIRECTIONS

26 COSTS
the costs of this application be;
(a) in the case, or
(b) summarily assessed at £ and paid by , or
(c) the in any event to be the subject of a detailed assessment,
(d) the pay the the sum of £ on account of such costs on or before

Dated

# Index